COLLECTING TOYS

A Collector's Identification & Value Guide
5th Edition

by Richard O'Brien

BOOKS AMERICANA
INC

ISBN 0-89689-073-2

TABLE OF CONTENTS

ACKNOWLEDGEMENTS

One of the great pleasures of doing this book has been the number of people it has put me in touch with, virtually all of them cheery, bright and enthusiastic about doing whatever they could to make "Collecting Toys" better.

Some of the pitchers-in are now veterans at this sort of thing, but if they were feeling jaded, they didn't show it. Jim Harmon came through with his usual expertise and insights on radio-tv premiums. Ed Poole got the usual word that I needed photos, and as usual, came through. Charles W. Best, he of all the guns knowledge, continued to impart it, and Barbara and Jonathan Newman did the same re paper toys. Don Hultzman (with Ron Chojnacki assisting on photos) did so much work that I suspect he's the true author of this volume. Blossom Abell took time out to do a complete revamping of the Schoenhut Circus section, and John Murray, whose co-authorship of "Fisher-Price 1931-1963" resulted in one of the very best books on toys, came through again on this particular (and popular) subject.

I'd always been unhappy with the Aircraft section; it was just too skimpy. And then Perry Eichor popped up, with precisely the right credentials (Capt. USAF-Ret.). The result is impressively beefy, with additional heft given to it by Dick MacNary's specialized section on ID airplanes. At the last minute, Bill Bertoia came through, in a very busy year in which his name stood out in the field of mechanical banks.

There were plenty of others. Gary Linden breezed in with a slew of information and photos. Dave Leopard was approached about making the rubber vehicles section better, said "sure," and inundated me with absolutely great stuff. Dave's fever seemed to be contagious. Alfred R. Maxwell, when told I'd love to have information on an area that has long plagued and mystified collectors, went right to work, researched, wrote and photographed, and the result is that we now know virtually the entire story of those intriguing slush-cast toys from Kansas Toy & Novelty and Best Toys, with Fred casually slinging in a few bonus sections.

Also chipping in mightily in the area of vehicles were Calvin L. Chaussee, who lent his expertise to several sections, Phil Savino, who passed on a poor reproduction of the only known (and not known till then) Best Toys catalog, which enabled me to trace it back to Dee Buchanan, great granddaughter of John Best, who then furnished me (and via me, Fred Maxwell) with some very pertinent information on that company (as well as a much improved photocopy). Chic Gast furnished photos and information on various wheeled toys, and Joe and Sharon Freed were more than generous; providing reams of knowledge and photos on Walt Reach-Courtland, as well as other toys.

Not much has been known till now about all those pressed wood forts that were made in the 1930s and early 40s. If all goes well, and everything gets in, Ron Fink will earn a lot of gratitude from collectors for all the information, written and visual, that he's provided. Joe Stern, once of Banner Toys, furnished the history of that company.

News continued to be made in the toy soldier area, as one discovery after another tumbled forth. Contributing to the flow were Sam Speers, who was in on the origin of G.I. Joe (and who also contributed a number of significant toy company catalogs, amassed during his years of designing toys), Bill Nutting, whose dedication to the early American toy soldier has led to all sorts of new information (and photos), the ever helpful Hank Anton, Steve Balkin (ultra-knowledgeable owner of New York's Burlington Antique Toys), Bill Cardiff, Ron Steiner, John Stetson, Monty Mitzelfeld, Gordon Gee, Marvin Sussman, Fred Wilhelm, Pete Ferguson, Don Pielin, Davis H. King, Verne Johnson, Bertel Bruun, A. J. Mergenthaler and Jack Matthews (paper toys, too), and Orville Britton, who was provided with a jot of information on Sheila, Inc., and promptly ran with it.

Cast iron toys, antique toys and animal-drawn toys all fall into Ed Hyers' realm of high-level knowledge, and he generously shared what he knows, in addition to providing some excellent photos of some notable toys. Ron Smith, equally expert in the exotic field of Japanese, etc., tin toys, provided the same high level of help in an area that has become increasingly popular, and until the advent of his contribution, rather fuzzily defined.

A number of other people contributed photos. Richard and Rex Gray of Toy Collector News absolutely deluged me, as did the equally generous Heinz Mueller of Continental Hobby House. Barbara Niman was generous, too, with photos from the Wilkinson Collection of the Detroit Antique Toy Museum, and Mark Schulz graciously allowed me to use information he'd developed on the Plasticville toy line. Excellent photos also came in from Brad Krewson, Charles D. Richards, Dick and Nancy Dice, Scott Smiles, Mrs. Clint Seeley, Roger Sanders (where'd you disappear to, Roger?) and Superman fan extraordinaire, Danny Fuchs.

Gracious, too, were ever-helpful Henry Kurtz of Phillips, New York and super-efficient Dana Hawkes of Sotheby's New York, as well as Pennsylvania's John Wright Co. For new information on the toy companies he wrote about, Fred Maxwell would like to thank the following: Bob Bostoff, Perry Eichor, Chic Gast, Louis Hertz, Ernest Istas, Dr. Carl Natter, Kennie Nudson, Don Veta, John West, Gates Willard and Minnie Best Nelson.

Finally, I'd like to thank all of those who've contributed in the past (and whose contributions are still very much a part of this book), anyone I've forgotten (as I smite myself on the forehead!), my agent Al Zuckerman and Books Americana publisher Dan Alexander, for his continuing courtesy, friendliness and professionalism.

INTRODUCTION

A little more than ten years have passed since the first edition of this book, and nearly five since the last. There have been a number of changes along the way. The first edition listed almost 4000 toys. The second added 1500, the third another 2000, and the fourth brought the total up to something over 8000. This edition lists over 12,000.

There has also been a substantial increase in company histories. Many collectors, once hooked, want to know everything they can about the firms that made their favorite toys. The fourth edition had approximately thirty-five histories; this one has almost ninety. Necessarily, these are brief. However, some are shorter than need be; I simply had no more information. Since this seems to be an ongoing project, I'd appreciate receiving additional intelligence for future editions, whether on these firms or on ones not yet mentioned.

Some other things have changed since the earlier editions. The collectible toys field has exploded, particularly since the last volume. More and more collectors are entering the field, a wealth of magazines and newsletters have sprung up, and prices, particularly in the past two years, have soared. For this latter reason, I've confined virtually all the price changes to those recorded on lists and in auctions and shows of the past year. I've also relied far more heavily this time out on other collectors for price information. And for the first time, because of this enormous inflation, I've extrapolated where I had no price information, and brought up the prices to what would appear to be the current floor.

Another enormous change since earlier editions has been the startling increase of interest in relatively recent toys. Plastic, once sneered at, has become highly collectible. And the thirty or more years gap that once existed between a toy's being new and its becoming collectible has been shortened dramatically. Even some toys made in the early 1980s are now sought after. This condition, incidentally, is not restricted to the toys area. A lot of veteran collectors would have begun years before they did if they'd been able to find the items they yearned after. Today, with much readier information, and the obvious money to be made from collectibles, far less remains in hiding.

One thing hasn't changed. As always, it should be stressed that when it comes to prices, this book is a **guide**. It is **not** the absolute last word on the price of a toy. Nothing could be. Prices may inflate or deflate in the months it takes to publish a book. And even on the same day a toy can vary in price, depending on the dealer, the buyer, the geographical area in which it's being sold, and whether it's being offered in the first moments of a toy show or in the last, draggy minutes, when the dealer finds himself having to pack up all that stuff again. Used by itself, "Collecting Toys" should at least prevent very serious mistakes being made. Used with the assistance of a few current prices found on lists or on dealer tables, it can get the prospective buyer or seller much nearer to the current (always fuzzily defined) market price.

Finally, for those who wish to consider this field as an investment, and it can be a good one, it should be stressed that mint or near-mint condition provides considerably more financial safety than any of the other conditions, as this is the only condition sure to attract all collectors and dealers of any particular toy.

Richard O'Brien
October, 1989

Note: Due to numerous collector requests, the former G-VG-M grading system has, at the last minute, been changed in most sections to the numerical grading that seems to have become more favored in recent years. The Toy Soldier section still retains the G-VG-M classification.

CONDITION OF A TOY
AND ITS RELATION TO PRICE

> **CONDITION CODE:**
> C5 – Good, wear evident overall, shows that has been played with
> C6 – Fine, shows some wear in spots, but taken care of
> C7 – Very Fine, minor wear overall, very clean
> C8 – Excellent, minor wear on edges only
> C9 – Near Mint, no noticeable flaws, close inspection may show minute marks
> C10 – Mint (like new)
> Note: Mint in Box does command higher price

VEHICLES
(See also Tin Wind-Up)

Average mint price of vehicles in the last edition was $159.36, this edition it is $363.85, an increase of 128%.

CAST IRON AUTOMOTIVE TOYS
by C. B. C. Lee

The manufacture of cast iron toys began shortly after the Civil War and had about reached its zenith by the beginning of the twentieth century. The first toy automobiles began to appear soon after their real life prototypes began chugging along the horse-carriage roads, by which time some of the great 19th century toy makers had already gone out of business. Among those that continued into the automotive era were Hubley, Dent, Wilkins, and Kenton. During the first three decades of this century, others came to the forefront, such as Arcade, Kilgore, A. C. Williams, and Champion. Others also made toy cars and trucks in smaller numbers or for a short period of time, such as Grey Iron, Freidag, and North and Judd. Many of these firms made no identifying marks on their toys, and it has only been in recent years that many very familiar toys have been correctly attributed, as catalogues, patents, and old advertisements have gradually come to light. Probably the greatest American toymaker of all was Ives, but this firm is thought to have made only one toy car, a clockwork-driven horseless carriage runabout with figure, measuring 6½" long and 6" to the top of the jockey-cap on the driver.

Value does not have much relationship to either age or size, however, having more to do with scarcity, complexity and nicety of design, detail, and "desirability". As with anything else in a free market, it is simply the rule of supply and demand.

Demand and "desirability" are affected by a number of factors. One of these is nostalgia.

As a general guide to factors affecting desirability, there are a few broad easy clues, however. Accuracy of scale and proportion, the use of many different cast parts, cast-in or decal logos and details, hand-painting (by the original maker, but NOT by some later child or collector!!), etc. all enhance the value. In most cases, a 4-inch roadster with a separate chassis, separate nickel-plated radiator and headlights, and a separate cast figure will be worth much more than a two-piece one with the halves riveted together.

Values are very volatile, both up and down, and may be badly obsolete even by the time this is printed. The lawyers long ago defined the "fair market value" as that price paid by a (knowledgeable) willing buyer to a (knowledgeable) willing seller.

A WORD OF CAUTION!!!

In recent years several American makers have begun to make cast-iron or brass copies of old toys, and more recently many more have been coming in from Taiwan and perhaps other sources. These are marketed as decorator pieces, and sell quite cheaply. Many unscrupulous dealers are using these pieces to cheat unwary new collectors. They usually rust them hurriedly – and sometimes make other modifications of tip-off parts (axles or screws) to fool the uninitiated. The Makers, "IRON ART", "UTEXIQUAL" and others here and abroad are running an honest enough business, but the dishonest dealers are using the products to turn a quick profit at the expense of naive buyers.

The fakes are usually easy to spot once one has gained a little experience. They are usually held together by a long screw, which is threaded all the way up to the hub, as are standard stove bolts in your local hardware store (only a few genuinely old toys are asembled with a screw rather than a long peaned rivet, and the few screws used often had only about ¼-inch threaded at the tip (the Hubley Packard is an important exception). Modern axles are usually a hollow rolled piece of sheet-metal, much like a long shear-pin, though a few are rods with threaded ends and sheet-metal acorn nuts. The castings themselves are the most dependable give-away, but require a little experience; a blind-man could tell in an instant. The old castings are thinner, lighter, and smoother; the modern ones being gritty, thick and coarse of detail.

CLINT SEELEY (8/28/27—3/6/84), a New England doctor, used the pen-name C.B.C. LEE when writing about toys, which he did prolifically. He contributed to books and magazines not only in this country but also in England, France, Italy, New Zealand, Australia and Japan and was in touch with collectors on five continents. His extensive research on the subject, and his generosity in sharing what he'd learned, will keep his name alive as long as interest remains in the hobby he so loved.

TOOTSIETOYS, DIE-CAST AND SLUSH
by C. B. C. LEE

Die-casting was an outgrowth of the invention of the Linotype machine, introduced at the Columbian Exposition at Chicago in 1893. A trade-journal publisher in that city named Samuel Dowst began to adapt the type-casting machine to making small promotional miniatures, collar buttons, and so on related to the Laundry Journal he also published. By the turn of the century, however, the die-casting business had become his principal business, and he was producing a myriad of small party favors, candy premiums, political items and penny jewelry. Amongst these were several charms and miniatures of automotive, trains, and aircraft. By 1911, he produced a small 477 mm. limousine with free-turning wheels. By 1914 a 77 mm. Ford touring car was marketed, and a matching pick-up truck was made two years later. All three of these stayed in the catalogue until the late 20s, and the truck as late as 1932. In 1922 a line of doll furniture was developed, and was trade-named Tootsietoy after the daughter of the company's president at that time, Tootsie Dowst. The name later was used to identify nearly all of the toys the company sold. However, it continued to make items for other buyers, and still makes the metal marker pieces used in the deluxe Monopoly game. Tootsietoys continue to be made today, the present name of the Company being the Strombecker Corporation.

As with other collectibles, the value of obsolete toys today is not greatly related to age. The oldest Tootsietoys were made in such large numbers and for so long a period that they are not hard to find today. Others, some of which were unpopular in their day, were not sold in great numbers and are rare today. The 1932 Funnies series of six pieces drawn from the contemporary comic strips is an example of this. These were made in a boxed set of 6, having cams on the axles, which imparted action to the figures as the toy was pushed along the floor, and having details and figures hand-painted in up to seven different colors. This boxed set sold for $1.00. The six pieces were also made in simplier non-action versions with simple paint and sold for 10¢ each. For reasons hard to understand today, these toys were not popular. Consequently they are very hard to find, and are more valuable. Some of the individual pieces must have been better liked by their owners and were played to death or lost, making them even scarcer. So, though all were made in about equal numbers, some are rarer than others. Uncle Walt Wallet in a roadster is the most valuable. Uncle Willie and Mamie in a boat is at the other end, worth about half as much.

In regular production cars, LaSalles and a sort of pseudo-Lincoln have the greatest value, while other Fords, Yellow Cabs, and early Mack trucks are about one-third of that. A 1925 delivery truck, often called "Federal" by collectors, was made in stock versions having legends on the side panels saying: MILK, MARKET, LAUNDRY, GROCERY, BAKERY, and FLORIST. Their rarity is in about that order, MILK being worth the least. This same line of small trucks were also made in small numbers with custom private liveries, and over a dozen such versions with store names on the sides are presently known to exist. There were probably more. These, too vary in value according to scarcity, the most common being HORSCHSCHILD KOHN & CO. One which had the J.C. Penney logo is worth twice that, and a few might find a buyer at even higher prices.

Other manufacturers also made die-cast toys, and a few of these are desirable enough to have some value. Barclay made a small series of separate body/chassis vehicles in the late 1930s, and a west coast firm, TIP-TOP Toys, which are of fair value. So are a few of the finer die-cast Manoils and ERIEs. Many others are in little demand, such as JANE FRANCIS, GOODIE, METAL MASTERS and IT'S A BEAUT.

Slush casting was a process simple enough to be done in tiny factories, and even in home-industries during the depression. A few large manufacturers made toys in this way, most notably Barclay, Manoil, Savoye, Kansas Toy and Novelty, and others, but many were made by anonymous and small unidentifiable and local operations, using molds made and marketed by a few firms. Many slush-cast toys are of very little value today, but there are exceptions. Foremost among these were dealer promotional replicas of real cars, made by Banthrico and National Products. Other very accurate and detailed slush models, similar in size and scale to the contemporary Tootsietoys, can be valuable, most notable among these being certain nicely cast models of the Reo Victoria, Packard, Chrysler Imperial, Cord coupe, late 20s, Buick and Model A Ford; these, and others made with an extra moldpart resulting in detailed radiator grilles, were made by the Lincoln White Metal Works. Other small accurate replicas, with the names cast on the door sides, were made by Tommy Toy.

As with other toys, condition is very important. The values quoted here are for those in like-new condition. Paint-wear can drop the value to half, and broken or missing parts can drop it to nearly nothing. Repairing can occasionally partially rescue an exceptionally rare piece, but more often depresses the value. Reproductions are beginning to appear on the market, and will also tend to depress the values of the real thing. As with anything else in a free market, cost is largely a matter of supply and demand, both of which can wax and wane cyclically. Let the buyer beware.

RUBBER TOY VEHICLES
by Dave Leopard

For about 20 years (roughly 1935-1955), American kids enjoyed playing with rubber toys and Moms were told that these toys would not mar the furniture or floors. Then, almost as suddenly as they came on the market, they disappeared again, but left a rich legacy for toy collectors.

The Auburn Rubber Company of Auburn, Indiana was not the first to introduce rubber toys to the American market but they were no doubt the largest and had the greatest impact on the toy field. After introducing some toy soldiers in 1935, Auburn brought out its first vehicle in 1936 – a beautiful coffin-nosed Cord sedan. Today, the Auburn Cord is one of the most highly prized rubber toys and is seldom seen offered for sale. Auburn followed the Cord with a wealth of vehicles, including trucks, farm tractors and implements, motorcycles, racers, fire engines, military vehicles, aircraft, ships, and trains. In all, I have catalogued about 90 different varieties of Auburn rubber vehicles and I'm sure there are more than that. To my knowledge, 1952 was Auburn's last year of marketing rubber toys exclusively. The 1953 Auburn catalog contained a vinyl motorcycle, which I believe was their first vinyl toy. By 1955, their toy line was mostly vinyl with a few rubber varieties hanging on. The 1956 catalog is exclusively vinyl, except for two rubber fire engines, which were no doubt the last rubber toys to be marketed by Auburn. Auburn continued in the toy business in Auburn, Indiana and later in Deming, New Mexico until they went out of business in 1969.

The Sun Rubber Company of Barberton, Ohio was the second largest producer of rubber toys and, like Auburn, produced a full line of toys, in addition to vehicles, including dolls, balls, and baby squeak toys. I have catalogs that confirm Sun's line of rubber toy vehicles, beginning in 1936 and ending in 1955, which pretty well puts them on the same course with Auburn - about 20 years of rubber toys. The Sun 1936 catalog contains a good selection of cars, trucks, and racers. In later years, they added a few airplanes and military vehicles but unlike Auburn never produced any motorcycles, ships, or trains. Among the most famous of the Sun Rubber vehicles are the Walt Disney characters, Mickey Mouse and Donald Duck driving a tractor, firetruck, roadster, or airplane. The Disney tractor and firetruck are the only examples of each produced by Sun. By 1955, Sun's catalog line largely consisted of athletic balls, with the Disney toys included as the only vehicle toys. I'm not sure how long Sun existed as a company, but it's safe to say they did not manufacture rubber toy vehicles much past 1955. I have catalogued 33 varieties of Sun Rubber toy vehicles, which I believe accounts for all of the toys they made.

Auburn and Sun made the vast majority of rubber toys we see today but there were a significant number of rubber toys made by other companies, mostly prior to World War II. Several companies from the rubber industry produced some rubber toy vehicles, including Firestone, Seiberling, Barr, and Rainbow. All of the Rainbow, Barr, and Seiberling toys appear to have been made in 1935-1936, or at least based on real cars from those years. All of the Seiberling or Barr toys I have seen are 1935 Fords. The Firestone toys include a 1935 Ford, a 1936 Ford, and a 1939 Mercury. Rainbows are mostly based on a 1935 Oldsmobile. Some of these toys were mass-marketed via dimestores, just like Auburn and Sun toys were, but some were sold (or given away?) at expositions and exhibits. All of the Firestone toys seem to be marked with some significant event being celebrated, like the Texas Centennial in 1936. I have catalogued only 12 varieties of toys produced by these four companies.

Many rubber toys were produced as "promotionals" for the automobile industry and are not marked to indicate who manufactured them. A number of Chrysler, DeSoto, Dodge, and Plymouth vehicles were produced during the mid-thirties as promotionals and are highly prized as collectibles.

A few rubber vehicles were produced as very inexpensive toys, perhaps sold in sets, and can take the form of either a solid rubber or hollow vehicle. These toys often had the wheels molded in, so they could not turn. Some of these solid rubber toys are two-dimensional and are referred to as 'flat" toys. Although they were originally sold as cheap toys, they are actively sought by collectors and constitute a small but important segment of the field.

DAVE LEOPARD is a retired Air Force Colonel, now employed by the State of South Carolina Budget and Control Board, Division of Human Resource Management. Dave is a collector of small, American made toy cars and trucks and is an authority on rubber toys. He currently writes the "Little Wheels" column monthly for "U.S. Toy Collector Magazine" and is engaged in research for his own book on rubber toy vehicles.

A.C. WILLIAMS (see WILIAMS, A.C.)

ACME

Many Acme vehicles are exactly like Thomas Toys. The reason is that New York's Ben Shapiro was a financial partner in Thomas Toys, and Thomas Toys' Islyn Thomas made up toys for Shapiro at his request, with the Acme imprint substituted for that of Thomas.

	C6	C8	C10
Acme No. 138 Airline Limousine, plastic, 4" long	5.00	7.50	10.00

ALL AMERICAN TOY COMPANY: All American was located in Salem, Oregon, and made its products of aluminum and heavy steel. The company seems to have been in business in the late 1940s and early 1950s.

	C6	C8	C10
All American C-5 Cattle Liner	160	240	320
All American CL-8 Cargo Liner	180	275	360
All American HH-9 Heavy Hauler, early versions came without logs, later logs were optional	300	525	700
All American Dump Truck	140	210	280
All-Nu "Field Kitchen," approx. 2½" long, "Made in USA," slush lead	No Price Found		
All-Nu Searchlight, approx. 2¾" long, "Made in USA", slush lead	No Price Found		
All-Nu Sound Detector, approx. 2¾" long, "Made In USA", slush lead	No Price Found		
All-Nu Tank "USA", 3" long, "Made In USA", slush lead	No Price Found		

	C6	C8	C10
American National Army Truck, Mack "Giant," 26½" long	500	750	1000
American National "Juvenile Auto" dump truck pedal car, red and yellow tin, 57" long	1500	2250	3000
American National Packard Coupe, 30" long, 1920s, steerable front wheels	900	1400	2000
American National Velie, child's pedal car, circa 1918	1000	1400	2000
Animate Toy "Baby Tractor", friction, "patented June 20, 1916"	35.00	52.50	70.00

ALL-NU Searchlight, "Field Kitchen", Sound Detector, Tank. (Head of soldier missing on Field Kitchen) Photo by Bill Kaufman. Courtesy Evelyn Besser.

ANIMATE TOY "Baby Tractor", circa 1916. Courtesy Good Old Days Store. Photo by Bill Kaufman.

ARCADE MANUFACTURING COMPANY
A Brief History
by C. B. C. Lee
(based on information from Dave Davison)

In 1869 a foundry in Freeport, Ill. was organized as a two-man partnership under the name of Novelty Iron and Brass Foundry, but was dissolved in 1885, when a new, larger factory was incorporated under the name of Arcade Manufacturing Co. It made industrial castings and household items, but no toys. After a disastrous fire in 1892 and management changes in 1893, toys began to appear in its catalogue, and by the early 1900s the line had become so extensive that a 50-page catalogue was issued showing a large line of notions and novelties, small stoves, banks and a few trains, including a unique pile-driver. But it was not until an enterprising young lawyer married the daughter of one of the officers and joined the firm in 1919 that the firm rapidly became one of the major makers of cast iron toys. Struck by the large number of Yellow Cabs in the streets of Chicago (my reference doesn't say he was hit or injured by them), the young man approached the Yellow Cab Company with a novel proposition: in return for the sole right to make toy replicas of the cab, the Yellow Cab Company would have the exclusive right to use the toy in its advertising. Success was instantaneous.

Arcade went on to duplicate this pattern with miniature Buicks, Chevrolets, Ford cars, McCormack-Deering and Harvester farm equipment, and several makes of trucks and buses. Arcade's slogan "They look real" was well justified by its products. In the booming 1920s the company's sales swelled so much that a new and larger plant was built in 1927. Two years later, the stock market crash heralded the great depression, and hard times hit the small car business just as it did the large ones. Cheap competition and dwindling demand for toys costing more than a dime had brought the company to the brink of bankruptcy by 1933. But, once again, the enterprising management gave the firm new life with an exclusive arrangement to provide souvenir replicas of the fairground buses made by G.M.C. for the Chicago Century of Progress. The depression caused a cheapening of quality, but World War II gave the firm business in military material. After the war, the company returned to making industrial and household hardware and a few toys, but cheaper toys of die-cast zamac, plastic, rubber and lithographed tin eclipsed the costlier cast iron toys. In 1946 the firm was sold to Rockwell Manufacturing Co. of Pittsburgh. Death and retirement soon finished the change of the old firm, and it followed its guiding directors into oblivion when Rockwell moved to Alabama.

Though the source is gone, the toys live on in collections across the land. Arcade is a prestigious name in cast iron automotive toys exceeded by none and approached by very few of its old competitors. No serious collection of cast iron toy cars, trucks, buses, or farm and construction equipment can pretend to be representative without its inclusion.

	C6	C8	C10		C6	C8	C10
Arcade A.C.F. Bus	1250	1875	2500	Arcade Bus, 12" long, early 1930s, dual rear wheels, driver	300	450	600
Arcade Allis-Chalmers Tractor trailer, approx. 12" long, circa 1937	90	135	180	Arcade Bus, with driver, cast iron, 13" long	1000	1500	2000
Arcade "Allis-Chalmers" tractor and wagon, white rubber tires, 9½" long	50	75	100	Arcade No. 316x bus, double-decker coach, 1932, rear stairway to top, 8¼" long	250	375	500
Arcade "Allis Chalmers" tractor and wagon, 12¾" long	350	525	700	Arcade No. 311 Bus, approx. 6" long, 1920s	75.00	112.50	150.00
Arcade Ambulance, "City Ambulance", 6" long, 1920	125.00	187.50	250.00	Arcade No. 312 Bus	100	150	200
Arcade Andy Gump car, No. 348 on license plate	800	1200	1600	Arcade Bus, double-decker, rear stairway to top, circa 1928, 8" long	300	450	600
Arcade Anthony Company Dump Truck, reads "Anthony Company Inc., Streater, Illinois" in raised gold embossed letters on tailgate	1000	1500	2000	Arcade Bus, double-decker, rear stairway to top circa 1938	300	450	600
Arcade Auto No. 1481, Plymouth, 3½" long	35.00	52.50	70.00	Arcade Bus, double-decker, 10" long	100	150	200
Arcade auto, looks like 1933 Plymouth, white rubber tires, approx. 4¾" long	50	75	100	Arcade "Caterpillar Tractor", No. 268 x, 1932, chair caterpillar treads, approx. 5½" long	75.00	112.50	150.00
Arcade auto, four-door hard top, 6" long	300	450	600	Arcade Caterpillar Tractor 8" long, steel tracks, diesel	300	450	600
Arcade Avery Tractor circa 1920s, 4¾" long	80	120	160	Arcade No. 269 very early Caterpillar tractor	800	1200	1600
Arcade Brinks Armored Truck	2500	3750	5000	Arcade Century of Progress Bus, 1934, 6" long	45.00	67.50	90.00
Arcade Bugatti Racer, 5½"	100	150	200	Arcade Century of Progress Bus 7⅞" long	65.00	97.50	130.00
Arcade Buick Sedan, 8½" long, rubber tires, 1920	3000	4500	7500	Arcade Century of Progress Greyhound bus, 10½" long, circa 1933	100	150	200
Arcade Buick, coupe, circa 1928, 8" long, spare tire on rear	1500	2250	3000	Arcade Century of Progress Greyhound bus, 12" long, circa 1940	125.00	187.50	250.00
Arcade Bus, 4" long, 1920s, 5 windows on each side	50	75	100	Arcade Century of Progress sightseeing bus, 14½" long, 1933	500	750	1000
Arcade Bus, 1930, 6¼" long, metal wheels	125.00	187.50	250.00	Arcade Chevrolet utility coupe, 1924, rubber tires, black with gold belt line, silver headlights, 6¾" long, with chauffeur	250	375	500
Arcade Bus, 8" long, seven side windows, circa 1930	200	300	400	Arcade Chevrolet Coupe 1928, 8" long, white rubber tires, spare tire on rear	750	1125	1500
Arcade Bus, circa 1940, 8¾" long	150	225	300				
Arcade Bus, 9" long, circa 1940	150	225	300				
Arcade Bus, 9½" long, early 1930s, dual rear wheels	200	300	400				

ARCADE "Fageol Safety Coach" with metal wheels, approx. 12" long. Photo by Bill Kaufman. Courtesy Good Old Days Store.

ARCADE Allis-Chalmers Tractor Trailer, circa 1936. Courtesy Dick & Nancy Dice.

ARCADE "New York World's Fair" tourist train, 1939. Photo by Bill Kaufman.

ARCADE Bus, Double-Decker, 10" long. Courtesy Mapes Auctioneers & Appraisers.

ARCADE "Yellow Cab", 9" long, circa 1928, no driver. Courtesy Mapes Auctioneers & Appraisers.

ARCADE Steamroller, "Austin Autocrat Worm Drive", 7" long. Courtesy Mapes Auctioneers & Appraisers

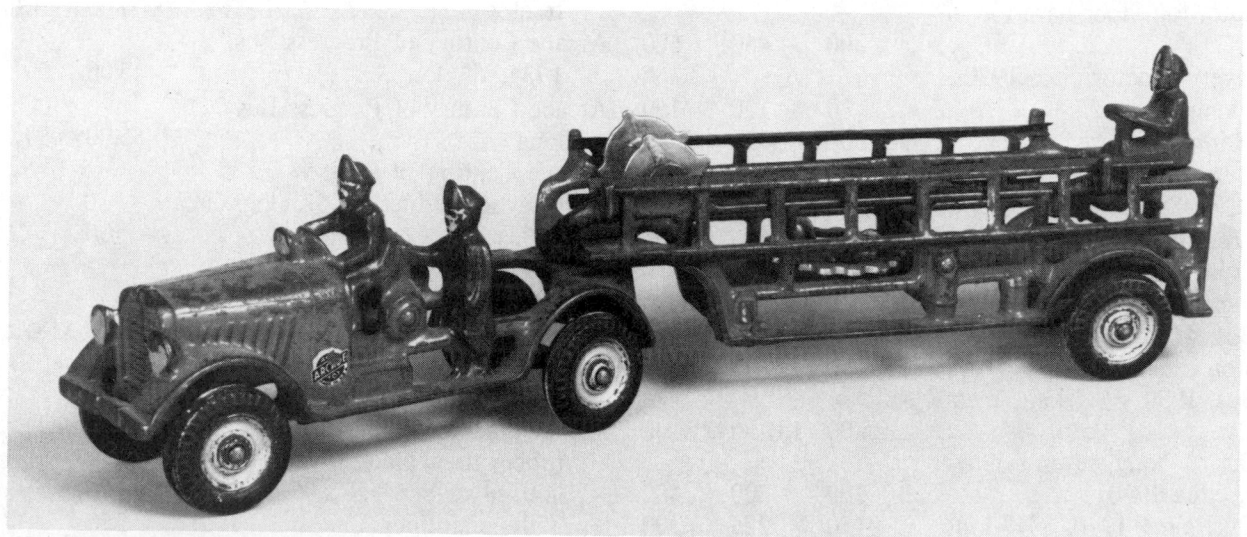

ARCADE Fire Truck, hook and ladder, 18" long. Courtesy Mapes Auctioneers & Appraisers.

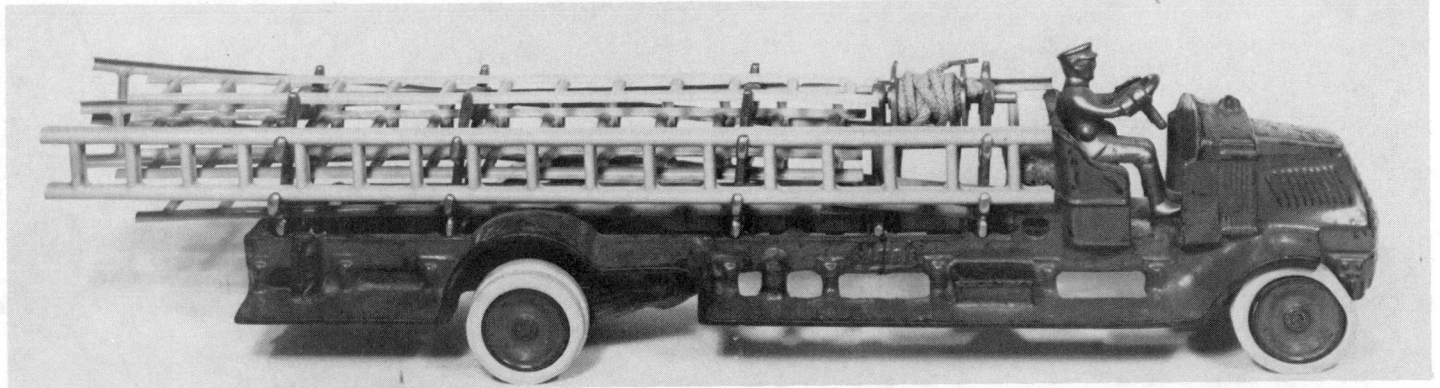

ARCADE Fire Hook and Ladder, Mack, 21" long.   Courtesy Phillips New York

ARCADE Delivery Van, circa 1925, 8¼" long.
Courtesy Phillips New York

ARCADE Model T Ford Sedan with door in middle
Courtesy Ed Hyers Antique Toys

ARCADE Model A Coupe, rumble seat.
Courtesy Ed Hyers Antique Toys

ARCADE Model A Coupe, rumble seat, driver
Courtesy Ed Hyers Antique Toys

ARCADE Bus, double-decker, rear stairway to top, circa 1938.
Courtesy Ed Hyers Antique Toys

ARCADE Chevrolet Sedan, about 4 inches long and ARCADE Chevrolet Coupe with rumble seat, about 4 inches long, both mid-1930s. Courtesy Chic Gast

ARCADE Coupe, 7½" long.
Courtesy Mapes Auctioneers & Appraisers.

ARCADE Mack "Gasoline" truck, 13½" long.
Courtesy Mapes Auctioneers & Appraisers.

	C6	C8	C10
Arcade Chevrolet Coupe with rumble seat, approx. 4" long, mid-1930s..	30	45	60
Arcade Chevrolet Sedan, approx. 4" long, mid-1930s...............	25.00	37.50	50.00
Arcade Coast to Coast bus, 10" long.	500	750	1000
Arcade Corn Cutter and binder......	108	150	200
Arcade Corn Planter, rubber wheels..	40	60	80
Arcade Coupe, circa 1937, 3¾" long.	60	90	120
Arcade Coupe, 5" long, 1920s, two side windows.................	120	180	240
Arcade No. 116 coupe with working rumble seat, 1920s, approx. 5" long........................	75.00	112.50	150.00
Arcade Coupe, 5¼" long, circa 1920, metal wheels.................	70	105	140
Arcade Coupe (Ford?), 6½" long, one side window, 1920s............	100	150	200
Arcade Coupe, 6¾" long, two side windows, early 1920s..........	200	300	400
Arcade Coupe, 7½" long...........	200	300	400
Arcade Coupe, 9" long, circa 1920s, spare tire on rear, two windows on side........................	500	750	1000
Arcade Delivery Van, circa 1925, 8¼" long........................	750	1125	1500
Arcade disk harrow...............	40	60	80
Arcade double-decker bus, open, 18 tin seats on roof, dual wheels on rear, "Made by Arcade Mfg. Co. Freeport, Ill." on each side, 13¾" long, circa 1930s	1100	1650	2200
Arcade dump hay rake, 5".........	30	45	60
Arcade dump hay rake, 7".........	50	75	100
Arcade dump truck, 6" long, circa 1927........................	100	150	200
Arcade dump truck, 7", 1920s or early 30s........................	150	225	300
Arcade dump truck, open cab, 8" long, early 1920s................	175.00	262.50	350.00
Arcade dump truck with driver, 10½" long........................	400	600	800
Arcade dump truck, Red Baby, 11" long, 1920s.................	500	750	1000

	C6	C8	C10
Arcade dump truck, Mack, 12" long..	325.00	487.50	650.00
Arcade Dump Truck, Mack, with hoisting rod and pulley, 12" long.	600	900	1200
Arcade Dump Truck, Mack, 13".....	500	750	1000
Arcade Fageol Coach (bus), circa 1932, 6" long.................	125.00	187.50	250.00
Arcade Fageol bus, 8" long, 7 windows on each side, 1920s........	200	300	400
Arcade Fageol bus, 12½" long, dual wheels, circa 1930s............	400	600	800
Arcade "Fageol Safety Coach", with metal wheels, approx. 12" long...	175.00	262.50	350.00
Arcade Fageol Safety Coach, 1920, 12½" long, rubber tires........	350	525	700
Arcade Farm Mower..............	60	90	120
Arcade Farmal Tractor, Model B....	200	300	400
Arcade Fire Apparatus Truck, Mack, 21" long.....................	900	1350	1800
Arcade Fire Engine, 9" long, 1930s..	125.00	187.50	250.00
Arcade Fire Hook & Ladder Truck, 16" long, articulated...........	400	600	800
Arcade Fire Hook and Ladder Truck, 18" long....................	350	525	700
Arcade Fire Hook and Ladder, Mack, 21" long....................	350	525	700
Arcade Fire Pumper, 13" long, six figures	300	450	600
Arcade Fire Truck, circa 1936, 13½" long, rubber tires, removable hose reel, bell, six firemen in blue coats, steam boiler.............	450	675	900
Arcade Fire Truck, 15"...........	300	450	600
Arcade Ford Coupe with rumble seat No. 106.....................	125.00	187.50	250.00
Arcade Ford Coupe with rumble seat No. 116.....................	200	300	400
Arcade Ford gondola, 13" long, circa 1927........................	350	525	700
Arcade Ford stake truck, 7" long....	140	210	280
Arcade Ford Tractor, 4"..........	80	120	160
Arcade "Fordson" tractor, 1920s, 3½" long........................	60	90	120
Arcade Fordson Tractor, 4" long....	60	90	120

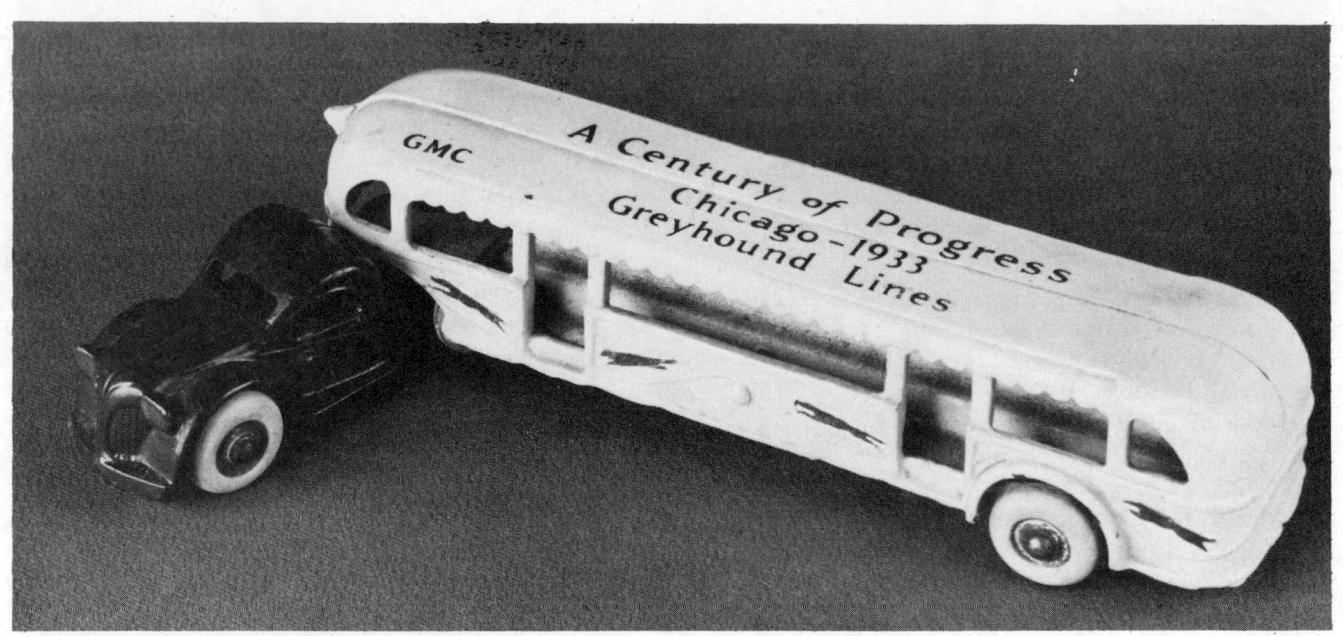

ARCADE "Century of Progress" Greyhound bus, 10" long, 1933.
Courtesy Mapes Auctioneers & Appraisers.

	C6	C8	C10
Arcade Fordson Tractor with driver, cast iron 5¾".................	85	125	170
Arcade Gasoline Truck, 5" spoked wheels	150	225	300
Arcade "Gasoline" Truck, Mack, 5" long........................	100	150	200
Arcade "Gasoline" Truck, Mack, 13" long........................	800	1200	1600
Arcade "Gasoline" truck circa 1920s, 13" long, tin operating tank, rubber hose......................	1000	1500	2000
Arcade "Gasoline" truck, Mack, 13½" long, circa 1925..............	200	300	400
Arcade Gasoline Truck, Mack, "Independent Oil", 13½" long......	2000	3000	4000
Arcade GMC Bus, 7½" coast to coast	200	300	400
Arcade Greyhound bus, 1938, rubber wheels, 8½".....................	250	375	500
Arcade Greyhound GMC Bus, 7½" .	200	300	400
Arcade Greyhound 1939 World's Fair bus, rubber wheels, 6½"........	250	375	500
Arcade "Ice" Truck, 6½" long with ice and tongs..................225.00		337.50	450.00
Arcade Ice Truck, circa 1930s.......225.00		337.50	450.00
Arcade Industrial Derrick...........	750	1125	1500
Arcade International Dump Truck, 1939, 11" long, rubber wheels....	450	675	900
Arcade International Harvester Caterpillar tractor.................	500	750	1000
Arcade International Harvester Caterpillar tractor, large.............	1000	1500	2000
Arcade International Harvester dump truck, white rubber tires, circa 1929...........................	450	675	900
Arcade International pickup, circa 1939, rubber wheels, 9"........	250	375	500

	C6	C8	C10
Arcade International Stake Truck, No. 237-0	500	800	1100
Arcade International Truck 11" long,.	1250	1875	2500
Arcade John Deere thresher, mid-1930s	300	450	600
Arcade John Deere tractor..........	60	90	120
Arcade Ladder Truck, 4" long.......	50	75	100
Arcade Ladder Truck, 7"...........125.00		187.50	250.00
Arcade limousine (or bus), circa 1920s, 12½" long...................	300	450	600
Arcade "Lubrite Gasoline" truck, Mack, 13¼" long..............	750	1125	1500
Arcade Mack "American Oil Co.", circa 1928, 10½" long............	600	900	1200
Arcade Mack bus..................	3000	4500	6000
Arcade Mack Stake Truck, 7½".....	300	450	600
Arcade Mack Truck, 4¾"..........	50	75	100
Arcade Mack Truck, circa 1928, 8½" long	400	600	800
Arcade Mack Truck with dump body, driver, body cranks up and dumps, 1920s 8½" long...............	900	1350	1800
Arcade McCormick-Deering combine, 10", cast iron.................	220	330	440
Arcade 10-20 McCormick-Deering Farm Tractor.................	250	375	500
Arcade "McCormick-Deering", manure spreader with shaft.............	200	300	400
Arcade No. 450x McCormick-Deering thresher, 9½" long, 1932........	110	165	220
Arcade Model A convertible Coupe, 4".............................	90	135	180
Arcade Model A Coupe, 4¼", spare tire on back...................	120	180	240
Arcade Model A coupe, rumble seat, 5" long.........................	400	600	800

	C6	C8	C10
Arcade Model A Coupe, rumble seat, driver	300	450	650
Arcade Model A Ford 6½" long, circa 1928-1931, with driver	400	600	800
Arcade Model A Pickup, 8", metal wheels, circa 1928	450	675	900
Arcade Model A truck, stake sides, circa 1928-1931	140	210	280
Arcade Model A wrecker, circa 1929-31, 11" long	400	600	800
Arcade Model T Coupe, 4"	100	150	200
Arcade Model T Ford coupe, driver, two side windows, 6½" long, circa 1922	120	180	240
Arcade Model T Pickup, 8" long	600	900	1200
Arcade Model T Ford sedan with door in middle	125.00	187.50	250.00
Arcade Model T Ford sedan, two-door, with driver, 6¼" long	180	270	360
Arcade Model T Ford four-door car, 6"	450	675	900
Arcade Model T Ford touring car, 6¼" long, circa 1920, rubber tires, open-sided	500	750	1000
Arcade Model T, 6½" long, rubber tires	180	270	360

	C6	C8	C10
Arcade Model T Touring Car, 1920, 6½" long, nickel plated wheels	150	225	300
Arcade Motorcycle, Harley-Davidson, cop rider, 5½" long, 1930s	125.00	187.50	250.00
Arcade Moving Van	750	1100	1500
Arcade mower, rubber wheels	28	42	56
Arcade Nash, approx. 4" long	200	300	400
Arcade "New York World's Fair" Greyhound bus, 6½"	100	150	200
Arcade New York World's Fair bus, 10½" long	175.00	262.50	350.00
Arcade "New York World's Fair" 11" long (with two trailers) cast iron tourist train, 1939-40, tin litho canopy, price with one trailer, add $65 for each additional trailer in mint	175.00	262.50	350.00
Arcade No. 1 Farm Tractor	75.00	112.50	150.00
Arcade Oliver Tractor, black rubber wheels	50	75	100
Arcade Pickup Truck No. 1488, 3½" long	25.00	37.50	50.00
Arcade Pickup Truck, Chev., 1920s, 8½" long	275	410	550
Arcade Pile Driver, 10½"			
Arcade plow, one-gang, with black rubber tires	100	150	200

ARCADE Model T Touring 6¼" long
Courtesy Lloyd W. Ralston Auctions

ARCADE Rack Truck, Chevrolet, 1920s, 9" long
Courtesy Lloyd W. Ralston Auctions

ARCADE Yellow Cab, Zephyr, late 30's, 8¼" long.
Courtesy Lloyd W. Ralston Auctions

Top, L to R: Dump Truck, tin 5¾" long, Road Grader, 7½" long, cast iron, Truck, open back, cast iron, 4¼" long. Middle, L to R: Pickup Truck, 7¼" long, cast iron, 1920s, ARCADE "Allis Chalmers" tractor and wagon, 9½" long. Bottom, L to R: ARCADE "Allis Chalmers" tractor and wagon, 12¾" long, Coupe with rumble seat, tin, 5" long.
Courtesy Garth's Auctions Inc.

ARCADE Fageol Safety Coach, 1920, 12¼" long.
Courtesy Lloyd W. Ralston Auctions

	C6	C8	C10
Arcade plow, two-gang............	200	300	400
Arcade Plymouth Sedan, circa 1932, 4¾" long.................	70	105	140
Arcade Pontiac Sedan, 1935, 6 1/8" long......................	400	600	800
Arcade Race Car with two figures...	50	75	100
Arcade Racer 3¾", circa 1932, rubber wheels....................	25.00	37.50	50.00
Arcade Racer, solid wheels, 5½"....	100	150	200
Arcade Racer No. 1457, 5½" long, rubber wheels, circa 1935......	70	105	140
Arcade Rack Truck, Chevrolet, 1920s, 9" long....................	1100	1650	2200
Arcade Railroad spike driver, cast with small wheels, upright lever..	400	600	800
Arcade Reo Coupe, rumble seat, 9"..	600	900	1200
Arcade Reo Coupe, smaller........	200	300	400
Arcade Road Grader, 4½".........	150	225	300
Arcade Rumble Coupe with driver, 6¾"....................	210	315	420
Arcade "Safety Coach" tour bus, rubber tires, 12" long, with driver...	200	300	400
Arcade "Safety Coach" tour bus, steel wheels, driver, 12" long........	250	375	500
Arcade Sandloader, 8½" long, 1920s.	450	675	900
Arcade Sedan No. 2272...........	30	45	60
Arcade Sedan circa 1937, cast iron, 8" long.....................	200	300	400
Arcade Sedan, 3¾" high, circa 1940.	60	90	120
Arcade Sedan, No. 1511, 5".......	125.00	187.50	250.00
Arcade Semi-truck, cast iron, 1920s, blue.....................	100	150	200
Arcade sickle bar mower...........	100	150	200
Arcade "Silver Arrow" sedan, 7" long	140	210	280
Arcade stake truck, cast iron, blue, 7" long	140	210	280
Arcade stake truck, 1920s, 7½" long.	400	600	800
Arcade Steam Roller, 3½".........	90	135	180
Arcade Steam Roller, 4½".........	110	165	220
Arcade Steamroller, "Austin Autocrat Worm Drive", 7" long..........	200	300	400
Arcade Steam Roller, 7½" long.....	125.00	187.50	250.00
Arcade Steam Shovel, 4½".........	80	120	160
Arcade tank No. 3960, 1930s, 3" long, spring-firing cannon.......	125.00	187.50	250.00
Arcade taxi, 1920s, 7" long........	375	565	750
Arcade Tractor 273...............	100	150	200
Arcade Tractor 288OL, 2½"	20	30	40
Arcade Tractor No. 2738, 3½"......	50	75	100
Arcade Tractor, Ford and Trailer....	400	600	800
Arcade Tractor Trailer No. 289, 3½"	50	75	100
Arcade tractor with white rubber wheels....................	25.00	37.50	50.00

	C6	C8	C10
Arcade transport service semi-truck...	400	600	800
Arcade Truck and Trailer No. 233, 13½" long...................	300	450	600
Arcade truck, black rubber tires, 1930s.....................	50	75	100
Arcade red baby truck, with driver, open back, 11" long...........	300	450	600
Arcade White bus...............	2000	3000	4500
Arcade White dump truck, circa 1920s...................	2500	3750	5000
Arcade White moving van.........	2000	3000	4500
Arcade White panel truck........	2000	3000	4500
Arcade Wrecker, circa 1930s, 4½"...	100	150	200
Arcade Wrecker, circa 1930s, 6" long.	150	225	300
Arcade wrecker with driver and hard rubber wheels, 11" long........	300	450	600
Arcade wrecker with driver, 11½" long.....................	300	450	600
Arcade Wrecker, Mack, 13" long, 1920s...................	600	900	1200
Arcade "Yellow Cab," 5" long	400	600	800
Arcade "Yellow Cab", 7½" long, 1920s, with driver...........	400	650	900
Arcade "Yellow Cab" 8" long, 1920s.	425	650	850
Arcade "Yellow Cab", 9" long, circa 1928, no driver.............	500	750	1000
Arcade "Yellow Cab", No. 155, 1930s, actually orange and black, 8 1/8" long, nickel-plated driver, white rubber tires, lead cowl lights	600	900	1200
Arcade Yellow Cab, 1934, "A Century of Progress", 6½".........	750	1200	1500
Arcade Yellow Cab with driver, 9" long, 1920..............	600	900	1200
Arcade Yellow Cab 15" long, circa 1924......................	500	750	1000
Arcade Yellow Cab 3, small........	60	90	120
Arcade Yellow Cab, Zephyr, late 1930s, 8¼" long..............	400	600	800
Arcade Yellow coach bus.........	1200	1800	2400
Arcade Yellow coach bus, double-decker, 1925, 14" long..........	2000	3000	4000
Army Truck, pressed steel, cloth top, black wooden wheels, approx. 10" long......................	80	120	160

AUBURN RUBBER

This company also manufactured rubber tires for other companies, including Wyandotte. The following list and its codings were compiled by David Leopard. Vehicles are broken down by types.

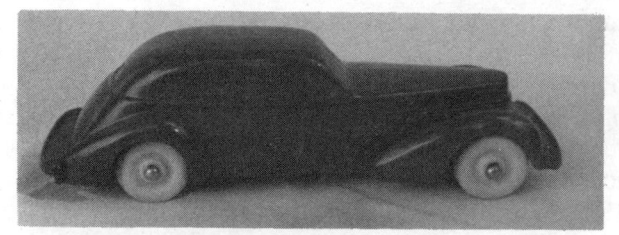

AUBURN AA01
Photo by Dave Leopard

AUBURN AT01, AT03
Photo by Dave Leopard

	C6	C8	C10
AA01 '36 Cord, four door coffin-nose scdan 6" long	No Price Found		
AA02 '37 Olds, 4 door sedan, 4½" long	10	12	15
AA03 '38 Olds, 4 door sedan, 5¾" long	12	15	18
AA04 '40 Olds, 4 door sedan, open fenders, 6" long	12	15	18
AA05 '40 Olds, 4 door sedan, fender skirts, 6" long	12	15	18

	C6	C8	C10
AT04 Same as above with rounded bumper, minor variations	10	15	20
AT05 '37 International cabover stake truck, 3¾" long	10	15	20
AT06 Same as above with rounded bumper, minor variations	10	15	20
AT07 '37 International cabover stake truck, milk version, 4¼" long	No Price Found		
AT08 '37 International cabover stake truck, ambulance version	No Price Found		
AT09 Cab-Forward box truck, smooth sides, futuristic, 5½" long	10	12	15
AT10 Cabover box truck, smooth sides, futuristic, 4-1/8" long	10	12	15
AT11 '47 Chevy Cab Forward Box Truck, 5¾" long	10	12	15
AT12 c. '50 Pickup truck open fenders, 4½" long	10	12	15
AT13 c. '50 Pickup truck, fender skirts, 4½" long	10	12	15

AUBURN AA06
Photo by Dave Leopard

	C6	C8	C10
AA06 '48 Buick, 2 door sedanette, fastback, 7¼" long	20	28	35
AA07 '39 Buick, Y Job Experimental Roadster, 9¾" long	No Price Found		
AA08 '35 Ford Coupe, 4" long	10	15	20
AA09 '35 Ford 2 door slantback sedan, 4" long	10	15	20
AA10 '50 Cadillac, 4 door sedan, 7¼" long	20	27	35
AA11 '50 Cadillac, 4 door sedan, 5¾" long	20	27	35
AA12 '39 Plymouth, 2 door trunkback sedan, 4¼" long	10	12	15
AA13 '46 Lincoln convertible, 2 door, square headlights, 4½" long	10	12	15
AA14 '46 Lincoln convertible, 2 door, round headlights, 4½" long	10	12	15
AA15 Late 40's Futuristic Sedan, fin down back, 5" long	10	12	15
AT01 '37 International cabover stake truck, 5-3/8" long	10	15	20
AT02 Same as above with rounded bumper, minor variations	10	15	20
AT03 '37 International cabover stake truck, 4¼" long	10	15	20

AUBURN AT14
Photo by Dave Leopard

	C6	C8	C10
AT14 '38 GMC "Carry Car" Auto Transport, 11½" long	30	45	60
AT15 '38 GMC Cab/Open Squared-off Trailer, 9" long	20	30	40
AT16 Updated Carry Car Transport, cab changed, trailer same, 11¾" long	No Price Found		
AT17 '35 Ford Stake Body Truck, 4¾" long	No Price Found		
AE01 Ahrens-Fox Fire Engine, 5½" long	30	40	50
AE02 c. 40s Fire Engine, hose and ladders, 7¾" long	20	27	35

AUBURN AE03
Photo by Dave Leopard

	C6	C8	C10
AE03 c. 40s Pumper, boiler, 7¾" long	20	27	35
AE04 c. 40s Fire Engine, ladders, no hose, 7¾" long	20	27	35

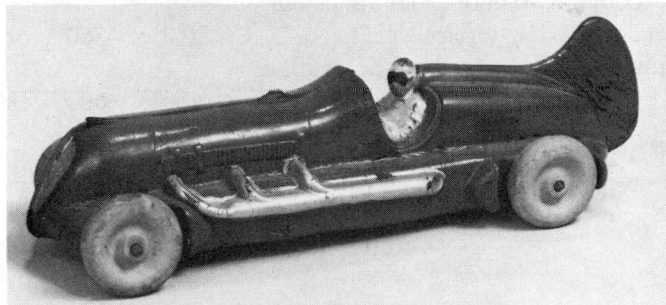

AUBURN AR01
Courtesy Mapes Auctioneers & Appraisers

	C6	C8	C10
AR01 Open racer, V-6, high fin, 10½" long	30	40	50

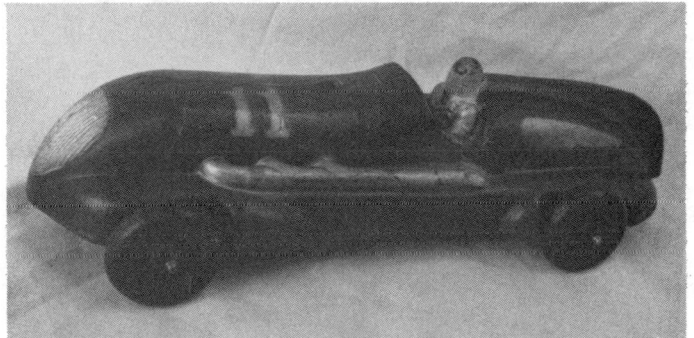

AUBURN AR02   Photo by Dave Leopard

	C6	C8	C10
AR02 Open racer, V-6, low fin, 10½" long	20	30	40
AR03 Open racer, short, tapered tail, large tires, 10½" long	30	40	50
AR04 Open racer, short, boat tail, 6½" long	20	27	35
AR05 Open racer, boat tail, 4¾" long	10	15	20

AUBURN AR06
Photo by Dave Leopard

	C6	C8	C10
AR06 Open racer, small fin, 6¼" long	10	15	20

	C6	C8	C10
AR07 Open racer short, boat tail, early, 6½" long	20	27	35
AR08 Open racer, no fenders, low fin, long back, 5¼" long	10	15	20
AR09 Open racer, midget type, late, 6-1/8" long	10	15	20
AR10 Open racer, boat tail, no side pipes, 4¾" long	10	15	20
AF01 Farm Tractor, John Deere "A", 5" long	15	17	25
AF02 Farm Tractor, John Deere, 4¼" long	15	17	25

AUBURN AF01   Photo by Dave Leopard

AUBURN AF03   Photo by Dave Leopard

AUBURN AF05   Photo by Dave Leopard

	C6	C8	C10
AF03 Farm Tractor, Minneapolis-Moline "Z", 4" long	15	17	25
AF04 Farm Tractor, Minneapolis-Moline "R", early style, 7½" long	20	30	40

	C6	C8	C10
AF05 Farm Tractor, Minneapolis, Moline "R", later style, 7¼" long	20	30	40
AF06 Farm Tractor, Oliver Row Crop "70", 8" long............	20	30	40
AF07 Farm Tractor, Oliver Row Crop "70", 6½" long.........	20	30	40
AF08 Farm Tractor, McCormick-Deering IH Farmall "M", 4" long	15	20	25
AF09 Farm Tractor, make unknown, 3-7/8" long.................	15	20	25
AF10 Farm Tractor, Graham-Bradley, 4¼" long.................	15	20	25
AT01 Trailer, 2 wheel, Graham-Bradley, 5¾" long	No Price Found		
AT02 Trailer, 4 wheel, Graham-Bradley, 4¾" long............	No Price Found		
AT03 Harvester, open top, 5½" long.	No Price Found		
AT04 Manure Spreader, David Bradley, 4¾" long..........	No Price Found		
AT05 Reliable Front-Lift Seeder, 5" long.....................	No Price Found		
AT06 Plow Seeder, 3½" long......	No Price Found		
AT07 Side-Cutter Sickle Bar Mower, David Bradley, 3¾" long........	No Price Found		
AT08 Two Furrow Plow, David Bradley, 4¾" long...........	No Price Found		
AT09 Cultipacker (Disc Harrows?), David Bradley, 4-3/8" long......	No Price Found		
AT10 Harrow, 4½" long...........	No Price Found		
AM01 Tank, Marmon-Harrington, 4½" long.....................	15	20	25
AM02 Tank, Marmon-Harrington, 3¼" long.....................	10	15	20

	C6	C8	C10
"Austin", cast iron, early 1930s	100	150	200
Austin Racer, 4" cast iron	20	30	40
"Austin" stakebody, 3¾" long, 1920s, cast iron	100	150	200
"Austin" wrecker, 4" long, 1920s, cast iron (Arcade).............	100	150	200
Auto Express 546, 6" long with drivers and barrels............	250	375	500
Auto Express 546, 7" long, cast iron.	125.00	187.50	250.00
Auto, raked cab, cast iron, early 1930s, approx. 4" long........	70	105	140
Auto Trailer, 12½" long, carries three cars, all two-door, circa 1932....	80	120	160
Auto Trailer, 1920s, 22" long, with coupe, two-door sedan, and four-door sedan on trailer..........	240	360	480
Auto with house trailer, late 1930s, cast iron, 13½"..................	400	600	800

AUBURN AM03
Courtesy Don Pielin

	C6	C8	C10
AM03 Tractor and Cannon, 11½" long, olive green..............	No Price Found		

Arcade Buicks and Chevrolets: on top are Chevy 1924 coupe and 1928 sedan and coupe. The latter were later made with double-striping around the waistline, rarer and more valuable. Bottom row, the famous Arcade Buicks, Sedan and 4-passenger coupe.
Photo by C.B.C. Lee.

Arcade made other brands of cars and trucks; Top, 1922 Dodge coupe; 1931 Reo Royale coupe 9¼"; Mach high-lift coal truck, one of a very large range of various trucks; bottom: Yellow panel truck; White panel delivery; International-Harvester panel truck; each of these vans was issued in various private liveries, the best known being the I-H Hathaway Bakery, which was done in versions using either decal transfers or colored rubber stamping.
Photo by C.B.C. Lee.

Other toy makers also made some nice trucks and cars; Top: Champion panel truck; Dent Police Patrol (they also made a similar parcel delivery); and Freidag delivery truck; Bottom: Vindex Pontiac coupe, Hubley Chrysler Airflow, Dent sedan.
Photo by C.B.C. Lee.

Among the most valuable large iron toys are several non-Arcades; rear, Kenton touring car, Kilgore Model T Ford with moving figures; Dent Red Devil touring car (Kenton made a very similar Franklin); bottom, the famous Hubley Packard and Kilgore Stutz, both assembled from multiple castings and very choice items amongst advanced automotive toy collectors.
Photo by C.B.C. Lee.

Choicer small cast iron pieces include: Top row, A.C. Williams 1934 Ford (series included coupe and sedan); A.C.W. 1936 Ford (series included coupe, sedan, roadster and panel truck and in a simpler single-piece casting only three, omitting the roadster); A.C.W. generic take-apart (series included coupe, sedan and stake truck). Bottom row shows Arcade 1933 Nash (coupe and sedan); Arcade 1935 Ford (sedan and stake truck); Dent 1935 LaSalle (sedan, coupe, roadster, pick-up truck, wrecker and panel truck).
Photo by C.B.C. Lee.

Smaller realistic slush-mold cars. The center car in bottom row is marked Cord on door and "A TOMMY TOY" along the rocker panel on each side.
Photo by C.B.C. Lee.

Some desirable slush-cash include top row, Reo Victoria, Chrysler coupe, L29 Cord coupe. Bottom, a selection of late 20s models, some marked with car names "CHEVROLET", "CHRYSLER".
Photo by C.B.C. Lee.

These are a rare make of toy, evidently manufactured through most of the twenties and thirties in San Francisco by the TIP TOP TOY CO.
Photo by C.B.C. Lee.

These are by various English makers. There were many makers of die-cast, poured lead, slush, etc. in Europe, some of them highly desirable and costly.
Photo by C.B.C. Lee.

15

BANNER

BANNER was begun by Emanuel M. Pressner (8/4/99–1/1/74) around 1945, in the Bronx, New York. Pressner had been a toy importer before the war. When the war cut off imports, he went to work for Columbia Protektosite, which, among other things, cast Beton's plastic toy soldiers. (Through his family has no recollection of this, in 1942 Pressner was noted in a toy trade magazine as being secretary of Beton.) Banner moved to 80 Beckwith Avenue in Paterson, New Jersey in 1950, where it remained. The firm's original toys seem to have been small plastic cars and trucks, with the leading items for years being tea sets and metalicized plastic forks, knives and spoons. Other items included plastic sand molds. The stamped steel Banner used was made up of "off-falls" – the blanks formed when holes were cut in steel to allow for car windows and television tubes.

The company, which at its peak periods had as many as 200 employees, went into Chapter 11 bankruptcy in 1965, came out of it, and then was sold in 1967 to Tal-Cap, a toy conglomerate in Minnesota. During its heyday, Banner produced at least tens of thousands of toys a week, according to former vice-president Joseph Stern. Banner got its name, according to Stern, because Pressner (his father-in-law) wanted a company with a name "high up in the alphabet".

	C6	C8	C10		C6	C8	C10
Banner American Express Truck, tin, 11" long	60	90	120	Banner Service Station (cardboard) with 3 plastic trucks, circa late 40s–early 50s	19.00	27.50	38.00
Banner Dodge, 1950, 4", plastic	5.00	7.50	10.00	Banner Stake Truck, GMC, 4" plastic	5.00	7.50	10.00
Banner Garbage Truck, Ford. plastic, 1954, 4"	5.00	7.50	10.00	Banner Station Wagon, 1948 Oldsmobile, plastic, 4"	5.00	7.50	10.00
Banner International Harvester Metro 1950 van, plastic, 4"	5.00	7.50	10.00	Banner Tractor, Wheelhorse, 3" plastic	5.00	7.50	10.00
Banner LaFrance Fire Truck, plastic, 4", 1950	5.00	7.50	10.00	Banner Wonder Bread Truck, circa 1950s 11" long, tin litho	30	45	60
Banner North American Van Lines Truck & Trailer, 15" long	65.00	97.50	130.00				

BARCLAY VEHICLES

Barclay vehicles can be roughly dated by their tires. The earliest are metal. About 1934 rubber tires on wooden hubs were introduced. About 1936 nail axles began to replace the wooden hubs. Black tires are post War (after 1945).

A number of unmarked vehicles were in the possession of the late Barclay-All Nu designer Frank Krupp. Most of these were too early to have been All-Nu and were checked with four early Barclay employees. The number of Xs in parenthesis after the toy's description indicate how many thought it had been Barclay. However, it is possible, since these are based on memories of several decades, that not all are Barclay, An X? indicates the employee believed it was Barclay but was not sure. Those not marked with Xs have been identified in other ways.

	C6	C8	C10		C6	C8	C10
(BV 1) Ambulance, No. 50, 3½" long, small cross	15.00	22.50	30.00	(BV 11) Auto Carrier, circa 1941, 2-piece, "Barclay Made in U.S.A." on each piece	17.50	26.25	35.00
(BV 2) Ambulance No. 50, 3½" long, large cross	25.00	37.50	50.00	(BV 12) "Beer" truck, circa 1940, No. 376, approx. 3¾"	12.50	18.75	25.00
(BV 3) Ambulance No. 50, 4¾" long.	15.00	22.50	30.00	(BV 13) Beer Truck No. 377, with barrels	14	21	28
(BV 4) No. 151 Army Truck with Gun, 2¾" long	12	18	24	(BV 14) Bus, futuristic, "Made in U.S.A."	10	15	20
(BV 5) Anti-aircraft gun vehicle, 2½" long, post WW II, black rubber tires	6	9	12	(BV 15) Cannon Car, 3¼" long, gunner low	5.50	8.75	11.00
(BV 6) Armored car, circa 1937, two protruding weapons	7.00	10.50	14.00	(BV 16) No. 198, Anti-Aircraft Gun Truck, in 1931 Barclay catalog, 3-1/8" long	6.50	9.75	13.00
(BV 7) No. 197 Army tank truck, circa 1935-36	8	12	16	(BV 17) Cannon Car, 3¼" long, slight casting differences from headlight version	6	9	12
(BV 8) Army Car with two silver bullhorns, approx. 2½" long	10	15	20	(BV 18) Cannon Car, battery-powered headlight, 3½" long	40	60	80
(BV 9) Army Tractor (Minneapolis-Moline "Jeep"), 2¾" long	7.50	11.25	15.00	(BV 19) No. 48 Anti-Aircraft Gun Truck, 4" long	20	30	40
(BV 10) Austin Coupe, circa 1931, 2" long, No. 43	22.50	33.75	45.00				

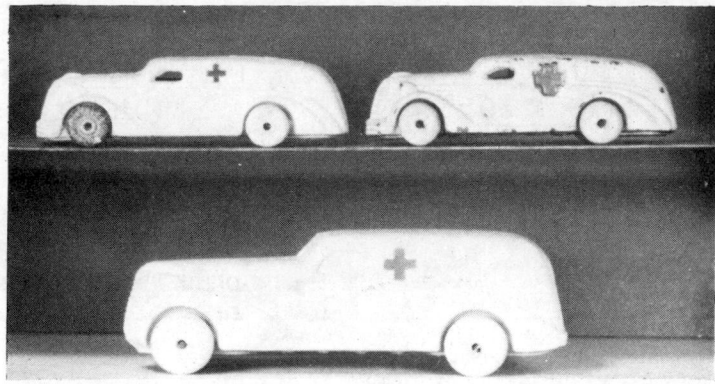

Top, L to R: BARCLAY BV1, BV2. Bottom BV3.
Photo by Ed Poole.

BARCLAY, top, L to R: BV 60; BV 63; BV 25; BV 28; BV 71;
    bottom, L to R: BV 37; BV 61; BV 55; BV 24.
Photo by Bill Kaufman. Courtesy George Buhler.

BARCLAY, L to R; BV 64; BV 72; BV 40.
Photo by Bill Kaufman. Courtesy Evelyn Besser.

BARCLAY, L to R: BV 54, BV 30, BV 81.
Photo by Bill Kaufman. Courtesy Evelyn Besser.

BARCLAY L to R, top: BV 11; BV 49; BV 14; BV 13.
    Bottom, L to R: BV 82; sedan for BV 61 set; BV 47.
Photo by Bill Kaufman. Courtesy George Buhler.

BARCLAY, L to R: BV 65; BV 52.
Photo by Bill Kaufman. Courtesy Evelyn Besser.

BARCLAY, L to R: BV 80; BV 10; BV 26; BV 59.
Photo by Bill Kaufman. Courtesy Evelyn Besser.

BARCLAY: Top, L to R: BV 15; BV 6; BV 4; BV 9.
    Middle, L to R: BV 56; BV 19; BV 20.
    Bottom, L to R: BV 16; BV 18; BV 17.
Photo by Ed Poole

BARCLAY, top, L to R: BV57, BV 21 (cannon missing), BV 39.
    Middle, L to R; BV67, BV66, BV70.
    Bottom, L to R: BV 68, BV 5, BV 69, cannon 4" long, Post WWII.
Photo by Ed Poole

BARCLAY, top row, L to R: Howitzer, 4 wheels, loop hitch horozontal,
Howitzer, 4 wheels, loop hitch vertical; BV 78 with wire hitch; BV 78 with
peg hitch.
    Bottom row, L to R: BV 7; BV 76, wire hitch; BV 76, no hitch.
Photo by Ed Poole.

BARCLAY, L to R: BV 32; BV 33, BV 41.
Photo by Bill Kaufman. Courtesy Evelyn Besser.

In 1984, 45 plaster castings retained by Barclay's chief of maintenance when he cleaned out the shut-down factory in 1971 were shown to the author in the course of his research. Included were soldiers, Disney figures, vehicles and an autogiro, many never produced. Some of the toys in this photo may now identify previously unmarked vehicles as being made by Barclay.

	C6	C8	C10
(BV 20) **No. 48, Anti-Aircraft Gun Truck,** 4"long	7.50	11.25	15.00
(BV 21) Cannon Truck, 4" long, with moveable cannon	12.50	18.75	25.00
(BV 22) Cannon Truck, more streamlined version	9.00	13.50	18.00
(BV 23) Chrysler Airflow, 4" long, circa 1936	10	15	20
(BV 24) "Coast to Coast" diecast bus, "Barclay Toy," two-piece, **No. 405**	37.50	56.25	75.00
(BV 25) Coupe, 1930s, "Made in U.S.A."	10	15	20
(BV 26) Coupe, approx. 2½" long, slush lead, circa 1935, XXX	10	15	20
(BV 27) Coupe, 1934, 4¼" long, XXX	40	60	80
(BV 28) Coupe, 2-piece, 1930s, "Barclay Toy"	32.50	48.75	65.00
(BV 29) (Unused)			
(BV 30) Coupe, 1934, 4¼" long, XXX	40	60	80
(BV 31) **No. 40 Cord Front Drive Coupe, circa 1931, 3-5/8" long**	**12.50**	**18.75**	**25.00**
(BV 32) No. 302, Streamline Car, circa 1936	10	15	20
(BV 33) "Delivery" Truck, **No. 309,** 2-7/8"long, XXX	9.00	13.50	18.00
(BV 34) Double Decker Bus, 4"	15.00	22.50	30.00
(BV 35) **Double Transport Set No. 440,** four cars on upper and lower racks, 1960s, hinged for unloading	12.50	18.75	25.00
(BV 36) Esso Gas Truck, approx. 6" long	10	15	20
(BV 37) "Express" stake truck, 1930s	10	15	20
(BV 38) Fire Engine No. 390?, moveable ladder, circa 1950s	7.50	11.25	15.00
(BV 39) Field Kitchen, 2" long	10	15	20
(BV 40) Fire Engine, approx. 2¾" long, 2 firemen, black metal wheels, 1930s, **No. 41,** 2- 1/16"	7.50	11.25	15.00
(BV 40A) **No. 46** Wrecker, 3½" circa 1931	15.00	22.50	30.00
(BV 41) Fire Engine, 4" long, French-looking (Barclay often copied foreign toys), XXX	12.50	18.75	25.00
(BV 42) Ford, 1931, 2¼"	10	15	20
(BV 43) "Golden Arrow Racer", approx 4½" long, slush lead, X?X	12.50	18.75	25.00
(BV 44) Mack Pick Up Truck, 3½"	12.50	18.75	25.00

BV45
Courtesy Toy Soldier Review

BV83
Photo by Ed Poole

	C6	C8	C10
(BV 45) Milk Truck **No. 377** with cans	15.00	22.50	30.00
(BV 46) Motorcycle with flat rider, full-dimensioned sidecar, **No. 55,** 2¾"	12	18	24
(BV 47) "Oil-Fuel" truck, **No. 308,** circa 1936	7.50	11.25	15.00
(BV 48) "Parcel Delivery", approx. 3-5/8" long, slush lead, **No. 45** circa 1931	15.00	22.50	30.00
(BV 49) Police Car **No. 317,** slush mold, approx. 3¾" long, circa 1930s	17.50	26.25	35.00
(BV 49A) Police Car **No. 317,** diecast	12.50	18.75	25.00
(BV 50) Race Car, 3"	10	15	20
(BV 51) Racer, 5½"	14	21	28
(BV 52) Racer, closed cockpit, approx. 7" long, circa 1939, slush lead	12.50	18.75	25.00
(BV 53) Racer, **No. 53,** early slush lead, 1920s-30s	10	15	20
(BV 54) Racer, two passengers, approx. 4¼" long, XXX	12.50	18.75	25.00
(BV 55) Racer with tail fin, "Made In U.S.A."	12.50	18.75	25.00

	C6	C8	C10
(BV 56) Renault Tank, circa 1938, **No. 47**	12.50	18.75	25.00
(BV 57) Searchlight Truck, white rubber tires, circa 1940	12.50	18.75	25.00
(BV 57A) Searchlight Truck, second version	20	30	40
(BV 58) Sedan, 4 door, approx. 5" long, maybe Chrysler, circa 1936	12.50	18.75	25.00
(BV 59) Sedan, two door, approx. 3-1/8" long, rubber wheels, slush lead, circa 1935, XX	12.50	18.75	25.00
(BV 60) Sedan, two-piece, **No. 401** 2-door, 1930s, "Barclay Toy", diecast	32.50	48.75	65.00
(BV 61) Sedan and "Tourist Trailer", Made in U.S.A.," 1930s	17.50	26.25	35.00
(BV 62) Silver Arrow Race Car, 5½".	11.00	16.50	22.00
(BV 63) Station Wagon, **No. 404,** diecast, 1930s, 2-piece, "Barclay Toy", approx. 3"	35.00	52.50	70.00
(BV 64) Steam-Roller, 3¼" long, traction type, slush lead with tin roof, **No. 44,** (Circa 1931)	15.00	22.50	30.00
(BV 65) **No. 363 Large Streamline Racer,** approx. 6¾" long, in 1935 catalog	12.50	18.75	25.00
(BV 66) Tank "4562", one man in turret, 3¾" long	17.00	25.50	34.00
(BV 67) Tank "4562", two men in turret, 3¾" long	17.00	25.50	34.00
(BV 68) Tank T41, 4¼" long	11.00	16.50	22.00
(BV 69) Tank, 2½" long, man in turret	11.00	16.50	22.00
(BV 70) Tank 2¼" long (based on US M2 light tank)	8	12	16
(BV 71) Taxi, 3¼" long, circa 1940s, slush	7.50	11.25	15.00
(BV 72) Tractor, approx. 2½" long, caterpillar type, slush lead, XX	17.50	26.25	35.00
(BV 73) Tractor, circa 1940	10	15	20
(BV 74) Trailer Truck variously "Railway Express", or with Moving Company name, circa 1950s	5.00	7.50	10.00
(BV 75) **Transport Set No. 330,** 2 cars, 1960s	17.50	26.25	35.00
(BV 76) **No. 204 U.S. Army Truck,** 2½" long, slush lead	6	9	12
(BV 77) "U.S. Army" truck, white rubber tires	8	12	16
(BV 78) Truck "U.S. Motor Unit", circa 1940, white rubber tires	8	12	16
(BV 79) Wheel-A-Rific speedway track, two lead racers, black rubber wheels, 10' of plastic track, sold for $1.00 circa 1970	5.00	7.50	10.00
(BV 80) Wrecker, approx. 3¾" long, circa 1935, slush lead, XX	17.50	26.25	35.00
(BV 81) Wrecker, 4½" long, circa 1934, XXX	17.50	26.25	35.00

	C6	C8	C10
(BV 82) Wrecker, two-piece, **No. 403,** diecast 1930s, "Barclay Toy"	37.50	56.25	75.00
(BV 83) Cannon Truck, moveable cannon, 4" long	37.50	56.25	75.00
(BV 84) Milk truck in shape of bottle, **No. 567**	40	60	80

BV85

	C6	C8	C10
(BV 85) "Milk" truck (closed top), 5" long, bottle on side	12.50	18.75	25.00
(BV 86) Officer's car (small) with megaphone on top	22	33	44
(BV 87) Side dump	2	3	4
(BV 88) Convertible with vacationers.	15.00	22.50	30.00
(BV 89) **100/4 Build & Paint Auto Set,** 6 vehicles, parts, paints, 1930s	No Price Found		
(BV 89A) No. 5004 Build and Paint Auto Set, circa 1934	No Price Found		

BV90   another view, showing from L to R: BV140, BV145, BV144a
Courtesy Roger Sanders

	C6	C8	C10
(BV 90) **2004 Build & Paint Set,** truck, coupe, sedan, parts, paints, early	No Price Found		
(BV 91) "U.S. Mail" truck, 1960s	4	6	8
(BV 92) Moving Truck, circa 1960s	4	6	8
(BV 93) Log Truck, circa 1960s	4	6	8
(BV 94) Dump Truck, circa 1960s	4	6	8
(BV 95) Racing Car, circa 1968	3.00	4.50	6.00
(BV 96) "Police" car (like BV86 and BV97)	4	6	8
(BV 97) "Chief" police car (like BC86 and BV96)	4	6	8

BV91
Courtesy Toy Soldier Review

BV92   BV92   BV94   BV87
Courtesy Toy Soldier Review

BV95   BV96   BV97   **BV98**
Courtesy Toy Soldier Review

BV99   BV100   BV101   BV102
Courtesy Toy Soldier Review

BV103   BV104   BV105   BV106
Courtesy Toy Soldier Review

BV107
Courtesy Toy Soldier Review

	C6	C8	C10
(BV 102) Volkswagen, 1960s........	3.00	4.50	6.00
(BV 103) U.S. Army truck, circa 1968	6.	9	12
(BV 104) Hospital Truck, circa 1968..	6	9	12
(BV 105) Army truck, open bed, circa 1968....................	6	9	12
(BV 106) Army oil truck, circa 1968..	6	9	12
(BV 107) Double transport truck, circa 1968....................	15.00	22.50	30.00
(BV 108) Two-door sedan, 1960s.....	3.00	4.50	6.00
(BV 109) **No. 203 Tractor**..........	11.00	16.50	22.00
(BV 110) Open coupe with driver in cap, early 30s................	10	15	20
(BV 111) "Esso Gas" truck, 1930s, large.....................	7.50	11.25	15.00
(BV 112) **No. 361 Streamline Large Coupe**....................	12.50	18.75	25.00
(BV 113) 1935 DeSoto Airflow, large.	12.50	18.75	25.00
(BV 114) Car Carrier, two small cars, early 1930s................	20	30	40
(BV 115) **No. 371 Racing Car**, large, 1930s.....................	15.00	22.50	30.00
(BV 116) **No. 7 Tractor**, circa late 20s-early 30s.................	12.50	18.75	25.00
(BV 117) **No. 1105 (or 1705)** "Towing Service" truck, large...........	17.50	26.25	35.00
(BV 118) 1929 Buick Sedan?, 3".....	10	15	20
(BV 119) **No. 312** "Towing" truck, in 1936 catalog................	15.00	22.50	30.00
(BV 120) **No. 306 Racer**, in 1936 catalog.....................	11.00	16.50	22.00
(BV 121) **No. 303 Steamline Racer**...	10	15	20
(BV 122) **No. 208 Hook and Ladder**, in 1935 catalog................	14	21	28
(BV 123) **No. 301 Coupe Streamline**..	7.50	11.25	15.00
(BV 124) **No. 207 Stake Truck**, in 1935 catalog................	15.00	22.50	30.00
(BV 125) **No. 362 Streamline Sedan Large**, in 1935 catalog.........	12.50	18.75	25.00
(BV 126) **No. 368 Fire Truck**, 1930s..	12.50	18.75	25.00
(BV 127) **No. 1703** 1935 Chrysler Airflow sedan, large...........	15.00	22.50	30.00
(BV 128) **No. 42** small tractor, in 1931 magazine, 2-3/16" long........	10	15	20
(BV 129) **No. 39 New Imperial Chrysler Coupe**, circa 1931......	11.00	16.50	22.00
(BV 130) **No. 5 Racer**, in 1931 magazine, Golden Arrow........	12.50	18.75	25.00

	C6	C8	C10
(BV 98) Vintage Car..............	3.00	4.50	6.00
(BV 99) Oil Truck, circa 1960s......	4	6	8
(BV 100) Pepsi-Cola truck, 1960s.....	5,00	7.50	10.00
(BV 101) Racing car, circa 1968, no fenders.....................	3.00	4.50	6.00

	C6	C8	C10
(BV 131) No. 206 Delivery Truck "Bakery Fine Cake Pies", circa 1934	13.00	19.50	26.00
(BV 132) **No. 51** Coupe, circa 1931, 2-3/16" long	10	15	20
(BV 133) **No. 210** Fire Truck, circa 1934	11.00	16.50	22.00
(BV 134) **No. 209 Fire Engine,** circa 1934	12.50	18.75	25.00
(BV 135) **No. 311** Sedan, circa 1936	11.00	16.50	22.00
(BV 136) **No. 309** "Delivery" truck, circa 1936	11.00	16.50	22.00
(BV 137) **No. 50** Fire Truck, circa 1931, 2¼" long	10	15	20
(BV 138) **No. 56** Double-Decker Bus, circa 1931	20	30	40
(BV 139) **No. 58** Auburn Speedster, circa 1931	15.00	22.50	30.00
(BV 140) Sedan, circa 1934	15.00	22.50	30.00

	C6	C8	C10
(BV 141) **No. 205 Tow Car,** in 1935 catalog	17.50	26.25	35.00
(BV 142) **No. 338 Contractor Set,** tractor, two hoppers, 1930s	No Price Found		
(BV 143) Large Streamline Coupe, 1930s	12.50	18.75	25.00
(BV 144) "Gasoline" Truck, small, circa 1931, 2¼" long	11.00	16.50	22.00
(BV 144A) Gas Truck, circa 1935, 200 series?	15.00	22.50	30.00
(BV 145) Coupe, cast rear tire, circa 1935, 200 series?	17.50	26.25	35.00
(BV 146) Coupe, removable spare tire, large, in 1935 catalog	25.00	37.50	50.00
(BV 147) Dump Truck, spring action, ratchet, in 1935 catalog, 4¼" long	20	30	40
(BV 148) Sport Coupe, 3" long, removable spare tire, in 1935 catalog	25.00	37.50	50.00
(BV 149) Racing Car, large, raised exhaust pipe, driver, in 1935 catalog	15.00	22.50	30.00

BV108
Courtesy Toy Soldier Review

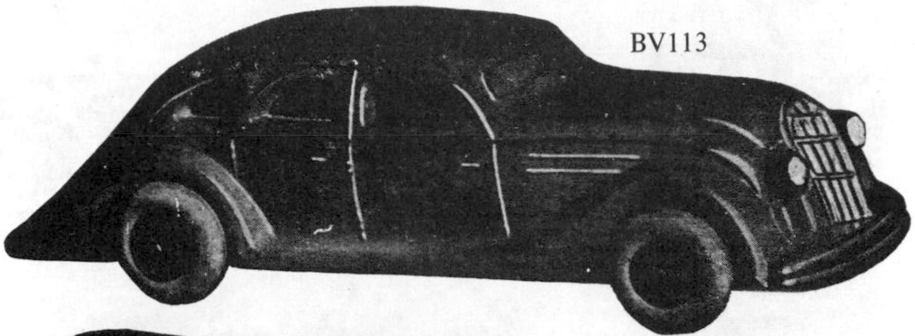

BV109

BV116

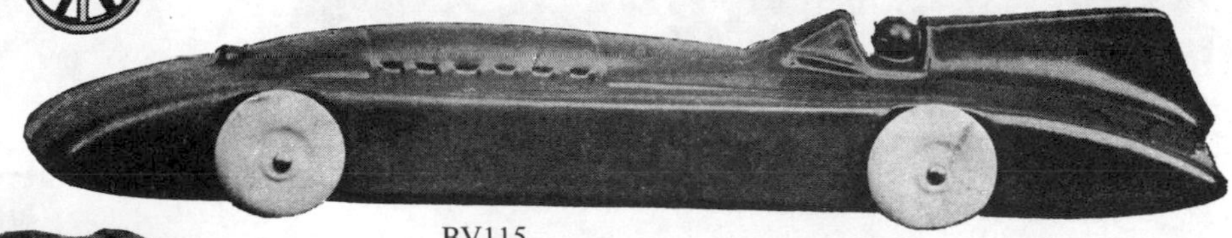

BV111

BV112

BV113

BV114

BV115

BV119

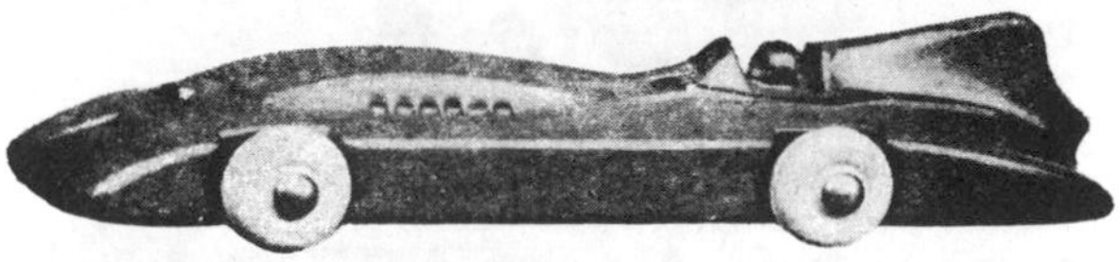

BV120

BV121

BV135

BV122

BV136

BV138

BV123

BV139

BV141

BV124

BV142

BV129

BV130

BV143

BV131

BV132

BV133

BV144

BV144a

BV134

BARCLAY, L to R: BV148, BV147
Photo by Fred Maxwell

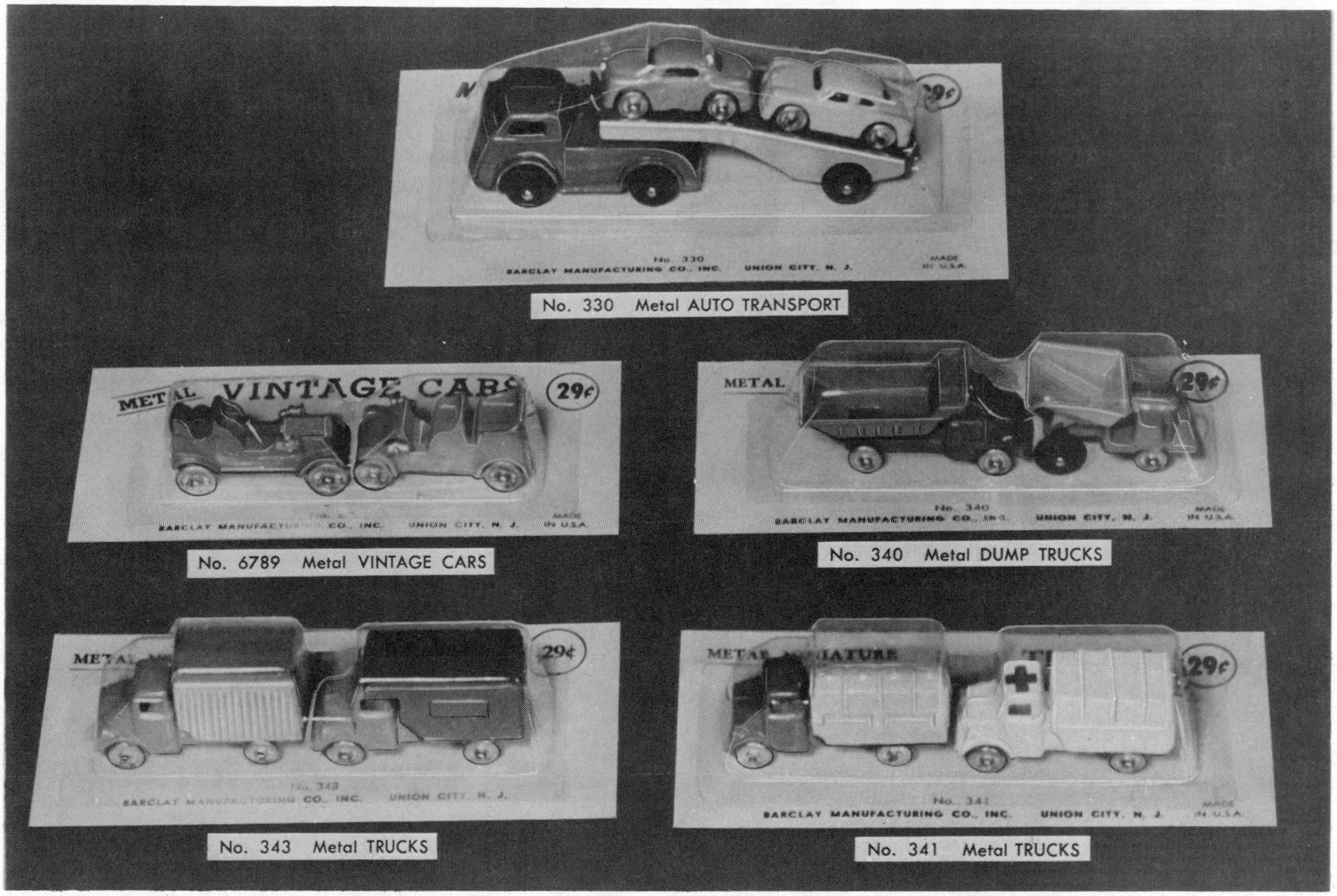

No. 330 Metal AUTO TRANSPORT

No. 6789 Metal VINTAGE CARS

No. 340 Metal DUMP TRUCKS

No. 343 Metal TRUCKS

No. 341 Metal TRUCKS

BARCLAY blister pack sets, circa 1968. **The No. 330 Auto Transport (BV75) is worth about $35 in mint. The others are worth about $20 in mint.**
Courtesy Toy Soldier Review

BARCLAY'S trucks in "Bottle" blister packs sell for about $15 in mint. Photo from the Barclay files.
Courtesy Toy Soldier Review

325 TRAILER TRUCK

339 MINIATURE AUTOS

349 MINIATURE FOREIGN CARS

347 SPORTS CARS

BARCLAY blister pack vehicles, circa 1968. Value is about $15 in mint, except for the No. 339 pack of seven autos, which would go for about $30 in mint. Photo from the Barclay files.   Courtesy Toy Soldier Review

BV79   Courtesy Toy Soldier Review

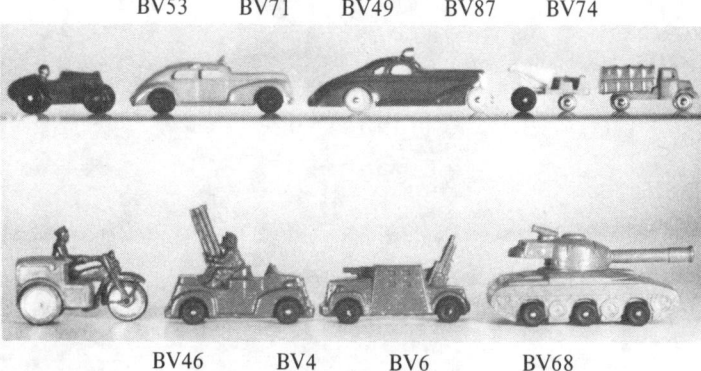

BV53   BV71   BV49   BV87   BV74

BV46   BV4   BV6   BV68

BV31   BV48   BV43

24

BARR RUBBER

Barr Rubber was located in Sandusky, Ohio. The following list, with its codings, was compiled by Dave Leopard. Vehicles are broken down by type.

BARR BA01
Photo by Dave Leopard

RUBBER TOY CARS

Miniature reproductions in molded rubber of the famous V-8 in four different models. Tiny details such as door handles, radiator grills, etc., are all skillfully reproduced. Wheels are sturdily mounted on plated hubs; colors are varied; and finishes are sparkling and non-cracking. Due to their rubber construction, these beautiful little cars cannot harm the child or mar the furniture.

Write for samples and literature.

WORLD'S LARGEST MANUFACTURER OF TOY BALLOONS
The **BARR RUBBER PRODUCTS CO.** SANDUSKY OHIO

BARR RUBBER ad from the November 1935 Playthings magazine
Courtesy Playthings

	C6	C8	C10
BA01 '35 Ford Coupe, 4" long......	10	15	20
BA02 '35 Ford 2 door slantback sedan, 4" long......................	10	15	20
BT01 '35 Ford Stake Body Truck, 4 ¾" long......................	15	20	25
BT02 '35 Ford Panel Truck/Ambulance, 4¼" long.............	15	20	25

BEAUT MFG. CO.

Beaut Mfg. Co., North Bergen, New Jersey, was founded in 1946 by Eugene Buhler and Irving Reader, former machinist and salesman, respectively, for Barclay Mfg. Co. The company put out five toys: a taxicab, a police car, a fire engine, a sedan and a child's wagon. The company was successful at first, employing ten people, and selling to Woolworth's and many overseas buyers. It ceased its toy-making activities (it continued until 1982 as a general machine shop) around 1950, because of competition from plastic toys.

BEAUT "Police" car (left) and "Taxi". Photo by Bill Kaufman. Courtesy George Buhler.

	C6	C8	C10
BEAUT Fire Engine...............	7.50	11.25	15.00
BEAUT "Police" car, approx. 3¾"...	7.50	11.25	15.00
BEAUT Sedan, approx. 3¾"........	7.50	11.25	15.00
BEAUT "Taxi", approx. 3¾"........	7.50	11.25	15.00

BEST TOY & NOVELTY FACTORY

By Fred Maxwell and Margaret Rice

Best Toy & Novelty occupied the hot seat in the middle of the 1930's and the Great Depression, as it tried to market a once profitable line of potmetal toys originally molded by Kansas Toy & Novelty – a line still being made today by Eccles Bros. Memories are tricky from this distance and many of the participants are gone, so the exact boundaries defining Best's production between Kansas Toy and Ralstoy are uncertain. Best was a small enterprise operated by John Best, Sr. in Manhattan, Kansas in the heartland of USA. The molding or casting of toys must have seemed a natural sideline to Mr. Best, who was a printer by profession. Although they must have produced at good volume for wholesaling to the dimestores and toy distributors, it was a family-run business thought of as a hobby, according to his daughter, Minnie Best Nelson. Other known personnel were John Best, Jr. and his family. Conrad Morsch was a molder.

Started about 1933, its growth was probably disappointing, for in 1939 it was sold to Ralstoy, a Ralston, Nebraska company. In one sense, the history of Best Toy is a chapter in the story of molds obtained from its betterknown predecessor, Kansas Toy & Novelty Company, which had gone out of business about 1931.

Of great assistance was a donation by Dee Buchanan, a granddaughter of Mrs. Nelson, of a faded copy of a Best Toy brochure. Although this appears to be a prepublication printer's draft catalog, undated, its 42 illustrations are adequate to identify most of the Best and many of the Kansas Toys in collections. With the publication of this edition much of the confusion and hearsay errors of this family of toys can be eliminated. Many thanks to all who helped.

The only other catalog used in this research was a page from Butler Bros. (a distributor), April 1933. This showed five "new" 4 in. toys: No. 75d, No. 76, No. 77, No. 79, and No. 81, probably molded by Best, although No. 75 and No. 81 do not appear in the printer's draft we have. Kansas Toy had produced toys and parts in mold numbers probably up to No. 75.

Best Toy reissues (with mold numbers) can usually be distinguished from K. T. & N. versions if they are equipped with white rubber tires or wheels; or are those higher numbered miniatures of prototype vehicles of the 1930's; or are marked "Made in USA". However, some of the toys such as No. 17, were made with the metal wheels of the Kansas originals. It is also quite possible that some of the Best molds were modified or rebuilt versions of the earlier Kansas molds. The earlier type Best wheels were hard rubber, shapely realistic discs, sometimes painted in two colors. We don't know if this type was inherited from Kansas Toy. The wood hub-rubber balloon tire wheels were probably a Best innovation. The ugly soft rubber white "balloon" wheel, often out-of-scale, was a Best trademark.

We also include a few unnumbered vehicles said by experienced collectors to belong in this family of molds.

(O'Brien: Dee Buchanan, great granddaughter of John Best, has contributed a history in 1988 that may be of interest to readers: "About fifty-five years ago, John Milner Best Sr. and his wife, Roseanna, purchased a company from Kansas Toy and Novelty Company located in Vining, Kansas – actually a suburb of Clifton, Kansas. The Bests owned a newspaper, printing plant and book-bindery in Manhattan, Kansas. They moved the Toy Company to a building in back of their home at 530 Fremont Street, Manhattan, Kansas. The family, in-laws and friends, all worked making the lead cars produced by the Toy Company and were shipping them all over the world. There were also farm implements, tractors, airplanes, buses and trains as well as all types of cars.... One of the Best's grandchildren, Rosemary, remembers the Toy Factory well, as when she was about three years old and was playing about the toy factory, she fell into one of the lead melting pots head-first. Very fortunately the lead was not hot – so she just had a bad bruise on her head, whereas if the lead had been hot and melted it would indeed have been a tragedy.")

	C6	C8	C10		C6	C8	C10
(BE 1) Best **Medium Racer: No. 10,** 3¼", Indy boattail type, 4 cyl. r. side exhaust, driver (See No. 31, No. 67), (also unnumbered version)	No Price Found			(BE 4) Best **Racer****: "26", 4", Strip-down type, long hood, motometer, r. exh., 3 circular 1. louvers, driver (See K. T. & N. No. 33)...	No Price Found		
(BE 2) Best **All Metal Tractor: "17"**, 3", "Fordson" farm type, visible engine, large rear small front wheels with 4 circular openings, driver	No Price Found			(BE 5) Best **Racer: "31"**, 2 1/8", Indy type, 4 cyl., r. exh., driver. HO*** (Popular toy similar to other makers', incl. K. T. & N.) (See No. 10, No. 67)	4	6	8
(BE 3) Best **Country Tank Wagon: No. 20**, 3¼", Truck, Ford (?), 3 tanks, oil & gas	No Price Found			(BE 6) Best **Coupe: "35"**, 2¼". Convertible, '34 Nash?, HO, horiz. louvers, open window, plain grille, rearmount, windshield visor (See different K. T. & N. versions & UV)	5.00	7.50	10.00

No. 100 – 4 inches

No. 99 – 4 inches

No. 86 – 4 inches

No. 96 – 3½ inches

No. 91 – 3½ inches

No. 95 – 3½ inches

No. 92 – 3¾ inches

No. 90 – 3½ inches

No. 97 – 4½ inches

No. 85 – 4 inches

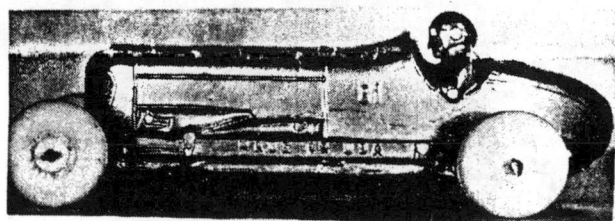

No. 81 – 4½ inches

No. 26 – 4 inches

No. 76 – 4¼ inches

No. 10 – Medium Racer

No. 55 – Truck - Detachable Trailer

No. 46 – Small Racer - 3 inches

No. 47 – Seaplane - 4 inches

No. 78 – Concrete Mixer - 4 inches

No. 43 – Road Roller - 3¼ inches

No. 17 – All Metal Tractor - 3 inches

No. 36 Engine - 4½ inches

No. 39 Oil Tanker - 3¼ inches

No. 41 – Box Car - 3¼ inches

No. 40 – Caboose - 2¾ inches

No. 37 – Pullman Car - 3½ inches

Box from a BEST TOYS Farm Set. All the toys illustrated are from molds believed to have originated with Kansas Toys.
Photo by Perry Eichor   Courtesy Fred Maxwell

	C6	C8	C10
(BE 7) Best **Engine: No. 36**, 4½". Locomotive-Tender, 10 metal wheels, 0-6-4, "K. T. & N. RR 3600"	No Price Found		
(BE 8) Best **Pullman Car:** "37", 3½", "K. T. & N. RR", "Pullman"	No Price Found		
(BE 9) Best **Oil Tanker:** "39", 3¼", "K. T. & N. RR"	No Price Found		
(BE 10) Best **Caboose:** "40", 2¾", "K. T. & N. RR"	No Price Found		
(BE 11) Best **Box Car:** "41", 3¼", "K. T. & N. RR"	No Price Found		
(BE 12) Best **Dump Truck: No. 42**, 3½", "42 diamond" logo. Ford? String pull, open cab, driver. (See K. T. & N. "42" and a new Best '33 International COE "42" with tin dump box)	7	10	15
(BE 13) Best **Road Roller:** "43", 3¼", steam, wooden rollers, driver	15	20	30
(BE 14) Best **Small Racer:** "46", 3", Streamlined record car, 1929 Golden Arrow, large square tail fin, driver, metal wheels	8	12	16
(BE 15) Best **Coach:** "49", 2 3/8", Double-decked 1928 Pickwick "Nite Coach", string pull. (See No. 59)	5.00	7.50	10.00
(BE 16) Best **Pickup:** "51", 2¾", Ford, cab, no windshield. Metal wheels or rubber	5.00	7.50	10.00
(BE 17) Best **Sport Coupe:** "54", 2 3/8". Open, rumble seat roadster, sidemounts, trunk	10	15	20
(BE 18) Best **Truck, Detachable Trailer:** "55", 4". Ford (cab same as No. 51) semi-stake trailer	8	10	16

	C6	C8	C10
(BE 19) Best **Tractor: No. 57**, 1-⅞". Fordson, visible engine, lge. rear wh., driver	No Price Found		
(BE 20) Best **Jillopi:** "58", 2¼". Austin Bantam 2 dr. sedan, "rooster" outline on doors	10	15	20
(BE 21) Best **Large Coach Bus:** "59", 3½". 1929 Pickwick Nite Coach. RDW. (See No. 49)	10	15	20
(BE 22) Best **Racer*:** "67", 1 5/8". Midget, 4 cyl; r. exh, driver HO (See No. 10, No. 31)	4	6	8
(BE 23) Best **Fire Engine:** "70", 2¼". Seagrave (?) steam pumper, driver .	7	10	15
(BE 24) Best **Engine: No. 71**, 2½". Steam tractor, Case, lge. r. wh., two drivers. (See No. 25)	No Price Found		
(BE 25) Best? **Tank*:** "74", 2 1/8". "U. S. Army", 2 gun turret. May be new toy	5.00	7.50	10.00
(BE 26) Best? **Coupe*: No. 75a**, 4¼" in 1933 catalog. '33 Duesenberg (?), WHRT	15.00	22.50	30.00
(BE 27) Best? **Sedan*: No. 75b**, 4". 2 dr. (may be same as above)	No Price Found		
(BE 28) Best? **Coupe*: No. 75c**, 3½" Desoto (?)	No Price Found		
(BE 29) Best **Racer**:** "76", 4¼". Auburn speedster, oval fin, string pull, driver, WHRT or RDW, in 1933 catalog	15.00	22.50	30.00
(BE 30) Best **Large Sport Coupe:** "77", 4". '30 Duesenberg roadster, top and windshield down, WHRT, in 1933 catalog	15.00	22.50	30.00
(BE 31) Best **Concrete Mixer;** "78", 4". Truck w/tank, mixer, WHRT. (Sometimes called a fuel tanker) . .	12	18	25

29

	C6	C8	C10		C6	C8	C10
(BE 32) Best **Sedan with spare tire:** "79", 4¼". 5 rubber tires, WHRT, in 1933 catalog	15.00	22.50	30.00	(BE 49) Best Coupe**: **No. 96,** 3½". Cadillac? Not produced? See remarks No. 93	No Price Found		
(BE 33) Best? Coupe*: "80", 3½". Chrysler? Packard? RDW	20	30	40	(BE 50) Best Record Car**: "97", 4½". '35 Bluebird No. 5, V-12, triangular fin, driver, RDW	15.00	22.50	30.00
(BE 34) Best Racer**: "81", 4½". Miller FWD, 8 cyl., r. exh., WHRT, driver, in 1933 catalog	12	18	25	(BE 51) Best? Coupe: No. 98, ?". Hupmobile?	No Price Found		
(BE 35) Best? Sedan: **No. 82,** 4". Streamlined	No Price Found			(BE 52) Best Coupe**: **No. 99,** 4". Streamlined '35 Chevy or '37 Stude? Rearmount	No Price Found		
(BE 36) Best? Racer*: "83", 4½". R. side exh., driver, Indy type	No Price Found			(BE 53) Best Sedan**: "100", 4". Roomy 2 dr. '36 Pontiac, HO, trunk	No Price Found		
(BE 37) Best? Sedan*: "84", 3 5/8". DeSoto airflow, 4 dr., RDW, HO	No Price Found			(BE 54) Best Cab Unit: **No. 101,** Oil Transport (semi): No. 102. Total 6¾". "Gasoline", International K-line?, sleeper cab, HO, slanted grille	15.00	22.50	30.00
(BE 38) Best Record Car**: "85", 4". Streamlined, square fin, 12 ports, driver, WHRT	12	18	25				
(BE 39) Best Sedan**: "86", 4". Fastback Olds?, Lincoln?, rear wheel skirts	No Price Found			Big Bang carbide armored car, cast iron, 9½" long	100	150	200
(BE 40) Best? Sedan: **No. 87,** ?". Brewster-like, similar No. 92 but data poor	No Price Found			Big Bang motor tank, 9" long, circa 1933	60	90	120
(BE 41) Best Sedan**: "90", 3½". Airflow, no grille pattern but center trim	12	18	25	Big Boy Fire Hook and Ladder, 38" long. (Kelmet)	750	1125	1500
(BE 42) Best Sedan**: "91" 3½". 2 dr. Cadillac? airflow, high style V grille behind fenders which are horiz. fairings	No Price Found			Boattail Speedster, cast iron, 5" long, blue with nickel wheels, driver, circa 1920s	100	150	200
(BE 43) Best Coupe**: "92", 3¾". Chopped top, Brewster-like heart-shaped grille, long streamlined front fenders. HO	12	18	25				
(BE 44) Best Coupe*: "93", 3 5/8". Cadillac?, streamlined, same front end as No. 91, RDW. Same toy as No. 96, Best "catalog"	No Price Found						
(BE 45) Best? Sedan*: "94", 4½". Fastback 2 dr., taxi light on roof. (Same car as No. 95)	No Price Found						
(BE 46) Best Sedan**: **No. 95,** 3½". Airflow 2 dr., no grille but spotlight in center, shallow airflow trunk. Chrysler-Briggs 1933 dream car?	No Price Found						
(BE 47) Best? Sedan*: "95b", 3½". Same as above, but "Police Dept." in shield on doors. Or is it a siren on grille?	No Price Found						
(BE 48) Best? Sedan*: **No. 95c,** 3½". Another version, "Police" painted on top	No Price Found						

The top of a BEST TOYS set. The drawings on the boxtop offer good representations of BEST vehicles and cannon. All or most of the toys shown appear to have originated with Kansas Toy & Novelty.
Courtesy Margaret Rice and Fred Maxwell

Footnotes:
* Not shown in Best Toy draft "catalog", but have Best characteristics; we have no evidence linking them to Ralstoy.
**Shown but not named in Best "catalog".
***Abbreviations used: HO – hood ornament, RDW – realistic rubber disc wheels; WHRT – wood hubs, rubber tires.

BUDDY "L"

BUDDY "L": Buddy "L" toys were first manufactured by the Moline Pressed Steel Company, Moline, Illinois, in 1921, and were named after the son of the owner, Fred Lundahl. Lundahl had started the company about eight years earlier, manufacturing auto and truck parts (fenders, etc.). The toys were originally made as special items for his son, but as Buddy Lundahl's playmates began to clamor for similar toys of their own and their fathers began asking Lundahl senior to make duplicate toys for their sons, Lundahl went into the toy business. Buddy "L" toys were large, typically 21 to 24 or more inches long for trucks and fire engines. Construction was of very heavy steel, strong enough to support a man's weight. These were made until the early 1930s, when the line was modified and lighterweight materials were employed. Before this time, Fred Lundahl had died, having already lost control of the company. The company has changed names several times, being known as the Buddy "L" Corp., Buddy "L" Toy Co., etc., in recent years dropping the quotes around the L. Continuing to make toys till the present day, the company even put out a few wooden toys during World War II, when its main plant made nothing but war-related items. The early Buddy "L" trains are also popular, and tend to be worth even more than the vehicles. Buddy "L" material from the pre-1932 period is almost indestructible and as a consequence, 50% of the pieces found are either very rusty or have been repainted at some point. The basic metal seems to hold up forever, but repainting and rust drops the price well below "good".

Following is a list of pre-1932 Buddy "L" toys compiled by Thomas W. Sefton.

	C6	C8	C10		C6	C8	C10
Large Trucks				Buddy L 210B Flivver Coupe 1925-30	750	1125	1500
Buddy L 200 Express Truck 1921-31.	400	750	1100	Buddy L 211 Ford Dump Cart			
Buddy L 201 Dump Truck (Ratchet)				1926-30	850	1200	1700
1921-30	500	750	1000	Buddy L 211A Ford Dump Truck			
Buddy L 201A Hydraulic Dump				1926-30	750	1125	1500
Truck 1926-31	400	675	950	Buddy L 212 Ford Express Truck			
Buddy L 202 Coal Truck 1926-31	650	975	1250	1929-30	750	1250	1800
Buddy L 202A Sand & Gravel Truck				Buddy L 212A One-Ton Ford			
1926-31	850	1150	1450	Delivery Truck 1929-30	600	1100	1850
Buddy L 203 Stake Truck 1921-24,				**Construction Equipment**			
1926-28	650	975	1250	Buddy L 220 Steam Shovel 1921-31	100	200	300
Buddy L 203A Lumber Truck 1925-30	800	1250	1700	Buddy L 220A Heavy Steam Shovel			
Buddy L 203B Baggage Truck				1929-30	500	800	1100
1929-31	300	550	725	Buddy L 220AB Heavy Shovel (on			
Buddy L 204 Moving Van 1924-30	600	950	1400	Treads) 1929-30	450	700	950
Buddy L 204A Railway Express				Buddy L 230 Sand Loader 1925-31	500	750	1000
1926-31	800	1300	2000	Buddy L 240 Small Derrick 1922-31	170.00	262.50	350.00
Buddy L 206, 206B Street Sprinkler				Buddy L 241 Large Derrick 1922-31	350.00	562.50	700.00
Truck 1924-31	650	1350	1950	Buddy L250 Overhead Crane 1924-27	750	1125	1500
Buddy L 206A Oil Truck 1925-30	875	1350	2000	Buddy L 250A Traveling Crane			
Buddy L 207 Ice Truck 1926-31	600	1100	1850	1928-30	750	1125	1500
Buddy L208 Coach 1928-31 (Lt.				Buddy L 260 Pile Driver 1926-28	550	825	1100
Green Motorbus)	550	1050	1800	Buddy L 270 Dredge (Clamshell)			
Buddy L 209 Auto Wrecker 1928-31				1926-30	550	825	1100
(Tow Truck)	800	1150	1500	Buddy L 270A Tractor Dredge (on			
Fire Trucks				Treads) 1929-30	600	900	1200
Buddy L 205 Hook & Ladder 1924-31	450	800	1100	Buddy L 280 Concrete Mixer 1926-30	300	450	700
Buddy L 205A Pumper 1925-30	500	1100	1600	Buddy L 280A Mixer (on Treads)			
Buddy L 205AB (Working) Pumper				1929-31	400	600	800
1930-31	475	825	1450	Buddy L 290 Road Roller 1929-31	1200	1800	2400
Buddy L 205B Aerial Ladder 1926-30	475	850	1450	Buddy L 300 Sand Screener 1929-30	600	900	1200
Buddy L 205C Insurance Patrol				Buddy L 350 Hoisting Tower 1929-31	1000	1500	2000
1926-30	450	800	1000	Buddy L 360 Aerial Tramway			
Buddy L 205D Water Tower Truck				1929-30	1000	1500	2000
(Working) 1930-31	500	950	1500	Buddy L 400 Trencher 1928-31	500	700	1300
				End listing by Thomas W. Sefton			
Model T Series							
Buddy L 210 Flivver Truck 1925-30	650	1150	1650				
Buddy L 210A Flivver Roadster							
1925-27	750	1125	1500				

BUDDY L Coca Cola Truck, wooden.
Courtesy Dick MacNary.

BUDDY L 201A Hydraulic Dump Truck.
Courtesy Mapes Auctioneers & Appraisers.

BUDDY L 205 Hook and Ladder.
Courtesy Mapes Auctioneers & Appraisers.

BUDDY L 220 Steam Shovel
Courtesy Mapes Auctioneers & Appraisers.

No. 230 BUDDY "L" Sand Loader

No. 204-A BUDDY "L" Railway Express Truck

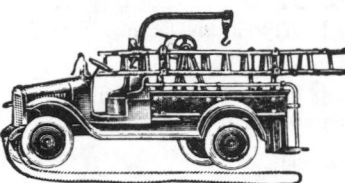

No. 205 BUDDY "L" Fire Truck

No. 207 BUDDY "L" Ice Truck

No. 201-A BUDDY "L" Hydraulic Dump Truck

No. 203-B BUDDY "L" Baggage Truck.

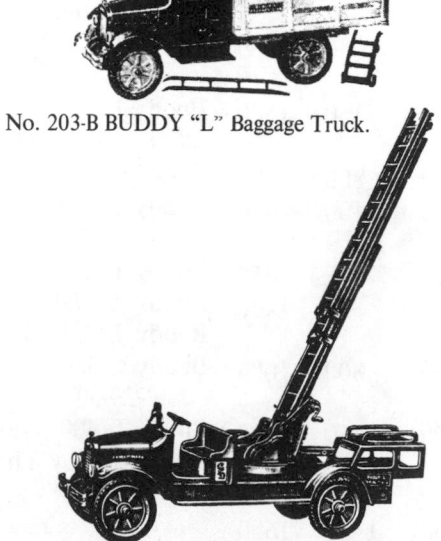

No. 205-B BUDDY "L" Hydraulic Aerial Truck

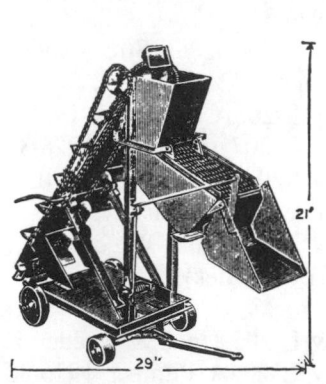

No. 300 BUDDY "L" Sand Screener

No. 205-AB BUDDY "L" Pumping Fire Engine

No. 209 BUDDY "L" Auto Wrecker   No. 220 BUDDY "L" Steam Shovel   No. 2005 Junior BUDDY "L" Steam Shovel

Buddy L 1932 on

	C6	C8	C10
Buddy L "Allied Van Lines" moving van No. 366, 31" long	250	375	500
Buddy L "Army Signal Corps" Truck, 1941-42, 12" long	90	135	180
Buddy L Army Transport, 27" with towed cannon, 6-spoke wheels	100	165	220
Buddy L "Army Truck 21", circa 1940, cloth top	100	150	200
Buddy L Army Truck No. 506, 20½" long	125	195	250
Buddy L Baggage Truck No. 11, 26½" long, 1933	225	385	500
Buddy L Baggage Truck No. 41	65.00	97.50	130.00
Buddy L City Baggage Dray No. 439, 1934, 19" long	100	185	310
Buddy L City Baggage Dray No. 839, 1939, 20¾" long	125.00	187.50	250.00
Buddy L Coca Cola Truck, wooden, 19" long, circa WWII, only 3 known, worth $4200 in mint in 1984.			
Buddy L Concrete Mixer with Truck No. 54, 34½" long, 1937	75	115	150
Buddy L Concrete Mixer No. 832, 1950-51 with Motor Sound, 10¾" long	75	125	175
Buddy L Country Squire Station Wagon, 15" long	70	105	140
Buddy L Dairy Truck No. 2002 (Junior Line), 1930-32, 24" long	240	360	480
Buddy L Dandy Digger No. 33	120	180	240
Buddy L Delivery Truck, Deluxe Rider No. 803, 1945-48, 22¾" long	60	100	145
Buddy L Dump Truck No. 434, 1936	120	195	275
Buddy L Dump Truck No. 634, 20½" long	100	150	200
Buddy L Emergency Auto Wrecker No. 3317	100	150	200
Buddy L Excavator Truck and Shovel Set No. 948, 27½" long, 1940	80	125	175
Buddy L Express Trailer Truck No. 35, 1934	200	300	400
Buddy L Fast Delivery Truck No. 3313	75.00	112.50	150.00
Buddy L Engine No. 29, 1933-34, 25½" long	150	275	450

	C6	C8	C10
Buddy L Greyhound Bus with Bell No. 481, wooden, 18½" long	250	375	500
Buddy L Hose Truck No. 38, 1933, 21¾" long	150	240	325
Buddy L Hook and Ladder Truck No. 859, wooden, 21½" long	75	115	150
Buddy L Hydraulic Aerial Truck No. 27, 1933-34, 40" long with ladders down	150	300	550
Buddy L Hydraulic Dump Truck No. 10, 24¾" long, 1933-34	200	325	450
Buddy L Ice Truck No. 12, 1933-34, 26½" long	175	275	375
Buddy L International Delivery Truck No. 51, 1935, 24½" long	200	300	400
Buddy L Merry-Go-Round Truck	40	60	80
Buddy L Mister Ice Cream Van	24	36	48
Buddy L Repair-It, 24" long	110	165	220
Buddy L Robotoy Dump Truck with driver, operates on remote control	700	1050	1400
Buddy L Sand & Gravel Truck No. 3312	50	75	100
Buddy L Scarab No. 211, no wind-up mechanism	No Price Found		
Buddy L Scarab No. 711, winds up	90	135	180
Buddy L Service Truck, 1953	75.00	112.50	150.00
Buddy L Siren Pull-n-Ride	120	180	240
Buddy L Steam Shovel and International Truck No. 16, 1937, 29½" long, 13½" high	110	165	225
Buddy L Steam Shovel, Mechanical, No.30, 1935, 17½" long, 13½" high	150	245	350
Buddy L Steam Shovel on Treads (Junior Line) No. 2005, 1930-32, 24" long	150	275	400
Buddy L Tank Truck No. 438, 19¼" long, 1935	150	200	250
Buddy L Tank Truck No. 938, 21½" long, 1941	200	325	450
Buddy L "Texaco" tanker, 25" long, promo sold at gas stations	60	90	120
Buddy L Utility Delivery Truck No. 946, 25" long, 1941-42	75	125	155
Buddy L Water Tower No. 28, 1936	800	1250	1800
Buddy L Wrecker No. 13, 31" long, 1933	110	180	300

BUDDY L Delivery Truck, Deluxe Rider No. 803
Courtesy Joe and Sharon Freed

	C6	C8	C10
Buddy L Wrecker No. 37, 1933, 24" long	100	180	300
Buddy L Wrecker No. W37, 25¼" long, 1939	40	60	100
Buddy L Wrecker No. 437, 1934, 24" long	110	180	300
Buddy L Wrecker No. 503, 1940, 19¼" long, 1941-42	60	90	135
Buddy L No.647, 1949, 26¼" long	110	165	200
Buddy L Wrecker No. 813, 1938, 32" long	80	140	200
Buddy L Wrecker, Emergency Towing Rider No. 903, 1949, 33" long	70	115	150
Buddy L Wrecker No. 903, 33" long, 1950, "Buddy L Emergency Towing"	100	160	225
Buddy L Wrecker No. 937, 1939, 25¼" long	80	120	200
Buddy L Wrecker No. 937, 1941-42 version, 25" long	50	95	135
Buddy L "Wrigley's Spearmint" Railway Express Truck No. 835, 25" long, 1938	90	135	180
Buffalo Toys Silver Bullet Racer, 26" long	100	150	200
Bus, 1930s, 15½" long, aluminum	300	450	600
Bus, late 1920s, 23½" long, six side windows	150	225	300
Bus, cast iron, approx. 3½" long, A.C. Williams?	20	30	40
Bus, cast iron, 4" long	20	30	40
Bus, cast iron, 4½" long, five side windows, circa 1928	100	150	200
Bus, cast iron, 4¾" long, circa 1920s	75.00	112.50	150.00
Bus, cast iron, with driver, rubber tires, 13" long	500	750	1000
Bus, double-decker, cast iron, four figures, 8" long	200	300	400
Bus, cast iron, double-decker, 9½" long	400	600	800
"C2 to C Co." semi-trailer, cast iron steel wheels, small	30	45	60

	C6	C8	C10
"C. W. Brand Coffee" Dump Truck, approx. 11¼" long, 1930s (Metalcraft?)	300	450	600
Cabriolet with rumble seat, cast iron, circa 1920s	200	300	400
"Cannonball Express" child's pedal car, red-painted, 37" long	500	750	1000
Car, cast iron, 1½" long, maybe Cracker Jack. Possibly smallest cast iron car	50	75	100
Car, cast iron, 4" long	75.00	112.50	150.00
Car, cast iron, with people, 3" long	35.00	52.50	70.00
Caterpillar tractor, cast iron, red, with driver, chain treads	150	225	300
Century of Progress cast iron Greyhound bus, 11" detachable trailer	175.00	262.50	350.00
Champion Coupe, Reo type, 7½" long	400	600	800
Champion Gas and Motor Oil truck, 8" long, cast iron, circa 1930s	120	180	240
Champion four-casting nickeled radiator car, approx. 4" long	175.00	262.50	350.00
Champion Mack Dump, 7" long, circa 1930s	250	375	500

"Champion" Wrecker, 7½" long.
Courtesy Good Old Days Store   Photo by Bill Kaufman

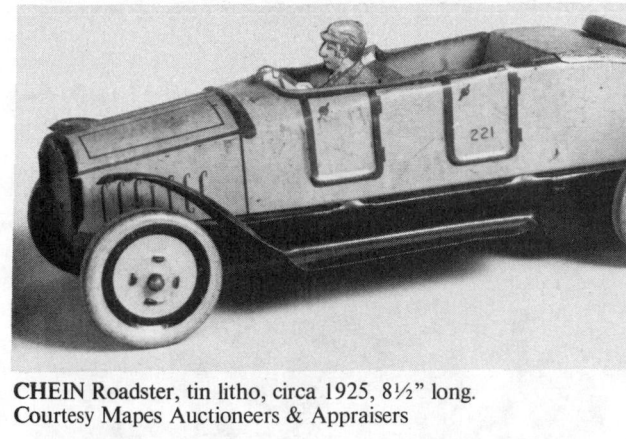

CHEIN Roadster, tin litho, circa 1925, 8½" long.
Courtesy Mapes Auctioneers & Appraisers

"Champion", policeman on motorcycle
Courtesy Mapes Auctioneers & Appraisers

CLEVELAND TOY racer, aluminum, 13" long.
Courtesy Mapes Auctioneers & Appraisers

	C6	C8	C10
Champion Mack Stake Truck, 7½" long	350	525	700
Champion Race car, 6" long, cast iron, detachable driver	100	150	200
Champion Race car, 9" long, circa 1930s	150	225	300
"Champion" motorcycle and rider, 4½" long, cast iron	40	60	80
"Champion" motorcycle, cast iron, circa 1930, 7¼" long, rubber tires on wood hubs	150	225	300
Champion policeman on motorcycle, 7" long, rubber tires	150	225	300
"Champion" Wrecker, 7½" long, cast iron	140	210	280
Checker Cab, circa 1920s, with driver, thin white rubber tires, with rear tire	1000	1500	2000
Chein Army Truck, cannon on back, 8½" long, tin, early	75.00	111.25	150.00
Chein Army Truck, open bed, 8½" long, tin, early	75.00	111.25	150.00

	C6	C8	C10
Chein Hercules Motor Express, tin litho, 19½" long, Mack	400	600	800
Chein "Junior Oil Tank" truck, 8½" long, 1920s	62.50	93.75	125.00
Chein Mack Tanker Truck, 19" long, circa 1928	200	300	400
Chein Roadster, tin litho, circa 1925, 8½" long	300	450	600
Chein "Royal Blue Line Coast to Coast Service"	600	900	1200
Chein Touring car, tin litho, 7" long	250	375	500
Chrysler Airflow, heavy sheet metal with wind-up motor. Tin grill, headlights and bumper, wooden wheels, 4" long	150	225	300
Chrysler Airflow, cast iron, 4½" long, 1930s	40	60	80
Chrysler Airflow, pressed steel, 6" long, circa 1937	50	75	100
Circus Band Wagon, plays record and moves, 17" long, comic musicians on top, circa 1922	1000	1500	2000
"City Fire Dept. Truck", 1930, pressed steel, rubber tires, 26" long	450	675	900
Clark friction auto, produced in 1894, 10½" long, wood, iron and tin	500	750	1000
Clark friction auto, circa 1901, wood body covered with steel	600	900	1200
Cleveland Toy Racer, aluminum, steel wheels, circa 1935, 13" long	175.00	262.50	350.00
Converse Auto with fringe on top, 3-seat, 1905, painted, pressed steel, clockwork, rubber tires	600	900	1200

CLARK friction auto, produced in 1894, 10½" long, wood, iron and tin
Photo by Joe and Sharon Freed

	C6	C8	C10
Converse Fire Engine ladder truck, bell, wooden headlight, 10", 1915	1250	1875	2500
Converse Pick-Up Truck, very early, open cab	500	750	1000
Converse Touring Auto, 1910, pressed steel, canvas roof	900	1350	1800
Convertible, futuristic, 1930s, with large streamlined fenders, black wooden wheels, heavy pressed steel, large size	75.00	112.50	150.00
Cor-Cor Bus	200	300	400
Cor-Cor dump truck, dumps back or side to side, 23" long	300	450	600
Cor-Cor Graham Paige sedan, 20" long, electric	350	525	700
Cor-Cor Van, painted metal, circa 1928, 23" long	175.00	262.50	350.00
Coupe, cast iron, 6" long, 2-piece body	45.00	67.50	90.00
Coupe, tin friction 17½" long	40	60	80
Coupe with rumble seat, tin, 1920s, 5" long	30	45	60
Coupe with rumble seat, possibly Plymouth, circa 1920s, cast iron, 6" long	110	165	220

"City Fire Dept. Truck", 1930, 26" long.
Courtesy Lloyd W. Ralston Auctions

COURTLAND (WALT REACH)
Non- Powered Vehicles
List by Joe and Sharon Freed

400 Courtland Open Van tractor-trailer. L-13", W-3" H-3¼"	15	30	45
500 Courtland Side dump tractor-trailer. L-13", W-3", H-3¼"	16	35	50
600 Courtland Open Van tractor-trailer. L-13", W-3", H-3¼"1946 retail price 49 cents	15	30	45

CONVERSE Auto with fringe top, 3-seat, 10½" long.
Courtesy Lloyd W. Ralston Auctions

COURTLAND Non-Powered Vehicle No. 610 side dump tractor-trailer
Photo courtesy Joe and Sharon Freed

610 Courtland Side dump tractor-trailer. L-13", W-3", H-3¼", 1946 retail price 49 cents	20	35	50
620 Courtland Log Truck tractor-trailer. L-13", W-3", H-3¼", 1946 retail price 59 cents	25	40	55

Auto with house trailer, late 30s, cast iron 13½".
Courtesy Lloyd W. Ralston Auctions

COURTLAND Non-Powered Vehicles, L to R: No. 900 Fire Patrol truck,
No. 900 Moving and Storage truck
Courtesy Joe and Sharon Freed

COURTLAND Friction-Powered vehicle. No. 4000 Woody sedan
Courtesy Joe and Sharon Freed

COURTLAND (WALT REACH)
Friction-Powered Vehicles
List by Joe and Sharon Freed

	C6	C8	C10
3875 Courtland Mechanical "Gulf" Gasoline tractor-trailer. L-13", W-3", H-3¼"	50	70	100
4000 Courtland Woody Sedan. L-7¼", W-3¼", H-2¾"	25	35	45
4000 Courtland Woody Sedan. L-7¼", W-3¼", H-2¾", Note: This is one of only four Courtland styled toys stamped "A Walt Reach Toy by Courtland Toy Co. Phila. Pa. Made in U.S.A." The only known Courtland styled toys marked with the Courtland Toy Company, Philadelphia stamping is this No. 4000 sedan, a non-powered "Fire Chief" car, a private garage similar to No. 9075 and a mechanical parking meter bank	50	75	100
4060 Courtland Space Rocket Patrol Car. L-7¼", W-3¼", H-2¾", 1952 retail price 98 cents	75	100	135
7500 Courtland Mechanical State Police Car with siren. L-7¼", W-3¼", H-2¾"	25	35	45
7500 Courtland Mechanical Fire Chief Car with siren. L-7¼", W-3¼", H-2¾"	25	35	45
7600 Courtland FBI Riot Squad Car. L-7¼", W-3¼", H-2¾"	40	50	60
XXXX Courtland "Pop-Up" Ladder Fire Truck. L-13", W-3", H-3¼"	45	60	80
XXXX Courtland Mechanical Military Gun Car. L-7½", W-3¼", H-2½"	50	75	100

	C6	C8	C10
700 Courtland Side dump tractor-trailer. L-13", W-3", H-3¼", 1946 retail price 49 cents	15	30	45
900 Courtland Ice Cream Truck. L-9", W-3", H-2¾" 1946 retail price 39 cents	45	60	75
900 Courtland Moving and Storage Truck. L-9", W-3", H-2¾", 1946 retail price 39 cents	50	70	85
900 Courtland Fire Patrol No. 2 Truck, L-9", W-3", H-2¾", 1946 retail price 39 cents	45	60	75
900 Courtland Express and Hauling Truck. L-9", W-3", H-2¾", 1946 retail price 39 cents	45	60	75
1050 Courtland Logging Camp Train Set. L-26¾", W-3", H-3¼", 1946 retail price $1.79	No Price Found		
1060 Courtland Trailer Truck Parade. L-13", W-3", H-3¼", 1946 retail price $1.79	No Price Found		
1070 Courtland Big 4 Truck Parade. The four 900 L-9½", W-3¼", H-3", 1946 retail price $1.79	No Price Found		
1200 Courtland Side Dump tractor-trailer. L-13", W-3", H-3¼"	20	35	50
Courtland tractor-trailer. Same tractor as No. 2000 except marked, "Loft-Fresh Candies." however, it is unknown what type trailer as only the tractor has been located. No reference to Courtland or Walt Reach Toys but unquestionably a Courtland	No Price Found		

CRAFTOY

By Ron Eccles and Fred Maxwell

CRAFTOY, a small Omaha, Nebraska firm, had a brief career producing potmetal toys. Since it presumably got started on slush molds obtained from the faltering Ralstoy Co. about 1940, it is not certain whether they commenced operation then or after World War II. Whichever era, the war's need for lead was no doubt decisive. The surviving molds are now owned by Eccles Brothers (see Leading Collectors and Dealers).

On a surviving Craftoy sales sheet we spot reissues of Best, Kansas and Ralstoy as well as new issues. Because our information on Best Toys is much more authoritative than on Ralstoy, it is not certain whether Ralstoy or Craftoy made the "new" molds of the listing below. The farm tractor no. 17 and the freight train no. 3600 (except the stock car) show Kansas and Best ancestry. The tractor of the no. 102 semi is the same as Ralstoy's; it is not the Best version, although the gasoline semi-trailer is the same as Best no. 102. All the Craftoys in the company's sheets have black rubber tires. Bold words are Craftoys' own description. Words in quotes appear on the toys.

	C6	C8	C10
Craftoy Tractor: "17", 2½". "Fordson", "Made in USA" farm tractor, rear wheels larger. Driver (See Kansas, Best toys. Differences in length due to wheels used.)	No Price Found		
Craftoy Cement Mixer: **No. 78, 3¾".** (See Best No. 78)	No Price Found		
Craftoy Racer: **No. 81, 4½".** Miller FWD Indy type. (See Best No. 81)	No Price Found		
Craftoy Sedan: **No. 92, 4".** (Not a sedan version of Best No. 92 coupe.	No Price Found No Price Found		
Craftoy Racer with Removable Hood: **No. 100, 4¼".** Miller? Indy type. Tin hood. New issue?	No Price Found		
Craftoy Fire Truck: **No. 101, 4½".** New issue?	No Price Found		

	C6	C8	C10
Craftoy Gasoline Transport: **No. 102,** 6¾". 1938 International K-line(?) semi. (Tractor probably Ralstoy or a Best redesign. Trailer is B-102.).	No Price Found		
Craftoy Speed Car: **No. 103, 4¼".** Streamlined coupe, body grooved or trimmed in fantasy streamlines, new issue	10	15	20
Craftoy Oil Truck: **No. 104, 3¾".** 1938 International C.O.E.(?), "gas" "oil" tanker. (Probably Ralstoy or Best redesign.	No Price Found		
Craftoy Station Wagon: **No. 105,** 3¾". Looks like a sedan. Was it produced?	No Price Found		

DAYTON FRICTION WORKS

DAYTON was owned by D.P. Clark of Dayton, Ohio. Clark's wood and metal "Hill Climber" friction toys were his best-known. Clark was in business from 1898, and his company was one of the first to use a friction motor, which is activated by moving the toy by hand against a surface and then releasing it. William Schieble, who joined the company in the early 1900s, left in 1909 and formed the Schieble Toy and Novelty Company, using the "Hill Climber" name, which he felt was legally his, while Clark continued to use it, despite Schieble's lawsuits. Thus the parentage of some "Hill Climbers" is uncertain.

	C6	C8	C10
Dayton Coal and Ice Truck, tin friction circa 1920	150	225	300
Dayton Coupe, 12", 1928, pressed steel	125.00	187.50	250.00
Dayton Coupe, 12½" long, circa 1920	150	225	300
Dayton "Dayton Friction", pressed steel, rubber tires, 1920s, 14¼" long.	250	375	500
Dayton Fire Ladder Truck, 18" long.	200	300	400
Dayton Fire Pumper, 1920s	100	150	200
Dayton Ladder Truck, 1920s	200	300	400

	C6	C8	C10
Dayton open touring car, dated 1909, friction motor, driver	250	375	500
Dayton touring car, 13½" long, friction motor	440	660	880
Dayton touring car, 13½" long, unpowered	350	525	700
Delivery Truck, 3½" long, cast iron	60	90	120
Delivery Truck, 10½" long, with driver, friction	100	150	200
Delivery Truck, "Packard", 28" long steel	400	600	800

DENT HARDWARE COMPANY

DENT, of Fullerton, Pennsylvania, was in business from 1895-1973. Henry H. Dent, with four partners, was the owner. Cast iron toys seem to have first emerged in 1898. Dent is known for particularly fine castings in its vehicles. It was also one of the first manufacturers to try (with little success) aluminum toys (in the 1920s). Toys seem to have been phased out during the hard times of the Depression.

	C6	C8	C10
Dent "American Oil Co.", cast iron truck, approx. 10½" long.......	750	1125	1500
Dent bus, cast iron, 6¼" long.......	100	150	200
Dent Coast to Coast Bus, 7½" long..	125.00	187.50	250.00
Dent "Coast to Coast" bus, circa 1925, 15" long...............	750	1000	1500
Dent "Express J & B" stakebed truck, 14½", 1915, driver.............	500	800	1100
Dent fire truck, cast iron, 7" long....	150	225	300
Dent fire ladder truck, 8½" long, with driver.......................	450	675	900
Dent fire truck with ladder and men, cast iron, 18" long.............	900	1350	1800
Dent hose reeler with men, cast iron, large.....................	500	750	1000
Dent "Interurban" bus, cast iron, 9" long.......................	250	375	500
Dent La Salle, approx. 4" long......	125.00	187.50	250.00
Dent Ladder truck, 10" long, two drivers.....................	250	375	500
Dent Mack Dump Truck, 4½" circa 1925, iron wheels...............	55.00	82.50	110.00
Dent Model T two door sedan, iron wheels, circa 1925...........	125.00	187.50	250.00
Dent "Patrol", 6½" long, circa 1920s.	125.00	187.50	250.00
Dent "Police Patrol," 8¾" long	750	1125	1500

	C6	C8	C10
Dent "Public Service" Bus, circa 1926, 13½" long.............	600	900	1200
Dent Sedan, 7½" long, spare tire, has stop and go light, full bumpers on front......................	900	1350	1800
Dent Steam Roller, cast iron, 6" long.	100	150	200
Dent Yellow Cab, approx. 7¾" long.	600	900	1200
"Dept. of Street Cleaning" dump truck, 10½" long, circa 1935....	50	75	100

DINKY

	C6	C8	C10
Dinky No.? Humbler two-door sedan.	35.00	52.50	70.00
Dinky 14c Coventry Fork Lift.......	30	45	60
Dinky 23H Ferrari racer..........	17.50	26.25	35.00
Dinky 27f 1948 Plymouth Station Wagon......................	17.50	26.25	35.00
Dinky 30r Fordson Truck..........	17.50	26.25	35.00
Dinky 34 Royal Mail Van..........	32.50	48.75	65.00
Dinky 36b Bentley...............	40	60	80
Dinky 36c Humber, 1936..........	30	45	60
Dinky 38c Lagonda..............	30	45	60
Dinky 38d Alvis................	30	45	60
Dinky 40a Riley 4DS.............	25.00	37.50	50.00
Dinky 106 Thunderbird 2 space.....	17.50	26.25	35.00
Dinky 112 Triumph Purdey.........	17.50	26.25	35.00
Dinky 130 Ford Corsair...........	17.50	26.50	35.00
Dinky 134 Triumph Vitesse.........	17.50	26.25	35.00
Dinky 135 Triumph 2000..........	17.50	26.25	35.00
Dinky 137 Plymouth, 1963.........	17.50	26.25	35.00
Dinky 151 Austin Devon..........	20	30	40
Dinky 154 Ford Taurus..........	17.50	26.25	35.00
Dinky 157 Jaguar XK120.........	30	45	60
Dinky 172 Studebaker Land Cruiser..	20	30	40
Dinky 174 Hudson Hornet Sedan....	32.50	48.75	65.00
Dinky 200 Matra 630.............	17.50	26.25	35.00
Dinky 201 Plymouth Rally, 1976	17.50	26.25	35.00
Dinky 207 Triumph TR7 Leyland...	17.50	26.25	35.00
Dinky 227 Beach Buggy...........	17.50	26.25	35.00
Dinky 241 Austin taxi............	17.50	26.25	35.00
Dinky 252 1968 Pontiac..........	22.50	33.75	45.00
Dinky 267 Dodge Fire Rescue......	37.50	56.25	75.00
Dinky 278 Bedford Dump..........	17.50	26.25	35.00
Dinky 308 Leyland Tractor........	17.50	26.25	35.00
Dinky 344 Estate Car............	20	30	40

DENT "Public Service" Bus, circa 1926. 13½" long.
Courtesy Phillips New York

DENT Sedan, 7½" long, late 1920s.
Courtesy Lloyd W. Ralston Auctions

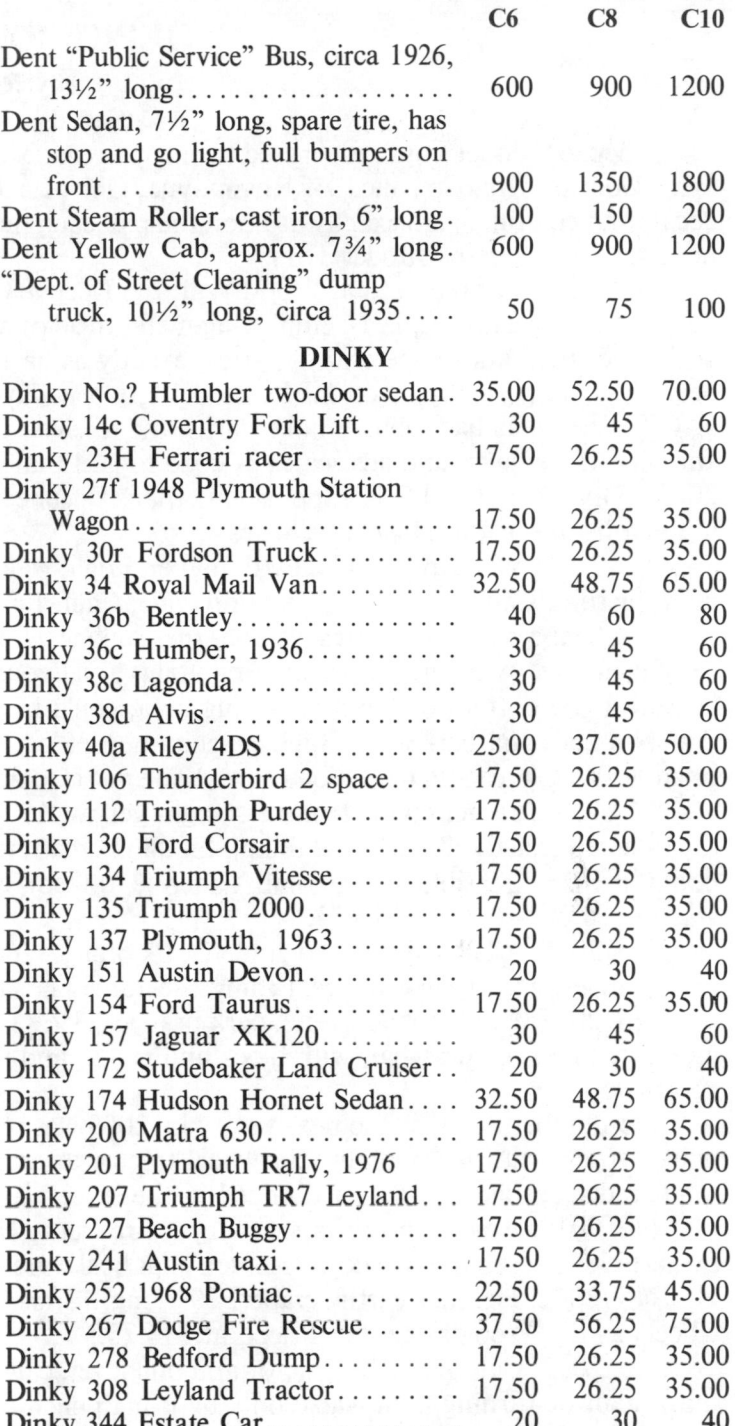

DINKY Top L to R: 157 Jaguar KX120 Coupe, 334 Estate Car.
Bottom: 174 Hudson Hornet Sedan, 172 Studebaker Land Cruiser Courtesy Phillips New York

DOEPKE "MODEL TOYS"

by Ray Funk
(See also Miscellaneous)

Doepke "Model Toys" advertised their toys as outlasting all others 3 to 1. The company's full title was the "Charles Wm. Doepke Mfg. Co., Inc." of Rossmoyne, Ohio. Each toy was an authorized replica of the actual thing and the decals and coloring were exactly as upon the real equipment or trucks, with the exception of the manufacturer having his own, in this case "Model Toys."

At the end of the Second World War, the Doepke Corp. hit the market with five models, first in a line of heavy duty metal operating replicas, employing metal tread or authentic miniature tires, either Goodyear or Firestone, with authentic tread and name and tire sizes, exactly as on the real tires. This, to the best of my knowledge, has never been done so perfectly, even in the model kits of today.

These toys all had rubber smoke stacks, and received the approval of Parents Magazine, P.T.A., Boy's Life Magazine, and all other experts and advocates of good toys at that period. The first five numbers were 2000, 2001, 2002, 2006, 2007. Why not 3, 4 and 5, I cannot say. Perhaps Doepke had toys planned for these numbers that fell through. Following is a listing of the Doepke vehicles.

No. 2000, Wooldridge H.D. earth hauler, bright yellow, four huge tires, 25" long, and weighing 10 lbs. The actual manufacturer's address is listed as Sunnyvale, Calif. I'm sure most of you have seen the John Wayne movie, "The Fighting Seabees", which used several of these, along with caterpillar bulldozers and road graders. These Wooldridge's caught my eye with their maneuvering ability, and could traverse the roughest terrain easily. Two long doors, the length of the bottom of the dirt-hauling area, could be released to deposit a load. Price was $14.75 new in 1945.

No. 2001, Barber-Greene high-capacity bucket loader, 13" high, 10 lbs., dark green, all steel and rolling on steel tread, was designed as a toy to load earth haulers. Handcrank operated, operated exactly as the real thing. Price $14.75.

No. 2002, Jaeger concrete mixer, bright yellow, 15" long, 8 lbs. on four wheels, steerable via draw bar (all model toys steered exactly like the real thing), though perhaps the best-detailed, was the poorest-selling toy, as although you could, it wasn't feasible to really mix concrete in them, due to small amound received versus cleaning time. This toy was priced at $10.75 to $13.75.

No. 2006, Adams diesel road grader, dark orange, 26" long, 14 lbs., all six wheels, three axles, and blade adjustable to all angles, exactly like the real thing, steerable via steering wheel, priced at $14.75.

No. 2007, Unit Mobile Crane, dark orange, 11½" long, 19½" boom, eight lbs. and eight ounces, adjustable side jacks, steered via a drawbar, with block and tackle, and removable operating clam shell as standard accessory. Priced at $14.75

No number 2008, as the next year, No. 2009 was released and No. 2000 dropped. No. 2009 was a Euclid earth-hauler truck, with uncoupling four-wheel tractor to use to tow other toys. 27" long, 11 lbs., Euclid green, or light road-grader orange, the trailer dumped in the same way as the Wooldridge. Priced $14.75.

No. 2010, American-LaFrance pumper fire truck, 18" long, 7 lbs., bright red with chrome trim, ladder, bell, fire extinguisher, hoses and nozzle, a reservoir that held water for hand-operated pressure pump. A beautiful toy at $16.75.

No. 2011, Heiliner earth scraper, 29" long, 13 lbs., bright dark red, loaded and dumped and operated on four wheels as the Wooldridge did. Priced at $16.75.

No. 2012, Caterpillar D6 tractor and bulldozer, caterpillar yellow, 15" long, 7 lbs., with real bulldozer treads for sharp realistic turning (removable only by using punch and hammer to remove connecting pin from between two of the pads) and adjustable bulldozer blade, plus heavy draw bar. Truly a beautiful toy at $13.75. Diesel motor was cast metal.

No. 2013 eliminated and replaced No. 2001. No. 2013, Barber-Green mobile high-capacity bucket loader, 22" long, 12" high, 10 lbs., buckets on chains and rubber conveyor belt, adjustable and steered by steering wheel, priced at $19.75.

No. 2014, American La-France aerial ladder truck, 23" long, 42" extended ladder height, 11 lbs., bright red and chrome, bell, red light, adjustable side jacks, single unit truck steered by steering wheel, priced at $20.75.

Doepke "Model Toys" were doomed to extinction by lower-priced, lighter-constructed imitators of lesser quality, some of which were started in the 1920s, and others that came into being in the 1950s, several of which are still around today, but none ever containing, before or after, the heavy-duty constructed realism and operating qualities as had the one and only "Model Toys".

Of the Doepke Model Toys that were mass produced, several had variations in their basic construction from time to time. Usually these changes were an elimination of the more intricate operating procedures, and had little or no effect on the toy's overall outward appearance.

In Antique Toy World, Philip Sayer wrote a two part article on the Doepke Co., and featured pictures of nearly all toys ever manufactured by the firm. The ones that were produced in such limited numbers (only one to a few), are mentioned and often times described. Also listed are nearly all of the slight changes in the mass produced toys, though I could not (perhaps overlooked it) find mention of the change in the D-6 Caterpillar. The first models to hit the market have the front axles held tightly forward by springs, so when being pushed forward and they strike a solid object to climb over, there is some give to absorb the shock and protect the tract pads. Later models eliminated this and opted for simple axle wells as in the rear wheels. Had I not had both types, this slight change would have easily gone unnoticed.

It would seem that the Doepke Co. would accept orders to make model toys of the real thing for the actual producers, and the toys with the most allure, playability, and feasible mass production design, and greatest entertainment to be provided to the child that received one, would be mass produced. Of the others that would not withstand rough handling by young hands, or because of cost and time required to produce them, there were only one to a few produced as previously mentioned. This is no doubt the explanation for the number gaps between the marketed items.

Among the scarcer articles produced, were even a few automobiles, avidly sought after by collectors that have delved into this company's past history to any depth. Of these, perhaps there were catalogs or brochures about them, though all I have ever seen are the ones dealing with the mass produced toys I have listed.

RAY FUNK is a leading collector and authority on trains and other toys, as well as a collector and authority on comic books and Western literature.

DOEPKE Catalog Illustrations of Nos. 2009 and 2011. Photo by Bill Kaufman. Courtesy Ray Funk.

DOEPKE Catalog illustration of Model No. 2012. Photo by Bill Kaufman. Courtesy Ray Funk.

DOPEKE Catalog illustration of Model No. 2010. Photo by Bill Kaufman. Courtesy Ray Funk.

An ad for DOEPKE Model Toys Photo by Bill Kaufman Courtesy Ray Funk

41

	C6	C8	C10
Doepke No. 2000 Wooldridge H.D. Earth Hauler, 25" long.........	270	405	540
Doepke No. 2001 Barber-Greene high capacity bucket loader, 13" high..	250	375	500
Doepke No. 2002 Jaeger Concrete Mixer, 15" long.............	300	450	600
Doepke No. 2006 Adams Diesel Road Grader, 26" long.........	120	180	240
Doepke No. 2007 Unit Mobile Crane, 11½" long..................	300	450	600
Doepke No. 2008 American La France Aerial Ladder Truck.....	250	375	500
Doepke No. 2009 Euclid Earth Hauler Truck, 27" long..............	220	330	440
Doepke No. 2010 American-La France pumper fire truck, 18" long......................	200	300	400
Doepke No. 2011 Heiliner Earth Scraper, 29" long.............	300	450	600
Doepke No. 2012 Caterpillar D6 tractor and bulldozer, 15" long......	180	270	360
Doepke No. 2013 Barber-Green mobile high-capacity bucket loader 22" long......................	240	360	480
Doepke No. 2014 American-La France aerial ladder fire truck, 23" long.....................	300	450	600
Doepke No. 2015 Clark Airport Tractor and Baggage Trailers........	400	600	800
Doepke No. 2015 MG, 1954........	170	255	350
Doepke No. 2018 Jaguar, 1955......	160	240	320
Doepke No. 2023 Searchlight Truck, 1955..................	480	720	960
Drudge "Hyster" lumber carrier.....	175.00	262.50	350.00
Dump Truck, 4½" long, cast iron, "2205"........................	65.00	97.50	130.00
Dump Truck, tin, 5¾" long, wooden wheels	20	30	40
Dump Truck, 6" long, pressed steel, circa 1939..................	50	75	100
Dump Truck, 7" long, cast iron, driver	90	135	180
Dump Truck (Beck), steers via horn on top of cab, late 1940s, large...	60	90	120

Dunwell: Dunwell was the trade name given to its toys by Metal Products Co. of Clifton, New Jersey. Its trucks seem to have been sold circa 1953-1958. Their line resembles Tonka's rather closely, and is rare.

	C6	C8	C10
Dunwell "Grain Hauler"..........	200	300	400
Dunwell Log Truck...............	400	600	800
Dunwell "Red Star Express Lines" truck	300	450	600
Dunwell "Snowcrop" Refrigerator Semi	280	420	560
Dunwell "Steel Carrier Co." semi....	220	330	440

Dyna-Model Products Company (Dyna-Mo)
by Fred Maxwell

Dyna-Model Products Co., 93 South Street, Oyster Bay, Long Island, New York, may have pioneered the scale models industry dominating today's markets with their "Dyna-Mo" brand of HO toys to be used in train layouts. They are rather high quality pot-metal toys, identified by their method of assembling body parts, clamping axles between small posts and the standardized appearance of the undersides of the whole line.

Probably produced in the 1930's, and perhaps in the post-war era, the toys were made by a coarse diecasting process. The earlier vintage cars were made in two to five parts, exclusive of wheels and axles, to be pinned, clamped or glued together: body, frame, steering wheel, top and windshield. Some were packaged as kits, with instructions printed on the box: "Pinch ends of axel (their spelling) after installing wheels" (R-26). The toys were factory painted in as many as 4 colors per toy.

DYNA-MODEL, Top, L to R: D1, Ford T Roadster, 1-7/8", D7, D3, Franklin steam touring 2-1/8". Middle, L to R: D5, D6, D9, D10, D8. Bottom, L to R: D11, Cadillac sedan 2", D23, D16
Photo by Fred Maxwell

DYNA-MODEL, Top, L to R: D14, D20?, D12, Cadillac 2-door sedan, 2-3/8". Middle, L to R: D15, D18, D21. Bottom, L to R: D22, D23, D24
Photo by Fred Maxwell

	C6	C8	C10
D1 Dyna "R-26 HO Surrey, 35c": 1¾". Horseless carriage, tiller steering, 3 colors, 3 pc. body, kit..	4	6	8
D2 Dyna Touring Car: 2". Antique Stanley Steamer, open tonneau, rt. hand steering, 4 colors, 4 pc.....	4	6	8
D3 Dyna Speedster: 2". Antique Mercer, rt. hand steering, 4 colors, 4 pc........................	4	6	8
D4 Dyna Roadster: 1 7/8". Antique Buick? Open, rt. hand steering, 4 pcs., 3 colors..............	4	6	8
D5 Dyna Touring Car: 1 7/8". Antique. Realistic folded top attachable with hinge pins, left hand steering, 5 pcs., 2 colors........	4	6	8
D6 Dyna "R-61 HO Model T Ford 1914 touring with top 60c": 1 5/8". One piece body, top up, 3 colors. "Cut plastic windshield to fit, darken edges with ink or paint and glue top and windshield in place, in slots provided."........	4	6	8
D7 Dyna Touring car: 1¾". 1914 Ford, top down cast in one-piece body, glued windshield, 3 colors..	4	6	8
D8 Dyna Roadster: 2". 1920's Packard convertible, top down, rumble seat, one piece body, glued windshield, spoked wheels, 3 colors......................	6	9	12
D9 Dyna Roadster: 2". Packard, same as above, top up, 3 colors.......	6	9	12
D10 Dyna Touring: 2". Packard, same as above, top down, 3 colors.....	6	9	12
D11 Dyna Roadster: 2". Model A Ford? Top down, open rumble seat, disc wheels, one piece body, unpainted....................	2	3	4
D12 Dyna Sedan: 2". Buick sedan, 1930's. Open windshield and windows. 2 colors.................	4	6	8
D13 Dyna "R-68 HO Buick convertible 55c": 2 3/8". Late 1930's. Open, 2 dr. sedan, top down, one piece body, solid cast windshield, disk wheels..................	6	9	12
D14 Dyna Sedan: 2 3/8", Buick 2 dr. airflow, open windshield and windows......................	6	9	12
D15 Dyna Taxi: 2 3/8". Buick sedan, late 1930's. Open windshield and windows, 2 colors..............	6	9	12
D16 Dyna Convertible, 2 3/8". Cadillac 2 dr. sedan, late 1930's..	6	9	12
D17 Dyna Sedan: 2 3/8". Cadillac 2 dr. sedan, open windshield and windows, incl. rear, late 1930's...	6	9	12

	C6	C8	C10
D18 Dyna Taxi: 2 3/8". Cadillac sedan, late 1930's, open windshield and windows including rear, 2 colors........................	6	9	12
D19 Dyna Sedan: 2 3/8". Pontiac 4 dr. airflow, open windshield and windows incl. rear............	6	9	12
D20 Dyna Limousine: 2½". Cadillac, late 1930's, open windows as above.....................	6	9	12
D21 Dyna Delivery Van: 2 3/8". Pontiac, late 1930's, open windshield and door windows.............	4	6	8
D22 Dyna Pickup Truck: 2½". GMC?, late 1930's, open windows, spoked wheels, 2 piece, 3 colors..	4	6	8
D23 Dyna Wrecker: 2¾", GMC?, late 1930's, open windows, 3 piece, 4 colors......................	6	9	12
D24 Dyna Dump Truck: 2¾". Open windows, hinged body with realistic load of coal. 3 pieces, 2 colors, dual rear wheels........	8	12	16
D25 Dyna Pickup Truck: 2". GMC?, 1930's, one piece, open windows, one color.....................	4	6	8
D26) Dyna Pickup Truck: 2". Mack? "US Army", Air Corps star decals, late 1930's, 2 pc. body, 2 colors..	4	6	8
D27 Dyna Truck: 2". Mack? Same chassis as above, but tarpaulin covered, 2 pc. body...........	4	6	8
Electric car cast iron 3¾" long......	150	225	300
"Electric Powered Rider Convertible", lithographed tin, circa 1950, 29" long, riding toy...............	75.00	112.50	150.00

ERIE (PARKER WHITE METAL)

According to James Apthorpe, Erie toys were made by Parker White Metal Company, which apparently began in Erie, Pennsylvania, but moved to Fairview (West of Erie), Pa. in the early 1960s. However, according to company officials he contacted, the firm made toys only prior to World War II. It printed no catalogs.

	C6	C8	C10
Erie Ford, "Servel Body," 5" long, 1936	25.00	37.50	50.00
Erie Lincoln Zephyr, 3" long, 1940s .	25.00	37.50	50.00
Erie Packard (?) 115-C or 120 convertible, circa 1937	25.00	37.50	50.00

ERTL

Ertl was begun by Fred Ertl Sr. in 1945, working out of his Dubuque, Iowa home. As business expanded, the firm moved to Dyersville. Ertl had learned about using sand molds in his native Germany, and very early in the company's history began working directly from the original blueprints to make his toy tractors, trucks and other wheeled toys. Ertl's specialty is farm toys, with rights obtained from such manufacturers as International Harvester and John Deere. Today Ertl is the largest manufacturer of toy farm equipment in the world, and in addition makes a number of other toys, such as cars, trucks and airplanes.

Fire Pumper, cast iron, 11" long
Photo by Bill Kaufman
Courtesy Good Old Days Store

	C6	C8	C10
Ertl Firetruck No. 9, 22" long	15.00	22.50	30.00
Ertl Firetruck No. 9 with Fire Chief's car	20	30	40
Ertl Harvester, first Ertl	175.00	262.50	350.00
Ertl International Harvester btm. plow	12.50	18.75	25.00
Ertl IHC Scout Pickup Truck	15.00	22.50	30.00
Ertl Spreader with metal beater	20	30	40
Ertl Velveeta Trailer Truck	26	39	52
Farm truck, "Speed," with driver, 7" cast iron	150	225	300
Fire ENgine "9608" die cast, 6" long, Post-War	35.00	52.50	70.00
Fire Engine Pumper, friction, gear shift lever, with drivers	200	300	400
Fire Pumper, 5" long, cast iron, circa 1935	70	105	140
Fire Pumper, approx. 6½" long, cast iron	100	150	200
Fire Pumper, 8" long, cast iron	85.00	112.50	170.00
Fire Pumper, 11" long, cast iron	125.00	187.50	250.00
Fire Truck, cast iron, 7" long	70	105	140
Fire Truck, friction, with driver, metal and wood, pat. Nov. 2, 1897	600	900	1200
Fire Truck, pressed steel friction toy 10½" long, early with driver	350	525	700

Fire Pumper, cast iron, 5" long, circa 1935.
Courtesy Mapes Auctioneers & Appraisers

FIRESTONE

The following list, with its codings, was compiled by David Leopard.

	C6	C8	C10
FA01 '39 Mercury fastback 4 door sedan, 4¾" long	30	40	50
FA02 '35 Ford 2 door humpback sedan, 4⅞" long	30	40	50
FA03 '36 Ford 2 door humpback sedan, 4⅞" long	30	40	50

FIRESTONE FA03
Photo by Dave Leopard

	C6	C8	C10
Ford coupe, 4" long, 1924	80	120	160
Ford coupe, blue, chrome wheels, 5" long	80	120	160
Ford coupe, cast iron, black, chrome wheels, circa 1920s, 5" long	80	120	160
"Fordson" tractor with driver, cast iron, 5¾" long	140	210	280
Fordson tractor with hay rake, cast iron, 1930s	150	225	300
Friction car, cast iron and wood, with figures	125.00	187.50	250.00
Friction car, 7¼", 1910	900	1350	1800
Friction toy with two riders, 1897	150	225	300
GMC "Greyhound Lines" cast iron bus, 7½" long, circa 1934	200	300	400
"Gasoline" truck, circa late 30s, red, approx. 2¾" long, slush	10	15	20
Gibbs "Gibbs No. 701" truck	150	250	350

GIRARD	C6	C8	C10
Girard Fire Chief Car, 15" long	125.00	187.50	250.00
Girard "Fire Chief Siren Coupe," 14½" long	100	150	200
Girard Fire truck, 12" long, 1920s ..	90	135	180
Girard Pump Truck, battery operated, headlights, 10" long	75.00	112.50	150.00
Girard Roadster, 14½" long, electrified	150	225	300
Girard Stake Truck, 10", electric headlights	120	180	240
Girard Tank Truck, 11½" long, wood wheels	75.00	112.50	150.00

HILLCLIMBER Horseless Carriage, woman driver, 7" long.
Courtesy Mapes Auctioneers & Appraisers

GIRARD Touring Bus
Courtesy Mapes Auctioneers & Appraisers

	C6	C8	C10
Girard Touring Bus, painted tin, circa 1920, 12" long	150	225	300
Girard Truck with Trailer, 1930s, 17"	100	150	200
Goodie Cadillac Convertible, 1957?, 3" long	6	9	12
"Guided Missile Unit No. 10" truck, tin litho, circa 1960	60	90	120
Happy Sam driving wood truck, circa 1920s, 8" long	80	120	160
Hillclimber "Ambulance", 10½" long, very early....................	600	900	1200
Hillclimber Armored Truck, 11" long, pressed steel friction...........	600	900	1200
Hillclimber Auto, woman driver, friction, very early, 6" long........	500	750	1000
Hillclimber hook and ladder wagon, painted pressed steel friction, driver, 20" long................	200	300	400
Hillclimber Horseless Carriage, woman driver, cast iron and wood, very early, 7" long................	400	600	800
Hillclimber Racer with track, 7½" long	375	525	750
Hillclimber Touring car, 11" long....	85.00	127.50	170.00
Hoge Fire chief car, 15" long.......	350	525	7.00
Hook and ladder, aluminum, with driver, 13" long................	100	150	200
Hook and ladder truck, tin friction, 21" long.....................	100	150	200
Hose Wagon, 1897, two riders, friction toy	125.00	187.50	250.00

HUBLEY

HUBLEY: The Hubley manufacturing company was founded at least as early as 1894 by John Hubley, and made iron toys from the start at its plant in Lancaster, Pennsylvania. All toys at the beginning were cast iron, and some early toys included coal ranges, circus wagons and mechanical banks. Hubley's cast iron toys were popular almost from the start, and have long been collector's items, as they were well-made and attractive. By 1940, however, the cast iron toy, due to the increased cost of freight and foreign competition, was slowly becoming a thing of the past. At this time, when Hubley was the largest producer of cast iron toys and cap pistols in the world, it began to introduce die cast zinc alloy toys. During the Second World War, Hubley was 98% engaged in war production, turning out over five million M-74 bomb fuses, which the Hubley engineers played a large part in developing. Since the war, Hubley manufactures die cast toys and plastic toys exclusively. In 1952, Hubley manufactured 9,763,610 toys and 11,184,878 cap pistols, about ten times the amount of toys and pistols they produced in 1930, but with a line of toys 80% smaller than in 1930. It is the combination of the relative scarcity (and multiplicity) of the older toys, plus the preference by collectors for cast iron over die cast zinc alloy and plastic toys that makes the pre-World War II toys the most attractive to collectors. Hubley was acquired by Gabriel Industries in late 1965, and puts out holster sets, cap pistols, vehicles, hobby kits and a number of other toys.

HUBLEY Caterpillar 3¼" long.
Courtesy Mapes Auctioneers & Appraisers

HUBLEY Stake bed truck, 7" long.
Courtesy Mapes Auctioneers & Appraisers

	C6	C8	C10
Hubley Auto Express, 9" long, cast iron	900	1350	1800
Hubley Avery tractor, 4¾" long, very early	120	180	240
Hubley auto circa 1950s, black plastic wheels, die cast	12.50	18.75	25.00
Hubley Bell Telephone Truck, 3¾" long	50	75	100
Hubley Bell Telephone, 5¼"	300	450	600
Hubley "Bell Telephone", 12" long, with tools	60	90	120
Hubley Bell Telephone truck, 12½" long, 1940s	150	225	300
Hubley Bell Telephone truck, 10" long, No. 41, 1936, with derrick and windlass, auger, trailer with 10" pole, three digging tools, and two loose ladders	500	750	1000
Hubley "Bell Telephone", 13" long, just ladders as equipment	250	375	500
Hubley Bell Telephone Truck, 9" long, implements	400	600	800
Hubley "Borden's Milk Cream", deluxe version, 7½" long, rubber tires, clicker	1250	1875	2500
Hubley "Borden's Milk Cream", standard version	1000	1500	2000
Hubley Bulldozer, die-cast, front scoop, circa 1950, 10¼" long, rubber treads	15.00	22.50	30.00
Hubley bus, (futuristic type), 3½", circa 1935	25.00	37.50	50.00
Hubley bus, 5½", circa 1938, rubber wheels	90	135	180
Hubley bus, 8" long, 1930s	60	90	120
Hubley Bus, 9" long, diecast, circa 1950s	20	30	40
Hubley Cadillac, 7" die cast	16	24	32
Hubley 2278 car and 2279 house trailer, circa 1939	150	225	300
Hubley Caterpillar Tractor, 3¼" long, driver in cab	35.00	52.50	70.00

	C6	C8	C10
Hubley Army Motor Truck No. 807 with driver, 15" long	500	750	1000
Hubley Auto, 6½"	80	120	160
Hubley Auto, 9", 1922, Chevy?	400	600	800
Hubley Auto carrier, 10" long, with three cars and one pickup truck, circa 1939	400	600	800
Hubley Cement Mixer, 18" long	400	600	800

	C6	C8	C10
Hubley Champion Stake Truck, 8½" long, 1930s, white rubber tires ...	140	210	280
Hubley Chemical Truck with ladders, 13" long...	200	300	400
Hubley Chevrolet 1932 Phaeton Kit, 1960s...	17.50	26.25	35.00
Hubley Chevrolet 1932 Roadster Kit, 1960s...	17.50	26.25	35.00
Hubley Chrysler airflow, 4½" long, take-apart body...	100	150	200
Hubley Chrysler Airflow, 6¾" long, take-apart body...	55.00	82.50	110.00
Hubley Chrysler Airflow, 8" long, electrified, white rubber tires on wood hubs...	600	900	1200
Hubley Chrysler Airflow racing car, circa 1938...	100	150	200
Hubley Coal Truck, cast iron, with driver, 16¾"...	1500	2250	3000
Hubley "Coast to Coast" bus, cast iron, 1927, 13" long...	450	675	900
Hubley Corvette...	200	300	400
Hubley Coupe, 1933 Ford...	90	135	180
Hubley Coupe roadster, rumble seat, 11" long, rubber tires...	125.00	187.50	250.00
Hubley Crash Car, three-wheel motor-cycle, chrome wheels...	100	150	200
Hubley Crash Car, circa 1937, 4¾" long, white rubber tires...	100	150	200
Hubley Digger, Mack General, 10" long...	250	375	500
Hubley Dump Truck, 5½"...	30	45	60
Hubley Dump Truck, circa 1938, 7½" long...	200	300	400
Hubley Dump Truck, Mack, 1930s, 6 tires, 10¾" long...	300	450	600
Hubley Fire Engine Pumper, circa 1920, 12½" long, cast iron, black rubber tires, driver, boiler-tender .	100	150	200
Hubley Fire Engine pumper, early, No. 504...	375	525	750
Hubley Fire Engine No. 526, 10½" long, circa 1936...	175	265	350
Hubley Fire Engine, die cast, white rubber tires with wooden rims, circa 1941...	15.00	22.50	30.00
Hubley Fire Ladder Truck, 8½", early	100	150	200
Hubley Fire Ladder Truck, 19½" long	500	750	1000
Hubley Fire Truck with searchlight, white rubber tires with wooden rims...	30	45	60
Hubley Fire Truck, 5"...	40	60	80
Hubley "5 Ton Truck", 17" long, 8 wooden barrels, circa 1920...	700	1050	1400
Hubley Ford Coupe, 1936...	40	60	80
Hubley Ford Model A Coupe Kit, 1960s...	22.50	33.75	45.00
Hubley Ford Model A Phaeton Kit, 1960s...	17.50	26.25	35.00

	C6	C8	C10
Hubley Ford Model A Pickup Kit, 1960s...	22.50	33.75	45.00
Hubley Ford Model A Station Wagon Kit, 1960s...	17.50	26.25	35.00
Hubley Ford Model A Town Car Kit, 1960s...	20	30	40
Hubley Ford Model A Victoria Kit, 1960s...	17.50	26.25	35.00
Hubley Hook & Ladder No. 463....	28	42	56
Hubley Hook & Ladder Truck, 19½" long, cast iron...	200	300	400

Hubley Huber Steam Roller, 8" long.
Courtesy Mapes Auctioneers & Appraisers

	C6	C8	C10
Hubley Huber Road Roller, 15" long.	2400	3600	4800
Hubley Jaguar Roadster, 9", 1950s ...	22.50	33.75	45.00
Hubley Kiddietoy No. 432 MGTD Roadster, 6" long...	20	30	40
Hubley Kiddietoy No. 457 Racer, 6½" long, diecast, rubber tires...	20	30	40
Hubley Kiddietoy, "Patrol" stake truck, circa 1937...	20	30	40
Hubley Ladder Truck circa late 1930s, 5"...	45.00	67.50	90.00
Hubley Ladder Truck, terraplane front, 1930s, 6" long...	70	105	140
Hubley Ladder Truck, 13½" circa 1940...	200	300	400
Hubley Life Saver Truck, circa 1930, hole in rear is large enough to hold pack of Life Savers...	125.00	187.50	250.00
Hubley Life Saver Truck, small hole in rear, can't hold Life Savers....	400	600	800
Hubley Limousine, 7" long, six-door, 1920s...	70	105	140
Hubley Lincoln Zephyr, 7¼" long...	125.00	187.50	250.00
Hubley Lincoln Zephyr and House Trailer, cast iron, 14" long overall	125.00	187.50	250.00
Hubley Log Truck No. 469...	35.00	52.50	70.00
Hubley Log Truck with five chained logs, black rubber tires, die-cast, approx. 19" long...	50	75	100

L to R: HUBLEY "Merchants Delivery," ARCADE Ambulance, "City Ambulance," 6" long.
Courtesy Chic Gast

	C6	C8	C10
Hubley Mack Truck Steam Shovel-Digger, circa 1920, nickel wheels and scoop, 7" long	300	450	600
Hubley "Merchants Delivery" 1920s, approx. 6" long	No Price Found		
Hubley "Milk and Cream" truck, 1920, cast iron, 3½" long, white rubber tires	125.00	187.50	250.00
Hubley Monarch tractor, 5½" long	150	225	300
Hubley Motor Express tractor and trailer, black rubber tires, 500 series, approx. 19" long	80	120	160
Hubley 2287 "Motor Express" truck and trailer, 8" long	70	105	140
Hubley Motorcycle, Armored, with sidecar and removable riders, 9" long	1300	1950	2600
Hubley Motorcycle, 6" has light in front and place for battery	100	150	200
Hubley Motorcycle and rider, 4"	125.00	187.50	250.00
Hubley Motorcycle, "Harley Davidson", Civilian Rider	200	300	400

	C6	C8	C10
Hubley Motorcycle, Harley-Davidson, with policeman, 1930s, 6½" long, swivel head, small wheels near feet	175.00	262.50	350.00
Hubley Motorcycle, Harley Davidson, with policeman, white rubber wheels	200	300	400
Hubley Motorcycle, Harley Davidson, with side car and rider	350	525	700
Hubley Motorcycle No. 649 Hill Climber, 1936, 6¾" long	200	300	400
Hubley Motorcycle, Indian, 9½" long, policeman rider, nickel-plated cylinder	180	270	360
Hubley Motorcycle policeman with side-car 4" long, 1920s	60	90	120
Hubley Motorcycle policeman with sidecar, 5" long	70	105	140

HUBLEY Motorcycle, Harley-Davidson with policeman, 1930s.
Courtesy Lloyd W. Ralston Auctions

	C6	C8	C10
Hubley Motorcycle with detachable cop, 4¼" long, cast iron, "Made USA", circa mid 1930s	50	75	100
Hubley Motorcycle, policeman rider, 5", circa 1936	35.00	52.50	70.00
Hubley Motorcycle with policeman, 1920s, 5" long	70	105	140
Hubley Motorcycle with side car, 8½" long, No. 46-F, two demountable policeman, 1936	175.00	262.50	350.00
Hubley Motorcycle, two-cylinder Indian, with side car, no riders	150	225	300

HUBLEY Motorcycle, Harley-Davidson with policeman, 1930s, 6½" long, swivel head, small wheels near feet.
Courtesy Mapes Auctioneers & Appraisers

HUBLEY Motorcycle "Traffic Car"
Courtesy Continental Hobby House

	C6	C8	C10
Hubley Motorcycle "Traffic Car", four-cylinder Indian with stake sides on two-wheel cart.........	400	600	800
Hubley Motorcycle, Parcel Post delivery, with two-wheel cart....	400	600	800
Hubley Motorcycle, four-cylinder P.D.Q. delivery...............	400	600	800
Hubley Motorcycle, three-wheel with stake sides, rider, chrome wheels..	90	135	180
Hubley Motorcycle, "U.S. Mail", 9" long......................	350	525	700
Hubley Motorized Steam Pumper, 4" long, circa 1930s..............	30	45	60

HUBLEY Night Coach, 3½" long, metal wheels, went on "Nu Car" carrier, 1930s.
Courtesy Chic Gast

	C6	C8	C10
Hubley Nite Coach, 3½" long, metal wheels, went on "Nu-Car" carrier, 1930s........................	30	45	60
Hubley "Nucar Transport" with trailer 17" long, 4 cars...............	500	750	1000
Hubley Packard, 15 parts, 1929, 11" long......................	5000	7500	10,000

HUBLEY "Panama" digger, 13" long
Courtesy Joe and Sharon Freed

	C6	C8	C10
Hubley "Panama" Digger, approx. 3½" long (hard to find)........	300	450	600
Hubley "Panama" digger, Mack, 13" long......................	1100	1650	2200
Hubley Parcel Post motorcycle and sidecar, Harley Davidson........	4000	6000	8000
Hubley "Patrol," 15½" long, driver, policeman	1400	2100	2800
Hubley Pipe Truck No. 803, 9½" long, c. 1950s.............	35.00	52.50	70.00
Hubley Power Shovel, 14".........	50	75	100

	C6	C8	C10
Hubley Pumper, circa late 1930s.....	100	150	200
Hubley Pumper, terraplane front, 1930s, 6¼" long..............	75.00	112.50	150.00
Hubley Race Car, "1790", 5" long approx......................	70	105	140
Hubley Race Car, driver, 7" long....	175	265	350
Hubley Race Car, 2241, 7½" long, 1930s......................	75.00	112.50	150.00
Hubley Racer No. 5, early wheels....	900	1350	1800

HUBLEY Racer No. 5, 9½" long.
Courtesy Lloyd W. Ralston Auctions

	C6	C8	C10
Hubley Racer No. 5, painted and nickeled iron and aluminum, 9½" long, raise hood-see motor.......	900	1350	1800
Hubley Racer 629, 1936 6¾" long...	60	90	120
Hubley Racer "No. 1", 8" long......	80	120	160
Hubley Race Car, driver, rubber tires, 8" long........................	125.00	187.50	250.00
Hubley Race Car, die-cast, black rubber tires...................	15.00	22.50	30.00
Hubley Race Car, animated exhaust stacks, 8" long, driver..........	300	450	600

HUBLEY "Railway Express" truck, 5" long.
Courtesy Mapes Auctioneers & Appraisers

	C6	C8	C10
Hubley "Railway Express" Truck, 5" long, rubber tires.............	100	150	200
Hubley Road Grader, 12"	30	45	60
Hubley Road Roller, late 1920s, 8" long, driver..................	300	450	600
Hubley Road Scraper No. 481......	45.00	67.50	90.00
Hubley Sedan, 1920, cast iron, 7" long......................	100	150	200

HUBLEY Huber Road Roller
Courtesy Lloyd W. Ralston Auctions

	C6	C8	C10
Hubley Sedan, 1928, cast iron, 7" long	125.00	187.50	250.00
Hubley Sedan, circa 1938, 2-door, 3½", looks like Ford, rubber wheels	60	90	120
Hubley Service Car, 4¼" long	60	90	120
Hubley Service Car, 5" cast iron, including wheels, 1930s	200	300	400
Hubley 726 Shovel Truck, 10" long, circa 1930			
Hubley Sport Car No. 485	70	105	140
Hubley Stake Truck, circa late 1930s	150	225	300
Hubley No. 614 Stake Truck, circa 1930s	75.00	112.50	150.00
Hubley Stake Bed Truck, cast iron, 3½" long	30	45	60
Hubley Stake bed truck, 7" long	90	135	180
Hubley Stake Truck with trailer - No. 927. Two pieces, 21" long	90	135	180
Hubley No. 452 stake-type truck, black rubber tires, circa post WW II	30	45	60
Hubley Station Wagon, circa 1940s, 1950s	75.00	112.50	150.00
Hubley Steam Roller, 5"	150	225	300
Hubley Steam Shovel, "General", 9" long, rubber tires on hubs	350	525	700
Hubley Steam Shovel, "General", 15" long	425.00	637.50	850.00
Hubley Street Sweeper, 8" long, "The Elgin", cast iron, 1931	3000	4500	6000
Hubley Studebaker Roadster, frame and body separate	300	450	600
Hubley Touring Auto, 1915, 9½" long, cast iron, chauffeur and rider	750	1125	1500
Hubley Tow Truck, 8¾" long, cast iron, circa 1930s	125	190	250
Hubley T-Bird	45.00	67.50	90.00
Hubley Tractor No. 472	50	75	100
Hubley Tractor, Ford 6000	20	30	40
Hubley Tractor, steam boiler in front, 4¾" long, circa early 1920s	125.00	187.50	250.00
Hubley Tractor, 5", 1930s	90	135	180
Hubley Tractor Trailer and Road Scraper No. 506	100	150	200
Hubley Trailer Truck, crica 1936-38	100	150	200
Hubley Transitional Fire Patrol, 12" cast iron, driver, firemen, 1920	1000	1500	2000
"Hubley U.S.A." Airflow type, circa 1937, approx. 3½" long	20	30	40

	C6	C8	C10
Hubley Wrecker, chrome wheels, Service Car	60	90	120
Hubley Wrecker, 3½"	30	45	60
Hubley Wrecker, 4½", rubber wheels, 1930	70	105	140
Hubley Wrecker, 4¾"	70	105	140
Hubley Wrecker, 6", circa 1940, white wheels on large hubs	100	150	200
Hubley Wrecking Truck, 1930, cast iron, rubber tires, 7½" long	100	150	200
Hubley Yellow Cab, 8"	300	450	600
"Ice" Stake Truck, circa 1940, streamlined fenders, pressed steel	60	90	120
Ice Cream Truck, cast iron, 8" long	300	450	600
Ideal Atomic Cannon, 13" long	35.00	52.50	70.00
Ideal Barracuda coupe, 1964, plastic, 4"	7.50	11.25	15.00
Ideal Cadillac, four door, 1948, plastic, 4"	6	9	12
Ideal Car Trailer, circa 1945, plastic, 3"	6	9	12
Ideal Pickup Truck, American, 1948, 4" plastic	6	9	12
Ideal Pickup Truck, Ford, 1940, 4" plastic	6	9	12
Ideal Tractor, 1948, plastic, 4" long	12.50	18.75	25.00
International Diesel Crawler, Product Miniature, Inc., 11", plastic with black rubber treads, 1950s	300	450	600
Irwin Ford Sunliner, 9" plastic friction	50	75	100
Ives horseless carriage runabout, 6½" long, 6" high to the top of jockey cap on driver	2500	3750	5000
Ives steamer, cast iron, 19½" long, two drivers	500	750	1000

Jaeger cement mixer.
Courtesy Mapes Auctioneers & Appraisers

	C6	C8	C10
Jaeger Cement Mixer, cast iron	600	900	1200
Jane Francis Wrecker, 6"	35.00	52.50	70.00

	C6	C8	C10
Jeep, glass candy container, 4" long..	20	30	40
"Jeepster", rubber tires, 14¼" long...	20	30	40
Jones Tank, throwing flame, flame touching hull..................	40	60	80
Jones Tank, throwing flame, flame not touching hull..............	45.00	67.50	90.00
Jones Tank, throwing flame, "No. 25"	60	90	120
Jones Tank, "22" on side...........	50	75	100

CONDITION CODE:
C5 – Good, wear evident overall, shows that has been played with
C6 – Fine, shows some wear in spots, but taken care of
C7 – Very Fine, minor wear overall, very clean
C8 – Excellent, minor wear on edges only
C9 – Near Mint, no noticeable flaws, close inspection may show minute marks
C10 – Mint (like new)
Note: Mint in Box does command higher price

KANSAS TOY & NOVELTY COMPANY
by Fred Maxwell
with assistance of
Clifton Historical Society, Bob Condray and L. D. Morgison

Among collectors one of the unsung sagas of the potmetal toy industry is that of Kansas Toy of Clifton, Kansas, a small town in the heart of our country. Until recently, Kansas Toy was believed to be the maker of most of those "slush-mold toys with the numbers" (numbers plainly embossed on the outsides of the toys). With this edition we are able to show that Kansas Toy founded the dynasty, a line that consisted of at least four other companies stretching from 1923 through the ups and downs of the exhilarating 1920s, the Great Depression, and World War II, to today. The Eccles Brothers are still casting toys and novelties for collectors from surviving molds.

The line, as now understood, went from Kansas to Best Toy and Novelty Factory to Ralstoy to Craftoy to Eccles Bros. Surviving molds include new designs from each of the middle three companies, although the boundary lines have become diffused over these 65 years. Although neither presence nor absence of numbers is final proof, they are the strongest clue throughout the line and its several makers. Although to adult eyes, numbers and labels cast on the outsides may be disfiguring, in some cases they could have been deliberate: "KT & N RR" is obvious. Numbers on taxis and racers are realistic; in some cases they may have been on the "real" cars.

Except for a short news clipping and old snapshots we have little physical, except the toys and their molds, to reconstruct this report. We have been greatly helped by serious insiders, neighbors and collectors from all over the country; as well as by research on Best, Craftoy and Ralstoy.

Authur Haynes, the founder of Kansas Toy & Novelty, was an auto mechanic machinist who started molding toys in his shed for local stores in 1923. One day his full mold dropped and spilled its hot metal. To his delight he had a perfect, hollow auto toy, with promise of saving of metal and shipping costs. Mr. Haynes, with clever hands and the eye of an artist, charmed his friends and townspeople with his bright colored toys. His patterns were designed from advertising pictures of known road and farm vehicles. Later, he branched out into race cars making a splash in the world; into aircraft, including Lindy's, making national and international records; and into a few figures, animals and novelties.

This was a town enterprise from the first. Jess Foster, the local editor, helped him with metal mixtures; Mr. Hadsell of the Union pacific (see No. 38, an early RR promotional?) suggested they send samples to Woolworth's in New York. From this grew an industry founded on sales to the dimestores, including Kresge and Kress. Expansion was helped by Clayton D. Young, a traveling salesman, who helped with sales and financing and became a partner. At its peak of national and international sales in the late 1920s the growing factory employed as many as 65 in two shifts during the Christmas order season in the early fall.

Fred Maxwell, collector and occasional author, has been collecting antique aircraft and vehicle toys for 25 years. This retirement hobby was started from scratch, for his lead soldiers were missing when he returned home from college. He founded Capitol Miniature Auto Collectors Club 20 years ago to promote interest in the Central Atlantic states. He felt challenged by the lack of public knowledge and the ambiguity of that orphan category: Pot Metal or Slushmold Toys.

The employees were young people who had grown up together, a happy gang who talked and sang at their work. This informality was reflected in the local name, "the Hoopie factory", for some of the early toys were based on familiar vehicles: autos, tractors, trucks, (and the jalopies and stripdowns they raced locally?). (See No. 26, No. 33, and No. 58). Whether "whoopee" (see No. 48) was a local spelling of "hoopie" or whether it reflected a particularly happy season is not known. Certainly a lot of happy stories must have floated from the "hoopie factory".

Teamwork there must have been, for a molder (according to Ernest Istas, one of them) could produce 2000 toys a day. Helen Istas, his wife, was the bookkeeper, showing the family nature of the work force, with its clippers, painters, assemblers, and boxers. "Butch" Morgison was variously each of these during his long career with the company.

At some point Mr. Young left, and moved back to his hometown in Kansas City, Missouri. Whether it was the loss of his assets or the onset of the Great Depression, by 1930 the company was in trouble. George Hoeffner reorganized it in 1931 and moved it down the road. This effort lasted only a few months.

According to ex-employees there were about 175 molds in use. We assume that KTN got up to mold numbers around 70 to 75. The difference can be explained by novelties, parts molds (cannon No. 23 included barrel, dolly mount, and wheels), defective molds and castings without numbers. In 1939 Ralstoy reported acquiring 140 molds (including new molds made by Best). Today, our premier mold collector and the current molder of these toys, Ron Eccles, has only found about 50, including some of the parts molds. This illustrates the frustrations and challenges facing the collector in correctly identifying toys from this line, but with this report we believe major progress has been made.

In spite of much progress we are still frustrated in our identifications. It is helpful to know that Kansas Toy often made toys in two or three sizes. There were many unnumbered (some duplicates, and some not). This may have been a customer requirement, or a change in company policy. If the latter, which company? Kansas Toys were probably all metal-wheeled, in several types and sizes, although we are not sure of the wheels on their largest pieces. Metal wheels were disc, wire and spoked. Some wires had plain back sides; assemblers could turn either side out. Spoked were solid or open. The tractor No. 17 and cannon No. 23 used discs with 4 circular openings. Bottom pan construction was not standard, as in Barclay. Apparently they were an afterthought, used where rigidity was important.

The finish also may help identification. The earliest toys were not painted, but remember that surplus sales could also have been unpainted. Then an Egyptian lacquer was used which gave a glittery semi-transparent appearance. This was followed by enamel, both dipped and sprayed, in many colors including black. Colors used were blue, green, light green, yellow, light yellow, orange, red, violet, gilt and bronze. Finishing nails, cut and clamped at the cut end, were a trademark of this line.

Kansas Toy, in the happy 1920s, had the longest run, produced the most designs and had a larger factory than its followers. The followers capitalized on the popularity of Kansas with reissues, and were more timid about introducing new pieces.

The following list has been carefully sifted, but may contain errors. All items, unless noted "unnumbered" (UV), have mold numbers cast somewhere on the toy, sometimes prominently. All other cast labels such as "KT & N" or "Whoopee" are shown in quotes. "Made in USA" labels were probably not required in this era, so are clues to later makers.

Abbreviations used are:

HG – horizontal grille
HO – hood ornament
"KTN" – Kansas Toy & Novelty
LI – laundau irons
MW – metal wheels
MWW – metal wire wheels
MSW – metal spoke wheels

RM – rearmount spare
SM – sidemount spares
SP – stringpull knob in front
T – trunk
UV – unnumbered version
VG – vertical grille
WV – windshield visor

KANSAS TOY K32
Photo by Fred Maxwell

KANSAS TOY, etc., Top, L to R: K31, Craftoy?, K39. Middle, L to R: K20, K17, K34. Bottom, L to R: K49, K14, K50
Photo by Fred Maxwell

KANSAS TOY & NOVELTY, etc. Racers. Top, L to R: K4, K35, BEST BE34. Middle L to R: BEST BE38, KANSAS TOY No. 67 (unlisted), BEST BE?36. Bottom L to R: Craftoy? K21, BEST BE50.
Photo by Fred Maxwell

	C6	C8	C10
(K1) Kansas Racer: Some doubt about the first toy; believed to be an Indy type, larger than No. 10, without driver	No Price Found		
(K2) Kansas Roadster: **8a**, 3¼", '28 Cadillac?, top up, SM,T, UV (similar to no. 14)	No Price Found		
(K3) Kansas Coupe: **8b**, 3¹⁄₁₆". RM	No Price Found		
(K4) Kansas Racer: **10**, 3¼". Indy type, 4 cyl. r. side exhaust, motometer, HG, SP, driver. Also UV	No Price Found		
(K5) Kansas Roadster: **14a**, 3¼". "Chrysler", RM, SP, HO, plain grille, VL, HG, driver	No Price Found		

	C6	C8	C10
(K6) Kansas Convertible (roadster?): **14b**, 3¼". "Chevrolet", MW, driver	No Price Found		
(K7) Kansas Coupe: **14c**, 3¼". "Chrysler", LI, WV, HG, HO, RM	No Price Found		
(K8) Kansas Coupe: **14d**, 3¼". "Chrysler", SM, T	No Price Found		
(K9) Kansas Coupe: No. ?, 3¼". "Ford"	No Price Found		
(K10) Kansas Sedan: No. ?, Buick, 4 open windows, WV	No Price Found		
(K11) Kansas Sedan: No. ?, "Chevrolet," L1, 6 windows, VL, RM, MSW, WV	No Price Found		
(K12) Kansas Sedan: No. ?, Ford, checkered grille, 6 open windows, MWW, WV	No Price Found		
(K13) Kansas?: Also other marques and unnumbered, but bearing **14** mold family resemblance. Local collectors believe they are Kansas, but they are an anomaly in the line.			
(K14) Kansas Tractor: **17a**. 3". "Fordson", visible engine, large rear, small front, wide-rimmed disc wheels w/4 circular holes, tow hook, driver	10	15	20
(K15) Kansas Tractor: **17b**, 2⅝". "Fordson", visible engine, large 6 spoke rear wheels, small 4 spoke front wheels, driver	No Price Found		
(K16) Kansas Truck, tank: **20**, 3¼", Ford, 3 tanks oil & gas, 2 open windows, MW, (sim. solid tires)	12	18	24
(K17) Kansas Tractor engine: **25** and UV, 3⅛". Case steam, large rear small front MSW, flywheel high on engine, crew of 2. (See no. 71) (There may be a one-driver version)	16	24	32
(K18) Kansas Racer: **26**, 4", Stripdown, long hood, driver. (See no. 33)	15	23	30
(K19) Kansas Tractor: **26**, 1.?, "Caterpillar", "Whoopee". (See no. 48)	No Price Found		
(K20) Kansas Harvester/Thresher: **27** and UV, 3⅛", Tow hook, 6 or 8 spoke MSW. (See no. 72)	15	23	30
(K21) Kansas Racer: **31**, 2⅛", Indy boattail, 4 cyl. r. exhaust, MWW, driver. (See no. 10, no. 67) (And UV?)	6	9	12
(K22) Kansas Racer: **33**, 3⅛", "Bearcat" stripdown, 4 cyl. l. exhaust, large "33", driver. (See no. 26)	16	24	32
(23) Kansas Coupe: **35a** and UV, 2¼", '31 Nash?, no louvers, NWW	6	9	12

	C6	C8	C10
(K24) Kansas Coupe: **35b** 2¼", HO, VG, verticle louvers, LI, MWW, RM, WV	6	9	12
(K25) Kansas Locomotive: **36**, 4½", Tender, 10 wheel 0-6-4, "KT & N RR"	10	15	20
(K26) Kansas "Pullman": **37**, 3½", "KT & N RR"	6	9	12
(K27) Kansas Box Car: **38**, 3¼", "KT & N RR", Union Pacific shield. (a promotional?)	12	18	24
(K28) Kansas Tank Car: **39**, 3¼", "KT & N RR"	6	9	12
(K29) Kansas Caboose: **40**, 2¾", "KT & N RR"	5	8	10
(K30) Kansas Stock Car or Box Car: 41, 3¼", KT & N RR"	6	9	12
(K31) Kansas Dump Truck: **42a**, 3½", Ford, open cab, "42 diamond" logo on hinged box, SP, driver	10	15	20
(K32) Kansas Dump Truck: **42b**, 3½", Ford, open cab, "42" on frame, tin hinged box, driver	8	12	16
(K33) Kansas Truck, Flatbed or Tractor: **42c**, 3½". COE type	6	9	12
(K34) Kansas Road Roller: **43**, 3¼", Steam, wood rollers, driver	16	24	32
(K35) Kansas Record Car: **46**, 2⅞", '29 Golden Arrow, large fin, driver. May be an UV, 2¼"	10	15	20
(K36) Kansas Tractor: **48**, 3". "Caterpiller" crawler w/rubber track, "Whoopee", SP, driver	20	30	40
(K37) Kansas Bus: **49**, 2⅜". '28 Pickwick two deck "Nite Coach", SP. (See no. 59). Also UV with dual wheels	6	9	12
(K38) Kansas Truck: **51a**, 3⅝", Ford dump, driver (see no. 42)	No Price Found		
(K39) Kansas Truck: **51b**, 2¾", Ford pickup, open cab	8	12	16
(K40) Kansas Roadster: **54a**, 2¼". Buick, plain grille, rumble seat, SM, driver	12	18	24
(K41) Kansas Sport Coupe (Roadster): **54b**, 2⅜", Plain grille, SM, T, driver. May be an UV	12	18	24
(K42) Kansas Truck: **55**, 4", Ford, semi-stake detach, trailer, MSW (tractor similar to no. 51)	9	14	18
(K43) Kansas Coupe: **56**, 2¾". Closed 3 wheeler, little known	No Price Found		
(K44) Kansas Tractor: **57**, 1⅞", Fordson, visible engine, driver (see no. 17)	No Price Found		
(K45) Kansas Sedan: **58a**, 2¼", American Austin 2 dr. Bantam, "rooster" on doors, 4 open windows, MWW	12	18	24
(K46) Kansas Sedan: **58b**, 2¼", Bantam w/o rooster image; probably a smaller version also	10	15	20
(K47) Kansas Bus: **59**, 3½", '29 Pickwick Nite Coach, arched shape grille	12	18	24
(K48) Kansas Sedan **60**, 3½", Chrysler?, 2 dr., 4 open windows, SM (sim. disc covers), T	20	30	40
(K49) Kansas Planter: **61**, 4", "KTN no. 61", towed V blade plow w/seed hopper, hinged frame, 6 spoke 1¼" wheels	No Price Found		
(K50) Kansas Plow: **62**, Single blade plow towed on same frame	No Price Found		
(K51) Kansas Harrow: **62**, 8 discs towed on same frame	No Price Found		
(K52) Kansas Dirt Scoop or Tumble: 64, Towed on same frame	No Price Found		
(K53) Kansas Scraper: **65**, Towed blade 1⅞" wide, on same frame	No Price Found		
(K54) Kansas Fire Engine: **70**, Steam pumper, Seagrave?, driver	8	12	16
(K55) Kansas Traction Engine: **71**, 2¼" or 2½", Case steam, crew of 1 or 2? (See no. 25)	No Price Found		
(K56) Kansas Harvester: **72**, 2⅜", Thresher (see no. 27)	No Price Found		

Higher numbers not verified for Kansas. (See Best Toy)

UNNUMBERED KANSAS TOY & NOVELTY VEHICLES

The following are believed by collectors to be Kansas Toys. Some are reported as duplicates of those with numbers. Values should be the same as of comparable numbered toys.

	C6	C8	C10
(K?57) Coupe, unnumbered, 3⅛", probably mid-1920s, squarish cab on streamlined racing body, no fenders, 4 side windows, small rear window, trunk shallow, sloping, cab roof slopes slightly to rear, prominent hood ornament or knob, stringpull knob below grille, metal disk wheels, blue japaned finish	No Price Found		
(K?58) Race car: 1", Solid casting. A premium or marker? (See no. 31, no. 67)	No Price Found		
(K?59) Race car: 1½", Version of no. 67?	No Price Found		
(K?60) Tractor: 1¾", Fordson, driver. Version of no. 57?	No Price Found		
(K?61) Midget cabin racer: 2", Open windows, no windshield	No Price Found		
(K?62) Portable engine: 2¼", Witte brand	No Price Found		

KANSAS (cont.)

(K?63) Sedan: 2½", Buick, 4 open
    windows, SM, NWW, T, (similar
    to no. 60)..................... No Price Found

(K?64) Bus: 2½", Blimp shape w/tail
    fins, propeller in tail........... No Price Found

(K?65) Fire truck: 3¼", Driver...... No Price Found

(K?66) Truck: 3½", Tanker, oil or gas No Price Found

(K?67) Speed car: 4", (Speedster no.
    26, or Best record car no. 85?)... No Price Found

(K?68) Coupe: 4½"................. No Price Found

(K?69) Tractor: 5", John Deere?,
    metal spoked wheels, large rear
    with pleated wide rims and
    fenders, no driver............. No Price Found

(K?70) Racer, 6", company's first toy?
    With driver, metal wheels, Indy
    type .... No Price Found

Kelmet No. 501, White Dump Truck,
    25" long.................... 400   700   1000

KELMET No. 501 White Dump Truck, "Big Boy"
Courtesy Joe and Sharon Freed

KENTON Fire Pumper, 18" long, has gong.
Courtesy Mapes Auctioneers & Appraisers

KENTON

	C6	C8	C10		C6	C8	C10
Kenton Auto, 6" long, cast iron.....	140	210	280	Kenton Bus, Double-Decker, 6" long, 1920s.......................	400	600	800
Kenton Boat-tail cut-down speedster, 1910, 7" long.................	120	180	240	Kenton Bus, Double Decker, 1920, 7¼" long....................	1100	1650	2200
Kenton Buckeye Ditching Machine...	800	1200	1600	Kenton Bus, double-decker, 9½" long	500	750	1000
				Kenton Bus, 8" long, cast iron......	340	510	680

KENTON Bus, double-decker, 9½" long.
Courtesy Phillips New York

	C6	C8	C10
Kenton Bus, 1920s, 10¾" long	375.00	525.50	750.00
Kenton Cement Mixer, rubber wheels, marked "Jaeger", 7" long, cast iron	200	300	400
Kenton Cattle Truck, 8" long, cast iron, circa 1938	150	225	300
Kenton Cement Mixer	120	180	240
Kenton "Coal" dump truck, 8½" long	140	210	280
Kenton "Coast-to-Coast" bus	100	150	200
Kenton Emergency Truck, circa 1930s, black rubber tires, takes batteries for headlights and spotlight	180	270	360
Kenton Fire Apparatus Truck	400	600	800
Kenton Fire Pump truck, early, with driver	350	525	700
Kenton Fire Pumper, 14½" long, 1920s	450	675	900
Kenton Fire Pumper, 18" long, circa 1920, has gong	350	525	700

	C6	C8	C10
Kenton Fire Truck, 15" long with pumper	400	600	800
Kenton Ice Truck, tongs and glass ice, 7½"	300	450	600
Kenton Jaeger cement mixer, 6½" long, iron wheels	250	375	500
Kenton Jaeger cement mixer, 8" long	300	450	600
Kenton Jaeger "Mixer", cast iron cement truck, 9" long	600	900	1200
Kenton Ladder Truck, approx. 7½" long, cast iron	200	300	400
Kenton Ladder Truck, pressed steel ladders, 16" long	300	450	600
Kenton Ladder Truck, 17¼" long	300	450	600
Kenton Overland Circus cage truck with driver, 7½" long	300	450	600
Kenton Overland Circus with lion, 9" long	900	1350	1800
Kenton Patrol Wagon, marked "Patrol" on side, circa 1920s-1930s	325	500	650
Kenton Phaeton touring car, 12"	350.00	562.50	700.00
Kenton Pontiac, approx. 4" long	150	225	300
Kenton Road Grader, cast iron, 7½" long, rubber tires, nickel-plated moveable blade	200	300	400
Kenton Runabout Auto, 5" long, 1900	350	525	700
Kenton Runabout Auto, cast iron, 7" long, resembles a 1910 Franklin, has driver	700	1050	1400
Kenton Sedan, 7" long, late 1930s, rubber tires, take apart body	1400	2100	2800
Kenton "Speed" stake truck, circa 1927, 5½" long	50	75	100
Kenton Sprinkler Truck, early, 8"	300	450	600

KENTON Bus, double-decker 1920s, 7¼" long.
Courtesy Lloyd W. Ralston Auctions.

KENTON Tow Auto, 1920s, 9½" long.
Courtesy Lloyd W. Ralston Auctions

KENTON "Jaeger" Cement Mixer Truck, 8" long.
Courtesy HAKE'S Americana & Collectibles

KENTON, boat-tail, cut-down speedster, 1910, 7" long.
Courtesy Lloyd W. Ralston Auctions

KENTON Ladder Truck, pressed steel ladders, 16" long.
Courtesy Lloyd W. Ralston Auctions

KENTON Sedan 7" long, late 30s.
Courtesy Lloyd W. Ralston Auctions.

	C6	C8	C10
Kenton Steam Roller, "Gallon Master", 6½" long	150	225	300
Kenton Steam Shovel, Marion, 7¼" long	600	900	1200
Kenton Tank, cast iron, 2½" long . . .	80	120	160
Kenton Touring Car, open, driver and passenger, 8½" long	300	450	600
Kenton Tow Auto, 1920s, 9½" long.	1600	2400	3200
Kenton Yellow Cab, 1950s, 6⅜" long.	300	450	600

KEYSTONE "Moving Van Long Distance Hauling"
Courtesy Mapes Auctioneers & Appraisers

KEYSTONE

Keystone, of Boston, Massachusetts, had an odd assortment of products; movie projectors, steel trucks, wooden boats and pressed wood forts and garages. Founded in June, 1922 or 1923 by Chester Rimmer and Arthur Jackson, it was first located in a small shop in Malden, Mass. under the name Jackrim, using parts of the partners' last names. Rimmer retired in 1958 and sold out to various companies. Address in Boston was 288 A Street. All numbers and descriptions in bold type are Keystone's own.

	C6	C8	C10
Keystone No. ? "Dugan Brothers" "ridem" truck	150	225	300
Keystone **No. 41 Dump Truck**, 26½" long	250	550	850
Keystone **No. 43 American Railway Express**, 26" long	650	1100	1650
Keystone **No. 44 Truck Loader**, 17¾" high	150	275	350
Keystone **No. 45 U.S. Mail Truck**, 26" long	600	1100	1575
Keystone **No. 46 Steam Shovel**, 26" long when arm is extended	150	300	450
Keystone **No. 47 Steam Shovel**, 34½" long when arm is extended	175	545	500
Keystone **No. 48 U.S. Army Truck**, 26" long	400	700	1000
Keystone **No. 49 Fire Truck**, 27½" long hose truck	600	1000	1480
Keystone **No. 51 Police Patrol**, 27½" long	575	850	1175
Keystone **No. 52 Fire Truck**, 27½" long	400	825	1250

KEYSTONE No. ? "Dugan Brothers" "ridem" truck
Courtesy Joe and Sharon Freed

KEYSTONE No. 43 American Railway Express

KEYSTONE Packard Dump Truck 26" long.
Courtesy PB Eighty-Four New York

KEYSTONE No. 48 U.S. Army Truck
Courtesy Joe and Sharon Freed

	C6	C8	C10
Keystone **No. 53 Sprinkler Truck,** tank 12" long....................	650	1000	1450
Keystone **No. 54 Koaster Truck,** with skids, hoist cable, windlass, 26" long when skids retracted........	800	1350	1825
Keystone **No. 55 Koaster Truck,** without skids and windlass......	800	1225	1650
Keystone **No. 56 Water Pump Tower,** 29" long...................	650	1000	1375
Keystone **No. 57 Chemical Pump Engine,** 27½" long...........	800	1150	1575
Keystone **No. 58 Moving Van,** 26" long.......................	600	1200	1750
Keystone **No. 62 Hydraulic Dump Truck,** 26" long..............	300	650	975
Keystone **No. 73 Ambulance,** military, 27" long...................	550	900	1250
Keystone **No. 78 Wrecking Car,** 27" long........................	500	750	1000
Keystone **79 Aerial Ladder,** 30½" long........................	600	1050	1425
Keystone **No. ?? Steam Roller,** red and black, air pressure whistle, brass bell, 20" long............	300	450	600
Keystone **No. ?? "World's Greatest Circus" Truck,** 26" long, circa 1930s....................	1500	2250	3000

KEYSTONE No. 58 Moving Van
Courtesy Joe and Sharon Freed

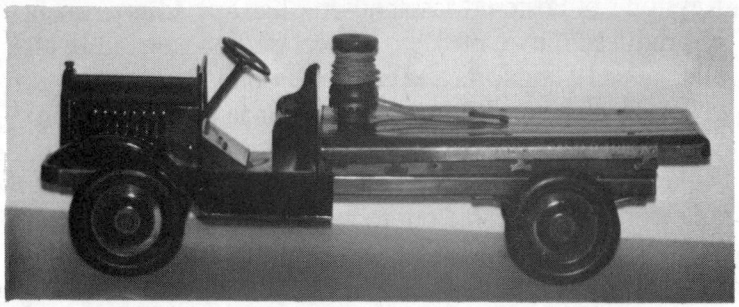

KEYSTONE No. 55
Courtesy Joe and Sharon Freed

KEYSTONE No. 49 Fire Truck
Courtesy Joe and Sharon Freed

KILGORE

Kilgore, of Westerville, Ohio, appears to have begun toymaking in the 1920s. Its toys were cast iron and low-priced, with cap pistols its most popular line. But it also did well with a number of attractive trucks, fire engines and cars, as well as scattered aircraft and ships. Some subsidiary manufacturing was done in Lancaster, Pennsylvania and Canada. In 1937 Kilgore began making plastic cars, trucks, planes and buses, and later added plastic cap pistols, placing it among the first (if not the first) companies to produce plastic toys. Kilgore seems to have remained in business until World War Two, and perhaps beyond.

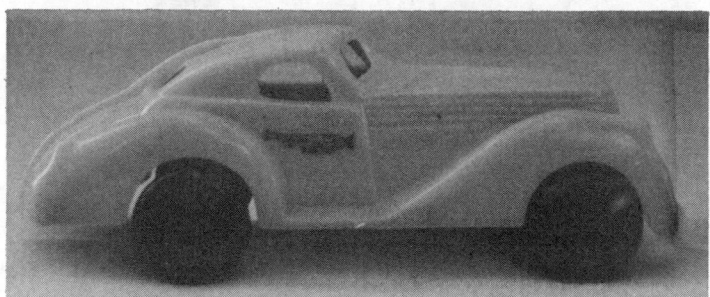

KILGORE Coupe, streamlined, plastic
Photo by Dave Leopard

KILGORE "Taxi", plastic
Photo by Dave Leopard

LAPIN Sedan, 6 side windows
Photo by Dave Leopard

LAPIN Coupe, plastic
Photo by Dave Leopard

KILGORE Arctic Ice Cream Truck
Courtesy Chic Gast

	C6	C8	C10
Kilgore Arctic Ice Cream Truck, 8" long	700	1050	1400
Kilgore "Arctic Ice Cream" truck, 9" long	500	750	1000
Kilgore Auto, "LF 1300A", with driver	180	270	360
Kilgore Bus, plastic, advertised in 1937, 4"	10	12	15
Kilgore Convertible with Rumble Seat, 7" long, early 1930s, with driver	160	240	320
Kilgore Coupe, streamlined, plastic, 4", advertised in 1939	10	12	15
Kilgore Dump Truck, cast iron, circa 1934, 5¾" long	160	240	320
Kilgore Dump Truck, 7" long, 1930s	180	270	360
Kilgore "Express" Truck, plastic, 4", advertised in 1937	10	12	15
Kilgore "Fire Chief" sedan, plastic, 4" advertised in 1937	10	12	15
Kilgore Livestock Truck, 7" long, 1930s	700	1050	1400
Kilgore Livestock Truck, 9" long	500	750	1000
Kilgore Motorcycle, 4" long, single rider	80	120	160
Kilgore Motorcycle, 4¼" long, double rider	100	150	200
Kilgore Packard Luxury Sedan, 8¼", take-apart body	800	1200	1600
Kilgore Pierce-Arrow Roadster, 6⅛" take-apart body	250	375	500
Kilgore Roadster, 6" long, driver, rumble seat	230	345	460
Kilgore Sedan, 3¼" long	70	105	140
Kilgore Stutz Roadster, 13 parts	500	750	1000
Kilgore "Taxi", plastic, 4", advertised in 1937	10	12	15
Kilgore "Toy Town Delivery" truck, 6⅛" long	200	300	400

KINGSBURY

Kingsbury had its origins in 1886 in Keene, New Hampshire. Its owner was Harry T. Kingsbury, who bought the Wilkins Toy Company, apparently not changing that firm's name till after World War One. Steel and spring motors characterize Kingsbury's toys, with cars, fire engines, farm equipment and racing cars its primary output. Kingsbury is still in business, but seems to have given up toy production in 1942.

KINGSBURY Phaeton Auto, 1900, 9¼" long.
Courtesy Lloyd W. Ralston Auctions

	C6	C8	C10
Kingsbury Aerial Ladder Truck, pressed steel windup circa 1941, 24" long, ladder rises automatically to height of 38 inches when the truck runs into any obstruction, fireman on ladder climbs up and down by turning crank at base of ladder, early version new in 1905.	150	225	300
Kingsbury Airflow, circa 1934, pressed steel, rubber tires, 14" long.....	190	275	380
Kingsbury Airflow, clockwork, 14" long..........	250	375	500
Kingsbury auto, very early, 9¾" long, steel windup.................	350	525	700
Kingsbury Brougham Sedan, 13" long, pressed steel windup..........	450	675	900
Kingsbury Bus, 18" long, pressed steel	400	600	800
Kingsbury Cannon Truck, very early, 11" long, clockwork............	140	210	280
Kingsbury Caterpillar, 8½" long, wind-up......................	150	225	300
Kingsbury Cattle Truck, 19" long, 1930s......................	90	135	180
Kingsbury De Soto, 14½" long, pressed steel windup, circa 1938..	75.00	112.50	150.00
Kingsbury Dump Truck, tin, driver, 10" long	225.00	337.50	450.00
Kingsbury Dump Truck, early 30s, 16" long, clockwork...........	350	525	700
Kingsbury Fire Pumper, 11" long, very early, clockwork iron and steel....................	250	375	500
Kingsbury Fire Pumper, 1920s, 23" long......................	450	675	900
Kingsbury Fire Truck, 18" long.....	150	225	300
Kingsbury Ford Sedan & House Trailer, 1937, 23" long, pressed steel....................	200	300	400
Kingsbury Golden Arrow Racer, 20" long, pressed steel windup.......	275	375	450
Kingsbury Greyhound Bus..........	150	225	300
Kingsbury Ladder Truck, steel, driver, 22"......................	150	225	300
Kingsbury ladder wagon fire truck, tin, rubber tires, 23½" long.....	75.00	112.50	150.00
Kingsbury Phaeton Auto, 1900, rubber slip tires, 9½" long.........	750	1125	1500
Kingsbury Rack Truck, 16" long, pressed steel windup..........	350	525	700

	C6	C8	C10
Kingsbury Roadster, 13" long, electric headlights, spring motor, luggage rack	250	375	500
Kingsbury Sedan, two-door, with trailer, 22½" long, 1930s, clockwork	175.00	262.50	350.00
Kingsbury Sunbeam Racer, sheetmetal, red with rubber tires on steel wheels, clockwork motor, 19" long	375	565	750
Kingsbury Tractor, mechanical, 8" with driver..............	150	225	300
Kingsbury Tractor and cart, tin, with iron driver, white rubber wheels, circa 1930s.................	110	165	220
Kingsbury Transit Truck, 1930s, 19" long	150	225	300
Kingsbury Truck with C Cap, 10" long, tin..................	175.00	262.50	350.00
Kingsbury Wind-Up Car, curved dash, driver, 9" long.................	225.00	337.50	450.00
Kingsbury Wrecker, 13" long, pressed steel, windup.............	250	375	500
Ladder Truck, driver front and rear, cast iron, 5" long..............	45.00	67.50	90.00
Ladder Truck approx. 14" long, battery operated lights, wind-up.....	150	225	300
Laketoy "John Wanamaker" delivery van, 10½" long, wooden.......	180	270	360
Lansing Slik-Toy 7" aluminum passenger sedan, circa 1940s.....	12.50	18.75	25.00
Lapin Cadillac, 1948, 4 doors, 6" long	5.00	7.50	10.00

LAPIN Coupe, plastic 1939 Hudson?   Photo by Dave Leopard

	C6	C8	C10
Lapin Coupe, plastic, 1939 Hudson?..	10	12	15
Lapin Sedan, six side windows, plastic, 1939 Hudson?.................	10	12	15
Lapin Stake Truck, Chevrolet, plastic, 1947, 4"......................	5.00	7.50	10.00

	C6	C8	C10
Lindstrom Lumber Truck no. 160, steerable front wheels, tin, with driver, 10" long	125.00	187.50	250.00
Lindstrom Steam Roller No. 181, mechanical, 12" long	50	75	100
Log Truck (Beck), steers via horn on top of cab, late 1940s, large	60	90	120

Mack Dump truck, cast iron, 1930s.
Courtesy Mapes Auctioneers & Appraisers

Mack Stake Truck, cast iron, 7" long.
Courtesy Mapes Auctioneers & Appraisers

	C6	C8	C10
Mack Dump Truck, cast iron, 12" long	120	180	240
Mack Dump truck, cast iron, 1930s	75.00	112.50	150.00
"Mack" Ladder Truck, 18" long, cast iron	300	450	600
Mack Stake Truck 4¼" long, cast iron (A.C. Williams)	90	135	180
Mack Stake Truck, 5" long, cast iron wheels, circa late 1920s	65.00	97.50	130.00
Mack Stake Truck, 5" long, white rubber wheels, circa 1930s	70	105	140
Mack Stake Truck, cast iron, 7" long	70	105	140

MANOIL

Manoil: List compiled by Terry Sells, Numbers and words in bold are Manoil's own description. 701-706 began production in 1934.

	C6	C8	C10
Manoil **700 Sedan**, futuristic	45.00	67.50	90.00
Manoil **701 Sedan**, futuristic	45.00	67.50	90.00
Manoil **702 Coupe**, futuristic	45.00	67.50	90.00
Manoil **703 Wrecker**, futuristic	70	105	140
Manoil **704 Roadster**, futuristic, Pa.. No. 95791	45.00	67.50	90.00
Manoil **705 Sedan**, futuristic, Pat. No. 95792	45.00	67.50	90.00
Manoil **706 Rocket**, futuristic bus-like vehicle, Pat. No. 95793	40	60	80
Manoil **70 Soup Kitchen**, large number	9.00	13.50	18.00
Manoil **70A Soup Kitchen**, small number	7.50	11.25	15.00
Manoil **71 Shell Carrier With Soldier On Shell Box**, has loop	11.00	16.50	22.00
Manoil **71A** Same as above, no loop	11.00	16.50	22.00
Manoil **72 Water Wagon**, large number	9.00	13.50	18.00
Manoil **72A** Same as above, small number	7.00	10.50	14.00
Manoil **72B** No number	5.00	7.50	10.00
Manoil **73 Tractor**, loop front	9.00	13.50	18.00
Manoil **73A Tractor**, plain front	8	12	16
Manoil **74 Armored Car with Anti-Tank Gun**	12.50	18.75	25.00
Manoil **75 Armored Car with Anti-Aircraft Gun**	20	30	40
Manoil **75A Armored Car with Siren**, siren cast separately	25.00	37.50	50.00
Manoil **75A Armored Car With Siren**, siren cast with vehicle	16	24	32
Manoil **95 Tank**	7.50	11.25	15.00
Manoil **96 Large Shell on Truck**	9.00	13.50	18.00
Manoil **97 Pontoon on Wheels**	15.00	22.50	30.00
Manoil **98 Torpedo on Wheels**	9.00	13.50	18.00
Manoil **103 Gasoline Truck**	9.00	13.50	18.00
Manoil **104 Chemical Truck**	15.00	22.50	30.00
Manoil **105 Five Barrel Gun on Wheels**	11.00	16.50	22.00
Manoil **(MC5) Tank**, composition	12.50	18.75	25.00

Manoil Post War Vehicles

	C6	C8	C10
Manoil **707 Sedan**	12.50	18.75	25.00
Manoil **708 Roadster**, horizontal radiator	12.50	18.75	25.00
Manoil **708A Roadster**, vertical radiator	12.50	18.75	25.00
Manoil **709 Fire Engine**	9.00	13.50	18.00
Manoil **710 Oil Tanker**	7.50	11.25	15.00
Manoil **711 Aerial Ladder**	No Price Found		
Manoil **712 Pumper**	No Price Found		
Manoil **713 Bus**	12	18	24
Manoil **714 Towing Truck**	10	15	20
Manoil **715 Commercial Truck**	10	15	20

704 ROADSTER

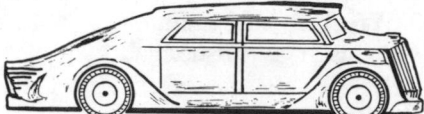

705 SEDAN

706 ROCKET

MANOIL Pre-World War II vehicles
Courtesy Peter and Marjorie Ruben

No. 713   BUS

No. 710 - OIL TANKER

No. 709 - FIRE ENGINE

No. 707 - SEDAN

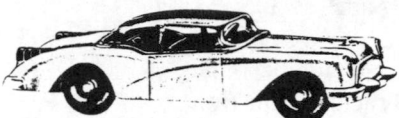

No. 716 - SEDAN

No. 717 - HARD TOP CONVERTIBLE

No. 718 - CONVERTIBLE

No. 715 - COMMERCIAL TRUCK has removable panels, as
shown above

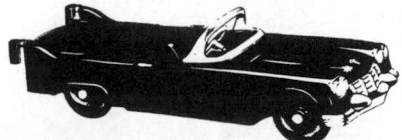

No. 719 - SPORT CAR

No. 714 - TOWING TRUCK

No. 720 - RANCH WAGON

MANOIL Postwar Vehicles
Courtesy Peter and Marjorie Ruben

No. 708 - ROADSTER

MANOIL Post-War Vehicles
Courtesy Peter and Marjorie Ruben

No. 700 - SEDAN

No. 701 - SEDAN

No. 702 - COUPE

No. 703 - WRECKER

MANOIL, circa 1935
Courtesy Peter and Marjorie Ruben

MANOIL 69 cannon, metal wheels, wood wheels, wood wheels variant.
MANOIL Vehicles, top row, L to R: 70,   71. Middle row,   71 with variant
on wheel support, 72, 73 with front tow loop, 74. Bottom row: 75,   75A
with siren cast separately, 75A siren cast integrally.
Photo by Ed Poole

	C6	C8	C10
Manoil 716 Sedan.................	10	15	20
Manoil 717 Hard Top Convertible...	12	18	24
Manoil 718 Convertible...........	10	15	20
Manoil 719 Sport Car	10	15	20
Manoil 720 Ranch Wagon..........	10	15	20
MANOIL Plastic Vehicles			
Manoil P-7 Roadster.............	2.50	3.75	5.00
Manoil P-8 Sedan...............	2.50	3.75	5.00
Manoil P-9 Pick-Up.............	2.50	3.75	5.00
Manoil P-10 Towing Truck........	2.50	3.75	5.00
Manoil P-11 Road Scraper........	2.50	3.75	5.00
Manoil P-12 Tractor.............	2.50	3.75	5.00
Manoil P-13 Dump Cart..........	2.50	3.75	5.00

MANOIL, top L to R: 713,   716,   P-7
  Bottom, L to R: 714,   P-10,   P-11,   P-9
Courtesy Marjorie and Peter Ruben

MANOIL, Top L to R: 705,   708 early,   708 later
  Bottom L to R: 707,   710,   709
Photo by Norbet Schachter
Courtesy Marjorie and Peter Ruben

95   96   97   98
103   104   105   200
MANOIL Vehicles and "Metal Action Cannon" No. 200.
Photo by Ed Poole

MANOIL 712 Pumper (top); 711 Aerial Ladder (bottom).
Photo by Norbert Schachter.
Courtesy Marjorie and Peter Ruben

	C6	C8	C10
Marx Air Force truck, "Air Defense Group", ridem toy, 32" long, No. 3290	130	195	260
Marx Air Force Truck, canvas top, 20" long	105.00	157.50	210.00
Marx Ambulance No. 8500, approx. 14" long, 1930s	240	360	480
Marx Ambulance No. 8600, approx. 14" long, 1930s	240	360	480
Marx "American Railroad Express Agency Inc.," early 1930s, open cab, 7"	120	180	240
Marx American Truck Co. No. 65 moving truck, friction	65.00	97.50	130.00
Marx Army Corps of Engineers, 20", canvas top	125.00	187.50	250.00
Marx Army Jeep with Searchlight Trailer, steel	120	180	240
Marx Auto Transport, 1950s with Tin Litho cars (2 of them), 34" long	100	150	200
Marx "Auto Transwalk" No. T-50447B, 1930s truck with three cars	130	195	260
Marx "Big Shot" Cannon Truck, plastic, 22" long, fires cap-loaded missile	30	45	60
Marx "Chief-Fire Dept. No. 1", "Friction Drive", circa 1948	40	60	80
Marx "City Sanitation Dept. Help Keep Your City Clean", circa 1940, 12¾" long	27.50	41.25	55.00

MARX Coca-Cola Truck, 20" long.
Courtesy Richard MacNary

MARX Convertible Roadster, 1930s, 11" long.
Courtesy Lloyd W. Ralston Auctions

MARX Lonesome Pine trailer and convertible sedan, 19" long.
Courtesy Lloyd W. Ralston Auctions

	C6	C8	C10
Marx Coca Cola truck, 20" long, sprite decal, stamped steel, late 1940s to early 1950s	150	225	300
Marx Convertible Roadster, 1930s, nickel plated tin, 11" long	150	225	300
Marx Dump Truck, 17" long, No. 695B	50	75	100
Marx Dump Truck, two-color, No. T751, circa 1930s	100	150	200
Marx No. 1084 Dump Truck	30	45	60
Marx "Electrically Lighted Truck and Trailer Set" No. T-5715, circa 1930s, 15" long	150	225	300
Marx Falcoln with plastic bubble top, black rubber tires	60	90	120
Marx Fire Truck, friction, 15", long	125.00	187.50	250.00
Marx G-Man Pursuit car, No. 7000, 15" long, 1930s	100	150	200
Marx Gang Buster Car No. 7200, approx. 14" long, 1930s	200	300	400
Marx Grocery Truck, 1950s, 14½" long	60	90	120
Marx Guided Missile Truck No. 4488	60	90	120
Marx "High-Boy Climbing Tractor" No. 950, 10½" long	60	90	120
Marx "Heavy Gauge Tractor" No. 926	45.00	67.50	90.00
Marx Hi-way Express Truck	150	225	300
Marx Jeep	30	45	60
Marx Lazy-Dazy Dairy Farm Pick-Up Truck and Trailer, 22" long	32.50	48.75	65.00
Marx Lonesome Pine trailer and convertible sedan, 1930s, 19" long	125.00	187.50	250.00
Marx "Lumar Contractors" 962 dump truck	62.50	93.75	125.00
Marx "Lumar Contractors" Steam Shovel	27.50	41.25	55.00
Marx M.D. War Dept. Ambulance, 1930s	180	270	360
Marx No. 1016 Machinery Moving Truck	60	90	120
Marx "Mammoth Truck Train" No. T-50-12345, circa 1930s, truck with five trailers	175.00	262.50	350.00
Marx "Motor Market"	50	75	100
Marx Mystery Taxi, circa 1930s, press down to operate	80	120	165
Marx Navy Jeep No. 1078	65.00	97.50	130.00
Marx Navy Jeep with Searchlight Trailer	125.00	187.50	250.00
Marx Panel Wagon	40	60	80
Marx Pepsi-Cola Truck, 11" long, 1950s	50	75	100
Marx "Pet Shop Delivery", 1950s, 10" long	40	60	80

MARX Power Grader
Courtesy Continental Hobby House

Metal Cast Tank
Photo by Ed Poole

	C6	C8	C10
Marx "Power Grader" No. 1759, black or white wheels, 17½" long	50	75	100
Marx Pure Milk Dairy Truck with glass bottles, pressed steel, tin wheels, circa 1940	100	150	200
Marx REA Express Truck No. 1021	125.00	187.50	250.00
Marx Road Grader, heavy-duty	50	75	100
Marx Rocker Dump No. 1752, 17½" long	60	90	120
Marx Side Dump Truck, four-color No. T-475, circa 1940	60	90	120
Marx Side Dump Truck and Trailer, No. T-4045, circa 1930s	100	150	200
Marx "Siren Fire Chief", circa 1930, "F.D. 1st Batt.", 15" long	150	225	300
Marx Siren Police Car No. 8300, 1930s, approx. 14" long	150	225	300
Marx "Sparkling Hot Rod Racer", 1950s plastic wind-up, 8" long	20	30	40
Marx Sports Coupe, 1930s, 15"	125.00	187.50	250.00
Marx Stake-type truck, 3-color, No. E-271, circa 1941	50	75	100
Marx No. 1008 Stake Truck	40	60	80
Marx "Tricky Taxi", friction, 4½" long	62.50	93.75	125.00
Marx "U.S. Mail" truck, 14" long	200	300	400
Marx "USA 41573147" Army Truck, circa 1952, 13¾" long	60	90	120
Marx Willys Jeep, steel, circa 1938, 12" long, hood opens, windshield folds down	50	75	100
Marx Willys Jeep and trailer, circa 1940s	70	105	140
Marx Wrecker Truck No. T-16, circa 1930s	150	225	300
McCormick-Deering Spreader, "Made in USA", steel, 10½" long, black rubber, 1950s	60	90	120
Metal Cast Tank, slush lead, circa 1946	33.00	49.50	66.00
Metal Masters Ambulance wind-up, circa 1940	40	60	80
Metal Masters Bus, 7" long, 1930s	30	45	60
Metal Masters Bus, black rubber tires	18	27	36
Metal Masters Bus, black plastic wheels, circa WW II, approx. 7" long	20	30	40

	C6	C8	C10
Metal Masters pickup truck with black plastic wheels, approx. 7" long	17.50	26.25	35.00
Metal Masters station wagon, like model 100, but not wind-up	30	45	60
Metal Masters station wagon, model 100, wind-up, circa 1940	50	75	100
Metal Masters Tow Truck No. 600, circa 1940, "Towing ABC Service"	30	45	60
Metal Masters Tow Truck with spring wind-up motor, like No. 600 otherwise	60	90	120
Metalcraft "Bunte Candies" 12" truck	175.00	262.50	350.00
Metalcraft Coca Cola Truck, 11" long, pressed steel, rubber tires, circa late 20s-early 30s, 10 bottles in rack, "Every Bottle Sterilized"	600	900	1200
Metalcraft Coca Cola Truck, 10 bottles, 10½" long, 1930s	300	450	600

METALCRAFT Coca-Cola truck, late 1930s, 12" long.
Courtesy Richard L. MacNary

	C6	C8	C10
Metalcraft Coca Cola Truck, 12" long, 10 bottles, late 1930s, long nose, stamped metal	No Price Found		
Metalcraft Coca Cola Truck, circa 1928, with bottles in racks	400	600	800
Metalcraft CW Coffee wrecker	300	450	600
Metalcraft Delivery Truck Van, 11" long, steel	200	300	400
Metalcraft "Goodrich Silvertone Tires" wrecker	125.00	187.50	250.00
Metalcraft "Heinz" truck, circa 1932 "Baked Beans, Bottled Vinegar", "Rice Flakes", 12" long	300	480	650

	C6	C8	C10		C6	C8	C10
Metalcraft "Meadow Gold Butter" truck 13" long, battery lights....	300	450	600	Motorcycle "Cop", 3¾" long, cast iron	40	60	80
Metalcraft "Sunshine Biscuits" truck..	250	375	500	Motorcycle, cast iron, white rubber tires, 3" long.	30	45	60
Metalcraft "White King Delivery" truck 12" long.	250	375	500	Motorcycle, Harley-Davidson, rider, 6" long	125.00	187.50	250.00
Model A Ford, coupe with spare tire on back, cast iron.	80	120	160	Motorcycle, Harley-Davidson, cast iron, 9" long, cop rider	200	300	400
Model A Tow Truck, cast iron, no maker imprinted, 7" long.	175.00	262.50	350.00	Motorcycle with sidecar, policeman rider, 4" long, cast iron.	60	90	120
Model T Ford, cast iron, 5" long....	175.00	262.50	350.00	Neff-Moon Groceries Van.	175.00	262.50	350.00
Model T, cast iron 6" long.	300	450	600	Neff-Moon Tow Truck, 16", circa 1925.	200	300	400
Model T Ford, cast iron, 8½" long..	225.00	337.50	450.00	Nonpareil Ambulance.	30	45	60
Model T Ford coupe, gray, with animated figures, cast iron, 1920s.	325.00	487.50	650.00	Nonpareil Dry Goods.	30	45	60
Model T Ford, tin.	100	150	200	Nonpareil Police Patrol.	30	45	60
Model T Ford "C" Cab Truck, cast iron, circa early 1920s, 8½" long.	200	300	400	Nonpareil Toyville Express.	30	45	60
Model T Speedster, 10" long.	125.00	187.50	250.00				

NORTH & JUDD. Research by collector C.B.C. Lee suggests that this company, located at the time in New Britain, Connecticut, made cast iron toys for only one year, probably 1930, for S. H. Kress. Their original designs appear to have been marked with the company's name, but their copies for the most part are unmarked. The company is still in business, making quality hardware.

	G	VG	M		G	VG	M
Austin Convertible, open top, marked "North & Judd"		No Price Found		"Anchor Truck Co." (an anchor is North & Judd's trademark)		No Price Found	
Austin Sedan, two-door, marked "North & Judd".		No Price Found		Motorcycle cop, like Hubley's "Cop", separate nickeled driver is held by mushrooms at front of handlebars and on driver's feet		No Price Found	
Bus, looks like Dent, 4.667" long.		No Price Found					
Ford Model A Coupe, looks like Arcade, length of left cab 1.528", has driver in window, trunk at rear. . .		No Price Found		Semi-Trailer Stake Truck, marked "North & Judd".		No Price Found	
Ford Model T stake truck, like Arcade's, but marked				Tractor, looks like Arcade, but has nickeled driver, 2.988" long.		No Price Found	

NYLINT

Nylint began in Rockford, Illinois in 1946. The following list was compiled by Calvin L. Chaussee, showing the period each group of toys was introduced.

NYLINT No. 2200 Michigan Shovel
Courtesy Continental Hobby House

1949

Nylint No. 100 Amazing Car (Turns-Parks-Corners), 13¾" long.	100	150	200
Nylint No. 800 Scootcycle (windup), 7¼" long.	120	180	240
Nylint No. 1000 Deliverall (windup), 10" long.	110	165	220
Nylint No. 1100 Street Sweeper (wind-up), 8¼" long.	180	270	360
Nylint No. 1200 Pump Mobile (wind-up), 8⅝" long	120	180	240
Nylint No. 1400 Roadgrader, 19¼" long	50	75	100
Nylint No. 1600 Payloader, 18" long.	110	165	220
Nylint No. 2000 Speed Swing, 19". . .	55.00	82.50	110.00
Nylint No. 2100 Tournadozer, 20" long	80	120	160
Nylint No. 2200 Michigan Shovel, 31½" long.	120	180	240

	C6	C8	C10
Nylint No. 2400 Electric Cannon, 22½"long	150	225	300
Nylint No. 2500 Telescoping Crane, 27"	66	99	132
Nylint No. 2600 Missile Launcher, 31½"	180	270	360
Nylint No. 2700 Uranium Hauler, 22½" long	170	255	340
Nylint No. 2800 Guided Missile Carrier, 15½" long	160	240	320
Nylint No. 2900 Junior Jack Hammer, 19½"	66	99	132
1952-52-53			
Nylint No. 1300 Tourna Rocker, 18".	120	180	240
Nylint No. 1500 Tournahopper, 22½"	160	240	320
Nylint No. 1700 Tourna Hauler, 30¼" long	120	180	240
Nylint No. 1800 Traveloader, 30" long	240	360	480
Nylint No. 1900 Tourna Tractor-Dozer, 14¾"	80	120	160
1956-59			
Nylint No. 2500 Telescoping Crane, 35¾"	160	240	320
Nylint No. 2600 Missile Launcher	160	240	320
Nylint No. 2800 Guided Missile Carrier	170	255	340
Nylint No. 3000 Grader-Loader, 23¾"	160	240	320
Nylint No. 3100 Payloader Tractor-Shovel, 17⅝"	64	96	128
Nylint No. 3200 Power and Light Lineman Truck, 35¾"	160	240	320
Nylint No. 3300 Power and Light Truck, Posthole Digger, 35¾" long	180	270	360
Nylint No. 3400 Highway Emergency Truck, 18⅝" long	64	96	128
Nylint No. 3500 Count Down Rocket Launcher, 21"	66	99	132
Nylint No. 3600 Ford Rapid Delivery, 18¼" long	100	150	200
Nylint No. 3700 Street Sprinkler Truck, 18" long	240	360	480
Nylint No. 3800 Ford Sales and Service, 13⅝" long	64	96	128
Nylint No. 3900 Ford Platform Tilt Truck, 15¾"	85.00	127.50	170.00
Nylint No. 4000 Ford Speedway Truck with Racer, 24¾"	80	120	160
1960-61			
Nylint No. 4100 U-Haul Truck and Trailer, 22" long	50	75	100
Nylint No. 4200 Bulldozer, 14" long.	34	51	68
Nylint No. 4400 Camper on Pickup, 13½" long	50	75	100
Nylint No. 4600 Construction 4 Wheel Platform Dump, 15¾" long	100	150	200

	C6	C8	C10
Nylint No. 4700 Happy Acres truck with Horses, 14"	90	135	180
Nylint No. 48-4900 (2) U-Haul Trailers, 3 piece set, 33¼" long	150	225	300
1962			
Nylint No. 5000 Dump Truck w/ Cement Mixer, 20½" long	64	96	128
Nylint No. 5100 Dump Truck, 13½" long	30	45	60
Nylint No. 5200 Pickup Truck (Econoline), 11¼" long	34	51	68
Nylint No. 5300 Custom Camper on above, 12½" long	44	66	88
Nylint No. 5400 Custom Camper on above with boat, 23½" long	150	225	300
Nylint No. 5500 Pepsi Truck, 16½" long	110	165	220
1963			
Nylint No. 5800 Ford Econoline Van, 12" long	50	75	100
Nylint No. 6000 American Oil Emergency Truck, 11¼" long	70	105	140
Nylint No. 6200 Kennel Truck with dogs, 11¼" long	125.00	187.50	250.00
Nylint No. 6300 Horse Van, 23½" long	66	99	132
1964			
Nylint No. 6600 Mobile Home, Semi Type, 30" long	110	165	220
Nylint No. 6700 Ambulance, 12" long	90	135	180
Nylint No. 6800 Jalopy, 9⅝" long	30	45	60
Nylint No. 6900 Airport Courtesy Van, 12" long	160	240	320
Nylint No. 7100 Fun on Farm Econoline Truck, 11¼" long, 29 pieces	190	285	380
1965			
Nylint No. ???? Race Team V. Racer, 21"	120	180	240
Nylint No. 1100 Digger Power Shovel, 27" long	80	120	160
Nylint No. 1200 Lawn and Garden Service Truck, 20" long, 12 piece set	170	255	340
Nylint No. 6100 Hydraulic Dump Truck, 13½" long	44	66	88
Nylint No. 6801 Jalopy w/Top, 9⅝" long	44	66	88
Nylint No. 7300 Army Ambulance, 12" long	66	99	132
Nylint No. 7900 Road Grader, 15" long	24	36	48
Nylint No. 8000 Pony Farm Van, 11¼" long, 7 piece set	100	150	200
Nylint No. 8100 Suburban Fire Pumper, 12½" long	85.00	127.50	170.00
Nylint No. 8200 Bronco, 12½" long	64	96	128
Nylint No. 8300 Texaco Service Van, 12" long	85.00	127.50	170.00

	C6	C8	C10
Ohio Armored Car, circa WW I, friction, 7¼" long	225.00	337.50	450.00
Ohio Coupe, 2-door, 17" long pressed steel	150	225	300
Ohio Delivery Truck, 1920s, painted pressed steel, friction, 12" long	260	390	520
Ohio Fire Ladder Truck, 13½" long, 1920s	300	450	600
Ohio Fire Patrol, 9¾" long, pressed steel, cast iron, wood, very early	500	750	1000
Ohio Fire Truck, 10½" long, pressed steel, cast iron, wood, very early	300	450	600
Ohio Fire Truck, 19½", friction	250	375	500
Ohio Pickup Truck, 13" long, 1920s, friction	125.00	187.50	250.00
Ohio Roadster, 7½" long, cast iron and wood, friction, very early	350	525	700
Ohio Roadster, 13" long, 1920s	175.00	262.50	350.00
Ohio Roadster, 18" long, 1920s, friction, pressed steel	250	375	500
Ohio Touring Auto, friction	100	150	200
Ohlsson & Rice, midget race car, aluminum body, rubber tires, circa 1940s	50	75	100
Oil and Gas Truck, cast iron, 8" long	200	300	400
Oil Truck circa 1936, pressed steel 10¾" long	100	150	200
Packard Van Truck, 27" long, screen side, pressed steel	500	750	1000
"Patrol" Motorcycle and rider, circa 1940, 6¼" long, cast iron	100	150	200
"Patrol" stake truck, Wyandotte? pressed steel, 4⅞" long	40	60	80
Pedal Car, "American National Company Toledo Ohio, USA", sheet metal and wooden, dashboard with dials, rubber tread on wheels, 46" long	350	525	700
Pedal Car, "AMF", Hook and Ladder, late 1970s	75.00	112.50	150.00
Pedal Car, circa 1905, chain driver, wooden spoke wheels	1250	1875	2500
Pedal Car, Cadillac, circa 1915 Toledo Metal Wheel Co. lithographed dashboard	500	750	1000
Pedal Car, Chrysler Airflow	500	750	1000
Pedal Car, Fire Truck, Mack, Steel-Craft	400	600	800
Pedal Car, "Ford, 1896", Tubular frame with wire wheels, sheet metal seat with wooden back rest and steering lever, plate under seat has diagram of motor, 39" long	1000	1500	2000
Pedal Car, "Ford" emblem on radiator, painted steel	350	525	700
Pedal Car, green and yellow-painted, metal	350	525	700

OHIO Fire Truck, 19½" long, 1910. Courtesy Lloyd W. Ralston Auctions.

OHIO Armored Car, C. WW I, 7¼" long. Courtesy Lloyd W. Ralston Auctions

OHIO Delivery Truck, 1920s, 12" long. Courtesy Lloyd W. Ralston Auctions

OHIO Roadster, 18" long, 1920s. Courtesy Lloyd W. Ralston Auctions

	C6	C8	C10
Pedal Car, Hudson, wood and steel, folding windshield, tilt-up steering wheel	400	600	800
Pedal Car, Lincoln, 1931	1500	2250	3000
Pedal Car, Mercer Raceabout, 1920	2000	3000	4000
Pedal Car, Nash Sideway, 34" long, 1920s	1000	1500	2000
Pedal Car, Open Coupe, 1920s or early 1930s, Glendron, 36" long	200	300	400
Pedal Car, Packard Dual Cowl Phaeton, 6' long, American National	3000	4500	6000
Pedal Car, Packard Roadster, 1920s, American National, 45" long	1200	1800	2400
Pedal Car, "Packard", early, wire wheels	300	450	600

	C6	C8	C10
Pedal Car, "Pioneer" race car, metal and wood	700	1050	1400
Pedal Car, Steelcraft Buick, late 1920s, 36" long	1500	2250	3000
Pedal Car, Winner, circa 1906	1000	1500	2000
Pickup Truck, cast iron, 3½" long, 1920s, white rubber tires on wooden wheels	40	60	80
Pickup Truck, cast iron, 4" long	80	120	160
Pickup Truck, 7¼" long, cast iron, 1920s	125.00	187.50	250.00
Pickup Truck, tin friction toy, 19" long, 1920s	200	300	400
Pickup Truck, tin or pressed steel, circa 1937-38, 6", wood wheels	40	60	80
Playboy Dump Truck 22" long, tan	150	225	300
Playboy "Intercity Bus", long, cream color	300	450	600

Pedal Car, "Ford"
Courtesy Mapes Auctioneers & Appraisers

PYRO

Pyro began in 1939 in Pyro Park, Union City, New Jersey. The owner was William Lester. At its height, the company had 400 employees.

	C6	C8	C10
Pyro Range Patrol Truck	6	8	10
Pyro "U.S. Army" Truck	6	8	10
Pyro "U.S.M.C." Truck	6	8	10
Pyro "U.S. Navy" Truck	6	8	10
Race Car, cast iron, 9"	125.00	187.50	250.00
Racer "Parker Special," simple body of heavy steel with steel wheels, 11" long	75.00	112.50	150.00
Race Car, friction, with driver, circa 1925	150	225	300
Race Car, 8" long, circa 1918	150	225	300
Racer, 7½" pressed steel with driver, white rubber tires, rubberband and gear powered	17.50	26.25	35.00
Racing Car, cast iron, 6½" long, with figure	75.00	112.50	150.00
Racing Car, cast iron, with driver, full figure, spiked wheels, early 1920s	75.00	112.50	150.00
Racing Car, cast iron, 7¼"	150	225	300
Racing Set, 1930s, 3 tin racing cars, small tin garage	125.00	187.50	250.00
"Radio Police" slush mold police car coupe, white rubber tires, circa 1940	17.50	26.25	35.00
"Railway Express" truck, cast iron, early 1930s, 5" long	110	165	220

CONDITION CODE:
C5 – Good, wear evident overall, shows that has been played with
C6 – Fine, shows some wear in spots, but taken care of
C7 – Very Fine, minor wear overall, very clean
C8 – Excellent, minor wear on edges only
C9 – Near Mint, no noticeable flaws, close inspection may show minute marks
C10 – Mint (like new)
Note: Mint in Box does command higher price

RAINBOW

The following list, with its codings, was compiled by David Leopard. Vehicles are broken down by types.

	C6	C8	C10
RA01 '35 Oldsmobile Coupe, 3¾" long	20	30	40
RA02 '35 Oldsmobile 4 door sedan, 3¼" long	25	35	45
RA03 '35 Oldsmobile 4 door sedan, 5" long	25	35	45
RT01 '35 Studebaker (?) stake side pickup, 5¼" long	25	35	45
RR01 Open Racer, tapered tail, 4" long		No Price Found	

RAINBOW RA01

Photo by Dave Leopard

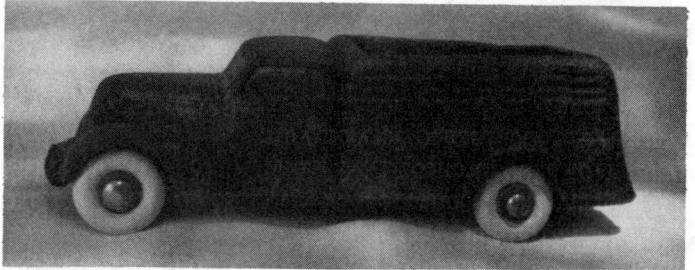

RAINBOW RT01

Photo by Dave Leopard

RALSTOY (Ralston Toy and Novelty Company)
by Fred Maxwell and Ferd Zegel

Ralstoy was formed in July 1939 to manufacture potmetal or slush-mold toys and novelties. It was formed by Dr. Despecher, A. M. Erickson and Henry C. Nestor to acquire the assets of Kansas Toy & Novelty Co. of Clifton, Kansas and Best Toy of Manhattan, Kansas. These assets included John M. Best, his "mold-builder", Conrad Morsch, and about 140 molds from these pioneering slush-mold companies. This continued a low-cost toy line and a number of toys familiar to collectors since Kansas Toy was formed in 1924.

With the death of its founder, Dr. Despecher, a few months later, Ralstoy was forced into reorganization and perhaps the end of its potmetal toys. Paul Massey reorganized the company and turned to production of wood toys, including the famous Army jeep, due to the war's need of lead. After the war the company turned to diecast novelties and is still there today producing a well known line of promotional vans and trucks. But that is a story for other researchers.

RALSTOY (none imprinted with company name)
Top: Transporter with tank, Cannon No. 34, Plane, 9" overall.
Middle: "U.S. Army Antiaircraft Unit," 5½" long, Cannon No. 23, 2¾" long.
Bottom: Tank 3" long, "U.S. Army," Cannon 3¾" long.
Photo by Ed Poole

	C6	C8	C10
Ralstoy Mayflower Moving Van	4.50	6.75	9.00
Ralstoy Tank, medium, "107," 3⅛", "U.S. Army", 2 gun turret, wood grooved wheels, OD color	5.00	7.50	10.00
Ralstoy Tank, small, "74" 2¼", "U.S. Army" 2 gun turret, dark OD, white rubber wheels (either Kansas Toy or Best No. 74 mold)	4	6	8
Ralstoy Transporter set, 9" long tractor-semi-trailer with modified Best Toy No. 101 tractor (Ford?), steel semi carrying tank "74," civil war cannon "34" (Kansas Toy mold), small Army transport plane "32" (Kansas Toy)	20	45	60
Ralstoy "U.S. Army Anti-Aircraft Unit", 5⅝", six-wheel vehicle with gun, 3 attached soldiers, searchlight	25	40	50
Ralstoy wooden Tank "U.S.A. W-356," marked "Ralstoy" underneath	37.50	56.25	75.00

	C6	C8	C10
Rehrberger "David" Moving Van, circa 1924, 7¼" long	1500	2250	3000
Remco Bulldog Tank	25.00	37.50	50.00
Renwal Pickup Truck, diecast, black rubber tires, approx. 7" long	22.50	33.75	45.00
Renwal TV Truck No. 260, with camera, mike, working spotlight, 18" long	75.00	112.50	150.00
Republic Roadster, 1920s, 10" long ..	200	300	400
Republic Taxi Cab with driver, sheetmetal, friction motor, circa 1926	200	300	400
Road Grader, 7½" long, cast iron, rubber wheels	100	150	200
Roadster, cast iron, early, driver, 7" long	125.00	187.50	250.00
Roadster, pressed steel, circa 1936, rumble seat	60	90	120
Roadster Tow Truck, cast iron, 5" long	60	90	120
"Rocket Launcher" truck, "U.S.A.F.", friction, pressed steel and plastic, circa 1960	60	90	120

RUBBER VEHICLES
– Unknown Manufacturers

The following list, with its codings, was compiled by Dave Leopard. Vehicles are broken down by types.

	C6	C8	C10
UA01 '35 Ford 2 door slantback sedan, 4" long (Auburn?)	10	15	20
UA02 '35 Ford Coupe, 4" long (Auburn?)	10	15	20
UA03 '35 Ford 2 door slantback sedan, 4" long (Sieberling?)	10	15	20
UA04 '35 Ford Coupe, 4" long (Sieberling?)	10	15	20
UA05 '36 Pontiac 2 door slantback sedan, 4" long (Rainbow?)	20	30	40
UA06 '35 DeSoto 4 door Airflow Sedan, 5" long	20	30	40
UA07 '35 Chrysler 4 door Airflow Sedan, rear spare, 4¾" long, ad on roof	20	30	40
UA08 '34 Chrysler 2 door Airflow Sedan, 5⅛" long (Barr?)	20	30	40
UA09 '36 Plymouth 4 door trunkback sedan, 4⅞" long	25	35	45
UA10 '37 Plymouth 4 door trunkback sedan, 4⅞" long	No Price Found		
UA11 c. '39 Ford 2 door Fastback Sedan, hollow, molded tires, 4" long	10	12	15
UA12 c. '39 Dodge (?) 2 door fastback sedan, solid, w/tires, 4" long	10	12	15
UA13 c. '36 LaFayette (?) Sedan, solid, w/tires, 4"? long	15	20	25

RUBBER VEHICLES UA11
Photo by Dave Leopard

RUBBER VEHICLES UA12
Photo by Dave Leopard

RUBBER VEHICLES, L to R; UT02, UT01
Photo by Dave Leopard

RUBBER VEHICLES UT03
Photo by Dave Leopard

	C6	C8	C10
UA14 Sedan, 2 dimensional (part of set), solid rubber, 5"? long, flat ..	15	20	25
UA15 '35 Ford 2 door slantback sedan, 5" long	No Price Found		
UT01 '35 Ford Stake Truck, 4¾" long (Sieberling?)	15	20	25
UT02 '35 Ford Stake Truck, Army version with canvas cover, 4¾" long (Sieberling?)	25	32	40
UT03 '35 Ford Panel Truck or Ambulance (paint variations), 4¼" long (Sieberling?)	15	20	25
UT04 '34 Dodge Rack Truck, 4⅞" long	No Price Found		
UT05 Mid 30s Pickup, solid, 2 dimensional, 5¼" long	15	20	25

	C6	C8	C10
UR01 Open Racer, left side Header pipes, solid rubber, 3½" long	No Price Found		
UR02 Open Racer, V-8, solid, large tires on wood hubs, 4" long	No Price Found		
UF01 Farm Tractor, solid, 2 dimensional, 5"? long	15	20	25
UM01 Crawler Tractor pulling 155mm Field Piece, 24¼" long ..	No Price Found		

SAVOYE

Little is known about Savoye. In 1931 the Savoye Pewter Toy Co., Inc., manufacturer of "pewter toys" (pewter was often the word used for lead alloy) was listed in a directory as being located at 69 Paterson Plank Road in North Bergen, New Jersey, with six male and three female employees. In 1934 the address was the same, with the workforce breakdown now seven male and two female employees. The names of the owners may have been Selma and Joseph Wigh. Slush lead toys were probably their only product. Collectors call a toy a Savoye if it has a somewhat coarse appearance, heavy slushmolded body and white rubber tires on oversized red wooden hubs that are smooth on the outside surface (no axle showing through), but whether that is accurate or simply lore isn't known at present. The son of one of the owners of Tommy Toy thinks some Savoye-looking vehicles were made by Tommy Toy. If so, it's possible Savoye sold its molds to nearby Tommy Toy, but at present nothing is really certain. Savoye was incorporated August, 1930. The following list was composed by Fred Maxwell.

	C6	C8	C10
SA1 Fire truck, ladder, length 4⅜", crew of two	20	30	40
SA2 "Beer Truck," 4½" long, 6 wood barrels	18	27	36
SA3 Coupe, 3½" long, Graham (?) as in Tootsietoy	16	24	32
SA4 "Police Patrol" (like Tommy Toy, but with large wood hubs), 4¼" long, cop on back	40	60	80
SA5 Roadster, 3½", Graham (?)	16	24	32
SA6 Roadster, 3½", Graham (?), realistic open rumble seat	16	24	32
SA7 "Motorcoach", 8" long, bi-level, double axle semi-trailer (tractor in photo lacks Savoye hubs)	40	60	80
SA8 Bus, double deck, open deck, 4¾", late 20s	20	30	40
SA9 Stake Truck, 5¾", hinged tail gate with chains	20	30	40
SA10 Tow Truck, 5¾", crude model, detachable hook	No Price Found		

	C6	C8	C10
SA11 Fire Truck, 3⅞", driver and rear-step rider, 2 detachable ladders on roof rack	20	30	40
SA12 Tractor, 2⅞", Case, similar to Tommy Toy tractor	No Price Found		

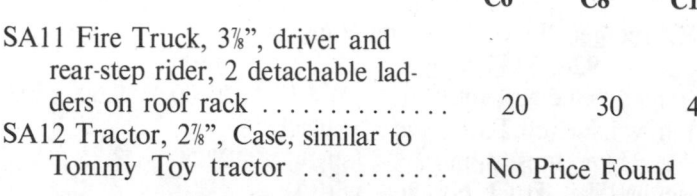

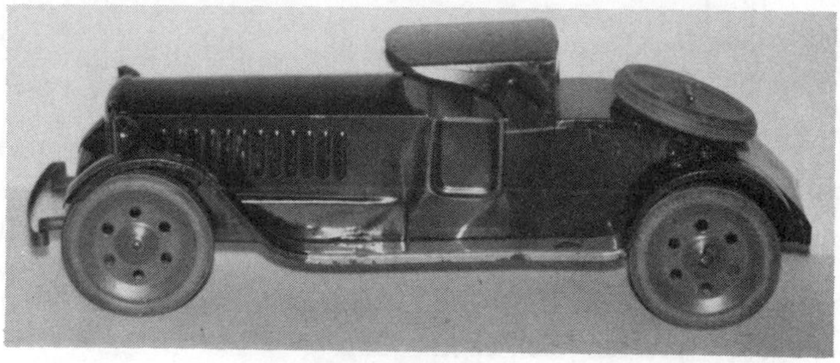

SCHIEBLE ROADSTER, 18¼" long
Courtesy Joe and Sharon Freed

	C6	C8	C10
Schieble Roadster, 18¼" long, spare tire on back	200	300	400
Schieble Sedan, 17" long	200	300	400
Schoenhut "Every Boy Auto Build 5 in 1 Toy" wood set to build, boxed	45.00	67.50	90.00

SEIBERLING RUBBER

compiled by Dave Leopard

SEIBERLING GA01
Photo by Dave Leopard

SEIBERLING GA02
Photo by Dave Leopard

	C6	C8	C10
GA01 '35 Ford 2 door slantback sedan, 5" long	20	30	40
GA02 '35 Ford 2 door slantback sedan, 4" long	15	20	25

"SMITTY TOYS"
by Ray Funk

A line of large cast metal and aluminum toy trucks hit the market in 1945, the Smith-Miller "Smitty Toys", "Famous Trucks in Miniature", produced in Santa Monica, California. These trucks were doomed from the beginning, as they were entering a highly competitive market, one that had toy producers of trucks dating back to the 30s and earlier, such as Buddy "L", Structo, Marx, Hubley, and in 46 Ny-lint, Tonka, in early 50s, and in the mid-1950s, Eldon plastics. However, despite the heavy competition, they fought to stay on the market for a full ten years, into 1955, outclassing virtually all toy trucks before and after, by far, although the last year they changed their profile from Mack Trucks to Auto-Car diesels, with opening doors and steering wheels that actually steered like the real thing. Their first trucks had two different classes, expensive replicas, and, still not cheap, though not actually true replicas, of a smaller type of truck of no name that looked to be a half-breed Ford. I will list the cheaper line first.

No. 401 Tow Truck, 15" long, No. 402 Dump Truck 11½" long, No. 403 Scoop Dump, 14" long (same dump with scoop), all complete cast, cast wheels and rubber tires.

The larger scale models were cast and aluminum, such as No. 404 Lumber Truck (six wheels), 19" long, $10.75; No. 404T Lumber Trailer, 17" long, $6.95; No. 405 Silver Streak, 28" long (14 wheels) six wheel tractor and eight wheel bogey'd heavy duty grain trailer, $15.95; No. 406 Bekins Van, 29" long, six wheel tractor and four-wheel trailer (single axle); No. 407 Searchlight Truck, long (six wheel) based frame 18½" long with platform that has diesel motor (to hold batteries) and huge searchlight, at $16.95; No. 408 Blue Diamond ten wheel huge dump truck, last double set of duals bogey'd, 18½" long, $17.95; No. 409 Pacific Intermountain Express (P.I.E.) six wheel tractor semi with eight wheel bogey'd aluminum trailer, 29" long, $19.75; No. 410 Aerial Ladder semi, six wheel tractor, and four wheel single axle trailer, 36" long, ladder extends to 48" high, $27.95. By 1950 some mid-West stores had the aerial ladder priced at $37.50, and various of the other higher-priced.

Later, various modifications were produced, one a straight Box bed truck, using the searchlight truck with metal box and rear double doors. Then yet another variation was the box truck employing the eight wheel bogey set-up, and the log trailer base with a same box to make a ten wheel straight truck and eight wheel trailer, as there were many on the California highways. Then the long base tractor (ten-wheeler) with bogey on rear eight wheels, hooked to Silver Streak and P.I.E. trailers, and yet other variations such as the P.I.E. eight wheel trailer minus top and raising rear door, as high-side grain hauler, and finally a long refrigerator trailer with small side door, all using ten-wheel tractors.

At the same time the company was putting the smaller wheels on the P.I.E. and Silver Streak trailers, and using the small six-wheeled cast "Half-Breeds" tractors, priced at lower competitive prices.

Their first Mack trucks were of the older 1940s types with running boards, old-type fenders and raised separate headlights, and all had fuel tanks, the later Mack trucks being 1954 Macks with air horn on top.

The final year saw a complete change, Smith dropping out and Ironson coming in, changing the name to M.I.C. toys, Miller-Ironson Corporation, and to the best of my knowledge they produced only four different, all cast trucks, and though no truck company name, definitely Auto-Car diesels. One was a heavy-duty tow truck as tows large semis, a flat bed with removable side racks, and turn-down hydraulically lowering tailgate (up and down), door handles that worked to open doors, seat, steering wheel and front wheel which were steered like on the "model toy" fire trucks and others of the "model toy" line, the last, fire truck #410 with Mack Tractor, I cannot say, as I only have the cab and no catalog or advertisement of this toy.

Honorable mention must be made, before closing, that one company in Minnesota, owned by Teamsters President Beck's son (in the late 1940s) put out a huge cast metal truck, mostly loggers and dumpers, which steered via a horn on top of the cab, and two, Wyandotte put out in 1950, a very realistic cab over semi six wheel tractor of cast and eight wheel bogey'd long aluminum trailer, with beautifully realistic cast center replica wheels and rubber tires. The fifth wheel on the tractor was operational to couple and uncouple from the trailer, and though of no name, the cast tractor was finely detailed, fuel tanks and all. The Wyandotte sold at $10 while the aforementioned, name unknown, and very short-lived trucks, sold at $20 each, a much too high price for the 1940s. All are now gone, but live on in the minds of those who played with them. There were a few minor variations of the Smith-Miller which I did not mention, and no doubt possibly some on all items that I do not know about, nor have catalogs depicting. Any added information would be appreciated.

Evidence via photographs, etc., has unearthed the fact that there are more in this toy truck line than I had listed.

An early Smitty truck is an all pot metal truck, mostly painted as an armored bank truck with square box and locking doors.

I received a picture of a tanker, using the small bastard six wheel tractor, and trailer having the dual-tandem setup. As by the pictures there did not seem to be any spare room in the wheel wells, I must assume that this was only produced with the small wheels and tractor. It is bright yellow, and has "SHELL" on the trailer.

Still yet another produced in the early years, a cattle hauling truck. This one was large as the largest S.M. and had the large early Mack with long frame. I have found this truck, minus wheels, so I can only assume that it was produced as many others with similar tractor frames as an 18 and also 14 wheeler. The enclosed trailer features double doors on the rear with latch, slotted vented sides and truck was same yellow as tanker, other than frame and fenders (all actually one piece on the early 'Macks') were gloss black, making an eye catching toy, colorwise. Eventually I hope to restore this item and have it pictured for your enjoyment.

How many different trucks, or variations Smitty produced, I have no idea, as I begin to suspect that like Doepke, at times they too made up a one, or few of a kind.

(NOTE: New versions of SMITTY vehicles, using original and new parts, are currently being produced — See Leading Collectors and Dealers)

SMITTY GMC Coca-Cola Truck
Courtesy R. L. MacNary

SMITTY MIC Aerial Ladder (Truck in photo restored)
Photo courtesy Ed Stivers

SMITTY "Bank of America" Armored Truck
Courtesy Good Old Days Store

SMITTY Catalog illustrations of Models 402, 401.
Photo by Bill Kaufman.   Courtesy Ray Funk.

SMITTY Catalog illustration of models 408, 404 and 404T.
Photo by Bill Kaufman.   Courtesy Ray Funk.

SMITTY Catalog illustration of Models 406 and 405.
Photo by Bill Kaufman.   Courtesy Ray Funk.

	C6	C8	C10
Smitty (Smith-Miller) No. 201-L Lumber Truck, 60 boards, 6 wheel, 14" long	60	90	125
Smitty No. 202-M Material Truck, 3 barrels, 3 cases, 18 boards, 4 wheels, 14" long	100	160	210
Smitty No. 203-H Heinz Grocery Truck, 6 wheels, 14" long	180	300	400
Smitty No. 204-A Arden Milk Truck, 12 milk cans, 4 cases, 4 wheels, 14" long	150	250	325
Smitty No. 205-P Oil Truck, 4 drums, 6 wheels, 14" long	90	150	200
Smitty No. 206-C Coca-Cola Truck, 16 Coca-Cola cases, 4 wheels, 14" long	320	500	750
Smitty No. 208-B Bekins Vanliner, 14 wheels, 22½" long	200	325	450
Smitty No. 209-T Timber Giant, 3 logs, 14 wheels, 23½" long	90	150	200
Smitty No. 210-S Stake Truck, 14 wheels, 23½" long	135	225	300
Smitty No. 211-L Sunkist Special, 14 wheels, 23½" long	150	250	325
Smitty No. 212-R Red Ball, 14 wheels, 23½" long	100	160	220
Smitty No. 301-W GMC Wrecker, 4 wheeler	80	125	160
Smitty No. 302-M GMC Materials Truck, 4 barrels, 3 timbers	125	195	250
Smitty No. 303-R GMC Rack Truck, 6 wheels	100	160	220
Smitty No. 304-K GMC Kraft Foods, 4 wheels	250	400	545
Smitty No. 305-T GMC Triton Oil, 3 drums	140	225	300
Smitty No. 306-C GMC Coca-Cola, 4 wheels, 16 Coke cases	300	480	625
Smitty No. 307-L GMC Redwood Logger Tractor-Trailer, 3 logs ...	120	190	250
Smitty No. 308-V GMC Lyon Van Tractor-Trailer, 14 wheels	200	300	400
Smitty No. 309-S GMC Super Cargo Tractor-Trailer, 14 wheels, ten barrels	200	300	400
Smitty No. 310-H GMC Hi-Way Freighter Tractor-Trailer, 14 wheels	100	175	250
Smitty No. 311-E GMC Silver Streak Express Tractor-Trailer, 14 wheels	150	250	325
Smitty No. 312-P GMC Pacific Intermountain Express ("P.I.E.") Tractor-Trailer	200	325	450
Smitty No. 401 Tow Truck, 15" long	90	145	190
Smitty No. 402 Dump Truck, 11½" long	100	160	220
Smitty No. 403 Scoop Dump, 14" long	160	250	350

	C6	C8	C10
Smitty No. 404 Lumber Truck, 19" long	350	600	750
Smitty No. 404T Lumber Trailer, 17" long	90	145	190
Smitty No. 405 Silver Streak 6-wheel tractor, 28" long	110	175	250

SMITTY Catalog illustrations of models 407, 403, 409.
Photo by Bill Kaufman.   Courtesy Ray Funk.

SMITTY Catalog illustration of Model 410.
Photo by Bill Kaufman.   Courtesy Ray Funk.

SMITTY Box Truck with Box Trailer, ten-wheeler
Courtesy Ray Funk

	C6	C8	C10
Smitty No. 406 Bekins Van, 29" long, six-wheel tractor and four-wheel trailer	180	300	400
Smitty No. 407 Searchlight Truck, 18½" long, "Hollywood Filmad"	110	175	250
Smitty No. 408 Blue Diamond 10-wheel dump truck, 18½" long	225	395	500

Item	C6	C8	C10
Smitty No. 409 Pacific Intermountain Express (P.I.E.) six-wheel tractor semi with eight wheel aluminum trailer, 29" long	150	250	320
Smitty No. 410 Aerial Ladder semi, six-wheel tractor and four-wheel trailer, 36" long, "SMFD"	300	480	675
Smitty No. 401-W GMC Wrecker, 6 wheels	200	300	400
Smitty No. 402-M GMC Material Truck, 4 barrels, 2 timbers	150	225	300
Smitty No. 403-R GMC Rack Truck, 6 wheels	100	160	210
Smitty No. 404-B GMC Bank of America, lock and key, 4 wheels	150	250	350
Smitty No. 405-T GMC Triton Oil, 6 wheels, 3 drums	100	160	250
Smitty No. 406-L GMC Lumber Tractor-Trailer, 14 wheels, eight timbers	100	160	250
Smitty No. 407-V GMC Lyon Van Tractor-Trailer, 10 wheels	250	375	500
Smitty No. 408-H GMC Machinery Hauler, 13 wheels	120	200	280
Smitty No. 409-G GMC Mobilgas Tanker, 14 wheels, 2 hoses	150	250	350
Smitty No. 410-F GMC Transcontinental Tractor-Trailer, 14 wheels	160	250	325
Smitty No. 411-E GMC Silver Streak Tractor-Trailer, 14 wheels	150	225	300
Smitty No. 412-P GMC P.I.E. 14 wheels	200	350	450
Smitty "B" Mack "Associated Truck Lines," 14 wheels	No Price Found		
Smitty "B" Mack Bekins Van, 10 wheel	350	600	800
Smitty "B" Back Blue Diamond Dump, 10 wheels	250	450	600
Smitty "B" Mack Jr. Fire Truck, warning light, battery-operated, 4 wheel	180	300	400
Smitty "B" Mack Lumber Truck, 6 wheels, 9 timbers	200	320	450
Smitty "B" Mack Lumber Truck & Trailer, 12 wheels, 18 timbers	280	450	625
Smitty "B" Mack Orange Dump, 10 wheels	275	440	600
Smitty "B" Mack P.I.E., 14 wheels	320	475	680
Smitty "B" Mack P.I.E., 18 wheels	320	475	680
Smitty "B" Mack Searchlight, 6 wheels, battery powered light	300	425	625
Smitty "B" Mack Silver Streak, 14 wheels	300	425	625
Smitty "B" Mack "Watson Bros." 18 wheels	325	500	700
Smitty "Bank of America" Armored Truck, No. 602B, 14½" long	No Price Found		
Smitty Chevy Bekins Van, 14 wheels, plain tires, hubcaps	200	325	450
Smitty Chevy Coca-Cola, 4 wheels, plain tires, early	300	485	675
Smitty Chevy Flatbed Tractor-Trailer, 14 wheels, unpainted wood trailer, plain tires, hubcaps, early	100	160	235
Smitty Chevy Milk Truck, 4 wheels, plain tires, hubcaps, early	180	300	400
Smitty Ford Bekins Van, 14 wheeler, plain tires, hubs. Earliest Smitty?	150	265	380
Smitty Ford Coca-Cola, 4 wheels, wood soda cases, early	450	750	1000
Smitty GMC Be Mac 14 wheel T-Trailer	175	250	350
Smitty GMC Coca-Cola Truck, 24 plastic bottles in 6 cases, 4 wheels	280	475	600
Smitty GMC "Drive-O" Steerable Dump, 6 wheels, cable with hand control	150	250	350
Smitty GMC "Furniture Mart" Pick-Up, 4 wheels	110	195	250
Smitty GMC Heinz Grocery Truck	180	300	400
Smitty GMC Machinery Hauler, 10 wheels	110	195	250
Smitty GMC Marshall Field & Company Tractor-Trailer, 10 wheel T-Trailer	180	300	400
Smitty GMC Peoples First National Bank and Trust Company armored truck; lock and key	225	385	500
Smitty GMC Rexall Drug, 4 wheels	225	375	480
Smitty GMC Searchlight Truck, "Hollywood Film Ad" with trailer	250	375	500
Smitty GMC Silver Streak, 14 wheels	110	195	250
Smitty GMC Triton Oil, 3 drums	110	195	250
Smitty GMC U.S. Treasury Truck armored truck, with lock and key	200	350	450
Smitty "L" Mack Aerial Ladder, "SMFD," 8 wheels	325	500	650
Smitty "L" Mack Army Materials Truck, 3 barrels, 2 boards, 1 large crate, 1 small, 10 wheel	325	500	700
Smitty "L" Mack Army Personnel Carrier, 10 wheels	310	485	680
Smitty "L" Mack Bekins Van, all white, 10 wheels	500	825	1100
Smitty "L" Mack Blue Diamond Dump, 10 wheels	275	440	600
Smitty "L" Mack International Paper Co., 10 wheels	300	425	625
Smitty "L" Mack Lyon Van, 6 wheels	450	750	1000
Smitty "L" Mack Material Truck, 2 barrels, 6 timbers, 6 wheels	325	500	700
Smitty "L" Mack Merchandise Van, 6 wheels	225	385	500
Smitty "L" Mack Merchandise Van & Trailer, 12 wheels	275	440	600
Smitty "L" Mack Mobil Tandem Tanker, 12 wheels	350	625	800

	C6	C8	C10
Smitty "L" Mack Orange Hydraulic Dump, 10 wheels	275	440	600
Smitty "L" Mack Orange Material Truck, 10 wheels, 3 barrels, 2 boards, one large crate, one small	275	440	600
Smitty "L" Mack Orange Utility Truck, 4 wheels	325	550	775
Smitty "L" Mack P.I.E., 14 wheel . . .	225	385	500
Smitty "L" Mack "Sibley's" Van, 6 wheels (rare)	350	625	800
Smitty "L" Mack Tandem Timber, 6 wheel, 18 or 24 timbers (varies) . .	225	375	490
Smitty "L" Mack Telephone Truck, 6 wheels	300	425	625
Smitty "L" Mack West Coast Transport, 6 wheel	225	375	500
SMitty MIC Aerial Ladder	300	425	625
Smitty MIC "Fruehauf Road Star" tractor-trailer, 14 wheels	235	400	520
Smitty MIC House Trailer	225	375	500
Smitty MIC Hydraulic Dump, 10 wheels	275	400	550
Smitty MIC Life-O-Matic, 6 wheels, 2 barrels	275	440	600
Smitty MIC Lincoln Capri (for MIC House Trailer), steerable	275	400	550
Smitty MIC Lumber Truck, 6 wheels, 9 timbers	225	375	500
Smitty MIC P.I.E. Tractor-Trailer, 14 wheels	275	440	600
Smitty MIC "Teamsters" Hydraulic Dump, 10 wheels	275	440	600
Smitty MIC "Teamsters" Tow Truck, 6 wheels	No Price Found		
Smitty MIC "Teamsters" Tractor-Trailer, 14 wheels	325	500	700
Smitty MIC Tow Truck, "Official Tow Car," 6 wheels	225	375	500
Smitty MIC Tow Truck, 6 wheels, unpainted, polished	225	375	500
Smitty MIC Tractor-Trailer, polished aluminum trailer, no decals, 14 wheels	225	375	500

SONNY "USA 1120" Anti-Aircraft Truck, 24" long
Courtesy Joe and Sharon Freed

	C6	C8	C10
Sonny Army Truck "U.S.A. 1120" . .	200	300	400
Sonny "USA 1120" Anti-Aircraft Truck	250	375	500
Sonny "US 1120" Artillery Truck, 26" long	250	375	500
Steam Pumper, "Boston," with lamp, cast iron wheels, 15½" long	2500	3750	5000
Stake Truck, cast iron, white rubber tires	120	180	240
Steam Pumper fire truck, cast iron, 5"	25.00	37.50	50.00
Steam Pumper truck, cast iron, hard rubber wheels, driver, 12" long . .	150	225	300
Steam Pumper, tin and wooden chain and friction drive with driver, "National," 10"	200	300	400
Steam Pumper, tin and wooden friction drive, 11" long	70	105	140
Steam Roller, steam-engine powered .	200	300	450
Steam Roller, cast iron, 4¾" long, circa early 1930s	75.00	112.50	150.00
Steam Shovel, "Sand Digger," 28" long	150	225	300
Steelcraft Army Truck, Mack, circa 1930, 22" long	150	225	300
Steelcraft Coca-Cola Truck, 12 bottles on side	600	900	1200
Steelcraft Dump Truck, Airflow	1750	2625	3500
Steelcraft Fire Truck, 25" long	450	675	900
Steelcraft GMC Scissor Dump Truck	500	750	1000
Steelcraft "Heinz, Rice Flakes, Baked Beans, Bottle Vinegar" truck . . .	200	300	400
Steelcraft Inter City Bus, 24"	450	675	900
Steelcraft Model T Roadster pedal car, 50" long, Lic. #65-287	450	675	900
Steelcraft Railway Express Truck, 26" long	450	675	900
Steelcraft Shell Motor Oil truck with oil barrels	300	450	600
Steelcraft Steam Shovel	200	300	400
Steelcraft Tank truck, sheet metal, 25½" long	100	150	200
Steelcraft "U.S. Mail," 27¼" long circa 1928	1000	1500	2000

SONNY "US 1120" Artillery Truck, 26 inches long
Courtesy Joe Freed

77

STRUCTO

Structo, of Freeport, Illinois, was founded in 1908 by three men: brothers Louis and Edward Strohacker and C.C. Thompson. They initially manufactured Erector Construction Kits, and about 1919 they started making toy vehicles. In 1935 J.G. Cokey bought a majority of the business, and when he died in 1975, the toy patents and designs were taken over by the Ertl Company. (Numbered Structos are found at the end of this listing.)

STRUCTO Tank, 11" long, No. 48
Courtesy Mapes Auctioneers & Appraisers

STRUCTO Dump Truck, open cab
Courtesy Joe and Sharon Freed

STRUCTO Tank, olive drab with orange turret, ten metal wheels, 12½" long
Courtesy Joe and Sharon Freed

	C6	C8	C10
Structo Army Truck with canvas top, 21" long	70	105	140
Structo Army Van, 17½" long, pressed steel and canvas	170	255	340
Structo Bearcat Racer, 12¼" long, clockwork	350	525	700
Structo Camper with cloth top, 12"	10	15	20
Structo Coupe, convertible, circa 1920s	160	240	320
Structo Caterpillar Tractor with Trailer, heavy spring clockwork motor, steel treads	140	210	280

	C6	C8	C10
Structo Caterpillar Whippet Tank, 12" long, heavy spring clockwork motor enameled green, red and black, may read "Patented 1920," on sale in 1929, No. 48	130	195	260
Structo Delivery Truck, tin electric lights	150	225	300
Structo Dump Truck, open cab, circa 1930, 18" long	150	225	300

	C6	C8	C10
Structo Fire Dept. Emergency Patrol Truck, red bubble light, 12" long 1950s	50	75	100
Structo Garbage Truck, 21" long	100	150	200
Structo Gasoline Truck No. 912, 1950s, 13" long	40	60	80
Structo Guided Missile Launcher, No. 906 with plastic launcher, missiles of wood and vinyl, 13" long	40	60	80
Structo Guided Missile Launching Truck, truck metal, missiles, etc., plastic, rubber tires	34	51	68
Structo Moving Van, 16" long, open cab, circa 1929	175	265	350
Structo Pick Up Truck, 13"	70	105	140
Structo Police Patrol Truck, 17" long	100	150	200
Structo Renault Tank, clockwork, green with red turret	260	390	520
Structo Roadster, 16" long, 1920s, clockwork	500	750	1000
Structo Sand Loader, 12" high, circa 1928	22	33	44
Structo Searchlight Truck, truck metal, light and generator plastic, uses batteries, has rubber tires ...	40	60	80
Structo Steam Shovel, 14" x 11"	80	120	160
Structo Steam Shovel, 16"	70	105	140
Structo Steam Shovel, 21" x 18"	60	90	120
Structo "Structo Telephone Co.", 12" long, circa 1948	50	75	100
Structo Tank, 11" long, #48	120	180	240
Structo Tank, olive drab with orange turret, ten metal wheels, 12½" long	120	180	240
Structo Tractor 8½" long with cast iron driver, early, caterpillar type	140	210	280
Structo Truck Assortment No. 317: Dump truck, blue, Stake truck, Lumber truck. Each 9" long, 3½" wide, 3½" tall. Heavy gauge metal, rubber wheels, original box folds to form garage. 1920s. Price per set	60	90	120
Structo U.S. Mail Delivery Truck, tin	200	300	400
Structo Wrecker, "Toyland Garage" .	30	45	60
Structo No. 601 Motor Express stake truck, early 1950s	110	175	230
Structo No. 603 Package Delivery, early 1950s	150	225	300
Structo No. 605 Shovel Dump, early 1950s	100	150	200
Structo No. 607 Machinery Truck, early 1950s	170	255	340
Structo No. 609 Barrel Truck, early 1950s	250	375	500
Structo No. 700 Transport Trailer, early 1950s	120	180	240
Structo No. 702 Steel Cargo Trailer, early to mid-1950s	100	150	200

	C6	C8	C10
Structo No. 704 Overland Freight Trailer, early 1950s	140	210	280
Structo No. 704 Grain Trailer, early and mid-1950s (replaced Freight Trailer)	100	150	200
Structo No. 706 Auto Transport Trailer, sold 1953-54	No Price Found		
Structo No. 708 Cattle Trailer	90	135	180
Structo No. 811 Barrel Truck wind-up, early 1950s	200	300	400
Structo No. 822 Wrecker Truck, wind-up, early-mid 1950s	160	240	320
Structo No. 844 Hi-Lift Dump, wind-up, early 1950s	140	210	280
Structo 866 Gasoline Truck, wind-up, early 1950s	260	390	520
Sturditoy Ambulance, 26" long, open cab, circa 1929	140	210	280
Sturditoy American Railway Express Truck, circa 1920s	115.00	172.50	230.00
Sturditoy Dump Truck, 1920s, 25" long	400	600	800
Sturditoy Dump Truck, 1920s, 26½" long	700	1050	1400
Sturditoy Pumper, 26" long, circa 1930	300	450	600

SUN RUBBER

Sun Rubber of Barberton, Ohio was founded in 1923. Toymaking started in 1924 and autos were introduced in April, 1935. Owner was Tom W. Smith Jr.

	C6	C8	C10
SA01 Coupe, external exhaust pipes, from 1936, 4" long, No. 515	10	12	15
SA02 '34 Desoto Airflow, four door sedan, 4" long No. 500	10	15	20
SA03 '40 Dodge, 4 door sedan, 4½" long No. 12001	10	12	15
SA04 circa 1936 "Teardrop" Sedan, 5½" long, No. 1010 (1936)	10	15	20
SA05 Art Deco Housetrailer, fits SA04, 4⅜" long	No Price Found		
SA06 Town Car, Brewster type limo, exposed driver, 5⅜" long, No. 1015	15	20	25
SA07 Station Wagon, woody, mid-30s, 3¾" long, No. 12007	10	12	15

L to R: Sun SM02, SM01   Photo by Ed Poole

SUN SA01
Photo by Dave Leopard

SUN SA02
Photo by Dave Leopard

SUN SA03
Photo by Dave Leopard

SUN SA04
Photo by Dave Leopard

SUN SA06
Photo by Dave Leopard

SUN SA07
Photo by Dave Leopard

SUN ST03
Photo by Dave Leopard

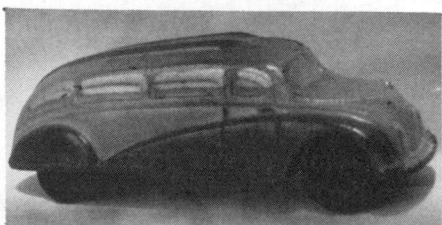

SUN ST08
Photo by Dave Leopard

SUN ST04, ST05   Photo by Dave Leopard

SUN SR02

Photo by Dave Leopard

SUN SR01 (both)

SUN ST09

	C6	C8	C10
ST01 Pickup Truck, stake sides, streamlined, 4½" long, **No. 510**	10	12	15
ST02 Open Truck, stake sides, streamlined (White?), 5¼" long **No. 1005**	15.00	17.50	20.00
ST03 Tractor/trailer, one-piece, 3 axles, futuristic, 5⅛" long, **No. 12013**	10	12	15
ST04 Open Truck, futuristic, 4½" long, No. **12003**	10	12	15
ST05 Open "Master" truck, futuristic, 5½" long	12	15	18
ST06 Open "Master" truck, futuristic, 5⅝" long, **No. 12111**	12	15	18
ST07 Open "Master" truck, futuristic, 6⅝" long, **No. 12011**	15	20	25

	C6	C8	C10
ST08 '36 White Bus, streamlined, 4¼" long, **No. 520** (1936)	10	12	15
ST09 Ambulance, c. late 1930s, 3¾" long, **No. 12006**	10	12	15
SR01 Open racer, 2 drivers, 4⅜" long, **No. 505** (1936)	10	12	15
SR02 Open racer, full fenders on rear, 6½" long, **No. 1000** (1936)	15	20	25
SR03 Open racer, boat tail, "Super" racer, 6¾" long, **No. 12012**	15	20	25
SM01 Tank, revolving turret and gunner, 6" long, **No. 12015** (1947)	20	27	35
SM02 Scout Car, 4 gunners, 6¾" long, **No. 12014** (1947)	20	27	35

80

THOMAS TOYS

Thomas Toys was founded by Islyn Thomas in 1944. Located from first to last at 80 Clinton Street, Newark, New Jersey, at its peak it had 350 employees. The company's first toys were plastic jeeps, planes and vinyl dolls. In 1960 Thomas sold the firm to Banner.

	C6	C8	C10
Thomas Toys No. 133 Buick Torpedo Sedan, plastic, 11" long	5.00	7.50	10.00
Thomas Toys No. 140 Loudspeaker Van, plastic, 4" long	5.00	7.50	10.00

TIP TOP TOY CO.

The Tip Top Toy Co. was located in San Francisco, and produced slush cast vehicles through most of the 1920s and 30s. The firm embossed its name inside some of its toys, but not all.

	C6	C8	C10
Tip-Top Coupe	16	24	32
Tip Top Wrecker, metal wheels	16	24	32

TOLEDO METAL WHEEL COMPANY
("Blue Streak")

The Toledo Metal Wheel Company was located in Toledo, Ohio during at least the early and late 1920s. It manufactured a large range of pedal cars as well as toy trucks. Its trade name for its products was "Blue Streak."

	C6	C8	C10
Toledo **No. 45 "Bull Dog" Truck,** 26" long, open cab	500	1000	1500
Toledo **No. 46 "Bull Dog" Dump Truck,** 26½" long	600	1000	1475
Toledo **No. 47 "Bull Dog" Sprinkler Truck,** 27½" long	600	1100	1510
Toledo **No. 48 "Bull Dog" Moving Van,** 26" long	550	1050	1550
Toledo **No. 50 "Bull Dog" Coal Truck,** 25" long	800	1350	1875
Toledo Fire Pumper Pedal Car, red-painted, 59" long	1250	1875	2500

TOMMY TOY

The following vehicles have been identified by Charles E. Weldon Jr., son of one of the owners of Tommy Toy. He is sure these are Tommy Toy, but admits there is always a chance he could be mistaken on some. Certainly the Cannon Truck, aside from the hubs, looks just like Barclay's, which was produced in the same years. Some others resemble Metal Cast, Savoye and other companies' vehicles. However, since slush molds did tend to change hands, production of a vehicle by one company would not preclude later manufacture of the same toy by another company. American Alloy is known to have produced copies of Tommy Toy's soldiers using new molds. The only vehicle known to bear the Tommy Toy trademark is the 810 Cord.

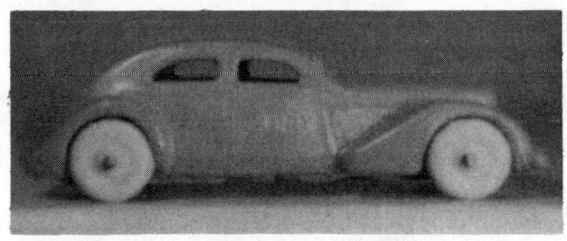

TOMMY TOY TTV8
Courtesy C.B.C Lee

	C6	C8	C10
TTV1 Aerial Ladder Truck (like Savoye), late 20s type	20	30	40
TTV2 Airflow type auto (like Kansas Toy), circa 1935	32.50	48.75	65.00
TTV3 "Ambulance," late 20s-early 30s type	16	24	32
TTV4 "Beer Truck" with wooden barrels, late 1930s	14	21	28
TTV5 Cannon Truck, mid-30s (like Barclay; Barclay's had wooden hubs)	5.50	8.75	11.00
TTV6 Convertible no driver, mid-late 30s	8	12	16
TTV7 Convertible with driver, mid-late 30s, 1935 Oldsmobile	10	15	20
TTV8 Cord, 810 (1935)	40	60	80

	C6	C8	C10
TTV9 "Delivery Deluxe" delivery truck (like Savoye), late 30s	18	27	36
TTV10 Double-Decker Bus, closed top, early 30s	16	24	32
TTV11 Double-Decker Bus, open top, extended hood (like Savoye), late 1920s	20	30	40
TTV12 Double-Decker Bus, open top, no hood (like Barclay), late 1930s	16	24	32
TTV13 Dump Truck, late 1930s (resembles Kansas Toy, Best Toy, Manhattan Toys)	16	24	32
TTV14 "General Trucking," late 30s	12.50	18.75	25.00
TTV15 Ladder Truck, mid 30s	20	30	40
TTV16 "Milk" truck, late 1930s	15.00	22.50	30.00
TTV17 "Milk Truck," grilled window, circa late 1930s	15.00	22.50	30.00
TTV18 "Milk Truck," smooth window, circa late 30s	15.00	22.50	30.00
TTV19 "Motorcoach," mid-30s (like Savoye)	No Price Found		
TTV20 "Oil" tanker, "Cap 80000" (like Metal Cast, which has different capacity number), 1930s, attaches to Tommy Toy Towing Car Coupe	8	12	16
TTV21 "Packard," coupe, mid-30s ...	17.50	26.25	35.00

TTV23 TTV22 TTV3
Photo by Bill Kaufman
Courtesy Charles E. Weldon Jr.

TTV20 TTV5 TTV7 TTV21

TTV4 TTV18 TTV6
Photo by Bill Kaufman
Courtesy Charles E. Weldon Jr.

TTV27 TTV28

TTV2 TTV30 TTV32
Photo by Bill Kaufman
Courtesy Charles E. Weldon Jr.

TTV24 TTV1 TTV15

TTV25 TTV26
Photo by Bill Kaufman
Courtesy Charles E. Weldon Jr.

TTV18 TTV17 TTV14 TTV16

TTV10 TTV11 TTV12
Photo by Bill Kaufman
Courtesy Charles E. Weldon Jr.

TTV31 TTV33 TTV13

TTV9 TTV29 TTV30
Photo by Bill Kaufman
Courtesy Charles E. Weldon Jr.

	C6	C8	C10
TTV22 "Police Patrol," open windows, late 20s-early 30s type	40	60	80
TTV23 "Police Patrol," solid windows, late 20s-early 30s type	35.00	52.50	70.00
TTV24 Pumper, mid 1930s	12.50	18.75	25.00
TTV25 Pumper, large, red hubs, late 30s	11.00	16.50	22.00
TTV26 Pumper, small, late 30s	8	12	16
TTV27 Racing Car, large, circa mid-30s	16	24	32

	C6	C8	C10
TTV28 Racing Car, small, circa mid-30s	12.50	18.75	25.00
TTV29 Sedan, four-door, circa 1935 .	17.50	26.25	35.00
TTV 30 Sedan towing "Tourist" trailer, circa 1936-37	20	30	40
TTV31 Towing Car Coupe (like Savoye), early 30s type	16	24	32
TTV32 Tractor	8	12	16
TTV33 Wrecker, late 1930s	10	15	20

TONKA

Tonka was incorporated in Mound, Minnesota, in September, 1946. The firm had secured the tooling for a steam shovel and crane and clam from Streator Industries, which had unsuccessfully introduced those toys at the Toy Fair in February, 1946. Tonka, which means "great" in Sioux-French, was located on the banks of Lake Minnetonka (and is now situated in Minnetonka itself). In 1948, Tonka introduced a lift fork with trailer, and in 1949 premiered its line of trucks, including a dump and wrecker. The firm had originally been incorporated as Mound Metal Crafts, with a line of tie racks and garden tools. Most of the following list was compiled by Calvin L. Chaussee, grouping the toys by period.

1947	C6	C8	C10
Tonka No. 50 Steam Shovel, 20¾" long	100	150	200
Tonka No. 150 Crane and Clam, 24" long	140	210	280
Tonka Coca-Cola Truck ('47 or '48 special order of 100 for a bottler)	300	450	650
1948			
Tonka No. 200 Lift Truck and Cart	No Price Found		
1949			
Tonka No. 100 Steam Shovel Deluxe, 22" long	No Price Found		
Tonka No. 120 Tractor and Carry-All Trailer with No. 50 Steam Shovel	160	240	320
Tonka No. 125 Tractor & Carry-All Trailer with No. 100 Steam Shovel	No Price Found		
Tonka No. 130 Tractor-Carry-All Trailer, 30½" long	75.00	112.50	150.00
Tonka No. 140 Transport Van, 22¼" long	140	210	280
Tonka No. 170 Tractor & Carry-All Trailer with No. 150 Crane & Clam	200	300	400
Tonka No. 180 Dump Truck, 12" long	50	75	100
Tonka No. 190 Loading Tractor, 10½" long	No Price Found		
Tonka No. 250 Wrecker Truck, 12½" long	120	180	240
1951 (1950 almost identical to 1949 line with minor color and decal changes.)			
Tonka No. 145 Street Carrier Semi, 22" long	150	225	300
Tonka No. 175 Utility Hauler, 12" long	140	210	280
Tonka No. 400 Allied Van Semi, 23½" long	150	225	300
1952			
Tonka No. 500 Livestock Hauler Semi, 22¼" long	140	210	280
Tonka No. 550 Grain Hauler Semi, 22¼" long	180	270	360
1953			
Tonka No. 575 Logger semi, 22¼" long	140	210	280
Tonka No. 600 Road Grader, 17" long	40	60	80
Tonka No. 650 Green Giant Transport Semi, 22¼" long	240	360	480

	C6	C8	C10
Tonka No. 675 Trailer Fleet Set, two tractors (five interchangable trailers)	350	525	700
1954 Newer Style Trucks - Rounded Fenders			
Tonka No. 580 Pickup Truck	50	75	100
Tonka No. 700 Aerial Ladder Semi Fire Truck, 32½" long	150	225	300
Tonka No. 725 Minute Maid Delivery Van, 14½" long	260	390	520
Tonka No. 725 Star Kist Van, 14½" long	200	300	400

TONKA No. 750
Courtesy Lloyd W. Ralson Auctions

	C6	C8	C10
Tonka No. 750 Carnation Milk Step Van, 11¾" long (rare)	160	240	320
Tonka No. 750 Parcel Delivery Van, 11¾" long	120	180	240
Tonka No. 775 Road Builder Set - 5 pc. set - Road Grader (Semi T&T - Crane and Dump Truck)	340	510	680
1955			
Tonka No. 725 Minute Maid Orange Juice Van	120	180	240
Tonka No. 750 Carnation Milk Delivery Van	120	180	240
Tonka No. 880 Pick Up Truck	100	150	200
Tonka No. 0850 Lumber Truck, 6 wheel	100	150	200
Tonka No. 0860 Stake Truck, 6 wheel	100	150	200
1956			
Tonka No. 990 Suburban Pumper, 17" long	140	210	280
Tonka No. 991 Farm Stake Truck, 13" long	66	99	132
Tonka No. 992 Aerial Sand Loader Set, Loader and Dump Truck	120	180	240
Tonka No. 994 Sand Loader Set, Loader and Dump Truck	120	180	240

	C6	C8	C10
Tonka No. 996 Wrecker (white color), 12" long	120	180	240
Tonka No. 998 Lumber Truck, 18¾" long	120	180	240
Tonka Fire Dept. Set. - Aerial Ladder Semi, Rescue Squad Van and Pumper	240	360	480
Tonka State Highway Department Set - Road Grader Dump Truck, Side Dump Hydraulic Truck, Pickup Truck and six Highway Signs and 2 Road Barriers	340	510	680
1957			
Tonka Big Mike Dual Hydraulic Dump Truck, 14" long	80	120	160
Tonka Gasoline Truck, 15" long (rare)	270	405	540
Tonka Parcel Delivery Van, 12" long	120	180	240
Tonka Pickup w/Box Trailer, 20½" long	90	135	180
Tonka Pickup w/Stake Trailer, 20½" long	90	135	180
Tonka Stock Rack Truck with Animals, 16¼" long	160	240	320
Tonka 3 in 1 Hiway Service Truck, w/2 snowblades, 13" long	200	300	400
Tonka Thunderbird Express Semi, 24" long	180	270	360
1958 Next Generation Cars			
Tonka Deluxe Sportsman w/Boat Trailer, 22¾" long	120	180	240
Tonka Farm Stake w/Horse Trailer, 21¾" long	100	150	200
Tonka Nationwide Moving Semi, 24¼" long	100	150	200
Tonka Sportsman Pickup w/topper, 12¾" long	66	99	132
1959			
Tonka No. 14 Dragline, 20" long	50	75	100
Tonka No. 30 Tandem Platform Stake w/Trailer, 28¼" long	140	210	280
Tonka No. 36 Tandem Air Express w/Trailer, 24¾" long	270	405	540
Tonka No. 41 Boat Transport Semi, 5 pc., 28" long	200	300	400
Tonka No. 42 Hydraulic Land Rover, big tires, 15" long	100	150	200
Tonka No. 44 Dragline and Semi Trailer, 3 pc., 26¼" long	100	150	200
Tonka B-203 Sanitary Service Truck, 22¾" long	140	210	280
Tonka Service Truck, 12¾" long	60	90	120
Tonka Sportsman w/topper and Boat, 12¾" long	110	165	220
1960			
Tonka No. 100 Bulldozer, 8⅞" long	50	75	100
Tonka No. 105 Rescue Squad Van, 13¾" long	80	120	160
Tonka No. 110 Fisherman Pickup, 14" long	52	78	104

	C6	C8	C10
Tonka No. 115 Power Boom Loader, 18½" long	100	150	200
Tonka No. 120 Cement Mixer Truck, 15½" long	120	180	240
Tonka No. 125 Bulldozer and Low Boy Semi, 3 pc., 26¼" long	160	240	320
1961			
Tonka No. 105 Golf Club Tractor, 12½" long	54	81	108
Tonka No. 116 Dump Truck and Sand loader, 23¼" long	80	120	160
Tonka No. 136 Houseboat Set with Truck, 29" long	140	210	280
Tonka No.. 142 Mobile Clam on Truck, 27¼" long	120	180	240
Tonka No. 145 Tanker Semi, 28" long	160	240	320
1962			
Tonka No. 201 Servi-Car, 9⅛" long	50	75	100
Tonka No. 249 Jeep Universal, 9¾" long	34	51	68
Tonka No. 250 Airport Tractor, 8⅝" long	110	165	220
Tonka No. 250 Jeep Surrey, Stripe Top, 10½" long	66	99	132
Tonka No. 301 Utility Dump Scooter, 12½" long	50	75	100
Tonka No. 402 Bulldozer Loader, 11½" long	35.00	52.50	70.00
Tonka No. 410 Jet Delivery, 14" long	100	150	200
Tonka No. 420 Luggage Service - Tractor and Trailer, 16⅝"	100	150	200
1963			
Tonka No. 251 Military Jeep, 10½" long	26	39	52
Tonka No. 422 Backhoe on Truck, 17½" long	80	120	160
Tonka No. 425 Jeep Pumper, 10¾" long	80	120	160
Tonka No. 524 Bulldozer w/Packer, 18¼" long	270	405	540
Tonka No. 530 Truck w/Camper, 14½" long	16	24	32
Tonka No. 534 Trencher, 18¼" long	16	24	32
Tonka No. 640 Ramp Hoist Flat Bed, 19¼" long	120	180	240
1964			
Tonka No. 375 Jeep Wrecker, 11" long	80	120	160
Tonka No. 384 Jeep w/Box Trailer, 19⅜" long	50	75	100
Tonka No. 720 Terminal Train, 33⅜" long, 4 pc.	160	240	320
1964 Two series of toys introduced. Smaller versions first, Junior Size follows:			
Tonka No. 50 Pickup (Jeep style), 9½" long	12	18	24
Tonka No. 56 Stake Truck, 9½" long	20	30	40
Tonka No. 68 Wrecker, 9½" long	16	24	32

	C6	C8	C10
Tonka No. 70 Camper, 9½" long ...	35.00	52.50	70.00
Tonka No. 60 Dump, 9½" long	10	15	20
Tonka No. 76 Road Grader, Open, 10¾" long	16	24	32
Tonka No. 77 Cement Mixer, 9" long	20	30	40
Tonka No. 86 Van, Semi, 16" long ..	24	36	48
Tonka No. 90 Livestock Semi, 16" long	26	39	52
Tonka No. 96 Car Carrier Semi, 18½" long	24	36	48

TOOTSIE TOY
(Compiled by C.B.C. Lee)

	C6	C8	C10
Tootsietoy 4528 Limousine circa 1910, in 1911-1928 catalogs	15.00	22.50	30.00
Tootsietoy 4570 Ford, Model T, open tourer, 1914, in catalog 1915-1926	22.50	33.75	45.00
Tootsietoy 4610 Ford Model T pick-up truck, 1914, in catalog 1919-1932	22.50	33.75	45.00
Tootsietoy 4629 (Yellow Cab) sedan, 1921, in catalog 1923-1933	17.50	26.25	35.00
Tootsietoy 4630 (Federal) "Grocery" delivery van, 1921, in catalog 1924-1933	45.00	67.50	90.00
Tootsietoy 4631 (Federal) "Bakery" delivery van, 1921, in catalog 1924-1933	70	105	14^
Tootsietoy 4632 (Federal) "Market" delivery van, 1921, in catalog 1924-1933	40	60	80
Tootsietoy 4633 (Federal) "Laundry" delivery van, 1921, in catalog 1924-1933	40	60	80
Tootsietoy 4634 (Federal) "Milk" delivery van, 1921, in catalog 1924-1933	30	45	60
Tootsietoy 4635 (Federal) "Florist" delivery van, 1921, in catalog 1924-1933	100	150	200

Tootsietoy Vans in the 4630s made in special custom liveries for private department stores, including "Boggs & Buhl," "Watt & Shand," "Pomeroy's," "Hochschild Kohn & Co.," "Bamberger's," "Alling Rubber Co.-Toys," "Jordan Marsh Co.," etc. Prices range on these from $125 to $350 in mint condition.

04638

Courtesy Phillips New York

	C6	C8	C10
Tootsietoy 4636 coupe, 1921, in catalog 1924-1933	30	45	60
Tootsietoy 4638 Mack stake truck, 1922, in catalog 1925-1933	30	45	60
Tootsietoy 4639 Mack coal truck, 1922, in catalog 1925-1933	30	45	60
Tootsietoy 4641 closed tourer, 1924, in catalog 1925-1933	30	45	60
Tootsietoy 4642 cannon, in catalog 1931-1941	6	9	12
Tootsietoy 4643 Mack AA Gun Truck, 1922, in catalog 1931-1941	30	45	60
Tootsietoy 4644 Mack searchlight truck, 1922, in catalog 1931-1941	30	45	60
Tootsietoy 4645 Mack "US Mail - Airmail Service," 1922, in catalog 1931-1933	40	60	80
Tootsietoy 4646 Caterpillar tractor, in catalog 1931-1939	12.50	18.75	25.00
Tootsietoy 4647 (Renault) tank, 1915, in catalog, 1931-1941	40	60	80
Tootsietoy 4648 steamroller, in catalog 1931-1934	100	150	200
Tootsietoy 4651 (Faegeol) safety coach circa 1927, in catalog 1927-1933 .	25.00	37.50	50.00
Tootsietoy 4652 Fire Engine - hook and ladder, in catalog 1927-1933 .	25.00	37.50	50.00
Tootsietoy 4653 Fire Engine - water tower, in catalog 1927-1933	40	60	80
Tootsietoy 4654 Farm Tractor, in catalog 1927-1932	25.00	37.50	50.00
Tootsietoy 4655 Ford, Model A Coupe, 1928, in catalog 1928-1933	30	45	60
Tootsietoy 4656 (Buick) coupe in tinplate garage, 1930, in catalog 1931-1932	90	135	180
Tootsietoy 4657 (Buick) sedan in tinplate garage, 1930, in catalog 1931-1932	90	135	180
Tootsietoy 4658 Mack insurance patrol in garage, in catalog 1931-1932	90	135	180
Tootsietoy 4665 Ford Model A Sedan	30	45	60
Tootsietoy 4666 Bluebird I Daytona record car, 1927, in catalog 1932-1941	22.50	33.75	45.00
Tootsietoy 4670 Mack tractor and two semi-trailers, 1927, "A&P", "American Express," in catalog 1929-1932 ....125.00		187.50	250.00
Tootsietoy 4680 "Overland Bus Lines," in catalog 1929-1933	70	105	140

4670

4680

4651

4634

These Tootsietoys are Durable as Well as Colorful

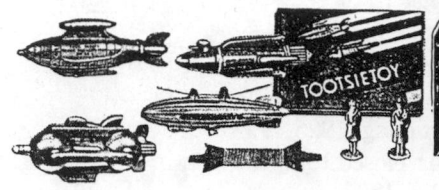

Buck Rogers Set. Three futuristic rocket ships and one modern Zeppelin and full figured models of Wilma and Buck. This set contains a spool of twenty feet of cable cord by which the ships sail through the air on their concealed pulleys. Attractively packed in a beautiful lithographed box.

No. 4N264. Per Set.................$0.70

Silvertoys. Contains four different types of aeroplanes and two automobiles. Has the non-tarnishable finish and packing is most attractive as a sales aid.

No. 4N249. Per Set.................$0.70

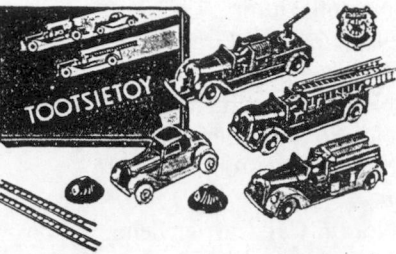

Fire Department Set. Consists of a Hook and Ladder, Hose Car, Insurance Patrol and Fire Chief Car plus fire-fighting equipment. Fire Trucks and Chief's Car finished in red and silver, ladders in gold and Firemen Hats in red. The attractively designed Chief's Badge is finished in gold. Packed in a sales appealing colorful box.

No. 4N245. Per Set.................$0.70

Playtime Set. Contains 10 outstanding 5c values. Autos, Trucks, Camping Trailer and U. S. Army Plane finished in brilliant colors and equipped with rubber tires. Star finished in a bright silver plate. Attractively packed in a newly designed box.

No. 4N254. Per Set.................$0.70

Interchangeable Truck Set. Is a set of five trailer type truck bodies that are interchangeable with two Mack type tractor engines attractively finished and packed in a brilliant colored box.

No. 4N259. Per Set.................$0.70

Aeroplane Set. Consists of five different types of aircraft. Each finished in bright colors. New Pilot Pin included in this set, finished in bright gold. Attractively packed in a new modern designed box.

No. 4N258. Per Set.................$0.70

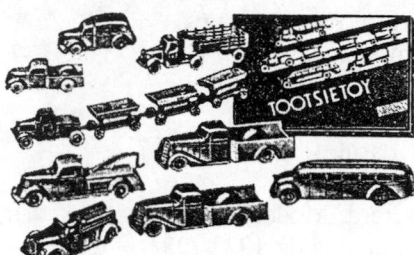

Truck Set. Consists of various commercial types of vehicles seen on the roads today and are "loadable" which adds play value to this popular set. Finished in bright colors and packed in a newly designed box.

No. 4N269. Per Set.................$1.50

Army Set. This set of 14 pieces contains various known types of cannon and anti-aircraft equipment, aircraft and armored tanks. Cannons actually shoot, Anti-Aircraft and Searchlight elevate and rotate. Finished in appropriate colors and attractively packed in a brilliantly colored box.

No. 4N261. Per Set.................$1.50

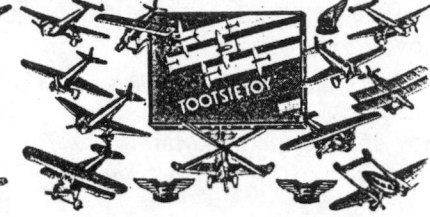

Round-the-World Set. Has practically every type of aeroplane imaginable: autogyro, amphibians, transports, bombers, cruiser and others. Added to this are the new Pilot, Co-Pilot and Stewardess Pins; finished in a bright gold. Complete set attractively packed in a colorful labeled box.

No. 4N262. Per Set.................$1.50

Jumbo Set. Is a set made up of the Jumbo-sized trucks and automobiles. They are not only brightly colored but unusual values plus a tool kit. Dressed in a new and attractive box measuring 15x10x2½ inches.

No. 4N267. Per Set.................$1.50

Motor Set. Is our interpretation of modern methods of travel. Latest model Bus, Aeroplane and Automobiles brightly finished and attractively packed in a newly designed brilliantly colored box.

No. 4N265. Per Set.................$1.50

Highways and Skyways. Consists of a modern Streamline Train, Zeppelins, Buses, Camping Trailer, Douglas Airliner and Automobiles. Finished in bright colors and packed in a newly designed box.

No. 4N268. Per Set.................$1.50

A TOOTSIETOY display of its sets in a Johnson-Smith catalog circa Christmas 1938.   Courtesy Don Pielin

TOOTSIETOY 0192

TOOTSIETOY 0806

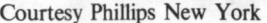

TOOTSIETOY 0802
Photo by Bill Kaufman
Courtesy Good Old Days Store

TOOTSIETOY 0805
Photo by Bill Kaufman
Courtesy Good Old Days Store

TOOTSIETOY Jeep CJ3, 3", 1950
Photo by Ed Poole

6-01 ROADSTER

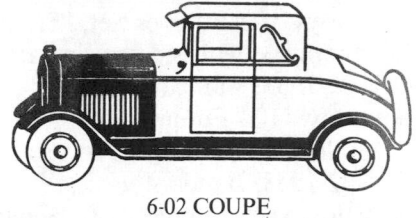

6-02 COUPE

6-03 BROUGHAM

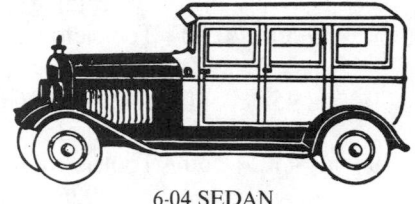

6-04 SEDAN

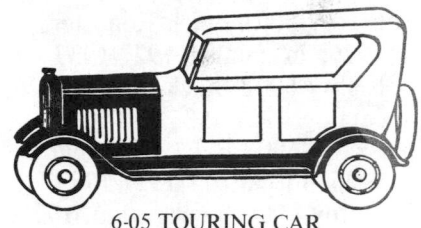

6-05 TOURING CAR

6-06 DELIVERY TRUCK

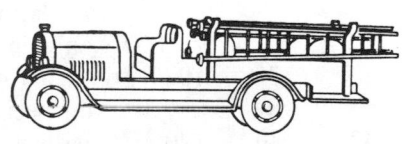

No. 4652 HOOK AND LADDER

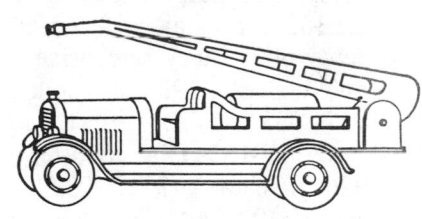

No. 4653 WATER TOWER

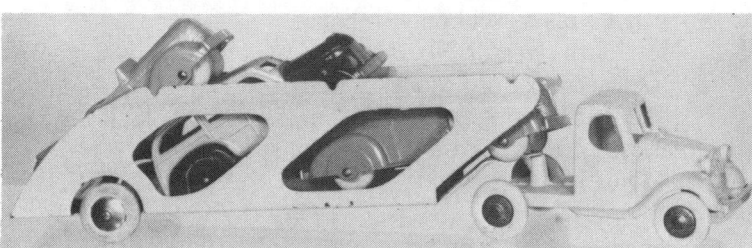

No. 187 Auto Carrier.

Courtesy Phillips New York

4665, 5655, unnumbered "U.S. Mail" (sold only in sets), 0716 "Doodlebug".

	C6	C8	C10
Tootsietoy 23 racer with driver, in catalog 1927-1933	40	60	80
Tootsietoy 190 Mack auto transport (3 Buicks), 1922 in catalog 1931-1933	125.00	187.50	250.00
Tootsietoy 190 Mack auto transport (4 Buicks) 1922, in catalog 1933-1936	175.00	262.50	350.00
Tootsietoy 5101 Funnies Set, "Andy Gump" roadster, in catalog 1932-1933, standard version	225.00	337.50	450.00
Tootsietoy 5102 Funnies Set, "Uncle Walt" roadster, in catalog 1932-1933, standard version	300	450	600
Tootsietoy 5103 Funnies Set, "Smitty" motorcycle with sidecar, in catalog 1932-1933, standard version	140	210	280
Tootsietoy 5104 Funnies Set, "Moon Mullins" police wagon, in catalog 1932-1933, standard v	250	375	500
Tootsietoy 5105 Funnies Set, "Kayo" ice wagon, in catalog 1932-1933, standard v	275.00	412.50	550.00
Tootsietoy 5106 Funnies Set, "Uncle Willie" rowboat in catalog 1932-1933, standard v	140	210	280
Tootsietoy 6001 Buick Roadster, 1926, in catalog 1927-1933	35.00	52.50	70.00
Tootsietoy 6002 Buick coupe, 1926, in catalog 1927-1933	30	45	60
Tootsietoy 6003 Buick Brougham, 1926, in catalog 1927-1933	30	45	60
Tootsietoy 6004 Buick sedan, 1926, in catalog 1927-1933	30	45	60
Tootsietoy 6005 Buick closed touring car, 1926, in catalog 1927-1933	35.00	52.50	70.00
Tootsietoy 6006 Buick screenside panel delivery, 1926, in catalog 1927-1933	50	75	100
Tootsietoy 6101 Cadillac roadster, 1926, in catalog 1927-1933	40	80	120
Tootsietoy 6102 Cadillac coupe, 1926, in catalog 1927-1933	40	80	120
Tootsietoy 6103 Cadillac Brougham, 1926, in catalog 1927-1933	40	80	120
Tootsietoy 6104 Cadillac Sedan, 1926 in catalog 1927-1933	40	80	120
Tootsietoy 6105 Cadillac closed Touring car, 1926, in catalog 1927-1933	75.00	112.50	150.00
Tootsietoy 6106 Cadillac Panel Delivery van, 1926, in catalog 1927-1933	27.50	41.25	55.00
Tootsietoy 6201 Chevrolet Roadster, 1926, in catalog 1927-1933	40	60	80
Tootsietoy 6202 Chevrolet Coupe, 1926, in catalog 1927-1933	40	60	80
Tootsietoy 6203 Brougham, 1926, in catalog 1927-1933	40	60	80
Tootsietoy 6204 Chevrolet Sedan, 1926, in catalog 1927-1933	40	60	80
Tootsietoy 6205 Chevrolet closed touring car, 1926, in catalog 1927-1933	100	150	200
Tootsietoy 6206 Chevrolet panel delivery van, 1926, in catalog 1927-1933	40	60	80
Tootsietoy 6301 Oldsmobile Roadster, 1926, in catalog 1927-1933	40	60	80
Tootsietoy 6302 Oldsmobile Coupe, 1926, in catalog 1927-1933	40	60	80
Tootsietoy 6303 Oldsmobile Brougham, 1926, in catalog 1927-1933	40	60	80
Tootsietoy 6304 Oldsmobile Sedan, 1926, in catalog 1927-1933	40	60	80
Tootsietoy 6305 Oldsmobile closed touring car, 1926, in catalog 1927-1933	75.00	112.50	150.00
Tootsietoy 6306 Oldsmobile panel delivery van, 1926, in catalog 1927-1933	40	60	80
Tootsietoy 6-01 Roadster, 1926, in catalog 1933 only	75.00	112.50	150.00
Tootsietoy 6-02 Coupe, 1926, in catalog 1933 only	75.00	112.50	150.00
Tootsietoy 6-03 Brougham, 1926, in catalog 1933 only	75.00	112.50	150.00
Tootsietoy 6-04 Sedan, 1926, in catalog 1933 only	75.00	112.50	150.00
Tootsietoy 6-05 Closed Touring Car, 1926, in catalog 1933 only	110	165	220
Tootsietoy 6-06 Panel Delivery Van, 1926, in catalog 1933 only	75.00	112.50	150.00
Tootsietoy, unnumbered, Ford Model A Van marked "U.S. Mail," sold only in sets	45.00	67.50	90.00
Tootsietoy 4654 Farm Tractor made in special version for Army Field Battery Set No. 5071, with cannons	65.00	97.50	130.00
Tootsietoy Box Trailer and road-scraper raker, sold only in boxed set Farm Tractor No. 7003	135	200	270
Tootsietoy 6665 Ford Model A Sedan, 1928, in catalog 1929-1933	32.50	48.75	65.00
Tootsietoy 101 Buick Coupe (see no. 4656), 1930, in catalog 1932-1934	15.00	22.50	30.00
Tootsietoy 102 Buick Roadster, 1930, in catalog 1932-1934	15.00	22.50	30.00
Tootsietoy 103 Buick Sedan (see no. 4657) 1930, in catalog 1932-1934	15.00	22.50	30.00
Tootsietoy 104 Mack Insurance Patrol (see 4658) in catalog 1932-1934	20	30	40
Tootsietoy 105 Mack tank truck, in catalog 1932-1934	15.00	22.50	30.00
Tootsietoy 108 Caterpillar Tractor, in catalog 1932-1934	12	18	24

	C6	C8	C10
Tootsietoy 109 Ford? Stake pick-up truck, in catalog 1932-1934	25.00	37.50	50.00
Tootsietoy 110 Bluebird I Daytona record car, 1927, in catalog 1932-1934	20	30	40

In the 1933 catalog, rubber tires were introduced, and many earlier models became available with optional rubber tires. Their catalog number was then preceded by the digit "0" so that the "Yellow Cab" with rubber tires, for example, was designated as 04629. New models with rubber tires only were also shown with a prefix of "0", so that the 1932 Macks, Grahams, etc., are thus listed below. However, all "0" prefixes were dropped in the 1937 and later catalogs. Also in the 1933 catalog, use of the new alloy (Zamac) was announced. Earlier models had been of lead and lead alloys. Some lead contamination in later castings resulted in the deterioration of the zamac. Lead-free zamac endures well.

	C6	C8	C10
Tootsietoy 0191 Mack dumper train, 3 carts, 1932 in catalog 1933-1941	100	150	200
Tootsietoy 0192 Mack "Tootsietoy Dairy" train semi-trailer plus two full trailers, 1932, in catalog 1933-1941	115	172	230
Tootsietoy 0198 Mack car transport (three Fords), 1932, in catalog 1935-1941	95	140	180
Tootsietoy 0801 Mack "Express" stake semi-trailer, 1932, in catalog 1933-1941	25.00	37.50	50.00
Tootsietoy 0802 Mack "Domaco" tank semi-trailer, 1932, in catalog 1933-1939	50	75	100
Tootsietoy 0803 Mack "Long Distance Hauling," cargo van, semi-trailer, 1932, in catalog 1933-1936, tin top	60	90	120
Tootsietoy 0804 "City Fuel," four wheels only, in catalog 1936-1938	75.00	112.50	150.00
Tootsietoy 0805 Mack "Tootsietoy Dairy" semi-trailer truck, 1932, in catalog 1933-1939	60	90	120
Tootsietoy 0806 Graham Wrecker, 1932, in catalog 1933-1939	50	75	100
Tootsietoy 0807 delivery motorcycle (adapted from 5103), in catalog 1933-34	65.00	97.50	130.00
Tootsietoy 0808 Graham "Tootsietoy Dairy" van, 1932 in catalog 1933-1938	70	105	140
Tootsietoy Graham "Commercial Tire & Supply Co." delivery van was sold only in sets. 05300 set is shown in 1935 catalog	100	150	200
Tootsietoy 0809 Graham ambulance, 1932, in catalog 1935-1941	40	60	80

	C6	C8	C10
Tootsietoy 0810 Mack "Railway Express Co." van (with Wrigley's ad), 1932, in catalog 1935-1939	70	105	140

The larger 1932 Macks were first issued in two-piece castings and dual wheels. In 1936 they were issued as one-piece castings with single rear wheels, worth about $20 less in mint. The tractor for the dumper train was never cast in the later one-piece (set 0191), and the car transport (0198) was never issued in the earlier two-piece casting. Tootsietoy Graham Series: There were several minor changes in chassis castings. Initially, there were none without spare tire on either sides or the rear. The "convertible" coupes and sedans listed below are castings identical to the non-convertible coupe and sedan, but painted two-toned with tan top. The same applies to the later 1934 Fords and 1935 LaSalles.

	C6	C8	C10
Tootsietoy 0511 Graham Roadster, five wheel, 1932, in catalog 1933-1935	60	90	120
Tootsietoy 0512 Graham Coupe, five-wheel, 1932, in catalog 1933-1935	50	75	100
Tootsietoy 0513 Graham Sedan, five-wheel, 1932, in catalog 1933-1935	40	60	80
Tootsietoy 0514 Graham convertible coupe, five-wheel, 1932, in catalog 1933-1935	40	60	80
Tootsietoy 0515 Graham Convertible sedan, five-wheel, 1932, in catalog 1933-1935	40	60	80
Tootsietoy 0516 Graham Town Car, five-wheel, 1932, in catalog 1933-1935	45.00	67.50	90.00
Tootsietoy 0611 Graham Roadster, six-wheel, 1932, in catalog 1933-1935	50	75	100
Tootsietoy 0612 Graham coupe, six-wheel, 1932, in catalog 1933-1935	40	60	80
Tootsietoy 0613 Graham Sedan, six-wheel, 1932, in catalog 1933-1935	55.00	82.50	110.00
Tootsietoy 0614 Graham Convertible Coupe, six-wheel, 1932, in catalog 1933-1935	45.00	67.50	90.00
Tootsietoy 0615 Graham Convertible sedan, six-wheel, 1932, in catalog 1933-1935	75.00	112.50	150.00
Tootsietoy 0616 Graham Town Car, six-wheel, 1932, in catalog 1933-1935	45.00	67.50	90.00
Tootsietoy (number not known) Graham Roadster, four-wheel, 1932	62.50	93.75	125.00
Tootsietoy (number not known) Graham Coupe, four-wheel, 1932, in catalog 1935?-1939 (Build-A-Car)	40	60	80
Tootsietoy (number not known) Graham Sedan, four-wheel, 1932, in catalog 1935?-1939 (Build-A-Car)	90	135	180

	C6	C8	C10
Tootsietoy 0712 LaSalle Coupe, 1935, in catalog 1936-1938	110	165	220
Tootsietoy 0713 LaSalle Sedan, 1935, in catalog 1936-1938	100	150	200
Tootsietoy 0714 LaSalle Convertible Coupe, 1935, in catalog 1936 only	110	165	220
Tootsietoy 0715 LaSalle Convertible Sedan, 1935, in catalog 1936 only	110	165	220
Tootsietoy 0716 (Briggs Lincoln) prototype "Doodlebug" 1933, in catalog 1936-1937	45.00	67.50	90.00
Tootsietoy 6015 Lincoln (only the grille is accurate, the rest of the body being the same as the Briggs prototype, which was never publicly sold) Zephyr, 1936, in catalog 1937-1939	125.00	187.50	250.00
Tootsietoy 6016 Lincoln Wrecker, 1936, in catalog 1937-1938	175.00	262.50	350.00

Tootsietoy Ford Series

The coupe and sedan in single color and convertible versions and the wrecker were issued in 1935 as 1934 Fords, having a separate grill-piece like the Grahams, the rubber tires mounted on metal hubs. The following year they were recast in one piece as 1935 Fords with slight changes also to the hood louvres and fender skirts and fitted with solid rubber wheels. The roadster, pick-up truck, etc., were not in the 1934 series.

	C.B.C.	Lee	
Tootsietoy 0111 Ford V-8 sedan, 1934, in catalog 1935 only	35.00	52.50	70.00
Tootsietoy 0111 Ford V-8 sedan, 1935, in catalog 1936-1939	25.00	37.50	50.00
Tootsietoy 0112 Ford V-8 coupe, 1934, in catalog 1935 only	35.00	52.50	70.00
Tootsietoy 0112 Ford V-8 coupe, 1935, in catalog 1936-1939	25.00	37.50	50.00
Tootsietoy 0113 Ford V-8 wrecker, 1934, in catalog 1935 only	40	60	80
Tootsietoy 0113 Ford V-8 wrecker, 1935, in catalog 1936-1941	22.50	33.75	45.00
Tootsietoy 0114 Ford V-8 convertible coupe, 1934, in catalog 1935 only	40	60	80
Tootsietoy 0115 Ford V-8 convertible sedan, 1934, in catalog 1935 only	40	60	80
Tootsietoy 180 set, Lincoln Zephyr and Roamer house-trailer issued in 1938 with clockwork motor, in 1939 without motor, 1936, in catalog 1938-1939	250	375	500
Tootsietoy 187 Mack car transport (up-tilted), 1932, in catalog 1941	90	135	180
Tootsietoy 4634 Army supply truck (adapted from 1042), in catalog 1939-1941	50	75	100
Tootsietoy 4635 Armored Car, in catalog from 1938 to at least 1941	45.00	67.50	90.00

	C6	C8	C10
Tootsietoy 0116 Ford V-8 roadster, 1935, in catalog 1936-1939	22.50	33.75	45.00
Tootsietoy 0117 Zephyr railcar, in catalog 1935-1936	37.50	56.25	75.00
Tootsietoy 0118 DeSoto Airflow sedan, 1935, in catalog 1935-1939	30	45	60
Tootsietoy 0120 Oil Tank Truck, in catalog 1936-1939	15.00	22.50	30.00
Tootsietoy 0121 Ford pick-up truck, 1935, in catalog 1936-1939	22.50	33.75	45.00
Tootsietoy 0123 Ford "Special Delivery" van, 1936, in catalog 1937-1939	30	45	60

This "camelback" van was also issued in several custom liveries by use of a tin-plate insert on the side panels. Price on these in mint condition is $5 and up.

	C.B.C.	Lee	
Tootsietoy 1006 "Standard" oil truck, in catalog from 1939 to at least 1941	30	45	60
Tootsietoy 1007 "Sinclair" oil truck, in catalog from 1939 to at least 1941	30	45	60
Tootsietoy 1008 "Texaco" oil truck, in catalog from 1939 to at least 1941	30	45	60
Tootsietoy 1009 "Shell" oil truck, in catalog from 1939 to at least 1941	25.00	33.75	50.00
Tootsietoy 1010 "Wrigley" box van, in catalog from 1940 to at least 1941	40	60	80
Tootsietoy 1011 Farm tractor, in catalog 1941	40	60	80
Tootsietoy 1016 (Auburn) roadster "torpedo", 1934, in catalog 1936 to at least 1941	12	18	24
Tootsietoy 1017 torpedo coupe, in catalog from 1936 to at least 1941	10	15	20
Tootsietoy 1018 torpedo sedan, in catalog from 1936 to at least 1941	22.50	33.75	45.00
Tootsietoy 1019 pick-up truck, in catalog from 1936 to at least 1941	22.50	33.75	45.00
Tootsietoy Greyhound bus (see 1045), in catalog 1941	30	45	60
Tootsietoy (no number known) Transamerica bus, in set only, in 1941 catalog	120	180	240
Tootsietoy 1027 wrecker, in catalog 1938-1941	9.00	13.50	18.00
Tootsietoy 1040 hook & ladder, in catalog 1937-1941	30	45	60
Tootsietoy 1041 hose car, in catalog 1937-1941	30	45	60
Tootsietoy 1042 Insurance patrol with open rear, in catalog 1937-1938	30	45	60
Tootsietoy 1042 Insurance patrol with single rear ladder and rear fireman in catalog 1939-1941	35.00	52.50	70.00
Tootsietoy 1043 Ford and small house trailer, 1935, in catalog 1937-1941	40	60	80

	C6	C8	C10
Tootsietoy 1044 Roamer house-trailer (see 180 set), in catalog 1937 only	80	120	160
Tootsietoy 1045 Greyhound deluxe bus, 1935, in catalog 1937 to at least 1941	26	39	52
Tootsietoy 1046 station wagon, circa 1939, in catalog 1940 to at least 1941	30	45	60
Tootsietoy 230 (LaSalle) sedan, circa 1939, in catalog 1940 to at least 1941	22.50	33.75	45.00
Tootsietoy 231 coupe, circa 1939, in catalog 1940 to at least 1941	24.00	36.00	48.00
Tootsietoy 232 open touring car, circa 1939, in catalog from 1940 to at least 1941	24	36	48
Tootsietoy 233 boat-tail roadster, circa 1939, in catalog from 1940 to at least 1941	15.00	22.50	30.00
Tootsietoy 234 box van, in catalog from 1940 to at least 1941	7.50	11.25	15.00
Tootsietoy 235 oil tank truck, in catalog from 1940 to at least 1941	7.50	11.25	15.00
Tootsietoy 236 fire engine, hook & ladder, in catalog from 1940 to at least 1941	25.00	37.50	50.00
Tootsietoy 237 fire engine, insurance patrol, in catalog from 1940 to at least 1941	12.50	18.75	25.00
Tootsietoy 239 station wagon, circa 1939, in catalog from 1940 to at least 1941	12.50	18.75	25.00

Tootsietoy 260 Paramount Air-N-Lite taxi "Yellow," 261 Paramount Air-N-Lite taxi "Checker", 262 fire engine and 263 hook & ladder were a "Giant Series," shown in 1941 catalog but never released.

End of List by C.B.C. Lee

POST-WAR TOOTSIETOYS

	C6	C8	C10
American LaFrance Pumper, 3", 1954	10	15	20
Austin-Healy 100-6 4-passenger roadster, 1956, 6"	17.50	26.25	35.00
Austin-Healy 100-6, 1955, 9"	No Price Found		
Buick Century Estate Wagon, 1954, 6"	20	30	40
Buick LeSabre Experimental Roadster, 1951, 6"	25.00	37.50	50.00
Buick Roadmaster 4-door sedan, 1949, 6"	No Price Found		
Buick special experimental coupe, 1954, 6"	15.00	22.50	30.00
Buick Special Fastback, 1947, 4"	20	30	40
Buick Super Estate station wagon, 1948, 6"	10	15	20
Buick Y Experimental Roadster, 4", 1938 (postwar release)	22.50	33.75	45.00
Cadillac 60 special 4-door sedan, 1948, 6"	18	27	36

	C6	C8	C10
Cadillac 62 4-door sedan, 6", 1954	18	27	36
Caterpillar Bulldozer, 1956, 6"	9.00	13.50	18.00
Same as above, with blade	11.00	16.50	22.00
Caterpillar Scraper 1956, 6"	9.00	13.50	18.00
Chevrolet Ambulance, 1950	25.00	37.50	50.00
Chevrolet Bel Air four-door sedan, 3", 1955	10	15	20
Chevrolet Cameo Pickup, 4", 1956	15.00	22.50	30.00
Chevrolet Coupe, 1947	25.00	37.50	50.00
Chevrolet Deluxe Panel Truck, 1950, 4"	20	30	40
Same as above, as Army Ambulance	25.00	37.50	50.00
Chevrolet Deluxe Panel Truck, 1950, 3", civilian	8	12	16
Chevrolet El Camino camper truck with boat atop, 1960, 6"	No Price Found		
Chevrolet El Camino pickup truck, 1960, 6"	18	27	36
Chevrolet Fleetline 2-door sedan, 1950 fastback, 3"	10	15	20
Chevrolet Semi with Gooseneck Trailer, 6", 1959	No Price Found		
Chrysler New Yorker 4-door sedan, 1953, 6"	20	30	40
Chrysler 300 2-door hardtop, 1955, 6"	12.50	18.75	25.00
Chrysler Thunderbolt experimental roadster, 1942, (postwar), 6"	25.00	37.50	50.00
Chrysler Windsor convertible, 1941 (released postwar), 4"	20	30	40
Chrysler Windsor convertible, 1950, 6"	12	18	24
Chrysler Windsor convertible, 1960, 4"	14	21	28
Corvette Roadster, 1954-55, 4"	14	21	28
Dodge D100 Panel Truck, 6", 1956	25.00	37.50	50.00
Dodge Pickup Truck, 1950, 4"	20	30	40
Ferrari Racer, 6", 1956	9.00	13.50	18.00
Ford B Hot Rod, 1931 (made 1960), 3"	8	12	16
Ford C600 Oil Tanker, 1956, 3"	8	12	16
Ford C600 Truck, 1962, 6"	7.50	11.25	15.00
Ford Country Sedan Station Wagon, 6", 1959	11.00	16.50	22.00
Ford Country Sedan Station Wagon, 1960, 3"	12	18	24
Ford Country Sedan Station Wagon, 1962, 6"	25.00	37.50	50.00
Ford Custom Convertible, 3", 1949	12	18	24
Ford Custom 4-door sedan, 1949, 3"	12	18	24
Ford Customline V-8 2-door sedan, 3", 1955	10	15	20
Ford Econoline Pickup, 1962, 6"	10	15	20
Ford F1 Pickup, 1949, 3"	7.00	10.50	14.00
Ford F6 Oil Tanker, 1949, 6"	25.00	37.50	50.00
Ford F6 Oil Tanker, 4", 1949	6	9	12
Ford F6 Stake Truck, 4", 1949 (no stakes, looks like long pickup)	7.00	10.50	14.00
Ford F100 Styleside Pickup, 3", with rear window, 1957	9.00	13.50	18.00

	C6	C8	C10
Ford F100 Styleside Pickup, 3", without rear window	3.00	4.50	6.00
Ford F-600 Stake Truck with tin cover, 1955, 6"	14	21	28
Ford Fairlane 500 convertible, 1957, 3"	8	12	16
Ford Falcon, two-door sedan, 1960, 3"	8	12	16
Ford Farm Tractor, 1956, 6"	No Price Found		
Ford LTD 2-door hardtop, 4", 1960 (last metal Tootsietoy)	12	18	24
Ford Mainline four-door sedan, 1952, 3"	10	15	20
Ford Ranch Wagon, 1954, 4"	14	21	28
Ford Ranch Wagon, 1954, 3"	9.00	13.50	18.00
Ford Special Deluxe convertible, 1940 (sold 1960), 6"	10	15	20
Ford V-8 Hot Rod, 1940 (made 1960), 6"	10	15	20
GMC 3571 Greyhound Bus, 1948, 6"	25.00	37.50	50.00
GMC Greyhound Scenicruiser Bus, 1957, 6"	25.00	37.50	50.00
Hook and Ladder Truck, No. 1040 (postwar release), 4"	15.00	22.50	30.00
Hose Car No. 1041 (postwar), 4"	25.00	37.50	50.00
International K1 panel truck, 1941, 4" (postwar release)	10	15	20
International K11 Oil Tanker, 1946, 6"	20	30	40
International Metro Van, 1960, 6"	30	45	60
International RC 180, 1955, 6", gooseneck Army version with launcher	10	15	20
Same as above, gooseneck	9.00	13.50	18.00
Same as above, grain trailer	10	15	20
Same as above, oil	9.00	13.50	18.00
Same as above, moving van	12	18	24
Same as above, boat transport	No Price Found		
Same as above, car transport	20	30	40
Jaguar type D 1957, 3"	8	12	16
Jaguar XK120 roadster, 3", 1954	7.00	10.50	14.00
Jaguar XK 140 coupe, 1956, 6"	20	30	40
Jeep, CJ3, Army version, 4", 1950	6	9	12
Same as above, civilian version	7.00	10.50	14.00
Same as above, 3", Army	9.00	13.50	18.00
Same as above, 3", Civilian	10	15	20
Jeep CJ5, 1960, 6"	8	12	16
Same as above, Army version	10	15	20
Same as above, snowplow version	No Price Found		
Jeepster, 1947, 3"	20	30	40
Kaiser Sedan, 6", 1947	30	45	60
Lancia Racer, 1956, 6"	7.50	11.25	15.00
Lincoln Capri 2-door hardtop, 1952, 6"	20	30	40
Mack B Line, 1955, 6", Cement Mixer	12.50	18.75	25.00
Same as above, Hook and Ladder	25.00	37.50	50.00
Same as above, Moving	10	15	20
Same as above, Log	No Price Found		
Mack B Line, 1955, 6", Oil	20	30	40
Same as above, Open Stake	12.50	18.75	25.00
Same as above, Pipe	No Price Found		
Mack L-Line Dump, 1947, 6"	8	12	16
Mack L-Line Fire Pumper, 6", 1947	25.00	37.50	50.00
Mack L-Line with fire trailer (ladder), 1947, 6"	10	15	20
Mack L-Line Truck, 6", 1947, Log	No Price Found		
Same as above, Moving Van	8	12	16
Same as above, Pipe	No Price Found		
Same as above, Stake, closed side	10	15	20
Same as above, stake trailer	20	30	40
Same as above, "Tootsietoys Coast to Coast" trailer truck	10	15	20
Same as above, Tow	12	18	24
Mercedes 190SL Coupe, 1956, 6"	30	45	60
Mercedes 300SL Gullwing Coupe, 1955, 9"	No Price Found		
Mercury custom sedan, four-door, 1952, 4"	20	30	40
Mercury Fire Chief car, 1949, 4"	22	33	44
Mercury Sedan, four-door, 1949, 4"	17.50	26.35	35.00
Metro Van, HO series	20	30	40
MG TF Roadster, 6", 1954	20	30	40
Same as above, 3"	17.50	26.25	35.00
Nash Metropolitan Convertible, 3", 1954	14	21	28
Offenhauser Hill Climber Racer, 1947, 3"	8	12	16
Oldsmobile 88 convertible, 4", 1949	15.00	22.50	30.00
Oldsmobile Dynamic 88 convertible, 6", 1959	15.00	22.50	30.00
Oldsmobile 98 Holiday 2-door hardtop, 1955, army version, 4"	15.00	22.50	30.00
Same as above, civilian version	18	27	36
Packard Patrician 4-door sedan, 1956, 6"	20	30	40
Plymouth Belvedere 2-door hardtop, 1957, 3"	9.00	13.50	18.00
Plymouth Special Deluxe 4-door Sedan, 3", 1950	12	18	24
Pontiac Chieftain Deluxe Coupe Sedan, 4", 1950	20	30	40
Pontiac Chieftain Fire Chief Coupe Sedan, 4"	20	30	40
Pontiac Safari Station Wagon, 2-door, 1955, 9"	7.50	11.25	15.00
Pontiac Star Chief 4-door sedan, 1959, 4"	14	21	28
Porsche Spyder Roadster, 1956, 6"	20	30	40
Rambler Super Cross-Country 6-cylinder station wagon, 4", 1960	18	27	36
School Bus, HO series	9.00	13.50	18.00
Studebaker Champion Coupe, 1947	18	27	36
Studebaker Lark custom convertible, 3", 1960	8.50	12.75	17.00
Thunderbird Coupe, 4", 1955	12	18	24
Thunderbird Coupe, 3", 1955	11.00	16.50	22.00

	C6	C8	C10
Triumph TR3 Roadster, 3", 1956 ...	6	9	12
Twin Coach Bus, 1950, 3"	17.50	26.25	35.00
Volkswagen 113 Beetle, 1960, 6"	12	18	24
Same as above, 3"	5.00	7.50	10.00
White Army Half Track, 1941 (postwar), 4"	16	24	32

End TOOTSIETOY

Tow Truck, cast iron, 6" long.
Courtesy Mapes Auctioneers & Appraisers

L to R: TOOTSIETOY Moon Mullins Police Patrol Car. TOOTSIETOY Uncle Willie and Mamie in Boat. TOOTSIETOY Kayo Ice Truck.
Courtesy PB Eighty-Four, New York

L to R: TOOTSIETOY Herbie & Smitty motorcycle and sidecar. TOOTSIETOY Andy Gump in Roadster.
Courtesy PB Eighty-Four, New York

	C6	C8	C10
Touring Car, tin, friction, 6"	24	36	48
Touring Car, tin and wooden friction drive, with cast iron driver and two cast iron women, 10½" long	250	375	500
Tow truck, cast iron, 6" long	70	105	140
Tow truck, cast iron, 7½", rubber wheels	125.00	187.50	250.00
Tractor, cast iron, 3"	65.00	87.50	130.00
Tractor, cast iron with wooden wheels, 4"	25.00	37.50	50.00
Tractor, cast iron with driver, 4½" long	125.00	187.50	250.00
Tractor with front loader and driver, cast iron, rubber wheels, 9½" long	450	675	900
Trailer truck, wooden, plastic wheels, "Coast to Coast Fast Freight," approx. 8¼" long	7.00	10.50	14.00

	C6	C8	C10
Trailer Truck Cab, slush cast, possibly Metal Cast, late 1930s	10	15	20
Trailer Truck "C to C C Co.," circa 1929, approx 6¾" long ...	45.00	67.50	90.00
Traveleer Land Coach Traveler, Trailer Co., L.A., 1927	180	270	360
Truck, cast iron, flat back, 1920s, approx. 4¼" long, looks like Model A Ford semi-tractor	40	60	80
Truck, open back, 4¼" long, cast iron, wheels marked "Hamilton Corhart"	35.00	52.50	70.00
Truck cab with interchangeable flat bed and tank, sheet metal with wooden wheels, 10¾"	16	24	32
Turner Bulldog Mack closed cab dump truck, red and green steel, 23" long	140	210	280
Turner Dump, friction, 15½" long, circa early 1930s	240	360	480
Turner Dump, 26" long	250	400	550
Turner Fire Engine Pumper, 15" long	200	300	400
Turner Hook and Ladder, 15" long, circa 1930s	150	225	300
Turner Lincoln Sedan, 26" long	1000	1500	2000
Turner Packard Roadster, 16½" long, 1920s	400	600	800
Turner Speedster, 1920s, 17" long, circa late 1920s, early 1930s	500	750	1000
Turner Steam Shovel	85.00	127.50	170.00
Turner Tow Truck	125.00	187.50	250.00
"U.S. Army Shooting Tank," 6" wood, pre WW II, 6" long, metal action	22.50	33.75	45.00
U.S. Army truck, boat and cement carrier, three pieces	9.00	13.50	18.00
U.S.A.W. No. 60118 half-track, black wooden wheels, die-cast, approx. 4¾"	10	15	20
Vindex Coast to Coast Bus, cast iron, circa 1930, 12" long	1250	1875	2500
Vindex Hay Loader	1600	2400	3200
Vindex "P&H" power shovel, cast iron, 12" (17" extended), wheels in caterpillar base, handle revolves rig	2000	3000	4000
Vindex Pick-Up Truck, cast iron, 7½" long	300	450	600
Vindex Racer, cast iron, "2" 11½" long, circa 1920s	200	300	400
Wannatoy Convertible, 6" long	7.00	10.50	14.00
Weeden Auto, live steam, 8¾" early	500	750	1000
Weeden Steam Road Roller, 1920s, 7" long, brass, tin, cast iron, steam toy fired by alcohol	180	270	360

WILKINS Hook and Ladder open truck, steel, windup motor, 9¾" long
Courtesy Phillips New York

	C6	C8	C10
Wilkins Fire Engine, circa 1900, with driver, steam boiler	125.00	187.50	250.00
Wilkins Hook and Ladder open truck, steel, wind-up motor, 9¼" long	150	225	300
Wilkins, Olds, 1904, curved dash, wind-up, 10"	400	600	800

A.C. WILLIAMS

A. C. Williams was founded in 1886 when Adam Clark Williams (1/22/1848-6/15/32) bought the J.W. Williams Company from his father. After a fire the firm was moved in 1893 from Chagrin Falls, Ohio to Ravenna. Toy production began about this time. Small cast iron toys were Williams' specialty, with banks, cars and aircraft predominant. A.C. Williams retired in 1919, but the firm continued to make toys until 1938, after which it continued in business in a non-toys capacity. Williams marked few, if any, of its toys. Two clues to an A.C. Williams toy are turned steel hubs and starred axle peens.

WILLIAMS Sedan, 6½" long
Courtesy Phillips New York

	C6	C8	C10
Williams Car Carrier, with three Austins, 1920	500	750	1000
Williams Coupe, rumble seat, side mounts, 1930, cast iron, rubber tires, 6¾" long	175.00	262.50	350.00
Williams four-casting nickeled radiator car, approx. 4" long	75.00	112.50	150.00
Williams "Gasoline" truck, circa 1920, 5½" long, cast iron	125.00	187.50	250.00

	C6	C8	C10
Williams Lincoln Touring Car, 7" long	150	225	300
Williams Model T Coupe, 6" long	125.00	187.50	250.00
Williams Racer, boat-tailed, 6½" long	175.00	262.50	350.00
Williams Sedan, circa 1930, cast iron, 6½" long, streamlined rear fender	225.00	337.50	450.00
Williams Sedan, 6¾" long, circa 1931, cast iron, interchangeable body	170	255	340
Williams Stake Truck 7" long, circa 1931, interchangeable body	170	255	340
Williams Steamroller, 5½", 1930s	75.00	112.50	150.00
Williams Studebaker, circa 1933-34, approx. 4" long, two tone sedan	110	165	220
Williams Touring Car, 9½" long, cast iron	500	750	1000
Willys Knight, cast iron, 8" long, 1920s, with driver	120	180	240
Wolverine Car & Trailer, 27" long, press down to operate	75.00	112.50	150.00
Wolverine "Mystery Car," press down to make car move, circa 1938	100	150	200
Wolverine Speeding Bus "5 Via Main St." tin litho, driver and occupants, 14" long, "19302," press down on rear to move	50	75	100
Wood Commodities Corp. Army Jeep and Cannon, 23" long	62.50	93.75	125.00

WYANDOTTE (All Metal Products Company)

Wyandotte seems to have been formed in the early 1920s, with pistols and rifles its main product. But by 1935 the Wyandotte, Michigan firm became best known for its simply built, streamlined, art deco steel cars and trucks, almost all of them employing wooden wheels. During WW II it made clips for the M-1 rifle, and after the war moved to Piqua, Ohio. In an attempt to diversify, it bought the Hafner trains line, but went out of business in 1956. Wyandotte's heavy gauge steel toys with baked enamel finish also included aircraft, doll buggies, musical toys, wagons and games.

	C6	C8	C10
Wyandotte Ambulance, 11¼" long, swinging rear door	90	135	180
Wyandotte Army Truck, 10" long, steel with wood wheels	25.00	37.50	50.00
Wyandotte Auto Transport, circa 1950s	60	90	120
Wyandotte boattail racer, 8½" long, steel, red with white rubber tires, electric headlamps	50	75	100
Wyandotte Car Carrier, early 1930s .	80	120	160
Wyandotte Car Carrier, late	50	75	100
Wyandotte Circus Truck, 10¾" long	110	165	220
Wyandotte Circus Truck, No. 503, 11" long	130	195	260
Wyandotte Circus Truck with Trailer, 19" long	160	240	320
Wyandotte Coffin Nose Cord, 13" long, pressed steel, rubber tires . .	200	300	400
Wyandotte Coffin Nose Cord, Fire Dept. version, red	350	525	700
Wyandotte Convertible (open) Roadster, 10" long, 1930s	90	135	180
Wyandotte Coupe, 2-door, about 1930, 6"	25.00	37.50	50.00
Wyandotte Coupe, 6", circa 1940 . . .	15.00	22.50	30.00
Wyandotte Coupe, 6" circa 1935, red with white rubber tires, electric headlights, 8½" long	60	90	120
Wyandotte Dairy Truck, 1930s, 12" long	100	150	200
Wyandotte Dump Truck No. 122 . . .	45.00	67.50	90.00
Wyandotte Dump Truck No. 124 . . .	50	75	100
Wyandotte Dump Truck, 6", 1930s . .	150	225	300
Wyandotte Dump Truck, pressed steel, approx. 6½" long, circa 1940	40	60	80
Wyandotte Dump Truck, steel, 7" long, circa 1937	35.00	52.50	70.00
Wyandotte Dump Truck, 12"	80	120	160
Wyandotte Dump Truck, circa mid-1930s, 15" long, white rubber tires	80	120	160
Wyandotte Dump Truck, 1930s, 12½" long	60	90	120
Wyandotte "Express" trailer truck, tin wheels	35.00	52.50	70.00
Wyandotte Fire Truck, 12", with ladder, ringing bell	25.00	37.50	50.00
Wyandotte Hydraulic Dump Truck, rear and side tip, 20" long	150	225	300

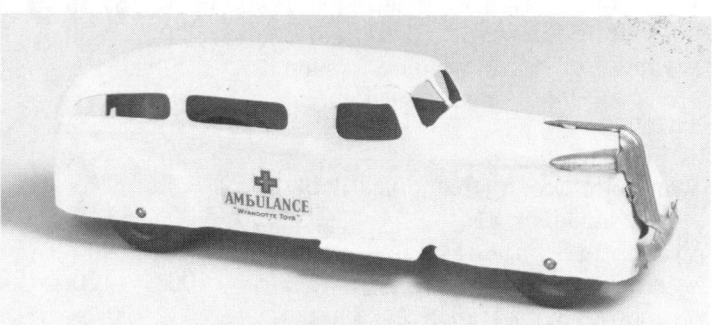

WYANDOTTE "Ambulance"
Courtesy Mapes Auctioneers & Appraisers

WYANDOTTE Stake Truck, 10" long, battery-operated headlights.
Courtesy Mapes Auctioneers & Appraisers

WYANDOTTE Circus Truck, 10¾"

	C6	C8	C10
Wyandotte Ice Truck, marked "ICE" on sides, circa 1940	55.00	82.50	110.00
Wyandotte LaSalle car with trailer, 25½" long, 1930s	250	375	500
Wyandotte Motor Express Trailer Truck, circa 1950s	70	105	140

	C6	C8	C10
Wyandotte Pickup Truck, 6" long, circa late 1930s	25.00	37.50	50.00
Wyandotte Race Car, 8½" long, pressed steel, rubber tires, circa 1937	50	75	100
Wyandotte School Bus, 1930s, 24" long	100	150	200
Wyandotte Sedan, 4" long, circa 1940	35.00	52.50	70.00
Wyandotte Sedan, 6", circa 1940	20	30	40
Wyandotte Sedan & House Trailer, 25½" long, pressed steel, circa 1939	250	375	500
Trailer alone	50	75	100
Wyandotte Sedan streamlined (looks like LaSalle), 15"	175.00	262.50	350.00
Wyandotte Semi, Grey Lines, cast wheels	100	150	200
Wyandotte Semi-Trailer Stake Truck "Valley Farms Livestock Produce" 2-piece, 8½" long, 1940s	100	150	200
Wyandotte Stake Truck, 5½" long, rubber wheels	22.50	33.75	45.00
Wyandotte Stake Truck about 1930, 6¾"	20	30	40
Wyandotte Stake Truck 1930s, 7½", white rubber wheels	20	30	40
Wyandotte Stake Truck, 10" long, battery-operated headlights	80	120	160

	C6	C8	C10
Wyandotte Stake Truck, 12" long, circa 1930s	100	150	200
Wyandotte Stake Truck, 20"	125.00	187.50	250.00
Wyandotte Station Wagon, Cadillac, 1941, Woody model, 21" long, metal	170	255	340
Wyandotte Steam Shovel	30	45	60
Wyandotte Sunshine Dairy Truck, 12"	50	75	100
Wyandotte Tow Truck, late	35.00	52.50	70.00
Wyandotte Town & Country Chrysler convertible, 1940s, 12" long	125.00	187.50	250.00
Wyandotte Trailer truck, 1950, extruded aluminum trailer	55.00	82.50	110.00
Wyandotte Wrecker, 1930s, wooden wheels, 10" long	22.50	33.75	45.00
Wyandotte "Wyandottey," pressed steel two-door sedan, sweeping long fenders, circa WW II black plastic wheels	15.00	22.50	30.00
Yellow Cab, 1930s, 7½" long, white rubber tires, rear suitcase rack	650	975	1300
Yellow Cab, cast iron, with driver, 7¾" long	220	330	440
Yellow Cab, 9" long, cast iron	250	375	500

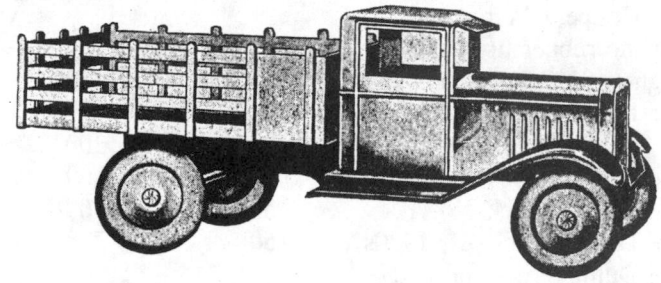

A WYANDOTTE ad from December, 1931, in Toys and Novelties magazine.

MATCHBOX

Matchbox began in London, England, with the partnership of longtime friends Leslie and Rodney Smith, who in 1947 combined portions of their first names to form Lesney Products. Business began in a former pub, and consisted of industrial zinc diecastings. Toys were added as a sideline, and in 1952 England's Woolworth's encouraged the Smiths to expand their toys line. In 1953 the 1-75 series began, and in 1954 the firm began using the Matchbox name. Sales to Japan began in 1958, and to the U.S. in 1959. Lesney was acquired by Universal holdings (since 1986 known as Matchbox Toys) in 1982. In 1987 Matchbox, of Moonachie, New Jersey, was one of the top three toy car makers, selling 77 million vehicles. Matchboxes are modeled to a one-sixty-fourth scale. (Moses Kohnstadt was the firm's first agent and sold the toys under his own label, Moko, using portions of his name. Lesney later acquired Moko.)

	C6	C8	C10
No. 1 Diesel Road Roller, 1953 .	20	30	40
No. 1 Aveling Barford Road Roller, 1964	15.00	22.50	30.00
No. 1 Mercedes Benz Lorry, 1968 ...	4.50	6.75	9.00
No. 1 Mod Rod, 1971	5.00	7.50	10.00
No. 1 Dodge Challenger, 1976	2.50	3.75	5.00
No. 2 Dumper, 1953	22.50	33.75	45.00
No. 2 Muir-Hill Dumper, 1962	6.00	9.00	12.00
No. 2 Mercedes Trailer, 1968	4.50	6.75	9.00
No. 2 Hot Rod Jeep, 1971	3.00	4.50	6.00
No. 2 Hovercraft, 1976	4.50	6.75	9.00
No. 3 Cement Mixer, 1953	20	30	40
No. 3 Bedford Ton Tipper, 1961	10	15	20
No. 3 Mercedes Benz Ambulance, 1968	5.00	7.50	10.00
No. 3 Monteverdi Hai, 1973	4.50	6.75	9.00
No. 3 Porsche Turbo, 1978	4	6	8
No. 4 Tractor, 1954	25.00	37.50	50.00
No. 4 Triumph Motorcycle and Sidecar, 1959	25.00	37.50	50.00
No. 4 Stake Truck, 1967	4	6	8
No. 4 Gruesome Twosome, 1971	3.00	4.50	6.00
No. 4 Pontiac Firebird, 1976	3.00	4.50	6.00
No. 4 '57 Chevy, 1981	2.50	3.75	5.00
No. 5 London Bus, 1954	12.50	18.75	25.00
No. 5 Lotus Europea Sports Car, 1969	10	15	20
No. 5 Seafire, 1976	2	3	4
No. 5 U.S. Mail Truck, 1981	2	3	4
No. 6 Quarry Truck, 1955	17.50	26.25	35.00
No. 6 Euclid 10-Wheel Quarry, 1964	12.50	18.75	25.00
No. 6 Ford Pick-Up, 1969	4	6	8
No. 6 Mercedes Tourer, 1974	3.00	4.50	6.00

	C6	C8	C10
No. 7 Horse Drawn Milk Cart, 1955	30	45	60
No. 7 Ford Anglia, 1961	10	15	20
No. 7 Ford Refuse Truck, 1967	4	6	8
No. 7 Hairy Hustler, 1971	4.50	6.75	9.00
No. 7 VW Golf, 1976	4.50	6.75	9.00
No. 8 Caterpillar Tractor, 1955	10	15	20
No. 8 Ford Mustang Fastback, 1966 .	5.00	7.50	10.00
No. 8 Wildcat Dragster, 1971	6	9	12
No. 8 De Tomaso Pantera, 1975	10	15	20
No. 9 Dennis Fire Engine, 1955	25.00	37.50	50.00

MATCHBOX No. 9 Merryweather Marquis Fire Truck
Courtesy Gary Linden

	C6	C8	C10
No. 9 Merryweather Marquis Fire Engine, 1959	10	15	20
No. 9 Boat & Trailer, 1967	4	6	8
No. 9 Javelin, 1972	4.50	6.75	9.00
No. 9 Ford Escort RS2000, 1978 ...	2.50	3.75	5.00
No. 10 Mechanical Horse & Trailer, 1955	20	30	40
No. 10 Sugar Container Truck, 1961	17.50	26.25	35.00
No. 10 Pipe Truck, 1967	10	15	20
No. 10 Piston Popper, 1973	4.50	6.75	9.00
No. 10 Plymouth 'Gran Fury' Police Car, 1980	2	3	4
No. 11 Petrol Tanker (Esso decal), 1955	20	30	40

MATCHBOX No. 7 Horse-Drawn Milk Cart
Courtesy Gary Linden

MATCHBOX No. 12 Land Rover
Courtesy Gary Linden

	C6	C8	C10
No. 11 Jumbo Crane (Taylor), 1964 .	4	8	12
No. 11 Scaffolding Truck (Mercedes), 1969	5.00	7.50	10.00
No. 11 Flying Bug, 1972	4.50	6.75	9.00
No. 11 Car Transporter, 1977	4	6	8
No. 12 Land Rover, 1953	10	15	20
No. 12 Safari Land Rover, 1965	10	15	20
No. 12 Setra Coach, 1971	7.50	11.25	15.00
No. 12 Big Bull, 1975	4.50	6.75	9.00
No. 12 Citroen CX, 1981	4.50	6.75	9.00
No. 13 Bedford Wreck Truck, 1955 .	12.50	18.75	25.00
No. 13 Thames Wreck Truck (MB Garages), 1959	20	30	40
No. 13 Dodge Wreck Truck (BP Label), 1961	10	15	20
No. 13 Baja Buggy, 1971	4.50	6.75	9.00
No. 13 Snorkel Fire Engine, 1977	2	3	4
No. 14 Daimler Ambulance, 1955	20	30	40
No. 14 Bedford Lomas Ambulance, 1962	10	15	20
No. 14 Iso Grifo Sports Car, 1968	4	6	8
No. 14 Mini Ha Ha, 1975	4.50	6.75	9.00
No. 15 Prime Mover, 1955	20	30	40
No. 15 Dennis Refuse Truck, 1963	10	15	20
No. 15 Volkswagen 1500 Saloon, 1968	7.50	11.25	15.00
No. 15 Fork Lift Truck, 1972	4.50	6.75	9.00
No. 16 Low-Loading Trailer, 6 wheels, 1955	12.50	18.75	25.00
No. 16 Low-Loading Trailer, 8 wheels, 1955	12.50	18.75	25.00
No. 16 Scammel Mountaineer Dump with Plough, 1961	10	15	20
No. 16 Case Tractor Bulldozer, 1969	4	6	8
No. 16 Badger, 1974	4.50	6.75	9.00
No. 16 Pontiac, 1981	2	3	4
No. 17 Bedford Removal Van, 1955 .	15.00	22.50	30.00

	C6	C8	C10
No. 17 Austin Taxi, 1960	20	30	40
No. 17 8-Wheel Tipper "Hoveringham", 1964	5.00	7.50	10.00
No. 17 Horse Box "Ergomatic Cab", 1969	4.50	6.75	9.00
No. 17 Londoner, 1973	4.50	6.75	9.00
No. 18 Caterpillar Bulldozer, 1955	25.00	37.50	50.00
No. 18 Field Car, 1969	10	15	20
No. 18 Hondarora, 1975	4.50	6.75	9.00
No. 19 MG Midget Sports Car, 1955	17.50	26.50	35.00

MATCHBOX No. 19 MGA, Sports Car
Courtesy Gary Linden

	C6	C8	C10
No. 19 MGA Sports Car, 1959	12.50	18.75	25.00
No. 19 Aston-Martin F.1, 1961	22.50	37.50	45.00
No. 19 Lotus Racing Car, 1965	3.50	5.25	7.00
No. 19 Road Dragster, 1971	3.50	5.25	7.00
No. 19 Cement Truck, 1976	3.00	4.50	6.00
No. 20 E.R.F. Lorry Truck, 1955	12.50	18.75	25.00
No. 20 Taxi Cab (Chevrolet Impala), 1965	10	15	20
No. 20 Lamborghini Marzel, 1969	4.50	6.75	9.00
No. 20 Police Patrol, 1975	2.50	3.75	5.00
No. 21 Long Distance Coach "London To Glasgow", 1955	12.50	18.75	25.00
No. 21 Commer Milk Truck, 1961	10	15	20
No. 21 Foden Concrete Truck, 1969	4	6	8
No. 21 Road Roller, 1973	4.50	6.75	9.00
No. 22 Vauxhall Cresta, 1955	17.50	26.25	35.00
No. 22 Pontiac 'Grand Prix' Sports Coupe, 1964	4	6	8
No. 22 Freeman Inter City Commuter, 1970	4.50	6.75	9.00
No. 22 Blaze Buster, 1975	2	3	4
No. 23 Caravan Trailer, 1956	5.00	7.50	10.00
No. 23 House Trailer Caravan, 1967	10	15	20
No. 23 Volkswagen Camper, 1970	3.50	5.25	7.00
No. 23 Atlas, 1975	3.00	4.50	6.00
No. 24 Excavator, 1956	10	15	20

MATCHBOX No. 25 Bedford "Dunlop" Van
Courtesy Gary Linden

MATCHBOX No. 28 Bedford Compresssor Truck
Courtesy Gary Linden

	C6	C8	C10
No. 24 Rolls Royce Silver Shadow, 1967	5.00	7.50	10.00
No. 24 Team 'Matchbox', 1973	3.00	4.50	6.00
No. 24 Diesel Shunter, 1979	2.00	3.00	4.00
No. 25 Bedford 'Dunlop' Van, 1956	17.50	26.25	35.00
No. 25 Volkswagen 1200 Sedan, 1958	20	30	40
No. 25 B. P. Tanker, 1960	10	15	20
No. 25 Ford Cortina G.T., 1968	4	6	8
No. 25 Mod Tractor, 1972	3.00	4.50	6.00
No. 25 Flat Car & Container, 1979	3.00	4.50	6.00
No. 26 Ready Mix Concrete Truck, 1956	15.00	22.50	30.00
No. 26 G.M.C. Tipper Truck, 1968	4	6	8
No. 26 Big Banger, 1972	3.00	4.50	6.00
No. 26 Site Dumper, 1976	2.50	3.75	5.00
No. 27 Bedford Low Loader, 1956	17.50	26.75	35.00

	C6	C8	C10
No. 27 Cadillac Sedan, 1960	15.00	22.50	30.00
No. 27 Mercedes Benz 230SL, 1965	4.50	6.75	9.00
No. 27 Lamborghini Countach, 1974	3.50	5.25	7.00
No. 28 Bedford Compressor Truck, 1956	13.00	19.50	26.00
No. 28 Thames Compressor Truck, 1959	10	15	20
No. 28 Mark Ten Jaguar, 1964	7.00	10.50	14.00
No. 28 Mack Dump Truck, 1968	4	6	8
No. 28 Stoat, 1974	2.50	3.75	5.00
No. 28 Lincoln Continental, 1980	2.50	3.75	5.00
No. 29 Bedford Milk Delivery Van, 1956	10	15	20
No. 29 Austin A55 Cambridge, 1961	15.00	22.50	30.00
No. 29 Fire Pumper Truck, 1965	7.50	11.25	15.00
No. 29 Racing Mini, 1971	3.00	4.50	6.00
No. 29 Shovel Nose Tractor, 1976	2.50	3.75	5.00
No. 30 Ford Prefect with Towbar, 1956	15.00	22.50	30.00
No. 30 German Crane Truck, 1961	14	21	28
No. 30 Favin Crane, 8 wheel, 1965	4.50	6.75	9.00
No. 30 Beach Buggy, 1971	2.50	3.75	5.00
No. 30 Swamp Rat, 1977	2.50	3.75	5.00
No. 30 Articulated Truck, 1981	2	3	4
No. 31 Ford Customline Station Wagon, 1956	15.00	22.50	30.00
No. 31 Ford Fairlane Station Wagon, 1959	20	30	40
No. 31 Lincoln Continental, 1964	6	9	12
No. 31 Volks Dragon, 1971	4.50	6.75	9.00
No. 31 Caravan, 1977	2.50	3.75	5.00
No. 32 Jaguar XK 140 Coupe, 1956	15.00	22.50	30.00
No. 32 Leyland Tanker, 1968	10	15	20
No. 32 Excavator, 1981	10	15	20
No. 33 Ford Zodiac MKII, 1956	10	15	20
No. 33 Ford Zephyr 6 MKIII, 1963	4.50	6.75	9.00
No. 33 Lamborghini Muira P400, 1969	4.50	6.75	9.00
No. 33 Datsun 126X, 1973	3.50	5.25	7.00
No. 33 Police Motorcyclist, 1977	2	3	4
No. 34 Volkswagen Microvan 'Matchbox' Express, 1956	12	18	24
No. 34 Volkswagen Camper, 1961	17.50	26.25	35.00
No. 34 Formula 1 Racing Car, 1971	4	6	8
No. 34 Vantastic, 1976	5.00	7.50	10.00
No. 34 Chevy Pro Stocker, 1981	2	3	4
No. 35 Marschall Horse Box, 1956	20	30	40
No. 35 Snow-Trac Tractor, 1961	9.00	13.50	18.00
No. 35 Merryweather Marquis Fire Engine, 1970	4	6	8
No. 35 Fandango, 1975	4.50	6.75	9.00
No. 36 Austin A50 with Towbar, 1956	15.00	22.50	30.00
No. 36 Lambretta & Sidecar, 1960	30	45	60
No. 36 Opel Diplomat, 1966	4	6	8
No. 36 Hot Rod Draguar, 1971	4.50	6.75	9.00
No. 36 Formula 5000, 1975	3.00	4.50	6.00
No. 36 Refuse Truck, 1981	2.50	3.75	5.00
No. 37 Coca-Cola Truck, 1956	25.00	37.50	50.00
No. 37 Cattle Truck (Dodge), 1967	4.50	6.75	9.00

MATCHBOX No. 36 Lambretta Motorcycle with sidecar
Courtesy Gary Linden

MATCHBOX No. 37 Coca-Cola Truck
Courtesy Gary Linden

MATCHBOX No. 38 Darrier Refuse Collector
Courtesy Gary Linden

	C6	C8	C10
No. 37 Soopa Coopa, 1973	4.50	6.75	9.00
No. 37 Skip Truck, 1976	2	3	4
No. 38 Darrier Refuse Collector	15.00	22.50	30.00
No. 38 Vauxhall Estate, 1963	12	18	24
No. 38 Honda Motorcycle with Trailer, 1968	6	9	12
No. 38 Stingeroo, 1973	4.50	6.75	9.00
No. 38 Armoured Jeep, 1976	2.50	3.75	5.00
No. 38 Camper, 1981	2	3	4
No. 39 Ford Zodiac Convertible, 1956	12.50	18.75	25.00
No. 39 Pontiac Convertible, 1962	20	30	40
No. 39 Ford Tractor, 1967	4.50	6.75	9.00
No. 39 Clipper, 1973	4.50	6.75	9.00
No. 39 Rolls-Royce Silver Shadow MKII	3.50	5.25	7.00
No. 40 Bedford 7 Ton Tipper, 1956	15.00	22.50	30.00
No. 40 Hay Trailer, 1967	3.00	4.50	6.00
No. 40 Leyland 'Royal Tiger' Coach/Long Distance, 1961	8	12	16
No. 40 Guildsman, 1971	4.50	6.75	9.00
No. 40 Horse Box, 1977	2.50	3.75	5.00
No. 41 'D' Type Jaguar Racing Car, 1956	20	30	40
No. 41 Ford G.T. 40 (Sports Racer), 1965	4.50	6.75	9.00
No. 41 Siva Spyder, 1972	4.50	6.75	9.00
No. 41 Ambulance, 1978	2.50	3.75	5.00

MATCHBOX No. 42 Bedford "Evening News" Van
Courtesy Gary Linden

	C6	C8	C10
No. 42 Bedford 'Evening News' Van, 1956	22.50	33.75	45.00
No. 42 Studebaker Lark Wagonaire, 1965	10	15	20
No. 42 Iron Fairy Crane, 1969	4	6	8
No. 42 Tyre Fryer, 1972	4	6	8
No. 42 Container Truck, 1977	2	3	4
No. 43 Hillman Minx, 1957	25.00	37.50	50.00
No. 43 Aveling-Barford Shovel, 1962	6	9	12
No. 43 Pony Trailer, 1968	6	9	12
No. 43 Dragon Wheels, 1972	3.50	5.25	7.00
No. 43 Steam Loco, 1978	2	3	4

	C6	C8	C10
No. 44 Rolls-Royce Silver Cloud, 1957	17.50	26.25	35.00
No. 44 Refrigerator Truck GMC, 1967	4	6	8
No. 44 Boss Mustang, 1972	2	3	4
No. 44 Passenger Coach, 1978	2	3	4
No. 45 Vauxhall Victor, 1957	10	15	20

MATCHBOX No. 46 Morris Minor 1000
Courtesy Gary Linden

MATCHBOX No. 47 Trojan "Brooke Bond Tea" van
Courtesy Gary Linden

	C6	C8	C10
No. 45 Ford Corsair with Green Boat, 1959	5.00	7.50	10.00
No. 45 Ford Group Six, 1970	4.50	6.75	9.00
No. 45 BMW, 1976	4.50	6.75	9.00
No. 46 Morris Minor 1000, 1957	20	30	40
No. 46 Pickfords Removal Van, 1960	12	18	24
No. 46 Mercedes-Benz 300SE, 1968	5.00	7.50	10.00
No. 46 Stretcha Fetcha, 1972	2.50	3.75	5.00

	C6	C8	C10
No. 46 Ford Tractor, 1978	2	3	4
No. 47 Trojan 'Brooke Bond' Van, 1957	22.50	37.50	45.00
No. 47 Neilson Ice Cream Van, 1963	9.00	13.50	18.00
No. 47 Daf Tipper Container Truck, 1968	5.00	7.50	10.00
No. 47 Beach Hopper, 1973	4.50	6.75	9.00
No. 47 Pannier Loco, 1980	1.50	2.25	3.00
No. 48 Sports Boat & Trailer, 1957	17.50	26.25	35.00
No. 48 Dodge Dumper Truck, 1967	4.50	6.75	9.00
No. 48 Pi-Eyed Piper, 1973	3.00	4.50	6.00
No. 48 Sambron Jack Lift, 1977	2.00	3.00	4.00

MATCHBOX No. 49 Army Half Track MK III
Courtesy Gary Linden

	C6	C8	C10
No. 49 Army Half Track MKIII, 1958	12.50	18.75	25.00
No. 49 Mercedes Unimog Truck, 1967	4	6	8
No. 49 Chop Suey, 1973	4.50	6.75	9.00
No. 49 Crane Truck, 1976	1.50	2.25	3.00
No. 50 Commer Pick-up Truck, 1958	12.50	18.75	25.00
No. 50 John Deere-Lanz Tractor, 1963	8	12	16
No. 50 Ford Kennel Truck, 1969	4.50	6.75	9.00
No. 50 Articulated Truck, 1973	4.50	6.75	9.00
No. 50 Harley Davidson Motorcycle, 1981	2	3	4
No. 51 Albion Truck 'Portland Cement', 1958	12.50	18.75	25.00
No. 51 Tipping Farm Trailer, 1963	10	15	20
No. 51 8 Wheel Tipper Truck, 1969	4	6	8
No. 51 Citroen SM, 1972	4	6	8
No. 51 Combine Harvester, 1979	2.50	3.75	5.00
No. 52 Maserati 4 CLT, 1958	25.00	37.50	50.00
No. 52 BRM Racing Car, 1965	5.00	7.50	10.00
No. 52 Dodge Charger MKIII, 1970	3.50	5.25	7.00
No. 52 Police Launch, 1976	2	3	4
No. 53 Aston-Martin DB2/4, 1959	7.00	10.50	14.00
No. 53 Mercedes-Benz 220SE, 1968	10	15	20
No. 53 Ford Zodiac MKIV, 1968	4	6	8

MATCHBOX No. 54 Army Saracen Personnel Carrier

	C6	C8	C10
No. 53 Tanzara, 1972	3.00	4.50	6.00
No. 53 C.J. 6 Jeep, 1977	2	3	4
No. 54 Army Saracen Personnel Carrier, 1959	10	15	20
No. 54 Cadillac Ambulance, 1965 ...	5.00	7.50	10.00
No. 54 Ford Capri, 1971	4	6	8
No. 54 Personnel Carrier, 1976	2.50	3.75	5.00
No. 54 Mobile Home, 1981	2	3	4
No. 55 D.U.K.W. (Army Amphibian), 1959	18	27	36
No. 55 Ford Police Car, 1963	15.00	22.50	30.00
No. 55 Mercury Parkland Police Car, 1969	10	15	20
No. 55 Mercury Police Car (Station Wagon), 1970	6	9	12
No. 55 Hell Raiser, 1975	2.50	3.75	5.00
No. 55 Ford Cortina, 1980	5.00	7.50	10.00
No. 56 London Trolley Bus, 1959 ...	25.00	37.50	50.00
No. 56 Fiat 1500, 1965	4.50	6.75	9.00
No. 56 BMC 1800 Pininfarina, 1970	4.50	6.75	9.00
No. 56 Hi Trailer, 1975	3.00	4.50	6.00
No. 56 Mercedes 450SEL, 1980	2	3	4
No. 57 Wolseley 1500, 1959	12.50	18.75	25.00
No. 57 Chevrolet Impala, 1966	15.00	22.50	30.00
No. 57 Eccles Caravan, 1970	5.00	7.50	10.00
No. 57 Wild Life Truck, 1973	4.50	6.75	9.00
No. 58 British European Airways Coach, 1959	12.50	18.75	25.00
No. 58 Drott Excavator, 1963	12.50	18.75	25.00
No. 58 Daf Girder Truck, 1968	4.50	6.75	9.00
No. 58 Woosh-N-Push, 1972	4.50	6.75	9.00
No. 58 Faun Dumper, 1976	1.50	2.25	3.00

MATCHBOX No. 55 Ford Police Car

MATCHBOX No. 56 Fiat 1500

MATCHBOX No. 59 Ford "Singer" Van
Courtesy Gary Linden

	C6	C8	C10
No. 59 Ford 'Singer,' Van, 1959	22.50	33.75	45.00
No. 59 Ford Fairlane Fire Car, 1964	10	15	20
No. 59 Fire Chief Car, 1966	5.00	7.50	10.00
No. 59 Planet Scout, 1975	10	15	20

MATCHBOX No. 60 Morris Omnitruck J-2 Pick Up
Courtesy Gary Linden

	C6	C8	C10
No. 59 Porsche 928, 1981	2.50	3.75	5.00
No. 60 Morris Omnitruck J2 Pick-up .	12.50	18.75	25.00
No. 60 Truck with Site Office, 1967 .	4	6	8
No. 60 Lotus Super Seven, 1971	4	6	8
No. 60 Holden Pick-Up, 1977	2	3	4
No. 61 Military Scout Car (Ferret), 1959	9.00	13.50	18.00
No. 61 Alvis Stalwart, 1967	4.50	6.75	9.00
No. 61 Blue Shark, 1971	2.50	3.75	5.00
No. 61 Wreck Truck, 1978	2.50	3.75	5.00
No. 62 General Army Lorry, 1959 ..	12	18	24
No. 62 TV Service Van, 1964	9.00	13.50	18.00
No. 62 Mercury Cougar, 1969	5.00	7.50	10.00
No. 62 Rat Rod Dragster, 1971	4	6	8
No. 62 Renault 17TL, 1974	3.50	5.25	7.00
No. 62 Chevrolet Corvette, 1980	2	3	4

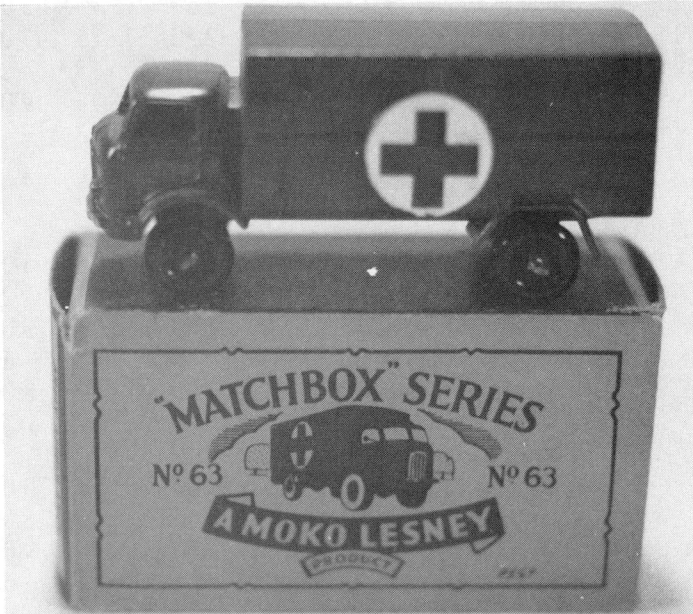

MATCHBOX No. 63 Army Ambulance
Courtesy Gary Linden

MATCHBOX No. 64 Scammell Army Wreck Truck
Courtesy Gary Linden

	C6	C8	C10
No. 63 Army Ambulance, 1959	10	15	20
No. 63 Airport Fire Fighting Crash Tender, 1964	9.00	13.50	18.00
No. 63 Dodge Crane Truck, 1968 ...	4.50	6.75	9.00
No. 63 Freeway Gas Tanker, 1973 ..	4.50	6.75	9.00
No. 64 Scammell Army Wreck Truck, 1959	15.00	22.50	30.00
No. 64 MG 1100, 1966	4.50	6.75	9.00
No. 64 Slingshot Dragster, 1971 ...	3.00	4.50	6.00
No. 64 Fire Chief Car, 1976	2	3	4
No. 64 Caterpillar Tractor, 1981	2	3	4
No. 65 Jaguar 3.4 Litre Saloon, 1959	12	18	24
No. 65 Claas Combine Harvester, 1968	4	6	8
No. 65 Saab Sonnet, 1973	3.00	4.50	6.00
No. 65 Airport Coach, 1977	2	3	4
No. 66 Citroen DS19, 1959	13.00	19.50	26.00
No. 66 Harley Davidson Motorcycle & Sidecar, 1963	35.00	52.50	70.00
No. 66 Greyhound Bus, 1967	10	15	20
No. 66 Mazda RX500, 1972	4.50	6.75	9.00
No. 66 Ford Transit, 1977	5.00	7.50	10.00
No. 67 'Saladin' Armoured Car, 1959	10	15	20
No. 67 Volkswagen 1600 T.L., 1968 .	4.50	6.75	9.00
No. 67 Hot Rocker, 1973	2.50	3.75	5.00
No. 67 Datsun 260Z, 1978	2	3	4
No. 68 Army Austin MKII Radio Truck, 1959	10	15	20
No. 68 Mercedes Coach, 1965	4.50	6.75	9.00
No. 68 Porsche 910, 1970	4.50	6.75	9.00
No. 68 Cosmobile, 1975	10	15	20
No. 68 Chevrolet Van, 1980	12	18	24
No. 69 Commer 30 Cwt. Van 'Nestles', 1959	20	30	40
No. 69 Hatra Tractor Shovel, 1965 ..	4.50	6.75	9.00
No. 69 Rolls-Royce Silver Shadow, 1970	10	15	20
No. 69 Turbo Fury, 1973	4.50	6.75	9.00

MATCHBOX No. 68 Army Austin MK II Radio Truck
Courtesy Gary Linden

MATCHBOX No. 69 Commer 30 CWT. Van "Nestle's"
Courtesy Gary Linden

	C6	C8	C10
No. 69 Wells Fargo Security, 1978 ..	2	3	4
No. 70 Ford Thames Estate Car, 1959	10	15	20
No. 70 Atkinson Grit-Spreading Truck, 1965	6	9	12
No. 70 Dodge Dragster, 1971	6	9	12
No. 70 S.P. Gun, 1977	1.50	2.25	3.00
No. 70 Ferrari, 1981	2	3	4
No. 71 Army Water Truck, 1959 ...	10	15	20
No. 71 Jeep Pick-Up Truck, 1964 ..	9.00	13.50	18.00
No. 71 Ford Heavy Wreck Truck, 1968	7.00	10.50	14.00
No. 71 Jumbo Jet, 1973	2.50	3.75	5.00
No. 71 Cattle Truck, 1976	2	3	4

	C6	C8	C10
No. 72 Fordson Tractor (Power Major), 1959	20	30	40
No. 72 Standard Jeep, 1967	10	15	20
No. 72 Hovercraft SRN6, 1972	4.50	6.75	9.00
No. 72 Bomag Road Roller, 1980 ...	2	3	4

MATCHBOX No. 73 R.A.F. 10 Ton Pressure Refueler Tanker
Courtesy Gary Linden

	C6	C8	C10
No. 73 RAF 10-Ton Pressure Refueler Tanker, 1959	17.50	26.25	35.00
No. 73 Ferrari Racing Car, 1963	10	15	20
No. 73 Mercury Station Wagon (Commuter), 1969	4.50	6.75	9.00
No. 73 Weasel, 1974	2	3	4
No. 73 Model 'A' Ford, 1981	2	3	4
No. 74 Mobile Refreshment Bar (Canteen), 1959	17.50	26.25	35.00
No. 74 Daimler Bus, 1966	6	9	12
No. 74 Toe Joe, 1972	2	3	4
No. 74 Cougar Villager, 1978	2.50	3.75	5.00
No. 75 Ford Thunderbird, 1959 ...	22.50	33.75	45.00
No. 75 Ferrari Berlinetta, 1965	10	15	20
No. 75 Alfa Carabo, 1971	4.50	6.75	9.00
No. 75 Helicopter, 1976	2	3	4

MATCHBOX 'MODELS OF YESTERYEAR'
(With Year of Introduction)

	C6	C8	C10
Y-1 1925 Allchin 7 N.H.P. Traction Engine, 1955	32.50	48.75	65.00
Y-1 1911 Model 'T' Ford, 1964	10	15	20
Y-1 1936 Jaguar SS100, 1977	4.50	6.75	9.00
Y-2 1911 'B' Type London Bus, 1955	30	45	60
Y-2 1911 Renault 2-Seater, 1963 ...	9.00	13.50	18.00
Y-2 Prince Henry Vauxhall, 1970 ...	6	9	12
Y-3 1907 London 'E' Class Tramcar, 1955	35.00	52.50	70.00
Y-3 1910 Benz Limousine, 1965 ...	9.00	13.50	18.00
Y-3 1934 Riley MPH, 1972	4.50	6.75	9.00
Y-4 Sentinel Steam Wagon, 1955 ...	30	45	60
Y-4 1905 Shank-Mason Horse-Drawn Fire Engine, 1960	11.00	16.50	22.00

MATCHBOX Y-5 Talbot Van
Courtesy Gary Linden

MATCHBOX Y-12 1912 Model T Ford
Courtesy Gary Linden

MATCHBOX Y-6 1913 Cadillac
Courtesy Gary Linden

MATCHBOX Y-14 1931 Stutz Bearcat
Courtesy Gary Linden

	C6	C8	C10
Y-4 1909 Opel Coupe, 1966	9.00	13.50	18.00
Y-4 1930 Dusenberg Model J, 1976 .	4.50	6.75	9.00
Y-5 1929 LeMans Bentley, 1955	32.50	48.75	65.00
Y-5 1929 Supercharged 4:1/2 Litre Bentley, 1960	12.50	18.75	25.00
Y-5 1907 Peugeot, 1968	9.00	13.50	18.00
Y-5 1927 Talbot Van, 1978	10	15	20
Y-6 1916 A.E.C. "Y" type Lorry Truck, 1955	30	45	60
Y-6 1926 Type "35" Bugatti, 1961 ..	22.50	33.75	45.00
Y-6 1913 Cadillac, 1967	9.00	13.50	18.00
Y-6 1920 Rolls-Royce Fire Engine, 1978	4.50	6.75	9.00
Y-7 1914 4-Ton Leyland, 1955	35.00	52.50	70.00
Y-7 1913 Mercer Raceabout Sportcar, 1961	24	36	48
Y-7 1912 Rolls-Royce, 1967	9.00	13.50	18.00
Y-8 1926 Morris Cowley "Bullnose", 1955	17.50	26.25	35.00
Y-8 1914 Sunbeam Motorcycle with Sidecar, 1962	27.50	41.25	55.00
Y-8 1914 Stutz Roadster, 1968	9.00	13.50	18.00
Y-8 1945 MC TC Sports Car, 1978 .	4.50	6.75	9.00
Y-9 1924 Fowl "Big Lion" Showman Engine, 1955	35	52	70
Y-9 1912 Simplex, 1967	4.50	6.75	9.00

	C6	C8	C10
Y-10 1908 Grand Prix Mercedes Racing Car, 1957	10	15	20
Y-10 1928 Mercedes-Benz 36/220, 1963	32.50	48.75	65.00
Y-10 1906 Rolls-Royce Silver Cloud, 1968	9.00	13.50	18.00
Y-11 1920 Aveling & Porter Steam Roller, 1957	35.00	52.50	70.00
Y-11 1912 Packard Landaulet, 1963 .	12.50	18.75	25.00
Y-11 1938 Lagonda Drophead Coupe, 1972	4.50	6.75	9.00
Y-12 1899 Horse-Bus (London), 1957	20	30	40
Y-12 1909 Thomas Flyabout, 1967 ..	9.00	13.50	18.00
Y-12 1912 Model "T" Ford, 1979 ...	4.50	6.75	9.00
Y-13 1862 American 4-4-0 Locomotive	25.00	37.50	50.00
Y-13 1911 Daimler, 1965	10	15	20
Y-13 1918 Crossley Truck, 1972	4.50	6.75	9.00
Y-14 1903 "Duke of Connaught" Locomotive, 1957	32.50	48.75	65.00
Y-14 1911 Maxwell Roadster, 1965 .	9.00	13.50	18.00
Y-14 1931 Stutz Bearcat, 1972	4.50	6.75	9.00
Y-15 1907 Rolls-Royce "Silver Ghost", 1960	12.50	18.75	25.00

	C6	C8	C10		C6	C8	C10
Y-15 1930 Packard Victoria, 1969 ...	9.00	13.50	18.00	Y-18 1937 Cord 812, 1979	4.50	6.75	9.00
Y-16 1904 Spyker Veteran Automobile, 1961	12	18	24	Y-19 1935 Auburn 851, 1980	4.50	6.75	9.00
Y-16 1928 Mercedes SS, 1971	4.50	6.75	9.00	Y-20 1938 Mercedes 540K, 1981	4.50	6.75	9.00
Y-17 1938 Hispano Suiza, 1972	4.50	6.75	9.00	Y-21 1929 Woody Wagon, 1981	4.50	6.75	9.00

MATCHBOX Accessory Pack A-1 BP Gas
Pump and BP sign, with box.
Courtesy Gary Linden

MATCHBOX 1966 Collector's Guide front
cover, U.S.A. edition.
Courtesy Gary Linden

Box cover for MATCHBOX service station
Courtesy Gary Linden

JAPANESE (ETC.) TIN CARS
by Ron Smith

Tin toy cars have been manufactured since the first horseless carriages roamed the streets of the United States and Europe. They ranged in size and price from the tiny one-inch penny toy to the 28" Eldorado which sold at the ten dollar mark. Although there are German, Spanish and French toy cars listed here, our concentration will be the 1950's Golden Era of Japanese tin toy cars. These examples enjoy much popularity today and prices have been raised by the limitlessness of some people's insanity. Keep one thing foremost in your mind when trying to sell a toy at the mint listed price; the person who paid that price already has one.

RON SMITH has always loved toy cars and planes. He can still show you his first Dinky Toy bought for him in 1940 by his aunt in Fred Harvey's Toy Store inside Cleveland's Terminal Tower Building. Born and raised in Shaker Heights, Ohio, Ron served in the United States Navy, attended John Carroll University, and for the last 14 years has been employed by Arrow Distributing of Solon, Ohio as Vice President of Sales. He has collected die cast cars, trucks and planes, cast iron toys, plastic promotional cars and, for the last 10 years, specialized in tin plate cars and planes. Ron lives in Solon, Ohio with his wife Joan and their two cats, Trouble and Bogart.

CONDITION CODE:
C5 – Good, wear evident overall, shows that has been played with
C6 – Fine, shows some wear in spots, but taken care of
C7 – Very Fine, minor wear overall, very clean
C8 – Excellent, minor wear on edges only
C9 – Near Mint, no noticeable flaws, close inspection may show minute marks
C10 – Mint (like new)
Note: Mint in Box does command higher price

No.	Year	Model	Manufacturer	Power	Size	C6	C8	C10
J1	1960's	Aston-Martin DB5 (James Bond)	Gilbert	Friction	11½"	50	75	150
J2	1960's	Aston-Martin DB6	Asahi Toy Co.	Friction	11"	50	100	300
J2A	1959	Austin Healey 100 Six Coupe	Bandai	Friction	8"	40	80	150
J2B	1959	Austin Healey 100 Six Convertible	Bandai	Friction	8"	40	80	150
J3	1953	Buick	Marusan	Friction	7"	75	125	250
J4	1954	Buick Station Wagon	Unknown	Battery	8"	75	150	200
J5	1955	Buick Roadmaster	Yoshiya	Friction	11"	100	150	350
J6	1958	Buick Century	Yonezawa	Friction	12"	300	400	800
J7	1958	Buick Century	Bandai	Friction	8"	80	110	130
J8	1959	Buick	TN.	Friction	11"	90	150	300
J9	1959	Buick	Ichiko	Friction	12"	100	275	350
J10	1960	Buick	Ichiko	Friction	17½"	150	250	600
J11	1961	Buick	T.N.	Friction	11"	50	100	175
J12	1961	Buick Emergency Car	T.N.	Friction	14"	50	95	125
J13	1963	Buick Wildcat	Ichiko	Friction	15"	100	200	300
J14	1966	Buick Le Sabre	Asahi Toy Co.	Friction	19"	100	150	275
J15	1968	Buick Sportswagon	Asakusa	Friction	15"	75	125	175
J16	1950	BMW 600 Isetta	Bandai	Friction	9"	150	200	250
J17	1950	BMW Isetta (three wheels)	Bandai	Friction	6½"	75	125	150
J18	1950	Cadillac	Marusan	Friction	11"	200	300	500
J19	1950	Cadillac	Marusan	Battery	11"	300	500	800
J20	1952	Cadillac	Alps	Friction	11½"	100	200	350
J21	1952	Cadillac	T.N.	Battery	13"	75	150	350
J22	1954	Cadillac	Gama	Friction	12"	200	300	400
J23	1954	Cadillac	Joustra	Battery	22"	200	300	500
J24	1959	Cadillac Sedan	Bandai	Friction	12"	50	75	150
J25	1959	Cadillac Convertible	Bandai	Friction	12"	50	75	150
J26	1960s	Cadillac	Bandai	Friction	17"	125	175	375
J27	1960	Cadillac	Yonezawa	Friction	18"	150	200	350

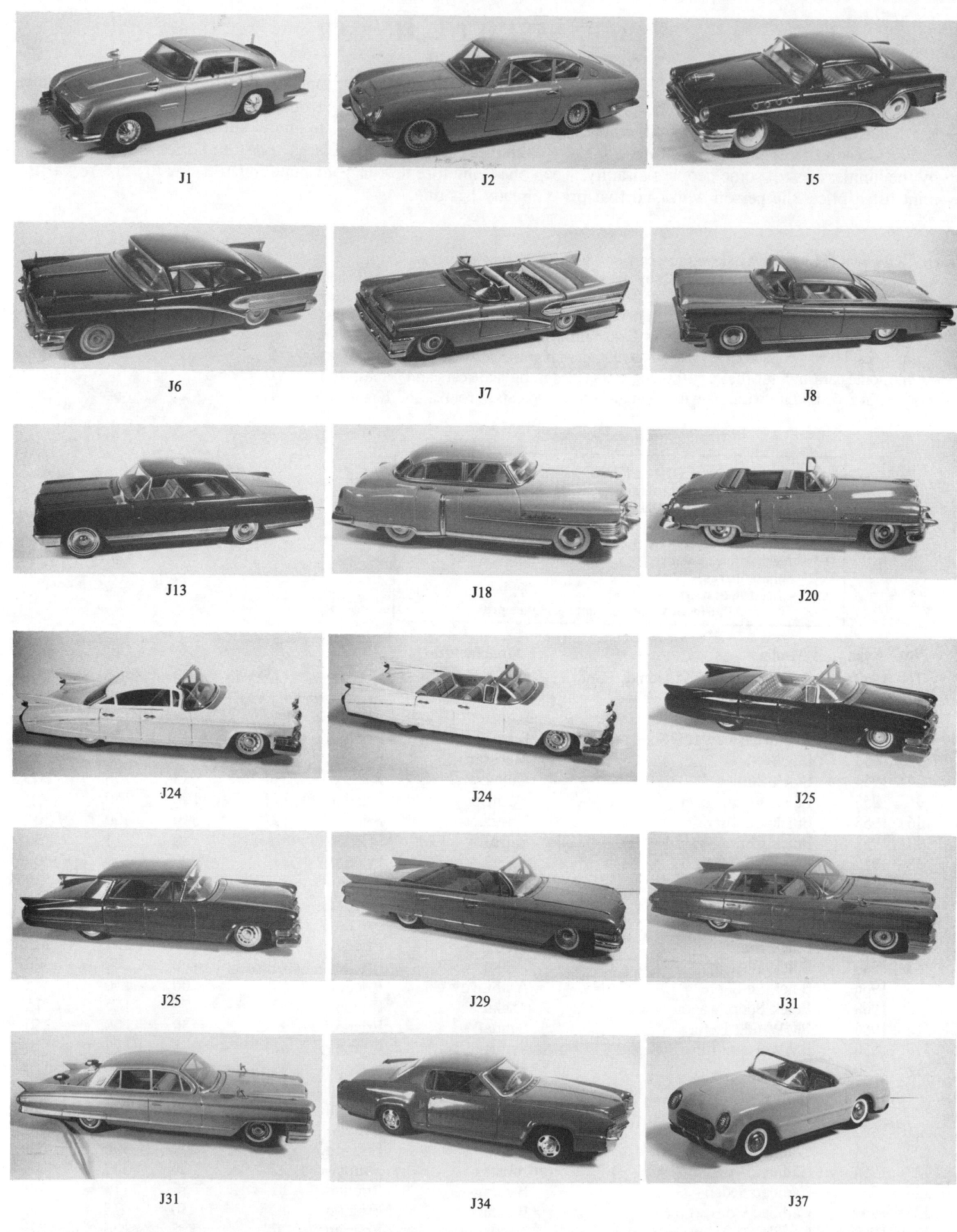

J1

J2

J5

J6

J7

J8

J13

J18

J20

J24

J24

J25

J25

J29

J31

J31

J34

J37

Photos by Ron Smith

108

J38   Photos by Ron Smith

No.	Year	Model	Manufacturer	Power	Size	C6	C8	C10
J28	1953	Cadillac 60	Unknown	Friction	9"	95	125	150
J29	1961	Cadillac Fleetwood	SSS	Friction	17½"	125	175	300
J30	1962	Cadillac	Yonezawa	Friction	22"	100	250	350
J31	1963	Cadillac	Bandai	Friction	17"	125	200	350
J32	1965	Cadillac	Asahi Toy Co.	Friction	17"	100	200	300
J33	1965	Cadillac	Ichiko	Friction	22"	200	300	450
J34	1967	Cadillac	K.O.	Friction	10½"	75	100	150
J35	1967	Cadillac	Unknown	Friction	10¾"	75	100	125
J36	1967	Cadillac El Dorado	Ichiko	Friction	28"	175	250	375
J37	1953	Chevrolet Corvette	Bandai	Friction	7"	75	100	150
J38	1958	Chevrolet Corvette	Yonezawa	Friction	9½"	150	200	300
J39	1962	Chevrolet Corvette	Bandai	Friction	8"	50	75	100
J40	1965	Chevrolet Corvette	Bandai	Friction	8"	65	90	125
J41	1964	Chevrolet Corvette	Ichida	Battery	12"	150	225	350
J42	1968	Chevrolet Corvette	Taiyo	Battery	9½"	35	50	75
J43	1960s	Chevrolet Corvair	Bandai	Friction	8"	50	65	90
J44	1963	Chevrolet Corvair	Ichiko	Friction	9"	50	65	95
J45	1967	Chevrolet Camaro	Taiyo	Friction	9½"	15	30	45
J46	1967	Chevrolet Camaro	T.N.	Friction	14"	100	150	225
J47	1967	Chevrolet Camaro	Modern Toys	Friction	11"	25	50	75
J48	1971	Chevrolet Camaro Rusher	Taiyo	Battery	9½"	10	20	35
J49	1954	Chevrolet	Marusan	Friction	11"	200	275	500
J50	1955	Chevrolet	Marusan	Battery	10¾"	200	375	600
J51	1956	Chevrolet Station Wagon	Bandai	Friction	9½"	75	125	175
J52	1956	Chevrolet Pick Up	Bandai	Friction	9½"	75	125	175
J53	1956	Chevrolet Convertible	Bandai	Friction	9½"	100	150	225
J54	1958	Chevrolet Red Cross Ambulance	Bandai	Friction	8"	20	30	50
J55	1958	Chevrolet Pick Up Truck	Bandai	Friction	8"	50	65	90
J56	1958	Chevrolet Convertible	Bandai	Friction	8"	60	90	125
J57	1958	Chevrolet Station Wagon	Bandai	Friction	8"	50	60	85
J58	1958	Chevrolet Sedan	Bandai	Friction	8"	75	100	125
J59	1959	Chevrolet Sedan Convertible	SY	Friction	11½"	150	200	350
J60	1960	Chevrolet	Marusan	Friction	11½"	125	175	300
J61	1959	Chevrolet Wagon	SY	Friction	12"	60	90	115
J62	1961	Chevrolet Impala Sedan	Bandai	Friction	11"	100	150	225
J63	1961	Chevrolet Impala Convertible	Bandai	Friction	11"	100	150	225
J64	1962	Chevrolet Secret Agent	Unknown	Battery	14"	50	75	125

J41

J42

J46

J49

J48

J50

J57

J59

J60

J62

J63

J64

J65

Photos by Ron Smith

110

J72

J71

J73

J74

J77

J86

J86

CONDITION CODE:
C5 – Good, wear evident overall, shows that has been played with
C6 – Fine, shows some wear in spots, but taken care of
C7 – Very Fine, minor wear overall, very clean
C8 – Excellent, minor wear on edges only
C9 – Near Mint, no noticeable flaws, close inspection may show minute marks
C10 – Mint (like new)
   Note: Mint in Box does command higher price

Photos by Ron Smith

J103

J87

J93

J96

J97

J99

J100

J102

J106

J107

Photos by Ron Smith

112

No.	Year	Model	Manufacturer	Power	Size	C6	C8	C10
J65	1962	Chevrolet	Unknown	Friction	11"	125	250	350
J66	1963	Chevrolet Impala	Unknown	Friction	18"	150	225	375
J67	1960	Citroen DS 19 Convertible	Bandai	Friction	12"	100	150	200
J68	1960	Citroen DS 19 Sedan	Bandai	Friction	12"	100	150	200
J69	1960	Citroen ID 19 Station Wagon	Bandai	Friction	12"	100	150	200
J70	1950	Chrysler	Guntherman	Friction	11"	75	100	150
J71	1955	Chrysler	Yonezawa	Friction	8"	75	100	150
J72	1957	Chrysler New Yorker	Alps	Friction	14"	300	500	800
J73	1958	Chrysler	Unknown	Battery	13"	150	250	350
J74	1959	Chrysler Imperial Convertible	Bandai	Friction	8"	75	90	125
J75	1959	Chrysler Imperial Sedan	Bandai	Friction	8"	75	90	125
J76	1960	Chrysler Valiant	Bandai	Friction	8"	20	45	65
J77	1962	Chrysler Imperial	Asahi Toy Co.	Friction	16"	300	500	800 +
J78	1960	DKW 1000 Convertible	Bandai	Friction	8"	75	85	125
J79	1960s	Datsun Bluebird 1200	Bandai	Friction	8"	60	75	125
J80	1950s	Divco Dugans Bakery Truck	Unknown, Jap.	Friction	7½"	300	400	500 +
J81	1930s	Desoto	Masudaya	Friction	8"	300	400	600 +
J82	1958	Dodge Sedan	T.N.	Friction	11"	150	175	250
J83	1959	Dodge Truck	Unknown	Friction	24"	350	500	600 +
J84	1959	Dodge Pick Up	Unknown	Friction	18½"	350	500	600 +
J85	1968	Dodge Yellow Cab	T.N.	Friction	12"	90	125	175
J86	1958	Edsel Convertible/Sedan	Haji	Friction	10½"	300	400	500 +
J87	1958	Edsel Wagon	Haji	Friction	10½"	200	250	300
J88	1958	Edsel Ambulance	Haji	Friction	11"	200	250	300
J89	1958	Edsel Station Wagon	T.N.	Friction	11"	150	200	250
J90	1958	Edsel H.T.	Asahi	Friction	10¾"	300	400	500 +
J91	1958	Edsel H.T.	Toy Nomura	Friction	8½"	100	125	225
J92	1958	Edsel	Yonezawa	Friction	10½"	300	400	500 +
J93	1949	Ford Sedan	Guntherman	Wind Up	11"	125	250	350
J94	1951	Ford Sedan	Guntherman	Wind Up	11"	125	250	350
J95	1950	Ford Good Humor Ice Cream Trk.	KTS, Japan	Friction	10¾"	150	250	350
J96	1955	Ford Pick Up	Bandai	Friction	12"	150	250	300
J97	1955	Ford Station Wagon	Bandai	Friction	12"	75	125	150
J98	1955	Ford Ambulance	Bandai	Friction	12"	150	250	300
J99	1955	Ford Panel Truck	Bandai	Friction	12"	200	300	400 +
J100	1955	Ford Convertible	Bandai	Friction	12"	200	300	400 +
J101	1956	Ford H.T.	Yonezawa	Friction	12"	300	400	500 +
J102	1956	Ford Convertible	Haji	Friction	11½"	350	500	800 +
J103	1956	Ford Sedan	Marusan	Friction	13"	500	800	1,000 +
J104	1956	Ford Wagon	Nomura	Friction	10½"	100	150	250
J105	1957	Ford Fairlane Sedan	Ichiko	Friction	10"	100	175	225
J106	1957	Ford H.T.	T.N.	Friction	12"	75	125	175
J107	1957	Ford Sedan/Conv./Wagon/Pick Up	Joustra	Friction	12"	175	225	275
J108	1957	Ford Sedan/Conv./Wagon/Pick Up	Bandai	Friction	12"	175	250	300
J109	1957	Ford Station Wagon	Monura	Friction	7½"	60	80	95
J110	1958	Ford Retractable Top	K. Japan	Friction	10"	65	90	125
J111	1958	Ford Retractable Top	T.N.	Battery	11"	90	125	150
J112	1958	Ford Country Squire Station Wagon	Bandai	Friction	8"	60	80	96
J113	1958	Ford Fairlane H.T./Conv.	Bandai	Friction	8"	60	80	95
J114	1958	Ford Fairlane H.T./Conv.	Sankei Gangu	Friction	9"	90	115	125
J115	1959	Ford Fairlane Skyliner	Sankei Gangu	Friction	9"	65	85	100
J116	1959	Ford Station Wagon	T.N.	Friction	12"	90	125	175
J117	1959	Ford Retractable	T.N.	Friction	11"	90	125	150
J118	1960s	Ford Falcon	Bandai	Friction	8"	30	40	60
J119	1960	Ford	Haji	Friction	11"	125	150	225
J120	1961	Ford Country Sedan	Bandai	Friction	10½"	125	150	175
J121	1962	Ford Country Sedan	Asahi	Friction	12"	200	250	400
J122	1964	Ford H.T.	Ichiko	Friction	13"	125	150	200

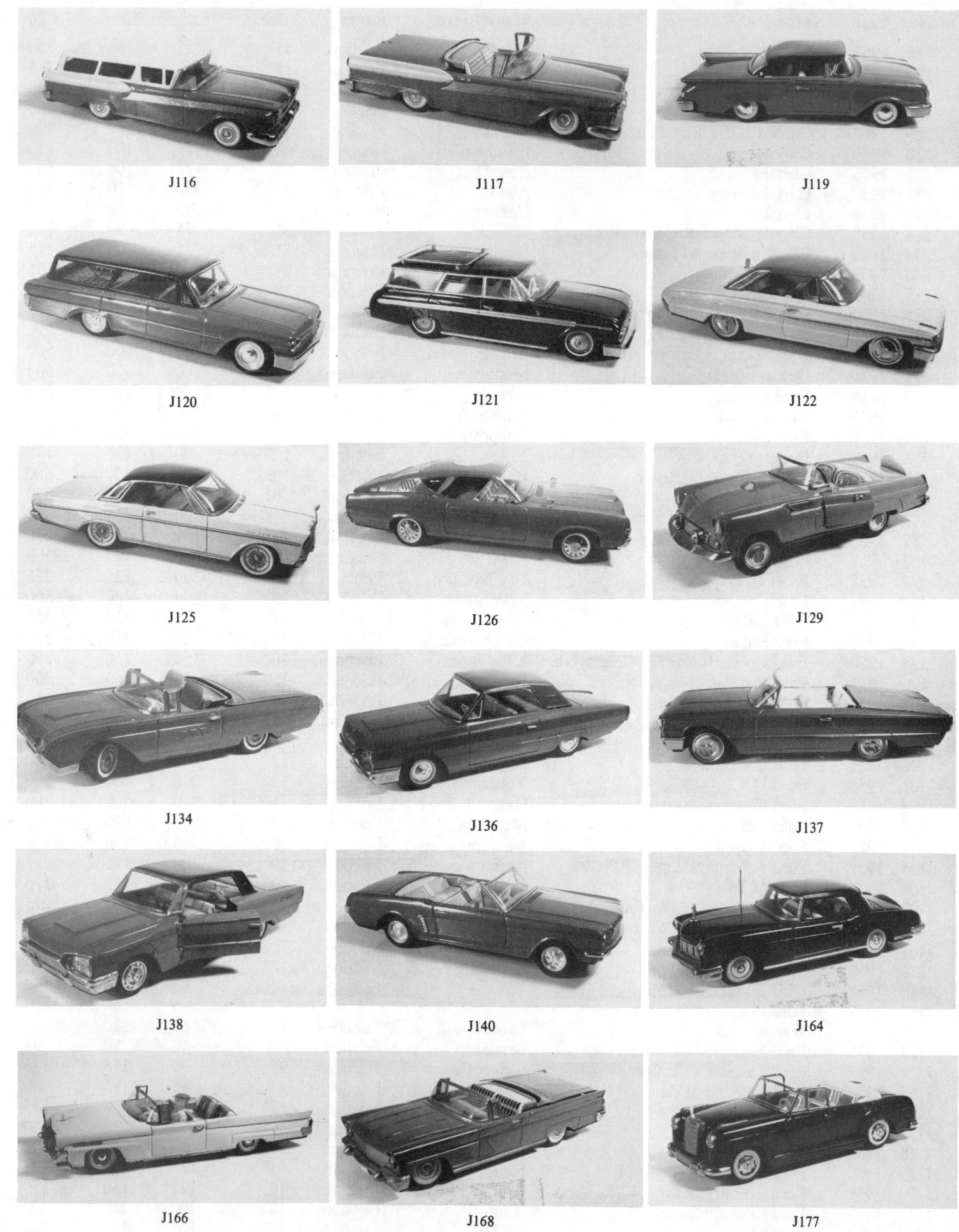

J116 J117 J119

J120 J121 J122

J125 J126 J129

J134 J136 J137

J138 J140 J164

J166 J168 J177

114

Photos by Ron Smith

No.	Year	Model	Manufacturer	Power	Size	C6	C8	C10
J123	1964	Ford H.T.	Rico	Friction	17"	100	200	300
J124	1964	Ford Convertible	Rico	Friction	17"	100	200	300
J125	1965	Ford Galaxie H.T.	MT	Friction	11"	125	150	175
J126	1968	Ford Torino	S.T.	Friction	16"	200	250	300
J127	1956	Ford Thunderbird	T.N.	Friction	11"	275	325	375
J128	1956	Ford Thunderbird H.T. Clear Top	T.N.	Friction	11"	275	325	375
J129	1956	Ford Thunderbird	T.N.	Battery	11"	275	350	400
J130	1959	Ford Thunderbird Sedan	Bandai	Friction	8"	50	60	75
J131	1959	Ford Thunderbird Convertible	Bandai	Friction	8"	50	60	75
J132	1961	Ford Thunderbird Retractable	Yonezawa	Battery	11"	90	120	150
J133	1962	Ford Thunderbird Retractable	Yonezawa	Battery	11"	90	120	150
J134	1963	Ford Thunderbird Retractable	Yonezawa	Battery	11"	90	120	150
J135	1964	Ford Thunderbird Convertible	Asahi	Friction	12½"	125	150	250
J136	1964	Ford Thunderbird H.T.	Asahi	Friction	12"	125	150	250
J137	1964	Ford Thunderbird	Ichiko	Friction	16"	100	175	275
J138	1965	Ford Thunderbird H.T.	Bandai	Friction	10¾"	60	85	125
J139	1965	Ford Mustang F.B.	Bandai	Friction	11"	45	65	90
J140	1965	Ford Mustang H.T./Conv.	Bandai	Fric/Bat	11"	75	125	150
J141	1965	Ford Mustang (FBI)	Bandai	Friction	11"	75	100	125
J142	1965	Ford Mustang Convertible	Yonezawa	Battery	13½"	90	125	175
J143	1966	Ford Mustang F.B.	T.N.	Friction	17"	100	175	250
J144	1967	Ford Mustang	Bandai	Battery	13"	45	65	95
J145	1960s	Ford Taunus 17M Convertible	Bandai	Friction	8"	30	40	60
J146	1960s	Ford GT	Bandai	Battery	10"	65	85	125
J147	1957	Ferrari 250 G. Convertible	A.T.C.	Friction	9½"	100	250	375
J148	1958	Ferrari	Bandai	Battery	11"	90	125	175
J149	1960	Ferrari SuperAmerica Coupe	Bandai	Friction	12"	100	200	300
J150	1960s	Ferrari SuperAmerica Convertible	Bandai	Friction	12"	100	200	300
J151	1960s	Fiat 600 Sedan	Bandai	Friction	8"	50	65	95
J152	1950s	International Cement Mixer	SSS	Friction	19"	275	300	400
J153	1950s	International Grain Hauler	SSS	Friction	23"	275	300	400
J154	1960	Jaguar XK150 H.T./Conv.	Bandai	Friction	9½"	75	125	175
J155	1960s	Jaguar XKE Convertible	T.T.	Friction	10½"	95	125	175
J156	1960s	Jaguar XKE Coupe	Lendolet Auto	Friction	10½"	75	100	125
J157	1960s	Jaguar XK140	Bandai	Friction	9½"	40	60	90
J158	1960s	Jaguar XKE	Bandai	Battery	10"	90	125	175
J159	1960s	Jaguar 3.4 Sedan	Bandai	Friction	8"	50	60	85
J160	1960s	Jaguar 3.4 Convertible	Bandai	Friction	8"	50	60	85
J161	1965	Jaguar XKE 120	Alps	Friction	6½"	65	85	95
J162	1954	Lincoln	Unknown	Friction	12"	175	275	375
J163	1955	Lincoln Sedan	Yonezawa	Friction	12"	250	325	425
J164	1956	Lincoln Continental Mark II	Line Mar	Friction	12"	400	600	800 +
J165	1956	Lincoln	Ichiko	Friction	16½"	150	250	375
J166	1959	Lincoln Continental Mark III Conv	Bandai	Friction	12"	90	125	150
J167	1959	Lincoln Continental Mark III Sedan	Bandai	Friction	12"	90	125	150
J168	1960	Lincoln H.T./Convertible	Yonezawa	Friction	11"	75	100	150
J169	1964	Lincoln	Unknown	Friction	10½"	90	175	275
J170	1950s	Lotus Elite	Bandai	Friction	8½"	25	35	45
J171	1960s	Land Rover "88" Station Wagon	Bandai	Friction	8"	30	40	60
J172	1950s	Mercedes Limousine	Tipp & Co.	Friction	14"	500	600	800 +
J173	1950s	Mercedes Benz Racer	Line Mar	Friction	9½"	95	150	185
J174	1950s	Mercedes Benz Racer W196	Marusan	Battery	10"	150	200	250
J175	1960s	Mercedes	Ichiko	Friction	12½"	115	155	185
J176	1960s	Mercedes Benz 219 Sedan	Bandai	Friction	8"	40	60	75
J177	1960s	Mercedes Benz 219 Convertible	Bandai	Friction	8"	40	60	75
J178	1960s	Mercedes Benz 230 SL	Modern Toys	Battery	15"	175	210	250
J179	1960s	Mercedes Benz 230 SL	Alps	Battery	10"	65	75	95
J180	1960s	Mercedes Benz 230 SL	Yanoman	Battery	14½"	125	155	185
J181	1960s	Mercedes Benz 250 SE	Ichiko	Battery	13"	110	140	185

J193

J195

J197

J208

J209

J210

J215

J216

J219

J222

J223

J224

J225

No.	Year	Model	Manufacturer	Power	Size	C6	C8	C10
J182	1960s	Mercedes Benz 250 S	Daiya	Friction	14"	110	155	175
J183	1950s	Mercedes Benz 300 SL	T.N.	Battery	11"	125	150	200
J184	1950s	Mercedes Benz 300 SL	KS	Battery	7"	45	65	85
J185	1950s	Mercedes Benz 300 SL	Dist. Cragstan	Battery	9"	65	95	125
J186	1950s	Mercedes Benz 300 SL	Bandai	Friction	8"	65	95	125
J187	1957	Mercedes Benz 300 SL	Marusan	Friction	8½"	150	250	325
J188	1960s	Mercedes Benz 600	Unknown	Friction	10"	95	125	175
J189	1960s	Mercedes Benz Taxi	Bandai	Battery	10"	75	100	125
J190	1962	Mercedes Benz	SSS	Battery	12"	200	250	350
J191	1970	Mercedes Benz	Ichiko	Friction	24"	125	150	200
J192	1954	Mercury H.T.	Rock Valley Toys	Battery	9½"	100	125	150
J193	1956	Mercury H.T.	Alps	Friction	9½"	400	500	600 +
J194	1958	Mercury Station Wagon	Bandai	Friction	8"	60	70	90
J195	1958	Mercury H.T.	Yonezawa	Friction	11½"	250	325	375
J196	1967	Mercury Cougar H.T.	Taiyo	Battery	10"	25	45	65
J197	1967	Mercury Cougar H.T.	Asakusa Toys	Friction	15"	175	225	275
J198	1952	MG TF	Unknown	Friction	8½"	50	75	95
J199	1954	MG TD	SSS	Friction	6½"	35	65	85
J200	1955	MG TF	Bandai	Friction	8"	95	125	150
J201	1957	MGA	A.T.C.	Friction	10"	175	250	375
J202	1960s	MG Magnette Mark III Sedan	Bandai	Friction	8"	95	125	150
J203	1960s	MG Magnette Mark III Convertible	Bandai	Friction	8"	95	125	150
J204	1960s	Messerschmitt 4 Wheels Convert.	Bandai	Friction	8"	200	250	300
J205	1960s	Messerschmitt 4 Wheels Sedan	Bandai	Friction	8"	200	250	300
J206	1950s	Nash	MSK	Battery	8"	40	70	90
J207	1956	Nash Ambassador	Sankei Gangu	Friction	8"	100	125	150
J208	1956	Oldsmobile Sedan	Ichiko/Kanto	Friction	10½"	150	250	350
J209	1956	Oldsmobile Super 88 Sedan	Masudaya	Friction	16"	250	325	400
J210	1958	Oldsmobile Sedan	A.T.C.	Friction	12"	150	250	350
J211	1958	Oldsmobile Super 88 Sedan	A.T.C.	Friction	13"	250	325	375
J212	1958	Oldsmobile Sedan	Y	Friction	16"	300	400	600 +
J213	1959	Oldsmobile Sedan	Ichiko	Friction	12½"	75	125	175
J214	1961	Oldsmobile Convertible	Yonezawa	Friction	12"	75	125	175
J215	1966	Oldsmobile Toronado	Bandai	Battery	11"	65	110	150
J216	1968	Oldsmobile Toronado	Ichiko	Friction	17½"	250	350	450
J217	1950s	Opel Sedan	Yonezawa	Battery	11½"	70	90	125
J218	1954	Pontiac Star Chief	Asahi	Friction	11"	250	350	450
J219	1967	Pontiac Firebird	Akasura	Friction	15½"	90	150	275
J220	1967	Pontiac Firebird	Bandai	Friction	10"	30	55	75
J221	1967	Pontiac Firebird (w/wipers)	Bandai	Battery	9½"	40	55	75
J222	1953	Packard Convertible/Sedan	Alps	Friction	16"	300	500	800 +
J223	1957	Packard Hawk Convertible	Schuco	Battery	10¾"	300	400	500 +
J224	1956	Plymouth H.T.	Unknown	Friction	8½"	125	175	275
J225	1956	Plymouth H.T.	Alps	Battery	12"	300	350	400 +
J226	1957	Plymouth Fury H.T.	Y	Friction	11½"	300	350	400 +
J227	1958	Plymouth Fury	Bandai	Friction	8"	75	90	125
J228	1959	Plymouth Hardtop	A.T.C.	Friction	10½"	100	150	275
J229	1959	Plymouth Convertible	A.T.C.	Friction	10½"	100	150	275
J230	1961	Plymouth Sedan	Ichiko	Friction	12"	125	250	350
J231	1961	Plymouth Station Wagon	Ichiko	Friction	12"	125	165	195
J232	1961	Plymouth T.V. Car	Ichiko	Battery	12"	125	175	250
J233	1964	Plymouth Fury H.T.	Kusama	Friction	10"	60	80	100
J234	1960	Porsche 911	Bandai	Battery	10"	65	95	125
J235	1950s	Porsche Speedster	Distler	Battery	10½"	350	400	500
J236	1960	Rolls Royce "Silver Coupe" Conv.	Bandai	Friction	12"	75	150	225
J237	1960s	Rolls Royce "Silver Coupe" Sedan	Bandai	Friction	12"	75	150	225
J238	1960s	Rolls Royce (with Electric Lights)	Bandai	Battery	12"	100	200	300 +
J239	1960	Rolls Royce	T.N.	Friction	10½"	175	250	375
J240	1960s	Rambler Rebel Station Wagon	Bandai	Friction	12"	50	85	125

J227

J232

J235

J236

J237

J240

J242

J243

J252

J260

J265

J276

J286

J287

J288

Photos by Ron Smith

No.	Year	Model	Manufacturer	Power	Size	C6	C8	C10
J241	1960	Renault	Bandai	Friction	7½"	95	150	200
J242	1960s	Studebaker Avanti	Bandai	Friction	8"	125	175	250
J243	1954	Studebaker	Yoshiya	Friction	9"	150	200	250
J244	1960s	Saab 93B	Bandai	Friction	7"	50	70	90
J245	1960s	Subaru 360	Bandai	Friction	7"	75	100	125
J246	1960s	Triumph TR-3 Convertible	Bandai	Friction	8"	50	75	125
J247	1960s	Triumph TR-3 Coupe	Bandai	Friction	8"	50	75	125
J248	1960s	Toyopet Crown	Bandai	Friction	9"	40	50	75
J249	1960s	Toyota	Ichiko	Friction	16"	150	275	325
J250	1967	Toyota 2000 GT	A.T.C.	Friction	15"	150	275	325
J251	1960s	Vespa	Bandai	Friction	9"	50	75	125
J252	1960	VW Karmann-Ghia	Bandai	Friction	7"	90	125	150
J253	1960s	Volkswagen Bus	A.T.C.	Friction	12"	125	175	350
J254	1960s	Volkswagen Pick Up Truck	Bandai	Friction	8"	50	60	75
J255	1960s	Volkswagen Bus	Bandai	Friction	8"	50	60	75
J256	1960s	Volkswagen Bus	Bandai	Bat/Fric	9½"	75	125	175
J257	1950s	Volkswagen Bus	Tipp & Co.	Battery	9"	250	375	450
J258	1950s	Volkswagen Convertible	T.N.	Friction	9½"	100	150	225
J259	1960s	Volkswagen Convertible	Bandai	Battery	7½"	50	70	90
J260	1960s	Volkswagen Convertible	Bandai	Battery	11"	110	145	185
J261	1960s	Volkswagen Convertible	Taiyo	Battery	10½"	50	100	140
J262	1960s	Volkswagen	Bandai	Friction	8"	20	30	50
J263	1960s	Volkswagen	Bandai	Battery	10½"	25	50	75
J264	1960s	Volkswagen	Bandai	Battery	11"	25	50	75
J265	1960s	Volkswagen with/without Sun Roof	Bandai	Friction	15"	90	125	150
J266	1960s	Willys Jeep FC-150 Pick Up	T.N. Toy Nomura	Friction	11"	50	75	95
J267	1950s	Zuendapp Janus	Bandai	Friction	8"	125	150	200
J268	1950s	Mazda Auto Tricycle K 360	Bandai	Friction	6"	75	100	150
J269	1950	Daihatsu Midget	Kokyu Shokai	Friction	5"	75	100	150
J270	1950s	Daihatsu Midget	Yonezawa	Friction	7"	75	100	150
J271	1950s	Mitsubishi Auto Tricycle Leo	Bandai	Friction	5"	75	100	150
J272	1950s	Mitsubishi Auto Tricycle	Bandai	Friction	11"	100	150	200
J273	1950s	Orient Auto Tricycle	Yonezawa	Friction	9"	75	100	150
J274	1950s	Mazda Auto Tricycle	Bandai	Friction	8"	75	100	150
J275	1950s	Daihatsu Auto Tricycle	Nomura	Friction	11"	100	150	200
J276	1950s	Buick Futuristic Le Sabre	Yonezawa	Friction	7½"	100	200	300 +
J277	1963	Corvair Bertone	Bandai	Battery	12"	75	150	200
J278	1950s	Dream Car Buick Phantom	Tipp & Co.	Friction	12"	300	400	500 +
J279	1960s	Dream Car Firebird III	Alps	Friction	11"	75	100	150
J280	1960	Ford Gyron	Ichida	Battery	11"	75	100	150
J281	1956	GM's Gas Turbine Powered Firebird II	Ashahi	Friction	8½"	100	200	300 +
J282	1950s	Pontiac Dream Car	Mitsubishi	Friction	10"	100	200	300 +
J283	1950s	Atom Jet Car	Y	Friction	30"	300	500	800 +
J284	1950s	Atom Car	Yonezawa	Friction	17"	200	400	600 +
J285	1950s	Record Racer NSU	Bandai	Friction	18"	75	100	150
J286	1950s	Agajanian Racer No. 98	Y	Friction	18"	500	800	1,200 +
J287	1950s	Champion's Racer No. 98	Y	Friction	18"	500	800	1,000 +
J288	1950	Champion Racer No. 42	Gem	Friction	18"	500	750	900 +
J289	1950	Champion Racer No. 15	German	Friction	18"	500	750	900 +

JAPANESE TIN AIRPLANES
by Ron Smith

No.	Type	Manufacturer	Power	Wing-span	C6	C8	C10
A1	Cessna	T.N.	Friction	25"	75	125	250
A2	Jenny Biplane	S&E	Friction	14½"	75	125	200
A3	Jenny Biplane	S&E	Friction	14½"	75	125	200
A4	Bristol Bulldog	S&E	Friction	14½"	60	90	175
A5	Cessna	W. Ger.	Friction	12"	50	80	150
A6	Ford	T.N.	Friction	15"	60	90	175
A7	Jenny Biplane	Haji	Friction	11½"	40	60	90
A8	Ryan Spirit of St. Louis	HTC	Friction	12"	75	125	200
A9	U.N. Hospital Plane	HTC	Friction	12"	70	120	210
A10	WWII Fighter	?	Friction	14½"	65	115	160
A11	Constellation	Ingap	Friction	15"	90	150	180
A12	F3F Biplane	Cragstan	Battery	11½"	100	200	300
A13	Bluebird Seaplane	S&E	Friction	13"	50	75	125
A14	B 50	Bandai	Friction	7½"	40	60	90
A15	Sky Bird "Spirit of St. Louis"	Bandai	Friction	9"	50	75	100
A16	Spitfire	HTC	Friction	10"	70	125	175
A17	P-51 Mustang	HTC	Friction	10"	70	125	175
A18	P-47 Thunderbolt	HTC	Friction	10"	70	125	175
A19	Zero	?	Friction	15½"	New	Issue	50
A20	De Havilland Comet	Rico	Wind Up	13"	100	150	200
A21	WW II Fighter	Spain	Wind Up	8½"	75	150	225
A22	F-80	Bandai	Friction	7½"	30	60	90
A23	Disney Comic Plane	Linemar	Friction	10"	75	100	150
A24	WW II Fighter	Spain	Wind Up	9"	50	75	150
A25	WW II Tri-Motor	Spain	Wind Up	9"	50	75	150
A26	Hospital Plane	Tekno	—	14"	200	400	500 +
A27	German Biplane	Tipp	Bat/W U	20"	200	400	500 +
A28	Construction	England?	—	22"	75	150	300
A29	30⁹ German	Tipp	W.U.	16"	200	400	500 +
A30	Fiat CR-42	Ingap	W.U.	10"	200	400	500 +
A31	Stuka	Dux	—	12"	200	400	500 +

A1

A2

Photos by Ron Smith

A3

A7

A4

A8

A5

A9

A6

Photos by Ron Smith

CONDITION CODE:
C5 – Good, wear evident overall, shows that has been played with
C6 – Fine, shows some wear in spots, but taken care of
C7 – Very Fine, minor wear overall, very clean
C8 – Excellent, minor wear on edges only
C9 – Near Mint, no noticeable flaws, close inspection may show minute marks
C10 – Mint (like new)
Note: Mint in Box does command higher price

A10

A11

A12

A16

A13

A14

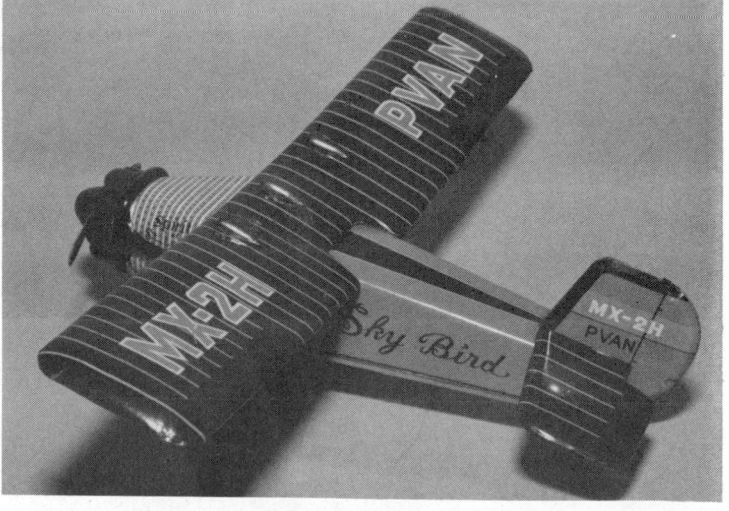

A15

Photos by Ron Smith

A18

A21

A19

A22

A20

A23

A24

A25

A26

A27

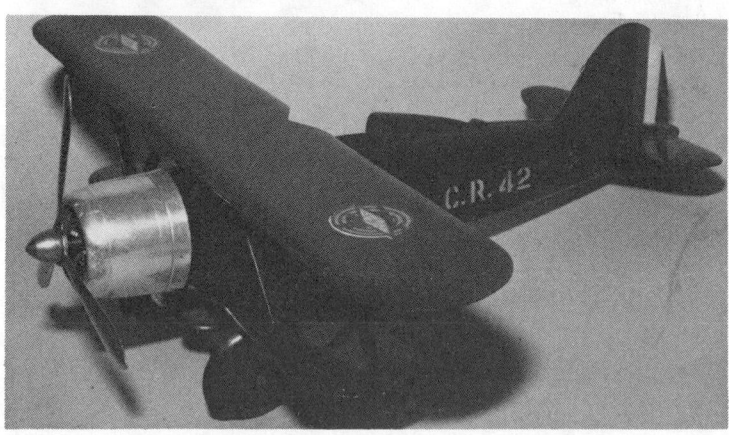

A30

A28

A29

A17

Photos by Ron Smith

ANIMAL-DRAWN

The average mint price in this section in the last edition was $354.19, with the average mint price in this edition $1244.89, an increase of 251%.

In this category, the toys generally commanding the highest prices are horse-drawn cast iron pieces. One reason for the eye-opening prices is that horse-drawn cast iron toys have considerable value apart from their lure as toys. There is an air of genuine Americana about them, and they are likely to attract the interest of many who otherwise pay no attention to toys (decorators figure largely in this area).

Since prices are often so high, reproductions, whether honest or dishonest, can be a problem. Things to look for when a reproduction is suspected include a rougher surface than an old toy would have (recastings are invariably rougher), uneven fit of pieces, a blurring of details, and "aging" that doesn't have the patina of age. Since at least one company, John Wright (formerly Grey Iron), is still manufacturing turn-of-the-century horse-drawn vehicles, some of them from the original molds, it is wise to become familiar with the field before investing heavily.

Carpenter Doctor's Cart
Courtesy Ed Hyers Antique Toys

ALTHOF, BERGMANN

Althof, Bergmann began in 1867, when L. Althof teamed with the brothers Bergmann, forming a jobbing firm (the brothers were already jobbers). In 1874 the New York company received two patents, one for a bell toy with three soldiers. In addition to bell and animal-drawn toys, they made (or jobbed out) toy furniture, banks, hoop and clockwork toys.

	C6	C8	C10
"Alderney Dairy" Milk Truck two-horse wood and lithographed paper	175.00	262.50	350.00
All-Nu Trotter, lead alloy, 1941, approx. 4" long	22.50	33.75	45.00

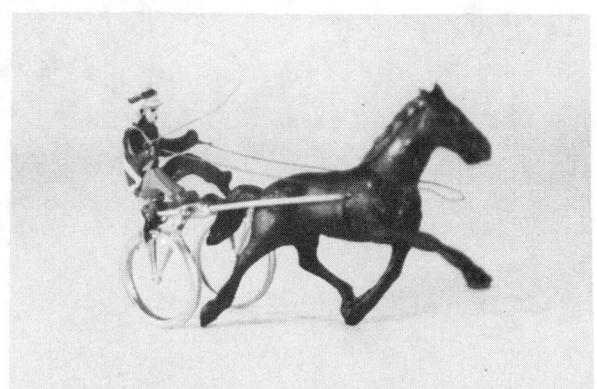

ALL-NU Trotter.
Photo by Bill Kaufman
Courtesy Evelyn Besser

ALTHOFF, BERGMANN "Fruits and Vegetables"
Courtesy Ed Hyers Antique Toys

	C6	C8	C10
Althof, Bergmann "Fruits and Vegetables", 17½" long	5000	7500	10,000
Althof, Bergmann Milk Cart, "Pure Milk," 14" long, c. 1880	500	750	1000

ARCADE "Contractors Dump Wagon"
Courtesy Mapes Auctioneers & Appraisers

BARCLAY Coach and Four, approx. 10¼" long.
Photo by Bill Kaufman   Courtesy Evelyn Besser

	C6	C8	C10
"Barnum and Bailey" circus cage, elephant drawn, 1930, painted, stained and litho wood, 35" long .	400	600	800

"Barnum and Bailey" Circus Cage, 35" long.
Courtesy Lloyd W. Ralston Auctions

ARCADE (ALL ARCADE TOYS ARE CAST IRON)

	C6	C8	C10
Arcade Bakery wagon, 13"	300	450	600
Arcade "Big Six Circus & Wild West" wagon, 14½" long (see Movies - "Tom Mix Big Six Circus," appears to be the same except for name)	225.00	337.50	450.00
Arcade Cart, wicker, horse, driver, cast iron	100	150	200
Arcade Coal car with horse	150	225	300
Arcade Contractors Dump Wagon, 14" long, horse team, driver	125.00	187.50	250.00
Arcade "Contractors Dump Wagon," 13¼" two-horse driver, 1930s ...	100	150	200
Arcade Farm Wagon, two-horse, driver	250.00	337.50	500.00

ARCADE McCormick Deering Spreader.

	C6	C8	C10
Arcade McCormick Deering Farm Wagon, two-horse	125.00	187.50	250.00
Arcade McCormick Deering manure spreader, with team of horses ...	250	350	500
Arcade Sulky plow, one horse, 10½"	150	250	350
Bakery Wagon, one horse, 13" long, cast iron	100	200	350
Barclay "Animal Cage" circus wagon, circa 1930s, lead and tin, approx. 9⅞" long, slush lead	25.00	37.50	50.00
Barclay Coach and Four, approx. 10¼" long, slush lead, circa 1930s	40	60	80
Barclay Covered Wagon with Oxen, under 6½" long, 1930s, "1849" ..	25.00	37.50	50.00

BLISS

Bliss was founded about 1832 by Rufus Bliss. Toymaking may not have begun till the late 1860s or early 1870s in its Rehoboth, Mass., plant. But by 1871 its toys were being advertised. Most were made of wood, and the range was wide; from dollhouses to trains, Noah's arks and ships. In 1883 Bliss made what might have been the first toy telephone set. The brilliant color lithography on Bliss's toys has made many of them prime collectibles.

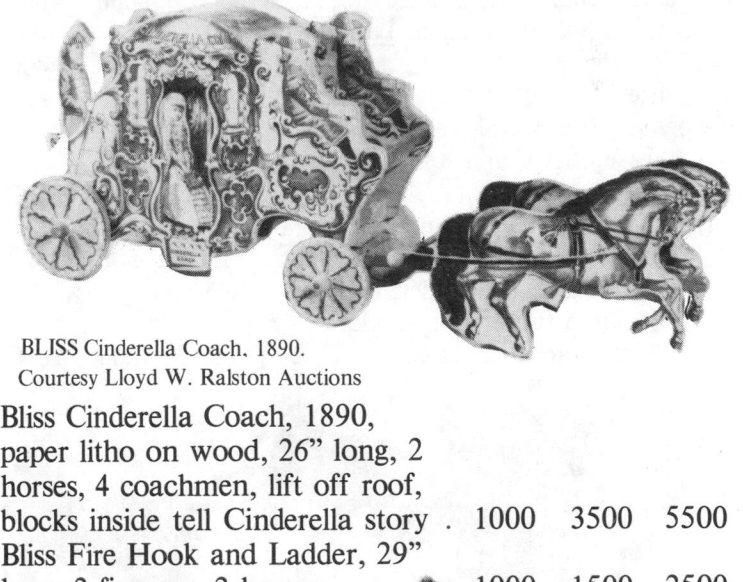

BLISS Cinderella Coach, 1890.
Courtesy Lloyd W. Ralston Auctions

	C6	C8	C10
Bliss Cinderella Coach, 1890, paper litho on wood, 26" long, 2 horses, 4 coachmen, lift off roof, blocks inside tell Cinderella story .	1000	3500	5500
Bliss Fire Hook and Ladder, 29" long, 2 firemen, 2 horses	1000	1500	2500

BARCLAY Covered Wagon
Photo by Don Pielin

BLISS Pansy 4-horse stagecoach, 1890. Courtesy Lloyd W. Ralston Auctions

	C6	C8	C10
Bliss Fire Hook and Ladder, 31" long, paper litho on wood	1200	2000	3500
Bliss Pansy 4 horse stagecoach, 1890, paper litho on wood, 31" long	1000	1500	2500
"Borden's Farm Products," wood, horse-drawn wagon pull-toy with articulated legs	200	300	400
Bread Wagon "Bread and Cakes" with driver, tin horse, 12½"	350	525	700
Brewery Wagon, cast iron and pressed steel, two horse with driver, 20½" long	350	525	700
Buckboard, cast iron, 14" long, one horse and driver	200	300	400
Buggy and Horse, tin	100	150	200
Buggy, pressed steel, cast iron wheels and horse	40	60	80
Buggy with driver, cast iron, 6½" long	70	105	140

CARPENTER

Carpenter (Francis W.) of Harrison and Port Chester, New York, was in business from 1844-1925. Malleable iron was its trademark; malleable iron being a type that has a bit of give, making it less fragile. Its two predominant lines were horse-drawn toys and trains.

	C6	C8	C10
Carpenter Cart, animated, pat. 1883, cast iron	150	225	300
Carpenter Cart, two-wheel, one horse, no driver, pat. 1882	250	400	600
Carpenter Dump Cart, 2-horse	350	600	1000
Carpenter Coal Cart, iron	2000	3000	4000
Carpenter Delivery Wagon, Pat. 1881, 12" long	200	300	400
Carpenter Doctor's Cart	400	600	800
Carpenter Fire Patrol, cast iron, 2-horse, driver and 3 figures, 1885, 16½" long	1000	2000	3500
Carpenter Fire Wagon, one horse, one fireman	350	500	750
Carpenter Hook and Ladder, two-horse, two firemen in standard helmets, early	800	1200	1600

CARPENTER Horse and carriage, 1880, 14" long.
Courtesy Lloyd W. Ralston Auctions

	C6	C8	C10
Carpenter Hook and Ladder, cast iron, 2-horse with driver and rear man, ladders, circa 1883-1890, 26½" long	700	1050	1400
Carpenter Horse and Carriage, 1880 painted cast iron, 14" long	750	1000	1500
Carpenter Iron Coal Cart	2000	3000	4000
Carpenter Ox Cart, 2 oxen, cast iron, circa 1880-1903, 11" long	400	600	800
Carpenter Pumper, 2-horse 18" long No. 33	1500	2500	3500
Carpenter Tally Ho, 27½" long, 4-horse, cast iron, seven festive riders in coach	4000	9500	12,000
Carriage, cast iron, one-horse, 7½" long, Doctor's Cart	400	600	900
Carriage, metal and wood, one horse, malleable iron horse with articulated legs and tail, carriage made of wood	300	450	600
Cart, bull-pulled, cast iron two-wheeled cart	100	150	200
Cart, cast iron lion, two wheels, 8" long	125.00	187.50	250.00
Cart, one horse, cast iron, 9" long ...	50	75	100
Cart, one horse, 8" long, early tin ...	125.00	187.50	250.00
Cart, one horse, painted tin, 1890, 15" long	250	500	750
Cart with driver and buffalo, 7½" long, cast iron	400	600	800

CARPENTER "Tally-Ho", 27½" long.
Courtesy PB Eighty-Four, New York

Cart one Horse, tin 15" long.
Courtesy Lloyd W. Ralston Auctions

CONDITION CODE:
C5 – Good, wear evident overall, shows that has been played with
C6 – Fine, shows some wear in spots, but taken care of
C7 – Very Fine, minor wear overall, very clean
C8 – Excellent, minor wear on edges only
C9 – Near Mint, no noticeable flaws, close inspection may show minute marks
C10 – Mint (like new)
Note: Mint in Box does command higher price

DENT Hook and Ladder, 1915, 14" long. Courtesy Lloyd W. Ralston Auctions

DENT Pumper, 1915, 14½" long.   Courtesy Lloyd W. Ralston Auctions

	C6	C8	C10
Cart with cast iron woman and prancing horse, 10¼" long	500	750	1200
Cart with elephant, cast iron, 7" long	125.00	187.50	250.00
Cart, stake sides, 1-horse, 7" long, early cast iron	150	225	300
Chariot drawn by tin horse, highly decorated, 13½" long	125.00	187.50	250.00
Chein "Dispatch" Wagon, 1-horse, 11½" long	90	135	180
Chief's Wagon, cast iron "Chief," one horse, circa 1915-1920, 12" long .	150	225	300
"Chief" fire chief wagon, cast iron, one-horse, 15½" long	200	300	400
Circus Wagon, iron and tin, two horses, lion cage, 9" long	200	300	400
Circus Wagon, cast iron and wood, containing carved wood bear, 13" long	250.00	337.50	500.00
"City Sprinkler" 8¼" long, cast iron .	No Price Found		
Coal Wagon, cast iron, small	50	75	100
"Coal" Wagon, cast iron with driver and coal shovel, 9¼" long	150	225	300
Conestoga Wagon, cast iron, with cloth cover and two horses, 12½"	50	75	100
Conestoga Wagon, lithographed walking horses, iron wheels, 18" long .	140	210	280
Confectionary Wagon, early 1-horse .	500	750	1000
Courtland Circus Parade No. 300, "Monkeys" on side	45	70	100
Courtland Circus Parade No. 400, "African Lions" on side	45	70	100
Courtland Circus Parade No. 500, "Circus Band" on side (all Circus Parades 11⅝" long	60	85	125
Courtland Easter Rabbit pulling van, 11⅝" long, No. 200	15	20	25
Covered Wagon, 13" long, cast iron, cloth top, one horse, driver	170	255	340
Covered Wagon, tin, driver and horse, Indian head lithographed on side .	40	60	80
Dent buckboard, rider, one horse, very early, primitive looking	125.00	187.50	250.00
Dent Cart, horse and driver, 10" long	125.00	187.50	250.00
Dent Cart, lady driver, horse, 11" long	150	225	300
Dent Cart, mule, driver	250	375	500
Dent Contractors Dump Wagon, two horse, 15" long	150	225	300
Dent Coupe, one horse, driver, 9¾" .	125.00	187.50	250.00
Dent Dump Cart, black man, mule ..	300	450	600
Dent Fire Engine Pumper, silver with white horses, two horse, 21" long	400	750	1000
Dent Fire Engine steam pumper, three horses, 21" long	400	750	1200
Dent Fire Hook & Ladder, 27" long .	1200	1800	2400
Dent Fire Patrol, 15½" long, 3-horse, firemen figures	400	1000	2000
Dent Fire Patrol, "Patrol," circa 1905, 3-horse, 22" long, cast iron, driver, 6 riders	600	1200	2500

	C6	C8	C10
Dent Fire Pumper, circa 1908, 15½" long, 3-horse, driver, paint and nickel plate	250	400	750
Dent Fire Snorkle Wagon, 3-horse, driver	300	450	600
Dent Hansom Cab, 14" long, cast iron, circa 1905, lady passenger, driver	300	500	850
Dent No. 57 Hansom Cab, two-wheeled, one horse	175.00	262.50	350.00
Dent Hook and Ladder, three-horse, extra large	500	1000	1500
Dent Hook and Ladder, painted cast iron, 1915, 14" long, mechanized horses	250	400	800
Dent Hose Reel, three-horse, 24", 10" horse, figures	600	1000	1800
Dent Horse and Cart, cart is tin	150	225	300
Dent Horse and Cart, low sides, all cast iron	125.00	187.50	250.00
Dent "Ice" wagon, two horse, 12" ...	100	200	300
Dent "Ice" wagon, one horse, 14" long	300	500	750
Dent "Ice" Wagon, cast iron, black horse pulling yellow and orange ice wagon, with driver, circa 1910, 15½" long	600	800	1200
Dent Ladder Wagon, 1890, 43½" long, 4-horse, may be longest cast iron toy made	3000	4500	6500
Dent Ox Wagon, 2 oxen, driver, 16" long, cast iron	250	500	600
Dent Ox Cart, stake sides, one ox ...	125.00	187.50	250.00
Dent Police Patrol, three horses, driver and four patrolmen, 21" long	500	1000	1500
Dent Pony Cart No. 20, has driver, team of horses, stake sides on cart	125.00	187.50	250.00
Dent Pumper, painted cast iron, 1915, 14½" long, moving horses	300	450	600
Dent Road Cart, 1-horse, driver in top hat, 2 seats, 16" long	450	675	900
Dent small truck wagon, stake sides .	200	300	400

	C6	C8	C10
Dent one horse truck wagon, stake sides, with driver, 16" long	200	300	400
Dent Sulky with jockey	150	225	300
Dent Surrey, horse has wheel attached to one leg	200	300	400
Dog Cart (baby carriage), black cloth top, 5½" long, tin	75.00	112.50	150.00

Dog Cart, tin, 10" long, circa 1875
Courtesy Mapes Auctioneers & Appraisers

	C6	C8	C10
Dog Cart, tin, 10" long, circa 1875 ..	400	600	800
Donkey and Cart, cast iron, with driver	250	375	500
Donkey and Cart, tin, 8" long, iron star wheels	300	450	600
Donkey and Cart, tin, 8½" long	250	375	500
Dray, cast iron, one horse, black horse pulling yellow dray	200	300	400
Dray Wagon, cast iron, driver and two horses, 18" long	250	375	500
"Dry Goods" cloth and wood two-horse drawn wagon pull-toy, circa 1860, 26" long	400	600	800

Dump Cart, "Hard and Soft Coal- Coke and Kindlings"
Courtesy Lloyd W. Ralston Auctions

	C6	C8	C10
Dump Cart, "Hard and Soft Coal – Coke and Kindlings," tin, 19" long	500	750	1000
"Dump Cart," horse pulling cart pull toy, 7¾" long	80	120	160
Dump Truck, cast iron and tin, one horse	200	300	400

FALLOWS Streetcar, "4th Avenue"
Courtesy Ed Hyers Antique Toys

FALLOWS

James Fallows was a foreman at the very early American tin toy company, Francis, Field and Francis. In 1874 he formed James Fallows & Company in Philadelphia. His toys were often marked "IXL" which may have stood for "I excel". Most of Fallows' toys were tin, though often with cast iron wheels. Papier mache was another prime material, in a toy line that was made up of over 200 items.

FALLOWS Covered Wagon, 12" long
Courtesy Lloyd W. Ralston Auctions

FALLOWS Horse and Carriage, 1890, 12½" long
Courtesy Lloyd W Ralston Auctions

FALLOWS "Pure Milk" wagon, 12½" long.
Courtesy Lloyd W. Ralston Auctions

	C6	C8	C10
Fallows Cart, tin, 12" long	500	750	1000
Fallows Cart and Horse, painted tin, 1870, 8½" long	100	200	400
Fallows Covered Wagon painted tin, litho paper scenes on sides, 12" long	800	1000	1500
Fallows "Dump Cart," 1-horse, 16" long, tin, circa 1890	600	1000	1200
Fallows "Fancy Goods and Toys," 21" long	7500	11,250	15,000
Fallows "Fine Groceries" delivery wagon, 7½" long	1250	1875	2500
Fallows Fire Pumper, 18" long, two horse, very early	5000	8500	10,000

	C6	C8	C10
Fallows Fire Pumper, 24" long, tin, very early	5000	10,000	15,000
Fallows Horse and Carriage, 1890, American painted and stenciled tin, 12½" long	500	750	1000
Fallows "Pure Milk" wagon, 1895, painted and stenciled tin, 12½" long	800	1200	2000
Fallows Streetcar, "4th Avenue," one-horse tin	500	750	1000
Fallows Streetcar, 10" long, two-horse	350	500	800
Farm Wagon and Donkey, cast iron, 10½" long	175.00	262.50	350.00
Farm Wagon, cast iron, two horse, 10"	200	300	400
Farm Wagon, cast iron, 14" long, two unusual horses, with driver	250	375	500
Farm Wagon, cast iron, large heavy horses, body wood, 25½" long	300	450	600
Farm Wagon, tin, with horse, 10½" long	40	60	80
"Fine Groceries," tin wagon, two horses, 14" long	400	600	800
Fire Hose Reel, cast iron, horse-drawn, 6"	150	225	300
"Fire Patrol" cast iron three horse wagon contains two firemen and driver, 17" long	900	1350	1800
"Fire Patrol" three-horse, 18¾" long, driver, riders	1000	1500	2000
"Fire Patrol" cast iron, two horse, three firemen and driver, circa 1910, 19" long	1250	1875	2500
"Fire Patrol," cast iron, two-horse, three firemen, one driver, 20½" long, circa 1890	500	750	1000
Fire Pumper, cast iron, three horse, 11¼"	500	750	1000
Fire Pumper, cast iron, two horse with driver, 13" long	600	900	1200
Fire Pumper, cast iron, three horse, 14½" long	650	975	1300
Fire Pumper, cast iron, two horse, driver, 19¾" long	500	750	1000

	C6	C8	C10
Fire Pumper, circa 1910, cast iron, three horse, 17½" long	500	750	1000
Fire Pumper, cast iron, three horse with driver, fireman, circa 1910, 18¼" long	600	900	1200

GEORGE BROWN

In 1856, George W. Brown, with Chauncey Goodrich, founded George W. Brown and Company, toymakers. Brown, an innovator, introduced the American clockwork toy (he'd spent 11 years in the clockmaking business). He invented many of his toys' mechanisms and may also have designed all or most of his toys. Brown worked primarily in tin, jobbing some of the work out to companies like Clinton, Connecticut's Union Manufacturing Company. Necessarily simple because of the material and manufacturing techniques employed, Brown's toys made up for it with brilliant hand-painted color and stenciling. Tops, rattles, flutes, wagons, fire engines, swords, trains and toy buckets were among the many items put out by the firm. The company merged with Stevens in 1868 and was dissolved in 1880.

	C6	C8	C10
George Brown Cab, driver, one-horse, 8½" long	560	840	1120
George Brown Cart and Horse, 1880, painted and stenciled tin, 7½" long	200	300	500
George Brown Doctor's Buggy, 14" long, tin and cast iron	650	975	1300
George Brown Dump Cart, painted tin, 1885, 8¼" long	100	150	200
George Brown Dump Cart, 1880, 13" long, tin, back gate lifts out for dumping	150	225	300
George Brown "Eagle Chariot," painted tin, 1870, 11" long	500	1000	2500
George Brown "Fine Groceries" cart and horse	1250	1875	2500
George Brown Gig, tin, 9" long	150	225	300
George Brown Gig, tin, 10" long, 1-horse	150	225	300
George Brown Goat Cart, 7" long	300	450	600

Fire Pumper, cast iron, two horse, driver, 19¾" long.
Photo courtesy Garth's Auctions Inc.

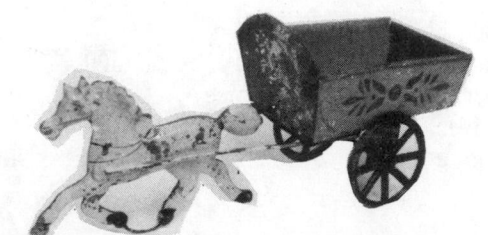

GEORGE BROWN Cart and Horse, 1880, 7½" long.
Courtesy Lloyd W. Ralston Auctions

GEORGE BROWN Dump Cart, 1885, 8¼" long.
Courtesy Lloyd W. Ralston Auctions

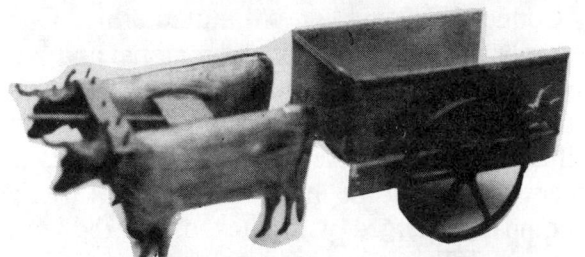

GEORGE BROWN Ox Cart, 9" long.
Courtesy Lloyd W. Ralston Auctions

GEORGE BROWN Eagle Chariot.
Courtesy Lloyd W. Ralston Auctions

	C6	C8	C10
George Brown Horse Cart, 1870, tin 11½" long	125.00	187.50	250.00
George Brown Ox Cart, 1880, painted tin, 9" long	500	1000	2000
George Brown Peddle Wagon, tin, circa 1880, 20" long, two wheeled, horses, driver, awning	1000	2500	5000
George Brown Rockaway, passenger cart, 2-horse, 13" long	1850	2500	4500
George Brown Sulky, 8¾" long	250	375	500
George Brown Yankee Notions Peddler Wagon, 16½" long	3000	7000	10,000

GIBBS

Gibbs Manufacturing Company of Canton, Ohio began turning out toys in 1896 (after previously, from about 1830, manufacturing wooden barrels and tubs and metal plows). The company's first toy was a political giveaway for William McKinley. (McKinley was from Canton.) It was a spring-operated top, and variations of it remained in the firm's catalogs till 1969, when it stopped making toys. Most Gibbs toys were wood or tin, with much use made of lithographed paper for decoration. Many of Gibbs' playthings were of the push and pull variety. Lewis Gibbs was the original owner.

	C6	C8	C10
Gibbs Cart and Horse, paper litho on wood, 13" long	150	225	300
Gibbs Chariot, horse 7½"	150	225	300
Gibbs "Delivery 14," one-horse, articulated	150	225	300
Gibbs "Groceries The Great Atlantic and Pacific Tea Co." mule-drawn cart, 12"	350	500	1000
Gibbs Gypsy Wagon, two-horse	250	375	500

GIBBS Hay Cart, 1910, 19" long.
Courtesy Lloyd W. Ralston Auctions

	C6	C8	C10
Gibbs Hay Cart, paper litho and painted wood, iron wheels, 1910, 19" long	150	225	300
Gibbs pony cart, Shetland pony, paper litho on wood, cart tin, 7" long	100	150	200
Gibbs "Pony Circus" wagon, two-horse, 13¾" long, paper litho on tin and wood, cast iron wheels	200	300	400
Gibbs Tea Co. Mule Cart	350	500	1000
Gibbs "Yankee" cart and horse, wood and tin, 18¾"	250	375	500
Girard Wagon, 2 tin horses, stake sides	125.00	187.50	250.00
Goat Cart, 7½" long, iron goat and wheels, tin cart	100	150	200
Goat Cart, 10½" long, tin, early	150	225	300

"Golden Pasture Farm Products, Milk and Cream"
Courtesy Lloyd W. Ralston Auctions

	C6	C8	C10
"Golden Pasture Farm Products, Milk & Cream" 1915, horse-drawn milk wagon, steering mechanism for child to ride, painted and stenciled wood, 30" long	500	750	1000
Grass Cutter, two horse, driver, two-wheeled cart, cast iron	1000	1500	2000
Hansom Cab, cast iron, no horse or figures	1500	2250	3000
Hansom Cab, 8" long	150	225	300

GIBBS TOYS

The best selling and most attractive toys on the market. Children cannot resist them. You have only to put Gibbs Toys on your counters and they sell themselves. All jobbers carry Gibbs Toys.

TO RETAIL AT 5c., 10c., 25c., 50c.

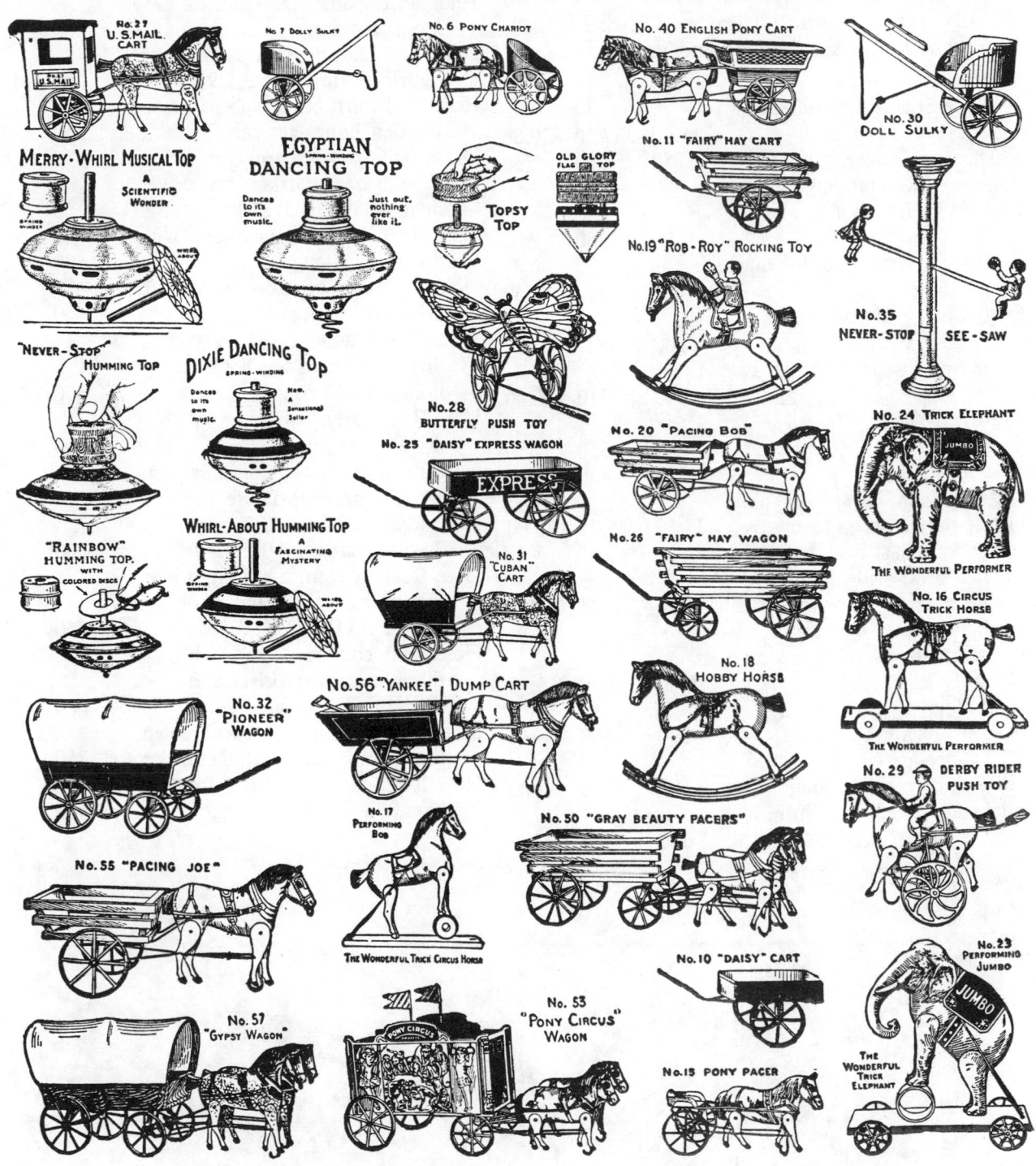

Gibbs Toys are always on display at our New York Agents

THE GIBBS MFG. CO. CANTON OHIO

NEW YORK AGENTS
The Owens-Kreiser Co.
The Strobel & Wilken Co.
Geo. Borgfeldt & Co.
Baker & Bennett Co.

An April, 1914 Gibbs ad.

	C6	C8	C10
Hansom Cab with driver, cast iron, 9½" long	125.00	187.50	250.00
Hansom Cab, one horse, driver, 10" long, cast iron	250	375	500

HARRIS

Harris Toy Company of Toledo, Ohio seems to have begun production of cast iron toys during the late 1880s. The firm, which also jobbed for Dent, Hubley and Wilkins, stopped making toys in 1913.

	C6	C8	C10
Harris Brownie Shell Cart, 1903, cast iron	225.00	337.50	450.00
Harris Cart, mule, driver, 10" long	250	500	750
Harris, Gloomy Gus standing in tin cart pulled by iron horse, 7½" long	200	350	500
Harris Goat Cart, shell-type, 5" long, cast iron, driver	100	250	350
Harris Goat Cart, two goats, cast iron, driver	1000	2500	3000
Harris Hook and Ladder, 3 horse, cast iron, 19" long	140	210	280
Harris Transfer Wagon, 1903, 18½" long, 3-horse	400	650	850
Harris Wagon, mule, 12" long	300	450	600
"Hood's Milk," Rich Toys; wood and tin, horse-drawn wagon pull-toy	37.50	56.25	75.00
Hook and Ladder, cast iron, tin and wood, two-horse with driver and three ladders, 16½" long	150	225	300
Hook and Ladder, cast iron and tin, three horse, two firemen, ladders, 21" long	175.00	262.50	350.00
Hook and Ladder, cast iron, two-horse, 22¾" long	200	300	400
Hook and Ladder, cast iron, three-horse, with driver, 25" long	500	750	1000
Hook and Ladder truck, cast iron, three-horse, 25½" long	600	900	1200
Hook and Ladder truck, cast iron, three-horse, two drivers, four ladders, circa 1910-1914, 31¼" long	1000	1500	2000
Hook and Ladder, pressed steel and iron, figures, ladders, unusual hanging horses	250	375	500
Hook and Ladder, three horses, 27½" long, driver	750	1125	1500
Hook and Ladder, wood ladder with figurines, three-horse, 29½" long	750	1125	1500
Hook and Cart, lithograph paper on wooden horse, tin cart	150	225	300
Horse pulling two wheel cart, tin	400	600	800
Horse with open carriage and driver in top hat, tin 5½" long	150	225	300
Hose Reel, cast iron, one horse with driver, 11" long	400	600	800
Hose Reel, cast iron, one horse with driver, 12" long	400	600	800
Hose Reel Wagon, cast iron with driver and cord fire hose, one horse, 12½" long	500	750	1000
Hose Reel, early, two-horse with driver, cast iron, 14¼"	500	750	1000
Hose Reel, early, two-horse, cast iron, 14½" long, with figure	500	750	1000
Hose Reel, cast iron, 19" long, 3-horse, circa 1910	600	900	1200
Hose Reel, Wagon, cast iron, driver, two horses, man standing on rear bumper, 21" long	750	1125	1500
Hose Reel, cast iron, circa 1910-1914, three horse with driver and fireman, 21" long	1000	1500	2000
Hose Wagon, cast iron, two firemen, three horses and bell, 21½" long	750	1125	1500
Hose Reel, early, cast iron, unusual horse	500	750	1000

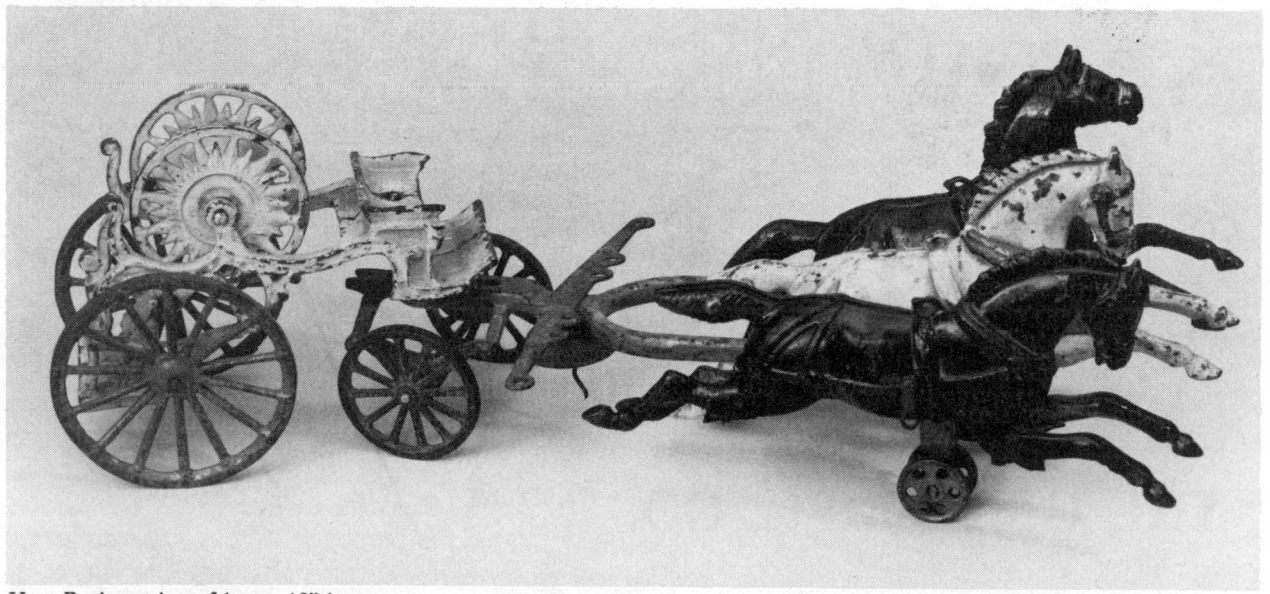

Hose Reel, cast iron, 3-horse, 19" long.
Courtesy Mapes Auctioneers & Appraisers.

	C6	C8	C10
Hubley Brake, four-seated, 4-horse, 8 articulated passengers, 28" long ..	5000	10,000	12,000
Hubley Brake, 3-seated, 18" long, 2 plumed horses, cast iron	3000	8500	10,000
Hubley Brake, 2-seat, 16½" long, driver, 3 women passengers	2500	5000	7500
Hubley Brougham, 16" long, cast iron and nickeled, horse and driver ...	300	1000	1500
Hubley Brougham, top-hatted driver, 1-horse, 17" long	300	900	1500
Hubley Cane Wagon, 15" long	600	900	1200
Hubley Cart, 5½" long, driver	150	225	300
Hubley Cart, 8" long, horse and driver	175.00	262.50	350.00
Hubley Cart, wood, iron wheels, iron horse, 10½" long, 1910	175.00	262.50	350.00
Hubley Chariot, cast iron, 8¾"	500	750	1000
Hubley Chariot, 9½" long, 2-horse, driver	600	900	1200
Hubley Chariot with Clown, early, cast iron, three horse, 12½" long	800	1200	1600
Hubley Chariot, Roman, with driver, 3-horse	700	1050	1400
Hubley Coal Wagon, 9" long, mule ..	250	375	500
Hubley Eagle Milk Wagon, 12" long .	300	750	1000
Hubley Essex Trap, 13" long, 1890, cast iron, driver and horse	500	1500	2500
Hubley Expandable Wagon with wood bed, 26" long, cast iron, 2-horse driver	750	1125	1500
Hubley Farm Wagon, 12½" long, 1-horse, circa 1915, cast iron	400	600	800
Hubley Fire Patrol, 13" long, driver, four riders, all in standard helmets	500	750	1000
Hubley Fire Patrol, 21", driver, 4 firemen, prancing horse team	500	1200	2000
Hubley fire pumper, cast iron, two horses with driver, circa 1910, 14" long	200	400	600
Hubley fire pumper, cast iron, two horse, white-painted, circa 1906-1910, 19" long	750	1125	1500
Hubley fire pumper, two horse, cast iron, with driver and two firemen, 20" long	750	1125	1500
Hubley fire pumper, three-horse with driver, circa 1906-1910, 20½" long	800	1200	1600
Hubley fire pumper, two horses, cast iron with American Eagle, circa 1905-1910, 21" long	500	1000	1500
Hubley Gig, lady driver, 15" long, horse drawn	350	650	950
Hubley Hansom Cab, driver cast in window, horse	300	500	750
Hubley Hook and Ladder, three-horse, two firemen, two wooden ladders, circa 1906-1910, 27¾" long	400	700	1200

HUBLEY Sleigh, one-horse, 15" long.
Courtesy Lloyd W. Ralston Auctions

HUBLEY Sleigh, two-horse, 15" long.
Courtesy Lloyd W. Ralston Auctions

HUBLEY Sleigh, one-horse, 14½" long.
Courtesy Lloyd W. Ralston Auctions

HUBLEY Landau Carriage, 1905, 16½" long.
Courtesy Lloyd W. Ralston Auctions

HUBLEY "Ice" Wagon, 9½" long, 1920s.
Courtesy Lloyd W. Ralston Auctions

	C6	C8	C10
Hubley Hook and Ladder, 2-horse, 28" long, cast iron	500	850	1500
Hubley hook and ladder wagon, three-horse, 33" long with eagle and shield on side	750	1500	2500
Hubley Hose reel, cast iron, three-horse with driver, circa 1906, 19" long	500	1000	1500
Hubley "Ice Wagon," 1920s, 9½" long	125.00	187.50	250.00

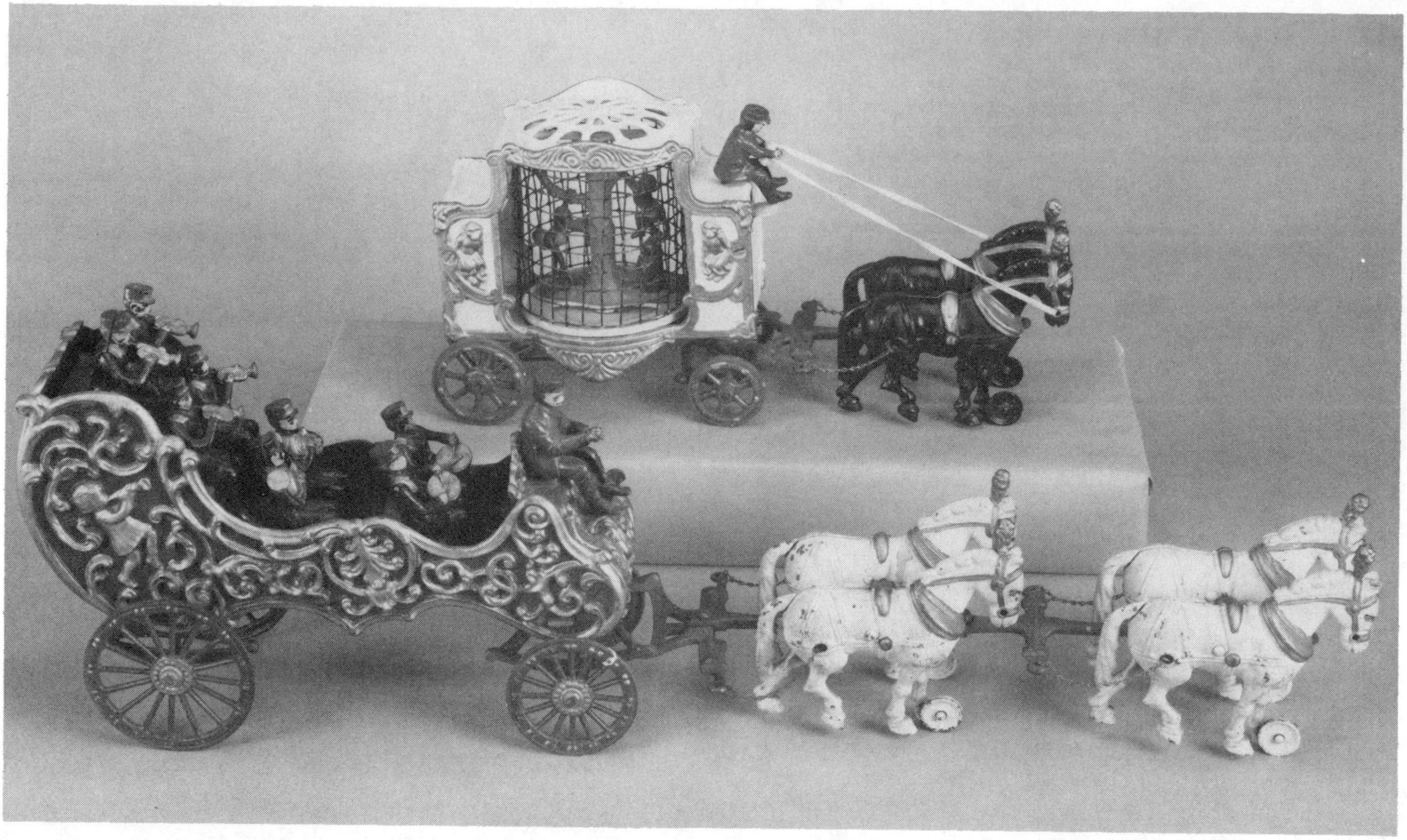

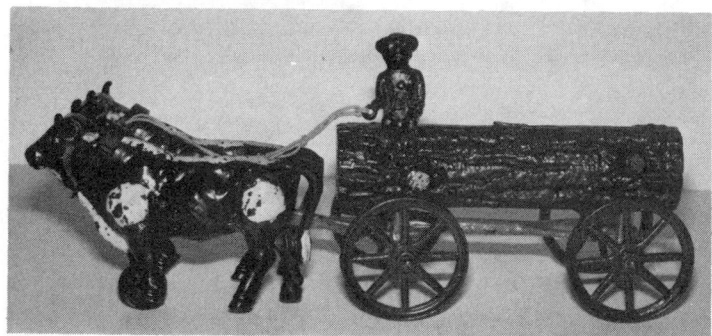

L to R: HUBLEY Royal Circus Bandwagon, 30" long, HUBLEY Revolving Monkey Cage (extremely rare) Courtesy Sotheby's New York

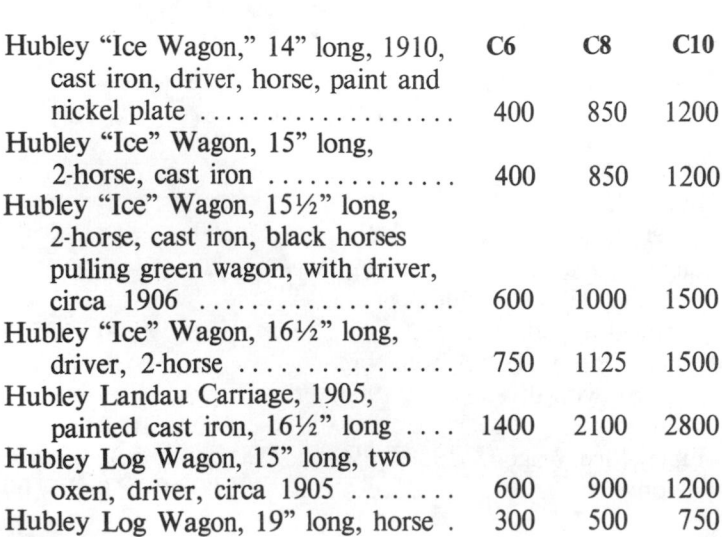

HUBLEY Log Wagon, 15" long, two oxen, driver
Courtesy Ed Hyers Antique Toys

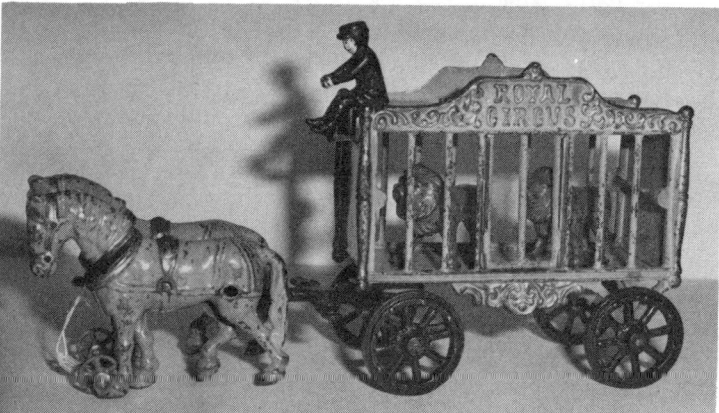

HUBLEY "Royal Circus" Lion Wagon, 15¾" long with rare grey horses and wagon
Courtesy Ed Hyers Antique Toys

	C6	C8	C10
Hubley "Ice Wagon," 14" long, 1910, cast iron, driver, horse, paint and nickel plate	400	850	1200
Hubley "Ice" Wagon, 15" long, 2-horse, cast iron	400	850	1200
Hubley "Ice" Wagon, 15½" long, 2-horse, cast iron, black horses pulling green wagon, with driver, circa 1906	600	1000	1500
Hubley "Ice" Wagon, 16½" long, driver, 2-horse	750	1125	1500
Hubley Landau Carriage, 1905, painted cast iron, 16½" long	1400	2100	2800
Hubley Log Wagon, 15" long, two oxen, driver, circa 1905	600	900	1200
Hubley Log Wagon, 19" long, horse .	300	500	750

CONDITION CODE:
C5 – Good, wear evident overall, shows that has been played with
C6 – Fine, shows some wear in spots, but taken care of
C7 – Very Fine, minor wear overall, very clean
C8 – Excellent, minor wear on edges only
C9 – Near Mint, no noticeable flaws, close inspection may show minute marks
C10 – Mint (like new)
Note: Mint in Box does command higher price

HUBLEY "Royal Circus Calliope"

HUBLEY "Royal Circus Giraffe Cage"

HUBLEY "Royal Circus Clown on Trapeze Van"

HUBLEY "Royal Circus Lion Cage"

	C6	C8	C10
Hubley lady in sleigh, circa 1900, 15" long	500	1000	2000
Hubley Monkey Trapeze circus mirror van, 12½" long	500	1000	1500
Hubley "Police Patrol," 13" long, driver, 3 riders, early	500	750	1000
Hubley Revolving Monkey Cage, auctioned for $30,000 in 1988.			
Hubley Roman Chariot, three small horses	425.00	637.50	850.00
Hubley Roman Chariot, three large horses	600	900	1200
Hubley Royal Circus, animals, driver, 2 horses, 15" long	500	1000	1200

	C6	C8	C10
Hubley Royal Circus Bandwagon, 22" long, 4-horse, 7 riders, cast iron	800	1500	2500
Hubley Royal Circus Bandwagon, circa 1920, 22½" long, cast iron, 2 horses, 7 riders	2500	3500	5000
Hubley "Royal Circus" Band Wagon, 30" long, 8 musicians and driver, 1920s	1500	2250	3000
Hubley "Royal Circus" Calliope, 12¾" (medium)	600	900	1200
Hubley "Royal Circus" Clown on Trapeze van, 16½" long, 1920, oval-mirrored sides	1500	2500	3500
Hubley "Royal Circus" Farmer Van, 1920, 16" long, head revolves and disappears in top of wagon as toy pulled	2000	3500	5500
Hubley "Royal Circus" Giraffe Cage with large and small giraffes, driver, 1920, 27" long	4000	7500	12,000
Hubley Royal Circus Lion Cage, 9" long	300	500	750
Hubley "Royal Circus" Lion Wagon, 15¾" long with rare grey horses and wagon	900	1350	1800
Hubley Royal Circus Polar Bear Cage, 1920s, 11¾" long	600	900	1500
Hubley Royal Circus Rhino Wagon, 16" long	1000	2000	3000
Hubley "Royal Circus" Tiger Wagon Cage, 1920, 16" long, driver, 2 tigers	350	750	1000
Hubley Santa Claus Sleigh, 16" long, 1910, 2 reindeer, cast iron	800	1200	1800
Hubley Santa Claus, Sleigh, 17" long, early	500	1000	1500
Hubley Shell Cart and Horse, 7", 1905	250	375	500
Hubley Sleigh, one horse, painted cast iron, 1910, 14½" long	500	750	1000
Hubley Sleigh, one-horse, woman with movable arms, 14¾", early	500	800	1200
Hubley Sleigh, one horse, 1900, painted cast iron, nickel plated, 15" long	250	375	500
Hubley Sleigh, 2 horse, 1910, painted and nickel plated cast iron, 15" long	250	375	500
Hubley Spring Wagon, horse, driver, cast iron	200	300	400
Hubley Sulky, 8½" long	150	225	300
Hubley Surrey, clockwork, 1894, 9" long, cast iron, brass works, five colors	500	1000	1500
Hubley Surrey, two-horse, woman driver, 13¾" long	750	1125	1500
Hubley Surrey, 18" long, 2-horse, driver	400	600	800

HUBLEY Chariot with clown, early, cast iron, three-horse, 12½" long
Courtesy Ed Hyers Antique Toys

HUBLEY "Royal Circus" Calliope, 12¾" (medium)
Courtesy Ed Hyers Antique Toys

	C6	C8	C10
Hubley Surrey, tin and cast iron, two-seat with driver and woman passenger, two horse	600	900	1200
Hubley Surrey, two-seat, 13¾" long, driver, woman passenger, two horse	600	900	1200
Hubley Trotter, 1900, 8¾" long, cast iron, horse and driver	200	300	400
Hubley Trotter Gig, lady driver, 11" long	150	225	300
Hubley Wagon, 12" long, horse, cast iron	150	225	300
Ice Cart, tin horse-drawn	200	300	400
"Ice" Wagon, one horse, 12", cast iron	500	750	1000
Ice Wagon, cast iron, two-horse, 12" long	600	900	1200
Ideal Fire Pumper, 2-horse, 20½" long, cast iron, 2 riders	250	500	750
"Ideal Fire Department" 30" long, 3-horse, cast iron	500	1000	1500

IVES

Ives is one of the fabled companies in American toy history. It was founded by Riley Ives as a metal stamping shop by at least the late 1850s. About 1865 the company made tin whistles for New York Rubber's squeak toys. This seems to have led to Ives' first true toys, hot air playthings, which were put in motion by the hot air from stoves, lanterns, etc. These were first sold in 1868. Son Edward Ives joined about 1860. Edward's son, Harry, took over the reins in 1895. He was ousted in 1929, and the firm was dissolved in 1932. During its heyday, which lasted about 40 years, the firm put out a deluge of toys of every type, with quality its watchword. Toymaking was carried on from about 1870 till the end in Bridgeport, Connecticut.

	C6	C8	C10
Ives Coal Dump Cart, donkey, black driver	500	750	1000
Ives Coal Dump Wagon, donkey, black driver	375.00	562.50	750.00
Ives Doctor's cart, two wheels, 10¼"	400	600	1000
Ives dog pulling stake cart	200	300	400
Ives Donkey Cart, one of 4 walking animal toys by Ives, circa 1890, 15" long, cast iron	750	1500	2500
Ives "Fast Mail" wagon, 17" long, cast iron, walking horses	750	2000	3500
Ives "Fire Patrol", 19" long, circa 1890, 1 horse, 5 riders, driver . . .	750	1200	2000
Ives Fire Patrol, 20½" long, 2-horse, driver, 6 firemen, cast iron, circa 1880-1910	750	1200	2000
Ives Gig, 1890s, driver with top hat, 5½" long	500	750	1000
Ives Hansom Cab with walking horse, oversized	4500	6500	10,000
Ives Hook and Ladder, circa 1890, 29" long, 2 horse, 2 riders, cast iron	600	1100	1500
Ives Horse Cart, 1883, 17½" long, 2 horse	750	1200	2500
Ives Hose reel, cast iron, one horse, driver, "Phoenix," circa 1880-1910, 15" long	1600	2400	3200
Ives Hose Reel Wagon, one horse, driver	750	1125	1500
Ives Ice Wagon with mules, 1896 . . .	750	1500	2500
Ives Phoenix Pumper, circa 1890, 19" long, cast iron, rarest of Ives pumpers (clockwork)	1000	1500	2500
Ives Police Patrol Wagon, 1890s, 20½" long, 6 patrolmen, driver . .	1000	2000	3000
Ives Steam Pumper, two-horse, 20½"	4000	6000	8000
Ives Walking Horse, pull toy, late 19th century, horse which walks by means of wheel mechanism under it, pulling a two-wheeled cart	500	1000	1500
Ives and Blakeslee Fire Pumper, 1893, 25" long, cast iron, largest cast iron pumper made by Ives	1500	3000	5500

KENTON: Kenton Lock Manufacturing Co. was incorporated in May, 1890, in Kenton, Ohio. In November of 1894, it became the Kenton Hardware Manufacturing Company, and around this period, began producing toys. It ceased production of horse-drawn toys in the early 1920s (except for a 1930s beer wagon), but in 1939 introduced a completely new line of horse-drawn pieces, running through 1954.

KENTON Plantation Cart, 1910.
Courtesy Mapes Auctioneers & Appraisers

	C6	C8	C10
Kenton Bakery Wagon, marked "Bakery," 1941	250	375	500
Kenton Band Wagon, musicians, driver, rider on horse	150	225	300
Kenton Boar Cart, 8" long, circa 1910, cast iron, Egyptian driver	350	500	750
Kenton Cabriolet, painted cast iron, 2nd series made into 1950s, 15" long	200	350	500
Kenton Cement Mixer, driver, horse, 14" long	350	750	1000
Kenton Chariot, 6" long, cast iron	150	225	300
Kenton Chariot, 7½" long with comic driver, 1910, cast iron	250	375	500
Kenton Chariot, 3-horse, cast iron	600	900	1200
Kenton "Chief" wagon, one-horse, driver, 12¼" long	500	800	1500
Kenton Circus Cage Wagon, two horses, two riders, driver, animal in cage	150	225	300
Kenton "Coal" cart, donkey pulling, black driver	250	375	500
Kenton Contractor's Wagon, with black driver, 15½"	400	600	800
Kenton covered wagon, cast iron, two-horse	500	750	1000
Kenton Delivery Wagon No. 5 with driver and 2 horses	400	600	800
Kenton Delivery Cart, donkey, cast iron	150	225	300

	C6	C8	C10
Kenton Dog Cart, 7" long, greyhound pulling dog riding	250	375	500
Kenton Dray, 13¼" long	100	150	200
Kenton Dray, cast iron, two horse, black and white horses pulling green dray, with driver, 13½" long	300	450	600
Kenton Dray No. 5 painted cast iron, 1930, 14½" long	200	300	400
Kenton Dray Wagon with horse and driver, cast iron, 14¾"	200	300	400
Kenton Dray, cast iron, two-horse, two dark horses pulling a green cart, with driver, 14¾" long	200	300	400
Kenton Dump Cart, mule	125.00	187.50	250
Kenton Dump Wagon, 10¼" long, early 1900s	150	225	300
Kenton Dump Wagon, two-horses, lever releases bottom wagon	200	300	400
Kenton Egyptian Cart, elephant-drawn	300	450	600
Kenton Express Wagon, horse, driver, cast iron	225.00	337.50	450.00
Kenton Express Wagon, 11" long	225.00	337.50	450.00
Kenton Farm Wagon, 14" long, driver, 1 horse	500	750	1000
Kenton Farm Wagon, two horse, cast iron, 14½" with figure	500	750	1000
Kenton Farm Wagon, 15" long, driver, 1 horse, early	500	750	1000
Kenton Farm Wagon, two horse, 15" with driver	500	750	1000

139

KENTON Hook & Ladder, 1915, 26" long.
Courtesy Lloyd W. Ralston Auctions

KENTON Hose Reel, 1920, 13½" long.
Courtesy Lloyd W. Ralston Auctions

KENTON Dray No.5, 14½" long.
Courtesy Lloyd W. Ralston Auctions

KENTON Cabriolet, 2nd series made into the 1950s, 15" long.
Courtesy Lloyd R. Ralston Auctions

	C6	C8	C10
Kenton Fire Ladder Wagon, front driver only, 12" long	150	225	300
Kenton Fire Ladder Wagon, horse-drawn, 17" long, drivers front and rear	135.00	202.50	270.00
Kenton Fire Pumper, 20" long, 2 horse, driver	175.00	262.50	350.00
Kenton Fire Pumper, cast iron, 26½" long, horses 11" long	250	375	500
Kenton Fire Wagon, 23" long, 2 horse, driver, equipment, bell, wagon nickel-plated	200	300	400
Kenton goat cart, 7", figure with large ears	250	375	500
Kenton gravel wagon, 13" with two horses	150	225	300
Kenton Hansom Cab, lady rider, driver in top hat, cast iron	700	1050	1400
Kenton Hansom Cab, 10" long, one horse, top-hatted driver	1000	1500	2000
Kenton Hansom Cab, 12" long	500	750	1000
Kenton Hansom cab, 15½" long, figures, horse	450	750	1200
Kenton Hook and Ladder Wagon, 20" long, 2 horse, driver	250	375	500
Kenton Hook and Ladder Wagon, 20" long, nickel-plated, 2-horse, driver	200	300	400
Kenton Hook and Ladder, 16" long, 3-horse, cast iron	150	225	300
Kenton Hook and Ladder, wagon, three horses, 17" long	250	375	500
Kenton Hook and Ladder, cast iron, three-horse, circa 1910, 19" long	150	225	300
Kenton Hook and Ladder, 1915, painted cast iron, ladders, 26" long	300	450	600
Kenton Hose Reel, 1920, painted cast iron, 13½" long	500	750	1000
Kenton Hose Reel, cast iron, 14½" long, circa 1905, two-horse	600	900	1200

	C6	C8	C10
Kenton "Ice" wagon, 15" long, 2-horse, driver, 1920s, cast iron	250	375	500
Kenton landau, cast iron, white horse pulling green carriage with driver, circa 1910, 15" long	600	900	1200
Kenton Log Wagon, one horse with driver, 14½" long	450	675	900
Kenton Log Wagon, 15" long, black man, 2 oxen, early 1900s, cast iron	300	500	750
Kenton "Milk" Wagon, with horse and driver	300	450	600
Kenton, "Overland Circus" Calliope Wagon	250	375	500
Kenton "Overland Circus" two-horse, cast iron with driver, cage containing bear, circa 1940s-1950s, 13¾" long	150	225	300
Kenton "Overland Circus" cast iron, two-horse with driver, cage containing cloth bear, 14" long	500	750	1000
Kenton Overland Circus Wagon, 6 musicians and driver, 15" long	400	600	800
Kenton "Overland Circus" cast iron, two-horse with driver, cage containing cast iron bear, 14" long, 1940s	350	525	700
Kenton Ox Cart, 5" long, cast iron	100	150	200
Kenton Ox Cart, 7"	110	165	220
Kenton Ox Cart, 12½" long	150	225	300
Kenton Ox Wagon, two oxen, 18" long	400	600	800
Kenton "Patrol" No. 526, 2-horse, driver, riders, 17" long	350	525	700
Kenton Plantation Cart, 1910, 10" long, black driver, mule	225.00	337.50	450.00
Kenton "Polar Ice" wagon, 2-donkey	500	750	1000
Kenton Police Patrol with mule team, 16"	500	750	1000
Kenton Pumper, 3 horses, 18"	400	600	800
Kenton Rabbit, 5" long, pulling cart with two wheels and seat, cast iron	200	300	500
Kenton Rhino Cart, 8" long	100	200	300

KENTON Bakery Wagon

	C6	C8	C10
Kenton Sand and Gravel dump wagon, 15" long, driver, 2 horses	175.00	262.50	350.00
Kenton two horse stake wagon, 15" long, driver with reins	200	300	400
Kenton Sulky, driver cast to sulky, 6" long	75.00	112.50	150.00
Kenton Sulky, two-wheel race cart with jockey and horse, 6"	75.00	112.50	150.00
Kenton sulky and driver, cast iron, 7" long	125.00	187.50	250.00
Kenton surrey, two-horse, cast iron with driver and passenger, 12½"	150	225	300
Kenton Surrey with fringe top, driver and passenger, two-horse (circa 1943?), 13" long	200	300	400
Kenton Surrey, one horse, approx. 1940, 16" long	150	225	300
Kenton team of horses with log and black driver	500	750	1000
Kenton Transfer Wagon, two horse, driver	650	975	1300
Kenton 3.2 Beer Delivery Wagon, 14½" long, 1930s, cast iron, 2-horse, driver, 10 wooden kegs	350	525	700
Kenton Victoria Cab and horse, cast iron, with driver and woman, 15½" long	200	300	400
Kenton No. 3, one-horse wagon, with driver, 15" long	125.00	187.50	250.00
Kenton No. 5 wagon, one horse, 15" long	125.00	187.50	250.00
Kenton wagon with driver, two-horse, 10¼" long	100	150	200
Kingsbury Dray, 2-horse, cast iron, 20¼"	300	450	600
Kingsbury Ladder Truck, 13", 1900, cast iron, tin and wood	300	450	600
Kingsbury Hook & Ladder, 25½" long, 3-horse, 2 riders, rubber covers on wheels, cast iron and pressed steel	400	600	800
Kingsbury Hook and Ladder, 2-horse, driver, 3 ladders, 27" long	600	900	1200
"The Klondike Ice Co., New York" tin ice wagon, two-horse, 17½" long	350	525	700
Ladder Wagon, cast iron, two ladders and three galloping horses, 13½" long	150	225	300
Ladder Wagon, cast iron, with two horses, three sections of ladder, bell, 25½" long	250	375	500

	C6	C8	C10
Ladder Wagon, cast iron with two drivers, four sections of ladder and three horses, Dart type, 30½" long	200	300	400
Lancaster Hook and Ladder, two-horse cast iron, 25" long	150	225	300
Lancaster Hook and Ladder, cast iron, 28" long, two horses, two drivers	200	300	400
Lancaster Hook and Ladder, 28" long, iron, three horses, two drivers	250	375	500
Lancaster Hubley No. 58 Surrey, no driver	75.00	112.50	150.00
Lancaster Hubley No. 174, surrey with one seat, driver, horse	150	225	300
Landau, four-horse, 24" with driver	300	450	600
Lehmann "Africa" tin friction toy, ostrich pulling cart	400	600	800
Lehmann "Duo" Rooster pulling egg cart with a rabbit perched on top, tin friction	500	750	1000
Lincoln Logs No. 30 Covered Wagon Set	62.50	93.75	125.00
Log Wagon, cast iron with driver and two oxen, 15¼" long	450	675	900
Mail Cart, tin, horse-drawn	100	150	250
Marx Covered Wagon, tin litho, 9" long, friction	60	90	120

MASON & PARKER Buckboard, one-horse, 31" long.
Courtesy Lloyd W. Ralston Auctions

MASON & PARKER Cart and horse, 13" long.
Courtesy Lloyd W. Ralston Auctions

	C6	C8	C10
Mason & Parker, buckboard, one-horse, 1910, pressed painted steel, 31" long	500	750	1000
Mason & Parker Cart and Horse, 1910, painted pressed steel, 13" long, mechanical action from axle	500	750	1000
McCormick Deering farm wagon, two-horse, 12½" long, cast iron	125.00	187.50	250.00

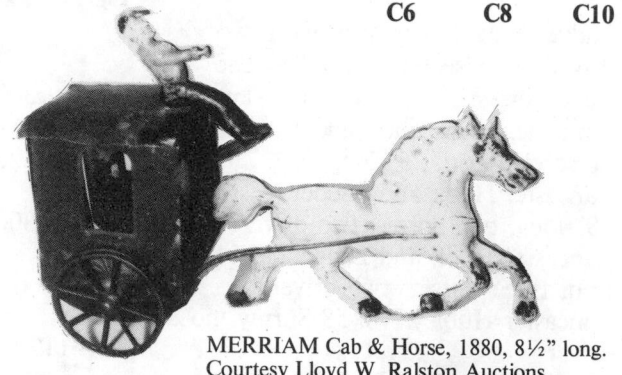

MERRIAM Cab & Horse, 1880, 8½" long.
Courtesy Lloyd W. Ralston Auctions

MERRIAM Wagon and Horse, 1890, 19¼" long.
Courtesy Lloyd W. Ralston Auctions

	C6	C8	C10
Merriam, cab and horse, 1880, painted and stenciled tin, 8½" long	1000	1500	2000
Merriam Wagon and Horse, American painted & stenciled tin, 1890, 19½" long	2500	3375	5000
Mess Cart, WW I-type, tin, two horse drawn, painted	100	150	200
Milk Wagon, goat-drawn, possibly George Brown, painted tin, 6" long	150	225	300
"Milk" wagon, driver and one horse, 12¾" long	100	150	200
Mower, two horses and driver, cast iron, 10" long	150	225	300
"National Express" wagon, tin litho, horse, 15" long	250	375	500
Omnibus, "People's" tin, with two horses, driver, circa 1880s-1890s	4000	6000	8000
Ox Cart, cast iron, 5" long, with ox	90	135	180
Ox Cart, cast iron, 11½" long	250.00	337.50	500.00
"Pansy" Stage Coach, Reed, 28" long, 4 horse, driver, lithographed alphabet blocks	1000	1500	2000
Phaeton, one-horse with driver, 16" long	400	600	800
Plow, one horse, cast iron, 10¾"	150	225	300
Police Patrol Wagon, cast iron, 11½" long, figures and driver, one horse	100	150	200
"Police Patrol," cast iron, one-horse, 12"	150	225	300
"Police Patrol" wagon, cast iron, with driver and five policemen and two horses, 15"	1000	1500	2000

PRATT & LETCHWORTH

Pratt and Letchworth was in business from about 1880 into the 1890s. The Buffalo, New York firm sold its toys under the name Buffalo Toy Works. Iron and steel were its main materials, and all of its most prominent toys seem to have been horse-drawn.

	C6	C8	C10
Pratt & Letchworth Artillery, 34" long, circa 1890, cast iron, hand-painted, 4-horse caisson, cannon, 4 riders, one sold in excellent condition for $9500 about 1981.			
"Pratt & Letchworth" Cart, 10" long	150	225	300
Pratt & Letchworth Chief's Wagon	1100	1650	2200

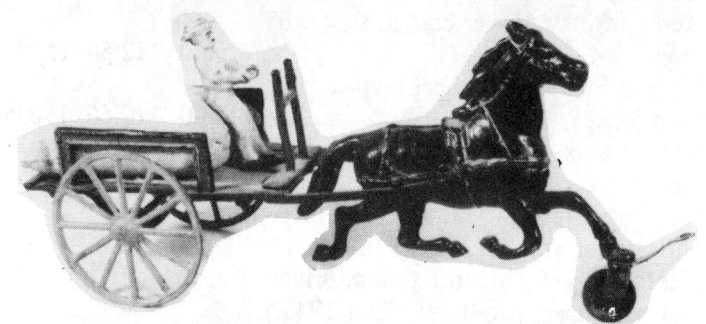

PRATT & LETCHWORTH Dray, one-horse, 12" long.
Courtesy Lloyd W. Ralston Auctions

	C6	C8	C10
Pratt & Letchworth Dray, one horse, cast iron and wood, 1890, 12" long	250	500	750
Pratt & Letchworth Gig, cast iron and pressed steel, 10½" long, seven colors, one horse, one rider	400	600	800
Pratt & Letchworth Hansom Cab, circa 1892, cast iron, 13" long	400	750	1200
Pratt & Letchworth Hay Cart, 10½" long	500	750	1000
Pratt & Letchworth Hose Reel, small, one-horse, driver in standard helmet	900	1350	1800
Pratt & Letchworth Hose Reel, one horse, 14¼"	900	1350	1800
Pratt & Letchworth Pumper, two horse	1750	2625	3500
Pratt & Letchworth Sulky, 8½" long	300	450	600
Pratt & Letchworth-Welker & Crosby Dray, 14½" long, one-horse, driver	500	850	1500
Pull Toy, tin, horse and cart, iron wheels, 11" long	250	375	500
Pull Toy, horse and covered delivery wagon, tin, 5¼" long	150	225	300
Pull Toy, horse and wagon, two wheels, tin, 9¼" long	125.00	187.50	250.00
Pull Toy, horse pulling water wagon, tin, iron wheels, 6¾" long	350	525	700
Pull Toy, horse-drawn carriage, tin, 12" long	150	225	300
Pull Toy, horse pulling water wagon, tin, iron wheels, 7¼" long	125.00	187.50	250.00

	C6	C8	C10
Pumper, 15½" long, driver part of casting, 2-horse, early	200	300	400
Pumper, cast iron, with driver and two horses	200	300	400
Pumper, cast iron, three horses with figure, 13" long	120	180	240
Reed "Band Chariot", 28½" long, 14 bandsmen	800	1200	2000

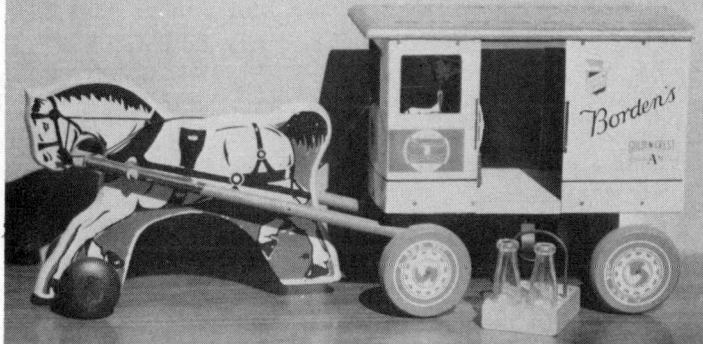

RICH TOYS "Borden's Golden Crest" wooden dairy cart
Courtesy Joe and Sharon Freed

	C6	C8	C10
Rich Toys "Borden's Golden Crest" wooden dairy cart, 18" long	50	80	120
"Sand and Gravel," wagon with driver, cast iron, 9½" long	150	225	300
Sand and Gravel Wagon, cast iron, 10" long, two horses	150	225	300
Sand and Gravel Wagon, single horse with driver, cast iron, 10½" long	175.00	262.50	350.00
"Sand and Gravel" Wagon, cast iron, driver, two-horse, 14¾" long	100	150	200
"Sand and Gravel" Wagon, with driver and two horses, cast iron, 15"	150	225	300
Santa and Sleigh, cast iron, 16x7"	500	750	1000

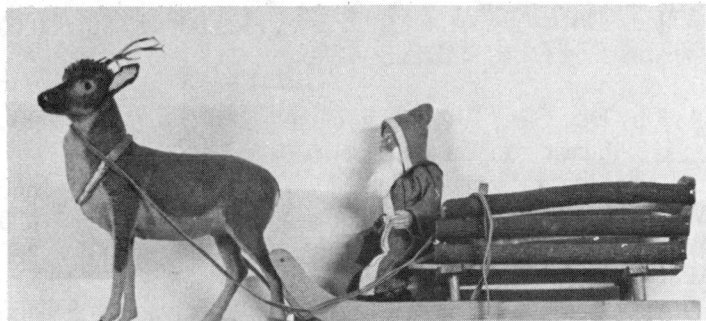

Santa Claus in wooden sleigh pulled by reindeer, 25" long.
Photo Courtesy Garth's Auctions Inc.

	C6	C8	C10
Santa Claus in wooden sleigh pulled by reindeer, 25" long, Santa composition, reindeer plush with cast pewter antlers, early	1500	2250	3000
Santa Claus, reindeer pulling sled, two reindeer pulling white sled containing black-painted Santa Claus	500	800	1200
Sheep, cast iron, pulling two-wheeled tin wagon, 8" long	125	200	300

	C6	C8	C10
"Sheffield Farms Company," wooden horse-drawn milk wagon, horse has articulated legs, 21" long	250	400	650
Shimer Surrey, woman driver	375.00	562.50	750.00
Spring Wagon, cast iron with driver, horse, 11"	150	225	300
Spring Wagon, cast iron, driver, one horse, 14½" long	150	250	350
Spring Wagon, driver and two horses, cast iron, 14½" long	150	275	400
Spring Wagon, driver and two horses, miniature pick, shovel, sledge-hammer, 14¼" long, cast iron	600	900	1200
Spring Wagon, cast iron, two horses, 15"	150	225	300
Stagecoach with cowboy driver and two horses, 11" long, cast iron	110	165	220
Stagecoach, 6-horse, 27" long, cast iron	60	90	120
Stake Bed Wagon, cast iron, one horse, 14¾"	400	700	1000
"Stanley" surrey with driver, lady passenger, two-horse, 14¾" long	90	135	180
Steam Pumper with stationary driver, two horses, cast iron, 9¼" long	100	150	250
Steam Pumper, cast iron, stationary driver, three horses, 10½" long	150	225	300
Steam Pumper, cast iron, 15" long with stationary driver and two horses	500	750	1000
Steam Pumper, cast iron, two horses, stationary driver, 15¼" long	500	750	1000
Steam Pumper, cast iron, driver, three horses, bell, 17½" long	600	900	1200
Steam Pumper, two-horse, cast iron with driver, 18" long	600	1000	1500
Steam Pumper, cast iron, driver and two horses, 20½" long	600	900	1500
Steam Pumper, cast iron, three horses and bell, 21¼" high	500	750	1000
Steamer with driver, two horses, 17" long	600	900	1500

STEVENS Black Man in cart whipping mule, 9" long.
Courtesy Lloyd W. Ralston Auctions

	C6	C8	C10
Stevens Black Man in cart whipping mule, painted cast iron, mechanical, 1890, 9"	400	600	900
Sulky, cast iron, horse and rider, cart mounted with four bells, 6½"	200	300	400

143

	C6	C8	C10
Sulky, cast iron, with driver, 7¼" long	150	225	300
Sulky, cast iron, with driver, circa 1890s, 8½" long	250	400	550
Sulky, cast iron, with rider, 8¾"	100	150	200
Sulky Rig, horse and driver pull toy, comic style, 10" long, 8" high, 1¼" thick	100	150	200
Surrey, cast iron, two-horse, 13" long	150	225	300

"Teddy Bear" Enclosed Cart, 9" long.
Courtesy Lloyd W. Ralston Auctions

	C6	C8	C10
"Teddy Bear" enclosed cart, painted litho tin, 1915, 9" long	600	900	1200
Transfer Wagon, cast iron, two-horse, driver	400	600	800
"Transfer Wagon", three horses and driver, cast iron, wagon bolted to team, 19" long	400	650	850
"Transfer" Wagon, cast iron, driver and two horses, 19½" long	400	600	800
"Trotter, jockey and horse", cast iron, 6" long	30	45	60
"United States Transfer Co. No. 7," wood wagon with cast iron wheels, 2 stuffed horses, 31" long	300	450	600
U.S. Mail Wagon, tin, two-horse, 17" long	500	750	1000
Wagon, two-wheeled, with driver, cast iron, 7¼"	100	150	200
Wagon, cast iron, mule, driver, two-wheeled wagon, 9½" long	350	525	700
Wagon, two-seater, cast iron, one horse	150	225	300
Walking Horse and Sulky Cart, horse of wood, moving legs and cart of tin, wheels cast iron, 7" long	250	375	500
Water Tower with three horses, cast iron and pressed steel, 43" long, horse 11" long	1000	1500	2000
Welker & Crosby Ox Cart, two oxen, black driver	600	900	1200

WILKINS TOY COMPANY

Wilkins, of Keene, New Hampshire, was begun by James S. Wilkins as the Triumph Wringer Company. But the tiny model Wilkins produced to promote his product proved so intriguing to prospective customers and their children that requests for them poured in. The real thing was quickly forgotten as Wilkins turned to toymaking. Its toys were generally cast iron and steel. The firm was acquired in 1894 by Kingsbury, which is still in business, though now as a tool and die maker.

	C6	C8	C10
Wilkins Aerial Fire Wagon, 43" long, cast iron, 3-horse, driver	1200	1800	2400
Wilkins Artillery, 10" long, circa 1895, 2-horse, rider on caisson, seat top lifts off, cannon	1000	1500	2000
Wilkins Buckboard, cast iron	120	180	240
Wilkins Caisson, horse-drawn, 18" long	700	1050	1400
Wilkins Cane Wagon, mule, driver, 11" long	300	450	600
Wilkins Carriage, driver in derby, 1-horse, passenger	1000	1500	2000
Wilkins Cart, animated, 6"	250	375	500
Wilkins Cart and Horse, 10" long	450	700	1000
Wilkins Cart and Horse, 12" long, driver	750	1200	1600
Wilkins Chariot, 7" long, four-horse	180	270	360
Wilkins "City Truck," cast iron, two-horse with driver	1000	1500	2000
Wilkins "Coal and Wood" wagon	750	1125	1500
Wilkins Delivery Wagon, 21" long, driver, prancing horse team	600	900	1200

WILKINS Doctor's Cart
Courtesy Ed Hyers

	C6	C8	C10
Wilkins Doctor's Cart	325.00	487.50	650.00
Wilkins Dog Cart, 7½" long, 1890, cast iron	150	225	300
Wilkins Dog Cart, 10½" long, circa 1890, cast iron, large St. Bernard-type dog, rider in cap	750	1200	1600
Wilkins Donkey Cart, 13¼" long	500	750	1000
Wilkins Dray, 15" long, cast iron	400	600	800
Wilkins, Dray, 16" long, 2-horse, cast iron	450	675	900
Wilkins Dray, 17½" long, two mules, driver	600	900	1200
Wilkins Dray, cast iron and tin barrel, drawn by two horses, driver in derby hat, circa 1910, 20½"	300	450	600
Wilkins Fire Chief buggy, one horse with rider	150	225	300

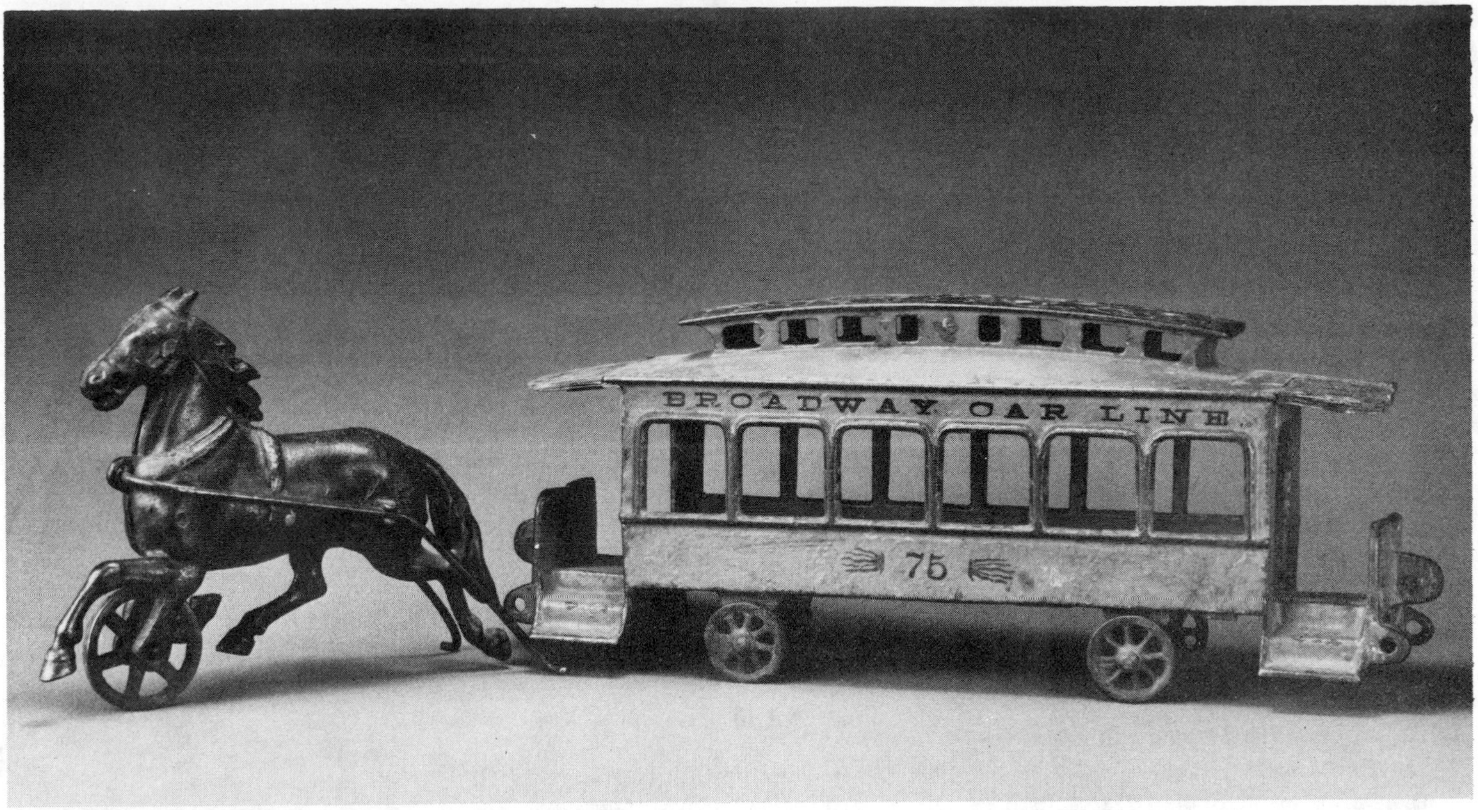

WILKINS Streetcar, "Broadway Car Line 75", horse-drawn
Courtesy Mapes Auctioneers & Appraisers

WILKINS Fire Ladder Truck, cast iron, 3-horse, 20" long, circa 1910.
Courtesy Mapes Auctioneers & Appraisers

WILKINS Hose Reel, two horse, two firemen in standard helmets
Courtesy Ed Hyers Antique Toys

WILKINS Hook and Ladder, two horse, two firemen
Courtesy Ed Hyers Antique Toys

WILKINS Pumper, two-horse, two firemen
Courtesy Ed Hyers Antique Toys

WILKINS Aerial Fire Wagon, cast iron, 43" long. Circa 1895, and believed to be the largest cast iron toy made during the 19th century. Courtesy Phillips New York

	C6	C8	C10
Wilkins Fire Chief Engine Pumper, two horses, 19" long	500	750	1000
Wilkins Fire Hose Reel, 10½" long .	350	550	750
Wilkins Fire Ladder Truck, cast iron, 20" long, 3-horse, circa 1910, two firemen	400	600	800
Wilkins Fire Patrol Wagon, four firemen in wagon, 12" long	250	375	500
Wilkins Fire Patrol, 2-horse, 2 men, cast iron	200	300	400
Wilkins Fire Pumper, 20" long, 2-horse, driver	600	900	1200
Wilkins Gentleman's Cart, 1900, 10" long, gentleman driver, white horse	300	450	600
Wilkins Gig, fancy, and driver, 10" long	150	225	300
Wilkins "Groceries" wagon, one-horse, 13½" long, circa 1900	200	300	400
Wilkins Hansom Cab, cast iron	150	225	300
Wilkins Hook and Ladder, 24" long .	500	750	1000
Wilkins Hook and Ladder, 27" long, prancing team, cast iron	750	1125	1500
Wilkins Hook and Ladder, two-horse, horses sit on pegs, has ladders, figures	1000	1500	2000
Wilkins Hook and Ladder, two horse, two firemen	1000	1500	2000
Wilkins Hose Reel, two horse, two firemen in standard helmets	750	1125	1500
Wilkins Hose Reel, 18" long, circa 1890, 1-horse, cast iron	1000	1500	2000
Wilkins Huckster's Wagon, two-horse, driver	900	1350	1800
Wilkins Ice Wagon, horse, tin and cast iron, 10" long	150	225	300
Wilkins Landau	2000	3000	4000
Wilkins Ox Cart, cast iron	300	450	650

WILKINS Stake Wagon, 1907
Courtesy Ed Hyers Antique Toys

	C6	C8	C10
Wilkins Phaeton, woman driver, 16" long, late 1800s	500	750	1000
Wilkins Plantation Cart, 1910, cast iron and pressed steel, tilt dump, 11" long	400	600	800
Wilkins Plow, one horse, driver, 10½" long	1500	2400	3200
Wilkins Pony Cart, 7½" long, one horse, driver	400	600	800
Wilkins Pumper, two-horse, two firemen	1100	1650	2200
Wilkins Spring Wagon, driver, horses	300	450	600
Wilkins Stake Wagon, 1907	625.00	937.50	1250.00
Wilkins Steam Engine, two-horse, with driver, 17" long	600	900	1300
Wilkins Streetcar, "Broadway Car Line 75," horse-drawn	700	1100	1400
Wilkins Wagon, driver, mule, 9" long	300	450	600
Williams Sulky, 8" long, circa 1920, cast iron	150	225	300

MECHANICAL BANKS
by Bill S. Bertoia

The average mint price in this category in the last edition was $1460.80 and in this edition it is $7383.91, an increase of 405%.

After trains, mechanical Banks are perhaps the most avidly pursued of all the toys cataloged in this book, and the most collectible remain those which were produced in cast iron from around 1870 to 1908, over three hundred different types being produced during that period. One factor that adds to their interest is that many were manufactured with an eye to adult trade as well as to that of children (the "Tammany" bank, for instance). As a result, prices are high, and have been so long before any of the other toys in this book were thought of as collector's items. With prices of this sort, the problem of counterfeiting arises, and care is urged in the purchase of any high-priced bank. Briefly, counterfeits tend to be rougher, to fit together less smoothly, and to not have the patina or "look" of age.

CONDITION CODE:
C5 – Good, wear evident overall, shows that has been played with
C6 – Fine, shows some wear in spots, but taken care of
C7 – Very Fine, minor wear overall, very clean
C8 – Excellent, minor wear on edges only
C9 – Near Mint, no noticeable flaws, close inspection may show minute marks
C10 – Mint (like new)
    Note: Mint in Box does command higher price

BILL S. BERTOIA is a recognized authority in the field of antique toys and banks. As an avid toy and bank collector, he is a member of the Antique Toy Club of America, the Mechanical Bank Collectors of America and the Still Bank Collectors of America. As an active antiques dealer specialist in the field, he handled the sales of the Perelman Antique Toy Museum, the Atlanta Toy Museum and the Hegarity Mechanical Bank Collection. He is married to Jeanne Bertoia, the author of the Doorstop book, and they have two young children who are starting to share their interest in collecting. They reside in Vineland, New Jersey.

ALWAYS DID DESPISE A MULE
Courtesy PB Eighty-Four, New York

BUILDING SAVINGS
Courtesy PB Eighty-Four, New York

AMERICAN BANK.
Courtesy Lloyd W. Ralston Auctions

CAT AND MOUSE
Courtesy PB Eighty-Four, New York

ACROBAT
Courtesy PB Eighty-Four, NY

ALLIGATOR IN TROUGH
Courtesy Sotheby's New York

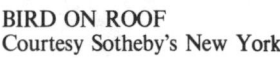

BIRD ON ROOF
Courtesy Sotheby's New York

	C6	C8	C10
Acrobat Bank, 5" high	1500	3500	6000
Alligator In Trough patented 1867 ..	10,000	20,000	35,000
Always Did Despise A Mule, black jockey on mule, 1879, 10" long ..	300	700	1200
Always Did Despise A Mule, black on bench being kicked by mule, 1897	300	800	1500
American Bank sewing machine	3000	6000	10,000
Artillery Bank, Union officer with mortar firing at fort, 1877	500	900	1400
Astronaut's Bank – gold moon with rocket on stand, has rings showing orbit of space capsule, ring has astronauts' names: "Shepard, Grissom, Glenn, Carpenter, Schirra, Cooper," little plane up side of rocket shoots money into moon, 11" high, pot metal	25.00	37.50	50.00

	C6	C8	C10
Bad Accident, Mule and black on two-wheeled car, 1887	750	1300	2000
Bear Hugging Tree	150	400	600
Bill E. Grin	300	900	1500
Bird On Roof	500	1200	2500
Book of Knowledge Reproduction of Original Banks, circa 1950; Artillery Bank; Bulldog Bank; Creedmore; Eagle and Eaglets; Jonah & Whale; Magician; Man and Pig; Man Milking Cow; Teddy and the Bear; Trick Dog, Trick Pony, Tree Trunk and Buffalo. (Note – original markings sometimes filed away from bottom and sold as originals). Price per each	25	50	75

BAD ACCIDENT
Courtesy PB Eighty-Four, NY

BOYS STEALING
WATERMELONS
Courtesy PB Eighty-Four, NY

BOY SCOUT
Courtesy Sotheby's New York

BREAD WINNER
Courtesy Sotheby's New York

CALAMITY
Courtesy PB Eighty-Four, New York

COW KICKING
Courtesy Sotheby's New York

DENTIST
Courtesy PB Eighty-Four, NY

DOG ON TURNTABLE
Courtesy PB Eighty-Four, NY

GIANT
Courtesy Sotheby's
New York

INDIAN SHOOTING BEAR
Courtesy Sotheby's New York

MAMA KATZENJAMMER
AND THE KIDS
Courtesy PB Eighty-Four NY

INITIATING BANK
Courtesy Lloyd W. Ralston
Auctions

ORGAN GRINDER AND
BEAR
Courtesy PB Eighty-Four, NY

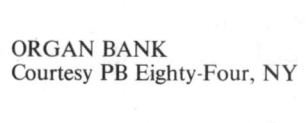

ORGAN BANK
Courtesy PB Eighty-Four, NY

	C6	C8	C10
Boy On Trapeze	300	850	1500
Boy Robbing Nest	1500	2500	4000
Boy Scout	1500	2500	4000
Boys Stealing Watermelons	750	1500	2500
Bread Winner	5000	8500	12,000
Buffalo, Bucking	1000	2000	3000
"Building Savings" patented August 13, 1878, dog springing forward grabs coin from man's hands	1500	2250	3000
Bull & Bear, brass model	1000	1750	2500
Bulldog, dog swallows coin	300	600	950
Bulldog, c. 1887, Judd	300	450	600
Butting Goat In Tree Stump, c. 1887, Judd	600	900	1200
Calamity, patented August 29, 1905, J&E Stevens Co., three football players	2500	6000	10,000
Cat And Mouse Bank	750	2000	3500
Charlie McCarthy, sitting with legs crossed on top of trunk, drop coin in back and mouth moves, pot metal, copyright 1938, 5¾" high	75	125	200
Chein Monkey, seated, tips hat when coin dropped in, tin litho, 5" high	25.00	37.50	50.00
Chief Big Moon, Indian in teepee, etc. 1899	500	1100	1800
Chimpanzee	1500	2200	3500
Chinese Reclining, 1882	1800	2800	4000
Circus Ticket Taker	350	700	1000
Clown & Harlequin, auctioned for $90,000 in 1988			
Clown On Box, auctioned for $45,000 in 1988			
Clown On Globe, 1873	500	1000	1500
Columbus	200	400	600
Confectionary	2000	5000	8000
Cow Kicking cow kicks over boy	2000	4500	8000
Creedmore Bank, man firing into tree, 1877, 10" long	200	500	750
Crowing Rooster	500	750	1000
Dapper Dan	200	400	600
Darktown Battery, black pitcher and catcher, 1888	600	1200	2000
Darky Football, auctioned for $245,000 in 1988			
Darky and Cabin, 1885	200	400	600
Dentist Bank, white dentist working on black patient, 1880	2500	4000	7500
Dinah, bust of black woman, 6½"	150	350	500
Dog Charges Boy, bronze finish	400	700	1000
Dog On Turntable, Judd Mfg. Co.	150	300	450
Dog Standing	150	350	500
Eagle And Eaglets, 1883	300	600	900
Elephant, late cast iron, Hubley	100	175	250
Elephant, Three Star, cast iron, trunk flips up to catch coin, 5" high	150	300	450
Elephant And Clowns	500	1000	1500
Elephant And Howdah, 1920	250	500	750
Elephant Howdah, circa 1934, Hubley	375.00	563.00	750.00

	C6	C8	C10
Ferris Wheel, Hubley/Bauer	1000	2000	3000
Fortune Teller patented February 19, 1901, safe, complete with roll of fortunes	400	600	800
The Forty-Niner, donkey moves ears and tail	100	225	400
Freedman, auctioned for $250,000.00 in 1988			
Frog And Snake In Pond lithographed tin mechanical bank in the form of a snake striking at a frog which opens its mouth to receive the coin	3000	4500	6500
Frog, Goat And Old Man	1200	2500	4000
Frog On Arched Track, auctioned for $35,000.00 in 1988			
Frog On Lattice, Stevens, 1870s	150	350	600
Frog On Rock, Kilgore Mfg. Co.	200	350	550
Frog On Stump, 1872	200	400	600
Frogs, two, J&E Stevens	600	900	1200
Gem, Dog and building	200	350	500
Giant, giant holding a club	10,000	15,000	20,000
Girl Skipping Rope, with key	5000	10,000	16,000
Globe Savings Fund Bank	250	375	500
Guessing Bank	1500	2500	3500
Hall's Excelsior Bank, monkey cashier	100	350	500
Hall's Lilliput, 1875	200	350	500
Hen And Chick, circa 1901, Stevens	1200	1800	2400
Hen Setting, J&E Stevens	650	975	1300
Hindu, 1882, Kyser & Rex	1000	1500	2000
Home building with two pillars, teller at window, tin	100	200	300
Horse Race	3500	5500	8500
Humpty Dumpty	250	650	1000
Independence Hall	150	325	500
Indian Shooting Bear, 1888	400	800	1200
Initiating Bank First Degree	3500	6500	10,000
Jolly Nigger, bust	100	250	400
Jolly Nigger, high hat, 8" high	150	350	600
Jolly Nigger, moves ears	75.00	112.50	150.00
Jonah And The Whale, cast iron (Jonah in boat)	700	1100	1600
Jonah And Whale (Jonah emerges)	15,000	22,000	30,000
Jumbo On Platform	800	1150	1500
Katzenjammer Kids	1000	2800	4500
"Keep 'Em Flying" dime register, tin	25.00	37.50	50.00

CONDITION CODE:

C5 – Good, wear evident overall, shows that has been played with
C6 – Fine, shows some wear in spots, but taken care of
C7 – Very Fine, minor wear overall, very clean
C8 – Excellent, minor wear on edges only
C9 – Near Mint, no noticeable flaws, close inspection may show minute marks
C10 – Mint (like new)
   Note: Mint in Box does command higher price

HUMPTY DUMPTY
Photo Courtesy PB Eighty-Four, New York

WILLIAM TELL
Courtesy PB Eighty-Four, New York

CLOWN ON GLOBE
Courtesy PB Eighty Four, NY

CHEIN Monkey
Courtesy Garth's Auctions Inc.

OWL, turns head.
Courtesy PB Eighty Four, NY

FORTUNE TELLER
Courtesy PB Eighty-Four, NY

CHIEF BIG MOON
Courtesy PB Eighty-Four, New York

JONAH AND THE WHALE
Courtesy Garth's Auctions Inc.

EAGLE AND EAGLETS
Courtesy PB Eighty-Four, New York

	C6	C8	C10
Kick Inn lithographed paper and wood mechanical bank, Presto, a mule standing in front of a small building	250	375	450
King Aqua, auctioned for $95,000 in 1988			
Leap Frog Bank, two boys, tree, 1891	750	1500	2000

	C6	C8	C10
Liberty Bell	200	350	500
Lighthouse Bank, 1891	300	500	750
Lion And Monkeys	200	400	650
Lion Hunter	2000	3000	4500
Little Jocko	150	225	300
Little Joe	150	225	300
Locomotive	300	600	900

TRICK PONY
Courtesy PB Eighty-Four, New York

NEW CREEDMORE
Courtesy PB Eighty-Four, New York

MASON AND HOD-CARRIER
Courtesy PB Eighty-Four, New York

TRICK DOG
Courtesy PB Eighty-Four, New York

LION HUNTER
Courtesy PB Eighty-Four, New York

DARKTOWN BATTERY
Courtesy PB Eighty-Four, New York

PRESTO-MOUSE ON ROOF
Courtesy PB Eighty-Four, New York

FROG AND SNAKE IN POND
Courtesy PB Eighty-Four, New York

HORSE RACE
Courtesy PB Eighty-Four, New York

PERFECTION registering
mechanical bank, STEVENS
Courtesy Lloyd W. Ralston
Auctions

PUNCH AND JUDY
Courtesy PB Eighty-Four, NY

**SANTA CLAUS AT THE
CHIMNEY**
Courtesy PB Eighty-Four, NY

SPEAKING DOG
Courtesy PR Eighty-Four, NY

GIRL SKIPPING ROPE
Courtesy PB Eighty-Four, New York

PADDY AND HIS PIG
Courtesy Garth's Auctions Inc.

FROG ON ROCK
Courtesy PB Eighty-Four, New York

TABBY
Courtesy PB Eighty-Four, New York

FROG ON LATTICE
Courtesy PB Eighty-Four, New York

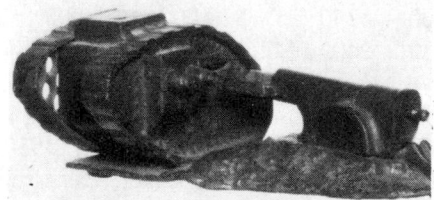

TANK AND CANNON
Courtesy PB Eighty-Four, NY

STUMP SPEAKER
Courtesy PB Eighty-Four, NY

MAMMY FEEDING CHILD
Courtesy Sotheby's New York

TEDDY AND THE BEAR
Courtesy PB Eighty-Four, New
York

PICTURE GALLERY
Courtesy Sotheby's New York

RED RIDING HOOD
Courtesy Sotheby's New York

ROLLER SKATING
Courtesy Sotheby's New York

	C6	C8	C10
Magic	250	700	1000
Magician Bank, 1882	1500	4000	6500
Mama Katzenjammer And The Kids, 5¾"	3200	5000	6500
Mammy Feeding Child	1500	2800	4000
Mason And Hod Carrier, 1887	1500	3000	4000
Merry Go Round, semi-mechanical	100	175	250
Meyers No. 84, Jumbo Elephant	100	250	350
Money Box Bank, hand-carved on wood base, 10¼"	800	1200	1600
Money Moves The World, Atlas Bank	750	1150	1850
Monkey And Coconut	500	1100	1600
Mosque	400	800	1200
Mule Bucking Black man riding a mule	500	750	1000
Mule Entering Barn	300	600	900
National Bank	1500	3500	5000
Naughty Girl Bank, modern	25	50	75
New Creedmore Meyer no. 54	200	300	400
New Bank, cast iron, circa 1875, brass policeman in building, 4½" long	200	350	500
North Pole, J&E Stevens Co., eskimos and dog sled	4000	7000	10,000
Novelty Bank, house-like bank, 1873	250	500	750
Organ Bank, monkey and revolving cat and dog, 7¼" high	250	500	750
Organ Bank, monkey only	150	250	400
Organ Boy And Girl, patented June 13, 1882, monkey flanked by boy and girl holding tambourine	350	700	1000
Organ Grinder And Bear	1500	2500	4000
Organ Grinder And Monkey, 1929	150	225	350
Owl, slot in back, cast iron	225.00	337.50	450.00
Owl, slot in head	150	300	500
Owl, turns head, cast iron	200	350	500
Paddy And His Pig	500	1000	1500
Panorama, building	1800	2800	4000
Patronize The Blind Man And His Dog, patented February 19, 1878, J&E Stevens Co.	1500	3000	4500
Pegleg Beggar	500	1000	1500
Pelican, cast iron, "boy thumbs nose"	500	1000	1500
Picture Gallery	3500	4800	6500
Pig, Bismarck	1500	3000	4500

	C6	C8	C10
Pig In High Chair	250	375	500
Preacher In Pulpit	25,000	30,000	35,000
Presto, shape of building	150	250	400
Presto-Mouse On Roof lithographed paper on wood	7500	12,000	17,500
Professor Pug Frog's Great Bicycle Feat	1500	3500	5000
Pump, Bucket	300	700	1000
Punch & Judy, Shepherd Hardware, Buffalo, NY, circa 1890	400	800	1200
Rabbit, tall	300	500	800
Rabbit, small, circular base	200	400	600
Rabbit In Cabbage Patch	175	300	450
Red Riding Hood	10,000	15,000	20,000
Roller Skating	15,000	22,000	30,000
Rooster	200	300	450
Perfection Registering Bank	3500	5000	6500
Santa Claus At Chimney	500	850	1200
See Him Frisk, auctioned for $55,000 in 1988			
Shoot The Chute	10,000	15,000	20,000
Speaking Dog Bank, J.E. Stevens, pat. 1885	500	1000	1500
Springing Cat, lead alloy, sold for $20,000 in 1988			
Squirrel And Tree Stump	500	850	1200
Standing Bear	100	165	220
Strato Bank, pot metal, rocket and planet, 8" long, 1950s	10	15	25
Stump Speaker, cast iron	500	1000	1500
Tabby	150	350	600
Tammany Bank, 1875, 5¾" high	100	250	400
Tank And Cannon, 1916	200	300	400
Teddy And The Bear, man firing at bear in tree, 1907	600	950	1400
Telephone	150	300	450
3-Star Elephant, brass	150	300	450
Trick Dog, clown with hoop, dog and barrel, 1888 version, has six part base	300	550	850
Trick Dog, clown with hoop, dark dog and dark barrel, 1929	150	225	300
Trick Pony	400	650	900

	C6	C8	C10
Turtle Bank, auctioned for $30,000 in 1988			
Two Frogs (see Frogs, Two)			
U.S. Building, circa 1878, boy and dog in windows, Stevens?	3100	4650	6200
U.S. And Spain	2000	3000	4000
Uncle Remus	2000	3100	4500
Uncle Sam, bust	300	450	600
Uncle Sam, has umbrella in left hand, 1886	900	1500	2000
Uncle Tom, with lapels and one star .	200	350	500
Uncle Tom, with lapels, one star	600	900	1200
United States Bank, Stevens	650	975	1300
Watchdog Safe	150	300	450
Weeden's, tin	600	1200	1800
William Tell, 1896	300	500	750
Wireless Bank, 1913	100	250	450
Woodpecker	1500	2800	4000
World's Fair	500	650	850
Zoo	400	700	950

UNCLE SAM, umbrella
Courtesy Sotheby's New York

WORLD'S FAIR
Courtesy Sotheby's New York

PAPER TOYS
(See also Premiums, Comic Character)

The average price for a mint paper toy in the last edition was $25.25, and in this edition it is $47.64, an increase of 89%.

AMERICAN PAPER TOYS
By Barbara and Jonathan Newman

The prices of paper toys have continued to climb rapidly, with celebrity paper dolls of the 40's and W.W. II military theme materials leading the pack.

This subject of paper toys is so vast that it continues to receive only superficial treatment even in books limited to just that medium. Some brief introduction, nevertheless, should be attempted. They have been called cut-outs, punch outs and press outs. By whatever name, forts, planes, trains, ships, paper dolls and much much more have been produced in paper. What adult does not have some memories (usually fond, often frustrating) of crisp booklets, shiny boxes, or just complicated sheets of paper and cardboard toys?

Throughout the period from the end of the last century to the period after World War II, paper was, if not king, certainly close to the throne. It was, in many ways, the plastic of its day. Every subject matter found in toys can be found in its own version in paper or cardboard.

No collector of military toys or toy soldiers can be unfamiliar with the whole world of paper soldiers, even though they were never quite as popular in this country as in Europe, where paper soldiers were born almost 200 years ago. American companies by the turn of the century were turning out paper troops by the thousands. The most popular was easily the McLoughlin Bros. Company which started out with paper toys in 1857 in New York City and was eventually bought out by Milton Bradley and moved to Springfield, Massachusetts in 1920. Their products included beautifully lithographed covered boxed sets of cardboard figures on wooden stands, or for the young boy with less resources, over a hundred different sheets of American and foreign armies to be cut out and mounted on little wooden stands.

During this same general time period, centered around the 10 years from 1895 to 1905, almost every major newspaper in the country (at least those big city ones with large Sunday editions) had Sunday "Art Supplements" which varied their "give away" fare from Armies or Navies of the world to historical panoramas illustrating our history, from political figures and personalities of the day to cut-out dolls of celebrities with vast wardrobes of clothes. Even the "Globe Quadruple Perfecting Press" itself was offered as a cut-out to construct a complete diorama as the Boston Sunday Globe's offering of August 6, 1896.

Paper houses and villages, a great favorite with little girls of the day, were sold by a wide variety of companies. The earlier ones included the ubiquitous McLoughlin Bros. and Milton Bradley (yes, they're still around) and more recent ones were World War II era giants in the field, Built-Rite and Megow.

In fact, while there was no shortage in the 20's and 30's, it's WW II that was really the Golden Age of paper toys in this country. The reason is obvious and the lack of any alternative material to paper caused the king of toy companies, Lionel, to produce as its only offering in the war, a complete train set in die-cut cardboard. Who would have thought such a poor substitute in 1943 would be a sought after and valuable rarity today? If you have one in mint condition you've got a real gem in both the world of toy trains and paper toys.

During these war years every conceivable type of toy, usually given a wartime, patriotic theme, was available. Punchout cardboard sets of "Rap-A-Jap," "Sink The Axis," "Camouflage Defense Force," books of punch out Naval Craft by Rigby, etc. were the birthday, Christmas or other presents of the forties. A whole range of Built-Rite forts, trenches, troops and doll houses are among our own fond memories. Celebrity paper dolls were at their zenith and, except for some vague awareness of the war and being forced to go to school against our wills, Barbara and Jonathan were having a great time playing.

The list and illustrations could go on and on and someday perhaps a reasonably definitive book will be written. For the meantime, just settle for a brief taste in words and pictures to either jog your own memory or kindle an interest in a lifetime passion for paper toys.

ARMY NURSE AND DOCTOR PAPER
DOLLS
Photo by Jonathan A. Newman
Courtesy Barbara and Jonathan Newman

ARMY AMBULANCE. BUILD FOR VIC-
TORY ACTION ON ROLLING
WHEELS.
Photo by Jonathan A. Newman
Courtesy Barbara and Jonathan Newman

ALL-NU Cardboard soldiers, No.111, 109,
106, 108
Photo by Jonathan A. Newman
Courtesy Barbara and Jonathan Newman

```
CONDITION CODE:
C5 – Good, wear evident overall, shows that has been played with
C6 – Fine, shows some wear in spots, but taken care of
C7 – Very Fine, minor wear overall, very clean
C8 – Excellent, minor wear on edges only
C9 – Near Mint, no noticeable flaws, close inspection may show
       minute marks
C10 – Mint (like new)
     Note: Mint in Box does command higher price
```

(Note: Where not specifically noted, paper toys listed are paper dolls.)

	C6	C8	C10		C6	C8	C10
Air-Hostess, 1947, Saalfield 2546	25	40	50	109 Charging with rifle, port arms, WW I helmet	3.00	4.50	6.00
Alice Faye, 1941, Merrill 4800	125	175	200	110 Seated machine gunner, WW I helmet	3.00	4.50	6.00
All-Nu decal sheet of soldiers, meant to be attached to heavy cardboard backing, circa 1942, by Frank Krupp	50	75	100	111 Flag-bearer, WW I helmet	3.00	4.50	6.00
				112 General McArthur	5.00	8.00	12.00
All-Nu soldiers, 5" high on heavy cardboard, circa 1942-3				113 Nurse	3.00	4.50	6.00
100 Officer marching with sabre	3.00	4.50	6.00	114 2 Men carrying wounded soldier on stretcher, WW II helmets	3.00	4.50	6.00
101 Marching, slope arms, WW I helmet	3.00	4.50	6.00	115 2 Men firing rifles from prone position, WW II helmets	3.00	4.50	6.00
102 Bugler, campaign cap	3.00	4.50	6.00	116 Soldier on wireless radio	3.00	4.50	6.00
103 Signalman, WW I helmet	3.00	4.50	6.00	117 3 Soldiers w/rifles leaving boat, WW II helmets	3.00	4.50	6.00
104 Officer kneeling with binoculars .	3.00	4.50	6.00	118 2 Paratroopers, one w/tommy gun, WW II helmets	3.00	4.50	6.00
105 Kneeling, firing rifle with WW I helmet	3.00	4.50	6.00	119 Ski trooper	3.00	4.50	6.00
106 Throwing grenade, WW I helmet	3.00	4.50	6.00	120 Soldier advancing w/rifle, WW II helmet	3.00	4.50	6.00
107 Fixed bayonet, WW I helmet ...	3.00	4.50	6.00	150 3 Men in jeep, WW I helmets ..	3.00	4.50	6.00
108 Charging with gas mask, WW I helmet	3.00	4.50	6.00				

	C6	C8	C10
151 5-man team with cannon, WW I helmets	3.00	4.50	6.00
152 2 men manning wheeled A-A gun, WW I helmets	3.00	4.50	6.00
153 Tank with 3 men	3.00	4.50	6.00
154 Ambulance	3.00	4.50	6.00
155 Truck w/soldiers in rear, WW II helmets	3.00	4.50	6.00
All-Nu boxed set of 24 of the above soldiers	No Price Found		
American Beauties, Paper Dolls, circa 1942, Reuben Lilja & Co., No. 917	9.00	15.00	22.00
American Beauty Paper Dolls with dresses worn by White House First Ladies 1789-1951, Merrill No. 154815, 1951	18.00	25.00	30.00
American Defense Battles Punch-out Book by George Trimmer, Merrill No. 3430, 1940	45.00	75.00	90.00
American Family Paper-Doll Book "Costumes for all the family from 1610 to now," Grinnell No. C1002	35.00	50.00	75.00
Amos & Andy – Cutout cardboard of just Andy, 8½" high, stand-up	4.00	6.00	8.00
Animal Paper Dolls to Dress, 1950, Saalfield 2598, Bear, Monkey, Pig, Kitten	8.00	15.00	20.00
Animals to Paint, 1910, Saalfield	8.00	15.00	22.00
Ann Blythe, 1952 Merrill No. 2550-25	35.00	60.00	75.00
Army Air Forces Aircraft Identification Silhouette Model – Feb. 1943, $\frac{1}{72}$ scale of Japanese fighter Najajima T-97, A.N.F. 7x11 envelope	7.00	15.00	18.00
Army Ambulance, circa 1942, Handi-Kraft	15.00	25.00	35.00
Army Cut Outs, 1937, Saalfield No. 245	35.00	60.00	75.00
Army Nurse and Doctor Paper Dolls, 1942, Merrill 3425	25.00	45.00	55.00
Around the World with Bob and Barbara, 1946, Children's Press No. 3000	7.00	12.00	15.00
Assemble 9 Model Warplanes, 4 Model Tanks, 1941, Fawcett Publications, Lowe	30.00	60.00	75.00
Ava Gardner, 1949, 1952 Whitman No. 119215	35.00	60.00	75.00
Baby Brother by Queen Holden, 1929, Whitman 920	50.00	75.00	85.00
Baby First Step, 1965, (Mattel) Whitman No. 1997	5.00	8.00	10.00
Babyland 1955, Merrill No. 3642	30.00	45.00	60.00
Baby Pat 1963 Whitman No. 2072	4.00	6.00	8.00
Baby Sitter Paper Dolls, Lowe No. 945	15.00	22.00	30.00

 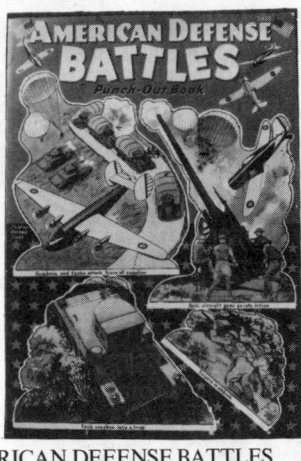

Left, ALICE FAYE. Right, AMERICAN DEFENSE BATTLES PUNCH-OUT BOOK.
Photo by Jonathan A. Newman
Courtesy Barbara and Jonathan Newman

	C6	C8	C10
Barbara Britton Paper Dolls with Magic Stay-On Costumes, 1954, Saalfield 5190, Boxed Set	32.00	45.00	55.00
Barbie and Ken 1962 Whitman No. 4797, 7"x12" boxed set	6.00	15.00	20.00
Barbie and Skipper 1964 Whitman No. 1957, Yachting outfits	6.00	15.00	18.00
Barbie Boutique 1973, Whitman No. 1954	4.00	9.00	11.00
Beautiful Paper Dolls by Betty Campbell, 1941, Saalfield No. 242, has some of same paper dolls as Little Miss American Paper Dolls	28.00	55.00	75.00
Belle of the Ball Paper Dolls, 1948, Saalfield 2702	18.00	32.00	40.00
Betsy McCall, 1971, Whitman No. 4744	6.00	10.00	12.00
Betsy McCall Around The World Paper Dolls, circa 1962	7.00	14.00	18.00
Betsy McCall Dress'N Play Paper Dolls, 1963, Standard / Toycraft /McCall No. 802 12"x18" boxed set	8.00	18.00	22.00
Betsy Ross and Her Friends – 1963, Platt and Munk No. 224B, 7"x11" boxed set	5.00	12.00	15.00
Betty and Joan, 1941, 1945, Whitman No. 1015, Joan also appears in Mary and Joan, Lois and Joan	15.00	35.00	40.00
Betty Bonnett – Her Family and Friends by Sheila Young, George W. Jacobs & Co., Phila. 1915. Each series with 6 sheets and folder. First series	100	150	180
Second series	90	145	175
Third series	90	145	175
Betty Grable, 1951, Merrill No. 1558	75	150	175
Betty Sue – A Cut Out Doll – circa 1940 No. 1010	12.00	18.00	22.00

BOB HOPE & DOROTHY
LAMOUR CUT-OUT BOOK

Top Right: BETTY BONNET
HER FAMILY AND FRIENDS
- Second Series
Photo by Jonathan A. Newman
Courtesy Barbara and Jonathan
Newman

BIRTHDAY PARTY STAND-
UP CUT-OUT DOLLS
Photo by Jonathan A. Newman
Courtesy Barbara and Jonathan
Newman

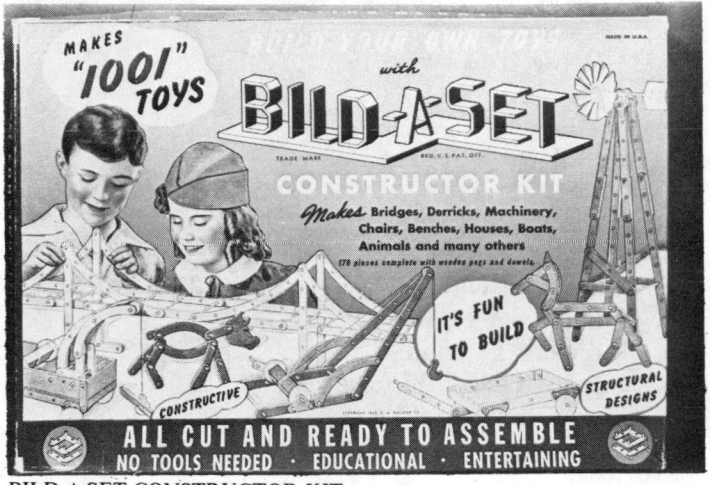

BILD-A-SET CONSTRUCTOR KIT
Photo by Jonathan A. Newman
Courtesy Barbara and Jonathan Newman

	C6	C8	C10
Birthday Party Stand-Up Cut-Out Dolls, 1944, National Syndicate Displays, Inc., 20 boys and girls	22.00	40.00	45.00
Blue Bonnet Paper Dolls by Florence Salter, Merrill No. 3444, 1942	22.00	35.00	40.00
Blue Feather and Silver Cloud, 1940s, Abbott No. 1356, Indian dolls	20.00	45.00	50.00
Boarding School Dolls and Clothes, 1942, Merrill No. 3492	25.00	45.00	55.00
Bob Hope and Dorothy Lamour, 1942, Whitman No. 976	125	175	200
Bobby Socks Cut Out Dolls designed by Doris Lane Butler, 1945, Whitman No. 988	25.00	45.00	55.00
Bombers by Schomburg, Whitman No. 961, 1943, B-17, B-25, B-24, Douglas A-20A, Short "Stirling"	35	75	100
Book of Airplanes, A, Whitman No. 923, 1930	10	15	20
Book of Paper Doll Cut-Outs, The, 1927, Saalfield No. 2051	40	65	75
The Brady Bunch, 1973, Whitman No. 1976	8.00	12.00	15.00
Brenda Lee Teenage Celebrity, 1961, Lowe No. 2785	7.00	12.00	15.00
Brenda Lee, 1964, No. 4360 De Journette, 6½"x10" boxed set, includes toy phonograph and records	18	40	45
Bridal Party, 1950, Whitman No. 1187, five dolls	12	20	25
Bride and Groom, 1949, Merrill No. 3443	30	60	70
Bride and Groom, 1949, Merrill No. 1555	30	60	70
Bride and Groom Military Wedding Party, 1941, Merrill No. 3411, 16 dolls	45	90	100
Bride Doll Cut-Out Book, 1940s, Samuel Lowe No. 1043	12	20	25
Brother and Sister Statuette Dolls, 1950, Whitman 1182-15, two heavy cardboard 7½" dolls	9	18	20
Buffy Paper Dolls ("Family Affair") 1968, Whitman No. 1955	9	15	18
Buffy and Jody, 1970 ("Family Affair"), Whitman 4764, Two magic dolls with Stay-On wardrobes	8	12	15

	C6	C8	C10
The Beverly Hillbillies – Jed, Jethro, Granny and Elly May, Whitman No. 1955, 1964	8.00	15.00	18.00
Big-Girl Paper Dolls, 1940, McLoughlin Bros. No. 707, actually Milton Bradley	12.00	20.00	25.00
Big Invasion Punch-Out Book, 1964, Whitman No. 1936, Punchout of beach landing	12.00	20.00	25.00
Bild-A-Set Constructor Kit No. 85, boxed, Erector-type set of cardboard	10.00	15.00	18.00
Binson-Freeman Pre Flight Trainer, cockpit and how to fly course	75.00	112.50	150.00

CONDITION CODE:
C5 – Good, wear evident overall, shows that has been played with
C6 – Fine, shows some wear in spots, but taken care of
C7 – Very Fine, minor wear overall, very clean
C8 – Excellent, minor wear on edges only
C9 – Near Mint, no noticeable flaws, close inspection may show minute marks
C10 – Mint (like new)
    Note: Mint in Box does command higher price

BUILT-RITE

BUILT-RITE began in 1922 as a manufacturer of cardboard boxes. Somewhere along the line, at least as early as 1934, it began to produce cardboard construction toys, and appears to have manufactured them into the 1950s, with its greatest period of success probably enjoyed during and just prior to WW II. The company remains in business as Warren Paper Products Co., making card games, games and puzzles. Numbers and words in bold print here are Built-Rite's own descriptions.

BUILT-RITE No. 20 Army Battery Set
Photo by Ed Poole

BUILT-RITE Airport No. 26.
Photo by Jonathan A. Newman
Courtesy Barbara and Jonathan Newman

BUILT-RITE Fort No. 25, with Barclay soldiers
Photo by Ed Poole

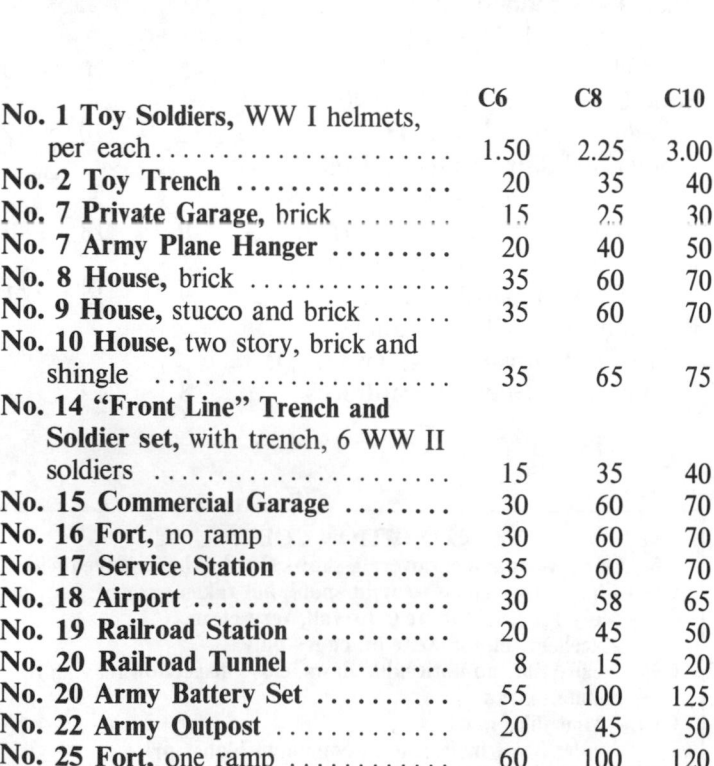

	C6	C8	C10
No. 1 Toy Soldiers, WW I helmets, per each	1.50	2.25	3.00
No. 2 Toy Trench	20	35	40
No. 7 Private Garage, brick	15	25	30
No. 7 Army Plane Hanger	20	40	50
No. 8 House, brick	35	60	70
No. 9 House, stucco and brick	35	60	70
No. 10 House, two story, brick and shingle	35	65	75
No. 14 "Front Line" Trench and Soldier set, with trench, 6 WW II soldiers	15	35	40
No. 15 Commercial Garage	30	60	70
No. 16 Fort, no ramp	30	60	70
No. 17 Service Station	35	60	70
No. 18 Airport	30	58	65
No. 19 Railroad Station	20	45	50
No. 20 Railroad Tunnel	8	15	20
No. 20 Army Battery Set	55	100	125
No. 22 Army Outpost	20	45	50
No. 25 Fort, one ramp	60	100	120

	C6	C8	C10
No. 25A 26-piece Fort and Soldier set same fort as 25, WW II soldiers, 2 sandbag foxholes and fibreboard pistol	75	125	150
No. 26 Airport	35	65	75
No. 28 Garage and Super Service Station	35	70	80
No. 33 Lokdwood Dolls, late 1940s, paper dolls	10	18	20
No. 33 House, Tudor type	35	65	75
No. 34 House, two story	35	65	75
No. 36 House	35	65	75
No. 36F 3-Room Furnished Doll House	35	65	75
No. 45 Living Room Furniture	25	45	55
No. 46 Dining Room Furniture	25	45	55
No. 47 Bedroom Furniture	25	45	55
No. 48 Bathroom Furniture	25	45	55
No. 49 Kitchen Furniture	25	45	55
No. 50 Army Raiders' Victory Unit, 28 pieces, truck, tank, AA gun, jeep, semitrack truck, 20 soldiers, WW II	35	65	75
No. 55 5 Miniature cardboard houses	30	55	60
No. 56 5 Miniature buildings, church, school, RR station, firehouse, drugstore	30	55	60
No. 57M 8 Piece Farm Set	20	30	40
No. 60 Navy Battle Fleet and Coast Artillery Gun	20	45	50
No. 66 3-Piece Kitchen	No Price Found		
No. 75 Living Room Furniture	30	55	65
No. 76 Dining Room Furniture	30	55	65
No. 77 Bedroom Furniture	30	55	65
No. 77 American Ranger Fighters, 8 vehicles, WW II soldiers	40	70	80
No. 78 Kitchen Furniture	30	55	65
No. 100A Fortress, circa 1938, two ramps	70	130	140

BUILT-RITE No. 22 "Army Outpost"
Courtesy John D. (Jack) Matthews

	C6	C8	C10
No. 300 Stock and Grain Elevator ..	10	15	20
No. 415 House, circa 1943, 13"x20" boxed set with 19" house and garage, 27 pieces of furniture, sedan, baby buggy, shrubbery, etc.	50	85	100
No. 460 Pocket Size Series of Miniatures Paperdoll Set	9	15	18
No. 566 Village	30	50	60
No. 1001 Modern Stock Farm	20	35	40
No. 1422 Fort and Soldiers (94 pieces, 2-ramp fort)	75	125	150
No. 2050 Country Estate, house, bushes, dog, cat, baby buggy	35	65	75

CAMOUFLAGE DEFENSE FORCE

	C6	C8	C10
– Airplane, soldiers, anti-aircraft guns all hidden within farm buildings. Heavy cardboard. Jay Line Manufacturing Co., 431, boxed. Circa 1943	35	50	60
Career Girls with Cloth-Like Clothes, 1944, Whitman No. 937 by Doris Lane Butler	15	20	30
Charmin' Chatty, 1964, Whitman No. 1959	6	8	12
Charming Paper Dolls, circa 1960, Saalfield No. 1357	4	6	8
Cheerleader – Teen age Doll, 1950? Stephens Publishing Co., No. 182, Mary and Elaine and four pages of clothes	4	6	8
Children From Other Lands, 1961, Whitman, No. 2089, 8 cut-out dolls and native costumes	7.50	12.00	15.00
Children In The Shoe, 1949, Merrill No. 1562	20	30	40
Cinderella Steps Out, Lowe No. 1242	9	12	18
Circus Day – 1946 by Art Tanchon, Stephens Printing No. 135, Animals, clown, circus cages and wagons	7	12	15
Circus Paper Dolls, 1952, No. 2610, Saalfield	5	8	10
Claire McCardell - designer of the American look, 1956, Whitman No. 2067	25	40	50
Claudette Colbert, 1943, Saalfield No. 2451	100	150	175

BUILT-RITE Fort No. 16
Courtesy John D. (Jack) Matthews

	C6	C8	C10
No. 105 Farm Set with 20 plastic animals	20	40	45
No. 111 Railroad Accessory Set	12	25	35
No. 112 American Fighters - includes 100A fortress with soldiers, cannons, etc., 55 pieces, no flag on tower	75.00	112.50	150.00
No. 115 Doll House, Garage Set (with car)	35	65	75
No. 119 Farm Set	30	50	60
No. 120 Five Room Suburban Doll House	40	65	75
No. 128 Miniature Village and Scenery Set	35	60	65
No. 156 Miniature Houses and Buildings	35	60	65
No. 201 26 Piece Guardsman Set, 2 trenches, artillery base, cannon, pistol, WW II soldiers	40	75	80
No. 202 Train Scenery (28 pieces, Terminal, Scenery, etc.)	30	65	75
No. 204F Furnished Country Estate .	35	70	75
No. 210 Railroad Station and Accessories	12	25	30
No. 212 Station and Railroad Accessories	25	40	50

CLAUDETTE COLBERT PAPER DOLLS
Photo by Jonathan A. Newman
Courtesy Barbara and Jonathan Newman

COLLEGE STYLE PAPER DOLLS
Photo by Jonathan A. Newman
Courtesy Barbara and Jonathan Newman

CUT-OUT DOLLS PUPPIES AND KITTENS
Photo by Jonathan A. Newman
Courtesy Barbara and Jonathan Newman

	C6	C8	C10
Cloth-Like Clothes For 3 Cute Girls, 1949, Whitman No. 1178:15, Flocked clothes	15	25	30
Clothes Make A Lady, 1941, Lowe No. 1029	15	25	35
Coke Crowd, The, 1946, Merrill No. 3445, 8 teens, costumes	45	65	75
College Style Paper Dolls, 1941, Merrill 3400	45	65	75
Colorgraphic Statue-ettes, 1943, 3-Dimensional and stand-up paper dolls of Marine, Soldier, Sailor, Nurse, WAAC, WAVE, boxed	12	20	25
Comet Model Airplane Co. Die Cut Glider, 5½x8" sheet containing die cut U.S. Army fighter printed in 1942 by the Comet Model Airplane Co.	3	5	7
Commando Machine Gun 1940s. Thin cardboard cut-out makes model over 25" long	10	15	20
Connie Francis, 1963, Whitman No. 1956	20	32	40
Coronation Cut-Out Model Book	30	55	60
Coronation Glitter Model Book	20	35	40
Coronation Paper Dolls and Coloring Book, 1953, Saalfield No. 4450, 10½x15" book. Queen Elizabeth, Prince Philip, young Prince Charles and Princess Ann	35	60	75
Cowboy and Cowgirl Cut-outs, 1950, Merrill No. 3449	15	25	30
Cowboy Cutouts Circa 1930s, Platt and Munk	15	25	30
Cowboys and Indians Cutouts, 1937, Saalfield	15	35	40
Cowgirl Jill and Cowboy Joe, Merrill, No. 3459	15	25	35
The Cradle Crowd, 1948, Four doll babies with cloth-like clothes, Whitman No. 1173	25	40	50

	C6	C8	C10
Cut and Stick - Our Army and Navy in Action, Merrill No. 4835, 1942	20	35	45
Cut-Me Out Paper Dolls, 1940s, Abbott No. 1358	8	10	15
Cut-Out Dolls, Puppies and Kittens, Whitman No. 931, 1939	25	45	55

162

CIRCUS DAY Cut-Out Book. Photo by Jonathan A. Newman. Courtesy Barbara and Jonathan Newman

	C6	C8	C10
Cut-Out Dolls with Paints and Clothes to Color, by Avis Mac, Whitman No. 983, circa 1930s 11x18" book with four 17" children and 16 pages of clothing and sheet of paints	35	60	70
Cyd Charisse 1956, Whitman No. 2084	30	45	55
Dancing Dolls with famous costumes, Merrill No. 3448, 1954, ballet dancers	18	30	35
Davy Crockett Punch Out Book, 1955, No. 1943	25	40	45
Deanna Durbin, 1940, Merrill No. 3480	150	175	200
Debs and Sub Debs Paper Doll Book, 1941, No. 2361 Saalfield, 20 Punchouts	20	30	40
Decalco-Litho Co. Paper Dolls Sheets. Circa 1920s, 8x10½" sheets, 1. Woman and girl and 9 outfits. 2. Woman and girl and 10 outfits. 3. Two women and 7 outfits. Price per sheet	6	10	12
Dennison's Crepe Paper Doll Outfit No. 36	55	90	125
Dennison's Dolls and Dresses No. 37, circa 1930	55	90	125
Diane and Daphne The Round About Dolls Book, 1937, No. 545 McLoughlin Bros. Large cut-outs by Campbell	35	55	65
Diana Lynn Paper Dolls, 1953, Saalfield, 157910	30	45	55
Dick the Sailor, circa 1942, Samuel Lowe No. L1074	15	25	30
Disneyland Park Punch Out, 1960, No. 175	20	35	40
Dodie From My Three Sons TV Series, 1971, Artcraft No. 5115, Dodie and Dolly	9	15	18
Dolls From Storyland by Vivian Robbins, 1948, Merrill 1554	15	25	35

	C6	C8	C10
Dolls That Walk - "They Walk - They Dance - They Play," designed by Emily Sprague Wurl, Whitman No. 977, 1939, two identical girls and two identical boys	30	60	75
Donna Reed Paper Dolls, 1960, Saalfield/Artcraft No. 5197, 9x12" boxed set	25	35	40
Doris Day, 1952, Whitman No. 210325	25	50	55
Dorothy Provine, 1962, Whitman No. 1964	25	35	40
Double Date Cut-Out Dolls by Eileen Fon Vaughan, 1949, Whitman No. 962	20	35	45
Double Wedding, 1939, Merrill 3472	45	75	90
Down On The Farm, 1940s, Lowe 1056	12	18	25

DOUBLE WEDDING 15 PAPER DOLLS

Courtesy Barbara and Jonathan Newman

DENISON'S CREPE PAPER DOLL OUTFIT No.36
Photo by Jonathan A. Newman

	C6	C8	C10
Dr. Kildare and Nurse Susan, early 1960s, Lowe No. 2740	15	25	30
Dress-Up Doll Book, The, 1953 Treasure Books No. T-167	7	12	15
Dress Up For The New York World's Fair by Judy and Barry Martin, Spertus No. 700, 1963	6	9	12
Dress-Up Paper Doll Cut-Outs 1947, Reuben Lilja & Co.	7	12	15
Drum Major and Majorette Paper Dolls, 1941, Merrill No. 3415	30	50	60
8 Ages of Judy, The, by Fern Bisil Peat, 1941, Lowe L1025, Judy as baby and ages 1-7	35	60	75
Elizabeth Taylor, 1950, Whitman No. 973-10	35	55	60
Eskimo Cut Outs by Milo Winter, 1939, Whitman 1054	12	20	25
Esther Williams, 1950, Merrill 1563, 3 dolls	45	75	80
Eve Arden Paper Dolls, 1953, Saalfield 158510	25	45	50

163

FAIRY FOLK CUT-OUT PAPER DOLLS,
Little Bo-Peep.
Photo by Jonathan A. Newman
Courtesy Barbara and Jonathan Newman

**GRACE KELLY 2 CUT-OUT DOLLS
AND CLOTHES**
Photo by Jonathan A. Newman
Courtesy Barbara and Jonathan Newman

**GLENN MILLER MARION HUTTON
TURNABOUT DOLL BOOK**
Photo by Jonathan A. Newman
Courtesy Barbara and Jonathan Newman

	C6	C8	C10
Evelyn Rudy – Little Star of Screen and Television, 1958, Saalfield No. 1745	20	40	45
Fabulous High Fashion Models, 1958, Bonnie Brooks/ChildCraft No. 2776	8	12	15
Fairy Folk Cut-Out Paper Dolls by Margaret Carlson, Still & Edwards Co., Inc., 1920s	12	20	25
Family Princess Paper Dolls, 1958, Merrill No. 1548	25	45	55
Family Affair, 1968, Whitman No. 4767	9	15	18
Family of Paper Dolls, 1947, Saalfield 2564	20	30	40
Family of Paper Dolls by Queen Holden, Whitman No. 991,, Mother, Father, Nurse, 6 kids	50	75	90
Farm Cut-Outs by Milo Winter, 1938, Whitman No. 1054, 6½x10½", six pages of heavy paper cut-outs	12	20	25
The Fashion Book of The Round About Dolls, 1936, McLoughlin Bros. Over an inch thick, eight stand-up dolls plus scissors and pack of paper dolls clothes in package by Betty Campbell	35	60	75
Fashion Cut-Outs with Sturdibilt Dolls, 1940s, Lowe No. 1243	12	18	25
Fifteen ABC Blocks to Play and Learn, 1933, Whitman No. 976, book containing 15 die-cut blocks to put together. Illustrations of nursery rhymes, alphabet letters, animals and numbers on each block	15	20	30

	C6	C8	C10
Fire Fighters in Action, Saalfield, 1938	20	45	50
Fire House P-18 by Megow, 1945, Brick firehouse. Boxed set	12	20	25
Five Little Peppers, Little Women and Annie Laurie, 1941, Lowe L1030, 3-book set	25.00	37.50	50.00
The Flying Nun, 1968, 1969, Artcraft No. 4417	10	18	20
Four Sisters Paper Dolls, 1943, Saalfield No. 269	12	20	25
Fourteen Dogs To Cut Out and Stand Up, Copyright 1930, Whitman, No. 935, 12 pages of dogs, cardboard punchouts	12	20	25
French Infantry – Milton Bradley? circa 1915, approx. 6" high. Single figure, each cardboard	2	4	5
Frontier Fort, 1952, Merrill No. 257225	7	12	15
Fun Farm, Reed and Associates	6	10	12
Gene Autry Melody Ranch Cut-Out Dolls, 1950, Whitman No. 990-10	35	65	75
Gene Autry Ranch cut-out book, 1940, Merrill	32	55	65
Gene Autry Ranch cut-out book, 1953	30	50	60
Gigi Perreau Paper Dolls, 1951, Saalfield 1542	20	40	45
Gigi Perreau, 1951, Saalfield No. 2605	20	40	45
Girl Friend - Boy Friend Paper Dolls, 1955, Saalfield, No. 1605	9	12	18
Girl Friends paper dolls, 1944, Whitman No. 974	12	20	25
Girl Pilots of the Ferry Command, 1943, Merrill 4852	50	75	90
Girls In Uniform Paper Dolls Book, circa 1942 No. L1048	22	40	45

	C6	C8	C10
Glamour Parade Cut-Out Dolls, Stephens Publishing Co., No. 184, 1950s? Four models and four pages of clothes	5	8	10
Glenn Miller, Marion Hutton Turnabout Doll Book, 1942, Lowe No. 21041	85	125	150
Gloria Jean Paper Doll Cut-Outs, 1940, Saalfield No. 1661	35	60	70
Gone With The Wind, 1940, Merrill No. 3404, 18 dolls	275	325	375
Gone With The Wind, 1940, Merrill, 3405, 5 dolls	250	300	350
Good Neighbor Paper Dolls, 1944, Saalfield No. 2487	12	20	25
Grace Kelly 2 Cut-Out Dolls and Clothes No. 2049 Whitman, 1955	30	50	60
Grace Kelly, 1956, Whitman No. 2069	28	45	55
Gulliver's Travels No. 1261 cut-outs, 1939, Saalfield	25	45	55
Hair-Do Dolls by Queen Holden, 1948, Whitman 991	35	60	70
Harry The Soldier, 1941, Samuel Lowe No. L1074	15	25	30
Hayley Mills, "The Moonspinners," 1964, Whitman No. 1960	12	20	25
Heavy Cruiser "This Is The Navy," circa 1943, Skyline Mfg. Co.	10	15	20
Hee Haw, 1971, Artcraft No. 5139	6	10	12
Heidi and Peter, circa 1970, Saalfield No. 1355	5	8	10
Here Comes The Bride, 1952, Whitman No. 118915	15	22	25
Here's The Bride, 1953, Whitman No. 2109	12	18	22
High School Girls, 1948, Merrill No. 1551	30	50	60
Historical Dolls To Cut Out And Dress, 1961, Platt & Munk No. 226B, 7"x11" boxed set. Mother, father, and two children of heavy cardboard, plus outfits	8	12	15
Holiday Paper Dolls, 1950s, Saalfield No. 1742	6	10	12
Hollywood Fashion Dolls 1939, Saalfield No. 397, 12 male and female dolls, clothes	28	45	55
Hollywood Fashions, 1949, Saalfield No. 1535	10	18	22
Hour of Charm Paper Dolls, 1943, women musicians, Saalfield No. 2481	35	65	75
House For Sale, 1962, Lowe No. 9042	15	25	30
House That Jack Built, circa 1895, Bliss, R.I. Paper litho, house and story's characters with stands	300	500	600

HOUSE FOR SALE.
Photo by Jonathan A. Newman
Courtesy Barbara and Jonathan Newman

LITTLE MARY MIXUP AND HER FRIEND PEGGY.
Photo by Jonathan Newman
Courtesy Barbara and Jonathan Newman

JAUNTY JUNIORS.
Photo by Jonathan A. Newman
Courtesy Barbara and Jonathan Newman

JUNE BRIDE.
Photo by Jonathan A. Newman
Courtesy Barbara and Jonathan Newman

	C6	C8	C10
Howdy Doody Puppet Show Punch-out Book Copyright 1952, Whitman No. 211129, Punchout cardboard puppets may be controlled by strings. Includes Howdy, Bluster, Inspector, Dilly Dally, Clarabell and Flubadub	25	45	50
Howdy Doody Sticker Fun, copyright 1951, Whitman No. 219525	9	15	18
Howdy Doody Sticker Fun, copyright 1953, Whitman No. 215825	9	15	18
Howdy Doody Sticker Fun Circus, copyright 1955, Whitman No. 2165	9	15	18
I Love Lucy - Lucille Ball and Desi Arnaz, 1953, Whitman No. 2101	25	50	55
Jack and Jill, 1962, Merrill No. 1561, 6 dolls and clothes from storyland	9	15	18
Jane Russell, 1955, Saalfield No. 2611	35	65	75
Janet Leigh Cutouts and Coloring Books, 1953, Merrill No. 2554	30	50	60
Janet Leigh, 1958, Abbott No. 1805	25	40	45
Jaunty Juniors, 1946, No. 903	12	20	25
Jean and Joan And Their Friends, Round About Dolls designed by Betty Campbell, 1934, boxed set, Milton Bradley No. 4396	50	65	100

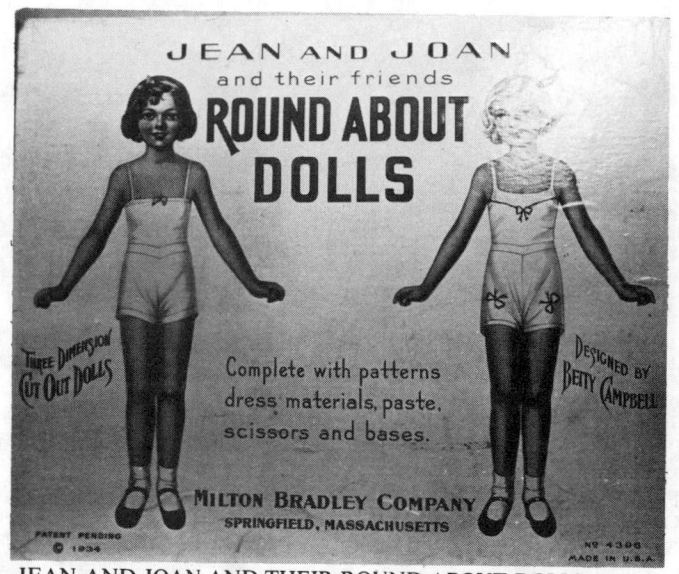

JEAN AND JOAN AND THEIR ROUND ABOUT DOLLS
Photo by Jonathan A. Newman
Courtesy Barbara and Jonathan Newman

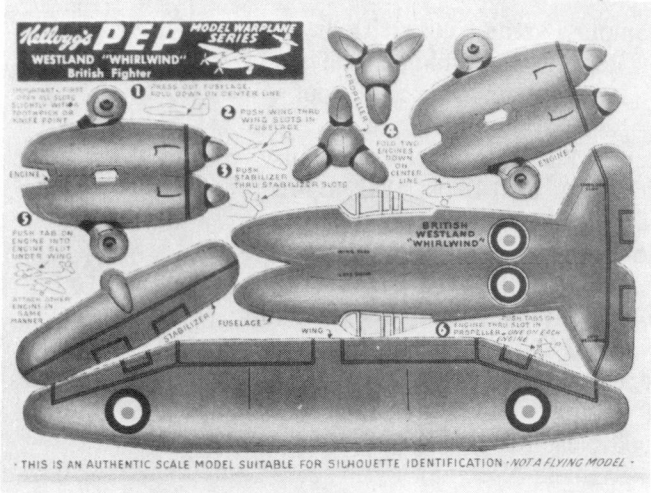

KELLOGG'S PEP Warplane, cardboard, circa 1944.
Courtesy HAKE'S Americana & Collectibles

	C6	C8	C10
Jeanette MacDonald, 1941, Merrill 3640	110	175	190
Jimmy & Jane Visit Gene Autry At Melody Ranch, 1951, Whitman No. 118415	30	55	65
Joan's Wedding by Florence Sarah Winship, clothes designed by Ruth M. Ruhman, 1942, Whitman No. 990	18	30	40
Judy and Jack/Peg & Bill Cut-Out Dolls by Pelagie Doane, 1940, Lowe No. L1024	20	35	40
"Julia" - Diahann Carroll, Julia, Corey, Marie and Earl J. Waggedorn, 1968, Artcraft No. 5140	12	20	25
Julia with Julia, Earl J. Waggedorn and Corey, 1969, Saalfield	12	20	25
June Allyson, 1950, 1952, Whitman No. 119015	25	45	55
June Allyson, 1953, Whitman 1173:15	25	45	55
June Bride by Art Tanchon, 1946, Stephens No. 136	9	18	20
Junior Bombardier, 1953, Einson & Freeman Co. No. 202	12.50	18.75	25.00
Junior Prom by Newman, 1942, Lowe 1042	14	22	28
Karen Goes To College! 1955, Merrill No. 1564	12	20	25
Kiddieland Village circa 1935, Whitman No. 2004, 11½"x15" boxed set, nine buildings and 65 cut-out figures	45	75	90
Kitty Goes To Kindergarten, 1956, Merrill No. 1548	12	20	25
Lennon Sisters, 1957, Whitman No. 1979	15	25	30
Lennon Sisters, 1961, Whitman, No. 1983	14	22	28

	C6	C8	C10
Lettie Lane Paper Family – Third Series, 1909, George W. Jacobs & Co. Original house folder and six sheets	110	150	170
Liberty Belles Paper Doll Book, 1943, No. 3477, Merrill	30	55	60
Little Ballerina, 1953, Merrill No. 154215	22	45	50
Little Ballet Dancers, 1950s? Saalfield No. 1743	6	10	12
Little Brothers and Sisters, 1953, Whitman No. 971:10, Tim, Kay Ann and Pete	6	10	12
Little Folks Friends, 1915, Saalfield No. 156	7	12	15
Little Friends From History by Muriel Wilhoite, Rand McNally No. 186, 1936	30	55	60
Little Friends Paper Dolls, 1950s, Saalfield No. 1746	6	10	12
Little Miss America Paper Doll Book, 1941, Saalfield No. 2358, 15 punchouts by Campbell	18	30	35
Little Nurse Cut-Out Book, early 1940s, Reuben H. Lilja and Co., Inc. No. 909	8	12	15
Little Red School House Kindergarten, The, by Margo Voight, McLoughlin Bros., 1940, 2 teachers, 23 children	30	55	60
Little Women, circa 1970, Artcraft No. 5127	7	12	15
Lois and Joan Cut-out Dolls, 1941, 1945, Whitman No. 1015 (Joan also appears in Betty & Joan and Lois & Joan)	9	15	18
The Lone Ranger Rides Again punch-out set, DeJournette Mfg. Co., makes fences, figures of LR and Tonto, horses, campfire	17	30	35

KIDDIELAND VILLAGE.
Photo by Jonathan A. Newman
Courtesy Barbara and Jonathan Newman

LITTLE FOLKS' FRIENDS
Photo by Jonathan A. Newman
Courtesy Barbara and Jonathan Newman

LITTLE FRIENDS FROM HISTORY
Photo by Jonathan Newman
Courtesy Barbara and Jonathan Newman

LOTS OF LITTLE PAPER DOLLS
Photo by Jonathan A. Newman
Courtesy Barbara and Jonathan Newman

	C6	C8	C10
Lots Of Little Paper Dolls by Angela Tuite Price, 1949, Saalfield No. 1537	12	20	25
Lucille Ball, Desi Arnaz Cut-Out Dolls With Little Ricky, 1953, Whitman 2116:25	22	40	45
Lucille Ball Paper Dolls, 1944, Saalfield 2475	45	75	90
Madame Hattie Fashions, 1940s, Reuben Lilja 908	17	30	35
Magic Mary, 1955, Milton Bradley No. 4010-1, 10½"x10½" boxed set, complete with magnetic doll and strips to put on clothes	7	12	15
Make Your Own Battle Set Mechanized Force, 1942, Electric Corporation of America	17.50	26.25	35.00
Marge and Gower Champion, 1959, Whitman	27	50	55
Martha Hyer Paper Dolls, 1958, Saalfield 4423	23	40	45
Mary and Joan, 1941, 1945, Whitman No. 1015 (Joan also appears in Lois & Joan and Betty & Joan)	9	15	18
Mary Belle Cut Out Doll by Fern Bisel Peat, Saalfield No. 2100, four separate sheets, 17" doll with three sheets of clothes, 1934	30	50	60
Mary Jane – A Cut Out Doll, by Florence Winship, 1939, 1941, Whitman No. 1010 with suitcase for accessories	22	40	45
Mary Lee – A Cut Out Doll Whitman No. 1010, circa 1939	17	30	35
Mary Martin, 1942, Saalfield 2427	90	150	175
Mary of the WACS – A Young American, by Hilda Miloche and Wilma Kane, Whitman No. 1012, 1943	25	45	50
Mary Poppins, 1973, Whitman No. 1977	9	15	18
Marybelle Mercer's Front and Back Dolls With Wrap-Around Dresses by Queen Holden No. 978	35	70	75

LUCILLE BALL DESI ARNAZ CUT-OUT DOLLS WITH LITTLE RICKY
Photo by Jonathan A. Newman
Courtesy Barbara and Jonathan Newman

THE LETTIE LANE PAPER FAMILY
Photo by Jonathan A. Newman
Courtesy Barbara and Jonathan Newman

	C6	C8	C10
Look-Alike Cut-Out Dolls, 1952, Whitman No. 97210, two mother and daughter pairs of dolls	8	12	15
Look Who I Am! 1952, Hart Publishing Co. by Doris Stelberg, 18" doll with 15 costumes. Spiral bound	7	12	15
Lori Martin in National Velvet 1962, Whitman No. 4612, 6"x11½" boxed set, paper dolls	11	20	22
Lost Horizon, 1973, Artcraft No. 5112	9	15	18

McLOUGHLIN BROS. OF BROOKLYN, NEW YORK

McLoughlin Brothers was the largest American producer of paper soldiers, and one of the earliest in the paper doll field. The firm, which traced its founding to 1828, began producing paper dolls at least as early as 1857. Among the other paper toys it sold were dollhouse furniture, toy theatres with actors and scenery, and blocks. The company was sold in 1920 to Milton Bradley.

	C6	C8	C10
McLoughlin Bros., circa 1884, mounted U.S. Cavalry, Hussar type, charging, several different poses. Price per figure	1.75	3.00	3.50
McLoughlin Bros. Infantry soldiers, printed 1857, price per each $5, complete set $150-175			
McLoughlin Bros., Infantry circa 1875, price per each	3.00	4.00	5.00
McLoughlin Bros., Zouaves, 1884, price per each	1.75	3.00	3.50
McLoughlin Bros. Brass Band, 1890, price per each	2.00	3.50	4.00
McLoughlin Bros. Grenadiers, 1890, price per each	1.75	3.00	3.50
McLoughlin Bros. Paper Dolls 1860-1890, price per cut set, $50 and up; uncut $100 and up, depending on title, date, etc.			
McLoughlin Bros. 100 Soldiers on Parade circa 1898	250	350	400
McLoughlin Bros. 100 Soldiers on Parade, second set, circa 1898	250	350	400
McLoughlin Bros. 260 series, circa 1889-1895; c. U.S. Regulars, spiked helmet, each			
d. U.S. Infantry	1.50	2.50	3.00
e. Mounted U.S. Cavalry, hussar type, charging	1.50	2.50	3.00
f. West Point Cadets	1.50	2.50	3.00
g. U.S. Regulars	1.50	2.50	3.00
h. U.S. Infantry	1.50	2.50	3.00
i. Bandsmen, various instruments, each	1.50	2.50	3.00
j. Navy – USS Boston	1.50	2.50	3.00
k. Grenadier Guards, each	1.50	2.50	3.00
l. Anapolis Cadets, each	1.50	2.50	3.00
McLoughlin Bros. Printed 1898, sailor 5¼" high, landing party for USS Texas	3.00	5.00	6.00
McLoughlin Bros. U.S. Infantry from Spanish-American War circa 1898. Approx. 6" high on wooden blocks. Price per figure	3.00	5.00	6.00
McLoughlin Bros. Circa 1898, small glossy series, 4½" high, West Point Cadets. Price per figure	2.50	4.00	5.00
McLoughlin Bros. Circa 1898, glossy series, g. U.S. Regulars, full dress, 5" high	2.50	4.00	5.00
McLoughlin Bros. circa 1898, British Infantry red coats, spiked helmets, 6" high on small wooden blocks. Price per figure	3.00	5.00	6.00

	C6	C8	C10
McLoughlin Bros. circa 1898, U.S. Zouaves, Civil War era, blue coats, red baggy trousers, 6" high on small wooden blocks	3.00	5.00	6.00
McLoughlin Bros. "02" series, circa 1905-1910 a. British Highlanders b. U.S. Zouaves c. U.S. Continentals d. U.S. Navy e. U.S. Infantry in Campaign Uniforms (Spanish American War) h. American Indians, kneeling and standing i. West Point Cadets. Price per figure	1.50	2.50	3.00
McLoughlin Bros. Same as above. g. West Point Cadets (round base), circa 1915	1.50	2.50	3.00
McLoughlin Bros. No. 0103 Dutch Paper Doll, boy of the Village of Vollendam. Circa 1910, 10½x10½" sheet	12	22	25
McLoughlin Bros. Circa 1915. Boy Scouts holding rifles across chests	3.50	5.00	6.00
McLoughlin Bros. Series No. 4026 10½x10½" Paper soldiers on sheet, seven soldiers plus officer (5½" high) in field uniform. Circa 1916. 1. Belgium. 2. France. 3. Italy. 4. Britain. Price per sheet	15	25	30
McLoughlin Bros. New Folding Doll House, 1897, boxed set, cardboard with lithographed paper	250	400	500
McLoughlin Bros. New Pretty Village – Church set 1897	60	90	120
McLoughlin Bros. New Pretty Village School Set, 1897	60	90	120
McLoughlin Bros. New Pretty Village, individual bldgs	9	15	18
Me and Mimi, 1957, A Bonnie Story Book Doll, 6"x8" in the style of the Little Golden Books. A Doll and Her Dolly Story Book, plus dolls and their dresses	12	20	25
Mexican Cut Outs by Milo Winter, 1938, Whitman 1054, six pages of people, animals, houses, etc	12	20	25
Mickey and Minnie Paper Dolls, 1930s 2 10" figures with clothes	90	150	175
Model Airplanes, Samuel Lowe No. 1069, 1941, WW II airplanes, international	35	65	75
Model Battleship by Reed, circa 1945, 7x10"	9	18	20
Model Flat-Top by Reed, circa 1945	9	18	20
Model Tanks, Samuel Lowe No. 1065, 1941	32	60	65

	C6	C8	C10
Model Tanks Construction Set, boxed set, 1942, Lowe No. 1267	35	65	70
Model War Planes Construction Set, boxed set, 1942, Lowe No. 1266 .	35	65	70
Modern Miss in Paper Dolls, 1942, by Van Swearingen, Saalfield 2397 ..	22	40	45
Molly Bee, 1962, Whitman No. 2091	12	20	25
Mommy and Me, 1954, Whitman No. 977:10.	8	12	15
Mother And Daughter by Patrie Winston, Grinnel Lithographic No. C-1005, 15" mother, 11" daughter, 2 Scotties, 1940	22	40	45
Mouseketeer Cut Outs, 1957, Whitman No. 1974	12	20	25
Movie Starlets, 1946, Whitman No. 960, Gail Russell, Diana Lynn, Olga San Juan, Marjorie Reynolds, Joan Caulfield	45	75	90
Movie Starlets Paper Dolls, circa 1949, Stephens Publishing Co. No. 178. Four dolls – Miss Premiere, Miss Stardust, Miss Hollywood, Miss Preview and four pages of costumes	10	18	20

McLOUGHLIN BROS. 100 SOLDIERS ON PARADE, Boxed Set
Photo by Jonathan A. Newman
Courtesy Barbara and Jonathan Newman

	C6	C8	C10
Mrs. Beasley Paper Doll Book, 1970 ("Family Affair" TV show) Whitman No. 1973	6	10	12
My Fair Lady, 1965, Ottenheimer Publishers No. 2960-2, by Evon Hartmann	15	25	30
My Paper Doll's Sewing Kit, 1940, by Margot Voight, Grinnell C-1018 .	22	40	45
My Twin Babies With Older Brother and Sister, 1940, Whitman 970 ..	22	40	45
My Very First Paper Doll Book, 1957, A Bonnie Book No. 4732, Samuel Lowe	6	10	12
Nancy and Her Dolls With Seven Busy Days of Fun, 1944, Saalfield No. 2478	20	40	45
Nanny And The Professor, 1971, Artcraft No. 5114	10	18	20
National Velvet, 1961, Whitman No. 1958	15	25	30
Navy Scouts Paper Doll Book, 1942, Merrill No. 3428	45	75	90
New Shirley Temple In Paper Dolls, The, 1942, Saalfield No. 2425 ...	90	150	175
New York World's Fair Make A Model, 1963, by Ottenheimer. Spertus No. 600-50. Includes Unisphere, Swiss Ride, N.Y. Port Authority, Heliport, etc.	10	20	25
Night Before Christmas With Cutouts Whitman No. 948	8	15	18
19 Farmyard Animals To Cut Out And Stand Up – Copyright 1930, Whitman No. 935, 12 pages	15	25	30
Oklahoma With Shirley Jones and Gordon MacRae, 1956, Whitman No. 1954	28	50	55
On Guard, 1942, Lowe No. L535 ...	25	40	45

McLOUGHLIN BROS. THE NEW PRETTY VILLAGE
Photo by Jonathan A. Newman
Courtesy Barbara and Jonathan Newman

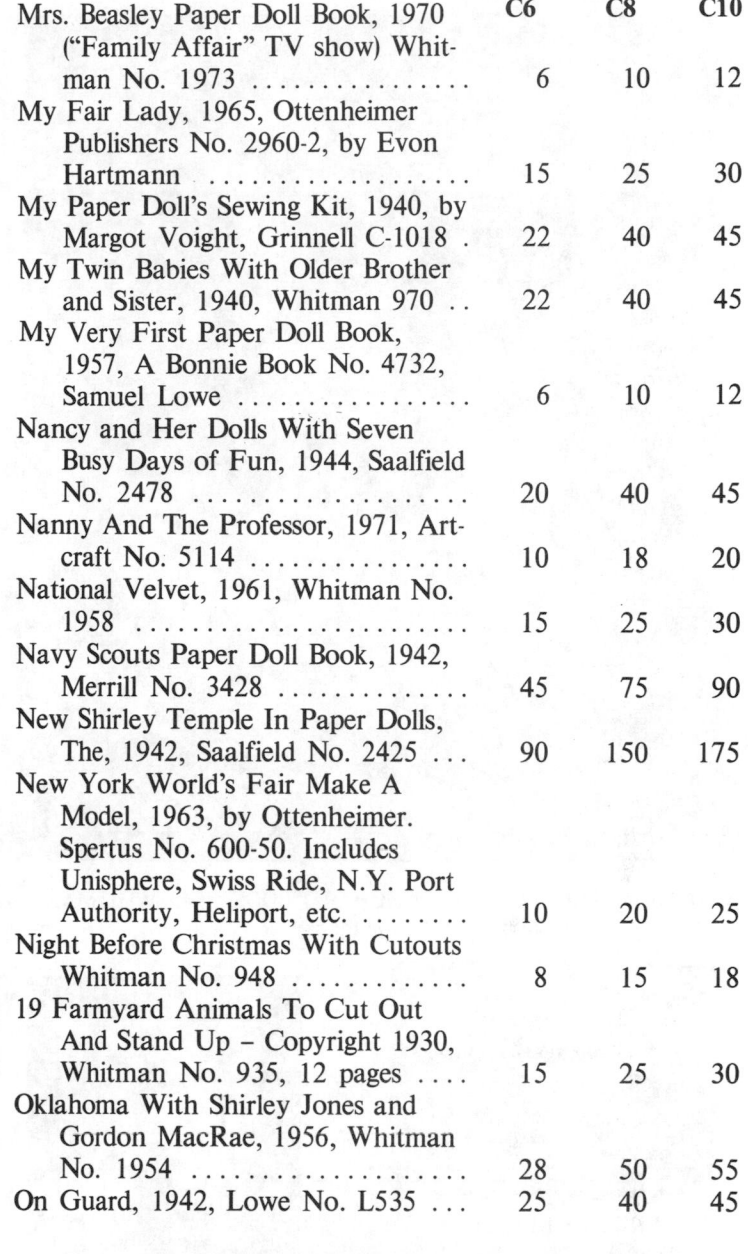

McLOUGHLIN BROS. Building from New Pretty Village
Photo by Jonathan A. Newman
Courtesy Barbara and Jonathan Newman

ONE HUNDRED SOLDIERS PUNCH-OUT BOOK, 1943, WHITMAN
999   Courtesy John D. (Jack) Matthews

MODEL TANKS CONSTRUCTION KIT
Photo by Jonathan A. Newman
Courtesy Barbara and Jonathan Newman

MODEL WAR PLANES CONSTRUCTION KIT
Photo by Jonathan A. Newman
Courtesy Barbara and Jonathan Newman

Make Your Own Battle Set
Mechanized Force
Photo by Jonathan A. Newman
Courtesy Barbara and Jonathan
Newman

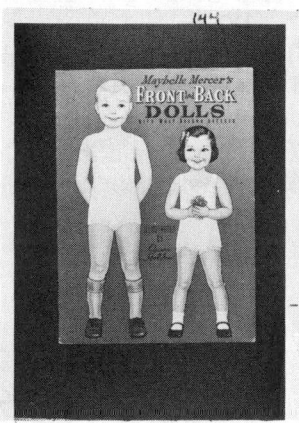

MAYBELLE   MERCER'S
FRONT AND BACK DOLLS
Photo by Jonathan A. Newman
Courtesy Barbara and Jonathan
Newman

	C6	C8	C10
One Hundred Soldiers Punchout Book, 1943, Whitman 999	27	50	55
Our Happy Family Cut-Out Sheets, 1928, Sam'l Gabriel Sons Co. No. D141	45	75	90
Our New Home, 1930, story by Susan S. Popper, pictures by Helen E. Ohrenschall, Sam'l Gabriel Sons, hardcover book, 6 pages of rooms, 6 gummed pages of people, furniture, etc.	60	100	125

	C6	C8	C10
Our Nurse Nancy – A Young American, by Hilda Miloche and Wilma Kane, 1943, cutouts, Whitman No. 1012	24	45	48
Our Sailor Bob, 10" doll with uniforms, Whitman, circa 1943 ..	15	25	30
Our Soldier Jim, 1943, Whitman No. 3980, designed by Hilda Miloche and Wilma Kane, 10½" standup doll with uniforms	15	25	30
Our Soldiers Cut Out Army Uniforms by Nat Falk, Dell, 1941, 4 cutout dolls and several uniforms	25	45	50
Our Wave Joan – A Young American, by Hilda Miloche and Wilma Kane, 1943, Whitman No. 1012	24	45	48
Outdoor Paper Dolls, 1941, Saalfield No. 1958, fourteen dolls and four pages of clothes	8	15	18
Over 80 Turn-About, Stand-Up Sailors, 1943, Lowe No. 141	25	40	45

OUR HAPPY FAMILY CUT-OUT SHEETS
Photo by Jonathan A. Newman
Courtesy Barbara and Jonathan Newman

OUR SOLDIERS CUT OUT ARMY UNIFORMS
Photo by Jonathan A. Newman
Courtesy Barbara and Jonathan Newman

OVER 80 TURN-ABOUT STAND-UP SOLDIERS
Photo by Jonathan A. Newman
Courtesy Barbara and Jonathan Newman

ON GUARD A PUNCH OUT BOOK
Photo by Jonathan A. Newman
Courtesy Barbara and Jonathan Newman

	C6	C8	C10
Over 80 Turn-About Stand-Up Soldiers, 1943, Lowe No. 140 ...	25	40	45
Paper Doll Family And Their House by Florence and Margaret Hoopes, 1934, Saalfield No. 4125.	35	70	75
Paper Doll Family And Their Trailer, Merrill No. 3436, 1938	50	80	90
Paper Doll "Joan" and Paper Doll "Bobby" by Queen Holden, 1928, Whitman 907	40	75	80
Paper Doll Outfit, American Toy Works No. 102, boxed set	40	60	75
Paper Doll Playmates, 1940, Saalfield No. 154, nurse, 19 children, costumes, toys	25	45	48
Paper Dolls From Mother Goose, 1957, Saalfield No. 2758, Mary, Bo-Peep, Boy Blue, Bobbie Shaftoe, Miss Muffett, Jack Horner ..	8	12	15
Paper Dolls Julia and Maria by Angela Tuite Price, 1958, Saalfield No. 1530	9	15	18
Paper Dolls Of All Nations - New York World's Fair, 1939, Saalfield, No. 227	25	45	48
Paper Dolls Of Eve Arden, 1956, Saalfield 1706	25	45	50
Paper Dolls Peter and Peggy, 1935, Whitman No. 965, 64 pages by Dixon. Very large punchouts on front and back	25	45	50
Paper Dolls To Cut Out And Paint, 1920s, Saalfield No. 1180	35	65	75
Paper Dolls - United We Stand by Margot Voight, Saalfield No. 113, 6 children with uniforms	24	45	48
The Partridge Family, 1971, Artcraft No. 5137	6	10	12
Partridge Family, 1972, Artcraft No. 5143	6	10	12
Pat Boone, 1959, Whitman No. 1968	15	25	30
Pat Crowley, 1955, Whitman No. 2050	22	42	45

MODEL AIRPLANES.
Photo by Jonathan A. Newman. Courtesy Barbara and Jonathan Newman

MODEL TANKS.
Photo by Jonathan A. Newman
Courtesy Barbara and Jonathan Newman

NEW SHIRLEY TEMPLE IN PAPER DOLLS.
Photo by Jonathan A. Newman
Courtesy Barbara and Jonathan Newman

	C6	C8	C10
Patience And Prudence, 1958, Lowe No. 2736 (Popular singers of the 1950s)	9	15	18
Patsy, 1946, Children's Press, No. 30002, Patsy, dog, doghouse, etc..	15	25	30
Patsy A Wooden Doll With Dresses (actually a 10" standup cardboard doll with wood backing) circa 1938, Whitman 3037	20	35	40

PAPER DOLL FAMILY AND
THEIR TRAILER
Photo by Jonathan A. Newman
Courtesy Barbara and Jonathan
Newman

PAPER DOLL OUTFIT
DRESSES AND HATS

Photo by Jonathan A. Newman
Courtesy Barbara and Jonathan
Newman

PILOT AND STEWARDESS
AIRLINER PAPER DOLLS
Photo by Jonathan A. Newman
Courtesy Barbara and Jonathan
Newman

PLAYHOUSE PAPER DOLLS
by Doris and Marion Henderson
Photo by Jonathan A. Newman
Courtesy Barbara and Jonathan
Newman

PAPER DOLLS TO CUT OUT
AND PAINT
Photo by Jonathan A. Newman
Courtesy Barbara and Jonathan
Newman

PAPER DOLLS JULIA MARIE
Photo by Jonathan A. Newman
Courtesy Barbara and Jonathan
Newman

PLAYHOUSE PAPER DOLLS.
Photo by Jonathan A. Newman
Courtesy Barbara and Jonathan
Newman

PAPER DOLLS OF ALL NA-
TIONS NEW YORK WORLD'S
FAIR, 1939.
Photo by Jonathan A. Newman
Courtesy Barbara and Jonathan
Newman

	C6	C8	C10
Patsy Ann And Her Trunk Full of Clothes by Queen Holden, 1939, Whitman No. 992	35	70	75
Patti Page 1958 book of paper dolls .	25	50	55
Patty's Party Paper Dolls, circa 1950, Stephens Publishing Co. No. 175	6	10	12
Pert And Pretty, 1948, Merrill No. 1552	25	45	50
Peter And Peggy, 1950, Whitman No. 99210	6	10	12
Peter And Peggy, Jerry And Joan Paper Dolls by Rachel Taft Dixon, 1935, Whitman No. 985	30	55	60
Photo Fashions, 1953, Whitman No. 973	6	10	12
Pig Tails, 1949, Merrill No. 344410 .	20	40	45
Pilot And Stewardess Paper Doll Book No. 3423, 1941, Merrill	25	45	50
The Pink Wedding, 1952, Merrill No. 1559	30	50	60
Piper Laurie, 1953, Merrill No. 2551	25	45	50
Playhouse Dolls 1949, Stephens Publishing Co. No. 1965. Four dolls and four pages of clothes . .	6	10	12

	C6	C8	C10
Playhouse Paper Dolls designed by Doris and Marion Henderson, Lowe No. 1028, 1941	17	30	35
Playhouse Paper Dolls, 1947, Saalfield No. 381	7	12	15
Playmates, 1952, Whitman No. 99510	6	10	12
Playthings To Cut Out And Stand Up, circa 1935, Whitman No. 934. Contains ventroliquist's dummy, floating ships, general's hat, lantern, animals, other moving toys	15	25	30
Play Time, 1952, Whitman 210525 . .	6	10	12
Playtime Pals, 1946, Lowe No. 1045	9	15	18

	C6	C8	C10
Polly Patchwork And Her Friends by Pelagie Doane, 1941, Lowe No. 1024	15	25	30
Polyanna Cut-Out Dolls, 1941, Whitman 995	28	50	55
Popular Paper Dolls, 1942, Saalfield No. 1973	15	25	30
Portrait Girls With Cloth-Like Clothes, 1947, designed by Hilda Miloche and Wilma Kane, Whitman No. 1170	20	35	40
Power Models Cut Out Dolls Book, 1942, Whitman No. 981, six dolls	23	40	45
Pressed Board Dolls And Their Dresses, boxed set, Lowe No. 1942	15	25	30
Pre-Teen Paper Dolls circa 1960s, Saalfield No. 1366	5	8	10
Prince And Princess Paper Dolls, 1949, Saalfield No. 2706	10	18	20
Prom Time, 1962, Whitman No. 2084, 2 dolls and party clothes	5	8	10
Queen Holden! Queen Holden! Betty and Bob, 1952, 12½" high children, Whitman 99110	30	55	60
Queen Holden! Queen Holden! Hair-Do Dolls, 1948, 3 dolls, clothes and 31 different hair-dos, Whitman No. 991	40	75	80

	C6	C8	C10
Quiz Kids Paper Dolls, 1942, Saalfield 2430	65	100	125
Raggedy Ann And Andy, 1953, by Ethel Hays, Saalfield 2719	16	24	32
Raggedy Ann And Andy Paper Dolls, 1944, Saalfield No. 2719-15	25	45	50
Raggedy Ann And Andy Paper Dolls, 1944, Saalfield No. 2741 by Ethel Hays	22	40	45
Raggedy Ann And Andy, 1968, Whitman No. 4740	9	15	18
"Rap-A-Jap," circa 1943, Woodburn Mfg. No. C1	25	45	50
Ready Cut Village, 1930s, no mfg. listed	45	75	90
Ricky Nelson paper dolls, 1959	25	40	45
Riders Of The West Paper Dolls, 1950, Saalfield No. 2716-15	8	12	15
Rigby's Book of Model Ships, 1953	45	75	90
Rigby's Easy To Build Models Of Fighting Planes	50	90	100
Rigby's Easier To Build Models Of Naval Craft, 24 models of warships, 27 pages, 11½"x14", designed by Wallace Rigby, 1944, includes Battleship North Carolina, aircraft carrier, cruiser, destroyer, etc	60	100	125

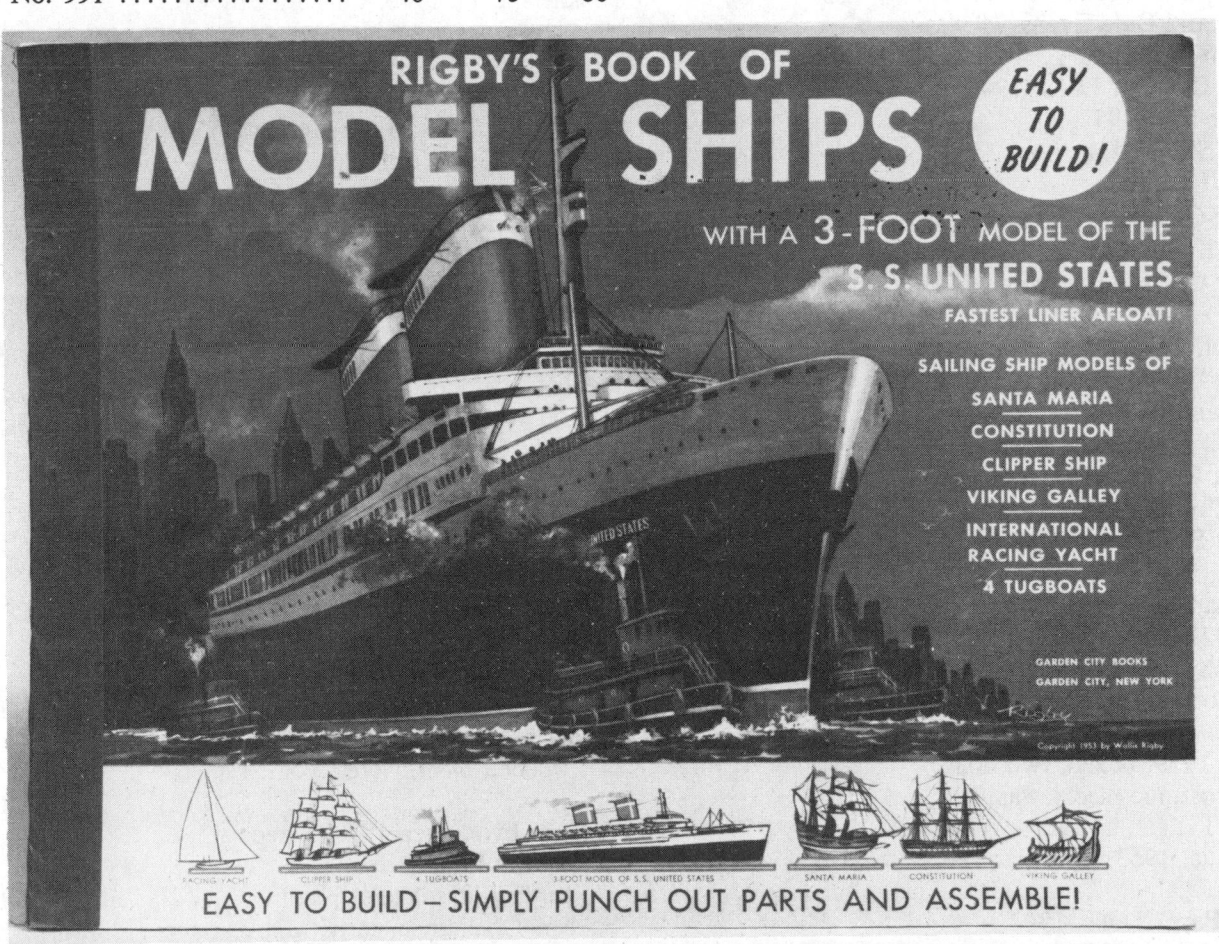

RIGBY'S Book of Model Ships. Courtesy Mapes Auctioneers & Appraisers.

	C6	C8	C10
Rigby Flying Models of Jet and Rocket Planes, ten planes, 1949, Garden City Books	45	75	90
Rigby's Model Book of Flying Clippers, 11"x14" book designed by Wallace Rigby, two scale models of Douglas DC-Jet Clipper and Douglas DC-7C, 1947	25	55	75
Rigby's Model Sports Cars of the World, 1954, includes 18" "sports-racer," Chevette, Jaguar, Mercedes-Benz, etc.	25	55	75
Robin Hood And Maid Marian, 1950s, Saalfield, No. 1761, paper dolls	9	15	18
Rock Hudson Paper Dolls, 1957, Whitman No. 2087	25	40	45
Rosemary Clooney, Samuel Lowe No. 1256	25	45	55
Rosemary Clooney, 1958, Samuel Lowe No. 2487	25	45	55
Rowan & Martin's Laugh-In Punch Out Paper Doll Book, 1969, Saalfield No. 1325, Rowan, Martin, Jo Ann Worley, Arte Johnson, Judy Carne and Goldie Hawn	10	20	22
Roy Rogers and Dale Evans, 1950, Whitman No. 1186	25	50	55
Roy Rogers and Dale Evans, 1954, Whitman No. 1950	25	50	55
Roy Rogers Cut Out Dolls, 1948, Whitman No. 995	30	55	60
Roy Rogers Sticker Fun Book, 1953, No. 2161	12	20	25
Royalty Cut-Out Books: A Procession Of The Knights Of The Garter	30	55	60
Royalty Cut-Out Books: Trooping The Colour	30	55	60
Ruth Newton's Cut Out Dolls and Animals "with over 80 pieces to cut out and play with," 1934, 11"x17"	35	65	75
Sally Ann A Cut Out Doll, circa 1940, Whitman No. 1010	20	35	40
Sally's Silver Skates, 1956, Merrill No. 1549	25	40	45
Sally The Standing Doll, 1940s, Lowe No. 1042	24	45	48
Sandra And Sue Statuette Dolls And Their Clothes, by Lee Lunzer, 1948, Whitman No. 1180	20	35	40
Sandra Dee, 1959, boxed, two dolls and 34 costume pieces, Saalfield No. 5511	25	50	55
Sandy and Sue, 1963, Whitman No. 1956	7	12	15
School Girl Paper Dolls, 1942, Saalfield No. 2400	17	30	35

	C6	C8	C10
Scissors Bird Paper Dolls, 1946, Stephens No. 137	7	12	15
Service Kit Of America's Armed Forces - On Land - On Sea - In The Air, 1942, Lowe No. 265	27	50	55
6 Good Little Dolls, no date, Stephens Publishing Co. No. 183	6	10	12
6 Movie Starlets, 1942, Anne Nagel, Peggy Moran, Jane Frazee, Anne Gwynne, Helen Parrish, Ann Gillis	90	150	175
Sharp Shooters, circa 1915, Milton Bradley No. 4103, boxed set with two sets of five cardboard soldiers and one officer on stands	60	90	125
Skating Party Paper Doll Book, 1941, No. 2328, Saalfield, 17 punchouts	20	35	40
Skating Stars, 1954, Whitman No. 2105	9	15	18
Smart Paper Dolls, 1940, Saalfield No. 1935	24	45	48
Smash The Axis, 1943, Electric Corp. of America	25	45	55
Snow White And The Seven Dwarfs Paper Dolls, 1938, 12"x17", Whitman No. 970	75	125	150
Snow White And The Seven Dwarfs, circa 1970, Whitman No. 1998	6	10	12
Soldiers, circa 1940, Concord Toy Co. boxed set contains 9 press-out soldiers, 3½" each, wooden cannon and ammunition	35	55	75
Soldier Set by J. Pressman and Co., Inc., New York. No. 1551, circa 1940, contains five cardboard soldiers, 4½" high and marbles	17	30	35
Soldiers, cardboard, approx. 6" high on wooden blocks, Navy, both officer and sailors circa 1920. Price per single figure	2	3	4
Soldiers, cardboard, approx. 6" high on wooden blocks. Sailor, U.S.	2	3	4
Soldiers, cardboard, approx. 6" high on wooden blocks. U.S. Infantry in campaign hats, mounted. Price per single figure	2	3	4
Soldiers, cardboard, approx. 6" high on wooden blocks. U.S. Infantry circa 1910, khaki uniforms with red trim. Officers, enlisted men. Price per single figure	2	3	4
Soldiers, cardboard approx. 6" high on wooden blocks, West Point Cadets	2	3	4
Soldiers Five, circa 1920, boxed set, Milton Bradley No. 4395, five cardboard soldiers, pistol	65	100	125
Soldiers On Parade, early, Milton Bradley No. 4518, set of 10	45	80	90

SERVICE KIT OF AMERICA'S ARMED FORCES ON LAND
ON SEA AND IN THE AIR
Photo by Jonathan A. Newman
Courtesy Barbara and Jonathan Newman

SOLDIERS FIVE WITH PISTOL
Photo by Jonathan A. Newman
Courtesy Barbara and Jonathan Newman

SHARPSHOOTERS, box and contents.
Photo by Jonathan A. Newman.
Courtesy Barbara and Jonathan Newman

SOLDIERS by Concord.
Photo by Jonathan A. Newman
Courtesy Barbara and Jonathan
Newman

STREAMLINE FLYER,
Photo by Jonathan A. Newman
Courtesy Barbara and Jonathan Newman

	C6	C8	C10
Spaceport, U.S.A. 1953, Whitman ...	8	10	15
Sports Time, 1952, Whitman No. 210525	6	10	12
Square Dance Paper Dolls, 1950, Saalfield No. 2717	9	15	18
Square Dance Paper Dolls, by J. Voelz, Lowe 968-10	6	10	12
Stage Door Canteen, 1943, Saalfield 2468	45	75	90
Stand-Up Dolls, Honey and Bunny, Merrill No. 3403, 1936	35	70	75
Statuette Dolls, 1943, Whitman No. 992, Two women	17	30	35
Statuette Dolls And Their Clothes, 1942, Whitman No. 998	17	30	35
Statuette Dolls And Their Clothes, 1946, Whitman No. 986, Two girls and a boy	17	30	35

	C6	C8	C10
Stencils Large and Small by Roy Best, circa 1935, No. 954 (Whitman?) folder of 30 animals to punch out and use as stencils. Comes with tiny box of crayons	12	20	25
Stock Farm Set, circa 1944, Concern No. 123, boxed 1200 die-cut pieces, including house, barn, silo, chicken house, tractor, etc.	20	45	55
The Story of Cinderella, A Fold-A-Way Toy Book designed by Will Pente. Circa 1925, Reilly & Britton Co.	9	15	18
Streamline Flyer, 10¾"x13½" boxed set, Concord Toy Co., No. 122, circa 1940. Contains engine, station, crossing gates, crossing signal, baggage truck, baggage and people	25	45	50
Style Shop Paper Dolls, 1943, Saalfield No. 1516	15	25	30
Sub-Deb Paper Dolls by Irving Nurick, 1941, Merrill No. 3408, 12 teenage boys and girls dolls, clothes	24	45	48

STATUETTE DOLLS AND
THEIR CLOTHES
Photo by Jonathan A. Newman
Courtesy Barbara and Jonathan
Newman

SALLY THE STANDING
DOLL

SUNSHINE CUT-OUTS
SPORTS SERIES - SPRING
Photo by Jonathan A Newman
Courtesy Barbara and Jonathan Newman

STAND-UP DOLLS HONEY
AND BUNNY
Photo by Jonathan A. Newman
Courtesy Barbara and Jonathan
Newman

	C6	C8	C10
Sue And Tom Cut-Out Dolls Book, The 1946, Lowe No. 149	12	20	25
Sunbonnet Sue, 1951, Whitman No. 2062-29	9	15	18
Sunshine Cut-Outs, Sports Series, Spring, by M&F Hoopes, 1926, 4-part foldout, Stoll & Edwards Co.	40	75	80
Susan Dey As Laurie ("Partridge Family" TV show), 1972, Artcraft, Fashions by Kate Greenaway	8	12	15
Sweetheart Paper Dolls, 1943, Saalfield No. 2458	22	40	45
Sweetie Pie Twins, 1949, Stephens Publishing Co. No. 166, Jane and Jean	7	12	15
Swing-A-Plane by J.L. Schilling Co., Model of a Flying Tiger, 1944, flies on string	7	12	15
Tammy, 1963, A Little Golden Story Book with paper dolls to cut out and dress. Illustrated by Ada Salvi	9	15	18
Tarzan Of The Apes, 1933 figure set	25	50	55
Teen Gal Cut Out Dolls, 1943, by Hilda Miloche and William Kane, Whitman No. 980	22	40	45
Teen Town, 1949, Merrill No. 3443 .	24	45	48
That Girl – Marlo Thomas, 1967, Saalfield No. 1351	11	18	22
That Girl – Marlo Thomas, 1967, Saalfield No. 1379	11	18	22
They Stand Up, by Avis Mac, 1939, Whitman No. 932, 13"x18" with five children	35	70	75
30 Toy Soldiers, circa 1943, Whitman No. 2950	25	45	50
This Is Bunny One Of The Five Cut-Out Dolly Sisters, 1939	24	45	48
This Is Dotty One Of The Five Cut-Out Dolly Sisters, Whitman, 1939	24	45	48
This Is Margie One Of The Five Cut-Out Dolly Sisters, Whitman, 1939	24	45	48

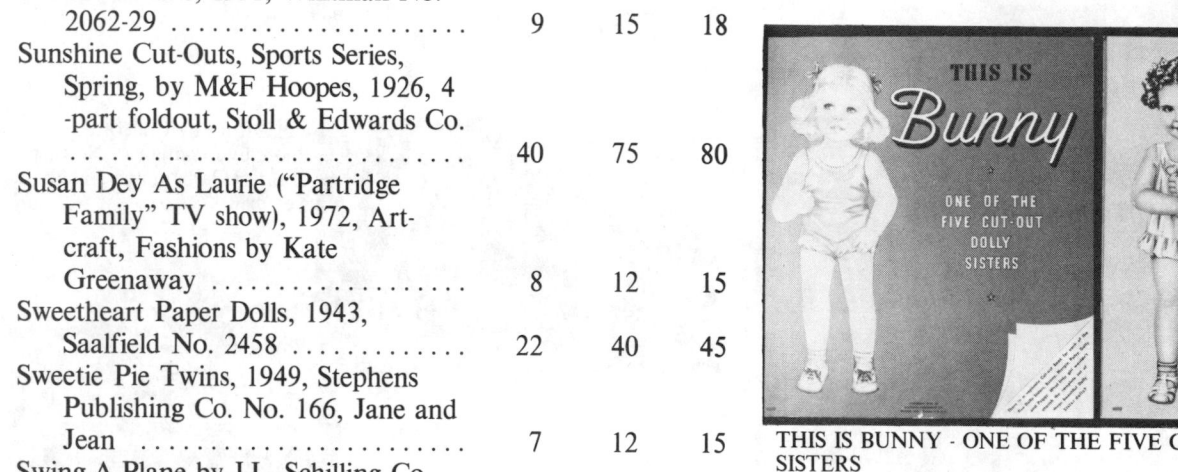

THIS IS BUNNY - ONE OF THE FIVE CUT-OUT DOLLY
SISTERS
THIS IS PATSY - ONE OF THE FIVE CUT-OUT DOLLY
SISTERS
Photo by Jonathan A. Newman
Courtesy Barbara and Jonathan Newman

	C6	C8	C10
This Is Patsy, One Of The Five Cut-Out Dolly Sisters, Whitman, 1939	24	45	48
This Is Peggy One Of The Five Cut-Out Dolly Sisters, Whitman No. 1002, 1939	24	45	48
This Is The Navy No. 500A Skyline Mfg., Destroyer and PT Boat, circa 1942	10	15	20
This Is The Navy No. 501 circa 1942, Skyline Mfg., Heavy Cruiser	10	15	20
Three Bears Cut Out Book, Copyright 1939, Whitman No. 1020, Goldilocks and 3 Bears	22	40	45
Three Flying Models of Famous Allied Fighting Planes by Judd Reed, 9"x12", contains Hell Cat, Spitfire and Stormovik planes. Included is "American Ace Spotter," with turning dial of 48 3-view silhouettes of 16 planes in little windows, 1944	20	35	40
Three Little Girls Who Grew And Grew And This Is How They Grew, 1945, Whitman No. 99410	18	35	38

TONI HAIR-DO
CUT-OUT DOLLS
Photo by Jonathan A.
Newman
Courtesy Barbara and
Jonathan Newman

	C6	C8	C10
Three Little Girls Who Grew And Grew and Grew And This Is How They Grew, with cloth-like clothes, flocked, 1945, Whitman No. 1176	18	35	38
Three Little Pigs Cut Out Book, Copyright 1939, Whitman No. 1020, Pigs and Big Bad Wolf	22	40	45
Three Sweet Baby Dolls To Cut Out And Dress, 1954, Whitman No. 975	7	12	15
Thrilltown Railroad, 1943, Reed, Pullman Passenger Set	45	80	90
Tiny Chatty Twins Paper Dolls, 1963, Whitman No. 1985	7	12	15
Toby Tyler Circus Playbook Punch Out, 1959, No. 1936	15	30	35
Tom Corbett Space Cadet Punch Out Book, 1952, Saalfield No. 4304, 14" long, 10½" wide	20	35	40
Tom The Aviator, circa 1942, Samuel Lowe No. L1074	15	25	30
Toni Hair-Do Cut-Out Dolls, Lowe No. 1284, 1950	25	45	50
Top Notch Paper Dolls, 1948, Saalfield No. 1504	17	28	35
Toy Models: Warplane and Tank Punchout, 1941, Fawcett Publications, Lowe	30	45	60
Toy Town, 1916, series of 50 different buildings by American Color Type Co. boxed set	65	100	125
Transfer Pictures, Copyright 1939, Whitman No. 1085, 100 decalcomanias	7.50	11.25	15.00
Treasure Hour Puppet Book, No. 4, 1968, Murray Sales and Service, The Rustlers of Rocky Ranch, a play of cowboys and Indians in five scenes. Cut-out section makes model theatre	12	20	25

	C6	C8	C10
Tricia, 1969, Artcraft No. 4248	12	20	25
Tricia Paper Dolls, 1970, Saalfield No. 1248, White House tour game, White House stand-up doll of Tricia Nixon and costumes	14	25	28
Trudy Phillips And Her Crowd, 1954, Whitman No. 2104	12	20	25
Tuesday Weld Paper Dolls, 1960, Saalfield No. 5112 boxed two dolls and 58 costume pieces	12	20	25
Turnabouts Dolls Book, The, 1940s, Lowe No. 1048, dolls printed front view on each side	24	45	48
TV Star Time Paper Dolls, circa 1950s, Abbott No. 1367	9	15	18
TV Tap Stars Paper Dolls, Lowe 99010	9	15	18
22 Animals To Cut Out And Stand Up, copyright 1930, Whitman, No. 935, rabbits, bears, owls, squirrels, etc.	15	30	35
Twiggy Paper Doll, 1967, Whitman No. 1999, with "plastilon" Twiggy dress for small girls	12	20	25
Tyrone Power & Linda Darnell, 1941, Merrill No. 3438	90	175	195
Umbrella Girls, 1956, Merrill No. 2562, wrap-around dresses	24	45	48
Uncle Sam's Little Helpers Paper Dolls by Ann Kovach, 1943, Saalfield 2450	22	40	44
United States Soldiers, 1942, Samuel Lowe No. L1063	25	45	50
U.S. Commandos Book, 1943, Lowe No. 1089	25	45	50
U.S. Infantry – Spanish American War, approx. 6" high soldier on small wooden block	2	3	4
Victory Girls - Arlene The Airline Hostess, circa 1940s, Lowe	22	40	45

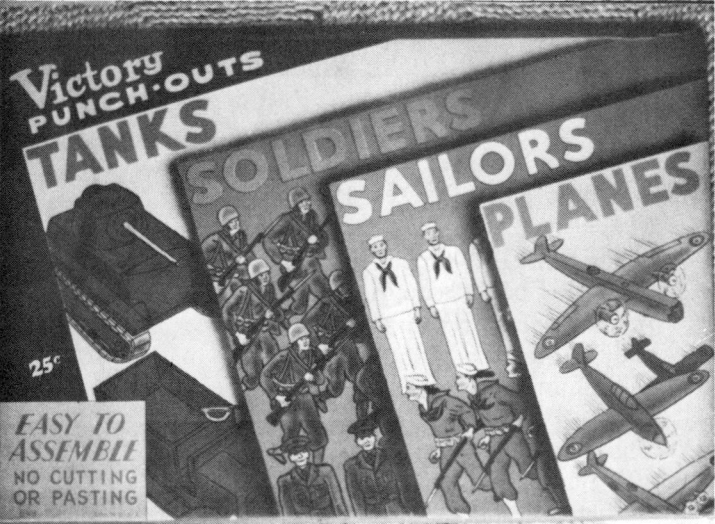

VICTORY PUNCH-OUTS TANKS SOLDIERS SAILORS
PLANES
Photo by Jonathan A. Newman
Courtesy Barbara and Jonathan Newman

	C6	C8	C10
Victory Punch-Out Tanks, Soldiers, Sailors, Planes circa 1943, Lowe No. 848	30	50	55
Victory Volunteers, 1942, dolls with uniforms by Merlin, Merrill No. 3424	45	75	90
Virginia Mayo, 1957, Saalfield, No. 4422	25	50	55
WACS And WAVES, 1943, Whitman No. 985	27	50	55
Walking Paper Doll Family No. 1074, Saalfield 1934	38	70	75
Walt Disney's Babes in Toyland 1961, Golden Punch-Out Book No. 10363	15	25	30
Walt Disney's Jane And Michael From Mary Poppins, 1963, Watkins / Strathmore 1892-6	9	15	18
Walt Disney's Let's Build Disneyland, 1957, Whitman No. 1986, forms sets for Adventureland, Frontierland, Tomorrowland and Fantasyland	15	25	30
Walt Disney's Mary Poppins, 1964, Whitman No. 1982	12	22	25
Walt Disney Match and Patch Sticker Fun, 1953, Whitman, Mickey Mouse, Donald Duck, Pluto, Goofy, etc	7	12	15
Walt Disney Presents Hayley Mills in That Darn Cat, 1965, Whitman No. 1955	12	20	25
Walt Disney Sticker Fun Book, 1951, Whitman	6	10	12
Walt Disney Sticker Fun With Peter Pan, 1952, Whitman	6	10	12
War Between The States, 1959, Golden Press No. GF152	25	40	45
War Plane Cut Outs, 1943, 10"x14", heavy stock, 8 different scale models	10	15	20
Wedding Paper Dolls, 1970, Whitman No. 1970	6	10	12
We're A Family Cut-Out Dolls, 1954, Whitman No. 1181	10	18	20
White House Party Dresses, 1961, Merrill No. 1550	17	30	35
Whitman No. 1146, little 3½"x7½" paper doll books, copyright 1939. A. Nancy and Tommy. B. Ann and Arthur. C. Kitty and Billy. D. Muriel and David. E. Cynthia and Bobby. F. Judy and Dick	30	50	60
Whitman Paper Doll Book, 1933, No. 3059, four dolls, ten sheets of clothes in folder	20	35	40
Winnie's New Wardrobe by Geraldine Cline, 1939, McLoughlin Bros. No. 555	17	30	35

	C6	C8	C10
Young Patriot Invasion Set, circa 1944, Colorgraphic No. 500, contains destroyer, amphibian tractor, tank, jeep, antitank gun, bomber and dive bomber, 10½"x13" boxed set	35	65	70
Young Patriot – Learn To Know Your Army, 1943, Colorgraphic No. 350, tank, howitzer, jeep, antitank gun, bomber, fighter and soldiers. Guns shoot, bombs drop, etc.	35	65	70
Young Patriot – Learn To Know Your Navy, 1943, Colorgraphic construction set No. 360, 10"x14" boxed set includes battleship, destroyer, aircraft carrier, mosquito boat, submarine, planes, depth charges, etc., with moveable parts	35	65	70
Ziegfeld Girl paper dolls, No. "1", 1941, Merrill No. 3466	150	175	200
Zoo Cut Outs by Milo Winter, 1938, Whitman No. 1054, six pages of heavy cut-out animals	12	25	30

TIN WIND-UP

(See also Movie, Comic Character, Disney)

The average mint price for tin wind-ups in the last edition was $163.55, and in this volume averages $346.22. an increase of 112%. Unlike most toys in this book, tin wind-ups do not "feel" particularly good in the hand, and depend more on the lure of motion and colorful lithography. Esthetically the most appealing, perhaps, are those of Lehmann, a Germany company which also patented a number of its toys in the United States, and which holds a strong attraction for a large number of collectors.

```
CONDITION CODE:
C5 – Good, wear evident overall, shows that has been played with
C6 – Fine, shows some wear in spots, but taken care of
C7 – Very Fine, minor wear overall, very clean
C8 – Excellent, minor wear on edges only
C9 – Near Mint, no noticeable flaws, close inspection may show
       minute marks
C10 – Mint (like new)
       Note: Mint in Box does command higher price
```

	C6	C8	C10
"Acrobatic Marvel" monkey on pole, with rocking base, circa 1937 ...	80	120	160
Aircraft Carrier, circa post WW II, tin litho, approx. 15" long, Japan ...	50	75	100
"Aircraft Carrier X53," with five jet planes, tin litho, circa 1950s	60	90	120

ANIMATE TOY CO.

In 1918 this firm was located at East 17th Street in New York City, and its president was L.T. Savage. By 1931 it has moved to 30 North 15th Street in East Orange, New Jersey, and employed ten men and forty women. In 1934 the president-vice president was George V. Turnbull and the secretary-treasurer was George H. Webb. Five men and eleven women made up the work force.

	C6	C8	C10
Animate Toy "U.S. Baby Tank," pat. 6/20/16, 2½" long, new in 1918 .	15.00	22.50	30.00
Automatic Toy Co. "Auto Speedway," circa 1930	50	75	100
Automatic Toy Co. Cross-Over Trolley Set	60	90	120
Automatic Toy Co. "Jungle Pete" No. 175, 15" long	50	75	100
Automatic Toy Co. "Mysterious Alpine Express," 1940s, 20" long, 14" wide, 2" high	60	90	120
Automatic Toy Co. "Rocket Space Ship," No. 305, 8½" long, sparks, 1940s	50	75	100

AUTOMATIC TOY COMPANY. Auto Speedway
Photo by Don Hultzman

Baby L. Racing Boat, 11" long.
Courtesy Lloyd W. Ralston Auctions

	C6	C8	C10
Automotive Toy Co., "Magic Crossroads" track, 2 wind-up cars, circa 1950	70	105	140
Baby L Racing Boat, 1930, 11" long, Lindstrom	100	150	200

	C6	C8	C10
"Barnum & Bailey," c. 1935, elephant pulling a four-wheeled cart loaded with a collapsible cage containing a camel, a monkey, a lion and a giraffe, each mounted on four wheels	150	225	300
Biplane, very early, Wright Bros.-like paper propellor blades, 6" long	400	600	800
Bird in Cage, 3½" high, German	60	90	120
Bird with flapping wings, 1930s, 6½" long, German	115.00	172.50	230
Black boy eating watermelon with dog biting his backside, 6½" high, Occ. Japan	210	315	420
Boy on St. Bernard on rocker, 6¾" long	150	225	300
Buffalo Bill, hand-painted, hand-soldered	250	375	500

Buffalo Toy Aero-Speeders

	C6	C8	C10
Buffalo Toys, "Aero Speeders," 1920s, carousel with 3 planes, screw-rod spring drive, 10" tall	120	180	240
Buffalo Toys, Dodgem Car	70	105	140
"The Cackling Hen of Paradise," 8" long, turn side handle and hen cackles; patented	30	45	60
"Cakewalk Dancers," short black man dancing with tall, heavy black woman	400	600	800
"Candy" cart driven by monkey in cap, also marked "candy," circa 1950s	40	60	80

	C6	C8	C10
Carousel with four biplanes and pilots, paper vanes, flag finial, 17" high, 1920s, German	1000	1500	2000
Carousel with four double horse and riders that alternate with four women in cars, velvet top with ball fringe, flag finial, 17" high	1300	1950	2600
Carousel with four men in canoes, propellors with paper vanes, 11" high	1200	1800	2400
Carter "Pan-Gee The Funny Dancer," 1920, 10" high	250	375	500
Cat pushing cage with two mice, 8¼" long	250	375	500

Caterpillar Tractor, "1916"
Photo by Bill Kaufman
Courtesy Good Old Days Store

	C6	C8	C10
Caterpillar Tractor, "1916," rubber treads, tin wind-up	100	150	200

CHEIN

Chein (pronounced "chain") was founded in 1903 by Julius Chein. The New Jersey company specialized in lithographed metal toys, the majority of them mechanical. In 1918 it was located at 310 Passaic Avenue, Harrison, New Jersey, with 250 employees. In 1934 it had 55 male and 92 female workers. In a 1946-47 directory it listed 148 male and 132 female employees. Chein made toys until 1979, and is still in business today in Burlington, New Jersey.

	C6	C8	C10
Chein Alligator with native on its back	100	150	200
Chein "Army Drummer," 1930s, plunger-activated, 7" high	100	150	200
Chein Barnacle Bill, looks like Popeye, 1930s	150	225	300
Chein "Barnacle Bill in a Barrel," 1930s, 7" high	200	300	400
Chein Bear with hat, pants, shirt, bow-tie, circa 1938	30	45	60
Chein "Ski-Boy," 8" long, 1930s	90	135	180
Chein Cabin Cruiser, 1940s, 9" long	15.00	22.50	30.00
Chein chick, brightly colored clothes and polka dot bowtie, 4" high	20	30	40

CHEIN "Barnacle Bill in a Barrel."
Courtesy PB Eighty-Four, New York

CHEIN Barnacle Bill.
Courtesy PB Eighty-Four, New York

CHEIN Bear with Hat
Courtesy Scott Smiles

Chein "Ferris Wheel" 1930's.

	C6	C8	C10
Chein Chicken pulling wheelbarrow, 6x3½", 1930s	30	45	60
Chein "Clown in Barrel," 1930s, 8" high	150	225	300
Chein Clown with umbrella	60	90	120
Chein "Dan-Dee Dump Truck"	200	300	400
Chein "Doughboy," 1920s, 6" high	150	225	300
Chein "Drummer Boy," 9" high, with shako, circa 1930s	110	165	220
Chein duck, 4" high, waddles, 1930	20	30	40
Chein duck, long-beaked, in orange sailor suit, not Donald Duck, but similar. Waddles, 6" high	40	60	80
Chein "Ferris Wheel," 16½" high, 6 compartments, ringing bell, 1930s	150	225	300
Chein Handstand Clown	50	75	100
Chein "Indian in Headdress," 1930s, 5½" high	40	60	80
Chein Marine, hand on belt	50	75	100
Chein "Mark 1" Cabin Cruiser, 8½" long, 1957	20	30	40
Chein "Mechanical Aquaplane" No. 39, boat-like pontoons, 1932, 8½" long, 7½" wingspan	110	165	220
Chein "Mechanical Aquaplane," post WW II	150	225	300
Chein "Mechanical Fish," 1940s, 11" long	40	60	80
Chein "Musical Aero Swing," 1940s, 10" high	110	165	220
Chein Pelican	20	30	40
Chein Penguin in tuxedo type jacket, circa 1940	20	30	40

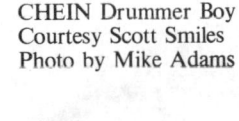

CHEIN Drummer Boy
Courtesy Scott Smiles
Photo by Mike Adams

CHEIN Duck
Courtesy Scott Smiles

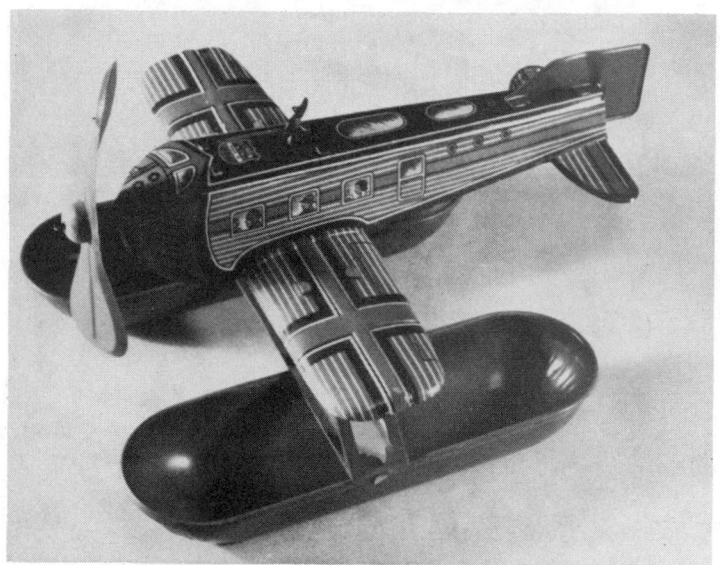

CHEIN Mechanical Aquaplane, 7½" wingspan
Courtesy Perry R. Eichor

	C6	C8	C10
Chein Pig	20	30	40
Chein "Playland Merry-Go-Round," 1930s, 9½" high	130	195	260
Chein "Playland Whip" No. 340, 4 bump cars, driver's head wobbles	150	225	300
Chein Rabbit in shirt and pants, circa 1938	20	30	40
Chein "Ride A Rocket" carnival ride, circa 1950s, 19"	200	300	400
Chein "Rocket Ride" No. 400, 18" high, base 11" diameter, 4 rockets	200	300	400
Chein "Roller Coaster," includes 2 cars, circa 1938	150	225	300
Chein "Roller Coaster," 1950s, includes 2 cars	130	195	260
Chein "Santa Elf," 1920s, 6" high ...	200	300	400
Chein Turtle with Native on back ...	120	180	240

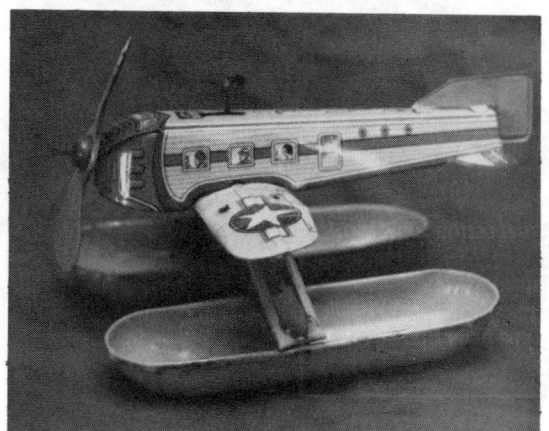

CHEIN "Mechanical Aquaplane," post WW II
Courtesy Calvin L. Chaussee

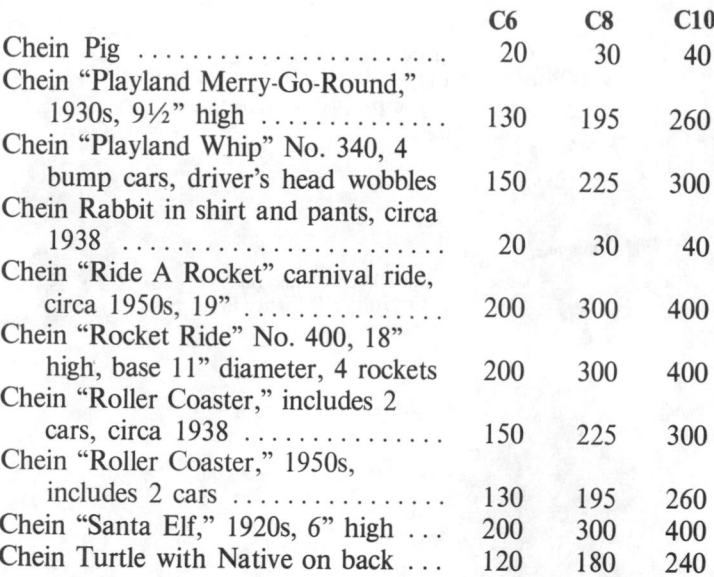

Chein "Roller Coaster" 1930s

CHEIN Penguin
Courtesy Scott Smiles
Photo by Mike Adams

CHEIN Pig
Courtesy Scott Smiles
Photo by Mike Adams

Chein "Roller Coaster" 1950's

	C6	C8	C10
Chicken pulling chick in cart, 7½" long, Wyandotte	40	60	80
Circus-type Trainer, baton in hand, revolves, with rooster on each side, 3½" long, musical, German	100	150	200
Clown in Donkey Cart, 7½" long ...	60	90	120
Clown in Hoop, 6½" high, Japan ...	150	225	300
Clown Musicians, four, on a pedestal, musical, 8" high	200	300	400

COURTLAND MFG. CO. - WALT REACH

(history based on information from Joe and Sharon Freed)

Walter Reach, owner of Courtland, had a burning desire to be known as the second Louis Marx. Also functioning as designer, he began production in 1944 with two die-cut cardboard toys (a rabbit and cart and horse and cart). Reach turned to tin litho toys after the war, a number of them non-wind-ups. At its height, Courtland, located first in Camden, New Jersey, and later in Philadelphia, had 600 workers and in 1947 its sales exceeded 1.5 million. But success was short-lived, and the firm lasted just seven years.

COURTLAND TOYS BY WALT REACH

List by Joe and Sharon Freed

	C6	C8	C10
No. 15 Mechanical Lawn Mower, 8¼"wide, 24" high, 3" wheels. 1950 retail price 79¢. 1951 retail - 98¢	20	30	45
No. 20 Mechanical Lawn Mower, 11¼" wide, 29" high, 5" wheels, 1950 retail - $1.29; 1951 retail - $1.49	25	35	50
No. 21 Mechanical Lawn Mower, 12" wide, 29" high, 5" wheels, 1951 retail - $1.98	30	45	70
No. 25 Mechanical Power Lawn Mower, 12" wide, 29" high, 5¾" wheels, 1951 retail - $2.98	50	70	90
No. 200 Easter Rabbit and Trailer, 11⅝" long, 3" wide, 3½" high, 1946 retail - 49¢	15	20	25
No. 300 Circus Elephant and "Monkeys" Cart, 11⅝" high, 3" wide, 3½" high, 1946 retail - 49¢	45	70	100
No. 400 Circus Elephant and "African Lions" Cart, 11⅝" long, 3" wide, 3½" high, 1946 retail - 49¢	45	70	100
No. 500 Circus Elephant and "Circus Band" Cart, 11⅝" long, 3" wide, 3½" high, 1946 retail - 49¢	60	85	125

COURTLAND VEHICLES
With Open Wind-Up Spring-Motors

	C6	C8	C10
No. 1070 Mechanical Big 4 Truck Parade, 9" long, 3" wide, 2¾" high, 1947 retail - $3.39	No Price Found		
No. 1200 Mechanical Trailer-Truck 13" long, 3" wide, 3¼" high, 1947 retail - $1.00	25	45	60
No. 1300 Mechanical Ice Cream Truck, 9" long, 3" wide, 2¾" high, retail - 79¢.	75	85	100
No. 1300 Mechanical Moving and Storage Truck, 9" long, 3" wide, 2¾" high, 1947 retail - 79¢. This truck is also reported to have No. 130 lithographed on the sides of the truck bed	75	95	110
No. 1300 Mechanical Fire Patrol No. 2 Truck, 9" long, 3" wide, 2¾" high, 1947 retail - 79¢	70	85	100
No. 1300 Mechanical Express and Hauling Truck, 9" long, 3" wide, 2¾" high, 1947 retail - 79¢	70	85	100
No. 1400 Mechanical "Automatic Ladder" Fire Truck, 9" long, 3" wide, 2¾" high, 1947 retail - $1.00	45	60	75
No. 1500 Mechanical Road Roller Truck, 9" long, 3" wide, 3¼" high	55	70	85
No. 1600 Mechanical Dump Truck, 7" long, 3" wide, 2¾" high	12	20	30
No. 2000 Mechanical "ESSO" Gasoline tractor-trailer, 13" long, 3" wide, 3¼" high			

Courtland Vehicles with "Motor Guaranteed For Life" Motor. (packed in individual boxes all with motor guarantee certificate)

COURTLAND Motor Guaranteed for Life No. 2000 Mechanical Gasoline tractor-trailer
Courtesy Joe and Sharon Freed

	C6	C8	C10
No. 2000 Mechanical Gasoline tractor-trailer, 13" long, 3" wide, 3¼" high	20	30	40

COURTLAND Motor Guaranteed For Life 2050 Mechanical Milk
Tractor-Trailer
Courtesy Joe and Sharon Freed

COURTLAND Motor Guaranteed For Life No. 2200 Mechanical Logging
tractor-trailer
Courtesy Joe and Sharon Freed

	C6	C8	C10
No. 2050 Mechanical Milk tractor-trailer, 13" long, 3" wide, 3¼" high, "American Dairies"	50	70	85

Note: 1951 catalog shows Milk trailer markings that read the same as above except 'Approved' is used in place of the words 'Vitamin D.' This variation is not known to have been produced.

COURTLAND Motor Guaranteed For Life No. 2100 Mechanical Hook and
Ladder tractor-trailer

COURTLAND Motor Guaranteed For Life No. 2150 Mechanical Emergency
Rescue Squad
Courtesy Joe and Sharon Freed

	C6	C8	C10
No. 2100 Mechanical Hook and Ladder tractor-trailer, 13" long, 3" wide, 3¼" high	25	35	45

	C6	C8	C10
No. 2150 Mechanical Emergency Rescue Squad tractor-trailer, 13", 3" wide, 3¼" high	25	35	45
No. 2200 Mechanical Logging tractor-trailer, 13" long, 3" wide, 3¼" high	25	35	45
No. 2250 Mechanical Logging Tractor-Trailer	25	35	45
No. 2300 Mechanical Open Van tractor-trailer, 13" long, 3" wide, 3¼" high	25	35	45
No. 2350 Mechanical Open Van tractor-trailer, 13" long, 3" wide, 3¼" high	25	35	45
No. 2375 Mechanical Heavy Duty Sand and Gravel tractor-trailer, 13" long, 3" wide, 3¼" high	25	35	45
No. 2400 Mechanical Trailer Tow Truck, 13" long, 3" wide, 3¼" high	25	35	45
No. 2600 Mechanical Freight Haulers tractor-trailer, 13" long, 3" high, 3¼" wide	25	35	45
No. 2700 Mechanical Side Tipper tractor-trailer, 13" long, 3" high, 3¼" wide	25	35	45
No. 2800 Assortment consists of 2 No. 2000 Gasoline Trucks, 2 No. 2050 Milk Trucks, 2 No. 2200 Log Trucks, 2 No. 2350 Open Van Trucks, 2 No. 2600 Freight Hauler Trucks and 2 No. 2700 Side Tipper Trucks - Wholesale Assortment Only..............	No Price Found		
No. 3000 Mechanical Road Roller Truck, 9" long, 3" wide, 3¼" high	45	60	75
No. 3100 Mechanical Dump Truck, 7" long, 3" wide, 3¼" high	15	25	35
No. 3200 Mechanical Stake Bed Truck, 7" long, 3" wide, 3¼" high	30	40	50
No. 3800 Assortment consists of 6 No. 3200 Stake Bed Trucks and 6 No. 3100 Dump Trucks - Wholesale Assortment Only	No Price Found		

	C6	C8	C10
No. 4000 City Meat Market Delivery Sedan, 7¼" long, 3¼" wide, 2¾" high	20	30	40
No. 4000 Modern Bakery Delivery Sedan, 7¼" long, 3¼" wide, 2¾" high	20	30	40
No. 4000 Fire Chief Car, 7¼" long, 3¼" wide, 2¾" high	20	30	40
No. 4000 Checker Cab Car, 7¼" long, 3¼" wide, 2¾" high	30	40	50
No. 4500 Express Service Pick-up, 7¼" long, 3¼" wide, 2¾" high .	20	25	35
No. 4500 Country Produce Pick-up, 7¼" long, 3¼" wide, 2¾" high .	20	25	35
No. 4500 Modern Decorators Pick-up, 7¼" long, 3¼" wide, 2¾" high .	20	25	35
No. 5000 Mechanical Operating No. 51 Crane Truck 13" long, 3⅝" wide, 5" high	45	60	75

COURTLAND "Motor Guaranteed For Life" No. 5100 "Black Diamond" Coal Truck
Courtesy Joe and Sharon Freed

	C6	C8	C10
No. 5100 Mechanical "Black Diamond" Coal Truck, 10½" long, 3" wide, 3⅜" high	45	60	75
No. 5200 Mechanical No. 51 Steam Shovel, 15½" long, 3¾" wide, 9½" high	25	35	45
No. 5300 Mechanical Combination Steam Shovel carried by low-boy tractor-trailer, 15½" long, 3⅞" wide, 10½" high	55	75	90

COURTLAND 5300
Photo by Joe Freed

	C6	C8	C10
No. 5800 Assortment consists of 3 No. 2300 Aluminum Open Van Trucks, 3 No. 2150 Emergency Rescue Squad Trucks, 3 No. 2375 Sand and Gravel Trucks and 3 No. 2400 Towing Service Trucks - Wholesale Assortment Only	No Price Found		
No. 6000 Mechanical Farm Tractor w/scraper, rear tires are large rubber and front are small rubber tires 8¾" long, 4¾" wide, 4½" high	30	37	45
No. 6050 Mechanical Farm Tractor w/o scraper. Rear tires are large rubber and front are small rubber tires, 7½" long, 4¾" wide, 4½" high	25	32	40
No. 6075 Mechanical Farm Tractor w/o scraper, rear tires are large tin litho while the front are small rubber tires, 7½" long, 4¾" wide, 4½" high	50	65	80
No. 6100 Mechanical Caterpillar Tractor with rubber treads, 6" long, 3" wide, 4½" high	55	70	85

COURTLAND Motor Guaranteed For Life No. 6500 Mechanical Ice Cream Scooter
Courtesy Joe and Sharon Freed

	C6	C8	C10
No. 6500 Mechanical Ice Cream Scooter, 6½" long, 3" wide, 4½" high	65	80	115
No. 7000 Mechanical Fire Chief Car with siren, 7¼" long, 3¼" wide, 2¾" high	25	35	45
No. 7500 Mechanical State Police Car with siren, 7¼" long, 3¼" wide, 2¾" high	25	35	45

	C6	C8	C10
No. 7500 Mechanical Parking Meter and Bank, Base 6"x6", 24½" high. Note: This is one of only four Courtland toys stamped "A Walt Reach Toy by Courtland Toy Co., Phila. Pa. Made in U.S.A." The only known Courtland styled toys marked with the Courtland Toy Company, Philadelphia stamping is this mechanical parking meter bank, a No. 4000 sedan, a non-power "Fire Chief" car, a private and a garage similar to No. 9075.	45	55	65
No. 8000 Mechanical "Rocking R Ranch" See-Saw, 17¾" long, 2⅛" wide, 6" high	20	30	40
No. 8500 Mechanical Chromed Trimmed Tow Truck, 8" long, 3¼" wide, 3½" high	30	40	50

END COURTLAND

	C6	C8	C10
Dancing dogs, two, and a boy with whip	200	300	400
Dancing horse, two small bells on top of bridle, 7½" high	100	150	200
Ferris Wheel carrying eight gondolas, the gondolas containing a total of 16 small bisque dolls, 33½" high	1200	1800	2400
Ferris Wheel, carved with figures and music box, 17"	400	600	800
Freight Cart pulled by man in cap, with luggage on cart, circa 1940 .	60	90	120

GIRARD Railroad Handcar
Courtesy Mapes Auctioneers & Appraisers

GIRARD Monoplane, high wing, one-engine, 1920.
Courtesy Lloyd W. Ralston Auctions

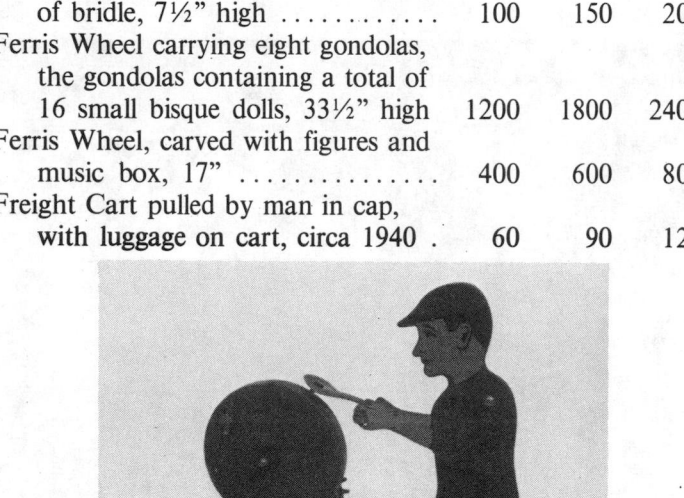

GIRARD "Flasho the Mechanical Grinder"
Courtesy Scott Smiles
Photo by Mike Adams

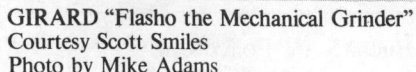

	C6	C8	C10
Girard Air Mail Biplane, 3-engine . . .	450	675	900
Girard bus with driver, 12½" long . . .	150	225	300
Girard Coupe, 1930s	200	300	400
Girard "Flasho The Mechanical Grinder," 1920s	120	180	240
Girard "Goble, The Gobbling Goose"	115	173	230
Girard Man pushing wheelbarrow, 5½"	60	90	120

	C6	C8	C10
Girard Monoplane, high wing, one engine, 1921-22, 13" long	150	225	300
Girard Railroad Handcar	70	105	140
"Ham and Sam," maker unknown, piano player and dancer	175	263	350
Hansom Cab, horse moves backward and forward as wheels rotate, driver atop cab, 5¾" long	100	150	200
Hy Line car, ultra-streamlined two-door coupe type, circa 1938	100	150	200
Hy-Lo, Buffalo Toys Ferris Wheel, 14½" high	150	225	300
Indian, like cigar store Indian, circa 1937	50	75	100

CONDITION CODE:
C5 – Good, wear evident overall, shows that has been played with
C6 – Fine, shows some wear in spots, but taken care of
C7 – Very Fine, minor wear overall, very clean
C8 – Excellent, minor wear on edges only
C9 – Near Mint, no noticeable flaws, close inspection may show minute marks
C10 – Mint (like new)
Note: Mint in Box does command higher price

"Ham and Sam" maker unknown, piano player and dancer
Courtesy Ed Hyers Antique Toys

IVES Destroyer, "3009". Courtesy PB Eighty-Four, New York

IVES Tugboat "King"
Courtesy PB 84 New York

	C6	C8	C10
Ives "Destroyer" "3009," 1923, painted, 9" long	400	600	800
Ives Submarine, 10½" long	300	450	600
Ives Tugboat "King"	150	225	300

	C6	C8	C10
Katz Toys NY "The Question Mark" airplane, 18" wingspan, high-wing, two motor	200	300	400
Kellerman "Armored Vehicle," 1930s, 4" long	45.00	67.50	90.00
Kingsbury Biplane, circa 1925, single engine, rubber wheels, 16" long	160	240	320
Kingsbury Convertible with rumble seat, electric headlamps, hard rubber wheels, 12½" long	150	225	300
Kingsbury fireman's ladder truck, hard rubber wheels, driver, 23½" long	150	225	300
Kingsbury Monoplane, high wing, single engine, wind-up wheels and spins prop via rubber band, 1930s, 11" long	250	375	500
Kingsbury Roadster, electric headlamps, 12½" long	250	375	500
Kingsbury Station Wagon, 1920s	150	225	300
Kingsbury "Streetcar," 1930s, No. 782, 9" long	70	105	140
Lehmann "Adam the Porter," 1920s, 9" high	650	975	1300
Lehmann "Ajax" Warrior with two clubs	1000	1500	2000
Lehmann "Alabama Coon Jigger"	300	450	600
Lehmann "Also"	225	338	450
Lehmann "Am Pol," Amundsen driving, figure behind with umbrella, map of North Pole	600	900	1200
Lehmann "Anxious Bride," chauffeur on tricycle, woman in car	800	1200	1600
Lehmann Balky Mule, 1930s, 7½" long	150	225	300
Lehmann "Bucking Bronco, Wild West," 6½" long	250	375	500
Lehmann "Climbing Miller," cardboard blades	300	450	600
Lehmann "Climbing Monkey," (Tom 385), 9" long, 1920s	200	300	400
Lehmann "Crawling Beetle, The", 1900s, 4" long	250	375	500
Lehmann "Dancing Sailor," 1920s, 7½" high	300	450	600
Lehmann "Daredevil" Zebra Cart	210	315	420
Lehmann "Duo"	500	750	1000
Lehmann "Express," porter pulling cart, circa 1927, 6" long	240	360	480
Lehmann "Galop" zebra cart	175	263	350
Lehmann, "Li La," early car with two excited women passengers, driver in top hat and dog with turning head, 5½" long	600	900	1200
Lehmann "Lu-Lu" bird	60	90	120
Lehmann "Masuyama," coolie pulling rickshaw	400	600	800
Lehmann "Mikado Family," 1920s, 6½" long	1500	2250	3000
Lehmann "Motor Coach," 1920s, 5½" long	200	300	400

187

Dancer, LEHMANN
Alabama Coon Jigger

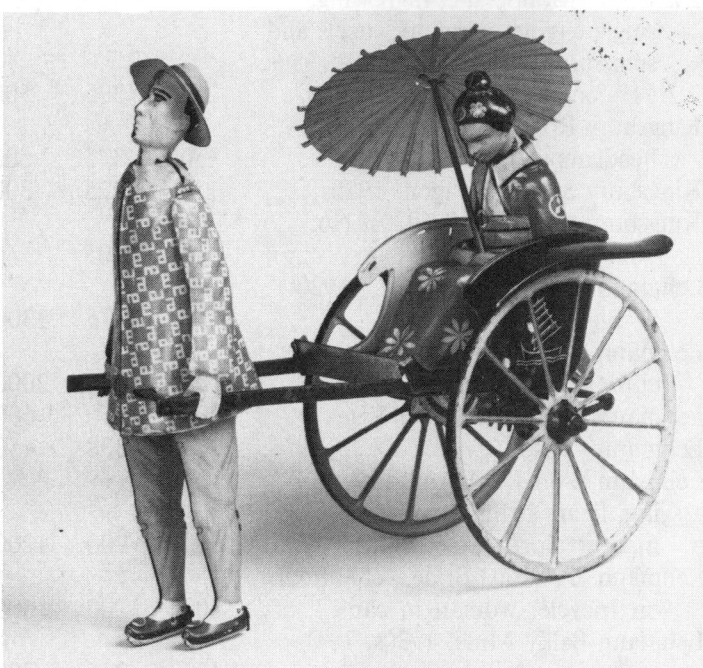

LEHMANN Masuyama
Courtesy Mapes Auctioneers & Appraisers

	C6	C8	C10
Lehmann "Naughty Boy"	600	900	1200
Lehmann "Na-Ob," man driving horse cart, wheels marked with elf, 6" long	350	525	700
Lehmann "Nu-Nu" No. 733, rickshaw with puller and rider, circa 1913, 4½" long	450	675	900
Lehmann "Oh My," 10" high	400	600	800
Lehmann "OHO" patented 1903	350	525	700
Lehmann "OnKel"	375	563	750
Lehmann "Paddy Pig" c. 1912, 6" long	400	600	800
Lehmann "Performing Sea Lion, The" 1900s, 7" long	200	300	400
Lehmann "Power Carriage"	300	450	600
Lehmann "Quack-Quack," mother duck pulling cart with three small ducks	200	300	400
Lehmann "Rad-Cycle," 5" long circa 1927	300	450	600
Lehmann "Rollo Chair"	500	750	1000
Lehmann Stubborn Donkey, clown in donkey cart, 7½" long	200	300	400

	C6	C8	C10
Lehmann Tap Tap, man pushing wheelbarrow	200	300	400
Lehmann "Tom" climbing monkey, 8" long	160	240	320
Lehmann "Tut-Tut," man in car with horn, 6¾" long	450	675	900
Lehmann Walking Couple	600	900	1200
Lehmann Walking Sailor, 7½" high	400	600	800
Lehmann "Zig Zag" patented 1903, 5" long	600	900	1200
Lehmann "Zulu," black man in cart pulled by ostrich	400	600	800
Lewco "See-Saw Circus"	60	90	120
Lindstrom Bird	60	90	120
Lindstrom "Betty," 1930s, 8" tall, shako walker	110	165	220
Lindstrom Bumper Car, 6½" long	100	150	200
Lindstrom "Dancing Lassie," 8" tall, shako, 1930s	110	165	220
Lindstrom "Delfine 7" motorboat, circa 1930	90	135	180
Lindstrom "Lindstrom's Ferry Boat," approx. 8¼", litho	90	135	180
Lindstrom "Lindstrom Flyer," 14" long	80	120	160
Lindstrom, "Mammy," 1930s, 8" tall, shako walker	150	225	300
Lindstrom "Miss America" speedboat	110	165	220
Lindstrom "Parcel Post No. 2" truck	200	300	400
Lindstrom Speedboat, circa 1950, 18½" long	130	195	260

Lindstrom Toys 1930's, Sweeping Mammy, Betty, Mammy (Shakos)

	C6	C8	C10
Lindstrom Sweeping Girl	110	165	220
Lindstrom "Sweeping Mammy," No. 1750, 1930s, 8" tall, shako walker while sweeping	200	300	400
Lupor Metal Products N.Y. Racer No. 8, 1930s	30	45	60

LOUIS MARX: By the 1950s, LOUIS MARX was the largest manufacturer of toys in the world; six large factories in the U.S., and ownership of interest in factories in seven other countries. Marx, born in Brooklyn in 1896, was working for "Toy King" Ferdinand Strauss when he was in his teens, and by the age of twenty his energy and enterprise had made him a director of that company. A falling out with Strauss persuaded him to go into business for himself, and in 1921 he and his brother began making their own toys, including some adaptations of items by the now-defunct Strauss. Marx's watchword seems to have been quality at the lowest possible price, and he was such a favorite with toy buyers that he had virtually no need for salesmen or advertising. Although Marx made virtually every type of toy with the exception of dolls, his tin wind-up toys are probably the most favored by toy collectors. Marx, in April, 1972, sold his company to the Quaker Oats Company, who in 1976 sold it to Europe's largest toy manufacturer, Dunbee-Combex-Marx. The company went into bankruptcy in 1980. Louis Marx died in 1982 at the age of 85.

	C6	C8	C10
Acrobatic Marvel, early	130	195	260
Acrobatic Marvel, late	120	180	240
Air Mail Biplane, 1930, 4-engine	160	240	320
Air Mail Monoplane, 1930, 2-engine .	155.00	232.50	310.00
Airplane, U.S. Army No. 6, 2-engine, no guns, 18" wingspan	100	150	200
Airplane No. 90, light fuselage	90	135	180
Airplane No. 90, medium fuselage ...	80	120	160
"American Tractor" with implements, 1920s, 10" long	150	225	300
"Ambulance" with siren, 1930s, 14½" long	150	225	300
Ambulance, "M.D. War Dept.," 1930s	130	195	260
"Army Dive Bomber" No. 482	120	180	240
Army Staff Car, 1930s, litho steel ...	200	300	400
"Army Staff Car," W-601158, with flasher and siren, 11" long, 1940s	210	315	420
Armored Trucking Co.	105.00	157.50	210.00

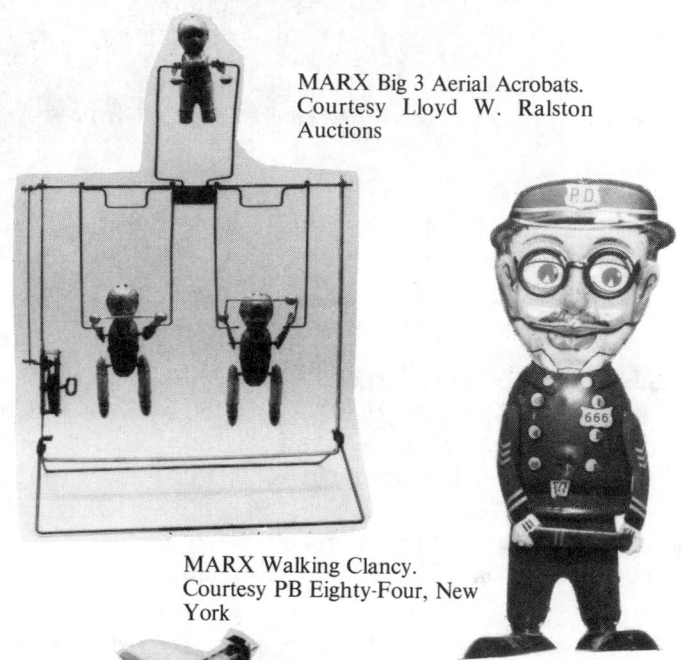

MARX Big 3 Aerial Acrobats. Courtesy Lloyd W. Ralston Auctions

MARX Walking Clancy. Courtesy PB Eighty-Four, New York

MARX Air Mail Biplane, 4-engine, 1930. Courtesy Lloyd W. Ralston Auctions

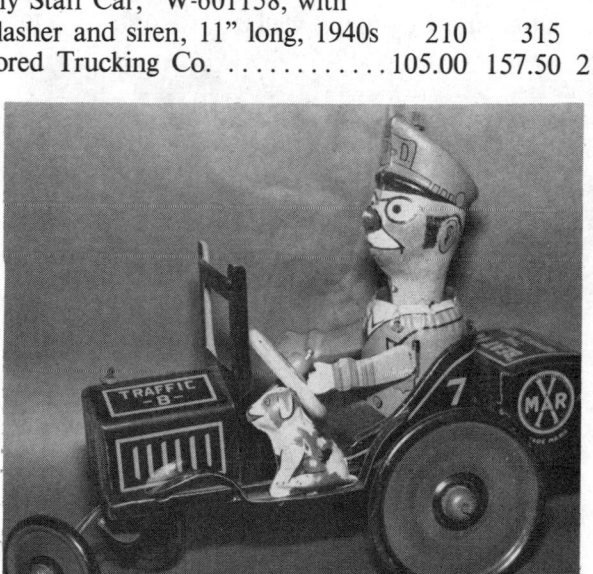

MARX "Beat It! The Komical Kop" Courtesy Ed Hyers Antique Toys

Balky Mule, pre-war	90	135	180
"Balky Mule," 1950s, 8" long	50	75	100
"Bear Cyclist," 1930s, 6" long	80	120	160
"Beat It" The Komikal Kop," 1930s ...	230	345	460
"Bi-Wing Airplane," 1930s, 18" wingspan	200	300	400
"Big Parade," moving vehicles, soldiers, tin airplane, etc., 1929, 24" long	300	450	600

MARX Balky Mule, post-War, with box Courtesy Scott Smiles. Photo by Mike Adams

MARX

MARX "Big Silver" Mack dump truck
Courtesy Ed Hyers Antique Toys

	C6	C8	C10		C6	C8	C10
"Big Silver," Mack Dump Truck	250	375	500	Bumper Auto, streamlined, circa 1939, large bumpers front and rear	90	135	180
Big Three Aerial Acrobats, 1920	160	240	320	"Busy Bridge," vehicles on bridge, 1935	300	450	600
Big Lizzie car, early 1930s, 7¼" long	150	225	300	"Busy Miners," 1930s, 16½" long, in-			
Bomber, two engine, 18" wingspan ..	90	135	180	cludes 2¼" tin litho miner's car .	150	225	300
Boy on Trapeze	80	120	160	"Butter & Egg Man," 1930s, 8" high	400	600	800
Bulldozer Climbing Tractor, caterpillar type, circa 1950s, 10½" long	80	120	160	"The Butter and Egg Man" walker ..	180	270	360

MARX "Busy Bridge"
Courtesy PB Eighty-Four New York

MARX Bulldozer Climbing Tractor
Courtesy Continental Hobby House

MARK "Ambulance" with siren
Courtesy Mapes Auctioneers & Appraisers

MARX "Royal Van Co."
Courtesy Mapes Auctioneers & Appraisers

MARX Cat with Ball
Courtesy Scott Smiles. Photo by Mike Adams

MARX Charleston Trio, one adult, child, dog
Courtesy Ed Hyers Antique Toys

	C6	C8	C10
Cadillac Roadster, 13" long, trunk with tools on luggage carrier, 1930	200	300	400
"Careful Johnnie," 1950s, 5½" long .	50	75	100
Cat with ball in front, two wheels in back, circa 1938	60	90	120
Caterpillar Climbing Tractor, circa 1950s, 10" long	60	90	120
"Charleston Trio," one black adult, dog, black kid dancer, 1921	400	600	800

	MARX		
	C6	C8	C10
Chicken Snatcher, black holding chicken, dog biting at the seat of his pants, circa 1927	450	675	900
Climbing Tractor, sparkling, 1960s, 8½" long	60	90	120
Climbing Tractor, late 20s, farm boy at wheel, detachable	70	105	140
"Climbing, Fighting Tank"	50	75	100
"Coast Defense," circular, with three cannon, revolving airplane, 1929 .	350	525	700
"Coke Coal City Coal Co." truck ...	250	375	500
"Coo Coo Car," 1920s, 7½" long ...	250	375	500
"Cowboy Rider," circa 1941, cowboy with lariat on dapple or black horse	140	210	280
Crazy Dora nodder head (also "Dan")	110	165	220
"Dapper Dan Coon Jigger," 1910 ...	260	390	520
Dare Devil Flyer, new in 1928	180	270	360
"Daredevil Motor Drome," 1930s, 5½" high, 9" diameter, 2" windup car	70	105	140
Donkey pulling cart, with rider, 1950s, 10" long	110	165	220
"Dottie the Driver," 1950s, 6½" long	50	75	100
Doughboy Tank, two side turrets, with top turret, 9¼" long, 1930, soldier with gun pops out	100	150	200

MARX Fireman
on Ladder
Courtesy Scott Smiles

	C6	C8	C10
"Fireman Joe," 8" tall, ladder 24" high, 1930s	200	300	400

MARX

	C6	C8	C10
"1st Batt. F.D. Chief's Car," 16", siren, battery headlights	110	165	220
"Flipo the Jumping Dog, See Me Jump," on hind legs, circa 1940, 3½x4"	90	135	180
"Flying Fortress 2905" sparkling aeroplane, 1940s, 4 engines	130	195	260
"Flying Helicopter Skyport," 1950s, 12x9"	70	105	140
"Funny Face," new in 1928	No Price Found		
"Funny Flivver" circa 1925	290	435	580

MARX G-Man Pursuit Car
Courtesy Gary Linden

MARX George the Drummer Boy with moving eyes
Courtesy Scott Smiles
Photo by Mike Adams

	C6	C8	C10
G-Man Pursuit Car, 1930s	200	300	400
"George the Drummer Boy," 1930s, 9" tall with moving eyes	110	165	220
"George the Drummer Boy," 1930s, 9" tall with stationary eyes	100	150	200
"Giant King Racer," circa 1930s, "711"	110	165	220
Giant Reversing Tractor Truck with tools, "Hauling," 14" long, circa 1950s	100	150	200
Golden Pecking Goose, 9½" long, dated July 8, 1924, hops along, pecking at ground	160	240	320

	C6	C8	C10
"Hee-Haw" balky mule, 1929, 10¾" long, six-color litho, goes backward, forward and rears, farmer and his dog on seat and 5 milk cans in cart	110	165	220
Highboy Climbing Tractor, circa 1950s, 10½" long	110	165	220
Highboy Tractor, sparkles, circa 1950s, 10" long	60	90	120
"Honeymoon Express," old-fashioned train on circular track, 1927	150	225	300

MARX "Honeymoon Express" circa late 1930s
Courtesy Phillips New York

	C6	C8	C10
"Honeymoon Express," circa late 1930s	140	210	280
"Honeymoon Express," circa 1940, circling train and plane, 9⅜" diameter	140	210	280
"Honeymoon Express," streamlined train on circular track, 1947, 9⅜" diameter	100	150	200
Jalopy Pickup Truck, 7"	60	90	120
"Jazzbo Jim," 1920s, 9" high	250	375	500
"Joy-Rider," 1929, 8" long, College Boy driver with bag, wording on car "goes backward, forward, circles and rears" head moves	130	195	260
Jumpin-' Jeep, circa WW II, 6"	80	120	160
"King Racer," 1920s	240	360	480
"Let The Drummer Boy Play," 1930s, 8½" high	150	225	300
"Limping Lizzie" car	180	270	360
"Looping Plane," No. 182	90	135	180
"Looping Plane," No. 382	90	135	180
Lucky Stunt Flyer	200	300	400
"Main Street," moving vehicles, traffic cop, etc., 1929	240	360	480
Mammy's Boy, eyes move, litho	170	255	340
"Mechanical Airplane," new in 1928	No Price Found		
"Mechanical Speedway Racer"	60	90	120
"Mechanical Tractor", 6" long, circa 1930s	90	135	180
Mechanical Tractor with Earth Grader, 21½" long, circa 1950s	100	150	200

MARX "Merrymakers" without marquee
Courtesy Phillips New York

MARX Motorcycle Policeman with side-car, "Police," "3"
Courtesy Phillips New York

	C6	C8	C10
Merrymakers, four mice, three in band, one a dancer, 1929, with marquee	600	900	1200
Same as above without marquee	500	750	1000
"Midget Climbing Fighting Tank," approx. 5½" long, circa 1935, Pat. No. 1,334,539	60	90	120
Midget Climbing Tractor, 5½" long, circa 1950	60	90	120

MARX "Midget Special"
Courtesy Scott Smiles

	C6	C8	C10
"Midget Special," race car - driver in old headgear and goggles, 5" long, No. 2 racer, 1930s	40	60	80
"Midget Special" race car driver in old headgear and goggles, 5" long No. 7 racer, 1930s	40	60	80
Minstrel figure, 11" high	160	240	320
"Monkey Cyclist," 1930s	75.00	112.50	150.00
"Moon Creature," 1950s, 5½" high (Japan)	120	180	240

MARX Mystic Motorcycle
Courtesy Scott Smiles   Photo by Mike Adams

	C6	C8	C10
Motorcycle Policeman with side-car "Police," "3" license plate reads "102D", approx. 8" long, 5¾" high, circa 1940	210	315	420
"Motorcycle Trooper," 1935	140	210	280
"Mountain Climber," 1960s (Japan), 32" long, 4" car	60	90	120
"Mysterious Kitty Kat," 1950s, 8" long	60	90	120
"Mystery Police Cycle," 1930s, 4½" long	80	120	160
Mystery Tunnel	60	90	120
"Mystic Motorcycle," circa 1930s	90	135	180
"New York," circular, with train, new in 1928	160	240	320
Nodding Goose	70	105	140

CONDITION CODE:
C5 – Good, wear evident overall, shows that has been played with
C6 – Fine, shows some wear in spots, but taken care of
C7 – Very Fine, minor wear overall, very clean
C8 – Excellent, minor wear on edges only
C9 – Near Mint, no noticeable flaws, close inspection may show minute marks
C10 – Mint (like new)
Note: Mint in Box does command higher price

MARX

MARX "Old Jalopy" large and small
Courtesy Ed Hyers Antique Toys

MARX "P.D." Police motorcycle w/sidecar.
Courtesy Gary Linden

	C6	C8	C10
"Old Jalopy"	130	195	260
"Old Jalopy," small	50	75	100
"P.D." Motorcyclist, "Pat. 2001625," approx. 4" long	90	135	180
"P.D." Police motorcycle w/side car, wood wheels, on-off lever, 1930s, 3½" long	100	150	200
"Parade Drummer," 1930s, "Let the Drummer Boy Play While You Swing and Sway"	300	450	600
"Parcel Post U.S. Mail," 8½" long, early	210	315	420
Peter Rabbit, eccentric car	60	90	120
"Piggy"	40	60	80
"Pinched" roadster, motorcycle cop in circular track, circa 1927, 9½"x9½"	380	570	760
"Play-Away-Piano," 1930s, 9x9", with songbook	40	60	80
"Police Patrol," motorcycle with sidecar, 1935	130	195	260
"Police Siren Motorcycle," 1930s, 8" long	150	225	300

	C6	C8	C10
"Power Snap Caterpillar Climbing Tractor," 1950s, 8" long	50	75	100
"Prone WW I Soldier," 1925, 8" long	70	105	140
Racer No. 2	42.50	63.75	85.00
Racer No. 3	42.50	63.75	85.00
Racer No. 5	40	60	80
Racing Car, 12" litho, circa 1940, two-man team	90	135	180
Racing Car, "27," litho, plastic driver circa 1950	140	210	280
"Range Rider," 1940s, 8½" high	90	135	180
"Range Rider," 1940s, 10½" high on rocker base	130	195	260
"Red Cap" Porter	200	300	400
Renfrew Tank	100	150	200

MARX "Reversible Coupe, The Marvel Car"
Courtesy Mapes Auctioneers & Appraisers

	C6	C8	C10
"Reversible Coupe" "The Marvel Car," circa 1938	120	180	240
Reversing Road Roller	80	120	160
"Reversing Tractor"	125.00	187.50	250.00
"Rex Mars Planet Patrol"	170	255	340
"Ride 'Em Cowboy"	45.00	67.50	90.00
"Ring-A-Ling Circus," early ringmaster and circus animals	400	600	800
"Roadside Rest Service Station," four pumps, car, garage, 1930	210	315	420
"Rocket Fighter" circa 1950s, complete with tail fin and sparking mechanism	250	375	500
Rocket Racer, 1930s	160	240	320
"Rodeo Joe," 1933	130	195	260
"Roll Over Plane," circa 1920s	110	165	220
"Rookie Cop," with siren, 1930s, 8½" long	150	225	300
Rookie Pilot, 7" long, No. 77, circa 1940	100	150	200
Rooster Pulling Wagon, 1930s	60	90	120
Royal Bus Line, 10" long	100	150	200
"Royal Coupe"	250	375	500
"Royal Van Co." "We Haul Anywhere," 9" long	160	240	320
"Running Scottie," 1940s, 5½" long	50	75	100
"Sam the City Gardener"	60	90	120
"Sand and Gravel Truck – Builders Supply Co.," 1920	90	135	180
Scenic Express Train Set, circa 1950s	90	135	180
"Service Station Pumps" (3?), 1920	140	210	280
"Sheriff Sam & His Whoopee Car," 1950s, 6" long	130	195	260

	C6	C8	C10
"Sheriff Sam & His Whoopee Car," 1960s, 6" long	90	135	180
"Single Track Speedway," 1938, 8 track sections, 4" long windup car	60	90	120
"Sky Hawk" airport tower, two planes, tower 7½" high	160	240	320
Skybird Flyer, new circa 1927	170	255	340
Soldier, prone, firing rifle, WW I helmet	60	90	120
"Space Mobile" 1960s (Japan), 32" long, 3 sections, 4" long car	80	120	160

MARX

Marx "Speed Boy Delivery"

MARX "Sparkling Climbing Fighting Tank," cannon recoils
Courtesy Charles D. Richards

MARX Sparkling Tank, 4" long
Courtesy Continental Hobby House

Marx "Subway Express", Chein "Boy Skier"

	C6	C8	C10
"Sparkling Climbing Fighting Tank," cannon recoils	160	240	320
"Sparkling Climbing Tank," 1939	90	135	180
Sparkling Climbing Tractor, 8½" long, circa 1950s	90	135	180
"Sparkling Climbing Tractor and Trailer," 16" long, circa 1950s	110	165	220
Sparkling Heavy Duty Bulldog Tractor with Road Scraper, circa 1950s, 11" long	100	150	200
"Sparkling Luxury Liner," 1950s, 14" long	60	90	120
Sparkling Soldier Motorcycle, circa 1940	160	240	320
Sparkling Super Power Tank, circa 1950s, 9½" long	110	165	220
Sparkling Tank, 4" long	80	120	160
"Sparkling Tractor," tractor with plow blade, 1939	120	180	240
Sparkling Tractor and Trailer Set, "Marbrook Farms," circa 1950s, 21" long	150	225	300
Sparkling Warship, 14" long	140	210	280
"Speed Boy Delivery," (Motorcycle delivery), 1930s, 9¾" long, battery operated lights	250	375	500
Same as above, no lights	200	300	400
Speedway coupe, battery to be inserted for headlights	110	165	220

	C6	C8	C10
"Spic and Span, the Hams What Am," drummer and dancer, 1924	450	675	900
"Spic Coon Drummer," 1924, 8½" high	500	750	1000
"Streamline Speedway," 1938 (tin figure 8 track, 2 windup cars, 31" long	70	105	140
Streamlined Coupe	160	240	320
"Subway Express," with plastic tunnel, 1950s, 9⅜" diameter	110	165	220
"Sunnyside Service Station," four pumps, car and garage, 1939	300	450	600
"Super Streamline Racer," 1950s, 17" long	120	180	240
"Tidy Tim" Streetcleaner, pushing wagon, 1933	210	315	420

MARX

	C6	C8	C10
"Tower Aeroplane," 1940s, 7½" high, two 3" tin airplanes	100	150	200
"Toyland Farm Products," 1930s, milk wagon, 10½" long	130	195	260
"Toytown Dairy," horsedrawn cart, 10½" long, 1930s	140	210	280
Tractor, early 1940s	90	135	180
Tractor and Trailer Set, 1930s, similar to climbing tractor set, but with rounded and radiator front and copper finish metal. Tin plow attaches to front, silver metal trailer attaches to rear; has tin, copper finish and "balloon" tires	150	225	300
Tractor and Trailer, 16½" long, circa 1950s	110	165	220
"Trans-Atlantic Zeppelin," 1930s, 10" long	200	300	400
"Tricky Motorcycle," 1930s, 4¼" long, non-fail action	120	180	240
"Tricky Taxi," 1940s, 4½" long	60	90	120
Trolley, headlight, bell, 9" long	170	255	340
"Tumbling Monkey," 1930s, 5" high, on two chairs	60	90	120
Turn Over Tank No. 3	50	75	100
"U.S. Army" bomber, post-War, 1940s, two-engine	130	195	260
"U.S. Army Fighter Plane," 1940, 8" wingspan	105.00	157.50	210.00

MARX Whoopee Car, laughing cows on wheels, driver looks like cowboy
Courtesy Scott Smiles, photo by Mike Adams

	C6	C8	C10
Whoopee Car, laughing cows on wheels, driver looks like cowboy, 1929	210	315	420
Whoopee Car, "Yale-Princeton" pennants on wheels	160	240	320
"Whoopee Car with Flappers," 7½" long	200	300	400
Xylophonist, 5"	100	150	200
Zeppelin, 27" long, 1930s	200	300	400
Zippo Monkey	80	120	160

END MARX

	C6	C8	C10
Merry-Go-Round, 11" high	160	240	320
"Movie Man" Touring Car, rare	2000	3000	4000
Newsboy, "Extra" with cap and bell, circa 1940s	110	165	220
Ohio Art Boat, 14" long	20	30	40
Ohio Art "Circus Shooting Gallery," 1950s, 12" high, 17" long	50	75	100
Ohio Art "Coast Guard Seaplane," 1950s, 10" wingspan	40	60	80

MARX "U.S. Mail" truck, 9½ inches long
Courtesy Phillips New York

	C6	C8	C10
"U.S. Mail" truck, 9½" long	150	225	300
"U.S.S. Washington" Battleship	60	90	120
"Uncle Wiggily, He Goes A Ridin'," 1935	See Comic Character		
Wacky Taxi	75.00	112.50	150.00
Walking Clancy	400	600	800
Walking Drummer Boy, "Let The Drummer Boy Play While You Swing and Sway," circa 1939	300	450	600
Wee Scottie, 5" long	90	135	180

OHIO ART Giant Ride Ferris Wheel Photo by Don Hultzman

196

"Skidoodle", NIFTY
Photo Courtesy PB
Eighty-Four

STRAUSS Hooligans Hack
Courtesy Mapes Auctioneers & Appraisers

	C6	C8	C10
Ohio Art "Giant Ride Ferris Wheel," 1950s, 16" high	130	195	260
Ohio Art Hot Job Floatplane	100	150	200
Ohio Art "Injun Chief," 1950s, 8" long	60	90	120
Ohio Art "Jungle Eyes Shooting Gallery," 1950s, 18" long, 14" high	50	75	100
Ohio Art "Traffic Control," 1950s wind-up cars, 3½" long, base 19x13"	40	60	80
Ori-O Tailspin 4" puppy	10	15	20
Orkin Coast Guard Cutter, 25" long	350	525	700
Pecking Bird, 5½" long, 1927	40	60	80
Pecking Chicken, 5½" high, 1927	40	60	80
"PT 10," tin litho PT boat, circa 1941	60	90	120
Roadster, orange and green	40	60	80
Santa Claus in red cloth suit and holding Christmas tree, 5½" high, (Occupied Japan)	110	165	220
Santa Claus with green sleigh, Christmas tree, presents and white celluloid reindeer, bell, sleigh on three wheels, 8½" long (Occ. Japan)	120	180	240
"Skidoodle," Nifty, circa 1920, family in odd-looking car	450	675	900
Speedboat, "G.E. 200," tin litho, circa 1930	40	60	80
Spinning Globe, tin litho, two tin planes circling it, circa 1930	140	210	280
"Spirit of America" airplane PNX211, NY to Paris litho on wings	160	240	320
Steam Roller, circa 1925	80	120	160

STRAUSS

Ferdinand Strauss was an immigrant from Alsace. He began as a toy importer in the early 1900s, and by 1914 had four New York toy shops. When war disrupted imports of toys, he began manufacturing them. In 1918 he was located in East Rutherford, New Jersey, with fifty employees. Eventually Strauss was known as "The Founder of the Mechanical Toy Industry in America." Strauss seems to have been wholly or partially out of business in the late 1920s, and then resumed turning out wind-ups and other toys until at least 1941-42. He is also famous for having given employment to the very young Louis Marx.

STRAUSS "Alabama Coon Jigger"
Courtesy Mapes Auctioneers & Appraisers

	C6	C8	C10
"Alabama Coon Jigger," 9¾"	300	450	600
"Alabama Coon Jigger - Tombo" 1918, 10½" high, 3"x5" base	350	525	700
"Big Trixo," climbing monkey, 10" long	120	180	240
Billiards Player	300	450	600
Black Porter Pulling wheelbarrow, 6¼"	150	225	300
"Bus Deluxe," 1920s, 12" long	400	600	800
Check-A-Cab	400	600	800
"Chicago Zeppelin," 1930s, 9" long	300	450	600
Circus Wagon, containing lion and tamer, 8½" long, no engine compartment	350	525	700
Circus Wagon, 10" long, has engine compartment	450	675	900
"Dizzie Lizzie"	140	210	280
"Ham and Sam The Minstrel Team," piano player and banjoist, 1921, 6½" long	600	900	1200

STRAUSS

STRAUSS Interstate Double-Decker Bus, 10½" long.
Courtesy Lloyd W. Ralston Auctions

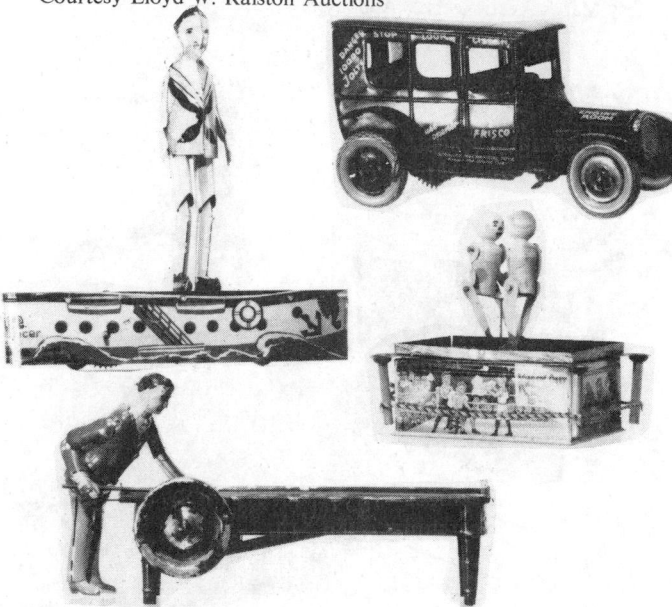

Top, L: STRAUSS Jackee the Hornpipe. Top, R: STRAUSS Leaping Lena. Middle R: Knockout Prize Fighters. Bottom: Billiards Player, STRAUSS.
Courtesy PB Eighty-Four, New York

STRAUSS "Jenny the Balky Mule"
Scott Smiles

	C6	C8	C10
"Haul Away Truck" No. 22, dump body	200	300	400
Hooligans Hack	300	450	600
Interstate Double Decker Bus, 1920	600	900	1200
"Jackee The Horn Pipe Dancer," 8½" long, No. 51	450	675	900
"Jazzbo Jim The Dancer on the Roof," 1910, 10" high	300	450	600

	C6	C8	C10
"Jenny the Balky Mule," 10" long, six-color litho, goes backward, forward and rears, farmer holding extended tin grain pail from his seat in front of mule's face to keep him moving vegetables in cart, No. 55	180	270	360
Joco the Golfer	200	300	400
Knock-Out Prize Fighters, ca. 1910, 7" high, No. 52	400	600	800
"Kraka Jack Car," 1920s, 5½" long	150	225	300
"Leaping Lena"	180	270	360
"Long Haulage Truck"	350	525	700
"Mailplane"	180	270	360
"Miami Sea Sled," 1920s, 10" long with 4" dinghy attached	200	300	400
Monkey driving 3-wheel cart pulled by bulldog, 1930s, 4½" high	200	300	400
"Play Golf"	350	525	700
"Red-Cap Porter," porter pushing a large trunk	300	450	600
"Red Star Van"	110	165	220

STRAUSS ROLLO CHAIR
Courtesy Phillips New York

	C6	C8	C10
Rollo Chair, black man pushing boardwalk chair, "Stock, DRGM, December 6, 1921"	600	900	1200
Santa Claus in Sleigh, 1921, 6" high, 2 reindeer	550	825	1100
"Speedwagon"	200	300	400
"Tip Tip" man with wheelbarrow	200	300	400
"Tip Top Porter," No. 40, 1920s, 6" long	170	255	340
Tippy Canoe	140	210	280
"Trikauto," No. 53	190	285	380
"What's It?" Car	800	1200	1600
"Yell-o Taxi"	350	525	700

END STRAUSS

	C6	C8	C10
Structo red and black painted tin wind-up automobile, 15" long ...	60	90	120
Structo Racer, early 1920s	90	135	180
Structo Steam Shovel, large size, rubber wheels, early	60	90	120
Structo Toyland Garage Truck	100	150	200
"Super Rocket Racer," tin litho, 1940s?	140	210	280
Sweetie Pie Boat, Lindstrom, 1920s ..	60	90	120
"Tip Top Toy Airplane," high wing, single engine, "Giant Flyer No. 200," 1930s, 23" long, 19½" wingspan	300	450	600
Tom Turkey, "B&S", 6" long, turkey struts, tail spreads, then moves up and down, German	160	240	320
Trolley, horse-drawn, German	150	225	300
Two rotating blimps and two cars, with passengers, that spin and rotate, 11¼" high, German	600	900	1200
"2001 Circus" 1930, 8" long	450	675	900
Train Set 1930s, three pieces, 20" long, wooden wheels	140	210	280
"U.S.A. Army" d-105 truck, 10½" long	80	120	160

UNIQUE ART MFG. CO.

Unique Art Mfg. Co. was in business from at least 1916, when it introduced its Merry Juggler and Charlie Chaplin. In 1931 it was located at Waverly and Peshine Avenues in Newark, New Jersey. Its president was Wm. Marbe, and there were 28 male employees (no females listed). In 1934 employees numbered 110 male and 165 female (same address). In a 1946-47 directory the address was 200 Waverly Avenue, Newark and the president was Samuel Burger (this last name may be incorrect; the handwriting in my notes is hard to read). Employees were equally divided: 125 male and 125 female. Unique was still manufacturing toys, mainly wind-ups, in 1952. Little else is known about the company, except that at some date, Louis Marx bought it.

UNIQUE "Bombo the Monk"
Courtesy Scott Smiles

UNIQUE "Dandy Jim"
Courtesy Ed Hyers Antique Toys

	C6	C8	C10
Unique Artie the Clown in his Crazy Car	190	285	380
Unique "Bombo the Monk," two-piece, tree 9½" high, monkey 5½" long, 1930s	110	165	220
Unique "Capitol Hill Racer," 1930s, 17½" long with 2" tin racing car	100	150	200
Unique "Casey the Cop," early	550	825	1100
Unique "Dandy Jim" dancer, 1921 ..	250	375	500
Unique "Daredevil Motor Cop," 8½" long, 1940s	150	225	300
Unique Flying Circus, elephant supports flying plane and flying clown	400	600	800
Unique "G.I. Joe and His Jouncing Jeep," post WW II, 7"	140	210	280
Unique "G.I. Joe and the K-9 Pups," circa 1941, 9" high	130	195	260
Unique "Gertie the Galloping Goose," 9½" long, 1930s	120	180	240
Unique "Hee Haw" donkey pulling milk cart, 10" long	110	165	220

UNIQUE Rodeo Joe Whoopie Car
Courtesy Mapes Auctioneers & Appraisers

L to R: UNIQUE Sky Rangers, MARX Skybird Flyer.
Courtesy Phillips, New York

Top: "2001" Circus. Bottom: UNIQUE
Krazy Kar, 1940.
Courtesy Lloyd W. Ralston Auctions

	C6	C8	C10
Unique Art, "Hillbilly Express," 1930s, 18" long, 3 pcs. and 3¼" tin locomotive	140	210	280
Unique Hobo Train, 8½" long, 1920s, dog biting pants of hobo atop train	160	240	320
Unique "Jazzbo Jim" dancer, new in 1921	300	450	600

	C6	C8	C10
Unique "Jazzbo Jim - The Dancer on the Roof," 1920s, 10" high, base 5x3x3"	200	300	400
Unique "Kid-Go-Round," Plastic horsemen and boat	140	210	280
Unique Art "Kiddy Cyclist," 1930s, 8¾" tall, steers figure 8 pattern and rings bell	180	270	360

200

UNIQUE G.I. Joe and his Jouncing Jeep
Courtesy Scott Smiles, photo Mike Adams

Walking Man, carrying red top hat over his head, head revolves to reveal three different faces. Photo courtesy PB Eighty-Four

	C6	C8	C10
Walking Man, carrying red top hat over his head, head revolves to reveal 3 different faces	450	675	900
Wilkins Roadster, early with driver, 9" long	300	450	600
Wilkins Auto, early, woman driver, 9" long	290	425	580

S.S. Wolverine Oceanliner

UNIQUE "G.I. Joe and the K-9 Pups"
Courtesy Scott Smiles

	C6	C8	C10
Unique Krazy Kar, new in 1921	210	315	420
Unique "Lincoln Tunnel," moving vehicles, cop, 1935, 24" long	180	270	360
Unique "Motorcycle Cop," 1930s, 9" long	80	120	160
Unique Musical Sail-Way Carousel with 3 kids in spinning plastic boats, 9" tall	140	210	280
Unique Pecking Goose, Witch and Cat	200	300	400
Unique Rodeo Joe Crazy Car	140	210	280
Unique "Rollover Motorcycle Cop," 1935	150	225	300
Unique "Sky Rangers" plane and zeppelin revolving from tower, 1933	230	345	460

	C6	C8	C10
Wolverine Acrobat	110	165	220
Wolverine "Drummer Boy," 14" high	130	195	260
Wolverine "Drum Major," No. 27, patent 1892546, 1930s, 13¼" tall on circular 4¼" base	170	255	340
Wolverine, "Drum Major," No. 27, pat. 1892546, 1930s, 13⅝" tall on rectangular 4½x6½" base	180	270	360
Wolverine Jet Roller, Coaster and small car, 21" long extended	100	150	200
Wolverine "Loop-A-Loop," 1930s, 19" long, includes small car	180	270	360
Wolverine Luxury Liner	70	105	140
Wolverine "Mechanical Man on the Flying Trapeze," 1930s, 8½" high	100	150	200
Wolverine "Merry-Go-Round," 1930s, 11" diameter, 12" high, includes four tin-litho flags	400	600	800
Wolverine Pontiac Mystery Car	100	150	200
Wolverine "S.S. Wolverine," 14½" long	110	165	220

WOLVERINE "Merry-Go-Round," 1930s No. 31A
Courtesy Ed Hyers Antique Toys

	C6	C8	C10
Wolverine "Sandy Andy Circus," dancing toy	140	210	280
Wolverine "Sunny Andy" Tank, 14" long	100	150	200
Wolverine "Zilotone" with six interchangeable records, 1930s	400	600	800
"The Wonder Cyclist" boy on tricycle, circa 1930, 8¾" high	200	300	400
Woodhaven "Robot Bus with the Mechanical Brain," 1940s, 13½" long	50	75	100
Woodhaven Tractor, 1916	60	90	120
World on base, wind-up plane circles it, German	100	150	200
Wyandotte Carousel, 5¼" high	130	195	260
Wyandotte Duck pulling tin Easter cart, 15" long, litho, wooden wheels	60	90	120
Wyandotte "Hoky-Poky" handcar with 2 clowns	160	240	320
Wyandotte "Red Ranger Ride 'Em Cowboy," circa 1930s, rocker base	180	270	360
Wyandotte "Ride 'Em Cowboy" No. 515, 6½" high	100	150	200

BATTERY-OPERATED TOYS
by Don Hultzman

The average mint price of Battery toys in the last edition was $100.26; this edition it is $198.28, an increase of 98%.

During the years preceding World War II, the Japanese toy industry was content with making cheap imitations of American and European toys, mostly out of recycled tin cans. Immediately after the war and through the 1960's, the Japanese came into their own with a new and different dimension in the toy world — the battery-operated toy.

Previously, early U.S. and European toy makers used batteries in their toys to add realism to their boats, cars, trains and airplanes by adding flashlight bulbs where headlights, spotlights, tail-lights and navigation lights were required. Later, batteries were used to power horns, buzzers and electromagnets as well as lights, but these early mechanical toys still depended on a spring or small flywheel to function as a mechanical toy should. There was just so much these early toys could do until the Japanese toy revolution opened up a whole new area with their clever automatons.

Starting in 1946, the Japanese toy makers began to replace the wind-up clockwork mechanisms and friction-drive mechanical toys with mini-electric motors powered by one or more batteries. These small electric motors could run much longer than the spring powered or friction drive mechanisms and with this advantage, the Japanese toy makers designed and manufactured the most ingenious and complicated automatons imaginable. There were able to simulate just about every conceivable type of human-animal motions and behavioral actions. This ingenuity carried over into a multitude of different types of novelty toys. Just how many different types of automata and vehicles were manufactured is unknown, but a conservative estimate would be around the 900 mark. Multiply this figure by the thousands and it was no wonder that Japan held the title of the leading toy maker for the next 20 years. About 95% of the battery-operated toys came from Japan during this period while the U.S. and other countries manufactured the remaining 5% of these toys.

Since most of the Japanese production was destined for the U.S. and European market, international distributorships were organized for the marketing of these thousands of toys. Cragstan, Linemar and Rosko were some of the largest distributors on an international scale, but a few American toy makers hopped on the band wagon in marketing these toys under their brand names, such as Marx, Ideal, Hubley and Daisy (the BB gun people). Therefore many of the trademarks stamped on Japanese battery-operated toys are not necessarily that of the original manufacturer, but of the distributor or marketer. Many Japanese toy shops and factories manufactured, assembled and sold their products through a central factory which in turn was under contract to an international marketer. As a result it is very difficult to pinpoint a specific designer or manufacturer of any battery-operated toy.

Some of the early Japanese toy makers such as the Masutoku Toy Factory (later Masudaya Toy Co.), founded in 1924 (which uses the "M-T" or "Modern Toy" trademark) and the Nomura Toys, Ltd., founded in 1923 (which uses the "T-N" trademark), are probably a couple of the original designers and manufacturers of many of the hundreds of different automations exported from Japan. "Alps", the trademark of the Alps Shoji, Ltd., (Alps Toy Midzuno Co.), founded in 1948 and "SAN", the mark of the Marusan Co., founded in 1946, can also be accountable for the creation of many original battery toys. In fact, Marusan Co., and Bandai, founded in 1950, as well as the Taijo Kogyo Co., founded in 1959, can be credited with some of the most spectacular scale model, battery-operated cars ever made in the batt-op category. "ATC", (Asahi Toy Co., founded in 1950), "T.P.S." (Toplay Ltd., founded in 1956), and "Haji", (founded in (1951), of the Mansei Toy Co., have their trademark on many more toys. The alphabet soup continues with many other toy companies using only a single letter or letters like "K", "S", "J", "KO", "Y", and "S&E", etc. Why only letters is a mystery, unless they represent many subsidiaries of the parent company. Besides being clever, the Japanese have left toy collectors very confused, but this is a small disadvantage compared to the fun of collecting battery-operated toys.

After peaking in the late 60's, the Japanese tin toy production began to decline due to increased labor costs, increased safety restrictions, inflation and competition from the cheaper die-cast and plastic toy makers. Many of the original toy companies either folded or diversified into the electronic field, using the IC-microchip the same way they used the mini-electric motor to develop new electronic products. It seems that presently, Japan has relinquished its toy monopoly to China, Hong Kong, Korea and Taiwan, in favor of its automotive and electronic industry. The battery operated toys now coming from these countries consist mostly of plastic, are higher priced, lack quality and are presently not very collectable. There is no comparison to the beauty of these toys with those from Japan. Tin and plastic just have never been compatible in a quality toy and this tends to "turn off" most serious toy collectors.

It is generally agreed upon by battery-operated toy collectors that the period of the 40's-60's should be considered as the "Golden Age of the Battery Operated Toy". During this 20 year period, most of the quality toy companies were founded and the most desirable and beautiful toys were produced. They were high in quality, most complex, and the detail and lithography most fascinating. These are the ones most sought after and in demand today. Prices of these toys are generally increasing as they become more scarce, and more and more toy collectors are beginning to focus on their desirability and are willing to pay as much for them as they have for many of the early classical tin wind-ups. Top prices go for the most complex toys, comic character, space, robots, scale-model cars, Blacks, and the older and earlier figurals.

The "Ball Playing Bear" is a good example of one of the first batt-op toys of the late 40's. As in most early toys, it uses one D-cell; is made of tin and celluloid, and has six actions going on and is very difficult to find complete with accessories.

Although tens of thousands of battery-operated toys were in circulation during this period, it is a rarity and a thrill to find one in mint condition, with original box, as the mortality rate of these toys was extremely high. Corrosion from leaking batteries left in them by their absent-minded owners took a high toll as well as deterioration of rubber parts due to age. (Rubber hoses of the water-drinkers and the rubber bellows of the bubble blowers were classic victims of aging and hardening of the rubber.) Rust was inevitable with the wet-toys that depended on water or bubble solutions to perform. Lubricants dried out or stiffened, rendering the toy inoperable, wires frequently worked loose or broke and electrical contacts corroded. Accidents, abuse, tampering and interfering with the toy while it was going through its cycle added enormously to the mortality rate. Reversing battery polarity by not following instructions burned out and ruined many a fine toy. Like a precision watch, the more complex the toy, the more delicate the mechanism and the more susceptible it becomes to damage due to negligence and abuse, such as physically interfering with the actions of the toy, and stopping it before it completes its cycle will damage the many levers and gears inside the toy, making it useless. Many toys require accessory parts to perform correctly and these were often lost, such as bowls for the bubble-blowers, trays, balls, umbrellas, discs, flags, clothes, etc. Top prices usually go for the complete toys with no parts missing.

The original box for battery-operated toys is extremely important, probably more so than other mechanical toys, because the intructions were often printed on the box lid. Also a picture or illustration of the toy showing any accessory parts the toy might need as well as the correct battery insertion was noted, if not on the actual toy's battery compartment. Finally, the name of the toy, if not lithographed on the toy itself, was printed on the box and very often, the name of the toy was nowhere near the actual appearance of the toy. Many times the name of the toy was given for its function rather than what it was supposed to be and since many toys did not have their identity stamped on them, the box lid was the only means of identifying the toy. The toy listing that follows are names of toys actually identified from their original boxes or the toy itself. Therefore the original box usually adds to the value of the toy.

The value of a battery-operated toy depends not only on its scarcity, desirability and condition, but also on the number of actions taking place during its performance cycle. These toys are classified as MAJOR or MINOR toys. Major action toys will have **three** or **more** actions taking place while performing, and will command top price, whereas minor action toys have only one or two actions and will have a correspondingly lower price. The actions of a major or minor toy include all the individual movements taking place during one cycle and include any lights, sound, or smoke effects. Also the major battery toys must have **all** actions functioning and in proper sequence. There should be no missing parts and the toy itself should be constructed mostly of tin, about 85-90%, and the rest plastic or vinyl such as heads, limbs, accessories, etc. Usually the more plastic, the lower the value of the toy, regardless of condition.

The following list of battery-operated toys are, for the most part, major action toys, and include, if known, the manufacturer or distributor derived from the box or lithographed on the toy itself. A "?" indicates that the name of this toy has not been verified by the author. Also the circa or year, if known, will follow, along with the most obvious or helpful dimensions and any special notes if necessary. The prices are the average market prices based on supply and demand, and not on "auction" or "will pay anything for this toy" price. Geographic area is another factor in their pricing and these were based on the going prices in the midwestern states.

A "RARE" toy is one that is difficult to find on the open market because: 1. It had a limited production, or; 2. It is of such a fragile nature that it is difficult to find complete or in operating condition, or; 3. They are so popular and highly collectible that they exist only in private collections.

DON HULTZMAN confesses he has always been a collector of toys, but didn't really get serious about the hobby until ten or so years ago, not only collecting but also repairing them. Born and raised in Cleveland, Ohio, he received a masters degree in Guidance and Administration at Kent State, and is currently employed by the Parma City School System as a school counselor. He does free-lance writing as a science consultant to the encyclopedia department of World Publishing Co. and lives in Brunswick Hills, Ohio. Many of his tin wind-up toys can be seen in the 1983 MGM movie "A Christmas Story".

CONDITION OF A TOY AND ITS RELATION TO PRICE

The value of a battery operated toy depends not only on its desirability, rarity and complexity, but very much on its condition. A toy in "mint" condition is generally worth twice as much as a toy in "good" condition. A toy in "very good" condition will be equally priced between "good" and "mint".

"Mint" means just that — the condition in which the toy was originally issued — **perfect** — regardless of age. It will also be in perfect mechanical condition, complete with all accessory parts when applicable, and will look "brand new". The cloth or fur (plush) covering on some battery toys may reveal some discoloration (yellowing) due to age, but this should not affect its value as a "mint" toy as long as it is clean. All toys in this category must be in perfect working condition. The original box in mint condition will significantly enhance the value of any "mint" toy.

"'Very good" indicates the condition of a battery toy that has seen some use and is starting to show its age. It will still be in perfect working order and have all its accessory parts where applicable. It will have some age-soiling, but will have no rust or corrosion. Overall, it will have an appearance of "freshness" and still be highly desirable to the fussy collector.

"Good" applies to a battery toy that has seen considerable use, wear and tear, some age soiling, but still in perfect working condition with no missing parts or accessories. The "wet" toys may show some slight surface rust that can be easily removed. A toy in "good" condition is still a welcome addition to any toy collection, but will be targeted for upgrading by a piece in better condition.

Any battery toy below the condition of "good" will reflect a drastic reduction in value. Toys in good shape, but missing accessory parts, will not lose as much value as those that are severely rusted, corroded, painted over, have parts broken off and are totally inoperable. These "poor" toys are usually collected for their "scrap value" by the toy repairer and seldom are they worth more than $10.00.

The key to grading is to use common sense and avoid wishful thinking. Since grading the condition of a toy may be difficult at times, consulting with an expert in the field, if possible, could clear up any lingering doubts. (See back section of this guide for references of toy collectors.)

GUIDELINES FOR THE CARE AND REPAIR OF YOUR BATTERY OPERATED TOY
by Don Hultzman

Your prized battery toy needs T.L.C. and when it stops working, you now have a frustrating disaster on your hands. To avoid this, the following suggestions should be of some help:

Battery toys, like other mechanical toys, should be operated periodically to keep them loosened up. A lightweight spray lubrication now and then will help considerably if the mechanism is accessible. Do not over-lubricate as the excess may stain any cloth or fur covering on some battery toys.

A good quality car wax or polish will keep the lithographed and bare metal parts looking like new — especially on the "wet" toys. Always test an obscure lithographed area to make sure the polish doesn't soften or dissolve the paint. Care should be exercised when polishing metal parts adjoining any cloth or plush covering, as the substance may stain the coverings. Light surface rust usually disappears with a careful polishing. Nothing can be done for deep rust or corrosion without ruining the value of the toy. Repainting will only further reduce the value and is not recommended.

Should your battery toy fail to operate, the following steps might be helpful:

1. Make sure it is not gunked-up and that no moving parts are binding.
2. Make sure the battery contacts are not dirty or corroded — if so then clean them with crocus cloth. ALWAYS USE FRESH BATTERIES!
3. Lightly tap the toy with your finger or **lightly** nudge one of the moving parts while the switch is "on".

If none of the above steps work, then your toy needs "major surgery". This means the toy must be completely torn down, repaired and reassembled. Most battery toys are repairable as long as they have not been destructively tampered with and no parts are missing or corroded beyond repair. This job is best left to an expert in toy repair and should never be attempted by one who doesn't know what he is doing. Expert repairs will not affect the value of a battery toy so long as the repair is **undetectable** and the toys looks and functions **exactly** as it did before the repair. Such repairs are acceptable in toy collecting circles. Expert repairs are also expensive but well worth the investment if it means the difference between a "mint" (and prized toy) and one below the grade of "good", since an inoperable toy is practically worthless, regardless of condition.

Accordion Bear
Photo by Don Hultzman

Air Defense Pom-Pom Gun
Photo by Don Hultzman

Automated Santa
Photo by Don Hultzman

American Airlines Electra
Photo by Don Hultzman

Arthur A-Go-Go
Photo by Don Hultzman

Antique Gooney Car
Photo by Don Hultzman

206

	C6	C8	C10
"A-B-C Fairy Train," 1950s, M-T Co., 14½" long, one pc., four actions	50	75	100
"Accordion Bear," 1950s, "Y" Co., 10½" tall, six actions	200	300	400
"Accordion Bear," 1950s, MST Co. (Flare Toy), 9¼" high, five actions	90	135	180
"Accordion Player Bunny," 1950s, Alps Co., 12" tall, 9" long, six actions	100	150	200
"Accordion Player Hobo With Baby Monkey Playing Cymbals," 1950s, Alps Co., six actions	100	150	200
"Acrobat Clown," 1960s, 9" tall, Y-M Co., minor toy	40	60	80
"Acro Chimp Porter," 1960s, Y-M Co., 8½" tall, minor toy	30	45	60
"Acrobat Robot," 1970s, S-H Co., 4½" tall, three actions	25	37.50	50
"Air Cargo Prop-Jet Airplane - Seaboard World Airlines," 1960's, Marx Co., 12" long, 14½" wingspan, five actions	110	165	220
"Air Control Tower," 1960s, Bandai Co., 11" high, 37" span (extended), four actions (includes detachable airplane and helicopter)	175	262.50	350
"Air Defense Pom-Pom Gun," 1950s, Linemar Co., 14" long, five actions	90	135	180
"Air Taxi Helicopter" 1960s, Haji Co., three actions	30	45	60
"Aircraft Carrier," 1950s, Marx Co., 20" long, eight actions	170	255	340
"Airport Saucer," 1960s, MT Co., 8" diameter, four actions	50	75	100
"Alley-The Exciting New Roaring Stalking Alligator," 1960s, Marx Co., 17½" long, five actions	120	180	240
"American Airlines - 4 Prop Airliner," 1960s, Waco Co., 12" long, 16½" wingspan, four actions	80	120	160
"American Airlines DC-7" (with automatic turnover propellers), ca. 1950s, Linemar, 7 action, 19" wingspan	200	300	400
"American Airlines DC-7C," 1960s, Yonezawa Co., 21" long, 23½" wingspan, seven actions	150	225	300
"American Airlines Airliner DC-7," 1960s, Linemar Co., 17½" long, 19" wingspan, seven actions	170	205	240
"American Airlines Electra," 1950s, Linemar Co., 18" long, 19½" wingspan	160	240	320
"American Airlines Flagship Carolyn," 1950s, Linemar Co., 18" long, 19½" wingspan, three actions	160	240	320

	C6	C8	C10
"Amphibian Navy Patrol Plane", circa 1950s, Alps Co., 15" wingspan, 3 actions	450	675	900
"Amtrak Locomotive" 1960s, ST Co., 16" long, minor toy	40	60	80
"Andy Gard - Brink's Armored Car - Bank," 1950s, General Molds & Plastics Corp. 6¾" long, minor toy	20	30	40
"Andy Gard Combat Knight No. 143," 1960s, General Molds & Plastic Corp., 10¼" high, three actions, includes lance, stanchion, 3 plastic rings and helmet plume	20	30	40
"Animated Santa on Rotating Globe," 1950s, HTC Co., 15" high, five actions	130	195	260
"Animated Squirrel," 1950s, S&E Co., 8½" tall, eight actions, rare	90	135	180
"Answer Game Machine" robot, 1960s, Ichida Co., 14½" tall, educational toy, eight actions	250	375	500
"Anti-Aircraft Jeep," 1950s, "K" Co., 9½" long, five actions	70	105	140
"Anti-Aircraft Unit No. 1," 1950s, Linemar Co., 12½" long, three electrical actions and three manual actions	70	105	140
"Antique Gooney Car," 1960s, Alps Co., 9" long, four actions	40	60	80
"Apollo Lunar Module," 1970s, DSK Co., 6" high, four actions, mostly plastic	60	90	120
"Apollo Space Ship USA-NASA", 1960s, M-T Co., 9" long, four actions	30	45	60
"Apollo Super Space Capsule," 1960s, S-H Co., 9" high, five actions	60	90	120
"Apollo-X Moon Challenger," rocket, 1960s, T-N Co., 16" long, six actions	50	75	100
"Armored Attack Set," 1960s, Marx Co., jeep 6¼" long and tank 5¼" long, plus 15 2" plastic figures	80	120	160
"Army Radio Jeep-J1490," 1950s, Linemar Co., 7¼" long, four actions	50	75	100
"Arthur A-Go-Go," 1960s, Alps Co., 10" high, six actions, (includes detachable cymbals and drum set)	80	120	160
"Astro Dog," 1960s, "Y" Co., 11" high, 2 cycles, five actions (looks like Snoopy)	70	105	140
"Astro Dog," 1960s, Y-M Co., 11" tall, three actions	40	60	80
"Astrobase" (motorized), 1960s, Ideal Co., 20" high, six actions	100	150	200
"Atom Motorcycle," circa 1950s, 11¾" long, 7 actions	400	600	800

	C6	C8	C10
"Atomic Fighter" robot, 1950s, S-H Co., 11" tall, five actions	50	75	100
"Atom Rocket 7", vehicle with fins, 1950s, M-T Co., 9½" long, four actions	50	75	100
"Attacking Martian Robot," 1950s, S-H Co., 11½" tall, 7 actions - two cycles	150	225	300
"Automated Santa," ca. 1960s, Santa Creations Co., 3 actions, 10¼" tall	60	90	120
"Ball Blowing Clown," 1950s, T-N Co., 11" tall, three actions with ball.........................	100	150	200
"Ball Playing Bear," 1940s, no marking, 10½" tall, six actions, includes five celluloid balls and one umbrella - rare	150	225	300
"Ball Playing Dog," 1950s, Linemar Co., 9" high, three actions	50	75	100
"Balloon Blowing Monkey," 1950s, Alps Co., 11⅛" tall, five actions with balloon	50	75	100
"Balloon Blowing Teddy Bear," 1950s, Alps Co., 11⅛" tall, five actions with balloon	50	75	100
"Balloon Vendor," 1960s, Y Co., 12" tall, four actions, includes four plastic balloons and tin tray	60	90	120
"Barber Bear," 1950s, T-N Co., (Linemar) 9½" tall, five actions ..	150	225	300
"Barking Boxer Dog," 1950s, Marx, 7" long, minor toy	10	15	20
"Barking Dog," 1950s, STS Co., 7" long, 7" high, four actions, two cycles	30	45	60
"Barking Spaniel Dog," 1950s, Marx, 7" long, minor toy	10	15	20
"Barney Bear Drummer," 1950s, Alps Co., 11" tall, five actions, resembles "Steiff" bear	80	120	160
"Barnyard Rooster," 1950s, Marx, 10" high, five actions	60	90	120
"Bartender," 1960s, T-N Co., 11½" tall, six actions	20	30	40
"Batmobile," 1972 National Periodical Publications, ASC Co., 12" long, three actions	100	150	200
"Battery Locomotive No. 123," 1950s, T-N Co., 10" long, three actions .	10	15	20
"Bear Chef" (Cuty Cook), 1960s, "Y" Co., 9½" tall, five actions, (includes chef hat and tin litho egg)	80	120	160
"Bear Target Game," 1950s, M-T Co., 9½" high and 4"x5" base (includes gun and rubber tipped darts), four actions	90	135	180
"Bear - the Cashier," 1950s, M-T Co., 7½" high, five actions	150	225	300
"Begging Puppy," 1960s, "Y" Co., 9" long, six actions	30	45	60
"Bengali - The Exciting New Growling, Prowling Tiger," 1961, Marx Co., Linemar Div., 18½" long from nose to end of tail, 2 cycles, three actions	60	90	120
"Betty Bruin - Cashier" 1950s, Linemar, 9" tall, six actions	200	300	400
"Beauty Parlor Bear," 1950s, S&E Co., 9½" high, seven actions, rare	300	450	600
"Big Hunter-Automatic Gun," 1950s, Tada Co., 21" long - extended, three actions	25	37.50	50
"Big John," 1960s, Alps Co., 12" high, three actions	50	75	100
"Big John - The Indian Chief," ca. 1960s, T-N Co., 5 actions, 12½" tall	70	105	140
"Big Ring Circus Truck," 1950s, M-T Co., 13" long, three actions	40	60	80
"Big Max Robot," 1958, Remco Co., 8" long, 7" tall, four action	80	120	160
"Big Shot Cadillac," 1950s, T-N Co., 10" long, four actions, Rare	70	105	140
"Big Wheel Coca Cola Truck," 1970s, Taiyo Co., three actions	50	75	100
"Biller Train No. 573," 1950s, T-N Co., 13" long, includes rubber cable track and two hopper cars, a minor toy - Rare	50	75	100
"Billy Blastoff Space Scout," Eldon Co., 1960s, 4 actions, 16" long ..	50	75	100
"Billy the Kid Sheriff," 1950s, "Y" Co., 10½" tall, 2 cycles, four actions	80	120	160
"Bimbo the Clown," 1950s, Alps Co., 9¼" tall, three actions (includes detachable hat)	150	225	300
"Bingo Clown," 1950s, T-N Co , 13" tall, three actions	80	120	160
"Bird Watching Bear" (?), 1950s, M-T Co., 10" tall, three actions - Rare	200	300	400
"Blacksmith Bear," 1950s, A-1 Co., 9½" tall, six actions	100	150	200
"Blink-A-Gear-Robot," 1960s, S-H Co., 14½" tall, five actions	300	450	600
"Blinky-the-Clown," 1950s, no marking, 10½" tall, five actions, includes multicolor paper hat	150	225	300
"Blow-Up-Ball Locomotive," 1950s, M-T Co., 9½" long, minor toy, includes celluloid ball	40	60	80
"Blushing Willie," 1960s, Y Co., 10" tall, four actions	40	60	80
"Bobby Drinking Bear," 1950s, Y Co., 10" tall, six actions	100	150	200
"Bobby the Drumming Bear," 1950s, Alps Co., 10" tall, four actions ..	130	195	260

Barking Spaniel Dog, Sleeping Baby Bear, Barking Boxer Dog, Papa Bear-Smoking

Ball Blowing Clown, Sammy Wong-the Tea Totaler, Nutty Nibs

Frankie the Rollerskating Monkey, Buttons -Puppy with a Brain, Jocko-the Drinking Monkey, Blushing Willie
Courtesy Don Hultzman.   Photos by Ron Chojnacki.

Big Wheel Coca-Cola Truck   Photo by Don Hultzman

	C6	C8	C10
"Boeing 727 Jet Liner," 1960s, Y Co., 17½" long, 16¼" wingspan, three actions	100	150	200
"Boeing 727 Jet Plane," 1960s, M-T Co., 12½" long, 10⅜" wingspan, three actions	100	150	200
"Bongo, Drumming Monkey," 1960s, Alps Co., 9½" high, three actions, includes plastic hat	50	75	100
"Bongo Player," 1960s, Alps Co., 10" tall, four actions	50	75	100
"Bowling Bank," 1960s, M.B. Daniel & Co., 10" long, three actions	60	90	120
"Brave Eagle," ca 1950s, T-N Co., 5 actions, 11" tall	60	90	120
"Brave Eagle," 1960s, TN Co., 12" tall, four actions	50	75	100
"Breakfast Chef," 1960s, K Co., 8¼" tall, minor toy (includes plastic egg and coffee maker	40	60	80
"Brewster the Rooster," 1950s, Marx Co., 9½" high, five actions	90	135	180
"Bristol Bulldog Airplane," ca. 1950s, S&E Co., lights, prop spins, stop & go, noise, 4 actions, 14½" wingspan	140	210	280
"Broadway Trolley," 1950s, M-T Co., 10½" long, four actions - two cycles	80	120	160
"Bruno the Accordion Bear", 1950s, "Y" Co., 10½" tall, five actions	100	150	200
"Bubble Blowing Bear," 1950s, M-T Co., 9½" high, 4"x5" base, four actions	100	150	200
"Bubble Blowing Boy," 1950s, "Y" Co., 7" high, four actions	60	90	120
"Bubble Blowing Bunny," 1950s, "Y" Co., 7" high, four actions	60	90	120
"Bubble Blowing Dog," 1950s, "Y" Co., 8" high, three actions	60	90	120
"Bubble Blowing Kangaroo," 1950s, M-T Co., 9" high (base to tip of ears), three actions	90	135	180
"Bubble Blowing Lion," 1950s, M-T Co., 7½" high, 3½"x7" base, four actions	60	90	120
"Bubble Blowing Magician," 1950s, "Y" Co., 11" tall, three actions	80	120	160
"Bubble Blowing Monkey," 1950s, Alps Co., 10" tall, four actions, includes plastic bowl for bubble solution	60	90	120
"Bubble Blowing Popeye," 1950s, Linemar Co., 11¾" tall, five actions	500	750	1000
"Bubble Blowing Washing Bear," 1950s, Y Co., 8" high, three actions, (includes plastic washtub)	100	150	200

Bartender
Photo by Bill Kaufman
Courtesy Good Old Days

Bubble Blowing Popeye
Photo by Don Hultzman

Busy Secretary
Photo by Don Hultzman

	C6	C8	C10
"Bubbling Bull," 1950s, Linemar Co., 6½" long, 8" high, five actions (plastic bowl)	50	75	100
"Bulldozer," 1950s, T-N Co., 7½" long, five actions	40	60	80
"Bulldozer," 1950s, M-T Co., 11" long, six actions	40	60	80
"Bunny-The Magician," 1950s, Alps Co., 14½" tall, five actions, (includes card-ribbon apparatus for card trick)	110	165	220
"Burger Chef," 1950s, "Y" Co., 9" tall, eight actions (includes chef's hat and tin-litho hamburger)	80	120	160
"Busy Bizzy Friendly Bug," 1950s, M-T Co., 6¼" long, three actions	40	60	80
"Busy Housekeeper, The," 1950s, Alps Co., 8½" tall, four actions	100	150	200
"Busy Housekeeper, The" (bunny) 1950s, Alps Co., 10" tall, four actions	80	120	160
"Busy Robot," ca. 1960s, S-H Co., 4 actions, includes plastic wheelbarrow, 11" high	150	225	300
"Busy Santa Bank," (with remote pay-phone), 1960s, S&E Co., 8" high, six actions	100	150	200
"Busy Secretary," 1950s, Linemar Co., 7½" high, 7¼" long, seven actions	100	150	200
"Busy Shoe Shining Bear," 1950s, Alps Co., 10" high, five actions	80	120	160
"Butt Stompin' Ashtray," 1977, Poynter Prod., 7¼" high, four actions (includes tin manhole cover, ashtray insert and 4½" high plastic shoe)	20	30	40
"Buttons-Puppy With A Brain", also called "Buttons The Push Button Pup", 1960s, Marx, 12" high, 8 actions	125	187.50	250

	C6	C8	C10
"B-Z Porter" Baggage truck, 1950s, M-T Co., 7½" long, 6½" high, minor toy, includes three pcs. of luggage (tin)	90	135	180
"B-Z Rabbit," ca. 1950s, M-T Co., 4 actions, 7" long	30	45	60
"Cabin Cruiser," ca 1950s, SGK Co., 3 actions, 21½" long	140	210	280
"Cabin Cruiser With Outboard Motor," 1950s, Linemar Co., 12" long, minor toy	70	105	140
"Cable Train," 1940s, T-N Co., 12" long, four pc. set, minor toy	50	75	100
"Cadillac" car, 1949, Ashai Toy Co., 10" long, three actions	100	150	200
"Calypso Joe," 1950s, Linemar, 11" tall, four actions	100	150	200
"Candy Vending Machine Bank," 1950s, Wonderful Toy Co., 9" high, five actions	100	150	200
"Capitol Airlines Viscount 321," 1950s, Linemar, 11" long, 14" wingspan, four actions	100	150	200
"Cappy the Baggage Porter Dog," 1960s, Alps Co., 12" high, 11" long, four actions	70	105	140
"Captain Blushwell," 1960s, "Y" Co., 11" tall, six actions	50	75	100
"Caterpillar," 1950s, Alps Co., 16" long, three actions	70	105	140
"Central Choo Choo," 1960s, M-T Co., 15" long, three actions	20	30	40
"Champion Weight Lifter," 1960s, Y-M Co., 10" tall, five actions	60	90	120
"Chaparral 2F," car, 1960s, Alps Co., 11" long, five actions	50	75	100
"Charlie The Drumming Clown," 1950s, Alps Co., six actions (includes detachable drum and cymbals)	90	135	180

210

Cragstan "Tootin-Chuggin Locomotive", Greyhound Bus Scenicruiser.

Cragstan Biplane 7F18
Photo by Don Hultzman

Charlie Weaver
Photo by Bill Kaufman
Courtesy Good Old Days

	C6	C8	C10
"Chimp With Xylophone," 1970s, Y Co., 12" long, 8" high, minor toy (includes 4 records and hammer) .	50	75	100
"Chimpy the Drumming Monkey," 1950s, Alps Co., 9" high, six actions, includes detachable drum and cymbals	60	90	120
"Chippy the Chipmunk," 1950s, Alps Co., 12" long (nosetip to tail tip), four actions	50	75	100
"Christmas Time," 1950s Murusan Co., 10" high, 7" base diameter, three actions	100	150	200
"Cindy the Meowing Cat," 1950s, Tomiyama Co., 12" high, (nosetip to tail tip), 2 cycles, four actions .	30	45	60
"Cine Bear," 1950s, Linemar Co., 11" tall, five actions	250	375	500
"Circus Elephant With Blowing Ball and Parasol," 1950s, T-N Co., 9¾" high, three actions (includes celluloid ball and tin litho umbrella), rare	120	160	240
"Circus Fire Engine," 1960s, M-T Co., 11" long, four actions	80	120	160
"Circus Lion," 1950s, Rock Valley Toy Co., (Via), 11" high, four actions, includes whip and flannel carpet with levers (2 cycles)	130	195	260
"Climbing Fireman," 1950s, TPS Co., 24" high assembled, five actions (includes 3 tin ladder sections)	110	165	220
"Climbing Fireman" (remote control), 1950s, T.P.S., 28" high assembled, five actions	120	180	240
"Climbing Linesman," 1950s, T.P.S. Co., 24" high when assembled, three actions, (includes 3 tin pole sections) Rare	150	225	300
"Clown Circus Car," 1960s, M-T Co., 8½" long, 9" high, five actions ..	90	135	180
"Clown and Monkey Car," 1960s, M-T Co., 10¼" long, 8" high, three actions	120	180	240
"Clown on Unicycle," 1960s, M-T Co., 10½" high, three actions ...	140	210	280
"Clown With Lion," 1950s, T-N Co., 12" high, four actions (includes spiral apparatus)	110	165	220
"Clowns Bank, The," 1940s, unmarked, 10" high, minor toy (all plastic)	50	75	100
"Clown-The-Magician No. 40244," 1950s, Alps Co., 12" tall, six actions includes card-ribbon apparatus for card trick	100	150	200
"Cock-A-Doodle-Doo Rooster," 1950s, Mikuni Co., 8" high, four actions	50	75	100
"Colonel Hap Hazard" Robot, 1968, Marx Co., 11¼" tall, four actions	200	300	400

	C6	C8	C10
"Charlie Weaver," 1962, T-N Co., 12" tall, six actions	30	45	60
"Charm the Cobra," 1960s, Alps Co., 6" high, three actions	50	75	100
"Chee Chee Chihuahua," 1960s, Mego Co., 8" high, five actions	20	30	40
"Chef Cook," 1960s, Y Co., 11½" tall with hat on, five actions (includes tin litho egg and hat)	90	135	180
"Chief Robotman," 1950s, K.O. Co., 12" tall, four actions	300	450	600
"Chimp and Pup Rail Car," 1950s, T-N Co., 8';' high, four actions	80	120	160

	C6	C8	C10
"Combi-O-Mixer," 1950s, Excelo Co., (mixer-blender), 9" long, 9" high, minor toy	20	30	40
"Comic Hungry Bug" VW auto, 1970s, Tora (S-T) Co., 7¾" long, five actions	20	30	40
"Comic Road Grader," 1950s, Bandai Co., 9" long, four actions	40	60	80
"Coney Island Penny Machine," 1950s, Remco Co., 13" high, minor toy, (includes plastic prizes)	90	135	180
"Coney Island Rocket Ride," 1950s, Alps Co., 13½" high, four actions	180	270	360
"Continental Blue Locomotive," 1960s, M-T Co., 12½" long, 4 actions	15	22.50	30
"Cowboy Riding Horse," 1950s, T-N Co., 7" high, three actions	40	60	80
"Cragstan Astronaut," 1950s, Daiya Co., 14" tall, four actions	400	600	800
"Cragstan Beep Beep Greyhound Bus," 1950s, Cragstan Co., 20" long, three actions	90	135	180
"Cragstan Biplane," 7F7, U.S. Navy, 1950s, T-N Co., 9½" long, 11½" wingspan, four actions	110	165	220
"Cragstan Biplane-7518," 1950s, T-N Co., 12" long, 14⅜" wingspan, five actions	120	180	240
"Cragstan Crapshooter," 1950s, Y Co., 9½" tall, four actions, includes pair of small dice	80	120	160
"Cragstan Crapshooting Monkey," 1950s, Alps Co., 9" tall, three actions, includes pair of small dice	60	90	120
"Cragstan Dishwasher-Automatic," 1960s, Alps Co., 9" high, (includes 24 pc. dish set, 2 dish baskets and metal tray), minor toy	25	37.50	50
"Cragstan Great Astronaut," 1960s, Alps Co., 14" tall, five actions	350	525	700
"Cragstan's Mr. Robot," 1960s, Y Co., 10½" tall, four actions	300	450	600
"Cragstan Mother Goose," 1960s, Y Co., 8¼" high, six actions	60	90	120
"Cragstan One-Arm Bandit," 1960s, Y Co., 6¼" high, three actions, includes 3"x3¼" sign	60	90	120
"Cragstan Peanut Vendor," 1950s, T-N Co., 8" tall, five actions (includes felt hat)	150	225	300
"Cragstan Playboy," 1960s, Cragstan Co., 13" high, five actions	70	105	140
"Cragstan Roulette - A Gambling Man," 1960s, Y Co., 9" tall, five actions, (includes steel ball, chips, tin table, game sheet)	100	150	200
"Cragstan Satellite," 1950s, Cragstan Co., 8" diameter, 5½" high	70	105	140

	C6	C8	C10
"Cragstan Smoking Jet Plane-U.S.A.F." 1950s, T-N Co., 11½" long, 7½" wingspan, four actions	100	150	200
"Cragstan Talking Robot," 1960s, Y Co., 10½" tall, three actions	200	300	400
"Cragstan Telly Bear," 1950s, S&E Co., 8" high, six actions	120	180	240
"Cragstan Tootin'-Chuggin' Locomotive," 1950s, Cragstan Co., 24" long, three actions (longest single piece battery toy made)	30	45	60
"Cragstan Tugboat," 1950s, San Co, 12¾" long, three actions	60	90	120
"Cragstan Vertol 1107 Helicopter," 1950s, T-N Co., 13½" long, four actions, includes rotors	70	105	140
"Cragstan Western Locomotive," 1950s, Cragstan Co., 12" long, four actions	50	75	100
"Cragstan's Two Gun Sheriff," 1950s, Y Co., 9½" tall, five actions (includes tin hat)	100	150	200
"Crane Tractor," 1950s, SKK Co., 7½" long, 11½" high extended	50	75	100
"Crawling Baby," 1940s, Linemar Co., 11" long, 8½" high, minor toy,	40	60	80
"Cry-Baby-In-Buggy" (?), 1950s, T-N Co., 11¾" long, 7" high, minor toy, includes plastic baby bottle to activate switch	50	75	100
"Cycling Daddy," 1960s, Bandai Co., 10" high, four actions	60	90	120
"Cyclist Clown," 1950s, M-T Co., 6½" high, six actions	80	120	160
"Cyclist Clown," 1950s, Alps Co., 9" high, five actions	90	135	180
"Cymbal Playing Turnover Monkey," 1960s, T-N Co., 8" tall, three actions	30	45	60
"Daisy-The Jolly Drumming Duck," 1950s, Alps Co., 9" high, seven actions, (includes detachable drum and cymbals, rare	110	165	220
"Dalmation One-Man Band No. 90262," 1950s, Alps Co., 9" high, six actions, includes cymbals and stand	90	135	180
"Dancing Merry Chimp," 1960s, Kuramochi Co., (C-K), 11" tall, five actions	50	75	100
"Dancing Sweethearts," 1950s, T-N Co., 7" tall, minor toy	70	105	140
"Dandy-The Happy Drumming Pup," 1950s, Alps Co, 8½" high, six actions, (includes detachable drum and cymbals)	60	90	120
"Dapper Jigger Dancer," 1950s, Haji Co., 12" tall, minor toy	70	105	140

Dentist Bear   Courtesy Don Hultzman.   Photos by Ron Chojnacki.

	C6	C8	C10
"Dennis the Menace" (Playing London Bridge), 1950s, Rosko, 9" high, 3 actions, includes xylophone	100	150	200
"Dentist Bear," 1950s, S&E Co., 9½" tall, 6¾"x4¼" base, seven actions, includes detachable head	210	335	420
"Desert Patrol Jeep," 1960s, M-T Co., 11" long, four actions, includes turret gunner	60	90	120
"Destroyer 206" boat, 1950s, Y Co., 14" long, six actions, includes detachable antenna and five depth charges	70	105	140
"Dino Robot," 1960s, S-H Co., 11" tall, five actions	200	300	400
"Dino the Dinosaur and Fred Flintstone," 1961, Marx, 22" long, eight actions	200	300	400
"Disney Acrobats" (Mickey, Donald & Pluto), 1950s, Linemar Co., 9" high, minor toys	300	450	600
"Disney Fire Engine", 1950s, Linemar Co., 11" long, four actions	400	600	800

Dynamic Fighter Robot
Photo by Don Hultzman

	C6	C8	C10
"Disneyland Fire Engine," 1950s, Linemar Co., 18" long, five actions	200	300	400
"Docking Rocket," 1960s, Daiya Co., 16" long, 24" extended, six actions, (includes plastic radar antenna)	70	105	140
"Dog Family," 1960s, Alps Co., 11" long, four actions	30	45	60
"Dog Sled," T-N Co., 14" long, four actions	110	165	220
"Dolly Dressmaker," 1950s, T-N Co., 7" high, ten actions, includes cloth sample ("Dolly Seamstress" on box) Rare	110	165	220
"Donald Duck," 1960s, Linemar Co., 8" tall, four actions	150	225	300
"Donald Duck Trolley," 1960s, M-T Co., 11" high, three actions	120	180	240
"Douglas C-124 Globe Master," ca. 1950s, Yonezawa Co., 8 actions, 20½" wingspan	250	375	500
"Doxie The Dog," 1950s, Linemar Co., 9" long, five actions	20	30	40
"Dozo-The-Steaming Clown," 1960s, T-N Co., Rosko Toys, 10" tall, five actions	120	180	240
"Dream boat Hot Rod," ca. 1950s, M-T Co. (?), 4 actions, 7" long	40	60	80
"Drill," 1950s, Linemar Co., 6" long, includes attachments, minor toy	20	30	40

"Mod Monster, Blushing Frankenstein", Hootin' Hollow Haunted House, Frankenstein Monster

Tricky Dog-House, Sky Taxi (Panam), Slurpy Puppy

B-Z Porter, Cragstan "Tugboat", Goodtime Charlie, Picnic Bunny

Treasure Chest Bank, Santa Bank, Hole-In-One Bank, Poverty Pup Bank.

Maxwell Coffee Loving Bear, Bird Watching Bear, Peanut Vendor

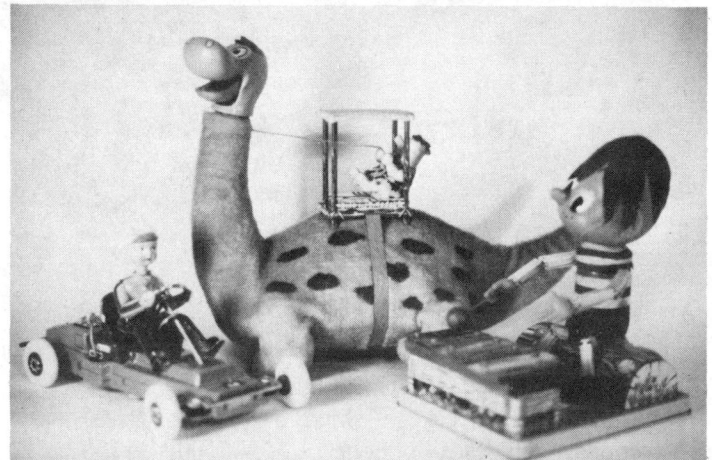

Go-Kart Dino the Dinosaur & Fred Flintstone, Pinnochio playing "London Bridge".

Bulldozer, Shaking Old-Timer Car, Tractor

Drinking Captain, Hi Jinks of the Circus, Cragstan "Playboy"

Courtesy Don Hultzman.   Photos by Ron Chojnacki.

214

Flower Watering Pup, Rock 'N Roll Monkey, Barney Bear Drummer

Puzzled Puppy, Shutter Bug, Popcorn Vendor

Silver Mountain Express, Spirit of 1776

Military Police Car, Desert Patrol Jeep

Happy Singing Bird in Cage, Cragstan-One Arm Bandit, Comic Hungry Bug, Mag-oo

Teddy-the Rhythmical Drummer, Major Tooty, McGregor, Cycling Daddy

Chimpy, Drumming Monkey, Happy Santa One-Man Band, Fred Flintstone's Bedrock Band, Dalmation One-Man Band
Courtesy Don Hultzman.

Pepi-Tumbling Monkey, Yo Yo Monkey, Jo Jo-the Flipping Monkey
Photos by Ron Chojnacki.

	C6	C8	C10
"Drinker's Savings Bank," 1960s, Illfelder Co., 9" high, minor toy .	40	60	80
"Drinking Captain," 1960s, S&E Co., 12" tall, six actions	70	105	140
"Drinking Dog," 1950s, Y Co., four actions	60	90	120
"Drinking-Licking Cat," 1950s, T-N Co., 10" high, 4"x4" base, six actions	50	75	100
"Drum Bear," ca. 1950s, Alps Co., 5 actions, walks, lights, beats drum, noise, 7¾" tall	90	135	180
"Drum Monkey," 1970s, Yada Co., 8" high, three actions	30	45	60
"Drummer Bear," 1950s, Alps Co., 10" tall, six actions	120	180	240
"Drumming Clown Charlie, The," 1950s, Alps Co., 9½" tall, six actions, includes drums and cymbals	100	150	200
"Drumming Mickey Mouse," 1950s, Linemar, 10" tall, four actions, Rare	500	750	1000
"Drumming Polar Bear," 1960s, Alps Co., 12" tall, three actions	60	90	120
"Ducky Duckling," 1960s, Alps Co., 8" high, four actions	30	45	60
"Dump Truck No. 7343," 1960s, T-N Co., 10¼" long, seven actions ...	40	60	80
"Dynamic Fighter Robot," 1960s, Junior Toy Co., 10" tall, five actions	40	60	80
"El Toro-Cragstan Bullfighter," 1950s, T-N Co., 9½" long, four actions, includes detachable tin matador ..	80	120	160
"Electric Powered TV and Radio Station," 1950s, Marx, 30" long, three actions	60	90	120
"Electric Remote Control Robot," 1950s, M-T Co., 7½" tall, four actions, Rare	400	600	800
"Electric Robot," 1950s, Marx, 14½" tall, five actions, Rare	200	300	400
"Electric School Bus," 1950s, M-T Co., 9½" long, minor toy	50	75	100
"Electric Vibraphone," 1950s, T-N Co., 7½" long, 5½" high, three actions	50	75	100
"Electro Special Racer," 1950s, Yonezawa Co., 10" long, three actions	60	90	120
"Electro Train Transcontinental," 1950s, "M" Co., 20½" long, (3 pcs.) three actions	50	75	100
"Electronic Countdown," 1959, Ideal Toy Co., 24" long, six actions ...	30	45	60
"Electronic Fighter Jet 4800," 1950s, 19" long, eleven actions	50	75	100
"Electronic Fire House," 1940s, Banner Co., 7" square, minor toy (includes plastic fire engine)	50	75	100

	C6	C8	C10
"Electronic Periscope (Nautilus) Firing Range," 1950s, Cragstan, 11" high on tripod, three actions	60	90	120
"Engine Robot," 1970s, S-H Co., 9½" tall, four actions	30	45	60
"Excavator Robot," 1960s, S-H Co., 10" tall, four actions	50	75	100
"Fairyland Loco," (locomotive), 1950s, Daiya Co., 9" long, four actions .	30	45	60
"Farm Truck," 1960s, Alps Co., 11" long, three actions	30	45	60
"F.D. Fire Engine," 1960s, Y-M Co., 10" long, 12" high when ladder is extended, four actions	40	60	80
"Feeding Bird Watcher," 1950s, Linemar, 9" high, five action, (includes detachable tin branch and bird), Rare	200	300	400
"Ferris Wheel Truck," ca. 1950s, Linemar Co. (?) 4 actions, 11" long	100	150	200

	C6	C8	C10
"Fido - The Xylophone Player," ca. 1950s, Alps. Co., body sways, head turns, arms activate lights, sound, 6 actions, 8¾" high, includes detachable xylophone	90	135	180
"Fighter," (airplane), 1960s, K-O Co., 10½" long, 9" wingspan, six actions	100	150	200
"Fighter Airplane," ca. 1960s, Marx Co., 4 actions, 7" wingspan	40	60	80
"Fighter Jet" ca. 1960s, Marx Co., 4 actions, 7" wingspan	40	60	80
"Fighting Bull," 1960s, Alps Co., 9½" long, five actions	40	60	80
"Fighting Bull, 1970s, Rock Valley Tech Co., 12" long, nose to tail tip, four actions, two cycles	50	75	100
"Fighting Spaceman," 1960s, S-H Co., 12" tall, five actions	120	180	240
"Fire Boat," 1950s, M-T Co., 15" long, five actions	40	60	80

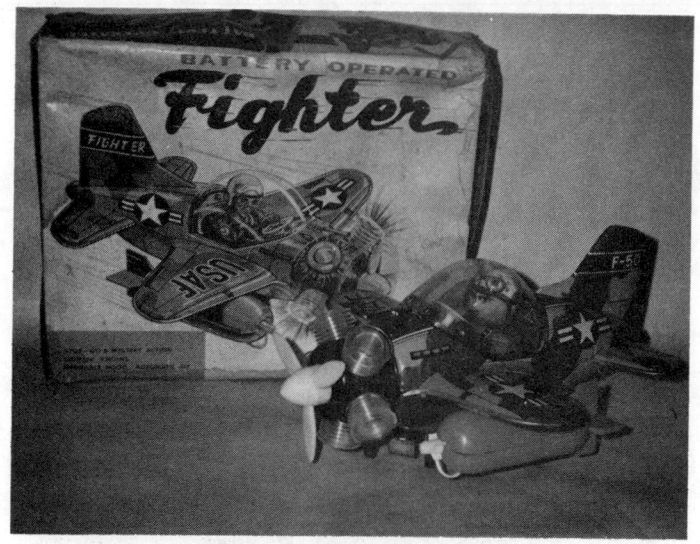
Fighter
Photo by Don Hultzman

Fighting Spaceman   Photo by Don Hultzman

Fishing Bear, three variations
Photo by Don Hultzman

	C6	C8	C10
"Fire Chief No. 8 Car," 1960s, Y Co., 11¼" long, three actions	20	30	40
"Fire Chief Mystery Action Car," 1960s, T-N Co., 9¾" long, four actions	70	105	140
"Fire Engine," 1950s, Y Co., 12" long, ladder extends 16", six actions	40	60	80
"Fire Engine," ca. 1950s, S-H Co., 3 actions, 8" long	40	60	80
"Fire Patrol Boat," 1950s, KKS Co., 12" long, three actions	70	105	140
"Fishing Bear," (also Fishing Panda Bear, Polar Bear, Forest Bear), 1950s, Alps Co., 10" high, six actions, (includes detachable pond, tin fish)	100	150	200
"Fishing Bears-Bank," 1950s, Wonderful Toy Co., 9½" tall, six actions, Rare	200	300	400
"Flashing Jet-FC-657 Airplane-U.S.A.F. 7452," 1950s, Marx Co., 7" long, 6" wingspan, four actions	50	75	100
"Flashy Ray Space Gun," 1950s, T-N Co., 18½" long, a minor toy	40	60	80
"Floating Satellite Target Game," 1960s, 8½" high, (includes tin gun, rubber tipped darts & celluloid ball)	70	105	140
"Flutter Birds," 1950s, Alps Co., 26½" high when assembled, six actions, includes detachable pulley assembly, Rare	150	225	300
"Flying Dutchman-PH-KLM Airliner," 1950s, T-N Co., 11" long, 14" wingspan, five actions	90	135	180
"Flying Jet Plane-Boeing 747P," 1960s, J Toy Co., 13" long, 12" wingspan, five actions	60	90	120
"Flying Tiger Airplane," 1960s, Marx Co., 7" long, 7" wingspan, four actions (remote control)	40	60	80
"Ford Model T," 1950s, Nihonkogei Co., 10¼" long, four actions (includes detachable tin roof)	50	75	100
"4 Prop Airplane," 1960s, Waco Co, 17" long, 16¼" wingspan, four actions	100	150	200
"Fork Lift Truck," 1960s, M-T Co., 11" long, five actions	40	60	80
"Frankenstein" (tin), 1950s, Marx Co., (Japan), 12" tall, five actions (remote control), rare	500	750	1000
"Frankenstein Monster," 1960s, T-N Co., 14" tall, six actions	110	165	220
"Frankie-The Rollerskating Monkey," 1950s, Alps Co., 12" tall	80	120	160

	C6	C8	C10
"Fred Flintstone Bedrock Band," 1962, Alps Co, 9½" high, four actions	200	300	400
"Friendly Jocko-My Favorite Pet," 1950s, Alps Co., 8" high, five actions (includes detachable cymbals, plastic cup	110	165	220
"Fruit Juice Counter," 1960s, "K" Co., 8" long, 8" high, three actions (includes plastic barrel, lid, glasses and tin tray)	80	120	160
"Funland Cup Ride," 1960s, Sonsco Co., 7" tall, 6"x6" base, three actions, includes 6" umbrella	70	105	140
"Galloping Cowboy Savings Bank," 1950s, Y Co., (Cragstan), 8" high, 6½" long, minor toy	100	150	200
"Gama Mercedes Benz 220 SE Sedan," 1960s, Mignon Co., 9" long, three actions	80	120	160
"Gear Robot" 1960s, "Y" Co., 10" tall, four actions	200	300	400
"Gino-Neapolitan Balloon Blower," 1960s, Tomiyama Co. (Rosko), 10" tall, five actions, includes bubble solution plastic tray	70	105	140
"Girl With Baby Carriage," 1960s, T-N Co., 8" high, three actions	60	90	120
"Go-Go Girl," (bar toy), 1969 Poynter Prod. Co., 15¼" tall, minor toy (risque toy - PG rated)	20	30	40
"Go Kart," 1960s, M-T Co., 6½" long, minor toy (includes control wire with steering key)	50	75	100
"Go Kart," 1950s, Rosko Co., 10" long, three actions, includes detachable head	60	90	120
"Godzilla Monster," 1970s, Marusan Co., 11½" tall, three actions	50	75	100
"Golden Locomotive," 1950s, Nihonkogei Co., 10½" long, minor toy	20	30	40
"Golden Roto Robot," 1960s, S-H Co., 8½" tall, five actions	90	135	180
"Good Time Charlie," 1960s, M-T Co., 12" tall, seven actions	70	105	140
"Grandpa Bear," (rocking chair), 1950s, Alps Co., 9" tall, five actions	100	150	200
"Grand-Pa Car," 1950s, Y Co., 9" long, four actions	40	60	80
"Great Garloo, The", 1960s, Marx Co., 23" tall, seven actions, (includes chain and medallion)	300	450	600
"Greyhound Bus-Scenicruiser," 1950s, I.Y. Metal Toy Co., 16" long, three actions	60	90	120
"Greyhound Bus with Headlights," 1950s, Linemar Co., 10¼" long, three actions	70	105	140

Great Garloo, The
Photo by Don Hultzman

	C6	C8	C10
"Guided Missile Launcher," 1950s, Irco Co., 8" long, 3" tall, 5" wide, three actions (includes plastic missiles)	80	120	160
"Hamburger Chef," 1960s, K Co., 8" long, 8" high, three actions, (includes tin frying pan, hamburger, plastic bottles)	90	135	180
"Handy Hank Mystery Tractor," 1950s, T-N Co., 9" long, four actions	30	45	60
"Happy Band Trio," 1970s, M-T Co., 12" high, seven actions	60	90	120
"Happy Clown Car," 1960s, Y Co., 6½" long, three actions	40	60	80
"Happy Clown Theater," (with Pinocchio-like puppet), 1950s, Y Co., 10" tall, three actions	90	135	180
"Happy Fiddler Clown, The" 1950s, Alps Co., 9½" high, four actions, includes tin litho violin, Rare	200	300	400
"Happy Miner," 1960s, Bandai Co., 11" tall, three actions	80	120	160
"Happy Naughty Chimp," 1960s, Daishin Co., 9½" high, assembled, four actions	40	60	80
"Happy 'n Sad Magic Face Clown," 1960s, Y Co., 10" tall, five actions	80	120	160

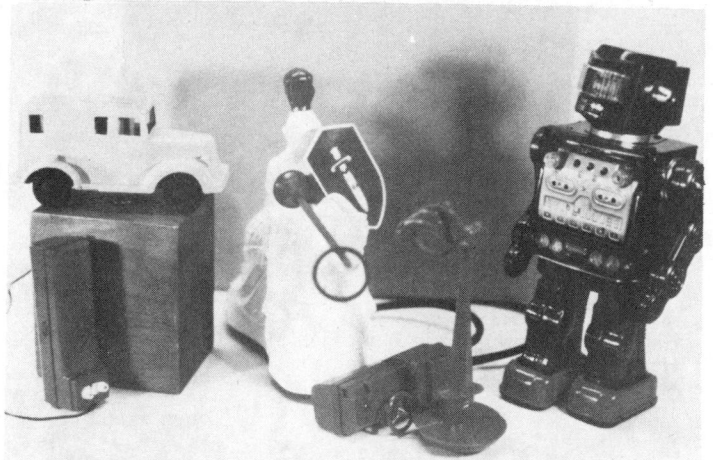

Andy Gard Brinks Armored Car Bank, Andy Gard Combat Knight, Swivel-O-Matic Robot

Surrey Jeep, Continental Blue Locomotive

Roaring Gorilla, Mighty Kong, Dancing Merry Chimp

Butt Stompin' Ashtray, Army Radio Jeep, Blow-Up Ball Locomotive
Courtesy Don Hultzman.   Photos by Ron Chojnacki

Railroad Handcar, Winner-25-Rocket, Biller Train No.573

Ray Gun, Universal Machine Gun, Big Hunter Automatic Gun, Flashy-Ray Gun

Balloon Vendor, Miss Friday, Sam the Shaving Man, Gino the Neapolitan Balloon Blower

Balloon Blowing Bear, Balloon Blowing Monkey, Bubble Blowing Monkey

219

Tank (M-4), Tank X-3), Tank (M-103)

James Bond's Aston-Martin

Dennis The Menace-Xylophone Player, Chimp-Xylophone Player

Bongo Monkey, Chef Cook, Cola Drinking Bear
Courtesy Don Hultzman.   Photos by Ron Chojnacki.

Happy Fiddler Clown, Roarin' Jungle Lion, Mama Dog Feeding, Hungry Baby Dog

Patrol Helicopter, Cragstan Biplane, T360-Monoplane

Western Badman-Red Gulch Bar, Drinker's Saving Bank

Happy the Clown Puppet Shown Drummer Mickey Mouse, Clown-the Magician

Smoking Grandpa in Rocking Chair, Rocking Chair Bear, Mama Bear & Hungry Baby Bear, Pop Drinking Bear

	C6	C8	C10
"Happy 'n Sad Face Cymbal Clown," 1960s, Y Co., 10" tall, five actions	80	120	160
"Happy Santa", 1960s, "Z" Co., 11" tall, three actions	90	135	180
"Happy Santa" (walking), 1950s, Alps Co., 11" tall, five actions	110	165	220
"Happy Santa-One Man Band," 1950s, Alps Co., 9" high, six actions, includes cymbals and stand	90	135	180
"Happy Singing Bird," 1950s, M-T Co., 9" high, bird 3" long, 5⅝" dia. base, three actions	40	60	80
"Happy the Clown" (with Pinocchio-like puppet), 1950s, Y Co., 10" tall, three actions	120	180	240
"Happy Tractor," 1960s, Daiya Co., 8" long, four actions	20	30	40
"Hasty Chimp," 1960s, Y Co., 9" high, four actions	30	45	60
"Haunted House Mystery Bank", 1960s, (Disneyland promotion), Brumberger Co., 7⅜" high, four actions	60	90	120
"Heavy Machine Gun," 1950s, T-N Co., 24" long, 13" high on tripod, four actions (includes detachable tripod and plastic ammo belt)	100	150	200
"Hi Bouncer Moon Scout" robot, 1968, Marx Co., 11¼" tall, five actions, includes five plastic balls, Rare	350	525	700
"High Jinks of the Circus," 1950s, T-N Co., 14" high, extends to 29", six actions			
"Highway Drive," 1950s, T-N Co., 15½" long, three actions (includes tin magnetic car)	40	60	80
"Highway Patrol Jeep," 1950s, Daiya Co, 10" long, four actions	40	60	80
"Highway Skill Driving," 1960s, K Co., 13" long, three actions	40	60	80
"Hiller Hornet Helicopter," 1950s, Alps Co., 12¼" long, 15" 2-pc. metal rotor, four actions	50	75	100
"Hippo Chef" (Cuty Cook), 1960s, Y Co., 10" tall, five actions (includes chef hat and tin litho egg)	80	120	160
"Hole-In-One Bank," 1960s, no marking, 8½" long x 3½" wide, minor toy, includes marked test coin and golfer	50	75	100
"Holiday Sink-Stove Combination," 1950s, T-N Co., 9" high, minor toy, includes 3 pc. pan set	30	45	60
"Hoop Zing Girl," 1950s, Haji Co., 11" tall, minor toy	80	120	160
"Hoopy-the Fishing Duck," 1950s, Alps Co., 10" high, seven actions (includes magnetic fish and detachable 'pond')	150	225	300
"Hootin' Hollow Haunted House," 1960s, Marx, 11" high, eight actions, Rare	350	525	700
"Hooty the Happy Owl," 1960s, Alps Co., 9" tall, six actions	50	75	100
"Hot Rod" car, 1950s, T-N Co., 10" long, minor toy	20	30	40
"Hungry Baby Bear," 1950s, Y Co., 9½" high, six actions	90	135	180
"Hungry Cat," 1950s, Linemar Co., 9" high, seven actions (includes tin tray and plastic fish	150	225	300
"Hungry Hound Dog," 1950s, Y Co., 9½" high, six actions	100	150	200
"Hungry Sheep," 1950s, M-T Co., 9" long, three actions, 2 cycles	80	120	160
"Hy Que Monkey," 1960s, T-N Co, 17" tall, six actions	150	225	300
"Hysterical Robot, The," (a.k.a. 'Hysterical Harry and Happy Harry'), 1960s, S-H Co., 13½" tall, seven actions	100	150	200
"Ice Cream Loving Bear" (?), 1950s, M-T Co., 9½" high, three actions, Rare	150	225	300
"Ice Cream Truck," 1960s, Bandai Co., 10½" long, five actions	70	105	140
"Indian Joe," 1960s, Alps Co., 12" tall, four actions	40	60	80
"Indian Signal Choo Choo," 1960s, Kanto Toys Co., 9½" long, four actions	30	45	60
"Interceptor," target game, 1950s, S&E Co., 13" high, 16" wingspan, four actions	100	150	200
"Interplanetary Rocket," 1960s, Y Co., 14¾" tall, five actions	80	120	160
"James Bond's Aston-Martin"	150	225	300
"James Bond-007 Car-M101," 1960s, Daiya Co., 11" long, seven actions, includes ejectable driver	100	150	200
"Jeep-USA," 1950s, TKK Co., 12½" long, a minor toy	40	60	80
"Jeep No. 10560," 1950s, Cragstan, 5½" long, a minor action toy	40	60	80
"Jet Airport with 4 Jet Airplanes," 1960s, Turnpike Lines (Sears), 12½" long, seven actions	100	150	200
"Jet Plane Base," 1950s, Y Co., 7¼"x11" base, plane 9" long, 7" wingspan, seven actions (includes crank)	200	300	400
"Jig-Saw-Matic," 1950s, Z Co., 7¼" high, 4½"x8½", a minor action toy	30	45	60

Jet Plane Base
Photo by Don Hultzman

Jungle Trio
Photo by Don Hultzman

	C6	C8	C10
"Jo-Jo the Flipping Monkey," 1970s, T-N Co., (Illfelder), 10" high, minor toy	30	45	60
"Jocko the Drinking Monkey," 1950s, Linemar, 11" tall, four actions, includes top hat	60	90	120
"John's Farm Truck," 1950s, M-T Co., 9½" long, seven actions	70	105	140

	C6	C8	C10
"Jolly Bambino," 1950s, Alps Co., 9" high, five actions, includes candy pieces, Rare	150	225	300
"Jolly Bear the Drummer Boy," 1950s, K Co., 7" tall, five actions	50	75	100
"Jolly Drummer Chimpy," 1950s, Alps Co., 9" high, 6 actions, includes cymbals and stand	50	75	100
"Jolly Drumming Bear," 1950s, T-N Co., 7" tall, four actions	40	60	80
"Jolly Penguin," 1950s, T-N Co., 7" tall, five actions	40	60	80
"Jolly Pianist," 1950s, Marusan Co., 8" high, five actions	90	135	180
"Jolly Santa on Snow," 1950s, Alps Co., 12½" tall, four actions, two cycles	100	150	200
"Josie The Walking Cow," 1950s, Daiya Co., 14" long, 8½" high, seven actions, two cycles	70	105	140
"Journey Pup," ca. 1950s, S&E Co., 4 actions, remote control, 7½" long	40	60	80
"Jumbo The Bubble Blowing Elephant," 1950s Y Co., 7¼" high, three actions, includes plastic bowl for bubble solution	40	60	80
"Jungle Jumbo," 1950s, B.C. Co., 9" high, five actions	70	105	140
"Jungle Trio," 1950s, Linemar, 8" high, eight actions, includes tin litho whistle, Rare	350	525	700
"Jupiter Robot," 1950s, Yonezawa Co., 12¾" tall, four actions	200	300	400
"Jupiter Rocket Launching Pad," 1960s, T-N Co., 8½" long, 7" high	160	240	320
"K-55 Electric Tractor", ca. 1950s, M-T Co., 3 actions, 7" long	40	60	80
"King Flying Saucer," 1960s, KO Co., 7½" diameter, three actions	50	75	100
"Kissing Couple," 1950s, Ichida Co., 10¾" long, five actions	140	210	280
"Kitchen-ette Stove and Sink," 1940s, no marking, 6½" long x 6¾" high, a minor toy, includes kitchen utensils and side tray and stoppers	30	45	60
"Knight in Armor Target Game," 1950s, M-T Co., 12" tall, three actions (includes crossbow and rubber tipped darts)	80	120	160

	C6	C8	C10
"Knitting Grandma," 1950s, T-N Co., 8½" tall, three actions	80	120	160
"Kooky-Spooky Whistling Tree," 1950s, Marx Co., 14¼" tall, six actions, (two color schemes) Rare	450	675	900
"Lady Pup Tending Her Garden," 1950s, Cragstan Co., 8" high, five actions	100	150	200
"Laughing Clown Robot," 1960s, S-H Co., 14" tall, seven actions	150	225	300
"Lectric Revolver," 1950s, Daisy Mfg. Co., 11½" long, three actions	30	45	60
"Leo- The Growling Pet Lion With Magic Face-Change," 1970s, Toyiyama Co., 9" long, 2 cycles, three actions	40	60	80
"Light House," 1950s, Alps Co., 8½" high, 6¾"x6¾" base, five actions (includes detachable spin-ball tower) Rare	250	375	500
"Lighted Freight Train," 1950s, Y Co., four actions, 25½" long, five pcs., 8 section track	40	60	80
"Lighted Space Vehicle with Floating Satellite," 1960s, M-T Co., 8½" long, three actions (includes cell. ball)	110	165	220
"Linda Lee Laundromat," washing machine, 1940s, T-N Co., 6½" high, a minor toy	20	30	40
"Lion," 1950s, Linemar, 9" long, four actions	50	75	100
"Lion Target Game," 1950s, M-T Co., 7½" high, four actions (includes dart gun and darts)	90	135	180
"Locomotive-Continental Blue," 1970s, 13" long, four actions, M T Co.	20	30	40
"Looping Airplane," ca. 1960s, "Y" Co., Sears (distribution), minor toy, 14½" high, airplane 5" long	30	45	60
"Los Walky - Son" 1960s, Geyper Co., 11½" high, 15" wide, includes detachable rifles and baton	100	150	200
"Lost in Space Robot," 1966, Remco Co., 13" tall, three actions	90	135	180
"Love- Beetle - Volks," 1960s, K.O. Co., 10" long, three actions	40	60	80
"Lucky Crane," 1950s, M-T Co., 8½" high, five actions (includes tin prizes)	90	135	180
"Lucky Seven - Dice Throwing Monkey," 1960s, Alps Co., 11½" tall, five actions (includes plastic straw hat, five dice, two game sheets, twenty chips)	70	105	140
"Lufthansa Jet Airplane," 1960s, GAMA Co., 19½" long, 18½" wingspan, three actions	80	120	160

Light House
Photo by Don Hultzman

Lucky Crane with box
Photo by Don Hultzman

	C6	C8	C10
"Lunar Loop/Swing and Orbiting Action," 1960s, Daiya Co., 14" high, 12" diameter hoop, three actions	80	120	160
"M-101 Aston Martin Secret Ejector Car," 1960s, Daiya Co., 11" long, six actions, (includes ejectable passenger)	110	165	220
"Mac the Turtle," 1960s, "Y" Co., 8" high, five actions	80	120	160
"Magic Color Moon Express," 1960s, S-H Co., 13" long, four actions	40	60	80
"Magic Man Clown," 1950s, Alps Co., 12" tall, five actions	100	150	200
"Magic Snowman," 1950s, M-T Co., (Santa Creations) 11¼" tall, four actions, (includes detachable tin broom, plastic pipe and styro ball)	110	165	220

223

M-101 Aston-Martin Secret Ejector Car
Photo by Don Hultzman

Mickey Mouse on Handcar
Photo by Don Hultzman

Magic Snowman
Photo by Don Hultzman

Mickey the Magician
Photo by Don Hultzman

	C6	C8	C10
"Magnet Rail Moon Orbiter," 1960s, "Y" Co., 14" high, 12" diameter, minor toy	40	60	80
"Mag-oo, Mr. Magoo Car," 1961, Hubley Co., 9" long, five actions, includes cloth roof top	90	135	180
"Major Tooty," 1960s, Alps Co., (R.F.), 14" tall, three actions, includes drum and hat	70	105	140
"Mambo-The Jolly Drumming Elephant," 1950s, Alps Co., 9½" high, six actions, includes cymbals and stand	80	120	160

	C6	C8	C10
"Man in Space - Astronaut," 1960s, Alps Co., 6" tall, a minor action toy	60	90	120
"Mars Explorer," robot, 1950s, S-H Co., 9½" tall, seven actions	150	225	300
"Mars King Robot No. 12101", 1960s, S-H Co., 9½" tall, four actions	180	270	360
"Marshall Wild Bill," 1950s, Y Co., 10½" tall, four actions, 2 cycles, includes tin cowboy hat	120	180	240
"Martian Robot," 1970s, SJM Co., 12" tall, four actions	40	60	80
"Marvelous Fire Engine," 1960s, "Y" Co., 11" long, four actions	20	30	40
"Marvelous Mike," 1950s, Saunders Co., 17" long, four actions	90	135	180
"Maxwell Coffee-Loving Bear," 1960s T-N Co., 10" tall, five actions	80	120	160

Mr. Mercury - Type I and Type II
Photo by Don Hultzman

Moon Globe Orbiter
Photo by Don Hultzman

Mystery Police Car
Photo by Don Hultzman

	C6	C8	C10
"McGregor," 1960s, T-N Co., 12" tall when standing, six actions	70	105	140
"Mechanic Robot," 1960s, "Y" Co., 12" tall, five actions	40	60	80
"Mechanized Robot, The," ("Robby"), 1950s, T-N Co., 13½" tall, four actions, Rare	500	750	1000
"Mercury Explorer," 1960s, T.P.S. Co., 8" long, five actions	80	120	160
"Mercury X-1 Space Saucer," 1960s, "Y" Co., 8" diameter, four actions	50	75	100
"Merry Ice Cream Truck", 1960s, Bandai Co., 10½" long, five actions	70	105	140
"Mexicali Pete-Drum Player," 1960s, Alps Co., 10½" high, three actions	50	75	100
"Mickey Mouse and Donald Duck Fire Engine," 1960s, M-T Co., 16" long, three actions	120	180	240
"Mickey Mouse on Handcar," 1960s, M-T Co., 9¾" long, 7¾" high, three actions	200	300	400
"Mickey Mouse Sand Buggy," 1960s, M-T Co., 11" long, four actions	100	150	200
"Mickey Mouse Trolley," 1960s, M-T Co., 11" high, three actions	110	165	220
"Mickey the Magician," 1960s, Linemar, 10" tall, four actions, includes celluloid rabbit, Rare	450	675	900
"Mighty Mike the Barbell Lifter Bear," 1950s, "K" Co., 10½" tall, four actions	100	150	200
"Mighty Kong," 1950s, Marx, 11" tall, five actions	150	225	300
"Mighty Robot," 1960s, K-O Co., 11½" tall, four actions	200	300	400
"Military Jet Plane," 1960s, Marx Co., 16" long, 14" wingspan, three actions	70	105	140
"Military Police Car," 1950s, Linemar, 8½" long, six actions	60	90	120
"Mimi Poodle with Bone," 1950s, T-N Co., 11" long, 10" high, five actions, two cycles, (includes plastic bone)	30	45	60
"Mischievous Monkey," 1950s, M-T Co., 18" tall, six actions, includes tree and monkey	90	135	180
"Mischievous Monkey with Bulldog," 1950s, T-N Co., 12" high, four actions	110	165	220
"Miss Friday - The Typist," 1950s, T-N Co., 8" tall, six actions, removable head	90	135	180
"Missile Robot - Mr. 45.", M-T Co., 17½" tall, five actions	40	60	80
"Mr. Atom - The Electronic Walking Robot," 1950s, Advance Doll & Toy Co., 17" tall, four actions	250	375	500

225

Santa Claus Sitting on Roof, Santa Copter, Royal Bunny in Buggy

Cragstan "Crapshooter", Tumbles-the Bear, Overland Stage Coach

Warpath Indian, Nutty Mad Indian, Indian Joe

Puffy Morris, Piggy Cook, Cragstan "Crapshooting Monkey"

Tank (M-81), Tank (M-35), Tank (M-56), Tank (M-197)

Pinky The Clown, Circus Elephant, Tom & Jerry Handcar (Tom)

Cragstan's Two Gun Sheriff, Bimbo the Clown, Mother Bear Sitting and Knitting in Her Old Rocking Chair.

Bear-the Cashier, Old Fashion Telephone Bear, Washing Bear, Ice Cream Eating Bear   Courtesy Don Hultzman   Photos by Ron Chojnacki

226

Circus Lion

Happy Santa-Walking, Santa on Hand Car

Cragstan "Schoolbus", Cragstan "Western Locomotive", New Bell Ringer Choo-Choo

Mr. Fox the Magician-blowing magic bubbles, Professor Owl, Mr. Fox the Magician with the Magical Disappearing Rabbit.

Peter-the Drumming Rabbit, Picnic Bear, Bunny-the Magician

Funland Cup Ride, Big Shot Cadillac

Bubble Lion, Wild West Rodeo, Cragstan "Bullfighter"

Courtesy Don Hultzman.

Trumpet Playing Monkey, Monkey On A Picnic, Busy Housekeeper
Photos by Ron Chojnacki.

227

	C6	C8	C10
"Mr. Atomic" robot, 1950s, Cragstan, 11" tall, three actions, rare	600	900	1200
"Mr. Baseball Junior," 1950s, T-N Co., 7" high, three actions	130	195	260
"Mr. Chief" Robot, 1950s, K-O Co., 12" tall, four actions	350	525	700
"Mr. Fox, the Magician - Blowing Magical Bubbles," 1950s, Y Co., 9" tall, four actions, includes plastic bowl for bubble solution	150	225	300
"Mr. Fox, the Magician - With the Magical Disappearing Rabbit," 1960s, Y Co., 9" tall, five actions, includes plastic rabbit	170	255	340
"Mr. Hustler Robot," 1960s, Taiyo Co., 11" tall, six actions	110	165	220
"Mr. MacPooch (Smoking)", 1950s, SAN Co., 9" tall, four actions	70	105	140
"Mr. Mercury" - Type I (all tin), 1960s, Marx Co., 13" tall, seven actions	400	600	800
"Mister Mercury" - Type II (lighted), 1960s, Marx Co., seven actions	400	600	800
"Mr. Strong Pup - Weight Lifting Dog," 1950s, "K" Co., 9" tall, five actions	100	150	200
"Mr. Zerox," 1960s, S-H Co., 9½" tall, four actions	130	195	260
"Mix-ette Mixer," 1940s, KDP Co., 9" high when assembled, a minor toy, includes mixer stand and bowl	20	30	40
"Mod Monster- Blushing Frankenstein," 1960s, T-N Co., 13¼" tall, five actions	100	150	200
"Monkey Artist," 1950s, Alps Co., 8" high, five actions	120	180	240
"Monkey Handcar," 1950s, T-N Co., 7" high, three actions	40	60	80
"Monkey On A Picnic," 1950s, Alps Co., 9½" high, seven actions	110	165	220
"Monorail Rocket Ship," 1950s, Lincmar Co., 10" long with supports and rail rods, minor toy	120	180	240
"Moon Astronaut," 1950s, Daiya Co., 9" tall, four actions	400	600	800
"Moon Explorer" Robot, 1960s, Bandai Co., 17½" tall (feet to antenna top), five actions, Rare	400	600	800
"Moon Globe Orbiter", ca. 1960s, "Y" Co. (Mego), 3 actions, rocket orbits globe, noise, lights, 10½" high	50	75	100
"Moon Orbiter," 1960s, Y Co., minor toy, 4" long, includes 6 sections of track and trestles	60	90	120
"Moon Traveler - Apollo Z," 1960s, T-N Co., 12" long, 15" extended, five actions	80	120	160
"Moon Patrol Space Rover," 1960s, Gakken Toy Co., 11½" long, five actions	100	150	200
"Mother Bear - Sitting and Knitting In Her Old Rocking Chair," 1950s, M-T Co., 9½" high, four actions	150	225	300
"Movieland Drive-In Theater," 1959, Remco Co., 14" long, minor toy (includes 6 small cars, ad cards, filmstrips)	100	150	200
"Multi Action Electra Jet - KLM Royal Dutch Airlines PH-DSF," 1960s, T-N Co., 14" long, 17" wingspan, three actions	70	105	140
"Mumbo Jumbo," (Hawaiian drummer), 1960s, Alps Co., 9¾" high, three actions	60	90	120
"Musical Bank Organ Grinder & Monkey," 1950s, HTC Co., 8" tall, four actions, includes test coin and detachable celluloid monkey, Rare	200	300	400
"Musical Bear" (Drum and Cymbals), 1950s, Linemar Co., 10" tall, six actions (including detachable tin horn)	110	165	220
"Musical Bulldog Playing Piano," 1950s, SAN Co., 8½" tall, 6"x9" base, four actions, Rare	400	600	800
"Musical Clown" (New Adventures of Clown), 1960s, T-N Co., 9" tall, three actions	120	180	240
"Musical Comic Jumping Jeep," 1970s, M-T Co., 12" long, six actions	40	60	80
"Musical Jackal," 1950s, Linemar Co., 10" tall, six actions	110	165	220
"Musical Jolly Chimp," 1960s, C-K Co., 10½" high, five actions, two cycles	30	45	60
"Musical Showboat," 1960s, Gakken Toy Co. 13" long, minor toy, (includes two detachable smokestacks)	40	60	80
"My Fair Dancer," 1950s, Haji Co., 10½" tall, minor toy	60	80	120
"Mystery Fire Chief Car No. 81," 1950s, Sanshin Co., 9¼" long, three actions	70	105	140
"Mystery Police Car," 1960s, T-N Co., 9¾" long, 6" wide, 4" high, three actions	70	105	140
"NAR Television Truck," 1950s, Linemar Co., 12" long, four actions (includes six strip film inserts)	150	225	300
"Nautilus SSN 571 Submarine," 1950s, Marusan Co., 15" long, three actions	90	135	180
"Neptune Tugboat," 1950s, M-T Co., 15" long, 7" high, four actions	60	90	120

228

	C6	C8	C10
"New Astronaut" robot, 1970s, S-H Co., 9½" tall, six actions	60	90	120
"New Bell Ringer Choo Choo," locomotive, 1960s, M-T Co., 10" long, three actions	30	45	60
"News Service Car," 1960s, TPS Co., 10" long, four actions	70	105	140
"Non-Stop Robot," 1960s, M-T Co., 15" tall, three actions, Rare	500	750	1000
"Nutty Mad Indian," 1960s, Marx, 12" tall, four actions	60	90	120

	C6	C8	C10
"Nutty Mads Car" (Drincar), 1960s, Marx Co., 9¼" long, three actions	120	180	240
"Nutty Nibs," 1950s, Linemar, 11½" tall, a minor action toy, includes litho bowl of nuts and steel ball, Rare	350	525	700
"007 Aston Martin," 1966, Gilbert Co., 11½" long, eight actions, (includes ejectable passenger)	150	225	300
"007 Secret Agent's Car," (Impala), 1960s, Spesco Co., (Joy Toy), 15" long, five actions	100	150	200

	C6	C8	C10
"Ol' Sleepy Head Rip," 1950s, "Y" Co., 9" long, seven actions, Rare	110	165	220

	C6	C8	C10
"Old Fashioned Car," 1950s, S-H Co., 10" long, four actions	30	45	60
"Old-Fashioned Telephone Bear," (?) 1950s, M-T Co., 9½" high, four actions	100	150	200
"Old Ford Touring Car," 1950s, Z Co., 10" long, four actions	30	45	60
"Old Time Automobile," 1950s, "Y" Co, 8¾" long, three actions (includes detachable tin litho driver and steering wheel)	40	60	80
"Oldtimer Automoball," 1950s, M-T Co., 10" long, three actions, includes celluloid ball	50	75	100
"Oldtimer Sunday Driver," 1960s, Daiya Co., 9" long, four actions .	40	60	80
"Overland Choo Choo Express" locomotive, 1950s, M-T Co., 14" long, a minor action toy	14	21	28
"Overland Stage Coach," 1960s, Ichida Co., 18" long, four actions	70	105	140
"Pacific Piping Express Locomotive," 1960s, Kanto Toy Co., 14" long, four actions	20	30	40
"Pan Am Sky Taxi - Helicopter," 1960s, Haji Co., 3 actions, 11" long	30	45	60
"Pan American World Airways 'Seven Seas' DC-7," 1950s, T-N Co., 15" long, 19" wingspan, five actions .	100	150	200
"Panda Bear," 1970s, M-T Co., (Masudaya Co.), 10" long, four actions, mostly plastic	20	30	40
"Papa Bear - Reading & Drinking in his Old Rocking Chair," 1950s, M-T Co., four actions, 10" high	90	135	180
"PaPa Bear Smoking," 1950s, SAN Co., 8" tall, four actions	60	90	120
"Passenger Bus," 1950s, "Y" Co., 16" long, four actions	130	195	260
"Pat O'Neill," 1960s, T-N Co., 12" tall, standing, six actions	90	135	180
"Pat the Roaring Elephant," 1950s, "Y" Co., 9" long with attached baby elephant, four actions	70	105	140
"Patrol Auto-Tricycle," 1960s, T-N Co., 19" long, 7½" high, four actions	90	135	180
"Patrol Helicopter No. 7," 1960s, Bandai Co., 11" long, four actions ...	40	60	80
"P.D. No. 5 - Police Patrol Car," (Buick), 1960s, Asakusa Toy Co., 11½" long, three actions	40	60	80
"Penguin on Tricycle," 1950s, T-N Co., 6½" high, three actions	60	90	120
"Pepi-Tumbling Monkey," 1960s, Yanoman Toy Co., 9½" high, minor toy	30	45	60

229

	C6	C8	C10
"Peppermint Twist Doll," 1950s, Haji Co., 12" tall, minor toy	60	90	120
"Peppy Puppy," 1950s, "Y" Co., 8" long, 6½" high, seven actions, two cycles, (includes tin litho bone)	40	60	80
"Pet Turtle," 1960s, Alps Co., 7" long, four actions, two cycles	60	90	120
"Pete the Space Man," 1960s, Bandai Co., 5" tall, minor action (Walking Mate Series)	30	45	60
"Peter The Drumming Rabbit," 1950s, Alps Co., (VIA-Cragstan), 13" tall, five actions	100	150	200
"Pick-Up Truck," T-N Co., 10" long, four actions	40	60	80
"Picnic Bear," 1950s, (with Coke, Pepsi and generic logo), Alps Co., 10" high, five actions	50	75	100
"Picnic Bunny," 1950s, Alps Co., 10" tall, four actions	70	105	140
"Picnic Monkey," 1950s, Alps Co., 4 actions, 10" high	60	90	120
"Picnic Poodle," 1950s, STS Co., 7" long, 7" high, four actions, two cycles	24	36	48
"Piggy Barbecue," 1950s, Y Co., 9½" tall, five actions, includes chef's hat and tin litho fried egg	90	135	180
"Piggy Cook," 1950s, Y Co., 9½" tall, 4"x6" base, five actions, includes chef's hat and tin litho fried egg .	90	135	180
"Pinkee the Farmer," 1950s, M-T Co., 9½" long, seven actions	70	105	140
"Pinky The Clown," 1950s, Rock Valley Toy Co., (Via) 10¼" tall, five actions, (includes tin litho propeller-ball on nose), Rare	120	180	240
"Pinocchio Playing London Bridge," 1962, T-N Co., (Rosko), 10" tall, three actions, includes xylophone	100	150	200
"Pioneer Covered Wagon," 1960s, Ichida Co., 14½" long, four actions (includes detachable canopy and driver)	70	105	140
"Pipie the Whale," 1950s, Alps Co., 12" long, minor toy	50	75	100
"Piston Action Bulldozer," 1960s, Linemar Co., 7½" long, two cycles	50	75	100
"Piston Robot," 1960s, S-H Co., 10½" tall, four action	90	135	180
"Pistol Pete," 1950s, Marusan Co., 5 actions, 10¼" high, includes tin hat	120	180	240
"Planet Rover," wheeled tank, 1960s, J Co., 9" long, 6½" high, six actions	80	120	160

Playful Puppy
Photo by Don Hultzman

Police Motorcycle
Photo by Don Hultzman

Power Shovel
Photo by Don Hultzman

	C6	C8	C10
"Playful Pup in Shoe," 1960s, "Y" Co., 10" long, three actions	30	45	60
"Playful Puppy," 1950s, M-T Co., 7⅞" long, 5" high, four actions	80	120	160
"Pluto," 1960s, Linemar Co., 10" long, five actions	100	150	200
"Polar Bear," 1970s, Alps Co., 8" long, three actions	20	30	40
"Police Auto Cycle," 1960s, (motorcycle and plastic driver), Bandai Co., five actions, Remote Control	60	90	120

Musical Bulldog

Animated Squirrel, Cock-A-Doodle-Doo Rooster, Josie-the-Cow, Sparky-the-Seal

Old Fashioned Telephone Bear, Cragstan Telly Bear, V.I.P. the Busy Boss, Telephone Bear
Courtesy Don Hultzman.   Photos by Ron Chojnacki.

Tom & Jerry Choo-Choo, Old Timer Automoball

Broadway Trolley, Battery Locomotive No.123, A-B-C Fairy Train, Smoking Pop Locomotive-the General

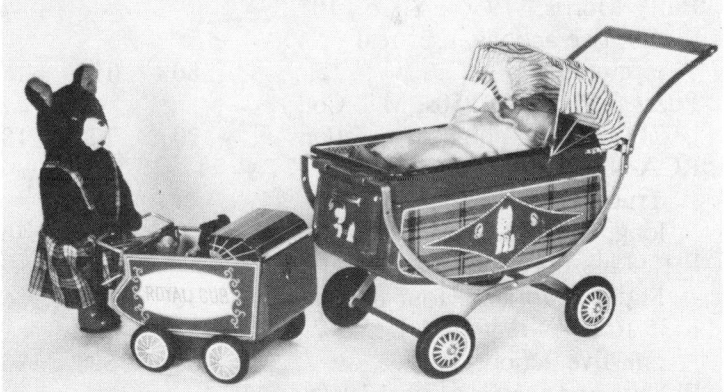

Royal Cub in Buggy, Cry-Baby-In-Buggy

Silver Streak Locomotive, Silver Bell Choo-Choo, Western Locomotive

231

	C6	C8	C10
"Police Motorcycle," 1950s, M-T Co., 11¾" long, seven actions	90	135	180
"Police Patrol Jeep," 1960s, T-N Co., 4 actions, lights, bump & go, noise, smoke, 9¼" long	50	75	100
"Policeman," 1950s, A-I Co., 14" tall, 6"x6" base, four actions	100	150	200
"Popcorn Eating Bear," 1950s, M-T Co., 9" high, five actions	90	135	180
"Popcorn Vendor," No. 4035, 1960s, S&E Co., 8" high, 7" long, six actions, includes litho umbrella	150	225	300
"Popcorn Vendor Truck," 1960s, T-N Co., 9" long, three actions	80	120	160
"Porsche With Visible Engine," 1964, Bandai Co., 10" long, three actions	40	60	80
"Poverty Pup," bank, 1966, Poynter Products Co., 6" long, 4¼" high, three actions	30	45	60
"Power Shovel," 1950s, Alps Co., 15" long, extended, six actions	70	105	140
"Pretty Peggy Parrot," 1950s, T-N Co., 12" long, four actions	200	300	400
"Princess the French Poodle," 1950s, no markings, 9" long, 8" high, five actions	30	45	60
"Professor Owl," 1950s, E-T Co., 8" high, five actions, includes two discs	120	180	240
"Project Yankee Doodle," 1959, Remco Co., 15" long, six actions (includes plastic missiles, rockets & accessories)	60	90	120
"Puffy Morris," 1960s, Y Co., 10" tall, five actions, uses real cigarette	80	120	160
"Puzzled Puppy," 1950s, M-T Co., 7½" long, 5" high, five actions ..	90	135	180
"RCA-NBC Mobile Color T.V. Truck," 1950s, Yonezawa Co., 9" long, four actions	250	375	500
"R.R. Line Locomotive," 1950s, Marx, 6½" long, four actions ...	30	45	60
"R-35 Robot," 1950s, M-T Co., 7½" tall, five actions	400	600	800
"Rabbits and the Carriage," 1950s, S&E Co., 9" high, three actions .	100	150	200
"Radar Robot," 1960s, T-N Co., 9" tall, three actions, remote robot-face control box	600	900	1200
"Radar Robot," 1970s, S-H Co., 12" tall, five actions	50	75	100
"Radio Rex," 1930s, Elmwood Button Co., 5"x7" dog house, minor toy (includes cell. dog)	50	75	100
"Railroad Hand Car," 1950s, KDP Co., 8" long, a minor toy, includes rubber track	60	90	120

River Boat
Photo by Don Hultzman

Roaring Gorilla Shooting Gallery
Photo by Don Hultzman

Root Beer Counter
Photo by Don Hultzman

	C6	C8	C10
"Railway Yard - Shuttle Train," 1950s, ATC Co., 8" long, track 28" long, three actions, includes locomotive boxcar and track	60	90	120
"Ranger Robot," 1950s, Daiya Co., 10½" tall, four actions	300	450	600
"Ray Gun," machine gun, 1950s, T-N Co., 17½" long, three actions, includes tripod	30	45	60
"Reading Bear," 1950s, Alps Co., 9" tall, five actions	70	105	140
"Reversible Diesel Electric Tractor," 1950s, Marx Co., minor toy	30	45	60
"Ricki - The Begging Poodle," 1950s, Rock Valley Toys (VIA), 9" long, 8" high, 5 actions	20	30	40
"Riverboat," 1950s, Marusan Co., 12¾" long, three actions (includes detachable tin smokestack	80	120	160
"River Queen Sidewheeler," 1950s, M-T Co., 13½" long, three actions .	60	90	120
"Road Construction Roller," 1950s, Daiya Co., 8½" long, four actions	50	75	100
"Road Grader," 1960s, T-N Co., 12" long, three actions	30	45	60
"Road Roller," 1950s, M-T Co., 9" long, four actions	50	75	100
"Roaring Gorilla," (white gorilla), 1950s, T-N Co., 9¼" tall, five actions	100	150	200
"Roaring Gorilla Shooting Gallery," 1950s, M-T Co., 9½" tall, three actions, (Includes fold-out target box, tin gun, plastic darts)	80	120	160
"Roarin' Jungle Lion," (?) 1950s, Marx Co., 16" long, nose to tail tip, four actions, 2 cycles	120	180	240
"Robbie Robot," 1950s, Yonezawa Co., 13" tall, five actions	600	900	1200
"Robert the Robot," 1950s, Ideal Toy Co., 14" tall, three actions	110	165	220
"Robot," 1960s, Y Co., 10½" tall, three actions	350	525	700
"Robot 2500," 1970s, Durham Industries, 10½" tall, four actions .	40	60	80
"Robotank-Z Space Robot," 1960s, T-N Co., 10¼" high, four actions .	200	300	400
"Rock 'N' Roll Hotrod," (Dreamboat), 1950s, T-N Co., 3 actions, 7" long	50	75	100
"Rock 'n' Roll Monkey, 1950s, Rosko Co., 13" tall, five actions, includes plastic hat (2 variations)	100	150	200
"Rocket Launching Pad," 1950s, "Y" Co., 8½" high, five actions (includes tin litho satellite and rocket)	100	150	200
"Rocking Chair Bear," (?) 1950s, M-T Co., 10" high, five actions	70	105	140

Santa Claus on Scooter
Photo by Don Hultzman

Santa Pay-Phone Bank
Photo by Don Hultzman

Sneezing Bear
Photo by Don Hultzman

233

Teddy-Go-Cart, Mambo-the Jolly Drumming Elephant.

F.D. Fire Engine, Fire Engine, Fire Chief Mystery Action Car,
Police Motorcycle Cop

Cragstan Automatic Dishwasher, Bengali Tiger, Holiday Sink/Stove
Combination

Ricki-the Begging Poodle, Picnic Poodle, Princess-the French
Poodle

Champion Weight Lifter

Fighting Bull, Breakfast Chef, Near Sighted Pup

Dump Truck No.7343, Bulldozer, Crane Tractor

Courtesy Don Hultzman. Photo by Ron Chojnacki.

234

	C6	C8	C10
"Rocking Santa," 1950s, Alps Co., 10" high, four actions, Rare	150	225	300
"Rollerskating Clown," 1950s, T.P.S. Co., 6" tall, minor toy	180	270	360
"Romance Car - M-841," 1950s, "M" Co., 8" long, three actions	50	75	100
"Rootbeer Counter," 1960s, "K" Co., 8" long, 8" high, three actions (includes plastic barrel & glasses & tin tray)	80	120	160
"Rotate-O-Matic Super Astronaut," 1960s, S-H Co., 11½" tall, six actions, two cycles	70	105	140
"Roy Rogers Western Telephone," Ideal, 1950s, 3 actions, 9" high	50	75	100
"Royal Cub In Buggy," (pushed by Mama Bear), 1940s, S&E Co., 8" long, 8" high, six actions, Rare	80	120	160
"Rudy the Robot," 1968, Remco Co., 16¼" tall, four actions	100	150	200
"Sam the Shaving Man," 1960s, Plaything Toy Co., 11½" tall, seven actions, includes metal mirror	100	150	200
"Sammy Wong - The Tea Totaler," 1950s, T-N Co., 10" tall, four actions	110	165	220
"Santa Bank," 1960, HTC Co., (Trim a Tree), 11" high, four actions	110	165	220
"Santa Claus - Bellringer," 1950s, Santa Creations Co., 13" tall, five actions	70	105	140
"Santa Claus," No. M-750 (Sitting on House), 1960s, H.T.C. Co., 8" high, four actions	70	105	140
"Santa Claus on Handcar," 1960s, M-T Co., 10" high, three actions	60	90	120
"Santa Claus on Scooter," 1960s, M-T Co., 10" high, four actions	60	90	120
"Santa Claus - Stands & Sits," 1960s, T-N Co., 10" tall, six actions	60	90	120
"Santa Copter," 1960s, M-T Co., 8½" long, three actions	50	75	100
"Santa in Rocker," 1950s, Alps Co., 21" high, from base to tree top, four actions (includes detachable tree and stocking)	110	165	220
"Santa Pay-Phone Bank," 1950s, S&E Co., 7 actions, 8" high, includes remote 4¾" high payphone	150	225	300
"Santa Sled," 1950s, T-N Co., 14" long, four actions	100	150	200
"Santa the Bellringer," 1950s, Chase Import Co., 7" high, minor toy (electro-magnet activated & Blinker bulb)	60	90	120
"Satellite Target Game," 1960s, S-H Co., 8" high, 10½" wide, minor toy (includes celluloid ball and special gun)	60	90	120
"Saxophone Playing Monkey," 1950s, Alps Co., 9½" high, four action	80	120	160
"School Bus," 1950s, Cragstan, 20½" long, a minor toy	40	60	80
"Secret Service Action Car" ("Green Hornet" motif), 1960s, ASC Co., 11" long, four actions, rare	100	150	200
"Serpent Charmer," 1950s, Linemar Co., 7" high, four actions	140	210	280
"Shaggy The Friendly Pup," 1960s, Alps Co., 8" long, three actions	20	30	40
"Shaking Classic Car," 1960s, T-N Co., 7" long, four actions	40	60	80
"Shaking Old-Timer Car No. 2511-1", 1960s, T-N Co., 9" long, four actions, includes plastic driver	50	75	100
"Shark-U-Control Racing Car," 1961, Remco Ind. Inc., 19" long, all plastic, minor toy	40	60	80
"Shoe Maker Bear," 1960s, T-N Co., 8½" high, three actions	70	105	140
"Shoe-Shaking Dog," 1950s, M-T Co., 8" long, 6" tall, five actions	24	36	48
"Shoe Shine Bear," 1950s, T-N Co., 9" tall, five actions	90	135	180
"Shoe Shine Joe," 1950s, Alps Co., 11" high, six actions	80	120	160
"Shoe Shine Monkey," 1950s, T-N Co., 9" high, five actions	80	120	160
"Shooting Bear," 1950s, SAN Co., 9½" tall, five actions	100	150	200
"Shooting Gorilla," 1950s, M-T Co., 12" high, four actions, includes gun and darts	80	120	160
"Shutterbug" photographer, 1950s, T-N Co., 9" tall, five actions	200	300	400
"Shuttling Train and Freight Yard," 1950s, Alps Co., 11" long, track 51" long, four actions, includes locomotive, baggage car, two platforms, litho luggage	100	150	200
"Sight Seeing Bus," 1960s, Bandai Co., 14½" long, four actions	80	120	160
"Silver Bell Choo Choo," 1950s, Kanto Co., 12" long, three actions	20	30	40
"Silver Mountain Express Locomotive," 1960s, M-T Co., four actions, 15¾" long	20	30	40
"Silver Mountain Locomotive," 1950s, M-T Co., 16" long, three actions	20	30	40
"Silver Ray Secret Weapon Space Scout," 1960s, S-H Co., 9" tall	100	150	200
"Silver Streak Locomotive No. 6682," 1950s, M-T Co., 16" long, four actions	20	30	40
"Singing Bird In Cage," 1950s, T-N Co., 9" high, 4"x6" rectangular base, four actions	60	90	120
"Skiing Santa," 1960s, M-T Co., 12" tall, four actions	100	150	200

	C6	C8	C10
"Skipping Monkey," 1960s, T-N Co., 9½" tall, minor toy	30	45	60
"Sky Patrol Flying Saucer," 1950s, K-O Co., 7½" diameter, seven actions, includes detachable antenna	70	105	140
"Sky Taxi-Panam-Boeing Vertol 107," 1970s, Haji Co., 12¾" long, three actions, includes 2 detachable rotors	60	90	120
"Sleeping Baby Bear," 1950s, Linemar, 9" long, six actions, includes detachable Alarm Clock	110	165	220
"Sleeping Pup," 1960s, Alps Co., 9" long, five actions	30	45	60
"Slurpy Pup," 1960s, T-N Co., 6½" long, 4" high, four actions	20	30	40
"Smokey Bear," 1950s, Marusan Co., 8½" tall, five actions	140	210	280
"Smokey Bill on Old Fashioned Car," 1960s, T-N Co., 9" long, four actions	60	90	120
"Smokey the Bear Jeep," 1950s, M-T Co., 10" long, four actions	200	300	400
"Smoking Bulldozer," 1960s, WKC Co., 9" long, four actions	50	75	100
"Smoking Bunny," 1950s, SAN Co., 10½" tall, four actions	60	90	120
"Smoking Elephant," 1950s, Marusan Co., 8¾" tall, four actions	90	135	180
"Smoking Grandpa," (in Rocking Chair), 1950s, SAN Co., 8" tall, four actions (Type I - eyes open)	110	165	220
"Smoking Grandpa" (in Rocking Chair), 1950s, SAN Co., 8" tall, four actions (Type II - eyes closed)	120	180	240
"Smoking Jet Plane," 1950s, T-N Co., 12" long, 11" wingspan, four actions	100	150	200
"Smoking Pop Locomotive - the General," 1950s, San Co., 10¼" long, four actions	40	60	80
"Smoking Popeye," 1950s, Linemar, 9" tall, five actions, Rare	400	600	800
"Smoking Robot," 1960s, M-T Co., 10" tall, four actions (all plastic)	50	75	100
"Smoking Spaceman," 1950s, Linemar Co., 12" tall, six actions, Rare	600	900	1200
"Smoking U.S.A.F. Jet," 1950s, T-N Co., 13" long, 12" wingspan, four actions	100	150	200
"Smoking Volkswagen," 1960s, Aoshin Co., 10½" long, four actions	40	60	80
"Smoky Joe - Fancy Mobile," 1960s, T-N Co., 4 actions, smokes, lights, bump & go, noise, 9" long	60	90	120
"Snake Charmer (And Casey the Trained Cobra)", 1950s, Linemar Co., 8" high, four actions	150	225	300
"Snappy the Dragon," 1960s, T-N Co., 30" long, six actions, Rare	500	750	1000
"Sneezing Bear," 1950s, Linemar Co., 9" high, five actions	150	225	300
"Snoopie the Non-Fall Dog," 1960s, Amico Co., 8" long, three actions	20	30	40
"Space Capsule," 1960s, M-T Co., 10" long, four actions, includes styrofoam saucer and astronaut	60	90	120
"Space Commando - Spaceman," 1960s, M-T Co., 7¾" tall, four actions	400	600	800
"Space Explorer," 1960s, S-H Co., 7¾" high, extends to 11½" high, six actions, Rare	400	600	800
"Space Fighter" robot, 1970s, S-H Co., 9" tall, six actions	40	60	80
"Space Frontier Saturn 5 Rocket," 1960s, K-Y Co., (Yoshino Toy Co.), 18" long, six actions	80	120	160
"Space Patrol 3 Saucer," 1950s, K-O Co., 7½" diameter, five actions	60	90	120
"Space Patrol Robot," 1950s, S-H Co., 11" tall, six actions	80	120	160
"Space Patrol Rocket," 1970s, M-T Co., 11" long, three actions	30	45	60
"Space Patrol - Snoopy," 1960s, M-T Co., 11" long, four actions	40	60	80
"Space Patrol Vehicle," 1950s, K Co., 9" long, four actions	60	90	120
"Space Patrol Vehicle," 1960s, M-T Co., 9½" long, three actions	50	75	100
"Space Robot Trooper," 1950s, K-O Co., 7½" tall, three actions, Rare	300	450	600
"Space Robot (X-70)," 1960s, T-N Co., 12" tall, five actions, rare	450	675	900
"Space Rocket - Blue Eagle," 1950s, Masuya Toy Co., 15" long (tail to probe tip)	90	135	180
"Space Rocket - Solar X," 1960s, T-N Co., 15½" tall, five actions	80	120	160
"Space Scooter," 1960s, M-T Co., 10½" high, 8" long, three actions	70	105	140
"Space Ship," 1950s, I.Y. Co., 9½" diameter, four actions	140	210	280
"Space Ship," 1970s, M-T Co., 9" long, three actions	60	90	120
"Space Ship X-5," 1970s, M-T Co., 8" diameter, four actions	40	60	80
"Space Ship X-8," 1960s, Tada Co., 8" long, four actions	90	135	180
"Space Station," 1950s, T-N Co., 9" diameter, four actions	80	120	160
"Space Station," 1950s, S-H Co., 11¾" diameter, five actions	400	600	800

	C6	C8	C10
"Space Tank," 1960s, K-O Co., 6" long, four action	150	225	300
"Space Tank," 1950s, Daiya Co., 8" long, four actions	80	120	160
"Space Tank – M41," 1950s, M-T Co., 9" long, four actions (includes detachable plastic antenna)	60	90	120
"Spaceman" robot, 1950s, T-N Co., 9¼" tall, four actions	300	450	600
"Spaceman" robot, 1950s, Linemar, 7½" tall, three actions	200	300	400
"Spad X111 S-7 Stunt Biplane," 1960s, T.P.S. Co., 9" long, 10⅜" wingspan, three actions	60	90	120
"Spanking Bear," 1950s, Linemar Co., 9" high, six actions	100	150	200
"Sparkling Mike The Robot," 1950s, Ace Co., 7½" tall, three actions, rare	500	750	1000
"Sparky Savings Bank," 1930s, Byron Co., 4" long, 4½" high doghouse, minor toy (electro magnet action - includes 4" long compo dog)	40	60	80
"Sparky the Seal," 1950s, M-T Co., 6" high, 7" long, four actions, two cycles, includes celluloid ball	60	90	120
"Spirit of 1776," locomotive No. 4406, 1976, M-T Co., 15¾" long, five actions	20	30	40
"Steam Roller (Road Roller), 1950s, T-N Co., (Rosko), 12" long with trailer, four actions	60	90	120
"Steam Roller," 1950s, "Y" Co., 8" long, four actions (includes tin trailer)	80	120	160
"Steerable Tank," 1950s, Linemar Co., 9" long, 5 actions	40	60	80
"Strange Explorer," 1960s, DSK Co., 7½" long, four actions	80	120	160
"Strato Jet U.S.A.F.," 1950s, T-N Co., 13" long, 14" wingspan, three actions	100	150	200
"Strutting My Fair Dancer," (Dancing Sailor Girl), 1950s, Haji Co., 12" tall, (two pieces), a minor toy	60	90	120
"Struttin' Sam," 1950s, Haji Co., 10½" tall, minor jigger toy	150	225	300
"Sunbeam Jeep No. 1," 1940s, 10" long, unmarked, three actions	80	120	160
"Sunday Driver," 1950s, M-T Co., 10" long, four actions (includes detachable driver)	50	75	100
"Super Astronaut," Robot, 1960s, S-H Co., 11½" tall, five actions, two cycles	80	120	160
"Super Astronaut" robot, 1960s, SJM Co., 12" tall, four actions			
"Super Giant Robot," 1960s, S-H Co., 15½" tall, six actions	60	90	120

	C6	C8	C10
"Super Space Capsule," 1960s, S-H Co., 9" high, four actions	90	135	180
"Super Space Commander," 1960s, S-H Co., 10" tall, three actions	40	60	80
"Superman Tank," 1950s, Linemar Co., 12" long, three actions, Rare	400	600	800
"Surrey Jeep," 1960s, T-N Co., 11" long, three actions	60	90	120

	C6	C8	C10
"Susie the Cashier Bear," 1950s, Linemar Co., 9" high, six actions	250	375	500
"Suzy-Q Automatic Ironer," 1950s, GW Co., 7" high, four actions	60	90	120
"Suzette the Eating Monkey," 1950s, Linemar Co., 8¾" high, 7"x5" base, five actions (includes tin litho steak) Rare	200	300	400
"Swingtail Airplane Flying Tigers," 1960s, Marx Co., 19½" long, 21" wingspan, seven actions	150	225	300
"Switchboard Operator" (?), 1950s, Linemar, 7½" high, four actions, Rare	150	225	300
"Swivel-O-Matic Astronaut" robot, 1960s, S-H Co., 11½" tall, five actions, 2 cycles	60	90	120
"T 360 Monoplane," 1950s, S&E Co., 12" long, 14½" wingspan, four actions	110	165	220

	C6	C8	C10
"Tank-Daisy-Matic No. 80," 1965, Daisy Mfg. Co., 8½" long, five actions, includes darts	60	90	120
"Tarzan," 1960s, SAN Co., 13" tall, three actions	150	225	300
"Taxi," (yellow cab), 1950s, Linemar Co., 7½" long, five actions	40	60	80
"Taxi Cab," 1950s, "Y" Co., 8½" long, five actions	40	60	80
"Teddy Bear Swing," 1950s, T-N Co., 18" high, minor toy	90	135	180
"Teddy-Go-Kart," 1960s, Alps Co., 10½" long, four actions	40	60	80
"Teddy the Artist," 1950s, Y Co., 8½" high, 5¼"x7" base, 3 actions, includes removable tray and 9 patterns	150	225	300
"Teddy the Boxing Bear," 1950s, "Y" Co., 9" tall, five actions	110	165	220
"Teddy the Rhythmical Drummer," 1960s, Alps Co., 11" tall, three actions	50	75	100
"Telephone Bear," 1950s, Linemar, 7½" high, six actions	90	135	180
"Telephone Bear - Ringing and Talking In His Old Rocking Chair," 1950s, M-T Co., 10" high, four actions	120	160	240
"Telephone Bunny - Ringing and Talking In His Old Rocking Chair," 1950s, M-T Co., 10" high, four actions	100	150	200
"Television Spaceman," 1960s, Alps Co., 14½" high to tip of antenna, six actions	400	600	800
"Television Truck," 1950s, Linemar Co., 14" long, three actions	150	225	300
"The Big Parade," 1963, Marx Co., 11½" tall, 15" wide, four actions (includes detachable guns and baton)	110	165	220
"The Loser," (Bar Toy), ca. 1971, Poynter Prod. Co., 3 actions, 13" high	30	45	60
"Thunder Jet Boat," 1950s, Bandai Co., 9¾" long, three actions	110	165	220
"Tin Man" Robot, 1960s, Remco Industries, Inc., 21" tall, all plastic, four actions	90	135	180
"Tiny Jeep," 1950s, WACO Co., 4¼" long, minor action	10	15	20
"Tiny Tank," 1950s, WACO Co., 4¼" long, minor action	10	15	20
"Tom and Jerry Car," 1960s, Rico Co., (Spain), 13" long, three actions, Rare	300	450	600
"Tom and Jerry Choo Choo," 1960s, M-T Co., 10¼" long, five actions	80	120	160

	C6	C8	C10
"Talking Parrot," 1950s, T-N Co., 18" high, six actions	200	300	400
"Talking Police Car - Mystery Action," 1960s, Y Co., 14" long, three actions	40	60	80
"Tank M-4 Combat Tank," 1960s, Taiyo Co., 11½" long, 13" with gun barrel extended, five actions .	30	45	60
"Tank M-35," 1950s, HTC Co., 8" long, three actions	50	75	100
"Tank-M-41," 1970s, J Co., 8¼" long, four actions	50	75	100
"Tank M-48-T," 1960s, T-N Co., 8¼" long, four actions	60	90	120
"Tank M-56," 1940s, M-T Co., 7½" long, wheel drive, seven actions ..	50	75	100
"Tank M-81," 1960s, M-T Co., 8½" long, seven actions	60	90	120
"Tank M-103," 1950s, M-T Co., 7" long, three actions	50	75	100
"Tank M-107-U.S. Army," 1950s, Y Co., 6" long, four actions, includes four missiles	70	105	140
"Tank M-X," 1950s, T-N Co., 8½" long, five actions	40	60	80
"Tank X-3" (explorer defense), 1950s, Cragstan Co., 7¾" long, five actions, includes six cartridge shells	90	135	180
"Tank-Daisymatic No. 64 Rapid Fire Tank," 1960s, Daisy Mfg. Co., 8" long, four actions	50	75	100

The Big Parade
Photo by Don Hultzman

Thunder Jet Boat
Photo by Don Hultzman

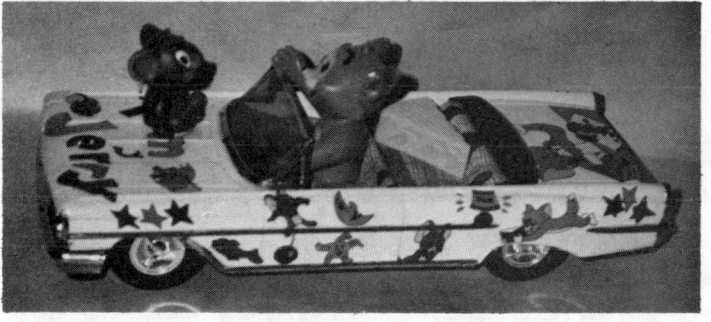
Tom and Jerry Car
Photo by Don Hultzman

	C6	C8	C10
"Tom and Jerry Handcar - Jerry," 1960s, M-T Co., 7¾" high, 7¾" long, three actions	90	135	180
"Tom and Jerry Handcar - Tom," 1960s, M-T Co., 9¾" high, 7¾" long, three actions	90	135	180
"Tom and Jerry Helicopter," 1960s, M-T Co., 9½" long, three actions	70	105	140
"Tom and Jerry Highway Patrol," 1960s, M-T Co., 8" long, three actions	110	165	220

	C6	C8	C10
"Tom and Jerry Jumping Jeep," 1960s, M-T Co., 9" long, three actions	110	165	220
"Tom-Tom Indian," 1961, Y Co., 10½" tall, four action	70	105	140
"Topo Gigio Playing the Xylophone," 1960s, T-N Co., three actions	250	375	450
"Torpedo Boat - PT 107," 1950s, Linemar 11½" long, three actions	90	135	180
"Tractor," 1950s, Showa Co., 7½" long, four actions, includes litho tin figure (driver)	30	45	60
"Tractor," 1960s, Y Co., 6" long, three actions	30	45	60
"Traffic Policeman, Mr." 1960s, A-1 Co., 13½" tall, eight actions	150	225	300
"Traveler Bear," 1950s, Linemar Co, 8" high, three actions	80	120	160
"Treasure Chest" Bank, 1960s, Ilfelder Co., 11" tall, five actions, two cycles, risque toy - pg rated	60	90	120
"Tricky Dog House," No. 673, 1960s, Y Co., 6¾" high, 7¼" long, 6¾" wide, four actions	50	75	100
"Trumpet Playing Bunny," 1950s, Alps Co., 10" high, four actions	100	150	200
"Trumpet Playing Monkey," 1950s, Alps Co., 9" high, four actions, includes tin horn	100	150	200
"Tubby the Turtle," 1950s, Y Co., 7" long, three actions	40	60	80
"Tugboat," 1950s, Marx, 6½" long, a minor toy	30	45	60
"Tugboat," 1950s, Marusan Co., 3 actions, 13½" long	80	120	160
"Tumbles the Bear," 1960s, Y-M Co., (Yanoman), 8½" tall, minor toy, includes porter's hat	50	75	100
"Turn-O-Matic Gun Jeep," 1960s, T-N Co., 10" long, five actions	60	90	120
"Turn Signal Robot," 1960s, T-N Co., 11" tall, five actions	150	225	300
"Turntable Xylophone Melody Train," 1960s, Cragstan Co., 29½" long assembled, three actions	30	45	60
"TWA Jet Plane - Douglass DC-9," 1960s, T-N Co., 17" long, 13" wingspan, three actions	60	90	120
"TWA Multiaction DC-7C Airliner," 1960s, Yonezawa Co., 22½" long, 23½" wingspan, seven actions	150	225	300
"Twist Dancer" (Let's Twist), 1960s, no mfr. mark, minor toy, 15" high	60	90	120
"Two Stage Rocket Launching Pad," 1950s, T-N Co., 7" long, 4" wide, 8" high, three actions	100	150	200

Trumpet Playing Bunny
Photo by Don Hultzman

Milk Drinking Kitty, Fishing Kitty, Shoe Shine Bear, Busy Shoe
Shining Bear, Knitting Grandma

Musical Jolly Chimp, Grand-Pa Car, Circus Fire Engine

Traffic Policeman
Photo by Don Hultzman

Mix-ette Mixer, Wash-O-Matic Washing Machine, Jig-Saw-Matic
Jigsaw Kitchen-ette Stove & Sink

	C6	C8	C10
"UFO-X05," 1970s, M-T Co., 7½" diameter, three actions	30	45	60
"Union Mountain Cable Lines," Monorail set, 1950s, T-N Co., car 8" long, 16 pc. oval track, 22"x32", minor toy	50	75	100

U.S. Air Force Smoking Jet
Photo by Don Hultzman

U.S. Royal Tire - Mechanical Toy
Photo by Don Hultzman

	C6	C8	C10
"U.S. Air Force Military Airlift Command Jet," 1960s, T-N Co., 14" wingspan, 4 actions	50	75	100
"U.S. Air Force Smoking Jet No. 75029," 1950s, (rare), T-N Co., 12" wingspan, 3 actions, smokes, eng. noise, bump & go	110	165	220
"U.S. Navy Pom Pom Gun," 1950s, Remco Co., 20" long, four actions	50	75	100
"U.S. Royal Tire - Mechanical Toy" (Ferris Wheel) souvenir for 1964-65 N.Y. World's Fair (now permanently located at Uniroyal Co. on rt. 94, west of Detroit), includes plastic figures, minor toy, 10" high, Ideal	100	150	200
"Video Robot," 1960s, S-H Co., 10" tall, three actions	40	60	80
"V.I.P. the Busy Boss," 1950s, S&E Co., 8" high, six actions	130	195	260
"Visible Ford Mustang," 1960s, Bandai Co., 10" long, four actions ...	40	60	80
"Vision Robot," 1960s, S-H Co., 11¾" tall, five actions	110	165	220
"Voice Control Astronaut Base," 1969, Remco Co., 19" long, four actions (includes plastic missiles and phonograph records)	60	90	120
"Volkswagen - Elektrik," 1950s, Mignon Co., 8½" long, three actions	40	60	80
"Volkswagen No. 7653," 1960s, Bandai Co., 10" long, three actions ..	50	75	100
"Volkswagen With Visible Engine," 1960s, K.O. Co., 7" long, three actions	40	60	80
"Volkswagen with Visible Engine No. 4049," 1960s, Bandai Co., 8" long, three actions	50	75	100

	C6	C8	C10
"United DC 7 Mainliner," 1950s, Yonezawa Co., 14" wingspan, five actions	150	225	300
"United Mainliner Stratocruiser," 1950s, Linemar, 19½" long, 13" wingspan, four actions	120	180	240
"United States Ocean Liner," 1950s, Linemar Co., 14" long, three actions	100	150	200
"Universal Machine Gun," 1950s, T-N Co., 14¾" long, three actions ...	40	60	80
"U.S. Army Machine Gunner," 1960s, unmarked, 10" long, 4 actions ...	50	75	100
"USA-NASA Apollo Space Ship," 1960s, M-T Co., 9" long, four actions	100	150	200
"USA-NASA Gemini Space Capsule," 1960s, M-T Co., 9" long, four actions (includes detachable astronaut)	80	120	160

Walky-Son (Los)
Photo by Don Hultzman

241

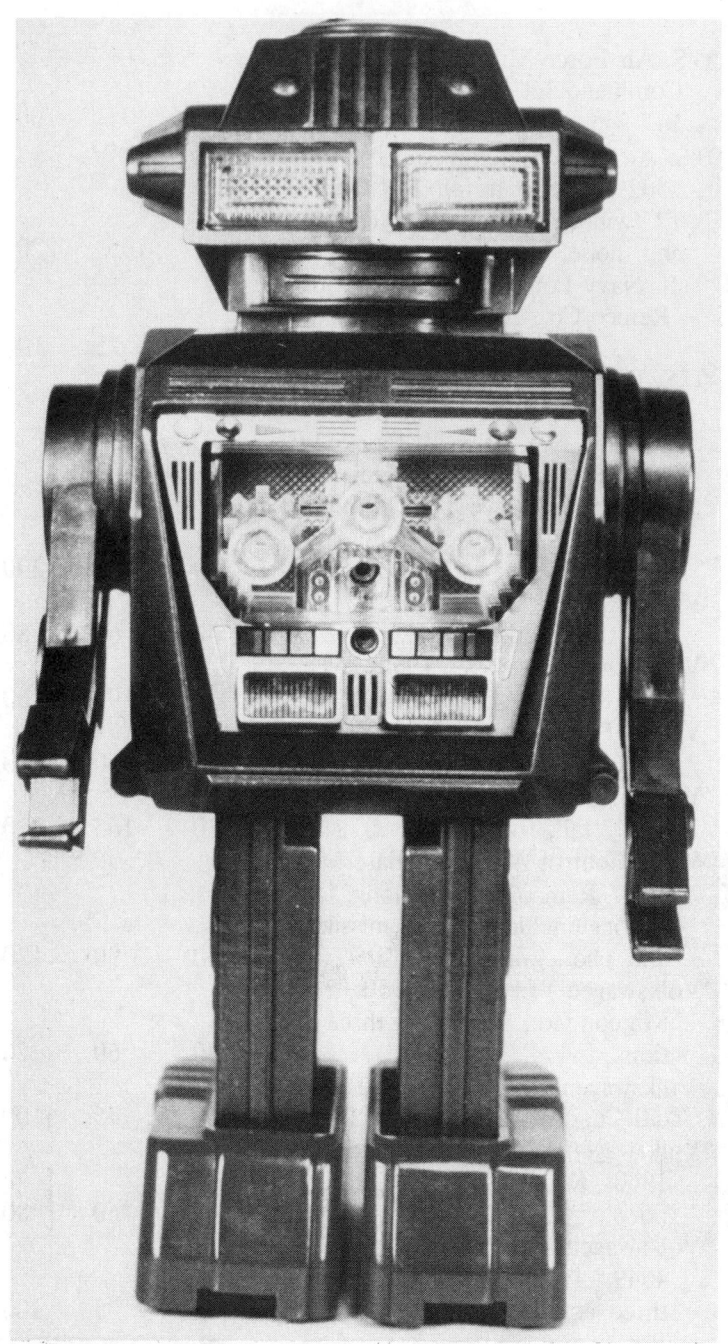

Smoking Robot   Courtesy Don Hultzman.

New Astronaut

Photos by Ron Chojnacki.

	C6	C8	C10
"Wagon Master," 1960s, M-T Co., 18" long, four actions	60	90	120
"Walking Bear with Xylophone," 1950s, Linemar Co., 10" high, seven actions	120	180	240
"Walking Elephant," 1950s, Linemar Co., 8½" long, three actions	60	90	120
"Walking 'Esso' Tiger," 1950s, Marx Co., 11½" tall, four actions	200	300	400
"Walking Itchy Dog," 1950s, Alps Co., 9" long, five actions	40	60	80
"Walky-Son" (Los), 1960s, rare, Geyper Co., 4 actions, 11½" high, includes detachable guns and baton	180	270	360

	C6	C8	C10
"Warpath Indian," 1950s, Alps Co., 12" tall, three actions	60	90	120
"Wash-O-Matic" washing machine, 1940s, T-N Co., 5¾" high, 4¼" diameter, a minor toy, includes lid	20	30	40
"Water Spouting Whale with Flopping Tail," 1950s, KKS Co., 13" long, minor toy	80	120	160
"Western Badman," (Red Gulch Bar), 1960s, M-T Co., 9¾" high, eight actions, includes 3 plastic bottles and 2 plastic glasses, rare	250	375	500
"Western Express" Locomotive, 1960s, Kanto Toy Co., 14" long, four actions	40	60	80

	C6	C8	C10
"Western Locomotive," 1950s, M-T Co., 10½" long, four actions	30	45	60
"Western Special Locomotive," 1950s, M-T Co., 12" long, five actions ..	30	45	60
"Wheel-A-Gear" Robot, 1960s, Taiyo Co., 14" tall, five actions	150	225	300
"WHOH-Skyway Patrol Helicopter," 1950s, M-T Co., 18" long, four actions	30	45	60
"Whirlybird Helicopter," 1960s, Remco Co., 25" long, three actions ..	40	60	80
"Whistling Showboat," 1950s, M-T Co., 14" long, three actions	60	90	120
"Wild West Rodeo," 1950s, Linemar, 6½" long, 8" high, five actions, includes plastic bowl for bubble solution	60	90	120
"Windy the Elephant" 1950s, T-N Co., 9¾" high, three actions, includes celluloid ball and tin litho umbrella	100	150	200
"Winner-23," Rocket, 1950s, KDP Co. (Excelo), 5½" long, minor action, includes rubber track	80	120	160
"Winston the Barking Bulldog," 1950s, Tomiyama Co., three actions, two cycles, 10" long	30	45	60
"Worried Mother Duck and Baby," 1950s, T-N Co., 11" long, 7" high, three actions	70	105	140

	C6	C8	C10
X-7 Space Explorer Ship," 1960s, M-T Co., 7" diameter, four actions ...	40	60	80
"X-70 Robot," 1960s, T-N Co., 12¼" tall, five actions, Rare	400	600	800
"X-1800 Space Vehicle," 1960s, M-T Co., 9" long, five actions (includes detachable plastic antenna	100	150	200
"X-F 160 Jet Airplane," 1960s, K-O Co., 8" wingspan	70	105	140
"Yeti the Abominable Snowman," 1960s, Marx, 12" tall, four action	200	300	400
"Yo-Yo Clown," 1960s, Alps Co., 9" high, three actions (includes plastic yo yo)	80	120	160
"Yo-Yo Monkey," 1960s, Alps Co., 9" tall, three actions (includes plastic yo yo)	80	120	160
"Yo-Yo Monkey," 1960s, Y-M Co., 12" tall, spring extension to 32", minor	40	60	80
"Yum Yum Kitty," 1950s, Alps Co., 9½" high, five actions	150	225	300
"Zero Fighter Plane," 1950s, Bandai Co., 12½" long, 15" wingspan, three actions	150	225	300
"Zoom Motorboat," 1950s, K Co., 12" long, three actions	30	45	60
"Zoomer the Robot," 1950s, T-N Co., 8" tall, three actions	150	225	300

"Bear The Magician"

Happy Plane
T.P.S. Co., 3 actions, mint price $200
Photos by Don Hultzman

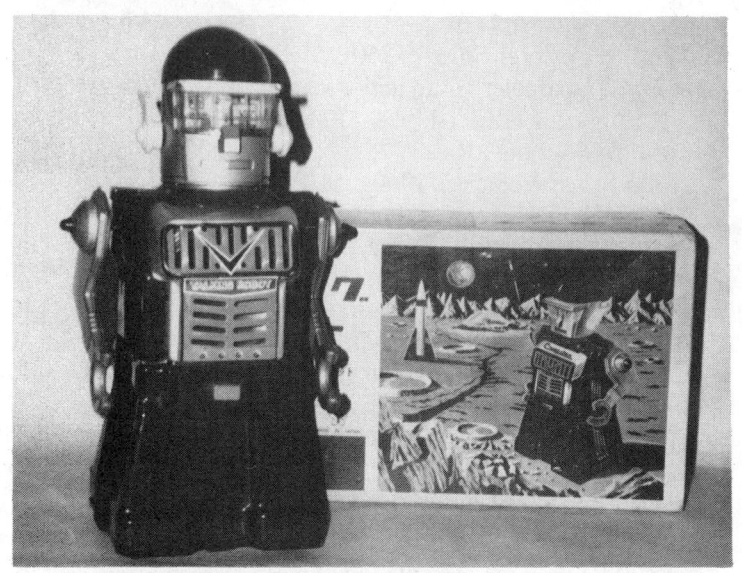

"Talking Robot"

Robert The Robot Mechanical Bulldozer. Rare, value $400 in mint.

American Circus Television Truck, 6 actions, worth $800 in mint.

"Lost In Space" Robot

Photos by Don Hultzman

SOLDIERS
(See also Paper)

The average price of American dimestore soldiers in the last edition was $31.58, and in this edition it is $55.35, an increase of 51%.

CONDITION OF A TOY SOLDIER AND ITS RELATION TO PRICE

The price of a toy soldier depends not only on its desirability, but on its condition.

"Mint" means just that; the condition in which it was originally issued — perfect, regardless of age, not the slightest blemish. Needless to say this is a fairly rare state of affairs, but enough soldiers exist in mint condition to make it an employable term. Many people, hoping to dispose of toys, are tempted to term them "mint" when they are really "near mint", "very good" or sometimes even just "good". Inevitably this can result in unhappiness all around, and not infrequently, in a cancelled sale.

"Very Good" indicates a soldier which has obviously seen use; with signs of wear and aging, but with most of its paint remaining and in general having a freshness to its appearance that makes it seem attractive and collectible to all but the most discriminating.

"Good" signals a soldier that has seen considerable wear, but has at least one half to one third of its original paint, and is basically sound. A collector will collect it, but will often not be wholly satisfied with it as an example of his collection, and thus prices are well below that which the same item in mint can command.

Condition below good results in another drastic drop in price, and figures with missing parts, although otherwise in excellent condition, will usually fall into this lower-priced category. At precent, a BARCLAY soldier minus its tin helmet (signalled by a large round hole in the top of its head) is worth about half of what it would otherwise bring. Rust, even small spots of it on the cast iron soldiers, can seriously lower their price, as can repainting of any of the soldiers. "Near-Mint," "Fine," "Very Fine" and similar terms often found in sellers' descriptions, denote conditions between Mint and Very Good, and are priced accordingly.

The key to grading is to avoid wishful thinking. Grading can sometimes be a problem for the uninitiated, but common sense will usually prevail, and when possible a consultation with an expert in the field can often clear up lingering doubts. A toy in its original box is worth up to 10 to 20% more if the box is in mint condition, with the price dropping as condition lessens.

BARCLAY
(See Vehicles, Animal-Drawn, Aircraft and Miscellaneous)

Barclay Mfg. Co. was the largest manufacturer of toy soldiers in the U.S. prior to World War II, selling millions of figures annually. The company, named after Barclay Street in West Hoboken, New Jersey (now 10th Street in Union City) began in 1924 or late 1923, owned by an elderly Frenchman, Leon Donze (1865-66–1950) and by Michael Levy (c. 1895–10/9/64), who became affiliated by buying a partnership. Levy eventually took over the company (around 1932) and it was he who turned it into a major one. From about five employees in 1924, the company expanded to a pre-War peak of 400 workers, and moved several times as it was forced to expand. Barclay's soldiers came in four styles prior to World War II. The first, which were probably produced almost from Barclay's beginning, were small, with the mounted figures having moving arms. The second, approximately 3¼" high, with a separate tin helmet, seem to have begun production in 1934, and were designed and sculpted by Barclay employee Frank Krupp. This figure (the tin helmet was subcontracted) was rather stiff and is known by collectors as "short stride" because its marching figures' feet were close together. The third style, again by Krupp, also had a separate tin helmet, was more realistic, and is known as "long stride." These were on sale as early as 1937. In 1937 or 1938, a clip was designed to hold on the tin helmets, as the formerly glued-on helmets frequently came off, and drew complaints from the chain stores such as Woolworth's, which sold Barclay toys. The fourth style, introduced about 1939-1940, when Barclay moved from slush casting to die casting its soldiers, was by free-lance artist Olive Kooken (1904-1964), and is known as "cast helmet", as the soldiers featured helmets that were an integral part of the figure. Barclay's soldiers were made of antimonial lead, consisting of about 13% antimony and the rest lead. When slush-molding was done, only one mold was made of each single figure. The lead would be poured into the mold, rocked, and immediately poured out, thus providing a hollow figure. Later, the die-cast molds produced a number of the same figures at the same time. During the Second World War BARCLAY laid off all but four of its employees, and did sub-contract work. It was never as successful after the war, and finally closed down in 1971, by this time employing only 50-75 people. Although BARCLAY assigned numbers to its figures from the beginning for its own records, many of the soldiers themselves bore no numbers. Figures listed with a question mark after the number are based on the memory of longtime BARCLAY employee George Fall, whose memory, judged against known BARCLAY numbers, is quite accurate, but not infallible. All short stride BARCLAYS have separate helmets.

BAC

BAD

Pre-1934
(All bold words and numbers are BARCLAY'S OWN DESCRIPTION)

Ba   Baa   Bb   Bba

Bc   Be   Bg   Bh

Photo by Ed Poole
Courtesy Tony Salamone

	C6	C8	C10
(Ba) 87? Mounted Officer, moving arm holding sword, on rearing horse ..	22.50	33.75	45.00
(Baa) 87? Same as above on cantering horse	22.50	33.75	45.00
(Bb) 87? Mounted Officer, moving arm holding bugle, on rearing horse ...	22.50	33.75	45.00
(Bba) 87? Same as above, on cantering horse	22.50	33.75	45.00
(Bc) 87? Mounted Officer, moving arm holding pistol on cantering horse .	30	45	60
(Bd) 88? Mounted Cowboy with lasso .	No Price Found		
(Be) 89? Mounted Indian, moving arm holding rifle	15.00	22.50	30.00
(BeA) Same as above, holding pistol ..	15.00	22.50	30.00
(Bf) 90? Mounted Cowboy with pistol .	25.00	37.50	50.00
(BfA) 90? Mounted Cowboy with moving arm, holding rifle (horse's tail missing in photo)	20	30	40
(Bfa) Indian chief on foot, 54mm high, blue and red-striped headdress, may look like Ideal I-14	No Price Found		

B1   BfA

(Bfb) Indian brave on foot, 54 mm high, carrying rifle across stomach ... No Price Found

(Bg) 186? Cavalryman mounted, 2¾" high, no moving parts, modeled on French toy soldier, circa late 1920s-early 30s 10 15 20

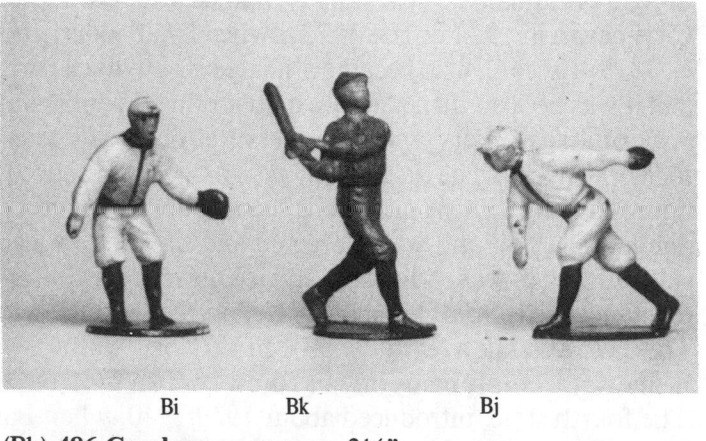

Bi   Bk   Bj

	C6	C8	C10
(Bh) **486 Cavalryman,** approx. 2¼" high, circa early 30s, no moving parts	9.00	13.50	18.00
(Bi) Baseball fielder, approx. 1⅞" high, circa 1920s	40	60	80
(Bj) Baseball pitcher, circa 1920s	40	60	80
(Bk) Baseball batter, circa 1920s	40	60	80
(Bl) Mounted Indian on rearing horse .	14	21	28
(Bm) **200 Jockey on Horse**	6	9	12
(Bn) **No. 87 Officer on Horse,** smaller size, circa 1931 (one known)	No Price Found		

	C6	C8	C10

1934 and After

(BA) **Paint Your Own Army Set No. 2003**, circa 1934, boxed 125.00 187.50 250.00

(BAa) **Paint Your Own Army Set No. 2003**, larger size than above, same toys, with compartment for one more. In set bought in September, 1980, compartment contained two two-dimensional lead elephants. Barclay employees queried don't remember these . . . . No Price Found

(BAC) **89 Indian on Horse** (on catalog sheet with Ethopians) 12.50 18.75 25.00

(BAD) **90 Cowboy on Horse** (on catalog sheet with Ethopians) 12.50 18.75 25.00

(B1) **89 Indian on Horse** 10 15 20

(B1a) **89 Indian on Horse** two feathers (earlier) 20 30 40

(B2) **90 Cowboy on Horse** 9.50 14.25 19.00

(B2A) **90 Cowboy on Horse** variation, thinner bullets in gunbelt, saddle not as long 11.00 16.50 22.00

(B2AA) **90 Cowboy on Horse**, variation, no bullets in gunbelt . . . . No Price Found

(B2AAA) **100 Masked Rider on Horse** (may not have been produced; in the order sheet the figure faces forward) . . . . No Price Found

(B2B) **100? Masked Rider on Horse**, horse's tail down 14 21 28

(B2C) **100? Masked Rider on Horse**, horse's tail up 16 24 32

(B3) **187? Mounted**, in grey, cap, intermediate size 30 45 60

(B3A) **87 Officer on Horse**, in cap, khaki or grey, larger black, grey or brown horse 12.50 18.75 25.00

(B4) **87? Mounted** in colored jacket and cap, may be Chinese or Japanese (horse's tail missing in photo) 16.50 24.75 33.00

(B5) **701 Flagbearer**, tin helmet, short stride 9.50 14.25 19.00

(B6) **701 Flagbearer**, tin helmet, long stride 7.00 10.50 14.00

(B7) **701 Flagbearer**, cast helmet 7.50 11.25 15.00

(B8) **701 Flagbearer**, Cuban flag variation painted for 10 Woolworth's in Cuba, cast helmet or pot helmet . . No Price Found

(B9) **701 Machine-Gunner**, kneeling, short stride 6.50 9.75 13.00

(B10) **702 Machine-Gunner**, kneeling, long stride 6 9 12

(B11) **702** Machine-Gunner, kneeling, cast helmet 9.00 13.50 18.00

(B12) **703 Sniper**, kneeling, firing, short stride 6.50 9.75 13.00

Photo by Ed Poole

B1a

Photo by Don Pielin

Photo by Bill Kaufman

247

	C6	C8	C10
(B12A) 703 Sniper, kneeling, firing, short stride, shorter rifle, in front of fingers fat portion of gun and thin portion of barrel about equal length	7.50	11.25	15.00
(B13) **703 Sniper,** kneeling, firing, long stride, tin helmet	6.50	9.75	13.00
(B14) **704 Soldier on Parade,** shoulder arms, short stride	6.50	9.75	13.00
(B15) **704 Soldier on Parade,** shoulder arms, long stride, tin helmet	5.50	8.25	11.00
(B16) **705 Soldier at Attention** (actually port arms)	6	9	12
(B17) **705** Soldier at Attention (actually port arms), cast helmet	9.00	13.50	18.00
(B18) **706 Soldier,** charging, short stride	8	12	16
(B18a) Same as above, with shorter rifle, sling around hand	No Price Found		
(B19) **706** Tall, tin helmet, solid puttees	300	450	600
(B20) **706** Soldier, charging, tin helmet, long stride	10	15	20
(B21) **706** Soldier, charging, cast helmet	10	15	20
(B22) **707** At Attention, cast helmet ..	8.50	12.75	17.00
(B23) **708 Officer** with sword, short stride	12.50	18.75	25.00
(B24) **723 Marine Officer,** same as above, in blue	11.00	16.50	22.00
(B25) **708 Officer,** with sword, tin helmet, long stride	5.50	8.25	11.20
(B25a) 708 Officer with sword, tin helmet, long stride, no chest strap .	50	75	100
(B25b) 723 Marine Officer with sword, tin helmet, long stride, no chest strap	50	75	100
(B26) **723 Marine Officer,** with sword, tin helmet, long stride	9.00	13.50	18.00
(B27) **708** Officer with sword, cast helmet	17.50	26.25	35.00
(B28) **708** Marine Officer with sword, cast helmet	22.50	33.75	45.00
(B29) **709 Bugler,** short stride	12	18	24
(B30) **709 Bugler,** long stride, tin helmet	6.50	9.75	13.00
(B31) **710 Drummer** short stride	10	15	20
(B32) **710 Drummer,** long stride, tin helmet	6	9	12
(B33) **711 Drum Major,** short stride ..	9.00	13.50	18.00
(B34) **711 Drum Major,** long stride, tin helmet	11.00	16.50	22.00
(B35) **743 West Point Officer,** short stride	6	9	12
(B36) **718 West Point Cadet,** with rifle, short stride	9.00	13.50	18.00
(B37) Same as above, but painted as wooden soldier, only three known	300	450	600
(B37a) Same as B36, with line-and-dot eyes, white pants, white gloves ...	9.00	13.50	18.00
(B38) **718 West Point Cadet,** long stride	6.50	9.75	13.00
(B39) **724 Ethiopian Soldier,** circa 1935-36	100	150	200
(B40) **725 Ethiopian Officer,** circa 1935-36 ....125.00		187.50	250.00
(B41) **727 Italian Officer,** circa 1935-36	75.00	112.50	150.00
(B42) **726 Italian Soldier,** circa 1935-36	100	150	200
(B43) Japanese, charging with rifle, circa 1937	40	60	80
(B44) Japanese Officer, circa 1937 (this is the original Ethiopian officer, painted as a Japanese)	100	150	200
(B45) Chinese or Mongolian Officer in steel helmet, circa 1937	100	150	200

B46   B46a
Variations noticed by Gordon Gee on Barclay B46. The figure at left has a wider face and a right breast pocket and appears to be less common. Photo by Gordon Gee

	C6	C8	C10
(B46) Chinese or Mongolian rifleman, circa 1937	75.00	112.50	150.00
(B46a) Same as above, narrower face, no right breast pocket	60	90	120
(B47) **717 Indian Brave,** rifle across waist	5.50	8.25	11.00
(B48) **716 Indian Chief**	6	9	12
(B49) **719 Sailor White Uniform,** marching, short stride	8	12	16
(B50) **720 Sailor Blue Uniform,** like above	8	12	16
(B51) **719** Sailor White Uniform, long stride, bell bottoms	7.50	11.25	15.00
(B51a) 720 Sailor in Blue Uniform, long stride, bell bottoms	7.00	10.50	14.00
(B52) **719 Sailor in White Uniform,** in puttees	6	9	12
(B52a) 720 Sailor Blue Uniform, in puttees	6.50	9.75	13.00
(B53) **756 Sailor, Flagbearer,** long stride	8	12	16
(B54) **721 Naval Officer,** short stride, tin top to a cap	32.50	48.75	65.00

B20 B21 B22 B23 B24 B25 B25a B26 B27 B28

B29 B30 B31 B32 B33 B34 B35 B36 B37

B25a Courtesy Bill Adams

Photo by Bill Kaufman

	C6	C8	C10
(B55) **721 Naval Officer,** short stride ..	8	12	16
(B55a) 721 Naval Officer, same as above, in blue	100	150	200
(B56) **721 Naval Officer,** long stride ..	7.50	11.25	15.00
(B57) **722 Marine,** short stride, tin top to cap	30	45	60
(B58) **722 Marine,** short stride	10.50	15.75	21.00
(B59) 722 Marine, long stride	6.50	9.75	13.00
(B59a) 722 Marine, long stride, white cap (probably post-War)	15.00	22.50	30.00
(B60) **757 Sailor with Signal Flags** ...	7.50	11.25	15.00
(B60a) 757 Sailor with Signal Flags, flat underbase, minor variations in cap	7.50	11.25	15.00
(B61) **728 Machine Gunner Lying Flat**	8	12	16
(B62) 728 Machine Gunner Lying Flat, cast helmet	8	12	16
(B63) 728 Machine Gunner Lying Flat, cast helmet, lip of base extends under gun barrel	5.50	8.25	11.00
(B64) **750 Soldier, Crawling**	8	12	16
(B65) **730 Soldier Signal Man with Flag**	8.50	12.75	17.00
(B66) **731 Soldier Pigeon Dispatcher** ..	7.00	10.50	14.00
(B67) **732 Soldier Telephone Operator**	6	9	12
(B68) **733 Soldier Bullet Feeder** (actually a shell)	6.25	9.38	12.50
(B69) **734 Soldier Ammunition Carrier**	8.50	12.75	17.00
(B70) **735 Soldier Range Finder**	7.00	10.50	14.00
(B71) **736 Soldier Sentry**	6	9	12
(B72) **737 Soldier Charging Machine Gunner,** tin helmet	6	9	12
(B73) 737 Soldier Charging Machine Gunner, cast helmet	9.00	13.50	18.00
(B74) **738 Soldier Bomb Thrower**	6.50	9.75	13.00
(B75) 738 Soldier Bomb Thrower, tall, tin helmet, solid puttees	No Price Found		

	C6	C8	C10
(B76) **738 Soldier Bomb Thrower,** rifle off ground, tin helmet	8.50	12.75	17.00
(B77) **738 Soldier Bomb Thrower,** rifle off ground, cast helmet	8	12	16
(B78) **739 Soldier Fifer**	7.00	10.50	14.00
(B79) **740 Soldier French Horn**	7.00	10.50	14.00
(B79a) Machine Gunner, seated, cast helmet, bandage-type puttees ..	12.50	18.75	25.00
(B80) **741 Aviator**	6.50	9.75	13.00
(B81) **745 Navy Doctor,** in white, flat underbase	6.50	9.75	13.00
(B81a) **746 Army Doctor,** in brown, flat underbase	6.50	9.75	13.00
(B81A&B) **746 Doctor,** as above, inverted base	No Price Found		
(B82) **767 Nurse,** kneeling	8.50	12.75	17.00
(B83) **744 Nurse,** hand on hip	6.50	9.75	13.00
(B83a) Same as above, in blue	No Price Found		
(B84) **751 Soldier, Sharpshooter,** prone position	9.00	13.50	18.00
(B85) **762 Wounded,** sitting, arm in sling	7.50	11.25	15.00
(B86) **707 Sharpshooter,** standing, firing, short stride	9.00	13.50	18.00
(B87) **747 Sharpshooter,** standing, firing, long stride	7.50	11.25	15.00
(B88) 747 Sharpshooter, standing, firing, cast helmet	7.00	10.50	14.00
(B89) **748 Soldier, Running** with rifle, tin helmet	6.50	9.75	13.00
(B90) 748 Soldier, Running, with rifle, cast helmet	10	15	20
(B91) **749 Soldier, Gas Mask,** charging with rifle	7.50	11.25	15.00
(B92) 749 Soldier, Gas Mask, charging with rifle cast helmet	7.00	10.50	14.00

249

B38 B39 B40 B42 B41 B43 B44

B45 B46 B47 B48 B49 B51 B52
Photo by Bill Kaufman

B12   B12a
Photo by K. Warren Mitchell

B53 B60 B54 B55 B56 B57 B58 B59

B61   B62   B63
B64 B65 B66   B67 B68 B69

B70 B71 B72 B73 B74 B75 B76
Photo by Bill Kaufman

	C6	C8	C10
(B93) 310 Army Motorcyclist	10	15	20
(B93a) **310 Cop** on motorcycle	11.00	16.50	22.00
(B93b) 310 Motorcyclist, head higher .	11.00	16.50	22.00
(B93c) 310 Cop on motorcycle, head lower	11.00	16.50	22.00
(B93d) 310 Motorcyclist, larger, markings on cycle, like B93A and B93B, but cruder	14	21	28
(B93A) **310 Army Motorcyclist,** post-War, dot eyes, or none at all, larger, motor variation	14	21	28
(B93B) **310 Cop on Motorcycle,** post-War, dot eyes, or none at all, larger, motor variation	19.00	27.50	38.00
(B94) **715 Cowboy** with tin hat brim . .	3.75	5.63	7.50
(B95) **752 Cowboy with lasso**	5.50	8.25	11.00
(B95A) 752 Masked Cowboy with lasso	5.50	8.25	11.00
(B95a) 752 Cowboy with lasso, Post-WWII version, lasso goes directly through hands	5.50	8.25	11.00
(B96) **753 Cowboy With Two Guns,** pointing one	6	9	12
(B97) **754 Indian Chief,** tomahawk and shield	4	6	8
(B97a) Same as above, flat base, some with fatter legs	4	6	8
(B98) **755 Indian, Bow and Arrow**	4.50	6.75	9.00
(B99) **756 Indian Chief,** long headdress, may only have been produced post-WW II	34	51	68
(B100) **757 Indian Brave,** standing with bow and arrow, may only have been produced post WW II	4	6	8
(B101) **758 Camera Man,** kneeling, tin helmet	11.50	17.25	23.00
(B102) **759 Soldier, Stretcher Bearer,** open hand	32.50	48.75	65.00
(B102a) 759 Soldier, Stretcher Bearer, closed hand	7.50	11.25	15.00
(B103) **760 Surgeon,** with stethoscope .	7.00	10.50	14.00
(B104) **761 Lying wounded,** tin helmet	7.00	10.50	14.00
(B105) **763 Raiding,** in crouch, tin helmet	7.00	10.50	14.00
(B106) **767 Advance,** raised rifle, tin helmet	9.00	13.50	18.00
(B107) **765 Bayoneting,** although no bayonet, thrusting with gun mussle; tin helmet	12	18	24
(B107a) **765 Bayoneting,** same as above, no bayonet, cast helmet . . .	50	75	100
(B108) **766 Clubbing** with rifle, tin helmet	16	24	32
(B109) **766 Clubbing** with rifle, cast helmet	60	90	120
(B110) **769 Cook** holding roast	8	12	16
(B110a) 769 Cook egg-timer, ...	10	15	20
(B111) **771 Peeling Potatoes**	7.00	10.50	14.00
(B112) Soldier eating	17.50	26.25	35.00

B77 B78 B79 B79a B80 B81a B81 B82 B83

B84 B85 B86 B87 B88
B89 B90 B91 B92 B93

B94 B95 B96 B97 B98 B99 B100
B101 B102 B102a B103 B104 B105 B106

B107 B107a B108 B109 B110 B111 B112
B107a Courtesy Jeff Maund
B113 B114 B115 B116 B117 B118

B119 B120 B121 B122 B124
Above photos by Bill Kaufman

	C6	C8	C10
(B113) 729 Soldier with Binoculars, long binoculars	7.00	10.50	14.00
(B114) **729 Soldier with Binoculars,** short binoculars	38	57	76
(B115) **760 Soldier Sitting Position**	12.50	18.75	25.00
(B116) **776 Officer Reading Orders** . .	8	12	16
(B117) **774** Soldier with AA gun, tin helmet	8	12	16
B(118) **774** Soldier with AA gun, cast helmet	7.00	10.50	14.00
(B119) **775** Wounded on crutches . . .	11.00	16.50	22.00
(B120) **776** Standing at searchlight, smooth lens, elevation wheel	50	75	100
(B120a) **776** Standing at searchlight, smooth lens, no elevation wheel .	50	75	100
(B121) **776** Standing at searchlight, ridges along base (this and following have ridged lenses)	11.50	17.25	23.00
(B122) **776** Standing at searchlight, smooth base connected to searchlight, no elevation wheel	14	21	28
(B123) **776** Standing at searchlight, low seat, not connected to searchlight	10	15	20
B(124) **776** Standing at searchlight, high seat, two rivets in front of left foot	11.00	16.50	22.00
(B125) **776** Standing at searchlight, high seat, no rivets in front of left foot	11.50	17.25	23.00
(B126) **777** Marching with pack, tin helmet	6.50	9.75	13.00
(B127) **777** Marching with pack, cast helmet	6.50	9.75	13.00
(B128) **778** Officer with gas mask, cast helmet	8.50	12.75	17.00
(B129) **779** Firing from behind wall, cast helmet	27.00	40.50	54.00
(B130) **780** Falling with rifle, cast helmet	15.00	22.50	30.00
(B131) **781** Digging, cast helmet . . .	19.00	28.50	38.00
(B132) **782** Leaning out, with field phone, antenna, cast helmet	31.00	46.50	62.00
(B133) **783** Crouching with binoculars, cast helmet	15.00	22.50	30.00
(B134) **784** Parachutist landing	8	12	16
(B135) **785** Skier in white, cast helmet, 1940, with separate metal skis. (Meant to be Finn)	11.00	16.50	22.00
(B136) **785** Skier in white, no skis . . .	7.50	11.25	15.00
(B137) **785** Skier in brown, no skis . .	22.50	33.75	45.00
(B138) 785 Skier in red, meant to be Russian, may not have been produced (listing based on memory) .	No Price Found		
(B139) **787** Diver with axe	225.00	337.50	450.00
(B140) **788** Marching with slung rifle, cast helmet	6.50	9.75	13.00
(B141) **789** Soldier with AA gun, cast helmet, sitting	9.00	13.50	18.00

251

B18a   B120a   B120   B177   B179   B180

B181   B190   B191   B192   B193
Photo by Don Pielin

B123   B125   B126   B127

B128   B129   B130
Photo by Bill Kaufman

B139
Photo by Ed Poole

B131   B132   B133   B134   B135   B140   B141

B142   B143   B144   B145   B146
Photo by Bill Kaufman

	C6	C8	C10
(B142) **790** Two soldiers on raft, cast helmet	27.00	40.50	54.00
(B143) **791** Two-man rocket team	9.00	13.50	18.00
(B144) **792** Mechanic with airplane engine, prop spins, brace on back of engine bulges	16	24	32

	C6	C8	C10
(B144a) Same as above, brace on back of engine doesn't bulge)	16	24	32
(B145) Soldier kneeling with anti-tank gun, cast helmet	12.50	18.75	25.00
(B146) **960 Surgeon and Soldier**	30	45	60
(B147) **951 Soldier Wireless Operator**	11.50	17.25	23.00
(B148) **952 Soldier, Dispatcher with Dog**	14	21	28
(B149) **953 American Legionnaire** in overseas cap, tall, made for 1937 Legion convention in New York, 12 known color combinations	120	180	240
(B150) **954?** American Legionnarie flag-bearer, tall, cloth flag, made in 1937, as above, five known	300	450	600
(B151) **961 At Typewriter,** with typewriter and table	27.50	41.25	55.00
(B151A) **770 At Mess,** typist alone, apparently meant to sit at mess table	6	9	12
(B152) **374 Army Motorcycle,** with side-car	26	39	52
(B153) **45** Two-man machine-gun car	17.50	26.25	35.00
(B154) **714 Pirate**	6.50	9.75	13.00
(B155) **713 Knight** with pennant	6	9	12
(B156) **712 Knight** with shield	5.50	8.25	11.00
(B157) **610 Woman Passenger,** with dog	6	9	12
(B158) **611 Man Passenger,** overcoat over arm	5.00	7.50	10.00
(B159) **614 Red Cap** with bags	7.00	10.50	14.00
(B160) **613 Porter,** with whisk broom	6.50	9.75	13.00
(B161) **612 Conductor**	5.50	8.25	11.00
(B162) **615 Engineer**	5.50	8.25	11.00
(B163) **616 Boy**	4.50	6.75	9.00
(B164) **617 Girl**	5.00	7.50	10.00
(B165) **618 Elderly Woman**	5.50	8.25	11.00
(B166) **619 Old Man**	5.50	8.25	11.00
(B167) **620 Minister walking**	17.50	26.25	35.00
(B168) **620 Minister holding hat**	7.00	10.50	14.00
(B169) **621 Newsboy**	5.50	8.25	11.00
(B170) **622 Shoeshine Boy**	8	12	16
(B171) **623 Detective with pistol**	35.00	52.50	70.00
(B172) **624 Burglar**	27.50	41.25	55.00
(B173) **625 Bride**	8	12	16
(B174) **626 Groom**	8	12	16
(B175) **627 Girl in Rocker**	6.50	9.75	13.00
(B176) **628 Boy Skater**	4	6	8
(B177) **629 Girl Skater**	4.50	6.75	9.00
(B178) **630 1/2 Man and Woman on Park Bench**	13.00	19.50	26.00
(B179) Seated man and woman in winter coats	12.50	18.75	25.00
(B180) **635 Man Speed Skater**	6	9	12
(B181) **636 Girl Figure Skater**	6	9	12
(B182) **801 Boy Scout Hiking**	14	21	28

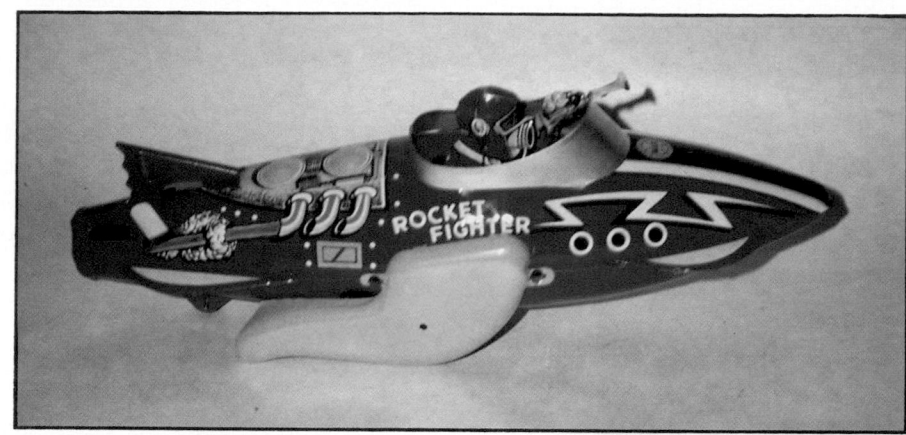

MARX Rocket Fighter.

*Courtesy Don Hultzman,
Photo by Ron Chojnacki.*

Buck Rogers Rocket Ship,
1934, MARX.

*Courtesy Wilkinson Collection,
Detroit Antique Toy Museum.*

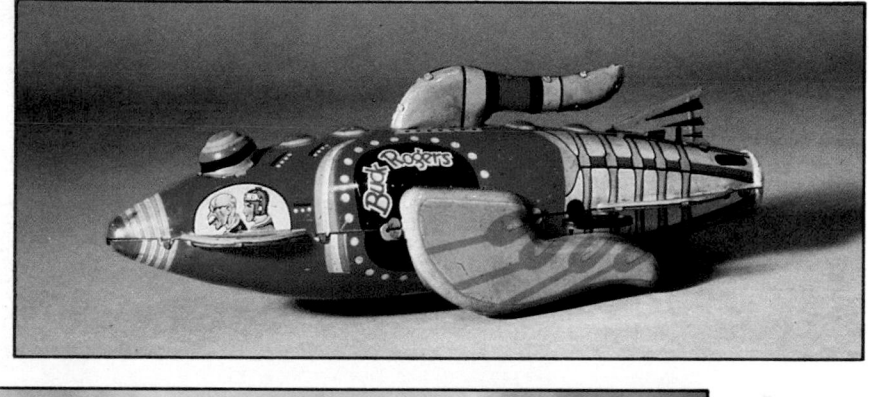

CHEIN Cathedral Organ.

Courtesy Don Hultzman, Photo Ron Chojnacki.

Disneyland Roller Coaster,
CHEIN.

*Photo by Ron Chojnacki,
Courtesy Don Hultzman.*

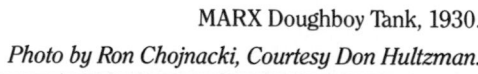

MARX Space Tank.

*Photo by Ron Chojnacki,
Courtesy Don Hultzman.*

MARX Doughboy Tank, 1930.

Photo by Ron Chojnacki, Courtesy Don Hultzman.

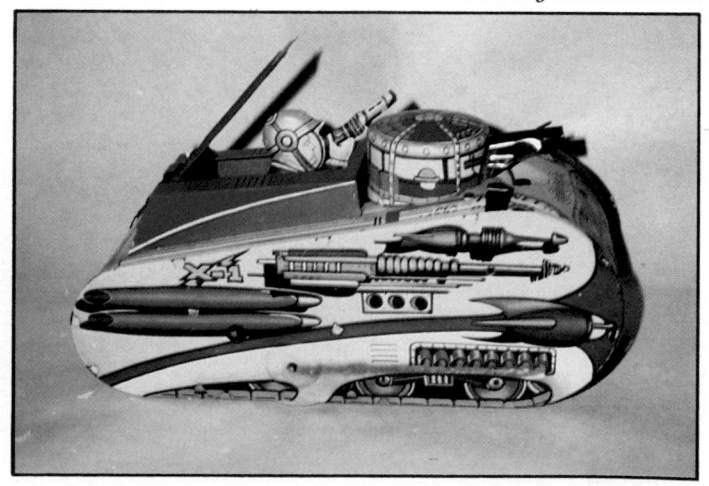

HUBER,
Steam Roller, cast iron,
8″ long.

*Photo courtesy of Dick and
Nancy Dice.*

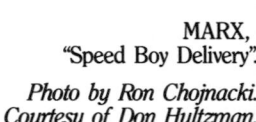

MARX,
"Speed Boy Delivery".

*Photo by Ron Chojnacki.
Courtesy of Don Hultzman.*

NY-LINT,
"Elgin Street Sweeper".

*Photo by Bill Kaufman.
Courtesy of the
Good Old Days Store.*

ARCADE Allis-Chalmers tractor pulling manure spreader. Total length about 12 inches.

Courtesy Dick and Nancy Dice.

KENTON Stake Wagon, two horse, No. 221.

Courtesy Orville C. Britton.

NYLINT Bulldozer.

Photo by Orville C. Britton.

NIFTY,
Toonerville Trolley.

*Photo courtesy of
Bob Black, Jr.*

MARX,
"Toytown Dairy", tin wind-up.

*Photo by Bill Kaufman.
Courtesy of the Good Old Days Store.*

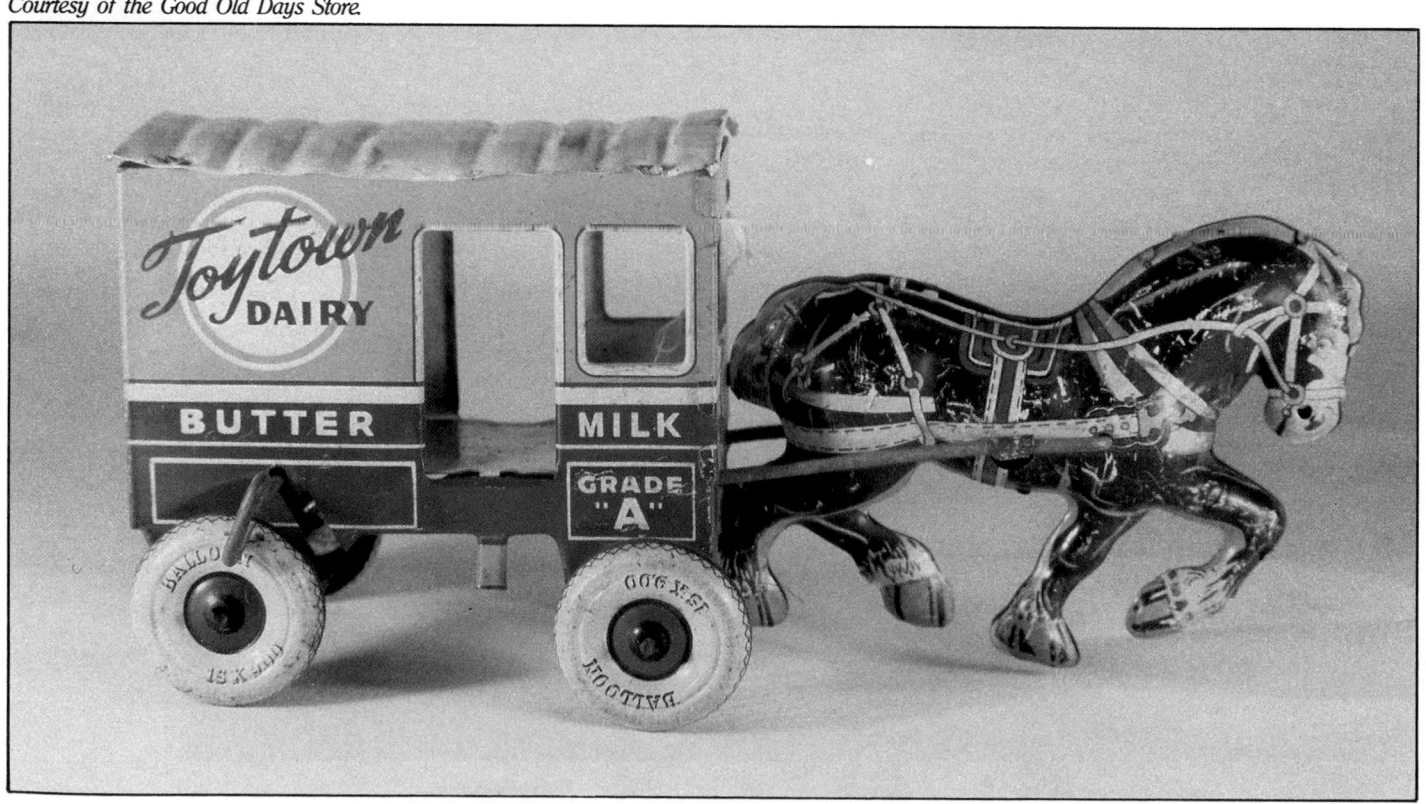

Fire Pumper, cast iron, 11″ long.

Photo by Bill Kaufman.
Courtesy of the Good Old Days Store.

OHIO,
Fire Truck, 10½″ long.

Photo by Bill Kaufman.
Courtesy of the
Good Old Days Store.

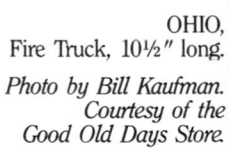

(Above)
MARX, "Reversible Coupe, The Marvel Car".

Photo courtesy of Dick and Nancy Dice.

(Above)
MANOIL, 702 Coupe and 703 Wrecker.

Photo by Bill Kaufman.
Courtesy of the Good Old Days Store.

(Below)
Pre-WW II, BARCLAY vehicles.

Photo courtesy of George Buhler

GREY IRON midget autos, copyright 1938. Since the company's cars are unmarked, this photo has been used to help collectors with identification. No prices found.

MacNary Collection, Photo: RLM.

KEYSTONE "Moving Van Long Distance Hauling."

Photo by Joe Freed.

HUBLEY "Panama" digger.

Photo by Joe Freed.

Superman Krypto-Raygun.

Courtesy Danny Fuchs

A.C. GILBERT Erector Set No. 1
from 1924.

Courtesy Charles Richards.

MARX "Sunny Side Service Station"
(Miscellaneous).

Photo by Ron Fink from his collection.

AUBURN RUBBER,
#231 "Infantry Set",
copyright 1939, sold
for $100.

*Photo by Bill Kaufman.
Courtesy of the
Good Old Days Store.*

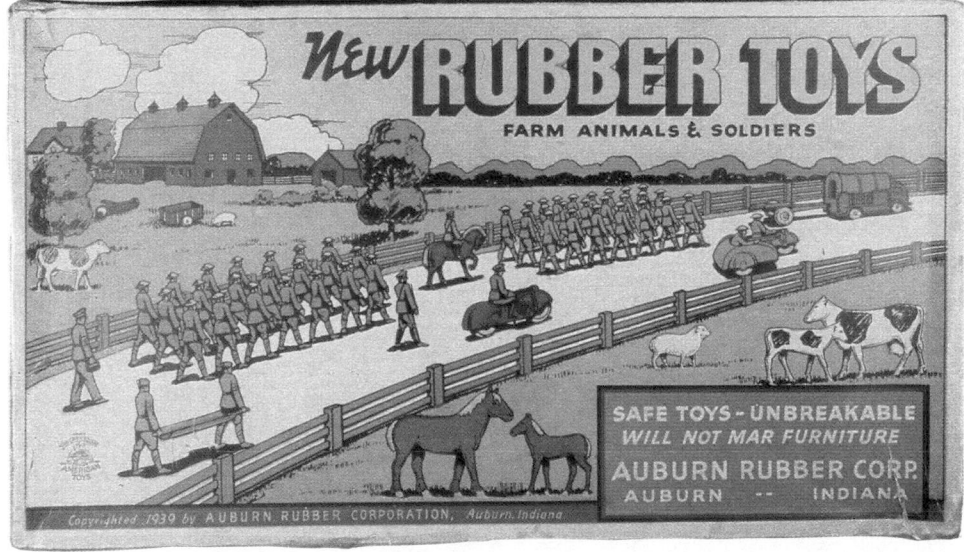

AUBURN RUBBER,
Toy Soldiers, boxed set,
sold for $60.

*Photo by Bill Kaufman.
Courtesy of the
Good Old Days Store.*

SOLJERTOYS,
boxed set, circa 1932.

Photo by Ed Poole.

IDEAL, Soldiers.

Photo by Bill Kaufman.
Courtesy of Hank Anton.

MARX, Castle Fort.
Photo courtesy of Bob Black, Jr.

BUILT-RITE, #100-A.
Photo courtesy of Ed Poole.

Toy Soldiers
made by TOY CREATIONS and
Two Guys from BARCLAY.

Photo Courtesy of Hank Anton.

Mint boxed set
from Two Guys from BARCLAY.

Photo Courtesy of Hank Anton.

IDEAL, Train Figures.

*Photo by Bill Kaufman.
Courtesy of Hank Anton.*

JONES,
Farmer and Wife with
BARCLAY Animals.

*Photo courtesy of
Bob Black, Jr.*

MARX Merrymakers.

Courtesy Wilkinson Collection,
Detroit Antique Toy Museum.

WILLIAM TELL mechanical bank.

Photo by Joe Freed.

CHEIN Monkey bank
(Mechanical Banks).

Courtesy Don Hultzman,
Photo by Ron Chojnacki.

LIONEL'S No. 43
wind-up speedboat.

Courtesy Wilkinson Collection,
Detroit Antique Toy Museum.

KEYSTONE, Riding Airplane.

Photo courtesy of Bob Black, Jr.

HUBLEY, Plane.

Photo courtesy of Bob Black, Jr.

STRAUSS, "Mailplane", tin wind-up.

Photo by Bill Kaufman. Courtesy of the Good Old Days Store.

TOOTSIETOY, 719 Crusader.

Photo by Bill Kaufman. Courtesy of the Good Old Days Store.

MARX
Four-Engine Bomber, plastic
or celluloid propellors. (Aircraft).
The figure is a MANOIL pilot
(M60).

Photo by Ron Fink.

CHEIN "Mechanical Aquaplane"
(tin wind-up).

*Courtesy Don Hultzman,
Photo by Ron Chojnacki.*

WYANDOTTE
twin engine passenger plane,
1935-40. 182 mm wingspan.

Photo by Perry R. Eichor.

MARX 4 engine bomber—
carries and drops bombs.
370 mm wingspan.

Photo by Perry R. Eichor.

Darth Vader Tie Fighter (SW-V1) with Darth Vader aboard (SW-A5).
Figures left to right: Ben (Obi-Wan) Knobi (SW-A1), Chewbacca (SW-A3), Han Solo (SW-A10),
Luke Skywalker (SW-A12), Princess Leia Organa (SW-A15), Yoda (ESB-A27), C-3PO (SW-A4),
R2-D2 (SW-A17), Lando Calrissian (ESB-A16), Stormtrooper (SW-A20).

B147 B148 B149 B150 B151

B152 B153 B154 B155 B156
Photo by Bill Kaufman

B157 B158 B159 B160 B161 B162 B163 B164

B165 B166 B167 B168 B169 B170 B171 B172
Photo by Bill Kaufman

B173 B174 B175 B176 B178 B182 B183 B184 B185

B186 B187 B188 B189
Photo by Bill Kaufman

	C6	C8	C10
(B183) **802 Boy Scout Saluting**	11.00	16.50	22.00
(B184) 803 Boy Scout Signaling	12.50	18.75	25.00
(B185) **804 Boy Scout Cooking**	18	27	36
(B186) **850 Policeman,** arm raised ...	7.00	10.50	14.00
(B186a) 850 Policeman, figure eight base	7.00	10.50	14.00
(B187) **851 Fireman,** with axe	9.00	13.50	18.00
(B187a) Fireman with axe, flat under-base	11.00	16.50	22.00

	C6	C8	C10
(B188) **852 Fireman** (with hose)	10	15	20
(B189) **853 Mailman**	5.50	8.25	11.00
(B190) **495 Man on skis**	8	12	16
(B191) **496 Girl on skis**	7.00	10.50	14.00
(B192) **497 Man on Sled**	7.00	10.50	14.00
(B193) **498 Girl on Sled**	7.50	11.25	15.00
(B194) **499 Santa Claus on Sled**	17.00	25.50	34.00
(B195) **500 Santa Claus on Skis**	20	30	40
(B195a) **500 Santa Claus on Skis,** no skis, or poles and no holes for them	55.00	82.50	110.00
(B196) Santa Claus with holly sprig ..	27.50	41.25	55.00
(B197) Santa Claus seated, bag of toys at side, made to ride in sleigh ...	100	150	200
(B198) **510 One Horse Open Sleigh** (Sleigh, horse, seated man and woman)	28	42	56
(B199) **530 Man Pulling Children on Sled**	16	24	32
(B200) **535 Young Man Putting Skates on Girl Sitting on Bench** .	48	72	96

Post World War II

	C6	C8	C10
(B201) **701** Flagbearer, pot helmet ...	15.50	22.15	31.00
(B202) **703?** Kneeling, firing rifle	15.00	22.50	30.00
(B203) **705** Port Arms	8	12	16
(B204) **707** Order Arms	8	12	16
(B205) **708** Officer with Sword	8.50	12.75	17.00
(B206) **728** Prone Machine Gunner ..	11.00	16.50	22.00
(B207) **737** Tommy-Gunner	8	12	16
(B208) **747** Standing Firing Rifle	8.50	12.75	17.00
(B209) **774** AA Gunner	6.50	9.75	13.00
(B210) **777** Marching at Slope	7.00	10.50	14.00
(B211) **788** Marching, rifle slung	7.50	11.25	15.00
(B212) **789** AA Gunner	7.00	10.50	14.00
(B212a) Cowboy, two pistols, one in air	23.00	35.50	46.00
(B213) Drum Major	25.00	37.50	50.00
(B214) Drummer	25.00	37.50	50.00
(B215) Bugler	25.00	37.50	50.00
(B215A) Bugler, buttons run down front of uniform	No Price Found		
(B216) Clarinetist	25.00	37.50	50.00
(B217) Tubist	25.00	37.50	50.00
(B218) Sailor, white	15.00	22.50	30.00
(B218A) **720 Blue Sailor**	15.00	22.50	30.00

BARCLAY POD FOOT SERIES
Circa 1950s to 1971

Most podfoot soliders came in khaki and later, green.

	C6	C8	C10
(B219) **81 Two soldier Crew at Radar Equipment**	9.00	13.50	18.00
(B220) **82 Three Soldier Crew at Range Finder**	10.50	15.75	21.00
(B221) **83 Two Soldier Crew at Searchlight**	18	27	36
(B222) **84 Two Soldier Crew at Mobile Cannon**	8.50	12.75	17.00

B194   B195   B196   B197

B198

Photo by Don Pielin

B199   B200   B205

B225   B227   B226
Photo by Don Pielin

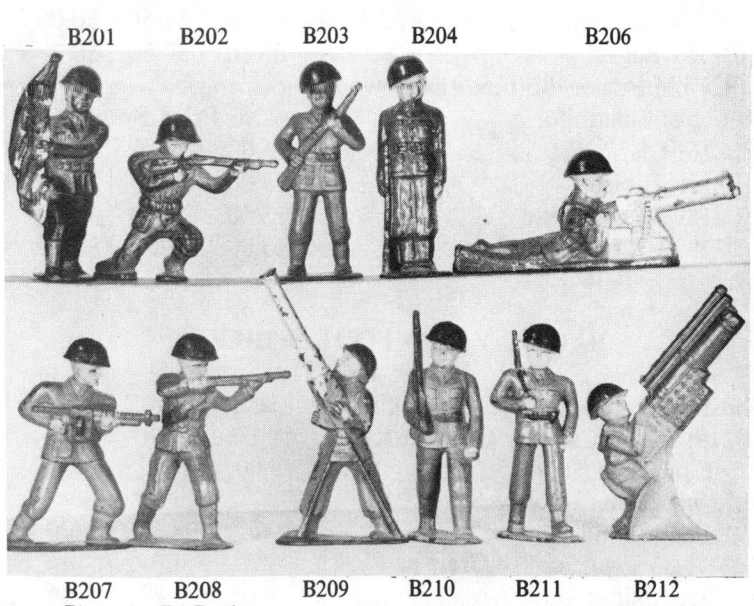

B201   B202   B203   B204   B206

B207   B208   B209   B210   B211   B212
Photo by Ed Poole

	C6	C8	C10
(B223) **85 Two Soldier Crew at A.A. Gun**	12.50	18.75	25.00
(B224) **187 Officer on Horse** (pot helmet)	33.00	49.50	66.00
(B225) **188 Cowboy on Horse** (lasso)	10	15	20
(B226) **189 Indian on Horse**	9.00	13.50	18.00
(B227) **190 Cowboy with Pistol on Horse**	8	12	16
(B228) **800 Black Knight w/Sword & Shield**	11.00	16.50	22.00
(B229) **801 Knight w/Red & Blue Shield & Sword**	15.00	22.50	30.00
(B230) **802 Knight w/Orange & Black Shield & Sword**	6	9	12
(B231) **803 Knight w/Red & Green Shield & Sword**	11.00	16.50	22.00
(B232) **901 Soldier Flag Bearer**	5.00	7.50	10.00
(B232A) Same as above, in red (not shown)	12.50	18.75	25.00
(B233) **903 Soldier Sniper** (kneeling)	6	9	12
(B233A) 903 same as above, in red	15.00	22.50	30.00
(B234) **906 Soldier Charging**	4.50	6.75	9.00
(B234A) Same as above, in red (not shown)	12.50	18.75	25.00
(B235) **908 Soldier Officer**	4	6	8
(B235A) Same as above, in blue	30	45	60
(B235B) Same as above, in red	12.50	18.75	25.00
(B236) **909 Soldier Bugler**	5.00	7.50	10.00
(B236A) Same as above, in red (not shown)	15.00	22.50	30.00
(B237) **919 Sailor White Uniform**	4.50	6.75	9.00
(B238) **920 Sailor Blue Uniform**	5.00	7.50	10.00
(B239) **922 Marine**	4	6	8
(B240) **928 Soldier Machine Gunner Lying Flat**	4	6	8
(B240A) Same as above, in red	12	18	24
(B241) **929 Soldier w/Pistol, Crawling**	11.00	16.50	22.00
(B241A) Same as above, in red	30	45	60
(B242) **937 Soldier, Charging Machine Gunner** (holding tommy gun)	4.50	6.75	9.00
(B242A) Same as above, in red	12.50	18.75	25.00
(B243) **938 Soldier Bomb Thrower**	5.00	7.50	10.00
(B243A) Same as above, in red	14	21	28
(B244) **941 Aviator**	4	6	8
(B244A) Same as above, in red	15.00	22.50	30.00
(B245) **947 Soldier Marksman**	4.50	6.75	9.00
(B245A) Same as above, in red	12.50	18.75	25.00
(B246) **948 Soldier Running**	4.50	6.75	9.00
(B247) **950 Cowboy w/Pistol Shooting**	5.00	7.50	10.00
(B248) **951 Cowboy w/Rifle**	3.50	5.25	7.00
(B249) **952 Cowboy w/Lasso**	3.50	5.25	7.00
(B250) **953 Cowboy w/Pistol** (upraised)	5.50	8.25	11.00
(B251) **954 Indian w/Shield & Tomahawk**	4	6	8
(B252) **955 Indian w/Rifle**	4	6	8
(B253) **956 Indian w/Knife & Spear**	4	6	8
(B254) **957 Indian w/Bow & Arrow**	4	6	8
(B255) **960 Soldier, Wounded, w/Crutches**	11.00	16.50	22.00
(B255A) Same as above, in red	20	30	40

254

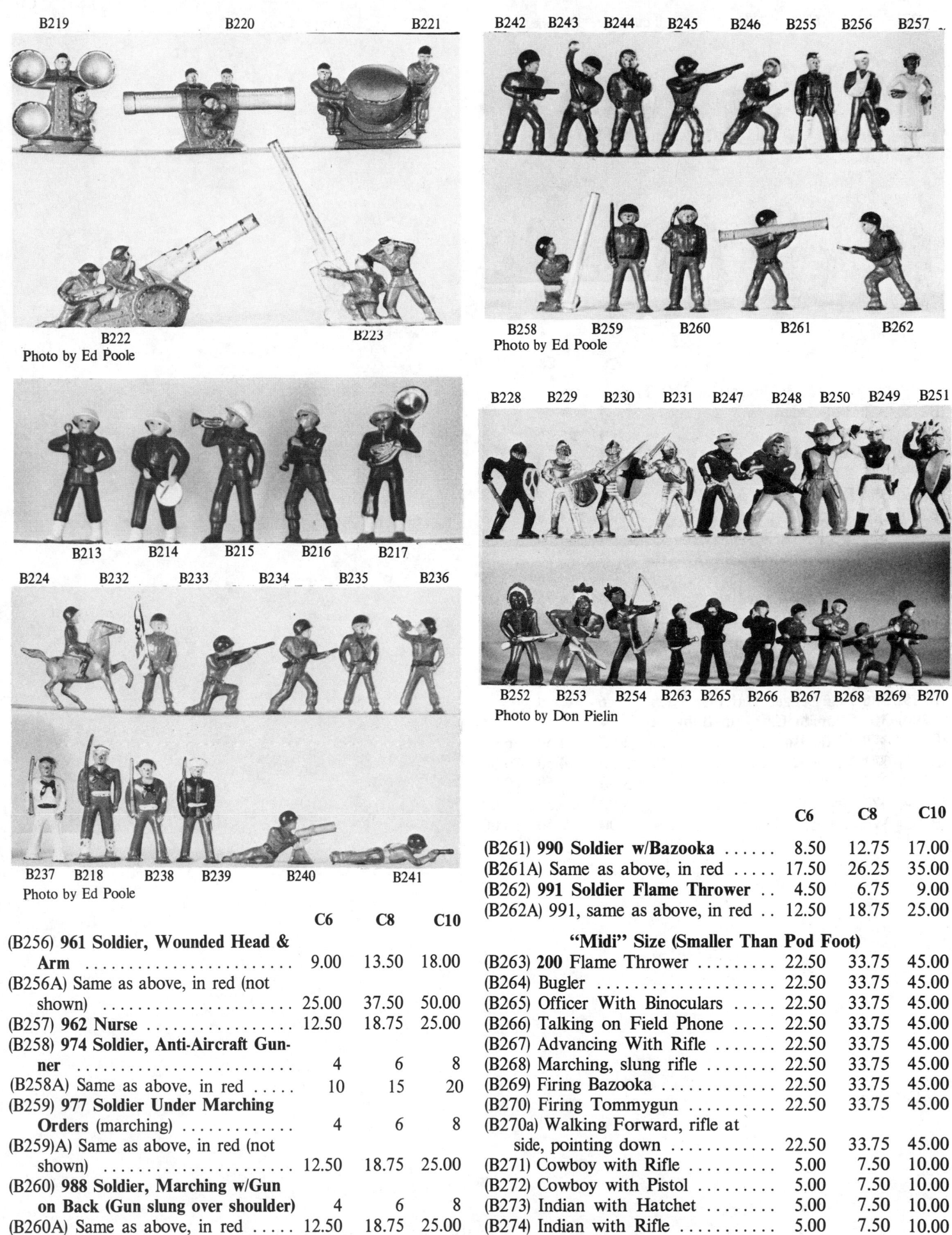

B219　　　　　B220　　　　　　B221

B222　　　　　　B223
Photo by Ed Poole

B242　B243　B244　B245　B246　B255　B256　B257

B258　　　B259　　　B260　　　B261　　　B262
Photo by Ed Poole

B213　　B214　　B215　　B216　　B217

B224　　B232　　B233　　B234　　B235　　B236

B237　B218　　B238　　B239　　B240　　B241
Photo by Ed Poole

B228　　B229　　B230　　B231　B247　B248　B250　B249　B251

B252　　B253　　B254　B263　B265　B266　B267　B268　B269　B270
Photo by Don Pielin

	C6	C8	C10
(B256) **961 Soldier, Wounded Head & Arm**	9.00	13.50	18.00
(B256A) Same as above, in red (not shown)	25.00	37.50	50.00
(B257) **962 Nurse**	12.50	18.75	25.00
(B258) **974 Soldier, Anti-Aircraft Gunner**	4	6	8
(B258A) Same as above, in red	10	15	20
(B259) **977 Soldier Under Marching Orders** (marching)	4	6	8
(B259)A) Same as above, in red (not shown)	12.50	18.75	25.00
(B260) **988 Soldier, Marching w/Gun on Back (Gun slung over shoulder)**	4	6	8
(B260A) Same as above, in red	12.50	18.75	25.00

	C6	C8	C10
(B261) **990 Soldier w/Bazooka**	8.50	12.75	17.00
(B261A) Same as above, in red	17.50	26.25	35.00
(B262) **991 Soldier Flame Thrower**	4.50	6.75	9.00
(B262A) 991, same as above, in red	12.50	18.75	25.00

"Midi" Size (Smaller Than Pod Foot)

	C6	C8	C10
(B263) **200 Flame Thrower**	22.50	33.75	45.00
(B264) **Bugler**	22.50	33.75	45.00
(B265) **Officer With Binoculars**	22.50	33.75	45.00
(B266) **Talking on Field Phone**	22.50	33.75	45.00
(B267) **Advancing With Rifle**	22.50	33.75	45.00
(B268) **Marching, slung rifle**	22.50	33.75	45.00
(B269) **Firing Bazooka**	22.50	33.75	45.00
(B270) **Firing Tommygun**	22.50	33.75	45.00
(B270a) **Walking Forward, rifle at side, pointing down**	22.50	33.75	45.00
(B271) **Cowboy with Rifle**	5.00	7.50	10.00
(B272) **Cowboy with Pistol**	5.00	7.50	10.00
(B273) **Indian with Hatchet**	5.00	7.50	10.00
(B274) **Indian with Rifle**	5.00	7.50	10.00

B271   B272   B273   B274   All others are 300 series

Photo by Don Pielin

	C6	C8	C10
HO Figures for HO Trains			
(B275) **350 Policeman**	4	6	8
(B276) **351 Man**	4	6	8
(B277) **352 Woman**	4	6	8
(B278) **353 Conductor**	4	6	8
(B279) **354 Redcap**	4	6	8
(B280) **355 Oiler**	4	6	8
(B281) **356 Brakeman**	4	6	8
(B282) **357 Engineer**	4	6	8
(B283) **358 Porter**	4	6	8
(B284) **359 Dining Steward**	4.50	6.75	9.00
(B285) **360 Hobo**	5.00	7.50	10.00
(B286) **361 Newsboy**	4	6	8
(B287) **362 Mailman**	4	6	8
(B288) **363 Fireman**	4	6	8
(B289) **366 Peg Legged Gateman**	6	9	12
(B290) **369 Woman Carrying Baby** ..	4	6	8
(B291) **370 Little Boy**	3.00	4.50	6.00
(B292) **371 Little Girl**	3.00	4.50	6.00
(B293) **372 Bride**	5.00	7.50	10.00
(B294) **373 Groom**	5.00	7.50	10.00
(B295) **Woman with Dog**	5.00	7.50	10.00

MANOIL

(See also Vehicles, Aircraft, Ships, Trains and Miscellaneous)

Manoil began production of toy soldiers in 1935. It was in business as early as 1927 under the name Jack Manoil, turning out metal lamps and novelties at 34 West Houston Street in New York City. The company changed its name to Man-O-Lamp Corporation on July 11, 1928, and was owned by Maurice Manoil (12/4/1893-9/15/74) and Jack Manoil (1/29/02-9/1/55), two brothers who had emigrated from Rumania in the early 1900s. The final name-change to Manoil Manufacturing Co., Inc. took place on July 7, 1934.

The two brothers were essentially partners, with Maurice handling the business end of the operation and Jack, who oversaw the creative area, working closely with Walter Baetz (1894-1978), who sculpted all the company's toys.

Manoil advanced firmly into toy-making in 1934, with seven vehicles, and moved to other addresses as it grew, leaving Manhattan in 1937 for Brooklyn, and then in June, 1940, moving to Waverly, New York (which afforded excellent shipping by rail), employing 225 people at its peak.

With the onset of World War II, Manoil shut down, but then resumed production of soldiers in a fine-grained composition form (employing sulphur) in January, 1944. Brittle, the pieces were ultimately unsuccessful, and their manufacture ended by the end of the year.

After the Second World War, the company introduced several new lines of soldiers, (also containing some of its pre-War soldiers and its appealing Happy Farm series), but they were no longer distributed as widely.

Manoil's soldiers have a distinctive jauntiness to them, at times veering on caricature, the latter trait becoming more pronounced as the years wore on. In 1953 the firm moved to a smaller location in Waverly, changing its name to Jack Manoil Specialty Company, but went out of business shortly after Jack's death. Baetz and Jack Manoil were both keenly interested in the company's soldiers and would work late into the night as they collaborated on ideas for them. One of Baetz's continuing concerns was to design the molds so that there was no structural weakness in the soldiers as a result of air bubbles. For this reason, many of Manoil's soldiers were redesigned a number of times, sometimes with subtle and sometimes with broad variations.

Unlike Barclay, Manoil also produced plastic toys, selling millions of vehicles and airplanes in its later years. Models of Manoil and Barclay soldiers are being reproduced (see Leading Collectors and Dealers), hollow-cast from the original molds. **All bold words and numbers are Manoil's own description.**

M1   M2   M3   M4   M5   M6   M7   M8   M9   M10

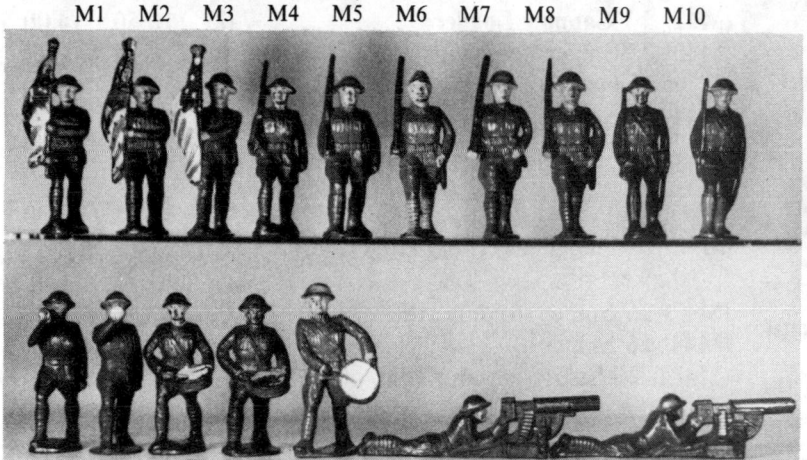

M58a
Photo by Don Pielin

M38b
Photo by Norbert Schachter
Courtesy Peter & Marjorie Ruben

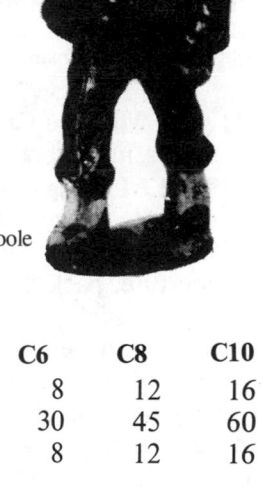

M23
Photo by Ed Poole

M11   M12   M13   M14   M15   M16   M17
Photo by Bill Kaufman

	C6	C8	C10
(M1) **7 Flag Bearer,** hollow base version	24	36	48
(M2) **7 Flag Bearer,** second version	9.50	14.25	19.00
(M3) **7 Flag Bearer**	7.50	11.25	15.00
(M4) **8 Parade,** hollow base version	15.00	22.50	30.00
(M5) **8 Parade,** stocky version	9.50	14.25	19.00
(M6) **8 Parade,** campaign cap straight on head	18	27	36
(M7) **8 Parade,** number on back	30	45	60
(M8) **8 Parade,** fifth version	7.50	11.25	15.00
(M9) **9 Officer,** hollow base version	34	51	68

	C6	C8	C10
(M10) **9 Officer,** second version	8	12	16
(M11) **10 Bugler,** hollow base version	30	45	60
(M12) **10 Bugler,** second version	8	12	16
(M13) **11 Drummer,** hollow base version	17.00	25.50	34.00
(M14) **11 Drummer,** stocky version	10	15	20
(M15) **11 Drummer,** vertical drum	15.50	22.75	31.00
(M16) **12 Machine Gunner** (Prone), grass on base	9.50	14.25	19.00
(M17) **12 Machine Gunner** (Prone), flat base, no grass	11.00	16.50	22.00

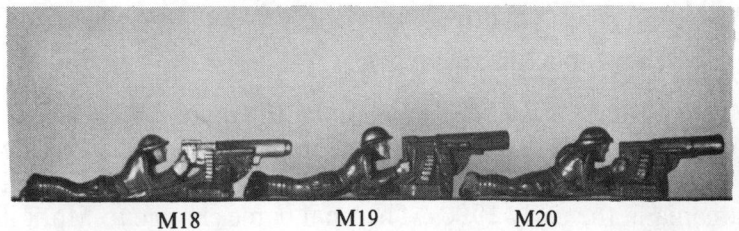

M18 M19 M20

M21 M22 M23 M24 M25 M26 M27a M27

Photos by Bill Kaufman

M28 M29 M30 M31 M32 M35 M36

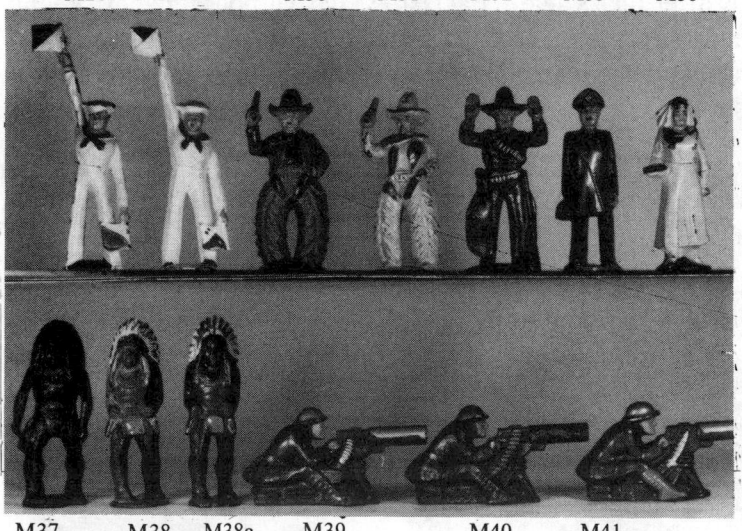

M37 M38 M38a M39 M40 M41

Photo by Bill Kaufman

	C6	C8	C10
(M30) **18 Cowboy**, hollow base version	14	21	28
(M31) **18 Cowboy**, second version . . .	7.00	10.50	14.00
(M32) **18A Cowboy With Hands Up** .	6	9	12
(M33) **18A Cowboy With Hands Up** (subtle variation)	6	9	12
(M34) **20 Doctor** (same as 20K, but in white)	8	12	16
(M35) **20K Doctor** (khaki)	6	9	12
(M36) **21 Nurse**	7.00	10.50	14.00
(M36a) **21 Nurse**, no hem in skirt, shorter, etc.	12.50	18.75	25.00
(M37) **Indian** with hatchet	42.50	63.75	85.00
(M38) **22 Indian** with knives	5.00	7.50	10.00
(M38aa) **22 Indian**, with knives, same as above, minor difference in hairline may be casting flaw	No Price Found		
(M38a) **22 Indian**, with knives, right toes off base	9.00	13.50	18.00
(M38b) **22 Indian**, with knives, sarong-like garment, only one known . . .	No Price Found		
(M39) **23 Machine Gunner Sitting**, seated on four pillows, bullets feed from ammo box	11.00	16.50	22.00
(M40) **23 Machine Gunner Sitting**, markings under base	13.00	19.50	26.00
(M41) **23 Machine Gunner Sitting**, squarer-looking, markings near right leg	9.50	14.25	19.00
(M42) **24 Cannon Loader**	7.00	10.50	14.00
(M43) **25 Sniper (kneeling)** hollow base, (may not be Manoil)	37.50	52.25	75.00
(M44) **25 Sniper (kneeling)** folding rifle	110	165	220
(M45) **25 Sniper (kneeling)** short thin rifle	8.50	12.75	17.00
(M46) **25 Sniper (kneeling)** longer, thicker rifle	9.00	13.50	18.00
(M47) **26 Sniper**, folding rifle	125.00	187.50	250.00
(M48) **26 Sniper**	8	12	16
(M48a) **26 Sniper**, shorter rifle, angle different on underside of rifle . . .	8.50	12.75	17.00
(M49) **27 Tommy Gunner**, bloated version	13.00	19.50	26.00

	C6	C8	C10
(M18) **12 Machine Gunner** (Prone), spaces under body	15.00	22.50	30.00
(M19) **12 Machine Gunner** (Prone), no aperture between hands and gun .	9.00	13.50	18.00
(M20) **12 Machine Gunner** (Prone), no aperture, pack on back	9.00	13.50	18.00
(M21) **13 Cadet**, hollow base, no buckle on belt	20	30	40
(M22) **13 Cadet**, second version	7.00	10.50	14.00
(M23) **14 Sailor**, hollow base	20	30	40
(M23a) Same as above, in blue	25.00	37.50	50.00
(M24) **Sailor**, second version	7.50	11.25	15.00
(M25) **15 Marine**, hollow base	32.50	48.75	65.00
(M26) **15 Marine**, second version	6.50	9.75	13.00
(M27) **16 Ensign**	10	15	20
(M27a) **16 Ensign**, hollow base	34	51	68
(M28) **17 Signal Man**, hollow base version	15.00	22.50	30.00
(M29) **17 Signal Man**, second version	7.50	11.25	15.00

M42 M43 M44 M45 M46 M47

M48 M49 M50 M51 M52 M53

Photo by Bill Kaufman

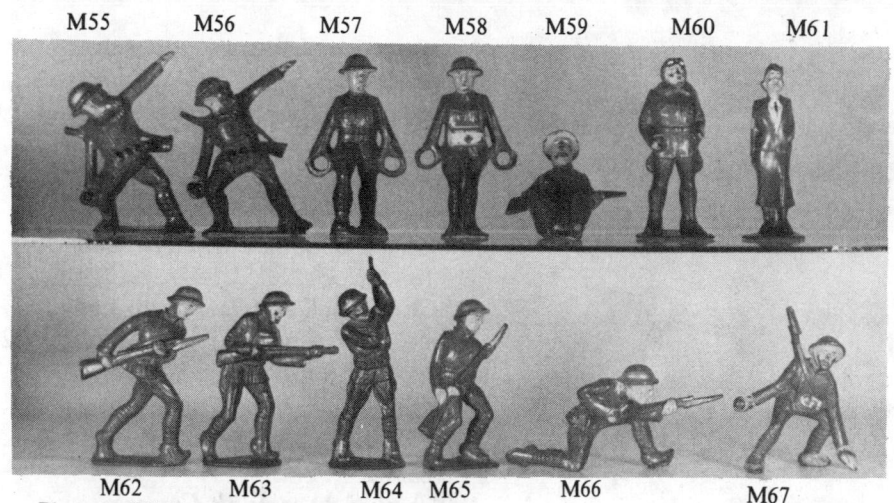

M55 M56 M57 M58 M59 M60 M61

M62 M63 M64 M65 M66 M67

Photo by Bill Kaufman

M 68 M69 M70 M71

M72 M73 M74 M75 M75b M76 M77

Photo by Bill Kaufman

M36a M36

Photo by K. Warren Mitchell

	C6	C8	C10
(M50) 27 Tommy Gunner, second version	9.50	14.25	19.00
(M51) 28 Observer	8	12	16
(M52) 29 Wounded Soldier (Walking).	7.00	10.50	14.00
(M53) 30 Wounded Soldier (Lying)...	7.50	11.25	15.00
(M54) 30 Wounded Soldier (Lying), number on back, shorter head ...	9.00	13.50	18.00
(M55) 31 Bomb Thrower, three grenades in pouch	7.50	11.25	15.00
(M56) 31 Bomb Thrower, two grenades in pouch	8	12	16
(M57) 32 Stretcher Carrier, no medical kit	7.00	10.50	14.00
(M58) 32 Stretcher Carrier, medical kit	8.50	12.75	17.00
(M58a) 32 Stretcher Carrier, medical kit, number on back, buttons on uniform, different pockets and collar from above	35.00	52.50	70.00
(M59) 33 Sitting Soldier	12	18	24
(M60) 34 Aviator	8	12	16
(M61) 35 Hostess, in white	40	60	80
As above, in green	27	40	54
(M61a) 35 Hostess in Khaki	No Price Found		
(M62) 36 Soldier With Bayonet Charging	16	24	32
(M63) 37 Soldier with Gun Charging	22	33	44
(M64) 38 Soldier With Gun Butting .	24	36	48

	C6	C8	C10
(M65) 39 Soldier With Bayonet Jabbing	22	33	44
(M66) 40 Soldier (Kneeling With Bayonet)	27.50	41.25	55.00
(M67) 41 Soldier (Crouching With Hand Grenade)	26	39	52
(M68) 42 Field Doctor (Crawling) ...	21.00	31.50	42.00
(M69) 43 Officer (Lying Down - Shooting Revolver)	20	30	40
(M70) 44 Crawling Scout With Gun, left leg high when right leg on ground (only three known)	42	63	84
(M71) 44 Crawling Scout With Gun, left leg lower	24	36	48
(M72) 45 Observer (With Periscope) .	12	18	24
(M73) 46 Anti-Aircraft Gunner, barrel of gun drops below arm	7.50	11.25	15.00
(M74) 46 Anti-Aircraft Gunner, barrel of gun ends at arm	7.50	11.25	15.00
(M75) 47 Anti-Aircraft Searchlight ..	8	12	16
(M75a) 47 like above, with tin lens ..	55.00	82.50	110.00
(M75b) 47 like M75, number on back, helmet looks as if it was adapted to look like WW II helmet	9.00	13.50	18.00
(M76) 48 Navy Gunner	8	12	16
(M77) 49 Policeman	8	12	16
(M78) 49 Policeman slightly larger ...	8	12	16
(M79) 50 Bicycle Dispatch Rider	11.00	16.50	22.00

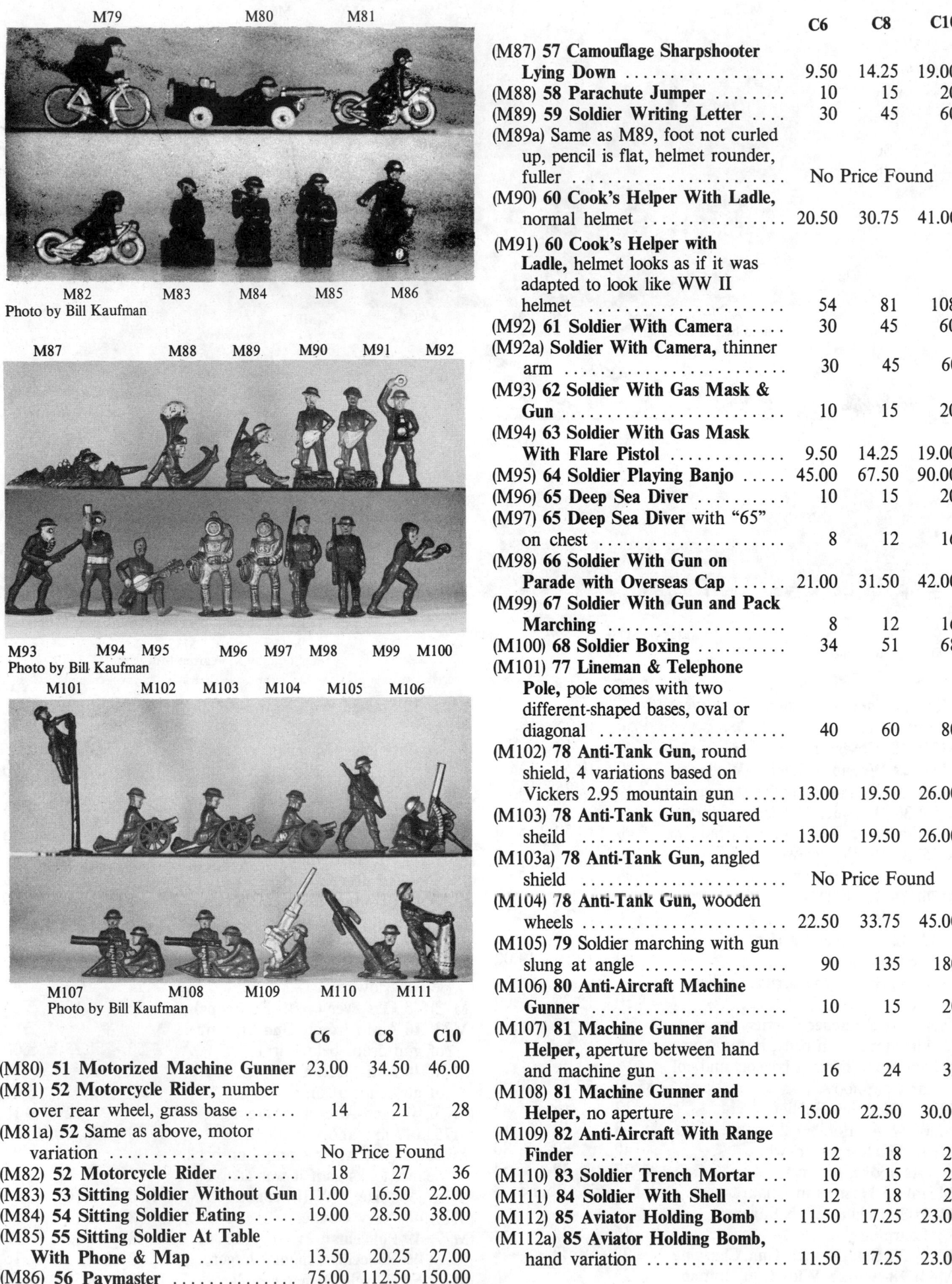

M79　　　　M80　　　　M81

M82　　　M83　　　M84　　　M85　　　M86

Photo by Bill Kaufman

M87　　　M88　　M89　　M90　　M91　　M92

M93　　　M94　M95　　　M96　M97　M98　　M99　M100

Photo by Bill Kaufman

M101　　　M102　　M103　　M104　　M105　　M106

M107　　　　M108　　　M109　　M110　　M111

Photo by Bill Kaufman

	C6	C8	C10
(M87) **57 Camouflage Sharpshooter Lying Down**	9.50	14.25	19.00
(M88) **58 Parachute Jumper**	10	15	20
(M89) **59 Soldier Writing Letter**	30	45	60
(M89a) Same as M89, foot not curled up, pencil is flat, helmet rounder, fuller	No Price Found		
(M90) **60 Cook's Helper With Ladle,** normal helmet	20.50	30.75	41.00
(M91) **60 Cook's Helper with Ladle,** helmet looks as if it was adapted to look like WW II helmet	54	81	108
(M92) **61 Soldier With Camera**	30	45	60
(M92a) **Soldier With Camera,** thinner arm	30	45	60
(M93) **62 Soldier With Gas Mask & Gun**	10	15	20
(M94) **63 Soldier With Gas Mask With Flare Pistol**	9.50	14.25	19.00
(M95) **64 Soldier Playing Banjo**	45.00	67.50	90.00
(M96) **65 Deep Sea Diver**	10	15	20
(M97) **65 Deep Sea Diver** with "65" on chest	8	12	16
(M98) **66 Soldier With Gun on Parade with Overseas Cap**	21.00	31.50	42.00
(M99) **67 Soldier With Gun and Pack Marching**	8	12	16
(M100) **68 Soldier Boxing**	34	51	68
(M101) **77 Lineman & Telephone Pole,** pole comes with two different-shaped bases, oval or diagonal	40	60	80
(M102) **78 Anti-Tank Gun,** round shield, 4 variations based on Vickers 2.95 mountain gun	13.00	19.50	26.00
(M103) **78 Anti-Tank Gun,** squared sheild	13.00	19.50	26.00
(M103a) **78 Anti-Tank Gun,** angled shield	No Price Found		
(M104) **78 Anti-Tank Gun,** wooden wheels	22.50	33.75	45.00
(M105) **79 Soldier marching with gun** slung at angle	90	135	180
(M106) **80 Anti-Aircraft Machine Gunner**	10	15	20
(M107) **81 Machine Gunner and Helper,** aperture between hand and machine gun	16	24	32
(M108) **81 Machine Gunner and Helper,** no aperture	15.00	22.50	30.00
(M109) **82 Anti-Aircraft With Range Finder**	12	18	24
(M110) **83 Soldier Trench Mortar**	10	15	20
(M111) **84 Soldier With Shell**	12	18	24
(M112) **85 Aviator Holding Bomb**	11.50	17.25	23.00
(M112a) **85 Aviator Holding Bomb,** hand variation	11.50	17.25	23.00

	C6	C8	C10
(M80) **51 Motorized Machine Gunner**	23.00	34.50	46.00
(M81) **52 Motorcycle Rider,** number over rear wheel, grass base	14	21	28
(M81a) **52** Same as above, motor variation	No Price Found		
(M82) **52 Motorcycle Rider**	18	27	36
(M83) **53 Sitting Soldier Without Gun**	11.00	16.50	22.00
(M84) **54 Sitting Soldier Eating**	19.00	28.50	38.00
(M85) **55 Sitting Soldier At Table With Phone & Map**	13.50	20.25	27.00
(M86) **56 Paymaster**	75.00	112.50	150.00

	C6	C8	C10

(M113) **86 Aviator Mechanic With Propeller,** away from head 150 225 300

(M114) **86 Aviator Mechanic With Propeller,** orange prop, flat lower hand 40 60 80

(M114a) **86 Silver prop** 60 90 120

(M114b) **86 orange prop, curved lower hand** 40 60 80

(M115) **87 Aviator carrying bomb sight** 13.00 19.50 26.00

(M115a) **87 Aviator carrying bomb sight, smaller base** .... No Price Found

(M116) **88 Radio Operator Standing** . 26 39 52

(M117) **89 Radio Operator (Lying Down)** 16 24 32

(M118) **90 Soldier Digging Trench** .. 25.00 37.50 50.00

(M119) **91 Soldier With Barbed Wire,** wide-faced version 15.00 22.50 30.00

(M120) **91 Soldier With Barbed Wire** 16 24 32

(M121) **92 Fire Fighter** in white 38 57 76

(M121a) **92 Fire Fighter** in grey 62.50 93.75 125.00

(M122) **93 Soldier On Guard Duty** .. 50 75 100

(M123) **94 Soldier Running With Cannon** marked "Manoil USA," "1" cannon slants to right when looked at from above 16 24 32

(M123a) **94 Soldier Running With Cannon,** no markings, cannon straight from above, face narrower 16 24 32

(M124) **94 Soldier Running With Cannon,** wood wheels, thin face 20 30 40

(M125) **99 Finn with Skis** 29.00 43.50 58.00

(M126) **100 Finn Machine Gunner** ... 21.00 31.50 42.00

(M127) **101 Soldier Jumping With Chute** 40 60 80

(M128) **102 Soldier Jumping With Machine Gun** 30 45 60

Happy Farm Series

According to the late Peter Ruben, a great number of color varieties and shades in this series exist, many of which can be related to the women who did the detail painting, and the season, as represented by 41/2 with long and short sleeve dresses. A number of Happy Farm figures were produced circa 1960 for the Smithsonian Museum, solid-cast with a patina or black finish.

(M129) **41/1 Bench** 5.00 7.50 10.00

(M130) **41/2 Girl** 4 6 8

(M131) **41/3 Young Man** 4 6 8

(M132) **41/4 Man Carrying Sack on Back** 10 15 20

(M133) **41/5 Farmer Pitching Sheaves** 12.50 18.75 25.00

(M134) **41/6 Farmer Sharpening Scythe** 9.00 13.50 18.00

(M135) **41/7 Blacksmith Making Horseshoes** 9.00 13.50 18.00

M112a M113 M114 M115 M116 M117 M118
Photo by Bill Kaufman

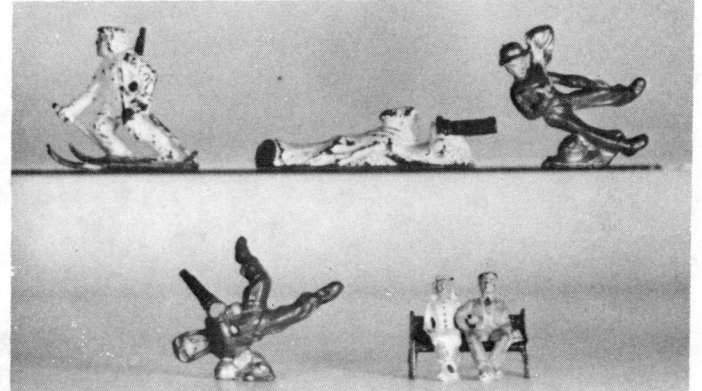

M119 M120 M121 M122 M123 M124
Photo by Bill Kaufman

M125 M126 M127

M128 M129-M131
Photo by Bill Kaufman

M132 M133 M134 M135 M137 M138 M139
Photo by Don Pielin

	C6	C8	C10

(M136) **41/8 Farmer Cutting With Scythe** 11.00 16.50 22.00

(M137) **41/9 Farmer Cutting Corn** ... 10.50 15.75 21.00

(M138) **41/10 Farmer Sowing Grain** . 9.00 13.50 18.00

(M139) **41/11 Man Carrying Sheaves Under Arm** 10 15 20

(M140) **41/12 Scarecrow With Top Hat** 9.00 13.50 18.00

(M141) **41/13 Farmer Carrying Pumpkin** 9.00 13.50 18.00

(M142) **41/14 Darky Eating Watermelon** 35.00 52.50 70.00

(M143) **41/15 Scarecrow With Straw Hat** 10 15 20

M141 M142 M143 M144 M145 M146

M147 M148 M149 M150 M151 M154
Photo by Don Pielin

M152 M153 M155 M156 M157 M158 M159 M160 M161

M162 M163 M164 M165 M166 M167 M168 M169
Photo by Don Pielin

M173

M170 M171 M172 M174 M175 M176
Photo by Ed Poole

M177 M178 M179 M180 M181 M182

M183 M184 M185 M186
Photo by Ed Poole

M187 M188 M189 M190 M191 M192 M193

M194 M195 M196 M197
Photo by Ed Poole

	C6	C8	C10
(M144) 41/16 Watchman Blowing Out Lantern	10.50	15.75	21.00
(M145) 41/17 Hod Carrier With Bricks	11.00	16.50	22.00
(M146) 41/18 Man Chopping Wood	10.50	15.75	21.00
(M147) 41/19 Mason Laying Bricks	12.50	18.75	25.00
(M148) 41/20 Man Dumping Wheel Barrow	10	15	20
(M149) 41/21 Old Man Fixing Shoe	13.00	19.50	26.00

	C6	C8	C10
(M150) 41/22 Blacksmith With Wheel	12	18	24
(M151) 41/23 Carpenter Carrying Door	16	24	32
(M152) 41/24 Hound	8.50	12.75	17.00
(M153) 41/25 Carpenter Sawing Lumber	13.50	20.25	27.00
(M154) 41/26 Carpenter With Square	20	30	40
(M155) 41/27 Sheperd With Flute	14	21	28
(M156) 41/28 Lady With Pie	11.00	16.50	22.00
(M157) 41/29 Lady With Child	14	21	28
(M158) 41/30 School Teacher	23.00	35.50	46.00
(M159) 41/31 Girl Watering Flowers	10	15	20
(M160) 41/32 Woman Lifting Hen From Nest	11.00	16.50	22.00
(M161) 41/33 Woman With Butter Churn	11.50	17.25	23.00
(M162) 41/34 Woman Laying Out Wash On Grass	11.50	17.25	23.00
(M163) 41/35 Woman Sweeping With Broom	12	18	24
(M164) 41/36 Man Juggling Barrel (double price in khaki)	15.00	22.50	30.00

M198   M199   M200   M201

M202   M203   M204   M205   M206
Photo by Ed Poole

	C6	C8	C10
(M164a) As above, in khaki	30	45	60
(M165) **41/37 Man Planting Tree** ...	14	21	28
(M166) **41/38 Girl Picking Berries** ...	21.00	31.50	42.00
(M167) **41/39 Farmer At Water Pump**	10	15	20
(M168) **41/40 Boy Carrying Wood** ..	11.50	17.25	23.00
(M169) **41/41 Stacks of Sheaves**	8	12	16
(M169) **41/41 Haystack** is a rare variant, easily distinguished by the bottle and jug by its side		No Price Found	
(M169a) Boxed Happy Farm Set (10 pieces) mint with box, no standard contents	150	225	300

End Happy Farm Listing

MANOIL COMPOSITION

(MC1) Prone machine-gunner	25.00	37.50	50.00
(MC2) Seated machine-gunner	24	36	48
(MC3) Motorcyclist	24	36	48
(MC3a) Motorcyclist, mirror variation of above	24	36	48
(MC4) Firing camouflaged AA gun ..	24	36	48

POST-WAR

M170 through M176 were the first new Post WW II series, and were produced only for a limited time. On a trial basis early production was also sold unpainted.

(M170) Flag Bearer (thin), circa late 1945	14.50	21.75	29.00
(M171) Parade (thin), circa late 1945 .	14	21	18
(M172) Tommy Gunner (thin, circa late 1945)	14.50	21.75	29.00
(M173) Machine Gunner Sitting (thin), circa late 1945	30	45	60
(M174) Machine Gunner Lying (thin), circa late 1945	50	75	100
(M175) Sniper (thin), circa late 1945 .	26	39	52
(M176) **45/6 Parade** (thin), circa late 1945	14	21	28
(M177) **45/7 Flag Bearer**	11.00	16.50	22.00
(M178) **45/8 Parade**	10	15	20
(M179) **45/9 Combat**	10	15	20

	C6	C8	C10
(M180) **45/10 At Attention** (present arms)	10.50	15.75	21.00
(M181) **45/11 Sniper**	11.00	16.50	22.00
(M182) **45/12 Tommy Gunner**	11.00	16.50	22.00
(M183) **45/13 Soldier With Bazooka Cannon** (some marked "45/18") ..	11.50	17.25	23.00
(M184) **45/14 Soldier With Shell For Bazooka** (some marked "46/14") .	12.50	18.75	25.00
(M185) **45/15 General** (some "46/15")	60	90	120
(M186) **45/16 Mine Detector** (some "46/16")	16	24	32
(M187) **521 Flag Bearer**, all 500s, circa 1950	15.00	22.50	30.00
(M188) **522 Parade**	13.00	19.50	26.00
(M189) **523 Soldier in poncho**	18	27	36
(M190) **524 Combat**	12	18	24
(M191) **525 Aviator holding bomb** ...	16	24	32
(M192) **526 Observer**	16	24	32
(**M193**) **527 Aircraft Spotter**	17.00	25.50	34.00
(M194) **528 Soldier with bazooka** ..	11.00	16.50	22.00
(M195) **529 Motorcycle rider**	25.00	37.50	50.00
(M196) **530 Machine gunner (lying)** ..	13.50	20.25	27.00
(M197) **531 Machine gunner sitting** ..	13.00	19.50	26.00
(M198) **532 Sniper (kneeling)**	13.50	20.25	27.00
(M199) **533 Soldier with gas mask with flare pistol**	16	24	32
(M200) **534 Sniper**	16	24	32
(M201) **535 Soldier throwing hand grenade**	12.50	18.75	25.00
(M202) **536 Anti-Aircraft gunner**	17.50	26.25	35.00
(M203) **537 Soldier with tommy gun** .	21.00	31.50	42.00
(M204) **538 Soldier firing up**	17.50	26.25	35.00
(M205) **539 Stretcher bearer**	37.50	56.25	75.00
(M206) **540 Wounded Soldier (lying)** .	40	60	80

My Ranch Corral Series

M207   M208   M209   M210
Photo by Don Pielin

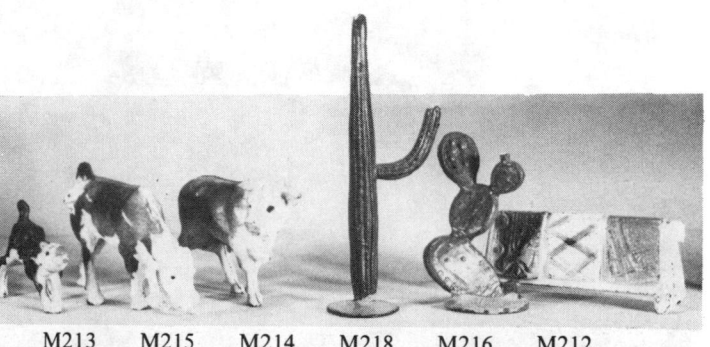

M213   M215   M214   M218   M216   M212

	C6	C8	C10			C6	C8	C10
(M207) **C-23 Cowboy Rider**	10	15	20	(M215) C19 Cow feeding	5.50	8.25	11.00
(M208) **C-24 Cowgirl Rider**	9.00	13.50	18.00	(M216) C28 Short Cactus	8	12	16
(M209) **C-29 Mounted Cowboy**	24	36	48	(M217) C14 Brahma Bull	8	12	16
(M210) **C-30 Mounted Cowboy**				(M218) C26 Large Cactus	9.00	13.50	18.00
Shooting	23.00	34.50	46.00	(M219) C1 Fence	5.50	8.25	11.00
(M211) C2 Ranch fence, gate	35.00	52.50	70.00	(M220) C25 Small Horse	7.00	10.50	14.00
(M212) C12 Blanket over Fence Section	15.00	22.50	30.00	(M221) Horse for Mounted Cowboy	9.50	14.25	19.00
(M213) C18 Small Calf	5.50	8.25	11.00	(M222) Horse for Mounted Cowgirl	11.00	16.50	22.00
(M214) C20 Bull, head turned	6	9	12	(M223) Small Gate	14.50	21.75	29.00
				(M224) Large Gate	14	21	28

GREY IRON

Grey Iron made the only 3¼" cast iron soldiers. The company began in 1840 as the Brady Machine Shop in Mount Joy, Pennsylvania, where it has remained to this day, and in 1881 was organized as the Grey Iron Casting Company, Limited. As early as 1903 it was manufacturing toy banks and stoves, cap pistols, wheeled toys and trains, as well as a number of non-toy items. On August 14, 1917, the company was granted two patents for their 40 mm solid cast iron Grey Klip Armies, which they then manufactured through 1941, the last of the series emerging in 1938 as "Uncle Sam's Defenders", painted khaki rather than nickel-plated, as the earlier versions had been. The soldiers were not successful at first, but with the advent of a new distributor, the company was swamped with orders, and in January, 1933, introduced a new line of thirty-five different cast iron soldiers, in an approximately 3" size (four Revolutionary War soldiers; an infantryman, a foot officer, a flagbearer and a mounted officer, may have been introduced earlier, as they are numbered lower, but were not part of the 1933 announcement).

The figures tended to be slight, and while apparently successful, were superseded in July 1936 by Grey's "Iron Men" series, a slightly larger, more robust model, which continued to be sold until World War II ended all toy production. Designers for the soldiers were at least two; Edward Musser and Samuel S. Schmidt. The soldiers were hand-poured and then painted on an assembly-line basis, and at least initially were sold for a dime, while their competitors charged a nickel. Grey is still in business today as the John Wright division of Donsco, and has recently been producing, on an erratic basis, some unpainted soldiers from its old molds. Some years ago, the author saw, at a Pennsylvania flea market, some crude, cast iron Continental Soldiers, about 2½" high, which he believes may be early Grey Iron, but none have surfaced since, and there is no evidence that Grey made them. However, they would be valuable to serious collectors, and in mint would probably bring about $30 apiece. **All bold words and numbers are Grey Iron's own description.**

Very rare Grey Iron set No. F114 "American Family on the Farm" boxed set. Traded in 1987 for estimated value of $325. Barn is part of set.
Courtesy K. Warren Mitchell

GREY IRON (GA) Set 1 Co.A
Courtesy the late Karl Zipple

GREY IRON (GB) Set 2, Company B
Courtesy the late Karl Zipple

GREY IRON (GC) Set 3   Company C
Courtesy the late Karl Zipple

GREY IRON (GD) Set 4 Troop D
Courtesy the late Karl Zipple

GREY IRON (GE) Set 5 Battery E
Courtesy Don Pielin

GREY IRON (GF) Set 6 Battery F
Courtesy Don Pielin

GREY IRON (GG) Set 5 Aviation Corps   (Above two photos)
Courtesy the late Karl Zipple

GREY IRON (GH) Uncle Sam's Defenders
Courtesy the late Karl Zipple

Greyklip Armies

	C6	C8	C10
(GA) Set 1/Company A, at attention, consists of bugler, officer, flag-bearer, drummer, rifleman, price per each	1.50	2.25	3.00
(GB) Set 2/Company B, marching, consists of bugler, officer, flag-bearer. drummer, rifleman, price per each	2	3	4
(GC) Set 3/Company C, charging, consists of bugler, officer, flag-bearer, drummer, rifleman, price per each	2	3	4
(GD) Set 4/Troop D, consists of four mounted troopers, one mounted officer, troopers all look alike, price per each	2.50	3.75	5.00
(GE) Set 5/Battery E, two-piece set, led by officer from Troop D, second piece is a gun limber with four horses, several attached soldiers, price for second piece ..	5.00	7.50	10.00
(GF) Set 6/Battery F, consists of shell stack, loader bending, loader standing, gunner, cannon, price per each, shells double	2.50	3.75	5.00
(GG) Set 5/Aviator Corps, consists of pilot (two of the same figure in set) and plane with detachable wing. Price for set	60	90	120
(GH) Uncle Sam's Defenders, consists of charging rifleman, machine gunner, charging officer, rifleman at attention, flagbearer, officer saluting, price per each (double the price on saluting officer and flagbearer)	2.50	3.75	5.00

End Greyklip Armies

	C6	C8	C10
(G1) 1 Colonial Soldier	10.50	15.75	21.00
(G2) 1A Colonial Foot Officer	10	15	20
(G3) 1B Colonial Color-Bearer	150	225	300
(G3a) 1B Colonial Color-Bearer, 1950s version, with rifle barrel drilled out for flag	10	15	20
(G4) 1MA Colonial Mounted Officer	19.00	28.50	38.00
(G5) 2 Cadet, early version	7.00	10.50	14.00
(G6) 2 Cadet	8.50	12.75	17.00
(G7) 2A Cadet Officer, early	7.00	10.50	14.00
(G8) 2A Cadet Officer	11.00	16.50	22.00
(G9) 3 U.S. Infantry, Shoulder Arms, early	7.00	10.50	14.00
(G10) 3 U.S. Infantry, Shoulder Arms	6	9	12
(G10a) Same as above, no tie	No Price Found		
(G11) 3/1 U.S. Infantry, Port Arms ..	6	9	12
(G12) 3A U.S. Infantry Officer, early	7.00	10.50	14.00
(G13) 3A U.S. Infantry Officer	6.50	9.75	13.00
(G14) 3AP Traffic Officer (same as above, in blue)	12.50	18.75	25.00

G1 G2 G3 G3a G4 G5 G6 G7 G8

G9 G10 G11 G12 G13 G15 G16 G17 G18
Photo by Ed Poole

G19 G20 G21 G22 G23 G24 G25

G26 G27 G28 G29 G30 G31 G32 G33
Photo by Bill Kaufman

G34 G35 G37 G38 G39 G40 G41

G42 G45 G46 G47 G48 G49 G50
Photo by Bill Kaufman

	C6	C8	C10
(G15) 3AR Red Cross Officer (same as above, with armband)	21.00	31.50	42.00
(G16) 4 U.S.Infantry, Port Arms, early	7.00	10.50	14.00
(G17) 4A U.S. Doughboy Officer With Field Glasses	10	15	20
(G18) 4/1 U.S. Doughboy Signaling ..	7.00	10.50	14.00

266

	C6	C8	C10
(G19) **4/2 U.S. Doughboy Combat Trooper**	10	15	20
(G20) **4/3 U.S. Doughboy With Range Finder**	37.00	55.50	74.00
(G21) **4/4 U.S. Doughboy Ammunition Carrier**	37.50	56.25	75.00
(G22) **4/5 U.S. Doughboy Sharpshooter**	10	15	20
(G23) **4/6 U.S. Doughboy With Bayonet**	8.50	12.75	17.00
(G24) **5 U.S. Infantry, Charging,** early	6.50	9.75	13.00
(G25) **6 U.S. Doughboy, Port Arms,** early	8.50	12.75	17.00
(G26) **6 U.S. Doughboy, Shoulder Arms**	5.00	7.50	10.00
(G27) **6A U.S. Doughboy Officer,** early	7.00	10.50	14.00
(G28) **6A U.S. Doughboy Officer**	6	9	12
(G29) **6/1 U.S. Doughboy Charging** ..	5.00	7.50	10.00
(G30) **6/2 U.S. Doughboy Sentry**	7.50	11.25	15.00
(G31) **6/3 U.S. Doughboy Bomber,** crawling	8	12	16
(G32) **6/4 U.S. Doughboy Grenade Thrower**	11.50	17.25	23.00
(G33) **7 U.S. Doughboy Charging,** early	6	9	12
(G34) **8M U.S. Cavalryman,** early ...	15.00	22.50	30.00
(G35) **8M U.S. Cavalryman**	12	18	24
(G36) **8M U.S. Cavalry Color Bearer With Silk Flag** (not shown, same as G34)	No Price Found		
(G37) **8MA U.S. Cavalry Officer,** early	17.50	26.25	35.00
(G38) **8MA U.S. Cavalry Officer**	16	24	32
(G39) **9 U.S. Marine,** early	6.50	9.75	13.00
(G40) **9 U.S. Marine**	7.00	10.50	14.00
(G41) **10 Royal Canadian Police,** early	7.00	10.50	14.00
(G42) **10 Royal Canadian Police**	7.00	10.50	14.00
(G43) **10M Royal Canadian Mounted Police** (same as G34)	15.00	22.50	30.00
(G44) **10M Royal Canadian Mounted Police** (same as G35)	17.50	26.25	35.00
(G45) **11 Indian,** with hatchet, early .	6	9	12
(G46) **11 Indian Chief,** with knife ...	7.50	11.25	15.00
(G47) **11/1 Indian Brave,** shielding eyes	10	15	20
(G48) **11/2 Chief Attacking,** upraised tomahawk	50	75	100
(G49) **11M Indian Mounted,** early ...	14	21	28
(G50) **11M Indian Mounted,** lying on horse	25.00	37.50	100.00
(G51) **11/1M Indian Scout, Mounted,** firing pistol rearward	100	150	200
(G52) **12 Cowboy,** early	5.50	8.25	11.00
(G53) **12 Cowboy**	5.00	7.50	10.00
(G54) **12/1 Hold-Up Man**	8.50	12.75	17.00
(G55) **12/2 Cowboy With Lasso,** with lasso price is 45.00 in mint	17.00	25.50	34.00

G51 G52 G53 G54 G55 G56 G57

G58 G59 G60 G61 G62

G64 G65 G66 G68 G69 G71 G72 G73 G74 G75

G76 G77 G78 G79 G80 G81 G82 G83 G84

Photo by Bill Kaufman

G85 G86 G87 G88 G89 G90 G91 G92

G93 G94 G95 G96 G97 G98

G99 G100 G101 G102 G103 G104 G105

Photo by Bill Kaufman

267

	C6	C8	C10
(G56) 12/3 Bandit, surrendering	45.00	67.50	90.00
(G57) 12M Cowboy Mounted, early .	13.00	19.50	26.00
(G58) 12M Cowboy Mounted	20	30	40
(G59) 12/1M Masked Cowboy Mounted	110	165	220
(G60) 13 U.S. Machine Gunner, early	6	9	12
(G61) 13 U.S. Machine Gunner	6.50	9.75	13.00
(G62) 13/1 U.S. Machine Gunner ...	7.00	10.50	14.00
(G63) 14 U.S. Sailor in blue, early ..	7.50	11.25	15.00
(G64) 14 U.S. Sailor in white, early .	6.50	9.75	13.00
(G65) 14 U.S. Sailor in blue	4	6	8
(G66) 14W U.S. Sailor, in white	7.50	11.25	15.00
(G67) 14A U.S. Naval Officer, early, in blue	6.50	9.75	13.00
(G68) 14AW U.S. Naval Officer, early, in white	6	9	12
(G69) 14A U.S. Naval Officer, in blue	6.50	9.75	13.00
(G70) 14 AW U.S. Naval Officer in white	5.00	7.50	10.00
(G71) 14/1W U.S. Sailor Signalman .	9.00	13.50	18.00
(G72) 15/1 Boy Scout Saluting, early	8.50	12.75	17.00
(G73) 15/2 Boy Scout Walking, early	7.50	11.25	15.00
(G74) 16/1 Pirate Boy (all pirates circa 1935, were also sold as a Treasure Island set, with either tent or treasure chest included, pirates meant to represent Jim, Captain Flint, Long John, Blind Pew, Billie Bones)	10.50	15.75	21.00
(G75) 16/2 Pirate Chief	8.50	12.75	17.00
(G76) 16/3 Pirate With Dagger	8	12	16
(G77) 16/4 Pirate With Hook	8	12	16
(G78) 16/5 Pirate With Sword	7.00	10.50	14.00
(G79) 17/1 Legion Drum Major, early	21.00	31.50	42.00
(G80) 17/1 Legion Drum Major	15.50	22.75	31.00
(G81) 17/2 Legion Bugler, early	6.50	9.75	13.00
(G82) 17/2 Legion Bugler	6	9	12
(G83) 17/3 Legion Drummer, early ..	8.50	12.75	17.00
(G84) 17/3 Legion Drummer	7.00	10.50	14.00
(G85) 17/4 Legion Color Bearer	8	12	16
(G86) 18/1 Ethiopian Tribesman, circa 1936	26	39	52
(G87) 18/2 Ethiopian Chief	17.00	25.50	34.00
(G88) 18/3 Ethiopian Soldier, Shoulder Arms	16	24	32
(G89) 18/3A Ethiopian Officer	25.00	37.50	50.00
(G90) 18/5 Ethiopian Soldier, Charging	21.00	31.50	42.00
(G91) Italian or English Desert Infantryman	112.50	168.25	225.00
(G92) Italian or English Desert Officer	75.00	112.50	150.00
(G93) 19 Knight In Armor	8.50	12.75	17.00
(G94) 20 Red Cross Doctor	10	15	20
(G95) 21 Stretcher Bearer	12.50	18.75	25.00
(G96) 22 Stretcher With Patient	12.50	18.75	25.00
(G97) 22/1 Wounded Sitting	41.00	61.50	82.00
(G98) 22/2 Wounded On Crutches ...	16	24	32

G106   G107   Courtesy Hank Anton

	C6	C8	C10
(G99) 23 Red Cross Nurse	8	12	16
(G100) 25 Aviator (24 is non-soldier) .	15.00	22.50	30.00
(G101) Ski Trooper, circa 1940, with skis four times the noted price ...	11.00	16.50	22.00
(G102) Greek Evzone	50	75	100
(G103) 75 Radio Set, Operator and Aerial	75.00	112.50	150.00
(G103A) 75 Radio Set, Operator Only	37.50	56.25	75.00
(G104) D26 Nurse and Wounded Soldier	90	135	180
(G105) D27 Doughboy Supporting Wounded Soldier	100	150	200
*(G106) U.S. Cavalryman, probably Grey Iron, like G34, but horse's head and left leg up	70	105	140
*(G107) U.S. Cavalry Officer, probably Grey Iron, like G37, but horse's head and left leg up	60	90	120
*These may not have been produced by Grey Iron, but instead by Distinctive Products, Inc.			
(G108) 6AF Foreign Legion Officr ..	15.00	22.50	30.00
(G109) 6F Foreign Legion - Shoulder Arms	15.00	22.50	30.00
(G110) 6/1F Foreign Legion Charging	15.00	22.50	30.00
(G111) 6/3F Foreign Legion Bomber .	20	30	40
(G112) 13F Foreign Legion Machine Gunner	17.00	25.50	34.00
(G113) 8A/F Foreign Legion Cavalry Officer	25.00	37.50	50.00
(G114) 8/F Foreign Legion Cavalryman	25.00	37.50	50.00

American Family Series
(approximately 2¼" high)

The American Family Travels

	C6	C8	C10
T-1 Man in traveling suit	3.00	4.50	6.00
T-2 Woman in traveling costume	4.50	6.75	9.00
T-3 Boy in traveling suit	3.50	5.25	7.00
T-4 Girl in traveling suit	4.50	6.75	9.00
T-5 Conductor	3.00	4.50	6.00
T-6 Engineer	3.50	5.25	7.00
T-7 Porter	4.50	6.75	9.00
T-8 Policeman	3.50	5.25	7.00
T-9 Postman	3.50	5.25	7.00
T-10 Newsboy	5.50	8.25	11.00
T-11 Preacher	6.00	9.00	12.00
T-12 Old Colored Man – sitting	7.00	10.50	14.00
T-13 Seat	3.50	5.25	7.00

T1 T2 T3 T4 T5 T6 T7 T8 T9 T10 T11 T12 T13

F1 F2 F3 F4　　F11 F7 F9 F8 F12 F7 F6　　F5
Photo by Don Pielin

B1 B2 B3 B4 B5 B6 B7 B8 B9　　B11 B10 B12

L to R: H1 to H11　　Photo courtesy Don Pielin

R1 R3 R6/R7 R10 R11　　R2/R8 R5 R4 R9
Photo by Don Pielin

	C6	C8	C10
The American Family on the Farm			
F-1 Farmer	4.50	6.75	9.00
F-2 Farmer's Wife	4.50	6.75	9.00
F-3 Girl	5.00	7.50	10.00
F-4 Hired Man digging	5.00	7.50	10.00
F-5 Horse	5.00	7.50	10.00
F-6 Cow	2.50	3.75	5.00
F-7 Calf	3.00	4.50	6.00
F-8 Pig	2.50	3.75	5.00
F-9 Sheep	3.00	4.50	6.00
F-10 Goat	3.00	4.50	6.00
F-11 Goose	3.00	4.50	6.00
F-12 Dog	2	3	4
F-13 Gate with Post	4.00	6.00	8.00
F-14 Fence	No Price Found		

The American Family At Home	C6	C8	C10
H-1 Man with watering can	4.50	6.75	9.00
H-2 Woman with basket	5.00	7.50	10.00
H-3 Boy flying kite	8	12	16
H-4 Girl skipping rope	7.00	10.50	14.00
H-5 Old man sitting	2.50	3.75	5.00
H-6 Old woman sitting	4	6	8
H-7 Colored cook	9.00	13.50	18.00
H-8 Colored man digging	8.50	12.75	17.00
H-9 Garageman	4.50	6.75	9.00
H-10 Delivery boy	5.00	7.50	10.00
H-11 Milkman	6	9	12
H-12 Dog	2	3	4
H-13 Lawn Seat	3.00	4.50	6.00

The American Family on the Beach	C6	C8	C10
B-1 Man in bathing suit	9.00	13.50	18.00
B-2 Woman in bathing suit	10	15	20
B-3 Boy in summer suit	5.00	7.50	10.00
B-4 Girl in slacks	9.00	13.50	18.00
B-5 Old Man Sitting	2.50	3.75	5.00
B-6 Boy with Life Preserver	9.00	13.50	18.00
B-7 Girl with Sand Pail	9.00	13.50	18.00
B-8 Boy with Ball	9.00	13.50	18.00
B-9 Girl Catching Ball	7.00	10.50	14.00
B-10 Life Guard	11.00	16.50	22.00
B-11 Life Guard's Chair	11.00	16.50	22.00

	C6	C8	C10
B-12 Life Boat	12	18	24
B-13 Bench	3.50	5.25	7.00
B-14 Cabana	No Price Found		
The American Family On The Ranch			
R-1 Cowboy with lasso	3.75	5.63	7.50
R-2 Cowboy Rider	10	15	20
R-3 Cowboy squatting	5.00	7.50	10.00
R-4 Boy in Cowboy Suit	5.00	7.50	10.00
R-5 Girl in Riding Suit	5.00	7.50	10.00
R-6 Cowgirl Rider	6	9	12
R-7 Stallion	4	6	8
R-8 Bucking Broncho	9.00	13.50	18.00
R-9 Colt	3.00	4.50	6.00
R-10 Burro	10	15	20
R-11 Calf	4.50	6.75	9.00
R-15 Rooster and Chickens	3.00	4.50	6.00
R-16 Three Ducks	4	6	8

The Champions On The Diamond
M69 Fielder in Position, approx 1½"
　high .... No Price Found

AUBURN RUBBER

Although AUBURN (also Aub-Rub'r) was founded in 1913, in Auburn, Indiana, as the Double Fabric Tire Corporation, making auto tubes and tires for Model T Fords, etc., it didn't produce its first toy until 1935, with five soldiers. The prototype was a Palace Guard, which AUBURN President and chief stockholder A. L. Murray had obtained in England. The model was taken to a local pattern-maker who made patterns from it, and then the company made the original molds from lead and molded sample toys for Murray. These samples were next taken to an artist and decorated per Murray's instructions. Presented to buyers, they immediately caught on. The soldiers were molded in 24" rubber presses, each containing forty to sixty soldiers, with cure time approximately 6-12 minutes. The soldiers, once trimmed, were dipped in a base laquer (advertised as "pure vegetable dyes") and then sent down a decorating conveyor, where as many as 24 women, using small camel hair brushes, added finishing touches, painting the faces, shoes, belts, buttons, medals, and finally eyes. After drying, each was wrapped individually in waxed paper and packed three dozen to a chipboard carton and twelve dozen to a corrugated carton for shipment. Design of the soldiers was credited to Edward McCandlish, a free-lance artist. The soldiers sold well from the beginning, with approximately 200 of the 400 AUBURN employees (AUBURN consistently made non-toy products as well) involved in them and other toys on a two-shift basis. Shortly after the first soldiers were introduced, animals and wheeled vehicles, the first a Cord automobile, were marketed, all successfully. AUBURN produced no soldiers during the war, and few after, though it continued to make toys in great quantity (70,000 wheeled items a day in 1962, for example). In 1960 the toys portion of AUBURN was purchased by the town of Deming, New Mexico, where it remained until it went out of business in 1969. AUBURN'S soldiers, all approximately the standard 3¼" length, went through three stages. The first were frail-looking, with long, thin bodies; the second, which emerged as early as September, 1936, were stockier and larger-headed, and the third, introduced in 1941, were more well-proportioned and realistic. Unlike its competitors, AUBURN produced no cowboys, Indians, sailors or civilians, except for baseball and football players and two farm workers. AUBURN'S infantry came in colors other than brown. There were several shades of blue, at least one of which was meant to represent U.S. Marines. It is speculated that the white were meant to represent the U.S. Navy, and the yellow, Italian Army in Ethiopia. At least two blue-grey soldiers have turned up, and these may have represented enemy troops or West Point cadets. It is thought that some Auburn Ethiopians remain to be discovered.

(All bold words and numbers are Auburn's own description)

	G	VG	M
(A1) Marching at port arms, early ...	6	9	12
(A2) **200 U.S. Infantry Private**	4.50	6.75	9.00
(A3) Bugler, early	8	12	16
(A4) **202 Bugler, U.S. Infantry**	8	12	16
(A5) **Foreign Legion,** also **White Guard** officer	9.00	13.50	18.00
(A6) **Foreign Legion,** infantryman ...	7.50	11.25	15.00
(A7) Ethiopian with shield and rifle ..	No Price Found		
(A7a) Ethiopian bugler	No Price Found		
(A7b) Ethiopian with rifle and shield, in robes	40	60	80
(A8) Officer, early	6	9	12
(A9) **204 U.S. Infantry Officer**	6	9	12
(A10) **Charging Soldier** with tommy gun, early	22.50	33.75	45.00
(A11) **238 Charging Soldier** with tommy gun	6	9	12
(A12) **232 Officer on Horse**	19.00	28.50	38.00
(A13) **230 Machine Gunner**	6.50	9.75	13.00
(A14) **224 Red Cross Doctor**	14	21	28
(A14a) Army Doctor, Khaki uniform	No Price Found		
(A15) **226 Red Cross Nurse** white or khaki uniform	16.50	24.75	33.00
(A16) **206 Stretcher Bearer**	12.50	18.75	25.00
(A17) **208 Wounded Soldier**	14	21	28
(A18) **216 Observer With Binoculars**	6	9	12
(A19) **236 Signalman**	10	15	20
(19a) **Signalman,** early smaller size, only two known	100	150	200

A14a
Photo by Ron Steiner

A35
Rough sketch from memory going back 40 years of A35. Note no box in hand, head tilted up toward left, left hand forward. None known.

Auburn A19a
Courtesy John Stetson

270

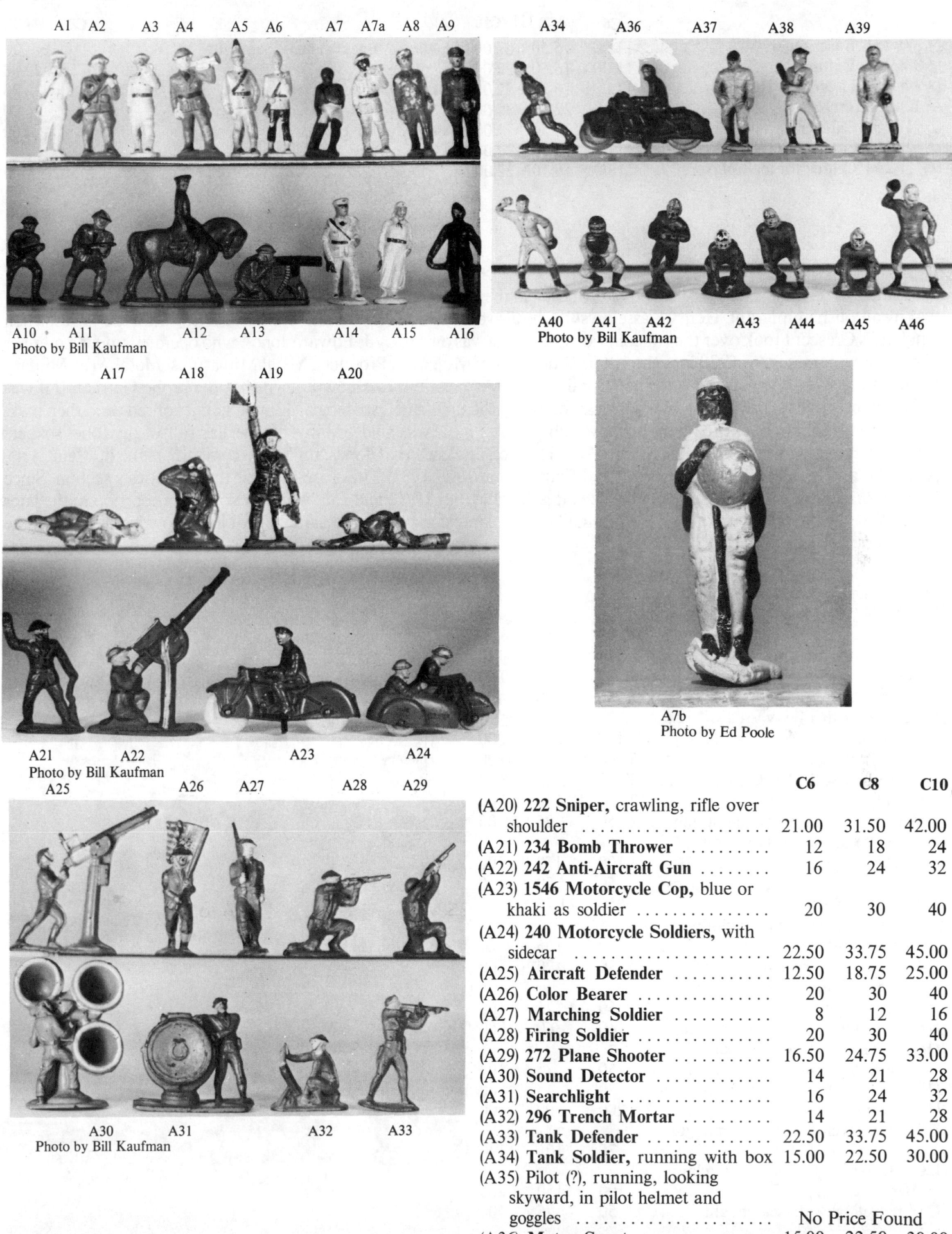

A1 A2 A3 A4 A5 A6 A7 A7a A8 A9

A10 A11 A12 A13 A14 A15 A16
Photo by Bill Kaufman

A34 A36 A37 A38 A39

A40 A41 A42 A43 A44 A45 A46
Photo by Bill Kaufman

A17 A18 A19 A20

A21 A22 A23 A24
Photo by Bill Kaufman

A25 A26 A27 A28 A29

A30 A31 A32 A33
Photo by Bill Kaufman

A7b
Photo by Ed Poole

	C6	C8	C10
(A20) **222 Sniper,** crawling, rifle over shoulder	21.00	31.50	42.00
(A21) **234 Bomb Thrower**	12	18	24
(A22) **242 Anti-Aircraft Gun**	16	24	32
(A23) **1546 Motorcycle Cop,** blue or khaki as soldier	20	30	40
(A24) **240 Motorcycle Soldiers,** with sidecar	22.50	33.75	45.00
(A25) **Aircraft Defender**	12.50	18.75	25.00
(A26) **Color Bearer**	20	30	40
(A27) **Marching Soldier**	8	12	16
(A28) **Firing Soldier**	20	30	40
(A29) **272 Plane Shooter**	16.50	24.75	33.00
(A30) **Sound Detector**	14	21	28
(A31) **Searchlight**	16	24	32
(A32) **296 Trench Mortar**	14	21	28
(A33) **Tank Defender**	22.50	33.75	45.00
(A34) **Tank Soldier,** running with box	15.00	22.50	30.00
(A35) Pilot (?), running, looking skyward, in pilot helmet and goggles		No Price Found	
(A36) **Motor Scout**	15.00	22.50	30.00

271

	C6	C8	C10			C6	C8	C10
(A37) **258 Baserunner**	11.00	16.50	22.00	(A44) **262 Backfieldman,** football				
(A38) **252 Batter**	11.00	16.50	22.00	player	11.00	16.50	22.00
(A39) **256 Fielder or Baseman**	11.00	16.50	22.00	(A45) **260 Lineman,** football player	11.00	16.50	22.00
(A40) **250 Pitcher**	15.00	22.50	30.00	(A46) **266 Passer,** football player	13.00	19.50	26.00
(A41) **254 Catcher**	11.00	16.50	22.00	(A47) Motorcycle Cop, large 5" high	25.00	37.50	50.00
(A42) **268 Carrier** football player	11.00	16.50	22.00	(A48) Cowboy, large, on wheeled			
(A43) **264 Center** football player	11.00	16.50	22.00	horse	20	30	40

JONES

Jones' 3¼" hollow lead soldiers probably began in the late 1930s, apparently cutting off in September, 1941. Sculpting was by a Polish immigrant, Henry Kasselowski, who also designed the toy soldiers for Lincoln Log until the 1950s, when England's Crescent took over the Lincoln Log line. Jones was owned by J. Edward Jones, who operated under a number of company names from 1930 into the 1960s, among them Miniature Products, Metal Miniatures, Metal Arts, Military Miniatures, World Miniatures and the Visual History Association. It is now known that the prone German (J3) was made directly over Barclay B61, Kasselowski removing the tin helmet, shaping a German helmet of red wax, then making a plaster cast of the entire figure, from which a bronze mold was made. Many, and perhaps all, of the Jones soldiers were also painted in gray, as "enemy". In 1982, research disclosed that Jones, under the company name of Metal Arts, produced an entirely different set of 3" lead figures from 1929-1931. These are listed at the end of this section. Since they seem to have been a slightly smaller size, it is possible that J1, J2 and J26, which are out of proportion to the later soldiers they were sold with, may have originally been planned as part of the earlier line. None, however, appear in the 1931 photos.

(J1) German, kneeling with rifle	70	105	140
(J1a) Same as above, short rifle	90	135	180
(J2) German, charging with rifle	75.00	112.50	150.00
(J3) German, prone machine gunner	70	105	140
(J4) Observer with binoculars and rifle	35.00	52.50	70.00
(J5) Wire-cutter, prone	200	300	400
(J6) Soldier with rifle, gassed or shot in neck	150	225	300
(J7) Stretcher-bearer	55.00	82.50	100.00
(J8) Kneeling with AA Gun	37.50	56.25	75.00
(J9) Charging, port arms	125.00	187.50	250.00
(J10) Firing machine gun on stump	27.50	41.25	55.00
(J10a) Same as above, No. 1 on pocket	100	150	200
(J11) Grenade thrower, no weapons	60	90	120
(J12) Seated with rifle	27.50	41.25	55.00
(J13) Officer in greatcoat, pointing, holding pistol	110	165	220
(J14) Prone with rifle, trunk upraised	80	120	160
(J15) Prone, firing double-barreled machine gun	50	75	100
(J16) Kneeling, firing anti-tank gun	40	60	80
(J16a) Same as above with barrel brace, "23" on wheel	50	75	100
(J17) Cook with chef's hat, frying pan	30	45	60
(J18) Ammunition Carrier	200	300	400
(J19) Motorcyclist with machine gun mounted on motorcycle	70	105	140
(J20) Flagbearer (similar to Barclay B7)	100	150	200
(J21) Kneeling with searchlight	50	75	100

J18   J26   J16a   J27   J28   J29
Photo by Don Pielin

J22   J12   J5

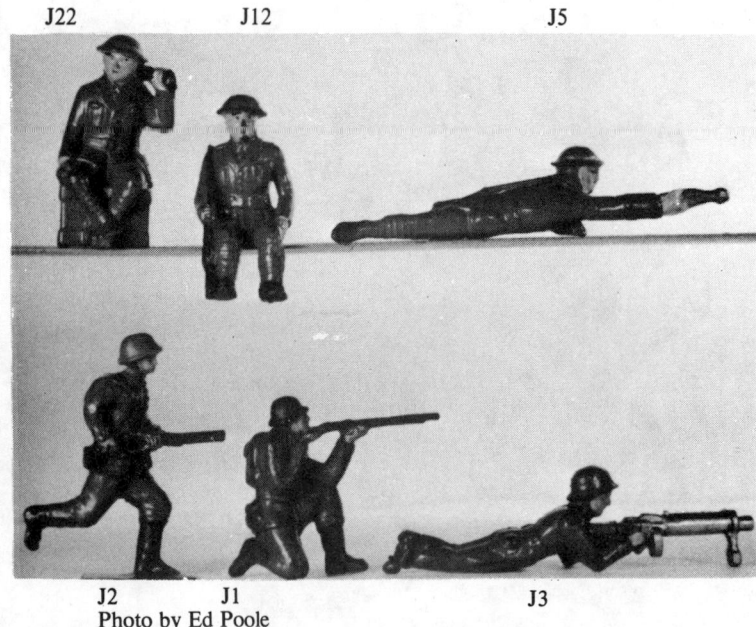

J2   J1   J3
Photo by Ed Poole

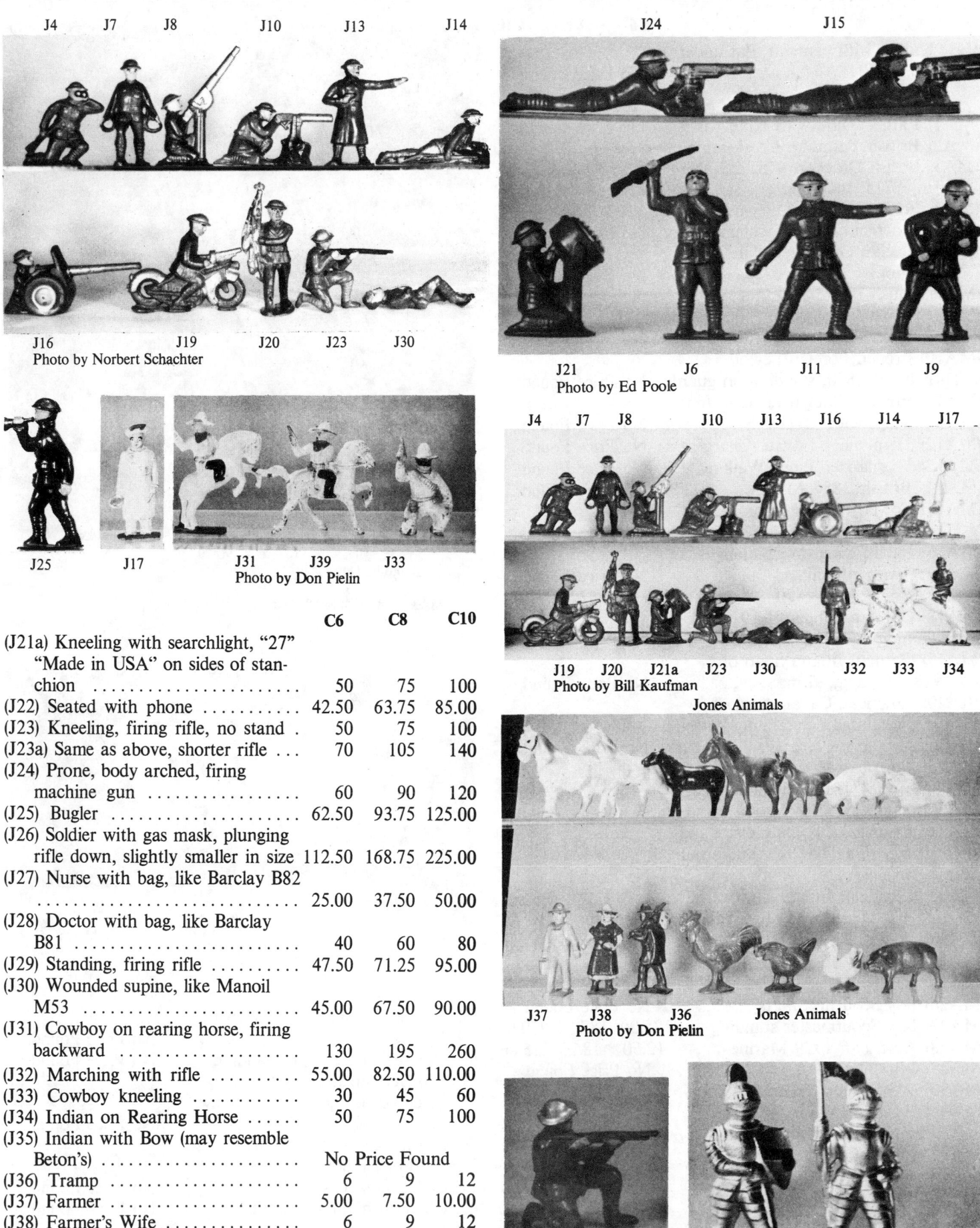

Photo by Norbert Schachter

Photo by Ed Poole

Photo by Don Pielin

Photo by Bill Kaufman

Jones Animals

Jones Animals

Photo by Don Pielin

J23a
Photo by Ron Eccles

Photo by Don Pielin

	C6	C8	C10
(J21a) Kneeling with searchlight, "27" "Made in USA" on sides of stanchion	50	75	100
(J22) Seated with phone	42.50	63.75	85.00
(J23) Kneeling, firing rifle, no stand	50	75	100
(J23a) Same as above, shorter rifle	70	105	140
(J24) Prone, body arched, firing machine gun	60	90	120
(J25) Bugler	62.50	93.75	125.00
(J26) Soldier with gas mask, plunging rifle down, slightly smaller in size	112.50	168.75	225.00
(J27) Nurse with bag, like Barclay B82	25.00	37.50	50.00
(J28) Doctor with bag, like Barclay B81	40	60	80
(J29) Standing, firing rifle	47.50	71.25	95.00
(J30) Wounded supine, like Manoil M53	45.00	67.50	90.00
(J31) Cowboy on rearing horse, firing backward	130	195	260
(J32) Marching with rifle	55.00	82.50	110.00
(J33) Cowboy kneeling	30	45	60
(J34) Indian on Rearing Horse	50	75	100
(J35) Indian with Bow (may resemble Beton's)	No Price Found		
(J36) Tramp	6	9	12
(J37) Farmer	5.00	7.50	10.00
(J38) Farmer's Wife	6	9	12
(J39) Cowboy on Prancing Horse, similar to Barclay B2	No Price Found		
(J40) Knight with shield, flat underbase	No Price Found		

273

(J41) Knight with pennant, flat underbase .... No Price Found

Jones' Metal Arts 3" Soldiers, 1929-31

(MA1) Father Time with large wings   No Price Found
(MA2) British Battalion Co. Marine .   30   45   60
(MA3) British Dragoon with movable
   arm, 1775, mounted 62.50 93.75 125.00
(MA4) British Light Infantryman   20   30   40
(MA5) American Backwoodsman ....   No Price Found
(MA6) Hessian Grenadier of 1777
   Charging .... No Price Found
(MA7) British Infantry Drummer ....   No Price Found
(MA8) British Grenadier 75.00 112.50 150.00
(MA9) American Marine of 1812 ...   No Price Found
(MA10) French Foreign Legion
   private of 1870, standing on guard   No Price Found
(MA11) French Foreign Legion, stand-
   ing firing, with neckcloth ......   No Price Found
(MA12) Highlander Private Charging   No Price Found
(MA13) Highlander Piper Walking ..   No Price Found
(MA14) British 1857 Marine ....   No Price Found
(MA15) Cowboy Mounted on Stand-
   ing Horse, 1870 ....   No Price Found
(MA16) Indian lying on galloping
   horse with rifle aimed ....   No Price Found
(MA17) Cowboy of 1870 .... 35.00 52.50 70.00
(MA18) German Officer of 1918,
   marching ....   No Price Found
(MA19) German Infantryman of
   1918, standing, firing ....   No Price Found
(MA20) American Cavalryman of
   1918, mounted on standing horse,
   movable arm ....   No Price Found
(MA21) American 1918 Doughboy
   Bomber (throwing grenade)......   40   60   80
(MA22) American 1918 Major, stand-
   ing in overcoat, holding pistol and
   pointing, resembles J13, but is not
   the same ....   No Price Found
(MA23) American Infantry in over-
   coat, 1918, appears to be at aten-
   tion .... No Price Found
(MA24) Seaman 1918 ....   No Price Found
(MA25) Boy Scout ....   No Price Found
(MA26) Boy Scout in Shorts ....   No Price Found
(MA27) Boy Scoutmaster standing ... 125.00 187.50 250.00
(MA28) American 1929 Marine 12.50 18.75 25.00
(MA29) Midshipman of 1932 ....   No Price Found
(MA30) West Point Cadet of 1929 ..   No Price Found
(MA31) German Infantry of 1918
   marching with movable arm ....   No Price Found
(MA32) Indian Creeping ....   No Price Found
(MA33) American Marine of 1776
   standing ....   No Price Found
(MA34) British Artillery Gunner of
   1776 .... No Price Found
(MA35) British Light Co. Marines ...   No Price Found

MA10   MA39   MA17   MA 14
Photo by Don Pielin

MA12   MA13   MA 9   MA8
Photo by Don Pielin

MA39 MA17 MA21? MA10

MA13   MA14   MA12   MA8 MA9   MA28
Photo by Don Pielin

(MA36) British Marine Officer with
   Sword .... No Price Found
(MA37) Artillery Ensign Standing ...   No Price Found
(MA38) German Infantry Charging
   (listed but not pictured; possibly
   J2) .... No Price Found
(MA39) Indian with Tomahawk (not
   listed or pictured, but seems to be
   from this series) ....   No Price Found
(MA40) British Infantry at Trail ....   No Price Found

MINIATURE TOY COMPANY - MOULDED MINIATURES
METAL-ART - METAL MINIATURES

Both before and after World War II, at least into the 1950s, J. Edward Jones also made hollowcast 54 mm figures. The following is a list of figures numbered to match the photos shown. Descriptions are provided where possible, with those in bold lettering Jones' own description. Since these photos have been matched against faint Xeroxes of Jones' sale lists, some may be identified incorrectly. Prices are erratic on these, as they have only recently come to be deemed collectible by more than a few. $15 in mint seems typical.

541 - Sailor, shoulder arms
542 - **West Pointer** parade rest No. 2907
543 - Annapolis Cadet with Guidon
544 - Annapolis Cadet at Port Arms
545 - **U.S. Marine**
546 - Crawling with Rifle, in Snow Camouflage
547 - German on Guard
548 - German Charging
549 - Charging in Pith Helmet, British
5410 - Parade Rest with Fixed Bayonet, Chinese Nationalist No. 2901
5411 - **1942 U.S. Infantry**
5412 - Highlander, WW I helmet, Shoulder Arms
5413 - U.S. Infantry (?)
5414 - **1948 U.S. Marine,** marching at shoulder arms
5415 - Private at Parade Rest
5416 - **1944 U.S. Cavalry**
5417 - **1190 Herald**
5418 - **1193 English Bowman**
5419 - Robinson Crusoe (prototype, probably never produced)
5420 - **1871 Cowboy**
5421 - Indian Chief, running with rifle
5422 - Indian Standing, Firing
5423 - Right Carry Arms - Italian WW II, running at trail
5424 - WW I Infantryman, Marching Shoulder Arms
5425 - **Pilot of the 17th Pursuit Squadron, 1937**
5426 - Officer with binoculars
5427 - Marching Highlander
5428 - **1944 U.S. Aimer**
5429 - Sailor Marching with Drum, British "Blue Jacket"
5430 - **1921 British Guardsman,** shoulder arms (also 1922)
5431 - Greek Evzone

5432 - Civil War (?) at attention
5433 - **1864 Militiaman**
5434 - **1861 Zouave of La.**
5435 - On Guard, circa 18th century
5436 - U.S. Marine of early 19th century, no pigtail
5437 - U.S. Marine of early 19th century, has pigtail
5438 - 1775 Soldier, modified port arms
5439 - Charging Highlander, circa 1775
5440 - Charging Highlander Officer, circa 1775
5441 - Officer circa 1775
5442 - Naval (?) Officer, circa 1775
5443 - Sailor circa 1775
5444 - French (?) soldier, circa 1775, modified port arms
5445 - Hessian (?) officer, marching
5446 - Hessian (?) soldier, on guard
5447 - Highlander, at ready, 1757 Scotsman, No. 270118
5448 - French (?) soldier circa 1775 at attention
5449 - American Marine, circa 1775-1797
5450 - **Highlander** of 1814, No. 1809GB
5451 - **Scotchman,** at ready
5452 - Piper
5453 - Soldier, Wayne's Legion, 1802, on guard
5454 - 1775 Officer, sword at side
5455 - 1775 Soldier (early American Marine?)
5456 - 1775 Officer, sword extended
5457 - 1775 Soldier, Rammer Drawn, British
5458 - **1775 British Ranger,** shoulder arms, 2701LB
5459 - **1775 British Marine,** firing at upward angle, 2705MB
5460 - **1775 Colonial Woman,** deluxe finish is PS 1383 **Belle of Baltimore,** ordinary finish is PT2389 **1776 Belle of New York**
5461 - **1775 Colonial Man,** deluxe finish is PL1390 **Dandy of Charleston,** ordinary finish is PX2390 **Dandy of Philadelphia**

541   542   543   544   545
Photo courtesy K. Warren Mitchell

546   547   548   549   5410
Photo courtesy K. Warren Mitchell

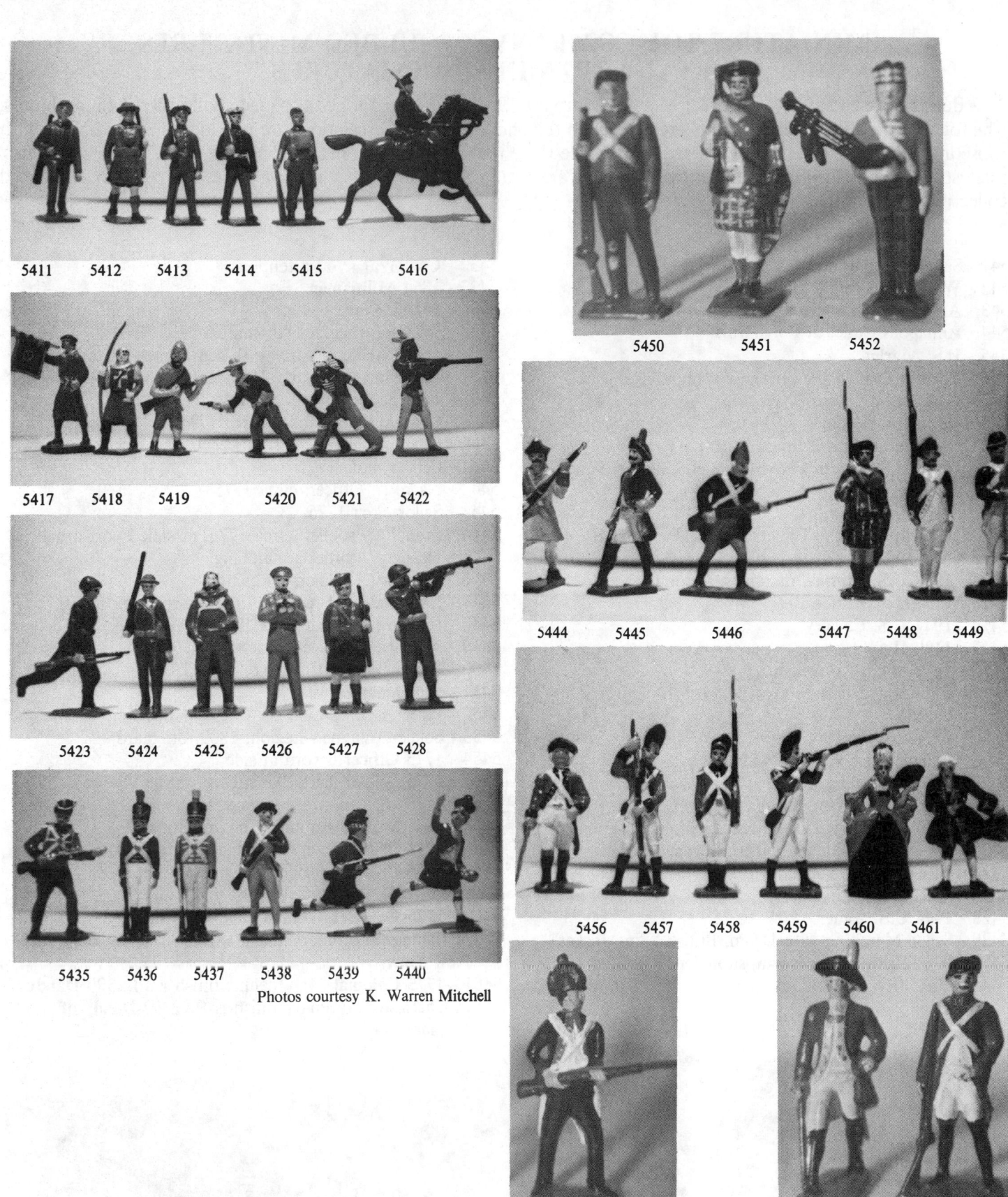

5411   5412   5413   5414   5415   5416

5417   5418   5419   5420   5421   5422

5423   5424   5425   5426   5427   5428

5435   5436   5437   5438   5439   5440

Photos courtesy K. Warren Mitchell

5450   5451   5452

5444   5445   5446   5447   5448   5449

5456   5457   5458   5459   5460   5461

5453

5454   5455

ALL-NU
(See also Vehicles, Animal-Drawn, Paper)

Frank Krupp (1/24/98-8/30/65), former sculptor and mold-maker for Barclay, was the owner of All-Nu, (his partner in the early stages was David Reader, brother of Barclay's chief salesman, Irving Reader), which was incorporated on February 16, 1938. Originally located at 55-57 Main Street, Yonkers, New York, the company later moved in the summer or fall of 1941 to a second-floor loft at 67 Irving Place in Manhattan. (The "Marching Majorettes" were produced in Yonkers as well as in Manhattan.) Krupp, a trained artist, designed all of All-Nu's toys as well as its novelties and souvenirs, and formed the company immediately upon leaving Barclay. Its first product was a lead souvenir horse, its two halves soldered together, and it is not known when All-Nu produced its first soldiers, which Krupp sculpted in clay over a wire armature without making preliminary sketches. The company was small, with about five or six pourers, six or seven women painters, and few other workers, and was just beginning to get off the ground (its "majorettes", which included all the girl musicians, were sold in 1941 at Woolworth's) when the advent of World War II ended all lead production. Krupp then drew, painted and produced cardboard soldiers and weapons, but they were not successful. Although All-Nu was not dissolved as a corporation until December 15, 1950, it was essentially out a business a year or two after the War began. Around 1946, Krupp resumed toy-making, this time with a new partner. The company, Faben Products, at 47 Walker Street in Manhattan, produced both new toys and novelties and continued All-Nu's prewar horses, mounted hunters, jockeys, and cowboy and cowgirl on bucking broncos. All known All-Nu soldiers are marked "All-Nu" on the underbase.

ALL-NU soldiers, as shown in the April, 1941, Toys and Novelties magazine. Courtesy Playthings Magazine.

ALL-NU Soldiers, photo by Bill Kaufman

	C6	C8	C10
(AN 1) "Newsreel" Cameraman in helmet, ten known	875.00	1312.50	1750.00
(AN 1b) like above, but helmet adapted to look WW II, only one known	No Price Found		
(AN 2) Seated machine-gunner, two known	225.00	337.50	450.00
(AN 3) Advancing with Tommy Gun, one known	No Price Found		
(AN 4) Grenadier, three known	No Price Found		
(AN 5) Bugler, three known	300	450	600
(AN 6) Signalman, two known	No Price Found		
(AN 7) Standing, firing rifle, seven known	40	60	80
(AN 8) Marching, slope arms, seven known	60	90	120
(AN 9) Advancing, fixed bayonet, three known	500	750	1000
(AN 10) Officer kneeling with binoculars, drawing pistol, only one known	No Price Found		
(AN 11) AA Gunner in campaign cap, four known	225	340	450
(AN 12) Prone, firing rifle, none known	No Price Found		
(AN 13) Running in Gas Mask, with Rifle, only one known	No Price Found		
(AN 14) Officer with sword, four known	50	75	100
(AN 15) 150? Majorette, baton in air	50	75	100
(AN 16) Majorette, baton held backward, cape-like cloth trailing behind, only one known (may be prototype, as underbase isn't finished)	No Price Found		
(AN 17) Majorette, ensign-type cap, with cape	160	240	320
(AN 18) 151? Girl flagbearer	40	60	80

	C6	C8	C10
(AN 19) 152? Girl fifist	40	60	80
(AN 20) 153? Girl bugler	40	60	80
(AN 21) 154? Girl saxophonist	40	60	80
(AN 22) 155? Girl drummer	40	60	80
(AN 23) Mounted Cowboy masked, firing pistol straight ahead	50	75	100
(AN 24) Football player throwing ball (probably All-Nu)	20	30	40

ALL-NU football players, Cowboy on Bucking Broncho, Cowgirl on Bucking Broncho (far right)
Photo by Bill Kaufman. Courtesy Evelyn Besser.

ALL-NU Dog Musicians. These sell for about $50 apiece in mint condition.
Photo by Bill Kaufman
Courtesy Evelyn Besser

ALL-NU, top row, L to R: Hunter on horse, Woman on horse, Jockey on horse, Mounted cowboy. Bottom row, L to R: ALL-NU "Marching Majorettes"
Photos by Bill Kaufman. Courtesy Evelyn Besser

ALL-NU Advancing with Tommy Gun (gun-tip restored, may not be accurate).
Photo by Ed Poole
Courtesy Gene Coffman

ALL-NU Majorette, with ensign-type cap, cape.
Photo by Don Pielin

AL-NU AN1b
Courtesy Monty Mitzelfeld

	C6	C8	C10
(AN 25) Football player running with ball (**probably** All-Nu)	No Price Found		
(AN 26) 501 (Faben's number) Cowboy on Bucking Bronco	30	45	60
(AN 27) 502 (Faben's number) Cowgirl on Bucking Bronco	21.00	31.50	42.00
(AN 28) 521 (Faben's number) Jockey on Horse	15.00	22.50	30.00
(AN 29) 526 (Faben's number) Hunter on Horse	22.50	33.75	45.00
(AN 30) Woman on Horse	15.00	22.50	30.00
(AN 31) Polo Player on Horse	15.00	22.50	30.00
(AN 31a) Male Jumper on Horse ...	15.00	22.50	30.00
(AN 32) Standing Horse	10	15	20
(AN 33) **619 Prancer** (Faben's number and description), large 4-1/8" high	No Price Found		
(AN 34) Jockey on Prancer, large ...	No Price Found		

TOMMY TOY
(See also Vehicles and Aircraft)

Tommy Toy was incorporated October 16, 1935, and recorded its first sale on November 13 of that year. The company was located on the second floor of a parking garage in Union City, New Jersey, on the southwest side of Palisade Avenue near 7th Street. In a 1938 business directory, Tommy Toy's officers are listed as "Pres. Albert D. Greene; V. Pres. Joseph Maulbeck; Sec. Treas. Chas. Weldon; Pur. Agt. Mgr. George Ganzkow," with employees noted as seven men and three women. Also involved was Leon Donze, former co-head of Barclay and presumably the inspiration for the formation of Tommy Toy. Olive Kooken, who did much of the sculpting for Barclay, and Margaret R. Cloninger are the two known to have designed the company's toys. The firm was not a success, and phonebooks of the time indicate it went out of business between August 1938 and May 1939, with Barclay veterans believing Tommy Toy was bought out by Barclay, which retained the molds, but did not use them. All Tommy Toy soldiers and nursery rhyme figures were marked under their bases with the company name and sometimes with the description of the toy as well. Most of their other toys bore no markings. Unmarked soldiers which appear to be Tommy Toys were actually produced by American Alloy and Toy Creations.

TOMMY TOY, Top row, L to R: "Doctor" in white, "Doctor" in brown, "Officer Gas Mask," "Stretcher Bearer," "Wounded," "Nurse" in brown, "Nurse" in white. Bottom row, L to R: "Officer," "Ground Arms," "Soldier Marching," "Port Arms," "Soldier Charging," "Hand Grenade," "Soldier Firing," "Machine Gunner." Photo by Bill Kaufman.   Courtesy Charles E. Weldon Jr.

TOMMY TOY, Top row, L to R: "Little Miss Muffet," "Puss In Boots," "Tom, Tom, The Pipers Son," "Jack & Jill," "Humpty-Dumpty." Bottom row, L to R: "Little Bo Peep," "Old Mother Hubbard," "Old King Cole," "Jack And The Bean Stalk," "Old Mother Witch."   Courtesy Don Pielin

	C6	C8	C10
(TT1) "Officer	100	150	200
(TT2) "Ground Arms"	90	135	180
(TT3) "Soldier Marching"	80	120	160
(TT4) "Port Arms"	100	150	200
(TT5) "Soldier Charging"	80	120	160
(TT6) "Hand Grenade"	100	150	200
(TT7) "Soldier Firing," kneeling firing rifle	125.00	187.50	250.00
(TT8) "Machine Gunner," standing firing tommy gun	100	150	200
(TT9) "Officer Gas Mask"	110	165	220
(TT10) "Stretcher-Bearer"	140	210	280
(TT11) "Wounded"	125.00	187.50	250.00
(TT12) "Doctor," brown uniform	140	210	280
(TT13) "Doctor," whte uniform	90	135	180
(TT14) "Nurse," white uniform, marked this way, she has a fine-grained partition between the legs	75.00	112.50	150.00
(TT15) "Nurse" brown uniform, same as above	75.00	112.50	150.00
(TT16) Nurse, white uniform, marked only "Tommy Toy," vinelike partition between the legs	No Price Found		
(TT17) Nurse, brown uniform, same as above	No Price Found		

	C6	C8	C10
(TT18) "Old Mother Hubbard" by Olive Kooken, copyright June 25, 1936	20	30	40
(TT19) "Tom, Tom, The Pipers Son," by Kooken, copyright June 25, 1936	27.00	40.50	54.00
(TT20) "Humpty-Dumpty" by Margaret R. Cloninger, copyright June 25, 1936	35.00	52.50	70.00
(TT21) "Little Bo Peep" by Cloninger, copyright June 25, 1936	30	45	60
(TT22) "Jack & Jill" by Kooken, copyright June 25, 1936 (much sought after by collectors)	400	600	800
(TT23) "Puss In Boots" by Cloninger, copyright June 25, 1936	24	36	48
(TT24) "Jack And The Bean Stalk," by Cloninger, copyright August 10, 1936	26	39	52
(TT25) "Old King Cole" by Cloninger, copyright August 10, 1936	37.50	56.25	75.00
(TT26) "Little Miss Muffet" by Kooken, copyright August 10, 1936	22	33	44
(TT27) "Old Mother Witch" by Kooken, copyright August 10, 1936	22.50	33.75	45.00

METAL CAST PRODUCTS CO.

The company began in 1899 as S. Sachs Toy Soldier Manufacturing Company, selling hand-casting molds. These originally were for solid cast toys, but by 1933 Sachs, now known as Metal Cast Products Company, offered, among other casting forms, eight hollow cast molds for soldiers. The company sold its slush cast molds to small businessmen in addition to manufacturing its own soldiers. Thus there appears to be no way of knowing which were made by Metal Cast and which by other individuals or companies, at least one of which is known to have imprinted its own name on molds supplied by Metal Cast. In 1946, Metal Cast was selling its soldiers with WW I helmets; however by the following year, it had updated its line, and its helmeted soldiers now had WW II pot helmets. Some of their soldiers appear to have been copied from Barclay and Manoil figures. On the other hand, Beton Plastic copied several of its pieces from Metal Cast. All bold words and numbers are the company's own description.

21A Flagbearer

33A Trumpeter

25A Signal Corps

26A Anti-Aircraft

29A Machine Gunner

34 Indian

33 Big Chief

32 Cowboy

30A Motorcycle Officer

28A Wounded

31 Bronco Bill

Circa 1933	C6	C8	C10
21 American Cavalry, mounted, wearing helmet, approx. 3" high	9.00	13.50	18.00
22 American Infantry Private, marching in helmet, rifle at slope, approx. 2½" high	6	9	12
23 American Infantry Officer, marching in cap, sword on shoulder approx. 2½" high	6	9	12
24 American Infantry Flag Bearer, wearing helmet	9.00	13.50	18.00
31 Bronco Bill, holding pistol, on bucking bronco	26	39	52
32 Cowboy holding rifle across waist .	No Price Found		
33 Big Chief mounted Indian in war bonnet, holding bow	10	15	20
34 Indian in war bonnet, holding Hatchet and shield	5.00	7.50	10.00
Circa 1941 and 1946 in WW I Helmets			
21A Flag Bearer 3⅝" high	60	90	120
22A Aviator (very similar to Barclay's) 3" high	37.50	56.25	75.00
23A Pilot With Bomb, 3⅛" high, similar to Manoil's	130	195	260
24A Suicide Squad, 3" high, very similar to Barclay's officer with gas mask and pistol	45.00	67.50	90.00
25A Signal Corps, with Semaphore Flags	No Price Found		

	C6	C8	C10
26A Anti-Aircraft Soldier, with searchlight	30	45	60
27A Bomb Thrower, gas mask, slung rifle, throwing grenade	No Price Found		
28A Wounded, lying down, head on hand, arm in sling, **none known** ...	No Price Found		
29A Machine Gunner, kneeling	No Price Found		
30A Motorcycle Officer on motorcycle, peaked cap	80	120	160
31A Cavalry Officer, 3¼" long	10	15	20
Metal Cast Circa 1947, WW II Helmets			
31A Cavalry Officer, in cap, 3¼" high	10	15	20
32A Flag Bearer, 3¼" high, in campaign cap	No Price Found		
33A Trumpeter, 3" high in campaign cap, **none known**	No Price Found		
34A Marching Private, 3" high, in campaign cap, no weapon	20	30	40
35A Infantryman, 3" long, similar to Manoil 44, pot helmet	6	9	12
36A Bomb Thrower, 2¾" high, similar to Manoil 31 and Metal Cast 27A, WW II pot helmet ...	6	9	12
37A Suicide Squad, 3" high, similar to Barclay 778 and Metal Cast 24A	75.00	112.50	150.00
38A Machine Gunner, 2½" high	8	12	16

27A   24A   31A

34A   35A   36A   37A

25A   24A   26   27A   29A

31A   34A   35A   38A
Photo by Ed Poole

21
METALCAST Soldiers

24 23 22
Photo by Don Pielin

32A
Photo by Don Pielin

34A 23A 22A
Photo by Don Pielin

METAL CAST No. 32
Courtesy Ron Steiner

AMERICAN ALLOY-TOY CREATIONS

American Alloy and Toy Creations had a common link: Louis Picco, former worker at Barclay (he began there in 1924). Picco was a partner in American Alloy and its president. The firm copied Tommy Toy's soldiers about 1941 and perhaps shortly after the second World War. About 1946 Picco was approached by Toy Creations to set up a toy soldier department for them. He seems to have continued some of the American Alloy line, added copies of two Barclays, and brought in a sculptor (probably Barclay's Olive Kooken) to design a new line of pot-helmeted soldiers, which seem to have debuted in early 1947. American Alloy was located in North Bergen, New Jersey, and Toy Creations in near-by Jersey City.

The following soldiers with a TC coding are known to have been produced by Toy Creations, but probably all in the listing were sold (if not produced) by the company, since American Alloy seems to have been tied to it virtually from the beginning. TC?7 has not been definitely identified as American Alloy or Toy Creations, but appears to be a transitional figure between Toy Creations' WWI and WWII figures.

American Alloy-Toy Creations

American Alloy-Toy Creations

	C6	C8	C10
AA1 Officer	65.00	97.50	130.00
TC1 Wounded	95.00	142.50	190.00
TC2 Grenade Thrower	85.00	127.50	170.00
TC3 Tommy Gunner	85.00	127.50	170.00
TC4 Charging with rifle	80	120	160
AA2 Doctor	80	120	160
AA3 Soldier Marching	60	90	120
TC5 Soldier on field phone	90	135	180
TC6 Prone machine gunner	25.00	37.50	50.00
TC?7 Charging with rifle, WW II helmet	No Price Found		
TC8 Soldier with Walkie-Talkie, WW II helmet	42.50	63.75	85.00
TC9 Soldier advancing with rifle, WW II helmet	40	60	80
TC10 Soldier with bazooka, WW II helmet	28	42	56
TC11 Grenade Thrower, WW II helmet	87.50	131.25	175.00
TC12 Marching, WW II helmet	30	45	60
TC13 Officer in gas mask with pistol, WW II helmet	67.50	101.25	135.00

"TWO GUYS FROM BARCLAY"

According to Barclay veteran George Fall, "two guys from Barclay" left the company at an undetermined time, and began producing soldiers that were close copies of Barclays. Fall remembers only a mounted cowboy and Indian, produced from an inferior alloy and coated with a substandard paint.

The owners may have been two brothers, Frank and Charlie Keller, and the company was probably located in a garage in West New York, although Fall is not positive about any of this.

The following list is based on the similarity of all the figures and on a boxed set that included other pieces, as well as the cowboy and Indian Fall remembers. All are either direct copies of Barclays or are slightly modified. Those I've examined are all made of a hard metal, perhaps some form of Zamac, which unlike lead alloys, doesn't scratch when a knife is dug into it. The paint is poor, tends to flake easily, and painted details are sparse. Most figures have no facial features; those that do have only two blurry dot eyes. The Two Guys From Barclay seem to have had some means of pantographing figures, as several (perhaps all) of their pieces come in two sizes.

Fall thinks the company began in pre-War days, and lasted only a year or two. It's more likely that the company was formed after the War, as only one pre-World War II soldier from this company has been found. Those which appear in the same boxed set (found, alas, minus the boxtop, which might have provided the company identification) are TG1, TG2, TG5 and TG8.

TG2   TG3   TG4   TG5

TG6   TG7   TG8   TG9

TG10a   TG12   TG13   TG14   TG14a   TG14b

TG15a   TG16   TG16a   TG16b   TG17   TG19

TG22   TG23   TG23a   TG24   TG24a   TG25

TG16   TG16a   TG16b
Photos by Ed Poole

	C6	C8	C10
TG1 Mounted Cowboy	15.00	22.50	30.00
TG2 Mounted Indian	15.00	22.50	30.00
TG3 Indian with rifle across waist, large	7.50	11.25	15.00
TG4 Indian with rifle across waist, standard size	7.50	11.25	15.00
TG5 Indian with knife	10	15	20
TG5A Same as above, larger (not shown)	10	15	20
TG6 Indian kneeling with tomahawk	10	15	20
TG6A Indian kneeling with tomahawk, larger (not shown) ...	10	15	20
TG7 Indian kneeling with bow and arrow	6	9	12
TG8 Cowboy, arms akimbo	8	12	16
TG9 Kneeling Cowboy firing pistol (some have braces under arm and/or between legs)	8	12	16

	C6	C8	C10
TG10 Marching Sailor	No Price Found		
TG10A Marching Sailor, smaller size	No Price Found		
TG11 Marching Marine	No Price Found		
TG12 Kneeling, firing, WW II helmet (two sizes)	28	42	56
TG13 Seated machine gunner, WW II helmet	32	48	64
TG14 Drummer, WW II helmet	15.00	22.50	30.00
TG14a Drummer, smaller size	15.00	22.50	30.00
TG15 Flagbearer, WW I helmet	20	30	40
TG15a Flagbearer, WW II helmet	20	30	40

	C6	C8	C10
TG16 Charging with rifle, WW II helmet, three sizes	15.00	22.50	30.00
TG17 Traffic Cop	10	15	20
TG18 Mailman	10	15	20
TG19 Standing Wounded, Tommy Toy copy	40	60	80
TG20 Fireman with Axe	10	15	20
TG21 Cowboy firing pistol	No Price Found		
TG22 Bugler in WW II helmet	15.00	22.50	30.00
TG23 Marching Soldier	15.00	22.50	30.00
TG24 Marching Officer	15.00	22.50	30.00
TG25 Copy of Grey Iron Officer	No Price Found		

SHEILA INC.

Sheila Inc. copyrighted its sports figures in 1937. Research by Orville C. Britton reveals the following: Sheila, of Cleveland, Ohio, was incorporated in 1936 as a cosmetics company. Edward Frantz was the president with the address 942 Prospect Avenue (in 1937 the address was 1104 Prospect, S.E.). In 1937 a directory listed the company as producing "toiletries". By 1938 the firm disappeared from the directories. The names listed in the copyrights of the figures were sculptors. Stephen Rebeck was a noted area sculptor and Jack Worthington was a student of sculpture at the Cleveland School of Art. Worthington has since become the sculptor for the Football Hall of Fame, doing their portrait busts (about 130 as of 1987). Worthington carved his Sheila figures out of blocks of plaster instead of wax, "thus their crudeness", he remembers. After the figures, Sheila made book ends and horse figurals, using Man-O-War and other race horses of the period as models. The only known Sheilas are two football players (back and lineman) which had labels marked "Sheila" pasted on them, and two other football players (center and passer) and baseball fielder which appear to be possible Sheilas.

Back   Lineman
Courtesy Hank Anton

Football Players (Jack Worthington)

	C6	C8	C10
Back, copyright 7/8/37	9.00	13.50	18.00
Ball Carrier, copyright 7/8/37	No Price Found		
Center, copyright 7/8/37	9.00	13.50	18.00
Lineman, copyright 7/8/37	9.00	13.50	18.00
Kicker, copyright 7/17/37	No Price Found		
Football Referee, copyright 7/17/37	No Price Found		

Baseball Players (Stephen A. Rebeck)
all copyright 7/7/37

A. Baseball Umpire ... No Price Found
B. Baseball Catcher ... No Price Found
C. Baseball Batter ... No Price Found
D. Baseball Pitcher ... No Price Found
E. Baseball Fielder ... No Price Found
F. Baseball Fielder ... No Price Found

Basketball Players (Jack Worthington)
all copyright 7/17/37

A. **Guarding** ... No Price Found
B. **Shooting** ... No Price Found
E. **Passer** ... No Price Found
F. **Pass Receiver** ... No Price Found
G. **Pass Receiver** ... No Price Found
I. **Punter** (listed with basketball players) ... No Price Found

The above were found in the N.Y. Public Library copyright directory. Collector-writer Edward Ryan has found additional figures in the Washington copyright office attributed to Keith Frazine, presumably another sculptor.

Sports Figures (Keith Frazine)
All copyright 6/15/37

H. **Baseball Batter** ... No Price Found
I. **Baseball Batter** ... No Price Found
G. **Baseball Catcher** ... No Price Found
M. **Baseball Fielder** ... No Price Found
N. **Baseball Fielder** ... No Price Found
J. **Baseball Pitcher** ... No Price Found
K. **Baseball Pitcher** ... No Price Found
L. **Baseball Pitcher** ... No Price Found

HISTORICAL MINIATURES

When a group of these were discovered a few years ago by collector-dealer Steve Balkin of New York's Burlington Antique Toys, he turned to toy soldier expert Gus Hansen for information. Hansen thought he recalled an article had been written about the company that produced them. Recently, in the files of J. Edward Jones, Hansen found, and passed on to Balkin, an illustrated article from the New York Sunday Mirror magazine section of January 11, 1942. This revealed the company's name to be Historical Miniatures Inc., and the sculptor Michael Gera (originally Gerashshenevsky, a Russian immigrant). Jones' accompanying penciled notes disclose that the firm was owned by Montgomery Evans, began "about June, 1941," and that the approximately 3¼" height of the figures was the same size as Jones himself made "back in 1932." The address of the company was 416 4th Avenue, New York City, and the soldiers were individually sold at fifty cents and seventy-five cents (the latter for drummers, flagbearers, etc.). Oddly, at almost the same time, James Miniatures of Garden City, New York began offering two representations of Winston Churchill which greatly resembled, in size and design, the Historical Miniatures figures. Historical Miniatures produced in composition during the second World War, and after the war sold at least a few G.I.s in pot helmets (first produced in composition). FAO Schwarz is known to have sold the metal G.I.s which suggests this could have been a continuing outlet for Historical Miniatures. The following list is incomplete, and contains figures not yet found.

HM5   HM6   HM7   HM8   HM9   HM10 HM11   HM12– HM13   HM14   HM15

Courtesy Steve Balkin - Burlington Antique Toys, NYC

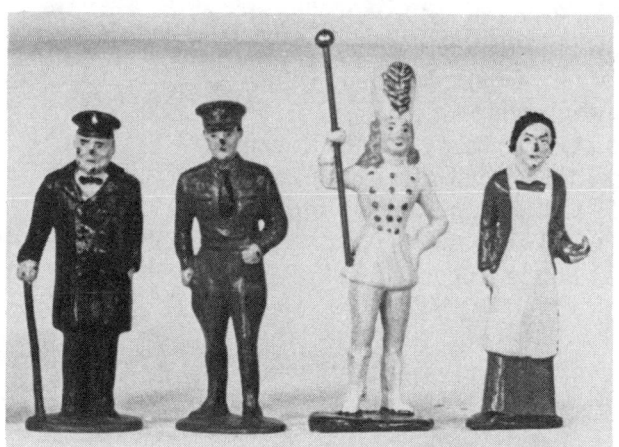

HM1   HM2   HM3   HM4

HM 18   HM17
The horse seen here is Elastolin.
Courtesy Bertel Bruun-Steve Balkin

	C6	C8	C10
HM1 Winston Churchill, with yachting cap, cane	17.50	26.25	35.00
HM2 General MacArthur	17.50	26.25	35.00
HM3 Majorette, with removable baton	17.50	26.25	35.00
HM4 Florence Nightingale	17.50	26.25	35.00
HM5 General Lafayette	17.50	26.25	35.00
HM6 Nathan Hale	17.50	26.25	35.00
HM7 General DeGaulle	17.50	26.25	35.00

	C6	C8	C10
HM8 Franklin Delano Roosevelt	17.50	26.25	35.00
HM9 Napoleon	17.50	26.25	35.00
HM10 Abraham Lincoln	17.50	26.25	35.00
HM11 Simon Bolivar	17.50	26.25	35.00

	C6	C8	C10
HM12 Josef Stalin	17.50	26.25	35.00
HM13 Chiang Kai-shek	17.50	26.25	35.00
HM14 Ben Franklin	17.50	26.25	35.00
HM15 Steuben	17.50	26.25	35.00
HM16 Gold Miner of 1849	17.50	26.25	35.00
HM17 George Washington, mounted, detachable	No Price Found		
HM18 George Washington, on foot, holding hat	17.50	26.25	35.00
HM19 Drummer Boy (Spirit of '76)	17.50	26.25	35.00
HM20 Fifer (Spirit of '76)	17.50	26.25	35.00
HM21 Drummer (Spirit of '76)	17.50	26.25	35.00
HM22 Flagbearer (Spirit of 76)	25.00	37.50	50.00
HM23 Colonial Soldier circa 1776 charging, plug-in rifle barrel	17.50	26.25	35.00
HM24 Colonial Soldier circa 1776, walking	17.50	26.25	35.00

	C6	C8	C10
HM25 Charging Highlander, plug-in rifle	17.50	26.25	35.00
HM26 Black Watch with Flag	25.00	37.50	50.00
HM27 John Paul Jones	17.50	26.25	35.00
HM28 Martha Washington	17.50	26.25	35.00
HM29 Churchill with Derby	17.50	26.25	35.00
HM30 Pulaski	17.50	26.25	35.00
HM31 Lee	17.50	26.25	35.00
HM32 Baden-Powell	17.50	26.25	35.00
HM33 Martin Luther	17.50	26.25	35.00
HM34 Greek Evzone (charging)	17.50	26.25	35.00
HM35 Greek Evzone with Flag	25.00	37.50	50.00
HM36 U.S. Legionnaire with Flag	25.00	37.50	50.00
HM37 Cossack, red uniform	22.50	33.75	45.00
HM38 Cossack, blue uniform	22.50	33.75	45.00
HM39 U.S. Soldier with Flag(s)	25.00	37.50	50.00
HM40 G.I. Charging with bayonet (composition)	22.50	33.75	45.00
HM41 G.I. Charging with bayonet (metal)	17.50	26.25	35.00
HM42 Stalin, composition	22.50	33.75	45.00
HM43 General MacArthur, composition	22.50	33.75	45.00
HM44 Churchill (naval uniform), composition	22.50	33.75	45.00
HM45 Franklin Delano Roosevelt, composition	22.50	33.75	45.00
HM46 Dwight D. Eisenhower, composition	No Price Found		
HM47 Montgomery, composition	22.50	33.75	45.00
HM48 G.I. Marching with Rifle, composition	No Price Found		
HM49 G.I. Prone with Rifle, composition (wood dowel barrel covered by composition)	22.50	33.75	45.00
HM50 G.I. Officer Marching with Sword, composition	22.50	33.75	45.00
HM51 G.I. Kneeling with Rifle, composition (metal rifle barrel)	22.50	33.75	45.00
HM52 G.I. Officer Running with Pistol, composition	22.50	33.75	45.00
HM53 Patton (?) composition	22.50	33.75	45.00

HM25

HM27
Courtesy Bertel Bruun

HM30
Courtesy Bertel Bruun

HM23   HM24   HM26   HM34   HM36
Rough sketch by the author of figures shown in 1942 newspaper article. Article courtesy Steve Balkin and Bertel Bruun.

286

HM35   HM37-HM38
Courtesy Bertel Bruun-Steve Balkin

HM42   HM45   HM44
Courtesy K. Warren Mitchell

HM40   HM52   HM40
The plug-in barrel and bayonet on HM40 are metal.
Photo by A. J. Mergenthaler

HM53   HM47
Courtesy K. Warren Mitchell

HM41 (rifle tip not correct)
Photo by Ed Poole

HM 49   HM50   HM51
The figures shown here were bought by A. J. Mergenthaler in late 1946 or early 1947 at F.A.O. Schwarz.
He remembers an extensive display with composition personality figures placed on a semi-circular tiered stand
with composition G.I.s below.
Photo by A. J. Mergenthaler

287

SOLJERTOYS - PEARLYTOYS

Soljertoys was the trade name for the toy soldiers produced by S. Rosenberg Toy Manufacturers, Inc., which incorporated January 14, 1930, for the purpose of manufacturing toys and novelties in lead. The company, which was located at, variously, 37 West 19th Street, 40 West 25th Street, 20 West 17th Street and 7 West 22nd Street, all New York, reorganized in 1934 as the Illfelder Corp. By 1936 the company appears to have ceased operations. In April, 1930, in a story on Soljertoys, Playthings Magazine showed a rifle-wielding charging doughboy along with an Indian doing a war dance, one leg raised. The single doughboy shown here resembles it in every way but is in a three-inch size. As all known Soljertoys are Britains-sized, there is no way of being sure that the doughboy is definitely a Soljertoy. In 1930, Soljertoys sold for ten cents apiece, with sets running 25¢ to $3.00. Later in the year, Rosenberg added "Paint-A-Toy" sets at $1.00 retail which contained 10 lead figures — U.S. Infantry and Cavalry, Cadets, Cowboys or Indians, plus paint. The foot Indians resembled Ideal's I-15. Recently, a boxed set (numbered "750") of Soljertoy doughboys, with a two-dimensional lead cannon, was found with the year "1932" written on the boxtop in crayon. These, like the Indians, are Britains-sized, and though crude-looking, some of the figures contain exceptionally sharp detail. In 1983, the boxed set sold for $80. Pearlytoys was an earlier version (1928) of this company.

	C6	C8	C10
SO1 Officer with sword, approx. 2¼" high	10	15	20
SO2 Marching left shoulder arms, approx. 2⅞" high	4	6	8
SO3 On Guard with fixed bayonet, approx. 2¼" high	4	6	8
SO4 Officer on horse, 2¼" high	7.50	11.25	15.00
SO5 Mounted Indian Chief	4	6	8

	C6	C8	C10
SO6 Indian on foot with rifle	3.00	4.50	6.00
SO7 West Point Cadet	5.00	7.50	10.00
SO8 Cowboy on foot	2.50	3.75	5.00
SO9 Mounted Cowboy	4	6	8
SO10 Indian doing war dance (3¼" type?)	No Price Found		
SO11 Doughboy advancing with rifle (3¼" type?)	40	60	80
SO12 Sailor	4.50	6.75	9.00
SO13 Marine	4.50	6.75	9.00

SO11 Soljertoy doughboy with rifle
Photo by Ed Poole

SO2   SO1   SO3
Photo by Ed Poole

Cannon from Soljertoy set. This cannon was produced by a number of manufacturers, both German and American.
Photo by Ed Poole

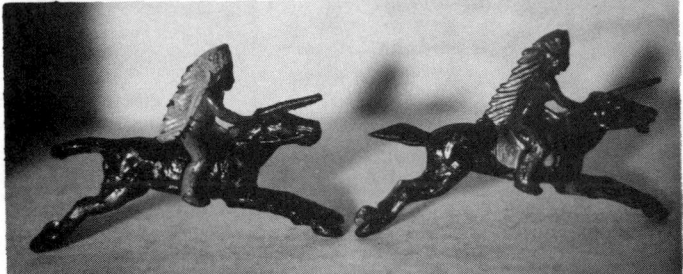

Soljertoy Indian on left, similar Indian on right (notice difference in horses' tails)
Photo by K. Warren Mitchell

Left, Soljertoy SO4, right Pearlytoy mounted officer. The only difference between the two figures is that the Soljertoy is less sharply defined in its details, and most of the "Pearlytoy" trademark found on the Pearlytoy horse's neck has been effaced on the Soljertoy.
Photo by Ed Poole.

SO10

SO8

SO9

SO7

SO12

ADDITIONAL SOLJERTOYS ART

All but SO 8 were traced from the art on a Soljertoys box. Judged by known Soljertoys, the art is very accurate. The foot cowboy is drawn from a murky 1932 Playthings illustration. The hat brim appears to be turned up.

Cosmo Novelty Co. Soldiers
Photo by Bill Kaufman

COSMO NOVELTY CO.

The Cosmo Novelty Co. was reported in the March 1931 Playthings Magazine as selling lead soldiers — including sailors, cadets, Indians and cowboys, boxed in various sets to retail from 25¢ to $5.00. Cosmo had previously been a manufacturer of rhinestone souvenirs. Located at 44 West 36th Street in New York, it appears to have been out of business by 1932, and was listed as a soldier manufacturer as early as 1930. The soldiers illustrated here greatly resemble the two shown in the Playthings article. In the Playthings photo, the rifles are on the right shoulder, but the photo may have been reversed. These pieces are extremely rare, and would probably be worth $20-40 in mint condition.

TOOTSIETOY

TOOTSIETOY produced a line of four flat 1½" high metal soldiers beginning in 1938. The figures were a Seated Machine-Gunner, Charging Soldier, Marching Rifleman, and Colorbearer. These were sold 10 on a card for a dime. Today, they sell for about $3.00 apiece in mint.

TOOTSIETOY Soldiers & Ambulance.
Photo by Ed Poole

ARCADE

Arcade's solid cast iron soldiers were oddly streamlined, in an art deco style. Five types are known, and appear to have been first produced in 1939. They came in at least two finishes, nickel and light bronze, as a way of forming separate armies. A set of 56 pieces included, in addition to the soldiers, an ambulance, an anti-aircraft gun and three planes, two with two engines, and one with four. In 1939, the set sold for $1.00. Despite being made of iron, and presumably near-indestructible, Arcade's soldiers turn up rarely, and sell for about $4 apiece in mint. The numbers and descriptions that follow are Arcade's own.

7721 Soldier "Sentry," 1⅝" high
7722 Soldier "Skirmisher," 1⅝" high
7723 Soldier "Sniper," 1¼" high

7724 Soldier "Marksman," 1⅝" high
7725 Soldier "Grenadier," 1¾" high

UNKNOWN MANUFACTURERS

Research since the last edition has considerably reduced the number of "Unknowns" in the 3¼" range, but some new ones have popped up.

U19

U20

U2

U38
Photo by Ed Poole

U41

E7   E5   E8   E1   E4
Courtesy Bill Cardiff

U44   U45

U43

	C6	C8	C10
U2 Indian with Rifle, hand shielding eyes	15.00	22.50	30.00
U19 Indian Kneeling with Rifle (may be Jones)	7.50	11.25	15.00
U20 Officer with Sword, copy of Manoil but larger (may be Two Guys from Barclay or American Lead Toy & Novelty)	9.00	13.50	18.00
U32 Santa on Sled (Two Guys From Barclay?)	18	27	36
U36 Doughboy Standing, shot, undersize	No Price Found		
U37 Doughboy Kneeling Firing, undersize	No Price Found		
U38 Doughboy Marching, rifle slung, undersize	No Price Found		
U39 Indian Firing Bow, standing (All-Nu or Barclay?)	4.50	6.75	9.00
U40 Diver, for fish bowls, copy of Manoil	5.00	7.50	10.00
U41 Cowboy on Horseback (All-Nu or Barclay?)	45.00	67.50	90.00
U42 Cast Iron Figures, Elizabethan Era (see photos with individual coding)	No Price Found		

U36   U37   U39   U40

U46

Former "Unknowns," these plastic copies of Barclay soldiers are known to have been made by at least two companies. Ajax and Thomas Toys (**not** Tommy Toy".) Prices average $4 apiece in mint.

During the World War II era, Breslin Industries produced these Manoil and Barclay copies in Canada. Though cruder than the originals, they are worth at least as much to collectors.
Photo by Don Pielin

U32

Photo by Don Pielin

	C6	C8	C10
U43 Marching with Rifle, like Manoil M5, but larger (Two Guys From Barclay or American Lead Toy & Novelty?)	8	12	16
U44 Indian Brave with Bow (Beton, Metal Cast or Jones?)	4	6	8
U45 Cadet (Beton or Metal Cast?) ...	4	6	8
U46 Mounted Colonial Officer (Metal Cast or Beton?)	30	45	60

MOLDED PRODUCTS INC.

Molded Products Inc. was incorporated November 29, 1941 by Leslie S. Steinau and his son, Leslie Steinau, Jr. In the advertising display business, with war approaching, they sensed coming shortages would leave them little to advertise, and they purchased the extruding equipment Lionel had employed in making the figures for its Mickey Mouse handcar. Barclay salesman Irving Reader, hearing of the purchase, urged the Steinaus to produce soldiers with the equipment, with Reader utilizing his ties to dimestores as their sales manager. Sculpting was done by Bill Zegel, with the factory employing about thirty people at 203 East 12th Street in Manhattan. The company was highly successful throughout the War, but foundered shortly after it ended, when they no longer had a competitive edge in materials. The figures were made of wood flour, starch, whiting and water, with the distinctive hole in the base and between the legs a result of the soldiers being placed on nails during the drying process. Descriptions in quotes are from a 1942-43 Butler Bros. catalog.

	C6	C8	C10		C6	C8	C10
C1 "Cowboy"	4.50	6.75	9.00	C9a Sitting at AA Gun, WW II helmet	3.50	5.25	7.00
C2 "Indian"	4.50	6.75	9.00	C10 Sailor marching, 3⅝" high "Sailor With Blue Uniform"	4.50	6.75	9.00
C3 Parachuting "Soldier with Parachute"	4.50	6.75	9.00	C10a Sailor marching 3¼" high, "Sailor With White Uniform"	4.50	6.75	9.00
C3a Parachuting, larger, inside of chute painted white	4.50	6.75	9.00	C11 "Marine" marching, 3½" high	4.50	6.75	9.00
C4 Aviator, "X" type front harness	4.50	6.75	9.00	C11a Marine marching, 3¼" high	4.50	6.75	9.00
C4a Aviator, square type front harness (not shown)	4.50	6.75	9.00	C12 "Flag Bearer"	5.00	7.50	10.00
C5 Soldier with gas mask, tommy gun and grenade, pot helmet	4.50	6.75	9.00	C12a Flag Bearer, WW II helmet	4	6	8
C6 "Soldier with Gas Mask" and pistol, WW I helmet	5.00	7.50	10.00	C13 Marching, slope arms, WW I helmet, "Marching Soldier"	3.00	4.50	6.00
C7 Soldier with gas mask and pistol, WW II helmet	4	6	8	C13a Marching, slope arms, WW II helmet	3.00	4.50	6.00
C8 Prone machine-gunner	4	6	8	C14 Officer on horse, WW II helmet	6	9	12
C8a Prone machine-gunner, WW I helmet, "Soldier with Machine Gun"	4	6	8	C15 Officer on horse, WW I helmet "Soldier on Horse"	7.00	10.50	14.00
C9 Sitting at AA Gun, WW I helmet, "Soldier with Anti-Aircraft Gun"	3.50	5.25	7.00				

C12a C13a C13 C11 C11a C10 C10a C10a

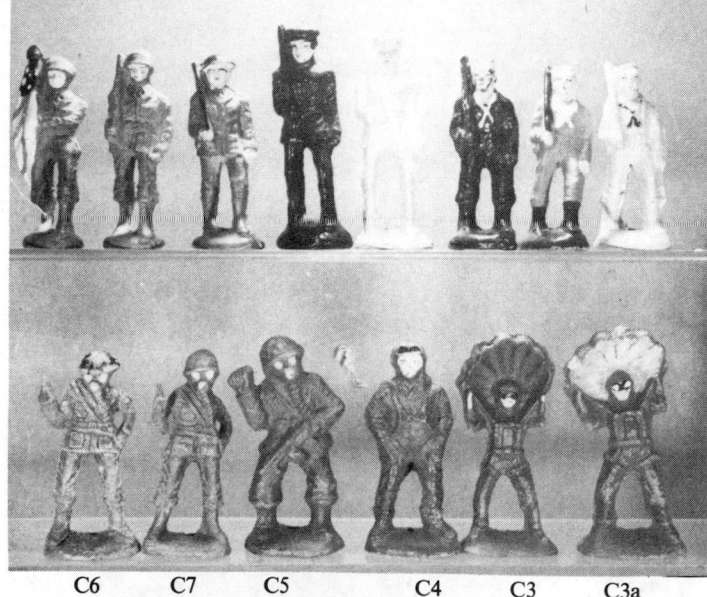

C6 C7 C5 C4 C3 C3a
Photo courtesy Don Pielin

Front and back of C2
Photo by K. Warren Mitchell

C8 C8a
Photo by Don Pielin

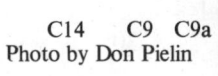

C14 C9 C9a
Photo by Don Pielin

PLAYWOOD PLASTICS

Playwood Plastics, a subsidiary of Transogram, began production in the spring or summer of 1942, with a factory at 133 Floyd Street, Brooklyn. Its soldiers, sculpted by Max Peinlich, were made of fine-ground sawdust, borax, flour and water. While the war lasted, the company was successful, employing 125 people, but never added to its original line of soldiers, partly because they had all the orders they could handle, and partly because finding metal for molds during war-time was too difficult. The soldiers were numbered in a 400 series, and marked with a P within a triangle. Descriptions in quotes are from a 1942-43 Butler Bros. catalog.

414 413 403 410 408 404

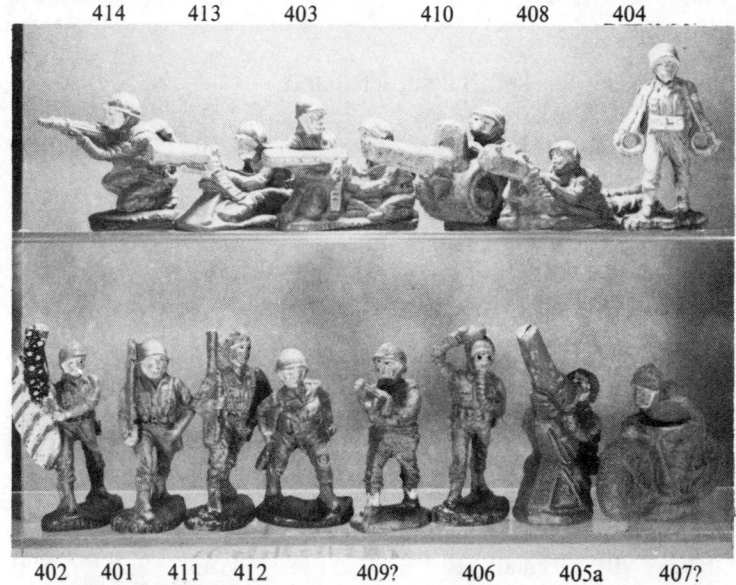

410a   410
Courtesy K. Warren
Mitchell

415

Courtesy K. Warren Mitchell.

402 401 411 412 409? 406 405a 407?
Photo by Don Pielin

407a   407?
Courtesy K. Warren Mitchell

	C6	C8	C10
408a Prone with Machine Gun, legs spread, "Machine Gun and Gunner (In Prone Position)"	4.50	6.75	9.00
409? Advancing with Tommy Gun "Sniper with Tommy Gun"	7.50	11.25	15.00
410 Kneeling with Anti-Tank Gun, square shield, spoked wheels "Anti-Tank Gun & Gunner"	5.00	7.50	10.00
410a Kneeling with Anti-Tank Gun, rounded shield, wheels not spoked ...	6.25	9.35	12.50
411 Marching at Slope in Campaign Cap "Soldier WIth Overseas Cap" ...	5.50	8.25	11.00
412 Paratrooper with Rifle, Parachutes	5.00	7.50	10.00
413 Seated at Machine Gun "Machine Gun & Gunner"	4.50	6.75	9.00
414 Kneeling Firing	4.50	6.75	9.00
415 Advancing with Rifle	No Price Found		
438 or 436? Motorcyclist, Leather-type Helmet (probably post-War) (see 407a)	No Price Found		

	C6	C8	C10
401 Marching at Slope in helmet "Parade Soldier With Pack"	3.50	5.25	7.00
402 "Flag Bearer"	4.50	6.75	9.00
403 2-Man Machine Gun Team "Machine Gun & 2 Gunners"	5.00	7.50	10.00
404 "Stretcher Bearer"	7.50	11.25	15.00
405 AA Gunner, triangle base	4	6	8
405a AA Gunner, plow base, "Anti-Aircraft Gun and Gunner"	7.00	10.50	14.00
406 In Gas Mask with Flare Gun overhead "Soldier with Gas Mask" ..	4	6	8
407? Motorcyclist with pot helmet, "Dispatch Rider on Cycle"	6.50	9.75	13.00
407a Looks exactly like "438 or "436?"	10.50	15.75	21.00
408 Prone with Machine Gun, crossed legs	4.50	6.75	9.00

BETON

Bergen Toy & Novelty Co. (later known simultaneously, and more informally, as Beton), incorporated in 1936, but was in business as early as 1935, producing slush lead soldiers from molds purchased from Metal Cast. In 1938, it became the first company to manufacture acetate plastic figures. The company, owned by Charles Marcak and his wife Elsie, was only marginally successful, though its figurines were ubiquitous in dimestores of the 1940s and 1950s, and about 1958 it was sold to Rel Plastics. It is not known who sculpted toys for the company, which was located variously in Carlstadt, Rutherford and Hackettstown (its last location), New Jersey.

BETON Plastic Soldiers   Photo by Ed Poole

PRE-1945

	C6	C8	C10
(BT1) **501 Machine Gunner**	2	3	4
(BT2) **502 Infantry Man, Charging** with bayonet	2	3	4
(BT3) **503 Hand Grenade Thrower**	2	3	4
(BT4) **504 Munitions Carrier**	2	3	4
(BT5) **505 Infantryman with gas mask**	2	3	4
(BT6) **506 Machine Gunner in prone shooting position**	2	3	4
(BT7) **507 Signaller,** left hand down	2	3	4
(BT8) **508 Bugler**	2	3	4
(BT9) **509 Rifleman, shooting position**	2	3	4
(BT10) **510 Rifleman marching position**	2	3	4
(BT11) **511 Infantryman with field glasses**	2	3	4
(BT12) **512 Rifleman, marching position** (somewhat heavier than 510)	2	3	4
(BT13) **513 Infantryman, saluting**	2	3	4
(BT14) **514 Signaller,** left hand across body	2	3	4
(BT15) **515 Infantryman, charging,** no bayonet	2	3	4
(BT16) **516 Drummer**	2	3	4
(BT17) **517 Machine Gunner, kneeling**	2	3	4
(BT18) **726 Indian Leader,** tomahawk away from head	1.50	2.25	3.00
(BT19) **727 Indian With Arrow,** carrying bow	1.50	2.25	3.00
(BT20) **728 Indian With Spear,** mohawk haircut	1.50	2.25	3.00
(BT21) **729 Indian Chief** with spear and headdress	1.50	2.25	3.00
(BT22) **730 Indian Warrior,** hatchet touching head	1.50	2.25	3.00
(BT23) **731 Indian With Drawn Bow**	1.50	2.25	3.00

	C6	C8	C10
(BT24) **830 Masked Bandit,** left hand pointing rearward	2.50	3.75	5.00
(BT25) **831 Cowboy With Lasso**	1.50	2.25	3.00
(BT26) **832 Highwayman,** pointing pistol, left hand on hip	1.50	2.25	3.00
(BT27) **833 Cowboy, Hand On Holster**	1.50	2.25	3.00
(BT28) **620 Cadet,** red coat, white pants	2	3	4
(BT29) **621 Cadet,** all grey coat and pants	2	3	4
(BT30) **622 Cadet,** all blue coat and pants	2	3	4
(BT31) **625 Cadet** blue coat, white pants	2	3	4
(BT32) **901 Fireman**	1.50	2.25	3.00
(BT33) **907 Traffic Officer,** hand raised	1.50	2.25	3.00
(BT34) **908 Patrolman,** walking his beat	1.50	2.25	3.00
(BT35) **950 Shoe Shine Boy**	1.50	2.25	3.00
(BT36) **951 Engineer**	1.50	2.25	3.00
(BT37) **952 Conductor**	1.50	2.25	3.00
(BT38) **953 Pullman Porter**	1.50	2.25	3.00
(BT39) **954 Red Cap**	1.50	2.25	3.00
(BT40) **955 Salesman,** coat over arm	1.50	2.25	3.00
(BT41) **956 Business Man**	1.50	2.25	3.00
(BT42) **957 Secretary,** case in right hand	1.50	2.25	3.00
(BT43) **958 Debutante,** in coat, purse in left hand	1.50	2.25	3.00
(BT44) **959 Matron** in coat, purse dangling from right hand	1.50	2.25	3.00
(BT45) **960 School Girl**	1.50	2.25	3.00
(BT46) **961 School Boy**	1.50	2.25	3.00
(BT47) **962 Newsboy**	1.50	2.25	3.00
(BT48) **M400 U.S. Cavalry, mounted on trotting horse,** steel helmet	3.00	4.50	6.00
(BT49) **M405 U.S. Cadet mounted on trotting horse,** assorted colors	2.50	3.75	5.00
(BT50) **M411 Indian, mounted on bronco,** with bow	2.50	3.75	5.00
(BT51) **M412 Cowboy mounted on bronco,** with lasso	2.50	3.75	5.00
(BT52) **M413 Road Agent mounted on Bronco,** with pistol	2.50	3.75	5.00
(BT53) **M416 U.S. Cavalry Officer, mounted on trotting horse,** peaked cap	3.00	4.50	6.00
(BT54) **M417 Royal Mounted mounted on trotting horse**	2.50	3.75	5.00

BETON Catalog, circa 1953
Courtesy Harold Frutchey

BETON Catalog, circa 1953
Courtesy Harold Frutchey

	C6	C8	C10
(BT55) **M418 Traffic Officer mounted on trotting horse**	2.50	3.75	5.00

Post-War Betons, with copyright dates (some pieces were in production long before these dates).

	C6	C8	C10
(BT56) **52 Baby Goat,** September 1, 1949	1.00	1.50	2.00
(BT57) **Bear,** January 2, 1952	1.00	1.50	2.00
(BT58) **2000 Bronco,** bucking	1.50	2.25	3.00
(BT59) **Buffalo,** June 5, 1952	1.50	2.25	3.00
(BT60) **508 Bugler,** WW II helmet, October 1, 1949	2	3	4
(BT61) **10 Bull,** September 1, 1949	1.00	1.50	2.00
(BT62) **620 Cadet,** White,	2	3	4
(BT63) **621 Cadet,** Grey	2	3	4
(BT64) **622 Cadet,** Blue	2	3	4
(BT65) **623 Cadet,** Red and White	2	3	4
(BT66) **624 Cadet,** Grey and White	2	3	4
(BT67) **625 Cadet,** Blue and White	2	3	4
(BT68) **M453 Cadet on running horse**	2.50	3.75	5.00
(BT69) **13 Calf,** September 1, 1949	1.00	1.50	2.00
(BT70) **Camel,** January 2, 1952	1.00	1.50	2.00
(BT71) **42 Chick**	.50	.75	1.00
(BT72) **41 Chicken,** September 1, 1949	.50	.75	1.00
(BT73) **Clown,** February 25, 1952 (See BT169)	2.00	2.50	3.00

	C6	C8	C10
(BT74) **1003 Colt**	1.00	1.50	2.00
(BT75) **Combat** Infantryman, January 15, 1952, holding rifle, butt upward	2.50	3.75	5.00
(BT76) **11 Cow,** standing	1.00	1.50	2.00
(BT77) **12 Cow,** running, July 1, 1949	1.00	1.50	2.00
(BT78) **M401 Cowboy on Bronco,** waving hat	2	3	4
(BT79) **M454 Cowboy on running horse, with lasso**	2	3	4
(BT80) **M412 Cowboy on bronco, with lasso**	2	3	4
(BT81) **M4027 Cowboy Rider with hat in hand,** May 1, 1950	2	3	4
(BT82) **Crocodile,** April 15, 1952	1.00	1.50	2.00
(BT83) **Dancer, Standing on one foot,** May 2, 1955	1.00	1.50	2.00
(BT84) **Z-5 Dancing Girl,** January 15, 1952	1.00	1.50	2.00
(BT85) **516 Drummer,** WW II helmet, October 1, 1949	2	3	4
(BT86) **72 Duck,** September 1, 1949	1.00	1.50	2.00
(BT87) **73 Duckling**	.50	.75	1.00
(BT88) **Z-2 Elephant,** February 1, 1952	1.50	2.25	3.00

	C6	C8	C10
(BT89) **22 Farm Boy,** July 1, 1949 ..	1.50	2.25	3.00
(BT90) **23 Farm Girl,**	1.50	2.25	3.00
(BT91) **20 Farmer,** July 1, 1949	1.50	2.25	3.00
(BT92) **21 Farmerette,** July 1, 1949 ..	1.50	2.25	3.00
(BT93) **M4036 Gentleman Rider,** large size	2	3	4
(BT94) **Giraffe,** January 15, 1952	1.50	2.25	3.00
(BT95) **50 Goat,** September 1, 1949 ..	1.00	1.50	2.00
(BT96) **51 Goat, Female**	1.00	1.50	2.00
(BT97) **70 Goose,** September 1, 1949	.50	.75	1.00
(BT98) **71 Gosling,** September 1, 1949	.50	.75	1.00
(BT99) **503 Hand Grenade Thrower,** WW II helmet, October 1, 1949 ..	2	3	4
(BT100) **Hippopotamus,** February 2, 1953	1.00	1.50	2.00
(BT101) **M452 Indian with tomahawk on running horse**	2.50	3.75	5.00
(BT102) **M452b Indian with bow on running horse**	2.50	3.75	5.00
(BT103) **M452s Indian with spear on running horse**	2.50	3.75	5.00
(BT104) **Indian Warrior holding Flag and Shield,** 5" high, January 2, 1952	2.50	3.75	5.00
(BT105) **Indian Warrior holding lasso,** 4" high, January 2, 1952	2.50	3.75	5.00
(BT106) **Infantryman Flagman (Marching w/Flag),** WW II helmet, July 16, 1951	3.00	4.50	6.00
(BT107) **Infantry Parachute Jumper (Paratrooper)** July 16, 1951	2	3	4
(BT108) **Infantry with Walkie-Talkie,** July 16, 1951	2	3	4
(BT109) **Infantry Flamethrower (Soldier),** August 10, 1951	2	3	4
(BT110) **502 Infantryman, Charging,** facing forward, rifle across waist, October 1, 1949	2	3	4
(BT111) **515 Infantryman, Charging,** facing sideways, rifle held out, October 1, 1949	2	3	4
(BT112) **Infantryman, holding Bazooka,** September 17, 1951 ...	3.00	4.50	6.00
(BT113) **513 Infantry Saluting,** WW II helmet, October 1, 1949	2	3	4
(BT114) **Infantryman wearing Gas Mask and** holding **Automatic,** August 10, 1951	2.50	3.75	5.00
(BT115) **511 Infantryman with Field Glasses,** kneeling, October 1, 1949	2	3	4
(BT116) **505 Infantryman with Gas Mask,** carrying rifle, October 1, 1949	2	3	4
(BT117) **Kangaroo,** April 15, 1952 ...	1.00	1.50	2.00
(BT118) **517 Machine Gunner Kneeling** October 1, 1949	2	3	4
(BT119) **62 Lamb,** head turned, September 1, 1949	1.00	1.50	2.00

	C6	C8	C10
(BT120) **4002 Large Running Horse with Saddle,** October 2, 1950	1.50	2.25	3.00
(BT121) **Leopard,** January 15, 1952 (not shown)	No Price Found		
(BT122) **Lion,** September 24, 1951 ...	1.00	1.50	2.00
(BT123) **501 Machine Gunner,** holding gun at waist, WW II helmet, October 1, 1949	2	3	4
(BT124) **506 Machine Gunner in Prone Shooting Position,** WW II helmet, October 1, 1949	2	3	4
(BT125) **Moose,** February 1, 1952 ...	1.50	2.25	3.00
(BT126) **504 Munitions Carrier,** WW II helmet, October 1, 1949	2	3	4
(BT127) **Panther,** January 15, 1952 ..	1.50	2.25	3.00
(BT128) **31 Pig,** September 1, 1949 ..	1.00	1.50	2.00
(BT129) **M4037 Polo Player,** August 24, 1951, large	3.00	4.50	6.00
(BT130) **4000 Prancing Horse,** large, no saddle, January 1, 1950 (not shown)	1.50	2.25	3.00
(BT131) **60 Ram,** September 1, 1949 .	1.00	1.50	2.00
(BT132) **Reindeer,** February 1, 1953 .	1.00	1.50	2.00
(BT133) **M4029-33 Rider, Cadet,** February 1, 1951	2.50	3.75	5.00
(BT134) **M4030 Rider, Canadian Mounted Policeman,** February 1, 1951	2.50	3.75	5.00
(BT135) **M4031 Rider, Cavalry Officer,** February 1, 1951	3.00	4.50	6.00
(BT136) **M4033 Rider, Cowgirl,** July 16, 1951....................	2.50	3.75	5.00
(BT137) **M4027 Rider, Cowboy Holding Hat,** February 1, 1951..	2.50	3.75	5.00
(BT138) **M4026 Rider, Hunter (Gentleman Rider)** February 1, 1951 (see BT 93).............	2.50	3.75	5.00
(BT139) **M4024 Rider, Huntress (Lady Hunter),** February 1, 1951.......	2.50	3.75	5.00
(BT140) **M4028 Rider, Jockey,** 3" high, February 1, 1951.......	2.50	3.75	5.00
(BT141) **510 Rifleman, marching position,** WW II helmet, October 1, 1949....................	2	3	4
(BT142) **M468 Rider, Jockey** 2" high, February 1, 1951..............	2.50	3.75	5.00
(BT143) **M4032 Police,** mounted, large........................	3.00	4.50	6.00
(BT144) **509 Rifleman, shooting position,** WW II helmet, standing firing, October 1, 1949............	2	3	4
(BT145) **M455 Road Agent on running horse, with pistol**..........	1.50	2.25	3.00
(BT146) **40 Rooster,** September 1, 1949........................	.50	.75	1.00
(BT147) **Running Horse**.............	1.00	1.50	2.00
(BT148) **1001 Saddled Standing Horse,** March 4, 1950	1.00	1.50	2.00
(BT149) **Seal,** April 15, 1952	1.00	1.50	2.00

	C6	C8	C10		C6	C8	C10
(BT150) **61 Sheep,** September 1, 1949	.50	.75	1.00	(BT159) **M465 Small Riders, Cowgirl,** 3" high, September 20, 1950.....	2.50	3.75	5.00
(BT151) **514 Signaller,** WW II helmet, October 1, 1949..............	2	3	4	(BT160) **1000 Small Running Horse,** 4" long, September 1950 (See BT147)......................	1.00	1.50	2.00
(BT152) Sitting Down Cow, August 21, 1950......................	1.00	1.50	2.00	(BT161) **1001 Small standing horse** (See BT148)...................	1.00	1.50	2.00
(BT153) **M455 Small cowboy,** holding pistol (mounted)..............	2.50	3.75	5.00	(BT162) **4001 Large standing horse,** February 21, 1950.............	1.00	1.50	2.00
(BT154) **M467 Small Cowboy Holding a Rifle (Mounted),** September 20, 1950......................	2.50	3.75	5.00	(BT163) **30 Swine,** September 1, 1949	.50	.75	1.00
				(BT164) **Tiger,** January 15, 1952.....	1.00	1.50	2.00
(BT155) **M454 Small Cowboy** mounted holding lasso..........	2.50	3.75	5.00	(BT165) **Trainer,** Holding a Whip, February 25, 1952..............	2	3	4
(BT156) **M466 Small riders, Cowboy** holding a Guitar, September 20, 1950......................	2.50	3.75	5.00	(BT166) **1002 Trotting Horse**.......	.50	.75	1.00
				(BT167) **80 Turkey** September 1, 1949	.50	.75	1.00
(BT157) **M452s Small Rider, Indian** with Spear, mounted..........	2.50	3.75	5.00	(BT168) **Zebra,** February 15, 1952...	1.00	1.50	2.00
				(BT169) **Clown**....................	1.50	2.25	3.00
(BT158) **M452t Small Rider, Indian** with tomahawk................	2.50	3.75	5.00	(BT170) **Rhinoceros**.................	1.00	1.50	2.00
				(BT171) **M4025 Lady Rider**........	2.50	3.75	5.00

PLASTIC TOYS INC.

Until 1982, when ads and articles regarding Plastic Toys Inc. were discovered in back issues of toy trade magazines, it was thought that the unmarked, integrally cast-base soldiers they produced were made by Beton. There was at least one tie to the latter company, aside from the fact that Plastic Toys Inc.'s soldiers were replicas of Beton's, and that was that O.J. Sharpe, the executive vice president of the firm, had previously served as sales manager for Beton. The company, originally located in Cambridge, Ohio, and later in Byesville, was formed in early 1944, and began delivering its soldiers to retailers in July of that year. By 1945, it had produced "several million", according to one of its ads. The company also manufactured three ships, farm animals, barnyard fowl, and later in its history, cowboys and Indians which bore no resemblance to Beton's figures. Prices for their soldiers are the same as for the Betons.

PLASTIC TOYS INC. Soldiers Set
Photo by Bill Kaufman

PLASTIC TOYS INC. Soldiers
Photo by Bill Kaufman

AUSLEY

Ausley Industries, Inc. began in 1943 in Atlanta, Georgia, and later moved to Thomasville, Georgia. Robert C. Ausley, its owner, founded it as a way of earning extra income. Its original soldiers were lead, and produced from home-casting sets. However, in 1948, when lead became too expensive, and soldiers no longer were as popular, Ausley turned to plastic figures, sculpting the company's single cowboy and Indian himself. The cowboys and Indians, which had movable arms, were produced in plastic injection molds, and sold well until the outbreak of the Korean War, when sales slackened drastically due to a renewed demand for soldiers. Ausley's other business precluded his putting any more time into the company, and it ended production in 1950. All told, Ausley produced about 250,000 lead and plastic figures. The cowboys and Indians retailed at a dime apiece. Today, their value is about $2.00 each.

AUS 1 - Cowboy with two moving arms
AUS 2 - Indian with two moving arms

Boxed set of Ausley Cowboys and Indians
Photo by Elizabeth Ausley

MILLER

Although cast in plaster, a fragile material, Miller soldiers were sold in the toy sections of 5&10s in 1950 and 1951 at 19 cents apiece. Five inches high, they were always marked on the top of the base "Miller 1950" or "Miller 1951". All the guns were plastic and separate.

	C6	C8	C10
(ML1) Stretcherbearer	8	12	16
(ML2) Wounded man on separate cloth and wire stretcher	10	15	20
(ML3) Nurse with Plasma	24	36	48
(ML4) General MacArthur	11.00	16.50	22.00
(ML5) Officer with Binoculars	8.50	12.75	17.00
(ML6) Soldier Kneeling with Sentry Dog	15.00	22.50	30.00
(ML7) Soldier Kneeling with Flame-Thrower	9.00	13.50	18.00
(ML8) Soldier Kneeling with Walkie-Talkie	8	12	16
(ML9) Soldier Prone with Bazooka	10.50	15.75	21.00
(ML10) Soldier Prone with Rifle	9.00	13.50	18.00
(ML11) Soldier in Foxhole Firing Rifle	8.50	12.75	17.00
(ML12) Soldier Walking with Flag	11.00	16.50	22.00
(ML13) Soldier Advancing with rifle (possibly also with tommy gun)	8.50	12.75	17.00
(ML14) Soldier throwing Grenade	7.50	11.25	15.00
(ML15) Soldier charging with Machine Gun	9.00	13.50	18.00
(ML16) Soldier planting flag	14	21	28
(ML17) Soldier marching with rifle	12.50	18.75	25.00
(ML18) Kneeling with Bazooka	10	15	20

	C6	C8	C10
(ML19) Kneeling with Submachine Gun	9.00	13.50	18.00
(ML20) Standing on guard with rifle, "Miller c. 1950"	9.00	13.50	18.00

ML8   ML11   ML14

ML15   ML13   ML16   ML6
Photo courtesy Don Pielin

298

LINCOLN LOG

These figures, about 2" high, were introduced in 1928. Beginning in 1933, some were also produced by Wright under the name Noveltoy Miniatures. The following listing is Lincoln Log's own description and numbering, if in bold type. The sets of 1918 U.S. Soldiers and both Mounties were introduced in 1932. The Og set came with a large color map.

LL31   LL32   Lincoln Logs animals and trees

LL13 LL14 LL1 LL12 LL22 LL23 LL19 LL16 LL17 LL18
Photo by Don Pielin

LL39   LL30 LL15 postwar   LL20   LL21

LL24 LL25 LL28 LL26 ; LL27 LL29 LL33 LL34 LL35 LL36 LL37 LL38
Photo by Don Pielin

	C6	C8	C10
LL1 **Foot Soldier of 1812 No. 201** ..	3.00	4.50	6.00
LL2 Indian with Gun	3.00	4.50	6.00
LL3 **Indian with Gun No. 225** (war-bonnet)	3.00	4.50	6.00
LL4 Indian with Bow	3.00	4.50	6.00
LL5 **Indian with Bow No. 226** (war-bonnet)	3.00	4.50	6.00
LL6 **Indian, Crawling No. 227**	3.00	4.50	6.00
LL7 **Cowboy - Foot No. 261** with lasso	3.00	4.50	6.00
LL8 **Cowboy - Foot No. 262,** firing pistol	3.00	4.50	6.00
LL9 **Indian - Mounted** with rifle	5.00	7.50	10.00
LL10 **Indian - Mounted No. 331** with bow	5.00	7.50	10.00
LL11 **Cowboy - Mounted No. 372** firing pistol	5.00	7.50	10.00
LL12 **Foot Soldier of 1776, No. 202** .	3.00	4.50	6.00
LL13 **Mounted Officer of 1776, No. 432**.....................	9.00	13.50	18.00
LL14 **Mounted Officer of 1776** larger casting	No Price Found		
LL15 **Pioneer - Foot No. 275** ...	3.00	4.50	6.00
LL16 **Foot Soldier of 1918 No. 203** marching	5.00	7.50	10.00
LL17 **Foot Soldier of 1918 No. 207** charging	5.00	7.50	10.00
LL18 **Machine Gunner No. 204** prone	5.00	7.50	10.00
LL19 **Mounted Officer, No. 314**	6	9	12
LL20 **Royal Canadian Police No. 280** foot	4	6	8

	C6	C8	C10
LL21 **Mounted Officer No. 381** (Mountie)	No Price Found		
LL22 **American Sailor at Attention No. 206**	3.00	4.50	6.00
LL23 **West Point Cadet No. 205** foot	3.00	4.50	6.00
LL24 **Og**	15.00	22.50	30.00
LL25 Nada	10	15	20
LL26 Big Tooth	7.50	11.25	15.00
LL27 Three Horn	10	15	20
LL28 Ru	No Price Found		
LL29 Rex	No Price Found		
LL30 **No. 276 Rail Splitter**	No Price Found		
LL31 **Farmer No. 282**	2	3	4
LL32 **Farm Wife No. 283**	2	3	4
LL33 **Conductor No. 293**	3.00	4.50	6.00
LL34 **Engineer No. 295**	3.00	4.50	6.00
LL35 **Red Cap No. 294**	3.00	4.50	6.00
LL36 **Telegraph Messenger No. 290** .	3.00	4.50	6.00
LL37 **Policeman No. 291**	3.00	4.50	6.00
LL38 **Traveling Man No. 292**	3.00	4.50	6.00
LL39 **Oxen Team**	4	6	8
LL40 **Poplar Tree No. 324**	3.50	5.25	7.00
LL41 Dog	2	3	4
LL42 Sheep	2	3	4
LL43 **Pig No. 502**	1.50	2.25	3.00
LL44 **Cow No. 316**	2.50	3.75	5.00
LL45 Cow feeding	2.50	3.75	5.00
LL46 **No. 315 Horse** feeding	No Price Found		
LL47 Horse feeding, short tail	No Price Found		
LL48 Large Cowboy, Noveltoy	No Price Found		
LL49 Large Indian, Noveltoy	No Price Found		

	C6	C8	C10
LL50 Cowboy on Rearing Horse	No Price Found		
LL51 Cowboy waving hat	No Price Found		
LL52 Masked Rider	No Price Found		
LL53 Tall Marching Doughboy	200	300	400
LL54 Tall Standing Firing Doughboy	200	300	400
LL55 Tall Kneeling Firing Doughboy	200	300	400
LL56 Tall Signalman Doughboy	250	375	500
LL57 Tall Flagbearer Doughboy	No Price Found		
LL58 Tall Machinegunner, Prone ...	No Price Found		

LINCOLN LOGS made a Snow White and the Seven Dwarfs set. Snow White was 6½ inches high, and the Dwarfs 3½-4 inches tall. Prices for the Dwarfs average $50 in Good, $75 in Very Good and $100 in Mint. Snow White averages $100, $150, $200. A complete set in mint might sell for $1000. All hollow lead. Information from Pete Ferguson. Photo by Marvin Sussman. Numbers shown elsewhere are Lincoln Logs' own.

LL56
(missing signal flags)
Courtesy Hank Anton

LL53   LL54   LL55
These tall Lincoln Logs doughboys were sold in 1940. The standing firing is 4⅜" high. All have the rifle tips off, and sold in this condition in 1983 for $125 apiece. J. Edward Jones unsuccessfully tried to market them for Lincoln Logs. Also in the series were a signalman, flagbearer and prone machine gunner.
Photo by Bob Klinedinst

No. 1   No. 2   No Number   No. 4
Courtesy Bill Nutting

No. 5   No. 6   No. 7
Photo by Bill Nutting

WILLIAM FEIX

William Feix was producing lead toy soldiers at least as early as 1903 at 58 Troutman Street, Brooklyn, New York. A 1903 ad, which may have been a generic drawing available to other manufacturers, shows a mounted officer, a drummer, a foot officer and a foot soldier on guard. The figures shown here greatly resemble those in the drawing and presumably are Feix. There is no question that Feix produced soldiers for a number of years, as he was still listed as a soldiers manufacturer in 1921. The likelihood is that he produced soldiers beyond that time, as a 1926-27 directory shows him still manufacturing metal toys. A 1908 ad using the same drawing (but with no manufacturer's name) lists fifteen sets of soldiers, including sailors, "volunteers," Indians and Japanese. The Japanese presumably would have been sold at one time with Russian soldiers, and each of those shown here greatly resembles the American soldiers which seem to have been made by Feix. A mounted Indian resembling the Barclay B1 has been found with its underbase stamped "Estb. 1859 Brooklyn N.Y.". Since Feix is known to have been a "pinmfr" at the same address in Brooklyn in 1901, it's possible a Feix business was established there in 1859, though as yet no documentation has been found.

	C6	C8	C10
WF?1 Soldier on guard position	6	9	12
WF?2 Officer with sword, free arm raised	7.50	11.25	15.00
WF?3 Drummer	5.00	7.50	10.00
WF?4 Marching with Rifle	5.00	7.50	10.00
WF?5 Mounted Officer	7.50	11.25	15.00
WF?6 Russian Soldier	No Price Found		
WF?7 Japanese Soldier	No Price Found		
WF?8 Sailor (not known what it looked like)	No Price Found		
WF?9 Volunteer (not known what it looked like)	No Price Found		
WF?10 Indian (not known what it looked like)	No Price Found		

WF?1
Photo by Bill Nutting

WF?2
Photo by Bill Nutting

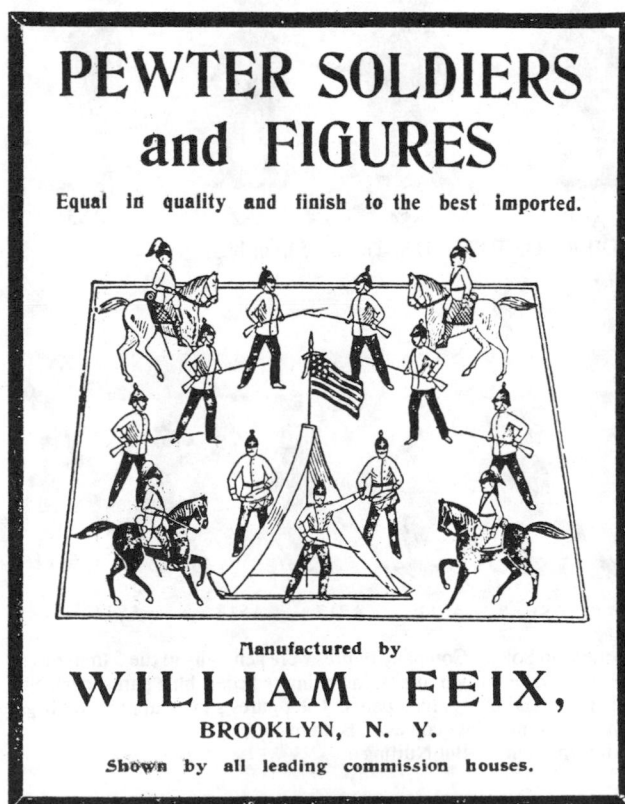
June 1903 Playthings ad
Courtesy Playthings Magazine

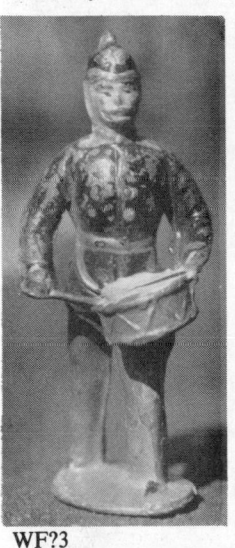

WF?3
Photo by Bill Nutting

WF?4

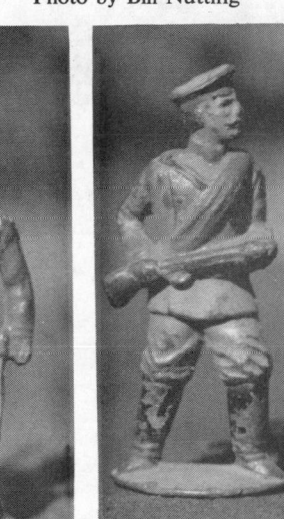

WF?6

WF?5   Photo by Bill Nutting

WF?7

301

AMERICAN SOLDIER COMPANY – EUREKA

The American Soldier Co. was founded in 1898 by C.W. Beiser and was probably the first commercial mass manufacturer of lead toy soldiers in the United States. Eureka seems to have been the first name of the company, with both names used for a while, and Eureka phased out in early 1903. Its advertising concentrated on its patented trays, first cardboard, later metal, which allowed the soldiers to be laid down or stood up en masse as well as individually. Rough Riders first appear in the 1904 ads, a running soldier with movable arms was added in 1907, and in 1908 corkshooting rifles debuted in the sets, with Indians and Phillipine Warriors sold at that time. Eureka's first address (in an 1898-9 directory) was 482 Hamilton Avenue in Brooklyn. It later moved to various Brooklyn locations with New York outlets (presumably showrooms) as well. The firm seems to have gone out of business about 1929, with Selchow and Righter, as announced in the September, 1930 Playthings, having "purchased all rights, patents, trademarks, machinery and stocks of and pertaining to the well-known 'American Hero' cowboy and Indian sets formerly manufactured by the American Soldier Company." The figures shown in the ad all appear to be Britains. (Britains supplied American Soldier with figures beginning about 1906.)

In December, 1987, a 21-piece set (with popgun) was sold for $990. In June, 1988, set No. 118 "Zulus" with a tent and six Britains Zulu Warriors (dated 1906) sold for $1200. Single pieces average $10 in very good condition.

AS1 AS1 AS1 AS5 AS2 AS16 AS15

AS4 AS4 AS4 AS2 AS3

AMERICAN SOLDIER COMPANY U.S. Troops, 54mm high
Photo by Ed Poole

A four-piece American Soldier Co. game sold June 1982 for $352 at Christie's.
Courtesy Christie's New York

AS5 AS6 AS7 AS8

AS9 AS10 AS11 AS12 AS13 AS14

These six American Soldier Company figures were generally in the 54mm range. Most came in several color variations, including red coats-blue pants; dark blue coats-blue pants; khaki coats-khaki pants. The figures shown apparently begin about 1907. Several are close copies of Britains.
Photo and information by Bill Nutting

American Soldier Company's No. 118 Zulus Set
Courtesy Phillips New York

An unusual American Soldier Company set, since the soldiers are solid, Germanic in style and 68mm, rather than 54. The rifle in the set establishes that this was sold no earlier than 1908. Auctioned in December, 1987 for $900. In June, 1988 an extremely rare set of Zulus was auctioned for $1200. Courtesy Phillips New York

McLOUGHLIN

Although many collectors had long considered McLoughlin to be the earliest of the American toy soldier mass manufacturers, recent research suggests that it didn't begin sales of its solid lead soldiers till about 1910 or 1911. Although its soldiers' uniforms suggest an earlier date, a number of American manufacturers were making soldiers in uniforms of this type right into the middle years of the First World War. McLoughlin is better known for its paper toys, including soldiers. In 1920 the firm was bought by Milton Bradley and moved to Massachusetts from New York. A set of 18 U.S. Infantry wearing spiked helmets, one of them a drummer, circa 1890, was offered for $300.00. A boxed set of "Soldiers On Parade," containing 19 West Point Cadets marching at slope, plus one officer, with a patent date of April 7, 1914, was offered in near mint condition for $125.00.

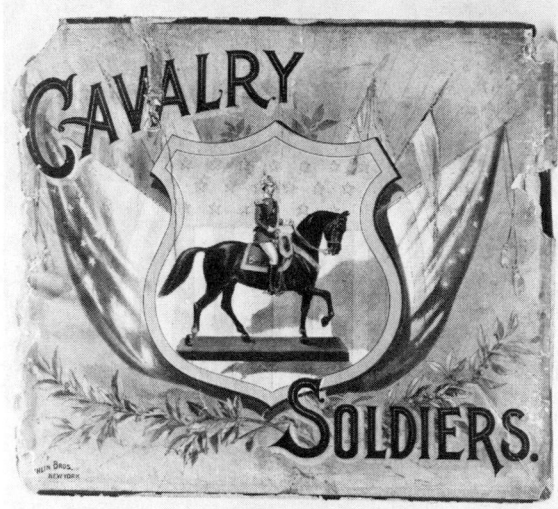

A twelve-piece "Cavalry Soldiers" turn of the century boxed set by McLoughlin Bros. sold at auction at Christie's for $460 in October, 1981. Photo courtesy Christie's New York

A 37-piece McLoughlin Bros. turn of the century "Infantry and Cavalry Soldiers" boxed set (see accompanying photo of box cover) sold for $480.00 at auction in October, 1981 at Christie's.
Courtesy Christie's New York

IDEAL

Ideal Toy Company of Bridgeport, Connecticut, produced toy soldiers circa 1920-1924, and was owned by Lewis David Christie. The soldiers, hollowcast of lead, were approximately 54mm high, and were crude in design. In 1923-24 there was a "Metal Toy & Soldier Co." located at the same address, 252 Middle Street. Whether this was Ideal is not known. It possibly may have been the name of the firm before Christie bought it. Ideal imported its molds from Germany. Apparently a number of other companies did, too, as soldiers exactly like or very similar to Ideal's are not uncommon. According to Bill Nutting, who specializes in early American soldiers, Ideals can be distinguished "by their combination of very metallic paints, such as for the blue tunics, and very flat paints, such as for the bases."

	C6	C8	C10		C6	C8	C10
(I-1) Infantryman with campaign hat .	5.00	7.50	10.00	(I-9) Sailor, rifle thrust out at angle ..	5.00	7.50	10.00
(I-2) Bugler, brown uniform	5.00	7.50	10.00	(I-10) Kneeling rifleman, steel helmet	3.00	4.50	6.00
(I-3) Bugler, blue uniform	5.00	7.50	10.00	(I-11) Train figure, conductor?	No Price Found		
(I-4) Officer with sword, grey uniform	5.00	7.50	10.00	(I-12) Train figure, signalman	No Price Found		
(I-5) Officer with sword, blue uniform	5.00	7.50	10.00	(I-13) Train figure, woman	No Price Found		
(I-6) Infantryman with rifle, cap, blue uniform	5.00	7.50	10.00	(I-14) Indian, arm raised	3.00	4.50	6.00
				(I-15) Indian, with rifle	3.00	4.50	6.00
(I-7) Officer, blue uniform, no weapons	5.00	7.50	10.00	(I-16) Charging soldier, steel helmet ..	4	6	8
(I-8) Sailor at slope arms	5.00	7.50	10.00	(I-17) Infantryman with campaign hat, rifle	4	6	8

I-1   I-2   I-4   I-5   I-6   I-3   I-7   I-8   I-9

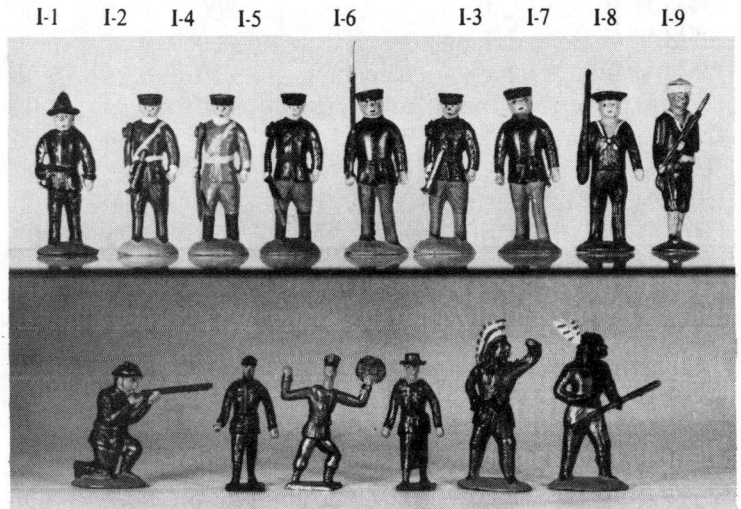

I-10   I-11   I-12   I-13   I-14   I-15
Photo by Bill Kaufman
Courtesy Hank Anton

I16   I17
Photo courtesy Bill Nutting

305

MARX

Marx produced a large number of 3½" flat tin lithographed soldiers in the 1930s and after which are attractive to collectors. The following list was compiled by collector Gene Parker.

	C6	C8	C10
(12MA) Italian Bersaglieri	3.00	4.50	6.00
(13MA) Kings Royal Rifle Corps	3.00	4.50	6.00
(14MA) Royal Scots Greys	3.50	5.25	7.00
(15MA) Seaman equipped for landing force	3.00	4.50	6.00
(16MA) Signalman, Navy	3.00	4.50	6.00
(17MA) Infantry Private, charging, two versions	3.50	5.25	7.00
(18MA) Infantry Private w/automatic rifle, lying prone, brown uniform	3.00	4.50	6.00
(19MA) Infantry Private w/automatic rifle, lying prone, blue uniform ..	3.50	5.25	7.00
(20MA) Sharpshooter w/rifle, green uniform	3.00	4.50	6.00
(21MA) French Infantry	3.00	4.50	6.00
(22MA) Indian Sikh	3.00	4.50	6.00
(23MA) Uhlan (Prussian Cavalry Soldier)	3.50	5.25	7.00
(24MA) Russian Infantry	3.00	4.50	6.00
(25MA) German Infantry	3.00	4.50	6.00
(26MA) Infantry First Lieutenant ...	3.50	5.25	7.00
(27MA) American Indian, standing ..	3.00	4.50	6.00
(28MA) Bandit, on horse	3.00	4.50	6.00
(29MA) Howitzer	3.50	5.25	7.00
(30MA) Ski Trooper on patrol	3.00	4.50	6.00
(31MA) Marine Corps Private	3.50	5.25	7.00
(32MA) Radio Operator	3.50	5.25	7.00
(33MA) Red Cross Nurse	3.00	4.50	6.00
(34MA) Machine Gun Unit, private w/30 cal m/g	3.00	4.50	6.00
(35MA) Tank Commander, standing .	3.00	4.50	6.00
(36MA) Infantry Captain	3.00	4.50	6.00
(37MA) Chief Petty Officer	3.00	4.50	6.00
(38MA) Parachute Trooper	3.00	4.50	6.00

	C6	C8	C10
(1MA) U.S. Cavalry	3.00	4.50	6.00
(2MA) Infantry Private, marching ...	3.00	4.50	6.00
(3MA) Infantry Private, attention ...	3.00	4.50	6.00
(4MA) Infantry Private, lying prone, fixing bayonet	3.50	5.25	7.00
(5MA) American Infantry "Doughboy"	3.00	4.50	6.00
(6MA) Air Force Mechanic	3.00	4.50	6.00
(7MA) American Cowboy standing ..	3.00	4.50	6.00
(8MA) American Cowboy on horseback	3.00	4.50	6.00
(9MA) Infantry Private kneeling firing rifle	3.00	4.50	6.00
(10MA) Infantry Sergeant	3.00	4.50	6.00
(11MA) Gordon Highlander	3.00	4.50	6.00

31MA 32MA 33MA 34MA 35MA 36MA 37MA

44MA 45MA 46MA 47MA

38MA 39MA 40MA 41MA 42MA 43MA

48MA 49MA 50MA 51MA

MARX Set with popgun, "Soldiers of Fortune"
Photo by Ed Poole

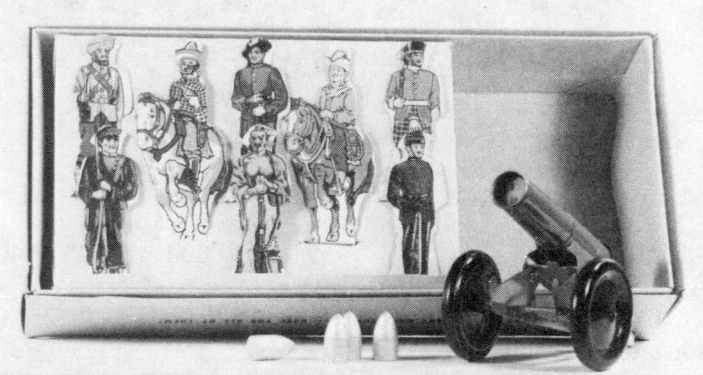

MARX Set with cannon, "Soldiers of Fortune"
Photo by Ed Poole

	C6	C8	C10
(39MA) 3-inch Anti-Aircraft Gun ...	3.50	5.25	7.00
(40MA) Marine Corps Officer	3.00	4.50	6.00
(41MA) Motorcycle Messenger	3.50	5.25	7.00
(42MA) Wounded Soldier	3.00	4.50	6.00
(43MA) Flame Thrower	3.00	4.50	6.00
(44MA) Pilot, with papers	3.00	4.50	6.00
(45MA) Pilot, adjusting gloves	3.00	4.50	6.00
(46MA) Sniper, camouflaged	3.00	4.50	6.00
(47MA) Infantry Colonel	3.00	4.50	6.00
(48MA) Captain Commands Battleship	3.00	4.50	6.00
(49MA) Officer in full dress uniform .	3.00	4.50	6.00
(50MA) General	3.50	5.25	7.00
(51MA) 50 cal. machine gun	3.00	4.50	6.00
(52MA) Fireman, sold with fire truck	3.00	4.50	6.00
(53MA) Fireman with Hose, sold with fire truck	5.00	7.50	10.00
Marx Soldiers of Fortune, set of eight with pop gun	75.00	112.50	150.00
Marx Soldiers of Fortune, set of eight with cannon	75.00	112.50	150.00
Marx Soldiers of Fortune, Fort Dix Barracks	50	75	100
Marx Soldiers of Fortune, set of 24 with pop gun	75.00	112.50	150.00
Marx Anti-Tank set, anti-tank gun, exploding tanks, soldiers circa 1940	200	300	400

52MA

53MA

MARX PLAYSETS

These sets, with plastic figures and metal buildings, were produced from the late 1940s through 1976, and have become increasingly popular in the past few years. The following list is not complete, but simply a compilation of those sets that appeared for sale recently. 90% of the sculpture was by Joe Ferriot of Ferrior Bros., of Akron, Ohio.

Mint with the Playsets means a boxed set that hasn't been opened, or if opened, the building hasn't been put together, and all the parts are in their original paper bags. Very Good signals that the building has been put together, that all the parts are there, and that everything is in excellent condition. In Good, the building shows wear, and some parts are missing.

Marx Castle Fort

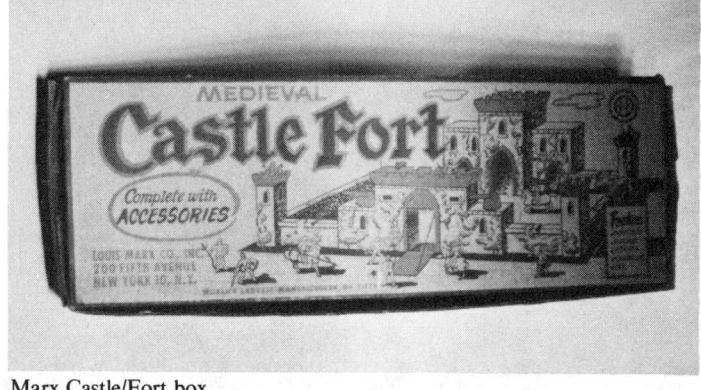

Marx Castle/Fort box

	C6	C8	C10
Alamo No. 3442	200	300	400
Alamo, Walt Disney Official Davy Crockett at the, No. 3520	125.00	187.50	250.00
Allstate Terminal and Warehouse . . .	150	225	300
Arctic Explorers	100	150	200
Atomic Cape Canaveral Missile Base .	90	135	180
Babyland Nursery	40	60	80
Bar-M Ranch	36	54	72
Battle of the Alamo, Sears No. 7959091	225.00	337.50	450.00
Battle of the Blue and Gray	112.50	168.75	225.00
Battle of the Little Big Horn	125.00	187.50	250.00
Battleground No. 4756	50	75	100
Ben Hur No. 4701 (extra large set) . .	1200	1800	2400
Ben Hur No. 4702	750	1125	1500
Blue and Gray, circa 1961	300	450	600
Cape Kennedy	30	45	60
Captain Gallant No. 4729	175.00	262.50	350.00
Cattle Drive No. 3983	112.50	168.75	225.00
Colonial Service Station No. 3450 . . .	35.00	52.50	70.00
Daniel Boone Frontier	120	180	240
Fort Apache No. 3681	34	51	68
Fort Apache No. 4202	62.50	93.75	125.00
Fort Apache No. 4685	20	30	40
Fort Dearborn	60	90	120
Freight Trucking Terminal No. 5422	125.00	187.50	250.00
Galaxy Command No. 4206	20	30	40
Horse Soldiers Cavalry Outfit, The No. 4962	40	60	80
International Airport No. 4816	70	105	140
Knight and Viking Set No. 4733	100	150	200

	C6	C8	C10
Lone Ranger Rodeo, no number, figures early, no bases, has Lone Ranger on Foot		See Movies	
Medieval Castle No. 4709	70	105	140
Midtown Service Station	80	120	160
Modern Farm Set	80	120	160
Modern Service Station No. 3471 . . .	75.00	112.50	150.00
Navarone	50	75	100
Operation Moonbase No. 4654	225.00	337.50	450.00
Prehistoric No. 3398	90	135	180
Prehistoric Animals No. 3399	75.00	112.50	150.00
Presidents of the U.S., seven figures .	12.50	18.75	25.00
Prince Valiant No. 4706	See Comic Character		
Red River Gang	50	75	100
Rex Mars Planet Patrol No. 7040 . . .	175.00	262.50	350.00
Rex Mars Space Drome No. 7016 . . .	150	225	300
Rifleman Ranch		See Movies	
Rin Tin Tin of Fort Apache		See Movies	
Roy Rogers Western Town No. 4258	190	285	380
Sons of Liberty	150	225	300
Stagecoach No. 3814	50	75	100
Star Station Seven	32.50	48.75	65.00
Super Circus	150	225	300
Tales of Wells Fargo	150	225	300
Trucking Terminal	140	210	280
Tom Corbett	200	300	400
U.S. Armed Forces Training Center No. 4149	40	60	80
Untouchables No. 4696	500	750	1000
Western Ranch Set	50	75	100
Western Town No. 4235	175.00	262.50	350.00
White House of the United States with 36 Presidential figures (Sears Heritage)	50	75	100

WARREN

Warren's soldiers are particularly prized by those who are attracted to Wm. Britain's soldiers, being roughly the same 54mm size, and equal in quality. The company, located in New York, New York, was in business from only 1936-1939, and thus its toys are rare. There were about 60 pieces in all, some possibly sculpted by owner John Warren, and the others by former Tommy Toy sculptress Margaret Cloninger, who later married Warren. Warren produced only American soldiers, infantry, cavalry and horse artillery. In 1936, the line was mainly U.S. Cavalry and light field artillery, with infantry being added in 1937. In 1936 the individual soldiers sold for fifty cents up, and the boxed sets from $2.50 to $20.00. In 1937, one-dollar boxed sets were added.

In June, 1988, Phillips N.Y. auctioned off several groups of Warrens. The U.S. Army Scout Car with three soldiers, machine gun and box sold for $900. The Army Staff Car with three soldiers and two flags went for $1200, six cavalrymen, in various conditions, went for $500, and 15 infantrymen and two horses, in various conditions, brought $550.

WARREN mounted troops
Courtesy Bob Kneale

WARREN Cavalrymen
Courtesy Ed Poole

(Above two photos) WARREN Horse Artillery.
Photo Courtesy PB Eighty-Four New York

Courtesy Ron Steiner

WARREN No. 5
Horse Galloping, solidcast

Warren U.S. Infantry
Photo courtesy Christie's New York

WARREN foot soldiers   Courtesy Bob Kneale

WARREN Officer's Car No.42 and Three Inch Gun No.34
Courtesy Bob Kneale

COMET

Comet Metal Products was founded in 1919 as a die-casting company by Abraham Slonim. Around 1940 he and his sons Joseph and Samuel began turning out solid-cast lead soldiers in a 54 mm size. Most had moving arms, and some were exact copies of other companies', such as Britains. These pieces are easily identified by the bases, which look like this:  The company, which was located in Queens, New York, produced ID models of planes, ships and vehicles during the War for the government, and in 1946 formed the Authenticast toy soldier company. The following is from what appears to be a summer, 1941 catalog put out by Comet. Prices for boxed sets of mint Comet figures average $60.00, individual foot soldiers $5.00 and mounted $8.00.

COMET Boxed Set of FR662 French Foreign Legion charging.
Photo by Bill Kaufman

C1 8 Chinese Infantry Charging
K10 8 Knights in Armor w/Shields
K11 7 Knights in Armor w/Shields (better painting)
K12 6 Knights in Armor w/Shields & Lances
GR50 7 Greek Evzones Marching
GR51 8 Greek Infantry Charging
GR52 8 Greek Evzones Marching (field uniform)
T70 8 Turkish Infantry Charging
T71 Turkish Machine Gun Set
D75 7 Danish Infantry Marching
D76 8 Danish Royal Guards Marching
A100 6 Arabs Running w/Swords
A101 6 Arabs Running w/Rifles
M200 8 Mexican Volunteers Marching
EG450 8 Egyptian Infantry Charging
G500 8 German Infantry Charging
G501 8 German Infantry (SS Troops) Charging
G502 8 German Infantry Marching
G503 German Machine Gun Set
G504 8 German Infantry Running
G505 8 German Infantry (SS Troops) Running
G506 8 German Sailor Marching
G507 8 German Infantry (SS Troops) Marching
G508 German Machine Gun Set (SS Troops)
G509 7 Austro-German Alpine Troops
G511 7 German-Alpine Troops
G514 6 German (SS) Shock Troops
FR650 8 French Infantry Charging
FR652 8 Turcos Charging
FR654 8 Zouaves Charging
FR656 8 Moroccans Charging
FR658 8 Tunisians Charging
FR661 French Machine Gun Set
FR662 8 French Foreign Legion Charging
FR664 8 French Infantry (Maginot Line) Chg.
FR665 8 French Infantry (Maginot Line) Mchg.

FR666 8 French Infantry Marching
SP700 7 Spanish Infantry Charging
E800 7 Black Watch Marching
E803 7 Indian Troops Charging
E804 8 British Navy Marching
E805 8 Australian Anzacs Charging
E806 8 New Zealand Infantry Charging
E807 8 English Infantry Charging
E808 8 British Marines Charging
E809 English Machine Gun Set
E810 8 English Royal Guards Marching
E811 8 English Infantry Running w/Gas Masks
E812 6 English General Staff
E813 7 R.A.F. w/Aeroplane
E814 8 R.A.F. without Aeroplane
E815 8 English Infantry Running
E816 8 English Infantry Marching Route Step
E817 New Zealand Machine Gun Set
E818 8 Canadian Infantry Marching Overseas Caps
E821 8 Sikhs Marching
E822 8 Indian Frontier Troops Marching
E823 6 Indian Malaca Troops Full Dress w/Lance
E824 7 Indian Troops Full Dress Marching
E827 8 Indian Army Marching
E828 Australian Machine Gun Set
I1000 7 Italian Colonial Troops Charging
I1001 8 Italian Infantry Charging
I1002 Italian Machine Gun Set
I1003 8 Italian Infantry Marching
I1004 Italian Infantry, Dress Uniform
J1050 8 Japanese Infantry Charging
USSR1100 7 Russian Infantry Charging
USSR1101 8 Russian Infantry Marching
USSR1102 7 Siberian Troops Marching
USA1250 8 U.S. Infantry Charging Steel Helmets
USA1251 8 U.S. Natl. Guard Charging Campaign Hats

G504
Courtesy Bill Nutting

FR656
Courtesy Bill Nutting

FR658
Courtesy Bill Nutting

E808
Courtesy Bill Nutting

E821
Courtesy Bill Nutting

E822
Courtesy Bill Nutting

E827
Courtesy Bill Nutting

I1003
Courtesy Bill Nutting

USSR1100 Officer
Courtesy Bill Nutting

I1001 Officer
Courtesy Bill Nutting

US1258 Officer
Courtesy Bill Nutting

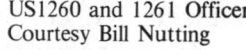

US1262 (two versions)
Courtesy Bill Nutting

US1260 and 1261 Officer
Courtesy Bill Nutting

US1252 8 U.S. West Point Cadets Marching
US1253 8 U.S. Marines Marching
US1254 8 U.S. Sailors Marching (white uniforms)
US1255 8 U.S. Sailors Marching (blue uniforms)
US1256 8 U.S. Infantry Marching Steel Helmet
US1257 8 U.S. Infantry Marching Overseas Caps
US1258 8 U.S. Panama Troops Charging
US1259 8 U.S. Philippine Troops Charging
US1260 8 U.S. Inf. Route Step Marching Steel Helmets
US1261 8 U.S. Inf. Route Step Marching Overseas Caps
US1262 U.S. Machine Gun Set Steel Helmets
US1263 U.S. Natl. Guard Machine Gun Set Campaign Hat
US1264 8 U.S. Infantry Crawling w/Gas Masks
US1265 7 U.S. Marine Band
US1276 U.S. Confederate Army
US1278 U.S. Northern Army (Civil War)
No. ? Italian Colonial Troops Marching
No. ? Italian Troops Machine Gun Set

US1277 - Unknown
DH300 - Unknown (Dahomey?)
DH301 - Unknown (Dahomey?)
B750 - Unknown
US1266 8 U.S. Infantry Band
US1267 6 American Indians w/Spears
US1268 8 U.S. Infantry Marching Overseas Caps
US1269 6 American Indians w/Tomahawks
US1274 U.S. Machine Gun Set Overseas Caps
US1275 8 U.S. Infantry Crawling Steel Helmets
S1300 7 Swedish Royal Guards Marching
US1776 6 "Spirit of 1776" (Price $8.40 dz.)
US2000 6 Colonial Infantry Marching (Revolution)
US2001 6 Colonial Infantry Marching (Revolution)
E2050 6 British Red Coats Marching (Revolution)
E2051 6 British Red Coats Charging (Revolution)
H2150 6 Hessian Troops Marching (Revolution)
H2151 6 Hessian Troops Charging (Revolution)

BRITAINS
by Joe Wallis

The most-collected of all toy soldiers are those manufactured by Englands' Britains Ltd. The firm was originally owned by William Britain, and in 1893 he introduced a hollow, three-dimensional lead soldier which was to revolutionize the toy soldier industry, and turn Britains into the largest toy soldier manufacturer in the world. Prices include the box.

JOE WALLIS is the author of the book *Regiments of All Nations* (see bibliography), a comprehensive 258 page study and identification guide of postwar Britains from 1946-1966. He helped conceive and organize *The Old Toy Soldier Newsletter* when he lived in Chicago. He is one of five owners and the Britains editor of the *OTSN* since its beginning in 1976. (*OTSN* now has over 1,000 subscribers worldwide; its address can be found in the bibliography.) His extensive collection of prewar and postwar Britains has been accumulated over a 20-year period. He was born and raised in West Texas and now works as a grants officer for the Historic Preservation Fund grants program administered by the National Park Service of the U.S. Department of the Interior. He also enjoys Victorian military history and researching the historical background of Britains production.

A WORD ABOUT PRICES AND THIS LISTING
by Joe Wallis

Price alone has not been the predominant factor in selecting items to be included in this guide. Widespread interest by collectors and reasonable availability have been the major criteria. Prices listed are based upon the average prevailing at the time this is written, with unrepresentative aberrations (whether extremely high or very low) being excluded. Truly esoteric items, such as the Civilian Autogiro, which are unlikely to regularly appear on the market have also been excluded.

The rationale for such exclusions is that simply compiling and averaging all the prices of all the items sold over a period of time, without taking into account widely varying defects of condition or completeness inevitably results in an inaccurate median price. A rare item in average condition will generally always command a higher price than a common item in mint condition. Particular care must be exercised with auction prices realized because of "auction fever"; a wealthy but uninformed collector may get carried away and bid far beyond the normal price for an item that has struck his fancy. Such an auction price may not be repeated for many years. By the same token, lack of interest at one particular auction may cause an item to sell for less than it usually brings. No one should expect to receive retail prices for items from a dealer who must pay "wholesale" to provide a profit margin for his business, or when selling an entire collection to one buyer for convenience.

Other factors that cannot be overemphasized with Britains are condition, completeness of sets as issued by the manufacturer, and age of items. As with all old toys, collectors of Britains prize original condition (preferably with original boxes). Repainting, significant paint scratches, broken or structurally repaired pieces, and sets missing pieces will invariably lower not only the price **but may even determine whether an item will sell readily at all.** The accompanying discussion on the importance of condition with toys found throughout this book **must** be kept in mind at all times when dealing with Britains.

The length of time a set was produced and the age of an item (older being harder to obtain in good condition) also affect prices. Some types of soldiers (such as Highlanders) were always produced, but are popular enough to maintain somewhat higher prices than their prevalence would otherwise dictate. Other sets have higher prices than their catalog records would seem to support (e.g. Set No.190, Belgian Chasseurs, which was always in the Britains catalog from 1913 to 1959, but does not seem to have been produced in great quantities.) There are also regional variations in which sets were available in different areas — probably connected with the idiosyncracies of hobby shop and department store orders being repeated without variation year after year.

With this background, the prices in this guide can be used as a general reflection of the market value of Britains sets with original boxes. Ultimately, however, the price of a Britains item, as with all hard-to-find toys, depends on how badly the seller wants to sell it, and how eagerly the buyer wishes to buy it.

BRITAINS No.2100, Republic of Venezuela.
Courtesy Phillips, New York

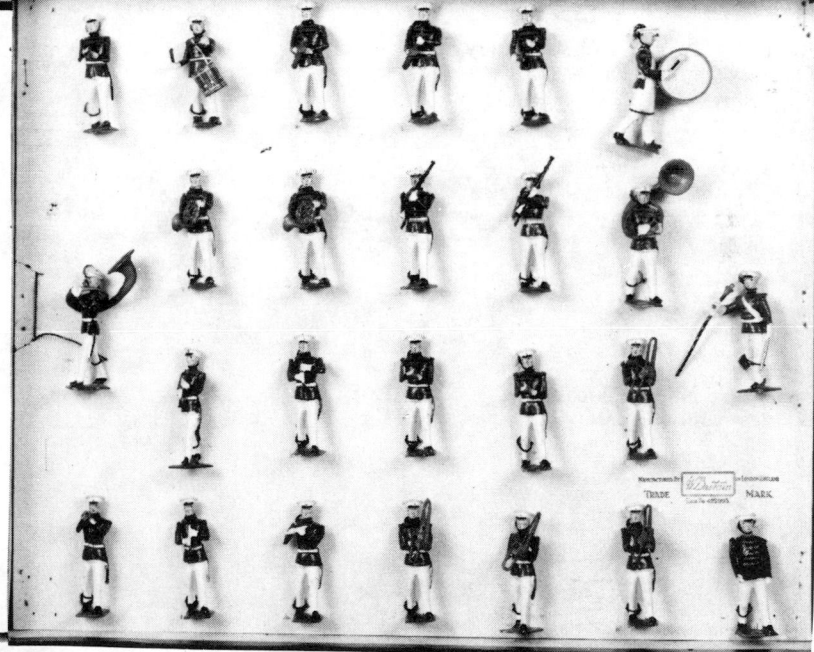

Britains No.2112 U.S. Marine Corps Band.
Photo Courtesy Phillips, New York.

BRITAINS No.2018 Danish Army, Guard Hussar Rgt.
Photo Courtesy Phillips, New York

313

BRITAINS No.49 South Australian Lancers
Courtesy Christie's East

BRITAINS No.153 Prussian Hussars
Courtesy Christie's East

BRITAINS No.167 Turkish Infantry
Courtesy Christie's East

BRITAINS No.191 Turcos
Courtesy Christie's East

BRITAINS NO.199 Motor Machine Gun Corps (soldier missing
on 3rd motorcycle)
Courtesy Phillips New York

BRITAINS BOXED SETS

Set No.	C6	C8	C10
1 The Life Guards - walking with tin swords, 1893 version may be first set of British hollow lead soldiers made	150	225	300
1953 version	70	105	140
2 Horse Guards - mounted with Aigulettes, 1953 version	75.00	112.50	150.00
8 Queen's Own Fourth Hussars, 1953 version	90	135	180
11 Black Watch - charging with piper, 1950 issue, 6 pcs.	55.00	82.50	110.00
12 Prince Albert's Own Eleventh Hussars - with carbines, 1930 issue	120	180	240
13 Third Hussars - Fred Whisstock label, officer on prancing horse	200	300	400
15 Prince Louise's Argyll & Sutherland Highlanders running	55.00	82.50	110.00
16 East Kent Regiment (The Buffs)	130	195	260
17 Somerset Light Infantry	65.00	97.50	130.00
19 West Indian Regiment	150	225	300
24 Queen's Royal Ninth Lancers, 1935	130	195	260
27 Infantry Band, 1955 issue	200	300	400
28 Mountain Artillery, 1950 issue	150	225	300
30 Drums and Bugles of the Line - 1908-1912	70	105	140
32 Scots Greys, 1950 issue	75.00	112.50	150.00
33 Sixteenth Lancers - officer turned to face troops, 1950 issue	120	180	240
35 Royal Marines, slope	100	150	200
36 Sussex Regiment, slope, 1950 issue	80	120	160
37 Coldstream Guard Band, 1950 issue	210	315	420
39 Royal Horse Artillery, 1950 issue	300	450	600
43 Second Life Guards - full gallop, 1930s painting	150	225	300
44 Second Dragoon Guards, 1935 issue	125.00	187.50	250.00
47 Indian Army cavalry - 1936 issue	100	150	200
48 Egyptian Camel Corps, 1960 issue	100	150	200
66 Thirteenth Duke of Connaught's Own Bombay Lancers, 1950 issue	100	150	200
68 Fourth Bombay Grenadiers, 1935	200	300	400
74 Royal Welsh Fusiliers - with goat mascot, officer, 1960 issue	62.50	93.75	125.00
76 Middlesex Regiment - at the slope	60	90	120
77 Gordon Highlanders - at slope with piper, postwar issue	50	75	100
79 Royal Navy Landing Party, 1960 issue	225.00	337.50	450.00
80 Royal Navy Whitejackets at trail	105.00	157.50	210.00
82 Scots Guards Pioneers - with axes, flag bearer	100	150	200
94 Twenty-first Lancers with steel helmets	270	405	540

Set No.	C6	C8	C10
98 King's Royal Rifle Corps - green uniforms, red facings, 1930 issue	130	195	260
100 Empress of India's Twenty-first Lancers	200	300	400
101 Life Guards mounted band in State Dress, 1960 issue	225.00	337.50	450
105 Imperial Yeomanry, 1901 issue	225.00	337.50	450.00
109 Dublin Fusiliers	140	210	280
112 Seaforth Highlanders - at slope, 1940	100	150	200
114 Queen's Own Cameron Highlanders - marching, 1930 issue	125.00	187.50	250.00
115 Egyptian Lancers, 1950 issue	100	150	200
117 Egyptian Infantry at attention, 1958	125.00	187.50	250.00
119 Gloucestershire Regiment firing	200	300	400
120 Coldstream Guards kneeling firing - officer with binoculars, 1950 issue	50	75	100
122 The Black Watch - firing	130	195	260
123 The Bikanir Camel Corps - with wire tails	150	225	300
127 Seventh Dragoon Guards - at trot	140	210	280
134 Japanese Infantry - Charging	175.00	262.50	350.00
136 Russian Cossack Cavalry 1935 issue	100	150	200
138 French Cuirassiers	100	150	200
141 French Infantry of the Line- light blue greatcoats, red trousers	100	150	200
142 French Zouaves - charging, post-War	55.00	82.50	110.00
144 Royal Field Artillery	800	1200	1600
145 The Royal Army Medical Corps - horsedrawn ambulance	200	300	400
145A Royal Army Medical Corps - horse and wagon, khaki	300	450	600
146 Army Service Corps Wagon - two horse team and crew	150	225	300
146A Royal Army Service Corps - active service wagon	175.00	262.50	350.00
147 Zulu Warriors	100	150	200
150 North American Indians - on foot	55.00	82.50	110.00
152 North American Indians - mounted, with rifles and tomahawks	40	60	80
153 Prussian Hussars - Types of the German Army	400	600	800
154 Prussian Infantry - marching, 1908	240	360	480
156 Royal Irish Regiment	100	150	200
157 Highlanders, firing	100	150	200
160 Territorial Infantry, 1915 issue	140	210	280
164 Bedouin Arabs of the Desert - mounted with scimitars and jezails	75.00	112.50	150.00
167 Turkish Infantry	150	225	300
169 Italian Bersaglieri, 1958 issue	90	135	180

	C6	C8	C10
178 Austrian - Hungarian Foot Guards	150	225	300
182 Eleventh Hussars - dismounted with horses, 1950 issue	100	150	200
183 Cowboys on foot - early painting	75.00	112.50	150.00
187 Bedouin Arabs - on foot	60	90	120
189 Belgian Infantry	130	195	260
190 Belgian Chasseurs	112.50	168.75	225.00
191 French Turcos	112.50	168.75	225.00
192 French Infantry of the Line - with shrapnel proof helmets	120	180	240
195 Infantry of the Line - with shrapnel proof helmets, officer with baton	100	150	200
196 Greek Evzones marching, 1950 issue	75.00	112.50	150.00
197 Gurkhas at the trail	90	135	180
199 Motorcycle Machine Gun Corps - with side car and detachable operator	150	225	300
201 Officers of the General Staff - mounted, Fred Whisstock label	110	165	220
202 Togoland Warriors - with bows and arrows	80	120	160
203 Royal Engineers' Pontoon Section	450	675	900
205 Coldstream Guards at Present	100	150	200
207 Officers and Petty Officers	150	225	300
212 Royals Scots - with piper at slope, 5 pcs.	75.00	112.50	150.00
213 Highland Light Infantry - at slope	275.00	412.50	550.00
214 Royal Canadian Mounted Police - marching in winter coats	200	300	400
216 Argentine Infantry - at slope	150	225	300
221 Uruguayan Cadets	240	360	480
224 Bedouin Arabs - mounted and dismounted and on camels, Fred Whisstock label, 11 pcs.	175.00	262.50	350.00
225 Kings African Rifles - at slope	90	135	180
227 U.S. WW I Doughboys - with campaign hats	90	135	180
228 U.S. Marines - winter dress	60	90	120
240 Royal Air Force - 1925, light blue uniforms	160	240	320
258 WW I British Infantry - Fred Whisstock label, with gas masks	95.00	142.50	190.00
299 West Point Cadets - in summer clothes	60	90	120
312 Grenadier Guards in greatcoats, 1955 issue	75.00	112.50	150.00
320 Royal Medical Corps	90	135	180
329 Scots Guards Sentry Box and Sentry	30	45	60
400 The Life Guards - in winter cloaks	100	150	200
429 Scots Guards and Life Guards in overcoats and cloaks	175.00	262.50	350.00
432 German Infantry, 1960 issue	75.00	112.50	150.00
1201 Royal Artillery Gun - 5½" long	20	30	40
1203 Tank of the Royal Tank Corps.	90	135	180
1250 Royal Tank Corps	160	240	320
1253 U.S. Navy, white jackets	70	105	140
1257 Yeoman of the Guard (Beefeaters) - with governor	112.50	168.75	225.00
1263 Royal Artillery Gun - thin wheels 3¾"	15.00	22.50	30.00
1265 18" Howitzer for Garrison work - 3 shell cases	90	135	180
1283 Grenadier Guards	50	75	100
1291 Band of Royal Marines	220	330	440
1292 Royal Artillery Gun	25.00	37.50	50.00
1301 U.S. Military Band, khaki	175.00	262.50	350.00
1307 16th Century Knights - in full armor, mounted and on foot	60	90	120
1318 Machine Gunners	55.00	82.50	110.00
1323 Royal Fusiliers, Seaforth Highlanders, Royal Sussex Regiment with 23 pcs.	250	375	500
1235B The Life Guards - trumpeter, regimental dress, Picture Pack box, 1 pc.	27.50	41.25	55.00
1330 Royal Engineers General Service Wagon galloping	205.00	307.50	410.00
1333B Life Guard, winter cape, white horse, Picture Pack box, 1 pc.	30	45	60
1334 Army Truck, metal wheels	90	135	180
1335 Army Truck - six wheels, 1955 issue	75.00	112.50	150.00
1337B Royal Horse Guard, trumpeter with grey horse in Picture Pack box	30	45	60
1343 Royal Horse Guards - mounted with cloaks	100	150	200
1432 Army Tender, with driver	110	165	220
1433 Army Tender split windshield and driver, caterpillar treads	100	150	200
1435 Italian Infantry, khaki green uniforms, 1955 issue	85.00	127.50	170.00
1436 Italian Infantry, foreign service dress, 1936	210	315	420
1437 Italian Carabinieri, 1958 issue	100	150	200
1448 Army Staff Car - twin windshields, 1955 issue	160	240	320
1470 George VI Coronation Coach	150	225	300
1475 Display Box, Beefeaters, Outriders, Footmen of the Royal Household	160	240	320
1512 Army Ambulance, Post War	130	195	260
1515 Coldstream Guards - at slope	65.00	97.50	130.00
1518 British Infantry of the Line, "1815"	100	150	200
1519 Waterloo Highlanders, "1815"	105.00	157.50	210.00
1542 New Zealand Infantry	110	165	220
1544 Australian Infantry	100	150	200
1554 Royal Canadian Police on foot, summer dress	55.00	82.50	110.00

	C6	C8	C10
1603 Republic of Ireland Infantry - marching, 1939 peak caps	130	195	260
1612 Gas Mask Infantry, service dress, bomb throwers	100	150	200
1614 Gas Mask Infantry Digging - assorted positions, 24 pcs.	100	150	200
1631 The Governor General's Horse Guards	70	105	140
1637 Governor-General's Horse and Foot Guards with officers	130	195	260
1638 Sound Locator	26	39	52
1639 Range Finder with operator, post war painting	18	27	36
1641 Underslung Heavy Duty Truck - 18 wheels, driver, white metal wheels	180	270	360
1711 French Foreign Legion - mounted officers and troops at slope	80	120	160
1715 Two-pound Light Anti-Aircraft Gun brass fixings	12.50	18.75	25.00
1717 AA two-pounder on mobile screw jack chassis	30	45	60
1720 Band of Royal Scot Greys - mounted	210	315	420
1722 Drums and Pipes of the Scot Guard	500	750	1000
1725 4.5" Howitzer	15.00	22.50	30.00
1726 Regulation Type Limber-rubber tires	12.50	18.75	25.00
1728 Predictor and Operator	22	33	44
1729 Height Finder and Operator	17.00	25.50	34.00
1730 The Royal Artillery	65.00	97.50	130.00
1731 Spotter and Chair	16	24	32
1759 Air Raid Precautions National Service Stretcher Party	150	225	300
1791 Royal Corps of Signals - dispatch riders	70	105	140
1855 Miniature Barrage Truck with winch and balloon	115.00	172.50	230.00
1858 British Infantry	85.00	127.50	170.00
1859 Sentry Box with Sentry at ease - steel helmet	55.00	82.50	110.00
1876 Bren Gun Carrier	20	30	40
1877 Beetle Truck with Driver	50	75	100
1893 Indian Army Service Corps - includes mule	125.00	187.50	250.00
1898 WW I British Infantry - Tommy Gunners	55.00	82.50	110.00
1901 Cape Town Highlanders	110	165	220
2010 Airborne Regiment - "Red Devils" marching with red berets	90	135	180
2019 Danish Livgarde	140	210	280
2021 U.S. Military Police, "Snowdrops,"	70	105	140
2022 Swiss Papal Guards	140	210	280
2026 25-Pounder Howitzer	12.50	18.75	25.00
2027 Red Army Guards in overcoats	90	135	180

	C6	C8	C10
2029 The Life Guards - mounted and on foot, 1953	60	90	120
2030 Australian Infantry - 1948, blue ceremonial dress	120	180	240
2033 U.S. Infantry - with steel helmets	50	75	100
2035 Swedish Lifeguards - ceremonial dress	90	135	180
2037 Ski Trooper, 1 pc.	50	75	100
2041 Trailer - universal clockwork unit with keys	55.00	82.50	110.00
2044 U.S. Air Corps, 1949 blue uniform, marching	62.50	93.75	125.00
2046 Arab Display, 12 pcs.	175.00	262.50	350.00
2051 Uruguayan Military School Cadets	140	210	280
2055 Confederate Cavalry	65.00	97.50	130.00
2056 Union Cavalry	65.00	97.50	130.00
2059 Union Infantry	45.00	67.50	90.00
2060 Confederate Infantry	45.00	67.50	90.00
2062 Seaforth Highlanders, 1953, with pipers	140	210	280
2063 Argyll and Sutherland Highlanders, firing	70	105	140
2064 155 mm Gun	48	72	96
2065 Her Majesty the Queen, mounted	48	72	96
2067 Sovereign's Standard & Escort	160	240	320
2075 Seventh Hussars - 1953	90	135	180
2076 Prince of Wales' 12th Royal Lancers	90	135	180
2078 Irish Guards - At "Present Arms"	80	120	160
2079 The Royal Company of Archers, 14 pcs.	300	450	600
2091 Glouchestershire Regiment at the slope	100	150	200
2094 Open State Landau - Duke of Edinburgh	190	285	380
2095 French Foreign Legion in Action	170	255	340
2102 Austin Champ jeep - detachable hood	48	72	96
2106 18" Heavy Howitzer for Garrison Work	54	81	108
2107 18" Heavy Howitzer on Tractor Wheels - 2 shell cases	50	75	100
2148 The Fort Henry Guard with goat mascot	60	90	120
2152 Waterloo Gunners	55.00	82.50	110.00
9158 Fort Henry Guards - with goat	60	90	120

March 1921 ad. Courtesy Playthings

THEODORE HAHN

Theodore Hahn was in business from at least 1921 through 1926 at 16-18 Hopkins Avenue, Jersey City, N.J.. In addition to soldiers, it made trains, cars, an airplane, a cannon and a canary whistle. Along with Ideal, it seems to have been the first American firm to make steel-helmet doughboys.

	C6	C8	C10
(TH1) Mounted Officer on rearing horse, moving arm	22.50	33.75	45.00
(TH2) Officer with Sword, movable arm	5.00	7.50	10.00
(TH3) Flagbearer	No Price Found		
(TH4) Bugler, movable arm	5.00	7.50	10.00
(TH5) Doughboy Charging, steel helmet	4	6	8
(TH6) Doughboy Advancing, rifle out at angle, steel helmet	4	6	8
(TH7) Doughboy Kneeling Firing, steel helmet	3.00	4.50	6.00
(TH8) Sailor (not known what it looked like, probably like Ideal I9)	No Price Found		

ACTION FIGURES

Though there had previously been similar toys, it was Hasbro's G.I. Joe which truly created the category of the Action Figure.

Don Levine, the Director of Development for Hasbro, conceived the idea of G.I. Joe while standing outside a Manhattan art supply shop in February, 1963. A licensing agent had suggested a military toy based on a t.v. series, "The Lieutenant." Levine had discarded the idea of a tie-in because the series was for adults, but the thought was in his mind as he looked at an artist's manikin in the shop window. The idea of a boy's soldier with movable parts came to him.

Sam Speers, who worked under Levine, came up with the engineering for G.I. Joe, both the mechanical and esthetic inventions (for which he received many patents), which included devising a way that enabled the toy to stand on its own (unlike artists' manikins) in various positions and while holding weapons or bearing equipment. Speers also thought of the added touch of the facial scar (the 11½" height was because the Barbie doll was that tall and a great success).

Noted artist Phil Kraczkowski sculpted the head, which was **not** a composite of 23 Medal of Honor winners, despite ad claims to that effect, and though Speers designed the parts and how they should go together, Walter Hansen and Norman Jacques did the sculpting of the body. It wasn't an easy sell to the Hasbro executives for Levine and Speers, but after the first year's enormous success, Levine was upped to Vice President and Speers moved up to Levine's job as Director of Development.

(Note: after the Hasbro-G.I. Joe listing, all Action Figures are listed alphabetically by company.)

1965 Catalog Illustrations

ACTION SOLDIER

	C6	C8	C10
7000 - GI Joe 5 Star Jeep, 106mm Rocket Launcher, ¼ ton trailer, tripod mounted searchlight and four 106mm shells	75.00	112.50	150.00
7100 - "Let's Go Joe" board game ...	15.00	22.50	30.00
7500 - GI Joe Action Soldier	30	45	60
7501 - Combat Set A - field jacket, M-1 rifle, bayonet, cartridge belt and six hand grenades	25.00	37.50	50.00
7502 - Combat Set B - back pack, canteen and cover, entrenching tool and cover, mess kit, utensils and single pouch cartridge belt	25.00	37.50	50.00
7503 - Combat Fatigue Shirt	12.50	18.75	25.00
7504 - Combat Fatigue Pants	12.50	18.75	25.00
7505 - Combat Field Jacket	12.50	18.75	25.00
7506 - Combat Field Pack - entrenching tool and cover	12.50	18.75	25.00
7507 - Combat Helmet, camouflage netting and foliage	12.50	18.75	25.00
7508 - Army Sandbags Set	12.50	18.75	25.00
7509 - Canteen with cover and mess kit, utensils	12.50	18.75	25.00
7510 - M-1 Rifle with bayonet and cartridge belt with six grenades ..	12.50	18.75	25.00
7511 - Camouflage Netting with poles and foliage	12.50	18.75	25.00
7512 - Bivouac Set A - zippered sleeping bag, M-1 Rifle, bayonet, cartridge belt, canteen with cover, and mess kit with utensils	25.00	37.50	50.00

	C6	C8	C10
7513 - Bivouac Set B - tent, stakes, poles, foliage, camouflage netting, entrenching tool with cover, 30 cal. tripod mounted machine gun and ammo box	25.00	37.50	50.00
7514 - 30 cal. tripod mounted machine gun, ammo box	12.50	18.75	25.00
7515 - Zippered Sleeping Bag	12.50	18.75	25.00
7517 - Command Post Set - Rain Poncho, .45 pistol w/belt and holster, field radio, field phone, wire roll, map and map case	25.00	37.50	50.00
7518 - .45 Pistol, holster, belt, ammo pouch, and six grenades	12.50	18.75	25.00
7519 - Rain Poncho	12.50	18.75	25.00
7520 - Field Phone, Field Radio, Wire Spool, map case and map	12.50	18.75	25.00
7521 - Military Police Set - "Ike" Jacket, trousers, ascot, white belt, nightstick, .45 pistol, holster, armband and duffel bag	50	75	100
7522 - Jungle Fighter Set - belt, entrenching tool, mess kit, utensils, canteen, cover, machete, sheath and Jungle knife	25.00	37.50	50.00
7523 - Duffel bag	12.50	18.75	25.00
7524 - "IKE" Jacket, ascot and MP armband	17.50	26.25	35.00
7525 - "IKE" Trousers	17.50	26.25	35.00
7526 - MP Helmet, white belt, .45 pistol, holster and nightstick	17.50	26.25	35.00
7527 - Ski patrol helmet, winter white cartridge belt, winter white M-1 rifle and six grenades	17.50	26.25	35.00
7528 - Bazooka and two shells	12.50	18.75	25.00

	C6	C8	C10
7529 - Snow Shoes, pick axe, climbing rope and sun goggles	15.00	22.50	30.00
7530 - Mountain Troops Set - Snow shoes, winter white belt, winter white field pack, pick axe, climbing rope and four grenades	32.50	48.75	65.00
7531 - Ski Patrol Set - two-piece white parka, gloves, boots, skis, poles and sun goggles	17.50	26.25	35.00
7532- Special Forces Set - uniform, beret, bazooka, two shells and four grenades	17.50	26.25	35.00
7533 - Beret, M-16 rifle and field radio	12.50	18.75	25.00
7536 - Green Beret Set - G.I. Joe action soldier dressed in special forces uniform, M-16 rifle, .45 pistol, belt, holster, six grenades and field radio	75.00	112.50	150.00
7537 - West Point Cadet Set - parade uniform, cap, feather, sword, scabbard, M-1 rifle and dress shoes ..	No Price Found		
7538 - Heavy Weapons Set - 81mm mortar, 3 shells, M-60 machine gun, tripod, ammo belt, bullet proof vest, bullet belt and 2 grenades	25	35	50
7590 - GI Joe talking action soldier ..	75.00	112.50	150.00
8000 - Official GI Joe footlocker	12.50	18.75	25.00
8030 - G.I Joe desert patrol jeep w/.50 cal. tripod mounted machine gun, radio antenna and GI Joe desert trooper	No Price Found		

ACTION SAILOR

	C6	C8	C10
7600 - GI Joe Action Sailor	30	45	60
7601 - Sea Rescue Set A - inflatable raft, oar, sea anchor, tow line, flare gun, knife, scabbard and first aid kit	22.50	33.75	45.00
7602 - Frogman Set - three pc. black scuba set, swim fins, face mask, oxygen tanks, depth gauge, knife, scabbard and depth charges	No Price Found		
7603 - Black scuba suit jacket and hood	17.50	26.25	35.00
7604 - Black scuba suit pants	17.50	26.25	35.00
7605 - Swim fins, face mask, knife, scabbard and depth gauge	17.50	26.25	35.00
7606 - Oxygen tanks	17.50	26.25	35.00
7607 - Navy Attack Set - life jacket, semaphore flags, hand held searchlight and binoculars	22.50	33.75	45.00
7610 - Navy attack helmet, hand held searchlight and binoculars	17.50	26.25	35.00
7611 - Life jacket	17.50	26.25	35.00
7612 - Shore Patrol Set - jumper, neckerchief, trousers, white belt, .45 pistol, holster, nightstick, armband, sailors cap and duffel bag .	30	45	60

	C6	C8	C10
7613 - Shore Patrol Jumper Set	20	30	40
7614 - Shore Patrol Pants	20	30	40
7615 - USN duffel bag	17.50	26.25	35.00
7616 - Shore Patrol helmet, white belt, .45 pistol, holster and nightstick	20	30	40
7618 - .30 cal. tripod mounted machine gun and ammo box	17.50	26.25	35.00
7619 - Dress Parade M-1 rifle, bayonet, white cartridge belt and white billyclub	20	30	40

| | 8200 | 8201 | 8202 | 8203 | 8204 | 8205 |

Courtesy of Sam Speers

	C6	C8	C10
7620 - Deep Sea Diver Set - divers' suit, gloves, helmet, breastplate, air pump, hoses, weighted belt, weighted shoes, signal float, line, knife, scabbard and sledge hammer	22.50	33.75	45.00
7621 - Landing Signal Officer Set - safety striped jumpsuit, cloth helmet with headphones, goggles, binoculars, signal paddles, clipboard, pad, pencil and flare gun	20	30	40
7622 - Sea Rescue Set B - same as Sea Rescue Set A also includes life jackets	20	30	40
7623 - Deep Freeze Set - fur parka, pants, boots, snow sled, flare gun and ice pick	25.00	37.50	50.00
7624 - Annapolis Cadet Set - dress parade jacket, cap, pants, belt, shoes, sword, scabbard and white M-1 rifle	100	150	200
7625 - Breeches Buoy Set - buoy, pulley, slicker jacket, pants, flare gun and hand held searchlight	20	30	40
7626 - LSO helmet w/headphones, signal paddles, flare gun, clipboard, pad and pencil	17.50	26.25	35.00
7627 - USN Life ring	17.50	26.25	35.00
7628 - White sailor's cap, boots and GI Joe dogtags	17.50	26.25	35.00
7690 - GI Joe talking action sailor	75.00	112.50	150.00
8050 - Official GI Joe Sea Sled - w/GI Joe frogman	140	210	280

ACTION MARINE

	C6	C8	C10
7700 - GI Joe Action Marine	30	45	60
7701 - Communications Set - M-1 carbine, camouflage poncho, field phone, field radio, wire spool, binoculars, map and map case	37.50	56.25	75.00
7702 - Camouflage poncho	12.50	18.75	25.00
7703 - Field radio, field phone, wire spool, map and map case	12.50	18.75	25.00
7704 - Flag Set - Old Glory, Army flag, Navy flag, Marine Corps flag and Air Force flag	37.50	56.25	75.00
7705 - Paratrooper Set - parachute pack, M-1 carbine, six grenades, knife, scabbard, belt, ammo pouch, canteen and cover	37.50	56.25	75.00
7706 - M-1 carbine, six grenades, knife, scabbard, belt, ammo pouch, canteen and cover	12.50	18.75	25.00
7707 - Camouflage helmet, foliage and helmet cover	12.50	18.75	25.00
7708 - Camouflage netting, foliage, poles and securing line	12.50	18.75	25.00
7709 - Parachute Pack	12.50	18.75	25.00
7710 - Dress Parade Set - traditional Marine "dress blues", cap and white M-1 rifle	50	75	100
7711 - Beachhead Set A - flame thrower, camouflage tent, poles, stakes, belt, ammo pouch, mess kit and utensils	30	45	60

	C6	C8	C10
7712 - Beachhead Set B - M-1 rifle, cartridge belt, six grenades, field pack, bayonet, entrenching tool, cover, canteen and cover	30	45	60
7713 - Field pack, entrenching tool and cover	12.50	18.75	25.00
7714 - Camouflage fatigue shirt	12.50	18.75	25.00
7715 - Camouflage fatigue pants	12.50	18.75	25.00
7716 - Mess Kit, utensils, canteen and cover	12.50	18.75	25.00
7717 - M-1 Rifle, bayonet, cartridge belt and six grenades	12.50	18.75	25.00
7718 - Flame thrower	12.50	18.75	25.00
7719 - Medic Set - stretcher, crutch, satchel, stethoscope, plasma bottle, IV tube, splints, bandage rolls, armbands and hospital flag	50	75	100
7720 - crutch, stethoscope, plasma bottle, I.V. tube, splints and bandage rolls	12.50	18.75	25.00
7721 - Medic's helmet, satchel and two armbands	12.50	18.75	25.00
7722 - Fatigue cap, boots and G.I. Joe dog tags	12.50	18.75	25.00
7723 - G.I. bunk bed	17.50	26.25	35.00
7727 - Weapons Rack with rack, M-1 rifle, M-1 carbine, M-16 rifle and 40 mm grenade launcher	30	45	60
7731 - Tank Commander Set - leather jacket, tanker's helmet, belt, .30 cal. M-60 machine gun, tripod, ammo box, radio and tripod	50	75	100
7732 - Jungle Fighter Set - green fatigue shirt, pants, campaign hat, AR-15 rifle, belt, knife, machete, sheath, canteen, cover, flame thrower and field phone	45.00	67.50	90.00
7790 - G.I. Joe talking action Marine	80	120	160

ACTION PILOT

	C6	C8	C10
7800 - G.I. Joe action pilot	30	45	60
7801 - Survival Set - inflatable raft, sea anchor, tow line, oar, knife, scabbard, flare gun, first aid kit and inflatable USAF life vest ...	42.50	63.75	85.00
7802 - Inflatable raft, sea anchor, tow line and oar	20	30	40
7803 - Dress Uniform - jacket, shirt, tie, pants, garrison cap, wings and captain's bars	50	75	100
7804 - Dress Jacket	17.50	26.25	35.00
7805 - Dress Pants	22.50	33.75	45.00
7806 - Dress Shirt and Cap	22.50	33.75	45.00
7807 - Scramble Set - gray flight suit, inflatable life vest, .45 pistol, holster, belt, clipboard, pad and pencil	42.50	63.75	85.00
7808 - Gray flight suit	17.50	26.25	35.00
7809 - Inflatable life vest, flare gun, knife, scabbard and first aid kit ..	17.50	26.25	35.00

	C6	C8	C10
7810 - Crash helmet w/oxygen mask .	17.50	26.25	35.00
7811 - Parachute pack	17.50	26.25	35.00
7812 - Communications Set - field radio binoculars, map, map case, clipboard, pad and pencil	17.50	26.25	35.00
7813 A. P. Helmet Set	17.50	26.25	35.00
7820 - Crash Crew Set - metallic heat suit, hood, gloves, boots, tool belt and CO_2 fire extinguisher	42.50	63.75	85.00
7822 - Colorado Air Cadet Set - uniform, sash, cap, dress shoes, M-1 rifle, sword and scabbard ...	42.50	63.75	85.00
7823 - Fighter Pilot Set - G-suit, boots, "Mae West" life jacket, helmet, oxygen mask, flashlight and working parachute	No Price Found		
7824 - Air Sea Rescue Set - three pc. orange scuba suit, mask, swim fins, air tanks, flare gun, first aid kit, rescue life ring and marker-buoy	No Price Found		
7890 - G.I. Joe talking action pilot ..	60	90	120
7900 G.I. Joe Action Soldier Colored (sic)	40	60	80
8020 - Official G.I. Joe Space Capsule - space suit, boots, gloves, helmet and recording of mercury control communications	200	300	400
8040 - Deluxe Crash Crew Set - fire truck, working water pump, working siren, blinking red light, fire axe, metallic heat suit, boots, gloves and hood	No Price Found		
G.I. Jane (1965) Army Nurse	400	600	800

"ACTION SOLDIERS OF THE WORLD"

	C6	C8	C10
8100 - German Storm Trooper - w/cartridge belt, luger pistol, holster, field pack, "Potato Masher" grenades, 9mm Schmeisser machine gun and iron cross medal	120	180	240
8101 Japanese Imperial Soldier w/field pack, Nambu pistol, holster, cartridge belt, Arisaka rifle, bayonet and Order of the Kite medal	120	180	240
8102 - Russian Infantryman - W/D.P. light machine gun, bi-pod, field glasses, case, anti-tank grenades, ammo box and order of Lenin medal	120	180	240
8103 French Resistance Fighter - w/ Lebel revolver, shoulder holster, knife, grenades, radio set, 7.65mm Mas submachine gun and Croix de Guerre medal	120	180	240
8104 - British Commando w/gas mask, case, canteen, cover, sten mark 25 submachine gun and Victoria Cross medal	120	180	240

	C6	C8	C10
8105 - Australian Jungle Fighter - w/ grenades, flame thrower, jungle knife, entrenching tool, bush machete, sheath and Victoria Cross medal	120	180	240
8200 - German storm trooper	90	135	180
8201 - Imperial Japanese soldier	50	75	100
8202 Russian Infantryman	90	135	180
8203 - French Resistance Fighter	90	135	180
8204 - British Commando	90	135	180
8205 - Australian Jungle Fighter	90	135	180
8300 - Equipment For German Storm Trooper - field pack, Luger pistol, holster, cartridge belt, 9mm Schmeisser machine gun, "Potato Masher" hand grenades and Iron Cross medal	42.50	63.75	85.00
8301 - Equipment For Japanese Imperial Soldier - cartridge belt, field pack, Arisaka rifle, bayonet, Nambu pistol, holster and order of kite metal	42.50	63.75	85.00
8302 - Equipment For Russian Infantryman - field glasses, case, D.P. light machine gun, bi-pod, belt, ammo box, anti-tank grenades and order of Lenin medal	42.50	63.75	85.00
8303 - Equipment For French Resistance Fighter - shoulder holster, Lebel revolver, 7.65 Mas submachine gun, grenades, radio, knife and Croix de Guerre medal	42.50	63.75	85.00
8304 - British Commando Equipment - canteen, case, cartridge belt, gas mask, case, stern mark 2-S submachine gun and Victoria Cross medal	62.50	93.75	125.00
8305 - Australian Jungle Fighter Equipment - flame thrower, jungle knife, grenades, bush machete, sheath, entrenching tool and Victoria Cross medal	42.50	63.75	85.00
Nazi Pilot Outfit, suit, vest, helmet, boots, light	150	225	300

NOTE - The Irwin Company of New York made three vehicles for G.I. JOE under license from Hasbro; an armoured car, a single seat helicopter and a jet fighter. The helicopter, early version, sells for $280 in mint.

G.I. JOE ADVENTURERS

	C6	C8	C10
Air Adventurer	19.00	28.50	38.00
Land Adventurer	19.00	28.50	38.00
Sea Adventurer	19.00	28.50	38.00
Talking Man of Action	90	135	180
Man of Action, likelike hair	25.00	33.75	50.00
Talking Adventure Team Commander	35.00	52.50	70.00
Talking Adventure Team Commander, lifelike hair, beard	60	90	120
Astronaut and Space Capsule Set With Equipment	125.00	187.50	250.00

	C6	C8	C10
Secret of the Mummy's Tomb Set with figure, vehicle, equipment	60	90	120
Adventure Team Helicopter	37.50	56.25	75.00
Adventure Team Training Tower	30	45	60
Adventure Team Headquarters	25.00	37.50	50.00
Adventure Team Outfit, pants, flare gun	8	12	16
Adventure Team Outfit, trenchcoat, walkie-talkie	8	12	16
Adventure Team Outfit, camouflage clothes, gun, holster	8	12	16

END G.I. JOE

	C6	C8	C10
Hasbro Charlie's Angels, Jaclyn Smith, 8" high	5.00	7.50	10.00
Hasbro Charlie's Angels, Kate Jackson, 8" high	5.00	7.50	10.00
Hasbro Charlie's Angels Outfits, each	6	9	12
Gabriel The Lone Ranger No. 23620, 9½" high, fully-jointed, cloth clothes		No Price Found	
Gabriel Tonto No. 23621, 9½" high, fully-jointed, cloth clothes		No Price Found	
Gabriel Scout No. 23626, jointed	9.00	13.50	18.00
Gabriel Silver plus 8-Way Action Saddle No. 27625, jointed	9.00	13.50	18.00
Gabriel Tonto and Scout No. 28691, cloth clothes		No Price Found	
Gabriel The Lone Ranger and Silver No. 28675, with 8-way trick Action Saddle, cloth clothes		No Price Found	

Gabriel The Lone Ranger No. 31630 (Legend of the Lone Ranger), 3¾" high, jointed, new in 1981 .... No Price Found

Gabriel Tonto No. 31631, 3¾" high, with pistol and knife, new in 1981 .. No Price Found

Gabriel Silver No. 31635, with removable saddle, bridle . . . .   No Price Found

Gabriel Scout No. 31636 for 3¾" Tonto, includes removable saddle and bridle . . . .   No Price Found

Gabriel Butch Cavendish No. 31632, 3¾" high, jointed, new in 1981, with pistol . . . .   No Price Found

Gabriel Smoke No. 31637 (Butch Cavendish stallion), with removable saddle and bridle . . . .   No Price Found

Gabriel General George Custer No. 31633, 3¾" high, with pistol . . . .   No Price Found

Gabriel Buffalo Bill Cody No. 31634, 3¾" high, jointed, comes with carbine . . . .   No Price Found

Gabriel Figure Assortment No. 31601, 3¾" high, Lone Ranger, Tonto, Butch Cavendish, General Custer, Buffalo Bill . . . .   No Price Found

Gabriel Horse Assortment No. 31602, includes Silver, Scout, Smoke (for 3¾" figures) . . . .   No Price Found

GILBERT James Bond 3½" figures 1-10
Courtesy Bill Nutting

	C6	C8	C10
Gilbert Honey West, 12" high, 1965 .	50	75	100
Gilbert James Bond, 12" high	50	75	100
Gilbert (James Bond) Odd Job, 1960s	60	90	120
Gilbert James Bond Action Toy Set No. 1, 1965 - figures of 007 as scuba diver, Domino and Largo with Disco Volante's yacht, display box	35.00	52.50	70.00
Gilbert James Bond Action Playset No. 2 - Bond, Goldfinger, Odd Job and spin-top pool table, display box	35.00	52.50	70.00
Gilbert James Bond Action Toy Set No. 3 in display box, 1965, - figures of 007 on Laser Table, Goldfinger, Odd Job and Dr. No.	35.00	52.50	70.00
Gilbert James Bond Action Playset No. 4 - Dr. No, Bond, Domino and firespitting Dragon Tank, display box	35.00	52.50	70.00
Gilbert James Bond Action Playset No. 5 - Bond with Beretta, Money Penny, M, and M's secret desk, display box	35.00	52.50	70.00
Gilbert James Bond No. 1, 3½" high, with Beretta pistol	7.50	11.25	15.00
Gilbert James Bond No. 2 with rifle, 3½" tall, 1965	6	9	12
Gilbert James Bond No. 3 in Scuba Suit with Spear Gun, 3½" tall, 1965	6	9	12

	C6	C8	C10
Gilbert James Bond No. 4 Odd Job, 3½" tall, 1965	4.50	6.75	9.00
Gilbert James Bond No. 5 M, Bond's boss	4.50	6.75	9.00
Gilbert James Bond No. 6 Goldfinger	4.50	6.75	9.00
Gilbert James Bond No. 7 Miss Moneypenny	4.50	6.75	9.00
Gilbert James Bond No. 8 Largo, 3½" tall, 1965, ...	4.50	6.75	9.00
Gilbert James Bond No. 9 Domino, 3½" tall, 1965	4.50	6.75	9.00
Gilbert James Bond No. 10 Dr. No with poison vial	4.50	6.75	9.00
Gilbert Man From Uncle **Ilya Kurayakin,** 12" high	35.00	52.50	70.00
Gilbert Man From Uncle **Napoleon Solo**	35.00	52.50	70.00
Hartland **Jim Bowie,** mounted	50	75	100
Hartland **Roy Rogers**	50	75	100
Hartland Lone Ranger on Horse	75.00	112.50	150.00
Hartland Tonto on Horse	75.00	112.50	150.00
Ideal **Captain Action No. 3400-9** - costumed figure, Lightning Sword, scabbard, gun, gun belt, 12" high	90	135	180
Ideal **Action Boy 3420-7,** new in 1967, 9" high, costumed, Panther, Space Helmet, utility belt, ray gun knife	80	120	160

Captain Action and Action Boy

Silver Streak Amphibian

Top, L to R: Flash Gordon Outfit, Spiderman Outfit, Steve Canyon Outfit, Green Hornet Outfit, Lone Ranger Outfit, Tonto Outfit. Bottom, L to R: The Phantom Outfit, Batman Outfit, Captain America Outfit, Aquaman Outfit, Buck Rogers Outfit, Superman Outfit.

	C6	C8	C10

Ideal **Dr. Evil No. 3465-2,** new in 1968, 12" high, costumed with laser gun 125.00 187.50 250.00

Ideal **Batgirl,** 12" high, 1967 . . . . 80 120 160

Ideal **Mera** (Aquaman's wife), 1967, 12" high 90 135 180

Ideal **Supergirl,** 12" high, 1967 . . . . . 80 120 160

Ideal **Wonder Woman,** 1967, 12" high 80 120 160

Ideal **Aqua Lad Outfit No. 3423-1** - costume, octupus, boots, belt with sea horse knife, sea shell axe, no figure included in outfits 200 300 400

Ideal **Aquaman Outfit No. 3408-2** - costume, swordfish sword, conch horns, fins, trident spear, knife with sheath, Aquaman face mask 110 165 220

Ideal **Bat Girl** - helmet, cape, batarang, boots, bat gloves, halter dress for alter ego Barbara Gordon . . . . No Price Found

Ideal **Batman** Outfit No. 3402-5 - costume, emblem, cape, boots, utility belt with 2-way radio buckle, flashlight, Batarang, laser-beam, Batrope, reel with grappling hook, hood, Batman face mask . . 125.00 187.50 250.00

Ideal **Buck Rogers Outfit No. 3416-5** - face mask, space belt, twin jet packs, space helmet, space gun, space light, space boots, canteen . 75.00 112.50 150.00

Ideal **Captain America Outfit No. 3409-0** - uniform, belt with holster, ultrasonic pistol, laser-beam gun, boots, shield, Captain America face mask 110 165 220

Ideal **Flash Gordon Outfit No. 3403-3** - silver astro-suit, space helmet, silver boots, space belt with holster and ray pistol, oxygen guidance "Zot" gun, Flash Gordon face mask 75.00 112.50 150.00

Ideal **Green Hornet Outfit No. 3413-2** - face mask, watch message receiver, gas pistol, hornet sting, TV scanner with phone, shoulder holster, gas mask, shoes, costume 135.00 197.50 270.00

Ideal **Lone Ranger Outfit No. 3406-6** - Wild West cowboy outfit, gun belt, two holsters, two pistols, boots with spurs, Winchester rifle, cowboy hat, Lone Ranger face mask 90 135 180

Ideal **The Phantom Outfit No. 3407-4** - costume, rifle with scope, belt, holster, pistol, knife, boots, Phantom face mask 110 165 220

Ideal **Robin Outfit No. 3421-5** - 2 suction grips, Bat-a-Rang Launcher, Bat-a-Rang, 2 Bat grenades 110 165 220

Ideal **Sgt. Fury Outfit** 125.00 187.50 250.00

Ideal **Spiderman Outfit No. 3414-0** - spray tank with hose, utility belt, spider hook with rope and handle, mask, light, boots 125.00 187.50 250.00

Ideal **Steve Canyon Outfit No. 3405-8** - uniform, 50 mission hat, parachute pack, garrison belt, holster, .45 automatic, helmet with oxygen mask, knife, boots, Steve Canyon face mask 75.00 112.50 150.00

Ideal **Super Girl** - cape, costume, boots, Krypto dog, halter dress for alter ego Linda Lee Danvers   No Price Found

Ideal **Superboy Outfit No. 3422-3** - uniform, belt, boots, cape, telepathic scrambler, interspace language translator, chem lab . . . 225.00 337.50 450.00

Ideal **Superman Outfit No. 3401-7** - costume, super shield, belt, flying cape, boots, arm shackles, block of Kryptonite, Superman face mask, Krypto the dog 125.00 187.50 250.00

Ideal **Tonto Outfit No. 3415-7** - face mask, gun belt, head band, pistol, knife, bow, quiver, 4 arrows, moccasins, eagle . . . . No Price Found

Ideal **Communicator Kit No. 3454-6** - Solar Power Pack, Rotating Antenna dome, Beam Projectors, Secret Sound Horn . . . . No Price Found

Ideal **Directional Communicator Set No. 3454-6** - Solar Power Pack, Rotating Antenna dome, power plugs, beam projectors, Secret Sound Horn . . . . No Price Found

Ideal **Dr. Evil Gift Set No. 3466-0** - Dr. Evil, lab coat, 2 disguise masks, Reducer, Hypnotic Eye, Ionized Hypo, Laser Ray Gun, Thought Control Helmet 175.00 262.50 350.00

Ideal **Dr. Evil Sanctuary No. 8701-5** - "space age" carrycase, storage bins, Dr. Evil figure . . . . No Price Found

	C6	C8	C10
Ideal **Jet Mortar No. 3452-0** - Mortar with Blaster Tripod, Radar Scanner, Ammo Carrier, two mortar missiles	90	135	180
Ideal **Parachute Pack** No. 3453-B - Parachute with Body Harness and Back Pack, Crash Helmet, jump boots	100	150	200
Ideal **Power Pack** No. 3455-3 - Thrust Ejector, Cosmic Boots, Cosmic Gloves, Flight Helmet	No Price Found		
Ideal **Silver Streak Amphibian** No. 3449-6 21¼" long	No Price Found		
Ideal **Survival Vest** No. 3450-4 Utility Vest with Fishing Kit, Mirror, First Aid Kit, Folding Spade, 3 pc. Extension Claw Hook, Machete, Utility Belt with Flare Pistol and holster, Flares, Dagger, Ammo and Hatchet	No Price Found		
Ideal **Weapons Arsenal** No. 3451-2 - Electronic Rifle, 2 Revolvers, Carbine, Automatic, 2 Grenades, Combat Knife, All-Purpose Knife, Ray Gun, Storage Rack	No Price Found		

KENNER

Kenner was formed in 1947 on Kenner Street in Cincinatti by three brothers; Al, Phil and Joe Steiner. In 1967 General Mills took it over. The "Star Wars" toys have probably been its most notable success, and follow Kenner's other action figures and toys in this listing.

	C6	C8	C10
Alien, 18" high, new in 1980, "Alien" move. Fully articulated jaws, tail moves, head glows in dark	50	75	100
Bionic Woman, 12" high	8	12	15
Captain Marvel (Shazam), (Super Powers)	5	8	10
Cyborg, (Super Powers)	10	15	20
Justice Jogger (Super Powers)	4	6	7
Lex Luthor (Super Powers)	4	6	7
Mantis (Super Powers)	5	8	10
Martian Manhunter (Super Powers) . .	4	6	8

	C6	C8	C10
Penguin (Super Powers)	4	6	8
Tyr (Super Powers)	5	8	10
Hall of Justice (Super Powers)	15	23	30

KENNER STAR WARS

ACTION FIGURES
By Whit Alexander and Neal Bates

The first set of 12 figures was introduced in 1977 and by 1984 over 80 different action figures were offered. Over the 7 year marketing period attention given to detail and variation of accessories increased.

STAR WARS ACTION FIGURES (SW-A)

The first set of action figures all read 1977 on their legs and included SW-A1, SW-A3, SW-A4, SW-A5, SW-A6, SW-A10, SW-A11, SW-A12, SW-A15, SW-A17, SW-A18, and SW-A20. The next set read 1978 and included the 5 cantina figures (SW-A8, SW-A9, SW-A19A, SW-A19B, SW-A21), plus 4 more (SW-A13, SW-A14, SW-A15, SW-A16, and SW-A7). Bobba Fett (SW-A2) was the only figure issued in 1979.

	C6	C8	C10
SW-A1 Ben (Obi-Wan) Knobi: 3¼" high, rust with removable brown cape and retractable blue light-saber, 1977	38	57	75
SW-A2 Boba Fett: 3¾" high; blue-gray with backpack and laser pistol (Weapon No. 1). Originally offered only through special mail order and was the only Empire Strikes Back character to be offered a year prior to the movie's release date. 1979.	38	57	75
SW-A3 Chewbacca: 4¼" high, brown with silver bandolier and laser rifle (Weapon No. 6). 1977.	20	26	32
SW-A4 C 3PO: 3¾" high, metallic gold with no accessories. 1977 . . .	38	57	75
SW-A5 Darth Vader: 4¼" high, black with removable black cape and retractable red light-saber. 1977. .	20	26	32
SW-A6 Death Squad Commander (Star Destroyer Commander); 3¼" high; gray with black helmet and laser pistol (Weapon No. 1). 1977.	20	26	32
SW-A7 Death Star Droid: 3¾" high, metallic silver with no accessories. 1978	17	23	30
SW-A8 Greedo: 3¾" high, green with laser pistol (Weapon No. 2) 1978.	17	23	30
SW-A9 Hammerhead: 4" high, brown with blue suit and laser pistol (Weapon No. 1). 1978	17	23	30
SW-A10 Han Solo: 3¾" high, white shirt with black vest and pants. Equipped with laser pistol (Weapon No. 2). 1977.	38	57	75
SW-A11 Jawa: 2¼" high, brown with brown cloth cape and laser rifle (Weapon No. 4). 1977	38	57	75

	C6	C8	C10

SW-A12 Luke Skywalker: 3¾" high; white shirt with beige pants. Equipped with retractable light-saber. 1977 .... **38 57 75**

SW-A13 Luke Skywalker X-Wing Pilot: 3¼" high, orange with white helmet and laser pistol (Weapon No. 2). 1978 .... **17 23 30**

SW-A14 Power Droid: 2¼" high, blue TV set shape with clicking legs. No accessories. 1978. .... **17 23 30**

SW-A15 Princess Leia Organa: 3½" high, white with removable white cape and laser pistol (Weapon No. 3). 1977 .... **38 57 75**

SW-A16 R5-D4: 2½" high, white trash-can shape with red detail. No Accessories. 1978. .... **17 23 30**

SW-A17 R2-D2: 2¼" high, white with blue detail and chrome-dome head which clicks when turned. No accessories. 1978. .... **38 57 75**

SW-A18 Sand People: 3¾" high, tan with removable tan cape and Gaffi Stick (Weapon No. 5). 1977 ... **38 57 75**

SW-A19A Snaggletooth: 3¾" high, blue with silver boots and laser pistol (Weapon No. 1). Offered only with Cardboard Cantina. 1978 **60 90 120**

SW-A19B Snaggletooth: 2⅞" high, red with laser pistol (Weapon No. 1). 1978 .... **17 23 30**

SW-A20 Stormtrooper: 3¾" high, white with white helmet and laser pistol (Weapon No. 1). 1977 .... **20 26 32**

SW-A21 Walrus Man: 3¾' high, blue with orange suit and green head. Equipped with laser pistol (Weapon No. 1). 1978 .... **17 23 30**

The Empire Strikes Back Action Figures

ESB-A1 AT-AT Commander: 3¾" high, gray with gray hat and laser pistol (Weapon No. 1). 1980 .... **16 22 29**

ESB-A2 AT-AT Driver: 3¾" high, light gray with white helmet and laser pistol (Weapon No. 7). 1980 **16 22 29**

ESB-A3A Bespin Security Guard: 3⅞" high, black man has navy uniform and laser pistol (Weapon No. 1). 1981 .... **23 30 37**

ESB-A3B Bespin Security Guard: 4" high, white man has navy uniform and laser pistol (Weapon No. 1). 1980 .... **16 22 29**

ESB-A4 Bossk: 4" high, yellow with olive head and laser rifle (Weapon No. 6). 1980 .... **16 22 29**

Left to Right: SW-A15, SW-A12, SW-A1, SW-A5

Left to Right: SW-A3, SW-A17, SW-A4, SW-A10

Left to Right: SW-A20, SW-A11, SW-A18, SW-A6

Left to Right: SW-A9, SW-A19B, SW-A19A, SW-A21, SW-A8

Photos courtesy of Whit Alexander and Neal Bates

Left to Right: SW-A7, SW-A16, SW-A14, SW-A2, SW-A13

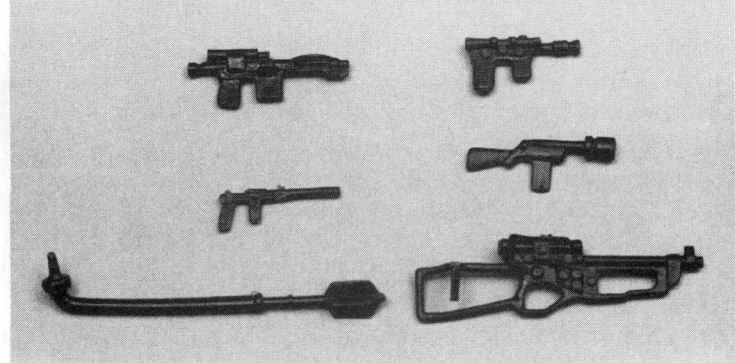

Star Wars Action Figures Weapons and Accessories. Top row, left to right: 1, 2; middle row, 3, 4; bottom row, 5, 6.

Photos courtesy of Whit Alexander and Neal Bates

	C6	C8	C10
ESB-A5 C-3PO: 4" high, metallic gold with removable limbs and papoose. (Acc. No. 13). 1980	23	30	37
ESB-A6 Cloud-Car Pilot: 3¾" high, white with orange and yellow helmet, with laser pistol (Weapon No. 9a) and walkie-talkie (Acc. No. 9b). 1981	20	23	26
ESB-A7 Dengar: 3⅝" high, white and brown with backpack and head wrap. Equipped with laser rifle (Weapon No. 2). 1980	16	22	29
ESB-A8 FX-7: 3⅜" high with head down, silver with 9 movable arms and retractable head. No accessories. 1980	16	22	29
ESB-A9 4-LOM: 3⅝" high, tan with removable tan cape and brown removable backpack. Equipped with laser pistol (Weapon No. 11). 1981	16	22	29
ESB-A10 Han Solo (Bespin outfit): 4" high, navy vest with brown pants and laser pistol (Weapon No. 3). 1980	16	22	29
ESB-A11 Han Solo (Hoth outfit): 4" high, blue fur-lined parka with brown boots and laser pistol (Weapon No. 3). 1980	16	22	29

	C6	C8	C10
ESB-A12 IG-88: 4⅝" high, gray with black bandolier and laser guns (Weapons No. 1 & 16). 1980	16	22	29
ESB-A13 Imperial Commander: 3⅞" high, black hat and laser pistol (Weapon No. 14). 1980	16	22	29
ESB-A14 Imperial Stormtrooper (Hoth Battle Gear): 3⅞" high, white with white veil and removable white skirt. Equipped with laser rifle (Weapon No. 2). 1980	16	22	29
ESB-A15 Imperial Tie-Fighter Pilot: 3¾" high, black with gray boots and gloves and laser pistol (Weapon No. 9a). 1982	16	22	29
ESB-A16 Lando Calrissian: 4" high, light blue with dark blue pants and removable cape. Equipped with laser pistol (Weapon No. 1). 1980	16	22	29
ESB-A17 Lobot: 3⅝" high, gray-brown with yellow sleeves and computerized head band. Equipped with laser pistol (Weapon No. 1). 1980	16	22	29
ESB-A18 Luke Skywalker (Bespin Fatigues): 3⅞" high, tan with brown boots. Equipped with laser pistol and light-saber (Weapons No. 3 & 5). 1980	16	22	29
ESB-A19 Luke Skywalker (Hoth Battle Gear): 3¾" high, white with brown vest and scarf and laser rifle (Weapon No. 17). 1981.	16	22	29
ESB-A20 Princess Leia Organa (Bespin Gown): 3½" high, brick red with pink cape and laser pistol (Weapon No. 4). 1980	16	22	29
ESB-A21 Princess Leia Organa (Hoth Outfit): 3¾" high, white with tan vest and laser pistol (Weapon No. 4). 1980	16	22	29
ESB-A22 R2-D2 (With Sensorscope): 2½" high, white with blue detail. One head panel extends into radar. No accessories. Bottom reads "1977" but new head was added circa 1980	16	22	29
ESB-A23 Rebel Commander: 3⅞" high, white with brown scarf and laser rifle (Weapon No. 7). 1980 .	16	22	29
ESB-A24 Rebel Soldier: 3⅞" high, white with brown vest and white hat. Equipped with laser pistol (Weapon No. 1). 1980	16	22	29
ESB-A25 2-1B: 3¾" high, blue with transparent middle and gas mask. Has medical stick (Acc. No. 12). 1980	16	22	29

329

	C6	C8	C10
ESB-A26 Ugnaught: 2¾" high, gray with blue apron and tool-purse (Acc. No. 8). 1980	16	22	29
ESB-A27 Yoda: 2" high, brown with light green head, has cloth tan robe, removable belt, orange snake and brown stick (Acc. Nos. 10a & 10b). 1980	18	24	31
ESB-A28 Zuckuss: 3¾" high, gray with blue fly-eyes and laser rifle (Weapon No. 15), 1982	16	22	29

Left to Right: ESB-A19, ESB-A11, ESB-A23, ESB-A24

Left to Right: ESB-A21   ESB-A10   ESB-A16   ESB-A5

Left to Right: ESB-A25, ESB-A21, ESB-A8

Left to Right: ESB-A18, ESB-A22, ESB-A27

Left to Right: ESB-A7, ESB-A28, ESB-A9, ESB-A12, ESB-A4

Left to Right: ESB-A14, ESB-A2, ESB-A15, ESB-A13, ESB-A1

Left to Right: ESB-A17, ESB-A6, ESB-A3B, ESB-A26, ESB-A3A

Photos courtesy of Whit Alexander and Neal Bates

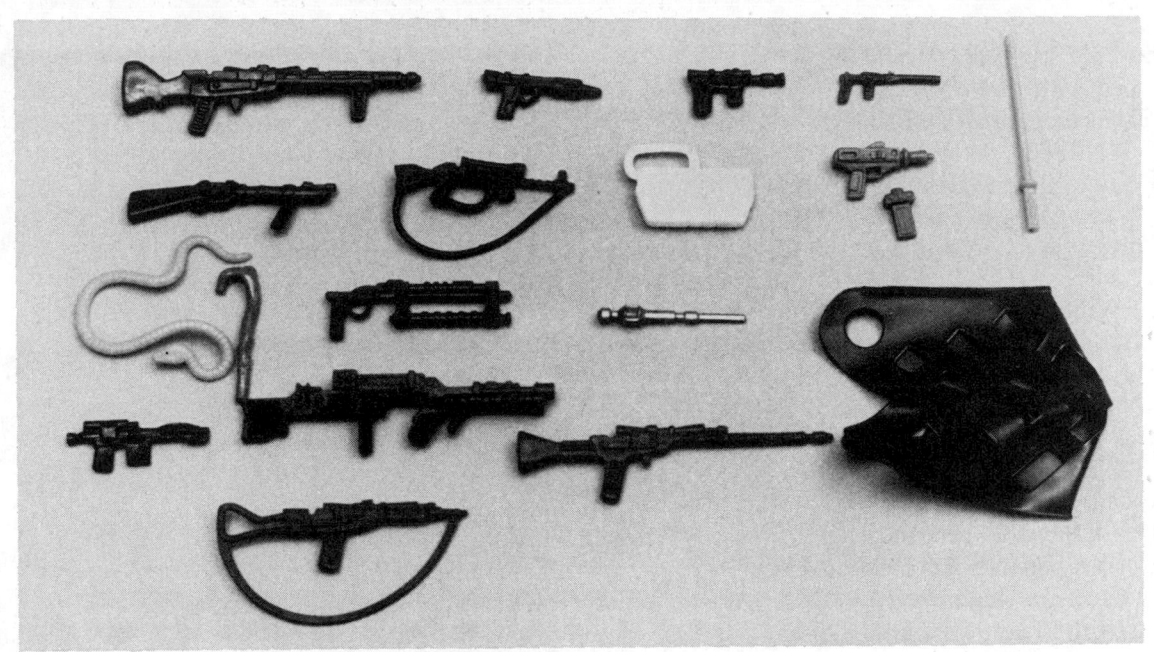

The Empire Strikes Back Action Figures Weapons and Accessories. Top row, left to right: 2, 1, 3, 4, 5. Second row: 6, 7, 8, 9a, 9b. Third row: 10a, 10b, 11, 12 13. Fourth row: 14, 15, 16. Bottom: 17.

Photos courtesy of Whit Alexander and Neal Bates

THE RETURN OF THE JEDI ACTION FIGURES

	C6	C8	C10
RJ-A1 Admiral Ackbar: 3⅞" high, white with tan vest and rust "lobster" head, black stick (Acc. No. 1). 1983	10	14	18
RJ-A2 AT-ST Driver: 3⅞" high, light gray with dark gray helmet and laser pistol (Weapon No. 2). 1984	10	14	18
RJ-A3 B-Wing Pilot: 3⅞" high, red with silver and brown helmet and laser pistol (Weapon No. 2). 1984	10	14	18
RJ-A4 Bib Fortuna: 4⅛" high, blue with removable beige cape and removable gray chestplate. Has wrap-around horn and staff (Acc. No. 6). 1983	10	14	18
RJ-A5 Biker Scout: 4" high, black with white armor and laser pistol (Weapon No. 4). 1983	10	14	18
RJ-A6 Boushh: 3⅝" high, beige and brown with silver armor. Has silver and orange removable helmet and laser stick. (Weapon No. 7). 1983	11	15	19
RJ-A7 Chief Chirpa: 3" high with removable brown hood and staff (Acc. No. 21). 1983	11	15	19
RJ-A8 8D8: White droid with silver and brown detail. No accessories. 1983	10	14	18

	C6	C8	C10
RJ-A9 Emperor's Royal Guard: Brick red and crimson cape and tunic with staff (Weapon No. 8). 1983 .	10	14	18
RJ-A10 Gamorrean Guard: 3⅞" high, olive with brown garment and battle-axe (Weapon No. 3). 1983 . . .	10	14	18
RJ-A11 General Madine: 4" high, light gray with black boots and gloves and blue sleeves and white wand (Acc. No. 16). 1983	10	14	18
RJ-A12 Han Solo (Trench Coat): 4" high, dark gray pants with light gray shirt and removable camouflage cape and laser pistol (Weapon No. 22). 1984	10	14	18
RJ-A13A Klaatu: 4" high, dark green with gray shirt and silver helmet. Has animal pelt skirt and skiff stick (Weapon No. 9). 1983	10	14	18
RJ-A13B Klaatu (Skiff Guard Outfit): 3⅞" high, dark green with off white garment and brown helmet with laser stick (Weapon No. 10). 1983	10	14	18
RJ-A14 Lando Calrissian (Skiff Guard Disguise): 3⅞" high, brown vest with armor. Has removable brown helmet and skiff stick (Weapon No. 9). 1982	11	15	19
RJ-A15 Luke Skywalker (Jedi Knight Outfit): 3⅞" high, black with removable olive cape. Has laser pistol and light-saber (Weapons No. 5a & 5b) 1983	11	15	19

331

	C6	C8	C10
RJ-A16 Logray: 3⅝" high, cream and brown striped with removable black hood, medicine bag and staff (Acc. No. 18). 1983	11	15	19
RJ-A17 Nein Nunb: 3⅞" high, red with navy vest, dark gray helmet and laser pistol (Weapon No. 17). 1983	10	14	18
RJ-A18 Nikto: White shirt with ice-blue vest and gray pants. Has brown head wrap and laser stick (Weapon No. 11). 1983	10	14	18
RJ-A19 Princess Leia Organa (Combat Poncho): 3⅝" high, gray with removable helmet and combat poncho. Has removable belt and laser pistol (Weapon No. 2). 1984	11	15	19
RJ-A20 Prune Face: 3⅞" high, lime green pants with cream shirt and removable tan cape. Has eyepatch and laser rifle (Weapon No. 15). 1984	10	14	18
RJ-A21 Rankor Keeper: 4" high, olive pants with no shirt. Has removable hood and stick (Acc. No. 23). 1984	11	15	19
RJ-A22 Rebel Commando: 4" high, olive uniform with green helmet, brown backpack and laser rifle (Weapon No. 24). 1983	10	14	18
RJ-A23 Ree-Yees: 3⅝" high, peach with three eyes and brick red garment and laser rifle (Weapon No. 13). 1983	10	14	18
RJ-A24 Squid Head: 4" high, white with white skirt, has removable belt and olive cape; head has 4 tentacles, has laser pistol (Weapon No. 14). 1983	10	14	18
RJ-A25 Teebo: 3⅞" high, light and dark gray striped. Has removable hood and horn on sling. Also has axe (Acc. No. 19). 1984	11	15	19
RJ-A26 The Emperor: 4" high, dark gray with staff (Acc. No. 12). 1984	10	14	18
RJ-A27 Weequay: 3⅞" high, ice blue shirt with beige pants and brown vest, gray ponytail and skiff stick (Weapon No. 9). 1983	10	14	18
RJ-A28 Wickett W. Warrick: 2" high, brown with creme belly, removable hood and spear (Weapon No. 20). 1984	11	15	19

Left to Right: FJ-A28, RJ-A7, RJ-A15, RJ-A25

Left to Right: RJ-A13A, RJ-A13B, RJ-A8, RJ-A18

Left to Right: RJ-A3, RJ-A11, RJ-A1, RJ-A17

Left to Right: RJ-A5, RJ-A22, RJ-A19

Photos courtesy of Whit Alexander and Neal Bates

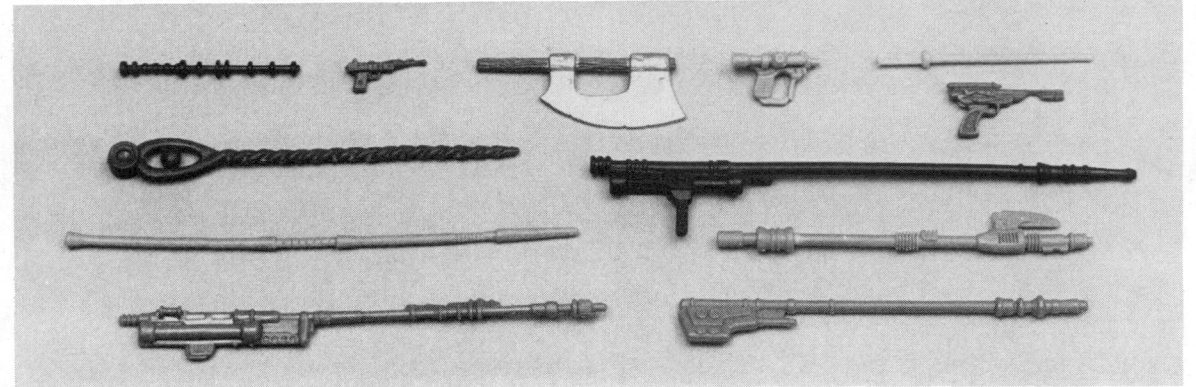

The Return of the Jedi Action Figures Weapons and Accessories. Top row, left to right: 1, 2, 3, 4, 5a, 5b. Second row: 6, 7. Third row, 8, 9. Bottom row: 10, 11.

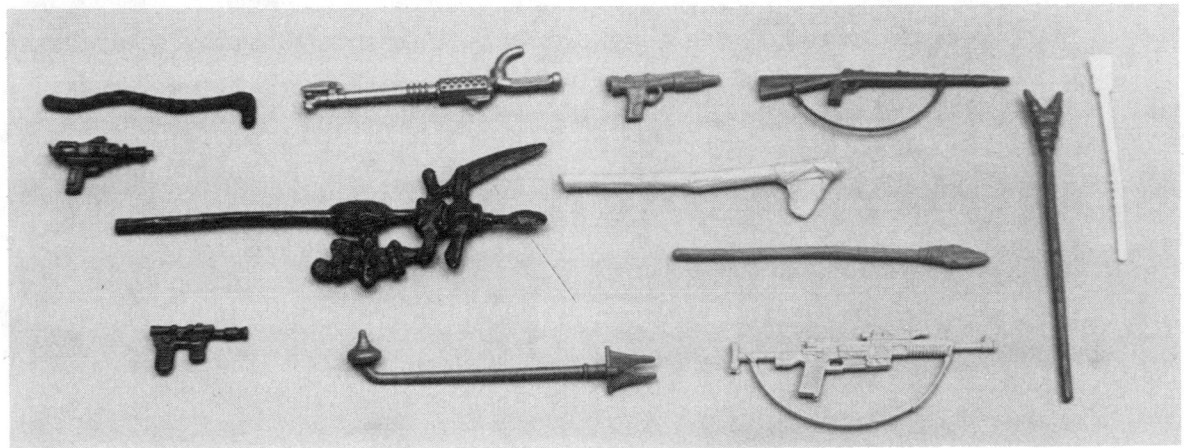

Top row, left to right: 12, 13, 14, 15. Second row, 17, 18, 19, 20, 21, 16. Bottom row: 22, 23, 24.

Photos courtesy of Whit Alexander and Neal Bates

VEHICLES

These vehicles are intended for use with the action figures and many are battery operated (B/O).

STAR WARS VEHICLES (SW-V)

	C6	C8	C10
SW-V1 Darth Vader Tie-Fighter (B/O), 9¾" long x 11¾" wide, dark gray with spherical cockpit and removable wing panels, red laser lights up and emits a whirring sound. 1978	60	90	120
SW-V2 Imperial troop Transport: (B/O), 10¼" long x 5¼" wide, gray with red stripes, has rear and 6 side compartments, dual cockpit and rotating laser cannons and radar, 2 prisoner holsters, 6 red buttons play a variety of recordings	80	120	160
SW-V3 Jawa Sandcrawler: 14½" long x 5⅝" wide, rust brown with wireless remote control. 1979	100	150	200

SW-V6, Tie-Fighter. Figure not included.

SW-V7, X-Wing Fighter. Figure not included.

SW-V1, Darth Vader Tie-Fighter. Figure not included.

SW-V4, Landspeeder. Figure not included.

SW-V2, Imperial Troop Transport. Figures not included.

SW-V5 Millenium Falcon. Figures not included.

Photos courtesy of Whit Alexander and Neal Bates

	C6	C8	C10
SW-V4 Landspeeder: 9½" long x 6" wide, brown with chrome grills, 3 jets and windshield, wheels can be lowered by shifter in cockpit. 1978	20	30	40

	C6	C8	C10
SW-V5 Millenium Falcon: (B/O) 20½" long x 16½" wide, off-white with gray laser cannon. Main compartment has chessboard, laser ball, floor panel and revolving laser cannon. Emits whirring sound when side button is pressed. 1979	75	100	125

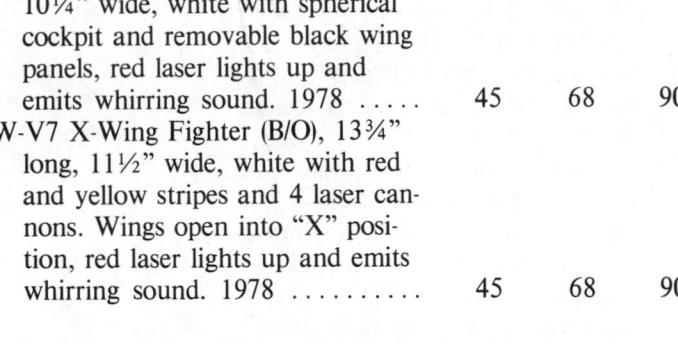
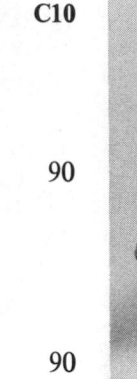

	C6	C8	C10
SW-V6 Tie Fighter (B/O) 7⅛" long, 10¼" wide, white with spherical cockpit and removable black wing panels, red laser lights up and emits whirring sound. 1978	45	68	90
SW-V7 X-Wing Fighter (B/O), 13¾" long, 11½" wide, white with red and yellow stripes and 4 laser cannons. Wings open into "X" position, red laser lights up and emits whirring sound. 1978	45	68	90

ESB-V7, Twin-Pod Cloud Car. Figure not included.

THE EMPIRE STRIKES BACK VEHICLES (ESB-V)

	C6	C8	C10
ESB-V1 AT-AT: (B/O), 17½" high, 22" long, light gray with black detail, 4 moveable legs and swiveling cockpit, 2 laser cannons light up and pulsate. 1981	75	100	125
ESB-V2 AT-ST (Scout Walker): 11¼" high, light gray, button on back moves legs. 1982	20	30	40
ESB-V3 Imperial Star Destroyer, swiveling laser cannon on bow and meditation chamber. 1981	30	40	50
ESB-V4A MCL-3: light gray with tank treads and dome top. 1981	15	20	25
ESB-V4B MTV-7: light gray with spring-loaded steamroller legs. 1981	15	20	25
ESB-V5 Slave 1: 15" long, 12¾" wide, gray with blue windshield, 2 swiveling wing flaps, black cargo door, gray side door, revolving laser cannons on tail. Han Solo in Carbonite. 1981	30	40	50
ESB-V6 Snowspeeder (B/O) 12¼" long, 12¾" wide, light gray with 2 light up laser cannons, rear harpoon gun with harpoon on string. 1980	40	60	80
ESB-V7 Twin-Pod Cloud Car: 10½" wide, 8¾" long, rust orange with dual pod cockpit. 1980	15	25	35

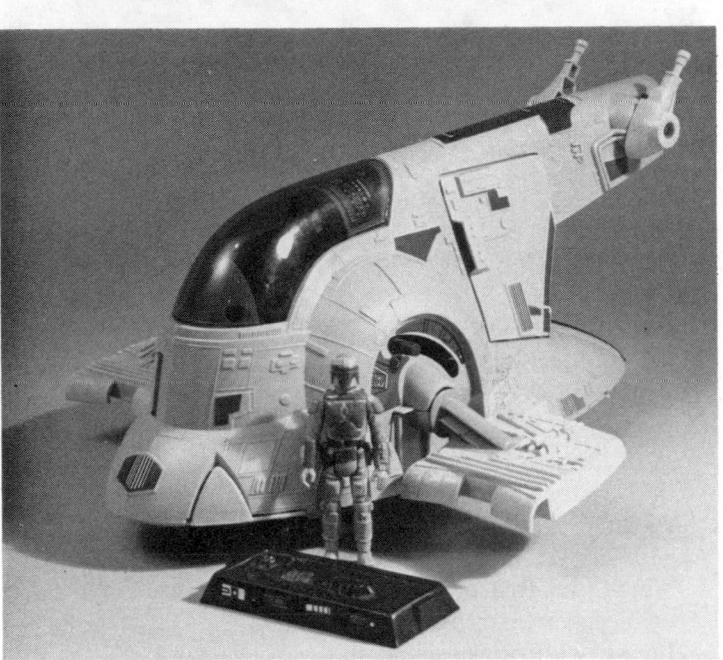

ESB-V5, Slave-1. Boba Fett not included.

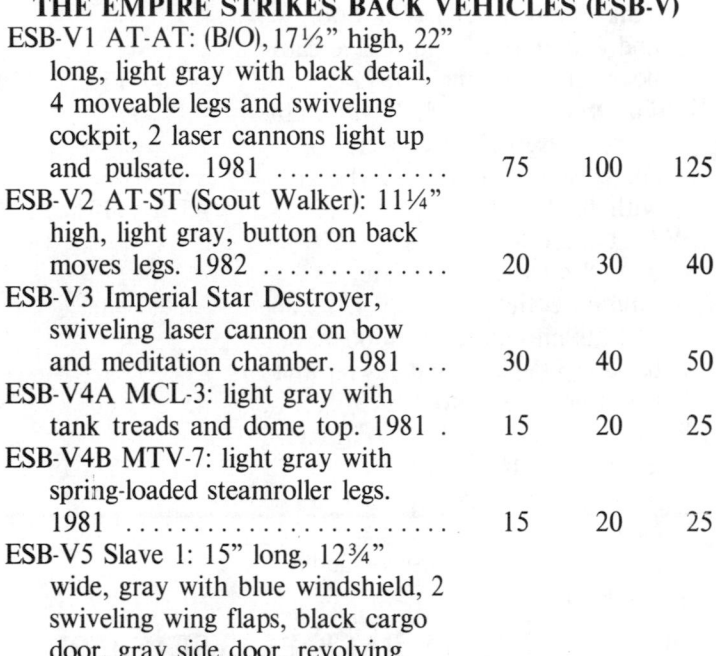

ESB-V6, Snowspeeder. Figure not included.

ESB-V2, AT-ST (Scout Walker). Figures not included.

ESB-P9, Taun-Taun. Figure not included.

Photos courtesy of Whit Alexander and Neal Bates

THE RETURN OF THE JEDI VEHICLES (RJ-V)

	C6	C8	C10
RJ-V1 B-Wing Fighter: light gray, cockpit on right side with fin-wing extending to the left. Circa 1985 .	35	45	55
RJ-V2 Ewok Combat Glider: brown with harness for one action figure and 2 stone-bombs. Circa 1984 ..	10	15	20
RJ-V3 Imperial Shuttle: light gray, stationary center fin and side wings that fold up. Circa 1984 ..	60	80	100
RJ-V4 Speeder Bike: 8¾" long, light brown with black engine and detail. Bike "explodes" when pack is pressed. 1983	10	15	20
RJ-V5 Y-Wing Fighter: light gray with twin hollow engines, 3 retractable landing skids. Circa 1984....	35	45	55

STAR WARS PLAYSETS (SW-P)

	C6	C8	C10
SW-P1 Action Figure Display Stand: 20" long, 5½" wide, gray base with moving discs for 12 action figures. Front has decal with the names of the 12 original action figures. Cardboard backdrop depicts a spaceship dogfight. Available through special mail order only. 1978	70	80	90
SW-P2 Cardboard Cantina: 18" long, 7" high, tan base has 11 action figure pegs. Backdrop has scene from Mos Eiseley city street. Available only with Cantina figure set which included SW-A8, SW-A9, SW-A19A and SW-A21. 1978	40	50	60
SW-P3 Collector's Case: 2 trays hold a total of 24 action figures. Case depicts scenes from Star Wars. ..	20	25	30

	C6	C8	C10
SW-P4 Creature Cantina; 13¾" long, 7¾" wide, tan-orange base has bar and table, 2 action levers and floor button which opens the doors. Also has cardboard backdrop depicting cantina scene. 1979	45	60	75
SW-P5 Death Star Space Station: 22¼" high, gray and black, 3 floors and basement trash compactor. Compactor has foam trash and green monster. Floors have drawbridge, grappling hook swing, "exploding" laser cannon and catwalk. Main tower has elevator and 2nd and 3rd floors have cardboard surface panels. 1977	100	150	200
SW-P6 Droid Factory: 13" x 11", tan-orange base holds 38 interchangeable droid parts and crane with hook. 1979	45	75	125
SW-P7 Land of the Jawas: 13½" long, 8¼" wide. Tan base has sand cave and action lever. Escape pod fits into crater. Cardboard backdrop depicts sandcrawler and has moving elevator. 1979	45	60	75
SW-P8 Patrol Dewback: 10½" long, green and white lizard has 4 posable limbs and trap door in back. Tail and head move together. Also has brown saddle and harness. 1979	20	30	40

EMPIRE STRIKES BACK PLAYSETS (ESB-P)

	C6	C8	C10
ESB-P1 Cardboard Bespin Set: 9" high, 11¾" wide, cardboard base has 6 action figure pegs. Backdrop depicts Cloud City scene and has protruding Carbonite Chamber. Available only with action figures ESB-A7, ESB-A10, ESB-A17 and ESB-A26. 1980	35	45	55
ESB-P2 Collector's Case: 2 trays hold a total of 24 action figures. Case depicts scenes from The Empire Strikes Back	18	23	28
ESB-P3 Dagobah Playset: gray with brown tree stump, 3 action levers, mud puddle and 2 storage containers. 1981	35	45	55
ESB-P4 Darth Vader Collector Case: 14½" high, 16" wide, black with room for 31 action figures and accessories. Circa 1980	48	72	96
ESB-P5 Hoth Ice Planet: 13½" long, 8¼" wide, white base has snow cave and action lever. Tank-radar sits in crater. Cardboard backdrop depicts AT-AT with moving elevator. 1981	35	50	65

	C6	C8	C10
ESB-P6 Hoth Wampa: 6" high, white with 4 posable limbs. Circa 1981.	18	28	38
ESB-P7 Imperial Attack Base: 17¼" long, 10" wide, white with revolving laser cannon and gray control room, 3 action levers make 2 part snowbridge fall, control room "explode" and action figure fall	35	45	55
ESB-P8 Probot and Turret: 15½" long, 9¼" wide, white base has action lever and post for gray probot. Turret has door and revolving laser platform. 1979	30	40	50
ESB-P9 Taun-Taun: 9¾" from head to tail, gray and white with brown horns, trap door in back and 4 posable limbs, brown saddle and harness. Circa 1980	18	28	38

RETURN OF THE JEDI PLAYSETS (RJ-P)

	C6	C8	C10
RJ-P1 C-3PO Collector Case: metallic gold with room for 31 action figures and accessories. Circa 1983	35	45	55
RJ-P2 Chewbacca Bandolier Strap: black, holds 10 action figures and accessories. Circa 1983	20	25	30
RJ-P3 Ewok Assault Catapult: brown logs with rotating winch and 2 gray boulders. Circa 1983	10	15	20
RJ-P4 Jabba the Hutt Playset: 11" long, 5¼" wide, grayish-brown platform with 2 doors, with Jabba, Salacious Crumb and a long-armed green monster. 1983	35	45	55
RJ-P5 Land of the Ewoks: 22" high, 16" long, tan platform supported by 3 trees, spit over the firering, stool, moving elevator, net and litter for carrying action figures. 1983	45	55	65
RJ-P6 Rancor Monster: 10" high, tan with 4 posable limbs. 1983	15	17	20
RJ-P7 The Jabba The Hutt Dungeon: 13" x 11", gray base, crane with hood and branding iron. Complete with action figures RJ-A13B, RJ-A18 and RJ-A8. 1983	25	30	35
RJ-P8 Sy Snootles and the Max Rebo Band: complete with blue keyboardist and keyboard, spotted singer and microphone, pink clarinet player and microphone. Circa 1983	25	30	35

LARGE FIGURES AND DOLLS

	C6	C8	C10
Ben (Obi-Wan) Knobi, 12" high, light-saber, removable cape	30	40	60
Boba Fett, 13¼" high, laser rifle, molded backpack	60	90	120
C-3PO, 12" high	25	38	50
Chewbacca, 18" high, stuffed	25	38	50
Chewbacca, 15" high, with laser crossbow	20	30	40
Chewbacca, 8" high, furry	18	27	35
Darth Vader, 15" high, light-saber and removable cape	38	57	75
Han Solo, 12" high, laser rifle	45	67	90
IG-88, 15" high, laser weapons	100	150	200
Jawa, 8¼" high, hooded cape and laser rifle	20	30	40
Luke Skywalker, 11¾" high, lever-like arm and grappling hook	60	90	120
Princess Leia Organa, 11½" high, combable hair	60	90	120
R2-D2, 7½" high, head clicks when turned	25	38	50
R2-D2, radio controlled	33	49	65
Stormtrooper, 12" high, has laser rifle	20	30	40
Yoda, large	15	23	30

DIE CAST VEHICLES

	C6	C8	C10
Kenner - Series 1, No. 38100, includes Darth Vader Tie Fighter, X-Wing Fighter, Land Speeder, Tie Fighter, each worth $75 in mint .	175.00	262.50	350.00
Kenner - Series II No. 39200, includes Millenium Falcon, Darth Vader's Star Ship Destroyer, Princess Leia's Command Ship, Tie Bomber, Y-Wing Fighter, prices volatile ($25-150)	No Price Found		
Kenner Series III, No. 39650, contains Snow Speeder, Slave I space ship, Twin-Pod Cloud Car, each worth $40 in mint	No Price Found		

CONDITION CODE:
C5 – Good, wear evident overall, shows that has been played with
C6 – Fine, shows some wear in spots, but taken care of
C7 – Very Fine, minor wear overall, very clean
C8 – Excellent, minor wear on edges only
C9 – Near Mint, no noticeable flaws, close inspection may show minute marks
C10 – Mint (like new)
　　Note: Mint in Box does command higher price

LJN "V" Action Figures (TV series),	C6	C8	C10
each	9.00	13.50	18.00
Marx Johnny Apollo Astronaut, 10" high	20	30	40
Marx Sgt. Stormy 4-Figure Deluxe Kit, 12" high, large assortment of equipment	250	375	500
Marx Stoney Smith, 12" high (new in 1964)	25.00	37.50	50.00

MATTEL

Mattel was founded in 1945 by Harold Mattson and Ruth and Elliot Handler (the "Matt" in Mattson and "El" in Elliott formed the firm's name). The business, created to make picture frames, began in a Los Angeles garage, with Mattson bowing out early due to poor health. Toys were made almost from the beginning, furniture fashioned from the plastic and wood scraps left over from the frames. Its most famous toy is the Barbie doll.

	C6	C8	C10
Major Matt Mason, figure only with helmet	12.50	18.75	25.00
Major Matt Mason Flight No. 6300, new in 1967, 6" high. Contains figure, Space Sled with control column, helmet, Jet Propulsion Pak .	62.50	93.75	125.00
Moon Suit Pak No. 6301, contains Moon Suit, air pump, 2-piece radiation detector, interior control console, screwdriver, rock hammer	42.50	63.75	85.00

MATTEL Major Matt Mason in flexible space suit with jet propulsion pack and space sled

MATTEL Major Matt Mason with moon suit

	C6	C8	C10
Major Matt Mason with Moon Suit No. 6303, contains figure, plastic Moon Suit, attachable air pump, two-piece Radiation Detector, wrench, screw driver, rock hammer, space labels, helmet, Space Sled, Jet Propulsion Pak	75.00	112.50	150.00
Space Crawler No. 6304	25.00	37.50	50.00
Rocket Launch Pak No. 6305, contains 2-piece remote control rocket launcher, with control column, cap-firing rocket, Roto-Jet Gun, pair of Walkie-Talkies, firing string, safe knife, sheath, belt, space labels	42.50	63.75	85.00
Space Probe Pak No. 6307, contains adjustable remote control launcher, with control console, 2 Space Probes, Chemical Decontamination Gun, chemical tank, flare signal gun, binoculars, space labels	No Price Found		
Space Station No. 6308, approx. 2 feet high	50	75	100
Space Station Deluxe Action Set No. 6310, contains Space Crawler, Space Station, Matt Mason figure, Space Sled, Jet Propulsion Pak, etc.	75.00	112.50	150.00
Space Crawler Action Set No. 6311, includes Matt Mason, Space Crawler, Space Sled, Jet Propulsion Pak, control column	No Price Found		
Sgt. Storm Flight Set No. 6317	20	30	40
Major Matt Mason No. 6318, includes figure, Lunar Tractor	12.50	18.75	25.00
Sgt. Storm No. 6319 with Lunar Trac (tractor)	25.00	37.50	50.00
Space Shelter Pak No. 6321, contains inflatable space tent with air pump, map case, compass	42.50	63.75	85.00
Capt. Lazer No. 6330, new in 1968 ("Major Matt Mason's Friend From Outer Space")	50	75	100
Callisto No. 6331, contains Callisto (alien), bellows-action Space Sensor	20	30	40
Jeff Long No. 6332, "Space Scientist-Rocketry" figure with helmet	20	30	40
Doug Davis No. 6333 "Space Scientist-Radiologist" figure with helmet	20	30	40
Space Mission Team No. 6337, gift set of Matt, Jeff, Callisto, Doug, Cat Trak, Space Sled, Space Sensor	125.00	187.50	250.00
Uni-Tred and Space Bubble No. 6339, Uni-Tred $115 in mint, Space Bubble $75 in mint	110	165	220
Gamma-Ray Gard No. 6342, contains automatic launch swivels	42.50	63.75	85.00

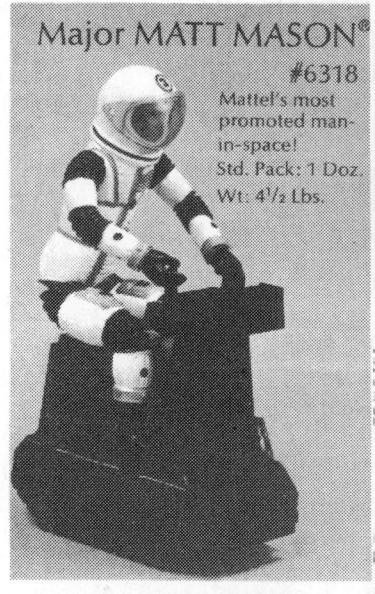

Major MATT MASON® #6318

Mattel's most promoted man-in-space!
Std. Pack: 1 Doz.
Wt: 4½ Lbs.

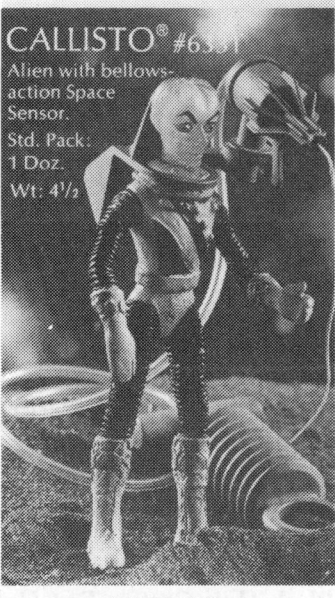

CALLISTO® #6331

Alien with bellows-action Space Sensor.
Std. Pack: 1 Doz.
Wt: 4½

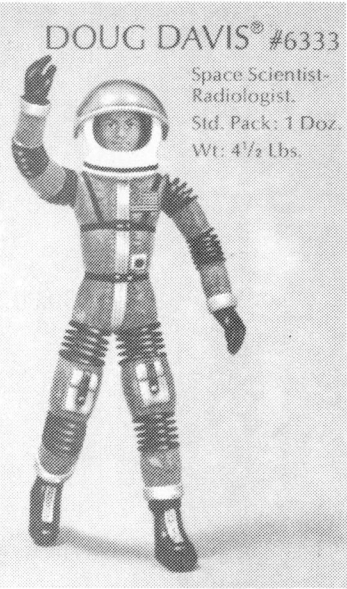

DOUG DAVIS® #6333

Space Scientist-Radiologist.
Std. Pack: 1 Doz.
Wt: 4½ Lbs.

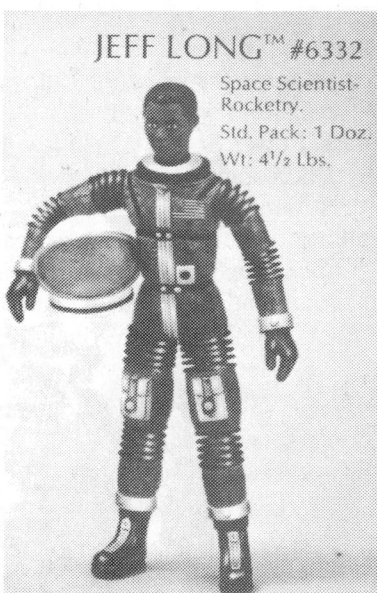

JEFF LONG™ #6332

Space Scientist-Rocketry.
Std. Pack: 1 Doz.
Wt: 4½ Lbs.

Major Mat Mason 6318   Callisto 6331   Doug Davis 6333   Jeff Long 6332

Reentry Glider 6360

Space Crawler 6304

#6339

Tinted SPACE BUBBLE rolls a full 360° behind powerful
UNI-TRED. Gyro-Seat Control Center always remains upright!
Dual Action Tow Yoke links the two rigs together.
2 "D" batteries and astronauts not included.
Std. Pack: ½ Doz.   Wt: 12 Lbs.

	C6	C8	C10
Supernaut Power-Limbs No. 6343, contains Robot scoop, alligator-clip arms and space stilts	42.50	63.75	85.00
Space Power Suit No. 6344, with Telescoping Power Claw and Hammer	42.50	63.75	85.00
Talking Major Matt Mason No. 6362, new in 1970, with voice command flight pak, helmet	65.00	93.75	130.00

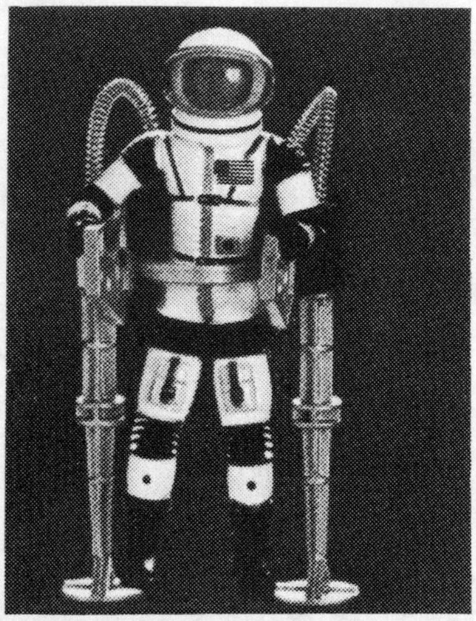

Famous spaceman with exclusive Voice Command Flight Pak. Says five things while "Flying on space cord." Removable VCF Pak may be used with all other Mattel astronauts as well.

	C6	C8	C10
Talking Matt Mason with XRG-1 Reentry Glider No. 6378 with Voice Command Pak	110	165	220
Major Matt Mason Super Power Equipment Set No. 6379 contains Matt Mason, Lunar Track, Power Limbs, Space Power Suit	62.50	93.75	125.00
Talking Space Station (number not known)	90	135	180
XRG-1 Reentry Glider No. 6360	40	60	80
End Major Matt Mason			
Captain Arak (Flash Gordon), 3¾", 1979	12.50	18.75	25.00
Dr. Zarkov (Flash Gordon), 3¾", 1979	7.50	11.25	15.00
Flash Gordon, 3¾", 1979	7.50	11.25	15.00
Lizard Woman (Flash Gordon), 3¾", 1979	7.50	11.25	15.00
Ming (Flash Gordon), 3¾", 1979	7.50	11.25	15.00
Ming's Space Shuttle w/Cannon No. 1, 3¾" range, 1979 (Flash Gordon)	20	30	40
Battlestar Galactica figures, all 3¾"			
Commander Adams	5.00	7.50	10.00
Daggit	5.00	7.50	10.00
Imperious Leader	5.00	7.50	10.00
Lt. Starbuck	5.00	7.50	10.00
Ovion	5.00	7.50	10.00
Cylon (Battlestar Gallactica), 12" high, 1978, lights up, battery-operated	25.00	37.50	50.00

	C6	C8	C10
Colonial Warrior (Battlestar Gallactica), 12" high, 1978, lights up, battery-operated	25.00	37.50	50.00
Space 1999, Bergman, 8" high	15.00	22.50	30.00
Space 1999, Russell 8" high	15.00	22.50	30.00
End MATTEL			

MEGO

	C6	C8	C10
Action Jackson, 8" high	4.50	6.75	9.00
Action Jackson Wild Mustang, radio controlled, 8" range	17.50	26.25	35.00
Black Hole Cygnus Security Robot, 3¾", 1979 (very rare)	25.00	37.50	50.00
Black Hole Harry Booth, 1979, 3¾"	2.50	3.75	5.00
Black Hole Dr. Alex Durant, 12" high, 1979	20	30	40
Black Hole Dr. Durant, 3¾", 1979	2.50	3.75	5.00
Black Hole Captain Dan Holland, 12", 1979	15.00	22.50	30.00
Black Hole Captain Dan Holland, 3¾", 1979	3.00	4.50	6.00
Black Hole Maximillian, 3¾", 1979	22.50	33.75	45.00
Black Hole Dr. Kate McRae, 3¾", 1979	3.00	4.50	6.00
Black Hole Charles Pizer, 12", 1979	15.00	22.50	30.00
Black Hole Charles Pizer, 3¾", 1979	3.00	4.50	6.00
Black Hole Dr. Hans Reinhardt, 12", 1979	15.00	22.50	30.00
Black Hole Dr. Hans Reinhardt, 3¾", 1979	3.00	4.50	6.00
Buck Rogers Ardella, 3¾", 1979	4	6	8
Buck Rogers, 12" range, 1979	12.50	18.75	25.00
Buck Rogers, 3¾", 1979	10	15	20
Buck Rogers Dr. Huer, 12", 1979	16	24	32
Buck Rogers Dr. Huer, 3⅜", 1979	4	6	8
Buck Rogers Draco, 12", 1979	12.50	18.75	25.00
Buck Rogers Draco, 3¾", 1979	4	6	8
Buck Rogers Draconian Guard, 3¾", 1979	6	9	12
Buck Rogers Killer Kane, 12"	12.50	18.75	25.00
Buck Rogers Killer Kane, 3¾"	4	6	8
Buck Rogers Tigerman, 1979, 3¾"	6	9	12
Buck Rogers Twiki, 7" high, 1979	20	30	40
Buck Rogers Twiki, 3¾" high	15.00	22.50	30.00
Buck Rogers Wilma Deering, 3¾", 1979	12.50	18.75	25.00
Buck Rogers Star Fighter Command Center No. 1, 1979, for 3¾" figures	20	30	40
Flash Gordon Dale Arden, 9"	30	45	60
Flash Gordon, 9"	30	45	60
Flash Gordon Ming, 9"	25.00	37.50	50.00
Flash Gordon Zarkov, 9"	25.00	37.50	50.00
One Million B.C. (1970s), 6" to 8"			
Grok (caveman), 8"	30	45	60
Orm (caveman), 8"	30	45	60
Trag (caveman), 8"	32	48	64

Planet of the Apes	C6	C8	C10
Astronaut, 8" high	5.00	7.50	10.00
Dr. Zaius, 8" high, 1974-76	12.00	18.00	24.00
Soldier Ape, 8" high, 1974-76	12.50	18.75	25.00
Soldier Ape, 5" high, 1976	3.00	4.50	6.00
Forbidden Zone Trap, 8" range, 1974-75	17.00	25.50	34.00
Throne With Trap, 8" range, 1974-75	12.50	18.75	25.00
Village for 8" figures	21.00	31.50	42.00

Star Trek	C6	C8	C10
Arcturian, 12" range, 1979	20	30	40
Captain Kirk, 12" range, 1979	20	30	40
Captain Kirk, 8" range, 1976	20	30	40
Captain Kirk, 3¾"	2.50	3.75	5.00
Cheron, 8", 1974-76	25.00	37.50	50.00
Decker, 12"	40	60	80
Gorn, 8", 1974-76	40	60	80
Ilia, 12" range, 1979	20	30	40
Ilia, 3¾"	3.50	5.25	7.00
Klingon, 8"	20	30	40
McCoy, 12"	17.50	26.25	35.00
McCoy, 8", 1974-76	17.50	26.25	35.00
Neptunian, 8", 1974-76	20	30	40
Scotty, 8", 1974-76	32.50	48.75	65.00
Scotty, 3¾"	3.50	5.25	7.00
Spock, 12" range, 1979	20	30	40
Spock, 8" range, 1976	20	30	40
Uhura, 8", 1974-76	25.00	37.50	50.00
Command Communications Console, 1976	30	45	60

MEGO Starsky & Hutch	C6	C8	C10
Chopper, 8", 1967	8	12	16
Dobey, 8", 1967	8	12	16
Huggy Bear, 8", 1967	8	12	16
Hutch	5.00	7.50	10.00
Starsky	5.00	7.50	10.00

MEGO Syperheroes and Villains	C6	C8	C10
Aqualad (Teen Titans)	50	75	100
Aquaman, 8", 1971	12.50	18.75	25.00
Bat Girl (World's Greatest Super Gals), 1974-79, 8" range	25.00	37.50	50.00
Batman, 1979, 12"	14	21	28
Batman, 8", 1974-79	12.50	18.75	25.00
Batman, 3½", 1975	12.50	18.75	25.00
Batmobile for 8" figures, 1974	12.50	18.75	25.00
Captain America, 12"	9.00	13.50	18.00
Captain America, 12", with flyaway action	20	30	40
Captain America, 8", 1971	12.50	18.75	25.00
Captain Marvel, 8", 1971	12.50	18.75	25.00
Catwoman, 8"	19.00	27.50	38.00
Conan, 8"	No Price Found		
General Zod (Superman), 3¾", 1979 .	7.50	11.25	15.00
Green Arrow, 8"	10	15	20
Green Arrow Car	42.50	63.75	85.00
Green Goblin, 8", 1974-79 (World's Greatest Arch Enemies)	37.50	56.25	75.00

	C6	C8	C10
Hulk, 12", flyaway action, 1978	12.50	18.75	25.00
Hulk, 8",, 1979 (World's Greatest Superheroes)	8	12	16
Hulk, 3¾" pocket hero	8	12	16
Hulk, 3½", 1975	12.50	18.75	25.00
Human Torch, 8"	10	15	20
Invisible Girl, 8"	11.00	16.50	22.00
Iron Man, 8"	20	30	40
Isis, 8", 1976	15.00	22.50	30.00
Joker, 8", 1974-79	21.00	31.50	42.00
Joker, 3½", 1975	15.00	22.50	30.00
Jor-El (Superman), 3¾", 1979	7.50	11.25	15.00
Kid Flash, 8"	12.50	18.75	25.00
Lizard Man, 8", 1974-79 (World's Greatest Arch Enemies)	15.00	22.50	30.00
Mr. Fantastic, 8"	7.50	11.25	15.00
Mr. Mxyzptlk, (World's Greatest Arch Enemies), 8", 1974-79, smirking face (first version)	15.00	22.50	30.00
Same as above, second version (open mouth)	15.00	22.50	30.00
Penguin, 8", 1974-79	15.00	22.50	30.00
Robin, 8" range, 1974-79	20	30	40
Robin, 3¾", 1979	7.50	11.25	15.00
Spidercar for 3¾" figures	11.00	16.50	22.00
Spiderman, 12", 1977-78	50	75	100
Spiderman, 8", 1979	12.50	18.75	25.00
Spiderman, 3¾", 1975	15.00	22.50	30.00
Supergirl, 8", 1974-79	24	36	48
Superman, 8", 1974-79	15.00	22.50	30.00
Superman, 3¾", 1979	7.50	11.25	15.00
Superman, 3½", 1975	12.50	18.75	25.00
Thing, 8", 1974-79	25.00	37.50	50.00
Thor, 8"	20	30	40
Wonder Woman, 12", 1976, first issue (separate cloth uniform), flyaway action	40	60	80
Wonder Woman, 12", 2nd issue (cloth pants, painted on uniform)	16	24	32
Wonder Woman, 3½", 1975	17.50	26.25	35.00
Wondergirl (Teen Titans)	50	75	100

> **CONDITION CODE:**
> C5 – Good, wear evident overall, shows that has been played with
> C6 – Fine, shows some wear in spots, but taken care of
> C7 – Very Fine, minor wear overall, very clean
> C8 – Excellent, minor wear on edges only
> C9 – Near Mint, no noticeable flaws, close inspection may show minute marks
> C10 – Mint (like new)
> Note: Mint in Box does command higher price

Pressman Tonto No. 7751

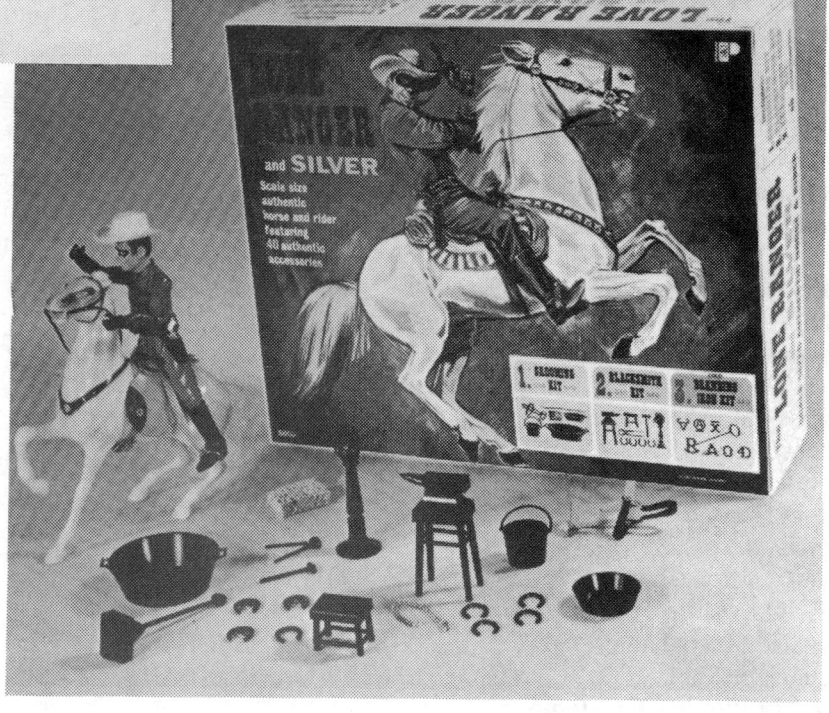

Pressman Lone Ranger No. 7750

Pressman Lone Ranger with his Horse, Silver, No. 7750 new in 1967, jointed, 40 accessories including working (cold) branding iron .... No Price Found

Pressman Tonto & his horse Scout No. 7751, new in 1967, jointed, 40 accessories including cold branding iron kit .... No Price Found

Remco Engergized Green Goblin, battery-operated, 12" 22.50 33.75 45.00

FIGURE KITS

Figure kits are meant, when assembled, to be viewed, rather than played with. But somehow they have fallen very decisively into the category of toys. The explosion in figure kits seems to have begun in 1961 when Aurora took advantage of the fad at the time for old monster movies. It began by depicting the famed monsters of Universal Pictures, with Frankenstein as its first plastic model kit. Dracula and the Wolfman made their appearance in 1962, and in 1963 the flood began, led by the Phantom of the Opera. As Aurora's monster kits became more and more gruesome, activitists began to protest, and when Nabisco took over Aurora the National Organization for Women picketed the parent company, which quickly ended the series.

Because it is the most popular of the figure kit companies, Aurora leads off this section, with the other firms following in alphabetical order.

Condition of a Figure Kit and its relation to Price

Condition of figure kits is rated differently from other toys. Thus, prices in this section are divided into MIB, BWB and BNB. MIB signifies a kit that is mint in the box with the original clear wrapping still untouched. BWB means that the kit has been built, and comes with the original box. BNB means that the kit has been built, and that there is no box.

AURORA	BNB	BWB	MIB
Addams Family House	425	600	850
Alfred E. Neumann, **802,** 1965	50	70	100
American Astronaut, **409,** 1967	20	30	45
Babe Ruth	125	175	250
Batboat	150	210	300
Batcycle, **810,** 1967	175	245	350
Batman No. **467,** 1964	50	70	100
Batman Comic Scenes **187,** 1974	10	14	20
Batmobile, **486,** 1966	160	225	320
Batplane **487,** 1966	50	70	100
Black Beauty (Green Hornet) **489,** 1967	150	210	300
Black Knight, Famous Fight Series, **K3,** 1956	25	35	50
Blackbeard	75	105	150
Blue Knight, Famous Fighter Series, **K2,** 1957	25	35	50
Bride of Frankenstein, **482,** 1964	300	420	600
Captain Action, **480,** 1966	100	140	200
Captain America, 1966, **476**	75	105	150
Captain America Comic Scenes	17.50	25.00	35.00
Captain Kidd **464,** 1965	20	32	40
Cave Bear, Prehistoric Scenes **738**	12.50	18.50	25.00
Chinese Girl, 1957 **416**	15	21	30
Chinese Mandarin, **415,** 1957	15	21	30
Chitty Chitty Bang Bang **828,** 1968	62.50	77.50	125.00
Creature From the Black Lagoon **426,** 1963	100	140	200
Creature From the Black Lagoon - Glow, 426	90	125	180
Cro Magnon Man, **730,** 1971	12.50	17.50	25.00
Cro Magnon Woman, Prehistoric Scenes No. **731,** 1971	17.50	25.00	35.00
Customizing Monster Kit No. 1, **463,** 1963	50	70	100
Customizing Monster Kit No. 2, **464,** 1963	50	70	100
Cyclops (Lost In Space)	225	315	450
D'Artagnan **410,** 1966	112.50	157.50	225.00
Dempsey vs. Firpo **861**	20	28	40
Dick Tracy	45	65	90

AURORA Store Display of its Monster Scenes, with Dr. Deadly, the Victim and Hanging Cage
Courtesy Toy Collector News
Photo by Rex Gray

	BNB	BWB	MIB
Dr. Jekyll **482,** 1969	90	130	180
Dr. Jekyll - Glow	40	55	80
Dracula **424,** 1962	75	105	150
Dracula - glow	55	77	110
Dracula's Dragster **466,** 1966	150	210	300
Dutch Boy, 1957	12.50	17.50	25.00
Dutch Girl **414,** 1957	12.50	17.50	25.00
Forgotten Prisoner **422,** 1966	140	200	280
Forgotten Prisoner - Glow	80	112	160
Frankenstein **423,** 1961	90	130	180
Frankenstein - Glow	25	35	50
Frankie's Flivver **465,** 1964	175	245	350
Frog, The	125	175	250
George Washington **852,** 1965	35	50	70
Gladiator **406,** 1964	75	105	150
Godzilla, 1964	175	245	350
Godzilla - Glow	70	100	140
Gold Knight on Horseback	100	140	200
Green Beret **413,** 1966	37.50	52.50	75.00
Guillotine **800** 1964	150	210	300

AURORA Phantom of the Opera and Napoleon Solo figure kits.
Courtesy Toy Collector News
Photo by Rex Gray

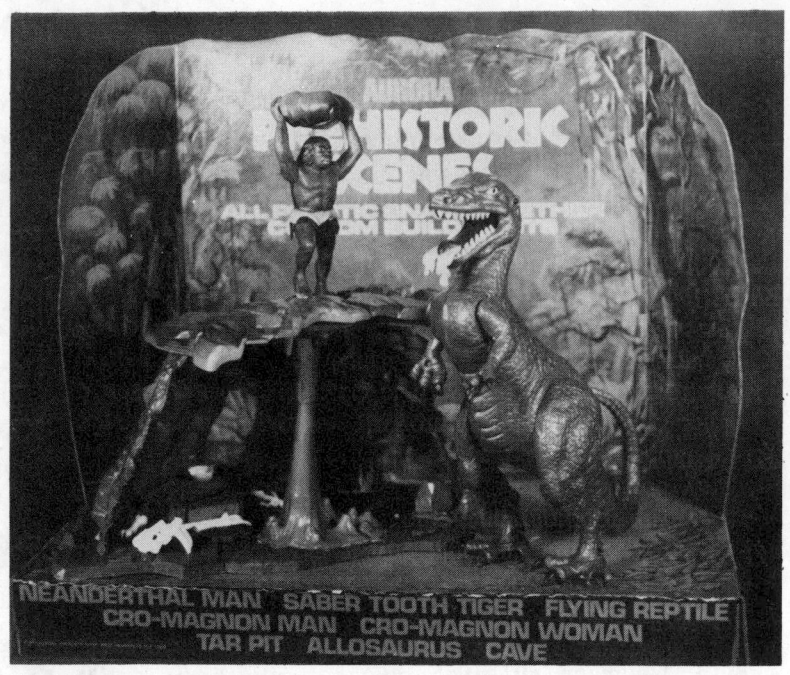

AURORA Store Display of its Prehistoric Scenes showing Cro-Magnon Man
Courtesy Toy Collector News
Photo by Rex Gray

	BNB	BWB	MIB		BNB	BWB	MIB
Hercules 481, 1965	100	140	200	Mummy - Glow 452, 1972	20	28	40
Hulk 421, 1966	100	140	200	Mummy's Chariot	212.50	297.50	425.00
Hulk Comic Scenes 184 1974	10	14	20	Munsters Family	400	560	800
Hunchback 461, 1964	62.50	87.50	125.00	Munsters Living Room	350	490	700
Hunchback - Glow	30	42	60	Napoleon Solo 411, 1966	100	140	200
Hunchback of Notre Dame 481, 1972	No Price Found			Neanderthal Man and Skeleton, 1959	30	42	60
Illya Kuryakin 412, 1966	75	105	150	Odd Job, 1966	100	140	200
Indian Squaw 418, 1957	35	50	70	Pain Parlor 635, 1971	25	35	50
James Bond, 1966	100	140	200	Penguin, 1967	150	210	300
Jerry West 865, 1965	40	56	80	Phantom of the Opera 428, 1963	100	140	200
Jesse James 408, 1966	100	140	200	Phantom of the Opera 451, 1972	12.50	17.50	25.00
Jimmy Brown	62.50	87.50	125.00	Phantom of the Opera - Glow	50	70	100
John F. Kennedy 851, 1965	37.50	52.50	75.00	Pushmi-Pullyu (Dr. Doolittle) 814,			
Johnny Unitas 864, 1965	37.50	52.50	75.00	1968	45	63	90
King Kong	150	210	300	Rat Patrol diorama 340, 1967	45	63	90
King Kong - Glow	37.50	52.50	75.00	Robin 488, 1966	20	28	40
Lone Ranger 808, 1967	50	70	100	Robin Comic Scenes 193, 1974	12.50	17.50	25.00
Lone Ranger Comic Scenes	10	14	20	Robot 418, 1968	600	840	1200
Lost in Space 419,	425	595	850	Scotch Lad 419, 1957	15	21	30
Lost in Space 420,	650	910	1300	Scotch Lassie 420, 1957	15	21	30
Mad Barber	850	1190	1700	Silver Knight - Famous Fighter Series			
Mr. Spock	100	140	200	K1-98, 1956	25	35	50
Monster Scenes Dr. Deadly 631, 1971	25	35	50	Snake Scene (Land of the Giants),			
Monster Scenes Dr. Deadly's				1964	150	210	300
Daughter 632, 1971	30	42	60	Space Coupe	40	56	80
Monster Scenes Frankenstein	37.50	52.50	75.00	Spartacus	75	105	150
Monster Scenes Gruesome Goodies				Spiderman 477, 1966	110	154	220
Kit 634, 1971	22.50	31.50	45.00	Spiderman Comic Scenes	17.50	24.50	35.00
Monster Scenes Hanging Cage Kit,				Steve Canyon	92.50	129.50	185.00
637, 1971	22.50	31.50	45.00	Superboy	40	56	80
Monster Scenes The Pendulum 636,				Superboy Comic Scenes	10	14	20
1971	20	28	40	Superman 462, 1963	62.50	87.50	125.00
Monster Scenes Vampirella 638, 1971	37.50	52.50	75.00	Superman Comic Scenes	10	14	20
Monster Scenes The Victim	30	42	60	Tarzan 820, 1967	35	49	70
Mummy 427, 1963	125	175	250	Tarzan Comic Scenes 181, 1974	10	14	20
Mummy 452, 1972	9	12	18				

AURORA Tarzan Figure Kit.
Courtesy Toy Collector News
Photo by Rex Gray

	BNB	BWB	MIB
Tonto **809,** 1967	45	63	90
Tonto Comic Scenes **183,** 1974	10	14	20
U.S. Marine **412,** 1956	65	90	130
Vampire	50	70	100
Wacky Back Whacker **807,** 1965	100	140	200
Witch **470,** 1969	80	112	160
Witch **470,** 1972	9	12	18
Witch - Glow **470,**	25	35	50
Wolfman **425,** 1962	50	70	100
Wolfman - Glow	50	70	100
Wolfman's Wolfwagon	225	315	450
Wonder Woman **479,** 1965	200	280	400
Zorro **801,** 1965	75	105	150

AMT

	BNB	BWB	MIB
Big Foot	15	21	30
Dragula **905,** 1964	90	126	180
USS Enterprise (small)	25	35	50
Enterprise Bridge	25	35	50
Exploration Set (Star Trek)	37.50	52.50	75.00
Gallileo Shuttle Craft	30	42	60
K-7 Space Station **955,** 1976	35	49	70
Klingon Battle Cruiser	25	35	50
Munster's Koach	100	140	200
Romulan Bird of Prey (Star Trek) . . .	37.50	52.50	75.00
Spock (original - short box)	55	77	110
Spock (original - long box)	50	70	100
Spock (movie)	15	21	30

HAWK

	BNB	BWB	MIB
Drag Hag	45	63	90
Endsville Eddie **537,** 1963	35	50	70
Francis the Foul **535,** 1963	20	28	40
Frantic Banana	45	63	90
Frantic Cats	45	63	90
Sling Rave Curvette **637,** 1964	5	7	10
Steel Pluckers	45	63	90
Wade a Minut **636,** 1964	6	8	12

MONOGRAM

	BNB	BWB	MIB
Batman Kit, 1985	5	7	10
Colonial Viper (Battlestar Gallactica) .	22.50	31.50	45.00
Cyclon Raider (Battlestar Gallactica) .	22.50	31.50	45.00
Draconian Marauder (Buck Rogers) . .	17.50	24.50	35.00
Frankenstein	10	14	20
Fred Flypogger as Speed Shift	75	115	150
Fred Flypogger as Flip Out	75	115	150
Gallactica Spaceship (Battlestar Gallactica)	50	70	100
Mummy, The **6010,** 1983	10	14	20
Superman, 1978	20	28	40
Wolfman	30	48	60

MPC

	BNB	BWB	MIB
Alien, The **1961,** 1979	40	56	80
Ape Man head	21.00	29.50	42.00
Barnabas Collins	90	126	180
Bionic Woman	15	21	30
C-3PO **1913,** 1977	7.50	11.50	15.00
Darth Vader **1916,** 1979, with glo light saber	20	28	40
Darth Vader breathing head **1921,** 1978	40	56	80
Darth Vader Tie Fighter **1915,** 1977 .	10	14	20
Escape From the Crypt	14	20	28
Fonz, The, on bike **0634,** 1976	27.50	38.50	55.00
Millenium Falcon **1933,** 1983	60	84	120
Play It Again Sam **5052,** 1974	17.50	24.50	35.00
R2-D2 **1912,** 1978	7.50	11.50	15.00
Road Runner on beep beep	20	28	40
Six Million Dollar Man - Evil Rider .	15	21	30
Six Million Dollar Man - Fight For Survival **0602,** 1975	15	21	30
"Star Wars" AT-AT (All-Terrain Armored Transport)	7.50	10.50	15.00
"Star Wars" AT-ST (All-Terrain Scout Transport)	5	7	10
"Star Wars" C-3PO	5	7	10
Vampire's Midnight Madness **5051,** 1974	14	20	28
Werewolf (Dark Shadows)	100	140	200
Yellow Submarine	100	155	220
Wile E. Coyote on skateboard	20	28	40
X-Wing Fighter **1914**	17.50	24.50	35.00

PYRO

	BNB	BWB	MIB
Der Baron	20	28	40
Gladiator, The	20	28	40
Lil Corporal	20	28	40
Rawhide	70	98	140
Restless Gun	70	98	140
Surf's Up	20	28	40
Wyatt Earp	70	98	140

345

REVELL

	BNB	BWB	MIB
Beatnik Bandit **1279**, 1963, "Big Daddy" Roth kit	25	35	50
Brother Rat Fink **1304**, 1964	20	28	40
Cat in the Hat	27.50	38.50	55.00
Flash Gordon & The Martian 1450, 1965	50	70	100
Dragnut **1303,** 1963	14	20	28
George Harrison	140	175	280
Gowdy (Dr. Seuss)	25	35	50
John Lennon	160	225	320
Jolly Roger pirate ship	15	21	30
Mr. Gasser in BRM - Roth Slot Car Model **1301**, 1964	20	28	40
Mother's Worry	25	35	50
Norvall (Dr. Seuss)	25	35	50
Outlaw - Daddy Roth kit	17.50	25.00	35.00
Paul McCartney	100	140	200
Phantom, The (comic strip hero)	50	70	100
Phantom Voodoo Witch Doctor	112.50	155.00	225.00
Ringo Starr **1351**, 1964	100	140	200
Sand Crawler **1776**, 1985	22.50	31.50	45.00
Sandworm **1778**, 1985	22.50	31.50	45.00

PREMIUMS

The average mint price of premiums was $43.63 in the last edition, rising to $61.34 in this, an increase of 41%.

TOYS FREE AS THE AIR
By Jim Harmon

Many radio premiums were nearly as free as the wonderful radio shows that advertised them.

We did have to pay the electric bill (or our folks did) to run the radio, and to get the offered toys we did have to send in a box-top from the sponsor's product.

Sometimes it was only that, a proof of purchase (Orphan Annie and Captain Midnight were particularly generous in responding with gifts for inner labels or inner seals from Ovaltine drink mix) and other times, usually only a dime was required "to handle the cost of handling and mailing". (That's really all it did do — the cost of the premium itself came from the advertising budget.)

The lure of the premium to kids then and for grown-up kids who are now collectors is difficult to explain to those who never lived through the era themselves. The ring or badge was more than the toy itself; it was our tangible link to those magical friends on the other side of the speaker cloth.

Those voices were wonderful out there — The rumbling bass of Brace Beemer as the Lone Ranger; the slightly "country" sound of Curley Bradley as Tom Mix; Bret Morrison, whom we recognized even as children was "sophisticated" as Lamont Cranston, alias The Shadow — but they were bodiless and yes, a bit remote.

It was the premium they offered, the same as the one they were using in the story, that put us in touch with them.

There were historic precedents for radio premiums. There were pictures of famous actresses in cigarette packages around the turn of the century, and early radio personalities, such as bandleader Vincent Lopez, offered their autographed pictures. But such footnotes to history aside, radio premiums began with **Little Orphan Annie** in 1931. The plucky little waif from the Sunday comics first gave away sheet music of her theme song ("Who's that little chatterbox with the pretty auburn locks?") and her own photo, but very shortly, she offered a drinking mug that could be used to shake-up Ovaltine powder with milk to make something resembling a soda fountain milk shake. The first significant radio premium, it was the only successful one that encouraged further use of the sponsor's product.

Many different models of the shake-up mug were offered by Annie, and later by Captain Midnight (on both radio and TV). So successful were the offers, shake-up mugs are not rare or high in dollar value. (The most sought after is the orange and blue, embossed — not decaled — Midnight mug.)

It took two more years after Annie came to radio for the fledgling medium to develop its really classic adventure heroes. In 1933, there appeared the Lone Ranger, Tom Mix and Jack Armstrong. Unlike Annie, the two Westerners and the All-American Boy were still around until the 1950s, when television began driving out all radio drama. In those nearly twenty years, these shows offered hundreds of give-away toys, which inspired similar premiums on dozens of other shows.

Any small toy that could be manufactured inexpensively enough might turn up as a premium. Those concerned with the great outdoors were popular. We had compasses, pedometers, telescopes, flashlights, pocketknives, signal mirrors, portable telegraph sets.

The secret society of childhood had its emblems and tokens. So had secret decoders and secret manuals of every size and description. It is these and other **paper** items that have the greatest dollar value. They were the most easily lost or used up in the rush to adulthood. A Captain Midnight Secret Manual is worth more than the metallic decoder it accompanied.

The rarest paper item is the Lone Ranger Frontier Town offered about 1947. To complete this model of a Western village, one had to get four different envelopes by mail, then augment this by buying several packages of Cheerios to cut out the model buildings from the packs. The complete set has been known to sell for hundreds of dollars and today might bring $1,000.00, the highest dollar premium.

Perhaps the most popular single type of premium was the ring. Rings let the listener show his loyalty to the fraternity of his favorite hero, but in a less officious and more "grown-up" way than the badge (although they were also highly popular). Besides . . . the rings looked neat, and many of them could **do** things — some of them pretty incredible things.

As with radio premiums in general, the Tom Mix show (and Ralston cereal's premium manufacturer, the Robbins Company) blazed the trail with ingenious ring designs. In 1937, Tom Mix Straight Shooters could get a Signet Ring with their own initial on it. (Years later, Captain Midnight would offer a ring that would ink-stamp your initial.) By 1938, Tom had a ring that let you look in a peep-hole and see a magnified picture of himself and his horse, Tony. (Technology had progressed so much that by the fifties, Straight Arrow offered a similar ring that put your own photo, if supplied, alongside radio's great Indian hero.)

After World War II and the ease in metal rationing, Tom Mix offered a Magnet Ring (good for picking up paper-clips — like the one on the stolen plans to the atomic bomb, in Tom's case). His spinning siren whistle ring was neat (but admittedly borrowed in design from Jack Armstrong's 1937 Egyptian Whistle Ring). Tom's Sliding Whistle Ring that played different musical notes (about 1948) was unique, however. His Look-Around Ring concealed an inner mirror that let you see behind you (sort of), a design rustled for a later Tennessee Jed ring.

The final Tom Mix ring looked attractive, sporting a glowing cat's-eye, but the Tiger-Eye Ring was only lightweight plastic in 1949, a far cry from the well-crafted metal rings of a decade earlier. But then, the decade was nearly over, and so was the era, fading in the light of another glowing eye in the living room.

The Shadow's own Glow-in-the-Dark Ring in 1939 had a band composed of two sculpted Shadow figures holding up a jagged blue stone — a proxy lump of his sponsor's product, Blue Coal. One of the very few Shadow premiums and the best-looking, this ring has sold for a record $400.00.

One glowing plastic ring — the identical mold — was used for several different radio shows. The band had two crocodiles holding a setting in their mouths. The oval "stone" was **green** when it was Jack Armstrong's Dragon Eye Ring in 1940. It stayed green for **Terry and the Pirates** in the mid-forties, but it was **black** for Carey Salt's Shadow ring in 1947 (not the rare Blue Coal model). The setting was **red** for Buck Rogers' Ring of Saturn in 1945. It is back to **black** in the slightly lumpy counterfeit being manufactured today, one of the handful of premiums of simple enough design to be faked for profit. The best way to authenticate these rings is by the accompanying paper instruction sheets, naming the famous character whose prize it is.

These rings, as are all radio premiums, are worth whatever you will pay to possess them. A fair average price is $60.00 with $200.00 a top price for very rare, complex and fragile items. No one who is not very familiar with the whole field should pay more. Even though $200.00 or more may be easier to come by today than a dime and a box-top were in those days of yesteryear.

```
CONDITION CODE:
C5 – Good, wear evident overall, shows that has been played with
C6 – Fine, shows some wear in spots, but taken care of
C7 – Very Fine, minor wear overall, very clean
C8 – Excellent, minor wear on edges only
C9 – Near Mint, no noticeable flaws, close inspection may show
     minute marks
C10 – Mint (like new)
     Note: Mint in Box does command higher price
```

PREMIUM UPDATE

There has been a radical change in the prices of radio and early TV premiums (and associated toys). For nearly twenty years, there had been no appreciable rise in premium prices. In fact, premium prices had not even kept up with inflation. You could have bought a Tom Mix Magnet Ring for $35.00 in 1967 and bought the same Magnet Ring for the same $35.00 in 1987. But now there has come a radical change in premium pricing, especially for rings. The Magnet Ring generally brings a minimum of $65.00 in 1989.

Part of the reason is the unnatural influence of "investor" types who have manipulated the market, much as they had the old comic book market for years. If events follow those in the comic book market, in a few years those interested in premiums for pleasure will be priced out of the market by manipulators interested only in holding them for a time as value accrues and selling them for profit. Now, if ever, is certainly the time to buy.

Events in the real world are also influencing the premium market. New stores of attic collections are no longer turning up; those in existence have already surfaced. Many of the good examples of the premiums have been sold and have disappeared into collections. More and more, premiums of secondary condition – frankly poor condition at times – are being offered at mint prices. **Condition** becomes more and more critical. A very rare premium in a battered, rusted, even broken condition is virtually worthless.

Slowly, a new source of premiums is becoming evident. Older collectors are retiring from their occupations, and sadly, selling their collections for needed money. Some die, and survivors sell. These collectors and families know the value of collectibles and sell for top market value. This pattern is bound to continue.

The items connected to once well-known characters, and some still well-known today, are going up fastest. The minor and unknown character items are not being given away, but probably won't increase in adjusted dollar value. **Rings** have a great appeal to many, and are the hottest ticket in the premium market – the rare ones are going up and up. The Shadow Blue Coal Ring, Green Hornet Seal Ring, and Captain Midnight Mystic Sun God Ring will probably go over the thousand dollar mark in the next few years (although the complete Lone Ranger Frontier Town is the only premium known to have sold for over one thousand dollars at this writing).

A new development is the rising prices on the old cereal boxes associated with famous characters. Any old box of Wheaties is worth money, but an offer of a Jack Armstrong premium can raise the price from a previous twenty-five dollars to a present seventy-five. The top of this line are complete boxes of the nine Lone Ranger Frontier Town Cheerios packs (about one hundred dollars each; the cut out complete backs with unassembled model buildings can go for twenty-five).

A few **new** authentic premiums have appeared in recent years: Boraxo offered a 20 Mule Team model in 1980 (similar to the **Death Valley Days** original of the '30s and '40s); Cheerios offered a Lone Ranger Deputy Kit in 1981 styled after the movie of that year but similar to earlier offers with mask, badge, etc. In 1982, Ralston began a limited Tom Mix revival with which the present author, Jim Harmon, was involved; offering a set of four Mix Ralston cereal bowls, a wind-up wrist watch, a Straight Shooters membership kit, a Tom Mix photo, a Mix in-box miniature comic book (edited by Harmon), and a Long Play recording with three old Mix radio episodes and one 1983 episode featuring Curley Bradley and produced by Harmon. In 1987, Ovaltine resurrected their original formula in jars, and instituted new premiums of their character, Captain Midnight of the Secret Squadron, with a tee-shirt that year, and with a Midnight digital watch in 1988. Already these new premiums are bringing high prices – the Mix wrist watch has sold for over one hundred dollars – and some dealers might try to represent them as being older and more valuable than they are. But they are valuable enough.

JIM HARMON is a writer of non-fiction (**The Great Radio Heroes**) and science fiction (including the often-authologized "The Place Where Chicago Was") magazine editor (**Monsters of the Movies**) and writer-producer-co-star with radio's Tom Mix in the 1970s **Curley Bradley, U.S. Marshal** radio and recording series. He has written virtually every imaginable category of fiction or non-fiction, has appeared in movies, radio drama and on many major TV talk shows. Harmon has produced several new radio episodes of **Tom Mix** for Ralston which have been both broadcast and offered on premium record albums. He has also edited a **Tom Mix** mini-comic book included in specially marked boxes of Hot Ralston. He is currently working on a book about radio drama and cowboy characters, and their adaptations to film. He lives with his wife, Barbara, a microbiologist, and daughter, Dawn, a U.C.L.A. student, in southern California.

	C6	C8	C10
Admiral Television Studio Giveaway – 1953 paper punchout TV studio and characters, features Sky King, Flight to Mars, Walt Disney's Peter Pan and Three Little Pigs. 15"x16"	47.50	71.25	95.00
Amos & Andy Pepsodent Give-away-Amos' Wedding	22.50	33.75	45.00
Amos & Andy Puzzle	12.50	18.75	25.00
Archie Comics Club Button	2.50	3.75	5.00
Aunt Jemima Breakfast Club Badge, metal	5.00	7.50	10.00
Barney Baxter Junior Birdmen of America wings, metal, circa late 1930s	7.50	11.25	15.00
Bendix Radio - 5½" WW II military figures circa 1944. Color photos with stands. a. Lt. (jg) Navy; b. Marine 1st Lt. (dress uniform); c. Commander-Coast Guard; d. Army Air Force officer with parachute harness; e. 2nd Lt. with modern Mae West; f. Flier with flying suit; g. Capt. Army Air Force; h. Air officer with fur-lined jacket and helmet. Price per each	2.50	3.75	5.00
Betty Boop face mask - 1931 theatre premium	10	15	20
Betty Boop pin "Roxy Theatre, New York," large	5.00	7.50	10.00
Blondie & Dagwood Go To Leisureland, 1940, Westinghouse .	6	9	12
Bobby Benson Code Rule 1935 cardboard decoder, Hecker H-O	30	45	60
Bobby Benson's Game Circus, 1934 .	17.50	26.25	35.00
Buck Jones Club Ring	17.50	26.25	35.00
Buck Jones Horseshoe Pin	17.50	26.25	35.00
Buck Jones Jr. Sheriff Badge	12.50	18.75	25.00
Buck Rogers Badge, enameled	27.50	41.25	55.00
Buck Rogers Birthstone and initial ring	47.50	71.25	95.00
Buck Rogers Chief Explorer Badge . .	32.50	48.75	65.00
Buck Rogers lead figures, solid, Cocomalt, Buck, Wilma, Killer Kane, per each	3.50	5.25	7.00
Buck Rogers Flight Commander Whistle Badge	35.00	52.50	70.00
Buck Rogers Girl's charm bracelet . . .	37.50	56.25	75.00
Buck Rogers Helmet	55.00	82.50	110.00
Buck Rogers Knife	37.50	56.25	75.00
Buck Rogers Morton Salt Punch-o-Bag, 1930s	17.00	25.50	34.00
Buck Rogers Morton Salt Spaceship (came in envelope)	50	75	100
Buck Rogers Pendant	20	30	40
Buck Rogers Pinback button, circa 1935, Whitehead and Hoag, "Buck Rogers in the 25th Century"	15.00	22.50	30.00

BUCK ROGERS Ring of Saturn
Courtesy Jim Harmon

BUCK ROGERS Chemical laboratory.
Courtesy HAKE'S Americana & Collectibles.

	C6	C8	C10
Buck Rogers Repeller Ray Ring (seal ring)	80	120	160
Buck Rogers Ring of Saturn, glows in the dark, with red stone	62.50	93.75	125.00
Buck Rogers Ring of Saturn Instruction Sheet	25.00	37.50	50.00
Buck Rogers Solar Scouts Badge, all brass color	17.50	26.25	35.00
Buck Rogers Solar Scouts Spaceship Commander Badge, 1936 Cream of Wheat premium	22.50	33.75	45.00
Buck Rogers Solar Scout Sweater Emblem	25.00	37.50	50.00
Buck Rogers Telescope	37.50	56.25	75.00
Buck Rogers items given away for Cream of Wheat green triangle (sold in stores also):			
Buck Rogers Films for projector	6	9	12
Buck Rogers Interplanetary Game . . .	45.00	67.50	90.00
Buck Rogers lead figures, hollow lead, Buck, Wilma, Huer, Robot, Kane, Ardala, average price per each, Britains	100	150	200
Buck Rogers Lite Blaster Flashlight . .	8	10	25
Buck Rogers Movie Projector	47.50	71.25	95.00
Buck Rogers Printing Set (12 rubber stamps)	25.00	33.75	50.00
Buck Rogers Super Dreadnaught, balsa wood	10	15	20
Buck Rogers Uniform	100	150	200
Buffalo Bill Bamby Bread Horseshoe Badge, late 1930s	5.00	7.50	10.00
Buffalo Bill Jr. brass ring, Buffalo in relief on top, TV premium	12.50	18.75	25.00
Buster Brown Gang (Smilin' Ed) Ring	12.50	18.75	25.00

350

	C6	C8	C10
Buster Brown Gang tab pins, assorted, price per each	2	3	5
Butter-Nut Bread premium, "Sail-Me" glider with 4½" wingspan, c. 1930	5.00	7.50	10.00
Captain Franks Air Hawks Ring	22.50	33.75	45.00
Captain Franks Air Hawks Wings, circa late 1930s, Post's 40% Bran Flakes premium	12.50	18.75	25.00
Captain Gallant Medal, c. 1950 dated 1939-1945 with an animal on it	10	15	20
Captain Gallant Medal, 1950s, this one is a cross with GRI on it	10	15	20
Captain Hawk Sky Patrol Propellor Badge, circa late 1930s	10	15	20
Captain Marvel Club button	15.00	22.50	30.00
Captain Marvel's Magic Whistle c. 1943, American Seed Co. Has full color picture of Captain Marvel on both sides and American Seed Co. ad on the inside	12.50	18.75	25.00
Captain Midnight Aerial Torpedo Bomber (Airplane), 1941	47.50	71.25	95.00
Captain Midnight American Flag Loyalty Badge, 1940	25.00	37.50	50.00
Captain Midnight Flight Patrol Wings Badge, 1941	17.50	26.25	35.00
Captain Midnight Flight Patrol Wings Badge, 1942	17.50	26.25	35.00
Captain Midnight Code-O-Graph Decoder Pin, 1941, Eagle on top	47.50	71.25	95.00

CAPTAIN MIDNIGHT Code-O-Graph Badge, 1942
Courtesy Jim Harmon

	C6	C8	C10
Captain Midnight Code-O-Graph Badge, 1942, with photo of Captain Midnight	55.00	82.50	110.00
Captain Midnight Code-O-Graph, 1945, magnifier	47.50	71.25	95.00

	C6	C8	C10
Captain Midnight Code-O-Graph, 1946, Mirromatic (best-looking, desirable)	55.00	82.50	110.00
Captain Midnight Code-O-Graph, 1947, works as a whistle	21.00	31.50	42.00
Captain Midnight Code-O-Graph, 1948, round, with mirror	37.50	56.25	75.00
Captain Midnight Code-O-Graph, 1949, Key-O-Matic (with key)	62.50	93.75	125.00
Captain Midnight Detect-O-Scope, 1941	30	45	60
Captain Midnight Flight Commander Commission, 1956	25.00	37.50	50.00
Captain Midnight Flight Commander Flying Cross, 1942	22.50	33.75	45.00
Captain Midnight Flight Commander Ring, 1941	75.00	112.50	150.00
Captain Midnight Flight Commander Signet Ring, 1957	82.50	123.75	165.00
Captain Midnight Flight Commander Ring, 1959	82.50	123.75	165.00
Captain Midnight Jumping Bean Target, 1939	12.50	18.75	25.00
Captain Midnight MJC-10 Plane Detector, 1942, distance-finder	45.00	67.50	90.00
Captain Midnight Magic Blackout Lite-Ups, 1942	22.50	33.75	45.00
Captain Midnight 1941 Manual for Decoder	50	75	100
Captain Midnight 1942 Manual for Decoder	100	150	200
Captain Midnight 1945 Manual for Code-O-Graph	32.50	48.75	65.00
Captain Midnight 1946 Manual for Code-O-Graph	32.50	48.75	65.00
Captain Midnight 1947 Manual for Code-O-Graph	42.50	63.75	85.00
Captain Midnight 1948 Manual for Code-O-Graph	42.50	63.75	85.00
Captain Midnight 1949 Manual for Code-O-Graph	30	45	60
Captain Midnight 1956 Manual for Decoder Badge	100	150	200
Captain Midnight 1957 Manual for Silver Dart decoder	100	150	200
Captain Midnight Marine Corps Ring, 1942	62.50	93.75	125.00
Captain Midnight medal, brass, pictures of cast, secret word, spinner, 1940	7.50	11.25	15.00
Captain Midnight Mystic Eye Detector Ring, 1942	62.50	93.75	125.00
Captain Midnight Mystic Sun God Ring, 1946	225.00	337.50	450.00
Captain Midnight Printing Ring, 1948	55.00	82.50	110.00
Captain Midnight Secret Squadron Decoder Badge, 1955	47.50	71.25	95.00
Captain Midnight Secret Squadron Decoder Badge, 1956	47.50	71.25	95.00

CAPTAIN MIDNIGHT Medal, 1940
Courtesy Jim Harmon

	C6	C8	C10
Captain Midnight Secret Squadron Insignia transfer, 1949	12.50	18.75	25.00
Captain Midnight Service Ribbon pin, 1944	17.50	26.25	35.00
Captain Midnight Silver Dart Decoder Badge, 1957	47.50	71.25	95.00
Captain Midnight Spy Scope, 1947 ..	32.50	48.75	65.00
Captain Midnight Surprise Package, 1942	17.50	26.25	35.00
Captain Midnight 3-Way Mystic Dog Whistle, 1942	12.50	18.75	25.00
Captain Midnight Trick and Riddle Book, 1939 Skelly Oil Premium, 64 pages	15.00	22.50	30.00
Captain Midnight Weather Wings, 1940, predicts weather	22.50	33.75	45.00
Captain Midnight Whirlwind Whistling Ring, 1941	55.00	82.50	110.00
Captain Sparks Airplane Pilot Training Cockpit, Sparkies	175.00	262.50	350.00
Capt. Tim Ivory Club Pin – Ivory Soap, circa 1936	5.50	8.25	11.00

	C6	C8	C10
Captain Video Flying Saucer Ring ..	37.50	56.25	75.00
Captain Video Rite-O-Lite	22.50	33.75	45.00
Captain Video Rocket Launcher and Ships, 1950s	30	45	60
Captain Video Secret Seal Ring, 1950s	47.50	71.25	95.00
Captain Video Space Fleet Ray Gun, 1952, TV premium – Powerhouse	32.50	48.75	65.00
Captain Video X-9 Rocket Balloon, 1950s	22.50	33.75	45.00
Chandu the Magician Galloping Coin Trick, 1930s	22.50	33.75	45.00
Chandu The Magician Hindu Cones, 1930s	22.50	33.75	45.00
Chandu Boxed Set of Tricks	162.50	243.75	325.00
Charlie McCarthy Puppet Doll – 21" high, cardboard, Chase & Sanborn mailer	17.50	26.25	35.00
Charlie McCarthy Radio Party Game – Giveaway by Standard Brands, 1938, 21 cardboard figures	32.50	48.75	65.00
Cinnamon Bear (annual Christmas show, circa 1940s) Silver Star ...	17.50	26.25	35.00
Cisco Kid Badge, western hat on chain, 1950s	10	15	20
Cisco Kid cardboard gun, 7" long, Harvest Bread giveaway, clicker sounds when handle squeezed ...	4	6	8
Cisco Kid and Pancho face masks, 1953, price per each	8.75	13.13	17.50
Cisco Kid Triple S Club Kit	17.50	26.25	35.00
Cisco Kid Picture Ring, 1950s	32.50	48.75	65.00
Coco Wheats Radio Club Badge shape of microphone	12.50	18.75	25.00

CRACKER JACK

Cracker Jack was first introduced in 1893 by the Ruckheim brothers, F.W. and Louis, at the Chicago World's Columbian Exposition. Toys first appeared in the boxes of popcorn and peanuts in 1912 and were bought from various manufacturers. Over 10,000 different have been produced over the years. From 1912 to 1930 they included whistles, tops, yo-yos, brooches and puzzles. From 1930 to 1940 the accent was on miniatures, such as irons, shoes, binoculars, trolley cars, trains, etc. 1940 to 1950 tended towards military items, with plastics being introduced in the late 1940s. Prices can range from $1.00 or less to $80.00. There are about thirty serious Cracker Jack collectors known in this country.

David Harding Counterspy, Junior Agent Badge	17.50	26.25	35.00
Davy Crockett goldplated ring	5.00	7.50	10.00
Dick Tracy Air Detective Ring	32.50	48.75	65.00
Dick Tracy Badge, "Capt."	32	48	64
Dick Tracy Badge, "Crime Stoppers"	6	9	12
Dick Tracy Badge, "Detective," picture of Tracy and Junior	9.00	13.50	18.00
Dick Tracy Badge, "Lt."	21.00	31.50	42.00
Dick Tracy Badge – Republic Pictures	12.50	18.75	25.00
Dick Tracy Badge – "Sgt."	20	30	40
Dick Tracy Decoder, green, 1948 ...	15.00	22.50	30.00
Dick Tracy Decoder, red, 1948	15.00	22.50	30.00

DICK TRACY Secret Service Patrol Member Pin
Courtesy Jim Harmon

Dick Tracy Detective Club Badge with secret money pouch in rear .	22.50	33.75	45.00
Dick Tracy Glider Airplane, 1938 ...	30	45	60

	C6	C8	C10
Dick Tracy Ring, in shape of Tracy's head	22.50	33.75	45.00
Dick Tracy Secret Compartment Ring	37.50	56.25	75.00
Dick Tracy Secret Service Patrol Member pin, early 1940s	10	15	20
Dick Tracy Secret Service 2nd Year Member pin	15.00	22.50	30.00
Dick Tracy's Secret Detective Methods & Magic Tricks. 1939 Quaker Oats, 68 pages	17.50	26.25	35.00
Dionne Quints "All Aboard for Shut-Eye Town" paper dolls, Palmolive Soap	10	15	20
Don Winslow Decoder Torpedo	37.50	56.25	75.00
Don Winslow Honor Badge	17.50	26.25	35.00
Don Winslow Magic Slate Secret Code Book	12.50	18.75	25.00
Don Winslow Ring	22.50	33.75	45.00
Don Winslow USN Secret Code Book, 1935, 16 page Oxydol giveaway, 7¾" x 4"	15.00	22.50	30.00
Donald Duck Punchout figure, circa late 1940s, Donald Duck Bread	5.00	7.50	10.00
Donald Duck Playboard, 1946, 9" high, Comics giveaway	9.00	13.50	18.00
Elsie The Cow, set of four figural buttons on color illustrated card, Borden 1949	4	6	8
Fighting Devil Dogs Ring, 1938, Republic Pictures serial ring, has bulldog head on top	32.50	48.75	65.00
Flash Gordon Ring, 1949 Post Toasties Corn Flakes	15.00	22.50	30.00
Fort Apache (Rin Tin Tin) plastic ring 1950s TV premium	7.50	11.25	15.00

FRANK BUCK Explorer's Sun Watch
Courtesy Jim Harmon

	C6	C8	C10
Frank Buck Explorer's sun watch, post WW II (offered by Jack Armstrong)	22.50	33.75	45.00
Frank Buck Leopard Ring	90	135	180
G.E. Punchout Circus – 65 pieces	22.50	33.75	45.00
G.E. Rodeo Punchout – 65 pieces	10	15	20
G-Man Badge	1.50	2.25	3.00
G-Man Official Signet Ring, 1933-35, G-man radio program premium, metal	17.50	26.25	35.00
Gabby Hayes Antique Cars, 1950s, set for:	22.50	33.75	45.00

	C6	C8	C10
Gabby Hayes Quaker Cannon Ring, 1950s	42.50	63.75	85.00
Gabby Hayes Western Gun Collection, 6 weapons, 3 pistols, 3 rifles, solid non-working, 1950s	22.50	33.75	45.00
Gabby Scoops Junior Press Club Card, 1954 Crackajack Comics	2.50	3.75	5.00
Gabby Scoops 1940-41 Press Card, Crackajack Comics	2.50	3.75	5.00
Gangbusters Pin	14	21	28
Goofy Playboard, 1946, 9" high, comics giveaway	9.00	13.50	18.00
Green Hornet Secret Compartment Ring, hornet seal, glows in dark	112.50	168.75	225.00
Gun, cardboard – Giveaway from Theatorium in Lykens, Pa. Pat'd Dec. 1914 by Spots Spec. Co. Lexington, Ky. Swoop downward to produce bang. "The Bang Gun For Young America"	2	3	5
H.C.B. Club Kit, contains badge, etc., early Cream of Wheat	12.50	18.75	25.00
Hop Harrigan Para-Plane, cardboard plane from Grape Nut Flakes plus two code signal blinders. Also in tail of plane is a small parachute that drops a cardboard "water" cannister	137.50	206.25	275.00
Hop Harrigan (unmarked) Sun Dial Ring	22.50	33.75	45.00
Hopalong Cassidy Bar 20 Compass ring	12.50	18.75	25.00
ring	12.50	18.75	25.00
Hopalong Cassidy Face Ring	12.50	18.75	25.00
Hopalong Cassidy tin badge, Post Raisin Bran giveaway, circa 1950s	3.00	4.50	6.00
Howdy Doody Climber – cardboard, with string, Welch's Premium, 1950s	12.50	18.75	25.00
Howdy Doody Face Flashlight Ring, 1950s	17.50	26.25	35.00
Howdy Doody Flicker Key Chain – 3D picture of Howdy Doody flicks to Poll Parrot (Poll Parrot Shoes), 1950s	7.50	11.25	15.00
Howdy Doody Flicker Ring – Poll Parrot Premium, flicks from Howdy to Poll	7.50	11.25	15.00
Howdy Doody 8" Howdy Doody flexible cardboard figure – Wonder Bread	15.00	22.50	30.00
Howdy Doody puppet, Mars Candy, cardboard, 15" high, 1950s	22.50	33.75	45.00
Howdy Doody Princess dancing puppet, 13" high, joints moveable, 1950s Snickers premium	7.50	11.25	15.00
Howdy Doody, Princess Spring, etc. cardboard figure, 14" high	7.50	11.25	15.00
I Am A Spy Smasher button, 1940, Fawcett Comics	10	15	20

	C6	C8	C10
Indian Chief tin badge, Post Raisin Bran, circa 1950s	2	3	4
Indian Gum Chief's Head Ring – Goudey Gum card premium, 1930s, silver	2.50	3.75	5.00
Jack Armstrong Crocodile Ring, glows in the dark, green stone	62.50	93.75	125.00
Jack Armstrong Big 10 Football Game	37.50	56.25	75.00
Jack Armstrong Explorer's Telescope	12.50	18.75	25.00
Jack Armstrong Flashlight	12.50	18.75	25.00
Jack Armstrong Hike-O-Meter	12.50	18.75	25.00
Jack Armstrong Magic Answer Box	27.50	41.25	55.00

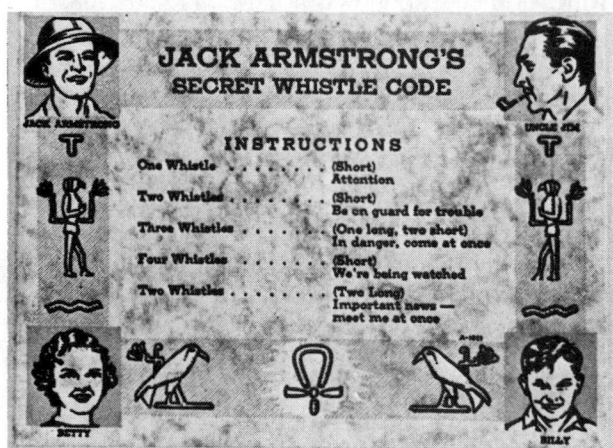

JACK ARMSTRONG Secret Whistle Code Card
Courtesy Jim Harmon

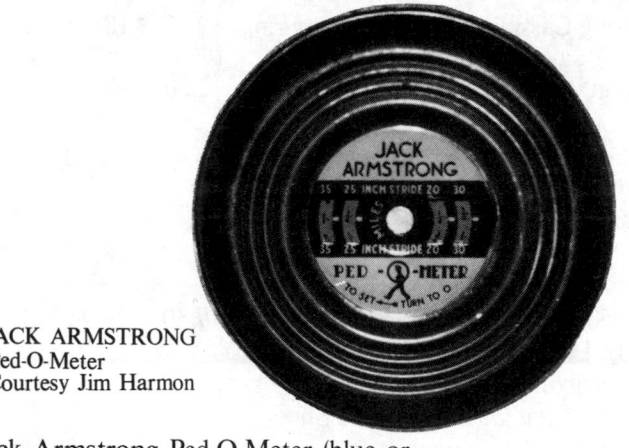

JACK ARMSTRONG
Ped-O-Meter
Courtesy Jim Harmon

	C6	C8	C10
Jack Armstrong Ped-O-Meter (blue or silver models)	17.50	26.25	35.00
Jack Armstrong, Secret Norden Bomb Sight, circa WW II with three bombs, paper target ships	137.50	206.25	275.00
Jack Armstrong paper airplane models, many different, price per each	9.50	14.50	19.00
Reprints of above (identified as such)	2.50	3.75	5.00
Jack Armstrong Secret Whistle Code Card for Secret Egyptian Coder Siren ring	12.50	18.75	25.00
Jack Armstrong Secret Egyptian Coder Siren Ring, late 1930s, Wheaties	32.50	48.75	65.00
Jack Armstrong 3-D viewer, filmstrip	17.50	26.25	35.00

JIMMIE ALLEN Richfield Hi-Octane Flying Cadet wings
Courtesy Jim Harmon

	C6	C8	C10
Jeff paper mask, 1933 Shell Oil	6	9	12
Jimmie Allen Colonial Gasoline Flying Cadet wings, late 1930s, bronze	10	15	20
Jimmie Allen High-Speed Gasoline Flying Cadet wings, late 1930s, bronze	10	15	20
Jimmie Allen Richfield Hi-Octane Flying Cadet wings, circa 1930s	10	15	20
Jimmie Allen Richfield Hi-Octane Pilot's Identification Bracelet, late 1930s, all metal	17.50	26.25	35.00
Jimmie Allen Skelly Oil Die-Cut Airplane cadet wings, late 1930s	10	15	20
Jimmie Allen Skelly Oil Flying Cadet Wings, late 1930s, bronze	10	15	20
Joe E. Brown pin	7.00	10.50	14.00
Junior G-Man Membership kit, circa mid-1930s	17.50	26.25	35.00
Junior G-Men of America, late 1930s, gold-plated tin badge	10	15	20
Junior Texas Ranger Badge, 1936 premium	7.50	11.25	15.00
Kellogg's Frogmen, 1950s, add baking soda and they swim undewater	6	9	12
Kellogg's Krumbles – Around-the-World paper dolls. Each cutout from box contains boy and girl, 10: Italy 11: Mexico 13: France 17: Czechoslovakia. Price per each	1.50	2.25	3.00
Kellogg's Nautilus Nuclear Submarine, 1950s	10	15	20
Kellogg's Pep Airplane Carrier, 6½"x10" cut-out sheet with airplane carrier, 5 planes with ¾" wingspan	15.00	22.50	30.00
Kellogg's Pep Warplanes circa 1945, balsa wood models, price per each	9.00	13.50	18.00
Kellogg's Pep Warplanes circa 1945, balsa, with Superman ad on envelope	6	9	12
Kellogg's Pep Warplanes – circa 1944, cardboard, price per each	6	9	12
"The Liberty Gun For Young America - McGrath's Big Store," 7" cardboard with photos of Charlie Chaplin	10	15	20

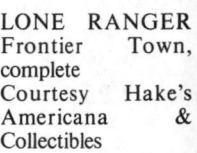

"The Liberty Gun For Young America-McGrath's Big Store", 7" cardboard with photos of Charlie Chaplin.
Courtesy HAKE'S Americana & Collectibles.

LONE RANGER Frontier Town, complete
Courtesy Hake's Americana & Collectibles

LONE RANGER Secret Compartment Ring
Courtesy Jim Harmon

	C6	C8	C10
Little Orphan Annie Necklace, circa 1936, metal enamel figure of LOA on metal chain	15.00	22.50	30.00
Little Orphan Annie pinback button, Little Orphan Annie, Member Funy Frosty's Club, mid-1930s	17.50	26.25	35.00
Lone Ranger, A Republic Serial – brass star badge	37.50	56.25	75.00
Lone Ranger Atom Bomb Ring (very common)	27.50	41.25	55.00
Lone Ranger Blackout Kit, 1942, Kix cereal glow in the dark material (two pieces), glow in the dark pledge to flag, glow in the dark Lone Ranger Volunteers armband, plus instruction	30	45	60
Lone Ranger Bond Bread Safety Club Badge, 1938	12.50	18.75	25.00
Lone Ranger Clicker Pistol, black, 1939 movie giveaway, Lone Ranger on one side and ruby on other, non-moveable silver cylinder	47.50	71.25	95.00
Lone Ranger Deputy Shield – brass with secret compartment	22.50	33.75	45.00
Lone Ranger Flashlight Ring	32.50	48.75	65.00
Lone Ranger Frontier Town – full set	625	937	1250
Lone Ranger Glow-in-the-dark Belt, 1941	40	60	80
Lone Ranger Hiyo Silver Pin, 1938	7.50	11.25	15.00
Lone Ranger Kix Air Base with cereal box cut-outs, precursor of Frontier Town - complete $450.00.			
Lone Ranger Lucky Piece – advertises 17th anniversary 1933-50	9.00	13.50	18.00
Lone Ranger Mask. About the last radio premium, c. 1953 or 1954, back of black mask promotes a personal appearance by "The Lone Ranger and Silver!"	12.50	18.75	25.00
Lone Ranger Movie Film ring, late 1940s Cheerios premium	37.50	56.25	75.00
Lone Ranger Pedometer, 1943 Cheerios	12.50	18.75	25.00
Lone Ranger Rubber Band Gun and 6 different targets, 1938 Morton Salt giveaway, cardboard	22.50	33.75	45.00
Lone Ranger Secret Compartment Ring, with picture of Lone Ranger and Silver	37.50	56.25	75.00

	C6	C8	C10
Lone Ranger Silver bullet, secret compartment compass	22.50	33.75	45.00
Lone Ranger Silver Saddle Film ring, late 1940s, Cheerios	37.50	56.25	75.00
Lone Ranger Chief Scout Badge, Silvercup Bread, early 1940s premium, red, blue and gold	37.50	56.25	75.00
Lone Ranger Safety Scout Badge, Silvercup Bread, 1935	12.50	18.75	25.00
Lone Ranger Silvercup Bread Safety Patrol, metal-silver and blue	12.50	18.75	25.00
Lone Ranger Six-Shooter Ring, gun ring with plastic and metal gun attached to top. Turn wheel and flint sparks	47.50	71.25	95.00
Lone Ranger Victory Corps Badge, 1942, Kix Cereal	17.50	26.25	35.00
Lone Ranger Weather Ring – color square stone on top with litmus paper. No markings to identify as Lone Ranger	17.50	26.25	35.00
Magic Show Kit, 1946 General Mills	12.50	18.75	25.00
Magician's Book of Cigarette Tricks, 1933, Camel Cigarettes	4	6	8
Major Bowes – Home Microphone	22.50	33.75	45.00
Maltex Health Club – pinback button	1.50	2.25	3.00
Melvin Purvis Junior G-Man Corps Badge, late 1930s	12.50	18.75	25.00
Melvin Purvis Junior G-Man Corps Roving Operative Badge, late 1930s	12.50	18.75	25.00
Melvin Purvis Law and Order Ring	22.50	33.75	45.00
Melvin Purvis Law & Order Patrol Lieutenant's Secret Operator Badge, mid-1930s	12.50	18.75	25.00
Melvin Purvis Law & Order Patrol Secret Operator Badge, late 1930s	12.50	18.75	25.00

	C6	C8	C10
Melvin Purvis Secret Operator, Girl's Division	17.50	26.25	35.00
Mickey and Donald's Race to Treasure Island, 1939, 12"x25" Standard Oil giveaway	47.50	71.25	95.00
Mickey and Donald's Race to Treasure Island, 1939, map of U.S. in full color 20"x27", Calco Gasoline giveaway, with stamps	150	225	300
Mickey Mouse Club Pinback Button, "Copyright 1928-30 by W.E. Disney," 1¼"	22.50	33.75	45.00
Mickey Mouse Globe Trotters Map, 28"x20", NBC Bread, 1937	175.00	262.50	350.00
Mickey Mouse Globe Trotters Map, 28"x22", NBC Bread, with all pictures pasted on	225.00	337.50	450.00
Mickey Mouse Globe-Trotters Map, 1930s, Pevely Milk premium	175.00	262.50	350.00
Mickey Mouse Official Money, 1930s Mickey Mouse Cones dollar bills Denomination is "1" (each)	7.50	11.25	15.00
Mickey Mouse Playboard, 1946, 9" high, comics giveaway	9.00	13.50	18.00
Morton Salt "Bat-O-Ball," 1939, features The Shadow (cartoon)	32.50	48.75	65.00
My-T-Fine Grocery Store folds into an 8"x3" full color grocery store with period products on the shelves, shoppers, workers, etc. Dated 1930	17.50	26.25	35.00
Nabisco Finger Puppet Rings, Slim Chants, horse Humbolt, gun, hand, Prairie Mary, Tagalong Boswell, Cold Deck Charlie, Sam Spiel, price per each figure	1.00	1.50	2.00
Nabisco Santa Fe Twin Unit Diesel Train, 1956, includes engine, train, tracks, ground, background	6	9	12
Nabisco Sound-Jet Glider	4	6	8
Nabisco Trailblazers of America cards, six cards make up horse-drawn van and open van, 1956	3.50	5.25	7.00
Nabisco Shredded Wheat Nabisco Flying Circus, 1948, designed by Wallace Rigby, 4"x7" cards, planes, once cut out, can glide. Series of 24. Price per each	2.50	3.75	5.00
The Nebbs – Detroit Times series No. 27544 (comic strip)	3.75	4.60	7.50
New York World's Fair Children's World G-Man Badge, giveaway, 3-color brass badge	12.50	18.75	25.00
Newsboy Brand Soups and Vegetables Official Booster Badge, late 1930s	3.00	4.50	6.00
Pep Pins – Little Orphan Annie	5.00	7.50	10.00
Pep Pins – Flash Gordon	10	15	20
Pep Pins – Felix the Cat	2.50	3.75	5.00
Pep Pins – The Phantom	5.00	7.50	10.00

	C6	C8	C10
Pep Pins – Popeye and Olive Oyl - each	3.00	4.50	6.00
Pep Pins – Superman	10	15	20
Pep Pins – Others, includes Smitty, Inspector, Harold Teen, Skeezix, Corky, Pop Jenks, Goofy, Spud, Andy Gump, Gravel Gertie, Punjab, Hans, Kayo, Smilin' Jack, Dagwood, B.O. Plenty, Mr. Bailey, Shadow, Moon Mullins, Flattop, Rip Winkle, Uncle Willie, Emma, Inspector, Chief Brandon, Vitamin Flintheart, Sandy, Uncle Bim, Sundown, Lillums, Tilda, Uncle Walt, Perry Winkle, Judy, Min Gump, Wilmer, Smoky Stover, Daisy, Ma Winkle, Tess Trueheart, Herbie, Mamie, Breezie, Pat Patton, Maggie, Barney Google, Fat Stuff, Chief Brandon, Toots, Nina, etc., average	2	3	4
Pep Rings – Jack Kramer, Dennis O'Keefe, Burt Lancaster, Sitting Bull, Pocahontas, Pan American Clipper, Douglas F-3D Sky Knight, Republic XF91 Thundercepter, each	1.50	2.25	3.00
Pepsodent's Moving Picture Machine shows Mickey Mouse, Donald Duck, Snow White and Seven Dwarfs in color	100	150	200
Pillsbury-Farina Complete Tel-A-Phone Set, 1938, two holders, mouthpieces, ear phones and 50 feet of line	9.00	13.50	18.00
Pinocchio Playboard, 1946 Disney Comics sub. giveaway	9.00	13.50	18.00
Popeye The Sailor Man Button, ¾" copyright 1935, theatre giveaway	7.50	11.25	15.00
Popsicle Movie Star coins – Aluminum coins circa early 1930s, includes Irene Dunne, Clark Gable, Marion Davies, Fredric March, Marie Dressler, Gary Cooper	2.50	3.75	5.00
Porcelain Enamel & Mfg. Co. 6" West Point Cadet on 3"x6" card with Pemco ad on back	.50	.75	1.00
Post Grape Nuts Flakes Playing-Filling Station, circa 1950s	2	3	4
Post Toasties 1939 Walt Disney cut-out figures, on box, Mickey the Traffic Cop, two types of Pinocchio, etc. Price per each box	7.50	11.25	15.00
Post Toasties Corn Flakes Comic Rings 1949, Fritz, Hans, Tillie the Toiler, Toots, Casper, etc.	3.75	4.60	7.50

	C6	C8	C10
Post's Cereal Junior Detective Club Sergeant Badge, late 1930s	5.00	7.50	10.00
Post's Explorer Ring, 1947, includes compass, sun watch, sunset predictor and star finder, plastic dome .	17.50	26.25	35.00
Post Cereal Rings – 1948, Perry Winkle, Winnie Winkle, Harold Teen, Skeezix, Lillums, Herbie, Smoky Stover, etc.	3.75	5.25	7.50
Post Cereal Rings – 1948 – Dick Tracy	7.50	11.25	15.00
Post Grape Nuts tin rings, Little King, Phantom, Skeezix, Lillums, Harold Teen	3.00	4.50	6.00
Post Raisin Bran Sheriff Badge	1.00	1.50	2.00

L. to R. RADIO ORPHAN ANNIE Decoder Badges, 1938 and 1939
Photo Courtesy Jim Harmon

RADIO ORPHAN ANNIE
Decoder Badge 1936
Courtesy Jim Harmon

	C6	C8	C10
Radio Orphan Annie – Annie and Joe Corntassel button, 1931	10	15	20
Radio Orphan Annie – Associated Membership Pin, 1934	10	15	20
Radio Orphan Annie Bandana, 1934 .	17.50	26.25	35.00
Radio Orphan Annie Birthstone Ring, 1935	17.50	26.25	35.00
Radio Orphan Annie Capt. Sparks Aviation Trainer	125.00	187.50	250.00
Radio Orphan Annie Circus Cut-Outs, 1935	47.50	71.25	95.00
Radio Orphan Annie Code Captain Belt and Buckle, 1940	40	60	80

	C6	C8	C10
Radio Orphan Annie Code Captain Pin, 1939	22.50	33.75	45.00
Radio Orphan Annie Manual, 1934 .	32.50	48.75	65.00
Radio Orphan Annie 1935 Decoder Manual	32.50	48.75	65.00
Radio Orphan Annie 1936 Decoder Manual	32.50	48.75	65.00
Radio Orphan Annie 1937 Decoder Manual	32.50	48.75	65.00
Radio Orphan Annie 1938 Decoder Manual	32.50	48.75	65.00
Radio Orphan Annie 1939 Decoder Manual	32.50	48.75	65.00
Radio Orphan Annie 1940 Decoder Manual	50	75	100
Radio Orphan Annie 1942 Decoder Manual and cardboard decoder ..	125.00	187.50	250.00
Radio Orphan Annie Decoder Pin, 1935	12.50	18.75	25.00
Radio Orphan Annie Decoder Badge, 1936	12.50	18.75	25.00
Radio Orphan Annie Decoder Badge, 1937	12.50	18.75	25.00
Radio Orphan Annie Decoder Badge, 1938	12.50	18.75	25.00
Radio Orphan Annie Decoder Badge, 1939	12.50	18.75	25.00
Radio Orphan Annie Decoder Badge, 1940	12.50	18.75	25.00
Radio Orphan Annie Foreign Coins, 1937	10	15	20
Radio Orphan Annie Goofy Circus, 1939	22.50	33.75	45.00
Radio Orphan Annie Identification Bracelet, 1934	17.50	26.25	35.00
Radio Orphan Annie Identification Bracelet, 1935	17.50	26.25	35.00
Radio Orphan Annie Identification Tag, 1939	20	30	40
Radio Orphan Annie Magic Transfer Pictures, 1935	17.50	26.25	35.00
Radio Orphan Annie Magic Transfer Picture, 1937	15.00	22.50	30.00
Radio Orphan Annie Mask, 1933 ...	30	45	60
Radio Orphan Annie Mystic Eye Ring, 1939	32.50	48.75	65.00
Radio Orphan Annie Package, 1942, includes Whirl-O-Matic Decoder, Whistle Badge, booklet, and order blanks	112.50	168.75	225.00
Radio Orphan Annie Pin, 1937	10	15	20
Radio Orphan Annie Portrait Ring, 1934, ring has head of Annie embossed on top	22.50	33.75	45.00
Radio Orphan Annie Premium Manual, 1937	17.50	26.25	35.00
Radio Orphan Annie Premium Manual, 1938	37.50	46.00	75.00
Radio Orphan Annie Punchouts, 1942	100	150	200

	C6	C8	C10
Radio Orphan Annie Ring, 1934	22.50	33.75	45.00
Radio Orphan Annie Ring, 1935	22.50	33.75	45.00
Radio Orphan Annie Roller Skates, 1938	30	45	60
Radio Orphan Annie Secret Egyptian Compass and Sundial, 1938	22.50	33.75	45.00
Radio Orphan Annie Secret Society Pin, 1934	15.00	22.50	30.00
Radio Orphan Annie Signet Ring, 1937	22.50	33.75	45.00
Radio Orphan Annie Silver Star Pin, 1934	15.00	22.50	30.00
Radio Orphan Annie Silver Star Pin, 1935	15.00	22.50	30.00
Radio Orphan Annie Secret Society Silver Star Ring, 1936	25.00	37.50	50.00
Radio Orphan Annie Silver Star Ring, 1937	25.00	37.50	50.00
Radio Orphan Annie Silver Star Ring, 1938	12.50	18.75	25.00
Radio Orphan Annie School Pin, 1939	10	15	20
Radio Orphan Annie Secret Guard Clicker, 1942	17.50	26.25	35.00
Radio Orphan Annie Shake-Up Game, 1931	10	15	20
Radio Orphan Annie Sun Watch, 1938	12.50	18.75	25.00
Radio Orphan Annie 3-Way Dog Whistle, 1940	17.50	26.25	35.00
Radio Orphan Annie Treasure Hunt Game, 1933	22.50	33.75	45.00
Radio Orphan Annie Treasure Hunt Game, 1935	22.50	33.75	45.00
Range Rider & Dick West button, Peter Pan bread, 1950s	5.00	7.50	10.00
Red Ryder Lucky Coin	4	6	8
Renfrew of the Mounted pin-back . . .	4	6	8
Rin Tin Tin "Ball-in-the-hole" Games (sealed coin-size games of Rinty, Rip Masters, Fort Apache, etc.) each	7.50	11.25	15.00
Rin Tin Tin Ring, plastic, 1950s	7.50	11.25	15.00
Rin Tin Tin set of plastic dinosaurs (Radio-TV 1954)	32.50	48.75	65.00
Rin Tin Tin Wonderscope (Telescope-Microscope-Compass) Radio-TV 1954), has "Rin-Tin-Tin" on face (Same item, without name, recently, perhaps currently, on sale in stores for under $1.00)	22.50	33.75	45.00
Rip Masters (Rin Tin Tin) plastic rings, 1950s	5.00	7.50	10.00
Rocky Lane's Explorer's Sun Watch, 1951, Carnation Milk	12.50	18.75	25.00
Roy Rogers Branding Iron Ring	32.50	48.75	65.00
Roy Rogers Deputy Badge	5.00	7.50	10.00
Roy Rogers Microscope Ring, 1947, Quaker Oats	32.50	48.75	65.00
Roy Rogers Paint Set, 1950s	7.50	11.25	15.00

	C6	C8	C10
Roy Rogers Signal Badge with mirror, secret compartment and whistle ..	32.50	48.75	65.00
Roy Rogers Silver Hat Ring	15.00	22.50	30.00
Roy Rogers - Trigger's Lucky Horseshoe, full size, black rubber	7.50	11.25	15.00
Roy Rogers Tuck-A-Way Gun	5.00	7.50	10.00
Scoop Ward News of Youth Official Reporter Badge, late 1930s, Ward's Soft Bun Bread giveaway	4.50	6.75	9.00
Secret Three Badge, with manual of secret codes	5.00	7.50	10.00
Sgt. Preston Distance Finder	22.50	33.75	45.00
Sgt. Preston Firefighting Set	22.50	33.75	45.00
Sgt. Preston Flashlight – Signals, has two filters	15.00	22.50	30.00
Sgt. Preston Klondike Land Pouch ..	10	15	20
Sgt. Preston Klondike Movie Film Viewer	37.50	56.25	75.00
Sgt. Preston Pedometer	15.00	22.50	30.00
Sgt. Preston Police Whistle with nylon cord, brass, 1950	17.50	26.25	35.00
Sgt. Preston Skinning Knife	22.50	33.75	45.00
Sgt. Preston Totem Pole Set	42.50	63.75	85.00
Sgt. Preston Trail Kit, rare, none known (probably the most complex of all premiums). Probably worth $150 in mint condition			
Sgt. Preston Yukon Village	175.00	262.50	350.00
Shadow Ring, Glow in Dark, "blue coal" jewel on white ring	200	300	400
Shadow "Carey Salt" Ring (same as J. Armstrong Crocodile ring except for black stone; this ring has been counterfeited; original is smoothly circular with clean-cut design	75.00	112.50	150.00
Shield G-Man Club Badge, 1942, Pep Comics premium, lithographed celluloid pinback	12.50	18.75	25.00
Skippy S.S.S.S. Captain, pinback button, all celluloid, 1930s	7.50	11.25	15.00
Skippy Compass, 1930s?	6	9	12
Sky Birds Propellor Ring, brass and silver, 1930s, Goudey Gum premium	2.50	3.75	5.00
Sky King Aztec Indian Ring	47.50	71.25	95.00
Sky King Detecto Microscope	17.50	26.25	35.00
Sky King Detecto Writer	32.50	48.75	65.00
Sky King Electronic Television Ring .	32.50	48.75	65.00
Sky King Magni-Glo Ring	22.50	33.75	45.00
Sky King Mystery Picture Ring (picture never works)	32.50	48.75	65.00
Sky King Navajo Indian Ring	47.50	71.25	95.00
Sky King – Small plastic statues of Sky King, Penny, Sky King's horse, Sky King's plane The Songbird, Nabisco giveaways in Wheat Honey and Rice Honey, 1950s, each	10	15	20
Sky King Signal Scope	30	45	60

SKY KING Teleblinker Ring
Courtesy Jim Harmon

	C6	C8	C10
Sky King Stamp Kit	17.50	26.25	35.00
Sky King Teleblinker Ring	32.50	48.75	65.00
Snow White Game, Tek Toothbrush	25.00	37.50	50.00
Space Patrol Binoculars, circa 1950s	22.50	33.75	45.00
Space Patrol Diplomatic Pouch, contains money, stamps, etc.	25.00	37.50	50.00
Space Patrol Goggles	10	15	20
Space Patrol 1951 Jet Glow Code Belt	50	75	100
Space Patrol Ring, with secret powder compartment, circa early 1950s	50	75	100
Space Patrol Smoke Gun, 1950s	45.00	67.50	90.00
Space Patrol Space Helmet, circa 1950s	47.50	71.25	95.00
Space Patrol 1952 Space-O-Phone	50	75	100
Space Patrol Space Ship, circa 1950s	50	75	100
Speed Gibson's Flying Police Badge, Dreikorn's Bread	11.00	16.50	22.00
Straight Arrow Magic Cave Ring, 1949 with original art	55.00	82.50	110.00
Straight Arrow Magic Cave Ring, reissued 1988 with new art and customer's photos	12.50	18.75	25.00
Straight Arrow Picture Ring, circa early 1950s	32.50	48.75	65.00
Straight Arrow Puppets and props, 1949, Nabisco radio premium	17.50	26.25	35.00
Straight Arrow Target Game, lithographed tin target board, 10"x14" National Biscuit Company copyright on the edge	25.00	37.50	50.00
Straight Arrow Tom-Tom, circa early 1950s	12.50	18.75	25.00
Straight Arrow Wrist Bracelet with secret compartment – circa early 1950s	29.00	43.50	58.00
Sunbrite "Junior Nurse Corps" brass badge	4	6	8
Sunbrite "Junior Nurse Corps" pinback button, pictures of Dorothy Hart	3.50	5.25	7.00
Superman Crusader Ring	75.00	112.50	150.00
Superman Kellogg's Gy Rocket	35.00	52.50	70.00
Superman Kellogg's Silver Jet Airplane Ring, plane flies off	20	30	40

	C6	C8	C10
Superman Pin, 1940s, "Read Superman Action Comics Magazine"	15.00	22.50	30.00
Superman Planes from Pep cereal, set of 8, 1948	22.50	33.75	45.00
Superman Premium Club Set – Certificate, Button and Decoder	62.50	93.75	125.00
Superman Tim Club Ring	35.00	52.50	70.00
Superman's Secret Code, circa 1939	20	30	40
Supermen of America Button – 1939 version, 1⅜" pinback button	25.00	37.50	50.00
Tarzan Gift Statues, Foulds, 1930s, Tarzan, Jane, Kala, etc. Price per set	400	600	800
Tarzan Jungle Map and Treasure Hunt Weston Biscuit, 1933	50	75	100
Tennessee Jed Look Around Ring, 1940s	22.50	33.75	45.00
Tennessee Jed Paper Gun, circa 1940s	17.50	26.25	35.00
Terry And The Pirates Glow in the Dark ring, crocodiles on sides	25.00	37.50	50.00
Terry And The Pirates Gold Detector Ring	30	45	60
Texas Longhorn tin badge, Post Raisin Bran, circa 1950s	2	3	4
Tom Corbett Space Cadet Badge, early 1950s	17.50	26.25	35.00
Tom Corbett Space Cadet Belt Buckle Decoder, early 1950s	37.50	56.25	75.00
Tom Corbett Decoder, cardboard, 1950s	15.00	22.50	30.00
Tom Corbett Rings, Kellogg's, 1950-55, 12 different including: Space Cruiser, Rocket Scout, Space Academy, Space Suit, Space Helmet, Corbett-Space Cadet, Cadet Dress Uniform, Girl's Space Uniform, Parallo-Ray Gun, Strate-Telescope, Sound Ray Gun, per each	7.50	11.25	15.00
Tom Mix Airplane and Parachute	62.50	93.75	125.00
Tom Mix Arm Patch (TM bar on checkerboard design) 1933-predominantly blue; 1947-predominantly red; 1983 - predominantly black (worth probably as much as older versions – only 1000 issued)	20	30	40
Tom Mix Badge – Ranch Box	27.50	41.25	55.00
Tom Mix Belt Buckle with Secret Compartment, belt glows in the dark (offered only on cereal boxes after radio show ended)	62.50	93.75	125.00
Tom Mix Bandana, has TM Brand	37.50	56.25	75.00
Tom Mix Baseball	17.50	26.25	35.00
Tom Mix Baseball bat	17.50	26.25	35.00
Tom Mix Baseball cap	17.50	26.25	35.00
Tom Mix Blowdart Game	42.50	63.75	95.00
Tom Mix Branding Iron, TM Brand	30	45	60
Tom Mix Bullet Flashlight	32.50	48.75	65.00

TOM MIX Look-Around Ring
Courtesy Jim Harmon

ANSWERS to TOM MIX mysteries!

THE TELEVISION MURDER: Photograph of Mint-more (Frame 3) shows he needed thick glasses. Why didn't he have them on if he was watching Television when shot? Window glass shows bullet was fired from inside room. Hole is always smaller on side wh... ...own hands to fake marks on neck. If someone had choked him, the little-finger mark would have been at the bottom of the neck . . . not at top.

TOM MIX Compass-Magnifying Glass, 1939
Courtesy Jim Harmon

TOM MIX Six-Shooter
Courtesy Jim Harmon

ANSWERS to TOM MIX mysteries!

THE TELEVISION MURDER: Photograph of Mint-more (Frame 3) shows he needed thic... glasses. Why didn't he have them on ... was watching Television when shot? ... dow glass shows bullet was fired from insi... room. Hole is always smaller on side wh... ...ed own hands to fake marks on ...meone had choked him, the little-...ould have been at the bottom ... not at top.

TOM MIX Compass-Magnifying Glass, 1937
Courtesy Jim Harmon

	C6	C8	C10
Tom Mix Bullet Telescope, bird-call device comes with it, approx. 4" long	17.50	26.25	35.00
Tom Mix Catalog of Straight Shooter Premiums, 8½"x11" b/w sheet with order form on reverse and descriptions and small pictures of premiums on the front. Includes sheepskin vest, rodeo rope, leather cuffs, wood gun, lucky spinner, etc.	12.50	18.75	25.00

	C6	C8	C10
Tom Mix Charm Bracelet with charm-steer head, gun, horseman, TM brand	30	45	60
Tom Mix Compass Magnifying Glass, 1937, silver color (Note: Originals have "Japan" written on the back. Imitations have the words "Comet-Japan" on the back)	22.50	33.75	45.00
Tom Mix Compass – Magnifying Glass, 1939, brass	32.50	48.75	65.00
Tom Mix Compass – Magnifying Glass, circa 1948, glows in the dark, plastic	32.50	48.75	65.00
Tom Mix Cowboy Shirt	47.50	71.25	95.00
Tom Mix Cowboy Vest	47.50	71.25	95.00
Tom Mix Cowgirl Skirt	62.50	93.75	125.00
Tom Mix Decoder Badge 1940 - moveable 6-shooter points to symbols	42.50	63.75	85.00
Tom Mix Decoder Buttons Instruction Sheet, 1946, Ralston	10	15	20
Tom Mix Decoder Pins – Tom, Tony, Jane, Sheriff, Wash. Price per pin	10	15	20
Tom Mix Decoder Pin "Curley Bradley"	15.00	22.50	30.00
Tom Mix Deputy Ring, 1934, chewing gum premium	37.50	56.25	75.00
Tom Mix Glow-in-the-Dark Arrowhead, 1946, has compass and magnifying glass	32.50	48.75	65.00
Tom Mix Gold Ore Badge	17.50	26.25	35.00
Tom Mix Gold Ore Charm, 1940, Ralston, contains genuine gold ore under plastic dome	17.50	26.25	35.00
Tom Mix "Good Luck" Spinner	15.00	22.50	30.00
Tom Mix Horseshoe nail ring, 1933 (can be verified only by accompanying papers)	25.00	37.50	50.00
Tom Mix Identification Bracelet	22.50	33.75	45.00
Tom Mix Initial Ring, 1935	37.50	56.25	75.00
Tom Mix Look-Around Ring, circa post 1945	27.50	41.25	55.00

TOM MIX Decoder Badge
Courtesy Jim Harmon

TOM MIX Magnet Ring
Courtesy Jim Harmon

TOM MIX Brand Ring

TOM MIX Sharpshooters Medal
Courtesy Jim Harmon

TOM MIX Straightshooters Medal
Courtesy Jim Harmon

TOM MIX Mystery Picture Ring ad
Courtesy Jim Harmon

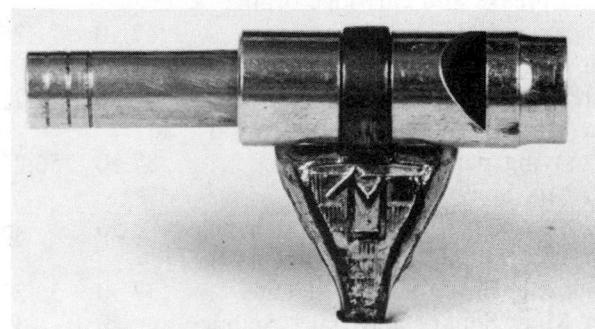

TOM MIX Whistle Ring
Courtesy Jim Harmon

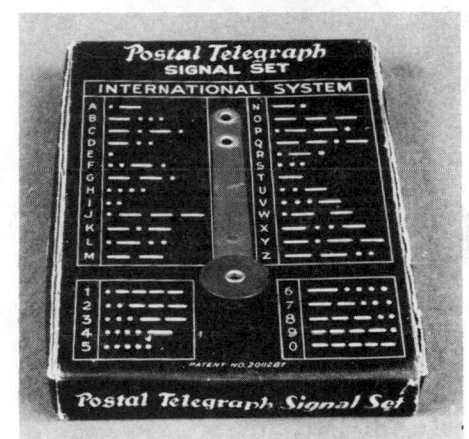

TOM MIX Postal Telegraph Set
Courtesy Jim Harmon

	C6	C8	C10
Tom Mix Lucky Wrist Band, 1936, Ralston premium, metal, TM bar brand, with leather strap and buckle	37.50	56.25	75.00
Tom Mix Magnet Gun and Signal Arrowhead bracelet, gun and arrowhead glow in the dark	44.50	66.75	85.00
Tom Mix Magnet Ring, 1945	32.50	48.75	65.00
Tom Mix Makeup kit (two grease-paint model, plus five grease-paint model)	125.00	187.50	250.00
Tom Mix 1941 Manual	30	45	60
Tom Mix 1944 Manual	34	51	68
Tom Mix 1946 Manual	27.50	41.25	55.00
Tom Mix Mask, cardboard	32.50	48.75	65.00
Tom Mix Mystery Picture Ring, 1939, with "look-in" picture of Tom Mix and Tony, viewed through one side of the ring	75.00	112.50	150.00
Tom Mix Parachute – 1936 Ralston premium	37.50	56.25	75.00
Tom Mix Periscope	32.50	48.75	65.00
Tom Mix Postal Telegraph Set – Blue, metal clicker, 1938	32.50	48.75	65.00

	C6	C8	C10
Tom Mix Premium Enclosures and Correspondence; Many picture postcards, letters on Straight Shooter stationery, etc. were sent out to listeners who wrote in to the radio show; these and various coupons, instruction sheets, contest entries are offered by dealers and collectors. Average value	10	15	30
Tom Mix Telegraph Set – red, uses batteries, 1940	100	150	200
Tom Mix Ralston Straight Shooters Pocket Knife, 1940	32.50	48.75	65.00

	C6	C8	C10
Tom Mix RCA TV set - shows photographs or comic strips (brown model or reddish model)	17.50	26.25	35.00
Tom Mix Secret Code Manual	27.50	41.25	55.00
Tom Mix Sharpshooters Medal, glows in the dark	27.50	41.25	55.00
Tom Mix Sheriff of Dobie County Siren Badge, 1946, Ralston	22.50	33.75	45.00
Tom Mix Signal Arrowhead, 1949 with magnifying glass and "whizzer" flute-type whistle, made of lucite	32.50	48.75	65.00
Tom Mix Signal Flashlight	32.50	48.75	65.00
Tom Mix Signature Ring, pre WW II	47.50	61.25	95.00
Tom Mix Siren Ring, 1945	37.50	56.25	75.00
Tom Mix Six-Shooter – wooden, barrel breaks and cartridge drum spins - 1933	47.50	71.25	95.00
Tom Mix Six Shooter – wooden, barrel spins, 1936	47.50	71.25	95.00
Tom Mix Six-Shooter – wooden, no moving parts, 1939	37.50	56.25	75.00
Tom Mix Spinning Rope, 1936, Ralston, hemp with wood handle	30	45	60
Tom Mix Spurs – metal, with plastic glow-in-the-dark rowels. Late	37.50	56.25	75.00
Tom Mix "Square and Fair" Spinner	20	30	40
Tom Mix Straight Shooters Campaign Medal, gold	22.50	33.75	45.00
Tom Mix Straight Shooters Campaign Medal, silver	22.50	33.75	45.00
Tom Mix Sundial Watch	37.50	56.25	75.00
Tom Mix Telephone Set	32.50	48.75	65.00
Tom Mix Telescope, TM brand on side	32.50	48.75	65.00
Tom Mix Tiger Eye Ring, 1949, Ralston	62.50	93.75	125.00
Tom Mix TM Brand ring, circa 1933	32.50	48.75	65.00
Tom Mix Tri-Color Flashlight	32.50	48.75	65.00
Tom Mix Western Movie Viewer – shows scenes from Tom Mix films, 1935	47.50	71.25	95.00
Tom Mix Whistle Ring, 1945	32.50	48.75	65.00
Tom Mix Wrangler Badge, 1936, Ralston	30	45	60
Toonerville Trolley cardboard village put out by Coca Cola	70	105	140
Trigger Button, ⅞", Post Grape Nut Flakes	2	3	4
Welch's Grape Juice Train; paper engine, box car, passenger car, caboose. Price for each	1.50	2.25	3.00
Complete Set above	7.50	11.25	15.00
Wheaties Jogometer	9.00	13.50	18.00
Wheaties Pedometer, circa late 1940s	5.00	7.50	10.00
Wild Bill Hickok Bunkhouse Set (cutout pin-ups of Bill, Jingles, guns, ropes, etc.)	20	30	40
Wild Bill Hickok Treasure Map & Guide, 1952, Kellogg's	17.50	26.25	35.00

WELCH'S GRAPE JUICE Engine and Box Car
Courtesy Gary Linden

WELCH'S GRAPE JUICE Passenger Car and Caboose
Courtesy Gary Linden

CONDITION CODE:

C5 – Good, wear evident overall, shows that has been played with
C6 – Fine, shows some wear in spots, but taken care of
C7 – Very Fine, minor wear overall, very clean
C8 – Excellent, minor wear on edges only
C9 – Near Mint, no noticeable flaws, close inspection may show minute marks
C10 – Mint (like new)
    Note: Mint in Box does command higher price

COMIC CHARACTER

(See also Premiums, Paper, Mechanical Banks, Vehicles – Arcade; Hubley; Tootsietoy)

Average mint price of these toys in the 4th edition was $162.99, and this year was $336.89, an increase of 107%.

Comic character toys are attractive to collectors as they are often colorful and eye-catching, as well as evocative of happy childhood memories. Popeye continues to be a magnet for collectors, with such as The Yellow Kid, Buck Rogers, Flash Gordon, Tarzan, Superman, Felix the Cat, Barney Google and Happy Hooligan also proving strong lures.

Alphonse, HUBLEY, two goats pulling wagon
Courtesy Kruse Auctioneers

	C6	C8	C10
Albert Alligator (Pogo) plastic, 1969, approx. 5" high ("Duz")	6	9	12
Alphonse, Hubley, in a goat-pulled cart, cast iron, 13¾" long, 7½" high, early 1900s, from comic strip team of Alphonse and Gaston, head-nodder, movable arms and hands	150	225	300
Alphonse, Hubley, mule pulling wagon, 6½" long	350	525	700
Alphonse, Hubley, two goats pulling wagon, cast iron, 13¾" long, 7½" high, early 1900s, head-nodder, movable arms and hands	150	225	300
Andy Gump wooden dancing doll 9" tin legs	125.00	187.50	250.00
B.O. Plenty holding Sparkle Plenty, circa mid-1940s, tin wind-up, Marx	140	210	280
Baby Snookums (The Newlyweds) fabric doll, 5½" high	150	225	300
Baby Sparkle Plenty paper dolls, Saalfield No. 1510	15.00	22.50	30.00
Barney Google, cloth and wood, Schoenhut	250	375	500

BARNEY GOOGLE cloth and wood doll, SHOENHUT. Courtesy Sotheby's, N.Y.

B. O. PLENTY holding SPARKLE PLENTY
Photo by Don Hultzman

363

	C6	C8	C10
Barney Google Doll, 9" high, wood with composition head, movable arms and legs	200	300	400
Barney Google glass candy container	180	270	360
Barney Google and Sparkplug pulltoy, tin litho, Sparkplug in barn	1450	2175	2900
Barney Google riding Sparkplug, wooden	100	150	200
Barney Google tin wind-up, circa 1923	400	600	800
Barney Google and Sparkplug, tin wind-up by Nifty	750	1125	1500
Batman "Batmobile - Batman Driver," 1966, Marx	50	75	100
Batman "Batmobile - Robin Driver," Marx, 4" long	50	75	100
Batman candy container, Pez, Mego head	7.50	11.25	15.00
Batman candy container, Pez, 1980 ..	5.00	7.50	10.00
Batman glasses, 1966	10	15	20
Batman Handpuppet, cloth body	12	18	24
Batman Handpuppet, vinyl, Ideal ...	10	15	20
Batman Helmet and cape, helmet fits over whole head, 1966, Ideal	70	105	140
Batman Thingmaker set, 1960s	50	75	100
Batman Utility Belt, 1941, with belt-radio buckle	110	165	220
Beauregard (Pogo), plastic, 1969	6	9	12
Beetle Bailey vinyl figure, 3"	6	9	12
Billy Batson (Capt. Marvel) Magic Box	36	54	72
Blondie "Blondie's Jalopy," actually has only Alexander and Dagwood in car, other characters lithoed on chassis, 16" long	450	675	900
Blondie, 1940, Whitman 982, paper cut-outs	30	45	60
Blondie, 1947, Whitman 967, paper cut-outs	20	30	40
Bonnie Braids (Dick Tracy), "Bonnie Braids Doll," Marx, 1950s wind-up, 9" long	150	225	300
Bonnie Braids Paper Dolls - Dick Tracy's daughter and wife Tess, Saalfield No 2724, 1951, cut-outs	25.00	37.50	50.00
Boob McNutt tin wind-up, Strauss ..	500	750	1000
Boots and Her Buddies Paper Dolls, 1943, Saalfield 2460	26	39	52
Bringing Up Father, hingee, 1944 ...	20	30	40
Brutus (Popeye) cardboard mask, 1940s	40	60	80
Brutus (Popeye) Dippy Dumper, celluloid figure, circa 1930, eccentric car	300	450	600
Buck Rogers Atomic Pistol, 1946, U-235, sparks and pops, Daisy ..	140	210	280
Buck Rogers Battle Cruiser, Tootsietoy, 1937, two grooved wheels on top to run on string	100	150	200
Buck Rogers binoculars, 1950s	60	90	120

	C6	C8	C10
Buck Rogers Casting Set, 1930s, Junior Caster, Rapaport Bros. ...	400	600	800
Buck Rogers Chemical Laboratory, Gropper Toys, 1937	1000	1500	2000
Buck Rogers Disintegrator pistol, 1936, Daisy	110	165	220
Buck Rogers figure, Tootsietoy, 1¾" high	37.50	56.25	75.00
Buck Rogers "Flash Blast" Attack Ship, Tootsietoy, 1937, two grooved wheels on top to run string, 4½" long	100	150	200
Buck Rogers Helmet, Daisy, 1933, leather	200	300	400
Buck Rogers lead figures – these are generally new, from early casting sets. Sell for $8.00 painted.			
Buck Rogers Liquid Helium water pistol, Daisy, 1936	160	240	320
Buck Rogers "Pop" pistol, 1930s	110	165	220
Buck Rogers Rocket Pistol, XZ-31, 1934, Daisy, 9½" long	120	180	240
Buck Rogers Rocket Police Patrol, wind-up, Marx, 1939	450	675	900
Buck Rogers Rocket Ship, Marx Wind-up, 12" long, 1934	500	750	1000

BUCK ROGERS Rocket Ship
Photo by Don Hultzman

BUCK ROGERS Rocket Police Patrol.

HENRY Celluloid and tin wind-up.

BUCK ROGERS Battlecruiser,

Flash Attack Ship,

Venus Duo Destroyer.

Courtesy PB Eighty-Four.

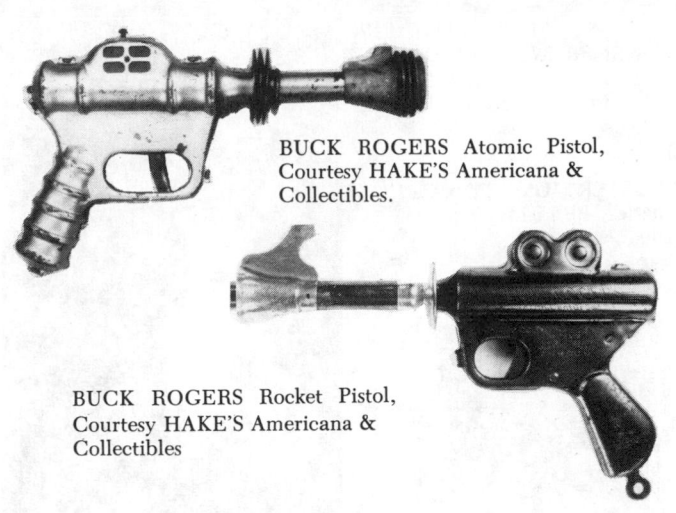

BUCK ROGERS Atomic Pistol, Courtesy HAKE'S Americana & Collectibles.

BUCK ROGERS Rocket Pistol, Courtesy HAKE'S Americana & Collectibles

Captain Marvel Buzz Bomb
Courtesy Continental Hobby House

	C6	C8	C10
"Buck Rogers Rubber Band Gun," 5"x10" punchouts card, 1940	100	150	200
Buck Rogers Sonic Ray Gun, yellow plastic, uses bulb and battery	60	90	120
Buck Rogers Strato Kite, 1946	30	45	60
Buck Rogers Super-Scope, 1953, Norton-Honer Mfg. Co., 8½" long, adjustable plastic telescope .	40	60	80
Buck Rogers Super Sonic Glasses (binoculars), 1953	40	60	80
Buck Rogers U-238 Atomic Pistol & Holster set, 1948	150	225	300
Buck Rogers U-238 Atomic Pistol & Holster set, with box, adventure book and coupon, 1948, Daisy ..	160	240	320
Buck Rogers "USN Los Angeles" Tootsietoy, 5" long dirigible	100	150	200
Buck Rogers Venus Duo Destroyer, Tootsietoy, two grooved wheels on top to run on string, 1937	100	150	200
Buck Rogers Walkie Talkie, 1950s ...	60	90	120
Buster Brown cast iron, painted	100	150	200
Buster Brown in cart pulled by Tige, cast iron	300	450	600
Buster Brown & Tige paper dolls, J. Ottman Lith. Co., N.Y. Envelope, doll, Tige, 4 suits, 4 hats, plus hat for Tige	60	90	120
Buster Brown & Tige ring, brass, 1930s	40	60	80
Buster Brown Doll, 23" high, 1920s .	110	165	220
Buster Brown figure, lead	6	9	12
Buster Brown Secret Agent Periscope, circa 1950	30	45	60
Buttercup (Toots & Casper) stuffed cloth doll, 18" high, jointed head, arms, legs, circa 1924	250	375	500
Buttercup & Spareribs, Nifty, Buttercup beats Spareribs with broom ..	700	1050	1400

	C6	C8	C10
Captain Marvel Buzz Bomb	10	15	20
Captain Marvel Comic Hero Punch-Outs, 1942, Samuel Lowe, has Captain Marvel (2), Capt. Marvel Jr., Bulletman, Bulletgirl, Spy Smasher, Ibis, Golden Arrow (2), Minute Man, Freddy Freeman, Mr. Scarlet, Commando Yank, Pinky, Bulletdog	210	315	420
Captain Marvel Gun, movie gun with film	175.00	262.50	350.00
Captain Marvel Magic Flute, copyright 1946, picture of Captain Marvel on side	60	90	120
Captain Marvel Lightning race car, 1948, Fawcett, tin wind-up, 4" long	70	105	140
Captain Marvel Toss Bag	10	15	20
Captain Marvel Jr. Ski Jump, 7"x10", circa 1946, paper, Reed & Associates, Chicago	24	36	48
Captain Marvel's Magic Picture, circa 1944, Reed	30	45	60
Captain Marvel's Magic Eyes, circa 1945, Reed	25.00	37.50	50.00
Captain Marvel's Rocket Raider, circa 1944-47, Reed	35.00	52.50	70.00
Charlie Brown composition bouncing head, 1950s, possibly first Peanuts toy	20	30	40
Chester Gump 12" high, oilcloth	60	90	120
Chester Gump 13" high oilcloth doll, circa 1920s	100	150	200
Chester Gump Cart, Arcade, 1920s, horse, open two-wheel cart, Chester driving	350	525	700
Comic Strip Rings, 1953, King Features, Phantom, Blondie, Barney Google, etc.	15.00	22.50	30.00
Churchy (Pogo) plastic, 1969, 4½" high	6	9	12
Cookie (Blondie), Syrocco, 1940s	15.00	22.50	30.00
Dagwood Aeroplane, 1935, Marx "Dagwood's Solo Flight"	350	525	700
Dagwood "Dagwood the Driver" Crazy Car, 1935, Marx, 8" long .	200	300	400

	C6	C8	C10
Dagwood Marionette, 15" wood body, plastic head, hands, feet, "Hazelle's," life-like hair, 1940s ..	60	90	120
Daisy Mae and Li'l Abner Paper Dolls with Mammy and Pappy Yokum, Saalfield No. 2360, 1941	45.00	67.50	90.00
Daisy Mae with Li'l Abner in Paper Dolls, Saalfield No. 280, 1942 ...	45.00	67.50	90.00
Dan Dunn Det. Corps Secret Operative 28 tin badge, circa 1930s	30	45	60
Denny Dimwit (Winnie Winkle) 11" composition doll	150	225	300
Dick Tracy Air Detective Wings, circa late 1930s	20	30	40
Dick Tracy and Junior Knife with Crimestopper whistle and clue detector	30	45	60
Dick Tracy Automatic, Hubley, with picture of Eagles	60	90	120
Dick Tracy click pistol, Marx No. 36	40	60	80
Dick Tracy Crimestoppers Set, badge, handcuffs, billy club	65.00	97.50	130.00
Dick Tracy detective badge with secret compartment, late 1930s, large, metal, leather pouch on back	70	105	140
Dick Tracy Detective Fingerprint Set, 1933	90	135	180
Dick Tracy Electronic Wrist Radio ..	30	45	60
Dick Tracy G-Man wind-up gun	60	90	120
Dick Tracy Hingee, paper figures, 1940s, set of six	15.00	22.50	30.00
Dick Tracy Inspector General badge .	70	105	140
Dick Tracy Pen-Lite, 1940s?	30	45	60
Dick Tracy "Police Station" with 7" long automatic siren car, 1950s ..	140	210	280
Dick Tracy Riot Car, circa 1946, Marx, heavy tin or sheetmetal litho, 7½" long, friction motor ..	90	135	180
Dick Tracy Siren Pistol, red with blue siren, circa late 1930s	70	105	140
Dick Tracy Siren Police Whistle No. 64, Marx, tin	30	45	60
Dick Tracy Sparkling Pop Pistol, tin litho, Marx No. 96	60	90	120
Dick Tracy Squad Car, convertible, heavy tin or sheetmetal, 20" long, Marx, circa 1948, friction motor with siren and battery-powered flashing light, Dick Tracy and Sam Catchum in plastic	100	150	200
Dick Tracy Squad Car No. 1, Marx, 11" long, friction	75.00	112.50	150.00
Dick Tracy Squad Car No. 1, Marx, 6¾" long, friction	50	75	100
Dick Tracy Sub-Machine Gun, 1946, "Raider"	80	120	160
Dick Tracy Target Game, Marx G25	40	60	80

DAISY MAE WITH LI'L ABNER IN PAPER DOLLS.
Photo by Jonathan A. Newman
Courtesy Barbara and Jonathan Newman

CHESTER GUMP Pony Cart. Courtesy PB Eighty-Four, New York.

DICK TRACY "Police Station"
Photo by Don Hultzman

DICK TRACY Riot Car
Courtesy Gary Linden

DICK TRACY Squad Car No. 1, MARX, 6¾" long
Courtesy Gary Linden

DICK TRACY Squad Car No. 1, MARX, 11" long
Courtesy Gary Linden

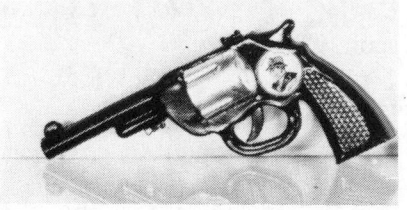

DICK TRACY Click
Pistol
Photo Courtesy PB 84
New York

	C6	C8	C10
Dick Tracy Target Game, Marx G34	50	75	100
Dick Tracy tin wind-up police car, 1949, 7" long	40	60	80
Dick Tracy viewer, 1940s, two films	30	45	60
Dick Tracy Jr. Click Pistol No. 78, Marx, aluminum	30	45	60
Dick Tracy's Handcuffs for Junior, circa 1946, John Henry Products No. 700	20	30	40
Dick Tracy Water Pistol, plastic, 1955	15.00	22.50	30.00
Don Winslow Flashlight Gun	70	105	140
Ella Cinders 17" high cloth and composition, 1925	100	150	200
Elmer Fudd Handpuppet, 1950s	20	30	40
Favorite Funnies large size rubber print set, Dick Tracy, Orphan Annie, etc. 14 stamps, pad, booklet	30	45	60
Felix The Cat, 2" high, cast iron, 1923	30	45	60
Felix The Cat, 2" high, pot metal nodding head figure, copyright Pat Sullivan on bottom of feet	70	105	140
Felix The Cat, 2¼" high, lead	40	60	80
Felix The Cat 2½" high, cast iron, circa 1930	100	150	200
Felix The Cat, 4" high, Schoenhut, 1925, jointed wood	200	300	400
Felix The Cat 6" high, 1924, wooden, George Borgfeldt Co., standup leather ears, jointed	100	150	200
Felix The Cat, 6½" rubber squeeze toy	20	30	40
Felix The Cat, 7" high, jointed wood figure, circa 1924	110	165	220
Felix The Cat, 8" high, tin with walking feet	130	195	260
Felix the Cat, 8" wood-jointed doll, 1924	160	240	320
Felix The Cat, 8" wood-jointed doll, 1930s	140	210	280
Felix The Cat, 9" wood-jointed, Schoenhut, 1923	350	525	700
Felix The Cat, 9" high, 1940s, wood, jointed with rubber head	70	105	140
Felix The Cat 12" high, wood	20	30	40
Felix The Cat, 13" high, composition, circa 1930s	140	210	280
Felix The Cat Doll, 15" high, stuffed, Gund, hands molded rubber, the rest cloth, circa 1950	80	120	160

FELIX THE CAT jointed wood figure, 7" high
Courtesy PB Eighty-Four, New York

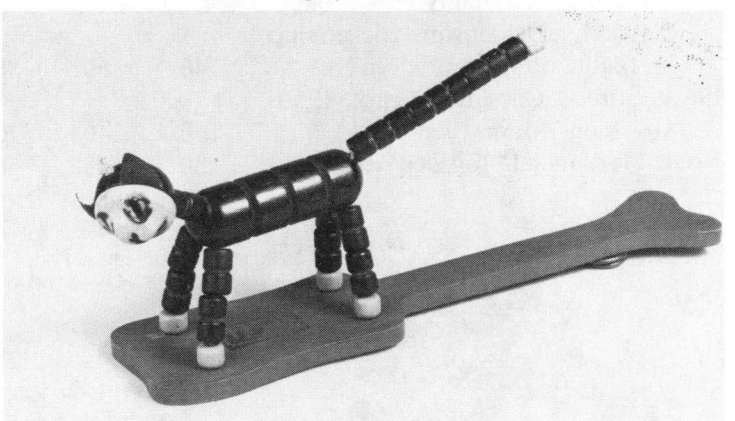

FELIX THE CAT "pop-up"
Courtesy Mapes Auctioneers & Appraisers

FELIX THE CAT on scooter
Courtesy Phillips New York

	C6	C8	C10
Felix The Cat, China Set	60	90	120
Felix The Cat flasher ring, plastic	15.00	22.50	30.00

	C6	C8	C10
Felix The Cat on fire truck, gong bell pull toy	70	105	140
Felix The Cat on scooter, Nifty	210	315	420
Felix The Cat on tricycle, gong bell pull toy	130	195	260
Felix The Cat "pop-up," jointed wood, string-operated, Fisher Price	10	15	20
Felix The Cat Pull Car, 12" long, Borgfeldt, 1925	300	450	600
Felix The Cat "Speedy Felix" in car	150	225	300
Felix The Cat Walker, painted wood and tin	200	300	400
Flash Gordon aluminum pistol, 10" long, shoots blast of air using rubber diaphragm	60	90	120
Flash Gordon Arresting Ray, Marx, 1936?, picture of Flash on handle	80	120	160
Flash Gordon Automatic Disintegrator, Hubley	100	150	200
Flash Gordon belt, many illos, large plastic buckle showing rocket ship in flight, 1950s	40	60	80
Flash Gordon Click Ray Pistol, 1950s, 10" long, Marx	160	240	320
Flash Gordon jet-propelled kite	30	45	60

FLASH GORDON Signal Pistol
Photo Courtesy PB 84 New York

FLASH GORDON
Rocket Fighter.
Courtesy PB Eighty-
Four, New York.

	C6	C8	C10
Flash Gordon Playsuit, Esquire Novelty, 1940s	75.00	112.50	150.00
Flash Gordon Radio Repeater clicker pistol, No. 58, Marx, 1950s, 10" long	180	270	360
Flash Gordon Rocket Fighter, Marx wind-up, 12" long, 1939	390	585	780
Flash Gordon Signal Pistol, tin litho, Marx No. 74	80	120	160
Flash Gordon Solar commando; three plastic space men and one ship, 1950s	20	30	40
Flash Gordon Space Cruiser, 1952	25.00	37.50	50.00
Flash Gordon Space Outfit	90	135	180
Flash Gordon Space Target, metal, standup, Alex Raymond illustration, 12x14	40	60	80

	C6	C8	C10
Flash Gordon Strat-O-Wagon, 9" long, Wyandotte	90	135	180
Flash Gordon Two way telephone, Marx, circa 1940	70	105	140
Flash Gordon water gun, plastic, 1950s	10	15	20
Flying Captain Marvel, 1944-47, Reed, 7"x10", paper	6	9	12

FOXY GRANDPA
A Roly-Poly.
Courtesy Lloyd W.
Ralston Auctions

FOXY GRANDPA
Jack In The Box.
Courtesy Lloyd W.
Ralston Auctions

FOXY GRANDPA clockwork figure
Courtesy PB 84 New York

	C6	C8	C10
Foxy Grandpa clockwork figure, tin, German, 8¼" high	300	450	600
Foxy Grandpa Jack in the Box, papier mache and paper litho on wood, 1900, 4" square	160	240	320
Foxy Grandpa Nodder, papier mache, 1900, 6" tall	120	180	240
Foxy Grandpa nodder, Hubley, circa 1910, cast iron, 6½", Grandpa large-headed in cart pulled by donkey	300	450	600
Foxy Grandpa Roly Poly, painted papier mache	110	165	220

HAPPY HOLLIGAN
Roly-Poly
Courtesy Lloyd W.
Ralston Auctions

HAPPY HOOLIGAN in cart, horse pulled.

	C6	C8	C10
Henry "Henry and his Swan," celluloid mechanical	450	675	900
Henry "Henry Eating Candy," 1950s, Linemar	400	600	800
Herby, 10" oilcloth doll	20	30	40
Herman (Harvey Comics Character) "Herman Nodder," 1950s, Linemar, 4½" high	150	225	300

HAPPY HOOLIGAN on a ladder, SCHOENHUT
Courtesy PB 84 New York

HI-WAY HENRY
Courtesy Phillips New York

	C6	C8	C10
"Gasoline Alley Garage and Auto Racer," 1924, Girard, tin litho garage and "Bearcat Racer" car	210	315	420
Gremlin (Gloom) T.E. Powers, in leather clothes, 1943	20	30	40
Happy Hooligan Donkey Cart, circa 1925, (possibly Wilkins), 10" long	200	300	400
Happy Hooligan in cart, Kenton, early 1900s, 10¼" long, 7½" high, horse-pulled, head nods, cast iron	450	675	900
Happy Hooligan on a Ladder, Schoenhut	200	300	400
Happy Hooligan Police Patrol, Kenton, 18" long, Happy hit by cop as Gloomy Gus drives	1700	2550	3400
Happy Hooligan Roly Poly	110	165	220
Happy Hooligan walking toy, Chein wind-up, 1932, 6" high	600	900	1200
Heckle, squeeze toy, 1950s	10	15	20
Henry, 9½" high rubber squeeze toy, 1950s	12	18	24
Henry celluloid and tin wind-up, Japanese, Henry sits on elephant's trunk	600	900	1200

	C6	C8	C10
Hi-Way Henry, wind-up, 1920s, jalopy with man, woman, laundry above roof	1600	2400	3200
Hoppy the Flying Marvel Bunny, circa 1944-47, Reed, paper	6	9	12
Howland Owl (Pogo), 1969, plastic, 4½" high ("Duz")	6	9	12
Humphrey Mobile (Joe Palooka) tin wind-up, circa mid-1940s, Wyandotte	300	450	600
Jane Arden, 1942, Saalfield 2408, paper dolls	30	45	60
Jeep (Popeye) wood-jointed, 1930s	60	90	120
Jeff 6" composition doll, ball joints, felt clothes	110	165	220
Jeff bendable figure, 1946	120	180	240
Jeff Stick Puppet, 12" high	40	60	80
Jiggs 3" high, hard plastic, 1960s	6	9	12
Jiggs 5" wood-jointed doll	40	60	80
Jiggs 7" high, wood-jointed doll, Schoenhut	450	675	900
Jiggs Stick Puppet, 12" high	40	60	80
Joan Palooka doll	50	75	100
Joe Palooka, 4" high, wood-jointed	20	30	40
Joe Palooka 5½" high wood-jointed doll	30	45	60

369

HUMPHREYMOBILE
Courtesy Mapes Auctioneers & Appraisers

KRAZY KAT on a Skooter. NIFTY used Felix the Cat's head for some reason
Courtesy Phillips, N.Y.

	C6	C8	C10
Joe Palooka Championship belt buckle, circa early 50s, heavy gold-plated brass buckle shows Palooka with hands raised in victory	12	18	24
Joe Palooka Filmatic, 12 different comic strips	20	30	40
Joe Palooka Punching Bag, circa 1950	10	15	20

KATZENJAMMER KIDS. Mama spanking kid, KENTON, 1911
Courtesy Ed Hyers Antique Toys

	C6	C8	C10
Katzenjammer Kids, Mama spanking Kid, other Kid standing, as Sailor drives mule cart, Kenton, 1911, 12" long	2000	3000	4000
Katzenjammer Kids See-Saw Bell Toy, Kenton	800	1200	1600
Kayo (Moon Mullins) 9¾" oilcloth doll	30	45	60
Kayo 10" high Sun Rubber circa 1937, head swivels	180	270	360
Komic Kamera – All metal viewer circa mid-1930s, used to view 35mm film strips. With set of five film strips	40	60	80
Komic Kamera, without film strips	20	30	40
"Krazy Kat On A Skooter," tin wind-up, Nifty, 1920s, 7¼" long	300	450	600

LI'L ABNER AND HIS DOGPATCH BAND, UNIQUE.
Courtesy Phillips New York

	C6	C8	C10
Li'l Abner Handpuppet	100	150	200
Li'l Abner and His Dogpatch Band, 1945, Unique, wind-up	350	525	700
Little Beaver Archery Set, 1951	30	45	60
Little King Walker, plastic, circa 1956	40	60	80
Little King, wooden pull toy, Jay-Mar, 1938, 4" high	80	120	160
Little Lulu 10" high felt doll	40	60	80
Little Lulu 14" high, Georgene Novelties, stuffed doll	150	225	300
Little Luli, 14" high, doll with mask face, 1944, M.H. Buell	55.00	82.50	110.00
Little Lulu "Shape Book," 1971, Whitman No. 1970	4	6	8
Little Mary Mixup And Her Friend Peggy, 1922, Saalfield No. 294, paper dolls	40	60	80
Little Orphan Annie 9½" printed fabric doll, 1930s	40	60	80

LITTLE MARY MIXUP AND HER FRIEND PEGGY
Photo by Jonathan Newman
Courtesy Barbara and Jonathan Newman

LITTLE ORPHAN ANNIE, jumping rope, tin-windup.

	C6	C8	C10
Little Orphan Annie Water Pistol ...	60	90	120
Little Orphan Annie Junior Commandos, 1943, Saalfield No. 299	30	45	60
Lonesome Polecat (Lil Abner), 1950s, rubber squeak toy, Reinert	30	45	60
Lucy 7¾" high squeeze toy, 1950s ..	10	15	20
Lucy 8¾" high, vinyl squeeze toy, 1950s	15.00	22.50	30.00
Maggie 3" hard plastic, 1960s	6	9	12
Maggie 9" high wood jointed doll, Schoenhut	450	675	900
Maggie & Jiggs, 1920s, Nifty, seated on 2-wheeled platform, 8" long ..	800	1200	1600
Maggie & Jiggs wind-up, Strauss, 1924, 7¼" long, German	600	900	1200
Mammy Yokum, doll, 21" high, rubber	30	45	60
Mandrake the Magician Magic Kit, 1949, Transogram	50	75	100
Mighty Mouse, rubber, 9" high, no mfr. listed	20	30	40
Moon Maid's Daughter (Dick Tracy) 16½" doll with space helmet, Ideal, 1965	60	90	120
Moon Mullins and Kayo on Hand Car, 1930s, 6" long, Marx tin wind-up	600	900	1200

MAGGIE & JIGGS, 1920s, NIFTY.
Courtesy PB Eight-Four, New York

MOON MULLINS and KAYO on Hand Car
Courtesy Phillips New York

LITTLE LULU doll
Courtesy Toy Collector News

	C6	C8	C10
Little Orphan Annie 16¼" oilcloth doll, circa 1920s	150	225	300
Little Orphan Annie Hingees, 1944, Annie, Sandy, Daddy, Punjab, price per set	60	90	120
Little Orphan Annie Skipping Rope, tin wind-up, 1930s	400	600	800
Little Orphan Annie and Sandy, tin wind-up, Marx, 1930s	350	525	700
Little Orphan Annie stove, 8" high, circa 1930s	90	135	180
Moon Mullins and Mamie Face Masks, 1933, each	10	15	20
Movie Komics, reels of film for toy viewers, circa 1940s	10	15	20
Mrs. Blossom (Gasoline Alley) 17" high oilcloth	80	120	160
Mutt 8" high composition doll with ball joints, felt clothes	100	150	200
Mutt bendable figure, 1946	120	180	240
Mutt Wooden Dancing Doll	20	30	40

	C6	C8	C10
Nancy 14" high stuffed doll, Georgene Novelties	90	135	180
Olive Oyl 11" Gund marionette	50	75	100
Olive Oyl Ballerina, Linemar tin mechanical	400	600	800
Olive Oyl Handpuppet, circa 1938, Gund	20	30	40
Olive Oyl Hingees No. 102, paper punchouts, Reed & Associates	10	15	20
Olive Oyl Mask, cardboard, 1940s	20	30	40
Olive Oyl Rubber Squeeze Toy, 1950s	20	30	40
Olive Oyl String and wood puppet, approx. 5" high, Jaymar circa 1940s	70	105	140
Olive Oyl and Sweepea Hand Car, Marx	210	315	420

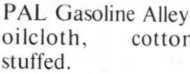

PAL Gasoline Alley, oilcloth, cotton stuffed.

	C6	C8	C10
Pal (Gasoline Alley) oilcloth doll, cotton-stuffed, 1923	80	120	160
Pappy Yokum Doll, 21" high, rubber	40	60	80
Peanuts figures: Charlie Brown, Lucy, Linus, Schroeder, Snoopy, Avon, price per each	6	9	12
Pete (the Tramp?) 1930s composition doll, strung	30	45	60
Pogo plastic, 1969, 4" high	6	9	12
Pogo Pogomobile	150	225	300
Popeye 3½" high, cast iron, circa 1930	100	150	200
Popeye 4" high, solid celluloid, 1930s	100	150	200
Popeye 7" high, hollow rubber, dated "1935" on back	90	135	180
Popeye, 8" high, celluloid, keywind, head spins, foreign	175.00	262.50	350.00
Popeye, 9" high, celluloid wind-up, neck goes up and down, circa 1930	450	675	900
Popeye 11" high, Chein, circa 1935	250	375	500
Popeye 14" high, "Cameo" hard rubber, jointed at neck, hips, shoulders	90	135	180
Popeye 14" high, composition, "Popeye 1935 King Features Syn"	400	600	800
Popeye 14" high, wood and composition, jointed arms and legs, "1935"	200	300	400
Popeye 15" high, composition, rolling up sleeve	60	90	120
Popeye 20" high, rubber arms and head, stuffed body, Gund, circa 1950s	50	75	100
Popeye Acrobat, Marx, tin wind-up	400	600	800

POPEYE "Boom Boom Popeye"
Courtesy Mapes Auctioneers & Appraisers

POPEYE Spinach Patrol
Photo by C.B.C. Lee
POPEYE Puncher
Courtesy Sotheby Parke Bernet

	C6	C8	C10
Popeye Basketball Player, Linemar tin wind-up	500	750	1000
Popeye "Bifbat" paddle toy, 1929	60	90	120
Popeye "Bo Lo Paddle," 1929	20	30	40
Popeye "Boom Boom Popeye," Fisher Price, drummer, 491 (see Fisher-Price)			
Popeye carrying parrots in cages, Marx wind-up, 1935, 7¾" high	210	315	420
Popeye "Dippy Dumper" truck, Marx	425.00	637.50	850.00
Popeye "Eccentric Plane," 1940, Marx wind-up, 8" long	350	525	700
Popeye Express – Marx, overhead airplane, 1935, flies over train	500	750	1000
Popeye Express – Marx, Popeye pushing box with parrot, wind-up, 1935	450	675	900

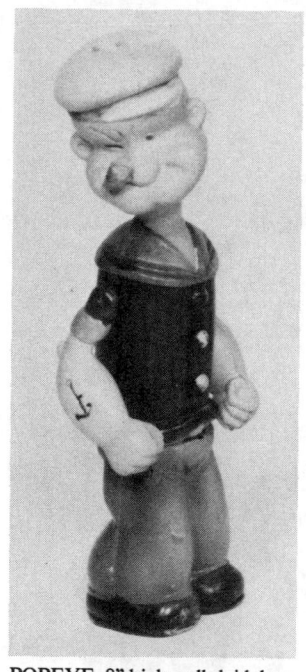

POPEYE, 8" high, celluloid, key-
wind, head spins, foreign.
Courtesy Phillips New York

POPEYE on a Unicycle.
LINEMAR
Courtesy Phillips New York

POPEYE in a Barrel
Photo by Don Hultzman

POPEYE Basketball Player box.
Courtesy Phillips New York

"POPEYE PATROL," HUBLEY, 8½ inches long
Courtesy Phillips New York

POPEYE the Pilot
Photo by Don Hultzman

	C6	C8	C10
Popeye Handcar, Marx, 1935, Popeye & Olive Oyl, composition	600	900	1200
Popeye Handpuppet	20	30	40
Popeye Hingee paper figures, No. 102, Reed, 1940s, price per each	10	15	20
Popeye in a barrel, Chein, 7" high	210	315	420
Popeye Jack-in-the-Box, Mattel Co., tin mechanical, Popeye pops out of spinach can	30	45	60
Popeye "Popeye Jigger" (on rooftop), Marx wind-up, 9½" high	300	450	600
Popeye mask, cardboard, 1940s	30	45	60
Popeye Moving Van, tin friction, Linemar	300	450	600
Popeye One-Man Band, pole with drum and cymbals, rubber Popeye head on top, 69" high	70	105	140
Popeye Pirate, click pistol, Marx No. 68	100	150	200
Popeye the Pilot, 1930, Marx wind-up	420	630	840

	C6	C8	C10
Popeye "Popeye & Olive Oyl Slinky Handcar" 1950s pulltoy, Linemar	300	450	600
Popeye "Popeye On A Unicycle," Linemar	300	450	600
Popeye "Popeye Patrol," Hubley, 8½" long	500	750	1000
Popeye Puncher, Chein, 1930, tin and celluloid	800	1200	1600
Popeye Pushing wheelbarrow, plastic walkie, Marx, circa 1950s	20	30	40
Popeye Rollerskating, Linemar	400	600	800
Popeye Roly-Poly, 3½" celluloid	40	60	80
Popeye in a Rowboat, 1935, Hoge	1500	2250	3000
Popeye rubber squeeze toy, 1950s	20	30	40
Popeye Sand Toy teeter-totter with Popeye, Sweepea, Olive Oyl, Jeep, tin litho	160	240	320

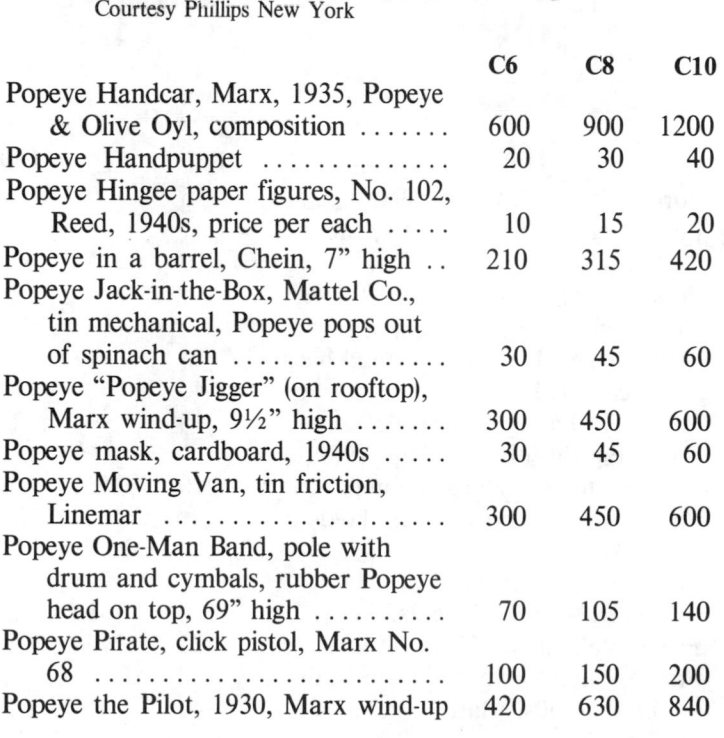

"Popeye The Champ," MARX
Courtesy Phillips New York

"POPEYE EXPRESS"
Photo Courtesy PB Eighty-Four

POPEYE
Rollerskating
Courtesy PB Eighty-
Four, New York

POPEYE Carrying
parrots in cages
Courtesy PB Eighty-
Four, New York

	C6	C8	C10
Popeye on Sparkplug, 1930s	See Fisher-Price		
Popeye "Popeye Spinning Olive Oyl in a Chair," 1950s, Linemar, 9" high	400	600	800
Popeye "Spinach Patrol" Hubley	360	540	720
Popeye Strength Tester, Holgate, 14"	60	90	120
Popeye String Puppet, approx. 5" high, wood, Jaymar, circa 1940s .	110	165	220
"Popeye" The Champ, Marx	500	750	1000
Popeye "Tumbling Popeye," Linemar, 5" high wind-up	750	1125	1500
Popeye Turnover Tank, Linemar tin wind-up, 1950s, 6" long	240	360	480
Popeye Whistle Pipe, Northwest Products of St. Louis, 3½" long, cardboard bowl with illos of Popeye characters, metal stem with whistle at base	70	105	140
Popeye Yazoo Pipe, Northwestern Productions, St. Louis Mo., 1934	80	120	160
Popeye & Olive Oyl Jiggers (Popeye dancing on roof, Olive Oyl playing concertina), Marx	800	1200	1600

	C6	C8	C10
Porky (Pogo) plastic, 1969	6	9	12
Porky Pig cowboy with lariat, Marx tin wind-up	210	315	420
Porky Pig squeeze toy, Sun Rubber, approx. 6" high, hollow with squeaker, has hands behind back, circa 1940	40	60	80
Porky Pig hand puppet, 1950s	6	9	12
Porky Pig tin litho wind-up, 1939, 8½" high, holding umbrella, Marx	210	315	420
Porky Pig tin litho wind-up, holds umbrella, raises hat	225.00	337.50	450.00
Prince Valiant Castle Fort, Marx, boxed set with knights, etc	110	165	220
Prince Valiant Shield, tin litho	30	45	60
Prince Valiant Sword and tin Scabbard, 1950s, Mattel	40	60	80

PORKY PIG, tin wind-up,
holding umbrella, MARX.

PORKY PIG cowboy with lariat
Courtesy Sotheby Parke Bernet

	C6	C8	C10
Sandy (Orphan Annie), 5" long, walks, tin wind-up	110	165	220
Sandy 10½" long oilcloth doll, circa 1920s	100	150	200
Sandy (Orphan Annie's dog) with suitcase in mouth, tin wind-up	220	330	440
Sandy (Orphan Annie) "Sandy Dog with Magic Tail," 1930s, Marx, 7" long	160	240	320
Schroeder (Peanuts) rubber squeeze toy, circa 1960	6	9	12
Secret Agent X-9 Gun and Billy Club	10	15	20
Shmoo (Lil Abner) doll, vinyl inflatable, 15" high	40	60	80
Skeezix oilcloth doll, cotton-stuffed, 1924	60	90	120
Smitty 9¾" oilcloth doll	30	45	60

RACHEL, Gasoline Alley,
oilcloth, cotton stuffed.

SKEEZIX, oilcloth, cotton
stuffed.

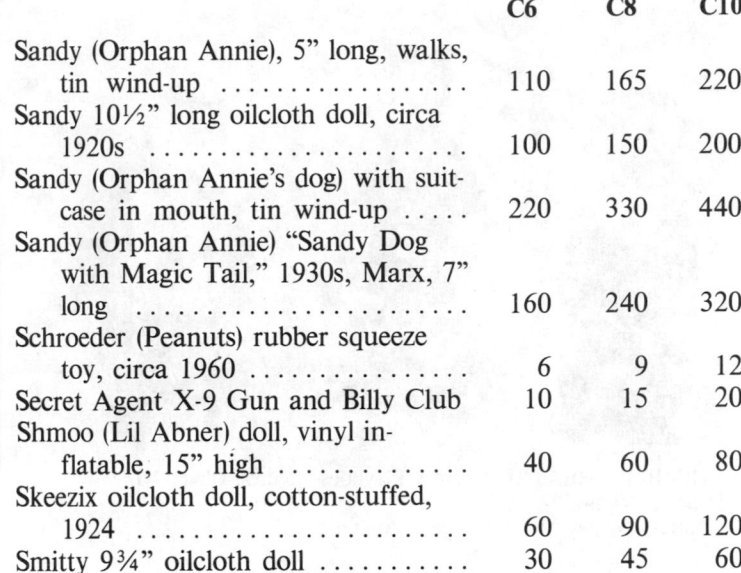

"Smitty On A Scooter"
Photo Courtesy PB Eighty-Four

SANDY with a suitcase in mouth
Courtesy PB Eighty-Four, New
York

SPARKPLUG, 1920s,
SCHOENHUT
Courtesy PB Eight-Four, New
York

	C6	C8	C10
Rachel (Gasoline Alley) oilcloth doll, cotton-stuffed, 1923	70	105	140
Red Ryder BB Gun No. 111, Daisy	80	120	160
"Red Ryder Cork Carbine," Daisy, plastic stock	40	60	80
Red Ryder gun and holster set, Daisy	60	90	120
Red Ryder Pop-Um shooting game, Daisy	70	105	140
Red Ryder Molding Set, 1948	40	60	80
Red Ryder Target Game, 1939	50	75	100
Sad Sack 15½" vinyl doll, 1950	40	60	80
Sad Sack 20" high vinyl doll, cloth uniform, Sterling Doll Co., circa 1952	50	75	100

	C6	C8	C10
"Smitty On A Scooter," tin wind-up, Marx, circa 1930, 8" high	600	900	1200
Smokey Stover, hard plastic, 3" high, 1960s	6	9	12
Snoopy rubber squeeze toy, 1958	6	9	12
Snuffy Smith Handpuppet, cloth, with rubber head, Gund, "King Features"	20	30	40
Sparkle Plenty Paperdoll Set, 1948, Saalfield No. 5160	18	27	36
Sparkle Plenty Washing Machine, Kalon Radio Corp., litho tin, crank action, circa 1947, 13" tall	90	135	180
Sparkplug, 1920s, Schoenhut jointed wood figure	220	330	440
"Sparkplug" (Barney Google), on wheels, 3¼" high	160	240	320

THIMBLE THEATRE Mystery Playhouse figures, Olive Oyl,
Popeye, Wimpy
Courtesy Mapes Auctioneers and Appraisers

"Toonerville Trolley" NIFTY tin wind-up
Courtesy PB Eighty-Four

TOONERVILLE TROLLEY, lead, circa
1923
Courtesy PB Eighty-Four, New York

	C6	C8	C10
Superman Handpuppet, Ideal, 1965 ..	12.50	18.75	25.00
Superman Holding Airplane, Marx tin wind-up, 1940	900	1350	1800
Superman Krypto-Ray Gun, Daisy No. 94, 1939, with seven film strips	120	180	240
Superman Krypton Rockets, circa 1939	100	150	200
Superman "Superman Cut-Outs," Saalfield No. 177, 1940	500	750	1000
Superman "Superman Rollover Airplane," 1940, No. 12 wind-up, 5" long	1400	2100	2800
Superman Tank, tin wind-up, Marx, 1940s	300	450	600
Superman Tank, Linemar, 1950s, 4" long	270	405	540
Sweepea Hingees No. 102, 1944, paper punchouts, Reed	6	9	12
Sweepea Mask, cardboard, 1940s	10	15	20
Tarzan, mask of Akut the Ape, Northern Paper Mills, 1933	60	90	120
Tarzan, mask of Numa the Lion, paper, 1933 by Northern Paper Mills	60	90	120
Tarzan, mask of Tarzan, 1933, Northern Paper Mills, paper	70	105	140
Tarzan In The Jungle dart board game, 1935, large	130	195	260

	C6	C8	C10
Sparkplug (Barney Google) stuffed cloth	110	165	220
Sparkplug Candy Container	130	195	260
Steve Canyon Glider Bomb Truck, Ideal	40	60	80
Steve Canyon Jet Helmet	20	30	40
Superman 13" high, wood and composition, Ideal, 1940	310	465	620
Supreme Cut-Out Adventure Book ...	60	90	120
Superman "Flying Superman", 1950s, plastic	40	60	80

376

	C6	C8	C10
Tarzan "Tarzan In The Jungle," 1935 battery-operated target game	120	180	240
Terry And The Pirates Hingees, 1944, set contains Terry, Flip Corkin, Pat Ryan, Burma, Taffy Tucker .	90	135	180
Thimble Theatre Mystery Playhouse "Starring Popeye with Wimpy and Olive Oyl," copyright 1939, Harding Products, Philadelphia, 12x10x3", figures composition, with wooden "Shuffle" feet, individual figures sell for $160 in mint	400	600	800
Three Flying Marvels (Captain, Jr., Mary), paper, circa 1944-47, Reed	50	75	100
Toonerville Trolley, lead, circa 1923 .	200	300	400
Toonerville Trolley, tin wind-up, "Copyright 1922 by Fontaine Fox," 7½" high, Skipper driving, Nifty	500	750	1000
Toonerville Trolley, 1921, Strauss wind-up	600	900	1200
Toonerville Trolley, 1⅞" high, sometimes called Crackerjack size	220	330	440
Toonerville Trolley – Dent, cast iron	600	900	1200
Toonerville Glass Candy Container, 3¼" long	400	600	800
Toonerville Trolley, "Powerful Katrinka," 6½" long, pushing boy in wheelbarrow, tin wind-up, Lehmann, 1923	1400	2100	2800
Tweety Bird rubber squeeze toy, 1950s	6	9	12
Uncle Walt (Gasoline Alley), oilcloth, 26" high	50	75	100
Uncle Wiggily, Marx, Crazy Car	400	600	800
Walter Lantz ink stamp character set, 12 different rubber stamps	10	15	20
Western Thrills with Billy The Kid, character from Funny Animals Comics, circa 1944-47, Reed, paper toy	12	18	24
Willie The Worm and Sammy in Car Trouble, paper toy, Fawcett Comics characters, Reed, circa 1944-47	6	9	12
Willie The Worm and Sammy Flying Machine	10	15	20
Willie The Worm and Sammy Fish-n Fun	6	9	12
Wimpy 3" hard plastic figure, 1960s .	8	12	16
Wimpy 3⅛" high, cast iron Hubley ..	120	180	240
Wimpy 4" high, wood-jointed, "by K.F.S."	80	120	160
Wimpy 8" high rubber squeeze toy ..	60	90	120
Wimpy Handpuppet, Gund	30	45	60
Wimpy mask, cardboard, 1940s	10	15	20
Wimpy Motorcyclist, Linemar	150	225	300
Wimpy rubber squeeze toy, 1950s ...	20	30	40
Wimpy String Puppet, approx. 5" high, wood, Jaymar, circa 1940s .	80	120	160

WIMPY Tricyclist, LINEMAR
Courtesy Phillips New York

	C6	C8	C10
Woody Woodpecker Handpuppet, Mattel, 1962, "W. Lantz" rubber head, cloth body	40	60	80
Woody Woodpecker, 6½" high, rubber, "Walter Lantz"	10	15	20
Yellow Kid in Cart, Kenton, early 1900s, 10" long, 6" high, pulled by mule, cast iron	800	1200	1600
Yellow Kid in Goat Cart, Kenton, 1890, painted cast iron, 7½" long	900	1350	1800
Yellow Kid papier mache and wood, Schoenhut, 11" high, early 1900s	400	600	800

Yellow Kid in goat cart, KENTON
Courtesy Lloyd W. Ralston Auctions

377

MOVIES, RADIO, TELEVISION

(See also Paper, Premiums, Banks, Miscellaneous, Comic Character, Marx Playsets, Action Figures, Figure Kits)

The average mint price in this category in the last edition was $103.48, and in this edition averages $202.47, an increase of 96%.

```
CONDITION CODE:
C5 – Good, wear evident overall, shows that has been played with
C6 – Fine, shows some wear in spots, but taken care of
C7 – Very Fine, minor wear overall, very clean
C8 – Excellent, minor wear on edges only
C9 – Near Mint, no noticeable flaws, close inspection may show
     minute marks
C10 – Mint (like new)
     Note: Mint in Box does command higher price
```

AMOS & ANDY FRESH-AIR TAXI
Photo Courtesy PB Eighty-Four

AMOS & ANDY tin wind-ups, 12" high, eyes move
Courtesy Lloyd W. Ralston Auctions

	C6	C8	C10
Amos Sparkler	500	750	1000
Amos tin wind-up, 1930	430	645	860
Amos and Andy in car, glass, 4½" long	350	525	700
Amos and Andy wood jointed dolls, 6" high, price for pair	190	285	380
Amos & Andy Fresh-Air Taxi, tin wind-up, Marx, 8" long, 1930s	600	900	1200
Andy Tin Wind-Up, 12" high	400	600	800
Barney Rubble (Flintstones) 10" high vinyl doll, 1960	20	30	40
Beany & Cecil Music Box, Mattel, 1950s (pops up)	30	45	60
Beany 15" stuffed doll, vinyl head, hands, feet, Mattel	30	45	60

	C6	C8	C10
Beany Doll, 16½" high, talks, Mattel, 1950s, stuffed cloth body, rubber head	40	60	80
Baby Huey Hand Puppet	10	15	20
Beatles, Ringo, John, Paul, George, 5" vinyl figures, 1964, Remco. Price per each	40	60	80
Ben Casey Play Hospital Set, Transogram	75.00	112.50	150.00
Ben Hur Sword, scabbard and shield, Marx, only produced in 1959, when movie was made	120	180	240
Betty Boop character doll, jointed, 9½" tall, 1930s	200	300	400
Betty Boop pinback button	30	45	60
Bob Burns Bazooka, brass kazoo-like toy, patterned after radio-movie comic Burns' famous musical invention (the Army weapon gets its name from it) metal sliding tube, M.M. Pochapia Toys, 13" long when not extended, 1930s	10	15	20
Bobba-Louie 14" stuffed doll, vinyl head, Knickerbocker, 1959	20	30	40
Bobba-Louie 18" stuffed doll, vinyl face, plush body, Knickerbocker 1959	22	33	44
"Bojangles Dances Again," tin litho and wood, 1930s, tap button on base and he dances	110	165	220
Buck Jones Rangers chaps	70	105	140

	C6	C8	C10
Buffalo Bill Jr. belt and buckle (TV), 1950s	20	30	40
Bugs Bunny & Porky Pig talking toy in original box, 1940s, has record that talks	80	120	160
"Bullet" (Roy Rogers' dog) stuffed doll, circa 1955	20	30	40
Captain Gallant Foreign Legion Holster outfit	75.00	112.50	150.00
Captain Kangaroo badge, tin shield	18	27	36
Casper The Friendly Ghost 11" stuffed doll, body is beanbag, 1960s	20	30	40
Casper the Friendly Ghost Turnover Tank, Linemar tin wind-up	180	270	360
Cecil Sea Serpent, 8" vinyl	20	30	40
Cecil Sea Serpent, 18" stuffed doll, Mattel	30	45	60
Cecil Sea Serpent, 22" stuffed doll, Mattel	34	51	68
Cecil Sea Serpent, stuffed talking doll	30	45	60
Charlie Chaplin Tin Wind-up, 8½" high	600	900	1200
Charlie Chaplin Bell Toy, cast iron, circa 1912	200	300	400
Charlie Chaplin, flat tin litho, he tips hat when string is pulled	110	165	220
Charlie Chaplin, 1920, Martin, clockwork, 7" high, papier mache, lead, wire cane, cloth clothes - Rare	700	1050	1400
"Charlie McCarthy" written on top hat, standing erect, tin wind-up, circa 1938	160	240	320
Charlie McCarthy rubber doll, Effanbee	40	60	80
Charlie McCarthy 13" high, composition mouth moves, 1930s	100	150	200

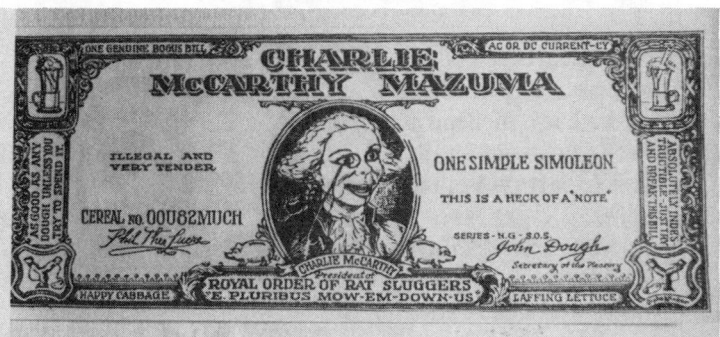

Charlie McCarthy paper money
Courtesy Toy Collector News

CHARLIE McCARTHY IN HIS BEN-ZINE BUGGY
Courtesy PB Eighty-Four, New York

CHARLIE McCARTHY, name written on top hat, tin windup.

	C6	C8	C10
Charlie McCarthy in his Benzine Buggy, Marx	400	600	800
Charlie McCarthy Car, wind-up, Marx, 1935	450	675	900
Charlie McCarthy Cardboard Puppet, 20" high	30	45	60
Charlie McCarthy Facemask, molded gauze, complete with separate monocle	40	60	80
Charlie McCarthy Handpuppet, composition head, circa 1939	60	90	120
Charlie McCarthy paper money	10	15	20

"CHARLIE McCARTHY and Mortimer Snerd Private Car"
Courtesy Phillips New York

	C6	C8	C10
Charlie McCarthy Ventriloquist doll, composition with cloth body, ring pull in back of head to activate lower jaw, 14½" tall	600	900	1200
Charlie McCarthy Ventriloquist Doll, 18"	200	300	400
Charlie McCarthy "Charlie McCarthy and Mortimer Snerd Private Car," Marx, two heads sticking out of top of car	1000	1500	2000
Cisco Kid Neckerchief with nickel sombrero slide	20	30	40
Cowardly Lion (Wizard of Oz) molded gauze facemask	30	45	65
Dale Evans holster outfit	60	90	120
Dale Evans & Horse Buttermilk, figures by Hartland	60	90	120
Deputy Dawg, 14" high stuffed doll, Ideal, 1961	20	30	40
Dick Van Dyke doll from Chitty Chitty Bang Bang, 1967, talks, Mattel	40	60	80
Dragnet Crime Lab, 1955, flashlight, signal gun, badge, handcuffs, fingerprint kit, etc.	60	90	120
Dragnet Jack Webb black police whistle	10	15	20
Dragnet Police Set, gun, handcuffs, badge	20	30	40
Dragnet Los Angeles Police No. 714 badge	10	15	20
Dragnet talking police car, Ideal Toys, circa 1954	80	120	160
Dragnet Water Pistol, circa 1955, 714 badge emblazoned on handle	20	30	40
Ed Wynn Fire Chief, litho on wood, pull toy, Schoenhut, 12" long ...	300	450	600
Fanny Brice (Baby Snooks), Ideal, composition and wire doll	200	300	400
Farmer Alfalfa (Terrytoons) circa 1950, 17½" high, stuffed body, vinyl head, hands	30	45	60
Flintstones "The Flintstones Bedrock Express Handcar," 1962, Marx wind-up playset 22x26"	180	270	360
Flintstones Choo Choo Train, Marx, "Bedrock Express," tin wind-up, Linemar Co., 13" long, 1950s ...	300	450	600
Flintstones "Flintstone Friction Cars," (Fred, Barney, Wilma, etc.), 1962, Linemar, 4" long, price per each .	60	90	120
Flintstones "Flintstone Pals" (Barney on Dino), Linemar, 1962, 8" long, wind-up	140	210	280
Flintstones "Flintstone Pals" (Fred on Dino), Linemar, 1962, 8" long, windup	140	210	280
Flintstones "Hopping Barney Rubble," 1962, Marx (Japan) windup, 4" high	110	165	220

FLINTSTONE PALS on Dino, Fred and Barney riders, MARX

	C6	C8	C10
Flintstones "Hopping Fred Flintstone," Linemar, 4" high	150	225	300
Flintstones "Hopping Dino," 1962, Linemar, 4" high	150	225	300
Flintstones Pebbles 7" jointed doll ...	12.50	18.75	25.00
Flintstones Turnover Tank, Linemar tin wind-up, 1950s, 4" long	220	330	440
Flub-A-Dub push puppet, plastic, felt, wood, 5" high	30	45	60
Flub-A-Dub (Howdy Doody) small plastic figure	10	15	20
Fred Flintstone, 5¾" tall, hollow vinyl figure	6	9	12

FROGGIE THE GREMLIN
Courtesy Toy Collector News

	C6	C8	C10
Froggie The Gremlin hollow rubber doll, squeeze toy, 5" high, of the Buster Brown radio with TV show, squeeze and tongue sticks out, 1950s	40	60	80

	C6	C8	C10
Froggie The Gremlin, 9¼" squeeze toy	50	75	100
Froggie The Gremlin, 10¾" squeeze toy	60	90	120
Groucho Marx "Ventriloquist Play Pal," Goldberger	50	75	100
Gulliver's Travels Boat, wooden (Paramount)	110	165	220
Gulliver's Travels Drum, tin, Chein, 1939	70	105	140
Gulliver's Travels Musical Top, Chein	30	45	60
Gulliver's Travels Sandpail, tin, Chein	40	60	80

HAROLD LLOYD Bell Toy
Courtesy Sotheby's New York

HOOT GIBSON Cowboy Outfit, WORNOVA CLOTHES, apparently new in 1935 and still on sale in 1939
Courtesy Heinz Mueller, Continental Hobby House

	C6	C8	C10
Harold Lloyd Bell Toy, German, 6½" high	300	450	600
Harold Lloyd "Funny Face," Marx wind-up walker, 1929	400	600	800
Harold Lloyd Policeman, 12" high, tin wind-up	180	270	360
Henry Fonda Texas Ranger Sheriff Badge, The Deputy, 1951	20	30	40
Highway Patrol "Highway Patrol Car," Broderick Crawford litho, 8" long	130	195	260
Hoot Gibson Cowboy Outfit, Wornova Clothes, 1935	50	75	100
Hoot Gibson lariat	30	45	60
Hoot Gibson Wornova Clothes (Squaw style), 1930s	40	60	80
Hopalong Cassidy Badge, tin with inset photo	40	60	80
Hopalong Cassidy Binoculars, circa 1950, plastic	12	18	24
Hopalong Cassidy compass	10	15	20
Hopalong Cassidy Cowgirl's outfit	50	75	100
Hopalong Cassidy dart board, 14"x17", stagecoach holdup and target practice, 1950	70	105	140
Hopalong Cassidy Field Glasses, 1940, metal	30	45	60

	C6	C8	C10
Hopalong Cassidy Flashlight Gun, plastic, 8" long, Hoppy's name on side	40	60	80
Hopalong Cassidy "Hop-A-Long Cassidy," 1938 Marx 10½" high (on "Range Rider" rocker base)	200	300	400
Hopalong Cassidy knife, circa mid-1940s, 3½" long	50	75	100
Hopalong Cassidy Photo Ring, circa late 1940s	30	45	60
Hopalong Cassidy Rocking Horse Cowboy, Marx	240	360	480
Hopalong Cassidy Shooting Gallery	60	90	120
Hopalong Cassidy Signet Ring, all metal, late 1940s	20	30	40
Hopalong Cassidy Spurs, leather and metal	40	60	80
Hopalong Cassidy Western Frontier set, with figures, stagecoach and buildings	130	195	260
Hopalong Cassidy woodburning set, 1950, American Toy and Furniture Co.	50	75	100
Hopalong Cassidy Wrangler Pin	10	15	20
Hopalong Cassidy Zoomerang Gun, shoots paper, Tigrett Enterprises, Chicago	40	60	80

HOWDY DOODY And BOB SMITH At The Piano
Courtesy PB Eighty-Four, New York

	C6	C8	C10
Howdy Doody 4" high plastic push-puppet, Hohner, has NBC mike	60	90	120
Howdy Doody 6" high, wall walker doll	30	45	60
Howdy Doody 7½" high, 1950s, plastic cloth clothes, eyes close, mouth opens	40	60	80
Howdy Doody 12" high, movable jaws, Goldberger Dolls	48	72	96
Howdy Doody 26" ventriloquist dummy	60	90	120
Howdy Doody Acrobat	80	120	160
Howdy Doody and Bob Smith at the piano, tin wind-up, Unique	450	675	900
Howdy Doody "Clarabelle Clown," 1950s, Linemar squeeze action cable, 6½" high	80	120	160

	C6	C8	C10
Howdy Doody "Clarabelle Clown," 1950s, Linemar, 5" high, Kagran Corp., wind-up	150	225	300
Howdy Doody, Clarabell's horn, 1950s	40	60	80
Howdy Doody, Cowboy Gloves, leather, 1950s	30	45	60
Howdy Doody hand puppets, no date, no mfr., rubber heads, cloth bodies	10	15	20
Howdy Doody "Howdy Doody Air-O-Doodle Circus Train," Kagran, 1950s, wind-up, 16" long	75.00	112.50	150.00
Howdy Doody "Howdy Doody Pump-mobile," 1950s wind-up, Nylint, 9" long	150	225	300
Howdy Doody Life Preserver, plastic, 1950s, show Howdy, Mr. Bluster, etc.	30	45	60
Howdy Doody Marionette, 17" high, wooden arms and legs, composition head	60	90	120
Howdy Doody Marionette, 16" high, composition head, hands and feet, handpainted features, 1950s	60	90	120
Howdy Doody Mask, rubber	10	15	20
Howdy Doody Piano, Howdy plays it	150	225	300
Howdy Doody plastic puppet toys, with levers in back of head to move mouths. Consists of Howdy, Bluster, Clarabell, Princess, Dilly Dally, Tee-Vee Toys No. 549. Price for set	100	150	200
Howdy Doody plastic Ukulele, Emenee, 1950s	40	60	80
Howdy Doody "Put-In-Head," similar to Mr. Potato Head, but with Howdy characters: Howdy, Bluster, Clarabell, Princess. Price for set	30	45	60
Howdy Doody "Pump-Mobile," Nylint, unauthorized Howdy, rides cart, 8½" long, 7" high	80	120	160
Howdy Doody Sand Forms, 1952, molds of Howdy, Bluster, Flub-A-Dub, Clarabell, plus shovel	10	15	20
Howdy Doody Squeeze Toy, 7" high	14	21	28
Howdy Doody TV Set with paper filmstrips, Lego, 1950s	20	30	40
Howdy Doody tin wind-up, circa 1950, Marx, 5" high, Howdy plays banjo and moves head	150	225	300
Howdy Doody tin wind-up circa 1950, Howdy does jig and Clarabell sits at piano, Marx, 5½" high	300	450	600
Howdy Doody wood-jointed doll, 13" high	300	450	600
Howdy Doody wood-jointed doll, 5½" high, holding NBC mike	140	210	280
Huckleberry Hound, 18" stuffed doll, 1959, Knickerbocker	20	30	40

	C6	C8	C10
Huckleberry Hound as Fireman, rubber squeeze toy, 1960s	6	9	12
Huckleberry Hound with top hat, rubber squeeze toy, 1960s	6	9	12
Huckleberry Hound 18" stuffed doll, 1959, Knickerbocker	30	45	60
Huckleberry Hound as Fireman, rubber squeeze toy, 1960s	6	9	12
Huckleberry Hound "Huckleberry Hound Car," 1962, Marx (Japan), wind-up, 4" long	40	60	80
Huckleberry Hound "Huckleberry Hound Hopper" 1962, Linemar, 4½" high	80	120	160
Hugh O'Brian-Wyatt Earp, Dodge City Western Town, Marx, 1950s	120	180	240
I Spy Ranger Pin	16	24	32
Jackie Coogan glass candy container, 5" high	800	1200	1600
Jackie Gleason "Away We Go" bus, 13"	225.00	337.50	450.00
Jackie Gleason "Story Stage Theatre," Utopia Enterprises, copyright 1955	75.00	112.50	150.00
James Bond Aston-Martin	See Battery-Operated		
James Bond 007 Attache Case, 11." Code Book, rifle, which converts to pistol, bullets, Code-O-Matic, billfold with money and James Bond business cards and instructions, circa 1965	100	150	200
James Bond Camera, shoots	60	90	120
Jerry Mahoney ventriloquist dummy	30	45	60
Jetsons "Astro- the Jetsons' Dog," 1963 Marx wind-up (Japan), 5" high	150	225	300
Jetsons "George Jetson" 1963 Marx, (Japan) squeeze action cable, 4" high	80	120	160

JETSON EXPRESS Choo Choo Train
Photo by Don Hultzman

JETSONS Turnover Tank, LINEMAR
Photo by Don Hultzman

	C6	C8	C10
Jetsons "Jetson Express Choo Choo Train," 1960s Marx (Japan), wind-up, 13" long	150	225	300
Jetsons Turnover Tank, Linemar tin wind-up	220	330	440
Joe Penner tin wind-up, Marx, circa 1930s, 8" high, tips hat, walks, "Wanna Buy a Duck?"	300	450	600
King Little (Gulliver's Travels), Ideal, 12" jointed composition	200	300	400
Lambchop Shari Lewis Handpuppet	20	30	40
Lone Ranger Acme Moviescope Set, 1948, includes 4 films: No. 1 Superman, No. 2 Lone Ranger, No. 3 Lone Ranger, No. 4 Lone Ranger. With pop-up box including films and viewer	110	165	220
Lone Ranger and Silver composition figure, 1938	80	120	160
Lone Ranger Chuck Wagon Lantern	60	90	120
Lone Ranger Deputy Badge, 1950s	40	60	80
Lone Ranger Doll, 20" high, 1938, very realistic composition head, hands, feet	160	240	320
Lone Ranger Flashlight	40	60	80
Lone Ranger Film Viewer, four films, 1953	50	75	100
Lone Ranger Harmonica, Magnus, 1950	20	30	40
Lone Ranger Hat, 1930s, official	40	60	80
Lone Ranger Hat, cowboy hat of white felt w/red trim. "Lone Ranger Hi! Yo! Silver!" inscribed, 1940s	50	75	100
Lone Ranger Official First Aid Kit with contents, 1938, tin litho	60	90	120
Lone Ranger "Official Outfit," 1939, mask, jail keys, badge, silver bullet, glow belt, Lone Ranger buckle, Lee Powell and Chief Thundercloud on belt	160	240	320
Lone Ranger "Lone Ranger Official Outfit," M.A. Henry Co., 1942 (belt, holster, guns, cuffs)	60	90	120
Lone Ranger 1938 Marx wind-up (on "Range Rider" rocker base), 10½" high	300	450	600
Lone Ranger 1938 Marx wind-up, chrome version, 8½" high from top of lariat	200	300	400
Lone Ranger 1938 Marx wind-up, litho version, 8½" high from top of lariat	100	150	200
Lone Ranger Picture Printing Set, 1939, 8 rubber stamps	40	60	80
Lone Ranger Rides Again movie viewer, 1939	50	75	100
Lone Ranger Rodeo, Marx set with metal bldgs., plastic figures, etc., 1950s	140	210	280

LONE RANGER, "Hiyo Silver, the Lone Ranger
Courtesy PB Eighty-Four, New York

	C6	C8	C10
Lone Ranger Signal Siren, Flashlight, 1950, with silver bullet secret code, United States Electric Mfg. Co.	80	120	160
Lone Ranger Silver Bullet Knife, length 3" closed	100	150	200
Lone Ranger "Stringless Marionette" handpuppet, cloth and vinyl	120	180	240
Lone Ranger Strongbox (coinbank)	100	150	200
Lone Ranger Target Game, 1938, Marx	150	225	300

LONE RANGER, L to R: 1938 MARX wind-up, litho version, 1938 MARX wind-up, chrome version
Photo by Don Hultzman

Milton Berle Car
Courtesy Mapes Auctioneers & Appraisers

	C6	C8	C10
Matt Dillon, U.S. Marshall badge (Gunsmoke)	10	15	20
Men Into Space space helmet, retractable visor, space mike, etc. From series starring William Lundigan as Col. McCaulety. Made of fortiflex	80	120	160
Milton Berle Car, two large wheels, two small, Marx, 1950s, "What the Hey," etc. written on car	180	270	360
Mortimer Snerd, 13" high, Ideal, composition and wire	130	195	260
Mortimer Snerd Band, Marx wind-up, 1935, "Hometown Band"	400	600	800
Mortimer Snerd, Jack In The Box, circa 1930s, 8" high	80	120	160
"Mortimer Snerd Teeth," plastic teeth and dental wax, circa 1950	10	15	20

MORTIMER SNERD tin wind-up, MARX,
Courtesy PB Eighty-Four, New York

	C6	C8	C10
Mortimer Snerd Tin Wind-up, Marx, circa 1939, Mortimer's hat tips as he walks	210	315	420
"Mortimer Snerd's Tricky Auto," 1939, Marx	170	255	340
Mr. Magoo Car, battery, tin litho....	See Battery Toys "MaGoo"		
Mr. Magoo Doll, Ideal, 15" high	40	60	80
My Favorite Martian "Martian Magic Tricks" Gilbert, 1964, magic set .	40	60	80

	C6	C8	C10
Oliver Hardy Handpuppet, Knickerbocker	30	45	60
Oliver Hardy Roly Poly, 10½" high, plastic	40	60	80
"Oswald, Universal Pictures, Irwin Prod." 18½" wind-up, wood and cardboard body with cloth clothes, stuffed arms and head, character created by Disney, early	350	525	700
Pinky Lee vinyl doll. Squeeze and his head pops up, 1950	120	180	240
Quick Draw McGraw "Quick Draw McGraw Hopper," 1962, Linemar, 4½" high	90	135	180
Rifleman (TV) Ranch, Marx	120	180	240
Rin Tin Tin and Rusty Knife, 1950s .	60	90	120
Rin Tin Tin - Marx Fort Apache Stockade, 1950s	160	240	320
Robin Hood Money Pouch, six foreign coins from Richard Greene TV series, 1953-54	40	60	80
Robin Hood Money Pouch, fifteen foreign coins, from Richard Greene TV series	40	60	80
Robin Hood Shield. Badge with embossed Robin Hood and gem stone, circa 1956	50	75	100
Rocky The Flying Squirrel Bendee figure, 1960s	20	30	40
Rootie Kazootie Marionette, 14" hard rubber head and hands, wooden shoes and body wearing clothes ..	60	90	120

ROY ROGERS "Stage Coach Wagon Train"
Courtesy Continental Hobby House

	C6	C8	C10
Roy Rogers bandana, large	10	15	20
Roy Rogers Branding Iron set	30	45	60
Roy Rogers Double R Bar Ranch, 1950s, tin litho ranch house, Marx	60	90	120
Roy Rogers Mineral City, town with hotel, music hall, cafe, bank, barber shop, trade goods, etc., tin	80	120	160
Roy Rogers Nellie Belle Jeep	100	150	200
Roy Rogers pocket flashlight	40	60	80
Roy Rogers Quickshooter Hat	20	30	40
Roy Rogers "Ranch Lantern," No. 90, metal, hurricane type with plastic chimney, 1950s, 7¾" tall	70	105	140
Roy Rogers Riders Lucky Piece	10	15	20
Roy Rogers Rodeo Ranch, Marx	110	165	220

	C6	C8	C10
Roy Rogers "Roy Rogers Buckboard," 1950s, Ideal, 16" long	80	120	160
Roy Rogers "Roy Rogers Chuck Wagon," Ideal, 1950s, 13" long	50	75	100
Roy Rogers "Roy Rogers Fix-It Stage Coach," 1950s, Ideal, 13" long	50	75	100
Roy Rogers "Roy Rogers Horse Trailer & Jeep," Ideal, 1950s, 15" long	80	120	160
Roy Rogers "Roy Rogers Stage Coach Wagon Train," wind-up, 14" long, plastic, 1950s	100	150	200
Roy Rogers Signal Flashlight	30	45	60
Roy Rogers Telescope	30	45	60
Roy Rogers and Trigger Pocket Knife	40	60	80
Roy Rogers Wagon Train, Marx	80	120	160
Scarecrow (Wizard of Oz) molded gauze facemask	60	90	120
Scrappy & Margie wooden pull toy, 13½" long, he plays xylophone, she revolves, Columbia Pictures	280	420	560
Sgt. Bilko Holster Set from the CBS TV series "You'll Never Get Rich," starring Phil Silvers. Photo-illustrated box contains leather holster and belt with realistic Army .45 made of silvered die cast metal. Sgt.'s arm patch and Sgt. Bilko hat with Badge, Halco Brand, 1956	80	120	160
Shirley Temple Playhouse	100	150	200
Small Fry Club Kit, 1949, button, etc., Dumont TV show (may be premium)	20	30	40
"Sneak" Facemask, molded gauze (Gulliver's Travels,) 1939	50	75	100
Soupy Sales dolls, 1965, Sunshine Doll Co.	20	30	40
Spanky of Our Gang 1930s pinback button	20	30	40
Stan Laurel Bendem Doll, 1960	25.00	37.50	50.00
Stan Laurel Handpuppet, Knicker-bocker	30	45	60
Sylvester, 1971, 15" high, cloth	25.00	37.50	50.00
Tales of the Texas Rangers Deputy Badge	10	15	20
Three Stooges handpuppet, Moe, Curley and Larry, price per each	16	24	32
Tim Holt Litho Target	10	15	20
Tinman Facemask (Wizard of Oz) molded gauze	50	75	100
Tom Corbett Space Cadet, 14 different figures, Marx, 1950s. Price per set	14	21	28
Tom Corbett, 7 different figures, same as above, price per set	10	15	20
Tom Corbett Cosmic Vision Space Helmet, one-way vision, plastic, early 1950s	80	120	160

TOM CORBETT "Polaris" Rocket Ship
Photo by Don Hultzman

	C6	C8	C10
Tom Corbett Space Cadet Molding and Coloring Set, Model Craft (All Tom Corbett toys 1950-55)	60	90	120
Tom Corbett Space Cadet Field Glasses, 3 power, Herald, 5½" long	30	45	60
Tom Corbett Space Cadet Flashlight with built-in signal siren, 7" long, metal, US Alite Corp	40	60	80
Tom Corbett Official Outfit, Yankiboy	80	120	160
Tom Corbett "Polaris" Rocket Ship, wind-up, Marx, 1952, 12" long, Tom, Astro and Rogers looking out of cockpit	230	345	460
Tom Corbett Space Hat, Lee	20	30	40
Tom Corbett Space Cadet official Space Pistol, Marx No. 105	60	90	120
Tom Corbett Space Cadet Rifle, Marx, No. 0239	80	120	160
Tom Corbett Space Station	40	60	80
Tom Corbett Space Cadet, 2-Way Space Phone, Zimmerman	40	60	80
Tom Corbett "Tom Corbett Space Cadet Atomic Rifle," Marx, 1950s, 24" long	50	75	100
Tom Corbett "Tom Corbett Space Cadet Official Space Pistol," 1950s, Rockhill, 9½" long	70	105	140
Tom Mix "Circus Wild West," Arcade circus wagon with driver, two horses, 14½" long, circa 1936. (See Animal Drawn, Arcade "Big Six")	No Price Found		
Tom Mix metal and leather spurs, 1934 (not a premium)	110	165	220
Tom Mix on Tony, Arcor Rubber, 1930s	35.00	52.50	70.00
Tom Mix Rodeorope, 1928, comes with box and instructions	80	120	160
Tonto (Lone Ranger) 20" high doll, 1938, very realistic, composition head, hands, feet	200	300	400
Wild Bill Hickock & Jingles TV Show, 42 piece Western Bunkhouse	140	210	280
Wild Bill Hickock Marshal Star Badge with picture of Hickock and Jingles in center	20	30	40

	C6	C8	C10
Wizard of Oz masks, set of five, Einson-Freeman Co., Inc., 1939, "Par-T-Mask"	160	240	320
Wizard of Oz, Mego, Glinda, 8", 1972	20	30	40
Wizard of Oz, Mego, Lion, 1972	25.00	37.50	50.00
Wizard of Oz, Mego, Scarecrow, 1972, 8" high	20	30	40
Wizard of Oz, Mego, Tinman, 8" high, 1972	25.00	37.50	50.00
Wizard of Oz, Mego, Wicked Witch, 8", 1972	27.50	41.25	55.00
Yogi Bear, 7½" high, stuffed, 1973, Knickerbocker	15.00	22.50	30.00
Yogi Bear Friction Car, Marx, 1962	40	60	80
Yogi Bear Go-Cart, Linemar	75.00	112.50	150.00
Yogi Bear "Yogi Bear Car," 1962 Marx (Japan), 4" long	40	60	80
Yogi Bear "Yogi Bear Hopper," 1962, Linemar, 4" high wind-up	50	75	100

DISNEY
(See also Paper, Premiums, Fisher-Price)

The average mint price of Disney toys in the last edition was $131.60, and in this edition it is $352.45, an increase of 168%.

Although Walt Disney was involved in animation as early as 1920, his first really notable character was Oswald the Rabbit, introduced in 1927. However, Disney did not own the rights, which eventually fell into the hands of another animator, Walter Lantz. Mickey Mouse first appeared in the 1928 short "Plane Crazy", but the third Mickey cartoon, "Steamboat Willie", seems to have been the first released, on November 18, 1928, and Mickey was a success from that point on. Minnie Mouse also appeared in the latter film, with Pluto emerging in 1930, though not called that till 1931, Goofy debuting in 1932, and Donald Duck in 1934. Mickey Mouse toys were first produced in 1930, and since then the stream of Disneyana has been unending, and apparently all of it deemed collectible.

```
CONDITION CODE:
C5 – Good, wear evident overall, shows that has been played with
C6 – Fine, shows some wear in spots, but taken care of
C7 – Very Fine, minor wear overall, very clean
C8 – Excellent, minor wear on edges only
C9 – Near Mint, no noticeable flaws, close inspection may show
      minute marks
C10 – Mint (like new)
      Note: Mint in Box does command higher price
```

	C6	C8	C10
Babes In Toyland, tin litho wind-up Indian on rollerskates, Linemar, 1950s, 6½" tall	160	240	320
Bambi "Jumping Bambi," Linemar, 1950s, trigger action, 6" high	130	195	260
Bashful 1½" lead figure, Britains	40	60	80
Bashful, approx. 12" high, 1938, Ideal	80	120	160
Bashful Party Mask, 1937	20	30	40
Bashful stuffed doll	60	90	120
Big Bad Wolf Halloween costume, 4' high	60	90	120
Big Bad Wolf celluloid pinback, 1¼"	20	30	40
Big Bad Wolf Stuffed toy in tux, with carnation, glass eyes, 20" tall	230	345	460
Cinderella wind-up 4¾" high, Irwin, umbrella, spins and dances	50	75	100
Cinderella and Prince - Dancing, No. 7000, Irwin Co., 1950s, plastic wind-up, 5" high	90	135	180
Cleo facemask, (Pinocchio) by Gillette, 1939	20	30	40
Cleo The Goldfish (Pinocchio) Sun Rubber squeeze toy	30	45	60

DAVY CROCKETT Powder Horn, DAISY
Courtesy Toy Collector News

	C6	C8	C10
Davy Crockett Auto-Magic Picture Gun	18	27	36
Davy Crockett Badge, 1950s	6	9	12
Davy Crockett Coonskin Hat	20	30	40
Davy Crockett doll, 8" high, Fortune Toy, 1950s	30	45	60
Davy Crockett Flying Arrows, balsa wood figures to be made into flying arrows. Copyright 1955	6	9	12

	C6	C8	C10
Davy Crockett "Frontierland Davy Crockett Outfit," gun, coonskin hat, etc.	80	120	160
Davy Crockett hand-gun, pop-action, tin litho, 1950s	40	60	80
Davy Crockett Play Knife, 1950s	20	30	40
Davy Crockett Powder Horn, Daisy .	30	45	60
Davy Crockett Prairie Wagon, 5" long	40	60	80
"Disney Television Playhouse," 1950s, Marx, 18½" wide, 12" high	100	150	200
Disneyland Ferris Wheel, circa late 1956, Chein, tin wind-up, 17" high	300	450	600

DISNEYLAND Roller Coaster, CHEIN
Courtesy Continental Hobby House

DISNEYLAND
Ferris Wheel
Courtesy HAKE'S
Americana &
Collectibles

	C6	C8	C10
Doc 1½" lead figure, Britains	60	90	120
Doc (Snow White), approx. 12" high, 1938, Ideal	100	150	200
Doc, 11½" high, stuffed molded oil-cloth face, Ideal	80	120	160
Doc Party Mask, 1937	14	21	28
Donald Duck, 4" high tin wind-up, Linemar	230	345	460
"Donald Duck," 5" high, 1930s, long-billed celluloid, Borgfeldt (Japan) .	1500	2250	3000
"Donald Duck," 6" high, 1950s, Linemar squeeze action	100	150	200
"Donald Duck," 6" high, Schuco wind-up, German	150	225	300
Donald Duck, 6" high drummer, mechanical	300	450	600
Donald Duck 6" high, Seiberling Rubber, long-billed	140	210	280
"Donald Duck" 7" high, 1960s, Marx wind-up, hard plastic	50	75	100
Donald Duck 10" high, Sun Rubber .	100	150	200
Donald Duck 13" stuffed doll, long-billed, Knickerbocker	150	225	300
Donald Duck, 13½" high, Gund, circa 1949	100	150	200
Donald Duck 13½" high, Character Novelty, 1940	110	165	220
Donald Duck 16" high, long bill, 1930s	80	120	160
Donald Duck Acrobat, Linemar, 1950s, 8½" high	175.00	262.50	350.00
Donald Duck "Choo Choo" No. 450 .	See Fisher-Price		

DISNEYLAND Happy Birthday Carousel
Photo by Don Hultzman

	C6	C8	C10
"Disneyland Happy Birthday Carousel," 1950s, Ross Co., 6" high	150	225	300
"Disneyland Jeep," 1960s, Marx, 10" long push toy	100	150	200
Disneyland Roller Coaster, Chein, 10" high	400	600	800

CONDITION CODE:
C5 – Good, wear evident overall, shows that has been played with
C6 – Fine, shows some wear in spots, but taken care of
C7 – Very Fine, minor wear overall, very clean
C8 – Excellent, minor wear on edges only
C9 – Near Mint, no noticeable flaws, close inspection may show minute marks
C10 – Mint (like new)
   Note: Mint in Box does command higher price

DONALD DUCK Xylophone Player
Courtesy Lloyd W. Ralston Auctions

DONALD DUCK, 6" high, SIEBERLING, rubber, long-billed
Courtesy HAKE'S Americana & Collectibles

DONALD DUCK AND PLUTO in Roadster, SUN RUBBER
Photo by Dave Leopard

DONALD DUCK Climbing Fireman   Photo by Don Hultzman

Donald Duck Duet
Courtesy Mapes Auctioneers & Appraisers

Donald Duck Dipsy Car
Photo by Don Hultzman

	C6	C8	C10
"Donald Duck Climbing Fireman," 1950s, Linemar, 13½" wind-up ..	300	450	600
Donald Duck Crazy Car, 1950s, Linemar, 5½" long wind-up	400	600	800
Donald Duck Delivery Tricycle, tin and plastic, 5", Marx	180	270	360
Donald Duck "Dipsy Car - Donald Duck," 1950s, Linemar wind-up, 6" long	250	375	500
Donald Duck Doctor Kit	60	90	120
Donald Duck Duet, small Donald, large Goofy, circa 1945, Marx tin wind-up	400	600	800
Donald Duck "Donald & His Nephew" 1950s, Linemar, pull string action, 5½" high	100	150	200
Donald Duck "Donald the Driver," 1950s Linemar friction car, 6½" long	200	300	400
Donald Duck "Donald the Drummer," 1950s, Marx wind-up, 9" tall	200	300	400
"Donald Duck Drummer," 1950s, Linemar wind-up, 6" high walker	90	135	180
"Donald Duck Drummer," 1950s Linemar wind-up, 6" tall, rocker .	200	300	400
"Donald Duck In His Convertible," 1950s, Linemar friction, 6" long .	150	225	300
Donald Duck Jigger, 11" high, papier mache wind-up	800	1200	1600
Donald Duck Mouseketeers Hat	10	15	20
Donald Duck on paddle, string-puller, long-billed	See Fisher-Price		
"Donald Duck on Tractor," 1950s, Marx friction, 3½" long, plastic .	40	60	80
Donald Duck pulltoy, baton-twirler, No. 400	See Fisher-Price		
Donald Duck pulltoy, No. 765, plastic feet, 1950s	See Fisher-Price		
Donald Duck pulltoy, 6½" long, long-billed, on platform	See Fisher-Price		
Donald Duck pull toy, No. 400, 1940, 10" tall, 7½" long, wooden figure with movable arms and legs, composition head	See Fisher-Price		

	C6	C8	C10
Donald Duck pull toy - wagon, circa 1940, No. 544	See Fisher-Price		
Donald Duck pull toy, with Xylophone, circa 1938, No. 185	See Fisher-Price		
"Donald Duck Railroad Car" with Pluto, Doghouse, 10" long, Lionel No. 1107	450	675	900
Donald Duck Rubber Boat, Sun Rubber Co., circa 1940s	30	45	60
Donald Duck Skier, Marx, 1940s, plastic Donald	210	315	420
"Donald Duck Straight Shooter," 1960s plastic wind-up, 6½" high	90	135	180
Donald Duck Teapot, Ohio Art	30	45	60
Donald Duck Tractor, Sun Rubber	75.00	112.50	150.00
Donald Duck Walker, celluloid wind-up, long-billed, 3½" high	320	480	640
"Donald Duck with Whirling Tail," 1950s, Linemar, tin wind-up, 5¼" high	200	300	400
"Donald Duck with Whirling Tail," 1950s, Marx plastic wind-up, 6½" high	70	105	140
Donald Duck and Pluto in roadster, Sun Rubber, 1930s, about 6½" long	20	30	40
Donkey (Pinocchio) rubber, Seiberling, 1940	50	75	100
Dopey 1½" lead figure, Britains	40	60	80
Dopey Doll, 9" composition with velvet clothes, Knickerbocker	130	195	260
Dopey, approx. 12" high, Ideal, 1938	150	225	300
Dopey Doll, Madame Alexander, 1938	150	225	300
Dopey Hand Puppet, composition, 1938, Crown Toys, bell, buckling belt	140	210	280
Dopey Marionette, circa 1952, Peter Puppet Playthings	30	45	60
Dopey Party Mask, 1937	20	30	40
Dopey 10" rubber squeeze toy, 1950s	10	15	20
Dopey tin wind-up, Marx, 1938	250	375	500

DUMBO tin windup, MARX, Dumbo flips over
Photo by Don Hultzman

ELMER ELEPHANT, rubber SEIBERLING, head moves. Courtesy Hake's Americana & Collectibles

DONKEY (Pinocchio) rubber, 4" high
Photo Courtesy HAKE'S Americana & Collectibles

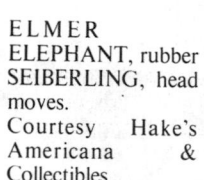
DOPEY Tin Wind-up, MARX
Courtesy PB Eighty-Four, New York

	C6	C8	C10
Dumbo tin wind-up, Marx, Dumbo flips over	230	345	460
Elmer Elephant 5" celluloid and string figure, 1930s	120	180	240
Elmer Elephant pull toy, 1936	See Fisher-Price		
Elmer Elephant, rubber, Seiberling, head moves	50	75	100
Ferdinand The Bull, Linemar	162.50	243.75	325.00
Ferdinand The Bull, copyright 1938, Marx, tail whirls, body shakes, wind-up	150	225	300
Ferdinand The Bull, late 1930s, Seiberling Latex Products, hard rubber, 6" long, 3½" high	50	75	100
Ferdinand The Bull, jointed, wood, 9"	100	150	200
Ferdinand and Matador, 1938, Marx tin wind-up	400	600	800
Figaro (Pinocchio) paper mask, 1939, Gillette	20	30	40
Figaro tin wind-up, Marx, 1940, 4¾" long	150	225	300

FERDINAND & MATADOR
Photo by Don Hultzman

	C6	C8	C10
"Flower," 1950s, Linemar, 3" long friction	60	90	120
Gepetto facemask (Pinocchio) by Gillette 1939	12	18	24
Gepetto 5½" wood figure holding his chin, Multi Products, 1940	90	135	180
Goofy 5¼" high tin wind-up, Linemar	210	315	420
Goofy - Pez container	7.50	11.25	15.00

Bashful, IDEAL, approx. 12" high, 1938
Courtesy HAKE'S Americana & Collectibles

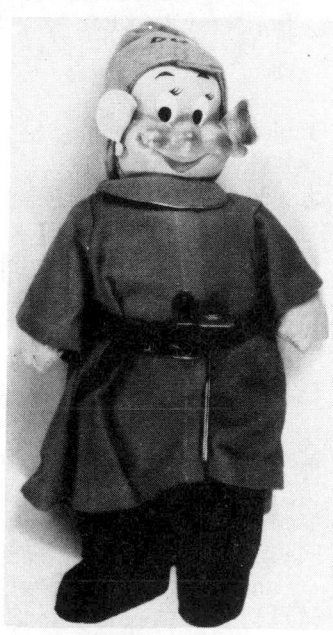

Dopey, IDEAL, approx. 12" high, 1938
Courtesy HAKE'S Americana & Collectibles

Grumpy, IDEAL, approx. 12" high, 1938
Courtesy HAKE'S Americana & Collectibles

Happy, IDEAL, approx. 12" high, 1938
Courtesy HAKE'S Americana & Collectibles

Doc, IDEAL, approx. 12" high, 1938
Courtesy HAKE'S Americana & Collectibles

Sneezy, IDEAL, approx. 12" high, 1938
Courtesy HAKE'S Americana & Collectibles

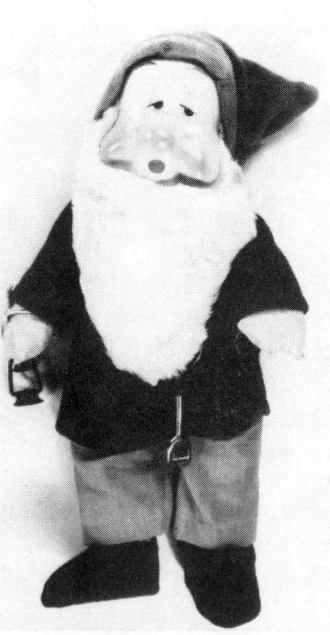

Sleepy, IDEAL, approx. 12" high, 1938
Courtesy HAKE'S Americana & Collectibles

Snow White, IDEAL, 15" high, 1938
Courtesy HAKE'S Americana & Collectibles

GOOFY the Walking Gardener
Courtesy Phillips New York

JIMINY CRICKET,
LINEMAR tin litho wind-up
Photo by Don Hultzman

LUDWIG VON DRAKE litho
tin windup, LINEMAR
Photo by Don Hultzman

	C6	C8	C10
Goofy "Goofy the Walking Gardener," Marx tin wind-up ...	600	900	1200
Goofy 1930 tin figure	400	600	800
"Goofy with Whirling Tail," 1950s, Marx plastic wind-up, 8" high ...	70	105	140
Grumpy lead figure, 1½" high, Britains	40	60	80
Grumpy Doll, stuffed, oilcloth face, velvet pants, 11" high, 1938	80	120	160
Grumpy, 11½" high, stuffed, molded oilcloth face, Ideal	90	135	180
Grumpy, Ideal, approx. 12" high, 1938	80	120	160
Grumpy Party Mask, 1937	40	60	80
Grumpy rubber squeeze toy, 1950s ..	10	15	20
"Gym Toys Acrobats," 1950s, Linemar, 8½" high (Mickey, Donald, Minnie, etc.) each priced at	150	225	300
Happy 1½" lead figure, Britains	40	60	80
Happy 3¼" high, Seiberling Rubber, 1938	60	90	120
Happy marionette, Madame Alexander, 9½" high, 1938	110	165	220
Happy party mask, 1937	40	60	80
Happy rubber squeeze toy, 1950s ...	10	15	20
Happy, approx. 12" high, Ideal, 1938	110	165	220
"Huey - Louie - Dewey Locomotive," 1950s, Marx friction, 3½" long, plastic	40	60	80
"Jiminy Cricket" 6" high, 1950s Linemar squeeze cable	200	300	400
Jiminy Cricket 12" approx. rubber head, wooden feet, cloth body, Gund	40	60	80
Jiminy Cricket 13" high, latex head, hands and feet, cloth body	60	90	120
Jiminy Cricket 14" high, Crown Toy, felt and cloth	140	210	280
Jiminy Cricket 15½" high, Crown Toy, felt and cloth	80	120	160
Jiminy Cricket facemask (Pinocchio) 1939 from Gillette	20	30	40
Jiminy Cricket Handpuppet, vinyl and cloth, Gund	30	45	60
Jiminy Cricket, Linemar, tin litho wind-up, 1950s, 5½" tall	240	360	480

	C6	C8	C10
Jiminy Cricket pushing bass fiddle, Marx walkie	30	45	60
Jungle Book Dancing Bear, Marx, plastic wind-up	40	60	80
Ludwig Von Drake, 7" rubber squeeze toy, circa 1960	10	15	20
Ludwig Von Drake, litho tin wind-up, Linemar, 1950s, 6" tall	240	360	480
Ludwig Von Drake rubber squeeze toy, 1960s	20	30	40
Mad Hatter puppet (Alice in Wonderland)	30	45	60
Mad Hatter's Taxi, Linemar, 5" long	200	300	400
Mickey and Donald on back of alligator, Marx, 1950s	330	495	660
Mickey and Donald Handcar, windup, plastic, 1948, Marx	400	600	800
Mickey and Donald in fire truck, late 1930s, rubber	30	45	60
Mickey and Minnie Mouse Tea Set, circa 1935, 13 pieces	180	270	360
Mickey and Minnie Mouse Swing Toy, celluloid with red and green flag, 11½" tall	420	630	840
Mickey On Pluto, rocks, tin windup, Linemar, 1950s	1200	1800	2400
Mickey Mouse, first toy made by Borgfeldt of NY in 1930, wooden Mickey with jointed hands, arms, legs and wire tail, leather ears. "Copyright 1928-1930 by Walter E. Disney"	550	825	1100
Mickey Mouse larger-size squeeze toy with clothes, 1950, Sun Rubber ..	40	60	80
Mickey Mouse with red shirt and yellow pants, squeeze toy, Sun Rubber, 1950	30	45	60
Mickey Mouse, 3½" high, Seiberling Rubber, 1930s	80	120	160
Mickey Mouse 5" high wood doll, Fun-E-Flex leather ears	160	240	320
Mickey Mouse 5½" high, vibrates, Linemar tin wind-up	340	510	680

MICKEY MOUSE, 5" high, wood doll, FUN-E-FLEX, leather ears
Courtesy HAKE'S Americana & Collectibles

MICKEY MOUSE 7" high, early, wood-jointed, BORGFELDT
Courtesy HAKE'S Americana & Collectibles

MICKEY MOUSE Mickey on Scooter, LINEMAR
Photo by Don Hultzman

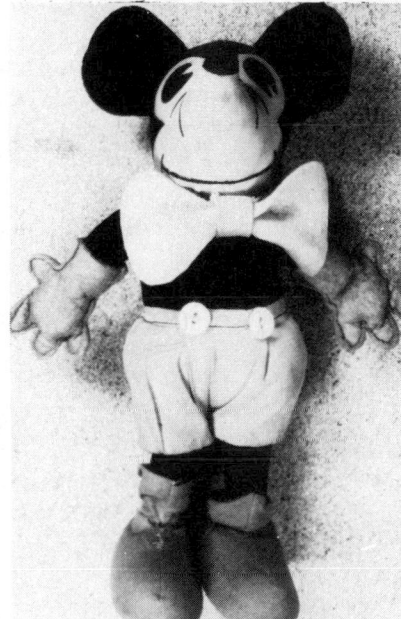

MICKEY MOUSE 11" high, cloth, "Walt Disney Mickey Mouse Geo. E. Borgfeldt & Company, New York" on bottom of one foot
Courtesy HAKE's Americana & Collectibles

MICKEY MOUSE Felt Doll, STEIFF, 12" high
Courtesy Lloyd W. Ralston Auctions

MICKEY'S TRACTOR, SUN RUBBER
Photo by Dave Leopard

	C6	C8	C10
Mickey Mouse 6" high, rubber, circa 1935, Seiberling	160	240	320
Mickey Mouse 7" high, wood jointed, early Borgfeldt	390	585	780
"Mickey Mouse," 7" high, 1960s Marx wind-up, hard plastic	50	75	100
Mickey Mouse 8" high, Sun Rubber .	60	90	120
Mickey Mouse 8" high, wooden, jointed arms and legs, circa 1933	600	900	1200
Mickey Mouse 9½" high, "Dell," rubber	40	60	80
Mickey Mouse 10" high, Sun Rubber, 1940s	20	30	40
Mickey Mouse 11" high, cloth "Walt Disney Mickey Mouse Geo. E. Borgfeldt & Company New York" on bottom of one foot	170	255	340
Mickey Mouse 12" high, 1930s, Knickerbocker	310	465	620
Mickey Mouse 12" high felt doll, early 1930s, Steiff	640	960	1280
Mickey Mouse 12" high, Borgfeldt ..	625	938	1250
Mickey Mouse 12" high, "Cowboy Mickey," Knickerbocker, 1936 ...	650	975	1300

MICKEY MOUSE Boat
Courtesy Continental Hobby House

MICKEY MOUSE
Acrobat
Photo Courtesy PB
Eighty-Four

MICKEY MOUSE Drum, OHIO ART, 6"
diameter, tin
Courtesy HAKE'S Americana & Collectibles

MICKEY MOUSE "Mickey-In-The-Box"
Photo Courtesy PB Eighty-Four,
NY

MICKEY MOUSE Circus Train Set
Courtesy PB Eighty-Four, New York

	C6	C8	C10
Mickey Mouse 17", rubber, Lakeside Mfg. Co.	80	120	160
Mickey Mouse 18" high, felt, Character Co., circa 1939-40	70	105	140
Mickey Mouse 21" high, circa 1933	350	525	700
Mickey Mouse 31" high, all felt dressed, opening in back for storing things, black jacket with yellow buttons, red pants, bells on toes of yellow shoes, 1950s	120	180	240
Mickey Mouse Acrobat, clockwork trapeze, celluloid Mickey	220	330	440
Mickey Mouse Airmail, rubber "Mickey's Airmail"	120	180	240
Mickey Mouse Banjo, 1930s, 17" long	140	210	280
Mickey Mouse Beverages felt soda jerk hat, shows Mickey from shoulders up saying "have one one me," 5"x11", circa 1930	60	90	120
Mickey Mouse Boat, 13"	250	375	500
Mickey Mouse Bubble Buster Gun, metal Mickey standing at gun sight. Cast iron	140	210	280
Mickey Mouse cardboard mask, circa 1935	60	90	120
Mickey Mouse Circus, Geo. Borgfeldt 6/3785, 1931, two wood figures revolving on swinging mechanism, 11" long	450	675	900
Mickey Mouse Circus Train Set, Lionel No. 1536, Engine, tender, containing Mickey, three carriage cars, dining car, Mickey Mouse Circus, Mickey Mouse Band, composition Mickey and track	1800	2700	3600

	C6	C8	C10
Mickey Mouse Circus Train, Mickey shoveling tender, three Disney Circus cars, wind-up train, red, circa 1931	1200	1800	2400
Mickey Mouse Clicker, tin litho, circa 1930, Mickey showing teeth while playing violin	90	135	180
Mickey Mouse "Climbing Mickey Mouse," 1930s, Dolly Toy Co., cardboard, 8" long	250	375	500
Mickey Mouse Club Auto-Magic Picture Gun, 1946, projects films	40	60	80
Mickey Mouse Club Newsreel	30	45	60
"Mickey Mouse and Donald Duck Handcar," 1950s Marx wind-up, 5" high, base 13x22"	300	450	600
Mickey Mouse Drum, Ohio Art, 6" diameter, tin	60	90	120
Mickey Mouse Drum Set, tin and cardboard, circa 1940, Minnie watching while Mickey juggles	240	360	480
Mickey Mouse Explorer's Outfit	87.50	131.25	175.00
"Mickey Mouse Express," 1950s Marx, 9" diameter (Mickey in airplane)	200	300	400
Mickey Mouse Express tin litho train set, 14" long, base 21x13", Marx, 1950s	400	600	800
Mickey Mouse Hand Car, orange base	550	825	1100
Mickey Mouse Hand Car, green base	500	750	1000
Mickey Mouse Hand Car, red base	450	675	900
Mickey Mouse holding flag, cast iron, 1930s	140	210	280
Mickey Mouse Jazz Drummer, finger-activated tin toy, Nifty, 4¾" high	80	120	160

Mickey Mouse Hand Car. Photo courtesy PB Eighty-Four

Mickey Mouse Circus
Courtesy PB Eighty-Four

MICKEY MOUSE
Racing Car
Courtesy PB Eighty-
Four, New York

	C6	C8	C10
Mickey Mouse Knickerbocker doll, 1935, 22" high	500	750	1000
Mickey Mouse, lead, 2½" high, 1933, Allied Toys	60	90	120
Mickey Mouse Marionette, circa 1930, 9½" high, felt body stuffed with cotton	160	240	320
Mickey Mouse Marionette, Peter Puppet Playthings Co., 1950s, 14" tall	90	135	180
"Mickey Mouse Meteor Five-Car Train, Walt Disneys" tin litho, Marx, 43" long	470	705	940
Mickey Mouse "Mickey-In-The-Box," 7" high jack-in-the-box	260	390	520
Mickey Mouse "Mickey on Scooter," 1950s, Linemar, 4½" high, all tin, Rare	1000	1500	2000
Mickey Mouse "Mickey on Unicycle," 1950s, Linemar, 5" high	400	600	800

	C6	C8	C10
Mickey Mouse "Mickey the Driver," 1950s Marx (Japan), 6½" long friction	200	300	400
Mickey Mouse "Mickey the Musician – I Play the Xylophone," 1950s Marx wind-up, 10" high	300	450	600
Mickey Mouse "Mickey's Delivery," Pluto on Tricycle-Cart, tin litho wind-up, celluloid head on Pluto, Linemar, 1950s, 5½" long	330	495	660
Mickey Mouse "Mickey's Service Truck," 1950s Marx friction, 3½" long, plastic	40	60	80
Mickey Mouse "Mickey's Tractor," Sun Rubber, 1930s, Mickey's head turns, 4½" long	45.00	67.50	90.00
"Mickey Mouse Motorcycle," 1950s Linemar friction, 3" long	150	225	300

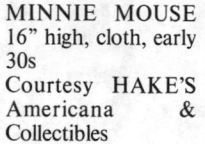

L to R: MINNIE MOUSE DOLL 14½" high, MICKEY MOUSE DOLL, 21" high
Courtesy PB Eighty-Four, New York

MINNIE MOUSE 16" high, cloth, early 30s
Courtesy HAKE'S Americana & Collectibles

	C6	C8	C10
Mickey Mouse Movie-Jecter, 1935 ..	90	135	180
Mickey Mouse Movie Projector No. E-18, Keystone, 1930s, 10" high .	225	375	450
"Mickey Mouse Newsreel," 1950s, Mattel, 9½" high, includes 3 records and 5 films	60	90	120
Mickey Mouse Organ Grinder, Minnie Mouse dancing on organ pushed by much larger Mickey, German .	1200	1800	2400
Mickey Mouse - Pez container	7.50	11.25	15.00
Mickey Mouse piano, wooden, grand, with decal showing Mickey playing, Minnie listening, circa 1935 .	200	300	400
Mickey Mouse Pocket Knife, 1935 ..	40	60	80
"Mickey Mouse Projector No. E-18", 1930s, Keystone Co. 7" long, 10" high, 9" wide	200	300	400
Mickey Mouse "Puddle Jumper," No. 310, circa 1950s	See Fisher-Price		
Mickey Mouse Puppet, approx. 10" high, "Gund"	20	30	40
Mickey Mouse Puppet, early 40s style, very large composition head, hands and feet, the rest of the body wood, cloth costume, felt ears	175	263	350
Mickey Mouse Puppet, Pelham 24" high, rubber legs and arms, wood body	250	375	500
Mickey Mouse Racing Car, red lithographed tin wind-up car with Mickey at the wheel, 4" long, 1930s	250	375	500
"Mickey Mouse Rollerskater," 1950s, Linemar, 6" high	300	450	600
Mickey Mouse Roly Poly, celluloid, early, 4" high	60	90	120
Mickey Mouse "Santa Car with Mickey Mouse and His Gift Pack" hand car, Lionel No. 1105, 1935	1100	1650	2200

	C6	C8	C10
Mickey Mouse "Scooter Jockey," Mavco Co., 1950s, all plastic, 6" high wind-up	160	240	320
"Mickey Mouse with Twirling Tail," 1950s Linemar, 5½" high	350	525	700
Mickey Mouse Sparkler Toy, 1930s, 5½" tall	300	450	600
Mickey Mouse Tambourine, Noble & Cooley Co., 1936, 9" heavy paper head, Mickey juggling while Minnie watches	310	465	620
Mickey Mouse Tea Service, 24 piece, tin	120	180	240
Mickey Mouse Tin Flute	40	60	80
Mickey Mouse Tin Washboard set, circa 1935	80	120	160
Mickey Mouse Tool Chest, 1935, Hamilton Metal	170	255	340
Mickey Mouse on Tricycle, tin litho, wind-up, celluloid Mickey, 1940s, 3½" long	320	480	640
Mickey Mouse Tumbling, 1947, Marks Bros., 8" high	120	180	240
Mickey Mouse Viewer, with film of "Brave Little Tailor," 1946	60	90	120
Mickey Mouse Washer, 1932 or 33 Ohio Art Co., tin litho washing machine, 7" high, two scenes with Mickey, Minnie, Pluto	90	135	180
Mickey Mouse Xylophone, tin wind-up, 1930s	600	900	1200
Mickey Mouse Xylophone Player, Linemar, tin wind-up, 1950s, 6" high	450	675	900
Mickey Mouse Club Bow and Arrow Set, circa 1955	20	30	40
Mickey Mouse Club Snap-on Ears, plastic, 1950s	10	15	20
"Mickey & Minnie Acrobats," 1934, Borgfeldt (Japan), 11" high	250	375	500
Minnie Mouse, wooden, June Flex ..	150	225	300

MINNIE MOUSE Knitter
Courtesy Don Hultzman

	C6	C8	C10
Minnie Mouse Knitter, tin litho wind-up, Linemar	250	375	500
Minnie Mouse Lead, 2½" high, 1933, Allied Toys	40	60	80
Minnie Mouse Marionette, circa 1930, 9½" high, felt body stuffed with cotton	230	345	460
Minnie Mouse Marionette, 13" wood and composition, 1950s	100	150	200
Minnie Mouse Puppet, Pelham, 24" high, rubber legs and arms, wood body	300	450	600
Minnie Mouse Roly Poly, celluloid, 4"	60	90	120
Minnie Mouse Washing Machine, 1950, Precision Specialties, Inc.	100	150	200
Mouseketeers Hat, 50% wool, 50% rayon, by Denayaluee, 1950s	30	45	60
Mouseketeers Outfit, Western Style	60	90	120
Oswald the Rabbit, circa 1927, 6½" long celluloid crib toy	250	375	500
"Parade Roadster" Marx lithographed tin wind-up, convertible car decorated with Mickey and other characters, with Donald at the wheel, Pluto and Mickey and Minnie Mouse as passengers, 1950s, 11¼" long	400	600	800

MICKEY MOUSE Xylophone Player, LINEMAR
Photo by Don Hultzman

	C6	C8	C10
Minnie Mouse 3" high, wooden, jointed, 1940s	80	120	160
Minnie Mouse, 7" high, Fun-E-Flex	280	420	560
"Minnie Mouse" 7" high, 1960s Marx wind-up, hard plastic	50	75	100
Minnie Mouse 10½" high, Sun Rubber, 1940s	40	60	80
Minnie Mouse 12" high, 1930, wearing dress, high heels, undies	225	338	450
Minnie Mouse 14½" high, early cloth figure dressed in a red and white polka dot skirt, wearing composition heeled shoes	300	450	600
Minnie Mouse 16" high, cloth, early 1930s	150	225	300
Minnie Mouse cardboard mask, circa 1935	40	60	80
Minnie Mouse cowgirl, Knickerbocker, 18" high, 1936	470	705	940
Minnie Mouse Handpuppet, Peter Puppet Playthings, circa 1952	40	60	80

PECOS BILL, MARX windup, plastic, 1950s
Photo by Don Hultzman

	C6	C8	C10
Pecos Bill, Marx wind-up, plastic, 1950s	140	210	280
Peter Pan 9¾" high, Sun Rubber, circa 1952	20	30	40

397

	C6	C8	C10
Peter Pan Marionette, circa 1952, Peter Puppet Playthings	60	90	120
Peter Pan Tea Set, circa 1953, 23 pieces	80	120	160
Pinocchio cloth and jointed wood figure, cloth tag	160	240	320
Pinocchio 2½" high, molded wood fiber figure, Multi Products, 1940	100	150	200
Pinocchio 5" high, molded wood fiber figure, Multi Products, 1940	150	225	300
Pinocchio 7½" high, jointed, circa 1940, Ideal	190	285	380
Pinocchio 8" high, Ideal	200	300	400
Pinocchio 10½" high, wood and papier mache wind-up, George Borgfeldt, 1940	350	525	700
Pinocchio 11" high, jointed, circa 1940	200	300	400
Pinocchio 12" high, Ideal jointed wood and composition	300	450	600
Pinocchio 19¾" high, jointed, circa 1940	100	150	200

PINOCCHIO tin wind-up, MARX, "Walking Pinocchio"
Courtesy Ed Hyers Antique Toys

Pinocchio, Cloth and Jointed Wood Figure, KREUGER Courtesy PB Eighty-Four, New York

PINOCCHIO Doll, IDEAL, 8" high Courtesy Lloyd W. Ralston Auctions

	C6	C8	C10
Pinocchio Handpuppet, Gund, 1950s	40	60	80
Pinocchio Paper Mask, Gillette, 1939	50	75	100
Pinocchio Express, pull toy, 1940, 11" long	See Fisher-Price		
Pinocchio on Donkey, pull toy, 1940, bell-ringer	See Fisher-Price		
Pinocchio The Acrobat, "Watch Him Go!" tin wind-up, 1939, Marx ...	230	345	460
Pinocchio tin wind-up, litho eyes, Marx, standing erect, circa 1940 .	200	300	400
Pinocchio tin wind-up, Marx, standing erect, moving eyes	300	450	600
Pinocchio, tin litho wind-up, Linemar Co., 1950s, 5½" tall	240	360	480
Pinocchio "Walking Pinocchio," Marx	150	225	300

PINOCCHIO, tin litho wind-up, LINEMAR Photo by Don Hultzman

PLUTO With Basket, 8" long Courtesy Lloyd W. Ralston Auctions

PLUTO, plastic wind-up, MARX, metal tail spins.

	C6	C8	C10
Pluto hand puppet, Gund, 1950s	20	30	40
Pluto lead cast, 1930s	10	15	20
Pluto, lead, 2½" high, 1933 Allied Toys	40	60	80
"Pluto" 1950s Linemar friction, 2¾" long	50	75	100

PLUTO Drum Major
Photo by Don Hultzman

PLUTO "Playful Pluto & Goofy"
Photo by Don Hultzman

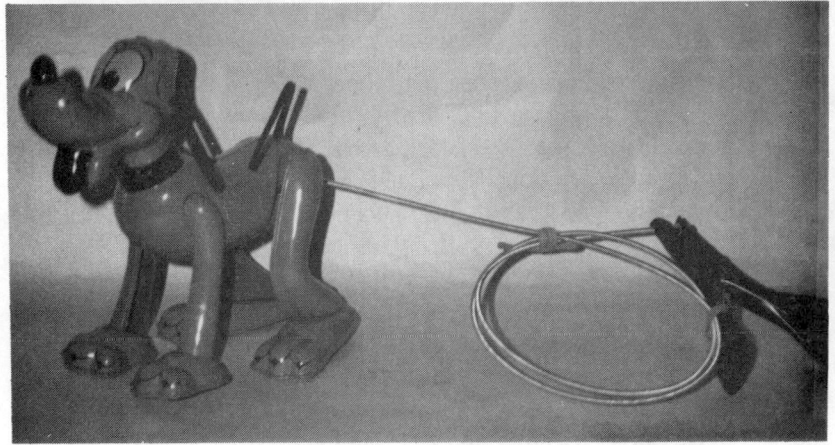

PLUTO tin litho squeeze-action with cable, LINEMAR
Photo by Don Hultzman

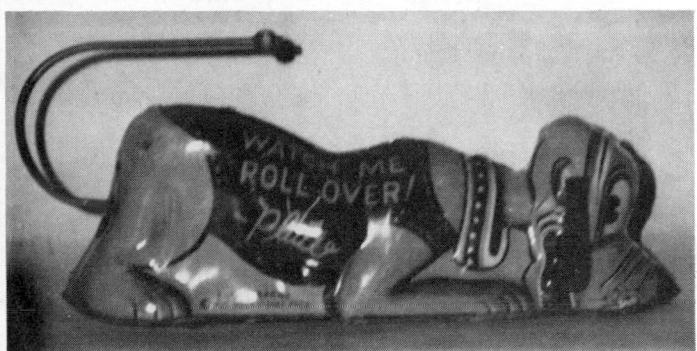

PLUTO "Watch Me Roll Over," MARX

	C6	C8	C10
Pluto tin wind-up, Marx, copyright 1939, sniffing, large wheels, tail ..	140	210	280
Pluto, plastic wind-up, Marx, metal tail spins, 1950s	110	165	220
Pluto 4" long Seiberling Rubber, circa 1935	60	90	120
"Pluto" 1960s Marx wind-up, hard plastic 6" long	50	75	100
"Pluto" Marx wind-up, 1960s plastic, 4½" high	40	60	80
Pluto, 7½" long, Seiberling Rubber ..	100	150	200
Pluto With Basket paper litho on wood, 8" long	See Fisher-Price		
Pluto 9" long, wood, jointed	150	225	300
Pluto, wooden, 3" bendable legs, circa 1934	100	150	200
Pluto "Begging Rollover Pluto," 1950s, Linemar, 6½" long	100	150	200
Pluto Drum Major, Marx tin windup, 1940s	240	360	480
Pluto "Drum Major" Linemar, 1950s, 6½" tall, tin litho wind-up	300	450	600
Pluto "Playful Pluto & Goofy" 1950s Linemar, 2 piece set, windups ...	750	1125	1500
"Pluto - Pulling Cart," 1950s Linemar friction, 8½" long	150	225	300
"Pluto with Whirling Tail," 1950s, Linemar wind-up, 4" high	150	225	300

	C6	C8	C10
Pluto Squeeze toy, Sun Rubber No. 11520, 1930s	40	60	80
Pluto, tin litho squeeze-action with cable, Linemar, 1950s, 4¼" tall .	210	315	420
Pluto, wooden, hand base, string-operated, many joints, marionette-type, 1936	See Fisher-Price		
Pluto on Rockers, wooden, circa 1930s	130	195	260
Pluto "Watch Me Roll Over," Marx, 1939	160	240	320
Pluto, sitting position, rubber squeeze toy, 1960s	20	30	40
Practical Pig, tin litho windup, Linemar	260	390	520
"Professor Von Drake Go Mobile," 1950s, 6" long, Linemar windup .	100	150	200
Sand Pail, 1938, Ohio Art tin litho, Mickey, Minnie and Goofy pictured	60	90	120
Seven Dwarfs, all, puppet-marionettes, Pelham	1500	2250	3000
Seven Dwarfs, all, Seiberling Rubber, 1938, 5½" high	350	525	700

SEVEN DWARFS, puppet-marionettes, PELHAM

	C6	C8	C10
Si-Am (Lady & Tramp) 16" high, stuffed, vinyl face, Gund, circa 1955	40	60	80
Sleeping Beauty squeeze toy, sitting with animals, 6½"	30	45	60
Sleepy 1½" lead figure, Britains	45.00	67.50	90.00
Sleepy, Ideal approx. 12" high, 1938	120	180	240
Sleepy party mask, 1937	20	30	40
Sneezy 1½" lead figure, Britains	45.00	67.50	90.00
Sneezy 3¼" high, Seiberling Rubber, 1938	60	90	120
Sneezy, Ideal, approx. 12" high, 1938	120	180	240
Sneezy Party Mask, 1937	20	30	40
Sneezy rubber squeeze toy, 1950s	10	15	20
Snow Shovel, 26" long, shows Mickey and Pluto building snowman	90	135	180
Snow White and the Seven Dwarfs lead figures by Lincoln Logs	See Soldiers, Lincoln Logs		
Snow White 2½" lead figure, Britains	45.00	67.50	90.00
Snow White doll, Seiberling Rubber	200	300	400
Snow White 13" high, Madame Alexander, 1938	120	180	240
Snow White, Ideal, 15" high, 1938	130	195	260
Snow White Party Mask	20	30	40
Snow White Washing Machine, circa 1950, Revell Plastics, 7½" high with wringer	80	120	160
Snow White and the Seven Dwarfs, 4½" dishes, china, with cups, creamer, sugar bowl, 6" plate	210	315	420
Snow White and The Seven Dwarfs musical top, Chein, 6½" across	80	120	160
Snow White and The Seven Dwarfs Sewing Set, Hasbro	10	15	20
Snow White Sink and Stove, Wolverine	60	90	120
Three Little Pigs clothes washer	50	75	100
Three Little Pigs Mask, 1933 Par-T-Mask	40	60	80
Three Little Pigs Sand Bucket, 3" tall	30	45	60

	C6	C8	C10
Three Little Pigs wooden pig, circa 1933, Borgfeldt, fiber arms and legs, 3¼" high	120	180	240
Thumper 6" friction, Marx, 1950s	100	150	200
Thumper 7" squeeze toy, Sun Rubber	30	45	60
Thumper 14" high, Gund, 1950s	38	57	76
Thumper 17" high, Gund, early 1940s	80	120	160
Timothy Mouse (Dumbo) stuffed, 17" high, Character Novelty, 1942	160	240	320
"Tramp The Dog," 1960s, Linemar friction, 4" high	90	135	180
Uncle Scrooge Handpuppet, 1960s? wearing high hat	20	30	40
Uncle Scrooge Limousine, "$" on back fender	110	165	220
Uncle Scrooge – Pez container	7.50	11.25	15.00
Uncle Scrooge vinyl squeeze toy bank, 7" high, circa 1960	40	60	80
Walt Disney Television Car, Marx, 1950s, 7½" long	210	315	420
"Walt Disney's Friction Delivery Wagon," 1950s, Linemar, 6" long, Mickey, Donald, Pluto, etc.	200	300	400
"Walt Disney's Friction Go-Mobile," 1960s Marx (Japan), 6" long, Mickey, Pluto, Donald, etc.	110	165	220
"Walt Disney's Mechanical Tricycle," 1950s Linemar, 4" high, Pluto, Mickey, Donald, etc.	140	210	280
Wendy (Peter Pan), handpuppet	10	15	20
Witch (Snow White) party mask	20	30	40
Zorro Handpuppet	30	45	60
Zorro Flintlock Pistol, Marx	40	60	80
Zorro Ring, black top with Z and 'Zorro' name	30	45	60

GUNS
(See also Premiums, Comic Character)

Average mint prices of guns in the fourth edition were $56.28 and in this edition they average $91.51, an increase of 63%.

SOME THOUGHTS ON TOY GUN COLLECTING
by Charles W. Best

Amid all the various toys in the world, the toy gun stands out as the one type most distinctly American and native to the United States, and with good reason. From the earliest days of our history up through the late 19th century, firearms were the primary tool that enabled us to survive, settle, explore, and subdue this land. Firearms gave us our freedom in 1776 and were instrumental in preserving that freedom throughout our first hundred turbulent years. Those years, as we now know, were to become an era of "romantic" wars when boys and young men dreamed of attaining fame and glory on the battlefield or out on the Western Frontier. The War of 1812, the Mexican War, the Civil War, and numerous Indian conflicts were all fought, basically, with small arms, so it is small wonder then that when toys first began to be mass produced after the Civil War, toy guns were among the first to appear on the market. Their success was instantaneous and toy guns remained among our most popular selling toys until as recently as the 1960's.

Although toy guns were patented in the late 1850's they were not manufactured in any quantity until a decade later due to the wartime shortages. These early toy guns were, for the most part, pea shooters and cork poppers and were usually made of wood with metal hardware although iron and lead types may occasionally be found among them. As you might suspect, these early examples are hard to find today and most are known only through their patent drawings. By 1870, inventors, trying to add realism to these toy guns, began using paper caps, a then new invention which had been developed just prior to the Civil War and was known as the Maynard Tape Primer. This tape primer was originally intended to detonate muzzle loading arms and closely resembled a roll of modern day paper caps. Now, for the first time, toy guns could make a loud noise yet still be relatively safe and harmless. Naturally, this spurred the demand for these new toys and designers worked overtime to create new and appealing guns. Their output was prolific and, today, the period from 1870 to 1900 is regarded as the "golden age" of the toy gun and especially the toy cap pistol, in America.

By 1880, the cast iron cap pistol had become the most popular type of toy gun by far and the various toy makers, primarily J. & E. Stevens and Ives, were competing among themselves to see who could produce the most unique and appealing designs. A glance at any collection of these early day toy pistols will show that, in those days, realism was secondary to artistic imagination. Many pistols from this period were literally covered with ornamentation and, in some cases, any resemblance to a real gun was purely coincidental. Leaf and scroll designs were the most popular but pistols can also be found with numerous other designs, including both two and three dimensional figures. Those guns with moving figures are now known as "animated" pistols and even though not as rare as some, are worth much more to a collector than an ordinary-looking pistol from the same period.

Another very desirable pistol from this same era is now known as the "head" pistol and featured a head, either animal or human, which was placed at the breech end of the barrel with the mouth open to receive the cap. Over two dozen varieties of head and animated pistols are known to exist but are so much in demand that they are seldom offered for sale.

The most popular material used to make these early toy pistols was, of course, cast iron, which continued to be used heavily into the 20th century, until the demands of World War II cut off the supply. Many varieties of old toy guns were, however, made of other materials than iron. I have seen examples made from such diverse materials as paper, wood, steel, tin, lead, rubber, zinc, glass, and even wax. During the Second World War, to meet the heavy demand, toy guns were even made of molded sawdust mixed with glue. After the war a few cast iron pistols were produced and assembled, using both new and old parts, but the cost proved to be prohibitive, and makers soon turned to less expensive metals such as steel and die cast zinc. By 1950, most toy pistols were being made of the die cast material and also plastic, both of which continue to be used today.

From almost the very beginning, toy gun makers have felt the need to personalize their products and literally hundreds of different names can be found embossed on these little guns. Some examples that come to mind are: EXCELSIOR, VICTOR, AMERICAN BULLDOG, ACORN, SUN, BOOM, DARB, ACE, DAISY, COWBOY KING, POLO, TRIUMPH, TERROR, etc. Many names were used only once on one particular gun and then dropped while others have reappeared time and again on different guns over the years. This custom of naming toy guns still goes on today and a visit to any toy store will turn up names such as: COWHAND, TOP GUN JR., 007, etc. Many of these names seem to reflect current events or personalities while on others, the meaning has become obscure.

For the toy collector, or would-be collector, the collecting of toy guns and especially pistols, not only offers a large diversity of models and styles but, because of their tremendous popularity in the past, also the opportunity to find and acquire interesting and unusual examples at an affordable price. Guns from as far back as the 1920's and '30's can still be found at flea markets, garage sales, and second hand stores, often at a price that is only a fraction of what other toys from these same years will sell for.

NOTE: Measurements given, in general, are from one end of the gun to the other, rather than on a diagonal from grip to muzzle. Much of the information on manufacturers, measurements, etc., comes from Charles W. Best's excellent book "Cast Iron Toy Pistols" (see bibliography). Dates of manufacture can vary within five years, though most of the later dates are considerably more accurate.

CHARLES W. BEST is a leading authority on toy weapons, and has been collecting them in earnest since 1966. His collection is regarded as one of the finest and most comprehensive in existence, and has won many awards at various gun shows. In addition to writing a number of articles on the subject in such magazines as Gun Report and Antique Toy World, he is the author of "Cast Iron Toy Pistols" (see Bibliography).

CONDITION CODE:
C5 – Good, wear evident overall, shows that has been played with
C6 – Fine, shows some wear in spots, but taken care of
C7 – Very Fine, minor wear overall, very clean
C8 – Excellent, minor wear on edges only
C9 – Near Mint, no noticeable flaws, close inspection may show minute marks
C10 – Mint (like new)
    Note: Mint in Box does command higher price

	C6	C8	C10		C6	C8	C10
Ace cast iron cap pistol, Stevens, "Made in U.S.A." 5" long, 1930 .	30	35	40	Aeromatic Glider Gun, steel automatic, circa 1940, shoots balsa airplanes	15	20	30
Ace cast iron cap pistol, 5" long, 1935	25	30	35	Agitator, The, cast iron cap and torpedo shooter, 1908, John Fox, 8¼"	100	130	150
Acme steel cap automatic, repeater, circa 1930	10.00	12.50	17.50				
Acorn cast iron pistol	75	100	125	Aim To Save, circa 1909	150	200	250
Admiral Dewey cast iron cap bomb .	100	125	150	Air Raid Warning signal pistol	30	50	75

	C6	C8	C10
America cap pistol with shield, pat. 1873	100	125	150
America, 1880	125	187.50	250
American cast iron cap pistol, Kilgore, 1940, 9⅝"	60	75	100
American Bulldog cast iron .22 cal. blank shooter, 1910, 4½" long, second trigger tips barrel to load, Kenton, handle projects outward	40	50	65
American Bulldog cast iron .22 blank shooter, 1920, 4½" long, Kenton, second trigger tips barrel to load, handle curves inward	40	50	65
Army cast iron cap pistol, 1910	40	50	65
Army 45 cast iron cap automatic, Hubley 1940 "Made in U.S.A." 6⅝"	40	50	65
Army 45 diecast zinc cap automatic, Hubley, 1940, plastic grips, "Made in U.S.A." 6½" long	15	20	25
Army pistol with revolving cylinder, tin litho, Marx no. 625	10.00	12.50	17.50
Army sparkling pop gun, Marx No. 197	12.50	17.50	25.00
Atomic Disintegrator cap pistol, Hubley	40	50	75
Auto Magic Picture Gun, projects film onto wall. 1936. Comes with film and instructions, in box	30	40	60
Automatic Repeater Paper Pop Pistol No. 74, Marx, aluminum	10.00	12.50	15.00
Bang cast iron cap pistol, Kilgore, "Made in U.S.A.," 6" long	25	30	35
Bang-O cast iron cap pistol, Stevens, 1938, "Made in U.S.A.," 7" long	15	25	35
Banner, blank-shooting mechanical cast iron pistol	100	150	200
Bell Pistol, Wyandotte	7.50	10.00	20.00
Benjamin Pump early BB gun, before 1910	50	75	125
Biff cast iron cap automatic, Kenton, 1935, "Made in U.S.A. Pat. Apld. For," 4½"	25	35	45
Biff Jr. cast iron cap automatic, Kenton 1935, "Made in U.S.A. Pat. Apld. For," 4⅛" long	25	35	45
Big Bill cast iron cap pistol, large hammer, "Made in U.S.A.," Kilgore 1935, 4⅞"	15	20	25
Big Bill cast iron cap pistol, Kilgore, 1925, 5½" long	15	20	25
Big Bill cast iron cap pistol, large hammer, "Made in U.S.A.," Kilgore 1930, 5¾"	15	20	25
Big Buster cast iron cap automatic, Kilgore 1915, "Patd Jul 2 1907, Made in U.S.A.," 5", two-piece trigger	60	75	100

Top, L to R: BIG BILL, PLUCK, DICK
Middle, L to R: ATOMIC DISINTEGRATOR, SURE SHOT SAFETY
Bottom, L to R: TIGER, GENE AUTRY 44
Photo Courtesy Garth's Auctions Inc.

	C6	C8	C10
Big Chief cast iron cap pistol, Kilgore, 1935, 6" long	20	25	35
Big Chief cast iron cap pistol, Kilgore, 1935, has star and "K", 6"	20	25	35
Big Chief cast iron cap pistol, early-looking, but made in 1930, 3½", Dent "Made in U.S.A."	12.50	15.00	20.00
Big Clip cast iron cap pistol, Stevens 1930, "Made in U.S.A.", 6¾"	25	30	35
Big Horn cast iron cap pistol, revolving cylinder, Kilgore, 1939, 8⅜"	45	55	75
Big Injun, hammerless	100	125	200
Big Scout, 1935	34	51	68
Big Scout, 1940, (engraved)	22.50	33.75	45.00
Bigger Bang large hammer cast iron cap pistol, Kilgore 1930, 6" long	30	40	50
Bill	40	50	60
Billy The Kid cast iron cap pistol, Kilgore 1930, 6¾"	40	50	60
Black Jack cast iron cap pistol, long barrel, Kenton 1930, "Pat. Sept. 11-23", 11"	60	75	90
Blaze Away Dart Pistol, Marx No. G23	7.50	10.00	15.00
Bob cast iron cap pistol, Kilgore, 1930, 5" long	25	30	35
Boom	120	180	240
Border Patrol cast iron cap automatic, Kilgore, 1930, 4¼" long	15	20	30
Border Patrol cast iron cap automatic, Kilgore, 1935, "Pat. Apld. For, Made in U.S.A.," 4½" long	15	20	30
Border Patrol, 1940	16	24	32

403

G-MAN GUN, MARX, tin litho with wood stock
Courtesy Gary Linden

	C6	C8	C10
Boss cast iron mammoth cap pistol, 1925, Kenton, 6¼"	20	25	35
Boy's Delight Pat. June 1891, cast iron cap pistol	100	125	150
Boy's Police Automatic 8" cardboard pop gun, circa 1940s	4	6	8
Brat cast iron cap pistol	30	40	50
Bravo	65	85	110
Brevet Depose	225	375	450
Bronc cast iron cap pistol, Kenton 1935, "Kenton, Made In U.S.A.," 6"	25	35	45
Buc-A-Roo cast iron cap pistol, Kilgore 1940, 7¾"	25	35	45
Buck cast iron pistol, Hubley 1930, looks earlier, 3¼"	25	35	45
Buck Jones Special Daisy Pump Repeater Rifle, with compass and sun dial in stock, 1937	35	50	75
Buddy, 1930	21.00	31.50	42.00
Buddy, 1935	21.00	31.50	42.00
Buffalo Bill, 1890	150	225	300
Buffalo Bill cast iron cap pistol, Kenton, 1925, "Pat. Sept. 11-23," 11⅜", very long barrel	50	65	90
Buffalo Bill cast iron cap pistol, Kenton, 1930, "Pat. Sept. 11-23," 13½", perhaps the longest-barreled cap pistol	65	85	110
Buffalo Bill cast iron cap pistol, Stevens, 1940, "Made in U.S.A.," 7¾" long	40	50	65
Bull cast iron cap pistol, Hubley, 1940, "Pat Appld. for, Pat. Mch. 25, '24," 6¼"	25	30	35
Bull Dog cast iron cap pistol, Hubley, 1935, "Pat. 1,488,046," 6¼" long	20	25	30
Bulldozer cast iron cap pistol, six-shooter, July 1874	150	200	250
Bull's Eye cast iron cap pistol, Kenton, 1940, "Gene Autry" signature on grips, 6½"	35	45	60
Bullseye Safety cast iron pistol, flare barrel, with spring	75	100	150
Bunker Hill cast iron cap pistol, National, 1925, 5¼" long	25	35	45
Buster cast iron cap automatic, 1910, Kilgore, 5½"	45	60	90

	C6	C8	C10
Butting Match mechanical pistol, cast iron	250	325	400
Cadet, 1930	24	36	48
Cal, 1925	30	45	60
Cannon - Animated Cap Pistol	250	350	450
Cap Bomb, cast iron, head shape	75	95	125
Cap Bomb, dog's head	75	95	125
Cap Pistol, cast iron, ornate, 1878 . . .	65	100	125
Cap Pistol, cast iron, revolving cylinder, 1887	95	135	175
Cap Pistol, cast iron, six-shot, dated 1895	95	135	175
Cast iron pistol, ornate, six shot, 1895	95	135	175
Cast iron pistol, shoots caps, embossed	20	25	30
Cast iron pistol, shoots caps, plated barrel	20	25	30
Cap pistol, steel, repeating, red, Wyandotte, 8" long	10	15	20
Captain cast iron cap automatic, Kilgore, 1940, 4¼" long	17.50	25.00	30.00
Cat (animated)	450	700	900
Cavalier cast iron cap automatic, Kilgore, 1935, "Pat. Appld. For, Made in U.S.A.," 4½"	25	35	45
Challenge, 1890	120	180	240
Champ Automatic 5", die cast, Hubley	4	6	8
Chief (1900-1910)	No Price Found		
Chief cast iron .22 cal. blank shooter, Kenton, 1915, 6" long, second trigger tips up barrel to load	40	50	65
Chief cast iron cap pistol, Hubley 1930, "Pat 1,488,046," 6⅛"	25	30	35
Chief cap pistol, aluminum single shot, Hubley	5.00	7.50	10.00
Chieftain cast iron cap pistol, National, 1920, 11" long	45	55	75
Chinese Must Go mechanical cap pistol	250	350	500
"Click Pistol" Marx No. 32	5.00	7.50	10.00
Click Pistol, Marx, approx. 7¾" long, pressed steel, with box	10	15	20
Click Pistol, tin litho, Marx No. 36 . .	7.50	12.50	17.50
Clicker Pistol, plain black, late 1930s, early 1940s	5.00	7.50	12.00
Clip Jr. cast iron cap pistol, Stevens, 1935, 5¼"	25	30	35
Clipper cast iron cap automatic, Kilgore, 1935 4⅛"	25	30	35
Clown and mule animated pistol	500	600	750
Clown (on a barrel)	300	400	500
Colt cast iron cap pistol, Stevens 1920, "Patented June 17, 1890, Made in U.S.A.," 5½"	35	45	60
Colt cast iron cap pistol, Stevens, 1935, 6½"	30	35	45
Colt .45 die cast Hubley	15	20	30

	C6	C8	C10
Columbia 1885 cast iron cap pistol ..	125	150	175
Columbia 1890 cast iron cap pistol ..	125	150	175
Columbia cast iron cap pistol, pat. June 1891	125	150	175
Columbian Junior Early BB gun	150	200	400
Comet, 1885, 5½", Stevens	120	180	240
Comet, 1925, 7⅛", Stevens	40	60	80
Cop cast iron cap pistol Hubley 1930 "Pat 1,488,046" or "Pat. Mch. 25 '24," 5"	25	30	35
Cork-popper pistol, Wyandotte, spur trigger	7.50	10.00	15.00
Cork-shooting rifle, Marx No. 206 ...	10	15	20
Corn Shooter cap pistol	45	55	65
Cowboy cast iron cap pistol, Ives, 1890, 7⅝"	60	75	100
Cowboy cast iron cap pistol, Stevens, 1935, "Made in U.S.A.," 3½" ...	12.50	17.50	25.00
Cowboy cast iron cap pistol, long barrel, Stevens, 1930, "Made in U.S.A."	40	45	50
Cowboy cast iron cap pistol, Hubley 1940 "Made in U.S.A.," 8"	30	40	50
Cowboy King, 1940	20	30	40
Coyote die cast Hubley	10	15	25
Crack, 1925, Stevens, 5"	40	60	80
Cupid, 1900, 5¼"	50	75	100
Dagger Derringer die cast Hubley ...	10	15	25

Typical Cast Iron Cap Pistols 1900-1910
Top Row, L to R: NEMO, LAS, TIGER 1915
Middle Row, L to R: GO, BUSTER 1910, SCOUT 1890
Bottom Row, L to R: unmarked; NATIONAL, Stevens 1920, unmarked
Courtesy Charles W. Best

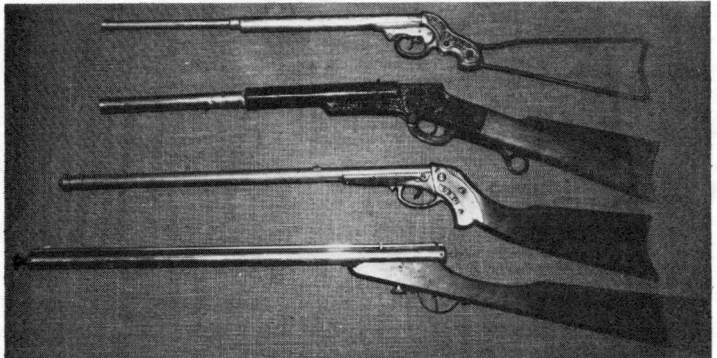

Typical B.B. Guns from the year 1900—Row 1: DAISY 3rd MODEL; Row 2: COLUMBIAN JUNIOR; Row 3: KING; Row 4: BENJAMIN (pump)
Courtesy Charles W. Best

DAISY No. 118 Targeteer
Photo by Bill Kaufman
Courtesy Good Old Days Store

Daisy 1895	80	120	160
Daisy 1925	20	30	40
Daisy Buzz Barton Special No. 195, BB gun	35	50	100
Daisy cast iron cap pistol, Pat. Apr. 1873	65	100	125
Daisy cast iron cap pistol, Hubley 1935, 4⅛"	20	25	30
Daisy "Daisy Mfg. Co. No. 80" water pistol, Pat. 1807839, approx. 7¼" long	10	15	20
Daisy Pump No. 25 BB gun (early) ..	25	35	55
Daisy Defender BB gun, No. 140 ...	75	100	200
Daisy early BB gun, 3rd model, with cast iron frame	150	200	350

Typical Cast Iron Cap Pistols, 1920-1930 — Top Row, L to R: OH BOY 1922, BUNKER HILL, BIG BILL 1925; Middle Row, L to R: FEDERAL 1920, RANGER 1920, NEW 50 SHOT INVINCIBLE; Bottom Row, L to R: IMPERIAL, MASTER 1922, NATIONAL No. 380.
Courtesy Charles W. Best

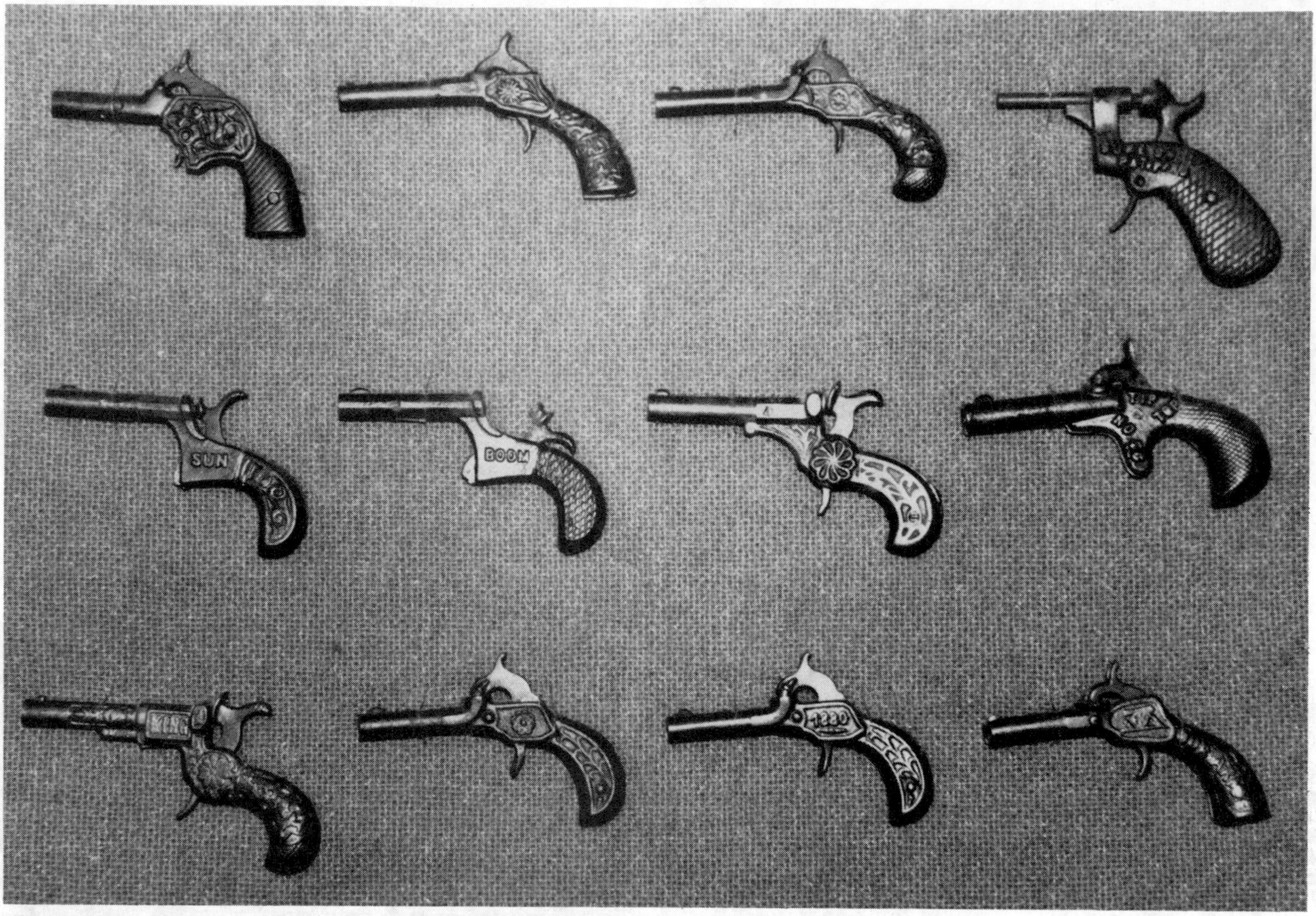

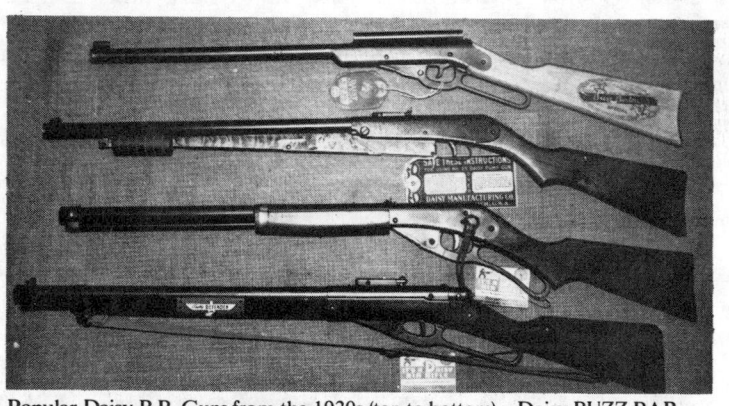

Typical Cast Iron Cap Pistols 1870-1880. Top Row, L to R: Unmarked, DAISY, Unmarked, SURE SHOT. Middle row, SUN, BOOM, Unmarked, TIP TOP NO. 50. Bottom row, KING, Unmarked, 1880, OUR ARMY FOREVER.
Courtesy Charles W. Best

Popular Daisy B.B. Guns from the 1930s (top to bottom)—Daisy BUZZ BARTON SPECIAL, No. 195; Daisy Pump No. 25; Daisy RED RYDER, No. 111; Daisy DEFENDER, No. 140
Courtesy Charles W. Best

	C6	C8	C10
Daisy Red Ryder BB gun No. 111 (see Comic Character)			
Daisy "Scout" No. 75 BB gun, circa 1955, plastic stock	15.00	22.50	30.00
Daisy No. 7 water pistol	7.50	10.00	12.50
Daisy No. 8 water pistol all metal, patent 1915	15	20	25
Daisy Targeteer Air Pistol, circa 1947, 1940s	10	15	20
Daisy "Daisy No. 118 Targeteer" automatic 10¼" long, target pistol	10	15	20

	C6	C8	C10
Daisy air rifle, cast iron and brass, early, 31" long	150	200	350
Daisy air rifle target, 1935, 4½x5"	1.00	1.50	2.00
Daisy Cinematic Picture Pistol, circa mid-1940s	30	40	50
Daisy Double Duty Pistol, pops and shoots water from separate barrel, very similar to Buck Rogers pistol (see Comic Character)	20	25	30
Daisy Zooka "Pop" Pistol, similar to Buck Rogers pistol	25	30	40
Dandy cast iron cap pistol, Hubley, 1935, can have variety of markings, 5¾"	30	40	50
Darb cast iron cap pistol, Kenton 1930, "Pat Sept. 11-23", 5½" long	25	30	40
Dart Pistol, Wyandotte, colorful, fancy lithographing	5	10	15
David	40	50	75
Dead Shot	50	70	90
Defence, 1896	50	75	100
Derby cast iron cap pistol, Hubley, 1930, 7"	30	40	50
Detroit cast iron cap pistol, 1910, 6⅝" long	45	55	65

DRAGNET - Detective Special Repeating Revolver Cap Gun, circa 1955
Courtesy HAKE'S Americana & Collectibles

DUDE
Courtesy Playthings Magazine

	C6	C8	C10
Dick cast iron cap pistol, Hubley 1930, 6"	25	30	35
Dick cast iron cap automatic, Hubley 1940, "Made in U.S.A.," 4⅛"	20	25	30
DIK cast iron cap pistol, Kenton 1935, "Pat. Sept. 11-23," 4¾" ...	25	30	35
Dixie (1888-1890)	50	75	100
Dixie cast iron cap pistol, Kenton 1935, "Made in U.S.A. Pat. Appld. For," 6¼"	30	40	50

	C6	C8	C10
Doc cast iron cap pistol, Kenton, 1940, "Pat. Sept. 11-23," 4½"	20	25	30
Dolphin animated cap pistol (may actually be Sea Serpent)	325	400	500
Double-barrel cast iron cap pistol, dated 1880	100	125	150
Double-barrel pop gun-rifle, Marx No. 230	15	20	25
Double-faced cap bomb, cast iron ...	60	75	90
Double trigger cast iron match-shooting pistol, large, Stephens, PA 1873 .	125	150	200
Doughboy cast iron cap automatic, Kilgore 1920, "Made in U.S.A.," 5"	30	35	40
Dragnet Detective Special repeating revolver cap gun, circa 1955	15	20	30
Dude cast iron cap pistol, Stevens 1887, "Pat. Mar. 22 '87," 3½" ..	75	125	150
Dude cast iron cap pistol, plastic grips, 1941, Kenton, 6½"	30	40	50
Eagle cast iron cap pistol, Stevens, 1895, "Pat. June 17, 1890," 7½"	100	125	150
Eagle, circa 1940	30	40	60
Echo cap pistol, six-shooter cast iron, 1881	150	250	400
Echo cast iron cap pistol, Stevens 1920, 4¼"	20	25	35
Echo cast iron cap pistol, Stevens 1930, "Made In U.S.A.", 4½" ...	10	15	20
Excelsior cast iron cap pistol, Stevens, 1875, "Pat'd Apr. 22, '73," 5¼" .	125	150	175
Federal cast iron cap pistol, Kilgore, 1920, 5½"	25	30	35

Typical Cast Iron Cap Pistols 1900-1910—Top Row, L to R: AMERICAN BULLDOG 1920, AGITATOR, THE, HANSON-LINDSBORG K.S.; Middle Row, L to R: MAGIC 1900, unmarked .22 blank shooter, unmarked; Bottom, L to R: COWBOY 1890, BOSS 1925, STAR 1910.
Courtesy Charles W. Best

	C6	C8	C10
Federal cast iron cap automatic, Kilgore 1940, 4⅞", has removeable clip to hold caps	25	35	45
Federal cast iron cap pistol, Kilgore 1920, "Pat. Dec. '14; Made in U.S.A."	30	35	40

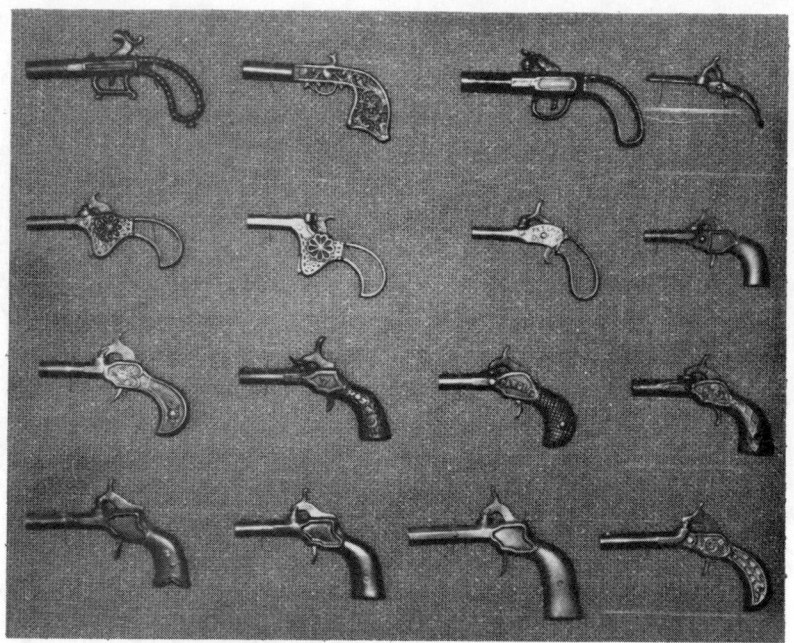

Typical Cast Iron Cap Pistols 1870-1880. Top row, L to R: Three Unmarked Firecracker Pistols, Unmarked Penny Pistol. Second row, L to R: Unmarked, Unmarked, GO BANG, Unmarked. Third row, L to R: Unmarked, "7", PAROLE, Unmarked. Bottom row, L to R; All Unmarked.
Courtesy Charles W. Best

Animated Cap Pistols, top to bottom: Cannon (KENTON, 1910), Lightning Express (KENTON, 1910), PUNCH & JUDY.
Courtesy Charles W. Best

	C6	C8	C10
Federal - Kilgore No. 1 cast iron cap pistol, 1925, 5¼", Kilgore	15	25	35
Federal No. 2 cast iron cap pistol, Kilgore 1925, 6⅜"	50	65	85
Fido, 4", 1910	50	65	85
Firecracker pistol, filigree handle, cast iron	85	100	125
First No. 1, 1920, 6¾"	125	175	250
Five-barrel firecracker pistol, iron and brass, 1877	550	700	850
5-Star steel dart pistol, Wyandotte	5.00	7.50	10.00
Flash cast iron cap pistol, Hubley 1934, "Pat'd" 6¼"	30	45	60
Flintlock die cast Hubley	10	15	25
Flintlock Junior die cast Hubley	10	15	20
Flintlock Midget, die cast, Hubley	9.50	10.00	15.00
Four Way cast iron cap pistol, Kenton 1930, "Pat. Appld. For", shoots pea or dart, rubber band and cap, all at same time	60	75	95
49-ER cast iron cap pistol, Stevens 1940, 9"	30	40	60
Fox cast iron cap pistol, Hubley 1935, 4½"	20	25	30
Frontier cast iron cap pistol, Ives, 1890, "Pat. June 21, 1887 and June 17, 1890," Dog's head atop the barrel facing hammer	175	225	300
G-Man cast iron cap automatic, Kilgore 1935, 6", looks like German Luger, removeable magazine holds caps	40	50	65

	C6	C8	C10
G-Man bakelite-framed cap automatic, Kilgore, 1940, 6"	20	25	35
G-Man clicker pistol, tin, black	10	15	20
G-Man wind-up steel spark pistol, painted finish	15	25	30
G-Man wind-up steel spark pistol, nickel finish with jewels on grip	15	25	30
"G-Man Automatic," Marx, sparkles when wound, 1930s	20	30	35
G-Man automatic sparkling pistol, Marx No. 43 aluminum	10	15	20
G-Man automatic sparkling pistol, Marx No. 44, tin	10	15	20
G-Man automatic sparkling pistol, Marx No. 85, tin	10	15	20
G-Man Gun, Marx, tin litho with wood stock	50	75	100
G-Man gun, Marx No. 707	10	15	20
G-Man Silent Alarm Pistol, Marx No. 54, tin	10	15	20
G-Man Tin Wind-up Machine Gun, 1940s, miniature	15	20	25
Gang Busters full size Marx Sub-Machine Gun	30	50	75

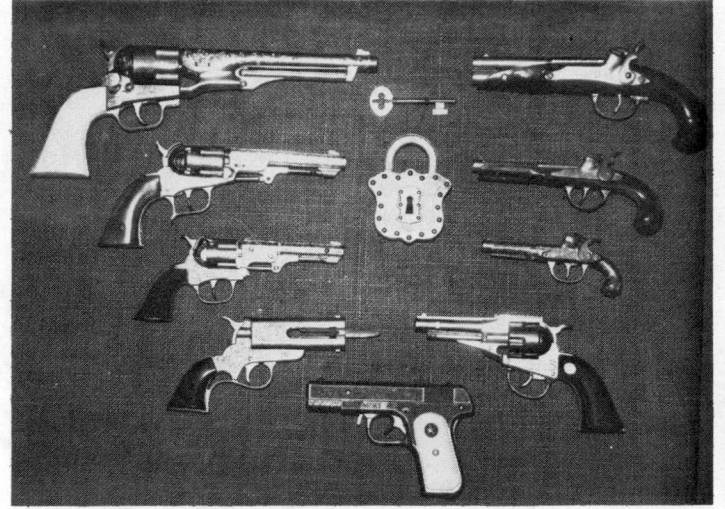

Some classic Hubley die-cast cap pistols from the 1950s:
Row 1: COLT .45; FLINTLOCK
Row 2: PIONEER; Padlock Pistol w/key; FLINTLOCK JR.
Row 3: COYOTE; FLINTLOCK MIDGET
Row 4: DAGGER DERRINGER; REMINGTON .36
Row 5: ARMY .45 (automatic)
Courtesy Charles W. Best

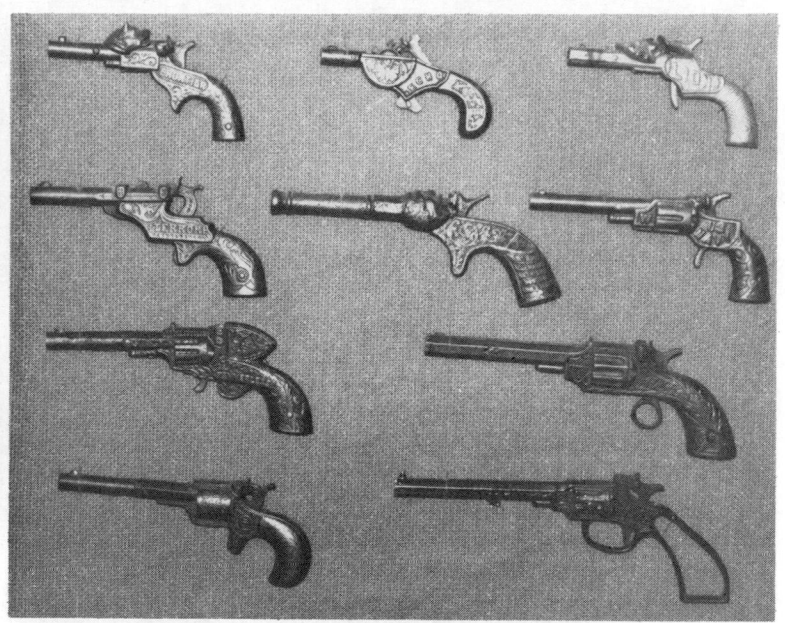

Typical Cast Iron Cap Pistols 1880-1890. Top row, L to R: FRON-
TIER, ECHO, LION. Second row, TERROR, BREVET
DEPOSE, US NAVY. Third row, HAMMERLESS, AMERICA.
Bottom row, Unmarked, TEXAS JACK.
Courtesy Charles W. Best

	C6	C8	C10
Gem cast iron cap pistol, Stevens, 1900, 3"	30	35	40
Gem 1925	20	30	40
Gene Autry cast iron cap pistol, Kenton 1939, 8⅜"	40	50	65
Gene Autry cast iron cap pistol, Kenton 1939, "Made in U.S.A. Pat. Appld. For," 6½"	35	40	50
Gene Autry cast iron cap pistol, Kenton 1940, "Made in U.S.A.," 6½", red grips	35	40	50
Gene Autry cast iron pistol (doesn't fire caps), Kenton, 1940, "Made in U.S.A.," 6½"	35	40	50
Gip, 1900	40	60	80
Go cast iron cap pistol, 1910, maker unknown, 6¾"	35	45	55
Go Bang	90	135	180
Guard cast iron cap pistol, Kilgore 1935, "Made in U.S.A.," 6¼"	30	35	40
H-Bar-O cast iron cap pistol, Kilgore, 1925, "Made in U.S.A.," 7½"	35	45	55
Halt	45	50	60
Hammerless cast iron cap pistol, Stevens, 1892, "Pat. Appld. For," 7¼", four revolving triggers, hammer concealed	125	175	250
Hanson-Lindsborg K.S. cast iron firecracker pistol, 1905, Hanson "Pat. Appld. For," 6⅜", fires firecracker	40	60	85
Hero cast iron cap pistol, Stevens, 1937, 5¼"	15	20	25
Hero, 1940	14	21	28
Hero Auto cast iron cap automatic, 1920, Stevens, 4¾"	35	45	60
Hi-Ho cast iron cap pistol, Stevens, 1940, "Made In U.S.A.," 7"	25	30	35

	C6	C8	C10
Hi-Ho cast iron pistol, can fire caps, Stevens, 1940, "Made in U.S.A.," 7"	25	30	35
Hi-Ho cast iron cap pistol, Kilgore, 1940, 6½"	25	30	35
Hi-Ho cast iron cap pistol, Kenton 1940, "Pat. Sept. 11-23," 5⅛"	25	30	35
Hi-Ranger cast iron cap pistol, Stevens, 1940, 7¾"	30	40	50
Hopalong Cassidy 9" revolver, Wyandotte, "Hopalong" on both sides of handle, with holster	25	30	50
Hopalong Cassidy 10" Revolver with bust of Hopalong, Schmidt	25	30	50
Hub cast iron cap pistol, Hubley, 1940, 6¼"	25	30	35
Hustler cast iron pistol	50	65	105
Ibex, 1895, Stevens, 4½"	45	60	90
Ideal, tin dart-shooter	10	15	20
Imperial cast iron cap pistol, Kilgore, 1935, 5¼"	35	45	60
Indian cast iron cap pistol	45	60	75
Invincible New 50 Shot, 1930	22	33	44
Invincible cast iron cap pistol, Kilgore 1935, 5¼", "Pat. Dec. 14"	20	25	35
Jack Armstrong airplane gun, Daisy, 1936	30	45	55
Jax cast iron cap pistol, Kenton 1930, "Pat. Sept. 11-23," 4"	20	25	30
Johnnie's Little Gun	150	220	280
Joker	120	150	180
Jumbo cast iron cap pistol, "Pat. June 17, 1890; Made in U.S.A.," 9½", Stevens 1895	85	125	200
Jr. Police Chief, cast iron cap automatic, Kenton, 1938, "Made In U.S.A.," 3⅞"	25	30	35

409

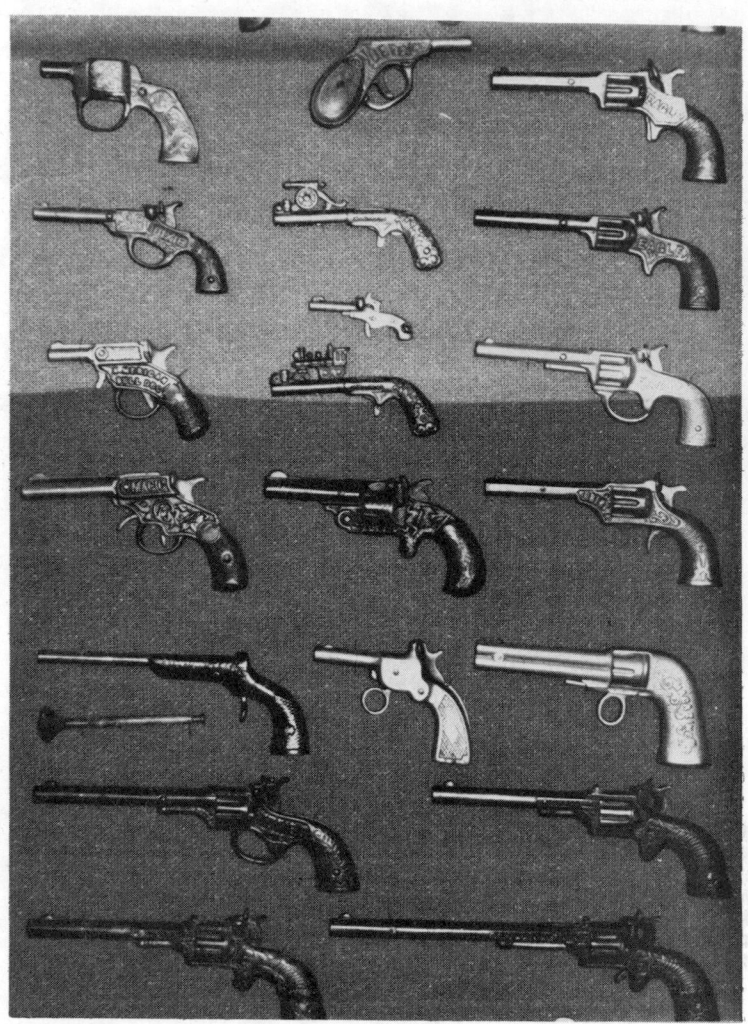

Typical Cast Iron Cap Pistols 1910-1920—Top, L to R: HERO AUTO, REX 1914, TERROR 1915, NATIONAL 1915; Middle, L to R: KILGORE 1910, KILGORE 1912, FEDERAL 1920, NEW 50 SHOT INVINCIBLE; Bottom, L to R: NATIONAL 1911, NATIONAL 1909, BIG BUSTER
Courtesy Charles W. Best

Typical Cast Iron Cap Pistols 1890-1900. Top row, L to R: KORKER, DEFENSE, EAGLE. Second row, DIXIE, Cannon (animated), EAGLE. Third row, Unmarked (small). Fourth row, AMERICAN BULLDOG, Locomotive (animated), EAGLE. Fifth row, MAGIC, ZULU, LIBERTY. Sixth row, Unmarked Dart Shooter, MEDRICK REPEATER, MAGAZINE. Seventh row, JUMBO, CHALLENGE. Bottom row, DEAD SHOT, BUFFALO BILL.
Courtesy Charles W. Best

	C6	C8	C10
Junior: Police 32 cast iron cap pistol, Hubley, 1940, "Hubley; Pat'd. 2088891" 5¼"	25	30	40
Jr. Ranger .32 cal. 1925	20	30	40
Junior Six-Shooter cast iron cap pistol, Kilgore, 1935, 5½"	25	30	45
Kid 1930	20	30	40
Kido cast iron cap pistol, Kenton, 1936, "Kenton, Made In U.S.A.," 5⅜"	25	30	35
Kilgore cast iron cap pistol, Kilgore, 1910, 5"	35	40	50
Kilgore cast iron cap pistol, Kilgore, 1912, 5¼"	35	40	50
King BB gun, early	75	100	175
King cast iron cap pistol, Pat. Aug. 1879	75	125	150
King cast iron cap pistol, Stevens, 1925, "Made In U.S.A.," 4¾"	20	25	30
King 1930	16	24	32

	C6	C8	C10
King Junior No. 10 cork rifle, Markham Rifle Co., "1909" 21" long	15.00	22.50	30.00
Kit Carson cast iron cap pistol, Kenton, 1928, "Pat. Sept. 11-23," 9"	40	50	75
Korker	120	150	180
L.F. & Co.	65	90	110
Las cast iron cap pistol	65	100	125
Lasso 'Em Bill cast iron cap gun, red rubies in handle, cylinder turns, 1930, 9"	40	50	65
Lawmaker cast iron cap pistol, Kenton, 1941, 8⅜"	45	55	65
Liberty 1875	100	150	200
Liberty, circa 1912, tin, ornate	30	40	55
Lightning Express, mechanical cap pistol, train slides forward along barrel to explode cap at end, 5", 1913, Arcade or Kenton	250	300	375
Lion, 1890, Stevens, 5¼"	150	180	240
Lion 1920	26	39	52
Lion head cast iron cap pistol, Pat. 1890, 5¼", Stevens	150	200	250
Little Bill cast iron cap pistol, Kilgore 1925, 5"	20	25	30
Little Chief Firefighter, water squirt gun	5.00	7.50	10.00
Lone Eagle cast iron cap pistol, Kilgore, 1929, 5¼"	35	50	65
Lone Ranger cast iron cap pistol, Kilgore, 1938, 8½"	50	75	100
Lone Ranger cast iron cap pistol, Kilgore 1940, 8½"	50	75	100
Lone Ranger click pistol, Marx	25	30	40
Lone Ranger 45 Flasher Flashlight Pistol, Marx	20	25	35
Lone Ranger Sparkling Pop Pistol, tin litho, Marx No. 096	30	40	60
Lone Ranger tin pop gun, 1950s, picture of Lone Ranger on handles	20	30	40

	C6	C8	C10
Lone Ranger Western Gun collection, circa 1939, six miniature guns mounted on card with history of guns on back	35	50	75
Long Boy cast iron cap pistol, Kilgore, 1922, 11" long, "Made in U.S.A."	40	50	7!
Long Tom cast iron cap pistol, Kilgore, 1939, 10⅜"	40	50	75
Look Out dog's head cast iron cap pistol	175	250	350
M&L water pistol, die-cast, rubber ball	5.00	7.50	10.00
Machine Gun, cast iron cap automatic, Kilgore, 1938, comes with crank, which when turned, fires the caps rapidly, "Ra-Ta-Ta-Tat," 5"	50	65	85
Magazine, 1892	90	135	180
Magic cast iron .22 cal. blank pistol, Kenton, 1900, "Pat'd. Oct. 17 '99," 6¼" long, ornate, has second trigger to open barrel for loading	50	65	85
Major	45	55	65
Mars, 1920	34	51	68
Mascot cast iron cap automatic, Kilgore, 1936, 3⅞"	25	30	35
Master cast iron cap automatic, 1922, Kilgore, 4⅝"	30	35	45
Master cast iron cap automatic, Kilgore, 1930, 4⅝"	30	35	45
Me and My Buddy, animated pistol with figure, steel, Wyandotte	25	35	40
Medrick Repeater	65	90	110
Mick 1930	24	36	48
Minute Man cast iron cap rifle, Kilgore 1936, "Pat. Appld. For," "Made in U.S.A.," 20"	100	125	200
Model, Pat. 1890, cast iron, 5⅜"	30	40	50
Model 1900	33.00	49.50	66.00
Monkey and Coconut animated cap pistol, 1878, 4¼", Stevens	350	425	600
Moonface capshooter, Stevens, circa 1880	500	650	800
National, 1915	24	36	48
National cast iron cap automatic, 1915, National, 3¾"	25	30	40
National cast iron cap pistol, National, 1909, 4⅞"	30	40	60
National cast iron cap pistol, National, 1911, 5"	30	40	50
National cast iron cap pistol, Stevens, 1920, 5⅜"	25	35	45
National cast iron cap automatic, National, 1925, "Made in U.S.A.," 5¼"	25	30	35
National No. 380 cast iron cap pistol, 1930s, National, 7"	30	35	45
Navy, 1878	110	165	220
Navy, 1910	33.00	49.50	66.00
Navy, 1925	18	27	36
Navy cast iron cap pistol, Kenton 1930, "Pat. Sept. 11-23," 5½"	30	35	45
Navy double barrel cap pistol	125	150	200
Nemo cast iron cap pistol, maker unknown, 1910, 6⅝"	35	45	60
New 50 Shot Invincible cast iron cap pistol, 1930, Kilgore, 5½"	25	35	45
Nigger Head cap pistol, cast iron, Ives, 1887, 4½"	150	200	250
"No. 71 Water Pistol" (Daisy?) automatic, approx. 5½" long	10	15	20
No. 500 (like Luger) 1935	44	66	88
Novelty cast iron cap pistol, Stevens, 1885, "Pat. Appld For," 5"	125	150	175
Nu-Matic Paper pop gun, 7" long	10	15	25
Officer Pistol, cast iron cap automatic, Kilgore, 1940, 6", modeled after German Luger	45	60	85
Official Detective-Type Sub-machine Gun, Marx, No. 2146	15	20	30
Oh Boy automatic cap, Kilgore, 1933, "Made in U.S.A.; Pat'd. Aug. 8, 1933," works both as automatic and crank-operated rapid-fire gun, 4⅛"	30	40	50
Oh Boy cast iron cap pistol, National, 1922, 5½"	20	25	30
Ohio cast iron cap pistol, Kenton 1930, "Pat. Sept. 11-23," 5⅛"	25	30	35
OK cast iron cap automatic, maker unknown, 1935, 3¾"	25	30	35
Old Ironsides cast iron cap pistol, 10¾"	45	60	75
Our Army Forever	160	240	320
"P"	60	75	100
P-38 steel clicker pistol, circa 1945	10	15	20
Padlock cap pistol, and key, Hubley, 4¼"	40	50	60
Pal cast iron cap pistol, Kilgore, 1930, 4"	25	30	35
Pal cast iron cap automatic, Kilgore, 1930, 4"	25	30	35
Parole	50	65	75
Pat cast iron cap pistol, Kenton, 1935, "Pat. Sept. 11-23," 6⅛"	25	30	35
Patrol cast iron cap pistol, Hubley, 1939, "Made in U.S.A.," 6"	25	35	45
Pawnee Bill, circa 1940	50	75	95
Pea Matic pea-shooting steel repeater	10	15	20
Pea Shooter	10	15	20
Pea shooter, pewter, highly embossed handle	25	35	45
Peacemaker cast iron cap pistol, Stevens, 1940, "Made in U.S.A.," 8½"	30	40	50
Peerless, 1905, 5½"	60	75	100
Persuader cast iron cap pistol, Kenton, 1939, "Made in U.S.A." Pat. Appld. For," 6⅜"	30	40	50

Top, L to R: "Teddy", "Chief"; Middle: "Buffalo Bill"; Bottom, L to R: "25 Jr.", "Pal", "Army 45"
Courtesy Mapes Auctioneers & Appraisers

	C6	C8	C10
Ranger cast iron cap pistol, Kilgore, 1920, 5⅜"	30	35	40
Ranger cast iron cap pistol, Kilgore, 1939, 8½"	35	45	60
Ranger cast iron cap pistol, Kilgore, 1940, 8½", hammer protrudes more than earlier version	35	45	60
Record	5.00	7.50	10.00
"Red Ranger," steel clicker pistol, Wyandotte, circa 1939, 8" long, black, red "jewel"	10	15	20
"Red Ranger," steel clicker pistol, Wyandotte, 8" long, circa 1941	10	15	20
Red Ranger steel click pistol, Wyandotte, 7¾"	10	15	20

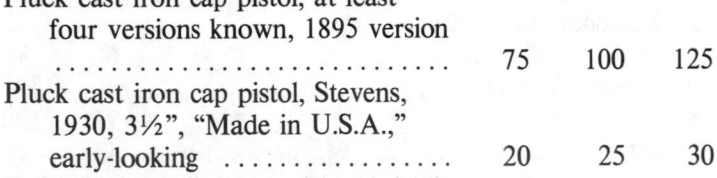

RED RYDER Daisy Air Rifle, circa 1950s
Courtesy HAKE'S Americana & Collectibles

RED RANGER Steel Clicker pistol, WYANDOTTE.
Courtesy Continental Hobby House

	C6	C8	C10
Pet, 4¼", Hubley, diecast	3.00	4.50	6.00
Ping-Pong rifle	10	15	20
Pioneer diecast Hubley	7.50	12.50	20.00
Pirate cap pistol die cast zinc with cast iron hammers and trigger, Hubley 1941, two-barrel, two hammers that cock, 9⅜"	20	25	40
"Pistol Packin' Mama," wood with cardboard sides, circa 1944, four revolving triggers, 8½" long, shoots wooden pegs	20	25	40
Pluck cast iron cap pistol, at least four versions known, 1895 version	75	100	125
Pluck cast iron cap pistol, Stevens, 1930, 3½", "Made in U.S.A.," early-looking	20	25	30
Police large steel automatic cap pistol, 8"	10	15	20
Police 1935 automatic	32	48	64
Police bakelite-framed cap automatic, Kilgore, 1940, 5¼"	25	30	35
Police Chief 1935	22	33	44
Police Chief gun and leather shoulder holster set, circa late 1940s, Wyandotte	25	30	35
Polo, 1878, Ives, 6"	40	50	65
Polo, later, Ives, has trigger guard	40	50	65
Pono cast iron cap pistol, Kenton 1936, "Pat. Sept. 11-23," 5⅛"	30	35	40
Powder keg cast iron cap bomb	75	100	125
Premier Safety, 1914	30	45	60
Presto cast iron cap automatic, Kilgore, 1940, 5⅛"	25	30	40
Punch & Judy cast iron animated cap pistol, 1880, 5" "Patented," Ives, Punch explodes cap with nose, on Judy's back	350	475	600
Pup 1930	19.00	27.50	38.00
Ranger (1890-1900)	65	85	100

	C6	C8	C10
Red Ranger steel six shooter repeater with plastic handles, Wyandotte, revolving cylinder	15	20	25
Red Ryder Air Rifle, 1940, Daisy with cast iron lever	35.00	52.50	75.00
Red Ryder Air Rifle, Daisy, circa 1950s	20	25	40
Remington .36 die cast Hubley	15	25	30
Repeating Cap Pistol, Marx No. G375, die cast	5.00	7.50	10.00
Rex cast iron cap automatic, 1914, Dent, 4⅛"	30	35	45
Rex cast iron cap automatic, Kilgore, 1939, 3⅞"	30	35	40
RIP, circa 1909	65	85	125
Rival 1920	45.00	67.50	90.00
Rob Roy, circa 1875	125	150	200
Rocket Ship Space Pistol. Late 1940s by Irwin	20	30	40
Rotor Fifty cast iron cap pistol, Kilgore, 6⅛" long, 1930	35	45	55
Roy Rogers cast iron cap pistol, 11"	65	95	125
Roy Rogers Forty Niner pistol and spurs set, 8½" long, 1940s	60	80	100

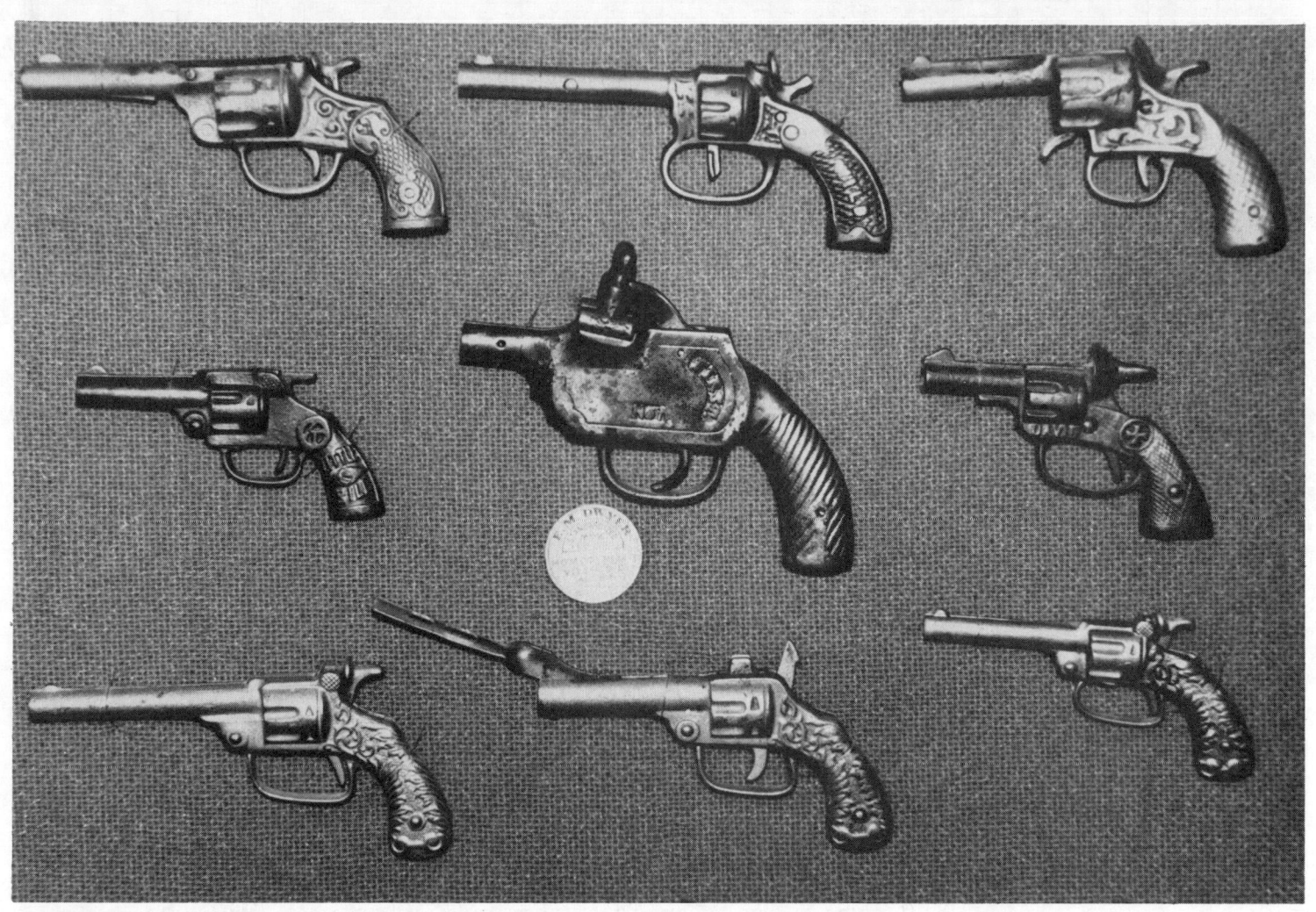

Typical Cast Iron Cap Pistols 1910-1920. Top Row, L to R: DETROIT, WILD WEST, Unmarked. Middle row, LITTLE BILL, FIRST NO. 1, DAVID. Bottom row, all unmarked with the middle a disk shooter.
Courtesy Charles W. Best

	C6	C8	C10
Roy Rogers Tuck Away Gun, 2½" derringer, circa early 1950s	15	25	35
Royal Pistol, The, 1878 cast iron cap mechanical pistol, fires spring-loaded top which is attached to bottom of the barrel, approx. 5", "Pat. Apr. 23 '78"	350	450	600
S&S 1880	90	135	180
Safety cast iron cap pistol, Hubley, 1924, "Pat. Mch 25, '24," 5"	25	30	35
Safety First cast iron cap automatic, 1920, "Safe," 3⅜", maker unknown	30	40	50
Sambo cast iron cap pistol, hammer hits head, 1887, Ives, "Pat. June 21, 1887," 4⅞"	150	225	275
Say I cast iron cap bomb	65	85	110
Scout cast iron cap pistol, Stevens, 1890, "Pat'd. June 17, 1890," 7" .	40	60	85
Scout cast iron cap pistol, Stevens, 1935, "Made In U.S.A.," 6¾" ...	25	30	40
Scout cast iron cap pistol, Stevens, 1940, 6⅛"	25	30	40
Scout cap pistol, tin, 1914, automatic	20	25	35

	C6	C8	C10
Scout Jr. cast iron cap pistol, Stevens, 1935, "Made In U.S.A.," 6"	30	35	40
Scoutmaster, 6¾", Dent	No Price Found		
Sea Serpent - see Dolphin			
Senator cast iron cap pistol, Kilgorc, 1925, 7" marked with star and "K"	30	35	40
1776-1876 cast iron cap pistol, Stevens, 1876, 5¼", produced for America's (100th) centennial	125	175	225
Shoo Fly cast iron cap pistol	100	125	150
Shoot The Hat cast iron mechanical cap pistol	450	650	850
Shotgun, double-barreled, steel, wood stock, 28", both barrels break down, cock and shoot	15	20	25
Siren Sparkling Airplane Pistol, tin litho, Marx No. 182	25	35	45
Siren Sparkling Pistol, tin litho, Marx No. 164	25	35	45
Six Shooter cast iron cap pistol, Kilgore, 1935, 6½"	30	40	50
Six Shooter cast iron cap pistol with plastic-type grips, Kilgore, 1935, 6½"	30	40	50

	C6	C8	C10
Six Shooter cast iron cap pistol, Kilgore, 1938, "Made in U.S.A." on hammer, 6½"	30	40	50
Six Shooter cast iron cap pistol, Kilgore, 1938, "Made in U.S.A." on hammer, plastic-type grips, 6½"	35	45	55
Six Shooter cast iron cap pistol, Kilgore, 1930, 7"	30	40	50
Six Shooter Automatic cast iron cap pistol (not an automatic), Kilgore, 1934, 6½"	30	40	50
6 Shot cast iron cap pistol, Stevens, 1895, "Pat'd. U.S.A., Jan. 22, 1895," 6¾"	95	135	175
Sliko cast iron cap pistol, Kenton, 1930, "Pat. Sept. 11-23," 6¼"	25	30	35
Snap, 1890	28	42	56
Snappy Jack, circa 1935, English	35	45	60
Sparkling Atom Buster, die cast Marx No. 46	10	15	20
Sparkling G-Man Sub-Machine Gun, Marx No. 2308	30	50	75
Sparkling G-Man Sub-Machine Gun, Marx No. 2310	30	50	75
Sparkling Pop Gun, Marx No. 198	15	20	25
Sparkling Space Gun, Marx	20	25	30
Sparkling Sure Shot	10.00	12.50	15.00
Spitfire cast iron cap automatic, Stevens, 1940, "Made in U.S.A.," 4⅝"	25	30	35
Sport cast iron cap pistol, Kilgore, 1930, "Made in U.S.A.," 7½"	25	30	35
Spud Gun, tin, automatic, circa 1940	15.00	17.50	20.00
Spud Gun No. 504, B.J. Cossman, Hollywood, Calif. die-cast	10.00	12.50	15.00
Spy cast iron cap pistol, Kilgore, 1936, "Made in U.S.A.," 4¼"	25	30	35
Star pot metal cap pistol, steer on handle	5.00	7.50	10.00
Star, circa 1878	100	125	150
Star cast iron cap pistol, 1910, Stevens, 6¼"	35	50	65
Stephans Pat, 1873, 5"	120	180	240
Stevens Repeater cast iron cap pistol, Stevens, 1930, 6¼", "Mammoth Cap; Made in U.S.A."	30	40	50
Stevens 6-Shot Rapid Load cast iron cap pistol, 1932, Stevens "Made in U.S.A.," 6½"	30	40	50
Streamline Siren Sparkling Pistol, tin litho, Marx No. 155	20	25	35
Sun cast iron cap pistol	100	125	150
S&W cast iron cap gun, 6"	15	20	25
Super cast iron cap pistol, Kenton 1930, "Pat. Sept. 11-23," 8¾"	35	45	60
Super Automatic Tom Gun, steel spark automatic	10	15	20
Super Nu-Matic Paper Buster Gun	10	15	20

	C6	C8	C10
Sure Shot 1870-1880	160	240	320
Sure Shot cast iron cap automatic, Hubley, 1940, 4¼"	30	35	40
Target cast iron cap pistol, Hubley, 1935, "Pat. 1,488,046," 8"	35	45	60
Teddy cast iron cap pistol, Hubley 1938, 5⅝"	25	30	35
Terror 1888	240	360	480
Terror cast iron cap automatic, Dent, 1915, "Pat. Jan 16' 15," 4¼"	25	30	35
Terror 1925	22	33	44
Terror, people embossed, cast iron cap pistol, 1882	150	200	300
Texan cast iron cap pistol, Hubley 1940, "Made in U.S.A.," 9¼" long	25	30	40
Texan Jr. cast iron cap pistol, Hubley 1941, "Made in U.S.A.," 8⅛"	25	30	40
Texas cast iron cap pistol, Kenton, 1936, Pat'd No. 1993916," 5¾"	25	30	35
Texas cast iron cap pistol, Kenton, 1930, "Pat. Sept. 11-23," 6⅝"	25	30	35
Texas Centennial, 1936, 11"	150	250	400
Texas Jack, 1886, Ives, 9⅜"	150	200	250
The Big Noise, circa 1922	40	50	65
The Forty Five cast iron cap pistol, unusual shape, National 1928, "Made in U.S.A.," 11⅛"	40	50	60
The Sheriff cast iron cap pistol, Stevens, 1940, 8½"	30	40	60
Tiger cast iron cap pistol, Stevens, 1915, 6¾"	30	40	50
Tiger cast iron cap pistol, Hubley, 1935, 6⅞"	30	35	40
Tin Tin Gun, 3x5", turn crank and it makes noise, Woodhaven Metal Stamping Co.	10	15	20
Tip Top cast iron cap pistol, 1878	125	150	200
Trainer	10	15	20
Trapper cast iron cap automatic, Kilgore, 1935, 4½", fires only single shot, but roll of caps can be carried in the grip	35	40	50
Triumph, 1878, 5⅛"	100	150	200
Trooper cast iron cap pistol, Hubley 1938, 5⅛"	25	30	35
Trooper Safety, 1925	30	45	60
Trooper Safety cast iron cap pistol, Kilgore, 1930, "Pat. Pend; Made in U.S.A.," 10" operates either as straight cap pistol, or can be fired with crank	40	50	65
Trooper Safety cast iron cap pistol, Kilgore, 1925, 10¼"	40	50	65
25 Jr. cast iron cap automatic, Stevens, 1930, "Made in U.S.A.; Patented," 4⅛"	15	20	25
25-50 cast iron cap automatic, Stevens, 1928, "Pat. Appld. For; Made in U.S.A.," 4½"	30	35	45

414

	C6	C8	C10
25-50, 1930	21.00	31.50	42.00
25-50 Cast iron cap automatic Stevens 1935, "Made in U.S.A.; Pat. Appld. For," 4½"	15	20	25
25-50 Cast iron cap automatic, Stevens 1935, "Oil Moving Parts; Made in U.S.A. Patented" 4½" .	15	20	25
25-50 Cast iron cap automatic, can be fired rapidly with crank, hole near muzzle holds removeable crank, Stevens, 1935, "Oil Moving Parts; Made in U.S.A., Patented"	35	50	65
25-50 Target cast iron cap automatic with "silencer" type barrel, Stevens, 1935, "Oil Moving Parts, Made in U.S.A.; Patented"	60	75	95
Two Dogs On Bench cap shooter (only two known, the one sold, condition unknown, sold for $3400 in 1981, its last sale).			
"2 in 1" cast iron cap pistol, 9¼" . . .	45	50	60

	C6	C8	C10
"2 Monkeys," 1882 cast iron animated cap pistol, 4½" maker unknown, monkey butts head against coconut held by another monkey	400	500	600
Two Time cast iron cap and rubber band pistol, 1930, Kenton, "Pat. Appld. For," 9¼"	50	60	75
Unxld Steel cap automatic, 6½", nickel plated	10.00	12.50	20.00
Urica	5.00	7.50	10.00
U.S.A. Liquid Pistol cast iron water pistol, Parker-Stearns, 1896, Pat'd. June 30, 1896," 4¾"	45	55	75
U.S. Navy, 1885, 6½"	50	75	100
Veteran 1935	35.00	52.50	70.00
Victor cast iron pistol	100	125	150
Villa cast iron cap pistol, Dent, 1934, "Made in U.S.A." 4¾"	30	40	50
Volunteer cast iron cap pistol, Stevens, 1873, "Pat'd April 22, '73"	100	125	150

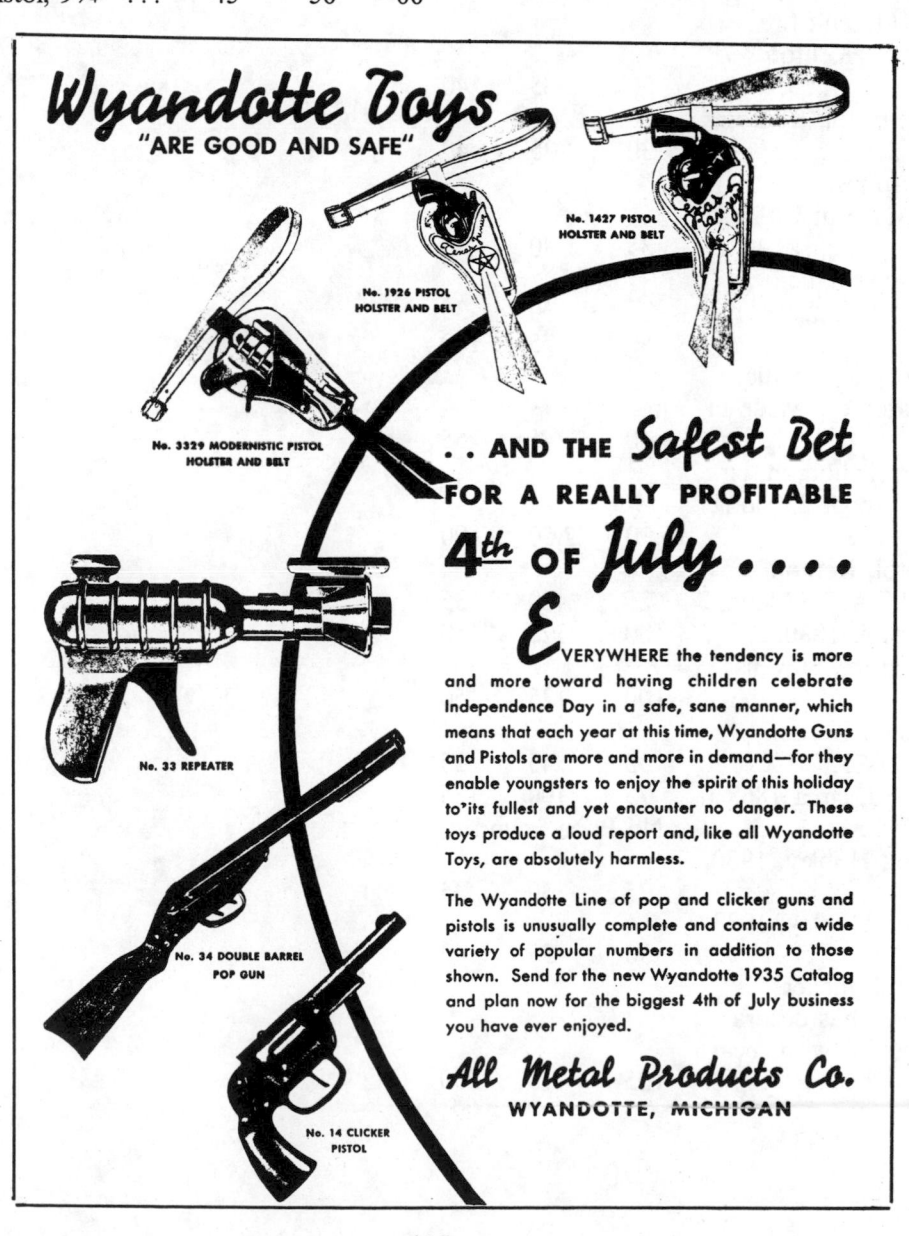

	C6	C8	C10
W on one side, S on other, cast iron cap pistol, nickel-plated, normal size barrel	10	15	20
W on one side, S on other, snub nose, single shot, cast iron nickel-plated	10	15	20
War cast iron cap pistol, Kenton, 1930, "Pat. Sept. 11-23," 4¼" ...	30	35	40
Warrior cast iron cap pistol, maker unknown, 1926, "Pat. Appld. For, 1926," 9"	60	75	90
Water Pistol, Wyandotte No. 41	5.00	7.50	10.00
Water Pistol, Wyandotte, unmarked .	5.00	7.50	10.00
Western cast iron cap pistol, Kenton, 1935, "Pat. Sept. 11-23," 7"	25	35	45
Western cast iron cap pistol, Kenton 1936, "Pat. Sept. 11-23," 7", has "jewel" over grips	25	35	45
Western cast iron cap pistol, Kenton, 1939, "Made in U.S.A.," 7½" ...	25	35	45
Westo cast iron cap pistol, Kenton, 1936, "Kenton," 7"	25	30	35
Westo cast iron pistol (doesn't fire caps), 1938, Kenton, "Kenton", 7"	30	35	40
Whoopie cast iron cap pistol, Kenton, 1932, 5⅞"	30	35	40
Wild West cast iron cap pistol, National, 1930, "Made in U.S.A," 6½"	35	40	45
Winner cast iron cap automatic, Hubley, 1940, 4⅜"	25	30	35
Wizard 1896	50	75	100
Woodsman cast iron cap automatic, Stevens, 1938, "Patented; Made in U.S.A.," 5¼"	40	45	55
Wyandotte double barrel shotgun, circa 1935, steel and wood, 25" long	15.00	22.50	30.00
Xtra cast iron cap pistol, Kenton, 1936, "Made in U.S.A.," 5" long .	25	30	35
Yank cast iron cap pistol, 1880	100	125	150
Yankee cast iron cap pistol, Stevens, 1895, 5½"	100	125	150
York cast iron cap pistol, Kenton, 1930, "Pat. Sept. 11-23," 7"	35	45	55
Young Sportsman, wood, circa 1868 .	75	100	135
Zip (1880-1890)	No Price Found		
Zip cast iron cap pistol, Hubley, 1930, 5"	25	30	35
Zip cast iron cap pistol, Hubley, 1938, 6"	30	35	40
Zulu cast iron cap pistol, maker unknown, 1890, 6⅝", has decoration of African warrior with spear pursuing bird	125	175	250

Aircraft in the last edition averaged $112.23 in mint condition, and this year averaged $107.34, a decrease of 4%.

AIRCRAFT
by Capt. Perry R. Eichor USAF, Ret.
(See also Tin Wind-Up, Comic Character, Premiums and Paper)

The airplane, until the last several years, was one aspect of toy collecting that attracted little interest and even less enthusiasm. Prices of toy airplanes generally reflected this lethargy.

Then, suddenly, those of us born and raised during 1920-1940 (the golden age of aviation) had the time, the inclination and the means to acquire those objects on which our fantasies were transported during childhood. The scramble began, and demand and prices have been climbing steadily ever since.

Collecting toy aircraft and memorabilia has finally come into its own. As an investment, they seem a good risk, although I find few true collectors who get any joy from acquiring only objects that are guaranteed to appreciate in value. True value lies in the ability of an object to rekindle the fires of our memories and bring to mind those halcyon days of our youth when our ambitions were great, our desires simple and our potential unlimited.

The majority of us would never fly, at least not in the pilot's seat, but the future and the unknown were not limiting factors for young minds. We had not been exposed to the harsh realities of the world, and our concepts of truth, justice, freedom and opportunity were not yet jaded. Naivete was a mantle we wore proudly, for we knew the future was ours for the taking.

Pick up a Hubley Airacuda, a Tootsietoy Army Pursuit, an ID model of a P-38, or any number of other types. Make sure no one is looking. Then, with the toy in your hand, let your inner self, the child within, take over. With toy aircraft, you need not be constrained by earthly bonds, deteriorating eyesight, shortness of breath, or any of the other myriad aches and pains that announce the onslaught of middle age.

Those interested in collecting toy aircraft can limit themselves to diecast and will choose from Tootsietoy, Hubley, Erie, Manoil, Barclay, Dinky, Mercury, S.R., Solido, Tekno, C.I.J., and a host of others. Cast iron was used by numerous companies before WWII and included Hubley, Arcade, Dent and Kilgore, to name a few. Pressed steel seemed to be dominated by Wyandotte and Marx for the smaller types, while Keystone, Kingsbury and Steelcraft, among others, produced the larger types. Tin is unlimited, ranging from the pre-war types, made by Marx, Strauss, Chein, Kingsbury, Girard, American Flyer and numerous European makes, up to the Japanese invasion of the 50's. Some of the later Japanese tin types were very accurate representations of actual aircraft, while others resembled real aircraft as much as Godzilla resembles Snow White.

Some of the nicest toy aircraft ever produced were the "Gnom" series made by Lehmann in the 1930's. These accurate small tin toys were based on two Heinkel aircraft and variations thereof. They are difficult to find and quite a nice display item.

In addition to the above, there are numerous examples of slush cast items from Barclay, Kansas Toy and Novelty, Tommy Toy, Ralstoy, etc., in addition to rubber facsimiles made by the Sun and Auburn companies. For obvious reasons, undistorted, well-preserved rubber toy aircraft are very rare.

CAPT. PERRY R. EICHOR, USAF, RET. was born in Oklahoma and is currently living in South Carolina. His interest in aircraft toys was reborn when he was a young officer in the Air Force and his mother sent him several toys that had been his as a boy. Twenty-one years in the Air Force only served to deepen his interest in the subject. Today, when he is not out collecting, researching or writing about aeronautical toys, he works as a Criminal Justice Administrator as well as an appraiser and auctioneer.

Some excellent plastic types were produced immediately after WW II and into the 50's. Some items such as the P-38, B-25, B-17 and P-40 by Renwal and the B-26 by Hubley were faithful copies, while others such as the P-39 by Ideal are so out of proportion that they lack even the symbiotic charm that often accompanies grotesqueness. Other toy manufacturers of plastic toy aircraft were Thomas, Acme, Premier, Lido and Reliable.

Of course, if one collects toy aircraft, it follows that they must be displayed, and they really look best on the numerous toy airports depicting structures of the same time period. In addition to airfields and hangars, there were numerous ground support personnel and vehicles. As with other toys, related memorabilia begin to encroach into the aircraft collector's acquisitions.

Interest in aviation is on the rise, and the flight of the Voyager, along with numerous other record-setting craft, will have a dramatic effect on the interest in things related to flight. Consequently, prices will rise and availability will decrease out of proportion to interest.

However, there will always be room for those of us who were excited during our youth by the sound of a rotary engine in a biplane passing overhead, doing slow rolls among cotton-ball clouds. We all still secretly yearn to fly with our youthful heros and perform daring feats of aerial combat. How many of you have a leather jacket in your closet? I rest my case.

Keep 'em Flying!

CONDITION CODE:
C5 – Good, wear evident overall, shows that has been played with
C6 – Fine, shows some wear in spots, but taken care of
C7 – Very Fine, minor wear overall, very clean
C8 – Excellent, minor wear on edges only
C9 – Near Mint, no noticeable flaws, close inspection may show minute marks
C10 – Mint (like new)
   Note: Mint in Box does command higher price

	C6	C8	C10
A. C. Gilbert "Erector" Biplane, with electric motor	120	180	240
Adam Bomb, circa 1946, wingspan approx. 11", wood and metal	110	165	220
Airford, small, cast iron, two-passenger, steel wheels, single engine	20	30	40
Airplane, early 1900s, single wing, prop behind tail, pilot, open fuselage	300	450	600
Airplane, wood, ride-on	20	30	40
Airport Set No. 88 T. Cohn Co., circa 1940s. Mechanical tin litho airport with early plastic planes that fly. Control tower controls for stunts, crash truck pumps water, airport bus, gasoline truck, etc.	37.50	56.25	75.00
American Flyer Spirit of America, 18" wingspan, 1928	100	150	200
American Flyer Spirit of Columbia, "555," pressed tin friction, 18" wingspan	500	750	1000
"Ancient Art Metal Co., Brooklyn, N.Y." Spirit of St. Louis, lead 5⅛" wingspan, circa 1927 "Pat. No. 74042"	24	36	48
Arcade Airplane No. 361 cast iron, twin engine, 4⅞" wingspan, "United Boeing"	25.00	37.50	50.00
Arcade Airplane No. 3620, cast iron, tri-motor, 4" wingspan, pressed steel props	37.50	56.25	75.00
Arcade Airplane No. 3630, cast iron body, twin engine, pressed steel wing, 7" wingspan	25.00	37.50	50.00

A.C. GILBERT "Erector" Biplane, incomplete in photo.
Photo by Bill Kaufman, courtesy Good Old Days Store

Adam Bomb
Courtesy Good Old Days Store, Photo by Bill Kaufman

418

"Ancient Art Metal Co." Lindy-type plane
Photo by Bill Kaufman,

	C6	C8	C10
Arcade Airplane, cast iron body, single engine, pressed steel wing, body resembles Corsair, red and yellow	50	75	100
Arcade Monocoupe, cast iron, 11" wingspan, pull toy	150	225	300

AA1   AA2

AA3   AA4

Photo by Ed Poole

	C6	C8	C10
AA1 Auburn Rubber **No. 1548** Boeing C-98 "Clipper," 8" wingspan	15.00	22.50	30.00
AA2 Auburn Rubber Consolidated A-11 light bomber, 4" wingspan	10	15	20
AA3 Auburn Rubber No. **586 Army Pursuit Plane,** "US 1X2755" on wings, Curtiss P-37	10	15	20
AA4 Auburn Rubber Douglas C32 Transport	10	15	20
Autogyro, 6" long, pressed steel, wheels turn blades via gear mechanism	21.00	31.50	42.00
Automatic Toy Co. Rocket and Space Ship, No. 305, friction, tin litho with rubber wheels, sparks, 9" long, 4½" wide, 3" tall, late thirties	25.00	37.50	50.00
Automatic Toy Co. Silver Eagle aluminum plane, 13" wingspan, wooden wheels, two-engine, 1930s	60	90	120

BARCLAY BA7
Photo by Bill Kaufman

BARCLAY BA2
Photo by Bill Kaufman

BARCLAY BA1, BA4a
Photo by Bill Kaufman, Courtesy Evelyn Besse

BARCLAY AIRCRAFT	C6	C8	C10
BA1 **307** Lindy-type plane, wingspan approx. 4⅜" long, early-mid 30s	10	15	20
BA1a **307** Monoplane, single engine	12	18	24
BA2 **Transatlantic Bremen,** circa 1928	12.50	18.75	25.00
BA3 Monoplane, single engine, high wing, Crackajack size, one-piece, sold with Aeroplane Carrier and piggy-backed on 195 Aeroplane	5.00	7.50	10.00
BA4 **No. 57 Giant Zeppelin**	12.50	18.75	25.00
BA4a Dirigible, 4⅜" long, early-mid 30s	12.50	18.75	25.00
BA5 **610 Rocket Ship**	25.00	37.50	50.00
BA6 **611 Rocket Ship**	25.00	37.50	50.00
BA7 **195 Aeroplane,** "U.S. Army" single engine transport, 3¾" wingspan	12.50	18.75	25.00
BA7a **195 Aeroplane** with BA3 monoplane piggy-backed on it	20	30	40

	C6	C8	C10
BA7b **195 Aeroplane** with clip of bombs attached to it............	18	27	36
BA8 "Old 307"	12	18	24
BA9 Airplane, slush cast, 3⅜" wingspan, single engine, low wing, cabin monoplane (Barclay?)	7.50	11.25	15.00
BA10 No. **52** Small Lindy-type plane	6	9	12
BA11 "Mister Mulligan" & "NR273Y" (Barclay?)	15.00	22.50	30.00

BARCLAY BA7b
Courtesy Hank Anton

BARCLAY (BA3) Monoplanes atop the firm's No. 372 Aeroplane Carrier
From The Barclay Catalog Book

BARCLAY (BA4) **No. 57 Giant Zeppelin**
From The Barclay Catalog Book

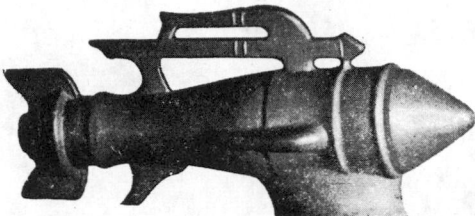
BARCLAY (BA5) **No. 610 Rocket Ship**
From The Barclay Catalog Book

BARCLAY (BA6) **No. 611 Rocket Ship**
From The Barclay Catalog Book

BARCLAY (BA1a) **307 Monoplane**
From The Barclay Catalog Book

BARCLAY (BA8) "Old 307"
From The Barclay Catalog Book

BEST - see KANSAS TOY & NOVELTY

	C6	C8	C10
Biplane, wooden, approx. 7½" wingspan, tin tail, aluminum propellor, pull plane, propeller spins .	35.00	52.50	70.00
Buddy L. No. **603 Transport Airplane** (Ford), 27" wingspan, circa 1946 .	300	450	600
Buddy L. No. **959 Army Tank Transport Plane,** 27" wingspan, two detachable tanks under wings, tanks have hum motor device, pressed steel, 1941	300	450	600
Buddy L. No. **2007** Monoplane and Catapult Hangar, 1930-31	450	675	900
Buddy L. No. **5000** single high wing monoplane, 1929-31	125.00	187.50	250.00
Buddy L. No. **5010** Triple Hangar and three planes, 1931, planes are monocoupes	450	675	900
Chein Helicopter-Toy Town Airways, litho 13" long, 5½" tall, 1950s ..	30	45	60

	C6	C8	C10
Dayton No. **700** high wing monoplane, 13" wingspan, open cockpit and pilot, red, yellow or blue, painted disc wheels	100	150	200
DC-4 type, four-motor passenger, circa 1930s, pressed steel	10	15	20

CONDITION CODE:
C5 – Good, wear evident overall, shows that has been played with
C6 – Fine, shows some wear in spots, but taken care of
C7 – Very Fine, minor wear overall, very clean
C8 – Excellent, minor wear on edges only
C9 – Near Mint, no noticeable flaws, close inspection may show minute marks
C10 – Mint (like new)
　　 Note: Mint in Box does command higher price

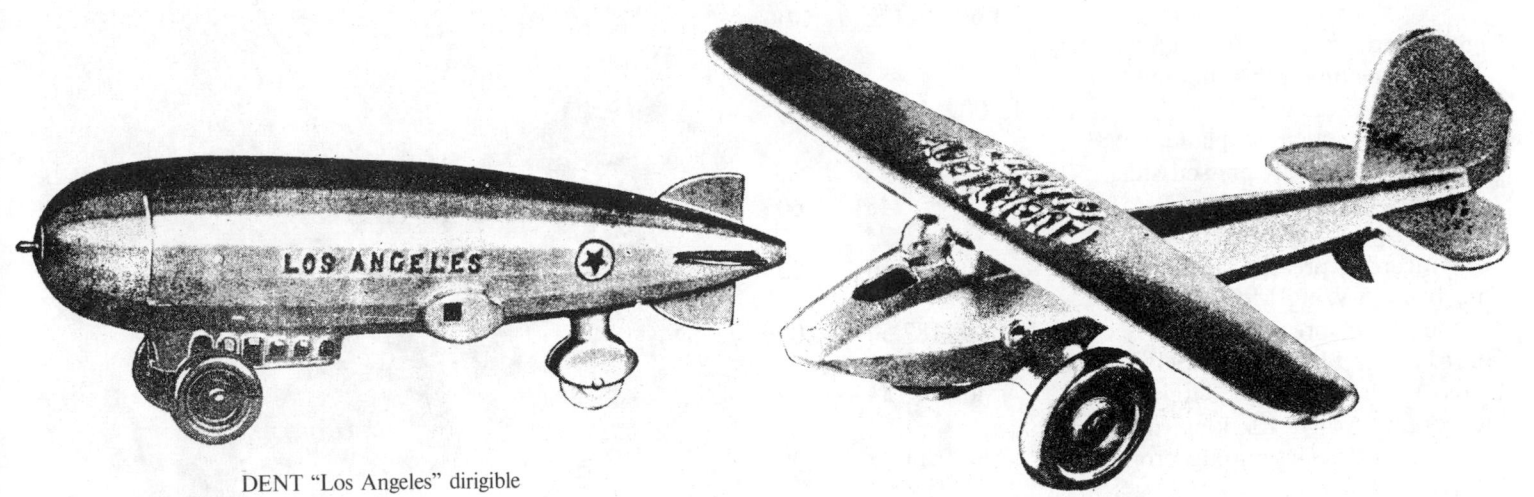

DENT "Los Angeles" dirigible

DENT "Lucky Boy" Glider

	C6	C8	C10
Dent "Air Express", cast iron, 12" wingspread	600	900	1200
Dent "Los Angeles" dirigible, 6¾", circa 1932	132.50	194.75	265.00

	C6	C8	C10
Dent "Los Angeles" dirigible, 8½", cast iron, circa 1925	112.50	168.75	225.00
Dent "Lucky Boy" glider, circa 1932	225.00	337.50	450.00

ERIE Northrup planes (not listed), L to R: Single seat Gamma, worth $50 in mint, 2-place E-2, worth $30 in mint, and Delta passenger plane, worth $40 in mint. The latter also comes with the wings marked "NC 17211". Photo by Perry R. Eichor

ERIE airplanes (not listed), L to R: Boeing 247, worth $30 in mint, and Boeing B-17, worth $40 in mint.
Photo by Perry R. Eichor

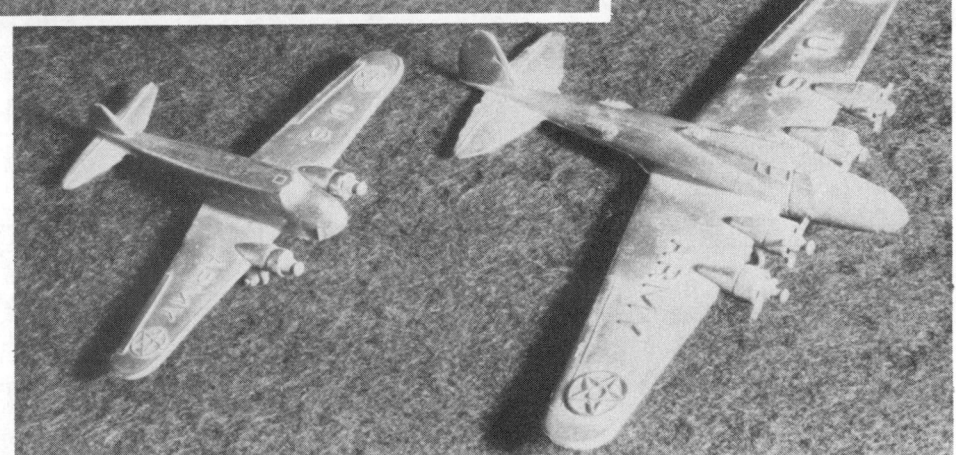

421

	C6	C8	C10
Fighter, tin, circa 1940, single engine, four machine guns mounted on wing	15.00	22.50	30.00
"Flagship America" airplane, metal Ford Tri-Motor, pressed steel, 1930s, 25" wingspan	30	45	60
Girard High-Wing Monoplane, 10" wingspan, pressed steel	100	150	200
Girard High-Wing Monoplane, 18" wingspan, pressed steel	125.00	187.50	250.00
Girard Whiz Skyfighter biplane, early	87.50	131.25	175.00
Glass Airplane, candy container	30	45	60
Helicopter, Army, 13" long, tin litho, friction drive, spinning prop	7.50	11.25	15.00

HUBLEY

	C6	C8	C10
H1 "America" cast iron, large, 17" wingspan, trimotor, open cockpit, pilot, copilot	1200	1800	2000
H2 Bell Airacuda, XFM-1, diecast, red and silver, folding landing gear, movable guns in front of twin pusher engines, 3-bladed props, new in 1941	100	150	200
H3 No. 377 "Lindy" cast iron, 3½" wingspan, single engine	25.00	37.50	50.00
H4 No. 431 U.S. Army Plane, diecast, 5½" wingspan, white rubber tires, enclosed in cast fairings, single engine, low wing monoplane	15.00	22.50	30.00
H5 No. 389 twin engine, cast iron, 5⅝" wingspan, painted and nickle plate, "TAT NC 431"	25.00	37.50	50.00
H6 Twin engine, 3⅜" wingspan, silver and red or green	12.50	18.75	25.00
H7 No. 430 jet, diecast, single engine, folding wings, retractable landing gear, 6" wingspan, cast cockpit, red and silver	12.50	18.75	25.00
H8 "U.S.N. 3-B-4" diecast, twin engine, 5⅛" wingspan, twin vertical stabilizer, retractable landing gear	10	15	20
H9 "Lindy," cast iron, 10" wingspan	250	375	500
H10 "Lindy," cast iron, 10" wingspan, prop turns via gear attached to wheel	350	525	700
H11 "Lindy" cast iron, with "Spirit of St. Louis" decals, ratchet drive action noisemaker, has wing struts	1000	1500	2000
H12 "Bremen", aluminum, 6½" wingspan	250	375	500
H13 "Bremen," cast iron, 6½" wingspan	200	300	400
H14 "Bremen," cast iron, 10" wingspan, "Junkers Bremen" on fuselage, open cockpit with 2 pilots, prop turned by wheels	350	525	700

HUBLEY H2
Photo by Perry R. Eichor

HUBLEY, L to R: H3, H5
Photo by Perry R. Eichor

HUBLEY H9
Photo by Perry R. Eichor

	C6	C8	C10
H15 "America," cast iron, single engine, 17" wingspan, wire spring drive, with 2 pilots in open cockpit	1250	1875	2500
H16 "Friendship," cast iron seaplane, "Fokker" embossed on fuselage, 13" wingspan	1000	1500	2000

HUBLEY, L to R: H7, H20, H22
Photo by Perry R. Eichor

HUBLEY H1

HUBLEY H19
Photo by Perry R. Eichor

HUBLEY H21, early and later versions
Photo by Perry R. Eichor

HUBLEY H24, two variations
Photo by Perry R. Eichor

HUBLEY, L to R: H25, H23
Photo by Perry R. Eichor

	C6	C8	C10
H17 "U.S. Army" diecast, 8" wingspan, low wing single engine monoplane, folding wheels, silver and red (early versions had red wood hubs with white rubber tires, later had large black rubber tires - cast cockpit may have openings or be cast or solid), introduced in 1939	15.00	22.50	30.00

	C6	C8	C10
H18 "U.S. Army," plastic, like above, folding wheels, 6" wingspan, "U.S. Army" embossed on horizontal stabilizer	5.00	7.50	10.00
H19 No. **326** Attack Bomber, plastic, retractable landing gear Martin B-26 Marauder copy, 7⅞" wingspan	10	15	20

HUBLEY, L to R: H28, H29, H8, H4
Photo by Perry R. Eichor

	C6	C8	C10
H20 P-39, diecast and tin, "U.S. Army" imprinted on rear horizon stabilizers, tin wings are 5½" ...	12.50	18.75	25.00

H21 No. **495** on wings, diecast, 11½" wingspan, single engine, folding wings, retractable landing gear, sliding plastic cockpit (numerous versions, and later packaged as "American Eagle" or "Flying Circus"):

	C6	C8	C10
Early - red & silver, 4-bladed prop, no airscoop on top of engine cowl	37.50	56.25	75.00
Mid - two tone blue, red cowl, large airscoop atop engine cowl, 4-bladed prop	25.00	37.50	50.00
Late - orange & yellow, large airscoop, either 4 or 2-bladed prop	15.00	22.50	30.00
H22 No. **433** Piper Cub, red, 7⅞" wingspan, also in olive drab L-4 version	7.50	11.25	15.00
H23 P-40, diecast, 8" wingspan, early version was silver & red with 3-bladed prop, later version orange & yellow with 2-bladed prop	17.50	26.25	35.00
H24 P-38, diecast, red & silver, 12⅝" wingspan, retractable landing gear, later versions are yellow & green camouflage	25.00	37.50	50.00
H25 No. **467** diecast, 8⅝" wingspan, folding wings, retractable landing gear, plastic cockpit, resembles Brewster Buffalo, red & silver with 4-bladed prop in early version, later version was green & yellow with 2-blade prop	15.00	22.50	30.00

	C6	C8	C10
H26 No. **751** folding delta wing jet, diecast, 6⅛" wingspan, retractable landing gear, red & silver plastic cockpit	12.50	18.75	25.00
H27 No. **427** Crusader, diecast, 5⅛" wingspan, twin engine, twin boom, "TAT NC-31"	12.50	18.75	25.00
H28 No. **303** cast iron, 5" wingspan, low wing single engine monoplane, nickel plate wings & prop with various colored body	20	30	40
H29 No. **305** cast iron, 3¾" wingspan, low wing single engine monoplane, nickel plate wings & prop	12.50	18.75	25.00
H30 No. **304** Giro plane, cast iron with nickel plate rotor, prop & engine	20	30	40
H31 **302** DO-X, cast iron, 4" wingspan, 6 engine, high wing seaplane	37.50	56.25	75.00
H32 DO-X, cast iron, 5" wingspan, larger version of above	50	75	100

H31 Hubley DO-X

424

I.D. PLANES

by Richard L. MacNary

The popularly called "black I.D. planes" were manufactured during World War II primarily as training aids initially for the U.S. Navy and then U.S. Army. The WW II airplanes covered in this section were all made in 1/72 scale (1" = 6'), all were colored black, and usually marked on the bottom in raised lettering with (1) the country of owner-ship/design (U.S., British, German, etc.), (2) the aircraft type (P-38, Spitfire, FW189, etc.), and date of model issue (7-42, 8-42, 5-42, etc.).

While the program reportedly started the day after Pearl Harbor, the earliest marking on any of the known models is 5-42. (The dates so marked on the planes are dates of model issue or copyright, not the date that the actual plane became operational.)

Some of the early WW II attempts at manufacturing these identification aircraft used materials such as reinforced plaster (too lumpy), paper-mache (too little detail), a hard rubber-like material (too pliable for long sections like wings), Wood's metal and even cast iron (too heavy for shipping and perhaps needed elsewhere).

The vast majority of these I-D aircraft were molded by the Cruver Company of Chicago. The master molds were made by either the Comet Engraving Company or H&H Specialty Company, also both of Chicago. A few models were produced (molded) by Design Center and Leominster as noted in the listing.

While these airplanes were manufactured for our Armed Forces, Polk's Hobbies of New York did sell some domestically under the Aristo-Craft name. Most of the surviving WW II types, though, were probably midnight requisitioned by pilot or gunner trainees. The quantity produced during the War was staggering *Flying* magazine of February, 1944 states that Cruver had manufactured over 2,000,000 model aircraft since the spring of 1941 (sic - they meant spring of 1942). Not many remain today.

The following listing of WW II model planes was taken from the most complete compilation known; it may not be totally inclusive nor may all of these planes have been made in quantity. The best story of all types of I.D. aircraft made from different materials and in different scales as well as those of the later Korean War vintage was well covered by Robert C. Mikesh in his excellent article in the May/June 1984 issue of *Fine Scale Modeler* magazine.

You will note in the guide that not much distinction is made between the values for similar size models. There is just not enough buying and selling nor large enough collections to accurately determine which plane is more rare than another. They could all be **equally** hard to find today.

As to grading, mint is just that – no scuffs, no warpage, no "prune-skin," no repainting or, in other words, a brand new 45-year-old airplane. Very Good covers models that are very nice; planes should be complete with wheels or floats if on originally; free of serious defects like "prune-skin" or missing parts, and not repainted (restored maybe). The Good grade covers everything else and likely includes the majority of those models still in existence.

A special thanks is due to master modeler Ray ".44 Magnum" Wheeler of Lilburn, GA for his help in identifying some of the more obscure types listed.

Comments and especially documented corrections are always welcome.

As previously reported in O'Brien's *Guide to Electric Trains*, RICHARD MAC-NARY had his first childhood outside of Chicago during WW II. While his wife and two children say he really never left his first, his second childhood has spanned the last 20 years while serving as the Atlanta District Manager for the Ohio Brass Company, the premier manufacturer of high voltage electrical equipment.

Dick's own WW II I.D. aircraft were the punch-out, three dimensional, black pressboard planes. These were sent back from the ETO by the Army son of his father's insurance partner. These cardboard models lasted about as long as his Built-Rite No. 25 forts in that damp Northern Indiana soil!

Punchout replacement aircraft along with some four dozen of the listed plastic WW II I.D. models are now hangered in Lilburn, GA, the home of MacNary Field (deactivated), U.S. Army Air Corps.

WW II IDENTIFICATION MODELS 1/72 SCALE
(Black I.D. Airplanes)

Each model is identified by type and date marked.

UNITED STATES	C6	C8	C10
A-20 Havoc, 6-42	20	30	40
A-24 Dauntless, SBD-3, 7-42	12.50	18.50	25.00
A-26 Invader, 2-44	20	30	40
A-29 Hudson (PBO-16), none	20	30	40
A-30 Baltimore, 2-43	20	30	40
A-31 Vengeance, 7-42	12.50	18.50	25.00
A-31 Vengeance, 7-44	12.50	18.50	25.00
A-35 Vengeance, 4-44	12.50	18.50	25.00
AT17 Bobcat*, 7-43	20	30	40
B-17 Flying Fortress, 7-42	40	60	80
B-24 Liberator, 7-42	40	60	80
B-25 Mitchell, 7-42	20	30	40
B-26 Marauder, 10-42	20	30	40
B-26 Marauder, none	20	30	40

ID PLANE, U.S. P-38 Lightning
MacNary Collection   Courtesy RLM

ID PLANE, U.S. B-29 Super Fortress, 9/44
MacNary Collection   Courtesy RLM

	C6	C8	C10
B-29 Super Fortress, 3-44	40	60	80
B-29 Super Fortress, 9-44	40	60	80
B-32 Dominator, 12-44	40	60	80
C-46 Commando, 3-43	20	30	40
C-47 Skytrain 3-43	20	30	40
C-47 Skytrain**, 5-43	20	30	40
C-54 Skymaster, 3-43	40	60	80
C60A Lodestar, 3-43	20	30	40
C69 Constellation, 4-44	40	60	80
C78 Bobcat, 6-44	20	30	40
C87 Liberator, 3-44	40	60	80
CG-4A Waco Glider, 6-43	12.50	18.50	25.00
F4F-4 Wildcat, 5-43	12.50	18.50	25.00
F4U-1 Corsair, 3-43	12.50	18.50	25.00
F6F Hellcat, 4-43	12.50	18.50	25.00
GH-1 Nightingale*, 5-43	20	30	40
J2F-4 Duck, 12-42	25.00	37.50	50.00
JRF OA-9 Goose*, 7-43	25.00	37.50	50.00
JRS-1 (S43), 11-42	25.00	37.50	50.00
JR2S-1 (S44) Excalibur, 11-44	50	75	100
L-1 Vigilant, 3-43	20	30	40
L-2 Grasshopper, 7-44	20	30	40
L-4 Grasshopper, 2-43	20	30	40
L-5 Sentinel, 1-44	20	30	40
OS2U (on floats)*, 2-43	20	30	40
OS2U (on wheels)*, 2-43	20	30	40

U.S. ID PLANE/JR2S1 (S44) Excalibur
MacNary Collection   Courtesy RLM

ID PLANES, British, L to R: Spitfire 9B (10/44), Spitfire 8/42
MacNary Collection   Courtesy RLM

	C6	C8	C10
OS2U-1 (on floats), 7-43	20	30	40
PBM-3 Mariner, 6-43	25.00	37.50	50.00
PBY-5 Catalina, 5-43	25.00	37.50	50.00
PB2Y-3 Coronado, 4-43	50	75	100
PV-1 (B-39) Ventura, 5-43	20	30	40
PV-2 Harpoon, 5-43	20	30	40
P-38 Lightning, 7-42	20	30	60
P-39 Airacobra, 6-42	12.50	18.50	25.00
P-40 Warhawk, 9-42	12.50	18.50	25.00
P-40 Warhawk, 4-44	12.50	18.50	25.00
P-43 Lancer, 5-43	12.50	18.50	25.00
P-47 Thunderbolt, 9-42	12.50	18.50	25.00
P-47(D) Thunderbolt, 2-44	12.50	18.50	25.00
P-47(N) Thunderbolt, 4-45	12.50	18.50	25.00
P-47 Thunderbolt*, none	12.50	18.50	25.00
P-51 Mustang, 6-42	12.50	18.50	25.00
P-51D Mustang, 4-45	12.50	18.50	25.00
P-61 Black Widow, 2-44	20	30	40
P-63 King Cobra, 5-44	12.50	18.50	25.00

* - molded by Design Center   ** - molded by Leominster   All others molded by Cruver

ID Plane, German. Focke Wulf FW189, with box
MacNary Collection   Courtesy RLM

	C6	C8	C10		C6	C8	C10
P-80 Shooting Star, 4-45	12.50	18.50	25.00	Maryland, 2-43	20	30	40
SB2A-2 Buccaneer, 5-43	12.50	18.50	25.00	Mosquito, 3-43	20	30	40
SB2C-1 Helldiver, 3-43	12.50	18.50	25.00	Roc, 8-42	12.50	18.50	25.00
SB2C-2 Helldiver, 2-45	12.50	18.50	25.00	Skua, 8-42	12.50	18.50	25.00
SB2C-2 Helldiver, (floats)*, 3-43	20	30	40	Spitfire, 8-42	12.50	18.50	25.00
SB2C-2 Helldiver, (wheels)*, 3-43	20	30	40	Spitfire, 1-44	12.50	18.50	25.00
SB2U-3 Vindicator, 6-43	12.50	18.50	25.00	Spitfire 9A, 10-44	12.50	18.50	25.00
SNJ-2 Texan, 7-42	12.50	18.50	25.00	Spitfire 9B, 10-44	12.50	18.50	25.00
SNJ-3 Texan, 7-42	12.50	18.50	25.00	Spitfire 22, 7-45	12.50	18.50	25.00
S03C-1 Seagull (floats), 3-43	20	30	40	Stirling, 5-42	40	60	80
S03C-2 Seagull (wheels), 3-43	20	30	40	Sunderland, 9-42	50	75	100
TBD-1 Devastator, 5-43	12.50	18.50	25.00	Swordfish, 9-42	25.00	37.50	50.00
TBF Avenger, 7-43	12.50	18.50	25.00	Tempest 2, 3-45	12.50	18.50	25.00
BRITISH				Tempest 5, 10-44	12.50	18.50	25.00
Albacore, 8-42	25.00	37.50	50.00	Typhoon, 6-43	12.50	18.50	25.00
Albemarle, 9-44	20	30	40	Walrus, 4-44	20	30	40
Barracuda, 2-43	12.50	18.50	25.00	Wellington 2, 9-42	20	30	40
Beaufighter 1, 9-42	20	30	40	Wellington 3, 9-42	20	30	40
Beaufighter 2, 9-42	20	30	40	Whirlwind, 8-43	20	30	40
Beaufighter 6, 5-44	20	30	40	Whitley, 9-42	20	30	40
Beaufort, 9-42	20	30	40	York, 9-44	40	60	80
Beaufort, none	20	30	40	**GERMAN**			
Blenheim IV, 8-42	20	30	40	Arado Ar196, 12-43	20	30	40
Boomerang (Aust.)*, none	12.50	18.50	25.00	Blohm & Voss BV138, 5-44	40	60	80
Botha, 8-42	20	30	40	Blohm & Voss HA139, 11-42	50	75	100
Defiant, 8-42	12.50	18.50	25.00	Blohm & Voss BV222, 2-44	50	75	100
Firefly, 2-43	12.50	18.50	25.00	DFS 230, 8-43	12.50	18.50	25.00
Fulmar, 8-42	12.50	18.50	25.00	Dornier DO 172, 9-42	20	30	40
Halifax, 9-42	40	60	80	Dornier DO 215, 9-42	20	30	40
Hampden, 8-42	20	30	40	Dornier DO 217E, 8-42	20	30	40
Hastings, none,	40	60	80	Fi 156 Storch, none	20	30	40
Horsa, 9-44	20	30	40	Focke Wulf FW 187, 8-42	20	30	40
Hotspur, 6-43	12.50	18.50	25.00	Focke Wulf FW 189, 5-42	20	30	40
Hurricane, 8-43	12.50	18.50	25.00	Focke Wulf FW 190, 7-42	12.50	18.50	25.00
Lancaster, 4-43	40	60	80	Focke Wulf FW 190, 12-42	12.50	18.50	25.00
Lerwick, 9-42	25.00	37.50	50.00	Focke Wulf 200, 3-44	40	60	80
Lysander, 7-43	20	30	40	Focke Wulf FW 200K, 9-42	40	60	80
Manchester, 8-42	20	30	40	Gotha Go 242, 7-42	20	30	40

* - molded by Design Center   ** - molded by Leominster   All others molded by Cruver

427

	C6	C8	C10
Heinkel He 111, 9-42	20	30	40
Heinkel He 112, 7-42	12.50	18.50	25.00
Heinkel He 113, 5-42	12.50	18.50	25.00
Heinkel He 113, 9-42	12.50	18.50	25.00
Heinkel He 113, 9-42	12.50	18.50	25.00
Heinkel He 115K, 9-42	25.00	37.50	50.00
Henschel Hs 126, 10-42	20	30	40
Henschel Hs 129, 8-44	20	30	40
Junkers Ju 52, 8-42	40	60	80
Junkers Ju 86K, 9-42	20	30	40
Junkers Ju 87B, 8-42	12.50	18.50	25.00
Junkers Ju 88, 9-42	20	30	40
Junkers Ju 90, 9-42	40	60	80
Junkers Ju 188, 7-44	20	30	40
Messers. Me 109E, 7-42	12.50	18.50	25.00
Messers. Me 109F, 7-42	12.50	18.50	25.00
Messers. Me 110, 8-42	20	30	40
Messers. Me 210, 7-43	20	30	40

ITALIAN

	C6	C8	C10
Cantiere Z.506B, 9-42	40	60	80
Cantiere Z.1007, 9-42	25.00	37.50	50.00
Caproni CA.133, 9-42	40	60	80
Fiat BR.20, 6-42	20	30	40
Fiat CR.42, 9-42	25.00	37.50	50.00
Fiat CR.42, 1-43	25.00	37.50	50.00
Fiat G.50, 8-42	12.50	18.50	25.00
Macchi C.200, 8-42	12.50	18.50	25.00
Macchi MC. 202, 3-43	12.50	18.50	25.00
Piaggio P.32 BIS, 9-42	20	30	40
Reggiane Rc.2000, 9-42	12.50	18.50	25.00
Reggiane Re.2001, 3-43	12.50	18.50	25.00
Savoia Marchetti 79, 9-42	25.00	37.50	50.00
Savoia Marchetti 81, 9-42	40	60	80
Savoia Marchetti 82 9-42	25.00	37.50	50.00
Savoia Marchetti 84, 4-43	25.00	37.50	50.00

JAPANESE

	C6	C8	C10
(Adam) Naka. 97, 11-42	20	30	40
(Ann) Mitsu. T-98, 7-42	20	30	40
(Babs) Mitsu. T-97, 6-42	20	30	40
Betty (G4M1), 9-43	20	30	40
Betty (G4M2), 4-45	20	30	40
(Claude) Mitsu. T-96, 6-42	20	30	40
(Dave) Naka. T-95-NOB, 7-42	20	30	40
Dinah (Ki46), 8-44	20	30	40
Emily (H8K2), 3-45	50	75	100
Francis (P1Y), 3-45	20	30	40
Frank (Ki84), 5-45	12.50	18.50	25.00
George (NIKI-J), 5-45	12.50	18.50	25.00
Hamp (T-00, Zeke 32), 7-43	12.50	18.50	25.00
Helen (Ki49), --44	20	30	40
(Ida) Mitsu. T-98 ALB, 6-42	20	30	40
Irving (J1N1)*, 5-45	20	30	40
Jack (J2M1), 12-44	12.50	18.50	25.00
Jake (E13A), 9-44	20	30	40
Jill (B6N)*, 5-45	12.50	18.50	25.00
Judy (D4Y), 3-45	12.50	18.50	25.00
(Kate) Naka. T-97, 6-42	12.50	18.50	25.00
Lily (Ki48), 9-43	20	30	40

	C6	C8	C10
(Mary) T-97 ALB, 6-42	20	30	40
(Mavis) Kawa., 11-42	50	75	100
Myrt (C6N), 3-45	12.50	18.50	25.00
(Nate) "97" Fighter, 9-42	20	30	40
(Nell) Mitsu. T-96, 6-42	20	30	40
Nell (G3M), 1-44	20	30	40
Nick (Ki45), 8-44	20	30	40
Oscar T-01 (Ki43), 9-43	12.50	18.50	25.00
Paul 14, Exp*, 12-44	20	30	40
Pete (F1M2), 6-43	25.00	37.50	50.00
Rufe (A6M2-N), 8-43	20	30	40
(Sally) Mitsu. T-97, 6-42	20	30	40
(Sonia) Mitsu. T-99, 7-42	12.50	18.50	25.00
Tojo (Ki44), 6-44	12.50	18.50	25.00
Tojo (Ki44), 3-45	12.50	18.50	25.00
Tony (Ki61), 7-44	12.50	18.50	25.00
Tony (Ki61), 4-45	12.50	18.50	25.00
(Topsy) Mitsu. MC-20, 10-42	20	30	40
(Val) Aichi T-99, 6-42	20	30	40
Val T-99 MK2, 8-43	20	30	40
(Zeke) Mitsu. 00, 9-42	12.50	18.50	25.00
Zeke 52 (A6M5)*, 12-44	12.50	18.50	25.00

NOTE: Japanese abbreviations used above:
Kawa. - Kawanishi   Mitsu. - Mitsubishi   Naka. - Nakajima

NETHERLANDS

	C6	C8	C10
Fokker T8W, 11-42	25.00	37.50	50.00

RUSSIAN

	C6	C8	C10
DB-3F, 9-42	20	30	40
DB-3F, 4-44	20	30	40
I-16, none	12.50	18.50	25.00
IL-2, 9-42	12.50	18.50	25.00
IL-2, 12-43	12.50	18.50	25.00
MiG-3, 8-42	12.50	18.50	25.00
I-18 (MiG-3), 2-43	12.50	18.50	25.00
MiG-3, 2-44	12.50	18.50	25.00
Pe-2, 9-42	20	30	40
SB-3, 11-43	20	30	40
TB-7*, 4-44	40	60	80

KANSAS TOY (Later BEST) List by Fred Maxwell

KANSAS TOY Seaplane
Drawing by Deb Eccles

KANSAS TOY "Glider"
Drawing by Deb Eccles

	C6	C8	C10
Kansas Toy No. 6 Airplane, Army "Stars" on wing, 3¾" long	7.50	11.25	15.00
Kansas Toy Cabin Monoplane, high wing, radial engine, large tin prop, Army "star insignia", small tail wheel, 2⅜" long	7.50	11.25	15.00

* - molded by Design Center   ** - molded by Leominster
All others molded by Cruver

KEYSTONE Riding Airplane, 28" wingspan, No.293 "Ride 'Em" Fighter.
Courtesy Bob Black Jr.

MARX Pan American 4-motor, 1940, 27" wingspan
Courtesy Lloyd W. Ralston Auctions

MANOIL Airplanes, L to R: 517, 518, 519, 520
Courtesy Peter and Marjorie Ruben

KINGSBURY "Trans Atlantic" Monoplane
Courtesy Lloyd W. Ralston Auctions

	C6	C8	C10
Kansas Toy Combat plane, as above, olive drab	7.50	11.25	15.00
Kansas Toy Zeppelin	10	15	20
Kansas Toy Fokker? airplane, high wing passenger monoplane, 3-blade prop, radial engine, "MUSA"	10	15	20
Kansas Toy "KTN 47," 3" long	7.50	11.25	15.00
Kansas Toy (Best?) Seaplane, 4" long	10	15	20
Kansas Toy "Glider," open frame fuselage, pilot on nose	7.50	11.25	15.00
Jet, USAF, 5" wingspan, friction-powered, tin litho	10	15	20
KD-1 Mak-a-plane – 4" long, mechanical, all metal with rubber wheels, 1940s	15.00	22.50	30.00
Kenton "Air Mail," wingspan approx. 8"	No Price Found		
Keystone Mail Plane, single wing, above fuselage, 24" long	90	135	180
Keystone riding plane, seat over tail, steering bar over cabin, single wing, high, one engine, 23½" long	150	225	300

	C6	C8	C10
Keystone riding plane, 28" wingspan, No. 293, "Ride Em" fighter	80	120	160
Kilgore, Seagull, high wing, pusher prop	250	375	500
Kingsbury Monoplane, high wing, trimotor, 15" wingspan, clockwork	200	300	400
Kingsbury Tin Goose, tri-engine, 21" wingspan, 1930s	600	900	1200
Kingsbury "Trans Atlantic" monoplane, painted pressed steel wind-up, 1930, 11" long	125.00	187.50	250.00
Kingsbury "U.S. Airmail" biplane, 15" long, steel windup	130	195	260
Lincoln White Metal Ford Trimotor, slush lead, tin propellors	No Price Found		
Lincoln White Metal (?) Batplane? (looks as if it were modeled after Batman's plane, 1930s slush lead	20	30	40
"Lindy" cast iron, nickel prop and wheels, 3½" wingspan	28	42	56
Lindy-type Plane, lead, 2¼" wingspan	2.50	3.75	5.00
Luscombe Airplane, 4" long	30	45	60
Manoil No. 517, Lockheed F90	10	15	20
Manoil No. 518 Navion	15.00	22.50	30.00
Manoil No. 519 Bonanza B-35	15.00	22.50	30.00
Manoil No. 520 Ercoupe	15.00	22.50	30.00
Marx "Army Bomber" No. 1025, tri-motor, 26" wingspan, circa 1935	75.00	112.50	150.00
Marx bomber, 18" wingspan, tin litho, sparkling mechanism, camouflaged, four-engine	40	60	80
Marx Curtiss Transport, 9½" wingspan, khaki, pressed steel	7.50	11.25	15.00
Marx DC-3 Transport, 10" wingspan, pressed steel, circa 1939	12.50	18.75	25.00
Marx Friction-powered 4-motor transport with whirling propellors, tin litho	25.00	37.50	50.00
Marx Futuristic Airport	225.00	337.50	450.00

	C6	C8	C10
Marx "Little Lindy Aeroplane," 1930s, friction, 6" wingspan	100	150	200
Marx Mainstream Airport, circa 1930s	110	165	220
Marx Pan American 4-motor, propellor-driven, also as PAA, 27" wingspan, 1940, pressed steel	50	75	100
Marx "Pioneer Air Express," 25½" wingspan, tin litho, high wing monoplane	50	75	100
Marx "Sky Cruiser" two-motored Transport Plane with siren and whirling propellors, Statoliner 700, 18" wingspan, rubber wheels, 1940s	37.50	56.25	75.00
Marx sparkling Rocket Fighter No. 1425, tin litho	37.50	56.25	75.00
Marx Universal Airport with two metal planes	55.00	82.50	110.00

METAL CAST No. 66 Aeroplane
Photo by Norbert Schachter

	C6	C8	C10
Metal Cast No. 66 Aeroplane, approx. 4½" wingspan, 2-engine, circa 1940s, lead (some marked "Fred Greene")	5.00	7.50	10.00

METALCRAFT Spirit of St. Louis, 9" long
Courtesy Mapes Auctioneers & Appraisers

	C6	C8	C10
Metalcraft Build-A-Zep, builds 21 different 18" zeppelins	100	150	200
Metalcraft Northrup Alpha Monoplane, wingspan approx. 17", "PURE the Pure Oil Company"	300	450	600
Metal Craft Riding Rocket, 24" long	35.00	52.50	70.00
Metal Craft Spirit of St. Louis, 9" long, came as kit	50	75	100
Ohio Art "Sea Patrol Plane," 9" long, pontoons, moves on water, early 40s wind-up	30	45	60
Ohio Art Seaplane "Hot Job" tin litho, checkerboard wings, spinning propeller, 10" wingspan, 3½" long, 1950s	14	21	28
P-38 glass candy container	15.00	22.50	30.00
Passenger Plane, high-wing, four-engine, approx. 9" wingspan, three wooden wheels	9.00	13.50	18.00
Pedal Car, Biplane, 2-motor, 54" long	300	450	600
"Pony Blimp," 1930, Kilgore, cast iron, 5¾" long, metal wheels	40	60	80

	C6	C8	C10
Pull-Toy, metal airplane	25.00	37.50	50.00
Ralstoy "Ralstoy 32," slush lead, tin prop, 2⅜" long	5.00	7.50	10.00
Renwal B-17, small	5.00	7.50	10.00
Renwal B-17, 9¼" wingspan, plastic, circa 1944	15.00	22.50	30.00
Renwal B-25, 6¾" wingspan, plastic, circa 1944	12.50	18.75	25.00
Renwal C54 Transport, large, plastic	7.50	11.25	15.00
Renwal P38, plastic	10	15	20
Renwal P40, plastic	6	9	12
Renwal P47, plastic	7.50	11.25	15.00
Renwal PB2Y Flying Boat	9.00	13.50	18.00
Savoye Blimp, 4" long, "U.S.N."	No Price Found		
Savoye Monoplane, 3" long	No Price Found		
Schieble Tri-Motor, 29½" long, steel	200	300	400
"Sky Cruiser" tin litho, 18" wingspan, 2-motor transport, engines turn with friction mechanism	25.00	37.50	50.00
"Spirit of America" pull toy aeroplane, 14" long, steel and litho	12	18	24
"Spirit of St. Louis," cast iron, 4"x4"	25.00	37.50	50.00
Spirit of St. Louis glass candy container, 4⅜" long	150	225	300
Spirit of St. Louis 11" wingspread, cast iron	75.00	112.50	150.00
Steelcraft "Akron" blimp pull toy, 25" long	75.00	112.50	150.00
Steelcraft "Army Scout Plane" single engine, 22½" wingspan, high-wing monoplane, 1920s	75.00	112.50	150
Steelcraft "Army Scout Plane," trimotor, single high wing, 1920s	150	225	300
Steelcraft Army Scout Plane, green and orange, 23" wingspan	75.00	112.50	150.00
Steelcraft "Graf Zeppelin," 30½" pressed steel pull toy	90	135	175
Steelcraft Graf Zeppelin, 32" long pull toy	150	225	300
Steelcraft Lockheed Sirius pull toy, 21½" wingspan	200	300	400
Steelcraft No. 79 pedal plane, high wing monoplane, 32" wingspan, 48" long	400	600	800
Steelcraft NX107, "Little Jim," 23" wingspan	125.00	187.50	250.00
Steelcraft NX130, blue eagles on wings, 23" wingspan	125.00	187.50	250.00
Steelcraft NX131, Tri-Motor, U.S. Mail plane, pull toy, 26½" wingspan	150	225	300
Strauss "Chicago" Dirigible, 10" tin litho	105.00	157.50	210.00
Strauss Graf Zeppellin, 16" long	240	360	480
Sun Rubber "Pursuit Ship," "25-P75," circa 1940-41, 4¼" wingspan	12.50	18.75	25.00
Sun Rubber No. **12008 Racing Plane,** circa 1947, also called "Scout," both same plane as "Pursuit Ship"	12.50	18.75	25.00

SUN RUBBER, L to R: No. 12009, Pursuit Ship, No. 12010
Courtesy Ed Poole

	C6	C8	C10
Sun Rubber No. **12009 Transport,** 4" long	15.00	22.50	30.00
Sun Rubber No. 12010 Dual-Control Plane, 4½" long	20	30	40
Tin Friction Plane, early, 6" wingspan	10	15	20
Tommy Toy Dirigible, "USN" slush lead, 1930s	15.00	22.50	30.00
Tootsietoy 106 Low-Wing Monoplane, 1932	10	15	20
Tootsietoy 119 Army Plane	12.50	18.75	25.00
Tootsietoy 125 Lockheed Electra	7.50	11.25	15.00
Tootsietoy 718 Waco Bomber	12.50	18.75	25.00
Tootsietoy 719 Crusader	20	30	40
Tootsietoy 721 Curtis P-40	50	75	100
Tootsietoy 722 Transport Plane, 1941	8	12	16
Tootsietoy 0001 P-38	15.00	22.50	30.00
Tootsietoy 0002 KOP-1 USN	10	15	20
Tootsietoy 0003 F9F-2 Panther	5.00	7.50	10.00
Tootsietoy 0007 2-engine airliner, 10 windows on each side	14	21	28
Tootsietoy 0008 S-58 Sikorsky Helicopter	10	15	20
Tootsietoy 0009 Navy Jet Cutlass	7.50	11.25	15.00
Tootsietoy 717 Douglas DC 2 TWA Airliner	15.00	22.50	30.00
Tootsietoy 720 Fly-N-Gyro, 1938	25.00	37.50	50.00
Tootsietoy 4482 Bleriot, 1910	20	30	40
Tootsietoy 4491 Bleriot, 1910 (smaller)	14	21	28
Tootsietoy 4649 Tri-Motor Plane	25.00	37.50	50.00
Tootsietoy 4650 Biplane, yellow and red, 58mm	30	45	60
Tootsietoy 4659 Autogyro	25.00	37.50	50.00
Tootsietoy 4660 Aero-Dawn	12.50	18.75	25.00
Tootsietoy 4660 Aero-Dawn seaplane	12.50	18.75	25.00
Tootsietoy 4675 Wings	12.50	18.75	25.00
Tootsietoy 4675 Wings seaplane	12.50	18.75	25.00
Tootsietoy 4850 Shooting Star	9.00	13.50	18.00
Tootsietoy "Atlantic Clipper," approx. 2" long	2.50	3.75	5.00
Tootsietoy Beechcraft Bonanza	7.50	11.25	15.00
Tootsietoy DC 4 Supermainliner	12.50	18.75	25.00
Tootsietoy Navion	7.50	11.25	15.00

TOMMY TOY "U.S.N." Dirigible
Photo by Bill Kaufman, Courtesy Charles
E. Weldon, Jr.

TOOTSIETOY Top Row, L to R: 4649 Tri-Motor Plane, 04460 Aero-Dawn, 4650 Biplane, 4675 Wings, High-Wing Floatplane, Middle Row: 04650 Autogyro, 718 Waco Bomber, 719 Crusader, Bottom Row L to R: 119 Army Plane, 125 Lockheed Electra, 0717 TWA Douglas Airliner, DC4 Super Mainliner.
Photo by Ed Poole

	C6	C8	C10
Tootsietoy Piper Cub	6.50	9.75	13.00
Tootsietoy P-39, diecast body, tin wings, 2-bladed prop	37.50	56.25	75.00
Tootsietoy "Tootsietoy Airport," hangar and two planes	220	330	440
Tootsietoy U.S. Moon Rocket, 3 types, all have 2 wheels to run on string, mid-1960s, replicas of original Buck Rogers spaceships (see Comic Character)	20	30	40
Tootsietoy "U.S.N. Los Angeles" dirigible, two grooved wheels on top to run on string (also was sold as part of Buck Rogers set)	37.50	56.25	75.00

TOOTSIETOY "U.S.N. Los Angeles" dirigible, also sold as part of Buck Rogers set, 1937
Photo by Ed Poole

	C6	C8	C10
Transport Plane, pressed steel, approx. 12" wingspan, four-engine	12.50	18.75	25.00
Turner High Wing Monoplane, 18½" wingspan, one engine, 1930s	100	150	200
"U.S." high-wing monoplane, single engine, 8" wingspan, open iron-work body, spool wheel works prop	200	300	400
UX83, cast iron, 3¼" wingspan	30	45	60
"UX-99" cast iron, wingspan approx. 4½"	37.50	56.25	75.00
"UX-166", Lindy-type plane, wingspan approx. 5¾", cast iron, nickeled engine and wheels	40	60	80
Watrous single engine biplane, pressed steel bell toy, 8¼" wingspan, circa 1915	162.50	243.75	325.00
Wyandotte Airacuda, 8½" wingspan, pressed steel, twin vertical stabilizers, twin pusher engines, blue or red,	17.50	26.25	35.00
Wyandotte Airliner, circa WW II, two engine, wooden wheels	7.50	11.25	15.00
Wyandotte American Airlines Flagship plane, 28" wingspan	44	66	88
Wyandotte Bomber, Army, pressed steel, two-engine	15.00	22.50	30.00
Wyandotte China Clipper, 13" wingspan	60	90	120
Wyandotte City Airport, American Airlines, two hangars, control tower, etc., lights up	40	60	80
Wyandotte High Wing Passenger monoplane, No. 2 Lockheed Vega, single engine, bullet nose, 18" wingspan	50	75	100
Wyandotte Military Air Transport, 13" wingspan	25.00	37.50	50.00
Wyandotte Crusader, 9¾" wingspan	12.50	18.75	25.00
Wyandotte Twin engine Airliner, early 4¾"	4	6	8

WYANDOTTE Crusader, two variations
Photo by Perry R. Eichor

WYANDOTTE, L to R: Airacuda, Airliner, circa WW II, two engine
Photo by Perry R. Eichor

WYANDOTTE high wing passenger monoplane, No. 2 Lockheed Vega
Photo courtesy Dick and Nancy Dice

	C6	C8	C10
Zeppelin, cast iron, approx. 3" long ..	20	30	40
Zeppelin, 5", cast iron	37.50	56.25	75.00
Zeppelin, "Akron," Marx, 28" long, 1930s	80	120	160
Zeppelin "EPL 1", Lehmann	300	450	600
Zeppelin "EPL 2," Lehmann, circa 1917?	225	375	450
Zeppelin, "Graf Zeppelin," small	12.50	18.75	25.00
Zeppelin "Los Angeles," cast iron, 12" long	200	300	400
Zeppelin, pull-toy, "Little Giant"	37.50	56.25	75.00
Zeppelin pull-toy, "Macon"	37.50	56.25	75.00
Zeppelin "Pony DE 107," cast iron, 5½" long	50	75	100
Zeppelin, "Sky Ranger," 9" long	7.50	11.25	15.00
Zeppelin "U.S. Akron," potmetal, circa 1932, 6" long	25.00	37.50	50.00
Zeppelin "ZEP," cast iron, 4" long ..	25.00	37.50	50.00
Zeppelin "ZEP," cast iron, 6¾" long, Dent	62.50	93.75	125.00
Zeppelin, "Goodyear" decals, 25" long, hatch opens	125.00	187.50	250.00
Zeppelin, 6" long, silver, pull toy, circa 1920-30s, cast iron	60	90	120
Zeppelin, metal, 25" long	42.50	63.75	85.00
Zeppelin, metal, 26½" long	45.00	67.50	90.00
Zeppelin, metal, 27½" long	50	75	100

SHIPS

(See also Tin Wind-Up, Paper)

Mint prices in this category averaged $287.84 in the last edition, and in this edition averaged $784.94, in increase of 173%.

CONDITION CODE:
C5 – Good, wear evident overall, shows that has been played with
C6 – Fine, shows some wear in spots, but taken care of
C7 – Very Fine, minor wear overall, very clean
C8 – Excellent, minor wear on edges only
C9 – Near Mint, no noticeable flaws, close inspection may show minute marks
C10 – Mint (like new)
    Note: Mint in Box does command higher price

	C6	C8	C10
"Adirondack" Sidewheeler, cast iron, approx. 13" long	500	750	1000
Admiral Dewey's Flagship from the White Fleet, wood and paper, 6" long	100	150	200
Admiral Dewey Flagship paper litho on wood, 30" long, c. 1900	300	450	600
Aircraft Carrier "65" tin litho, large, circa 1950s	50	75	100
Arcade "Showboat," cast iron, approx. 10¾" long, circa 1934	750	1125	1500
"Automatic Submarine," remote-controlled, tin litho	40	60	80
Atwood Motors, California "Amazon Side-Wheeler," plastic and metal, circa 1950s	200	300	400

AUBURN RUBBER Battleship and Submarine
Photo by Ed Poole

Aircraft Carrier "Libertania" (see Liberty Playthings)
Courtesy Mapes Auctioneers & Appraisers

	C6	C8	C10
Auburn Rubber Battleship, 8¼" long, circa 1941	6	9	12
Auburn Rubber Cruiser	6	9	12
Auburn Rubber Freighter, 8" long, circa 1941	5.00	7.50	10.00
Auburn Rubber Submarine, 6½" long, circa 1941	5.00	7.50	10.00
Authenticast French warships, including Richelieu, Algiers, Fantasque and others, each	30	45	60
Authenticast German Warships, scale models including Narvik, Galster and others, each	30	45	60
Authenticast Japanese Warships, including Fuso, Kaga, Mogani and others, each	30	45	60

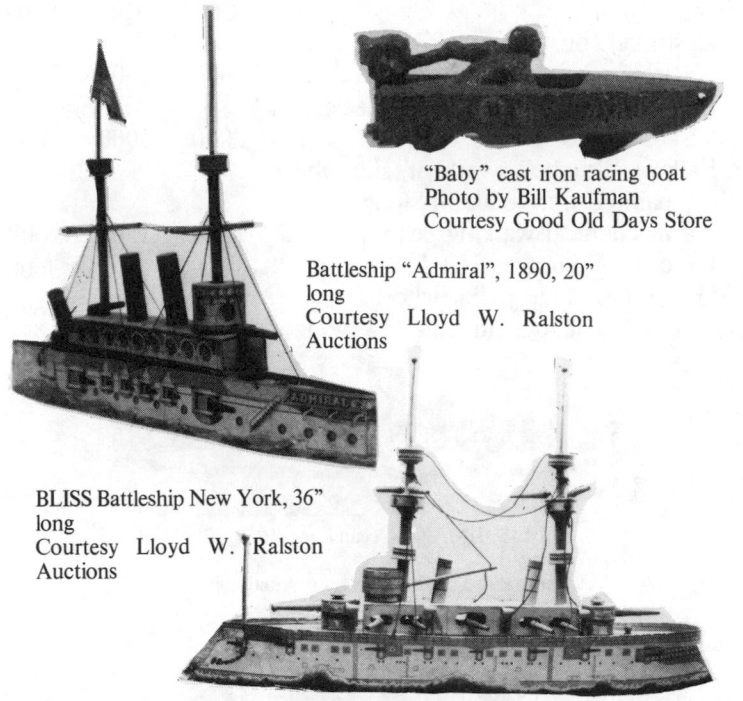

"Baby" cast iron racing boat
Photo by Bill Kaufman
Courtesy Good Old Days Store

Battleship "Admiral", 1890, 20"
long
Courtesy Lloyd W. Ralston
Auctions

BLISS Battleship New York, 36"
long
Courtesy Lloyd W. Ralston
Auctions

Top: BARCLAY 372 **Aeroplane Carrier**
Bottom: BARCLAY 373 **Battleship**
Photo by Ed Poole

	C6	C8	C10
Authenticast U.S. scale model war- ships, World War II including: Iowa, Enterprise, Sims and Farragut and submarine Sarge, each	30	45	60
B-LO submarine, metal, pat. no. 1318048	75.00	112.50	150.00
"Baby" cast iron racing boat, circa 1930, wheeled, 4½" long, Hubley?	60	90	120
Barclay **372 Aeroplane Carrier**	25.00	37.50	50.00
Barclay **373 Battleship**	30	45	60
Battleship "Admiral" paper litho, 1890, 20" long	600	900	1200
Battleship, cast iron, 14½" long	300	450	600
Battleship, glass, approx. 3" long, candy container	60	90	120

	C6	C8	C10
Battleship, Hillclimber, 15" long, pressed steel	200	300	400
Battleship Oregon, 25" long, paper litho and wood	700	1050	1400
Battleship "Rover" paper litho and wood, 20" long	600	900	1200
Battleship, Tin Friction, 9½" long, circa 1920s	200	300	400
"Big Bang Battleship," 8¼" long	125.00	187.50	250.00
Big Bang Gunboat, 8" long, cast iron, early	125.00	187.50	250.00
Bliss "Battleship New York" paper litho and stained wood, 1890, 36"x22"	450	675	900
Bliss "Conqueror"	900	1350	1800
Bliss "Marguerite" sailing schooner, 22" long	350	525	700
Bliss? "Union" ferry, sidewheel, c. 1900, 24" long	225	375	450
Boat, Hot Air, tin with driver, 9" long	100	150	200
Boat, pull motor, metal	100	150	200
Boat, tin friction, lithographed	100	150	200
Boat, tin friction, painted, early	100	150	200
Boat, tin friction, painted, early	150	225	300
Boat, tin friction, 13" long, two smokestacks, four lifeboats	90	135	180
Boucher "Gee Whiz" speedboat, painted sheetmetal, heavy clockwork motor, bronze pro- pellor, 25" long	550	825	1100
Bradley "Columbia" side paddle- wheeler, paper litho on wood, 24" long, c. 1890	400	600	800
Buddy L "49 LST," 12" long	42.50	63.75	85.00

Boat, tin friction, 13" long, two smokestacks, four lifeboats
Courtesy PB 84 New York

BUDDY L "49 LST"
Photo by Ed Poole

BUDDY L No. 3000 Tugboat
Photo Courtesy Thomas W. Sefton

"Columbia" riverboat, 1890, 2' long
Courtesy Lloyd W. Ralston Auctions

FALLOWS "Jumbo" riverboat, 14" long
Courtesy Lloyd W. Ralston

	C6	C8	C10
Buddy L No. 3000 Tugboat, 1929-30	1250	1875	2500
"C.C. JR." Brass-mounted Wood Boat, wind-up motor concealed within the rudder controlled from the wheel in the circular cockpit with a start-stop lever, 14½" long	90	135	180
Canoe, Wood, 6" long	15.00	22.50	30.00
"Columbia" riverboat, 1890, paper litho, tin litho, wood, working walking beam, 2' long	650	975	1300
Cruiser, glass, approx. 3" long, candy container	50	75	100
Dayton Battleship, 16" long, friction, circa 1920	200	300	400
Dent Adirondack, 15" long, cast iron	600	900	1200
Dent Battleship New York, circa 1900, 21", largest cast iron boat made	1250	1875	2500

	C6	C8	C10
Destroyer, on wheels, 12" long, cast iron	1000	1500	2000
Fallows "Constitution" sidewheeler, 10" long	2000	3000	4000
Fallows "Jumbo" riverboat, side-wheel, painted tin, 1880, 14" long, mechanical walking beam	1000	1500	2000
Fallows "Volunteer IXL," 16" long	1800	2700	3600
"Ferry Go" twin paddlewheel ferry boat pull toy, tin litho, 14" long	125	185	250

FLEISCHMANN Ocean Liner, 1930, 20½"
long
Courtesy Lloyd W. Ralston Auctions

GEORGE BROWN "Atlantic" sidewheel
riverboat, 14" long
Courtesy Lloyd W. Ralston Auction

	C6	C8	C10
Fleischmann Battleship	2000	3000	4000
Fleischmann Ocean Liner, 1930, painted tin clockwork, working, 20½" long	1300	1950	2600
George Brown "Atlantic" sidewheel riverboat, painted and stenciled tin, 14" long	2250	3375	4500
Gunboat, tin friction, large wheel rises above deck, circa early 1920s, smokestack	300	450	600
Gunboat, tin friction, rocks back and forth on wheels, 10" long	250	375	500
Gunboat, 19" long, friction	400	600	800
Gunboat, two guns, 2 small stacks, 2 stories above deck, wheeled, friction, 1920s or earlier	300	450	600
Hill Climber pressed steel battleship, 18" long	400	600	800
Hubley "Penn Yan" motorboat, 15" long, 5 people, very rare, unauthorized by Penn Yan, which stopped Hubley's production	2250	3375	4500
Hubley "Sea Horse" cast iron motorboat	1750	2625	3500
Ideal Pirate Ship, plastic, with six pirates	120	180	240
Ideal Varsity Racing Scull, 8 rowers, coxswain, 1890, 14" long, cast iron, oars move	1250	1875	2500
Ives "Miss Liberty" speedboat, 13½" long, steam-powered	750	1125	1500

HUBLEY "Sea Horse"
Courtesy Ed Hyers Antique Toys

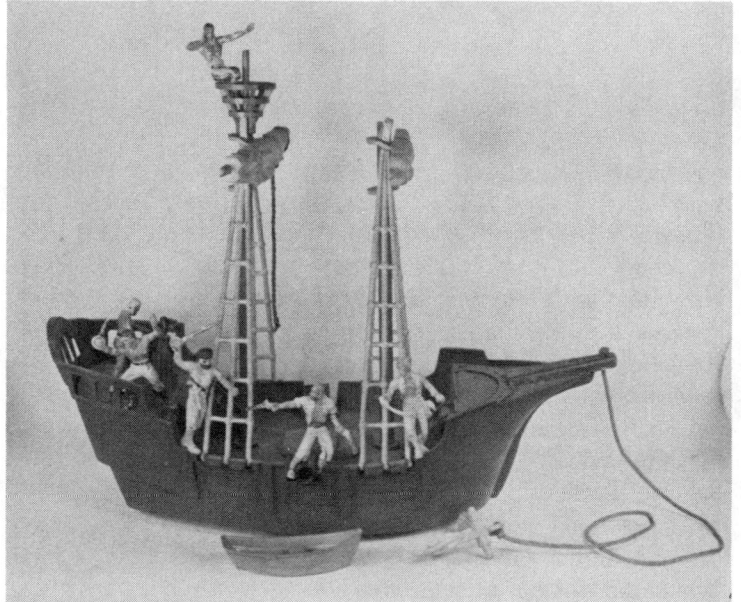

IDEAL Pirate Ship

"Kearsage" gunboat
Courtesy PB 84 New York

KEYSTONE Aircraft Carrier, wooden, 12" long
Courtesy Mapes Auctioneers & Appraisers

	C6	C8	C10
Keystone Ferryboat, wooden, circa 1930s, two wood cars, two wood trucks, 14" long	40	60	80
Keystone fishing boat, wooden, 12" long, circa 1940s	35.00	52.50	70.00
Kingsbury Boat, 10" long	100	150	200

LIBERTY PLAYTHINGS

Liberty Playthings was in business in the late 1920s and early 1930s in Niagara Falls, New York. All its toys, which were made of wood and metal, seem to have borne names with some variations of the word "Liberty," and all seem to have been sea-connected. Those advertised in 1929 were: No. 2 Tug and Scow; No. 5 Freighter; No. 6 Airplane Carrier; No. 7 Fire Boat; No. 8 Destroyer; No. 22 Seaplane. The carrier, which in the ad was called "Liberator" sold for $10. The "Libertania" aircraft seems to be the same ship, or a slight variation.

	C6	C8	C10
Liberty Playthings "Libertania" Aircraft Carrier, wood and tin litho with lead planes, 27¾" long	60	90	120
Life Boat, steel, 11" long by 5¼" wide, simple design, circa late 1930s	20	30	40

IVES, U.S. Merchant Marine, painted pressed tin clockwork.

	C6	C8	C10
Ives Ocean Liner, 13½" long	1000	1500	2000
Ives U.S. Merchant Marine Boat, painted pressed tin clockwork	1100	1650	2200
Ives "Vim" speedboat, 10½" long	650	975	1300
Ives "Vixen" speedboat, 12" long	650	975	1300
"Johnson's Sea Horse" cast iron speedboat with figure, 10½" long	1750	2625	3500
"Kearsage" gunboat, 13¾" long, cast iron	1000	1500	2000
Keystone Aircraft Carrier, wooden, 12" long	50	75	100
Keystone Battleship, wooden, approx. 2' long with guns, airplanes take off from a spring on deck of ship	50	75	100
Keystone Battleship, under 2' length, early 1940s	40	60	80

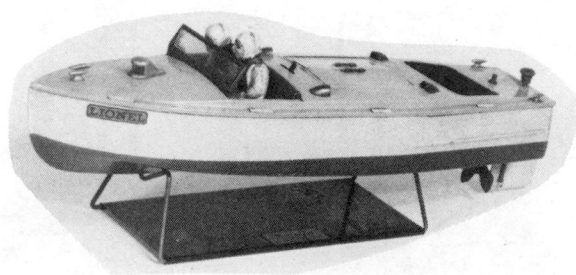

LIONEL NO. 43 Wind-up speedboat.
Courtesy Phillips New York

LIONEL No. 44 wind-up speedboat.
Courtesy Sotheby's New York

RENWAL Viking Ship

	C6	C8	C10
Lionel Craft No. 43 wind-up speedboat	450	675	900
Lionel Craft No. 44 wind-up speedboat	450	675	900
Manoil No. 79 Submarine, lead alloy	10	15	20
Marx "Caribbean" friction Luxury Liner, sparkling, 15" long, 3½" tall	55.00	82.50	110.00
Marx Mosquito Fleet Putt Putt Boat	80	120	160
"New York" warship, metal, 17", circa 1899	500	750	1000
Ohio Battleship, friction, 16" long, painted pressed steel	140	210	280
Orkin Craft speedboat, clockwork, 29" long	500	750	1000
"Priscilla" Side-Wheeler approx. 10" long, Dent or Wilkins, cast iron	500	750	1000
PT 107	37.50	56.25	75.00
Pull Toy boat by Hustilar Toy Corp., Sterling Ill., wood with some metal parts, oarsmen row in unison	75.00	112.50	150.00
"Puritan" Sidewheeler, cast iron, approx. 10½" long	480	720	960
Reed "Pilgrim" River Boat, 28½" long, paper litho	1000	1500	2000
Remco "Fighting Lady" battleship No. 710, 31" long	50	75	100
Remco "Mighty Matilda" aircraft carrier (nearly three feet long), complete with all accessories	100	150	200

	C6	C8	C10
Renwal Viking Ship No. 245, 17" long	75.00	112.50	150.00
Row Boat with four men and oars, cast iron, mechanical, 9" long	1250	1875	2500
Row Boat, tin rubber band driver, 9" long with man rowing	40	60	80
Schiebel Battleship, circa 1927, unpowered	1000	1500	2000
Schiebel Battleship, wood stacks and large wood guns and turrets, friction motor, circa 1920	1250	1875	2500
Schoenhut Submarine and Dreadnought Naval War Toy, pat. 4/6/15, torpedo explodes ship	100	150	200
Scull, 9-man crew, U.S. Hardware, 14" long, wheeled	1600	2400	3200
Shore Patrol, battery operated, tin boat, 9" long	10	15	20
Showboat, cast iron, 11" long	1000	1500	2000
Side-Wheeler Boat, "The Star," tin, height with stand, 21", length 14½"	3500	5200	7000
Side-Wheeler, cast iron, approx. 5½" long	125.00	187.50	250.00
Side-Wheeler, cast iron, 8" long	150	225	300
Side-Wheeler, cast iron, 10½" long	150	225	300
Side-Wheeler, tin clockwork, 11" long	90	135	180
"Sinking Battleship," Walbert Mfg., rubber band torpedo strikes die on ship and sinks it	250	375	500
"Speed Boat," 5¼" long	60	90	120
"Speed Boat," cast iron with rider, 4¾" long, early	120	180	240
Speed Boat, wood, rubber-band propelled	40	60	80
SS United States, tin friction, 6½" long	50	75	100
Steamboat, tin, self-propelled, 17" long	150	225	300
Steamer, lithographed paper on wood, 39" long, 22½" high	450	675	900

SIDE WHEELER BOAT, tin, "The Star", height, with stand, 21". Length 14½".

Steamship, alcohol burner, circa 1885, 19" long
Courtesy Mapes Auctioneers & Appraisers

U.S. HARDWARE Rowers, circa 1890
Courtesy Ed Hyers Antique Toys

WOLVERINE "Sandy Andy" Ferry

TOOTSIETOY, top L to R: 1037 Transport 1039 Tanker.
Bottom L to R: 129 Tender, 130 Yacht
Photo by Ed Poole

TOOTSIETOY, Top L to R: 1034 Battleship, 1036 Carrier.
Middle L to R: 1035 Cruiser, 1037 Liner.
Bottom l to R: 127 Destroyer, 128 Submarine
Photo by Ed Poole

	C6	C8	C10
Steamship, alcohol burner, ca. 1885, 19" long	200	300	400
Sterling 56" scale model, all wood and metal Battleship Missouri, radio control, with three electric motors	350	525	700
Submarine, "575," tin litho, remote-controlled, circa 1960	40	60	80
Submarine, steel, 6" long	40	60	80

	C6	C8	C10
Tillicum Convoy Set, Milton Bradley, 1940s, 2 destroyers, 3 freight boats, 3 ocean liners, 2 patrol boats, painted wood, destroyers 5½" long, others about 4½" long	50	75	100

TOOTSIETOY
(Compiled by Ed Poole)

	C6	C8	C10
1034 Battleship, 6" long, 1939 on, U.S.S. New York	4	6	8
1035 Cruiser, 5½" long, 1939 on, U.S.S. Portland	3.00	4.50	6.00
1036 Carrier, 6" long, 1939 on, Aeroplane Carrier Saratoga	3.00	4.50	6.00
1037 Transport, 6" long, 1939 on	3.00	4.50	6.00
1038 Freighter, 6" long, 1940 on	3.00	4.50	6.00
1039 Tanker, 6" long, 1940 on	3.00	4.50	6.00
127 Destroyer, 4" long, 1939	3.00	4.50	6.00
128 Submarine, 4" long, 1939 on	3.00	4.50	6.00
129 Tender, 4" long, 1940 on	3.00	4.50	6.00
130 Yacht, 4" long, 1940 on	3.00	4.50	6.00

Top to Bottom: "U.S.S. New Mexico, U.S.S. Narwahl"
Courtesy Hank Anton

TOOTSIETOY MIDGET SERIES

	C6	C8	C10
Battleship	1.50	2.25	3.00
Destroyer	1.50	2.25	3.00
Carrier	1.50	2.25	3.00
Cruiser	1.50	2.25	3.00
Tug (probably not Tootsie)	1.50	2.25	3.00
Submarine	1.50	2.25	3.00
Turbo Boat, pressed, tin, 10½" long	40	60	80
U.S. Naval Base, Superior	60	90	120
U.S. Hardware Rowers, circa 1890, 4-man crew and coxswain, cast iron, large wheels	1250	1875	2500
"U.S.S. Narwahl" submarine, lead, mfr. unknown, 1930s	20	30	40
"U.S.S. New Mexico" battleship, lead, manufacturer unknown, 1930s	20	30	40
"U.S. Submarine," 13" long, painted wood, fires torpedo for target set	20	30	40
U.S. Wasp, Carrier 27" long, wood storage under deck for planes	50	75	100

WOLVERINE Diving Submarine
Courtesy Mapes Auctioneers & Appraisers

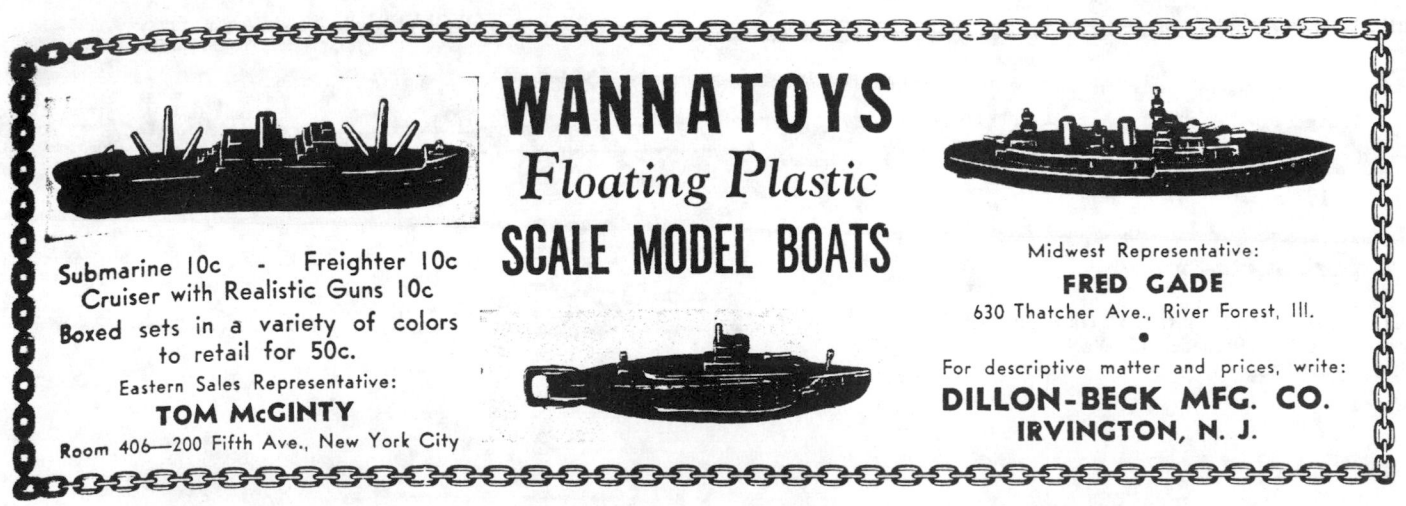

WANNATOYS (Dillon-Beck) plastic ships, advertised in the July, 1941 Playthings. Plastic Toys, Inc. copied the submarine a few years later. Courtesy Playthings Magazine

WANNATOYS were manufactured by Dillon-Beck Manufacturing Company of Irvington, New Jersey from 1941 on. They were plastic.

Wannatoys Cruiser	4	6	8
Wannatoys Freighter	4	6	8
Wannatoys Submarine	4	6	8

	C6	C8	C10
Weeden "Dewey" Steamboat, 15½" long, circa 1900	500	750	1000
Weeden Launch, steam-driven, 18" long	350	525	700
Weeden Steamboat, live steam, 15" long	300	450	600

WEEDEN Launch, steam-driven, 18" long
Courtesy Heinz Mueller, Continental Hobby House

WILKINS Riverboat, 10½" long. Courtesy Mapes Auctioneers & Appraisers

	C6	C8	C10
Wilkins Battleship, cast iron	1500	2250	3000
Wilkins "City of New York" riverboat, 15" long	750	1125	1500
Wilkins Riverboat, 5¾" long	140	210	280
Wilkins Riverboat, 7½" long, circa 1910, cast iron	300	450	600
Wilkins Riverboat, 10½" long, cast iron	450	675	900
Wilkins Rowers, circa 1890, 4-man crew and coxswain in 10" long, big-wheeled boat, cast iron	1250	1875	2500
Wolverine Diving Submarine, 13" long	80	120	160
Wolverine "Sandy Andy Ferry," tin litho, 13½" long	75.00	112.50	150.00
Wolverine Sandy Andy "Ferrygo," 11" long, tin and wood	150	225	300
Wyandotte Pocket Battleship, 7" long, tin litho, wheeled	60	90	120
Wyandotte, "S.S. America," 7" long, moves on metal wheels, 1930s	50	75	100
Wyandotte, "Sand-o'Land," 10" long, tin litho sandtoy, wood wheels, 1940s	40	60	80
Yacht-type ship, 28" long with spring-wind motor, either Ives or Bing	2000	3000	4000

FISHER-PRICE TOYS
by John Murray

⟨ Fisher-Price toys in the last edition averaged $75.34 in mint condition and this year averaged $183.38, an increase of 143%. ⟩

On October 1, 1930, in East Aurora, New York, the Fisher-Price Toy Company began operation. Uniquely located on a small side street in a small town atmosphere, it would grow and eventually be considered one of the major manufacturers of toys.

Herman Fisher and Irving Price shared their names in developing a name for their new company. Herman Fisher, a past employee of the FairChild Company, a manufacturer of games, and Irving Price, who had sound experience with the Woolworth Company, would form the guidelines by which they would run their new company.

The first manufacturing facility was located on Church Street in East Aurora, New York. To date it still exists, but was sold by Fisher-Price in the 1970s due to lack of use for the facility.

The Church Street facility would be considered a small area for any type of manufacturing today, but would serve as the main and only facility for Fisher-Price toys for the first twenty years.

The most important factor in constructing this new company was to create a work force that could contribute their efforts towards a smooth, profitable venture. Among the most important employees would be Helen M. Schelle and Margaret Evans Price.

Helen M. Schelle was the first secretary and treasurer of Fisher-Price toys. She developed her skills in the retail management field through a business in which she operated, the Walker Toy Shop, in Binghamton, New York. Given the opportunity to manage the early company's activities, Helen proved to be a great asset to the advancement of Fisher-Price toys.

Margaret Evans Price was the company's first artist and designer for their new line of toys. She developed her early skills as a writer and illustrator for Rand McNally and Harper & Brothers, and by creating children's art for Strecher Lithography Company of Rochester, New York. Many of Margaret Evans Price's art work can still be found on early post cards, valentines, and children's books. These early paper collectibles are most often marked "M.E.P."

Margaret created the early art work for the reproduction of color lithography for the toys. She was also talented in drawing, produced designs for early toys, and contributed in the development of her concepts to Fisher-Price's early line of toys. The Roycroft printers contributed their skills to produce the sales catalogs that prospective retailers would use to choose the toys that they would market.

The most important early development for the company was the forming of the labor force that would generate their efforts towards building the new toy line that would be sold to the public in 1931. The initial work force that first year was approximately 25 employees. As typical of any small town like East Aurora, most employees were neighbors, friends, and relatives, who contributed to a work force that took great pride in the product that they made, since many of the operations were done by hand labor.

Many of the early operations, such as band sawing, drilling, nailing, and painting were shared by these early employees. Quality control would be created by one employee checking the other and making any corrections immediately.

As Fisher-Price began toymaking, numbers were assigned to each toy. This number system started at Number 5 and went up into the thousands. To add to the confusion for collectors today, many of the numbers have been used more than once on various toys.

With the abundance of pine and its ease of workability, this was the main wood used in construction of Fisher-Price toys. During the 30s, another material was used, a heavy cardboard, in which brass eyelets were inserted to prevent wear from spinning axles.

Creating action from child power was of great importance. The use of bellows was common to produce sound, and, as time passed, the introduction of bells was added to create sound and action.

Because of the immense amount of time required to assemble various toys, cottage-type industries were set up by employees, families, and residents of East Aurora. Toys such as the Pop-up Kritter were completely hand assembled in area homes. Because of the large demand, this would prove to be a quick and efficient method of assembly.

As the demand for Fisher-Price toys consistently rose, they began to use the skills of a freelance designer, Edward Savage, a mechanical engineer from the University of Minnesota. He created some of Fisher-Price's most successful toys. In his home in Rochester, New York, Savage created such toys as the Pop-up Kritters, Snoopy Sniffer, and many of the wind-up toys. The most popular of the toys that he created was the Snoopy Sniffer, which was produced from the 30s to the 80s, in four different versions.

After well over a decade of positive growth for Fisher-Price toys in the 30s and 40s, Fisher-Price would meet a major challenge of limited production.

With the United States entering World War II, Fisher-Price, like many companies, served its patriotic duty in a quite different type of manufacturing.

Because of the type of manufacturing that Fisher-Price was set up for, the ability to create and produce wood products set the basis for essential goods needed for war production. Ship fenders, first aid kits, cots, bomb crates, and glider ailerons were among the items produced from 1943 - 1946.

During this time of near non-existent toy manufacturing, very limited toy production continued on a material-availability basis. These toys were made from scraps of wood, with bells and some metal parts painted instead of plated. Toys made during this time sometimes used parts from similar toys, leaving odd and sometimes unusual variations.

As the World War came to an end, normal production began to resume. Well into the 50s, Ponderosa Pine, with a proven durability, was the main source of material in Fisher-Price toys. As wood became more difficult to obtain, the experimentation with plastics as a new material began. The first toy to use this new material successfully was the Busy Bee. Because of the ease of molding, durability, and bright colors, plastic was more prevelant in toys of the 50s.

In 1951, Fisher-Price moved to its new manufacturing facility on Girard Avenue in East Aurora, New York. The Girard Avenue facility handled most operations well into the late 50s. In 1957, Tri Mold of Kenmore, New York, a plastics manufacturer, became a subsidiary of Fisher-Price and their main molding facility.

As the demand for plastics became greater and greater, a new molding facility was built in Holland, New York. This was completed in July 1962. The Holland plant produced many of the plastic parts used in the construction of a more plastic-dominated toy line.

As the 60s advanced, plastic would eventually take over as the main material used to produce toys.

In 1969, The Quaker Oats Company acquired Fisher-Price toys. Three years prior to this acquisition, Herman Fisher resigned as president of the company, and was chairman of the board until the Quaker Oats acquisition. Since Fisher-Price was taken over by Quaker Oats, a plant in Medina, New York, was built, and numerous plants and facilities both nationally and internationally were created.

Considered one of the oldest and largest manufacturers of toys, Fisher-Price has its main offices at the Girard Avenue address in East Aurora, New York.

JOHN J. MURRAY was born, raised and educated in the Buffalo, New York area and presently resides in Eden, a suburb of Buffalo. John, known to many as Jack, began his career in the printing industry and after serving in the Armed Forces, began his over 15-year career with Fisher-Price, in the Research and Development Art Production Department.
John admits that the joy of collecting wooden Fisher-Price toys is endless, as this area of toy collecting is rapidly on the rise. Their uniqueness, their bright and colorful litho, and their endless shapes and sizes all combine to make collecting them a hobby of real enjoyment.

CONDITION

There are many factors that may contribute to values of Fisher-Price toys. The most important factor to consider is the paper lithography. Most Fisher-Price toys found have what I call "edge wear." Edge wear may be considered as wear only around the outer corners or edge of the toy. Most toys found with edge wear may also be called normal-wear toys. Any toys with this type of wear most often fall in a value class of good/very good. When determining the condition of a toy, other areas of importance to the litho would be the amount of soil on the litho, and the extent to which it has faded and/or lost its color. These areas may be considered as less important, unless there is more than slight soiling or discoloration. When a Fisher-Price toy has advanced conditions of wear, soiling, or missing litho, the toy would be considered as less than good condition, and therefore, a value of less than good (poor) would be placed on it.

The next area that is of importance with regard to condition of the toy in determining value would be paint and originality. Toys with slight paint wear on wheels, bases, and handles would fall into the good/very good condition category, unless however, there is litho damage as stated above. Any parts missing also affect the value of the toy, especially lithography parts, such as arms, legs, and heads. These are especially important, since once the litho is gone, there is no means of replacement. Also lessening the value of a toy would be missing wheels and axles.

A toy which is mint is one that has absolutely no wear or damage on a complete basis. (Litho, paint, wheels, etc. in mint condition). These toys will reflect the highest of values. Boxes for older Fisher-Price toys may add up to 20% more for a mint toy, depending upon the condition of the box. Boxes from toys from the 1930s would be of the most value because of age, and are most often missing. Always consider condition of the box towards a value of a toy.

The last area that seems to have led the way demanding higher prices would be comic characters and the use of other company's names on Fisher-Price toys. Most often toys of this nature have much higher values placed on them than other Fisher-Price toys, due to the fact that there are many Disney, Popeye, and other comic-area collectors.

Because a toy may be a Disney, Popeye, or comic figure does not necessarily mean that it may be a rarer toy. There are many other Fisher-Price toys that are much rarer, since rarity is based on the amount of toys produced over a given period of time, and the amount still in existence.

Also, many toys that had accessories or figures that were often misplaced will bring higher values. Often these accessories and/or figures are difficult to locate separately from the toy itself. If a toy is found mint in the box with accessories, this most certainly will demand higher pricing.

The prices reflected in this guide for Fisher-Price toys were established by taking an average of toys seen at toy shows, flea markets, dealers, and collectors.

777 SQUEAKY THE CLOWN
Photo by Ross MacKearnin, Courtesy John Murray

770 DOC & DOPEY DWARFS
Photo by Ross MacKearnin, Courtesy John Murray

777 TEDDY ZILO
Photo by Ross MacKearnin, Courtesy John Murray

765 TALKING DONALD DUCK
Photo by Ross MacKearnin, Courtesy John Murray

	C6	C8	C10		C6	C8	C10
7 Looky Fire Truck	50	65	100	28 Bunny Egg Cart	50	65	100
8 Bouncy Racer	25	35	50	50 Baby Chick Tandem Cart	50	65	100
10 Bunny Cart	50	65	100	100 Musical Sweeper	125	135	150
11 Ducky Cart	50	65	100	120 Cackling Hen (white)	25	50	75
16 Ducky Cart	50	65	100	123 Cackling Hen (red)	25	50	75

491 BOOM BOOM POPEYE
Photo by Ross MacKearnin, Courtesy John Murray

480 LEO THE DRUMMER
Photo by Ross MacKearnin, Courtesy John Murray

494 PLUCKY PINOCCHIO
Photo by Ross MacKearnin, Courtesy John Murray

	C6	C8	C10
123 Roller Chimes (with push stick)	25	35	50
125 Uncle Timmy Turtle (with glasses) (see picture)	50	75	100
131 Toy Wagon	125	175	250
132 Dr. Doodle	50	75	100
137 Pony Chime	25	35	50
138 Pony Chime	25	35	50
139 Tuggy Turtle	33	55	75
140 Katy Kackler (see picture)	50	75	100
145 Musical Elephant (with original ears) (see picture)	125	165	250
150 Timmy Turtle	50	75	100
151 Happy Hippo	50	75	100
155 Moo-oo Cow	50	75	100
156 F/P Circus Wagon (see picture)	200	250	350
161 Looky Chug-Chug (with tender)	125	150	225
164 Mother Goose	35	50	65
166 Bucky Burro	125	165	200
168 F/P Chug Chug (with 2 cars)	35	50	60
168 Snorky Fire Engine (with all figures)	50	70	100
169 Snorky Fire Engine (with all figures)	50	70	100
170 American Airlines Flagship (with original propellors)	300	475	600
175 Gold Star Stage Coach (with baggage-two) (see picture)	125	175	250
177 Donald Duck Xylophone (see picture)	125	175	250
180 Snoopy Sniffer (see picture)	75	125	175
185 Donald Duck Xylophone	250	375	475
190 Molly Moo-Moo	100	125	175
191 Golden Gulch Express	50	75	100
192 Playland Express	50	75	100
195 Teddy Bear Parade	300	375	550
200 Winky Blinky Fire Truck	50	75	100
210 Pluto the Pup	200	275	350
211 Walt Disney's Elmer the Elephant	200	285	375
215 Streamliner Express	300	425	550
220 Looky Chug-Chug (see picture)	50	75	100
225 Musical Sweeper	50	75	100
230 Musical Sweeper	50	75	100

	C6	C8	C10
234 Nifty Station Wagon (with roof and four figures) see picture	125	175	250
237 Riding Horse (with original tail)	300	425	525
301 Bunny Basket Cart	25	35	50
302 Chick Basket Cart	25	35	50
303 Bunny Basket Cart	50	75	100
305 Walking Duck Cart	25	35	50
307 Bouncing Bunny Cart	25	35	50
310 Mickey Mouse Puddle Jumper	50	75	100
314 Queen Buzzy Bee (see picture)	25	35	50
325 Buzzy Bee	25	35	50
333 Butch the Pup	50	75	100
350 Go'n Back Mule (with original ears)	300	425	525
400 Donald Duck Drum Major	125	175	225
400 Tailspin Tabby (original pull loops) (see picture)	50	75	90
401 Bunny Cart	125	145	200
406 Bunny & Cart	25	35	50
407 Chick & Cart	25	35	50
410 Stoopy Storky (with original cardboard feet)	125	175	225
415 Lop-Ear Looie (see picture)	200	325	400
415 Super-Jet (see picture)	125	175	225
432 Mickey Mouse Choo-Choo (early version)	300	400	525
433 Dizzy Donkey (see picture)	50	75	100
434 Ferdinand the Bull (see picture)	300	475	600
440 Goofy Gertie	125	175	225
440 Pluto Pop-Up	60	75	110
444 Puffy Engine	50	75	100
444 Fuzzy Fido (see picture)	125	175	250
445 Hot Dog Wagon (see picture)	125	175	225
445 Nosey Pup (see picture)	25	35	60
450 Donald Choo-Choo	125	170	225
450 Jolly Jumper	50	75	100
454 Donald Duck Drummer (see picture)	125	175	250
455 Tailspin Tabby	50	75	100
462 Barky Dog	50	75	100
472 Peter Bunny Cart	125	190	250
472 Jingle Giraffe	125	175	225
473 Merry Mutt	50	70	90
476 Mickey Mouse Drummer	125	185	250
476 Cookie Pig	20	40	50

757 HUMPTY DUMPTY
Photo by Ross MacKearnin, Courtesy John Murray

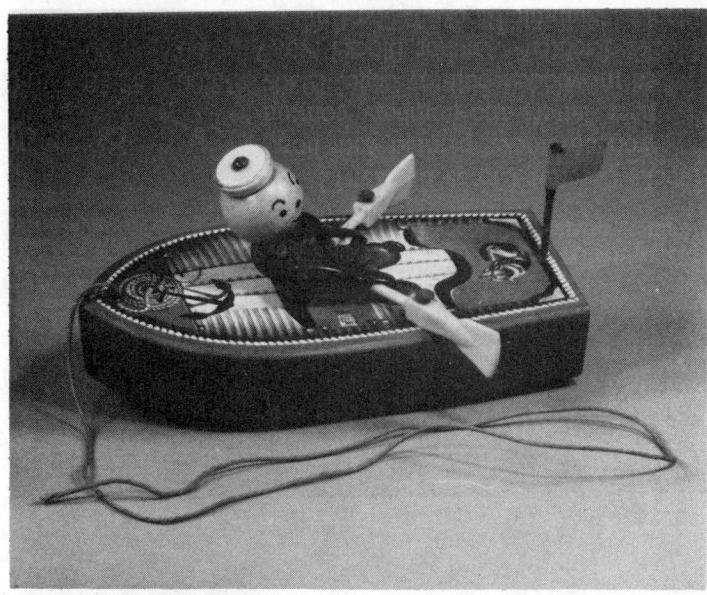

730 RACING ROWBOAT
Photo by Ross MacKearnin, Courtesy John Murray

703 POPEYE THE SAILOR
Photo by Ross MacKearnin, Courtesy John Murray

446

145 MUSICAL ELEPHANT
Photo by Ross MacKearnin, Courtesy John Murray

400 TAILSPIN TABBY
Photo by Ross MacKearnin, Courtesy John Murray

156 FISHER PRICE CIRCUS WAGON
Photo by Ross MacKearnin, Courtesy John Murray

415 LOP-EAR-LOOIE
Photo by Ross MacKearnin, Courtesy John Murray

177 DONALD DUCK XYLOPHONE
Photo by Ross MacKearnin, Courtesy John Murray

415 SUPER JET
Photo by Ross MacKearnin, Courtesy John Murray

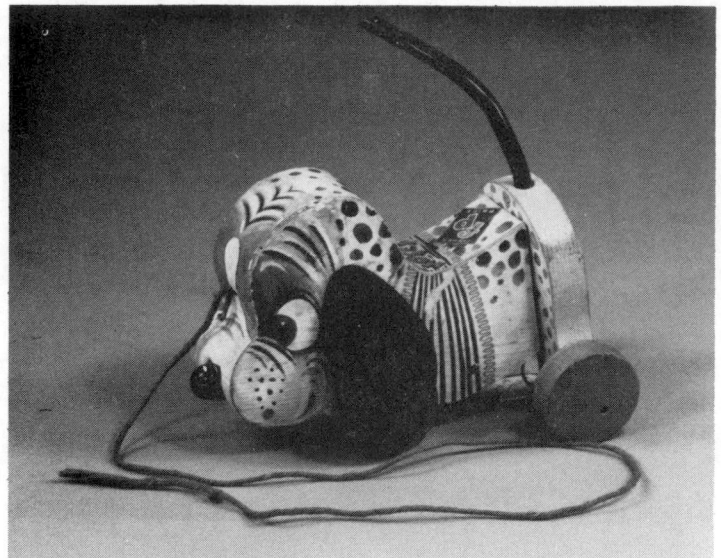

445 NOSEY PUP
Photo by Ross MacKearnin, Courtesy John Murray

454 DONALD DUCK DRUMMER
Photo by Ross MacKearnin, Courtesy John Murray

485 MICKEY MOUSE CHOO CHOO
Photo by Ross MacKearnin, Courtesy John Murray

678 KRISS KRICKET
Photo by Ross MacKearnin, Courtesy John Murray

472 PETER BUNNY CART
Photo by Ross MacKearnin, Courtesy John Murray

698 TALKY PARROT
Photo by Ross MacKearnin, Courtesy John Murray

166 BUCKY BURRO
Photo by Ross MacKearnin, Courtesy John Murray

125 UNCLE TIMMY TURTLE
Photo by Ross MacKearnin, Courtesy John Murray

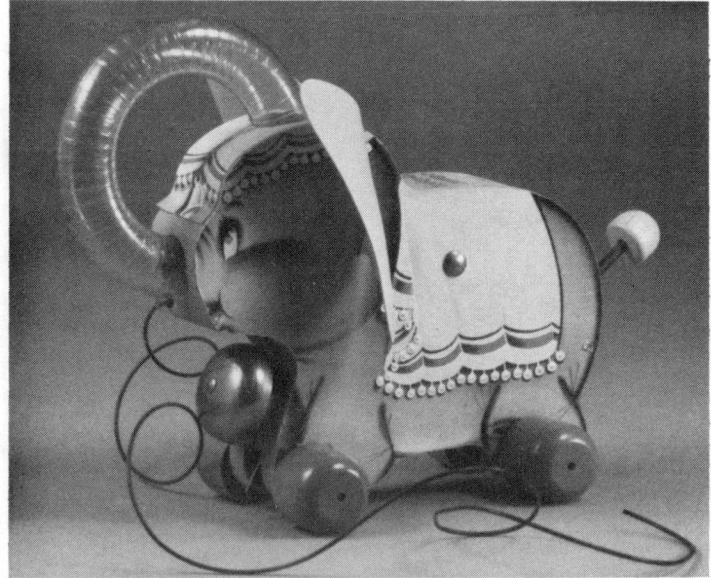

735 JUGGLING JUMBO
Photo by Ross MacKearnin, Courtesy John Murray

449

	C6	C8	C10
477 Dr. Doodle	125	140	200
478 Pudgy Pig	25	40	50
479 Donald Duck & Nephews (with 2 nephews)	200	300	400
480 Leo the Drummer (see picture)	125	160	225
485 Mickey Mouse Choo-Choo (see picture)	50	75	125
487 Bunny Cart	125	160	225
488 Popeye Spinach Eater	200	300	400
491 Boom-boom Popeye (see picture)	200	300	400
494 Plucky Pinocchio (see picture)	200	300	400
495 Sleepy Sue	25	35	50
498 Happy Helicopter	125	160	200
508 Bunny Bell Drummer	50	75	100
533 Thumper Bunny	200	300	400
544 Donald Duck Cart	125	160	250
600 Tailspin Tabby Pop-up	125	160	200
610 Tailspin Tabby	50	75	100
616 Chuggy Pop-Up	50	75	100
617 Whistling Engine	50	75	95
621 Suzie Seal (ball)	20	30	40
623 Suzie Seal (umbrella)	20	30	40
625 Playful Puppy	25	35	50
626 Playful Puppy	25	35	50
634 Tiny Teddy	35	50	75
635 Tiny Teddy	25	35	50
636 Tiny Teddy	35	40	70
640 Wiggily Woofer	40	60	80
642 Smokie Engine	15	30	40
653 Allie Gator	50	70	90
654 Tawny Tiger	50	75	90
656 Bossy Bell	20	30	45
658 Lady Bug	25	35	45
662 Merry Mousewife	25	35	45
674 Sports Car	50	75	100
678 Kriss Kricket (see picture)	50	75	100
686 Perky Pot	25	35	50
695 Pinky Pig	40	60	80
698 Talky Parrot	50	75	100
703 Popeye the Sailor (see picture)	300	450	650
707 Fido Zilo	50	75	100
712 Teddy Tooter	125	150	195
720 Pinocchio Express	200	300	400
721 Peter Bunny Engine	125	140	200
728 Buddy Bullfrog	50	70	90
730 Racing Rowboat (see picture)	125	150	225
733 Fisher-Price General Hauling	125	160	235
733 Mickey Mouse Safety Patrol	125	150	200

314 QUEEN BUZZY BEE
Photo by Ross MacKearnin, Courtesy John Murray

434 FERDINAND THE BULL
Photo by Ross MacKearnin, Courtesy John Murray

7 LOOKY FIRE TRUCK
Photo by Ross MacKearnin, Courtesy John Murray

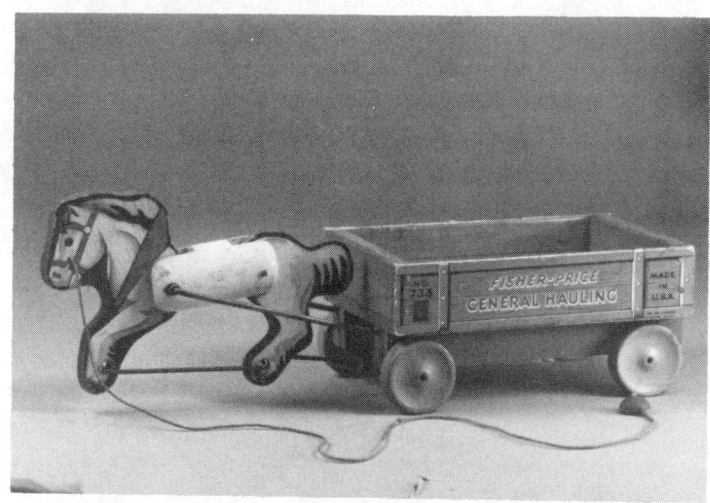

733 FISHER PRICE GENERAL HAULING
Photo by Ross MacKearnin, Courtesy John Murray

450 DONALD DUCK CHOO CHOO
Photo by Ross MacKearnin, Courtesy John Murray

479 DONALD DUCK & NEPHEWS
Photo by Ross MacKearnin, Courtesy John Murray

745 ELSIE'S DAIRY TRUCK
Photo by Ross MacKearnin, Courtesy John Murray

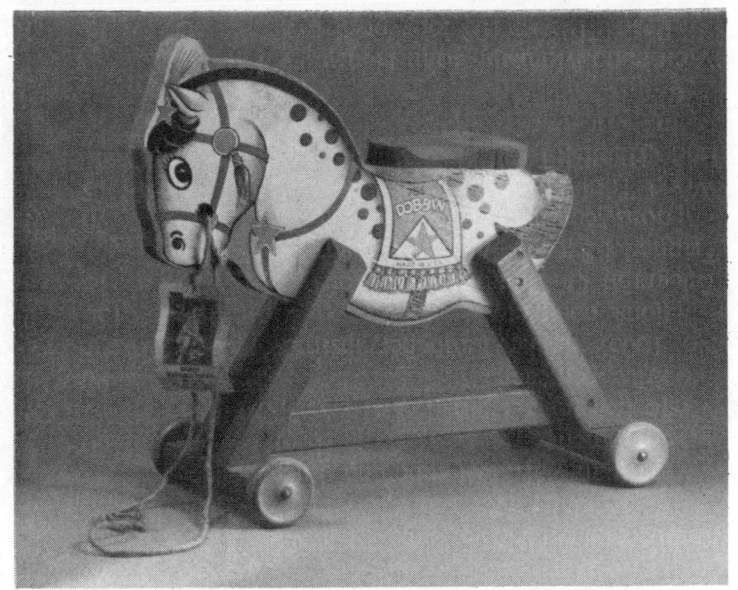

765 DANDY DOBBIN
Photo by Ross MacKearnin, Courtesy John Murray

445 HOT DOG WAGON
Photo by Ross MacKearnin, Courtesy John Murray

444 FUZZY FIDO
Photo by Ross MacKearnin, Courtesy John Murray

	C6	C8	C10
735 Juggling Jumbo (see picture)	125	150	225
738 Dumbo Circus Racer (original arms)	300	450	600
738 Shaggy Zilo	50	75	95
739 Poodle Zilo	50	75	90
742 Dashing Dobbin	200	300	400
745 Elsie's Dairy Truck (with 2 milk bottles-deduct $25.00 for each missing bottle) (see picture)	200	300	425
750 Hot Dog Wagon	200	350	450
750 Space Blazer	200	300	400
752 Teddy Xylophone	125	150	225
755 Jumbo Rollo	125	140	230
757 Humpty-Dumpty (see picture)	125	160	250
758 Pony Chime	125	150	200
765 Dandy Dobbin (see picture)	125	175	250
770 Doc & Dopey Dwarfs (see picture)	200	300	450

	C6	C8	C10
775 Gabby Goofies	25	30	50
776 Gabby Goofies	25	30	50
777 Teddy Bear Zilo	50	70	90
777 Squeaky the Clown (see picture)	125	160	200
785 Blackie Drummer	200	300	400
794 Big Bill Pelican (with cardboard fish-add $20.00)	40	60	80
795 Musical Duck	50	75	100
798 Chatter Monk	50	75	100
799 Quacky Family	25	35	50
810 Timber Toter	35	45	65
875 Looky Push Car (with steering wheel push stick)	35	45	65
900 Big Performing Circus (with all accessories)	125	175	300
926 Cement Mixer	125	150	300
983 Safety School Bus (with all figures)	125	160	200
984 Safety School Bus (with all figures)	125	160	200
999 Huffy Puffy Train (with 4 cars)	60	80	125

175 GOLD STAR STAGE COACH
Photo by Ross MacKearnin, Courtesy John Murray

220 LOOKY, CHUG, CHUG
Photo by Ross MacKearnin, Courtesy John Murray

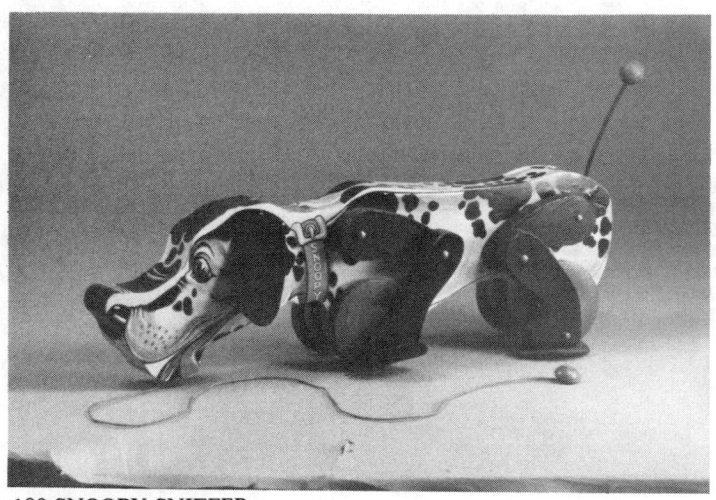

180 SNOOPY SNIFFER
Photo by Ross MacKearnin, Courtesy John Murray

234 NIFTY STATION WAGON
Photo by Ross MacKearnin, Courtesy John Murray

140 KATY KACKLER
Photo by Ross MacKearnin, Courtesy John Murray

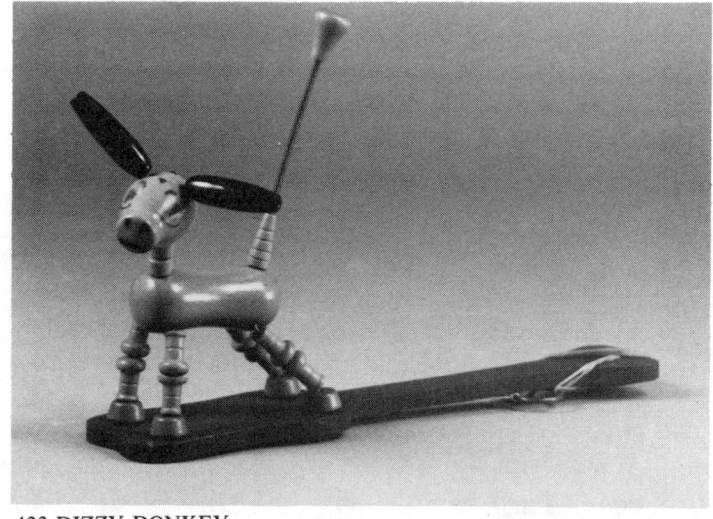

433 DIZZY DONKEY
Photo by Ross MacKearnin, Courtesy John Murray

MISCELLANEOUS

Average mint price in this category in the last edition was $187.61, and in this edition it is $430.96, an increase of 130%.

A.C. GILBERT

Alfred Carlton Gilbert, Jr. (1884-1961) began as a schoolboy magician who turned to producing magic kits under the name of Mysto Manufacturing Company. In 1916 his father bought out A.C.'s partner, and the firm became known as A.C. Gilbert Company, located on Erector Square in New Haven, Connecticut. The company produced non-toys as well as its various toy sets. Upon Gilbert's death, his son, Alfred Carlton Gilbert III took over, but died four years later. Since his death, the company has passed through several hands, with many of its items still being manufactured today, including what is probably its most famous product, the Erector Set.

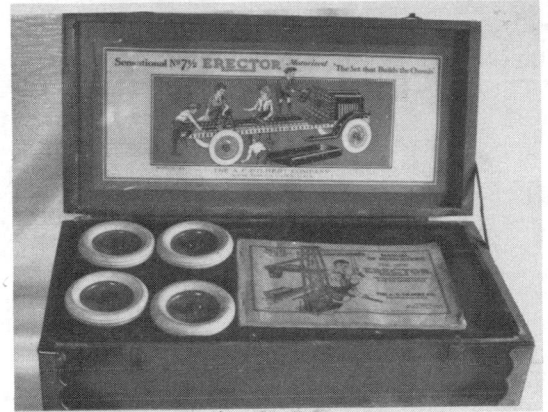

A. C. GILBERT Erector Set No. 7½, makes truck
Courtesy Continental Hobby House

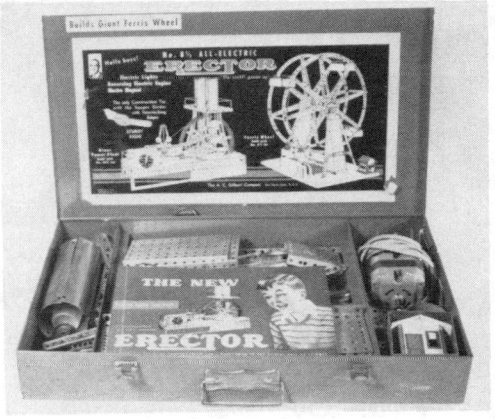

A. C. GILBERT Erector Set No. 8½
Courtesy Continental Hobby House

A. C. GILBERT Erector Set No. 10053 Rocket Launcher
Courtesy Continental Hobby House

A.C. GILBERT	C6	C8	C10		C6	C8	C10
Big Boy Tool Chest No. 6, with tools	20	30	40	Erector Set No. 4, 1919, price includes box, instructions, complete	30	45	60
No. 12052 Chemistry Experiment Lab, in three-piece metal box, complete	16	24	32	Erector Set No. 4, 1930, instructions, complete	130	195	260
"Electric Eye" early photoelectric toy, 1935, in metal box with original instruction booklet, complete	10	15	20	Erector Set No. 4, 1940, instructions, complete	170	255	340
				Erector Set No. 4½, copyright 1938 .	30	45	60
Erector Motor, early, 2½"x2"x3" ...	10	15	20	Erector Set No. 6½, electric engine .	15.00	22.50	30.00
Erector Set No. 1, complete	18	27	36	Erector Set No. 7, builds steam shovel, price includes wood box, complete	170	255	340
Erector Set No. 2, Junior, copyright 1949, complete	20	30	40				
Erector Set No. 2, 1919, "Patented Jan. 16th 1917, Patented May 6th 1918" includes box, complete	40	60	80	Erector Set No. 7½, makes truck, complete	100	150	200
Erector Set No. 2½, instructions and complete	20	30	40	Erector Set No. 8½, instructions, complete	40	60	80
Erector Set No. 3	20	30	40	Erector Set No. 9, price includes wood box, instructions, complete	80	120	160

A.C. GILBERT

	C6	C8	C10
Erector Set No. 10, giant deluxe set, includes box approx. 30x30", makes zeppelin (fabric included), Hudson and Tender, White Truck, etc. complete	1000	1500	2000
Erector Set No. 217, makes train engine and tender, price includes wood box, complete	80	120	160
Erector Set "The New Erector World's Greatest Toy, Copy. 1928," "A.C. Gilbert Co., New Haven, Conn. USA," complete set with box and directions	120	180	240
Erector How To Make 'Em Book, 1938, tells how to make various projects with Erector Set	6	9	12
Erector Hudson Locomotive	300	450	600
Erector Set Manual of Instructions for Set Number 4, 1928, illustrated	4	6	8
Erector, very large set, comes with big white truck, trains, crane, instructions, complete	100	150	200
Erector Set No. 10042 Radar Scope Set	17.50	26.25	35.00
Erector Set No. 10062 Steam Engine Set	17.50	26.25	35.00
Erector Set No. 10181 Action Helicopter	50	75	100
Microscope Set No. 6, circa 1938 with Polaroid Jr. microscope, original manual, vials, test tube and other equipment	40	60	80
Mysto Erector Set No. 1, 1A, 2A, 3A. Price per each	60	90	120
No. 10053 Rocket Launcher, instructions, complete	100	150	200
Telegraph Outfit and instructions	10	15	20
Trumodel Set No. 77, 1929, instructions, complete	60	90	120
Wood Tool Box and Tools, complete	10	15	20

End GILBERT

	C6	C8	C10
"Acrobatic Monkey" John Henry Prod., 1950s, 10" long push toy	50	75	100
Air Raid Warden Junior Kit, felt hat, arm band, gas mask, whistle, window sign, forms and street-plan sheets, stethoscope, book of instructions, WW II era	40	60	80
All-Nu Horse, not made to have rider	10	15	20
Alligator, cast iron, 9"	10	15	20
Alligator, cast iron, two-part, 9" long	20	30	40
American Badge ring, circa 1930s or 1940s, heavy metal, may have been premium	10	15	20
American Logs - similar to Lincoln Logs, circa WW II, price includes box, instructions	20	30	40

	C6	C8	C10
American Toy Co. Dancing Black Women, two	600	900	1200
Animate Toy Co. "Baby Haymaker," 1916 tin push toy playset	90	135	180
"Anti-Aircraft Rapid-Fire Machine Gun," cast iron, on wheels	40	60	80

ARCADE "Don't Park Here" sign, 1920, 5" high
Courtesy Lloyd W. Ralston Auctions

ARCADE Cast Iron Highway Signs
Courtesy Continental Hobby House

ARCADE Tools

ARCADE Weapons

	C6	C8	C10
Arcade Bathroom Set, 3-piece, cast iron tub, stool, sink	30	45	60
Arcade cast iron highway sign, "Men Working Ahead"	25.00	37.50	50.00
Arcade cast iron highway sign, "Road Closed"	30	45	60
Arcade "Don't Park Here" cast iron sign, 4½" high	20	30	40
Arcade "Don't Park Here" sign, painted cast iron, 1920, 5" tall	25.00	37.50	50.00

	C6	C8	C10
Arcade Farm Wagon, "Whitehead & Kales Co.," 6½"	125.00	187.50	250.00
Arcade Garage	100	150	200
Arcade Gas Pump, 6"	35.00	52.50	70.00
Arcade Grand Piano and bench, 3"	80	120	160
Arcade tools, cast iron, No. 779N, small, nickel finish, screwdriver, hammer, monkey wrench, pipe wrench, crescent wrench and S wrench, came in set of 6, 1938. Price per each	4	6	8
Arcade Weapons, cast iron, No. 778N, small nickel finish, cutlass, pistol, automatic, aerial bomb, tommy gun, airplane, came in set of six, 1938. Price per each	10	15	20
Arcade Pump and Tub	60	90	120
Arcade Windmill, cast iron, 15¼" high	125.00	187.50	250.00
Arkitoy Play Lumber by G.B. Lewis Co., 1926, No. 3	20	30	40
Artascope, optical toy, circa 1920, pressed steel, spin base with multi-colors, see thru mirrors	60	90	120
Auburn Rubber Calf, circa 1937	3.50	5.25	7.00
Auburn Rubber Chicken, circa 1937	2.50	3.75	5.00
Auburn Rubber Collie, circa 1937	3.50	5.25	7.00
Auburn Rubber Colt, circa 1937	4	6	8
Auburn Rubber Cow, circa 1937	4	6	8
Auburn Rubber Duck, circa 1937	5.00	7.50	10.00
Auburn Rubber Fence Section, circa 1937	4	6	8
Auburn Rubber Horse, circa 1937	5.00	7.50	10.00
Auburn Rubber Pig, circa 1937	2.50	3.75	5.00
Auburn Rubber Piglet, circa 1937	6	9	12
Baby Buggy, cast iron, 4¼" high	25.00	37.50	50.00
Baby Carriage, tin, with folding cloth top, 7¾" long	40	60	80
Badge, "Dick Steel News Service"	20	30	40
Badge, G-Man, lead	5.00	7.50	10.00
Badge, Jet Ranger	6	9	12
Badge, Junior Counter Spy Agent with picture, No. 161731	10	15	20
Badge, "Junior Detective," heavy six-pointed star badge with copper insert, nickel badge	10	15	20
Badge, Junior G-Man, circa late 1930s, brass, shield-shaped, eagle on top	10	15	20
Badge, Junior Secret Agent, metal	12	18	24
Badge, "The Purple Mask" detective badge	10	15	20
Badge, "Sheriff," six-pointed star, black oval insert and word "Oklahoma," nickeled metal	18	27	36
Badge, Wyatt Earp Marshall, six-pointed	10	15	20
Baggage Cart, cast iron, 5" high	36	54	72

BALDWIN

Baldwin was located in Brooklyn, New York at 361 State Street. Its material was pressed steel.

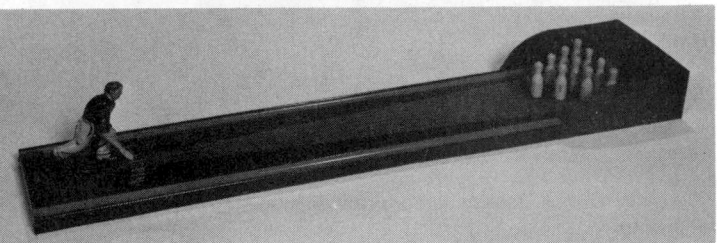

BALDWIN Kingpin, spring action.
Courtesy Scott Smiles, photo by Mike Adams

	C6	C8	C10
Baldwin Chicken on nest, marbles for eggs, 5" long	40	60	80
Baldwin Kingpin, spring action bowling	20	30	40
Baldwin "Little Red Hen," 1930s, crank action, 5" long	60	90	120
Barbed Wire (Army), 8" long, for toy soldiers	4	6	8
Barbed Wire, mesh, for toy soldiers	4	6	8
Barclay Searchlight, swivels on base, 3"	10	15	20

209   210   213   214

215   217   218   219   220   216?

	C6	C8	C10
Barclay No. 209 Work Horse	5.00	7.50	10.00
Barclay No. 210 Horse	5.00	7.50	10.00
Barclay No. 211 Grazing Horse	5.00	7.50	10.00
Barclay No. 212 Standing Cow	5.00	7.50	10.00
Barclay No. 213 Grazing Cow	5.00	7.50	10.00
Barclay No. 214 Lying Cow	5.00	7.50	10.00
Barclay No. 215 Bull	5.00	7.50	10.00
Barclay No. 216? Grazing Sheep	5.00	7.50	10.00
Barclay No. 217 Standing Sheep	5.00	7.50	10.00
Barclay No. 218 Resting Sheep	5.00	7.50	10.00
Barclay No. 219 Ram	5.00	7.50	10.00
Barclay No. 220 Pig	5.00	7.50	10.00
Barclay Mess Table, two benches (wooden)	20	30	40

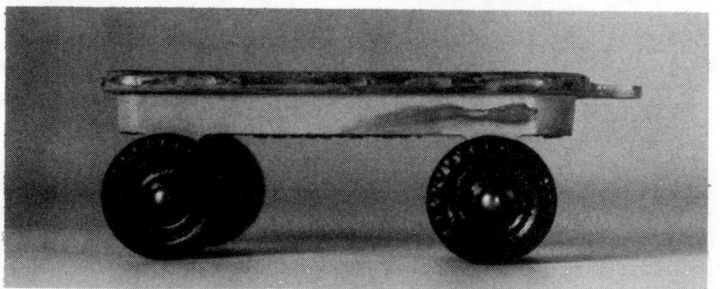

BEAUT MFG. CO. Wagon
Courtesy George Buhler, Photo by Bill Kaufman

	C6	C8	C10
Beaut Mfg. Co. Wagon No. 50	9.00	13.50	18.00
Bell Toy, Acrobats holding bells, Gong Bell No. 54	1400	2100	2800
Bell Toy, Alligator ridden by Black Boy, 5½" long, N. N. Hill, 1910, cast iron	1250	1875	2500
Bell Toy, Alligator Snapping at teasing boy, cast iron, 9¼" long	1300	1950	2600
Bell Toy, Althof Bergmann, tin "Chime & Design Patd. May 19th 1874," 3 women or boy soldiers, one with flag, two with rifles	1600	2400	3200
Bell Toy, bear, iron, bounces in air	400	600	800
Bell Toy, bear on tricycle, 4" long	150	225	300
Bell Toy, Billy Goat, Gong Bell No. 51, cast iron, goat mechanically butts bell, 7½" long, 1900	750	1125	1500
Bell Toy, bird and bell, tin and iron, 6" long	600	900	1200
Bell Toy, Boy and Goat, Althof Bergmann, tin 9" long	600	900	1200
Bell Ringer, Boy Scouts, iron, rest pressed steel, heart-shaped tin wheels, 13½" long	750	1125	1500
Bell Toy, Boys Eating Bananas, cast iron	700	1100	1400
Bell Toy, Cinderella Chariot, 9¼" long	750	1125	1500
Bell Toy, Clown and Pig, 1900, painted cast iron, 6¼" long	750	1125	1500
Bell Toy, Clown bell-ringers riding back to back on a mule	1000	1500	2000
Bell Toy, clown and black man on see-saw, circa 1905, 6½" long, six colors, Watrous, cast iron	600	900	1200
Bell Toy, Comic Characters, two, pressed steel and iron, 3 bells, pierced heart wheels	700	1125	1400
Bell Toy, "Ding Dong Bell, Pussy's Not In The Well," cast iron, c. 1880, 9½" long	600	900	1200
Bell Toy, Elephant on Platform, Fallows, 6¾" long	300	450	600
Bell Toy, Elephant with bell in trunk, N.N. Hill, circa 1905	600	900	1200
Bell Toy, "Eskimo & Bear," pressed steel body, iron figures	750	1125	1500
Bell Toy, Goat, Fallows, 1880, painted tin, 14" long x 14" tall	1100	1650	2200

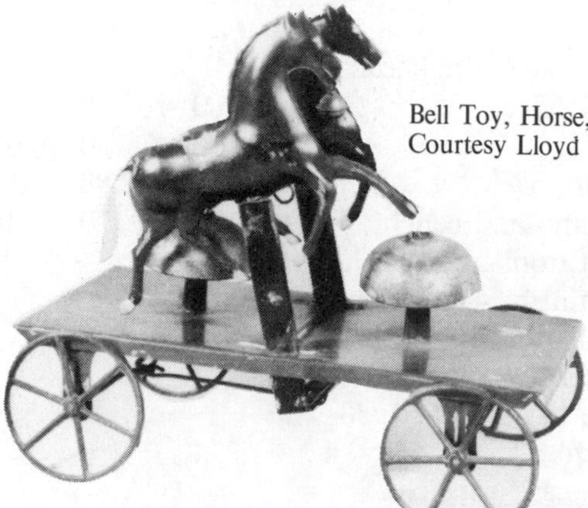

Bell Toy, Horse, FALLOWS, tin
Courtesy Lloyd W. Ralston Auctions

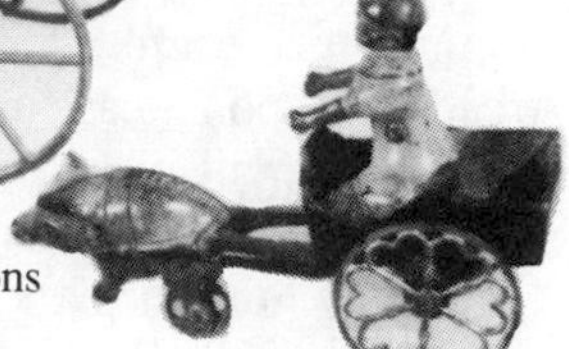

Bell Toy, Clown & Pig, 1900
Courtesy Lloyd W. Ralston Auctions

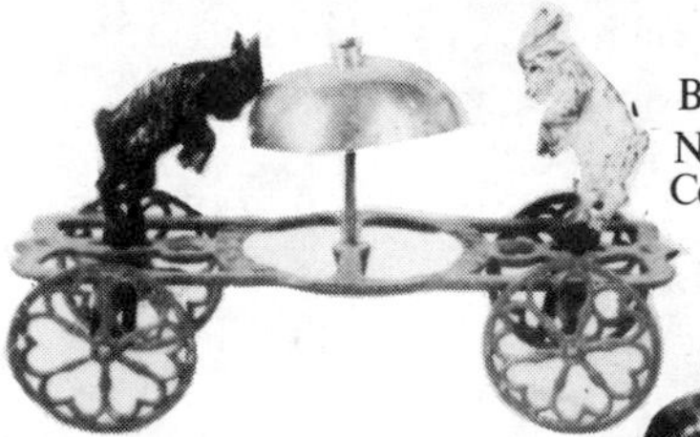

Bell Toy, Billy Goat, GONG BELL No. 51
Courtesy Lloyd W. Ralston Auctions

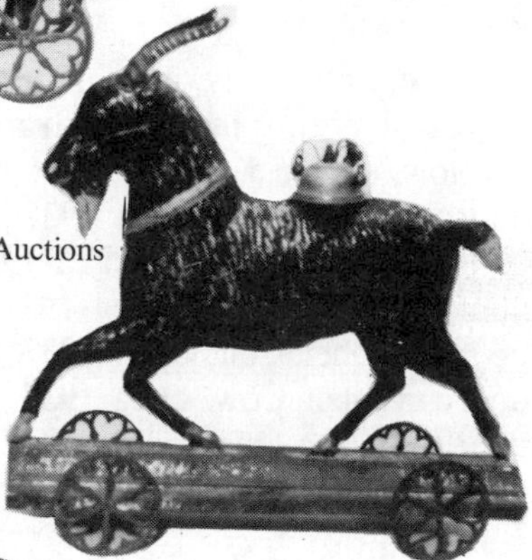

Bell Toy, Goat, FALLOWS
Courtesy Lloyd W. Ralston Auctions

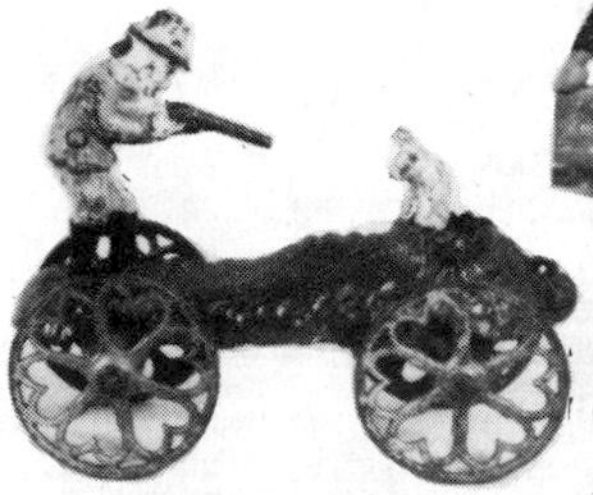

Bell Toy, Hunter and Rabbit, N.N. HILL
Courtesy Lloyd W. Ralston Auctions

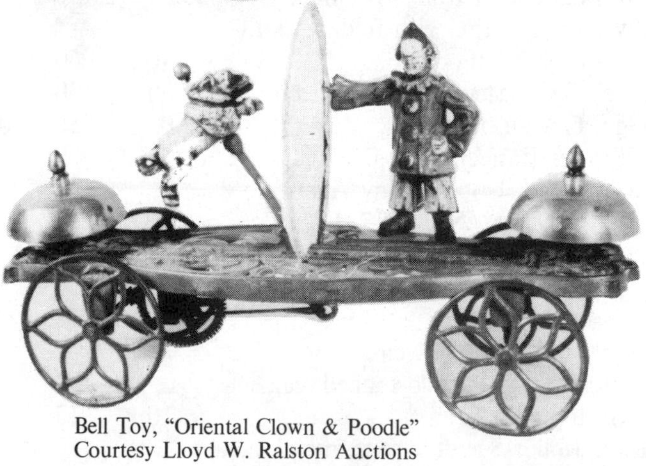

Bell Toy, "Oriental Clown & Poodle"
Courtesy Lloyd W. Ralston Auctions

CONDITION CODE:
C5 – Good, wear evident overall, shows that has been played with
C6 – Fine, shows some wear in spots, but taken care of
C7 – Very Fine, minor wear overall, very clean
C8 – Excellent, minor wear on edges only
C9 – Near Mint, no noticeable flaws, close inspection may show minute marks
C10 – Mint (like new)
Note: Mint in Box does command higher price

Bell Toy, Billy Goat, tin, circa 1890
Photo Courtesy PB Eighty-Four

Pull Toy, Sheep, tin, circa 1890
Photo Courtesy PB Eighty-Four

	C6	C8	C10
Bell Toy, Horse, tin, pulling heart-shaped wheels	200	300	400
Bell Toy, Ives, 9½" long, white horse pulling heart-shaped wheels, circa 1896	1000	1500	2000
Bell Toy, horse and rider, 9" long, heart-shaped wheels, tin	750	1125	1500
Bell Toy, Hunter and Rabbit, N.N. Hill, 1900, cast iron, rabbit pops out	750	1125	1500
Bell Toy, Jack and Jill on seesaw, 7½" long, cart iron and tin, Watrous	500	750	1000
Bell Toy, Jockey on Horse, early, 7½" long	200	300	400
Bell Toy "Landing of Columbus," 7" long	1000	1500	2000

Bell Toy, Monkey and Coconut, N.N. Hill
Courtesy Ed Hyers Antique Toys

Bell Toy, alligator ridden by black boy
Courtesy Ed Hyers Antique Toys

	C6	C8	C10
Bell Toy, Goat, Lamb and Girl on Platform, George Brown, tin, 11" long, early	750	1125	1500
Bell Toy, Goat, tin, circa 1890, small woman at left leg of goat, 7½" high, either Althof Bergmann or Ives	500	750	1000
Bell Toy, Horse, Fallows	450	675	900
Bell Toy, Horse, 9¼" long, tin	200	300	400

	C6	C8	C10
Bell Toy, Monkey and Coconut, N.N. Hill, 6" long "Monkey Mobile" . .	600	900	1200
Bell Toy, "Monkey and Dog," heart wheels, 7" long, cast iron and tin	500	750	1000
Bell Toy, Monkey on a Log, cast iron, Gong Bell Mfg. Co., circa 1900 . .	750	1125	1500
Bell Toy, Monkey on Tricycle, J&E Stevens, 8" high, cast iron	750	1125	1500
Bell Toy, Monkey Riding Elephant, Fallows, 10" long, tin, clockwork	1400	2100	2800
Bell Toy, Mule kicks bell, No. 42 . . .	600	900	1200
Bell Toy, nursery rhymes on drums, one horse	600	900	1200
Bell Toy, "Oriental Clown & Poodle," No. 44, painted cast iron, 1900, cloth in hoop, 13" long, poodle jumps through hoop and back . . .	1250	1875	2500
Bell Toy, Rough Rider, Watrous, 6½" long, early	90	135	180

457

Bell Toy, Clown and Pig, GONG BELL
Courtesy Ed Hyers Antique Toys

Bell Toy, Jack and Jill on seesaw, WATROUS
Courtesy Ed Hyers Antique Toys

Bell Toy, Monkey
Riding Elephant,
Fallows

Bell-Ringer, Trick Pony, GONG BELL CO., 1893
Photo Courtesy PB Eighty-Four

	C6	C8	C10
Bell Toy, Stevens, "Evening News Baby Quieter," 1890s cast iron, 8" long, man reading paper to baby .	2000	3000	4000
Bell Toy, "Teddy Roosevelt"	90	135	180
Bell Toy, Trick Pony, Gong Bell Co., 1893, "39," cast iron, 5¼" high .	600	900	1200
Bell Toy, Victory in a shell-form chariot, cast iron, mounted with bell and eagle	1500	2250	3000
Bell Toy, Watermelon, N.N. Hill Brass Co., circa 1905, 8½" long .	600	900	1200
Bell Toy, Wild Mule Jack, cast iron .	750	1125	1500
Bilt-E-Z Skyscraper Building Blocks, Scott Manufacturing, Chicago, circa 1925	90	135	180

	C6	C8	C10
Bliss Brooklyn Bridge, 1880s, 4' long x 11" tall, paper litho and stained wood, mechanical	600	900	1200
Blocks, Auburn Rubber building bricks, 1940s	35.00	52.50	70.00
Blocks, The Brownie, by McLoughlin Bros., 1891, 20 litho blocks	375	563	750
Blocks, Chautauqua Architectural Building No. 510, circa 1920s . . .	75.00	112.50	150.00
Blocks, Crandall's "Building Blocks" No. 3, pat. 1867	40	60	80
Blocks, Halsam American Plastic Bricks	12.50	18.75	25.00

458

Blocks, RICHTER'S ANCHOR BLOCKS No. 7
Courtesy Continental Hobby House

Bones Player
Courtesy Lloyd W. Ralston Auctions

BLISS Brooklyn Bridge
Courtesy Lloyd W. Ralston Auctions

	C6	C8	C10
Blocks Leecraft Circus Blocks, 12 wooden blocks, painted with lion, tiger, letters and numbers, contained in wooden pull-toy cage, 1930s	35.00	52.50	70.00
Blocks, Richter's Anchor Blocks No. 7	60	90	120
Blocks, "Stabuilt Blocks," The Embossing Co., 1916, 20x12"	42.50	63.75	85.00
Blocks, "Union Building Blocks" No. 7, early	75.00	112.50	150.00
Blocks, set of six puzzle blocks depicting The Three Bears, Old Mother Hubbard, Little Bo-Peep, Puss in Boots, Jack the Giant Killer and Red Riding Hood. Copyright 1892	35.00	52.50	70.00
Blocks, nested, 6, paper litho on cardboard, picturing children and animals, 1920, Cramer Publishing Co.	20	30	40
Blocks, 16, embossed, wooden, 1¾" square, red and blue, alphabet and pictures, 7½" square box, Dutch scene on cover, The Embossing Company's Toy Blocks, USA, price includes box	20	30	40
Blocks, 64, wooden, 1¼" square, very colorful, letters and numbers on sides, box 6" square, price includes box	22.50	33.75	45.00
Bones Player, Secor, 1880, cloth-dressed, cast iron, wood and tin figure with hair, painted pot metal-head, clockwork mechanism in body	1250	1875	2500
Boo Berry, rubber squeeze toy	4	6	8
Boxers, Black, mechanical wind-up with Ives clockwork mechanism	1000	1500	2000
Boy climbing windmill, tin, weight driven, 16" high, 1900s	100	150	200

	C6	C8	C10
Boy on Sled friction toy, rear wheels have spokes	65.00	97.50	130.00
Boy on Tricycle, boy celluloid, trike tin, wind-up	125.00	187.50	250.00
Boy on Velocipede, papier mache, cloth and cast iron, wind-up, Stevens & Brown, or Althorp & Bergmann, circa 1870-1880, 10¾" long	500	750	1000
Boy Scout Five-In-One Mystery Hidden Compass	30	45	60
Bradley's Interchangeable Combination Circus in wooden box with label. Patented May 30, 1882. Contains 35 3"x5¼" interchangeable panels which make up a changeable 15¾"x9" circus scene	400	600	800
Brownies, Brownie Glass Candy Container	500	750	1000
Buddy L. tool chests, 1927-28, four different, per each, includes tools	125.00	187.50	250.00

BUFFALO TOYS Mother Duck
Photo by Don Hultzman

	C6	C8	C10
Buffalo Toys "Mother Duck," 1930s wind-up (figure 8s), 9" long	40	60	80
Bulldog, kid-covered wind-up, walks and turns head, 7½" long, German	150	225	300
Cackling Hen, cardboard, drum, 2¼"x3½", with brown plaster chicken standing on top of drum, metal side handle activates cackling, dated 1936	10	15	20
Candy Container, tin, shaped like cannon, candy comes out barrel when crank is turned, "West Bros. Co. Grapeville, Pa.," 7½" long	60	90	120
Candy Container shaped like a desk phone, glass base with cast pewter mouthpiece and wooden receiver, paper labels "lines busy," 4¼" high	10	15	20
Cannon, "Admiral Dewey," cast iron, c. 1890s, 11" long	110	165	220
Cannon, Arcade howitzer, 4" long, circa 1941	13.00	19.50	26.00
Cannon, Auburn Rubber (Aubrubr) Fieldpiece, 75mm, 7" long	12.50	18.75	25.00
Cannon, Auburn Rubber Howitzer, 155mm, 7" long	12.50	18.75	25.00
Cannon, Baldwin, No. 890, 16" long, wood and metal	20	30	40
Cannon, Barclay, barrel elevated, 2½" long	9.00	13.50	18.00
Cannon, Barclay, circa 1931 (may be first Barclay cannon, from 1924) .	20	30	40
Cannon, Barclay Coast Defense Rifle, 4½" long, 5-man	30	45	60
Cannon, Barclay, Howitzer, 4 wheels, loop hitch horizontal, 3" long ...	9.00	13.50	18.00
Cannon, Barclay Howitzer, 4 wheels, loop hitch vertical, 3" long	5.50	8.25	11.00
Cannon, Barclay Mortar, heavy, swivels on base, 3" long	20	30	40
Cannon, Barclay, 4" long, Post WW II, very large wheels	10	15	20
Cannon, Barclay, silver, black rubber wheels, 7¾" long	15.00	22.50	30.00
Cannon, Barclay, spoked wheels, 3" long	6	9	12
Cannon, Barclay, spring-firing, spoked wheels, 4" long	6	9	12
Cannon, Big Bang, 8½" long	20	30	40
Cannon, Big Bang, 9" long	20	30	40
Cannon, Big Bang, 12" long	30	45	60
Cannon, Big Bang, 13"	30	45	60
Cannon, Big Bang, 16" long	20	30	40
Cannon, Big Bang, No. 10, 18" long .	30	45	60
Cannon, Big Bang, 23" long	40	60	80
Cannon, Big Bang, 24" long	40	60	80
Cannon, Big Parade, cast iron	25.00	37.50	50.00

Cannon, "Big Bang", approx. 23" long
Photo by Bill Kaufman, Courtesy Good Old Days Store

Cannon, BARCLAY, circa 1931 (may be Barclay's earliest, from 1924)
Courtesy Ed Poole

BARCLAY, top row, L to R: Cannon, spring-firing, spoked wheels, 4" long, Cannon, barrel elevated, Cannon, spoked wheels, 3" long, Cannon, 7¾" long. Bottom row, L to R: Coast Defense Rifle, Mortar, heavy, Searchlight
Photo by Ed Poole

	C6	C8	C10
Cannon, "Boy Ranger," fires marbles, cast iron	66	99	132
Cannon, "Boy Scout Machine Gun," 19" with 8¼" wheels	40	60	80
Cannon, cast iron, 5" long	10	15	20
Cannon, cast iron on wood base, 5½" long	10	15	20
Cannon, cast iron, 6" long	15.00	22.50	30.00
Cannon, cast iron, 6½" long	18	27	36
Cannon, cast iron, 7" long, early	30	45	60
Cannon, cast iron, 7" long, pat. 1894	30	45	60
Cannon, cast iron, 8" long, unusual design	30	45	60
Cannon, cast iron, 9" long, Pat. 1888	40	60	80
Cannon, cast iron with turned barrel, "Hotchkiss," 9½" long	30	45	60
Cannon, cast iron, 10" long, black ...	32	48	64
Cannon, cast iron 11" long	40	60	80
Cannon, cast iron, 12" long, Ives?, works on black powder	60	90	120

	C6	C8	C10
Cannon, cast iron, 14" long	50	75	100
Cannon, cast iron, 14" long, on 4-wheel platform	30	45	60
Cannon, cast iron, 15½"	30	45	60
Cannon, cast iron, 15½", "Young America," "Rapid Fire Gun"	80	120	160
Cannon, Coast Defense Gun, 5" long, camouflaged, litho tin	30	45	60
Cannon, "Dainty" cast iron, on wood base, 10" long	100	150	200
Cannon, David Carlin mortar, circa WW I, 15" long, cast iron	60	90	120
Cannon, die cast, approx. 5½" long, old type, shoots	10	15	20
Cannon "Disappearing Coast Defense Gun," Thomas & Skinner, Indianapolis, 15"wood and steel, fires	40	60	80
Cannon, field, World War I, cast iron, 15¾"	32.50	48.75	65.00
Cannon, firecracker, cast iron, 4" long, "Pat. Apr. 23 1895"	40	60	80
Cannon, Grey Iron, 4½" long	7.00	10.50	14.00
Cannon – Howitzer, circa 1930, double-barreled, 9" long, wood-handled firing lever	15.00	22.50	30.00
Cannon, howitzer type, die cast, shoots, approx. 5" long, spring mechanism, pre WW II	9.00	13.50	18.00
Cannon, Ideal, 1920s	10	15	20
Cannon, Ives, muzzle-loader, 1900, cast iron, 2 wheels	75.00	112.50	150.00
Cannon, Ives, cast iron, brass barrel .	25.00	37.50	50.00
Cannon, Ives, red wheels, brass cannon, 7" long	50	75	100

Cannon. KANSAS TOY & NOVELTY. L to R: No. 34, No. 23. These are the same as the later Ralstoy cannons, but the platform on No. 23 is different and wheels on No. 34 different (metal here)
Photo by Fred Maxwell

	C6	C8	C10
Cannon, Kansas Toy "23"	6	9	12
Cannon, Kansas Toy "34"	6	9	12
Cannon, Kenton, Firecracker type ...	40	60	80
Cannon, Kilgore, 2" cast iron firecracker mortar, rubber cannon ball	40	60	80
Cannon, Kilgore, 4½" cast iron firecracker cannon, rubber cannon ball	50	75	100

	C6	C8	C10
Cannon, Manoil 19 Metal Action Cannon, early version, "USA" ...	5.00	7.50	10.00
Cannon, Manoil 69, metal spoked wheels, early	5.00	7.50	10.00
Cannon, Manoil 69, metal spoked wheels, marked "M" left side, early 2nd version	5.00	7.50	10.00
Cannon, Manoil 69, solid wood wheels	6	9	12
Cannon, Manoil 69, solid wood wheels, variant	6	9	12
Cannon, Manoil "Metal Action Cannon" No. 200, later version of 19, "Made in USA"	4.50	6.75	9.00

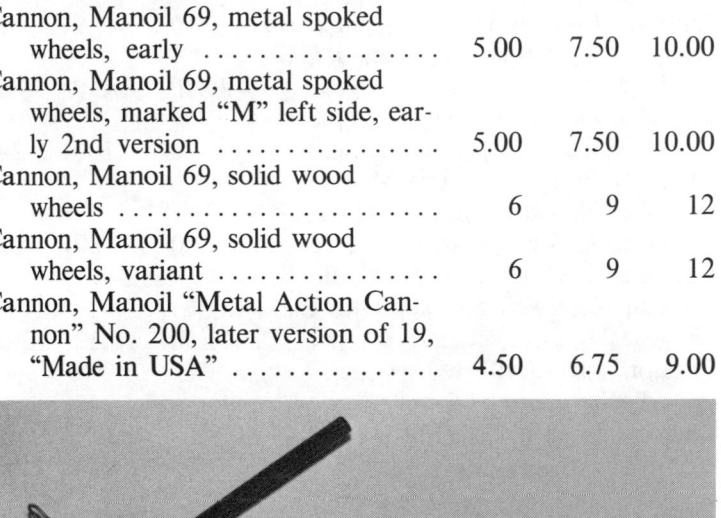

Cannon, MARX Anti-Aircraft Gun
Courtesy Joe and Sharon Freed

Cannon, MARX. 21" long, litho tin, shoots wooden balls
Courtesy Charles D. Richards

	C6	C8	C10
Cannon, Marx, 21" long, litho tin, shoots wooden balls	100	150	200
Cannon, Marx Anti-Aircraft Gun, No. 617	30	45	60
Cannon, Marx "Shell Shooting Long Tom Field Cannon," 1950s, 14" long, plastic	30	45	60
Cannon, "Phoenix," 8" long, brass barrel with touch hole	100	150	200
Cannon, Premier, large thick barrel, large wheels, cast iron	15.00	22.50	30.00
Cannon, pressed steel base, 9½"-	15.00	22.50	30.00

	C6	C8	C10
Cannon, Ralstoy No. 23	6	9	12
Cannon, Ralstoy No. 34	6	9	12
Cannon, Ralstoy 3¾" long	6	9	12
Cannon, Ranger Jr. cast iron, 10" long	45.00	67.50	90.00
Cannon, rapid fire, cast iron, embossed eagle	120	180	240
Cannon, "Remember The Maine," W.S. Hawkes Foundry, Dayton, Ohio, 13" long, circa 1900	120	180	240
Cannon, sheetmetal, shoots small marbles, 14" long, blue with red wheels	11.00	16.50	22.00
Cannon, silver, with red wooden wheels, approx. 3" long	6	9	12
Cannon, tin, pull lever for corks, 14" wood wheels	20	30	40
Cannon, tin, striped spring-loaded barrel with lever	20	30	40
Cannon, tin, two-wheel, 7¼", 4" high, circa 1915	30	45	60
Cannon, tinplate, 7" long, spring action	7.50	11.25	15.00
Cannon, Tootsietoy, approx. 3¾" long, pre WW II, shoots	6	9	12
Cannon, Tootsietoy, 40MM AA gun, pre WW II	6	9	12
Cannon, Tootsietoy, 155 MM gun, pre WW II	8	12	16
Cannon, Tootsietoy, 155 MM self-propelled howitzer, 1950s	6	9	12
Cannon, Tootsietoy, 1930s, approx. 5½" long, shoots	20	30	40
Cannon, Wyandotte, shoots marbles, 14"	20	30	40
Canoe, Kansas Toy and Novelty, slush lead, "50", two paddling Indians "Rain-In-The-Face" and "Chief Big Foot," 4 wheels	No Price Found		

Carousel, ALTHOF BERGMANN, 1870
Courtesy Lloyd W. Ralston Auctions

	C6	C8	C10
Carousel, Althof Bergmann, 1870, painted tin, wood base, cloth canopy, 20" tall, clockwork, bisque head doll, wood body, tin arms, turns, cranks and gives motion ..	1500	2250	3000

	C6	C8	C10
Carpet Sweeper, miniature Bissell ...	10	15	20
Cat, cardboard, standing on piece of wood, circa 1900	3.00	4.50	6.00
Catalog: Auburn Rubber, pre WW II	50	75	100
Catalog: Baltimore Price Reducer, 1928, illustrated with toys, games, etc.	15.00	22.50	30.00
Catalog: Barclay, pre-WW II	200	300	400
Catalog: Bilt E-Z, 1924	5.00	7.50	10.00
Catalog: Butler Bros. 1889, tin toys, squeak toys, etc.	30	45	60
Catalog: Butler Bros. 1891, illustrated with mechanical banks, toys, dolls, etc.	30	45	60
Catalog: Butler Bros. 1930, illustrated with toys, banks, etc.	40	60	80
Catalog: Dent Hardware Co., 1900, 40 pages	40	60	80
Catalog: Dent Hardware Co., 1905 ..	30	45	60
Catalog: Dent Hardware Co., Fullerton, Pa., undated	30	45	60
Catalog: Dent Hardware Co, Fullerton, Pa. iron toys	30	45	60
Catalog: "Dunham", Buckley & Co., New York, 1895, toys, etc.	40	60	80
Catalog: Ehrich Bros., New York, 1892, illus of banks, toys, dolls, etc.	40	60	80
Catalog: Eureka Trick & Novelty Co., circa 1875, 32 pages	20	30	40
Catalog: A.J. Fisher, N.Y. 1877, illustrating cap pistols, etc.	18	27	36
Catalog: Ives Yachts, Ships and Shipping, circa 1915, 24 pages	50	75	100
Catalog: Illustrated brochure of cap pistols and animated cap pistols by Ives and Williams	20	30	40
Catalog: Kenton Hardware Co., No. 16, 1920s, 112 pages	80	120	160
Catalog: Kenton Hardware Co., 1934, illus. in color	100	150	200
Catalog: Kingsbury Toys, Motor Driven, 1936, 16 pages	60	90	120
Catalog: Knapp Electric Toys No. 35	10	15	20
Catalog: Manoil, circa 1935-1939	100	150	200
Catalog: "McCadden & Bros." Philadelphia, llustrated iron and tin toys, banks, mechanical toys, dolls, games, etc.	50	75	100
Catalog: Mickey Mouse Merchandise Catalog, 1935, by Kay Kamen Co., 80 pages, hundreds of illustrations of Mickey Mouse items	300	450	600
Catalog: Nicol & Co., 1895, illustrating banks, etc.	10	15	20
Catalog: Popsicle Pete Radio News and Premium catalog, early	40	60	80
Catalog: Popsicle Pete's 1949 four-page gift list	10	15	20

	C6	C8	C10
Catalog: Schoenhut 1903	100	150	200
Catalog: Schoenhut 1918	80	120	160
Catalog: Schoenhut Circus, 1928	100	150	200
Catalog: Schoenhut Humpty Dumpty Circus Toys (other toys as well), circa 1915, many illustrations ...	100	165	220
Catalog: Selchow & Righter, 1894-5, games and toys, illustrated trains, boats, bell toys, mechanical banks, etc.	120	180	240
Catalog: Selchow & Righter, 1908-1909, 108 pages	80	120	160

Catalog: SMITH-MILLER (Smitty), 1954
Photo by Bill Kaufman
Courtesy Ray Funk

	C6	C8	C10
Catalog: Smith-Miller (Smitty) 1954 ..	40	60	80
Catalog: State, Adams & Dearborn Sts., Chicago, illustrated	10	15	20
Catalog: Carl P. Stern, illustrating cap pistols, etc.	15.00	22.50	30.00
Catalog: J.E. Stevens Co., 1906, illustrations of iron toys and mechanical banks	40	60	80
Catalog: J.E. Stevens Co., No. 51, Export	40	60	80
Catalog: Structo Toys, 1931, 8 pages	10	15	20
Catalog: Supplee-Biddle of Philadelphia, 1936, 180 pages, many toys	70	105	140
Catalog: Thorsen & Cassady, 1894, guns, etc.	20	30	40
Catalog: Tom Mix 1936 Premium Catalog	30	45	60
Catalog: Ward's 1953 Xmas Catalog, 318 pp	30	45	60
Catalog: Ward's 1955 Xmas Catalog, 296 pp	30	45	60
Catalog: A.C. Williams Co., Ohio, illustrating still banks, cast iron toys, airplanes, etc.	100	150	200
Catalog: Walt Disney Character Merchandise 1940-41	200	300	400
Catalog: Woolworth's Christmas Catalogs, pre WW II	30	45	60
Catalog: Woolworth's Christmas 1951	30	45	60

	C6	C8	C10
Cathedral Music Box, tin litho, of organ pipes and cherubs, plays loud or soft according to speed of cranking, 5x5x7" no markings, German	70	105	140
Charlie Tuna rubber squeeze toy	6	9	12

CHEIN "Busy Mike" sand seesaw.
Courtesy Calvin L. Chaussee

	C6	C8	C10
Chein "Busy Mike," sand seesaw, 7½" high, 1940s	90	135	180
Chein Cathedral Organ	70	105	140
Chein Drum, 6"x3½"	10	15	20
Chein Easter Egg with chicken on top, opens up to hold candy, circa 1938, tin, 5½"	8	12	16
Chein Helicopter, "Toy Town Airways," 1950s, 13" long, friction drive	40	60	80
Chein Sand-Toy, monkey bends and twists, 7" high	20	30	40
Chemcraft Beginners Chemistry Set No. 602 by Porter, 1956	20	30	40
Chicago Printing Press, No. 15, complete	20	30	40
Children's Telephone (set of two), 1920	10	15	20
Chimes Bell-Ringer with Elephant, 7" long	40	60	80
Climbing Monkey brings coconuts down from palm tree, tin, 18" high, "Monkey Shines, Emporium Specialists"	60	90	120
Clock, tin, transfer scene of coach and four, works with small pendulum, "Lux Clock Mfg. Co., Waterbury, Conn. USA," 7" high	40	60	80

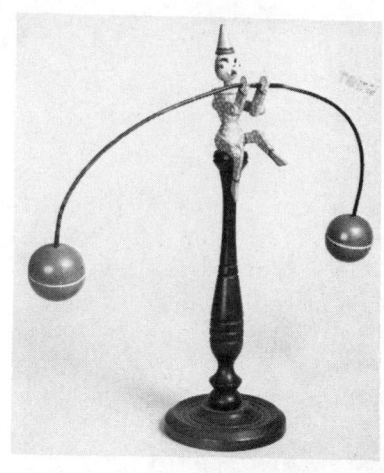

Clown, balancing on pedestal, painted wood, circa 1920, 15" high
Courtesy Mapes Auctioneers & Appraisers

COURTLAND 9050 Fire Department
Courtesy Joe and Sharon Freed

	C6	C8	C10
Clown, balancing, copper, clown holding arched balancing pole weighted at both ends with lead balls, standing on one leg on small round platform on stationary metal ladder 6½" high. Move clown in any direction and he won't fall off platform	50	75	100
Clown, balancing on pedestal, painted wood, circa 1920, 15" high	100	150	200
Clown, clockwork, early, cloth suit, 9½" high, German	300	450	600
Clown, wind-up, papier mache and cardboard, 43" high	90	135	180
Coffee Grinder, cast iron, 4" high ...	40	60	80
"Consul," the educated monkey, tin hand toy, monkey automatically adds, subtracts, multiplies and divides, 5½"x6", dated June 27, 1916	40	60	80
Cot, Army, canvas with steel frame, circa early 1940s	5.00	7.50	10.00
Count Chocula, rubber squeeze toy ..	5.00	7.50	10.00

COURTLAND TOYS
(Numerical Order)
List by Joe and Sharon Freed

	C6	C8	C10
800 Zylo-P-ano. 13¼" long, 5½" wide, 1946 retail - 79¢; 1947 retail - 69¢	35	65	100
1000 Walt Reach Toys G-Man Pocket Siren Signal, 3½" long, 2⅜" wide, 1¾" high	20	25	35
1050 Courtland Walt Reach Toys Halloween Pocket Siren Signal, 3½" long, 2⅜" wide, 1¾" high ..	30	40	55
1060 Courtland Walt Reach Toys New Years Pocket Siren Signal, 3½" long, 2⅜" wide, 1¾" high ..	20	25	35
9000 Mechanical 3 pc. Train set, 24" long, 2¼" wide, 3¼" high	45	60	80

	C6	C8	C10
9050 Fire Department with automatic garage door. 7¾"x10⅛"x6¾"; found to have a non-powered fire chief car with the Courtland Toy Co., Phila. Pa., markings, it is quite possible that some of the 9050 garages were also manufactured in Philadelphia	25	35	45
9075 Private Garage with automatic door, 7¾"x10⅛"x6¾". Since the non-powered car which accompanies this garage is found with Courtland Toy Co., Phila. Pa. markings, it is quite possible that some of the 9075 garages were also manufactured in Philadelphia.	15	25	35
Crackle (Kellogg's Rice Krispies) hand-puppet	10	15	20
Crackle (Kellogg's Rice Krispies) squeeze toy, 8½"	6	9	12

> **CONDITION CODE:**
> C5 – Good, wear evident overall, shows that has been played with
> C6 – Fine, shows some wear in spots, but taken care of
> C7 – Very Fine, minor wear overall, very clean
> C8 – Excellent, minor wear on edges only
> C9 – Near Mint, no noticeable flaws, close inspection may show minute marks
> C10 – Mint (like new)
>   Note: Mint in Box does command higher price

CRANDALL "Crandall's District School", circa 1875
Courtesy Ed Hyers Antique Toys

	C6	C8	C10
Crandall "Crandall's District School," circa 1875	375.00	562.50	750.00
Cupboard, cast iron, open work has diamond and heart pattern, two doors and one drawer	40	60	80

Dancers, black, AUTOMATIC TOY WORKS, 1870
Courtesy Lloyd W. Ralston Auctions

	C6	C8	C10
Dancers, black Automatic Toy Works, New York City, 1870, on box, clockwork, carved wood and jesso bodies, clothes, 6¼"w x 10¼"t	600	900	1200
"Davy Crockett Alamo Express Fix-It Stage Coach," 1950s, Ideal, 13" long push toy	50	75	100
Davy Crockett Indian Target set by Keystone Wood Company. David Crockett rifle, all wood and hardboard litho set that pre-dates Davy popularity of the 50s, made about 1949. Wood stagecoach and horses, wood covered wagon and horses, Indians, bear, etc.	20	30	40

	C6	C8	C10
Doctor's Set, Transogram, 1948, Little Country Doctor, full doctor set, chest and bag	20	30	40
Doepke No. W-11 Freddie Fireplug, wooden, comes apart	No Price Found		
Drum, metal body, litho, red white and blue design, varnished wooden hoops, leather "ears," sheepskin head and fiber bottom, with wooden drumsticks, circa 1910	20	30	40
Drum, about 1920, circus decor, tin litho	40	60	80
Drum, 13" diameter, metal with drumsticks	10	15	20
Drum, 13" diameter, wooden, with harness	10	15	20
Electric Stove, works, 1930s	20	30	40
Ferris Wheel, "DRGM," 11½" high, four figures, tin, 1895, sold for $2500 in July, 1988			
Ferris Wheel, made for World Columbian Exposition in Chicago, 1893, 20" high, clockwork motor, lead passengers	1000	1500	2000
Flagpole, wooden, with flag that raises and lowers, approx. 8" high	20	30	40
Flying Propellor Ring, heavy metal, circa 1930s-40s, could have been a premium	10	15	20
Fort, Keystone No. 523 U.S. Coast Defense Fort	35	50	70
Fort, Keystone No. 525 U.S. Coast Defense Fort, with accessories, circa 1942	40	55	80

465

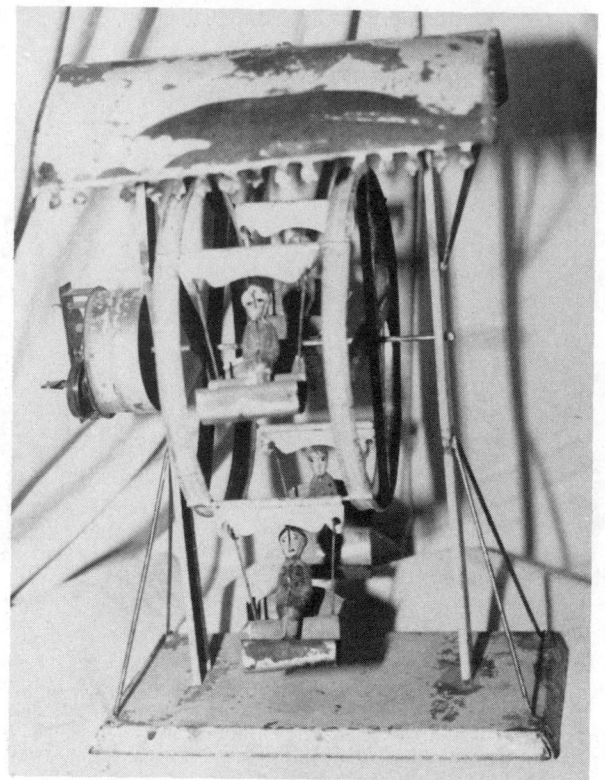

	C6	C8	C10
Fort, Keystone No. 527 U.S. Coast Guard Defense Fort, with accessories, circa 1942	40	70	100
Fort, Keystone No. 531, 12" long ...	40	60	85
Fort, Keystone No. 533, same as 531, but two electric lights at entrance	50	75	100
Fort, Keystone No. 535, 20" long, with two electric lights at entrance	60	90	120
Fort, Rich Toys No. 245 Siege Gun with Stone Fort	25	40	75
Fort, Rich Toys No. 246 Siege Gun with Stone Fort, two guns	30	50	80
Fort, Rich Toys No. 247 Siege Gun with stone fort, three guns	40	60	80
Fort, Rich Toys No. 260, 26¾" long	35	50	75

Ferris Wheel, "DRGM", 11½" high. First bought in 1895.
Courtesy Calvin L. Chaussee

WOOD SOLDIER FORTS
WITH SHOOTING CANNONS
WITH AND WITHOUT ELECTRIC LIGHTS

Shipped all
set up

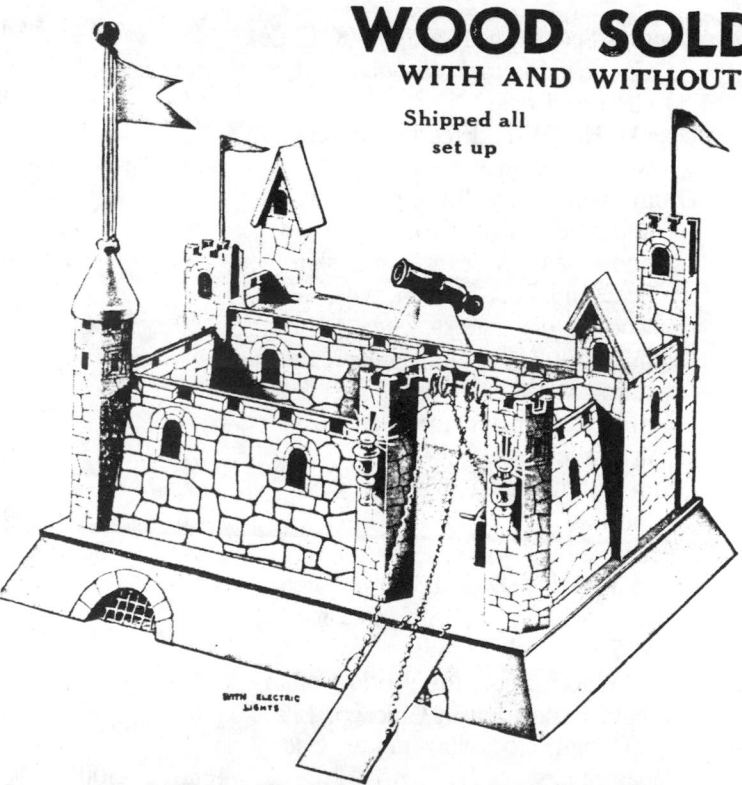

NO. 535—FORT 20" LONG with Electric Light

An all wood fort mounted on wood base, decorated in gray stone walls and towers, green base, orange roof and colored turrets tops and shield. Equipped with draw-bridge, winch, swivel shooting cannon, pennants, movable flag, fire step in court yard, moat gratings and electric entrance lamps connected to batteries and operated by switch in tower tops. Size: 20" long, 17" wide and 19" high. Weight when packed in Mullen-test carton 12 lbs. No battery furnished.

NO. 531—FORT 12" LONG

An all wood fort decorated in gray stone walls and towers, orange roof and colored coat of arms. Equipped with detachable chain barrier, pennants and shooting swivel cannon on roof. Size 12" long, 7½" wide, 11" high. Weight when packed for shipment 4 lbs.

NO. 533—FORT with Electric Light

Same as No. 531 with **electric entrance lamps** connected to battery and operated by switch on the roof. Weight when packed in Mullen-test carton 5 lbs. No battery furnished.

KEYSTONE MFG. CO., BOSTON, MASS.   **New York Showroom, 200 Fifth Avenue**

Forts by KEYSTONE, showing No. 535 and 533.   Original catalog illustration courtesy Ron Fink

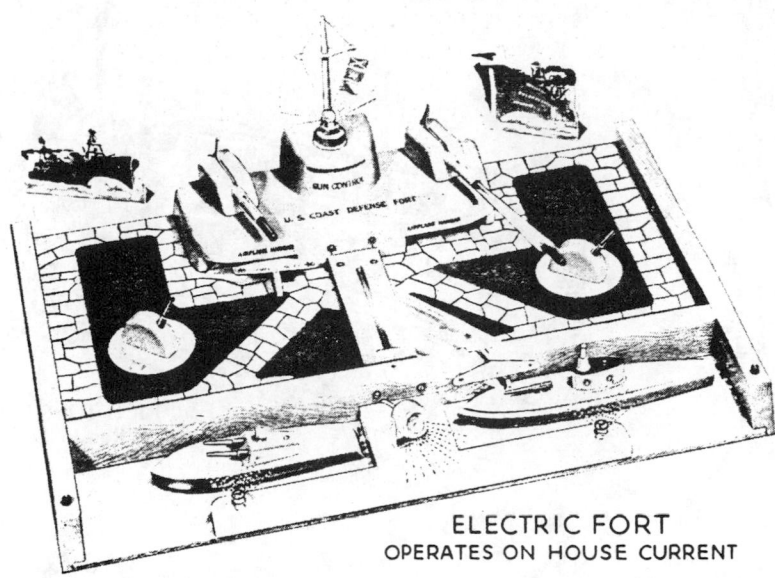

ELECTRIC FORT
OPERATES ON HOUSE CURRENT

- *Planes That Fly!*
- *Swivel Guns That Shoot!*
- *Electric Flashing Signals!*
- *Electric Searchlight!*
- *Electric Pier Lights!*
- *Turret Guns That Turn!*
- *Two Boats That Float!*
- *Two Airplane Hangars!*
- *Soldier Housing in Rear!*
- *Played From Front or Back With or Without Soldiers!*

No. 527 — U. S. COAST DEFENSE FORT

Two Flying Planes operated with catapult. *Pier and signal lights work off regular house current A.C.* Target and patrol ships and shells furnished for shooting cannons. Made of wood and fibre board. No assembling. Finished in gray, tan, green base and blue trim. Each boxed in shipping carton. Weight 175 lbs. per dozen. Size 24 x 17.

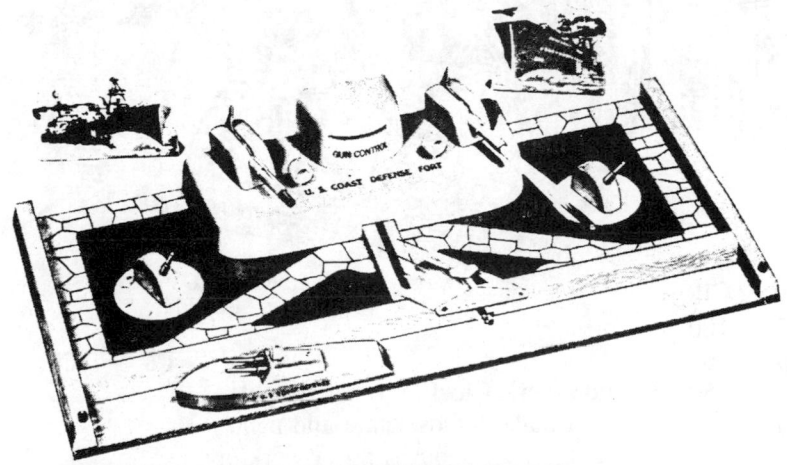

- *Plane That Flies!*
- *Swivel Guns That Shoot!*
- *Turret Guns That Turn!*
- *Boat That Floats!*
- *Soldier Housing in Rear!*
- *Battleship Target for Cannons!*
- *Play From Front or Rear With or Without Soldiers!*

No. 525 — U. S. COAST DEFENSE FORT

One Flying Plane operated with catapult. Target and scout ship and shells furnished for shooting cannons. Made of wood and fibre board. No assembling. Size 24 x 12. Finished in gray, tan, green and blue trim. Each in shipping carton. Weight 65 lbs. per dozen.

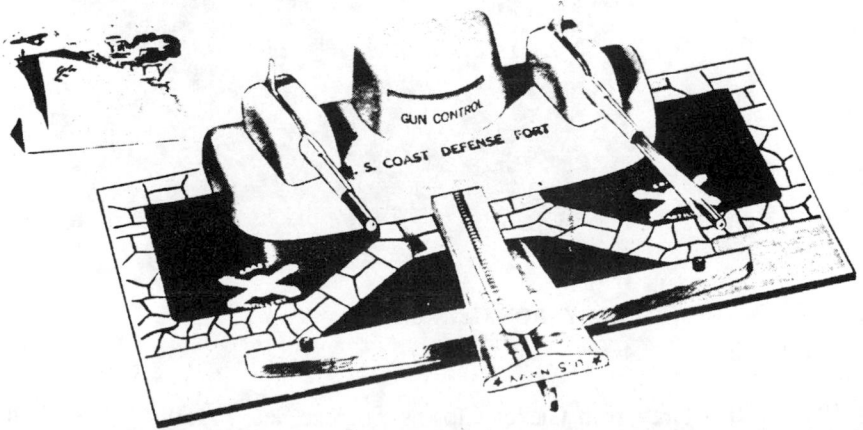

- *Plane That Flies!*
- *Swivel Guns That Shoot!*
- *Soldier Housing in Rear!*
- *Battleship Target for Cannons!*
- *Played From Front or Rear With or Without Soldiers!*

No. 523
U. S. COAST DEFENSE FORT

All wood and fibre board fort 16" x 8". Equipped with flying plane and catapult, ship target and shells for swivel shooting guns. All assembled each in a carton. Colors same as other models. Weight 30 lbs. per dozen.

KEYSTONE MFG. CO., BOSTON, MASS.
NEW YORK SHOW ROOM, 200 FIFTH AVENUE

Fort, RICH TOYS No. 260
Courtesy Ron Fink

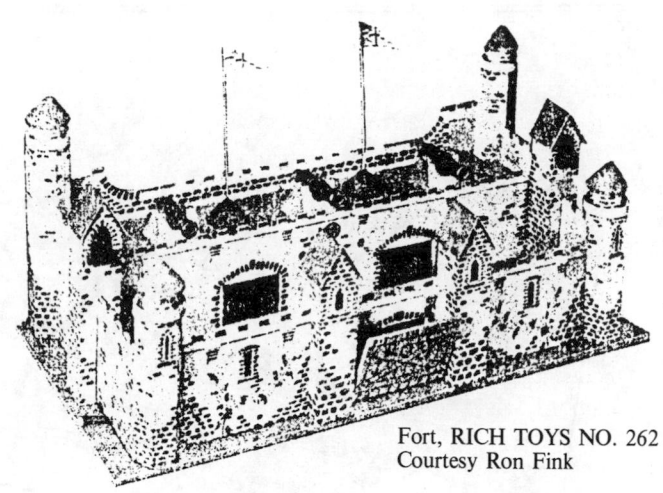

Fort, RICH TOYS NO. 262
Courtesy Ron Fink

Fort, RICH TOYS, No. 261
Courtesy Ron Fink

Fort, RICH TOYS No. 263
Courtesy Ron Fink

	C6	C8	C10
Fort, Rich Toys No. 261, 26½" long	50	75	100
Fort, Rich Toys No. 262, 27" long ..	100	200	300
Fort, Rich Toys No. 263, 29" long ..	150	250	350
Frankenberry rubber squeeze toy	4	6	8
Froggie, rubber squeeze toy, Rempel, 1940s	12	18	24
Fruit Brute, rubber squeeze toy	4	6	8
Girard "Knife Sharpener," crank action, 8" high, 1930s	60	90	120
Glass Candy Container, shaped like Biplane	500	750	1000
Glass Candy Container shaped like dog	40	60	80
Glass Candy Container, Dolly's milk bottle	4	6	8
Glass Candy Container, shaped like rabbit, Victory Glass	20	30	40
Glass Candy Container shaped like train engine, 3" long	10	15	20
Glass Candy Container shaped like a train lantern, 3½" high	10	15	20
Glass Candy Container, Stop and Go, glass, etc. traffic signal	100	150	200
Glass Candy Container, shaped like a train lantern, tin top and base, "Victory Glass Inc.", 3½" high ..	10	15	20

	C6	C8	C10
Grandfather's Clock, tin, has weights that make hands rotate and pendulum swing, but is not a working clock, transfer decorated, 8¾" high	40	60	80

GREY IRON Clever Clowns

	C6	C8	C10
Grey Iron Clever Clowns Trapeze Set	150	225	300
Grey Iron, Clever Clowns largest set .	500	750	1000

468

	C6	C8	C10
Grocery Store, tin, 14", scales, cash register, wrapping paper, order pad and pencil, "Little Toy Town Grocery Store," shelves with small boxes of products	100	150	200
Grocery Store, wood, "Pet's Grocery Store"	400	600	800
H.K. Electric Engine, patented 1908, uses D.C. current	50	75	100
Handwashing Machine with wringer	10	15	20
Hasbro, "Mr. Potato Head," 1950s, plastic car and boat trailer, plus all the parts to create different faces	10	15	20
Hasbro "Mr. Potato Head Funny-Face Kit," early 1960s	12	18	24
Hess Dynamobil	200	300	400
Hitch, Dent, two-horse, cast iron, 14¼"	50	75	100
Hobby Horse, "Black Beauty," wooden, 34" long	25.00	37.50	50.00
"Hometown Favorite Store," S.S. Kresge Co., Marx tin litho	100	150	200
"Home Town Movie Theatre," early 30s, Marx tin litho theatre with paper movie reel	50	75	100

Horse, American painted tin, 1870, 4½" long
Courtesy Lloyd W. Ralston

	C6	C8	C10
Horse, American painted tin, 1870, 4½" long	100	150	200
Horse in Hoop, George Brown, early	400	600	800
Horse, sheet metal, with cast iron jointed legs, full form, 10¾" long, 11" high	200	300	400
Horse Race, circular track within rectangular box, circa 1900, lever-activated	100	150	200

Horses in Hoops, ALTHOF BERGMANN Courtesy Lloyd W. Ralston Auctions

	C6	C8	C10
Horses in Hoops, Althof Bergmann, American painted tin, 1880, 4½" diameter	800	1200	1600
Hubley Ferris Wheel, early, cast iron, brass and tin, clockwork	500	750	1000
Hubley grasshopper pull toy, cast iron	400	600	800

HUBLEY Jantzen Surf Girl
Photo Courtesy Lloyd W. Ralston

	C6	C8	C10
Hubley Jantzen Beach Patrol, 8" long, circa 1932, man on surfboard riding through waves	750	1125	1500
Hubley Jantzen Surf Girl, 8" long, 1932, girl surf-board rider, cast iron	1000	1500	2000
Hubley Jumbo the Elephant, on wheels	25.00	37.50	50.00
Hubley Marathon Rider (bicyclist) cast iron	300	450	600
Hubley Old Dutch Cleanser Woman, cast iron	750	1125	1500
Hurdy-Gurdy, turn crank and play tune, shows animal playing cello	30	45	60
Ice Box, "Alaska" cast iron, has glass cube of ice in top, 5" high	30	45	60
Ideal "Mr. Machine," first version	17.50	26.25	35.00
Iron and Trivet, cast iron	20	30	40
Iron, tin, 5" high	7.50	11.25	15.00
Iron, tin, 3½" high	10	15	20
Irwin "Round-Up Tex the Whirling Cowboy," plastic wind-up, 1950s, 10" high	40	60	80
Ives Barrel Walkers, circa 1890, wood and paper litho balance toy, acrobat, ballerina, monkey	200	300	400
Ives Bear, mechanical wind-up	300	450	600
Ives Black Dancers circa 1873	900	1350	1800
Ives Black Dancers, clockwork, circa 1880, 11" high	600	900	1200
Ives Boy smoking cigar and holding stomach, cast iron	100	150	200
Ives Crawling Baby, circa 1871	300	450	600
Ives "Crawling Baby," 1893	1500	2250	3000

IVES Strukt-iron set, 1915
Courtesy Lloyd W. Ralston Auctions

IVES Mechanical Bear
Courtesy PB Eighty-Four, New York

IVES, BLAKESLEY & WILLIAMS Mule Dancers
Courtesy Lloyd W. Ralston Auctions

IVES Fire Engine House
Courtesy Lloyd W. Ralston Auctions

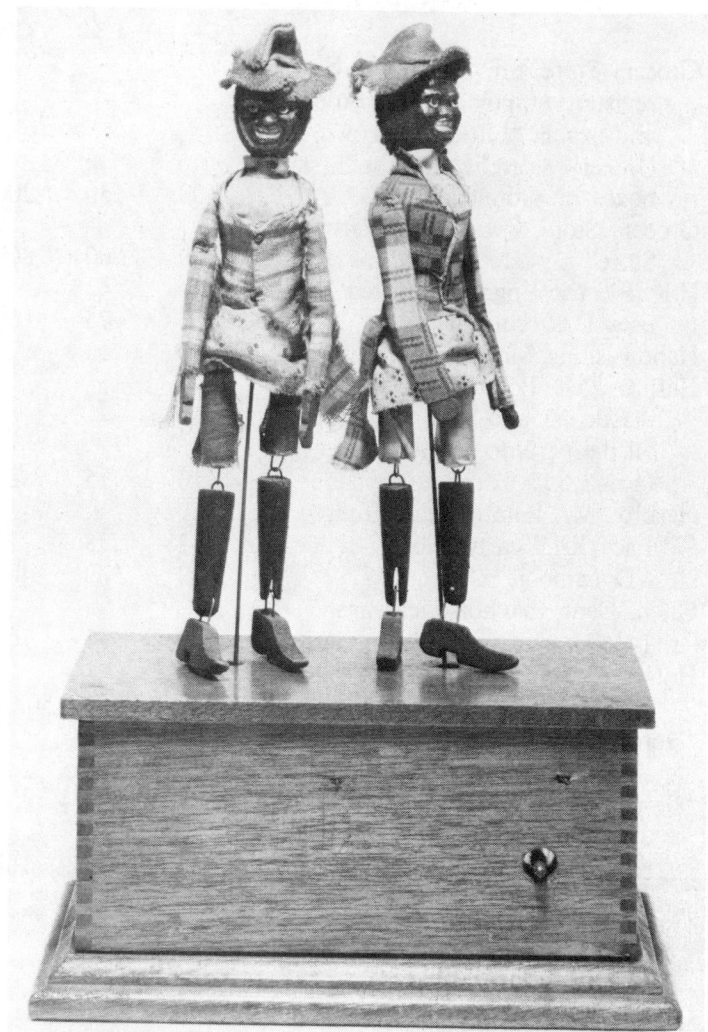

IVES Black Dancers, clockwork, circa 1880
Photo Courtesy PB Eighty-Four

	C6	C8	C10
Ives "Elephant Car," circus cage, cast iron, "serpent eggs" magic trick can be burnt in elephant's trunk, "Greatest Show on Earth"	790	1125	1500
Ives Fire Engine House, circa 1890, cast iron and wood, 16" long	1500	2250	3000
Ives General Grant, smoking, auctioned in 1988 for $150,000.			
Ives Juggler, clockwork, early	1000	1500	2000
Ives Mechanical Bear, patent 1872	300	450	600
Ives Struktiron set, 1915	100	150	200
Ives Struktiron, 1916, nonmotorized, with box	75.00	112.50	150.00
Ives Walking Elephant, "Pat. 1873," cast iron, 3½" long, walks down incline, moving legs and trunk	225.50	337.50	450.00
Ives, Blakesley & Williams, 1890, Mule Dancers, mechanical revolving, paper litho, painted tin, wooden box, clockwork, 8" tall	1600	2400	3200
"Jolly Jungleers," Milton Bradley, 1932, derringer type pistol shoots over animal targets	40	60	80

470

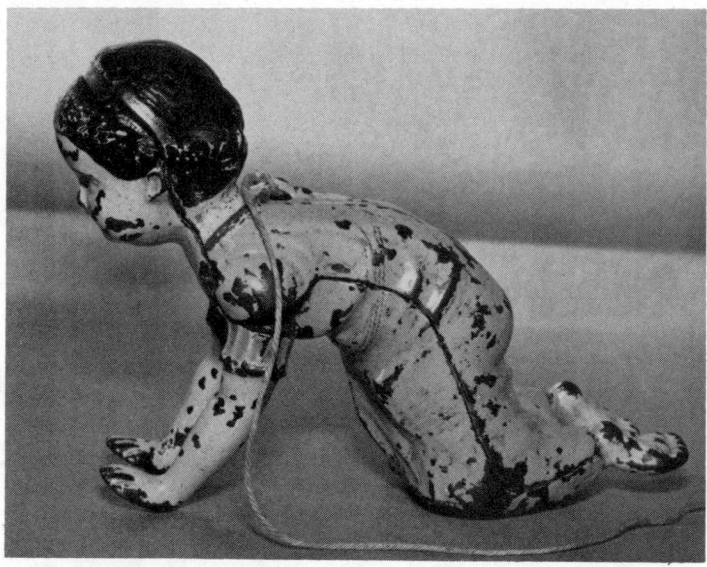

IVES "Crawling Baby," 1893
Courtesy Ed Hyers Antique Toys

IVES General Grant, Smoking
Courtesy Sotheby's New York

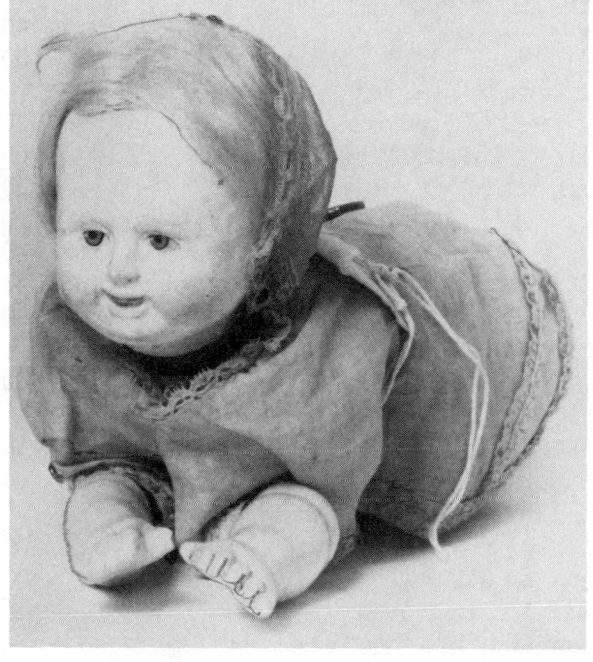

IVES Crawling Baby, circa 1871
Courtesy Phillips New York

Uncle Tom Walking Toy, IVES? Circa 1875
Courtesy Phillips New York

Uncle Tom Walking Toy,
IVES? Variation
Courtesy Phillips New York

471

J50   J51   J52

J53   J54   J55   J56

JONES Animals

"Kid Flyer"
Courtesy PB 84 NY

Jones Pillbox

	C6	C8	C10
Jones Animals, hollow lead, average price each	5.00	7.50	10.00
Jones Pillbox	48	72	96
Jumping Jack, composition and wood	70	105	140
Junior G-Man Whistle	20	30	40
Kaleidoscope "C. Bush, Prov. R.I. 1874," wood, brass & glass, 14" high	220	330	440
Kaleidoscope, Stevens	30	45	60
Kangaroo, cast iron, 6¼" long, "Jumps"	125.00	187.50	250.00
Kenton Baggage Cart, 6"	30	45	60
Kenton Drag Wagon, lithographed paper on sides, driver, 15½" long	200	300	400
Kenton Egyptian Toys – Rhino, Lion, Elephant, offered at $175 each, condition unspecified.			
Kenton Elephant – "Land-on Roosevelt 1936"	80	120	160
Kenton Stove, cast iron, marked "Oak" on door	30	45	60
Kenton Stove, with warming shelves and stove plates, high back for smokestack, "Royal" on door and shelves, 10" high	40	60	80
Keystone "Keystone Fire Department"	55.00	82.50	110.00
Keystone Service Station	100	150	200
"Kid Flyer" boy on scooter, tin litho, string-wound, 8½" long	200	300	400
Kingsbury Fire Station, No. 8, clockwork bell and door, 9"x10"x13"	150	225	300

	C6	C8	C10
"Knockout Champs," celluloid boxers in metal ring	375	563	750
"Knockout Target Shooting Gallery," lithographed tin with rifle, many targets	40	60	80
Ladder for fire trucks, cast iron	3.00	4.50	6.00
Ladders, stamped steel, from Hubley and Arcade trucks	10	15	20
Lawnmower, Arcade, circa 1920, iron and wood	20	30	40
Lehmann "Toy-Kadi," 1920s friction	500	750	1000
Lincoln Logs, Set No. 1A, John Wright, pat. 1920, complete	10	15	20
Lincoln Logs set 1C, post WW II	35.00	52.50	70.00
Lincoln Logs, Set No. 29, early	60	90	120
Lincoln Logs, 1923	10	15	20
Lincoln Logs 1930,	12.50	18.75	25.00
Lincoln Logs, in wooden box, complete	20	30	40
Lincoln Logs, pre WW II, large set, price includes box, complete	40	60	80
Lincoln Timbers, pre WW II, with box, complete	30	45	60
"Lindstrom's Little Show," cardboard and wood theatre with seven show strips	100	150	200
Lion in Hoop, tin 6¼" high	200	300	400
Lionel Science Kit, circa 1960	20	30	40
Machine Gun, Grey Iron, rapid fire, 9" long, cast iron, 1930s	60	90	120
Machine Gun, wood and steel, gravity fed, wooden bullets	10	15	20
Magic Lantern	60	90	120
Magic Lantern, Keystone, "Radio-ptocin"	40	60	80
Magic Lantern Projector, tin, embossed deer on door and side, 8" long	60	90	120
Man on Bicycle, animated, tin, high wheel bike, bell on top of bicycle, 10½" high	360	540	720
Man, smoking, clockwork mechanism	500	750	1000

Manoil Targets,
"4 5 6", "7 8 9"
Photo by Don Pielin

MARX Cat with Ball, cable operated
Courtesy Mapes Auctioneers & Appraisers

	C6	C8	C10
Marx Army and Navy Mechanical Target No. G169	20	30	40
Marx Army Code Sender, 9½" Morse key and phone, pressed steel	10	15	20
Marx Ballerina, 6" high, operated by sawtooth bar, pulled through, 1930s	80	120	160

MARX Ballerina
Courtesy Scott Smiles,
Photo by Mike Adams

	C6	C8	C10
Manoil Target, lead, either "4-5-6" or "7-8-9". "1-2-3" doesn't appear to exist, except in a version produced by collectors Ed Poole and Ron Eccles. Manoil's order number for the targets, without specifying which, was 76	35.00	52.50	70.00
Marky Maypo rubber squeeze toy, 1960s	6	9	12
Marx Air-Sea Power game	10	15	20
Marx Air-Sea Power Bombing Set	20	30	40
Marx "Allstate Terminal & Warehouse," Sears, 1960s, 23x15x4"	150	225	300

	C6	C8	C10
Marx Bear Cyclist, metal, lever action	100	150	200
Marx Bust 'Em Target Game No. G38	20	30	40
Marx Cat with Ball, cable-operated, tin litho	40	60	80
Marx "Champion Skater" ballet dancer, pull spinning rod out of motor, place skater in upright position and she spins	100	150	200
Marx "Climbing Fireman," tin and plastic	80	120	160
Marx Co. A Barracks, tin litho building, 6x8x12"	20	30	40

MARBLES

Marbles are known to date back as far as ancient Rome, when they were made of clay. Marbles are divided into types, such as "Indian Swirls," "Clambroth," "Lutz Type Swirls," etc. Size numbers range from 000, which equals ½ inch to 8, which equals 1⅛ inch. There are estimated to be 8-10,000 current collectors of marbles, about 600 of whom belong to the Marble Collectors' Society of America (see Leading Collectors and Dealers).

	C6	C8	C10
Antique, half gallon	17.50	26.25	35.00
Clay, 2 for	20	30	40
Sulphide Animal Centers, price per each marble	15.00	22.50	30.00
Glass, with spiral swirls, up to $20 apiece in mint.			
Swirl marbles, ¾", several	9.00	13.50	18.00

	C6	C8	C10
Swirl, 2" diameter	3.50	5.25	7.00
Swirl, 11 marbles	30	45	60
Bag of swirls	18.75	29.12	37.50
Bag of Swirls	16.25	24.12	32.50
Lot of assorted marbles	5.00	7.50	10.00

MARX "Climbing Fireman", tin and plastic
Courtesy Mapes Auctioneers & Appraisers

MARX "Pretty Maid Washing Machine"
Photo by Bill Kaufman
Courtesy Good Old Days Store

	C6	C8	C10
Marx Colonial Doll House No. 4052	40	60	80
Marx "Colonial Service Station," 1960s, 27" long, 15" wide, 4" high	40	60	80
Marx Deluxe Dial Typewriter, 1930s	14	21	28
Marx Dial Typewriter No. 1000A, 1930s	10	15	20
Marx Dishwasher K54, circa 1950s ..	10	15	20
Marx Doll House No. 4021	10	15	20
Marx Doll House No. 4030	20	30	40
Marx "Electric Lighted Filling Station," tin litho, 1930s, 10x13½" long	300	450	600
Marx "General Alarm Fire House," 1940s, 17" long, 11" wide, 3" high	130	195	260
Marx Headquarters, tin litho, U.S. Army Training Center, 5x8x11" .	20	30	40
Marx "Hometown Favorite Store," "F.W. Woolworth," tin litho, 5x2x3½"	120	180	240
Marx "Hometown Grocery Store," tin litho, 1930s, 5x2½x3½"	50	75	100
Marx "Hometown Savings Bank," tin litho building, 1930s, 5x2½x3½"	40	60	80

	C6	C8	C10
Marx "Honeymoon Cottage Village," 1930s tin litho, 17" long by 11" wide	50	75	100
Marx "Honeymoon Garage," 1930s tin litho, 6½"x7"x3"	20	30	40
Marx "Ice Skater," 1930s, 5½" high, sawtooth bar operates it	90	135	180
Marx Junior Dial Typewriter No. 2109, circa 1930s	10	15	20
Marx Kitchen Sink K47, circa 1950s	6	9	12
Marx "Loop the Loop" 1930s gravity toy, track 12" long, car 1½" long	50	75	100
Marx Newlywed Library, tin litho, 1930s, 5x2½x3½" long	40	60	80
Marx Practice Target Ranger, 1950s, 11" long	30	45	60
Marx "Pretty Maid Washing Machine," circa 1930s, 4½" high	30	45	60
Marx Refrigerator, K42, circa 1950s .	10	15	20
Marx Rex Mars Planet Patrol 45 Cal. machine-gun, tin and plastic, winds up, 22" long	40	60	80
Marx "Rex Mars Space Target Game," 1950s, 14" long	100	150	200
Marx Searchlight, tin litho, 3½" high	20	30	40
Marx Stove K39, circa 1950s	10	15	20
Marx "Sunnyside Service Station," 1930s	160	240	320
Marx Swinging Arm Target Game No. G52 and Gun	30	45	60
Marx Swinging Arm Target Game No. G55 and Gun	30	45	60
Marx Suburban Colonial Dollhouse, metal	20	30	40
Marx Tunnel, tin litho, 8"x10"x7" depicts farm scene, rolling hills, houses	10	15	20
Marx Typewriter No. 1110, metal and plastic, circa 1950s-1960s	10	15	20
Marx "Universal Gas Service Station," 1940s, 6½" high, base 12" long .	80	120	160

MATTEL "Farmer In The Dell", tin, crank, 7" high.
Courtesy Calvin L. Chaussee

	C6	C8	C10
Mattel "Farmer In The Dell," tin, crank, 7" high, 1951	150	225	300
Mattel Jack in the Music Box, circa 1950s	6	9	12
Meat Grinder with clamp, die cast	5.00	7.50	10.00
Meccano Set 0	10	15	20
Meccano Set 1	12.50	18.75	25.00
Meccano Set 1A	10	15	20
Meccano Set 1X	40	60	80
Meccano Set 2	25.00	37.50	50.00
Meccano Set 2A	10	15	20
Meccano Set 3	10	15	20
Meccano Set 3A	10	15	20
Meccano Set 4	50	75	100
Meccano Set 4A	25.00	37.50	50.00
Meccano Engineering Erector Set	10	15	20
Meccano Microscope Set, 1933	10	15	20
Merry-Go-Round, wind-up, lithographed paper and wood, with four bisque figures riding four fur-skinned papier mache horses	600	900	1200
Merry-Go-Round, wood and lithographed paper Jenny musical wind-up with five horse-form seats	200	300	400
Microphone, Ward toy	40	60	80
Monkey, mechanical, in red pants, red-checked shirt, squeeze metal lever attached to 34" spiral wire and monkey jumps alongside you, hitting cymbals, 10" high	20	30	40
Monkey on String, 8" high, Marx	15.00	22.50	30.00
Monkey string-climber, Lehmann	20	30	40
Monkey, stuffed, red felt cap and jacket, glass eyes, moveable arms and legs, move his tail and head moves from side to side, and up and down, circa 1910, 9½" high	30	45	60

	C6	C8	C10
Mound of Earth, tin litho, 4" long (for toy soldiers)	5.50	8.25	11.00
Mound of Rocks, tin litho (for toy soldiers)	6	9	12
Movie-Jector, hand crank	40	60	80
Movie Projector, "Flip Movies," turn crank and flip cards from "Midgette" movies, with film, circa early 1930s	56	84	112
"Movie Projector Gun," film only, 1937, Box 1 contains Chaplin, Gasoline Alley, Babe Ruth, Buffalo Bill, Harold Teen; Box 2 contains Dick Tracy, Terry & Pirates, Smitty, Orphan Annie, Winnie Winkle; Box 3 contains Clyde Beatty, Gumps, Little Joe, Tiny Tim, Buffalo Bill; Box 4 contains Gasoline Alley, Chaplin, Tracy, Lone Ranger, Harold Teen. Price per box	10	15	20
Movie Projector, "Uncle Sam," hand cranks, circa 1930s	30	45	60
Music Box, tin, shaped like coffee grinder, 3" high, German	80	120	160
Myrioptican, optical toy, Milton Bradley	100	150	200
Mysto Erector Set No. 1	75.00	112.50	150.00
Mysto Erector Set No. 1A	50	75	100
Mysto Erector Set No. 2, circa 1915	50	75	100
Mysto Erector Set No. 2A	50	75	100
Mysto Erector Set No. 3A	50	75	100

NOAH'S ARK
Courtesy Continental Hobby House

	C6	C8	C10
Noah's Ark, 6½" long, wooden, 12 animals, Noah	50	75	100
Noah's Ark, 11" long, 27 animals	75.00	112.50	150.00
Noah's Ark, Bliss, 13¼" long, 10 animals, wooden	150	225	300
Noah's Ark, cardboard, with animals, 14" long	20	30	40
Noah's Ark, Converse, 14" long, carved wooden animals	60	90	120
Noah's Ark with wooden village blocks	20	30	40

	C6	C8	C10
Noah's Ark, wood litho, 10" long with animals	30	45	60
Noise Maker, tin, shaped like old-fashioned phone mouthpiece, 2¼" high	6	9	12

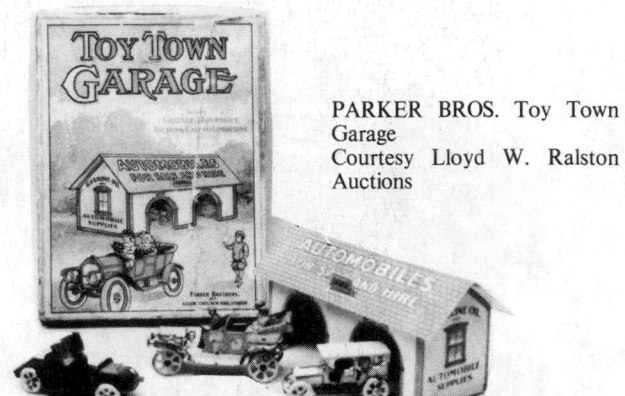

PARKER BROS. Toy Town Garage
Courtesy Lloyd W. Ralston Auctions

OHIO ART

Ohio Art was started in October, 1908 by a dentist, H.S. Winzeler. Originally its intent was to make metal picture frames (thus its name), but in 1917 the firm bought C.E. Carter (Erie Toy Plant) and began producing metal toys, including a climbing monkey on a string for Ferdinand Strauss. Winzeler later sold the plant to Louis Marx, but continued making tin toys, while Marx, according to Ohio Art history, used the former Carter plant as the foundation of his own company. Ohio Art is still making toys in Bryan Ohio.

	C6	C8	C10
Ohio Art Barrel Organ, musical, 5½" tall	15.00	22.50	30.00
Ohio Art Beach Toy Water Pumper, circa 1939, 8½" high, signed "Elaine Ends Hileman"	20	30	40
Ohio Art Children's Tea Set, tin, 14 pieces, 1950s	10	15	20
Ohio Art Drum, 6"x4"	6	9	12
Ohio Art "Fido's Musical Dog House," 1960s, 8" high	20	30	40
Ohio Art "Mini Farm Set," 1960s playset, 12" long, 5" high	30	45	60
Ohio Art "Realistic Farm Set" No. 197 1960s playset, 16" long, 7" high	40	60	80
Ohio Art Sandpail, 1940s, tin litho	6	9	12
Ohio Art Shooting Gallery, key wind	40	60	80
Ohio Art Sunnyfield Farms Barn and Silo Set with animals, tin litho, 1950s	40	60	80
Ohio Art Toyland Band, drums, bass and snare, cymbals, triangle and sticks, 7½" high	15.00	22.50	30.00
Ohio Art Washtub, tin litho, wood and metal scrubboard, 1940s	10	15	20
"Old Kentucky Home" wood litho action toy, six dancers, singer-musicians, moved by hand crank, 15½" long	366	549	732
Organ Grinder, monkey, 6" wooden, push bottom, squeaks and dances, Kohner Bros.	20	30	40
Paddle Wheel and Tower on base, tin, 14" high	20	30	40
"Paris Coaster," wood-wheeled cart	30	45	60
Parker Bros., 1910, Toy Town Garage, 3 litho tin penny cars, paper litho garage	550	825	1100

PEZ L to R: Robot, Santa
Courtesy Toy Collector News
Photo by Rex Gray

	C6	C8	C10
Parker Bros. "Toy Town Grocery Store"	110	165	220
Pez Astronaut, 1960s	7.50	11.25	15.00
Pez Frankenstein, 1960s	10	15	20
Pez Ogre, 1960s	7.50	11.25	15.00
Pez Pumpkin, 1960s	7.50	11.25	15.00
Pez Robot	7.50	11.25	15.00
Pez Santa	7.50	11.25	15.00
Pez Witch, 1960s	7.50	11.25	15.00
Phonograph, toy, Genola, cranks, with sound horn	100	150	200
Phonograph, toy, Nerona, cranks, sound comes from horn connected to needle, early	100	150	200
Pig and Piglet in cage, wood, cloth and lithographed paper, spring-loaded squeak toy	50	75	100
Pillsbury Poppin' Fresh, 5" high	6	9	12
Pillsbury Poppin' Fresh, 10" high	7.50	11.25	15.00
Pillsbury Poppie Fresh, 5" high	8	12	16
Plarola Corporation Organ, tin lithographed, with six organ rolls	300	450	600

PLASTICVILLE

(from information developed by Mark Schulz)

Plasticville Buildings and accessories were produced by Bachmann Bros., which dates back to 1833. In its early history Bachmann produced ivory cane handles and combs. In 1907 the firm purchased the second injection molding machine made, and began making eyeglass frames. After World War II, the growth in the toy train market led Bachmann to create plastic picket fences to enclose toy train platforms. This evolved into building kits, the first of which was the Log Cabin. Production continued into the late 1960s, with HO and N scale by then the main emphasis. In recent years, Bachmann has reintroduced some of the old O/S scale buildings. During its heyday the Plasticville line boasted over 100 items. C8 and C10 include box.

PLASTICVILLE Cape Cod House Kit
Photo by Gary Linden

PLASTICVILLE	C6	C8	C10
Airport Admin. Bldg.	10	15	20
Airport Hangar	8	11	15
Apartment House	30	38	45
Apartment Add-a-Floor	10	15	20
Autumn Trees	25	35	50
Bank	10	20	28
Barn	4	6	8
Barbecue	1	2	2

PLASTICVILLE Barnyard Animal Set
Photo by Gary Linden

PLASTICVILLE Fire House Kit
Photo by Gary Linden

PLASTICVILLE Billboard
Photo by Gary Linden

PLASTICVILLE Frosty Bar
Photo by Gary Linden

Barnyard Animal Set (18)	4	6	8
Billboard	.25	.50	1.00

PLASTICVILLE House Under Construction
Photo by Gary Linden

PLASTICVILLE Supermarket, large
Photo by Gary Linden

PLASTICVILLE Trailer
Photo by Gary Linden

	C6	C8	C10
Birdbath, Fence Section, Trellis	6	10	14
Bungalow	10	15	20
Cape Cod House Kit	2	4	6
Cathedral	12	16	20
Cattle Loading Pen	8	11	15
Church/Parish Church	4	6	8
Coaling Station	8	10	12
Colonial Church	8	12	15
Colonial Mansion	8	14	18
Corner Store	10	15	20
Country Church	3	4	6
Covered Bridge	4	6	8
Dairy Barn	5	8	10

	C6	C8	C10
Diner Kit	4	6	8
Factory	15	20	25
Fence and Gate (12 pcs.)	1	2	3
Fire House Kit	4	6	8
5 & 10	8	9	10
Frosty Bar	12	15	18
Gas Station, small	4	6	8
Greenhouse	18	23	28
Hobo Shacks (two bldgs.)	30	37	42
Hospital (w/furniture)	8	12	16
House Under Construction	15	20	25
Log Cabin Rustic Fence & Tree	2	4	6
Mobile Home	15	20	30
Motel	5	7	9
New England Ranch House	5	8	10
Outhouse	2	4	5
Pharmacy/Hardware	8	9	10
Plasticville Citizens (24 or 16) ...	2	4	5
Police Dept., HO scale	8	11	15
Police Dept., O scale	8	11	15
Post Office	6	8	10
Pump	1	2	2
Railroad Signal Bridge	4	6	8
Railroad Work Car	4	6	8
Ranch House	2	4	6
Roadside Stand	8	11	15
Schoolhouse	4	6	8
Split Level House	6	8	10
Street Accessories Unit (15 pcs.)	8	15	20
Suburban Station	3	4	6
Supermarket, large	8	10	12
Supermarket, small	4	6	8
Switch Tower (Railroad)	1	2	3
Telephone Booth	2	5	8
Town Hall	10	15	20
Trailer	15	20	30
TV station	6	9	12
Union Station	7	10	14
Water Tank (Railroad)	3	5	7
Well	2	4	5
Windmill	14	18	22
Roadrace Accessories			
Grandstand	15	20	25
Officials' Stand	8	11	15
Pit Stop	15	20	25
Sitting People	10	15	20

END PLASTICVILLE

	C6	C8	C10
"Play Store Register," tin and brass, Durable Toy and Novelty Co., 4" high	10	15	20
Pop (Kellogg's Rice Krispies) squeeze toy, 8½" high	5.00	7.50	10.00
Pop (Kellogg's Rice Krispies) hand puppet	10	15	20
"Preacher In The Pulpit" mechanical toy, all wood	500	750	1000
Pull Toy, Elephant, hide-covered with bisque head, native	150	225	300

Pull Toy, Rooster on
Platform
Courtesy Lloyd W.
Ralston Auctions

Pull Toy, Elephant tin
4½" long, 1870,
nothing on back
Courtesy Lloyd W.
Ralston Auctions

Pull Toy, horse on
platform, 6½" long
Courtesy Lloyd W.
Ralston Auctions

	C6	C8	C10
Pull Toys, Elephant, tin, 4½" long, 1870, nothing on back	140	210	280
Pull Toy, Elephant, tin, with blanket, iron wheels, 4½" long	60	90	120
Pull Toy, elephant with saddle, tin. Iron wheels, 4½" high	75.00	112.50	150.00
Pull Toy, Elephant, tin, 9" long, early	850	1275	1700
Pull Toys, Elephant with howdah, cast iron	600	900	1200
Pull Toy, Elephants, two, on platform, tin, 12" long	300	450	600
Pull Toy, Goat, 9½" long, tin, early	150	225	300
Pull Toy, four race horses and riders, tin with cast iron wheels, 8¼" long	400	600	800
Pull Toy, horse, galloping, tin, 7" long	75.00	112.50	150.00
Pull Toy, horse, tin, 8½" long, Harwood, circa 1876	2500	3750	5000
Pull Toy, horse, 13¼" high, leather reins, metal stirrups, felt saddle, circa 1880	125.00	187.50	250.00
Pull Toy, horse and animated figure with composition head and tin arms playing drum and cymbal. Horse is tin, wheels, wooden platform, 13½" long	500	750	1000
Pull Toy, horse and cart with chicken-shaped sides, iron wheels, tin, 5¼" long	125.00	187.50	250.00
Pull Toy, horse and covered delivery wagon, tin, 5¼" long	150	225	300
Pull Toy, horse and polo player on horse's back, tin, 4¼" long	75.00	112.50	150.00
Pull Toy, horse and rider, tin, iron wheels, 4½" long	80	120	160
Pull Toy, horse and rider, tin, iron wheels, 11" long	150	225	300
Pull Toy, horse (white) and water wagon, tin, 6¾" long	250	375	500

	C6	C8	C10
Pull Toy, horse (dark) and water wagon, tin, 7¼" long	150	225	300
Pull Toy, horse and wagon, tin, 9¼" long	150	225	300
Pull Toy, horse on platform, George Brown, 1880, American painted tin, 6½" long	250	375	500
Pull Toy, horse (race horse) in car, tin "Moxie," 8½" long	125.00	187.50	250.00
Pull Toy, horsewoman riding side-saddle on pony, cast iron	225.00	337.50	450.00
Pull Toy, jockey on dog, 10¼" long, tin, early	400	600	800
Pull Toy, Jockey on Horse, 9" long, tin, hair tail	600	900	1200
Pull Toy, Jumbo Elephant on wheels, Gibbs, 10" long	200	300	400
Pull Toy, rooster, tin, 3¼" long	40	60	80
Pull Toy, rooster on platform, 1890 painted tin, 4¾" long	100	150	200
Pull Toy, sheep, tin, 6¼" high, circa 1890	150	225	300
Pull Toy, three bears by Toycraft	30	45	60
Pull Toy, Two Frogs, 7½" long, painted tin	350	525	700
Pump, tin, with round trough, transfer of puppies, 7" high	15.00	22.50	30.00
Punch and Judy Puppet Theater with 6 puppets: Punch, Judy, Devil, Princess, Sailor, Workman	400	600	800
Push Toy, butterfly that flaps its wings	40	60	80
Push Toy, clown on log, bell toy, cast iron	500	750	1000
Push Toy, large running horses, tin, cast iron wheels, 14" high by 14½", horses' size	500	750	1000
Push Toy, horse, wooden, walks	40	60	80
Q.R.S. Playasax, uses paper rolls, Devry Corp., 12" long	87.50	131.25	175.00
Rabbit, moves ears, small	110	165	220
Rabbits, two, mashing ingredients in small bowl, tin, animated by squeezing, 6" high	15.00	22.50	30.00
Ranger Steel Co. "Gas Station - Auto Laundry," 1940s, 3x5x13", long	150	225	300
Refrigerator, cast iron, Hubley, 7" high, "GE"	150	225	300
Renwal Drawbridge, plastic, 2 plastic autos, 2 boats, cardboard river scene, 27" long, early 50s	125.00	187.50	250.00
Renwal Globe Trotter Set No. 305-150, 4 boats, 3 cars, train, jet plane	19.00	28.50	38.00
Ripley's Believe It or Not Disk-O-Knowledge, round piece of cardboard with another piece attached on top, turn to reveal questions and answers, 1932, 9½" diameter	10	15	20

	C6	C8	C10
"Rocket Ring," with futuristic rocket on top of ring, whistles, 1930s ...	15.00	22.50	30.00
Rocking Horse, hand carved, all wood, 1890s ...	425.00	637.50	850.00
Rocking Horse, "Shoo Fly" ...	100	150	200
Rocking Toy, tin, girl on horse, 3¾" long, German ...	100	150	200
Rolmonica, harmonica that plays rolls of tunes, "Blow, crank and play," with three songs, 1930s ...	60	90	120
Roly Poly, Boy on Horse, circa 1900	125.00	187.50	250.00
Roly Poly Clown, circa 1900, 10" high, papier mache ...	60	90	120

	C6	C8	C10
Roly Poly Clown, circa 1900, 13" high ...	190	285	380
Sand Toy Set, Chick Art Co., 1942, includes tin litho frog, sailboat, shovel and round sieve ...	36	54	78
Sandbags, variously marked, for toy soldiers ...	1.50	2.25	3.00
Sand Pail, tin litho, circa 1940 ...	6	9	12
Scales, cast iron, tin tray and four brass weights, 5¾" long ...	26	39	52
Scales, cast iron, "Dayton," 3½" high	40	60	80

SCHOENHUT
By Blossom Abell

Albert Schoenhut was a German emigrant toymaker. His company, founded in 1903, made many toys including "The Humpty Dumpty Circus," dolls, toy pianos, other musical instruments and a myriad of other toy items usually made of wood. The A. Schoenhut Co. closed its doors in 1933 though there were other Schoenhuts who made toys later. The last manufacturer of "Humpty Dumpty Circus" toys was Nelson Delavan of Seneca Falls, N.Y. Mr. Delavan bought the use of the name and manufacturing rights and operated from 1950 to 1953. We have not included pricing information on the Delavans here but they are generally lower priced than the reduced size Schoenhuts which they resemble.

Schoenhut produced many models of his animals and figures over the thirty years of production and invariably model changes had to do with reducing costs to hold established prices. Glass eyes and carved faces gave way to steam pressed heads and painted eyes. The glass-eyed earlier versions command 40 to 200% higher prices than the models with painted-eyes. In 1923 Schoenhut brought out the "Reduced Size" circus which were painted-eye with steam pressed heads, and had very little work or shaded paint. There is also a miniature clown, elephant and donkey.

Prices listed in this price guide are for examples (usually late models) that are most frequently found. **The glass eyed animals, early people with plaster faces (glued to a wooden head/neck), and other early models command an additional 40-100%. A few rare examples have even higher value. Painted eye animals that look exactly like glass eye examples (transition models) command only somewhat less than the earlier glass eye pieces.**

Bisque: Lion Tamer, Ringmaster, Lady Rider, or Lady Acrobat add 75-100%. Reduced size fancy head pig or camel or clown with cloth hat add 50%. Reduced Lady with bun commands an extra 20%.

Blossom Abell has been involved with antique toys for over twenty five years, and is a member of a number of collecting groups including the Schoenhut Collectors Club. This Club welcomes people interested in the Schoenhut Circus or the Schoenhut dolls. For information write the secretary: Barbara Black, 5865 N. River Forest Drive, Glendale, WI 53209.

SCHOENHUT, L to R: glass eyes, cloth mane Buffalo ($400 with worn mane), glass eyes carved mane Buffalo ($650). The cloth mane version was first.
Photo by Blossom Abell   Bruce Abell Collection

SCHOENHUT, L to R: very early plaster face Clown in sunburst suit ($140), later model all wood head (foreground), frequently found red on white suit ($75), all wood head Clown ($100). None of these clowns had ears.
Photo by Blossom Abell   Bruce Abell Collection

SCHOENHUT Camels. Top left, open mouth, one hump camel ($380), bottom left, fancy head (2 hump) reduced camel ($280). Right, full size, 2 hump camel, glass-eyed ($475).
Photo by Blossom Abell   Bruce Abell Collection

SCHOENHUT, L to R: painted eye Giraffe with carved head ($375), glass eye Giraffe with closed mouth ($500 in this condition, which is near mint)
Photo by Blossom Abell   Bruce Abell Collection

SCHOENHUT, L to R: Clown with wood hat and leather ears ($80), Clown with cloth hat (over wood cone), leather ears, rare model ($150), reduced Poodle ($275), Clown with molded ears ($75).
Photo by Blossom Abell   Bruce Abell Collection

	C6	C8	C10
Alligator	175	250	350
Brown Bear	140	175	250
Brown Bear - Reduced	180	240	350
Buffalo	175	210	300
Buffalo - Reduced	180	240	350
Bulldog	350	450	650

SCHOENHUT, L to R: Hobo, early version with plaster face ($400), Chinaman, early version with plaster face ($420). Whip with replaced string $30, damaged cane $25
Photo by Blossom Abell   Bruce Abell Collection

SCHOENHUTS, L to R: Glass-eyed Horse, missing leather belly strap ($200), two reduced horses ($185 each)
Photo by Blossom Abell   Bruce Abell Collection

SCHOENHUT, L to R: reduced Lady Rider with bobbed hair ($175), bisque Lady Rider ($450), very early plaster face Lady Rider, replaced skirt ($375).
Photo by Blossom Abell
Bruce Abell Collection

SCHOENHUT, L to R: early glass-eyed Lion with cloth mane ($500), early light face Monkey ($425)
Photo by Blossom Abell
Bruce Abell Collection

SCHOENHUT, L to R: glass-eyed Ostrich ($475), painted eyes earlier version Ostrich ($375)
Photo by Blossom Abell
Bruce Abell Collection

SCHOENHUT Piano, eight keys
Courtesy Continental Hobby House

	C6	C8	C10
Burro	250	350	550
Camel - Arabian 1 hump	150	190	300
Camel - Bactrian 2 hump	175	240	350
Camel - Bactrian - Reduced	140	180	260
Cat	350	450	650
Cow	200	275	375
Deer	230	300	450
Donkey	30	40	50
Donkey - Reduced	25	35	45
Elephant	50	75	100
Elephant - Reduced	40	60	85
Gazelle	450	600	1000

SCHOENHUT Negro Dude, 9" high
Courtesy Mapes Auctioneers & Appraisers

SCHOENHUT, L to R: Reduced Pig, rare fancy face ($400), Wheelbarrow ($90), glass-eyed pig, one-piece, neck-head, spotted paint ($375), glass-eyed Pig with ball joint head ($250, with body restoration)
Photo by Blossom Abell   Bruce Abell Collection

SCHOENHUT Circus Figures and equipment, circa 1904
Photo Courtesy Garth's Auctions, Inc.

SCHOENHUT, L to R: glass-eyed Leopard ($400), reduced Leopard (foreground, $225), painted eye Leopard ($225 because of worn paint on face)
Photo by Blossom Abell   Bruce Abell Collection

Barrels and Elephant
Courtesy PB Eighty-Four

	C6	C8	C10
Giraffe	150	180	300
Giraffe - Reduced	175	240	350
Goat	85	125	175
Goat - Reduced	175	240	350
Goose	200	325	450
Gorilla	700	950	1400

	C6	C8	C10
Hippopotamus	175	225	350
Hippopotamus - Reduced	175	240	350
Horse - Brown	90	125	190
Horse - Brown - Reduced	85	130	200
Horse - White	100	135	185
Horse - White - Reduced	100	135	230
Hyena	650	900	1500
Kangaroo	350	450	600
Leopard	180	240	375
Leopard - Reduced	150	190	280
Lion	140	170	240
Lion - Reduced	130	180	250
Monkey	160	200	275
Ostrich	210	260	400
Ostrich - Reduced	250	350	475
Pig	150	200	290
Pig - Reduced	250	325	425
Polar Bear	300	375	550
Poodle	70	100	130

SCHOENHUT golfer in skirt
Photo Courtesy PB84

SCHOENHUTS, Left, early painted-eye Polar Bear ($475), rear glass-eyed Polar Bear ($550), foreground later painted eye Polar Bear ($475), 10" Cage ($550), wooden head Lion Tamer ($240)
Photo by Blossom Abell   Bruce Abell Collection

	C6	C8	C10
Poodle - Reduced	160	225	350
Rabbit	300	425	625
Rhinoceros	175	260	400
Rhinoceros - Reduced	175	260	400
Sea Lion	350	425	550
Sheep	175	265	400
Tiger	140	190	280
Tiger - Reduced	130	180	260
Wolf	560	800	1400
Zebra	150	200	275
Zebra - Reduced	170	240	330
Zebu	500	750	1200

PERFORMERS

	C6	C8	C10
Chinaman Acrobat	150	240	360
Clown	50	75	125
Clown - Reduced	50	75	110
Gent Acrobat (Bisque)	270	350	450
Hobo	140	190	280
Hobo - Reduced	175	240	325
Lady Acrobat	175	225	325
Lady Rider	130	175	250
Lady Rider - Reduced	100	130	180
Lion Tamer	160	220	350
Negro Dude	210	285	425
Negro Dude - Reduced	210	285	425
Ringmaster	125	180	275
Ringmaster - Reduced	110	150	210

ACCESSORIES

	C6	C8	C10
Balls	30	40	60
Barrels	5	7	10
Bottle with label	30	45	65
Chairs	5	8	12

SCHOENHUT, L to R: Reduced Tiger ($225), painted-eyes Tiger, late ($225), early painted-eye Tiger (foreground, $400) that looks like the glass-eyed version)
Photo by Blossom Abell   Bruce Abell Collection

	C6	C8	C10
Flexible Cage	125	175	250
Goblet	5	7	10
Hoops	30	40	55
Horizontal Bar	125	175	250
Ladders	10	12	16
Pedestal - Tall	15	30	40
Pedestal - Short	10	18	25
Pedestal - Reduced	10	15	20
Tables	15	30	40
Tent - White Muslin	600	900	1600

	C6	C8	C10
Tent - Litho w/panels	2500	4500	7500
Tent - Reduced	400	550	900
Tubs	10	15	22
Weights, 50/100/200 lb.	40	55	75
Whips	20	30	40

End Schoenhut Circus listing
by Blossom Abell

	C6	C8	C10
Schoenhut Doll Cottage, 14½"x11" .	150	225	300
Schoenhut Golfer in Knickers	250	375	500
Schoenhut Golfer in Skirt	325	488	650
Schoenhut Hollywood Home buildings, set of six homes, 1928 .	150	225	300
Schoenhut Piano, 6"x6"x5"	42	63	84
Schoenhut Piano, 7"x6"x7", five keys	60	90	120
Schoenhut Piano, 9¾" long, 8" high, 7½" deep, 8 keys	50	75	100
Schoenhut Piano, 10"x10"x8"	45.00	67.50	90.00
Schoenhut Piano, 10"x11"x8"	45.00	67.50	90.00
Schoenhut Piano, 15½"x9¾"x8", 15 keys	70	105	140
Schoenhut Piano, symphony type, 15½"x10"x7½", 14 keys	44	66	88
Schoenhut Piano, 20"x16¾"x10½" . .	250	375	500
Schoenhut Railway Station	210	315	420
Schoenhut Roly Poly Cop, early	120	180	240
Schoenhut Teddy Roosevelt	1200	1800	2400
Schoenhut Trinity Chimes	100	150	200
Schoenhut Xylophone	30	45	60

	C6	C8	C10
Seiberling Latex Prod. Panda, rubber squeak toy	15.00	22.50	30.00
Sewing Machine, 6" high, circa 1920	50	75	100
Shooting Gallery Chickens, cast iron, 10¼" long	75.00	112.50	150.00
Signal Jr. R-70 Twin Wireless Practice Set, two beginner's sending keys, and one advanced key, circa 1920	25.00	37.50	50.00
Simplex Typewriter No. 300, tin	12.50	18.75	25.00
Snap (Kellogg's Rice Krispies) squeeze toy, 8½" high	5.00	7.50	10.00
Snap (Kellogg's Rice Krispies) hand puppet	10	15	20
Steam Engine, Big Giant Brass boiler Upright, 11¼"	80	120	200
Steam Engine, Doll & Co. upright, cast iron base, 11¼"	90	150	220
Steam Engine, Empire Horizontal, twin boiler and twin fly	250	375	500
Steam Engine, Empire, mounted on base board with transmission, concrete mixer, table saw, grinding wheel	110	165	220
Steam Engine, Empire vertical boiler, stationary, Metal Ware Corp., pat. Jan. 25, 1921	70	105	140
Steam Engine, Huber, 8"	150	225	300
Steam Engine, Weeden No. 49 with dual flywheels, cast iron base	200	300	400

Sewing Machine, 6" high, circa 1920
Photo by Bill Kaufman
Courtesy Good Old Days Store

Steam Engine, WEEDEN No. 49
Courtesy Heinz Mueller   Continental Hobby House

	C6	C8	C10
Steam Engine, Weeden, No. 42, 12" high	80	120	160
Steam Engine, Weeden No. 902, base 7¼"x9"	70	105	140
Steam Engine, Weeden dual flywheel, base 10", 11½" high	150	225	300
Steam Engine, Weeden, Early cast iron, deluxe model with cast iron boiler front, mounted on wood base inside wooden case, 1880 model	125	200	300
Steam Engine, Weeden Electric Steam Engine, 3½"x7¼" base	30	45	60

	C6	C8	C10
Steam Engine, Weeden, horizontal, 4" cast flywheel, mechanism on top of boiler	120	180	240
Steam Engine, Weeden, horizontal, 6" boiler, stationary	70	105	140
Steam Engine, Weeden, upright steam engine, 9½"x7" cast iron base, cast iron mechanism	70	105	140
Steam Engine, Weeden Upright Steam Engine on wooden base, 10" tall	45.00	67.50	90.00
Steam Engine, Weeden, Upright, early tin, 11"	60	90	120
Steam Engine, Weeden, Upright, early 11¼"	50	75	100
Steam Engine, Weeden, Upright, boiler only. Flywheel assembly mounted on base. Base is 8"x4"	100	150	200
Steam Engine, Wooden Dual Flywheel steam engine, base 10"x7"x11½"	150	225	300
Stitchwell Sewing Machine, child's floor model, circa 1920s	70	105	140
Stove, cast iron, "American"	100	150	200
Stove, "Daisy," cast white metal, 4¼" high	15.00	22.50	30.00
Stove, "Eagle," cast iron, 4¼" high	50	75	100

Stove, "Eagle," cast iron, 11½" high
Courtesy Mapes Auctioneers and Appraisers

	C6	C8	C10
Stove, "Eagle," cast iron, 11½" high	100	150	200
Stove, "Eagle," cast iron, 13½" high	125.00	187.50	250.00
Stove, cast iron, 13"x11½" high	75.00	112.50	150.00
Stove, cast iron, Ark, 4"x5"	25.00	37.50	50.00
Stove, electric, one burner, two ovens, chrome-finished steel, porcelain on oven doors, 16" wide, 14" tall	75.00	112.50	150.00
Stove, "Lancaster," "Eagle," on door and shelf, 10¾", cast iron	60	90	120

Teeter-Totter, GIBBS
Courtesy Garth's Auctions Inc.

	C6	C8	C10
Stove, wood-burning cast iron, "The Queen"	45.00	67.50	90.00
Stove, Roper, Arcade gas burner, cast iron, 6" high	100	150	200
Stove, wood-burning cast iron, "The Triumph Range"	100	150	200
Stove, tin, with four plate covers, four pans and one skillet, 5" high	60	90	120
Stretcher for 3" toy soldiers, pre-WW II	5.00	7.50	10.00
Structo Erector Set, 1910	50	75	100
Structo No. 3	70	105	140
Sulky, cast iron, single casting	30	45	60
Swing, animated, cast iron and pressed steel, for doll, with eagle, wheel	600	900	1200
Swinging Clown, tin, base marked "C.D. Kenny Co.," 4¼" high	100	150	200
"The Symmetroscope," wood and tin type of kaleidoscope, 6¼" high, F.P. Irving, Troy, N.Y.	60	90	120
Tea Kettle, cast iron, 3¼" long	30	45	60
Teeter-Totter, Gibbs Toys, 14½" high, when inverted, two children work their way down, tin, 1910	160	240	320
Tent, Army, two pole, two flags on top, approx. 5" long	7.50	11.25	15.00
Tent, "Bat. A," two flags	14	21	28
Tent, canvas, white, 9" long	7.50	11.25	15.00
Tent, Army, "Field Hangar, U.S. Aviation Corp Squadron 1," two flags atop tent, approx. 9" long	11.00	16.50	22.00
Tent, Army, "U.S. Battery B. Coast Artillery," two poles, two flags on top	14	21	28
Tent "Guard Tent Co. A" 4¼" high	5.00	7.50	10.00
Tent, "Inf. Co. C"	6	9	12
Tent, "Medical Unit"	12	18	24
Tent, "Mess Hall," wood base	15.00	22.50	30.00

	C6	C8	C10
Tent "Sail-Me" Co., 6 with box, c. 1931, paper	40	60	80
Tent, "U.S. Infantry Co. A," 4½" high, two flags on top	6	9	12
Tent "U.S. Infantry Co. B"	6	9	12
Tent, paper, 5" high, "State Camp Co. A"	1.50	2.25	3.00
Tent, No. 76, small pup, white with cardboard base, center support	4	6	8
Tin dog with boy rider, 13½" long, on wheeled platform	600	900	1200
Tinker Toys, round box, 12" high	12.50	18.75	25.00
Toledo Scales, 4x4", cast iron	25.00	37.50	50.00
"Tom Thumb" cash register, metal, 6½"x7½"x8¼" by Western Stamping Co.	17.50	26.25	35.00
Tools, Grey Iron, 1933, price per set	15.00	22.50	30.00
Tool Set, Greycraft (Grey Iron) 1940, cast iron, steel and wood	12.50	18.75	25.00
Tootsietoy Bathroom set	80	120	160
Tootsietoy Bedroom set	50	75	100
Tootsietoy Dining Room set	60	90	120
Tootsietoy furniture, six chairs, moveable bar, two side tables and a dining table	50	75	100
Tootsietoy living room set, two chairs, lamp, gramophone, sofa secretaire, table	50	75	100
Tootsietoy metal kitchen and bathroom furniture, sink, bathtub, toilet, stove, table and cupboard	45.00	67.50	90.00
Tootsietoy Music Room, set	110	165	220
Top, Carnival Whistling Top, tin litho circus decor, spring-wound,, 4" diameter, Lupor, 1930s	20	30	40
Top, gyro style, 1918	15.00	22.50	30.00
Top, tin	5.00	7.50	10.00
Top, wooden, circa 1940	4	6	8
Transworld Airlines, Jr. Pilot Wings	10	15	20
Tricycle, iron, Kilgore, 2¾"	60	90	120
Trix Rabbit, rubber squeeze toy	6	9	12
Turner Garage, heavy sheet metal, one window on each side, divided into four panes	50	75	100
The Twister, 12" high, in black cloth pants and red stripe shirt with porkpie hat, reminiscent of outfits worn at the Peppermint Lounge where the Twist was born. Stands on a 7" sq. platform, 3½" high, inscribed "Let's Twist!", which is exactly what he does, early 60s	75.00	112.50	150.00
Uncle Tom Walking Toy, Ives?, circa 1875, auctioned for $1300 in December, 1987.			
Uncle Tom Walking Toy, Ives?, variation, circa 1875, auctioned for $1200 in December, 1987.			
Waffle Iron, cast iron, Wagner	25.00	37.50	50.00

Water Tank Wagon, 1910
Courtesy Lloyd W. Ralston Auctions'

	C6	C8	C10
Wagon, Champion Express Coaster, 8" with handle	95.00	112.50	150.00
Wagon, "Express" wood spoke wheels	250	375	500
Wagon, Express Flyer, cast iron	125.00	187.50	250.00
Wagon, "Kiddie Kart," c. 1925, H.I. White, 20" long	50	75	100
Wagon, "Pony Express," 38" long	100	150	200
Wagon, wood, for child, 1900	75.00	112.50	150.00
Walking Horse, metal and papier mache wind-up, early 8¼"	400	600	800
Washing Machine, 1900, salesman's sample	100	150	200
Washing Machine, tin, works, circa 1940, seashore scene on side	30	45	60
Water Tank Wagon, 1910, painted pressed steel, 26" long	250	375	500
"Western Union" telegraph key, battery powered, code printed on front	25.00	37.50	50.00
Wheelbarrow, cast iron 4½", 1930	25.00	37.50	50.00
Wheelbarrow, cast iron, approx. 5½"	30	40	60
Wheelbarrow, cast iron, 6½" long	35.00	52.50	70.00
Wheelbarrow, cast iron, 7" long, with tools, 1915	50	75	100
Wheelbarrow, 9" long	25.00	37.50	50.00

Whirligig of Life
Courtesy Lloyd W. Ralston Auctions

	C6	C8	C10
Whiligig of Life, McLoughlin, 1870s, illusion of motion	600	900	1200
Wilkins Fire House No. 8, tin, 18½" long	600	900	1200
Wilkins Horse and Jockey, 1900, 10", cast iron, wheeled pull toy	600	900	1200
Windmill, metal, with pumping apparatus	75.00	112.50	150.00

WOLVERINE "Sunny Andy Kiddie Kampers"
Courtesy Mapes Auctioneers & Appraisers

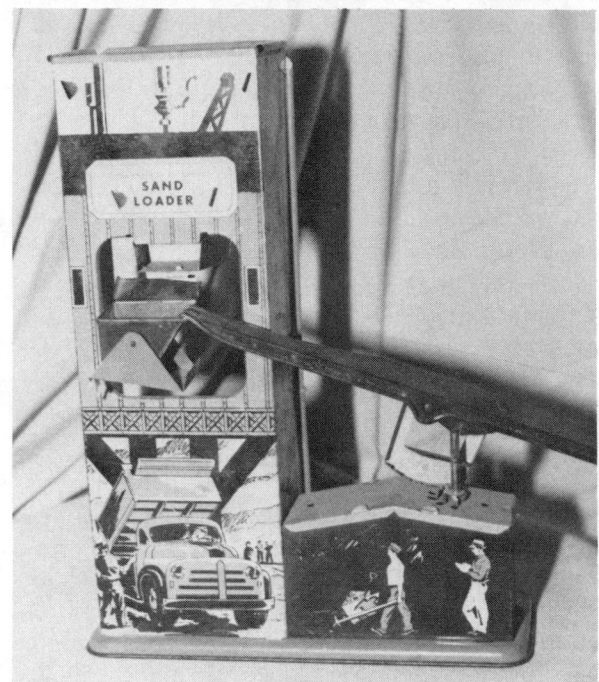

WOLVERINE Automatic Sand Loader, 1947
Courtesy Calvin L. Chaussee

WOLVERINE

Wolverine, of Pittsburgh, Pa., was founded in 1903 by B.F. Bain. The company got its name from Bain's Michigan hometown. In later years Wolverine became a subsidiary of Spang Industries, and in 1970 moved to Boonville, Arkansas. The "Sandy Andy," in all its variations, was probably Wolverine's most successful and famous toy.

	C6	C8	C10
Wolverine Auto Magic Sand Loader, 1947, 11" high	160	240	320
Wolverine "Automatic Coal Loader," 1940s, 10" high	50	75	100
Wolverine "Automatic Sand Crane," tin	50	75	100
Wolverine Bizzy Andy, 11" high sand toy, pat. 1914, steel and tin	60	90	120
Wolverine, Bizzy Andy Trip Hammer, 1917	60	90	120
Wolverine "Captain Sandy Andy" No. 63C sand toy, 1930s, 13" high	40	60	80

	C6	C8	C10
Wolverine "Dumping Sandy," 1916, 12" high	70	105	140
Wolverine Organ, tin, turn crank to make organ-like sounds	60	90	120
Wolverine "Post Office" with cardboard accessories	100	150	200
Wolverine "Sandy Andy No. 60 Automatic Sand Toy," Patented 1909 and 1911	60	90	120
Wolverine "Sandy Andy Full Back," 1920s	100	150	200
Wolverine "Ski Jumper," 1940s, 18" long, catapult action	60	90	120
Wolverine "Sunny Andy" Cable Car Set No. 53, 12" high, circa 1920-30s	60	90	120
Wolverine Sunny Andy "Kiddie Kampers," action toy, 5⅝" by 3½", color litho, three boy scouts and two girl scouts in backdrop camp setting; boys chop and saw wood and girls signal with flags, marbles drop down chute, circa 1929	110	165	220
Wolverine Sandy Andy sand loader, 1912	50	75	100
Wolverine "Texaco Service Station," 1960s, 25x15"	70	105	140
Wood Cage with horse, when gate is opened horse pops out and whinnies	125.00	187.50	250.00
Wood Cage, mechanical, rooster flies out when door is open	50	75	100
Wood Mechanical Dancing Figure, clockwork, on box base	125.00	187.50	250.00
Wooden Music Maker, "Auto Phone Co. H.B. Horton's Ithaca, N.Y.," 9½" high, uses player rolls	100	150	200

WYANDOTTE "Carnival"
Courtesy Joe and Sharon Freed

	C6	C8	C10
Wyandotte "Carnival," with ferris wheel, carousel and airplane ride, metal	125.00	187.50	250.00
Wyandotte hen, chubby, tin, lays egg when body pressed down, 8½" long, with eight eggs	50	75	100

WYANDOTTE
"Musical" Push Top
Photo by Bill
Kaufman
Courtesy Good Old
Days Store

Zoetrope.   Photo Courtesy Milton Bradley

WYANDOTTE "Posse" Shooting Gallery
Courtesy Good Old Days Store
Photo by Bill Kaufman

	C6	C8	C10
Wyandotte "Musical" push top, circa 1939	30	45	60
Wyandotte "Posse" Shooting Gallery, 14" wide, wind-up gallery	75.00	112.50	150.00
Wyandotte "Shooting Gallery," 1930s, wind-up, 14" long, 11" high	100	150	200
"Zoetrope," wood and cardboard, illusion of motion game, Milton Bradley	300	450	600
"Zulu Blow Gun," copyright 1925, 2' long, 4 arrows, target, instructions, etc. mfd. Battle Creek, Michigan	50	75	100
"Zulu Blow Gun" same as above, different coloring and target, no instruction sheet	45.00	67.50	90.00

CONDITION CODE:
C5 – Good, wear evident overall, shows that has been played with
C6 – Fine, shows some wear in spots, but taken care of
C7 – Very Fine, minor wear overall, very clean
C8 – Excellent, minor wear on edges only
C9 – Near Mint, no noticeable flaws, close inspection may show minute marks
C10 – Mint (like new)
   Note: Mint in Box does command higher price

BIBLIOGRAPHY

ANTIQUE TOY WORLD – $20.00 for one year subscription, payable to Dale Kelley, P. O. Box 34509, Chicago, Illinois 60634

TOY COLLECTOR NEWS – $12 for six issues, toys from 1950s up, P. O. Box 451, River Forest, Illinois 60305

COLLECTORS' SHOWCASE – $24.00 for one year subscription, P. O. Box 271369, Escondido, California 92027-9962

FISHER-PRICE 1931-1963 by John J. Murray and Bruce R. Fox (Books Americana)

A CELEBRATION OF COMIC ART AND MEMORABILIA by Robert Lesser, Hawthorn

CAST IRON TOY PISTOLS by Charles W. Best, Rocky Mountain Arms & Antiques (out of print)

DISNEYANA by Cecil Munsey, Hawthorn

JIM HARMON'S NOSTALGIA CATALOGUE by Jim Harmon, Tarcher/Hawthorn

THE AMERICAN DIMESTORE SOLDIER BOOK by Don Pielin, available at $12.50 from Don Pielin, 1009 Kenilworth, Wheeling, Illinois 60090

REGIMENTS OF ALL NATIONS (Postwar Britains) available at $20.00 from Joe Wallis, P.O. Box 2294, Washington, DC 20013

OLD TOY SOLDIER NEWSLETTER, $18.00 for one-year subscription, payable to Steve Sommers, 209 North Lombard, Oak Park, Illinois 60302

IT'S ALL IN THE GAME, Biography of Milton Bradley, by James J. Shea, Putnam

"The Grey Iron Casting Company of Mount Joy, Pa.," by Karl Zipple, published in Guidon Vol. 30 No. 4, 1972, Vol. 31 No. 2, 1973 and Vol. 32 No. 1, 1974

CAVALCADE OF TOYS by Ruth and Larry Freeman, 1942, Century House

TOYS IN AMERICA by Inez and Marshall McClintock, 1961, Public Affairs Press, Washington, D.C.

THE TOY COLLECTOR by Louis H. Hertz, 1969, Funk & Wagnalls

ANTIQUE TOYS by Gwen White, 1971, Arco

THE COMIC BUYER'S GUIDE – Comics, Premiums, Disney items and other toys. 26 issues $14.95. 700 E. State St., Iola, WI 54990

DICTIONARY OF TOYS SOLD IN AMERICA, Volumes I and II, by Earnest and Ida Long, P.O. Box 272, Mokelumne Hills, CA 95245, $10 plus postage per volume

MIDWEST PAPER DOLLS AND TOYS QUARTERLY by Janie Varsolona, Box 131, Galesburg, KS 66740, $12.50 for one year (four issues)

TOOTSIETOYS, WORLD'S FIRST DIECAST MODELS, by James Wieland and Edward Force, Motorbooks International, Osceola, Wisc.

"Schoenhut Wooden Toys" by Ann Soules AMERICAN COLLECTOR, April 1980, P. O. Drawer C-349, Kermit, TX 79745

"Black ID Planes," AMERICAN AIRCRAFT MODELER No. 54, September, 1973

TOY SOLDIER REVIEW, $12 for one-year subscription, Vintage Castings, Inc., 127-74th Street, North Bergen, NJ 07047

Ralstoy Information from July ___? 1939 Ralstoy Recorder.

Matchbox History from The Toy Book Magazine, November, 1987

THE BARCLAY CATALOG BOOK – Early Barclay catalogs, drawings, photos, etc. $16 from Richard O'Brien, 135 Stephensburg, Rd., RD2 Port Murray, NJ 07865

U.S. TOY COLLECTOR (Vehicles only) Sample issue $1.00, Box 4244, Missoula, MT 59806

THE TOY FARMER (Farm Toys only) $15 for 12 issues RR2 Box 5 - Sub. Dept., LaMoure, ND 58458

NOBLE HOUSE – Arcade, etc. catalog reproductions. SSAE for list. P.O. Box 964, Mundelein, IL 60060

TOY SHOP (Toy ads) Free copy on one-time basis, 700 E. State Street - Sample Copy Department, Iola, WI 54990

AUCTIONEERS

These are established firms experienced in disposing of large collections of toys by auction.

Sotheby's
1334 York Avenue
New York, NY 10021
(212) 606-7000

Philips New York
867 Madison Avenue
New York, NY 10021

Christie's East
219 East 67th Street
New York, NY 10021

Mapes Auctioneers & Appraisers
1600 Vestal Parkway West
Vestal, NY 13850
(607) 754-9193

Hake's Americana & Collectibles – Sample catalog $3.00
P.O. Box 1444N
York, Pennsylvania 17405
(717) 848-1333

Lloyd W. Ralston
447 Stratfield Road
Fairfield, Connecticut 06432
(203) 366-3399

Garth's Auctions Inc.
2690 Stratford Road
Delaware, Ohio 43015
(614) 362-4771

Continental Auctions (Mail)
P. O. Box 193
Sheboygan, Wisconsin 53082

New England Auction Gallery (Mail)
P. O. Box 2273
West Peabody, Massachusetts 01960

Ted Maurer
1931 N. Charlotte Street
Pottstown, Pennsylvania

Kruse Auctioneers
Kruse Building
Auburn, Indiana 46706

Gene Harris Antique Center
P. O. Box 476-203 So. 18th Avenue
Marshalltown, Iowa 50158
(515) 752-0600

Butterfield & Butterfield
1244 Sutter Street
San Francisco, CA 94109
(415) 861-7500

Ken Gooch
Dexter, IA 50070
(515) 789-4406

Philip B. Robinson
1010 Gray Street
St. Charles, IL 60174

LEADING COLLECTORS AND DEALERS

(It is suggested that, when writing to any of the following, you enclose a stamped, self-addressed envelope.)

JIM HARMON
Radio premiums and tapes, comic books and strips
634 So. Orchard Dr.
Burbank, CA 91506

BARBARA & JONATHAN NEWMAN
Paper toys, old and new
The Paper Soldier
8 McIntosh Lane
Clifton Park, NY 12065

CHARLES W. BEST
Old toy pistols, etc.
6288 South Pontiac
Englewood, CO

BIZARRE BAZAAR
Quality collectible toys
Place des Antiquaires
125 East 57th Street
New York, NY 10022   (212) 688-1830

JOHN MURRAY
Fisher-Price
Box 29
Eden, NY 14057

HANK ANTON
Buys, sells, trades, auctions toy soldiers, etc.
92 Swain Avenue
Meriden, CT 06450   (203) 237-5356

JOE WALLIS
Britains Soldiers
P. O. Box 2294
Washington, DC 20013

ED HYERS
Dealer in Antique toys
P. O. Box 18448
Asheville, NC 28814   (704) 252-2155

EDWARD K. POOLE
Toy soldiers, $\frac{1}{36}$ scale ID vehicles and
old wooden military vehicle kits
926 Terrace Mt. Drive
Austin, TX 78746

DON PIELIN
Toy Soldiers
1009 Kenilworth
Wheeling, IL 60090

JOE FREEMAN
Restorations of all Tin Toys
1313 North 15th Street
Allentown, PA 18102   (215) 434-0290

WHIT ALEXANDER & NEAL BATES
Star Wars
P. O. Box 2326
Florence, AL 35630

SECOND CHILDHOOD
Antique Toys
283 Bleecker Street
New York, NY

THE SOLDIER SHOP
Britains, other Soldiers
1222 Madison Avenue
New York, NY 10128   (212) 535-6788

GARY J. LINDEN
Marx and other plastic toys
P. O. Box 243
River Forest, IL 60305

MEMORABLE THINGS
American and foreign toy soldiers, vehicles, etc.
P. O. Box 10505
Towson, MD 21204
(Shop Address: 31 W. Allegheny Avenue, Towson
MD, 2nd floor)

BILL BERTOIA
Mechanical banks, antique toys
1217 Glenwood Drive
Vineland, NJ 08630   (609) 692-4092

RICHARD MacNARY
Marx Trains, Coca-Cola vehicles, wood, cardboard,
paper toys, soldiers
4727 Alpine Drive
Lilburn GA 30247

ECCLES BROTHERS
Comic Figures, Toy Soldiers and Vehicles from
original molds. Catalog $2.00
R.R. No. 1, Box 253-D
Burlington, IA 52601

BILL LANGO
Barclay vehicles, animals and soldiers from original
and new molds
127-74th Street
North Bergen, NJ 07047

K. WARREN MITCHELL
Soldiers of all types, Regular lists at no charge
1008 Forward Pass
Pataskala, OH 43062

STEVE BALKIN
Toy Soldiers including Warren
BURLINGTON ANTIQUE TOYS
1082 Madison Avenue
New York, NY 10028

STEVE LEONARD
Antique Mechanical Toys, etc.
Box 127T
Albertson, L.I., NY 11507   (516) 742-0979

HERMAN & FLORENCE LOTSTEIN
Trains, toys and books on toys
Cook's Antique Flea Market
Rt. 29, Lambertville, NJ

BLOSSOM ABELL
Schoenhut toys, including repairs
Christmas Past
P. O. Box 247
Algonquin, IL 60102

BOB LOWE'S TOONERVILLE JUNCTION
Classic American and European Toys
7 E. Church Street
Bethlehem, PA 18018   (215) 691-6736

LONDON BRIDGE COLLECTOR'S TOYS
Britains Soldiers, etc. and Britains replacement parts
1344 Rt. 100 S.
Trexlertown, PA 18087   (215) 395-2000

RON SMITH
Tin plate cars & planes, plastic promotional cars
33005 Arlesford
Solon, OH 44139

BUDDY K TOYS
Buddy L Toys, etc.
RD 9 Box 322, Bingen Road
Bethlehem, PA 18015

SANDY & DON MADDEN
Disneyana, Battery, Wind-ups
1315 Shanessey Rd.
El Cajon, CA 92019   (619) 444-8531

EXCALIBUR HOBBIES LTD.
Toy Soldiers, all types
63 Exchange Street
Malden, MA 02148-5523   (617) 322-2959

G.M. HALEY
Britains and other soldiers
"Hippins" Blackshaw head
Hebden Bridge, W. Yorks, England

DON HULTZMAN
Tin wind-up and battery-operated, also repairs, restorations
5026 Sleepy Hollow Road
Medina, OH 44256

SCOTT SMILES
Tin wind-ups, etc.
440 SW 5th Avenue
Boynton Beach, FL 33435

CONTINENTAL HOBBY HOUSE
Toys and Trains, Regular catalogs
P. O. Box 193
Sheboygan, WI 53082

FRED THOMPSON
New designs of Smitty vehicles
Smith-Miller Inc.
P. O. Box 139
Canoga, Park, CA 91305

REX MILLER
Premiums
Route 1, Box 457-D
East Prairie, MO 63845

JOHN D. (JACK) MATTHEWS
World War II toys, etc.
1255 23rd Street NW
Washington, DC 20037

DUTKINS' COLLECTABLES
Tin Toys, soldiers, etc.
1019 W. Route 70
Cherry Hill, NJ 08002   (609) 428-9559

DANNY FUCHS
Superman toys, games, etc.
209-80 18th Avenue
Bayside, NY 11360

DAVID M. LEOPARD
Old toy cars and trucks
2507 Feather Run Trail
West Columbia, SC 29169-4915

DARROW'S FUN ANTIQUES
Old toys of all types
309 E. 61st Street
New York, NY 10021   (212) 838-0730

FRED MAXWELL
Slush cars, planes, company catalogs, antique toys
4722 No. 33 Street
Arlington, VA 22207

CHARLES FRANCIS WILDING
Secretary, Capitol Miniature Auto Collectors Club
10207 Greenacres Dr.
Silver Springs, MD 20903

FERDINAND ZEGEL
Antique toys, postwar, Corgi, Dinky
Counterpane Toyland
P. O. Box 589
Ft. Belvoir, VA 22060

FRED & MARGARET WILHELM
Disney, Popeye, Comic, Barclay, Manoil soldiers
W & F Collectibles
Box 2054, Leucadia, CA 92024

JEFF AND SANDY ABRAMS
Cracker Jack Toys, tin wind-ups
3037 Boone Ave. So.
St. Louis Park, MN 55426

PERRY R. EICHOR
Aircraft toys and literature
P. O. Box 10171
Greenville, SC 29603

CLASSIC TOYS
New and old toys; military, vehicles, zoo, etc.
69 Thompson St.
New York, NY 10012

PHIL SAVINO
Mail Auctions in various toy categories - send SSAE
Rt. 2, Box 76
Micanopy, FL 32667

TONY AND JACKI GRECCO
Toy soldiers and related items
P. O. Box 3490
Poughkeepsie, NY 12603   (914) 462-8829

493

TOY MUSEUMS AND MUSEUMS THAT FEATURE TOYS

Auburn-Cord-Dusenberg Museum
Auburn, Indiana 46706
(Auburn toys and Cord and Dusenberg automobiles)

Museum of the City of New York
5th Avenue and 103rd Street
New York, NY

Smithsonian
Washington, DC

Daisy Gun Museum
U.S. 71 South
Rogers, Arkansas
(The world's most complete collection of air rifles, dating from the 18th century)

Nashville Toy Museum
2613 McGavok Pike
Nashville, Tennessee

Margaret Woodbury Strong Museum
One Manhattan Square
Rochester, New York, 14607

Lawrence Scripps Wilkinson Collection
c/o Detroit Antique Toy Museum
6325 West Jefferson
Detroit, Michigan 48209
(383) 843-9775
(Available only for traveling exhibitions)

Toy Train Museum
Paradise Lane
Strasburg, Pennsylvania

The Sterling Collection
Stone Castle
804 North Third Street
Bardstown, Kentucky

Museum of Childhood
8 Broad Street
Greensport, New York

Islip Town Museum
Montauk Highway
Oakdale, New York

San Francisco International Toy Museum
2801 Leavenworth St.
San Francisco, CA

Sullivan-Johnson Museum
(Kenton Toys exhibit)
223 North Main Street
Kenton, Ohio

Washington Dolls' House & Toy Museum
5236 44th Street, NW
Washington, DC 20015

The Toy Museum
42 Bridge St. Row
Chester, Cheshire
England

The London Toy & Model Museum
23 Craven Hill
London, England

Toy and Soldiers Museum
1100 Cherry St.
Vicksburg, Mississippi

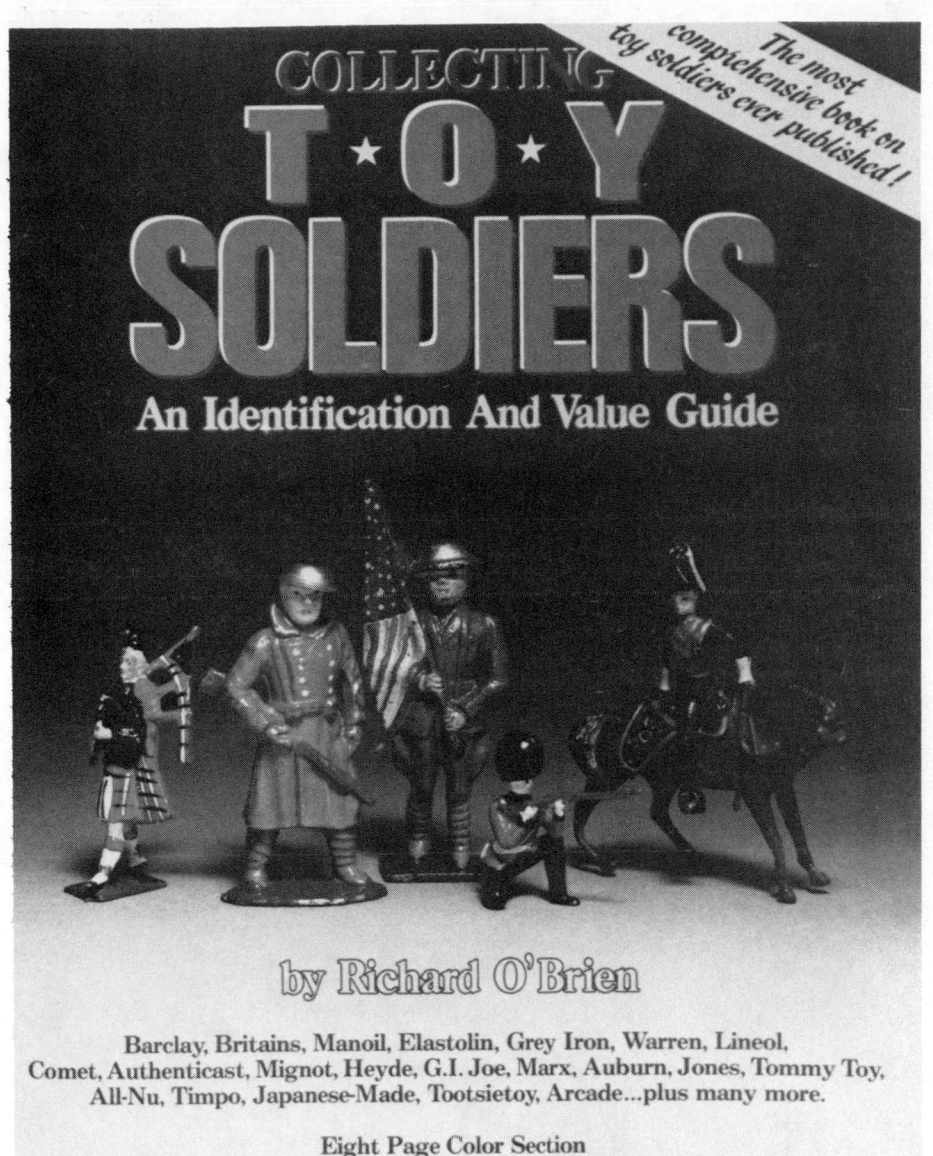